The Modern Gang Reader

The Modern Gang Reader

Edited by

Cheryl L. Maxson
University of California–Irvine

■

Arlen Egley, Jr.
National Gang Center

■

Jody Miller
Rutgers University

■

Malcolm W. Klein
University of Southern California

FOURTH EDITION

New York   Oxford
OXFORD UNIVERSITY PRESS

Oxford University Press is a department of the University of Oxford.
It furthers the University's objective of excellence in research, scholarship,
and education by publishing worldwide.

Oxford   New York
Auckland   Cape Town   Dar es Salaam   Hong Kong   Karachi
Kuala Lumpur   Madrid   Melbourne   Mexico City   Nairobi
New Delhi   Shanghai   Taipei   Toronto

With offices in
Argentina   Austria   Brazil   Chile   Czech Republic   France   Greece
Guatemala   Hungary   Italy   Japan   Poland   Portugal   Singapore
South Korea   Switzerland   Thailand   Turkey   Ukraine   Vietnam

For titles covered by Section 112 of the US Higher Education Opportunity
Act, please visit www.oup.com/us/he for the latest information about
pricing and alternate formats.

Published by Oxford University Press
198 Madison Avenue, New York, NY 10016
www.oup.com

Library of Congress Cataloging-in-Publication Data

The modern gang reader/[edited by] Cheryl L. Maxson, University of California—Irvine,
Arlen Egley, Jr., National Gang Center, Jody Miller, Rutgers University, Malcolm W. Klein,
University of Southern California.—[Fourth edition].
    pages cm
Includes bibliographical references.
ISBN 978-0-19-989539-7 (pbk. : alk. paper)   1. Gangs—United States.   2. Juvenile
delinquents—United States.   I. Maxson, Cheryl Lee, editor of compilation.
HV6439.U5M64 2014
364.106'60973—dc23

2012051030

Printing number: 9 8 7 6 5 4 3 2 1

Printed in the United States of America
on acid-free paper

Contents

---

*New to the Fourth Edition.

SECTION III: Gang Structures and Group Processes

SECTION IV: Race and Ethnicity

SECTION V: Gender

SECTION VI: Community Contexts

SECTION VII: Crime and Victimization

SECTION VIII: Responses to Street Gangs, Programs, and Policies

Acknowledgments

The editors gratefully acknowledge the scholars who wrote the articles included in this volume and conducted the important research on which they are based. We also appreciate the assistance provided by Daniel Scott, doctoral student in the Department of Criminology, Law and Society, University of California–Irvine in preparing the manuscript.

In addition, we would like to thank the following reviewers for their insights: Christian Bolden, Loyala University, New Orleans; Jean Marie McGloin, University of Maryland; Christopher Melde, Michigan State University; Dana Peterson, State University of New York at Albany; and Sean P. Varano, Roger Williams University.

About the Editors

Cheryl L. Maxson is Associate Professor in the Department of Criminology, Law, and Society at the University of California Irvine. She has studied various aspects of street gangs on regional, national and international levels. Her co-authored books include *Street Gang Patterns and Policies, Youth Gangs in International Perspective,* and *The Eurogang Paradox.*

Arlen Egley, Jr., is a Senior Research Associate at the National Gang Center (NGC), where he manages the National Youth Gang Survey (NYGS). He has authored or coauthored numerous publications pertaining to the NYGS, including Department of Justice and NGC reports as well as articles for academic journals and book chapters.

Jody Miller is a professor in the School of Criminal Justice at Rutgers University. Her research examines how inequalities of gender, race, and class shape young women's participation in crime and risks for victimization. She is author of *Getting Played: African American Girls, Urban Inequality, and Gendered Violence* and *One of the Guys: Girls, Gangs and Gender.*

Malcolm W. Klein is Professor Emeritus at the University of Southern California. As a psychologist and a sociologist, he has been involved in street gang research for 50 years. Twelve of his twenty books in criminology have been devoted to street gang issues in the US and Europe.

New to the Fourth Edition

The fourth edition of *The Modern Gang Reader* continues its tradition of orienting students to the study of gangs by—first and foremost—helping them to grapple with the key definitional concerns necessary for evaluating the field. As with past editions, the volume includes up-to-date research by leading scholars in the field, along with extensive coverage of contemporary policy and practice. To that end, the fourth edition includes 32 new chapters (with the retention of just five chapters from previous editions). In addition, it features several new sections and expanded coverage of several critical topics. New sections include three devoted to better understanding the relationships between gang membership and (1) racial inequality, (2) gender, and (3) community context. Each section is prefaced by introductory material that serves as a guidepost for the contents within and across sections. In addition, the new edition features updated and expanded discussion of several key issues, including:

- Methodological strategies for studying gangs

- New research on the demographic characteristics of gang members, including gender, race/ethnicity, and immigration status

- Extended coverage on group processes within gangs

- Research on victimization within gangs

- New research on gang desistance

- Consistent attention to international and comparative research on gangs

The Modern Gang Reader

Defining and Studying Gangs

This first section lays important foundations for the remainder of the book by tackling some of the thorniest and most divisive issues in gang research: how we define the topic, how we explain it, and how we study it. Definitions, theory, and methods are so intimately linked that the field's ability to come to terms with diverse views determines our progress in building a coherent understanding of gangs, their behavior, and their impacts. The lack of consensus on precisely what constitutes a gang or gang member limits theoretical advances even while the methods that we use to study gangs sometimes constrain how we define them. We can fully understand the diversity of gangs across places and times only when we are assured of the stability and consistency of the application of definitions and research methods.

The variety in definitional approaches often reflects the legitimate differences in perspectives among scholars, such as the debate as to whether or not involvement in criminal activity should be included as a defining element. This issue extends to defining gang crime as well, as, for example, whether or not a crime incident needs to be explicitly motivated by gang functions or whether any crime committed by or against a gang member is legitimately considered gang crime. This is more than just a matter of how we tabulate gang crime; at issue is what it is about gang participation, or what processes within the gang, that appears to substantially increase criminal activity and indeed make crimes committed by gang members quite distinct from those committed by other youth. How we understand gang crime—and develop adequate

responses to it—is intricately related to how we define gangs as groups.

Definitions are so important that generally, researchers begin reports of studies with a discussion on the topic, and this is readily illustrated by many articles in this volume. Scholars use definitions to distinguish the groups they are studying from other youth friendship groups, some of which engage in crime (delinquent youth groups) and others less so (peer groups derived from sports activity, religious groups, and school or community organizations). Gang researchers also draw a distinction between these primarily youth or young adult groups and more adult-oriented crime groups like motorcycle gangs, prison gangs, terrorist groups, drug cartels, or Mafia-like organized crime groups. One way they do that is by explicitly defining their object of inquiry as *street* gangs and leaving it to others to study the other groups. In order to enable advancement in comparative gang research, several international gang scholars have developed a definition reflecting the minimal elements that they consider necessary to call a group a street gang. According to the Eurogang collaborative, a street gang is "any durable, street-oriented youth group whose involvement in illegal activity is part of its group identity." This definition is described fully in the first article of this volume, but what is important here is the recognition that it was developed over the course of arduous discussions over several years; this is a consensus definition, but an uneasy consensus. While this definition has guided a wide range of studies both in the United States and in Europe, scholars continue to consider the propriety of definitional

1

elements in an international context where there is little common comprehension of "gangs" and how to recognize them. We neither want to fail to recognize an important emerging social problem, nor do we want to exaggerate it by promoting frightening stereotypical images of street gang behavior, as is readily apparent in popular media coverage of the topic, regardless of the location. This was the problem that Eurogang scholars tried to avoid by promoting a common gang definition—it remains to be seen whether studies in Europe and elsewhere will be able to avoid the fractured nature of gang studies conducted in the United States over the past several decades.

This lack of coordinated investigation has inhibited the advancement of gang theory because it is difficult to develop explanations of differences if you aren't sure whether they are real or an artifact of different definitions or methodological approaches. While many studies have tested theoretical constructs derived from more general crime or delinquency theories, relatively few specific gang theories have emerged since the classical period of the mid-century. The exceptions are Klein's framework for explaining the emergence and maintenance of street gangs advanced in *The American Street Gang* (1995); Hagedorn's application of underclass theory in *People and Folks* (1988);

Vigil's propositions deriving from the construct of multiple marginality, most recently portrayed in *Rainbow of Gangs* (2002); and Thornberry's interactional theory, detailed in his 2003 volume *Gangs and Delinquency in Developmental Perspective*. The influence of these theories can be seen in the gang research articles produced in this volume, yet none has gained the prominence that would accrue if tested in a coordinated, multisite study.

The Eurogang collaborative has tackled the definitional and methodological variability in existing gang research by offering their consensus definition and a unified, multimethod research design (see http://www.umsl.edu/ccj/eurogang/EurogangManual.pdf) that provides the framework for the type of planned, cross-national comparisons encouraged by Klein in the last article of this section. The Eurogang design promotes each type of comparison that Klein identifies: gang members, gangs as units, gang locations, and gangs over time. The increasing visibility of the Eurogang approach suggests a positive direction toward building broader knowledge about gangs and a deeper understanding of why gangs emerge and dissipate, why some youth participate and then leave them, and the types of impacts that gang activity has on neighborhoods and communities in thousands of locations throughout the world.

CHAPTER 1

A Brief Review of the Definitional Problem

Malcolm W. Klein ■ Cheryl L. Maxson

There is no universal consensus on a definition of street gangs, although these authors present a recent attempt that was crafted by a large group of U.S. and European scholars. The Eurogang definition has been employed successfully in many studies, and yet the groups identified by this method are likely somewhat different from those captured by other popular definitions and even from those that youth reference when they report that their own group of friends is a gang. This article describes the variations among gang definitions commonly used by researchers and contrasts these with a legal approach. While scholars disagree about the role that crime should play in defining street gangs, the legal community readily embraces this definitional feature. Many of the articles in this volume discuss gang definitions, and this overview alerts the reader to the most important definitional issues.

. . . We start with the difficult definitional issue: what *is* a street gang? Does it really matter how we define it? We answer, quite readily, that yes, it does matter. And to be as succinct as possible, we offer the following nominal definition of the street gang with an explanation of how we came to it:[1]

> A street gang is any durable, street-oriented youth group whose involvement in illegal activity is part of its group identity.

Reprinted from: Malcolm W. Klein and Cheryl Maxson, "A Brief Review of the Definitional Problem," *Street Gang Patterns and Policies*, 3–10. Copyright © 2006 by Oxford University Press, Inc. Reprinted by permission of Oxford University Press, Inc.

Point 1: *Durable* is a bit ambiguous, but at least an existence of several months can be used as a guideline. Many gang-like groups come together and dissipate within a few months. The durability refers to the *group*, which continues despite turnover of members.

Point 2: *Street-oriented* implies spending a lot of group time outside home, work, and school—often on streets, in malls, in parks, in cars, and so on.

Point 3: *Youth* can be ambiguous. Most street gangs are more adolescent than adult, but some include members in their 20s and even 30s. Most have average ages in adolescence or early 20s.

Point 4: *Illegal* generally means delinquent or criminal, not just bothersome.

Point 5: *Identity* refers to the group, not the individual self-image.

This is the consensus nominal definition agreed to by a consortium of more than 100 American and European researchers and policy makers from more than a dozen nations meeting in a series of eight workshops between 1997 and 2005 (the Eurogang program). It represents a minimal approach—the necessary and sufficient defining characteristics—that for most purposes allows us to distinguish street gangs from other troublesome youth groups (of which there are many more).

The components—durable, street oriented, youth group, identity with illegal activity—are definers of street gangs. They are the minimal necessary and sufficient elements to recognize a street gang. Many other characteristics are common descriptors but not definers. One thinks of leadership, cohesiveness, ethnicity, gender, and distinctive argot, clothing, tattoos, or hand signs, for instance. These are variables that help us to capture variations across gangs, but they are not necessary definers of a street gang. . . .

A Brief Review of the Definitional Problem

The definitional issue has probably been the stickiest one that gang scholars have had to confront in the almost eight decades since Frederic Thrasher's pioneering efforts in Chicago (1927). All of the attention paid to it has not until now yielded much consensus, a fact which in itself testifies to the complexity of the issue and the need felt by all gang scholars to find a useful and acceptable approach.

Suppose, for the sake of argument, that we were to assess the size and location of America's street gang problems and implicitly lay out the rationales for national gang policy by using a definition of gangs that had essentially no form, which said, essentially, that a gang is any group that you or other responsible people think is a gang. Using such an amorphous definition would make it very difficult to grasp our subject matter, wouldn't it?

Yet this is precisely what has happened. The National Youth Gang Center, on behalf of the U.S. Department of Justice's Office of Juvenile Justice and Delinquency Prevention, has carried out several national, annual surveys of thousands of police and sheriff's jurisdictions. In doing so, they have noted the locations of most gangs and provided a national estimate of the number of gangs and gang members in the United States. Relatively recent figures (National Youth Gang Center, 1999) put these numbers at 30,818 gangs and 846,428 gang members, a level of precision that defies credulity. The instructions to the law enforcement respondents to the gang survey are to include as a youth gang "a group of youths or young adults in your jurisdiction that you or other responsible persons in your agency or community are willing to identify or classify as a 'gang'" (1999: 45).

What sorts of problems does such a nondefinition yield? According to the NYGC report on the 1996 survey (National Youth Gang Center, 1998), 58% of respondents included taggers, 24% included satanic groups, 22% included "posses" and "crews,"

20% included stoners, and 5% included terrorist groups. Further, many respondents explicitly failed to exclude "unsupervised youth groups," a term that would include almost any friendship group at some point in its members' adolescence. Twenty-eight percent of respondents in large cities included these friendship groups, as did 33% in suburban counties, 38% in small cities, and 49% in rural counties.

Given these figures, it seems inevitable that the NYGC figures provide a substantial overestimate of gangs and gang members.[2] One would predict that the figures would be particularly suspect in small jurisdictions where minority populations are smaller and would therefore yield unusually high proportions of nonminority gangs. And this is exactly what happened: the figure for white gangs is 14%. Having been alerted to this problem, the NYGC added an item to its third annual national survey. At the very end of the questionnaire, NYGC asked its respondents how many of their gangs would fit under a modified definition that read as follows:

> A group of youths or young adults in your jurisdiction whose involvement in illegal activities over months or years marks them in their own view and in the view of the community and police as different from most other youthful groups. Do not include motorcycle gangs, hate or ideology groups, prison gangs, or other exclusively adult gangs.

This alternative definition adds durability and criminal identity. NYGC's preliminary analysis of the effect of adopting this modified definition suggests that its previous estimates were somewhat off base. The new data indicated that the number of jurisdictions with gangs was overestimated by 12%, and the number of gangs was overestimated by 26%. These are not trivial differences, and they alert us to the major effects that definitional disparities can yield.

There have been no other, comparable national surveys of the gang situation, although Miller (1980), Spergel (1995), Spergel and Curry (1990), and Maxson and Klein (1995) have used nonrepresentative samples for other research purposes. Thus we cannot know what figures might result from a more narrowly constructed definition of street gangs. Leaving aside antiscientific suggestions that the definitional problem is simply too difficult to merit attention (Horowitz, 1990), we offer what have probably been the most influential attempts to define gangs. Five, in particular, will set the stage for adopting the consensus Eurogang definition as a way to move forward.

The earliest of the five definitions was Thrasher's characterization of a gang as "an interstitial group originally formed spontaneously, and then integrated through conflict" (1927: 57). Thus marginalization, organizational informality, and violence (*conflict* meant intergang fighting here) were seen as central by Thrasher. All three themes are recurrent in more recent gang descriptions.

The second definition was offered by Klein (1971), based on his study of five large clusters of gangs in Los Angeles and on a review of gang structures described in the literature to that date. The definition is of juvenile gangs, specifically, and stresses a social-psychological framework:

[A juvenile gang is] any denotable adolescent group of youngsters who (a) are generally perceived as a distinct aggregation by others in their neighborhood, (b) recognize themselves as a denotable group (almost invariably with a group name), and (c) have been involved in a sufficient number of delinquent incidents to call forth a consistent negative response from neighborhood residents and/or enforcement agencies. (1971: 13)[3]

Twenty-five years later, Klein (1995) admitted to so much controversy over this or any other definition that he backed off from his earlier stance to approach the problem in two ways. Emphasizing the term *street gang*, he first excluded certain groups—terrorists, football hooligans, motorcycle gangs, and prison gangs, for instance—and then simply characterized gangs in terms of common descriptors: age, gender, ethnicity, territoriality, and criminal patterns and orientation.

The third much-cited definition was offered by Walter Miller (1980) based on his interviews with police officials, media, and others across the country in the mid-1970s. This definition was basically a distillation of the gang dimensions offered by his informants, almost a popularity poll to determine the most common elements:

A youth gang is a self-formed association of peers, bound together by mutual interests, with identifiable leadership, well-developed lines of authority, and other organizational features, who act in concert to achieve a specific purpose or purposes which generally include the conduct of illegal activity and control over a particular territory, facility, or type of enterprise. (1980: 121)

This definition captures many of the descriptors of gangs noted by various scholars in addition to Miller's respondents but attributes more formal organizational properties than most scholars might accept. The question of how well organized street gangs are has become one of the more contentious issues between scholars and practitioners.

The reader will note that Thrasher, Klein, and Miller all include involvement in illegal activities as one of their definitional components. This contrasts with the fourth of the commonly cited definitions, that of James F. Short, Jr.:

Gangs are groups whose members meet together with some regularity, over time, on the basis of group-defined criteria of membership and group-defined organizational characteristics; that is, gangs are non-adult-sponsored, self-determining groups that demonstrate continuity over time. (1996: 5)

Short emphasizes one element common to the Thrasher, Klein, and Miller definitions—self-determination of the group by its members—but significantly and deliberately avoids any connection to illegal activities. The rationale for this exclusion is that retaining illegal behaviors in the definition creates a tautology, a circular argument, in studying gangs in order to understand and predict their illegal behavior. Further, it overestimates the centrality of criminal activity to gang life and concerns.

We can accept the second of these concerns: gangs normally form for reasons of identity, status, need for belonging, and perceived protection, not primarily to commit crimes. But we cannot accept the tautological argument. First, because gangs vary so widely in their criminal orientations and involvement, these can be studied without circularity; i.e., one can readily predict to levels, types, and circumstances of criminal involvement. Second, crime is *not* the only aspect we study and predict. The dependent variables of gang research often include cohesiveness, leadership, organizational sophistication, size, gender, ethnic variations, community embeddedness, and so on. Including criminal involvement or orientation in the definition facilitates rather than hinders such research.

Common to all four of these attempts was a process of deriving definitions inductively from observations and experience with gangs. Each was concerned with specifying critical elements of *informal* groups: gangs don't normally come to us with constitutions and bylaws, charters, organizational charts, or written credos to which members subscribe. Thus, definitional approaches must to some extent be ad hoc and reflective of the definer's experience.

This contrasts starkly with the fifth definition, which was carefully crafted in the late 1980s to serve a specific purpose, the establishment of a *legal* category of gangs in order to enhance the ability of law enforcement to suppress gangs and incarcerate gang members. This definition has become widely accepted by public officials and the media as "real," with some unfortunate consequences. Since copied in many states, that law enforcement definition was originally embodied in the California Penal Code (section 186.22) and legislation known as the Street Terrorism Enforcement and Prevention (S.T.E.P.) Act (enacted January 1, 1993). It referred specifically to "the criminal street gang" as

> any ongoing organization, association, or group of three or more persons, whether formal or informal, having as one of its primary activities the commission of one or more of the criminal acts enumerated in paragraphs (1) to (8), inclusive, of subdivision (E), which has a common name or common identifying sign or symbol, whose members individually or collectively engage in or have engaged in a pattern of criminal gang activity.

The criminal acts referred to included felony assault, robbery, homicide, narcotics offenses, shooting into an inhabited dwelling, arson, witness (or victim) intimidation, and vehicle theft. The legal haziness of "youth gang" or "street gang" is replaced by the critical term *criminal street gang*, and this in turn is defined by reference to the most serious offenses and those that are stereotypical of gang activity. Thus the gang has become reified by police

and prosecutors' aims and concerns, with little reference to depictions accumulated over decades by gang research.[4]

As the public has come to accept this definition, street gangs have become demonized as purposefully criminal conspiracies, as violent organizations, and lost their informal, street-corner characterization. Further, any sense of the variations in gang structures and activities is lost in the definition in the S.T.E.P. Act. Reality is replaced by the goals of law enforcement: to label youth as gang members and to incarcerate them for as long as possible. Gangs may not have changed much, but their depiction most certainly has.

As a case in point, consider the suburban California county prosecutor in the case of three white boys who assaulted another during a confrontation at the beach in 1999. The prosecutor offered a plea bargain to the defendants, reducing the charges in exchange for an admission that they were members of a gang. To fit under the rubric of the criminal street gang, the prosecution had to invent a new term—"bully gang"—since the relationships among the defendants did not otherwise fit either the legal or scholarly depictions of street gangs.

These five definitional approaches are far from exhaustive. There are scores of attempts in the professional literature to define street gangs. These five, however, have probably been the most influential and illustrate the very broad dimensions that definitions can take. The consensus Eurogang definition, we think, captures the necessary minimal elements and avoids the complications of a myriad of gang descriptors. This is particularly important as we lay the groundwork for describing variations in gang structures and for encouraging cross-jurisdictional, comparative research and policy. Further, it is our experience to date that this definition, emphasizing durability, street orientation, youth, and self-identity involving illegal behavior, is largely acceptable to research scholars and working practitioners alike. This consensus among both researchers and policy folks is important to our purposes in this book. In this respect, it is our best answer to Ball and Curry (1995), who express their concern about these potentially divergent perspectives as follows:

Theorists may seek a definition that will provide a term logically integrated into a larger postulatory framework, while researchers seek sufficient standardization to guide them toward the same phenomena and allow for comparisons of findings. Administrators may care less about the theoretical power or empirical applicability of a definition than the fact that it is simple enough to impose bureaucratic standardization for purposes of record keeping, and police may be interested primarily in an expedient definition allowing them to hold the collectivity responsible for criminal acts of individual members or vice versa. (1995: 227) . . .

Notes

1. *Operational* definitions are a different matter. In Eurogang Program youth surveys, and in the multi-national second International Self-Report Delinquency Program (ISRD II), the following sequence of questions is used to establish gang affiliation. Number 1 is a funneling question, numbers 2 through 6 operationalize the consensus definition, and number 7 is a self-admission report that can be evaluated by reference to the first 6 questions.

   1. Some people have a certain group of friends that they spend time with, doing things together or just hanging out.

      Do you have a group of friends like that?

      __No

      __Yes

   2. Which one of the following best describes the ages of people in your group?

      __Under twelve

      __Twelve to fifteen

      __Sixteen to eighteen

      __Nineteen to twenty-five

      __Over twenty-five

   3. Does this group spend a lot of time together in public places like the park, the street, shopping areas, or the neighborhood?

      __No

      __Yes

   4. How long has this group existed?

      __Less than three months

      __Three months but less than one year

      __One to four years

      __Five to ten years

      __Eleven to twenty years

      __More than twenty years

   5. Is doing illegal things accepted by or okay for your group?

      __No

      __Yes

   6. Do people in your group actually do illegal things together?

      __No

      __Yes

   7. Do you consider your group of friends to be a gang?

      __No

      __Yes

2. At the same time, it is reasonable to assume that there is a counter-balancing undercount of members (not of gangs) because younger members don't enter into police files until they are detected and recorded (while older members may be retained in the files well after ceasing gang activity).

3. This rather wordy definition never sat well with police officials. Said one in direct response, "I'll tell you what a gang is: it's a group of thugs. They're hoodlums, they're crooks and criminals."

4. We leave as an aside the silliness of the term "three or more persons"; gangs don't come in groups of three. This is simply linguistic gimmickry for the sake of the legislation.

References

Ball, Richard and G. David Curry. 1995. The logic of definition in criminology: Purposes and methods for defining "gangs." *Criminology* 33(2): 225–245.

Horowitz, Ruth. 1990. Sociological perspectives on gangs: Conflicting definitions and concepts. In *Gangs in America*, ed. C. Ronald Huff, 37–54. Thousand Oaks: Sage.

Klein, Malcolm W. 1971. *Street gangs and street workers*. Englewood Cliffs, NJ: Prentice-Hall.

Klein, Malcolm W. 1995. *The American street gang: Its nature, prevalence, and control*. New York: Oxford University Press.

Maxson, Cheryl L. and Malcolm W. Klein. 1995. Investigating gang structures. *Journal of Gang Research* 3(1): 33–40.

Miller, Walter B. 1980. Gangs, groups, and serious youth crime. In *Critical issues in juvenile delinquency*, ed. David Shichor and Delos H. Kelly, 115–138. Lexington: D.C. Heath.

National Youth Gang Center. 1998. *1996 National Youth Gang Survey Program summary*. Washington, D.C.: Office of Juvenile Justice and Delinquency Prevention.

National Youth Gang Center. 1999. *1997 National Youth Gang Survey: OJJDP Summary*. Washington, D.C: Office of Juvenile Justice and Delinquency Prevention.

Pawloski, Randy and Bryan Brown. (n.d.). Gang expert testimony for S.T.E.P. act, penal code sections 186.22. *Prosecutor's Brief* 20(3).

Short, James F. Jr. 1996. *Gangs and adolescent violence.* Boulder: University of Colorado, Center for the Study and Prevention of Violence.

Spergel, Irving A. 1995. *The youth gang problem: A community approach.* New York: Oxford University Press.

Spergel, Irving A. and G. David Curry. 1990. Strategies and perceived agency effectiveness in dealing with the youth gang problem. In *Gangs in America*, ed. C. Ronald Huff, 288–309. Thousand Oaks: Sage.

Thrasher, Frederic M. 1927. *The gang: A study of 1313 gangs in Chicago.* Chicago: University of Chicago Press.

CHAPTER 2

Street Gang Theory and Research: Where Are We Now and Where Do We Go from Here?

Jane Wood ■ Emma Alleyne

Theoretical advances in the study of the emergence and persistence of gangs and gang involvement lag behind the explosion of empirical gang research that has occurred over the past few decades. This article embraces the challenging task of reviewing several theoretical explanations for gang participation and marshals the empirical evidence that supports their value and reveals their limitations. Wood and Alleyne argue that gang researchers would benefit by drawing more from the psychological literature to inject a better understanding of the social psychological processes of joining gangs. Moreover, they offer a new "unified" approach that integrates individual psychological factors and social cognition with criminological concepts. Interestingly, these authors include processes that might lead to desistance from gangs as a crucial stage in their framework.

Introduction

It is a universal given that street gang membership facilitates violent behavior over and above association with offender peers, even prolifically offending peers (Klein, Weerman & Thornberry, 2006). Consequently, the problems street gangs pose to any ordered society are considerable and worthy of research attention. The aim of our review is to draw attention to the significance of existing theories and research examining how street gangs form and the activities they are involved in. Criminologists and sociologists have

Reprinted from: Jane Wood and Emma Alleyne, "Street Gang Theory and Research: Where Are We Now and Where Do We Go From Here?" *Aggression and Violent Behavior*, 15: 100–111.

produced a bounty of excellent papers, but a broadening of discipline involvement will shape and expand knowledge in a way that can only benefit the area. And so, we also present the argument that psychologists need to become more involved in the study of gangs and suggest the way forward by suggesting a theoretical framework that integrates criminological and psychological concepts.

We cannot, in this review, cover all the research on gangs since the literature is so vast. Instead, we have selected the work we consider to be representative and relevant. Neither do we set date constraints. Early gang work such as Thrasher's (1927) and Short and Strodtbeck's (1965) is as relevant today as it was historically and should have a place in any review of gangs. Most of the research we examined was conducted in the U.S.A., and so we only state the country of origin of work conducted elsewhere. As is the case with any review, more questions are raised than resolved. However, we attempt to draw some cohesion into the ongoing debates surrounding literature relating to street gangs. And in doing so, we aim to produce ideas and directions that multidisciplinary approaches to gang research might embrace. . . .

Gang Membership: Criminological Theories

While we need a clear and comprehensive definition that clarifies what a gang is we also need a comprehensive theory to guide empirical work and provide synthesis in explaining why people

become members of a gang. Criminological theoretical explanations of gang membership span
almost a century and provide us with a vast literature. In this section, we review some of the most
influential theoretical propositions of involvement
in crime and consider their value in explaining
gang membership.

Theory of Social Disorganization

While, early interest in gangs was primarily descriptive. Thrasher (1927) paved the way for the explosion
of Chicago based research and theory development
with his account of why adolescent boys become
gang members. Thrasher argued that economic
destabilization contributed to *social disorganization*,
which in turn, led to the breakdown of conventional
social institutions such as the school, the church, and
most importantly, the family, which "failed to hold
the boy's interest, neglects him or actually forces
him onto the street" (p. 340). The gradual erosion of
conventional establishments meant they were weakened and unable to satisfy the needs of the people
such that they gradually lost the ability to control
the behavior of the area's populace. Thrasher maintained that one reason why social institutions failed
to satisfy the needs of the populace was because
so many people living in disorganized areas were
immigrants. Immigrant parents were unable to help
their children adapt to their new culture due to a
lack of familiarity with local customs. Furthermore,
a lack of support from established social orders such
as schools failed to compensate for this parental
ignorance. Thrasher (1927) neatly set the failure of
conventional institutions in opposition to the thrill
and excitement offered by unconventional institutions which offered children "the thrill and zest of
participation in common interests, more especially
corporate action, in hunting, capture, conflict, flight
and escape" (p. 32–33). For Thrasher (1927) a gang
existed when it became organized, adopted a formal structure, became attached to local territory
and involved itself in conflict. Conflict was a pivotal notion for Thrasher (1927), who argued that
it resulted in the formation of gangs who created
conflict with other gangs and with the conventional
social order which opposed them.

Theory of Cultural Transmission

Thrasher's (1927) observations of social disorganization threaded into the succession of gang
research that followed. Shaw and McKay (1931,
1942) developed Thrasher's (1927) concepts by
arguing that socially disorganized neighborhoods
culturally transmit criminal traditions which are as
transmissible as any other cultural elements. For
Shaw and McKay (1931), families in poor inner
city areas have low levels of functional authority
over children, who, once exposed to delinquent
traditions, succumb to delinquent behavior. In
such a cultural climate gang membership becomes
a satisfying alternative to unsatisfactory legitimate
conventions. If family, school, church and government all fail to adequately provide for young people
young people will form indigenous groups such as
gangs which provide a social support system in
socially disorganized communities (Hill, Howell,
Hawkins, & Battin-Pearson, 1999; Lane & Meeker,
2004; Papachristos & Kirk, 2006; Spergel, 1995).
This group formation and the criminality that ema-
nates from it are passed from generation to generation via socialization, motivating young people
to deviate from conventional norms. Conversely,
conventionality dominates middle class areas and
so middle class youth are *not* exposed to delinquent traditions and *are* adequately controlled by
parents in a stable environment. Consequently for
Shaw and McKay (1931) it is the *environment* and
not the ethnic identity of the individual that determines involvement in crime.

Theory of Differential Association

Although criticisms of the "Chicago school" of
gang research for its exclusive focus on working
class criminality (e.g., Cullen, 1984) are justified,
the exception to this accusation must be the ideas of
Sutherland (1937), Sutherland and Cressey (1960,
1974). Sutherland recognized that criminal behavior is prevalent across all classes and developed
a theory of *differential association* where young
people develop the attitudes and skills necessary to
become delinquent by associating with individuals

who are "carriers" of criminal norms (Sutherland, 1937). The essence of *differential association* is that criminal behavior is learned and the principal part of learning comes from within important personal groups (Sutherland & Cressey, 1960). Exposure to the attitudes of members of personal groups that either favor or reject legal codes influences the attitudes of the individual. And people will go on to commit crimes if they are: exposed more to attitudes that favor law violation than attitudes that favor abiding by the law; exposed to law-violation attitudes early in life; exposed to law-violation attitudes over a prolonged period of time; and exposed to law-violation attitudes from people they like and respect. Once the appropriate attitudes have developed, young people learn the skills of criminality in much the same way as they would learn any skills: or by example and tutelage. Sutherland argued that a principal part of this criminal learning process is derived from small social groups such as gangs.

The appeal of *differential association* is that it not only looks to the environment for explanations of criminal behavior to explain differences in populations that other researchers such as Shaw and McKay (1931, 1942) ignored, [but] Sutherland also considered the transmission and development of psychological constructs such as attitudes and beliefs about crime. However, Sutherland's ideas also have their critics. One is that they fail to specify how much individuals need to favor crime before they become influential in a pro-criminal sense since generally people hold beliefs that justify crime only in certain situations (Agnew, 1995; Akers, 1997). Differential association has also been criticized for stating simply that pro- or anti-criminal attitudes develop through the association with others without explaining *how* this process works (Akers, 1997). Expanding the ideas of differential association by drawing on psychological social learning processes, Akers (1997) proposes that crime is learned through: the development of beliefs that crime is acceptable in some situations; the positive reinforcement of criminal involvement (e.g. approval of friends, financial gains); and the imitation of the criminal behavior of others—especially if they are people the individual values.

Empirical Findings: Social Disorganization, Cultural Transmission, Differential Association: Empirical Evidence

A wealth of empirical evidence lends support to criminological propositions such as *social disorganization* (Shaw & McKay 1930, 1942; Thrasher, 1927), *cultural transmission* of criminogenic norms (Shaw & McKay 1930, 1942) and *differential association* (Sutherland, 1937). Where there are street gangs there is also likely to be poverty, victimization, fear, and social disorganization (Chin, 1996; Goldstein, 1991; Howell & Decker, 1999; Howell, Egley, & Gleason, 2002; Huff, 1996; Klein, 1995; Knox, 1994; Spergel, 1995) and low socio-economic status (Chettleburgh, 2007; Rizzo, 2003). Young people living in neighborhoods with high rates of delinquency are more likely to commit delinquent acts than are their counterparts living in areas of low delinquency (Hill et al., 1999; Hill, Lui, & Hawkins, 2001) and gang members have higher rates of delinquency than their non-gang counterparts *before* becoming involved in gangs (Eitle, Gunkel, & van Gundy, 2004; Esbensen, Huizinga, & Weiher, 1993; Gordon et al., 2004; Huff, 1998; Schneider, 2001; Spergel, 1995). There is also a positive relationship between gang membership and family members who are criminally involved (Eitle et al., 2004; Hill et al., 2001; Kakar, 2005; Maxson, Whitlock, & Klein, 1998; Sirpal, 2002; Sharp et al., 2006), and/or are gang members themselves (Spergel, 1995). Mixing with delinquent peers has been identified as a precursor to gang membership (Amato & Cornell, 2003; Esbensen & Weerman, 2005; Hill et al., 1999, 2001; Kakar, 2005; Maxson et al., 1998; Sharp et al., 2006), as has peer pressure to commit delinquent activities (Esbensen & Weerman, 2005). Also, children/youth that are unable to integrate into societal institutions are more likely to become delinquent and join deviant peer groups as a result (Dukes, Martinez, & Stein, 1997; Hill et al., 1999).

Street youth cultures provide criminal opportunities; provide skills, contacts, and a means of accessing illegal local markets in drugs and stolen goods (Webster, MacDonald, & Simpson, 2006). They also prove the greatest impediment to desisting from drug use and criminality (Webster et al., 2006). That gangs endure and develop comes from evidence that in many of the world's cities where governance is weak and insecurity and instability dominate, organized groups such as gangs "reign" (Sullivan, 2006). In many of these instances gangs have evolved into complex, third generation gangs who have sophisticated political and social agendas (Sullivan, 2006).

Although several studies seem to support the concepts proposed by the theories outlined above, critics are quick to point out the conceptual shortcomings of this school of thought. It has been accused of seeing people as motivationally empty, without choice, and as mere vessels to be filled with society's impositions (Emler & Reicher, 1995). That gang members exercise their ability to choose is indicated by evidence showing how they drift in and out of legitimate work over time (Hagedorn & Macon, 1998) as the lucrative illegal drug labor market, despite its dangerousness, competes with the low wages, and adverse working conditions of the legitimate labor market (Bourgois, 1995).

There is also evidence suggesting no link between low socio-economic status and gang membership (Eitle et al., 2004) and that gang members may just as easily come from wealthier backgrounds (Spergel, 1995). Having delinquent peers is also not an adequate explanation for gang membership (Thornberry, 1998) although involvement in a social network to which close friends and family members already belong is a key reason why gang members join a gang (Thornberry, Krohn, Lizotte, Smith, & Tobin, 2003). However, children raised in the same household are also "variably prone" to gang involvement, which Spergel (1995) maintains shows a *personal disorganization* perspective of gang membership. The concept of *social disorganization* is also accused of being tautological; explaining delinquency in terms of disorganization when delinquency is a criterion of disorganization (Emler & Reicher, 1995). Caulfield (1991) is particularly damning of the subcultural approach, arguing that it dictates who will be members of a subcultural society and where they will live, which in turn, determines where researchers will look and

thus selection bias. Caulfield (1991) argues that subcultural theorists create images of monsters and devils who must " . . . meet certain criteria— such as being at the lower end of class, race and gender hierarchies" (p 229). It is indeed an irony that subcultural theorists attempting to highlight the inequities of the social structure may also reinforce negative stereotypes of working class peoples and immigrants. Media accounts of gang activity largely ignore the activities of White gangs (Bursik & Grasmick, 1995; Spergel, 1995) and rely primarily on stereotypes (Jankowski, 1991). Consequently, the focus of research on relatively few gangs offers us little assurance that the locations where gangs are found are representative of gang locales or that similar places do not have gangs (Tita, Cohen & Engberg, 2005). As Sanday (1990) notes, in the U.S.A., a group of middle class youth apprehended on charges of a (gang) rape had many of the classic hallmarks of a gang including a name, regular criminal activities, and a "turf." At the trial the judge noted similarities between this group and other gangs and yet the Gang Crimes Unit showed no interest in this particular gang. This, Sanday (1990) argues, was due to the group emerging from a university fraternity. If social researchers concentrate on areas where the socio-economically deprived and ethnic populations live, there is a danger that explanations of gang membership will be framed solely by socio-economic deprivation and ethnicity. Clearly we need a broader perspective if we are to adequately explain why people join gangs.

Strain Theory

The central concept of *strain theory* is that society sets universal goals for its populace and then offers the ability to achieve them to a limited number of people. The resultant inequality of opportunity causes a strain on cultural goals. This, Merton (1938) proposes, leads to anomie (Durkheim, 1893); a breakdown in the cultural structure due to an acute division between prescribed cultural norms and the ability of members to act in line with them (Merton, 1938). The consequence of anomie is that people adapt to their circumstances by adopting a specific form of behavior (Merton, 1938). Cohen (1955) depicts gang members as working class youth who experience strain resulting in status frustration. Status frustration may be resolved by the youth associating with similar others in order to "strike out" against middle class ideals and standards. In turn, this leads to the formation of a delinquent subculture where instant gratification, fighting, and destructive behavior become the new values. It is a rebellion that is considered to be right precisely because it is wrong in the norms of the larger culture. Cohen argued that a child experiences frustration and tension due to the unequal opportunities offered in a meritocratic society that claims to operate on egalitarian principles of equal opportunity. Strain results when individuals are inadequately socialized to accept the legitimate means available to them. Inadequate socialization includes: unstructured leisure time, a failure in the educational system to provide sufficient resources, and the child's misunderstanding of what school requires of him or her. Further examples of inadequate socialization include meager community resources and educational toys and facilities in the home. The child experiencing these social deprivations gradually sinks to the bottom of the educational hierarchy and experiences feelings of status frustration involving self-hatred, guilt, loss of self-esteem, self-recrimination, and anxiety. The child blames him/herself for the failure and copes with it by seeking alternative avenues for status achievement such as street gang membership (Cohen, 1955).

Theory of Differential Opportunity

Taking a different perspective on the same issue, Cloward and Ohlin (1960) found that gang members blamed the system rather than themselves for their social failure, and "waged war" against society through expressions of anger and fighting, achieving honor through a form of "macho" bravado, and developing a formidable reputation. Although *differential opportunity* is often cited as a general theory of delinquency it began as a theory of gangs (Knox, 1994). In this theory, Cloward and Ohlin (1960), like Merton (1938), explain a class difference in opportunity, but unlike Merton (1938), Cloward and Ohlin argue that opportunity

for delinquency is also limited in availability. Such differential availability of *illegitimate* means to resolve strain means that middle class children lack the opportunity to learn how to offend. Lower class children do have this opportunity and so offend more frequently. Cloward and Ohlin (1960) argue that Shaw and McKay (1931, 1942) failed to observe a differential opportunity in learning how to offend and therefore simply assumed (wrongly) that middle classes had *less inclination* to offend. Cloward and Ohlin agree with Sutherland's (1937) ideas that young people learn how to offend from older, more experienced offenders. However, they point out that Sutherland failed to consider how access to "criminal schools" varied across the social structure while their theory unites two sociological traditions: *access to legitimate means* (Merton, 1938; Cohen, 1955) and *access to illegitimate means* (Sutherland, 1937). Agnew (1992) developed strain theory further by identifying specific forms of strain (irrespective of class): "(1) the actual or anticipated failure to achieve positively valued goals, (2) the actual or anticipated removal of positively valued stimuli, (3) the actual or anticipated presentation of negative stimuli" (p. 74). Each of these strains may have an increasing effect on delinquency and so there will be individual differences in response to the strain experienced (Agnew, 1992).

Strain Theory and Differential Opportunity: Empirical Evidence

Each of these strains threads through the gang literature. For instance, research shows that gangs compensate for strain by providing illegitimate means to achieve goals that are not achievable due to shortcomings in employment and education (Klemp-North, 2007). Gang members are likely to have lost positive role models since they often come from disorganized families and many have lost contact with a parent due to death, separation, or divorce (Klemp-North, 2007). Gang members are also more exposed to negative influences, such as drugs and delinquent peers (Sirpal, 2002; Klemp-North, 2007). Preteen stress exposure has been identified as a risk factor for gang membership (where deviance acts as a coping mechanism for unattainable goals, Eitle et al., 2004) as have poor parenting skills (Eitle et al., 2004; Hill et al., 1999; Sharp et al., 2006; Thornberry et al., 2003), and mental health issues (Hill et al., 1999). The inability to counteract any or all of the three types of strain with appropriate coping mechanisms may mean gang membership becomes a coping strategy for negative emotions such as anger, frustration, and anxiety (Eitle et al., 2004; Klemp-North, 2007), the need for personal development (Spergel, 1995), and a lack of confidence and self-esteem (Dukes, Martinez, & Stein, 1997). Some researchers claim there is no relationship between gang membership and self-esteem (Bjerregaard & Smith, 1993). However, other findings show that when the gang's esteem rises (due to success in delinquent and antisocial activities) so too does the self-esteem of previously low esteem gang members (Dukes et al., 1997).

One problem with strain theory is that although it explains some of the reasons why youth may join gangs it fails to explain why most lower class youth eventually lead law-abiding lives even though their economic status remains static (Goldstein, 1991) or why many youth who experience strain do not offend (Webster et al., 2006). Thirty three percent of youth living in deprived areas and who had never offended had experienced significant trauma such as, acrimonious parental divorce, domestic violence, parental institutionalization in prison or mental health units, family estrangement from siblings, and being bought up in the care system (Webster et al., 2006). Moreover, far from rebelling against middle class norms, many gang members actually endorse middle class values (Klein, 1995; Sikes, 1997). In an ethnographic study of female gang members, Sikes (1997) noted how most members expressed the wish to enter various professions such as nursing or teaching, despite a low attendance at school, a varied criminal record and a realistic chance of being killed while engaged in gang activity. Many gang members also spend a great deal of their time engaged in conventional pursuits by taking steps to find a job, taking part in sports, and making plans for the future such as enlisting in the Navy (Hughes & Short, 2005).

This research implies that many gang members are optimistic in their expectations for their futures and contrasts with the depressed outlook one might expect from working class youth who recognize that their chances of legitimate success are blocked by the unequal class system imposed on them. It would seem that strain theorists overestimate many deviant youths' philosophic consideration of their sociological reality. It seems more likely that delinquent youth act more in accordance with the current state of their lives than they do with perceptions of a future blocked by social inequity.

A further criticism of strain theory is that research shows that youth who have the most money supplied by their families (i.e., pocket money) are often those who become involved in gangs (Knox & Tromanhauser, 1991). This research questions the concept that the lower the economic status of the individual, the greater likelihood there is of their subcultural affiliation. Research also shows that families of non-gang youth are more likely to help their children with homework than are families of gang involved youth (Knox et al., 1992), which may mean that parental *time* rather than money is a protective factor in whether youth become gang involved.

Clearly, strain theory fails to account for many of the findings regarding gang membership. The notable (and often overlooked) work conducted by Short and Strodtbeck (1965) compared white gangs, black gangs, lower class youth, and middle class youth (over 500 in each group). Data was collected from multiple sources using a variety of methodologies, including: systematic observations, interviews with gang and non-gang members, and reports from gang workers. Not a single gang resembled any one of the theories proposed by Sutherland, Cohen, and Cloward and Ohlin. Short and Strodtbeck (1965) also raised the question of just which culture it is that delinquents presumably oppose. They also challenged the assumption that gangs oppose the middle class white American culture since so many ethnic minorities adhere to their own cultures.

Control, or Social Bond Theory

Control theory (Gottfredson & Hirschi, 1990; Hirschi, 1969) neatly diverts the attention of research away from why offenders offend, to why conformists *do not* offend? Where strain theory's central premise is the *presence* of negative relationships in the development of delinquency, control theory focuses on the *absence* of key relationships (Agnew, 1992; Klemp-North, 2007). Like strain theory and social disorganization theory, control theory posits that communities with a deteriorating social structure are a breeding ground for delinquency. The central contention of control theory is that people are inherently disposed to offend because offending offers short term gains (e.g., immediate money) and the central aim of those with criminal dispositions is to satisfy desires in the quickest and simplest way possible (Gottfredson & Hirschi, 1990). Offending is prevented by the social bond, which operates on psychological constructs such as the individual's conscience. However, a breakdown in social bonds during childhood leaves a child free to act on his/her natural inclinations without negative emotional repercussions.

Initially, control theory emphasized the restraining power the justice system had on delinquency (Gottfredson & Hirschi, 1990; Hirschi, 1969) and is therefore fundamentally tied up with deterrence theories. However, control theorists generally agree that conforming to legitimate social structures does not occur simply because social norms are *imposed on* people via societal processes (e.g., the justice system and deterrence). Social norms are effective because people *internalize* them through a socialization process where formal sanctions are reinforced by informal sanctions (Fagan & Meares, 2008). Hirschi (1969) noted that internalizing norms is mediated by attachment to others because adequately socialized children are concerned about the reaction of significant others to their behavior. The child is committed to others and does all s/he can to protect precious relationships, including internalizing significant others' rules in the form of self-control. "Insofar as the child respects (loves and fears) his parents, and adults in general, he will accept their rules" (Hirschi, 1969, p. 30). By abstaining from immediate gratification of desires to achieve long-term goals the child also shows commitment to a positive future.

Gottfredson and Hirschi (1990) developed this idea by explaining in their general theory of crime

that the cause of low self-control and hence delinquency is inadequate child rearing and can occur in any social class. Adequate child rearing includes: monitoring the child's behavior and recognizing and punishing deviant behavior. The result will be " . . . a child more capable of delaying gratification, more sensitive to the interests and desires of others, more independent, more willing to accept restraints on his activity and more unlikely to use force or violence to attain his ends" (p 97).

Adequate child rearing is vulnerable to impediments including: parents who do not care for their child, parents that care but who are unable to provide adequate supervision, parents able to provide both care and supervision but who are unable to identify a behavior as wrong, or parents who are disinclined or unable to provide punishment for the behavior (Gottfredson & Hirschi, 1990). To their credit, the authors emphasize that supervision and punishment should be conducted in a loving way and that parental disappointment is a more effective control mechanism than corporal punishment. Thus, they do not endorse the harsh and punitive sanctions that control theorists have been accused of favoring (e.g., Currie, 1985).

Gottfredson and Hirschi (1990) suggest that homes most at risk of producing delinquent children are those with criminal parents because they fail to recognize their children's criminal behavior and single parents because the lone parent is unable to adequately monitor the child's behavior and lacks psychological support from another adult. Introducing a stepparent may not improve the situation as the new family member may have little time or affection for the child which will create familial discordance and do little to alleviate child rearing problems. Working mothers also put children at risk because they cannot adequately supervise their children. Schools may help socialize children, but only if parents do not oppose any attempts to instill self-discipline into the child.

Control Theory: Empirical Evidence

Although Gottfredson and Hirschi (1990) do not directly address the involvement of young people in gangs, social control theory has been used to predict the onset of gang membership (Thornberry, 2006) and has been found to moderate and predict levels of self-reported delinquency (Huebner & Betts, 2002). A lack of commitment to a positive future is evidenced by gang members showing little or no commitment at school (Hill et al., 1999; Brownfield, 2003). However, more in line with strain theory, gang members *do* show commitment to delinquent peers (Esbensen et al., 1993). Gang members also experience an absence of parental role models and family disorganization (Klemp-North, 2007), and poor parental management skills (Eitle et al., 2004; Hill et al., 1999; Sharp et al., 2006; Thornberry et al., 2003) particularly if it occurs alongside a child's impulsivity and risk-seeking tendencies (Esbensen et al., 2001). Yet, since poor parental management is likely to be a causal factor for impulsivity and risk-seeking, it is pointless considering these variables separately (Gibbs, Giever, & Martin, 1998; Lattimore, Tittle, & Grasmick, 2006).

On the face of it evidence that youth from single parent families, families with one parent and other adults and youth with no parents are more likely to become gang members than are youth from two parent (even stepparent) households (Hill, Howell, Hawkins, & Battin-Pearson, 1999) seems to support control theory. However, family process variables have been found to play a much smaller role in gang membership (Thornberry et al., 2003) than control theory suggests. Research also shows that bonds with parents (attachment) and poor family management are not as strongly related to gang membership as family structure is (Hill et al., 1999). Even though parental supervision relates to gang membership, the relationship is only very modest (LeBlanc & Lanctot, 1998). This suggests that familial control is not as pivotal a factor in gang membership as control theory suggests. Even in families where parents attempt to control their children, discipline is not a simple solution to delinquency since it can lead to a greater likelihood of delinquency *regardless* of parental attachments (Wells & Rankin, 1988). Indeed, many gang members claim they were often physically punished by authoritarian fathers until they either left home, or retaliated with similar aggression (Klein, 1995).

There is also evidence that even within gangs legitimate social norms continue to be acknowledged. For example, gang members provide financial aid (albeit from drug trade profits) to disadvantaged communities and provide law and order services, security escorts for recreational programs and assist impoverished households by supplying groceries, free transportation and manpower (Venkatesh, 1997). It is also paradoxical that, while gang membership may be considered to occur because of a *breakdown* in formal and informal social control, research offers us examples of gangs that *provide* social control. For instance, the shared aims of gang leaders and upstanding citizens in middle class neighborhoods have resulted in a more stable and safe environment because gangs offer social control to the community and have been known to "police" neighborhood events even better than the police (Patillo, 1998).

Also, although control theory proposes that informal social control breaks down and offending results, the theory fails to adequately explain how informal social controls might be re-established. For instance, some social control theorists argue that a propensity for criminal involvement is stable throughout life and desistance from crime only occurs when there is a change in opportunity for crime (Gottfredson & Hirschi, 1990). However, evidence shows that it is the effect of social controls that urge people to stop offending. For instance, gang members leave the gang in favor of fatherhood (Moloney, Mackenzie, Hunt & Joe-Laidler, 2009) and employment, military service and marriage all contribute to a cessation of offending (Sampson & Laub, 2001). It therefore seems that social controls may be more flexible than control theory suggests and that even if informal social controls *break down* to the extent that youth become involved in delinquency, they *maintain* influence during the period of delinquency and can be *re-established* sufficiently to facilitate desistance. This supports the argument that conventional theories fail to incorporate a social contextual dimension to the study of gangs (Bursik & Grasmick, 1993; Jankowski, 1991; Spergel, 1995).

A Role for Psychology?

Overall, criminological theories used to explain gang membership pay scant attention to the social psychological processes involved in joining a gang (Thornberry et al., 2003). Some researchers have examined the psychological characteristics of gang members by, for example, looking at the interaction effects of neighborhood and personality traits of gang members. Youth who live in disorganized neighborhoods (i.e., with a high turnover of residents) and who have psychopathic tendencies (i.e. higher levels of hyperactivity and lower levels of anxiety and pro-social tendencies) are five times more likely to become gang members than youth without this configuration of traits (Dupéré, Lacourse, Willms, Vitaro, & Tremblay, 2007). Such youth are also less sensitive to parental attempts at supervision (Dupéré et al., 2007). Gang membership is even more likely if these youth live in an adverse family environment (Lacourse et al., 2006). We also know from research findings that gang members hold more negative attitudes to authority (Kakar, 2008) such as the police (Lurigio, Flexon & Greenleaf, 2008). Risk factors for gang membership also function on individual differences such as lower IQ levels (Spergel, 1995); learning difficulties and mental health problems (Hill et al., 1999) and low self-esteem (Dukes et al., 1997).

More recently, interactional theory (Thornberry, 1987; Thornberry & Krohn, 2001) has elaborated earlier criminological theories by proposing that gang membership results from a reciprocal relationship between the individual and: peer groups, social structures such as poor neighborhood and poor family, weakened social bonds, and a learning environment that fosters and reinforces delinquency (Hall, Thornberry, & Lizotte, 2006). Gang membership may result from *selection* where gangs select and recruit members who are already delinquent; from *facilitation* where gangs provide opportunities for delinquency to youth who were not delinquent beforehand (Gatti et al., 2005; Gordon et al., 2004; Thornberry, Krohn, Lizotte, & Chard-Wierschem, 1993), and *enhancement* where gang members are recruited from a population of high-risk youth who, as gang members, become more delinquent (Gatti et al., 2005; Thornberry et al., 1993).

Interactional theory also acknowledges that even within gangs, not all members are alike. For instance some gang members are transient and some are stable. High levels of delinquency before joining a gang positively relates to the length of time a member remains in a gang, whereas youth who were not delinquent before joining a gang are more likely to be temporary members (Gatti et al., 2005). Consequently, individual differences seem to be gaining conceptual importance in the development of gang theory and as such there is a role for psychology to add to this theoretical development.

There are many questions that psychology could address. Personality traits (e.g. Dupéré et al., 2007) already seem to be influential in determining who will join a gang. However, we also need to understand more about how and if, informal social controls are internalized and whether they may be either discarded in favor of new norms (such as gang rules) or adapted and used alongside new ones. As children grow they may seek a status that differs from the one prescribed by the legitimate social order taught by parents and teachers (Anderson, 1999). Young people may be tempted into gangs because they offer the potential to gain respect and status (Anderson, 1999). Knox (1994) described gangs as exerting two types of social power that attract youth: coercive power—the threat or actual use of force and violence; and the power to pay, buy, or impress, and to delegate status and rank to its members. As such, gangs reflect universal needs among young people for status, identity and companionship (Klein, 1995). However, people experience moral conflicts when they come across benefits requiring immoral behavior (Bandura, 1990). As a result, people engage in what Bandura (2002) described as moral disengagement strategies, "cognitive restructuring of inhumane conduct into benign or worthy behavior" (p. 101). We do know that youth will set aside their moral standards if by doing so they will be accepted by a chosen group (Emler & Reicher, 1995). As such, social cognitive processes such as moral disengagement may help explain the process of *how* youth disengage from the informal social controls they have learned in favor of the rewards gang membership offers. There is also the possibility of social learning aspects to gang membership. Young boys look up to gang members, mimic them, and aspire to gang membership (Hughes & Short, 2005) and gang films depicting characters rewarded for gang-like behaviors act as a blueprint for young aspiring gang members (Przemieniecki, 2005). Consequently, youth may adapt, modify, or discard their existing social controls in favor of what they *perceive* as the attractive or even "glamorous" attributes of gang membership. What is not clear is why gang membership continues to be attractive to youth when gang members, relative to non-gang members, have a greater chance of violent victimization, experience higher levels of sexual assault (for males and females), are more likely to experience violent dating victimization, and suffer serious injuries from fighting (Taylor, Freng, Esbensen, & Peterson, 2008; Gover, Jennings, & Tewksbury, 2009).

We clearly need to understand more about gang membership. For example, are female gangs mere satellites of male gangs as they are often regarded (Hagedorn & Moore, 2006) or are they independent entities who have their own set of motivations for membership? If so are these motivations similar or dissimilar to those of their male counterparts? Also, why is sexual assault in the home a greater antecedent to female gang membership than it is for male membership (Chesney-Lind, Sheldon & Joe, 1996)? Further, we need to understand more about the changing structure of gangs. For instance, why are many gangs becoming increasingly multi racial and multi ethnic (Howell, Egley & Gleason, 2002; cf Howell, 2007; Starbuck, Howell, & Lindquist, 2001)?

However, we must also be aware of the pitfalls of the gang myths (Howell, 2007) peddled out by sections of the media or even by gang members themselves who, for protective purposes, are intent on appearing more dangerous than they are (Felson, 2006). Such myths can mislead even the most conscientious researchers and undermine research findings (Howell, 2007). It also needs to be considered that individual differences do not apply *solely* at the individual level. No two gangs are alike and community experiences of gang problems vary widely. Such variance is frustrating to the media and others who thrive on simplicity and sweeping generalizations (Esbensen & Tuisinki, 2007). The only way we can counteract the perpetuation of myths and errors is by rigorous *theoretically derived* empirical work that includes psychological

factors relevant to street gang membership. So, yes, there is a definite role for psychology in street gang research.

The Role for Psychology

Too much research has ignored theory and launched itself into findings that offer some insight but do little to marry the literature and expand our overall understanding of the etiology of gang membership. Why do gangs form? They probably form to fulfill the needs that any adolescents have: peer friendship, pride, identity development, enhancement of self-esteem, excitement, the acquisition of resources, and goals that may not, due to low-income environments, be available through legitimate means (Goldstein, 2002). They may offer a strong psychological sense of community, a physical and psychological neighborhood, a social network, and social support (Goldstein, 1991). In short, gangs form for the same reasons that any other group forms (Goldstein, 2002). Social psychology offers a wealth of comprehensive theories explaining the dynamics of groups and each offers the potential for fruitful research into the question of gang formation (Goldstein, 1991, 2002). For instance *social comparison theory* (Festinger, 1954; Schachter, 1959) tells us that people group together because doing so provides useful comparisons of personal attitudes, behavior, etc. with those of others. *Social exchange theory* (Kelley & Thibaut, 1978; Thibaut & Kelley, 1959) is where group membership is valued according to its benefits and costs. *Self categorization theory* (Turner, 1987) explains how a person's sense of self is derived from learning what it means to be a member of a specific group. Other theories such as *social identity theory* (Tajfel & Turner, 1986), *social dominance theory* (Sidanius & Pratto, 1999) and *realistic conflict theory* (Sherif, 1966) offer us the potential to explain inter gang conflict (Goldstein, 2002). However, no *one* theory, either criminological or psychological, has the potential to fully explain the etiology of gang membership. A theoretical framework specific to gang membership that integrates sociological, criminological and psychological perspectives would do much to guide research and develop theory further.

Theory Knitting

A good theory should be able to explain and predict behavior (e.g., Newton-Smith, 2002). It should be coherent, consistent, and unify aspects of a phenomenon that appear to be diverse, to provide a clear and comprehensible account of the world. Theory knitting refers to integrating the best *existing* ideas into a new framework (Ward & Hudson, 1998). It involves identifying the common and unique ideas from existing theories so that good ideas are not lost (Ward & Beech, 2004). An integrated theory of gang membership should therefore bring together the good ideas contained in current theories into a model that provides explanatory power and *testable*

hypotheses. Such a model will facilitate the examination of specific aspects of gang membership and the further development of theory.

An Integrated Model of Gang Membership

With this in mind we present a *very preliminary framework* of the processes leading to and from gang membership. This framework draws together concepts from criminological theory and integrates them with relevant *psychological* factors (see Fig. 2.1). It includes concepts from similar models (e.g., Howell & Egley, 2005) to provide a more comprehensive framework with testable hypotheses which

Figure 2.1 A Unified Theory of Gang Involvement

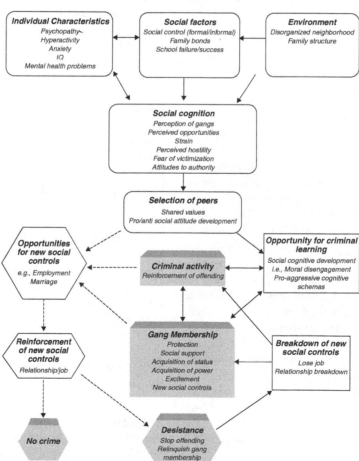

may be used to guide empirical examinations of why youth *may or may not* join gangs. By illustrating the pathway into criminality and/or gang membership together with alternative non-criminal pathways, and pathways out of criminality and/or gang membership, this model provides a more all-round conceptualization of criminality, gang membership and non-criminal involvement. And it is the inclusion of alternative pathways together with key psychological and criminological factors which distinguishes it from other similar models.

Social and Individual Factors

As the model shows, *social factors, individual characteristics* and *environment* are important starting points for a youth's social development. Family structure and type of neighborhood may go hand in hand since families with poor or unstable structures (i.e., frequent changes in parental romantic partners) are potentially more likely to live in disorganized neighborhoods. However, this model also allows for the consideration of *organized* neighborhoods as starting points for gang involved youth, since even if the neighborhood and family are stable, individual factors such as psychopathic personality traits, high levels of anxiety, hyperactivity, low IQ, low self-esteem, and/or mental health problems may influence an inclination for gang membership. Environmental factors will affect social factors such as the levels of formal and informal control. Disorganized neighborhoods may be difficult to police (formal control) and informal social controls such as parental supervision may be problematic depending on family structure, which, in turn, may weaken family bonds. If environmental factors influence levels of informal control then they will also have an indirect effect on school performance, since youth who are poorly supervised are less likely to succeed at school. Organized neighborhoods, on the other hand, may have higher levels of formal social control and more stable families. However, individual factors will affect social factors regardless of the type of neighborhood. Youth who: have psychopathic traits, are hyperactive, have high levels of anxiety, have low IQ, and mental health problems will present more social challenges for families, thus leading to a decrease in informal

social control, and a strain on family bonds. These individual factors will also affect the youth's ability to perform at school and the school's ability to manage the youth. In turn, school failure, weak family bonds, and social controls, may impact on a youth's levels of anxiety, mental health problems and self-esteem.

Social Perception

Individual factors and social factors will shape the youth's *social perception* of his/her world. The presence of gangs in the neighborhood will help shape a youth's attitudes and beliefs about gang membership and crime. If gangs are not active in the neighborhood, youth will develop perceptions of gang membership and crime from media images or from vicarious experience such as associating with youth from neighborhoods where gangs are active (e.g., at school). In conjunction with perceptions of gangs will be the youth's perception of the availability of legitimate opportunities. Personal failure at school and the likely associated low self-esteem will increase a youth's negative perceptions of the chance to take advantage of available legitimate opportunities, and may lead to strain. Neighborhoods peppered with gangs and crime may also make the youth fearful of victimization, which coupled with perceptions of limited opportunities, may lead to perceptions that the world is a hostile place. Negative attitudes to authority may develop if youth attribute their school failure to school officials rather than the self. And if crime is high in the neighborhood, and formal social control is low youth may develop hostile or even contemptuous perceptions of the police and see them as failing (or not bothering) to protect people in poor neighborhoods. Perceptions of social environment and shared values such as a mutual like/dislike of school, mutual attitudes to authority, and mutual fear of victimization will influence the youth's selection of peers.

Selection of Peers

The *selection of peers* will foster and strengthen the youth's existing attitudes and social cognitions. Youth who are doing well at school and who have a solid relationship with parents who supervise him/her will associate with peers who share these attributes (regardless of neighborhood structure and crime rates). These associations will strengthen the youth's pro-social moral standards which will make them less inclined to morally disengage. Youth who associate with pro-social peer groups are also likely to capitalize on further legitimate opportunities for informal social controls such as employment, solid romantic relationships and parenthood, and so they avoid criminal involvement. This legitimate pathway will strengthen legitimate informal social controls and provide youth with opportunities to progress, for example, in the workplace. On the other hand, even if youth are doing well at school and have solid familial backgrounds they may be tempted to associate with delinquent peers due to the lure of protection, excitement, status, and power. However, this association may be fleeting since there will be conflict between the youth's existing pro-social attitudes, morality, and school success, and the group ethos. These youth may also find that the rest of the group does not view them as "fitting in." In short, these youth may do little more than "flirt" with a more deviant lifestyle.

Opportunity for Criminal Learning

Association with delinquent peers means that the youth is provided with an *opportunity for criminal learning* and criminal involvement is likely to follow, which provides further criminal learning opportunities. The selection of delinquent peers will foster any existing anti-social attitudes the youth has. To become criminally active a youth will need to set aside any pro-social moral standards s/he may have so that harmful behavior is cognitively reconstructed into acceptable behavior (i.e. moral disengagement). In addition, by associating with delinquent peers, the youth is likely to develop pro-aggression beliefs and attitudes that, in the presence of pro-aggressive reinforcement (e.g., peer approval), will result in positive appraisal of personal aggression. These attitudes and beliefs, in turn, foster the development of information processing biases and deficits in a pro-aggressive direction, and are stored in memory as cognitive schemas to guide future behavior. These schemas

develop primarily during childhood (Huesmann, 1998), may have a lifetime influence and are resistant to change (Anderson & Bushman, 2002; see Collie, Vess, & Murdoch (2007) for a review). This implies that because the peer group's influence occurs at such a *critical* stage in the youth's life, it may well extend beyond shaping the youth's social cognitive *development* to exert an influence that is *lifelong*. As the youth becomes more involved in criminal activity he/she may also experience an increase in his/her self-esteem, and a strengthening of bonds with delinquent peers. In turn, this will all bolster his/her resolve for involvement in criminal activity.

Gang Membership

Our model shows how youth may take a pathway into criminal activity which does not necessarily include gang membership. Criminal activity may occur *independently of*, or *simultaneously to*, joining a gang. However, gang membership is likely to occur for reasons *over and above* those underlying involvement in criminal activity. Gang membership offers additional protection; possibly from threats stemming from competing criminal entities (e.g., rival drug dealers); it provides social support, offers elevated status, the chance to acquire power, and opportunities for excitement. Gang membership may also bring with it sets of rules or new social controls that members are expected to abide by—thus providing a form of familial environment. As a gang member, the youth is exposed to further opportunities for criminal learning, and s/he will become even more involved in criminal activity. Of course, hand in hand with these new opportunities for "personal enhancement" come additional chances of victimization and these may lead gang member youth to desire a gang-free life.

Desistance

As our model shows (see Fig. 2.1), desistance may occur at the criminal activity, or the gang member stage. The youth may relinquish his/her involvement in criminal activity or gang membership as they take up opportunities for informal social control such as employment and/or stable relationships. Of course these opportunities may be adversely affected if the youth has been caught and prosecuted for criminal acts. In this case the youth's criminal inclination will either dissipate (from fear of further legal repercussions) or strengthen (from the obstruction that prosecution puts in the way of legitimate opportunities). If, however, the newly acquired social controls are reinforced (e.g., opportunities to advance in employment) the youth's resolve to desist from crime may strengthen and desistance will continue. If, however, they break down (i.e., employment is lost or a relationship breaks up) then the youth may return to his/her previous lifestyle (i.e., criminal involvement and/or gang membership).

Although this model is in its *very early stages* it has the potential to expand research findings regarding gang membership and delinquency at both a psychological and a criminological level. Because it includes concepts of non involvement in crime and gangs and concepts of desistance, it allows us to make *meaningful comparisons*. As Klein (2006) so rightly observes, comparisons are all too rare in the gang literature. We can make comparisons between gang members, between abstaining and remaining gang members, and between gang and non-gang members. It is also possible to make comparisons between neighborhoods by examining the individual characteristics, social factors, and social cognitions of youth living in organized and disorganized neighborhoods. We do not suggest that this model is a panacea to all the gaps in the literature but it is a starting point and it can be developed and expanded as findings based on its concepts shed light on old and new ideas. Most importantly, it presents the integration of gang-related concepts into a coherent structure that integrates criminological and psychological ideas. Importantly, it provides us with *testable hypotheses* and we are currently engaged in research examining some of these.

Conclusion

This review considered the role of theory and research in understanding why youth join gangs and it has identified a large number of problematic issues that need to be overcome. It has shown that research is dogged by definitional difficulties and that current theoretical approaches have both value and limitations. As a result, empirical research that is guided by each of the theoretical approaches we have reviewed reflects both their value and their limitations. Nonetheless, street gang research has provided us with a wealth of empirical findings that presents us with much to consider. However, one of the problems with such a wealth of work is that confusion results as gang researchers strive to select the best theoretical path forward. This can result in what seems to be more of a competition between theories than a concerted effort to develop and merge the best theoretical propositions. The arguments we have presented show the gaps in the literature and we suggest how a multidisciplinary approach might plug them. There is a role for psychology in gang research, and if psychologists and criminologists work together to identify the reasons why youth join gangs, we will expand our knowledge and develop deeper and more meaningful explanations than are currently available. With this in mind we have presented a preliminary theoretical model of how youth may become involved in gangs. Gang research is vital and so it cannot afford to be marginalized by any discipline that might have light to shed on at least some of its multiple factors.

References

Agnew, R. (1992). Foundation for a general strain theory of crime and delinquency. *Criminology, 30,* 47–87.

Agnew, R. (1995). Strain and subcultural theories of criminality. In J. F. Sheley (Ed.), *Criminology: A contemporary handbook,* 2nd ed. Belmont: Wadsworth.

Akers, R. L. (1997). *Criminological theories: Introduction and evaluation,* 2nd ed. Los Angeles: Roxbury.

Amato, J. M., & Cornell, D. G. (2003). How do youth claiming gang membership differ from youth who claim membership in another group, such as crew, clique, posse or mob? *Journal of Gang Research, 10,* 13–23.

Anderson, E. (1999). *Code of the street: Decency, violence and the moral life of the inner city.* New York, NY: Norton and Company.

Anderson, C. A., & Bushman, B. J. (2002). Human aggression. *Annual Review of Psychology, 53,* 27–51.

Bandura, A. (1990). Selective activation and disengagement of moral control. *Journal of Social Issues, 46,* 27–46.

Bandura, A. (2002). Selective moral disengagement in the exercise of moral agency. *Journal of Moral Education, 31*, 101–119.

Bjerregaard, B., & Smith. C. (1993). Gender differences in gang participation, delinquency, and substance use. *Journal of Quantitative Criminology, 9*, 329–355.

Bourgois, P. (1995). *In search of respect: Selling crack in el barrio.* New York, US: Cambridge University Press.

Brownfield, D. (2003). Differential association and gang membership. *Journal of Gang Research, 11*, 1–12.

Bursik, R. J., Jr., & Grasmick, H. G. (1993). *Neighborhoods and crime: The dimensions of effective community control.* New York, NY: Lexington Books.

Bursik, R. J., & Grasmick, H. G. (1995). Defining gangs and gang behaviour. In M. W. Klein, C. L. Maxson, & J. Milher (Eds.), *The modern gang reader.* California: Roxbury Publishing Co.

Caulfield, S. L. (1991). Perpetuating violence through criminological theory: Subcultural theory as an ideological tool. In H. E. Pepinsky & R. Quinney (Eds.), *Criminology as peacemaking* (pp. 228–238). Bloomington, IN: Indiana University Press.

Chesney-Lind, M., Shelden, R., & Joe, K. A. (1996). Girls, delinquency and gang membership. In R. C. Huff (Ed.), *Gangs in America* (pp. 185–204). Thousand Oaks, CA: Sage Publications.

Chettleburgh, M. C. (2007). *Young thugs: Inside the dangerous world of Canadian street gangs.* Toronto, Canada: HarperCollins Publishers Ltd.

Chin, K. (1996). *Chinatown gangs.* New York, NY: Oxford University Press.

Cloward, R., & Ohlin, L. (1960). *Delinquency and opportunity.* NY: Free Press.

Cohen, A. K. (1955). *Delinquent boys: The culture of the gang.* Glencoe, IL: The Free Press.

Collie, R. M., Vess, J., & Murdoch, S. (2007). Violence-related cognition: Current research. In C. Hollin & M. McMurran (Series Ed.) & T. A. Gannon, T. Ward, A. R. Beech & D. Fisher (Vol Ed.), *Wiley series in forensic clinical psychology: Aggressive offenders' cognition theory research and practice* (pp. 179–197). Chichester, U. K.: Wiley.

Cullen, F. T. (1984). *Rethinking crime and deviance theory: The emergence of a structuring tradition.* New Jersey, US: Rowman and Allanheld Publishers.

Currie, E. (1985). *Confronting crime: An American challenge.* New York, NY: Pantheon.

Dukes, R. L., Martinez, R. O., & Stein, J. A. (1997). Precursors and consequences of membership in youth gangs. *Youth and Society, 29*, 139–165.

Dupéré, V., Lacourse, É., Willms, J. D., Vitaro, F., & Tremblay, R. E. (2007). Affiliation to youth gangs during adolescence: The interaction between childhood psychopathic tendencies and neighborhood disadvantage. *Journal of Abnormal Child Psychology, 35*, 1035–1045.

Durkheim, E. (1893). *The division of labor in society.* New York. NY: The Free Press.

Eitle, D., Gunkel, S., & van Gundy, K. (2004). Cumulative exposure to stressful life events and male gang membership. *Journal of Criminal Justice, 32*, 95–111.

Emler, N., & Reicher, S. (1995). *Adolescence and delinquency.* Oxford, UK: Blackwell Publishers Ltd.

Esbensen, F.-A., Huizinga, D., & Weiher, A. W. (1993). Gang and non-gang youth: Differences in explanatory factors. *Journal of Contemporary Criminal Justice, 9*, 94–116.

Esbensen, F.-A., & Tuisinki, K. (2007). Youth gangs in the print media. *Journal of Criminal Justice and Popular Culture, 14*, 21–28.

Esbensen, F.-A., & Weerman, F. M. (2005). Youth gangs and troublesome youth groups in the United States and the Netherlands: A cross-national comparison. *European Journal of Criminology, 2*, 5–37.

Esbensen, F.-A., Winfree, L. T., Jr., He, N., & Taylor, T. Jr. (2001). Youth gangs and definitional issues: When is a gang a gang, and why does it matter? *Crime and Delinquency, 47*, 105–130.

Fagan, J., & Meares, T. L. (2008). Punishment, deterrence and social control: The paradox of punishment in minority communities. *Ohio State Journal of Criminal Law, 6*, 173–229.

Felson, M. (2006). The street gang strategy. In M. Felson (Ed.), *Crime and nature* (pp. 305–324). Thousand Oaks, CA: Sage Publications.

Festinger, L. (1954). A theory of social comparison processes. *Human Relations, 7*, 117–140.

Gatti, E., Tremblay, R. E., Vitaro, F., & McDuff, P. (2005). Youth gangs, delinquency and drug use: A test of the selection, facilitation, and enhancement hypotheses. *Journal of Child Psychology and Psychiatry, 46*, 1178–1190.

Gibbs, J. J., Giever, D., & Martin, J. S. (1998). Parental management and self-control: An empirical test of Gottfredson and Hirschi's general theory. *Journal of Research in Crime and Delinquency, 35*, 40–70.

Goldstein, A. P. (1991). *Delinquent gangs: A psychological perspective.* Champaign, IL: Research Press.

Goldstein, A. P. (2002). *The psychology of group aggression.* West Sussex, UK: John Wiley & Sons Ltd.

Gordon, R. A., Lahey, B. B., Kawai, E., Loeber, R., Stouthamer-Loeber, M., & Farrington, D. P. (2004). Antisocial behavior and youth gang membership: Selection and socialization. *Criminology, 42*, 55–87.

Gottfredson, M. R., & Hirschi, T. (1990). *A general theory of crime.* Stanford, CA: Stanford University Press.

Gover, A. R., Jennings, W. G., & Tewksbury, R. (2009). Adolescent male and female gang members' experiences with violent victimization, dating violence and sexual assault. *American Journal of Criminal Justice, 34,* 103–115.

Hagedorn, J. M., & Macon, P. (1998). *People and folks: Gangs, crime and the underclass in a rustbelt city.* US: Lake View Press.

Hagedorn, J. M., & Moore, J. (2006). Female gangs: A focus on research. Retrieved June 10, 2009 from http://hdl.handle.net/123456789/4899

Hall, G. P., Thornberry, T. P., & Lizotte, A. J. (2006). The gang facilitation effect and neighbourhood risk: Do gangs have a stronger influence on delinquency in disadvantaged areas? In J. F. Short & L. A. Hughes (Eds.), *Studying youth gangs* (pp. 47–61). Oxford, UK: Altamira Press.

Hill, K. G., Howell, J. C., Hawkins, J. D., & Battin-Pearson, S. R. (1999). Childhood risk factors for adolescent gang membership: Results from the Seattle Social Development Project. *Journal of Research in Crime and Delinquency, 36,* 300–322.

Hill, G. H., Lui, C., & Hawkins, J. D. (2001). *Early precursors of gang membership: A study of Seattle youth.* Juvenile Justice Bulletin, Washington, DC: US Department of Justice, Office of Justice Program, OJJDP.

Hirschi, T. (1969). *Causes of delinquency.* Berkeley and Los Angeles, CA: University of California Press.

Howell, J. C. (2007). Menacing or mimicking? Realities of youth gangs. *Juvenile and Family Court Journal, 58,* 39–50.

Howell, J. C., & Decker, S. H. (1999). *The youth gangs, drugs, and violence connection.* Juvenile Justice Bulletin, Washington, DC: US Department of Justice, Office of Justice Program, OJJDP.

Howell, J. C., & Egley, A. (2005). Moving risk factors into developmental theories of gang membership. *Youth Violence and Juvenile Justice, 3,* 334–354.

Howell, J. C., Egley, A., Jr., & Gleason, D. K. (2002). *Modern day youth gangs.* Youth Gang Series Bulletin, Washington, DC: US Department of Justice, Office of Justice Program, OJJDP.

Huebner, A., & Betts, S. (2002). Exploring the utility of social control theory for youth development: Issues of attachment, involvement, and gender. *Youth & Society, 34,* 123–145.

Huesmann, L. R. (1998). The role of social information processing and cognitive schema in the acquisition and maintenance of habitual aggressive behavior. In R. G. Geen & E. Donnerrstein (Eds.), *Human aggression: Theories, research and implications for social policy* (pp. 73–109). San Diego, CA: Academic Press.

Huff, C. R. (1996). The criminal behavior of gang members and non-gang at-risk youth. In C. R. Huff (Ed.), *Gangs in America* (pp. 75–102). Thousand Oaks, CA: Sage Publications.

Huff, C. R. (1998). *Comparing the criminal behavior of youth gangs and at risk youth.* Research in Brief, Washington, DC: US Department of Justice, Office of Justice Program, OJJDP.

Hughes, L. A., & Short, J. F., Jr. (2005). Disputes involving youth street gang members: Micro-social contexts. *Criminology, 43,* 43–76.

Kakar, S. (2008). Gang affiliation and negative perceptions about authority, law enforcement, and laws: Is gang affiliation a precursor to becoming a threat to homeland security and terrorism? *Journal of Gang Research, 15*(4), 65–76.

Jankowski, M. S. (1991). *Islands in the street: Gangs and American urban society.* Berkeley, CA: University of California Press.

Kakar, S. (2005). Gang membership, delinquent friends and criminal family members: Determining the connections. *Journal of Gang Research, 13,* 41–52.

Kelley, H. H., & Thibaut, J. (1978). *Interpersonal relations: A theory of interdependence.* New York, NY: Wiley.

Klein, M. W. (1995). *The American street gang.* New York, NY: Oxford University Press.

Klein, M. W. (2006). The value of comparisons in street gang research. In J. F. Short & L. A. Hughes (Eds.), *Studying youth gangs* (pp. 129–143). Oxford, UK: Altamira Press.

Klein, M. W., Weerman, F. M., & Thornberry, T. P. (2006). Street gang violence in Europe. *European Journal of Criminology, 3,* 413–437.

Klemp-North, M. (2007). Theoretical foundations of gang membership. *Journal of Gang Research, 14,* 11–26.

Knox, G. W. (1994). *An introduction to gangs.* Bristol, US: Wyndham Hall Press.

Knox, G. W., & Tromanhauser, E. D. (1991). Gangs and their control in adult correctional institutions. *The Prison Journal, 71,* 15–22.

Knox, G. W., Tromanhauser, E. D., Jackson, P. I., Niklas, D., Houston, J. G., Koch, P., et al. (1992). Preliminary findings from the 1992 Law Enforcement Mail Questionnaire Project. *Journal of Gang Research, 1,* 12–28.

Lacourse, E., Nagin, D. S., Vitaro, F., Côté, S., Arseneault, L., & Tremblay, R. E. (2006). Prediction of early-onset deviant peer group affiliation: A 12-year longitudinal study. *Archives of General Psychiatry, 63,* 562–568.

Lane, J., & Meeker, J. W. (2004). Social disorganization perceptions, fear of gang crime, and behavioral precautions among Whites, Latinos, and Vietnamese. *Journal of Criminal Justice, 32,* 49–62.

Lattimore, T. L., Tittle, C. R., & Grasmick, H. G. (2006). Childrearing, self-control, and crime: Additional evidence. *Sociological Inquiry, 76,* 343–371.

LeBlanc, M., & Lanctot, N. (1998). Social and psychological characteristics of gang members according to the gang structure and its subcultural and ethnic makeup. *Journal of Gang Research, 5,* 15–28.

Lurigio, A. J., Flexon, J. L., & Greenleaf, R. G. (2008). Antecedents to gang membership: Attachments, beliefs, and street encounters with the police. *Journal of Gang Research, 4,* 15–33.

Maxson, C. L., Whitlock, M. L., & Klein, M. W. (1998). Vulnerability to street gang membership: Implications for practice. *Social Service Review, 72,* 70–91.

Merton, R. K. (1938). Social structure and anomie. *American Sociological Review, 3,* 672–682.

Moloney, M., MacKenzie, K., Hunt, G., & Joe-Laidler, K. (2009). The path and promise of fatherhood for gang members. *British Journal of Criminology, 49,* 305–325.

Newton-Smith, W. (2002). *A companion to the philosophy of science.* Oxford: Blackwell.

Papachristos, A. V., & Kirk, D. S. (2006). Neighbourhood effects on street gang behaviour. In J. F. Short & L. A. Hughes (Eds.), *Studying youth gangs* (pp. 63–83). Oxford, UK: Altamira Press.

Patillo, M. E. (1998). Sweet mothers and gang-bangers: Managing crime in a black middle-class neighborhood. *Social Forces, 76,* 747–774.

Przemieniecki, C. J. (2005). Gang behavior and movies: Do Hollywood gang films influence violent gang behavior? *Journal of Gang Research, 12,* 41–71.

Rizzo, M. (2003). Why do children join gangs? *Journal of Gang Research, 11,* 65–74.

Sampson, R. J., & Laub, J. H. (2001). Understanding variability in lives through time: Contributions of life course criminology. In A. Piquera & P. Mazerolle (Eds.), *Life-course criminology: Contemporary and classic reading* (pp. 242–258). Belmont, CA: Wadsworth/Thomson Learning.

Sanday, P. (1990). *Fraternity gang rape: Sex, brotherhood, and privilege on campus.* New York, NY: New York University Press.

Schachter, S. (1959). *The psychology of affiliation.* Stanford: Stanford University Press.

Schneider, J. L. (2001). Niche crime: The Columbus gangs study. *American Journal of Criminal Justice, 26,* 94–103.

Sharp, C., Aldridge, J., & Medina, J. (2006). *Delinquent youth groups and offending behaviour: Findings from the 2004 Offending, Crime and Justice Survey. Home Office Online Report 14/06.* London, UK: Home Office.

Shaw, C. R., & McKay, H. D. (1931). *Social factors in juvenile delinquency.* 2, 13. Washington DC: Government Printing Office.

Shaw, C. R., & McKay, H. D. (1942). *Juvenile delinquency and urban areas.* Chicago: The University of Chicago Press.

Sherif, M. (1966). *In common predicament: Social psychology of intergroup conflict and cooperation.* Boston: Houghton-Miffin.

Short, J. F., Jr., & Strodtbeck, F. L. (1965). *Group process and gang delinquency.* Chicago, IL: University of Chicago.

Sidanius, J., & Pratto, F. (1999). *Social dominance: An intergroup theory of social hierarchy and oppression.* New York, NY: Cambridge University Press.

Sikes, G. (1997). *8 ball chicks: A year in the violent world of girl gangsters.* New York, NY: Anchor Books.

Sirpal, S. K. (2002). Familial criminality, familial drug use, and gang membership: Youth criminality, drug use, and gang membership—What are the connections? *Journal of Gang Research, 9,* 11–22.

Spergel, I. A. (1995). *The youth gang problem.* NY: Oxford.

Starbuck, D., Howell, J. C., & Lindquist, D. J. (2001). *Hybrid and other modern gangs.* Youth Gang Series Bulletin, Washington, DC: US Department of Justice, Office of Justice Program, OJJDP.

Sullivan, M. L. (2006). Are "gang" studies dangerous? Youth violence, local context, and the problem of reification. In J. F. Short & L. A. Hughes (Eds.), *Studying youth gangs* (pp. 15–35). Oxford, UK: Altamira Press.

Sutherland, E. H. (1937). *The professional thief.* US: University of Chicago Press.

Sutherland, E. H., & Cressey, D. R. (1960). A theory of differential association. *Principles of criminology,* 6th ed. Chicago: Lippincott.

Sutherland, E. H., & Cressey, D. R. (1974). *Criminology.* New York: Lippincott.

Tajfel, H., & Turner, J. C. (1986). The social identity theory of inter-group behavior. In S. Worchel & L. W. Austin (Eds.), *Psychology of intergroup relations.* Chicago, IL: Nelson-Hall.

Taylor, T. J., Freng, A., Esbensen, F.-A., & Peterson, D. (2008). Youth gang membership and serious violent victimization: The importance of lifestyles and routine activities. *Journal of Interpersonal Violence, 23,* 1441–1464.

Thibaut, J. W., & Kelley. H. H. (1959). *The social psychology of groups.* New York, NY: John Wiley & Sons.

Thornberry, T. P. (1987). Toward an interactional theory of delinquency. *Criminology, 25,* 863–891.

Thornberry, T. P. (1998). Membership in youth gangs and involvement in serious and violent offending. In R. Loeber & D. P. Farrington (Eds.), *Serious and violent offenders: Risk factors and successful interventions* (pp. 147–166). Thousand Oaks, CA: Sage Publications.

Thornberry, T. P. (2006). Membership in youth gangs and involvement in serious and violent offending. In A. J. Egley, C. L. Maxson, J. Miller & M. W. Klein (Eds.), *The modern gang reader* (pp. 224–232). Los Angeles, CA: Roxbury Publishing.

Thornberry, T. P., & Krohn, D. (2001). The development of delinquency: An interactional perspective. In S. O. White (Ed.), *Handbook of youth and justice* (pp. 289–305). New York, NY: Plenum.

Thornberry, T. P., Krohn, M. D., Lizotte, A. J., & Chard-Wierschem, D. (1993). The role of juvenile gangs in facilitating delinquent behavior. *Journal of Research in Crime and Delinquency, 30,* 55–87.

Thornberry, T. P., Krohn, M. D., Lizotte, A. J., Smith, C., & Tobin, K. (2003). *Gangs and delinquency in developmental perspective.* Cambridge: Cambridge University Press.

Thrasher, F. (1927). *The gang: A study of 1,313 gangs in Chicago.* Chicago: University of Chicago Press.

Tita, G. E., Cohen, J., & Engberg, J. (2005). An ecological study of the location of gang "set space." *Social Problems, 52,* 279–299.

Turner, J. C. (1987). *Rediscovering the social group: A self-categorization theory.* New York: Basil Blackwell.

Venkatesh, S. A. (1997). The social organization of street gang activity in an urban ghetto. *American Journal of Sociology,* 82–111.

Ward, T., & Beech, A. R. (2004). The etiology of risk: A preliminary model. *Sexual Abuse: A Journal of Research and Treatment, 16,* 271–284.

Ward, T., & Hudson, S. M. (1998). The construction and development of theory in the sexual offending area: A meta-theoretical framework. *Sexual Abuse: A Journal of Research and Treatment, 10,* 47–63.

Webster, C., MacDonald, R., & Simpson, M. (2006). Predicting criminality? Risk factors, neighbourhood influence and desistance. *Youth Justice, 6,* 7–22.

Wells, E., & Rankin, J. (1988). Direct parental controls and delinquency. *Criminology, 26,* 263–285.

CHAPTER 3

Studying Youth Gangs: Alternative Methods and Conclusions

Lorine A. Hughes

Studies of gangs tend to use either quantitative or qualitative methods and rarely integrate multiple approaches. Hughes argues that this severely limits our understanding of gangs because while each approach has strengths, each also has limits. She describes three dominant quantitative methods utilized by gang scholars and finds that while this research has generated important information about general patterns of gangs, it can't explain how and why the correlates of membership increase risk for criminal involvement and other activity. On the other hand, the two qualitative approaches have produced significant understandings of daily gang life and the way it doesn't center on crime and violence, yet have failed to generate a representative picture of gangs. Hughes critiques both quantitative and qualitative studies for employing different definitional approaches, evidencing selection bias, and presenting the potential for distortion in data. Her call for integrated, multimethod studies that can generate comparative data dovetails with Klein's argument in the article that follows.

Methodological, as well as conceptual, issues are implied by the question: Why study youth gangs? How we study gangs affects our understanding of the phenomenon and determines what remains to be learned. This article reviews the major methods that have been used to study gangs and discusses the consequences of their use for what is known about the topic.[1]

Reprinted from: Lorine A. Hughes, "Studying Youth Gangs: Alternative Methods and Conclusions," *Journal of Contemporary Criminal Justice*, May 2005, 21(2): 98–119. Copyright © 2005 by Sage Publications. Reprinted by permission from Sage Publications.

Although qualitative and quantitative research traditions typically are described in oppositional terms, I argue that they should be used together. Each tradition is based on a variety of means of collecting data; however, quantitative research tends to be more structured in the interest of sampling criteria and statistical analysis of discrete variables. Qualitative research usually is more holistic, favoring specialized and in-depth accounts over broad summation and generalization to larger populations. Because critical disconnects exist between research in each of these two traditions, findings often contradict rather than inform one another.

The Quantitative Tradition

The popularity of quantitative studies of gangs and gang-related issues soared during the 1980s and 1990s, following renewed media and public interest, statistical advances, and increased government funding.[2] Quantitative studies have taken three major forms: (a) surveys of law enforcement officials (and at times other agency personnel) regarding gangs in their jurisdictions and actions taken to control them, (b) analyses of data compiled by law enforcement agencies and/or court officials, and (c) self-reports of samples of youth and/or young adults.

Because neither the *Uniform Crime Reports* nor the National Incident-Based Reporting System provides quality data on gangs or gang-related offenses, estimates of the so-called gang problem have been derived primarily from surveys of law enforcement officials.[3] Although many of these are of limited

Errors in authual agency

scope (e.g., Quinn, Tobolowsky, & Downs, 1994; Weisheit & Wells, 2001), the collection of nationwide data recently has been elevated to a top priority. Despite widely varying findings—due, in part, to differing definitions of gangs and sampling frames—national estimates based on these efforts consistently indicate that gangs are pervasive, disproportionately involved in delinquent and violent activities, and responsible for a substantial amount of official concern, particularly in the largest U.S. cities (see Curry & Decker, 2002; Egley, Howell, & Major, 2004; M. W. Klein, 1995; W. B. Miller, 1975, 1982, 2001). General consensus also exists concerning the most common social characteristics among gang members, as perceived by law enforcement. Of the roughly 500,000 estimated gang members (plus or minus 250,000), most are reported to be male, African American and/or Hispanic (but increasingly Asian), and between age 15 and 24 years (but probably aging).

Because law enforcement and court records contain little information on gangs (and are otherwise problematic; see C. L. Maxson, 1995), few researchers rely entirely on such data. However, secondary data analyses have been useful for uncovering general patterns in the participant and offense characteristics of officially defined gang incidents. Despite varying gang definitions, analyses of Chicago Police Department data (Block & Block, 1993; Block, Christakos, Jacob, & Przybylski, 1996; Spergel, 1986) and data from the Los Angeles police and sheriff departments (Hutson, Anglin, Kyriacou, Hart, & Spears, 1995; C. L. Maxson, 1995) found that substantial amounts of delinquent and violent offending are attributable to gang members, most of whom are described as minority male youth (Black or Hispanic) in their late teens or slightly older.[4] Compared to nongang incidents, gang incidents are more visible, more violent, more likely to involve a weapon, more likely to involve strangers, and more likely to involve fear of retaliation (Bailey & Unnithan, 1994; B. Cohen, 1969; M. W. Klein & Maxson, 1989; C. L. Maxson, 1995; C. L. Maxson, Gordon, & Klein, 1985; Rosenfeld, Bray, & Egley, 1999; Shelden, Snodgrass, & Snodgrass, 1993). They also are more homogeneous with respect to such offender and victim characteristics as age, sex, race or ethnicity, gang membership, and prior record

(Bailey & Unnithan, 1994; B. Cohen, 1969; Maxson et al., 1985; Rosenfeld et al., 1999). Although drug activity appears to be increasingly common in incidents involving gang members,[5] analyses of official data do not support widely disseminated claims regarding the dominance of gangs over the drug trade (M. Klein, Maxson, & Cunningham, 1991; C. L. Maxson, 1995; Meehan & O'Carroll, 1992).

Surveys of youth and/or young adults (hereafter, surveys of youth) also assess parameters of gang phenomena. Estimates of prevalence rates of gang membership ranging from 5% to 25% have been reported from major projects initiated by the Office of Juvenile Justice and Delinquency Prevention (Denver Youth Study, Pittsburgh Youth Study, and Rochester Youth Development Survey)[6] and by the Bureau of Alcohol, Tobacco, and Firearms (the National Evaluation of the Gang Resistance Education and Training; Bjerregaard & Smith, 1993; Esbensen & Osgood, 1997; Esbensen, Winfree, He, & Taylor, 2001; Lahey, Gordon, Loeber, Stouthamer-Loeber, & Farrington, 1999).[7] Findings from these and other surveys of youth are consistent with law enforcement surveys in showing a disproportionate involvement of gang members in various criminal and violent activities. Gang and nongang comparisons, primarily of at-risk minority youth drawn from institutionalized and noninstitutionalized settings, consistently reveal an association between admitted gang membership and self-reported crime or delinquency, including drug use and sales (Bjerregaard & Smith, 1993; Deschenes & Esbensen, 1999; Dukes, Martinez, & Stein, 1997; Esbensen, Peterson, Freng, & Taylor, 2002; Fagan, 1989, 1990; Huff, 1996; C. Maxson & Whitlock, 2002; C. L. Maxson, Whitlock, & Klein, 1998; Thornberry, Krohn, Lizotte, Smith, & Tobin, 2003; L. Zhang, Welte, & Wieczorek, 1999). However, these surveys raise important questions about law enforcement estimates of the sex and race composition of gangs. Although female youth are shown to be relatively underrepresented in gangs and gang activity, they self-report gang membership at a rate up to 4½ times higher (20% to 46%) than typically indicated in surveys of law enforcement (Esbensen & Huizinga, 1993; Esbensen & Osgood, 1997; Thornberry et al., 2003). Whites also self-report rates of gang membership in excess of law enforcement estimates—25%, compared to 12% to 15% in the National Young Gang Survey (NYGS) (Esbensen, Deschenes, & Winfree, 1999; Esbensen & Osgood, 1997; Esbensen & Winfree, 1998).

Surveys of youth also provide important information about the correlates and consequences of individual gang membership. Self-identified gang members typically express more antisocial attitudes and negative peer influences than their nongang counterparts and report less family, education, and childhood stability (Deschenes & Esbensen, 1999; Lahey et al., 1999; Thornberry et al., 2003; see Wyrick & Howell, 2004). Female gang members report higher offense rates than male and female nongang youth, but not as much criminal and drug involvement as their male counterparts (Fagan, 1990; Long, 1990), perhaps because of the tendency for male gang members to exclude them from gang-related activities (Bowker, Gross, & Klein, 1980). However, male and female gang members often attribute their involvement in gangs to similar factors, such as having gang-involved friends and family members or a desire for protection, a sense of belonging, status, and/or support in coping with boredom and the exigencies of growing up under harsh social and economic circumstances (Aiken, Rush, & Wycoff, 1993; M. I. Cohen, Williams, Bekelman, & Crosse, 1995; Fagan, 1990; Johnstone, 1981; C. L. Maxson, et al., 1998; but see C. Maxson & Whitlock, 2002). Gangs and gang banging have been described as a means by which members compensate for a strained home life and/or limited opportunities for economic and educational success (e.g., Dukes et al., 1997; see Short, Rivera, & Tennyson, 1965). Ironically, male and female gang members acknowledge that gang participation increases their vulnerability to other problems, such as greater contact with the criminal justice system and violent victimization (Johnstone, 1981; Maxson et al., 1998).

Studies that combine the main quantitative approaches and/or include some alternate form (e.g., detached worker ratings) confirm the relationship between gang membership and violent and other delinquent activities (Battin, Hill, Abbott, Catalano, & Hawkins, 1998; Chesney-Lind, Rockhill, Marker, & Reyes, 1994; Curry, 2000; Curry & Spergel, 1992; Friedman, Mann, & Friedmann, 1975; Strodtbeck, Short, & Kolegar, 1962). They also confirm the relationship between gang membership and social and economic disadvantage (Adler, Ovando, & Hocevar, 1984; Bowker & Klein, 1983; Chesney-Lind et al., 1994; Friedman et al., 1975; Hill, Howell, Hawkins, & Battin-Pearson, 1999; Rivera & Short, 1967); with few exceptions, individual-level variables such as self-esteem are found to be relatively unimportant among all but Hispanic male youth (Curry & Spergel, 1992). Quantitative studies of programs designed to ameliorate the problems of gang members and reduce their delinquency have not been encouraging (see Howell, 2000; Spergel, 1995; but see Adams, 1967). Perhaps the most pessimistic view is offered by M. W. Klein (1969), who claimed total failure for the Los Angeles County Group Guidance Project. Based on detached worker contact and activity reports, interviews with community adults, and probation records, M. W. Klein (1969) reported that (a) workers spent relatively little time in direct contact with the youth, (b) community support for the program was lacking, (c) workers had the most positive impact on those youth least in need of their services, and (d) workers inadvertently increased gang member recruitment and delinquency through programming efforts that enhanced group cohesiveness.

Reflecting the shift of emphasis during the 1970s from etiology to control (Short, 1990), quantitative studies focus primarily on the prevalence of gangs, characteristics of individual gang members, and gang crime and violence. Although such data do not permit assessment of the causal significance of gangs, they are useful for identifying important risk factors as a basis for the management of gang problems. Efforts to assess the extent to which descriptive findings concerning "gang location, diffusion, structure, ethnicity, age, gender, cohesiveness, and behavior patterns (including crime)" in the United States can be generalized to different social and cultural contexts are promising (M. W. Klein, 2002, p. 238; see also M. W. Klein, Kerner, Maxson, & Weitekamp, 2001).

Limitations

Neither surveys nor official reporting systems capture the complexity and dynamics of gang realities

(Hagedorn, 1990). By their very nature, studies based on such methods are designed to discover general patterns in data that have been extracted from their situational and interactional behavior contexts. As a consequence, they cannot explain how and why identified correlates increase the risk of gangs, gang membership, gang crime, and gang violence. Quantitative studies also have been relatively unsuccessful in reaching less conspicuous gang populations (e.g., female and Asian) and in reconciling conflicting findings. "We simply do not know whether the diversity in the findings of gang research reflects different characteristics of gangs and gang members in different places or is an artifact of research methods" (C. Maxson & Whitlock, 2002, p. 20). In addition to problems related to the use of inconsistent definitional approaches across studies, there are obvious difficulties in comparing research involving different sampling strategies (e.g., official records, incarcerated or school youth, law enforcement personnel in jurisdictions of a particular size, etc.), each of which is susceptible to an unknown amount of selection bias. Although it is generally agreed that gang members are disproportionately involved in delinquent activities, violence, and drug selling and abuse (Curry & Thomas, 1992; Huff, 1989; Johnson, Webster, Connors, & Saenz, 1995; Oehme, 1997; Rosenbaum & Grant, 1983; Spergel & Curry, 1990), perceptions of gangs, gang members, and gang behavior are influenced by prior experience with gangs, source of information, personal characteristics, and social position in the community (S. Decker & Kempf-Leonard, 1991; Pryor & McGarrell, 1993; Rosenbaum & Grant, 1983; Swetnam & Pope, 2001; Takata & Zevitz, 1990; R. G. Zevitz & Takata, 1992). Of equal concern is the potential for distortion, intentional and unintentional. Official records have been criticized for being incomplete, inaccurate, confusing, conflicting, outdated, and incapable of adequately representing the fluid nature of gang activities and membership. The veracity of survey data and reports from detached workers and other estimators also may be compromised, by ignorance, recall errors, or deliberate attempts to portray gangs and their members as more or less delinquent, dangerous, involved with drugs, or in need of some sort of organized response than is warranted. Gang member self-reports are particularly suspect, as they may be influenced by pressures to conceal delinquent and violent behaviors or to exaggerate them to confirm gang- and self-images.[8]

Despite such limitations, quantitative studies seem to be the only practical way to assess general patterns of gang prevalence and gang member characteristics and behaviors. Beyond such general patterns, however, qualitative data and studies are required to inform understanding of the nature of gangs and gang member behavior.

The Qualitative Tradition

Bursik and Grasmick (1995) observed that "the longest tradition of gang research is based on some variant of ethnographic fieldwork with gang members (or the combination of such research with supplementary forms of data collection)" (p. 154). Predictions of the declining value and use of such techniques (Bookin-Weiner & Horowitz, 1983) have not materialized. Increasingly, however, ethnographic research in the participant-observation tradition of the Chicago school (e.g., Thrasher, 1927) and other early gang studies (e.g., Whyte, 1943) is being replaced by studies that rely on in-depth interviews with former and/or currently active gang members (often the most criminally violent). When used to confirm quantitative analyses of the data, descriptions of gangs based on such accounts can be misleading, reinforcing stereotypical images of gangs. Field studies that go beyond static representations to explore the everyday realities of gang life portray gangs somewhat differently. These studies indicate that gangs and gang members are in many respects quite ordinary. Instead of being the defining characteristics of gangs, crime and violence are shown to be only a small part of gang life (Fleisher, 1998; Hagedorn, 1988; Horowitz, 1983; Suttles, 1968; Venkatesh, 2000; Vigil, 1988; Whyte, 1943). Although willingness to act violently (under appropriate circumstances) is often a valued source of status within the gang, gang members generally are not so preoccupied. Much of their time is spent in normal adolescent activities, such as hanging out, "doing nothing," "scoring," and drinking and partying.

Detailed qualitative descriptions tend to portray gangs as loosely structured groups that lack clear role expectations and stable leadership (Conquergood, 1994; Hagedorn, 1988; Harris, 1988; Jansyn, 1966; Mares, 2001; Short & Strodtbeck, 1965; Weisel, 2002; Yablonsky, 1962; R. Zevitz, 1993). Gang members often have only a vague understanding of the gang outside of their immediate ego-gang networks (Fleisher, 2002); in many cases, "the concept of the gang as a group [has] far exceeded the social nature of the group" (p. 205). Anticipation of a fight with a rival gang draws members together for collective violence, which can be especially dangerous should they all have to "throw down." Except for such episodic conflicts, however, the data suggest that gang members rarely are all together in the same place at the same time. Indeed, most so-called gang behavior takes place among cliques or other small groupings (Hagedorn, 1988; Short & Strodtbeck, 1965; Vigil, 1988; see Sanders, 1994; Suttles, 1968). Even the gangs that are reported to be organized hierarchically around the pursuit of entrepreneurial or political goals usually began as more amorphous street gangs (see Brotherton & Barrios, 2004; Jankowski, 1991; Padilla, 1992, 1993; Skolnick, Correl, Navarro, & Rabb, 1990; Taylor, 1990; Venkatesh & Levitt, 2000); arguably, such gangs are more appropriately classified as illegitimate business ventures ("crews," see Williams, 1989) or sociopolitical organizations (see Pfautz, 1961; but see M. W. Klein, 2002).

At the macro-social level of explanation, gangs have been attributed to diverse empirical contexts: social disorganization (see Thrasher, 1927), opposition to middle-class culture (A. K. Cohen, 1955), lower-class culture (W. B. Miller, 1958), opportunities associated with social structures (Cloward & Ohlin, 1960), a social order unique to slums (Suttles, 1968), "persistent and pervasive" poverty made worse by deindustrialization (Hagedorn, 1988; Moore, 1991), and multiple marginalities (Vigil, 1988; see also Conquergood, 1994). With the exception of a few studies that focus on the importance of group processes for individual or collective gang behavior (Jansyn, 1966; M. W. Klein, 1969; Short & Strodtbeck, 1965; see also Horowitz, 1983), the causal significance of gangs has not been addressed. Insofar as etiological issues are considered in

qualitative research, the tendency has been to point to individual-level characteristics, such as "psychological malaise" (Bloch & Niederhoffer, 1957), "violent pathology" (Yablonsky, 1962), masculinity, loyalty to peers, and a desire for immediate gratification (Karacki & Toby, 1962), and "defiant individualism" (Jankowski, 1991).

The lack of comparative research has stymied theoretical development (J. Katz & Jackson-Jacobs, 2004). No satisfactory explication of why youth become involved in gangs rather than other types of association has emerged. Qualitative descriptions suggest that, for many, gang membership represents an opportunity to enhance social capital as a means to cope with a multitude of problems. Although on balance gang life appears to be neither very rewarding nor satisfying (Hagedorn, 1988; Padilla, 1992; Short & Strodtbeck, 1965), identification with the gang is solidified in response to conflict—often with other gangs—as members pursue their individual and collective interests.

Although qualitative studies traditionally have concentrated on the most visible Black and Hispanic male gangs in major U.S. cities, recent field research has begun to focus on the nature of gang life among relatively understudied populations, especially female youth and Asians. Field researchers have been highly critical of the androcentric treatment of female gang involvement in earlier works (see Chesney-Lind, 1999; Curry, 1999), arguing that life in the gang for female youth is far more varied and complex than suggested by depictions of gang girls as tomboys and sex objects who group together to form small auxiliary units of male gangs (but see Jankowski, 1991; Spergel, 1995). Interview data indicate that female youth participate in a wide range of gang types, each of which influences the experiences and activities of its members. Differences have been noted between girls who belong to gangs of varying gender composition, for example. Female members of mixed-gender gangs tend to report only limited peer pressure to participate in criminal activities and frequently allude to alternative means of achieving status, such as through their relationships with high-ranking male members (Lauderback, Hansen, & Waldorf, 1992; J. Miller, 1998; J. Miller & Decker, 2001; cf. Harris, 1988). They also report facing numerous barriers to full participation in the gang (Brotherton & Salazar-Atias, 2003; see also J. Miller, 1998). In contrast, members of all-girl gangs report few such constraints and often are quite involved in property offending, drug use and sales, and even violence (Brown, 1977; Campbell, 1984; Hagedorn & Devitt, 1999; Lauderback et al., 1992; Taylor, 1993; see also Brotherton, 1996). Although some scholars interpret such findings in a manner consistent with the liberation hypothesis (see Chesney-Lind, 1999; Curry, 1998, 1999), there is much wider acceptance of the social injury perspective. Gangs generally are not described as a panacea to the troubled lives of the girls who eventually join (but see Quicker, 1983); rather, field researchers depict female involvement in gangs as a trade-off between prior problems and problems resulting from gang membership (see, e.g., Brotherton & Salazar-Atias, 2003; Fleisher, 1998; K. A. Joe & Chesney-Lind, 1995; J. Miller, 1998; Portillos, 1999).[9] For example, we are told that many girls seek in the gang refuge from random violence and abusive treatment at the hands of family members or male partners, only to find themselves and their female peers at increased risk of sexual and physical victimization by other gang members (J. Miller, 1998, 2000, 2002; J. Miller & Decker, 2001; Nurge, 2003; Portillos, 1999). We are also told of the gang being a social context in which girls can escape the gender expectations and constraints that exist in their homes and in the larger society but in which they face considerable devaluation and oppression (Brotherton & Barrios, 2004; Brotherton & Salazar-Atias, 2003; Campbell, 1984; Horowitz, 1983; Laidler & Hunt, 2001; Lopez & Mirande, 1990; J. Miller & Decker, 2001; Moore, 1991). Members of autonomous girl gangs may fare better; however, even they do not always present an entirely positive image of life in the gang and often move on to more conventional pursuits, especially motherhood (Hagedorn & Devitt, 1999; J. Miller, 2002). More research clearly is needed concerning the conditions under which female youth are more or less liberated or injured by gang participation. Hagedorn and Devitt's (1999) comparative work urges expanding the focus of research to include such factors as ethnicity, age, gang structure, and individual conceptions of gender.[10]

Knowledge of Asian gangs is not well developed; however, recent progress has been made. Descriptions of Asian gangs in many ways parallel those of Black and Hispanic gangs.[11] By all accounts, modern-day Asian youth gangs are loosely structured groups that gain their appeal by offering mutual support, protection, and friendship to their members, most of whom come from disadvantaged economic backgrounds and are confronted with adjustment problems in school, at home, and in the larger society (Hunt, Joe, & Waldorf, 1996; D. Joe & Robinson, 1980; Laidler & Hunt, 2001; Robinson & Joe, 1980; Vigil & Yun, 1996). Although status within these gangs is obtained largely through the demonstration of fighting prowess and/or material gain (D. Joe & Robinson, 1980; Robinson & Joe, 1980; Vigil & Yun, 1996), the evidence does not suggest a strong and sustained commitment to crime and violence. Contrary to popular belief, Asian youth gangs do not appear to play a central role in the trafficking of drugs (Chin, 1996; K. A. Joe, 1994); they rarely exact a significant profit from extortion of local businesses (Chin, Fagan, & Kelly, 1992); and they are at best only weakly allied with adult criminal organizations (Chin, 1996).

Overall, the picture of gangs that emerges from studies in the qualitative tradition provides important contrasts to quantitative findings. M. W. Klein, Maxson, and Miller (1995) noted that "[e]thnographers 'know' gangs in a way that survey researchers and analysts of official crime data cannot hope to achieve" (p. ix). Field research makes clear that gang life does not always center on crime and violence—a fact that can be easily missed when data are extracted from their relevant social contexts. Gangs and their members are hardly a wholesome bunch, yet their values and behavior are shown in many cases to be decent (see Anderson, 1999; see also Conquergood, 1994; Cureton, 2002; Fleisher, 1998; Hagedorn, 1988; Horowitz, 1983; Jankowski, 1991; Monti, 1994; J. W. Moore, 1991). There is considerable evidence that gang youth will avoid delinquent and violent behaviors when acceptable alternatives are available and unlikely to call their honor into question (e.g., Cureton, 2002; Fleisher, 1998; Hagedorn, 1988; Horowitz, 1983). Recent studies demonstrate the usefulness of observational data for the purpose of examining such processes, both qualitatively and quantitatively (e.g., Hughes & Short, in press).[12]

Limitations

Although qualitative studies have yielded rich descriptions of a variety of gangs and provided insight into the gang populations and issues that cannot be adequately addressed by official data or surveys, they are limited in their ability to provide general information about the scope of gangs and the extent to which gang membership is related to specific sociodemographic and behavioral characteristics. In addition, qualitative research is subject to methodological biases. Because field research is inherently difficult—requiring special investigative skills, a substantial amount of time and resources, and the cooperation of research participants—and may entail significant risks (Bookin-Weiner & Horowitz, 1983), researchers tend to restrict their attention to the limited number of gangs into which they are able to gain entree.[13] The representativeness of such gangs is questionable, however, particularly if they are selected based on preconceived notions about what gangs ought to look like, where they ought to be found, and what they and their members ought to be doing. Field researchers are beginning to appreciate Thrasher's (1927) dictum that no two gangs are exactly alike, sifting through the similarities and differences among gangs of varying organization, gender composition, and ethnicity. However, little is known about gang-community relationships (Sullivan, 1989) and the conditions under which gangs contribute to the maintenance of a stable social order, develop in suburban areas, or otherwise deviate from the currently popular so-called underclass perspective, which characterizes gangs as dysfunctional byproducts of socially disorganized slums (see Brotherton & Barrios, 2004; Monti, 1993, 1994; Spergel, 1995; Venkatesh, 1997, 2000).

Field researchers must exercise care to protect data from other biases. It is important that they interpret observational data cautiously, recognizing the various ways in which findings may be influenced by the presence of an observer and by observer-participant relationships (Sherif & Sherif, 1967). Interview data also need careful scrutiny. Field researchers often ignore potential selectivity in their samples, assuming that their respondents are representative of other gang members. This assumption is at best questionable when, for example, samples consist of incarcerated gang youth selected by corrections officials (e.g., Skolnick, 1990; Skolnick et al., 1990), students selected by their school principal (e.g., Monti, 1994), gang members selected because of their accessibility and willingness to provide information (e.g., Harris, 1988), or violent incidents selected because they are under investigation by police department gang units (e.g., Sanders, 1994).

Findings may be compromised in other ways, as well. In addition to the possibility of distortion stemming from recall errors and lack of knowledge, there may be problems of intentional misrepresentation. Underreporting is likely to be a serious threat to the validity of many studies, especially those that do not protect the confidentiality of respondents (e.g., Monti, 1994) or that solicit information that may reflect badly on respondents' ability to do their jobs. Of equal concern is the potential for "hyped-up" reports (Hagedorn, 1996). Despite the documented existence of a myth system within gangs (M. W. Klein, 1971) and the well-known inconsistency between words and deeds (Deutscher, 1966), many contemporary field researchers continue to report uncritically gang member accounts of violent and other deviant behaviors (e.g., S. H. Decker & Van Winkle, 1996; Jankowski, 1991; Skolnick et al., 1990). It is not surprising that their findings often are contradicted by evidence of conventional orientations among gang members found in studies that implement more rigorous checks (e.g., Hagedorn, 1994; see Hagedorn, 1996).

As is the case with quantitative studies, then, studies in the qualitative tradition provide, at best, a limited representation of gang phenomena. Sampling and data issues pose major challenges to substantive progress and to the development of theories that are capable of explaining the complexities of gang life. Nevertheless, qualitative studies enhance our understanding of gangs in ways that are not otherwise possible.

Discussion

Quantitative and qualitative studies have yielded important insights into the nature of gangs and their members' activities and have contributed to a substantial scholarly literature. Comprehensive understanding of the complexities of gang phenomena continues to be elusive, however. The lack of comparisons and inattention to etiological issues, particularly in quantitative studies, prevent us from knowing how—if at all—gangs contribute to crime and violence beyond individual and peer group influences. In addition, critical disconnects continue to exist between methodological approaches to gang studies. Although triangulation is the surest way to offset the limitations associated with each approach, relatively few gang researchers utilize quantitative and qualitative methods. At least part of the reason is that such methods vary in terms of the types of information that they allow researchers to obtain. Qualitative techniques clearly have been more effective in reaching so-called hidden gang populations, exposing the similarities and differences that exist between gangs and among their members, and achieving emic understandings of gang phenomena (see Vigil & Long, 1990). They also are more appropriate for investigations of the day-to-day life of gangs and gang members during long periods of time and for inquiries at the microsocial level, where interest centers on situational characteristics and interaction processes operative in the immediate contexts of behavior (see Short, 1998). In contrast, quantitative techniques emphasize breadth over depth and, therefore, are of greater value in the development of macrolevel summaries and large-scale gang and nongang comparisons. Given such differences, it is not surprising that gang researchers tend to favor one methodological approach over the other. However, future researchers must begin the complex task of integrating quantitative and qualitative techniques, allowing them to complement each other in ways that enable a fuller accounting of macro-, individual-, and micro-level properties of the gang phenomenon and the linkages between them. Gangs are likely to endure in the United States and elsewhere in the world (Covey, 2003) and, as such, will continue to elicit a variety of social responses. As part of this process, gang scholars may be called on to explain the causes of gangs and the effects they have on their members and on communities. It is imperative that research and theory accurately

reflect the realities of gangs and that understanding be simultaneously broad and deep.

Notes

1. Citations selected for inclusion are meant to be illustrative, not exhaustive.
2. See Savelsberg, Cleveland, and King (2004) for a discussion of political funding on criminological scholarship.
3. In some cases, however, staff members from other types of organizations (court and corrections, community service, and schools) are included in surveys along with law enforcement personnel (see, e.g., W. B. Miller, 1975, 1982, 2001).
4. Curry and Spergel's (1988) analysis of the gang homicide files maintained by the Gang Crime Unit of the Chicago Police Department (1978–1981 and 1982–1985) also indicates that the gang problem disproportionately affects low-income Black and Hispanic areas.
5. In a study of police gang intelligence in Mesa, AZ, C. M. Katz and colleagues (C. M. Katz, Webb, & Schaefer, 2000) found that officially documented gang members had significantly more arrests for drug and other offenses than did a matched sample of nondocumented offenders.
6. Although supplementary information was obtained from school, police, and juvenile court records, most—if not all—related studies have focused entirely on the youth self-report data.
7. Variations in the prevalence rate stem largely from the use of definitions with differing levels of restrictiveness. Studies that employ a minimally restrictive definition of *gang membership* (i.e., an affirmative answer to the question of having ever been a gang member) report much higher prevalence rates than those reported by studies that use a more restrictive definition (i.e., self-identification and admitted gang delinquency and organization).
8. However, Curry (2000) reported high levels of consistency between official and self-report data.
9. Curry (1999) proposed a dialectical perspective in which the gang is viewed as simultaneously "rewarding and destructive" (p. 152).
10. J. Miller & Brunson's (2000) analysis of data obtained from interviews with 58 male and female youth indicates that mode of entry into the gang also is important.
11. Several important differences have been noted, however. Unlike African American and Chicano gangs (S. H. Decker & Van Winkle, 1996; J. Moore, Vigil, & Garcia, 1983; Portillos, Jurik, & Zatz, 1996; Vigil, 1988; see also Lopez & Mirande, 1990; Skolnick, Correl, Navarro, & Rabb, 1990), Asian gangs are reported to

lack a strong orientation to turf, in part, because most of their members are recent immigrants (Hunt, Joe, & Waldorf, 1996; D. Joe & Robinson, 1980; K. A. Joe, 1994; Robinson & Joe, 1980; but see Chin, 1990, 1996). Members of Asian gangs also do not appear to participate in drug and drinking activity as frequently as do youth who belong to Chicano and African American gangs (Hunt et al., 1996; see also Hagedorn, 1994; Hagedorn & Devitt, 1999). In addition, the family and community ties reported to exist among Chicano/a gangs (Horowitz, 1983; Portillos et al., 1996; Skolnick et al., 1990) may not be as prominent among Asian gangs (S. X. Zhang, 2002).

12. Quantitative analysis of ethnographic observations is a new approach with clear implications in gang research. Although missing data problems tend to be especially serious when observational data are quantified, such an approach strengthens confidence in interpretive findings. A recent development involves the collection and analyses of quantifiable egocentric network data together with ethnographic observations and narrative interviews (see Fleisher, 2002).

13. Field researchers have employed a variety of techniques to gain entree into the gang (see Horowitz, 1990; Weisel, 2002).

References

Adams, S. (1967). A cost approach to the assessment of gang rehabilitation techniques. *Journal of Research in Crime and Delinquency, 4*, 166–182.

Adler, P., Ovando, C., & Hocevar, D. (1984). Familiar correlates of gang membership: An exploratory study of Mexican-American youth. *Hispanic Journal of Behavioral Science, 6*, 65–76.

Aiken, C., Rush, J. P., & Wycoff, J. (1993). A preliminary inquiry into Alabama youth gang membership. *Gang Journal, 1*, 37–47.

Anderson, E. (1999). *Code of the street: Decency, violence, and the moral life of the inner city*. New York: Norton.

Bailey, G. W., & Unnithan, N. P. (1994). Gang homicides in California: A discriminant analysis. *Journal of Criminal Justice, 22*, 267–275.

Battin, S. R., Hill, K. G., Abbott, R. D., Catalano, R. F., & Hawkins, J. D. (1998). The contribution of gang membership to delinquency beyond delinquent friends. *Criminology, 36*, 93–115.

Bjerregaard, B., & Smith, C. (1993). Gender differences in gang participation, delinquency, and substance use. *Journal of Quantitative Criminology, 9*, 329–355.

Bloch, H. A., & Niederhoffer, A. (1958). *The gang: A study in adolescent behavior*. New York: Philosophical Library.

Block, C. R., & Block, R. (1993). *Street gang crime in Chicago* (NIJ Research in Brief No. NCJ 144782). Washington, DC: U.S. Department of Justice, Office of Justice Programs, National Institute of Justice.

Block, C. R., Christakos, A., Jacob, A., & Przybylski, R. (1996). *Street gangs and crime: Patterns and trends in Chicago*. Chicago: Illinois Criminal Justice Information Authority.

Bookin-Weiner, H., & Horowitz, R. (1983). The end of the youth gang: Fad or fact? *Criminology, 21*, 585–602.

Bowker, L. H., Gross, H. S., & Klein, M. W. (1980). Female participation in delinquent gang activities. *Adolescence, 15*, 509–539.

Bowker, L. H., & Klein, M. W. (1983). The etiology of female juvenile delinquency and gang membership: A test of psychological and social structural explanations. *Adolescence, 18*, 739–751.

Brotherton, D. C. (1996). "Smartness," "toughness," and "autonomy": Drug use in the context of gang female delinquency. *Journal of Drug Issues, 26*, 261–277.

Brotherton, D. C., & Barrios, L. (2004). *The Almighty Latin King and Queen Nation: Street politics and the transformation of a New York gang city*. New York: Columbia University Press.

Brotherton, D. C., & Salazar-Atias, C. (2003). Amor de reina! The pushes and pulls of group membership among the Latin Queens. In L. Kontos, D. C. Brotherton, & L. Barrios (Eds.), *Gangs and society: Alternative perspectives* (pp. 183–209). New York: Columbia University Press.

Brown, W. K. (1977). Black female gangs in Philadelphia. *International Journal of Offender Therapy and Comparative Criminology, 21*, 221–228.

Bursik, R. J., Jr., & Grasmick, H. G. (1995). The collection of data for gang research. In M. W. Klein, C. L. Maxson, & J. Miller (Eds.), *The modern gang reader* (pp. 154–157). Los Angeles: Roxbury.

Campbell, A. (1984). *The girls in the gang: A report from New York City*. New York: Basil Blackwell.

Chesney-Lind, M. (1999). Girls, gangs, and violence: Reinventing the liberated female crook. In M. Chesney-Lind & J. M. Hagedorn (Eds.), *Female gangs in America: Essays on girls, gangs and gender* (pp. 295–310). Chicago: Lake View Press.

Chesney-Lind, M., Rockhill, A., Marker, N., & Reyes, H. (1994). Gangs and delinquency. *Crime, Law, and Social Change, 21*, 201–228.

Chin, K. (1990). *Chinese subculture and criminality: Non-traditional crime groups in America*. New York: Greenwood.

Chin, K. (1996). *Chinatown gangs: Extortion, enterprise, and ethnicity*. New York: Oxford University Press.

Chin, K., Fagan, J., & Kelly, R. J. (1992). Patterns of Chinese gang extortion. *Justice Quarterly, 9*, 625–646.

Cloward, R., & Ohlin, L. E. (1960). *Delinquency and opportunity.* New York: Free Press.

Cohen, A. K. (1955). *Delinquent boys: The culture of the gang.* New York: Free Press.

Cohen, B. (1969). The delinquency of gangs and spontaneous groups. In T. Sellin & M. E. Wolfgang (Eds.), *Delinquency: Selected studies* (pp. 61–111). New York: John Wiley.

Cohen, M. I., Williams, K., Bekelman, A. M., & Crosse, S. (1995). Evaluation of the National Youth Gang Drug Prevention Program. In M. W. Klein, C. L. Maxson, & J. Miller (Eds.), *The modern gang reader* (pp. 266–275). Los Angeles: Roxbury.

Conquergood, D. (1994). Homeboys and hoods: Gang communication and cultural space. In L. R. Frey (Ed.), *Group communication in context: Studies of natural groups* (pp. 23–55). Hillsdale, NJ: Lawrence Erlbaum.

Covey, H. C. (2003). *Street gangs throughout the world.* Springfield, IL: Charles C Thomas.

Cureton, S. R. (2002). Introducing Hoover: I'll ride for you, gangsta. In C. R. Huff (Ed.), *Gangs in America III* (pp. 83–100). Thousand Oaks, CA: Sage.

Curry, G. D. (1998). Female gang involvement. *Journal of Research in Crime and Delinquency, 35*, 100–118.

Curry, G. D. (1999). Responding to female gang involvement. In M. Chesney-Lind & J. M. Hagedorn (Eds.), *Female gangs in America: Essays on girls, gangs and gender* (pp. 133–153). Chicago: Lake View Press.

Curry, G. D. (2000). Self-reported gang involvement and officially recorded delinquency. *Criminology, 38*, 1253–1274.

Curry, G. D., & Decker, S. H. (2002). Defining and measuring the prevalence of gangs. In G. D. Curry & S. H. Decker (Eds.), *Confronting gangs: Crime and community* (2nd ed., pp. 1–31). Los Angeles: Roxbury.

Curry, G. D., & Spergel, I. A. (1988). Gang homicide, delinquency, and community. *Criminology, 26*, 381–405.

Curry, G. D., & Spergel, I. A. (1992). Gang involvement and delinquency among Hispanic and African-American adolescent males. *Journal of Research in Crime and Delinquency, 29*, 273–291.

Curry, G. D., & Thomas, R. W. (1992). Community organization and gang policy response. *Journal of Quantitative Criminology, 8*, 357–374.

Decker, S., & Kempf-Leonard, K. (1991). Constructing gangs: The social definition of youth activities. *Criminal Justice Policy Review, 5*, 271–291.

Decker, S. H., & Van Winkle, B. (1996). *Life in the gang: Family, friends, and violence.* New York: Cambridge University Press.

Deschenes, E. P., & Esbensen, F.-A. (1999). Violence among girls: Does gang membership make a difference? In M. Chesney-Lind & J. M. Hagedorn (Eds.), *Female gangs in America: Essays on girls, gangs and gender* (pp. 277–294). Chicago: Lake View Press.

Deutscher, I. (1966). Words and deeds: Social science and social policy. *Social Problems, 13*, 235–254.

Dukes, R. L., Martinez, R. O., & Stein, J. A. (1997). Precursors and consequences of membership in youth gangs. *Youth & Society, 29*, 139–165.

Egley, A., Jr., Howell, J. C., & Major, A. K. (2004). Recent patterns of gang problems in the United States: Results from the 1996–2002 National Youth Gang Survey. In F.-A. Esbensen, S. G. Tibbetts, & L. Gaines (Eds.), *American youth gangs at the millennium* (pp. 90–108). Long Grove, IL: Waveland Press.

Esbensen, F.-A., Deschenes, E. P., & Winfree, L. T., Jr. (1999). Differences between gang girls and gang boys: Results from a multisite survey. *Youth & Society, 31*, 27–53.

Esbensen, F.-A., & Huizinga, D. (1993). Gangs, drugs, and delinquency in a survey of urban youth. *Criminology, 31*, 565–589.

Esbensen, F.-A., & Osgood, D. W. (1997). *National evaluation of G.R.E.A.T* (NIJ Research in Brief No. NCJ 167264). Washington, DC: U.S. Department of Justice, Office of Justice Programs, National Institute of Justice.

Esbensen, F.-A., Peterson, D., Freng, A., & Taylor, T. J. (2002). Initiation of drug use, drug sales, and violent offending among a sample of gang and nongang youth. In C. R. Huff (Ed.), *Gangs in America III* (pp. 37–50). Thousand Oaks, CA: Sage.

Esbensen, F.-A., & Winfree, L. T. (1998). Race and gender differences between gang and nongang youths: Results from a multisite survey. *Justice Quarterly, 15*, 505–526.

Esbensen, F.-A., Winfree, L. T., Jr., He, N., & Taylor, T. J. (2001). Youth gangs and definitional issues: When is a gang a gang, and why does it matter? *Crime & Delinquency, 47*, 105–130.

Fagan, J. (1989). The social organization of drug use and drug dealing among urban gangs. *Criminology, 27*, 633–669.

Fagan, J. (1990). Social processes of delinquency and drug use among urban gangs. In C. R. Huff (Ed.), *Gangs in America* (pp. 183–219). Newbury Park, CA: Sage.

Fleisher, M. S. (1998). *Dead end kids: Gang girls and the boys they know.* Madison: University of Wisconsin Press.

Fleisher, M. S. (2002). Doing field research on diverse gangs: Interpreting youth gangs as social networks. In C. R. Huff (Ed.), *Gangs in America III* (pp. 199–217). Thousand Oaks, CA: Sage.

Friedman, C. J., Mann, F., & Friedman, A. S. (1975). A profile of juvenile street gang members. *Adolescence, 10*, 563–607.

Hagedorn, J. M. (with Macon, P.) (1988). *People and folks: Gangs, crime, and the underclass in a rustbelt city.* Chicago: Lake View Press.

Hagedorn, J. M. (1990). Back in the field again: Gang research in the nineties. In C. R. Huff (Ed.), *Gangs in America* (pp. 240–259). Newbury Park. CA: Sage.

Hagedorn, J. M. (1994). Homeboys, dope fiends, legits, and new jacks. *Criminology, 32,* 197–219.

Hagedorn, J. M. (1996). The emperor's new clothes: Theory and method in gang field research. *Free Inquiry in Creative Sociology, 24*(2), 111–122.

Hagedorn, J. M., & Devitt, M. L. (1999). Fighting female: The social construction of female gangs. In M. Chesney-Lind & J. M. Hagedorn (Eds.), *Female gangs in America: Essays on girls, gangs and gender* (pp. 256–276). Chicago: Lake View Press.

Harris, M. G. (1988). *Cholas: Latino girls and gangs.* New York: AMS Press.

Hill, K. G., Howell, J. C., Hawkins, J. D., & Battin-Pearson, S. R. (1999). Childhood risk factors for adolescent gang membership: Results from the Seattle Social Development Project. *Journal of Research in Crime and Delinquency, 36,* 300–322.

Horowitz, R. (1983). *Honor and the American dream: Culture and identity in a Chicano community.* New Brunswick, NJ: Rutgers University Press.

Horowitz, R. (1990). Sociological perspectives on gangs: Conflicting definitions and concepts. In C. R. Huff (Ed.), *Gangs in America* (pp. 37–54). Newbury Park, CA: Sage.

Howell, J. C. (2000). *Youth gang programs and strategies.* Washington, DC: U.S. Department of Justice, Office of Justice Programs, Office of Juvenile Justice and Delinquency Prevention.

Huff, C. R. (1989). Youth gangs and public policy. *Crime & Delinquency, 35,* 524–537.

Huff, C. R. (1996). The criminal behavior of gang members and nongang at-risk youth. In C. R. Huff (Ed.), *Gangs in America* (2nd ed., pp. 75–101). Thousand Oaks, CA: Sage.

Hughes, L. A., & Short, J. F., Jr. (in press). Disputes involving youth street gang members: Micro-social contexts. *Criminology.*

Hunt, G., Joe, K., & Waldorf, D. (1996). Drinking, kicking back and gang banging: Alcohol, violence and street gangs. *Free Inquiry in Creative Sociology, 24,* 123–132.

Hutson, H. R., Anglin, D., Kyriacou, D. N., Hart, J., & Spears, K. (1995). The epidemic of gang-related homicides in Los Angeles County from 1979 through 1994. *Journal of the American Medical Association, 274,* 1031–1036.

Jankowski, M. S. (1991). *Islands in the street: Gangs and American urban society.* Berkeley: University of California Press.

Jansyn, L. R., Jr. (1966). Solidarity and delinquency in a street corner group. *American Sociological Review, 31,* 600–614.

Joe, D., & Robinson, N. (1980). Chinatown's immigrant gangs: The new young warrior class. *Criminology, 18,* 337–345.

Joe, K. A. (1994). The new criminal conspiracy? Asian gangs and organized crime in San Francisco. *Journal of Research in Crime and Delinquency, 31,* 390–415.

Joe, K. A., & Chesney-Lind, M. (1995). "Just every mother's angel": An analysis of gender and ethnic variations in youth gang membership. *Gender & Society, 9,* 408–431.

Johnson, C. M., Webster, B. A., Connors, E. F., & Saenz, D. J. (1995). Gang enforcement problems and strategies: National survey findings. *Journal of Gang Research, 3,* 1–18.

Johnstone, J. W. (1981). Youth gangs and black suburbs. *Pacific Sociological Review, 24,* 355–375.

Karacki, L., & Toby, J. (1962). The uncommitted adolescent: Candidate for gang socialization. *Sociological Inquiry, 3,* 203–215.

Katz, J., & Jackson-Jacobs, C. (2004). The criminologists' gang. In C. Sumner (Ed.), *The Blackwell companion to criminology* (pp. 91–124). Malden, MA: Blackwell.

Katz, C. M., Webb, V. J., & Schaefer, D. R. (2000). The validity of police gang intelligence lists: Examining differences in delinquency between documented gang members and nondocumented delinquent youth. *Police Quarterly, 3,* 413–437.

Klein, M. W. (1969). Gang cohesiveness, delinquency, and a street-work program. *Journal of Research in Crime and Delinquency, 6,* 135–166.

Klein, M. W. (1971). *Street gangs and street workers.* Englewood Cliffs, NJ: Prentice Hall.

Klein, M. W. (1995). *The American street gang: Its nature, prevalence, and control.* New York: Oxford University Press.

Klein, M. W. (2002). Street gangs: A cross-national perspective. In C. R. Huff (Ed.), *Gangs in America III* (pp. 237–254). Thousand Oaks, CA: Sage.

Klein, M. W., Kerner, H.-J., Maxson, C. L., & Weitekamp, E. G. (Eds.). (2001). *The Eurogang paradox: Street gangs and youth groups in the U.S. and Europe.* Dordrecht, the Netherlands: Kluwer Academic.

Klein, M. W., & Maxson, C. L. (1989). Street gang violence. In N. A. Weiner & M. E. Wolfgang (Eds.), *Violent crime, violent criminals* (pp. 198–234). Newbury Park, CA: Sage.

Klein, M., Maxson, C. L., & Cunningham, L. C. (1991). "Crack," street gangs, and violence. *Criminology, 29,* 623–650.

Klein, M. W., Maxson, C. L., & Miller, J. (Eds.). (1995). *The modern gang reader.* Los Angeles: Roxbury.

Lahey, B. B., Gordon, R. A., Loeber, R., Stouthamer-Loeber, M., & Farrington, D. P. (1999). Boys who join gangs: A prospective study of predictors of first gang entry. *Journal of Abnormal Child Psychology, 27,* 261–276.

Laidler, K. J., & Hunt, G. (2001). Accomplishing femininity among the girls in the gang. *British Journal of Criminology, 41,* 656–678.

Lauderback, D., Hansen, J., & Waldorf, D. (1992). "Sisters are doin' it for themselves": A black female gang in San Francisco. *Gang Journal, 1,* 57–72.

Long, J. M. (1990). Drug use patterns in two Los Angeles barrio gangs. In R. Glick & J. Moore (Eds.), *Drugs in Hispanic communities* (pp. 155–165). New Brunswick, NJ: Rutgers University Press.

Lopez, J., & Mirande, A. (1990). The gangs of Orange County: A critique and synthesis of social policy. *Aztlan, 19,* 125–146.

Mares, D. (2001). Gangstas or lager louts? Working class street gangs in Manchester. In M. W. Klein, H.-J. Kerner, C. L. Maxson, & E. G. Weitekamp (Eds.), *The Eurogang paradox: Street gangs and youth groups in the U.S. and Europe* (pp. 153–164). Dordrecht, the Netherlands: Kluwer Academic.

Maxson, C. L. (1995). *Street gangs and drug sales in two suburban cities* (NIJ Research in Brief No. NCJ 155185). Washington, DC: U.S. Department of Justice, National Institute of Justice.

Maxson, C. L., Gordon, M. A., & Klein, M. L. (1985). Differences between gang and nongang homicides. *Criminology, 23,* 209–222.

Maxson, C., & Whitlock, M. L. (2002). Joining the gang: Gender differences in risk factors for gang membership. In C. R. Huff (Ed.), *Gangs in America III* (pp. 19–35). Thousand Oaks, CA: Sage.

Maxson, C. L., Whitlock, M. L., & Klein, M. W. (1998). Vulnerability to street gang membership: Implications for practice. *Social Service Review, 72,* 70–91.

Meehan, P. J., & O'Carroll, P. W. (1992). Gangs, drugs, and homicide in Los Angeles. *American Journal of Diseases of Children, 146,* 683–687.

Miller, J. (1998). Gender and victimization risk among young women in gangs. *Journal of Research in Crime and Delinquency, 35,* 429–453.

Miller, J. (2000). *One of the guys: Girls, gangs, and gender.* Oxford, UK: Oxford University Press.

Miller, J. (2002). Young women in street gangs: Risk factors, delinquency, and victimization risk. In W. L. Reed & S. H. Decker (Eds.), *Responding to gangs: Evaluation and research* (pp. 67–105). Washington, DC: U.S. Department of Justice, Office of Justice Programs.

Miller, J., & Brunson, R. K. (2000). Gender dynamics in youth gangs: A comparison of males' and females' accounts. *Justice Quarterly, 17,* 419–448.

Miller, J., & Decker, S. H. (2001). Young women and gang violence: Gender, street offending, and violent victimization in gangs. *Justice Quarterly, 18,* 115–140.

Miller, W. B. (1958). Lower class culture as a generating milieu of gang delinquency. *Journal of Social Issues, 14,* 5–19.

Miller, W. B. (1975). *Violence by youth gangs and youth groups as a crime problem in major American cities.* Washington, DC: U.S. Department of Justice, National Institute of Juvenile Justice and Delinquency Prevention.

Miller, W. B. (1982). *Crime by youth gangs and groups in the United States.* Washington, DC: U.S. Department of Justice, Office of Justice Programs, Office of Juvenile Justice and Delinquency Prevention.

Miller, W. B. (2001). *The growth of youth gang problems in the United States: 1970–98.* Washington, DC: U.S. Department of Justice, Office of Juvenile Justice and Delinquency Prevention.

Monti, D. J. (1993). Gangs in more- and less-settled communities. In S. Cummings & D. J. Monti (Eds.), *Gangs: The origins and impact of contemporary youth gangs in the United States* (pp. 219–253). Albany: State University of New York Press.

Monti, D. J. (1994). *Wannabe: Gangs in suburbs and schools.* Oxford, UK: Blackwell.

Moore, J., Vigil, D., & Garcia, R. (1983). Residence and territoriality in Chicano gangs. *Social Problems, 31,* 182–194.

Moore, J. W. (1991). *Going down to the barrio: Homeboys and homegirls in change.* Philadelphia: Temple University Press.

Nurge, D. (2003). Liberating yet limiting: The paradox of female gang membership. In L. Kontos, D. C. Brotherton, & L. Barrios (Eds.), *Gangs and society: Alternative perspectives* (pp. 161–182). New York: Columbia University Press.

Oehme, C. G., III. (1997). *Gangs, groups and crime: Perceptions and responses of community organizations.* Durham, NC: Carolina Academic Press.

Padilla, F. (1993). The working gang. In S. Cummings & D. J. Monti (Eds.), *Gangs: The origins and impact of contemporary youth gangs in the United States* (pp. 173–192). Albany: State University of New York Press.

Padilla, F. M. (1992). *The gang as an American enterprise.* New Brunswick, NJ: Rutgers University Press.

Pfautz, H. W. (1961). Near-group theory and collective behavior: A critical reformulation. *Social Problems, 9,* 167–174.

Portillos, E. L. (1999). Women, men and gangs: The social construction of gender in the barrio. In M. Chesney-Lind & J. M. Hagedorn (Eds.), *Female gangs in America: Essays on girls, gangs and gender* (pp. 232–244). Chicago: Lake View Press.

Portillos, E. L., Jurik, N. C., & Zatz, M. (1996). Machismo and Chicano/a gangs: Symbolic resistance or oppression? *Free Inquiry in Creative Sociology, 24,* 175–183.

Pryor, D. W., & McGarrell, E. F. (1993). Public perceptions of youth gang crime: An exploratory analysis. *Youth & Society, 24,* 399–418.

Quicker, J. C. (1983). *Homegirls: Characterizing Chicana gangs.* San Pedro, CA: International University Press.

Quinn, J. F., Tobolowsky, P. M., & Downs, W. T. (1994). The gang problem in large and small cities: An analysis of police perceptions in nine states. *Journal of Gang Research, 2,* 13–22.

Rivera, R. J., & Short, J. F., Jr. (1967). Significant adults, caretakers, and structures of opportunity: An exploratory study. *Journal of Research in Crime and Delinquency, 4,* 76–97.

Robinson, N., & Joe, D. (1980). Gangs in Chinatown: The new young warrior class. *McGill Journal of Education, 15,* 149–162.

Rosenbaum, D. P., & Grant, J. A. (1983). *Gangs and youth problems in Evanston: Research findings and policy options.* Evanston, IL: Center for Urban Affairs and Policy Research, Northwestern University.

Rosenfeld, R., Bray, T. M., & Egley, A. (1999). Facilitating violence: A comparison of gang-motivated, gang-affiliated, and nongang youth homicides. *Journal of Quantitative Criminology, 15,* 495–516.

Sanders, W. B. (1994). *Gangbangs and drive-bys: Grounded culture and juvenile gang violence.* New York: Aldine De Gruyter.

Savelsberg, J. J., Cleveland, L. L., & King, R. D. (2004). Institutional environments and scholarly work: American criminology, 1951–1993. *Social Forces, 82,* 1275–1302.

Shelden, R. G., Snodgrass, T., & Snodgrass, P. (1993). Comparing gang and non-gang offenders: Some tentative findings. *Gang Journal, 1,* 73–95.

Sherif, M., & Sherif, C. W. (1967). Group processes and collective interaction in delinquent activities. *Journal of Research in Crime and Delinquency, 4,* 43–62.

Short, J. F., Jr. (1990). Gangs, neighborhoods, and youth crime. *Criminal Justice Research Bulletin, 5,* 1–11.

Short, J. F., Jr. (1998). The level of explanation problem revisited—the American Society of Criminology 1997 Presidential Address. *Criminology, 36,* 3–36.

Short, J. F., Jr., Rivera, R., & Tennyson, R. A. (1965). Perceived opportunities, gang membership, and delinquency. *American Sociological Review, 30,* 56–67.

Short, J. F., Jr., & Strodtbeck, F. L. (1965). *Group process and gang delinquency.* Chicago: University of Chicago Press.

Skolnick, J. H. (1990). *Gang organization and migration: Drugs, gangs, and law enforcement.* Sacramento, CA: Department of Justice, Office of the Attorney General.

Skolnick, J. H., Correl, T., Navarro, E., & Rabb, R. (1990). The social structure of street drug dealing. *American Journal of Police, 9,* 1–41.

Spergel, I. A. (1986). The violent gang problem in Chicago: A local community approach. *Social Service Review, 60,* 94–131.

Spergel, I. A. (1995). *The youth gang problem.* New York: Oxford University Press.

Spergel, I. A., & Curry, G. D. (1990). Strategies and perceived agency effectiveness in dealing with the youth gang problem. In C. R. Huff (Ed.), *Gangs in America* (pp. 288–309). Newbury Park, CA: Sage.

Strodtbeck, F. L., Short, J. F., Jr., & Kolegar, E. (1962). The analysis of self-descriptions by members of delinquent gangs. *Sociological Quarterly, 3,* 331–356.

Sullivan, M. L. (1989). *"Getting paid": Youth crime and work in the inner city.* Ithaca, NY: Cornell University Press.

Suttles, G. D. (1968). *The social order of the slum: Ethnicity and territory in the inner city.* Chicago: University of Chicago Press.

Swetnam, J., & Pope, J. (2001). Gangs and gang activity in a non-metropolitan community: The perceptions of students, teachers, and police officers. *Social Behavior and Personality, 29,* 197–208.

Takata, S., & Zevitz, R. (1990). Divergent perceptions of group delinquency in a midwestern community: Racine's gang problem. *Youth & Society, 21,* 282–305.

Taylor, C. S. (1990). *Dangerous society.* East Lansing: Michigan State University Press.

Taylor, C. S. (1993). *Girls, gangs, women and drugs.* East Lansing: Michigan State University Press.

Thornberry, T. P., Krohn, M. D., Lizotte, A. J., Smith, C. A., & Tobin, K. (2003). *Gangs and delinquency in developmental perspective.* Cambridge, UK: Cambridge University Press.

Thrasher, F. M. (1927). *The gang: A study of 1,313 gangs in Chicago.* Chicago: University of Chicago Press.

Venkatesh, S. A. (1997). The social organization of street gang activity in an urban ghetto. *American Journal of Sociology, 103,* 82–111.

Venkatesh, S. A. (2000). *American project: The rise and fall of a modern ghetto*. Cambridge, MA: Harvard University Press.

Venkatesh, S. A., & Levitt, S. D. (2000). Are we a family or a business? History and disjuncture in the urban American street gang. *Theory and Society, 29*(4), 427–462.

Vigil, J. D. (1988). *Barrio gangs: Street life and identity in Southern California*. Austin: University of Texas Press.

Vigil, J. D., & Long, J. M. (1990). Emic and etic perspectives on gang culture: The Chicano case. In C. R. Huff (Ed.), *Gangs in America* (pp. 55–68). Newbury Park, CA: Sage.

Vigil, J. D., & Yun, S. C. (1996). Southern California gangs: Comparative ethnicity and social control. In C. R. Huff (Ed.), *Gangs in America* (2nd ed., pp. 139–156). Thousand Oaks, CA: Sage.

Weisel, D. L. (2002). *Contemporary gangs: An organizational analysis*. New York: LFB Scholarly Publishing.

Weisheit, R. A., & Wells, L. E. (2001). The perception of gangs as a problem in nonmetropolitan areas. *Criminal Justice Review, 26*, 170–192.

Whyte, W. F. (1943). *Street corner society: The social structure of an Italian slum*. Chicago: University of Chicago Press.

Williams, T. M. (1989). *The cocaine kids: The inside story of a teenage drug ring*. Reading, MA: Addison-Wesley.

Wyrick, P. A., & Howell, J. C. (2004). Strategic risk-based response to youth gangs. *Juvenile Justice, 9*, 20–29.

Yablonsky, L. (1962). *The violent gang*. Baltimore: Penguin Books.

Zevitz, R. (1993). Youth gangs in a small midwestern city: Insiders' perspectives. *Journal of Crime and Justice, 16*, 149–165.

Zevitz, R. G., & Takata, S. R. (1992). Metropolitan gang influence and the emergence of group delinquency in a regional community. *Journal of Criminal Justice, 20*, 93–106.

Zhang, L., Welte, J. W., & Wieczorck, W. F. (1999). Youth gangs, drug use, and delinquency. *Journal of Criminal Justice, 27*, 101–109.

Zhang, S. X. (2002). Chinese gangs: Familial and cultural dynamics. In C. R. Huff (Ed.), *Gangs in America III* (pp. 219–236). Thousand Oaks, CA: Sage.

CHAPTER 4

The Value of Comparisons in Street Gang Research

Malcolm W. Klein

In this article, Klein details several key ways in which the field of gang research can become more comparative and thus vastly improve our knowledge about street gangs. This author echoes Hughes's critiques of the diverse methods employed in gang research and also the damage wrought by scholars' use of the different gang definitions described in the first article. The reader might consider how the work reported in the remainder of this volume might be advanced if more of these scholars heeded Klein's call for planned, comparative gang research.

This article is based on a single assumption: street gang research is nowhere near as cumulative as it could be (or could have been). After many decades of studies of many kinds, largely uncoordinated, we have reached the point where we "know" much about the nature of street gangs and their contexts. In proof, I offer the knowledge syntheses available in Covey, Menard, and Franzese (1997), Spergel (1995), Curry and Decker (1998), and Klein (1995a, 2004). But it took us 6 decades to reach this point of cumulative knowledge. How might the process have been accelerated? How might it yet be accelerated?

My answer comes in many variations of a single theme: gang research would be far more productive if it were based on comparisons. The variations have to do with types of comparison—gang members,

Reprinted from: Malcolm W. Klein, "The Value of Comparisons in Street Gang Research," *Journal of Contemporary Criminal Justice*, 21(2): 135–152. Copyright © 2005 by Sage Publications. Reprinted with permission from Sage Publications.

gangs as units, gang locations, gangs over time, and gangs studied by coordinated rather than disparate methods. In the several sections of this article, I cite studies involving such comparisons, but the studies chosen are selected to be illustrative. This is not the place to be exhaustive.

It is the place, however, to be definitive about what I mean by the term *street gang*. For this article and for all my future writing, I have adopted the "consensus Eurogang definition" developed over 5 years and agreed on by more than 100 gang research scholars in the United States and Europe. It is a minimalist definition specifically designed to enhance comparative street gang research. It reads as follows: "A street gang is any durable, street-oriented youth group whose own identity includes involvement in illegal activity."

Point 1: "Durable" is a bit ambiguous, but at least several months can be used as a guideline. Many gang-like groups come together and dissipate within a few months. The durability refers to the group, which continues despite turnover of members.

Point 2: "Street-oriented" implies spending a lot of group time outside home, work, and school—often on streets, in malls, in parks, in cars, and so on.

Point 3: "Youth" can be ambiguous. Most street gangs are more adolescent than adult, but some include members in their 20s and even 30s. Most have average ages in adolescence or early 20s.

Point 4: "Illegal" generally means delinquent or criminal, not just bothersome.

Point 5: "Identity" refers to the group, to the collective identity, not the individual self-image.

These are four definers of street gangs, here the necessary and sufficient components: durability, street-orientation, youthfulness, and identity via illegal activity. All other gang characteristics we are accustomed to citing are not definers but descriptors (e.g., ethnicity, age, gender, special clothing and argot, location, group names, crime patterns, and so on). This consensus definition has now been employed with considerable success, and its history and applications can be reviewed in Klein, Kerner, Maxson, and Weitekamp (2001), Klein (2002), and Decker and Weerman (2005). It allows us to distinguish street gangs from prison gangs, terrorist groups, motorcycle gangs, and adult criminal organizations. Such distinctions are often blurred in media reports and law enforcement pronouncements. It also allows us to distinguish street gangs from the far more numerous informal and formal youth groups whose members may occasionally engage in illegal activities but for whom such activities or orientation are not definers of their gang's identity. There are far more youth groups than there are street gangs.

In the sections that follow, I spell out and illustrate a number of comparative areas of study in gang research, a larger number than we normally think about in generalizing about gang knowledge. The instigation for my discussion occurred many years ago, when I first became acquainted with gang research and read a few fascinating gang ethnographies. Both then and now, my question in each case has been, is this study part of a pattern, or is it an anomaly? Was the researcher attempting to build generalizeable knowledge or merely taking advantage of a fortuitous situation where a street gang was available and interesting?

Illustrative Case Studies

Let's consider several oft-cited case studies. Leon Jansyn (1966) studied a Chicago gang over a period of a year. He demonstrated that a major turning point in the group's life came when its solidarity or cohesiveness ebbed to a particularly low point. When that point was reached, remaining active members deliberately increased their criminal activity with a view to reenergizing the gang, reestablishing its solidarity. The process described by Jansyn makes sense conceptually; maintaining group cohesion is critical to gang maintenance. But whether Jansyn observed an exemplar of a larger pattern or a unique episode can't be known. One technical problem is that his observations over a 1-year period might have been merely an expectable seasonal pattern, as gangs tend to show activity patterns related to summer and winter periods.

More important, however, Jansyn was not able to place his case study in a wider array of cases, even though many Chicago gangs were under study at the time, with extensive recorded observations (Carney, Mattick, & Calloway, 1969; Short & Strodtbeck, 1965). What needs demonstration is not that gang cohesiveness or gang activity ebbs and flows but that this is deliberately fostered by gang members' activities (increasing at low points—again, deliberately). Such intentionality would be an antidote to the many descriptions of gang crime as merely the outcome of group processes (Klein, 1971; Thornberry, Krohn, Lizotte, Smith, & Tobin, 2003).

A second example arises from Chicago data of the same era. In 1995, Laura Fishman reported a delayed analysis of the activity of a Black female gang, the Vice Queens. The group included about 30 girls in a gang having auxiliary status to the famous Vice Kings. The ages ranged from 13 to 19, with about 19 of them described as "hard core." The group had functional rather than structural leadership, and a moderate level of cohesiveness. Members were largely out of school, unemployed, sexually active with the Vice Kings, and otherwise exhibiting versatile or "cafeteria-style" delinquency patterns.

Fishman declares that, to judge from these 1960s data, not much has changed about the nature of girl gangs, but she offers no modern comparisons. More to the point, we can in this case know that the Vice Queens were very similar to many other female auxiliary gangs in the 1960s and 1970s, as described by Klein (1971) and Moore (1978) in Los Angeles. Thus, the Fishman depiction makes sense, and we have the potential for a two-city, same-era pattern of findings. But how delicious it would have been way back then if the Chicago and Los Angeles projects could have joined forces to plan coordinated data collection on similarly defined and measured variables. What a quantum leap might have resulted in the then relatively barren area of female gang research.

A third example is provided by Sudhir Venkatesh's 1999 report on a traditional Chicago "super gang" heavily engaged in the drug trade. The gang numbered in several hundreds and was highly structured around the sale of crack cocaine. Venkatesh scored a research coup in gaining access to the gang's financial records of drug proceeds and expenditures (including amounts dedicated to wages, weapons, and funeral expenses).

This was obviously a unique opportunity and the author deserves credit for taking advantage of it. But is it a unique instance, part of a small, identifiable pattern among drug gangs, or something yet broader? Venkatesh claims that there has been a "dramatic transformation known as corporatization" in the 1970s, yet in support he cites only Taylor's troublesome work in Detroit about a project that started in 1980 (see Klein, 1995a, for a critique). Venkatesh clearly implies that he is describing a general pattern, and of course he may be correct. Nonetheless, most research on the organizational capacities of street gangs argues the opposite (Decker, 2001; Klein, 1995a; Weisel, 2002). How useful it would be to have a comparable set of drug gang studies that included data on how sales proceeds were spent.

In fact, a contrary case, also from Chicago, is offered by Felix Padilla (1992). He describes a Puerto Rican drug-dealing gang that is an offshoot of a larger traditional gang. About 24 members aged mostly between 15 and 18 work for distributors in their 20s. They seem less unstable than most street gangs in their criminal pursuits but more cohesive and more hierarchically organized. Conceptually, this makes sense for a gang "in business." Empirically, it fits the pattern for specialty gangs described first by Maxson and Klein (1995) and soon thereafter by Klein (2002) and Weitekamp (2001). But how much more solid would the pattern be if Padilla had been able to compare the same variables across several drug gangs? He reports that there were a dozen others around at the same time in the Chicago area he frequented. He also provides no description of the parent gang from which his evolved; was it similar to the one described by Venkatesh? Again, my purpose is not to fault ethnographies for undertaking single-case studies; they often have no other choice. Rather, the point is to suggest that a set of coordinated studies by several researchers would add generic knowledge to the rich case knowledge that single studies provide.

Finally, let me escape the confines of Chicago and move marginally southwest, to Kansas City. Mark Fleisher's (1998) ethnography of the Fremont Hustlers in that city is quite a departure from most gang studies, in part because it is truly an ethnography, not just an observational or field study. Fleisher got an inside look at the gang, its members, and the neighborhood and family setting in which they were embedded. He came to understand the gang culture from the inside out, as few of us do.

Fleisher describes a mixed gender, drug-oriented, amorphous street gang that, uniquely to date among ethnographies, illustrates the collective gang type described by Maxson and Klein (1995). But as rich and illuminating as the description is, it stands alone as an exemplar of the type (which was derived from police reports to structured inquiries). Maxson and Klein found collective gangs to be the least common of their five structural types, so it is not surprising that other depictions like Fleisher's are absent. To judge the type from the Hustlers may be appropriate, but we can't know this. Is Kansas City different? Was the time period unique? Does ethnography reveal an image that can't be captured by field observations or gang member surveys? A field that cannot adequately answer such questions has not yet achieved its potential; it has not grounded itself in generic knowledge.

These five good research studies illustrate the inherent limitations of unique attributes in time, location, and method. But what if such limitations could be reduced? Let's consider comparisons that could move us forward and faster; in some cases this has already happened.

Available Comparisons

Of all the comparative studies gang researchers have undertaken over the years, it is surprising to find that most types of comparison have been given relatively scant attention. Most surprising is the paucity of cross-gang comparisons, despite the obvious fact that gangs are groups, that groups are potential units of analysis, and that gangs proliferated at their peak to more than 4,000 jurisdictions (National Youth Gang Center, 2000). Instead, we have concentrated our efforts on gang member comparisons, so let's review these first.

Gang Member Comparisons

Examples of research cataloguing the different characteristics of gang members abound (Chin, 1996; Decker & Van Winkle, 1996; Klein, 1971; Miller, 2001; Short & Strodtbeck, 1965). Researchers have been able to document the wide ranges and central tendencies of members' ages, ethnicities, behavior patterns, familial and socioeconomic backgrounds, gang joining, participation levels, and leaving patterns. Two patterns among these seem to be so universal and yet surprising to the lay public that they deserve special attention, namely the versatility rather than the specialization of gang member crime (Klein, 1971; Robin, 1967; Short & Strodtbeck, 1965) and the dramatically changing level of criminal involvement associated with joining and leaving gangs (e.g., Thornberry et al., 2003, and replicated in studies in Denver, Pittsburgh, Seattle, Montreal, and Edinburgh).

Attention should also be drawn to gender differences, which have drawn increasing attention over time (Fagan, 1990; Klein, 1971; Maxson & Whitlock, 2002; Miller, 2001; Moore, 1991). Several descriptive facts stand out; gang girls are younger and leave earlier than boys, gang girls are not merely the sex objects and weapon carriers described in early research, and gang girls exhibit the same general illegal behavior patterns as the boys but at lower levels. A comparison between police reports of female gang participation on one hand and ethnographies and survey reports on the other makes it clear that the police greatly underestimate levels of female gang membership, which often reaches between 20% and 40% at younger ages (younger than 16). However, these statements are more cumulative than directly comparative. Studies looking at male and female members of the same group are uncommon (but see Fleisher, 1998; Klein, 1971; Moore, 1978, 1991).

Gang versus Non-Gang Members

Another important approach to understanding gang members is to compare them with non-gang youth. Preferably, such comparisons would encompass the same communities to control for broad contextual differences. Recent work by Maxson, Whitlock, and myself in San Diego and Long Beach, yet to be published, drew members and nonmembers from the same neighborhood where gangs were known to be present. The differences we are finding are fewer than those taken from less stringent comparisons (same schools, same communities) but nonetheless striking with respect to a subset of variables distinguishing members from nonmembers (see preliminary analysis in Maxson, Whitlock, & Klein, 1998). A few other gang/non-gang comparisons illustrate the sorts of findings that seem particularly instructive about the nature of gang members.

- A series of articles by Short and his colleagues explore comparisons between gang and non-gang youth on structural dimensions. One of these (Short, Rivera, & Tennyson, 1965) reports predictable differences in exposures to legitimate and illegitimate opportunities. A second (Short, Rivera, & Marshall, 1964) reports surprisingly few differences in the way gang and non-gang youth rate nine adult roles (politician, minister, policeman, etc.), suggesting a minor place for adult influence in explaining gang membership. Yet a third article (Rivera & Short, 1967) reports large differences between gang members and nonmembers in how the adults they know respond to them. Gang-nominated adults are far less responsive and more likely to "pin the blame" on the boys rather than on the conventional structure of opportunity.

- Huff (1996) reported that differences in social activities between members and nonmembers are far smaller than differences in illegal activities: gang members, contrary to popular conceptions, often engage in the same social and recreational activities as their non-gang peers. However, Huff's data show illegal activity differences to be significant in two thirds of all categories of crime, with ratios ranging from 3 to 1 up to 20 to 1, member to nonmember. It was the rare acts (e.g., forgery, kidnap, sexual assault) that showed nonsignificant differences.

- Fagan (1990) found ratios over 12 categories of crime to favor gang members between 2 to 1 and 4 to 1 among males. Female comparisons were almost equally large. As in the Huff (1996) analysis above, the more serious offenses showed the larger ratios.

- Esbensen, Huizinga, and Weiher (1995) advanced the issue with gang members and two categories of nonmembers, "non gang-street offenders" and "non-offenders" (relatively, that is). They, too, found no differences in levels of conventional activities but expectable major differences in crime rates. Unexpectedly, however, although there were significant differences in attitudes and perceptual variables between gang members and non-offenders, this was not true when comparing gang members and non-gang street offenders. Only 1 of 18 variables distinguished these two groups. Different but reasonable comparison groups provide different conclusions depending on the category of variables employed, in this case behavioral versus cognitive variables. More of this kind of work will inform our conceptualizations of what makes gang members different.

- Thornberry et al. (2003) added another comparative variation by comparing gang members with quartiles of non-gang groups who nonetheless had delinquent peers—another reasonable comparison. They found the highest quartile to be similar to the gang members in mean peer delinquency, but not in general delinquency rates. The gang processes were adding something beyond the effects of delinquent peers. These differences remained between eight waves of data collection in all quartiles, with violence differences being the greatest. Similar results were obtained for females across the first four waves, but then the female gang membership disappeared.

- Finally in this listing is the work of Jody Miller (2001) with gang and non-gang girls. She found major differences in self-reported delinquency on 20 of 26 items. In addition, she reported differences in exposure to or awareness of gang issues in the neighborhood, along with differences in family problems and gang membership within the families. The stability of the comparisons is established by drawing the gang respondents from two contrasting urban settings, Columbus and St. Louis.

In sum, there have been enough studies using comparison groups and analyses that a rather stable depiction of gang members has emerged, a depiction that allows us to speculate on factors that make gangs and gang members qualitatively different from non-gang youth. It is our historical emphasis on studying individuals that has permitted this to occur. This is less true of the other comparisons to which I turn next.

Cross-Gang Comparisons

When I started my career in gang research, I was fortunate to be presented with four large clusters of Black street gangs, which I later augmented with intensive exposure to a large Hispanic gang. I had five gangs to compare but did not appreciate until later how valuable this opportunity was. When, during this same period. I traveled to Chicago and Boston to compare notes with Jim Short and Walter Miller, I learned that they were studying gangs of much the same type, what we now call traditional gangs. Traditional gangs are large, self-regenerating clusters of subgroups with cafeteria-style crime patterns and territorial orientations. Joan Moore's gangs were of the same type (Moore, 1978), as were many described in New York, San Francisco, Philadelphia, and El Paso. This research took place largely before 1980, and although it provided wonderful data on traditional gangs, we didn't appreciate that such gangs were special. We could study them because they were stable over time, providing easy and continuing access. They were available; they were not necessarily typical.

Various attempts at typologizing gangs were undertaken, but they yielded different typologies, based on different methods (see Klein & Maxson,

2006, for a full exposition of the typological approach). Short and Strodtbeck (1965) had the luxury of gathering data from 16 Chicago groups, and the comparisons allowed them, among other things, to extract gang behavior patterns that failed to support popular typologies.[1]

The structural typology first described by Maxson and Klein (1995) was based on gang descriptions from 59 cities—one gang in each—and then validated in hundreds of others both in the United States and abroad (Klein, 2002). Traditional, neotraditional, compressed, collective, and specialty gangs account for between 74% and 95% of gangs studied, representing variations on durability, size, age structure, subgrouping, territoriality, and crime pattern. The strength of the typology rests on its stability when even statewide and national comparisons are made. And although it is based on male gangs for the most part, Miller (2001) has found it applicable to female gangs in Columbus and St. Louis as well.

Recent deliberately comparative studies have also helped lay to rest the stereotype of street gangs based on media reports of the mythical character of the Crips and Bloods of Los Angeles, and the super gangs of Chicago. Reports by Decker (2001) and Weisel (2002) compare the most serious gangs in San Diego, St. Louis, and Chicago (two gangs in each city) to search for the quasi-corporate structure that feeds both the public image and the claims of many enforcement agencies. Only one of the six gangs, the Black Gangster Disciples in Chicago, fits the bill. The others do not, based on organizational variables such as differentiated levels of membership, strong leaders, regular meetings, written rules, specialization of functions, organization of drug sales, profits used for gang purposes, owning legitimate businesses, engaging in local political activities, relationships with local businesses, and collaborative relationships with other groups. This important research dispels popular notions, just as the typological results clarify both the variety and patterns of gang structures.

One vital comparison is still missing: We know little about gangs, as defined in this article, as different from other youth groups. I am referring here specifically to using groups as units of analysis. If street gangs (by definition) are different from other youth groups—beyond the several defining characteristics—and different from such groups as prison gangs, motorcycle gangs, and drug cartels, what are the important differences and what do they tell us about street gang structure and street gang life? I cannot, offhand, think of a single comparative study that looks at these different group units.

Comparisons across Locations

Locations can refer to different neighborhoods in a given community, to different communities within a given city, to different cities, or even to different countries. Although there are a number of examples of the first three, it is often the case that data are aggregated across locations without specific comparisons between locations. My first four gang clusters in the early 1960s (Klein, 1971) were compared on gang structures in each of the four locations as well as on the cohesiveness of the four clusters, but the analysis of the offense patterns was aggregated across all four. Short and Strodtbeck (1965), with 16 gangs in several locations, aggregated most of their data analyses. So did Miller with his Boston gangs.

An exception to the aggregation pattern is provided by Dennis Mares's (2001) study of the gangs in three contrasting neighborhoods in Manchester, England. One of these was a downtrodden housing development area, the second a working-class area, and the third a changing suburban area. Dear to my heart is Mares's attempt to relate the different areas to differences in gang structure: neotraditional gangs in the first two areas and compressed gangs in the third. This was an ethnographic study, with no serious attempt to aggregate data across contrasting settings.

Across cities, Fagan (1989) drew gang members from Chicago, Los Angeles, and San Diego to illuminate a typology of social, party, conflict, and delinquent gangs, but otherwise aggregated his data across the three locations. Similarly, Huff's (1996) gang/non-gang comparisons were aggregated across several cities without intercity comparisons. Cross-city comparisons are difficult for two very practical reasons. First, it is a logistic nightmare to launch a sustained, multicity research project. It is expensive in finances, time, and effort. Second, a decent cross-city comparison is of limited value unless those cities (and neighborhoods) are described and studied to understand why one would expect differences and similarities between the gangs drawn from them. For example, Decker's (2001) commendable comparison of the most serious gangs in San Diego, St. Louis, and Chicago concentrated on the organizational capacities of the gangs, but not on what we might have expected given their very different urban and historical contexts.

I can think of only one cross-city study that deliberately selected contrasting cities, described their social, economic, and historical contexts, and then collected gang data to investigate in part what differences might emerge that made sense given those contrasting contexts. This was Jody Miller's study of female gang members in Columbus and St. Louis, cities with very different economic states of health and different histories of gang development. Miller provides a model that could easily be followed by others.[2]

One report stands out for its examination of cross-city data on a number of dimensions. As part of a program evaluation, Esbensen and Linskey (2001) compared school survey reports from young gang members in 11 cities. Included were responses about four topics: demographics, gang characteristics, self-report delinquency, and reasons for joining gangs. Although some notable differences emerge, the more striking pattern is that of similarities across most cities with respect to 28 items in the fourth category. This is all the more striking as the 11 sites ranged from rural to urban and small cities (less than 100,000 population) to major urban centers such as Philadelphia and Phoenix.

There is a way in which this situation could be further improved without great effort. The National Youth Gang Center (see National Youth Gang Center, 2000, and other yearly reports) has collected gang data from law enforcement agencies over about a decade, with literally thousands of communities included in the database. Although the material is necessarily somewhat superficial, it covers a number of areas of interest: percentage reporting gangs; numbers of gangs and gang members; distribution of age, gender, and ethnicity; use of member, motive, or other definitions of gang crime; various crime rates; approaches to gang control; and so on. Changes in levels of gang

crime per city are available over the 10-year period. What is required first is the melding of these data with census and other city databases to get at the patterns of gang prevalence. Then the stage would be set for adventuresome researchers to engage in both quantitative and on-site qualitative comparative studies.

Another stage-setting exercise has already taken place to add cross-national comparisons (with instrumentation equally applicable to neighborhood and city comparisons). The Eurogang Program (Klein, 2002) has since 1997 brought together more than 100 American and European gang scholars and policy officials in a series of seven international workshops. To date, two volumes of research reports have been produced (Decker & Weerman, 2005; Klein et al., 2001).[3] These include studies in the United States, Holland, England, Scotland, Norway, Denmark, Germany, France, Russia, Belgium, and Italy. Included are several comparative studies, employing the same instruments, by European and American gang researchers. The gang definitions employed in this chapter and described in its first pages derive from the Eurogang effort. The Decker and Weerman collection illustrates clearly how comparisons across countries are facilitated by the use of this definition in each contribution. Common terms cannot help but improve comparative efforts.

Historical Comparisons

Here, we are on even thinner ground. One of the reasons for needing historical comparisons is, of course, the enormous changes in gang prevalence, structure, and crime patterns that have taken place over the past several decades (Covey et al., 1997; Klein, 1995a; Spergel, 1995). In addition, gang activity has been shown to go through cycles, ranging from seasons to many years. These changes and cycles led me to comment some years ago (Klein, 1995b):

> With respect to changes in gang characteristics, it might be thought that the cyclical nature of gang activity would yield a picture of little linear change over time—that is, the back and forth swings of the pendulum would cancel each other out. But this is not the case. Through all the periodic cycles, gangs and gang problems have grown. The cycles end at

higher plateaus, on average, as if the pendulum seldom reverts to its original lower level, while often reaching a higher level on the upswing. Thus, over several decades, the upper age limit has increased; the variety of ethnic minority gangs has increased; the variety of gang structures has increased; associated gang violence has increased. (p. 233)

In the face of these sorts of changes, some continuity in the research process would be valuable, but this requires researchers who are willing and able to stay at the table over long periods of time or, at the very least, are interested in recapturing the past and comparing it with the present. Only a few examples present themselves. Taylor (1990) reported an evolution in gang structures from what he called scavenger to territorial to corporate gangs in Detroit. This analysis was low on data, but at least yielded testable hypotheses. Moore (1978, 1991) returned to East Los Angeles to assess changes in two traditional gangs. She found them to have become more institutionalized, with the groups coming to have more influence over members; greater drug involvement; violence cyclical rather than changing linearly; deviance generally but not dramatically increased; more isolation from other peer groups and less tolerated by community adults. These gangs, she noted, were "no longer just at the rowdy end of the continuum of local adolescent groups—they are now really outside the continuum" (Moore, 1991, p. 132).

Obviously, we can compare research findings from one period to another and assess aggregate changes. But such comparisons do not control for location or gang, and thus they give little sense for the dynamics of gang evolution within gangs or within locations. Models such as Taylor's (1990) or Moore's are far more promising in understanding such dynamics, but they are rare.

Methodological Comparisons

In the mid-1960s, I found myself in an odd argument with Walter Miller. We had both been collecting extensive data on gang delinquency from similar sets of traditional Black street gangs, he in Boston and I in Los Angeles. Miller reported quite a heavy level of violence among his gangs, whereas I was reporting a relatively light level of violence. Were Boston and Los Angeles gangs so similar in

type, yet so dissimilar in behavior? After considerable discussion, we discovered that the dissimilarities lay not in the gangs but in the researchers.

Miller's data were based on informal interviews and detached worker reports of gang member conversations. Miller was listening to violence. My data were based on street observations and detached worker reports of gang member behaviors. I was observing. Gang members, it seemed, talked a more violent game than they played. A listening researcher will find different levels of violence than an observing researcher. If Miller had taken his ears to Los Angeles and I had taken my eyes to Boston, the pictures likely would have been reversed.

The anecdote reminds us of the obvious fact of methodology: different methods may, or even must, yield variations on what we trust as independent reality. Further, entry into the gang world via different doors will probably yield different perspectives. There are important implications from starting out with gang member contacts, or street worker contacts, or school contacts, or police and correctional contacts. Different truths may emerge (see, for example, the data reported for Chicago by Curry, 2000). Only the application of different methods to the same phenomenon, in the same time and location, can lead us to a more comprehensive and interpretable reality.

A planned comparative methods approach can expose the limitations of the separate methods. It can give a rounder picture of gang realities. It forces a better appreciation of the ecology of gangs versus the nature of gangs that single methods can't provide. Too often, and for very understandable reasons of practicality and training, gang researchers have depended on a single method. This has been especially true of survey researchers whose data are most often taken from youth samples in school or household surveys, or occasionally from surveys of police respondents. It is also often true of archival researchers who dig into police, correctional, or court files and databases.

It has been somewhat less true of field observers and ethnographers where one finds an admixture of experiential, observational, and interview data (see, for example, Fleisher's 1998 depiction of the Fremont Hustlers in Kansas City). Yet, even in these instances, the combination of methods is not usually planned as a comparative methodological design. Perhaps the most comprehensive pattern of methods has been associated with researchers undertaking evaluations of gang intervention programs (Carney et al., 1969; Klein, 1971; Miller, 1962; Spergel, 1995). Still, this is not enough. A definitive statement of the street gang picture as seen from differently selected methods is not yet available. However, it might soon be possible.

After 6 years of interactions between U.S. and European scholars, a series of research instruments designed for comparative cross-national, multi-method research has emerged. To varying degrees, these instruments have been translated and back-translated into several languages, pretested and revised in a number of countries, and are now being employed by a variety of gang researchers here and abroad. They are publicly available and can now be used to assess the comparative gang pictures they produce. All of them are based on the consensus Eurogang definition introduced in the beginning of this article, and the three principal instruments incorporate operational measures of this definition. The instruments are as follows.

The Youth Survey

The survey protocol contains three levels of items as judged by the Eurogang researcher consortium. Core items are those necessary to establish a youth's group affiliations as gang or non-gang according to the program's definitional stance. Secondary items are those judged very important for basic comparisons of street gangs across different sites. Tertiary items are those of general interest to most gang researchers but not critical to establishing the nature of the gangs and gang members. Users of this interview protocol are required to use the core items, strongly urged to use at least the secondary set as well, and encouraged to use the tertiary set. They can, of course, add any items they deem useful for their research purposes.

The Ethnographic Guidelines

These are an explicit listing of information to be gathered in the course of an ethnographic street gang study. They correspond in content, although not of course in format, to the three levels of information gathered in the youth interview. They allow for systematic collection of the same information across gangs and across ethnographic study sites, as well as comparisons to data drawn from youth surveys in those sites. Nothing in the guidelines prevents an ethnographer from gathering additional data of interest in any form deemed feasible.

The Experts' Survey

This is an interview or questionnaire protocol designed for respondents who are knowledgeable about the street gang situations in their area or jurisdiction. It is appropriate to police, social service practitioners, teachers and school officials, local businessmen, crime reporters, neighborhood leaders, and even selected veteran or ex-gang members. It uses the same definitional items as the youth survey and then seeks structured information on known street gangs in the respondent's purview. Cross-site ecologies of street gangs are easily derived from the experts' survey.

Two other standardized instruments are also available. The first is a set of guidelines for city descriptions. Tested out for general availability of such information, it lists historical, cultural, geographic, and demographic data that can normally be collected about a research site to provide the broad social context within which to locate street gang problems. The fifth instrument is a survey of gang prevention and control programs with special emphasis on those that have been subjected to some evaluation effort.

It is my first fantasy that within a few years we will see planned, comparative method studies of street gangs using these standardized instruments. It is my second fantasy that we will see such studies in multiple sites—comparing gangs, gang neighborhoods, and gangs in different cities and countries. The technological means are now available through the Eurogang Program, and the opportunity as called for by Maxson (2001) in the first Eurogang collection of papers now exists. More comparisons means better knowledge and, for those so inclined, better practices in improving the worlds inhabited by street gangs.

Caveats and Conclusions

Fantasies such as these are easily come by. The realities of conducting comparative research teach hard lessons: It's difficult work and requires a good deal of tolerance, especially for the different perspectives of one's collaborators. Beyond this, good comparative research brings several requirements of particular note:

- It means using the same or similar definitions of the central concepts, such as "street gang" (thus, my use of the consensus Eurogang definition in this article).

- It means using the same or very similar forms of data collection procedures, be they ethnographic protocols, survey instruments, or archival coding schemes.

- But common definitions and common instruments do not necessarily yield common sample procedures. Comparative research should also mean careful attention to sample selection (members, gangs, locations) that yields either similar units, or units deliberately selected to compare the effect of their contrasts, for example, similar types of gangs or very different types, gang members from the same community or drawn from very different communities, gangs all in emergent or chronic gang areas, or gangs deliberately chosen to represent those two different contexts. In other words, we must know beforehand what the relevant parameters of comparison are.

- All of this, obviously, implies careful planning prior to launching comparative studies, and a commitment to resolving differences between collaborators' perspectives. In addition, it means that comparisons across types of data collection must also be carefully considered. The depth of ethnography, the breadth of surveys, and the selectivity of archives (police reports, court transcripts, news articles) must be appreciated and assessed for their differences. As a colleague remarked to me, "Quantitative factors have qualitative consequences."

- Finally, research on different gangs or in different locations, with several types of data collection methods, means that we are dealing with different contexts of knowledge

development. To be thorough, we must not only understand the elements of our methodological outputs but the contexts of those data sources as well.

My fear is that all the foregoing will discourage most readers from undertaking comparative gang research. I hope not; I hope it will instead be read as a challenge. I hope the challenge will appeal to researchers who thrive on complexity and the satisfaction of bringing order out of chaos. I write with them in mind.

Notes

1. They also employed another comparison of great merit, using their data to assess the validity of competing gang theories (Cohen, Cloward and Ohlin, Miller, and Yablonsky, inferentially).

2. It should be noted that Miller's design was derived from the distinction between emergent and chronic gang cities. Vigil's (2002) cross-ethnic comparison is not a cross-city comparison, but the model he uses is worth consideration because he searched for the connections between different ethnicities and gang characteristics for explanatory purposes, much as Miller did for different cities.

3. One should note as well the recent compendium of gang studies put together by Herbert Covey (2003). In this volume, Covey attempts secondhand comparisons of various sorts including the structures described in Maxson and Klein (1995).

References

Carney, F., Mattick, H. W., & Calloway, J. D. (1969). *Action on the streets*. New York: Association Press.

Chin, K. (1996). *Chinatown gangs: Extortion, enterprise, and ethnicity*. New York: Oxford University Press.

Covey, H. C. (2003). *Street gangs throughout the world*. Springfield, IL: Charles C Thomas.

Covey, H. C., Menard, S., & Franzese, R. J. (1997). *Juvenile gangs* (2nd ed.). Springfield, IL: Charles C Thomas.

Curry, G. D. (2000). Self-reported gang involvement and officially reported delinquency. *Criminology, 38,* 1253–1274.

Curry, G. D., & Decker, S. H. (1998). *Confronting gangs: Crime and community*. Los Angeles: Roxbury.

Decker, S. H. (2001). The impact of organizational features on gang activities and relationships. In M. W. Klein, H.-J. Kerner, C. L. Maxson, & E. G. Weitekamp (Eds.),

The Eurogang paradox: Street gangs and youth groups in the U.S. and Europe (pp. 21–39). Dordrecht: Kluwer Academic.

Decker, S. H., & Van Winkle, B. (1996). *Life in the gang: Family, friends, and violence*. Cambridge: Cambridge University Press.

Decker, S. H., & Weerman, F. (2005). *European street gangs and troublesome youth groups: Findings from the Eurogang Research Program*. Walnut Creek, CA: AltaMira Press.

Esbensen, F.-A., Huizinga, D., & Weiher, A. W. (1995). Gang and non-gang youth: Differences in explanatory factors. In M. W. Klein, C. L. Maxson, & J. Miller (Eds.), *The modern gang reader* (pp. 192–202). Los Angeles: Roxbury.

Esbensen, F.-A., & Linskey, D. (2001). Young gang members in a school survey. In M. W. Klein, H.-J. Kerner, C. L. Maxson, & E. G. Weitekamp (Eds.), *The Eurogang paradox: Street gangs and youth groups in the U.S. and Europe* (pp. 93–114). Dordrecht: Kluwer Academic.

Fagan, J. (1989). The social organization of drug use and drug dealing among urban gangs. *Criminology, 27*, 633–669.

Fagan, J. (1990). Social processes of delinquency and drug use among urban gangs. In C. R. Huff (Ed.), *Gangs in America* (pp. 183–219). Newbury Park, CA: Sage.

Fishman, L. (1995). The Vice Queens: An ethnographic study of Black female gang behavior. In M. W. Klein, C. L. Maxson, & J. Miller (Eds.), *The modern gang reader* (pp. 83–92). Los Angeles: Roxbury.

Fleisher, M. S. (1998). *Dead end kids: Gang girls and the boys they know*. Madison: University of Wisconsin Press.

Huff, C. R. (1996). The criminal behavior of gang members and nongang at risk youth. In C. R. Huff (Ed.), *Gangs in America* (2nd ed., pp. 75–102). Thousand Oaks, CA: Sage.

Jansyn, L. (1966). Solidarity and delinquency in a street corner group. *American Sociological Review, 31*, 600–614.

Klein, M. W. (1971). *Street gangs and street workers*. Englewood Cliffs, NJ: Prentice Hall.

Klein, M. W. (1995a). *The American street gang: Its nature, prevalence, and control*. New York: Oxford University Press.

Klein, M. W. (1995b). Street gang cycles. In J. Q. Wilson & J. Petersilia (Eds.), *Crime* (pp. 217–236). San Francisco: ICS Press.

Klein, M. W. (2002). Street gangs: A cross-national perspective. In C. R. Huff (Ed.), *Gangs in America III* (pp. 237–254). Thousand Oaks, CA: Sage.

Klein, M. W. (2004). *Gang cop: The words and ways of Officer Paco Domingo*. Walnut Creek, CA: AltaMira Press.

Klein, M. W., Kerner, H.-J., Maxson, C. L., & Weitekamp, E. G. (Eds.). (2001). *The Eurogang paradox: Street gangs and youth groups in the U.S. and Europe*. Dordrecht: Kluwer Academic.

Klein, M. W., & Maxson, C. L. (2006). *Street gang patterns and policies*. Oxford: Oxford University Press.

Mares, D. (2001). Gangstas or lager louts? Working class street gangs in Manchester. In M. W. Klein, H.-J. Kerner, C. L. Maxson, & E. G. Weitekamp (Eds.), *The Eurogang paradox: Street gangs and youth groups in the U.S. and Europe* (pp. 153–164). Dordrecht: Kluwer Academic.

Maxson, C. L. (2001). A proposal for multi-site study of European gangs and youth groups. In M. W. Klein, H.-J. Kerner, C. L. Maxson, & E. G. Weitekamp (Eds.), *The Eurogang paradox: Gangs and youth groups in the U.S. and Europe* (pp. 299–308). Dordrecht: Kluwer Academic.

Maxson, C. L., & Klein, M. W. (1995). Investigating gang structures. *Journal of Gang Research, 3*, 33–40.

Maxson, C. L., & Whitlock, M. L. (2002). Joining the gang: Gender differences in risk factors for gang membership. In C. R. Huff (Ed.), *Gangs in America III* (pp. 19–35). Thousand Oaks, CA: Sage.

Maxson, C. L., Whitlock, M. L., & Klein, M. W. (1998). Vulnerability to street gang membership: Implications for practice. *Social Service Review, 72*, 70–91.

Miller, J. (2001). *One of the guys: Girls, gangs, and gender*. New York: Oxford University Press.

Miller, W. B. (1962). The impact of a "total community" delinquency control program. *Social Problems, 10*, 168–191.

Moore, J. W. (1978). *Homeboys: Gangs, drugs, and prison in the barrios of Los Angeles*. Philadelphia: Temple University Press.

Moore, J. W. (1991). *Going down to the barrio: Homeboys and homegirls in change*. Philadelphia: Temple University Press.

National Youth Gang Center. (2000). *1998 National Young Gang Survey: Summary*. Washington, DC: U.S. Department of Justice, Office of Juvenile Justice and Delinquency Prevention.

Padilla, F. (1992). *The gang as an American enterprise*. New Brunswick, NJ: Rutgers University Press.

Rivera, R., & Short, J. F., Jr. (1967). Significant adults, caretakers, and structures of opportunity: An exploratory study. *Journal of Research in Crime and Delinquency, 4*, 76–97.

Robin, G. D. (1967). Gang member delinquency in Philadelphia. In M. W. Klein (Ed.), *Juvenile gangs in context: Theory, research, and action* (pp. 15–24). Englewood Cliffs, NJ: Prentice Hall.

Short, J. F., Jr., Rivera, R., & Marshall, H. (1964). Adult-adolescent relations and gang delinquency. *Pacific Sociological Review, 7,* 59–65.

Short, J. F., Jr., Rivera, R., & Tennyson, R. A. (1965). Perceived opportunities, gang membership, and delinquency. *American Sociological Review, 38,* 56–67.

Short, J. F., Jr., & Strodtbeck, F. L. (1965). *Group process and gang delinquency.* Chicago: University of Chicago Press.

Spergel, I. A. (1995). *The youth gang problem.* New York: Oxford University Press.

Taylor, C. J. (1990). *Dangerous society.* East Lansing: Michigan State University Press.

Thornberry, T. R., Krohn, M. D., Lizotte, A. J., Smith, C. A., & Tobin, K. (2003). *Gangs and delinquency in developmental perspective.* Cambridge: Cambridge University Press.

Venkatesh, S. (1999). The financial activities of a modern American street gang. *NIJ Research Forum, 1,* 1–11.

Vigil, J. D. (2002). *A rainbow of gangs: Street cultures in the mega-city.* Austin: University of Texas Press.

Weisel, D. (2002). The evolution of street gangs: An examination of form and variation. In W. L. Reed & S. H. Decker (Eds.), *Responding to gangs: Evaluation and research* (pp. 24–65). Washington, DC: National Institute of Justice.

Weitekamp, E. G. (2001). Gangs in Europe: Assessments at the millennium. In M. W. Klein, H.-J. Kerner, C. L. Maxson, & E. G. Weitekamp (Eds.), *The Eurogang paradox: Street gangs and youth groups in the U.S. and Europe* (pp. 304–322). Dordrecht: Kluwer Academic.

The Scope and Dynamics of Gang Involvement

The subject matter of this section follows directly from that discussed in Section I. Now that we have a better grasp of the many ways to conduct gang research and are aware of the challenging and ongoing definitional issues, we can begin to ask the basic descriptive questions regarding the characteristics of gangs, gang members, and gang activity. The articles that follow address three general questions:

1. What do we know about changes, if any, in gang activity across the U.S. in recent years?

2. What do we know about the demographic characteristics of the individuals who join gangs?

3. What do we know about the processes and factors that lead to joining and leaving gangs?

With regard to the first question, nationally, according to the FBI's Uniform Crime Reports, violent crime and homicide rates have declined by approximately 50 percent over the past 20 years. Yet, as Howell and colleagues report in this section, prevalence rates of gang activity show a dissimilar trend. Mirroring the start of the national crime drop in the early to mid-1990s, reports of gang activity also began to decline annually. But in the early 2000s these two trends noticeably diverged: while the overall crime rate, including violent crime, continued to fall, prevalence rates of gang activity began to slowly increase, such that these researchers find that gang activity is now more widespread—jurisdictionally speaking—than it was 10 years ago (though not as widespread as it was in the mid-1990s). What accounts for these findings? Maxson's article on gang member migration debunks one popular explanation: gang member relocation does *not* appear to cause most new gang problems. Gang-involved individuals move to new areas for a variety of reasons; some members' motives may be illegitimate in nature, but mainly gang members move for legitimate reasons (e.g., job opportunities, following family members), bringing along with them aspects of gang culture. Coupled with the diffusion of gang culture in movies and music and on the Internet, there exist many direct and indirect ways for gangs to proliferate without a corresponding increase in crime.

Concerning the second question about the characteristics of gang members, let us immediately dispense with the stereotypical image of gang members as principally urban, minority males (as was discussed in Section I). As Esbensen and Carson's chapter demonstrates, gang members are of both sexes and all races. Gangs typically emerge in the most socially disorganized and economically depressed areas, where social capital, collective efficacy, and access to resources are all severely lacking. The demographic characteristics of gang members, then, reflect the communities in which they reside. More will be said about each of these issues in Sections IV, V, and VI.

With regard to the third question of what we know about joining and leaving gangs, it is safe to say we know far more about the former (joining) than we do about the latter (leaving). The advent of large-scale, longitudinal risk factor studies (specifically, the Causes and Correlates studies; see Krohn and Thornberry's chapter in this section) have permitted examinations that are not only more comprehensive in scope, but also more methodologically sound, as they provide stronger evidence of a *causal* relationship—and not merely a correlational or associative relationship—between various risk factors and gang joining. Moreover, it is abundantly clear from existing research that no one, two, or three risk factors necessarily and sufficiently bring about gang involvement. Rather, it is the accumulation of various risk factors across the multiple social domains that influence youth to decide to join. This is illustrated for girls in Miller's qualitative investigation in this section. As noted, we are only now coming to a better understanding of the corollary of gang joining: the factors that can explain gang exit. The final article in this section provides a conceptual framework for understanding the process, methods, and motives behind leaving a gang.

CHAPTER 5

Gang Problem Prevalence Trends in the U.S.

James C. Howell ■ Arlen Egley Jr. ■ George E. Tita ■ Elizabeth Griffiths

Beginning in the mid-1990s, the National Gang Center has collected data annually from law enforcement agencies regarding the presence, trends, and activities of gangs nationwide. Two prominent findings presented in this article—perhaps surprising to those new to or unfamiliar with gang research—are changes in gang prevalence rates over the past 15 years across the U.S. and the rather transitory and unstable nature of gang activity in smaller cities and counties. In these less-populated areas, gang activity emerges and dissipates regularly, such that very few areas outside major cities (where gang problems are long-standing) have consistently experienced a gang problem. The myth that "once gangs appear, they are here for good" is just that: a myth.

Early Multicity Gang Surveys

... Miller's study (1982/1992) provides the national baseline of early multicity gang survey research. His studies were conducted against a backdrop of very limited knowledge of gangs in the United States. Only two previous efforts had been made to assess the gang problem in multiple cities. Bernstein (1964) examined gang problems in nine major cities in 1962, although not for the purpose of assessing gang characteristics; only to explore solutions. Simultaneous with Miller's 1982 survey, Needle and Stapleton (1983) surveyed 60 police departments in

1980, although the central purpose was to evaluate methods they were using to suppress and control gangs. Subsequent single-year gang surveys encompassed major cities (see Curry and Decker, 2003, pp. 17–30; Howell, 1994; Miller, 2001).

At the time of Miller's research, gang knowledge was based largely on a New York-centered picture of gang evolution: growth in the 1950s, demise in the 1960s, revival in the early 1970s, and dormancy in the later 1970s (Miller, 1982/1992, 2001). The popular perception was that the New York sequence of events applied to other cities. Miller's pilot study (1975) found this assumption to be seriously flawed. He found high levels of gang violence in 6 of the 12 largest cities in the United States. Hence, Miller's gang survey was expanded to encompass 26 cities (1982/1992). Based on this study, Miller (1990) recommended the creation of a federal center for statistically tracking and monitoring gang activity. The National Youth Gang Center (NYGS) was established in 1995 along with other federal anti-gang programming, following comprehensive reviews of gang research, programs, and policies (Howell, 1994; Kelley, 1994; Miller, 1990).

Gang Problem Prevalence Trends, 1996–2009

The National Gang Center (NGC)[1] has tracked the distribution and level of the gang problem in the United States since its first nationally representative National Youth Gang Survey (NYGS) in 1996. The NYGS is the first gang survey in any country that annually contacts a nationally

Reprinted from: James C. Howell, Arlen Egley, Jr., George E. Tita, and Elizabeth Griffiths, "U.S. Gang Problem Trends and Seriousness, 1996–2009," in the *National Gang Center Bulletin*, May 2011, 6: 2–6, 19–22. Published by the National Gang Center. Reprinted by permission of author.

representative sample of authoritative respondents in their respective jurisdictions regarding the prevalence and characteristics of gang activity using the same methodology each year. With the accumulation of 14 years of data, this report provides a long-term view of data generated in the NYGS, covering the time period from 1996 to 2009.[2]

The 14-year gang prevalence trend shown in Figure 5.1 demonstrates that gang activity remains a widespread problem across the United States. By 2009, prevalence rates were significantly elevated compared with recorded lows in 2000 and 2001. Approximately one-third of the jurisdictions in the NYGS study population experienced gang problems in 2009, compared with under one-quarter in 2002, an increase of more than 20 percent in the estimated number of gang-problem jurisdictions between 2002 and 2009.

Figure 5.2 shows the prevalence of gang activity within each of the four NYGS subsamples. Each subsample follows a similar trend over time, albeit at noticeably different levels. Larger cities consistently exhibit the highest prevalence rates of gang activity among the four groups, followed by, in order, suburban counties, smaller cities, and rural counties.[3] The rates of reported gang activity in suburban counties are closest to the rates for larger cities because of the relatively large populations in suburban counties (i.e., a high capacity to sustain gang activity, Egley et al., 2006), the shifting of previous inner-city slums and ghettos to ring-city or suburban areas (Miller, 1982/1992, pp. 75–76), and the growing popularity of gang culture in these areas (Miller, 2001). Mirroring the overall trend displayed in Figure 5.1, each of the subsamples shows uniform declines in the late 1990s, reaching a low point in 2001 and then steadily increasing before leveling off in recent years.

Grouping Jurisdictions by Gang-Problem Patterns

Gang-problem patterns within jurisdictions are further examined here through trajectory modeling, which groups jurisdictions that share similar trends in the outcome of interest (specifically, gang activity and gang-related homicides) and graphically illustrates those patterns over the 14-year survey period. For example, some jurisdictions may report a consistent presence of gangs, while others could experience no gang activity over time, rapid increases over time, rapid decreases, fluctuating presence of gang activity, or other more complex trends between 1996 and 2009.

The first trajectory model (Figure 5.3) displays *trends in the presence of gang activity* across the

Figure 5.1 Prevalence of Gang Problems in Study Population, 1996–2009

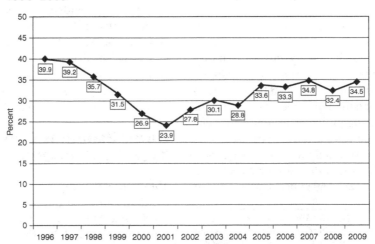

Note: Gang problems are measured by respondents' affirmative response that youth gangs were active in their jurisdictions during the past year.

Figure 5.2 Law Enforcement Agency Reports of Gang Problems by Area Type, 1996–2009

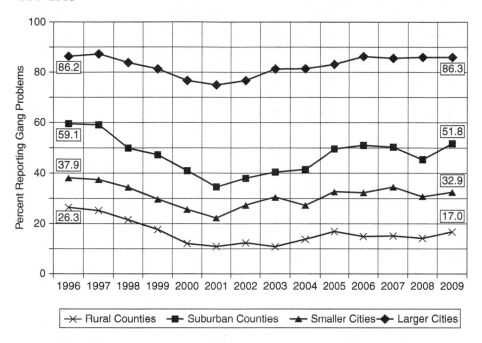

Figure 5.3 Trajectory Model: Presence of Gang Activity: Jurisdictions Included in the NYGS between 1996 and 2009 (*N* = 1517)

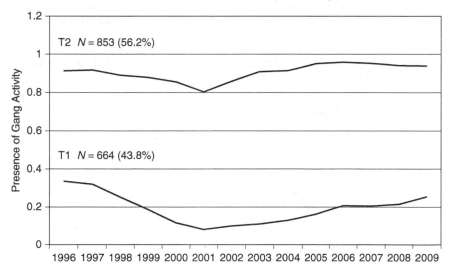

Notes: Data from the NYGS 1996 through 2009; best-fitting model includes two groups with quadratic polynomial functions (BIC = –7416.92). Jurisdictions reporting the presence of gang activity were coded as 1, and those reporting no gang activity were coded as 0 at each year.

1,517 jurisdictions included in both the first and current NYGS samples.[4] Of the total, 664 (43.8 percent) of the jurisdictions fall into the first trajectory (T1). This group exhibited a relatively lower prevalence of gang activity in 1996, which declined precipitously until 2001 before experiencing some growth that continued through 2009. By contrast, more than half ($N = 853$; 56.2 percent) of the jurisdictions reported a near-chronic presence of gang activity across the time period (T2). Thus, this trajectory model reveals that a small majority of all respondents reporting gang activity have a persistent gang problem which, apart from the minor deviation in 2001, has remained virtually constant over time.

Previous NYGS analysis has firmly demonstrated that gang activity—in terms of size of gang membership and the occurrence of gang violence—remains largely concentrated in the most populated areas in the United States (Egley, Howell, and Major, 2004, 2006; Howell and Egley, 2005; Howell, 2006). Therefore, the next analysis focuses only on jurisdictions with populations greater than 50,000. This permits an examination of areas with more persistent gang activity for distinctive trends—where gang activity is not only more prevalent, but also more serious, and thus more revealing with respect to common patterns.

Figure 5.4 displays the six identifiable groups uncovered in the analysis of this smaller sample of 598 localities (versus 1,517 in the previous analysis). The most predominant group is T5 (69.9 percent), which reported a persistent and chronic gang problem over the 14-year period. The remaining five groups showed widely varied trends in gang activity. Three of these groups (T3, T4, and T6) all showed substantial declines in gang activity from 1996 to 2000. However, each experienced a very different trend after year 2000. Among these three groups, one group (T4; 6.5 percent) continued to experience steady declines in gang prevalence which leveled off somewhat in recent years. Declines for the one group (T6; 5.4 percent) continued for two more years, to the point that by 2002, virtually no presence of gang activity remained.

In stark contrast, the reductions in the presence of gang activity evidenced between 1996 and 2000 for the last of these three unique trajectory groups (T3; 9.2 percent) were short-lived, since the presence of gang activity rose sharply thereafter to near saturation in recent years.

The remaining two groups of jurisdictions (T1 and T2) exhibit an opposite pattern, beginning with virtually no gang activity at the start of the 14-year period, and experiencing increases (at

Figure 5.4 Trajectory Model: Presence of Gang Activity: Jurisdictions with 50,000+ in 2002 and 1996–2009 Data ($N = 598$)

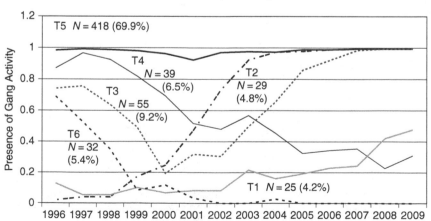

Note: Data from the NYGS 1996 through 2009; best-fitting model includes six groups with quadratic polynomial functions (BIC = −1892.99).

different rates) over time. More specifically, the first group (T1; 4.2 percent) exhibited small yet steady increases in gang activity. The second trajectory group (T2; 4.8 percent), however, started the period with virtually no reported gang activity but experienced a steep rise after onset in 1998 (similar to that of T3) that continued upward to complete persistence toward the end of the period.

Several conclusions can be drawn from this trajectory analysis. First, for most (over two-thirds) of the cities with populations of 50,000 or more, prevalence rates of gang activity have remained unchanged for the past decade and a half. By comparison, this observed consistency is rare in smaller localities (Howell and Egley, 2005), where gang activity is more transitory and less serious over time. Second, the remaining one-third of the large cities examined here exhibit widely varying trends. Some agencies have experienced substantial declines or the complete desistence of gang activity, while others have exhibited rather extraordinary increases since the turn of the century.

Unfortunately, at this point, explanations are not available for the trends observed above because of the novelty of this research. Our purpose in this initial application of trajectory analysis is to develop an understanding of the varied trends in persistent gang activity across cities.

Notes

1. The National Gang Center was formerly called the National Youth Gang Center.
2. For previous NGS publications covering relatively short time segments, see Egley, Howell, and Major (2004, 2006); Howell (2006); Howell and Egley (2005); Howell and Gleason (1999); Howell, Egley, and Gleason (2002); and Howell, Moore, and Egley (2002).
3. The upturn in suburban counties from 2008 to 2009 is the result of a group of agencies newly reporting gang problems in their jurisdictions to the NYGS. However, based on the initial data submitted by these agencies, the gang problem appears relatively small in size (e.g., fewer than 20 gang members) and magnitude (all of the agencies with the exception of one reported zero gang homicides) in these areas.
4. Both samples included all cities above 50,000 in population and all suburban counties, and randomly selected agencies from smaller cities and rural counties.

Thus, these analyses necessarily exclude agencies not participating in both samples.

References

Bernstein, S. (1964). *Youth on the Streets: Work with Alienated Youth Groups*. New York: Association Press.

Curry, G. D., and Decker, S. H. (2003). *Confronting Gangs: Crime and Community* (2nd ed.). Los Angeles, CA: Roxbury.

Egley, A. Jr., Howell, J. C., and Major, A. K. (2004). Recent patterns of gang problems in the United States: Results from the 1996–2002 National Youth Gang Survey. In F-A. Esbensen, S. G. Tibbetts, and L. Gaines (eds.), *American Youth Gangs at the Millennium* (pp. 90–108). Long Grove, IL: Waveland Press, Inc.

Egley, A. Jr., Howell, J. C., and Major, A. K. (2006). *National Youth Gang Survey: 1999–2001*. Washington, DC: U.S. Department of Justice, Office of Juvenile Justice and Delinquency Prevention.

Howell, J. C. (1994). Recent gang research: Program and policy implications. *Crime and Delinquency*, 40, 495–515.

———. (2006). The impact of gangs on communities. *NYGC Bulletin*, No. 2. Tallahassee, FL: National Youth Gang Center.

Howell, J. C., and Egley, A. Jr. (2005). Gangs in small towns and rural counties. *NYGC Bulletin*, No. 1. Tallahassee, FL: National Youth Gang Center.

Howell, J. C., Egley, A. Jr., and Gleason, D. K. (2002). Modern day youth gangs. *Juvenile Justice Bulletin*. Youth Gang Series. Washington, DC: U.S. Department of Justice. Office of Juvenile Justice and Delinquency Prevention.

Howell, J. C., and Gleason, D. K. (1999). Youth gang drug trafficking. *Juvenile Justice Bulletin*. Youth Gang Series. Washington, DC: U.S. Department of Justice, Office of Juvenile Justice and Delinquency Prevention.

Howell, J. C., Moore, J. P., and Egley, A., Jr. (2002). The changing boundaries of youth gangs. In C. R. Huff (ed.), *Gangs in America* (3rd ed., pp. 3–18). Thousand Oaks, CA: Sage.

Kelley, B. T. (1994). *A Comprehensive Response to America's Gang Problem*. Washington, DC: U.S. Department of Justice, Office of Juvenile Justice and Delinquency Prevention.

Miller, W. B. (1975). *Violence by Youth Gangs and Youth Groups as a Crime Problem in Major American Cities*. Washington, DC: U.S. Department of Justice, Office of Juvenile Justice and Delinquency Prevention.

———. (1982/1992). *Crime by Youth Gangs and Groups in the United States*. Washington, DC: U.S. Department of Justice, Office of Juvenile Justice and Delinquency Prevention.

———. (1990). Why the United States has failed to solve its youth gang problem. In C. R. Huff (ed.), *Gangs in America* (pp. 263–287). Newbury Park, CA: Sage.

———. (2001). *The Growth of Youth Gang Problems in the United States: 1970–1998*. Washington, DC: Office of Juvenile Justice and Delinquency Prevention.

Needle, J., and Stapleton, W. V. (1983). *Police Handling of Youth Gangs*. Washington, DC: U.S. Department of Justice, Office of Juvenile Justice and Delinquency Prevention.

CHAPTER 6

Gang Members on the Move

Cheryl L. Maxson

The proliferation of gangs nationwide is frequently touted as the product of gang members purposely seeking out "gang-free" cities and towns in order to expand their involvement in drug distribution. Often, this simplified explanation is based upon only one or a few instances and then hastily generalized for gang emergence everywhere, thus reinforcing stereotypes of the gang–drug connection. In this article the author reports solid evidence that gang member migration entails many different factors that oftentimes are not illegitimate and are essentially unrelated to the gang. The reader will note that while the data presented in this article are somewhat dated, subsequent research (most notably and broadly by the National Gang Center) strongly confirms that the findings presented here still hold today.

In recent years, local government officials, law enforcement officers, and community organizations have witnessed the emergence and growth of gangs in U.S. cities once thought to be immune to the crime and violence associated with street gangs in large metropolitan areas. Police chiefs, mayors, school officials, community activists, and public health officials have gone so far as to identify this proliferation as an epidemic. Reports of big-city gang members fanning out across the nation seeking new markets for drug distribution have added

Reprinted from: Cheryl L. Maxson, "Gang Members on the Move," *Juvenile Justice Bulletin*, October: 1–11. Copyright © 1998 by the U.S. Department of Justice, Office of Justice Programs, Office of Juvenile Justice and Delinquency Prevention. Reprinted by permission.

fuel to concerns about gang proliferation and gang migration.

The increase in gang migration has generated the need for the issue to be assessed based on empirical evidence. As local communities attempt to address gang-related problems in their areas, it is critical that they have a clear understanding of patterns of gang migration and an accurate assessment of local, or indigenous, gang membership.

This chapter explores how key terms such as *gang, gang proliferation*, and *gang migration* are defined; how and whether gang migration affects gang proliferation; and trends reported in research literature. This chapter is based in part on work supported by the National Institute of Justice (NIJ) and an article previously published in the *National Institute of Justice Journal* (Maxson, Woods, and Klein, 1996). Findings from a recent University of Southern California (USC) study on street-gang migration are also discussed (Maxson, Woods, and Klein, 1995).

Clarifying the Concepts

Defining the Terms "Gang," "Gang Proliferation," and "Gang Migration"

Gang. There has been much debate over the term "gang," but little progress has been made toward widespread acceptance of a uniform definition. Some researchers prefer a broad definition that includes group criminal and noncriminal activities, whereas law enforcement agencies tend to use definitions that expedite the cataloging of

61

groups for purposes of statistical analysis or prosecution. Variations in the forms or structure of gangs make it difficult to put forth one standard definition (Klein and Maxson, 1996). For example, researchers have attempted to draw a distinction between street gangs and drug gangs (Klein, 1995). Drug gangs are perceived as smaller, more cohesive, and more hierarchical than most street gangs and are exclusively focused on conducting drug deals and defending drug territories. Street gangs, on the other hand, engage in a wide array of criminal activity. Drug gangs may be subgroups of street gangs or may develop independently of street gangs. For the purposes of this chapter and the national surveys on gang migration conducted by USC, gangs were defined as groups of adolescents and/or young adults who see themselves as a group (as do others) and have been involved in enough crime to be of considerable concern to law enforcement and the community (Maxson, Woods, and Klein, 1995). In the USC survey, drug gangs were included in the overall grouping of gangs, but members of motorcycle gangs, prison-based gangs, graffiti taggers, and racial supremacy groups were excluded to narrow the focus to street gangs.

Another challenge in defining the term "gang" is the fluctuating structure of these groups. Over the course of adolescence and young adulthood, individual members move in and out of gangs, continually affecting the gangs' structure (Thornberry et al., 1993). The terms "wannabe," "core," "fringe," "associate," "hardcore," and "O.G." (original gangster) reflect the changing levels of involvement and the fact that the boundaries of gang membership are penetrable. Some researchers argue that the term "member" was created and used by law enforcement, gang researchers, and individuals engaged in gang activity with only a loose consensus of generalized, shared meaning.

Gang Proliferation. The term "gang proliferation" indicates the increase in communities reporting the existence of gangs and gang problems (Knox et al., 1996). While gangs have existed in various forms, degrees, and locations in the United States for many decades, the sheer volume of cities and towns documenting recent gang activity cannot be denied. Some of this increase may be attributed to

a heightened awareness of gang issues, redirection of law enforcement attention, widespread training, and national education campaigns. Nevertheless, gangs exist in locations previously unaffected and attract a larger proportion of adolescents than in the past.[1]

Gang Migration. The already difficult task of defining gangs is compounded when the relationship between gang migration and proliferation is addressed. Gang migration—the movement of gang members from one city to another—has been mentioned with increasing frequency in state legislative task force investigations, government-sponsored conferences, and law enforcement accounts at the federal, state, and local levels (Bonfante, 1995; Hayeslip, 1989; California Council on Criminal Justice, 1989; Genelin and Coplen, 1989; McKinney, 1988; National Drug Intelligence Center, 1994, 1996). For the USC study, migration was broadly defined to include temporary relocations, such as visits to relatives, short trips to sell drugs or develop other criminal enterprises, and longer stays while escaping crackdowns on gangs or gang activity. More permanent changes, such as residential moves (either individually or with family members) and court placements, were also included. Individuals in the study did not have to participate in gang activity in the destination city to be considered gang migrants. This broad definition of gang migration allowed researchers to investigate the degree of gang-organized and gang-supported expansion of members to other locations, of which little evidence was found. It also allowed researchers to examine variations in gang activity in the destination city and the many reasons for relocating. If the concept of migration was limited to individuals or groups traveling solely for gang-related purposes or at the direction of gang leaders, the patterns of migration would change drastically. Further, collective gang migration is rare, but the migration of individual gang members is not.

Another complication in defining gang migration is the distinction between migrant gang members (migrants) and indigenous gang members, which often fades over time. As migrants settle into new locations, sometimes joining local gangs, their identities may evolve to the point to which their prior gang affiliation no longer exists. This process of assimilation into local gang subcultures has not been addressed in research literature, because law enforcement officers and researchers have only recently begun to discuss gang migration. In future studies, researchers should consider at what point a migrant gang member is no longer perceived as a migrant but as a local gang member in the new location.

The Influence of Gang Migration on Gang Proliferation

The primary focus of this chapter is to assess whether gang migration has played a major role in gang proliferation. Migrant gang members may stimulate the growth of gangs and gang membership through a variety of processes, such as recruiting locals to establish a branch of the gang in previously unaffected areas. This approach, described as the importation model, involves efforts by gang members to infuse their gang into new cities, primarily to establish new drug markets and other money-making criminal enterprises (Decker and Van Winkle, 1996). This is also referred to as gang franchising (Knox et al., 1996) and gang colonization (Quinn, Tobolowsky, and Downs, 1994). Alternatively, migrants may establish a new gang without structural affiliation to an existing gang. Furthermore, if a sufficient number of individuals from a gang move to a new location, they may replicate a migrant subset of their former gang. No matter what process is used, new local gangs will most likely emerge in response to territorial challenges or perceived protection needs. The city with a single gang is a rare phenomenon (Klein, 1995). Regardless of the pattern of new gang initiation, gang member migration would create an increase in both the numbers of gangs and gang membership.

Another way migrant gangs may stimulate gang proliferation is by introducing new and exciting cultural distinctions from existing gangs. In a city in which gangs exist but are not firmly established, migrant gang members may act as cultural carriers of the folkways, mythologies, and other trappings of more sophisticated urban gangs. They may offer strong distinctions from other gangs and cause a rivalry with existing gangs, such as the rivalry between the Bloods and Crips in southern California and between the People and Folks in the Midwest. Most of the respondents in the 1993 USC phone survey reported that migrants influence local gang rivalries, gang dress codes, and recruiting methods (Maxson, Woods, and Klein, 1995). In addition, the solidification of local gang subcultures may increase the visibility or attractiveness of gangs to local youth. It may also influence the growth of rival gangs.

Conversely, there are a variety of circumstances in which migrant gang members have little or no impact on gang proliferation. If the geographic location allows, migrants may retain their affiliation with their original gangs by commuting to old territories or they may simply discontinue gang activity altogether. In cities with relatively large and established gangs, it is unlikely that migrant gang members would have a noticeable effect on the overall gang environment.

An important related issue is the impact of migrant gang members on local crime patterns.[2] Migrants are generally perceived as contributing to both increased levels of crime and the seriousness of criminal activity (Maxson, Woods, and Klein, 1995). The 1993 USC survey involved telephone interviews with law enforcement in 211 cities that experienced gang migration in 1992. Most of the cities involved in the survey (86 percent) reported that migrant gang members contributed to an increase in local crime rates or patterns primarily in theft (50-percent increase), robbery (35--percent increase), other violent crimes (59-percent increase), and, to a lesser extent, drug sales (24-percent increase). The small increase in drug sale activity can most likely be attributed to competition from established local drug markets. The survey also showed that the type of criminal gang activity was changing to include increased use of firearms and more sophisticated weapons (36-percent increase). Carjackings, firebombings, residential robberies, drive-by shootings, and advanced techniques for vehicle theft were also cited on occasion. Changes in the targets of criminal activity and the use of other technological advances were mentioned less frequently.

What Previous Studies Show

The following is a summary of the research literature on the relationship between migration and proliferation. Local law enforcement agencies have become increasingly aware of the usefulness of maintaining systematic information on gangs, yet such data bases hardly meet the scientific standards of reliability and validity. Therefore, the results of the studies described in this section should be viewed as exploratory.

Although a number of national studies dating back to the 1970s have documented an increase in the number of cities and smaller communities reporting street gang activity, the numbers reported by these studies vary (Miller, 1975, 1982; Needle and Stapleton, 1983; Spergel and Curry, 1990; Curry, Ball, and Fox, 1994; Klein, 1995; Curry, 1996). Variations in localities reporting gang activities are attributed to the use of different sampling frames in the national surveys. While the surveys are not compatible, each reports increased gang activity. Miller's 1996 compilation of data from several sources documents gang proliferation during the past three decades and shows that in the 1970s, street gangs existed in the United States in 201 cities and 70 counties (many with cities included in the former count) (Miller, 1996). These figures climbed to 468 and 247, respectively, during the 1980s and to 1,487 and 706 in the 1990s. A nationwide survey conducted by the National Youth Gang Center (NYGC) reported that in 1995 gangs existed in 1,492 cities and 515 counties (OJJDP, 1997). The figures reported by Miller and NYGC are considerably higher than the estimate of 760 jurisdictions reported by Curry and his associates (Curry, Ball, and Decker, 1996) and the projection of 1,200 gang cities derived from the 1992 USC national mail survey (reported in Maxson, Woods, and Klein, 1995). Similarly, the National Drug Intelligence Center (NDIC) reported a much smaller figure of 265 for cities and counties reporting gang activity in 1995 (NDIC, 1996). Of these 265 cities and counties, 182 jurisdictions reported gang "connections" to 234 other cities, but the nature of these relationships was not elaborated on (D. Mehall, NDIC, personal communication, August 20, 1996). With the exception of the Mehall report and that of Maxson, Woods, and Klein (1995), none of the studies addressed the issue of gang migration on a national scale.

With few exceptions, findings on gang migration reported in research literature contrast sharply with the perspectives presented by the media, government agencies, and law enforcement reports. Several researchers have studied gangs in various cities throughout the United States and examined their origin and relationships to gangs in larger cities (primarily Chicago) to examine correlations between gang migration and proliferation on a more regional scale.

Gangs in the Midwestern United States

In 1983, Rosenbaum and Grant identified three Evanston, IL, gangs as "satellites" of major Chicago gangs, but proceeded to emphasize that they "are composed largely of Evanston residents, and in a very real sense, are Evanston gangs" (p. 15). They also found that two indigenous gangs, with no outside connection, contributed disproportionately to levels of violence and were, therefore, "almost totally responsible for increasing fear of crime in the community and forcing current reactions to the problem" (Rosenbaum and Grant, 1983:21). In contrast, the Chicago-connected gangs maintained a lower profile and were more profit oriented in their illegal activities, aspiring "to be more like organized crime" (Rosenbaum and Grant, 1983:21). In other words, the gangs indigenous to Evanston seemed to be more of a threat to the community than the Chicago-based gangs. The conclusion can be drawn that in this particular study, the migration of gangs into Evanston only minimally affected the proliferation of gang activities.

In an extensive study of Milwaukee gangs in 1988, 18 groups were found to use the names and symbols of major Chicago gangs, including identification with such gang confederations as People versus Folk (Hagedorn, 1988). In questioning gang founders on the origins of the gangs, it was determined that only 4 of the 18 were formed directly by gang members who had moved from Chicago to Milwaukee. Further, these members maintained only slight ties to their original Chicago gangs.

Despite law enforcement claims to the contrary, no existence of a super-gang (i.e., Chicago) coalition was found in Milwaukee. Founding gang members strongly resented the idea that their gang was in any way tied to the original Chicago gangs (Hagedorn, 1988). In this study, Hagedorn concludes that gang formation in Milwaukee was only minimally affected by the migration of Chicago gangs. If anything, the influence was more cultural than structural, because gangs in smaller cities tend to follow big-city gang traditions and borrow cultural aspects from these gang images.

Further supporting the notion that gang migration only minimally affects proliferation is a 1989 study that determined that gangs in Columbus and Cleveland, OH, originated from streetcorner groups and breakdancing/rapping groups and also from migrating street-gang leaders from Chicago or Los Angeles (Huff, 1989). The study found no evidence that Ohio gangs were directly affiliated with gangs from other cities, particularly Chicago, Detroit, or Los Angeles.

In 1992, researchers examined the role that Chicago gangs played in the emergence of youth gangs in Kenosha, WI (Zevitz and Takata, 1992). Based on interviews with gang members, police analyses, and social service and school records, the study concluded that "the regional gangs in this study were products of local development even though they had a cultural affinity with their metropolitan counterparts. . . . We found no convincing evidence that metropolitan gangs had branched out to the outlying community where our study took place" (Zevitz and Takata, 1992:102). Regular contact between some Chicago and Kenosha gang members reflected kinship or old neighborhood ties rather than the organizational expansion of Chicago gangs.

These findings are echoed in a 1996 study of 99 gang members in St. Louis (Decker and Van Winkle, 1996). A minority (16 percent) of those interviewed suggested that gangs reemerged in St. Louis, MO, through the efforts of gang members from Los Angeles. Several of these migrants had relocated for social reasons, such as visiting relatives. The study also found that St. Louis gangs were more likely to originate as a result of neighborhood conflicts influenced by popular culture rather than from big-city connections.

The powerful images of Los Angeles gangs, conveyed through movies, clothes, and music, provided a symbolic reference point for these antagonisms. In this way, popular culture provided the symbols and rhetoric of gang affiliation and activities that galvanized neighborhood rivalries. (Decker and Van Winkle, 1996:88)

Another study on gang migration in 1996 surveyed 752 jurisdictions in Illinois (Knox et al., 1996). (Because only 38 percent of the law enforcement agencies responded, these findings should be interpreted cautiously.) The majority of respondents (88 percent) reported that gangs from outside their area had established an influence, that one-fifth or more of their local gang population was attributable to recent arrivals (49 percent), that parental relocation of gang members served to transplant the gang problem to the area (65 percent), and that some of their gang problem was due to gang migration (69 percent). The study concluded that, while the impact of migration varies, "it is still of considerable interest to the law enforcement community" (Knox et al., 1996:78).

Gangs in the Western United States

In a study of drug sales and violence among San Francisco gangs, 550 gang members from 84 different gangs were interviewed (Waldorf, 1993). Of these, only three groups reported relationships with other gangs outside San Francisco. The report concluded that

. . . most gangs do not have the skills or knowledge to move to other communities and establish new markets for drug sales. While it is true they can and do function on their own turf they are often like fish out of water when they go elsewhere. . . . They are not like organized crime figures (Mafia and Colombian cocaine cartels) who have capital, knowledge and power. . . . While it might be romantic to think that the L.A. Bloods and Crips are exceptional, I will remain skeptical that they are more competent than other gangs. (Waldorf, 1993:8)

To the contrary, a 1988 study of inmates in California correctional institutions and law enforcement and correctional officials suggested high levels of mobility among "entrepreneurial"

California gang members traveling long distances to establish drug distribution outlets and maintaining close ties to their gangs of origin (Skolnick et al., 1990; Skolnick, 1990). Among all the empirical studies conducted in this area, Skolnick's resonates most closely with the reports from law enforcement previously cited (Bonfante, 1995; Hayeslip, 1989; California Council on Criminal Justice, 1989; Genelin and Coplen, 1989; McKinney, 1988; National Drug Intelligence Center, 1994, 1996).

> Against a backdrop of escalating violence, declining drug prices, and intensified law enforcement, Los Angeles area gang-related drug dealers are seeking new venues to sell the Midas product—crack cocaine. . . . Respondents claim to have either participated in or have knowledge of Blood or Crip crack operations in 22 states and at least 27 cities. In fact, it appears difficult to overstate the penetration of Blood and Crip members into other states. (Skolnick, 1990:8)

But the sheer presence of Crips and Bloods in states other than California is a poor indicator of gang migration. The 1996 NDIC survey identified 180 jurisdictions in 42 states with gangs claiming affiliation with the Bloods and/or Crips. At the same time, the NDIC report cautions against assuming organizational links from gang names.

> It is important to note that when a gang has claimed affiliation with the Bloods or Crips, or a gang has taken the name of a nationally known gang, this does not necessarily indicate that this gang is a part of a group with a national infrastructure. While some gangs have interstate connections and a hierarchical structure, the majority of gangs do not fit this profile. (NDIC, 1996:v)

Gangs in the South Central United States

In a 1994 study of 9 states located in the south central United States, 131 municipal police departments were surveyed; 79 cities completed the mail survey (Quinn, Tobolowsky, and Downs, 1994). Respondents in 44 percent of small cities (populations between 15,000 and 50,000) and 41 percent of large cities (populations greater than 50,000) stated that their largest gang was affiliated with groups in other cities. It is unknown whether the perceived affiliation was based on structural links or on name association. Nearly three-fourths of the 792 gang cities that responded to the 1992 USC mail survey reported that at least some indigenous gangs adopted gang names generally associated with Los Angeles and Chicago (e.g., Bloods, Crips, Vicelords, Gangster Disciples, or Latin Kings). Approximately 60 of these cities had no gang migration.

The National Survey on Gang Migration

In 1992, the University of Southern California conducted a mail survey of law enforcement personnel in approximately 1,100 U.S. cities. The survey was distributed to all cities with a population of more than 100,000 and to more than 900 cities and towns that serve as likely environments for street gangs or gang migration.[3] Law enforcement officials suggested municipalities to include in the survey, and all cities with organizations that investigate gangs were included. To increase the survey pool, the survey asked respondents to list cities to which their local gang members had moved. This sample is best characterized as a purposive sample of gang cities—it is neither representative of all U.S. cities and towns, although all large cities are enumerated fully, nor all gang cities.[4] This survey captured data on the largest number of cities with gangs identified at the time (and a majority of the cities identified by the NYGC survey in 1995) and is the only systematic enumeration of U.S. cities experiencing gang migration to date. Repeated mailings and telephone follow up resulted in completion of the survey by more than 90 percent of those polled.

To develop descriptions about the nature of gang migration and local responses to it, extensive telephone interviews were conducted with law enforcement officers in 211 cities that reported the arrival of at least 10 migrant gang members in 1991. Interview participants were sampled from a larger pool of 480 cities that cited at least moderate levels of gang migration. Other facets of the study included interviews with community informants and case studies, including personal interviews with migrant gang members.[5]

A primary limitation of this research design is the necessity to rely on law enforcement for depictions of the scope and nature of gang migration. Locally based ethnographic approaches—based on the systematic recording of particular human cultures—would lend a more comprehensive view of the migration situation in individual cities. The USC case studies involved a range of informants whose depictions sometimes contrasted markedly with law enforcement's assessment of the issue. The attempt to extend beyond law enforcement to community respondents produced mixed results, because informants were generally less informed about migration matters in the city as a whole and tended to focus on particular neighborhoods of interest. It would seem that law enforcement is the best available source of information on national patterns of gang migration, but the reader should be wary of the limitations on law enforcement as a source of information on migration. These limitations include the occupational focus of law enforcement on crime (i.e., if migrants are not engaged in a lot of crime, they are less likely to come to the attention of law enforcement), the lack of local data bases with systematically gathered information about migration, and the definitional challenges described earlier in Clarifying the Concepts. Given these limitations, the results from this study should be viewed as exploratory until replicated by further research.

Study Findings

The National Scope of Gang Migration

Approximately 1,000 cities responded to the 1992 mail survey, revealing 710 cities that had experienced gang migration by 1992. The widespread distribution of these cities is reflected in Figure 6.1.[6] Only three states had not experienced gang migration by 1992—New Hampshire, North Dakota, and Vermont. The concentration of migration cities in several regions—most dramatically southern California and the Bay area, the area surrounding Chicago, and southern Florida—may obscure the geographic distribution. Forty-four percent of migration cities are located in the western region of the country, with slightly less prominence in the mid-western (26 percent) and southern (25

percent) portions of the country. Only 5 percent of the migration cities are situated in the northeastern region of the country.

Approximately 80 percent of cities with a population of more than 100,000 have migrant gang members. The overall sample cannot address the proportion of all smaller cities with migration, but the distribution of migration cities by population, shown in Figure 6.2, suggests that this is an issue confronting cities of all sizes. That nearly 100 towns with populations of 10,000 people or less experienced gang migration is striking. This phenomenon is a manifestation of the motivations to relocate and the potential influences of migrant gang members on small-town life and overtaxed law enforcement resources. Moreover, because smaller cities are less likely to have longstanding gang problems, gang migration could be a catalyst for the onset of local gang problems.

The sheer number of cities with migrant gang members and the widespread geographic distribution of these cities across the country is dramatic, but the volume of gang migration presents a far less alarming picture. Survey respondents provided an estimate of the number of migrants that had arrived in their city the year prior to survey completion.[7] Just under half (47 percent) of the 597 cities providing an estimate reported the arrival of no more than 10 migrants in the prior year. Only 34 cities (6 percent) estimated the arrival of more than 100 migrants during this period. The significance of such numbers would vary by the size of the city, but the large number of cities reporting insubstantial levels of migration suggests that gang migration may not represent a serious problem in many cities.

Survey respondents were asked to provide a demographic profile of migrant gang members. The typical age reported ranged from 13 to 30, and the mean and median age was 18. Female migrants were uncommon; more than 80 percent of the cities noted five or fewer. Compared with the ethnic distribution of gang members nationally, migrant gang members were somewhat more likely to be black. Approximately half of the cities polled in the survey reported that at least 60 percent of migrant gang members were black; predominantly Hispanic distributions emerged in 28 percent of the cities.

Figure 6.1 Cities Experiencing Gang Member Migration through 1992

Note: Number of cities = 694.

The predominance of Asian (14 cities or 7 percent) or white (2 cities) migrant gang members was unusual.

Gang Migration and Local Gang Proliferation

The potential for gang migration to have a harmful impact on local gang activity and crime rates may increase substantially if migrant gang members foster the proliferation of local gang problems in their destination cities. This is a pivotal issue, and data of several types are available for elaboration. The characteristics of cities with local gangs can be compared with those of cities with migrant gangs to establish the parameters of the relationship. Of particular interest are the dates of local gang formation and migration onset. Law enforcement perceptions about the causes of local gang problems are also relevant. Lastly, the motivations of gang members

to migrate and their patterns of gang activity upon arrival must be considered.

Through the survey of 1,100 cities, it was found that most, but not all, cities that have local gangs also have migrant gang members. Conversely, nearly all cities with gang migration also have local gangs. The 1992 survey identified 792 cities with local gangs; of these cities, 127 (16 percent) reported no experience with gang migration (Table 6.1). Only 45 of the 710 identified migration cities (6 percent) had no indigenous gangs. This simple comparison yields 172 cities (22 percent) in which migration could not have caused the emergence of local gangs, at least through 1992. The large proportion of cities with both local and migrant gang members made it difficult to detect any differences between local gang and migrant gang cities. Distributions across city size categories and geographic region are negligible (data not shown).

Table 6.1 Cities with Local Gangs or Gang Migration

	No Gang Migration	Gang Migration
Cities with no local gangs	182	45
Cities with local gangs	127	665
Source: Maxson, Woods, and Klein (1995).		

Another pertinent point of comparison from the survey is the date of onset of local gangs and the year in which migrant gang members first arrived in cities with local and migrant gang members. (These data are shown in Figure 6.3 with some loss of cases due to the respondents' inability to estimate at least one of the dates.) Only 31 of the cities with local gangs (5 percent) reported the onset of gang migration at least 1 year prior to the emergence of local gangs. Most cities (54 percent) had local gangs prior to gang migration. Adding these 344 cities (i.e., those with local gangs before migrants) to the prior figure of 172 cities that have just one or the other gang type yields a total of 516 cities that clearly challenge the notion of migration as the cause of local gang proliferation. While the picture for cities with coincidental onset of the two types of gang members is ambiguous, it seems reasonable to conclude that cities in which migration provides the catalyst for indigenous gang formation are the exception rather than the rule. The telephone interviews confirm this pattern; the majority of informants (81 percent) disagreed with the statement, "Without migration, this city wouldn't have a gang problem."

It can be argued that the concern over gang migration is most pertinent to emerging gang cities. The national gang surveys (Miller, 1996) discussed earlier have shown that the major proliferation of gang cities has occurred since the 1980s.[8] Nearly 70 percent of the 781 gang cities that could provide a date of emergence reported one after 1985. These cities can be characterized as "emergent" rather than "chronic" gang cities (Spergel and Curry, 1990). Emergent gang cities are equally as likely to report gang migration as chronic cities (84 percent of the cities in each group). However, cities with gang onset after 1985 are significantly less likely to report that local gangs preceded gang migration (40 percent versus 88 percent), as might be

Figure 6.2 710 Gang Migration Cities by Population

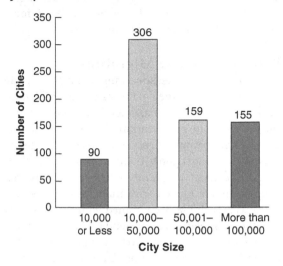

Figure 6.3 Dates of Onset of Local Gangs versus Migration

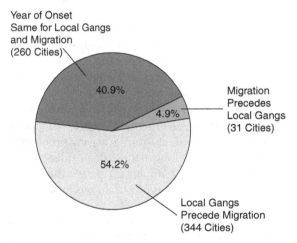

expected when they are compared with cities with longstanding local gang problems. Emergent cities are more likely to experience the onset of local gangs and migrants in the same year as opposed to chronic cities (53 percent versus 11 percent). The majority of respondents interviewed from emergent gang cities believed that migration was not the cause of local gang problems. This figure was significantly lower for emergent gang cities (73 percent) than for chronic gang cities (93 percent). This shows that the conclusion that migration is not generally the catalyst for gang proliferation holds up, but the exceptions to this general rule can most often be found in emergent gang cities.

Patterns of Gang Migration

Examination of the reasons gang members migrate to other cities and their patterns of gang affiliation in the new city show that migration is not a major catalyst of gang proliferation. Survey interviewers asked participating officers to choose from a list of reasons why most gang members moved into their cities. The most frequently cited reason was that gang members moved with their families (39 percent). When this was combined with the reason of staying with relatives and friends, 57 percent of the survey respondents believed that migrants relocated primarily for social reasons. Drug market expansion was the second most frequently cited motivation (20 percent of cities) for migrating. When this was combined with other criminal opportunities, it created a larger category of illegal attractions, or "pull" motivators, in 32 percent of cities reporting an influx of migrant gangs. "Push" motivators that forced gang members to leave cities, such as law enforcement crackdowns (8 percent), court-ordered relocation, or a desire to escape gangs, were cited in 11 percent of migrant-recipient cities.

Are these patterns of motivation for migrating different in cities with emergent gangs as compared with those cities with chronic local gang problems? The data shown in Table 6.2 provide evidence that they clearly are not. Emergent gang cities have nearly equal proportions of socially motivated gang

Table 6.2 Most Frequent Reasons for Migration Reported by Chronic and Emergent Gang Cities

Motivation	Chronic Gang Cities (n = 73)	Emergent Gang Cities (n = 111)
Social	41 (56%)	63 (57%)
"Pulls"	22 (30%)	37 (33%)
"Pushes"	10 (14%)	11 (10%)

Note: "Pull" motivators (e.g., drug markets) are those that attract gang members to relocate in specific locations. "Push" motivators, such as law enforcement crackdowns, are those that force gang members to leave cities and relocate elsewhere.

migration as chronic gang cities. "Pull" motivators (primarily drug market expansion) and "push" motivators are less frequent reasons for gang member relocation than social motivations in both types of city.

There are no differences between the two types of gang cities with regard to patterns of migrant gang activity. Approximately one-third (38 percent) of survey respondents stated that gang migrants established new gangs or recruited for their old gangs; 36 percent reported that gang migrants joined existing local gangs or exclusively retained affiliation with their old gangs. The proportions of each in chronic and emergent gang cities are quite similar (data not shown). Thus, data on motivations for migrating and on migrant patterns in joining gangs provide little support for the view of migrants as primary agents of gang proliferation and no evidence for differential impact on emergent gang cities.

Conclusion

The interpretation of these results should be tempered by an awareness of the limitations of the USC study methodology. The surveys used to collect data relied heavily on law enforcement as a source of information. A logical next step would involve using an array of informants, including courts, schools, and social service providers in addition to community residents and gang members. It should also be noted that the USC data are cross-sectional in nature and cannot adequately describe second- or third-order waves of migration, wherein some individuals may travel from city to city.[9] Another untapped dimension in the USC survey was termed "indirect migration," in which one gang is influenced by another gang that was influenced by a third gang. For example, Pocatello, ID, gangs were heavily influenced by Salt Lake City gangs, which were started by gang members from Los Angeles (R. Olsen, Pocatello Police Department, personal communication, September 24, 1996). Other patterns of sequential mobility were reported on during the USC interviews, but did not occur with sufficient frequency to warrant further analysis.

The findings from the 1992 and 1993 USC surveys provide evidence that gang member migration, although widespread, should not be viewed as the major culprit in the nationwide proliferation of gangs. Local, indigenous gangs usually exist prior to gang migration, and migrants are not generally viewed by local law enforcement as the cause of gang problems. This pattern is less evident in cities in which gangs have emerged more recently, but these municipalities are no more likely to experience gang migration than chronic gang cities. Moreover, the motivations for gang member relocation (i.e., more often socially motivated than driven by crime opportunities) and patterns of gang participation (equally likely to join existing gangs as to retain original affiliation in order to initiate new gangs or branches) do not distinguish migrants in the two types of cities. Proponents of the "outside agitator" hypothesis of gang formation as described by Hagedorn (1988) will find little support in the data available from the USC national study.

On the whole, the USC findings agree with the research literature on gangs cited earlier. Many of the researchers—Rosenbaum and Grant (1983), Hagedorn (1988), Huff (1989), Zevitz and Takata (1992), Decker and Van Winkle (1996), and Waldorf (1993)—found that gang formation was only minimally affected by the diffusion of gang members from other cities. The findings reported by some researchers—Skolnick et al. (1990) and NDIC (1994, 1996)—are less consistent with those reported in the USC study. The Skolnick et al. and NDIC studies focused heavily on drug issues and may have disproportionately represented cities with drug-gang migration or with migrants that moved for drug expansion purposes.[10] Such cities reflect a distinct pattern of gang migration—older gang migrants, traveling longer distances, staying for briefer periods (see Maxson, Woods, and Klein, 1995, for full presentation of these analyses). Research that focuses on drug matters may fail to capture more prevalent trends. Although more often the subject of media coverage, migration for drug distribution purposes is less common than other types of migration. The differential patterns of gang migration, and their effects on local communities, require more research.

In addition, the USC findings are difficult to compare with those reported by Knox et al. (1996). Respondents in the Knox et al. study presented a widespread perception of outside gang influence.

This may be the result of exposure to 'the media and products of the entertainment industry. Klein (1995) and others have suggested that the diffusion of gang culture in the media plays a key role in the proliferation of gang membership. Our nation's youth are hardly dependent on direct contact with gang members for exposure to the more dramatic manifestations of gang culture, which is readily accessible in youth-oriented television programming, popular movies, and the recent spate of "tell-all" books from reputed urban gang leaders. The nature of this influence and its impact on gang participation and expansion have not been investigated systematically but are crucial in understanding fully the dynamics of gang proliferation.

Cities with emerging gang situations should examine the dynamics of their own communities before attributing their gang problems to outside influences. Socioeconomic factors, such as persistent unemployment, residential segregation, and the lack of recreational, educational, and vocational services for youth, are more likely sources of gang formation or expansion than is gang migration.

Notes

1. Few studies attempt to assess the proportion and age of adolescent gang members within a given area. Recent information on self-identified membership from longitudinal projects for representative samples in Denver, CO, and Rochester, NY (Thornberry and Burch, 1997), is available from the OJJDP-funded Program of Research on the Causes and Correlates of Delinquency. Approximately 5 percent of youth living in "high-risk" neighborhoods in Denver indicated that they were gang members in any given year (Esbensen, Huizinga, and Weiher, 1993). In Rochester, 30 percent of the sample reported gang membership at some point between the beginning of the seventh grade and the end of high school (Thornberry and Burch, 1997). To address the issue of gang proliferation within Denver or Rochester, new samples would need to be examined to determine whether the proportion of youth joining gangs in these cities has increased since the initial sampling period (nearly 10 years ago).

   Prevalence estimates derived from law enforcement identification of gang members have been challenged, as when Reiner (1992) reported that, according to the gang data base maintained for Los Angeles County, 9.5 percent of all men ages 21 to 24 were identified gang members. However, this proportion increased to 47 percent when the analysis was limited to black males ages 21 to 24. This figure has been generally recognized as a vast overstatement of black gang membership.

2. Whether or not migrants provide a catalyst to local gang proliferation, their impact on local crime is of considerable concern to law enforcement.

3. It should be noted that incorporated cities (of all population sizes) were the unit of analysis in this study; unincorporated areas were not included. Whenever cities contracted law enforcement responsibilities to sheriff's departments or state police, such agencies were pursued as respondents. Letters were addressed to the head agency official with a request to pass the survey on to the individual in the department most familiar with the gang situation within the city jurisdiction.

4. A random sample of 60 cities with a population of between 10,000 and 100,000 was surveyed for gang migration or local street-gang presence. Projections from this sample indicate a much larger number of U.S. cities with gang migration than have been identified to date.

5. These data are not presented in this report. Also not included are data from interviews with law enforcement in 15 cities that reported drug-gang migration only. This report refers to street-gang, rather than drug-gang, migration. See earlier discussion under Clarifying the Concepts for the distinction between the two types.

6. A few cities with gang migration were not included in this map because respondents were unable to specify the year of the first arrival of gang members from other cities.

7. A separate estimate of the total number of migrants was discarded as less reliable than the annual estimate. Even the annual estimate should be considered with caution, as few departments maintained records on gang migration. Some officers had difficulty generalizing to the city as a whole, based upon their own experience, and many migrants presumably do not come to the attention of the police.

8. Klein (1995) provides a highly illustrative series of maps displaying dates of onset of local gang problems using data gathered in the migration study.

9. The interviews with migrant gang members gathered data on multiple moves, but there were too few instances from which to generalize. The author acknowledges Scott Decker for his observation of this limitation of the study design.

10. The Skolnick and NDIC studies employed purposive rather than representative sampling techniques.

Acknowledgments

Support was provided by the National Institute of Justice, grant #91-IJ-CX-K004. Malcolm Klein was co-principal investigator of the study and research assistance was provided by Kristi Woods, Lea Cunningham, and Karen Sternheimer. The author gratefully acknowledges the participation of personnel in hundreds of police departments and community agencies, along with several dozen gang members. Useful comments on an earlier draft were provided by Malcolm Klein, Walter Miller, James Howell, and Scott Decker.

References

Bonfante, J. 1995. Entrepreneurs of crack. *Time*, February 27.

California Council on Criminal Justice. 1989. *State Task Force on Gangs and Drugs: Final Report*. Sacramento, CA: California Council on Criminal Justice.

Curry, G. D. 1996. National youth gang surveys: A review of methods and findings. Unpublished. Tallahassee, FL: National Youth Gang Center, Institute for Intergovernmental Research.

Curry, G. D., Ball, R. A., and Decker, S. H. 1996. Estimating the national scope of gang crime from law enforcement data. In *Gangs in America*, 2d ed., edited by C. R. Huff. Thousand Oaks, CA: Sage Publications.

Curry, G. D., Ball, R. A., and Fox, R. J. 1994. *Gang Crime and Law Enforcement Recordkeeping*. Research in Brief. Washington, DC: U.S. Department of Justice, Office of Justice Programs, National Institute of Justice.

Decker, S., and Van Winkle, B. 1996. *Life in the Gang*. New York: Cambridge University Press.

Esbensen, F. A., Huizinga, D., and Weiher, A. 1993. Gang and non-gang youth: Differences in explanatory factors. *Journal of Contemporary Criminal Justice* 9:94–116.

Genelin, M., and Coplen, B. 1989. Los Angeles street gangs: Report and recommendations of the countywide Criminal Justice Coordination Committee. Unpublished report of the Interagency Gang Task Force. Los Angeles: Interagency Gang Task Force.

Hagedorn, J. 1988. *People and Folks: Gangs, Crime, and the Underclass in a Rustbelt City*. Chicago: Lakeview Press.

Hayeslip, D. W., Jr. 1989 (March/April). Local-level drug enforcement: New strategies. *NIJ Reports* 213:2–6. Washington, DC: U.S. Department of Justice, Office of Justice Programs, National Institute of Justice.

Huff, C. R. 1989. Youth gangs and public policy. *Crime & Delinquency* 35:524–37.

Klein, M. W. 1995. *The American Street Gang*. New York: Oxford University Press.

Klein, M. W., and Maxson, C. L. 1996. Gang structures, crime patterns, and police responses. Unpublished final report. Los Angeles: Social Science Research Institute, University of Southern California.

Knox, G. W., Houston, J. G., Tromanhauser, E. D., McCurrie, T. F., and Laskey, J. 1996. Addressing and testing the gang migration issue. In *Gangs: A Criminal Justice Approach*, edited by J. M. Miller and J. P. Rush. Cincinnati, OH: Anderson Publishing Company.

Maxson, C. L., Woods, K. J., and Klein, M. W. 1995. Street gang migration in the United States. Unpublished final report. Los Angeles: Social Science Research Institute, University of Southern California.

———. 1996 (February). Street gang migration: How big a threat? *National Institute of Justice Journal* 230:26–31. Washington, DC: U.S. Department of Justice, Office of Justice Programs, National Institute of Justice.

McKinney, K. C. 1988 (September). *Juvenile Gangs: Crime and Drug Trafficking*. Washington, DC: U.S. Department of Justice, Office of Justice Programs, Office of Juvenile Justice and Delinquency Prevention.

Miller, W. B. 1975. Violence by youth gangs and youth groups as a crime problem in major American cities. Unpublished. Washington, DC: U.S. Department of Justice, National Institute of Juvenile Justice and Delinquency Prevention.

———. 1982 (Reissued in 1992). *Crime by Youth Gangs and Groups in the United States*. Washington, DC: U.S. Department of Justice, Office of Justice Programs, Office of Juvenile Justice and Delinquency Prevention.

———. 1996. The growth of youth gang problems in the United States: 1970–1995. Unpublished. Tallahassee, FL: National Youth Gang Center, Institute for Intergovernmental Research.

National Drug Intelligence Center. 1994. *Bloods and Crips Gang Survey Report*. Johnstown, PA: National Drug Intelligence Center.

———. 1996. *National Street Gang Survey Report*. Johnstown, PA: National Drug Intelligence Center.

Needle, J. A., and Stapleton, W. V. 1983. *Police Handling of Youth Gangs*. Washington, DC: U.S. Department of Justice, Office of Justice Programs, Office of Juvenile Justice and Delinquency Prevention.

Office of Juvenile Justice and Delinquency Prevention. 1997. *1995 National Youth Gang Survey*. Summary. Washington, DC: U.S. Department of Justice, Office of Justice Programs, Office of Juvenile Justice and Delinquency Prevention.

Quinn, J. F., Tobolowsky, P. M., and Downs, W. T. 1994. The gang problem in large and small cities: An analysis of police perceptions in nine states. *The Gang Journal* 2(2):13–22.

Reiner, I. 1992. *Gangs, Crime, and Violence in Los Angeles*. Los Angeles: Office of the District Attorney of Los Angeles County.

Rosenbaum, D. P., and Grant, J. A. 1983. *Gangs and Youth Problems in Evanston*. Report. Evanston, IL: Northwestern University, Center for Urban Affairs and Policy Research.

Skolnick, J. H. 1990. *Gang Organization and Migration*. Sacramento, CA: Office of the Attorney General of the State of California.

Skolnick, J. H., Correl, T., Navarro, T., and Rabb, R. 1990. The social structure of street drug dealing. *American Journal of Police* 9(1):1–41.

Spergel, I. A., and Curry, G. D. 1990. Strategies and perceived agency effectiveness in dealing with the youth gang problem. In *Gangs in America*, edited by C. R. Huff. Newbury Park, CA: Sage Publications.

Thornberry, T. B., and Burch, J. H. II. 1997 (June). *Gang Members and Delinquent Behavior*. Washington, DC: U.S. Department of Justice, Office of Justice Programs, Office of Juvenile Justice and Delinquency Prevention.

Thornberry, T. B., Krohn, M. D., Lizotte, A. J., and Chard-Wierschem, D. 1993. The role of juvenile gangs in facilitating delinquent behavior. *Journal of Research in Crime and Delinquency* 30(1):55–87.

Waldorf, D. 1993. When the Crips invaded San Francisco: Gang migration. *The Gang Journal* 1(4).

Zevitz, R. G., and Takata, S. R. 1992. Metropolitan gang influence and the emergence of group delinquency in a regional community. *Journal of Criminal Justice* 20(2):93–106.

CHAPTER 7

Who Are the Gangsters? An Examination of the Age, Race/Ethnicity, Sex, and Immigration Status of Self-Reported Gang Members in a Seven-City Study of American Youth

Finn-Aage Esbensen ■ Dena C. Carson

The stereotypical image of gangs promulgated in the media is that they mainly comprise urban, minority males. Nearly 15 years ago the lead author in this article and his colleagues firmly disputed this image by presenting conclusive evidence that gang membership is not exclusive to one sex, one race/ethnicity, or one age. Moreover, gang members' offending rates across and within all demographic characteristics were found to be significantly higher when compared with their nongang counterparts. That is, gang membership trumps demography. Using newly collected data, this article reexamines these findings and provides confirmatory evidence that gang membership remains an equal opportunity promoter of delinquency.

Introduction

The past twenty years have witnessed considerable advancement in our understanding of youth gangs and their members (Bjerregaard & Smith, 1993; Esbensen & Huizinga, 1993). Qualitative studies continue to provide excellent descriptions of gang life (Decker & Van Winkle, 1996; Fleisher, 1998; Miller, 2001); law enforcement data have been used to document the existence of gangs in jurisdictions across the United States (Egley & Howell, 2011); and surveys (both cross-sectional and longitudinal) have identified risk factors associated with gang membership as well as the increase in delinquent activity that is associated with gang membership (Esbensen, Peterson, Taylor, & Freng, 2010; Hill, Howell, Hawkins, & Battin-Pearson, 1999; Thornberry, Krohn, Lizotte, Smith, & Tobin, 2003). In spite of these diverse research methodologies, there is a convergence of findings. Gangs can be found in cities and communities across the country, in large cities, small towns, suburban areas, and rural communities (e.g., Esbensen et al., 2010; Howell & Egley, 2005). Most of this recent research also highlights the fact that gang members tend to reflect the communities in which they live; that is, both boys and girls are gang-involved, gang membership is not the unique domain of racial and ethnic minorities or immigrants, and gang membership is not restricted to older adolescents and young adults. Despite this body of research, the common stereotype of the American gang member continues to be that of a young male from a racial/ethnic minority, and living in a deteriorating urban area (Esbensen & Tusinski, 2007). In this article, we rely on data from a recently completed five-year study of youth in seven cities across the USA to highlight the extent to which this common stereotype fails to be supported by research.

Our objectives in writing this article are modest; we seek to provide a descriptive account of youth gang members in the first decade of the 21st century in the seven cities across the USA. We believe that it is important, indeed essential, to accurately describe a social problem if we are

Reprinted from: Finn-Aage Esbensen and Dena C. Carson, "Who Are the Gangsters? An Examination of the Age, Race/Ethnicity, Sex, and Immigration Status of Self-Reported Gang Members in a Seven-City Study of American Youth," *Journal of Contemporary Criminal Justice*, November 2012, 28: 462–478. Copyright © 2012 by Sage Publications.

to understand it, to explain its presence and, importantly, to suggest strategies for addressing the problem. Politicians, practitioners, and the general public tend to rely upon media-generated stereotypical impressions of gangs and gang members, thereby failing to appreciate the true nature of the problem (Decker & Kempf-Leonard, 1991; Esbensen & Tusinski, 2007). This reliance on media accounts results in either 1) underestimating the magnitude of the problem (failing to identify the full range of youth involved in gangs), 2) misidentifying the problem (believing that the gang problem is primarily a minority male problem), or 3) over-reacting to the problem (the proverbial moral panic).

Gang Member Characteristics

In this article, we seek to replicate the prior work of Esbensen and Winfree (1998) in which they described the sex and race/ethnic composition of youth gangs (and their level of involvement in illegal activities) in an 11 city survey conducted in 1995. This work, and other studies described below, reveal a contrasting picture to those common stereotypes and provide the basis for our current study examining the extent to which this broader portrayal of young gang members is upheld using recent self-report data.

Sex

Prior to Esbensen and Winfree's (1998) work and that of several other surveys conducted in the late 1980s and early 1990s (Bjerregaard & Smith, 1993; Esbensen & Huizinga, 1993), girls were generally ignored and considered to comprise but a small fraction of gang-involved youth. Collectively, these publications questioned such assertions, revealing that girls comprised as many as half of all gang members in general samples of youth, a finding that has been replicated in a number of studies in the USA (Battin, Hill, Abbott, Catalano, & Hawkins, 1998; Esbensen & Deschenes, 1998; Maxson & Whitlock, 2002) as well as in Europe (Bradshaw, 2005; Haymoz & Gatti, 2010; Pedersen & Lindstad, 2012; Sharp, Aldridge, & Medina, 2006; Weerman, 2012).

Race/Ethnicity and Immigrant Status

Relying primarily on early ethnographic studies, law enforcement data, and surveys conducted on urban samples of high-risk youth, a long-standing belief has been that gang youth are racial and ethnic minorities. Beginning with the early work by Thrasher (1927/1963), gang members have regularly been described as members of primarily White national or ethnic minorities (e.g., Irish, Italian, Polish, Jewish) and membership was linked to immigration status. By the late 1950s, gangs and gang members were increasingly described as African American, Puerto Rican, and/or Hispanic to the extent that by the 21st century, the gang problem was viewed essentially as a racial/ethnic (rather than national/ethnic) minority problem. This trend can also be observed in European accounts of the gang problem (e.g., de Jong, 2012; Lien, 2008).

Age

Another question of interest is the extent to which gang membership is associated with age. According to the National Gang Survey of law enforcement, most gang members are over 18 years of age (NYGC, 2012). Based on youth surveys, however, a sizable portion of youth report gang affiliation and youth as young as 11 identify themselves as gang members. Several studies have reported that gang membership appears to peak around 14 and 15 years (e.g., Esbensen & Huizinga, 1993; Thornberry et al., 2003). Data from these studies were collected in the late 1980s and early 1990s, however, so the question remains as to whether this pattern still holds.

Delinquent Activity

Regardless of data source, one consistent finding is that gang-involved youth are more delinquent than their non-gang counterparts. Of interest, however, is whether all gang members are equally involved in illegal activity or are there distinct patterns based on sex and race/ethnicity? For instance, do gang boys offend more than gang girls; or are girls involved in violent offenses at the same level as boys? Or, do members of different racial/ethnic groups commit the same type and volume of crime? Esbensen and Winfree (1998) reported that gang boys and girls (and non-gang boys and girls) had similar rates of offending; the ratio of gang boy to gang girl offending was approximately 1.5:1 but importantly, the gang girls were considerably more delinquent than the non-gang boys (a ratio of 2.3:1 for violent offending). With respect to offending levels by race/ethnicity, that ratio of gang to non-gang offending was quite stable across all of the race/ethnic groups examined (generally in the range of 4:1).

While a number of sophisticated analyses examining trajectories of gang membership, life-course consequences of gang membership (e.g., Melde & Esbensen, 2011; Krohn & Thornberry, 2008), and factors contributing to leaving the gang (Pyrooz & Decker, 2011; Pyrooz, Decker, & Webb, in press) have been published in the recent past, basic description of gang members is lacking. In this article, we address this gap in the literature by providing a replication of the Esbensen and Winfree (1998) descriptive account. We frame our analysis and presentation of findings around the following seven research questions: 1) What percentage of gang members are female? 2) Are girls in the gang as delinquent as boys in the gang? 3) What is the race/ethnic composition of gangs? 4) Are members of racial/ethnic minorities in gangs disproportionately involved in delinquent activity? 5) Are youth not born in the US more involved in gangs than native born youth? 6) Are immigrant youth in gangs more delinquent than native born gang members? 7) Do these patterns vary by age of the gang sample?

Data and Methods

We utilize data collected as part of the second National Evaluation of the Gang Resistance Education and Training (G.R.E.A.T.) program conducted between 2006 and 2011 (Esbensen, Peterson, Taylor, & Osgood, 2012). Selection of sites for this longitudinal evaluation of a school-based gang prevention program was guided by three main criteria: 1) existence of an established G.R.E.A.T. program, 2) geographic and demographic diversity, and 3) evidence of gang activity. A total of 31 schools in the following seven cities were selected for inclusion: Albuquerque, NM; Chicago, IL; a Dallas-Fort

Worth area suburb; Greeley, CO; Nashville, TN; Philadelphia, PA; and Portland, OR. The sample consisted of sixth grade students in 26 schools and seventh grade students in the remaining five schools.

Active Parental Consent and Retention Rates

Active parental consent was obtained with close collaboration of the classroom teachers, who were recruited and compensated for their assistance in collecting the consent forms from their students. (For more detailed description of the active consent process, consult Esbensen, Melde, Taylor, & Peterson, 2008.) This strategy was quite successful, yielding consent from parents of 3,820 students (78%); 552 parents (11%) declined their child's participation; and 533 (11%) students failed to return a completed form. Students in this active consent sample were surveyed six times in the span of five years (pre- and post-tests during the first year of the study and four annual follow-up surveys). The current study utilizes data from the pre-test and four annual surveys; completion rates were 98, 87, 82, 75, and 73 percent, respectively.

Student Sample Characteristics

The overall sample is evenly split between males and females; most (55%) youths reported living with both biological parents; and the majority (88%) was born in the United States (see Table 7.1). The sample is racially/ethnically diverse, with Hispanic youths (37%), White youths (27%), and African American (17%) youths accounting for 81% of the sample. With the majority of study participants enrolled in 6th grade at the outset of the evaluation, approximately two-thirds of the youths (61%) were aged 11 or younger at the pre-test. Three of the six Chicago schools and two of four schools in Albuquerque taught G.R.E.A.T. in 7th grade; thus, students in these sites were somewhat older than students in the other sites.

Measures

Students participating in this longitudinal evaluation completed group, self-administered questionnaires each year for five years. The questionnaire, with the exception of some questions that were added after Wave 3, remained the same across all five years. Students required approximately 35 minutes to answer the more than 220 questions. The questionnaire contained a number of items intended to assess the effectiveness of the G.R.E.A.T. program. For the purposes of the current paper, we are interested only in the demographic questions, self-reported gang membership, and self-reported levels of offending. Students provided information regarding their sex, their racial/ethnic identity, their living arrangement, their age, and whether or not they were born in the US.

Following a number of attitudinal questions, students were asked about their involvement in 14 different illegal activities, ranging from truancy to robbery. To be consistent with Esbensen and Winfree's (1998) study, we created summary measures of property and violent crime and analyzed drug sales separately. We also asked respondents about four different types of substance use that we combined into a summary index. For property offenses, violence, and drug sales, students were asked how many times in the past six months they had committed each of the illegal acts, while for substance use they were asked how often they used each substance. Given the highly skewed nature of frequency measures of delinquency, we truncated the individual items at 10 before creating a summary score.[1] The property index consists of five items (purposely damaged or destroyed property that did not belong to you, illegally spray painted a wall or a building, stolen or tried to steal something worth less than $50, stolen or tried to steal something worth more than $50, gone into or tried to go into a building to steal something) and therefore had a range of 0 to 50. Violent crime was a composite of four behaviors (hit someone with the idea of hurting him/her, attacked someone with a weapon, used a weapon of force to get money or things from people, been involved in gang fights) and had a possible range of 0 to 40. Substance use included 1) tobacco products, 2) alcohol, 3) marijuana or other illegal drugs, and 4) paint, glue, or other inhalants. Response categories ranged from no use to daily use which resulted in a range of 0 to 16. Drug selling consisted of a single item measure asking youth how many times in the past six months they sold drugs. As with property and

violence, this index was truncated, resulting in a range of 0 to 10.

The past 20 years have provided a number of studies relying upon self-nomination techniques to identify gang involved youth (Esbensen & Huizinga, 1993; Esbensen, Winfree, He, & Taylor, 2001; Hill et al., 1999; Thornberry, Krohn, Lizotte, & Chad-Wiershem, 1993; Thornberry et al., 2003). Researchers have concluded that this technique is quite robust and results in classification of a group of youths who are substantively different on a number of indicators than youth who do not self-report gang affiliation. Drawing on past efforts examining the validity of the self-nomination approach, we use a single item (Are you now in a gang?) to classify youth as gang or non-gang members.

Analytic Plan

While the G.R.E.A.T. evaluation represents a longitudinal panel design (i.e., the same individuals are followed across time), we treat the five annual surveys as a series of cross-sectional studies, capturing the students at one point in time each year. Consequently, we do not control for length of gang membership (the vast majority are members for only one wave of data collection), we do not exclude students if they did not participate in all five years of data collection, and we do not attempt to test the effects of gang membership from a theoretical perspective (e.g., we are not interested in testing the selection/facilitation/enhancement effect); our objective is to provide a descriptive account of gang membership among a sample of American youth at five different points in time. As such, we utilize simple descriptive and bivariate statistics to highlight 1) differences between gang and non-gang youth both demographically and behaviorally and 2) differences and similarities among gang youth at five different ages (mean ages ranging from 11.5 to 15.5 years of age). Attrition analyses do reveal that by Wave 4, the sample experienced some differential attrition of higher risk youth and, therefore, differences between the gang and non-gang samples at Waves 4 and 5 are likely underestimates.

Chi-square measures of association, independent sample *t*-tests, and analyses of variance

Table 7.1 Demographic and Offending Variables across Gang and Nongang Youth

	Total Sample	Wave One		Wave Two		Wave Three		Wave Four		Wave Five	
		NG	G	NG	G	NG	G	NG	G	NG	G
N	3820	3476	168	3056	172	2869	151	2649	95	2610	74
Sex[b,c,d,e]											
Male	48.1	48.0	54.8	49.1	59.3	47.9	61.6	47.9	60.0	47.9	68.9
Female	51.7	52.0	45.2	50.9	40.7	52.1	38.4	52.1	40.0	52.1	31.1
Race[a,b,c,e]											
White	27.3	28.4	13.1	28.9	10.5	29.1	12.6	28.7	18.9	29.1	12.2
Black	18.0	17.0	38.7	16.5	25.6	17.2	21.9	16.4	21.1	16.6	21.6
Hispanic	39.7	39.7	36.3	40.0	49.4	39.3	52.3	40.9	49.5	39.9	54.1
Other	14.7	14.8	11.9	14.6	14.5	14.4	13.2	14.0	10.5	14.4	12.2
Living Arrangement[a,c,d]											
Single	19.2	19.4	25.9	21.6	20.5	22.9	25.7	24.5	17.0	25.4	23.0
Intact	53.2	56.2	38.6	55.4	49.1	54.8	37.8	53.9	43.6	52.9	44.6
Other	24.2	24.4	35.5	23.0	30.4	22.3	36.5	21.6	39.4	21.7	32.4
Foreign Born[e]	11.8	11.9	8.9	11.9	9.9	11.7	14.6	12.3	12.6	11.4	20.3
Age[a,b,c,d]	11.48	11.46	11.74	12.58	12.88	13.49	13.76	14.51	14.75	15.45	15.52
Property Crime[a,b,c,d,e]	1.23	0.95	6.85	1.57	13.34	1.51	12.87	1.62	12.71	1.49	10.82
Violent Crime[a,b,c,d,e]	1.28	0.96	8.27	1.28	10.24	1.19	10.88	1.13	11.05	1.07	9.05
Substance Use[a,b,c,d,e]	0.29	0.22	1.76	0.44	3.26	0.72	3.95	0.99	4.95	1.30	5.65
Drug Sales[a,b,c,d,e]	0.05	0.03	0.56	0.09	1.63	0.12	2.35	0.20	2.94	0.28	2.67

[a]Significant differences between gang and nongang youth at Wave 1; [b]significant differences between gang and nongang youth at Wave 2; [c]significant differences between gang and nongang youth at Wave 3; [d]significant differences between gang and nongang youth at Wave 4; [e]significant differences between gang and nongang youth at Wave 5.

(ANOVAs) were used, as appropriate, to determine differences between and among gang and non-gang members. Differences across the demographic variables, with the exception of age, were examined using chi-square analyses. Tests for differences between gang and non-gang members and between boys' and girls' offending and substance use were conducted using independent sample t-tests. Finally, race/ethnic differences in frequency of offending were examined using one-way ANOVA analyses.[2]

Results

Demographic Characteristics of Gang Members

The percent of the participating youth who report gang membership varies across time, with the peak of gang membership (5.3%) occurring during middle school (when the students were in grades seven and eight and aged 12 to 14). By tenth grade (average age of 15.5) only 2.8% of the sample reported gang affiliation. Across the five annual waves of data collection, the sample ranged in age from an average of 11.48 at Wave 1 (W1) to 15.52 at Wave 5 (W5); this longitudinal sample of youth therefore taps the lower age range of gang-involved youth. For the first four waves, gang members tend to be older than their non-gang counterparts.[3] As seen in Table 7.1, the difference in age of gang and non-gang youth declines as the sample ages so much so that the two samples are virtually the same age by W5.[4] With respect to sex, these findings are remarkably similar to findings reported in a number of other youth surveys during the past 20 years; girls comprise 45% of gang members at W1 (mean age of 11.5) but only 31% at W5 when the sample was aged 15.5 years.

Gang members' race/ethnicity, while fluctuating from year to year, remains relatively stable although white youth tend to be under-represented. White youth account for approximately 27% of the total sample at W1 but account for only 10.5% to 18.9% of gang youth across the five years. At younger ages (W1 & W2), black youth tend to be over-represented in the gang sample; while African Americans account for 18% of the total sample, they represent 38.7% of W1 gang members and 25.6% at W2. By W5, African Americans account for 21.6% of gang youth but only 16.6% of the non-gang youth. Hispanic youth, unlike the black youth, are under-represented in the gang sample in the first two waves but are over-represented among gang members at W3, W4, and W5. "Other" youth tend to be proportionately represented in the gang and non-gang samples.

In recent years, growing attention has been given to the role of immigration (both legal and illegal) on gang activity. Contrary to some reports (see Vigil, 2008) youth in this sample who were born outside of the USA are less likely to be gang-involved at younger ages but by W5 (when the youth are 15 years of age), they account for a disproportionate share of the self-identified gang youth (20.3% compared to 11.4% of non-gang youth).

Delinquent Activity of Gang Members

As in past research, the gang youth are significantly more delinquent than the non-gang youth, generally in the range of a ratio of 7:1 (see Table 7.1). At W1, the gang members reported committing 6.85 property offenses in the prior six months compared to 0.95 offenses by non-gang. Property offending for non-gang youth appears to peak at about W4 with a frequency score of 1.62 while it peaks at W2 (13.34) for gang members. The violent offending pattern for non-gang youth is remarkably stable, fluctuating from a low of 0.96 at W1 to a high of 1.28 at W2. The gang members report higher scores and greater absolute fluctuation across the five waves, ranging from 8.27 at W1, increasing to 11.05 at W4 and declining to 9.05 by W5. Substance use, contrary to the two forms of delinquency, continues to escalate for both groups, although at a sharper

incline for the gang members. The frequency score for non-gang members increases from a low of 0.22 to a high of 1.30, still reflecting a relatively low level of drug use among this group. In contrast, the gang members reported significantly higher rates of substance use, from a low of 1.76 at W1 to 4.95 and 5.65 at W4 and W5, respectively.

Delinquent Activity by Sex

As was the case in the earlier Esbensen and Winfree (1998) article, we find significant differences between gang and non-gang boys and girls. Table 7.2 reports the mean frequency score for property and person offenses as well as substance use and drug sales. The consistency of results, among both gang and non-gang members, across the five waves (i.e., ages) of the sample is noteworthy. To highlight the differences in offending, in addition to the mean scores, we also present the ratio of gang girls to non-gang boys offending for each category. The mean level of offending is quite similar for the gang boys and girls, although there are statistically significant differences on property offending at Waves 1 and 2 and on violence at Wave 1. As the gang members age, the differences between the sexes disappear. By contrast, significant differences between non-gang boys and girls are found across all waves for all types of offending except drug use. Importantly, and consistent with prior research, in all five data waves, the differences between the gang girls and non-gang boys are substantial. Depending on the wave and the particular behavior, gang girls commit from 3.93 (Wave 1 property) to more than 20 (20.7 for Wave 1 drug sales) times as many offenses as non-gang boys, with most of these ratios falling in the range of five to one. It is particularly noteworthy that gang girls commit nine times as many violent crimes at W3 relative to non-gang boys (see Figure 7.1).

Delinquent Behavior by Race/ Ethnicity

At W1, the rate of offending is virtually identical among the racial/ethnic categories (see Table 7.3). While there is some slight variation, the differences are not statistically significant for the gang youth. Among the non-gang youth, however, there are some significant differences with the African

Table 7.2 Sex Differences in Offending for Gang and Nongang Youth

	Gang				Nongang			
	Property Crime	Violent Crime	Substance Use	Drug Sales	Property Crime	Violent Crime	Substance Use	Drug Sales
Significance	a,b	a			a,b,c,d,e	a,b,d,e		b,c,d,e
Wave 1								
Male	8.47	9.95	1.75	0.52	1.23	1.22	0.24	0.03
Female	4.83	6.30	1.77	0.62	0.69	0.72	0.24	0.02
Ratio*								
GG to NGB	3.93:1	5.16:1	7.38:1	20.7:1				
Wave 2								
Male	16.19	11.50	3.42	1.79	1.98	1.52	0.45	0.12
Female	9.09	8.45	3.03	1.39	1.17	1.04	0.43	0.06
Ratio								
GG to NGB	4.59:1	5.56:1	6.73:1	11.58:1				
Wave 3								
Male	13.66	10.67	3.50	2.32	1.93	1.24	0.68	0.17
Female	11.63	11.21	4.64	2.40	1.13	1.14	0.75	0.07
Ratio								
GG to NGB	6.03:1	9.04:1	6.82:1	14.12:1				
Wave 4								
Male	14.00	11.95	4.79	3.18	2.29	1.38	0.97	0.30
Female	10.60	9.60	5.18	2.56	1.00	0.91	0.99	0.11
Ratio								
GG to NGB	4.63:1	6.96:1	5.29:1	8.53:1				
Wave 5								
Male	11.63	8.92	5.37	2.20	2.13	1.40	1.37	0.41
Female	9.04	9.35	6.26	3.73	0.91	0.77	1.23	0.16
Ratio								
GG to NGB	4.24:1	6.68:1	4.57:1	9.10:1				

*Ratio of gang girls to nongang boys; [a]significant difference at Wave 1; [b]significant difference at Wave 2; [c]significant difference at Wave 3; [d]significant difference at Wave 4; [e]significant difference at Wave 5.

American and Hispanic youth reporting higher rates of offending than white youth. Interestingly, the ratios of delinquent involvement of gang to non-gang youth within each racial or ethnic group are substantively important. For example, at W1 white gang members commit approximately 10 times as many property, person, and substance use offenses (9.8, 9.3, and 10.9 respectively) as the non-gang white youth. For drug sales, the rate is 105 to 1. The offending ratios of gang to non-gang members are less pronounced for African American and Hispanic youth but remain substantial; for instance, black gang members commit five times as many crimes against persons as do the non-gang youth while the ratio is 9.8:1 for the Hispanic youth. Across waves 1 through 4, this pattern holds; the white gang members are significantly more delinquent relative to their non-gang peers in comparison to African American and Hispanic youth. At W5, however, this pattern disappears and the white youth report levels more comparable to the African American and Hispanic youth. It is interesting to note that there are virtually no race/ethnic differences in the rates of offending among

Figure 7.1 Violent Offending of Female Gang Members versus Male Nongang Members

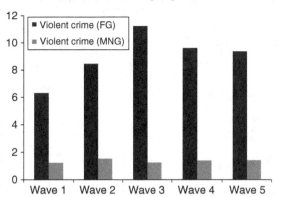

gang members at all five waves; regardless of race/ethnicity, all of the gang members report similar levels of involvement in property and violent offenses as well as drug sales. Black gang members report lower levels of substance use relative to the Hispanic gang youth at W1, W2, and W3.

Delinquent Behavior by Immigration Status

In the previous sections we have reported that there appear to be differences by sex, race/ethnicity, and age with regard to the delinquent behavior of gang and non-gang youth. We now turn our attention to the role of immigrant status.

Table 7.3 Racial/Ethnic Differences in Offending for Gang and Nongang Youth

	Gang				Nongang				Ratio of GM to NGM			
	Property Crime	Violent Crime	Substance Use	Drug Sales	Property Crime	Violent Crime	Substance Use	Drug Sales	Property Crime	Violent Crime	Substance Use	Drug Sales
Wave 1			d		a,b	a,d,e	b,d					
White	4.80	5.67	1.63	1.05	0.49	0.61	0.15	0.01	9.80:1	9.30:1	10.86:1	105.0:1
Black	6.90	8.96	0.94	0.16	1.29	1.78	0.15	0.02	5.35:1	5.03:1	6.27:1	8.00:1
Hispanic	7.91	8.85	2.77	0.97	1.20	0.90	0.31	0.04	6.59:1	9.83:1	8.94:1	24.25:1
Other	5.70	7.06	1.42	0.11	0.78	0.87	0.21	0.02	7.31:1	8.11:1	6.76:1	5.50:1
Wave 2			a,d		a,b	a,b,d,e	b,d,f					
White	18.41	11.50	5.29	2.89	0.91	0.84	0.35	0.05	20.23:1	13.69:1	15.11:1	57.80:1
Black	11.30	11.90	1.93	1.14	1.71	1.96	0.26	0.06	6.61:1	6.07:1	7.42:1	19.00:1
Hispanic	14.47	10.36	3.76	1.70	2.03	1.30	0.60	0.11	7.13:1	7.97:1	6.27:1	15.45:1
Other	9.33	5.96	2.52	1.32	1.43	1.29	0.37	0.13	6.52:1	4.62:1	6.81:1	10.15:1
Wave 3			d		b,d,f	a,b,e,f	b,d,f	b,d,f				
White	17.78	14.35	4.83	3.17	0.99	0.72	0.65	0.07	17.96:1	19.93:1	7.43:1	45.29:1
Black	8.36	8.88	2.21	1.45	1.43	1.71	0.43	0.06	5.85:1	5.19:1	5.14:1	24.17:1
Hispanic	14.04	11.52	4.64	2.57	2.07	1.42	0.94	0.21	6.78:1	8.11:1	4.94:1	12.24:1
Other	11.50	8.58	3.37	2.26	1.13	0.89	0.58	0.06	10.18:1	9.64:1	5.81:1	37.67:1
Wave 4					b,f	a,b,e,f	c,d,f	b,f				
White	12.22	11.72	5.89	2.94	1.29	0.84	1.08	0.12	9.47:1	13.95:1	5.45:1	24.50:1
Black	8.55	10.16	3.60	2.40	1.44	1.53	0.61	0.16	5.94:1	6.64:1	5.90:1	15.00:1
Hispanic	16.16	12.07	5.43	3.17	2.12	1.31	1.18	0.32	7.62:1	9.21:1	4.60:1	9.91:1
Other	6.70	7.00	3.70	2.90	1.03	0.76	0.68	0.06	6.50:1	9.21:1	5.44:1	48.33:1
Wave 5					b,d	a,b,e	a,c,d,f					
White	8.33	7.00	6.56	2.44	1.12	0.70	1.49	0.26	7.44:1	10.00:1	4.40:1	9.38:1
Black	12.38	12.75	5.19	2.81	1.00	1.69	0.74	0.21	12.38:1	7.54:1	7.01:1	13.38:1
Hispanic	10.65	8.38	6.10	2.71	1.95	1.22	1.50	0.36	5.46:1	6.87:1	4.07:1	7.53:1
Other	11.33	7.56	3.56	2.44	1.58	0.73	1.01	0.17	7.17:1	10.36:1	3.52:1	14.35:1

Significant differences across: ᵃwhite/black; ᵇwhite/Hispanic; ᶜwhite/other; ᵈblack/Hispanic; ᵉblack/other; ᶠHispanic/other.

Table 7.4 Immigration Status (Foreign Born) Differences in Offending for Gang and Nongang Youth

	Gang				Nongang			
	Property Crime	Violent Crime	Substance Use	Drug Sales	Property Crime	Violent Crime	Substance Use	Drug Sales
Significance	e	e				b,e	d	
Wave 1								
FB	13.87	11.50	3.86	0.79	1.10	1.00	0.24	0.02
Non-FB	6.12	7.97	1.55	0.54	0.93	0.95	0.22	0.03
Wave 2								
FB	15.18	9.82	4.13	0.82	1.35	0.91	0.43	0.09
Non-FB	13.12	10.29	3.17	1.72	1.60	1.32	0.44	0.09
Wave 3								
FB	14.00	9.32	3.90	1.86	1.67	1.03	0.66	0.11
Non-FB	12.67	11.16	3.96	2.44	1.49	1.21	0.72	0.12
Wave 4								
FB	11.64	9.73	5.67	3.25	1.48	0.98	0.78	0.19
Non-FB	12.85	11.23	4.84	2.89	1.64	1.16	1.02	0.20
Wave 5								
FB	5.53	4.27	4.87	1.43	1.11	0.66	1.14	0.64
Non-FB	12.17	10.27	5.85	2.97	1.54	1.13	1.32	0.29

[a]Significant difference at Wave 1; [b]significant difference at Wave 2; [c]significant difference at Wave 3; [d]significant difference at Wave 4; [e]significant difference at Wave 5.

Interestingly, while there are some minor differences in offending by gang and immigrant status, the most noticeable finding is the lack of an "immigrant effect" (see Table 7.4). The few statistically significant differences we did find tended to reveal lower rates of offending among the foreign-born gang members relative to the non-foreign born gang members.

Conclusion

The purpose of this article was to provide a current description of gang membership using a large sample of youth enrolled in public schools in seven cities across the USA. To do this, we drew on prior work by Esbensen and Winfree (1998) to examine demographic and offending behaviors across gang and non-gang youth. In addition, we expanded on this by examining these variables over five waves of data to determine if differences and similarities between gang and non-gang youth vary over time, at least at the bivariate level. At the outset of this article we identified seven descriptive research questions that guided our analyses. Overall, we find a depiction of youth involved in gangs that is remarkably similar to that which has evolved in both American and European research over the past twenty years. First, similar to Esbensen and Winfree (1998) as well as other research (Bjerregaard & Smith, 1993; Esbensen & Huizinga, 1993), this study found that girls comprise a substantial percentage of gang-involved youth, with 45 percent of gang members being female at Wave 1. This percentage decreases at later waves with 31 percent of gang members being female at Wave 5. This is consistent with Esbensen and Winfree's (1998) assertion that differences in the estimates of female gang participation can be attributed to the age of the sample. Second, it appears that female gang members participate in levels of offending similar to their male counterparts. This finding is fairly consistent across all time points, with males participating in more property offending at Waves 1 and 2. One of the most pronounced findings with regard to sex is the remarkable offending differences between gang girls and non-gang boys across time.

Third, gang-involved youth include a diverse constellation of youth from all racial/ethnic backgrounds but black and Hispanic youth are somewhat overrepresented, which is also similar to research by Esbensen and Winfree (1998). When looking over time, we see that the overrepresentation decreases in later waves for black youth in the gang sample, but increases for Hispanic youth. Fourth, when looking at offending behavior by race/ethnic composition, the ratio of offending for gang versus non-gang youth is more pronounced for white youth than for black and Hispanic youth. However, these differences decrease with time and the ratio of gang to non-gang offending is comparable for white, black, and Hispanic youth by Wave 5.

Fifth, this study was able to examine the relationship between immigrant status and gang membership. Findings demonstrate that immigrant status is not a major descriptor of gang youth—immigrants were less likely to be gang-involved in middle school years, although they were slightly more likely than non-immigrants to be involved by the time the youth were in high school. Sixth, there is also a lack of an "immigrant effect" when looking at the offending frequencies for these youth. Finally, youth are gang active at a relatively young age with the peak period of gang affiliation occurring in middle school (7th and 8th grade).

Regardless of age, sex, race/ethnicity, and immigrant status, gang involved youth are more delinquent than their non-gang counterparts. This finding remains stable over time for all illegal activity, including property and violent offending, substance use, and drug sales. While our objectives in examining demographics and offending across gang and non-gang youth were fairly modest, the findings are nonetheless informative. Gang-involved youth include: 1) boys and girls, 2) members of all racial/ethnic groups, 3) youth

from diverse family structures, and 4) represent both immigrant and native-born. As Esbensen and colleagues (2010:86) concluded, "Gang membership appears to provide an equal opportunity for all."

Notes

1. All of the analyses were replicated using variety scores (see Sweeten (forthcoming) for an excellent review of appropriate scaling techniques) with no substantive differences. For clarity in presentation, we report the frequency scores.
2. Given the small sample sizes we tested for equal variances using both Levene's test of equal variances and Welch's robust test. In terms of post-hoc analyses, Tukey's HSD was used when the assumption of equal variances was met. However, Games-Howell was used when the variances were not assumed to be equal. This is a modified HSD test that allows for unequal variances as well as unequal sample sizes.
3. Thanks to one reviewer who suggested that this may reflect the possibility that gang members do worse in school and are therefore more likely to be held back rather than age differences.
4. As one reviewer pointed out, this may be due to the effect of differential attrition.

References

Battin, S. R., Hill, K. G., Abbott, R. D., Catalano, R. F., & Hawkins, J. D. (1998). The contribution of gang membership to delinquency beyond delinquent friends. *Criminology, 36*, 93–115.

Bjerregaard, B., & Smith, C. (1993). Gender differences in gang participation, delinquency, and substance use. *Journal of Quantitative Criminology, 4*, 329–355.

Bradshaw, P. (2005). Terrors and young teams: Youth gangs and delinquency in Edinburgh. In S. H. Decker & F. M. Weerman (Eds.), *European Street Gangs and Troublesome Youth Groups* (pp. 193–218). Lanham: Altamira.

Decker, S. H., & Kempf-Leonard, K. (1991). Constructing gangs: The social definition of youth activities. *Criminal Justice Policy Review, 5*, 271–291.

Decker, S. H., & Van Winkle, B. (1996). *Life in the Gang: Family, Friends, and Violence*. New York: Cambridge University Press.

de Jong, J. D. (2012). Typically Moroccan? A group dynamic explanation of nuisance and group behavior.

In F.-A. Esbensen & C. L. Maxson (Eds.), *Youth Gangs in International Perspective: Results from the Eurogang Program of Research* (pp. 225–236). New York: Springer.

Egley Jr., A., & Howell, J. C. (2011). *Highlights of the 2009 National Youth Gang Survey. Juvenile Justice Fact Sheet*. Washington, D.C.: US Dept of Justice, OJJDP.

Esbensen, F.-A., & Deschenes, E. P. (1998). A multisite examination of youth gang membership: Does gender matter? *Criminology, 36*, 799–828.

Esbensen, F.-A., & Huizinga, D. (1993). Gangs, drugs, and delinquency in a survey of urban youth. *Criminology, 31*, 565–589.

Esbensen, F.-A., Melde, C., Taylor, T. J., & Peterson, D. (2008). Active parental consent in school-based research: How much is enough and how do we get it? *Evaluation Review, 32*, 335–362.

Esbensen, F.-A., Peterson, D., Taylor, T. J., & Freng, A. (2010). *Youth Violence: Sex and Race Differences in Offending, Victimization, and Gang Membership*. Philadelphia: Temple University Press.

Esbensen, F.-A., Peterson, D., Taylor, T. J., & Osgood, D. W. (2012). Results from a multi-site evaluation of the G.R.E.A.T. program. *Justice Quarterly, 29*, 125–151.

Esbensen, F.-A., & Tusinski, K. (2007). Youth gangs in the print media. *Criminal Justice and Popular Culture, 14*, 21–38.

Esbensen, F.-A., Winfree, J., L. Thomas, He, N., & Taylor, T. J. (2001). Young gangs and definitional issues: When is a gang a gang and why does it matter? *Crime & Delinquency, 47*, 105–130.

Esbensen, F.-A., & Winfree, L. T. (1998). Race and gender differences between gang and nongang youths: Results from a multisite survey. *Justice Quarterly, 15*, 505–526.

Fleisher, M. (1998). *Dead End Kids: Gang Girls and the Boys They Know*. Madison, WI: University of Wisconsin Press.

Haymoz, S., & Gatti, U. (2010). Girl members of deviant youth groups, offending behaviour and victimization: Results from the ISRD2 in Italy and Switzerland. *European Journal of Criminal Policy and Research, 16*, 167–182.

Hill, K. G., Howell, J. C., Hawkins, J. D., & Battin-Pearson, S. R. (1999). Childhood risk factors for adolescent gang membership: Results from the Seattle Social Development Project. *Journal of Research in Crime and Delinquency, 36*, 300–322.

Howell, J. C., Egley Jr., A. (2005). *Gangs in Small Towns and Rural Areas. NYGC Bulletin*. Washington, D.C.

Krohn, M. D., & Thornberry, T. P. (2008). Longitudinal perspectives on adolescent street gangs. In A. M. Liberman (Ed.), *A Long View of Crime: A Synthesis of Longitudinal Research* (pp. 128–160). New York: Springer.

Lien, I.-L. (2008). "Nemesis" and the Achilles heel of Pakistani gangs in Norway. In F. van Gemert, D. Peterson, & I.-L. Lien (Eds.), *Street Gangs, Migration and Ethnicity*. (pp. 227–240). Cullompton, Devon: Willan.

Maxson, C. L., & Whitlock, M. L. (2002). Joining the gang: Gender differences in risk factors for gang membership. In C. R. Huff (Ed.), *Gangs in America III* (pp. 19–35). Thousand Oaks, CA: Sage.

Melde, C., & Esbensen, F.-A. (2011). Gang membership as a turning point in the life course. *Criminology, 49*, 513–552.

Miller, J. (2001). *One of the Guys: Girls, Gangs, and Gender*. New York: Oxford University Press.

National Gang Center. (2012). *National Youth Gang Survey Analysis*. Retrieved April 4, 2012, from http://www.nationalgangcenter.gov/Survey-Analysis.

Pedersen, M. L., & Lindstad, J. M. (2012). The Danish gang-joining project: Methodological issues and preliminary results. In F.-A. Esbensen & C. L. Maxson (Eds.), *Youth Gangs in International Perspective: Results from the Eurogang Program of Research* (pp. 239–250). New York: Springer.

Pyrooz, D. C., & Decker, S. H. (2011). Motives and methods for leaving the gang: Understanding the process of gang desistance. *Journal of Criminal Justice, 39*, 417–425.

Pyrooz, D. C., Decker, S. H., & Webb, V. J. (In press). The ties that bind: Desistance from gangs. *Crime & Delinquency*. doi: 10.1177/0011128710372191.

Sharp, C., Aldridge, J., & Medina, J. (2006). *Delinquent Youth Groups and Offending Behaviour: Findings from the 2004 Offending, Crime, and Justice Survey. Home Office Online Report 14/06*. London.

Sweeten, G. (Forthcoming). Scaling criminal offending. *Journal of Quantitative Criminology*.

Thornberry, T. P., Krohn, M. D., Lizotte, A. J., & Chad-Wiershem, D. (1993). The role of juvenile gangs in facilitating delinquent behavior. *Journal of Research in Crime and Delinquency, 30*, 55–87.

Thornberry, T. P., Krohn, M. D., Lizotte, A. J., Smith, C. A., & Tobin, K. (2003). *Gangs and Delinquency in Developmental Perspective*. New York: Cambridge University Press.

Thrasher, F. M. (1927/1963). *The Gang: A Study of One Thousand Three Hundred Thirteen Groups in Chicago*. Chicago: University of Chicago Press.

Vigil, J. D. (2008). Mexican migrants in gangs: A second-generation history. In F. van Gemert, D. Peterson, & I.-L. Lien (Eds.), *Street Gangs, Migration and Ethnicity.* (pp. 49–62). Cullompton, Devon: Willan Publishing.

Weerman, F. M. (2012). Are correlates and effects of gang membership sex-specific? Troublesome youth groups and delinquency in Dutch girls. In F.-A. Esbensen & C. L. Maxson (Eds.), *Youth Gangs in International Perspective: Results from the Eurogang Program of Research* (pp. 271–287). New York: Springer.

CHAPTER 8

Getting into Gangs

Jody Miller

Miller's concern here is with issues of joining gangs. However, there are two important distinguishing features of her work: it specifically involves female gang members' pathways into gangs and her research strategy utilizes ethnography and personal interviews with females in two separate cities, facilitating comparative analyses and lending further validity to her findings. Miller finds neighborhood peer networks, serious family problems, and the influence of gang-involved family members to be of particular importance in the pathways to female gang membership. Note that it is the accumulation of these various factors that best explains gang membership, a point that will be elaborated and further discussed in the next article.

Gang membership doesn't happen overnight. Research shows that youths typically hang out with gang members for some time—often as much as a year—before making a commitment to join.[1] Moreover, there are pushes and pulls even earlier in life that increase the likelihood that young people will associate with gangs in the first place. The goal of this chapter is to explore girls' pathways into gangs by painting a picture of the broader contexts and precipitating events that lead young women to spend time with gang members and to join gangs.

On the whole, cities like Columbus and St. Louis have not had gang problems long enough to have intergenerational gang involvement within

families. Consequently gangs remain concentrated among adolescents and young adults. The young women in this study typically began hanging out with gang members when they were quite young—around age twelve on average—and they joined at an average age of thirteen. In fact, 69 percent of the girls in the sample described joining their gangs before they turned fourteen. . . . In considering girls' motives for joining gangs, it is important to keep their youthfulness in mind.

Three themes emerged in my research with regard to the life contexts that contribute to girls' gang involvement, at least among the kinds of gang girls in my sample. What's notable is that they emerged independently, both in the surveys—as factors distinguishing gang from nongang girls—and in the in-depth interviews, as contexts that young women attributed to their becoming gang-involved. First were girls' neighborhood contexts, and their exposure to gangs via both neighborhood peer and other friendship networks. A second theme that emerged for some young women was the existence of serious family problems, such as violence and drug abuse, which led them to avoid home, contributed to their weak supervision, and pushed them to attempt to meet social and emotional needs elsewhere. Finally, many young women described the strong influence that gang-involved family members—particularly older siblings in Columbus and siblings and cousins in St. Louis—had on their decisions to join.

While each young woman revealed her own trajectory into gang life, there were many common circumstances across girls' stories. In fact, the three themes noted above rarely stood alone in young women's stories of how they came to join their gangs. Instead they were overlapping in girls' accounts. As each told of individual life experiences, most recounted complex pathways into gangs that involved, in varying ways, the themes I've just described. Before I delve into each of these themes in greater detail, it is important to have a clear picture of the extent of their interrelationships, and how they differed for gang and nongang girls.

. . . Figure 8.1 illustrates how young women accounted for their gang involvement. Girls were classified as having neighborhood exposure to gangs when they said there was a lot of gang activity in their neighborhood, or they reported gang members living on their street. Gang-involved family members included girls with a sibling in a gang, with multiple family members in gangs, or girls who described another family member (e.g., a cousin or aunt) as having a decided influence on their decision to join. Girls with family problems included those with three or more of the following: violence between adults in the home, having been abused, drug or alcohol abuse in the family, or family members in jail. Four additional girls who did not report three of these were also categorized as

such because of their discussions of the impact of family problems. These included Heather, who was sexually abused by multiple members of her family; Rhonda and Latisha, who reported frequent abuse and witnessed physical violence among adults in the family; and Jennifer, whose parents were killed in a car crash, the loss of whom she felt was a turning point in her life.

What's striking about Figure 8.1 is the extent to which young women reported multiple dimensions of these risk factors. Taken individually, a majority of girls fit within each category: 96 percent described living in neighborhoods with gangs (of these, 69 percent explicitly described their neighborhood and peer networks as factors in their decisions to join). Likewise, 71 percent recognized family problems as contributing factors, and 71 percent had siblings or multiple family members in gangs, or described the influence of gang-involved family members on their decisions to join. In all, 90 percent of the gang members in the study report two or more dimensions of these risk factors, and fully 44 percent fit within the overlap of all three categories. . . . In Figure 8.1, the names of young women involved in ongoing serious delinquency are italicized. It is notable that only a third of the gang members were involved in serious offending. The majority of girls, despite their gang involvement, were not. . . .

Figure 8.2 provides a similar picture of nongang girls' exposure to the risk factors highlighted by gang girls. Nongang girls were classified using the same survey criteria as gang girls. . . . Young women listed outside the diagram met none of these criteria, though they nonetheless had some exposure to gangs. Several things are notable in comparing Figures 8.1 and 8.2. First, while the vast majority of gang girls (90 percent) fit in overlapping categories, only a third of the nongang girls experienced multiple of these risk factors for gangs, and only four nongang girls (9 percent, versus 44 percent of gang girls) reported all three dimensions. These data will be broken down individually in Tables 8.1 through 8.3. Those contexts most likely to be shared between gang and nongang girls were neighborhoods that exposed them to gangs, which 59 percent of nongang girls reported. However, only 26 percent of the nongang girls reported serious family problems,

Figure 8.1 Pathways into Gangs*

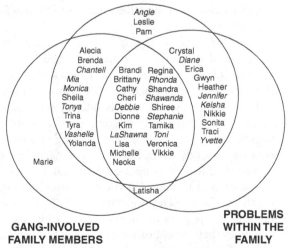

NEIGHBORHOOD EXPOSURE

*Girls whose names are italicized report regular involvement in serious delinquency.

Figure 8.2 Nongang Girls' Exposure to Risk Factors for Gangs

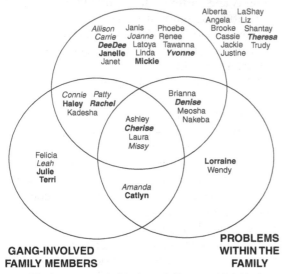

NEIGHBORHOOD EXPOSURE

Note: Girls whose names are italicized report half or more of their friends are gang members; girls whose names appear in boldface have considered joining gangs.

compared to 71 percent of gang girls. Likewise, 71 percent of gang members reported significant gang-involved family members, while only a third of the nongang girls had gang members in their immediate family or multiple gang members in their extended family. Thus, while the majority of nongang girls had gangs around them, most didn't have other experiences that could tip the scales in favor of gang involvement. . . .

Neighborhood Contexts and Networks

Scholars long have recognized factors such as neighborhood characteristics, poverty, and limited opportunities as being associated with the extent and nature of gangs in communities.[2] Recent studies of female gang involvement likewise have made the connection between these factors and young women's participation in gangs.[3] In fact, many scholars have pointed to the gang as a means for inner city youths—male and female—to adapt to the oppressive living conditions imposed by their environments. According to Karen Joe and Meda

Chesney-Lind, "the gang assists young women and men in coping with their lives in chaotic, violent, and economically marginalized communities."[4] . . .

In both [Columbus and St. Louis] there is substantial racial inequality, but on the whole Columbus is more socioeconomically stable than St. Louis. But what about the neighborhoods of the girls in my sample? . . . In both cities, the vast majority of girls in the study lived in neighborhoods that were economically worse off and more racially segregated than the city as a whole. Their neighborhoods had substantially lower median incomes and higher rates of poverty and unemployment than the citywide averages. . . . [Y]oung women in St. Louis were drawn from more [racially] segregated and economically devastated neighborhoods, on average, than young women in Columbus. In fact, two-thirds of the gang members in St. Louis lived in neighborhoods that were 80 percent or more African-American. . . .

Living in these neighborhoods means living in places with substantial amounts of crime.[5] In recent times, it often also means living in neighborhoods with street gangs. It goes without saying that in order to join a gang a young woman must have some exposure to gangs—at least the one she's joining. It's useful, then, to examine girls' descriptions of the extent of gang activity in their neighborhoods, but also the meanings they attribute to it. An important component of this is the extent to which they view gangs in the neighborhood as having facilitated or contributed to their decisions to join.

Table 8.1 illustrates girls' characterizations of the extent of gang activity in their neighborhoods. In both Columbus and St. Louis, the vast majority of young women described some exposure to gangs in their neighborhoods. . . . My interest here . . . is the extent and proximity of gang activity in girls' neighborhoods. As Table 8.1 shows, gang members were significantly more likely than nongang girls to report "a lot" of gang activity in their neighborhoods, and to note that there were other gang members who lived on their street.[6] While the vast majority of the gang members . . . described gang activity in their neighborhoods in these terms, just over half of the nongang girls did so. While all of the girls in the study could be characterized as at

Table 8.1 Exposure to Gangs

	Gang Members (N = 48)	Nongang (N = 46)
There is a lot of talk about gangs around the neighborhood	38 (80%)	31 (67%)
There is a lot of gang activity around the neighborhood	40 (83%)	25 (54%)*
There are other gang members living on the same street	39 (81%)	21 (46%)*
There are rival gangs close by	35 (73%)	26 (57%)

*$p < .05$

risk for problem behaviors and detrimental life consequences, only half of them had joined gangs. It appears then, that coupled with other factors, living in neighborhoods with gangs in close proximity increases the likelihood that young women will choose to become gang-involved themselves.

Documenting the existence of gang activity in girls' neighborhoods provides one piece of the puzzle. But what meanings do gang-involved girls attribute to gangs in their neighborhoods, and to what extent do they perceive neighborhood gangs as having had an impact on their decision to join? Because one goal of my study was to try to come away with an understanding of gang life from girls' points of view, this is an important line of inquiry. Other scholars have suggested that gangs can function to alleviate the boredom experienced by inner-city youths, who have few options for recreation or entertainment. John Quicker summarizes, "to be in a gang is to be part of something. It means having a place to go, friends to talk with, and parties to attend. It means recognition and respected status."[7] In addition, many scholars talk about the protective functions of gangs.[8] A number of the young women in my study had been victims of crime, prior to as well as after joining gangs. Many articulated a specifically gendered sense of protection that they saw resulting from being in gangs that were predominantly male. . . .

Not surprisingly, the majority of the gang girls suggested that their decision to become gang-involved stemmed in part from exposure to gangs through their neighborhood peer networks. Most often, they described a process in which they began to hang out with older gang-involved kids around the neighborhood as they reached adolescence, and these associations eventually led them to want to join. For instance, Angie was fifteen when we spoke, and had joined her gang at age eleven. She described how changes in her neighborhood shaped her desire to become a gang member:

> It's like, our neighborhood started changing a little bit, people started movin' in and out, and I was associating with the people who moved in and out, you know, and I was just, then, they was, a lot of 'em was in gangs, or things like that, and I wanted to be in a gang.

Because she was so young when she joined, it was a couple of years before she became actively involved. Instead, it appears that the older members thought it was cute that a young girl from the neighborhood wanted to be a member, but had few expectations for her participation. She explained:

> They was just like, "Hey, you wanna be a member?" I was like, one day, and I was like, "Yeah, yeah! I wanna be one, I wanna be one, I wanna be one!" Then they put me in and I was in, but then I, and as the years went by that's when I started really gettin' involved wid 'em, but then [at that time] I didn't, I didn't see them that much.

Chantell also described her neighborhood context as the overriding factor leading to her gang membership. She was fourteen when we spoke, and became gang-involved at age twelve. Chantell lived with her mother, grandmother, and siblings in a neighborhood where gangs were "just like everywhere." She described her childhood as one in which she grew up with gangs. She explained, "when I was little, I mean when I was young, I grew up around 'em. Just grew up around 'em, basically. Then when you grow up around 'em and you see 'em so much, until you want to get initiated."

At the time she decided to join, many of Chantell's neighborhood friends also were joining, as well as her older sister. "It was like a lot of gang-banging, I mean, it was just like, people were just like gettin' in it and having fun." Though she was somewhat torn about joining—"like wondering should I or shouldn't I, stuff like that, or what would happen if I did, or if I didn't"—eventually she decided to go ahead. "I was around 'em so much, the things they did I did," she explained, "so I said, since I grew up with 'em, I'm already hanging out with 'em, couldn't be no difference, so."

Chantell's comments about seeing other young people "gettin' in it and having fun" were echoed by a number of young women who described joining gangs in part because of their desire to belong to a neighborhood group, fit in, and have fun. This was especially the case for girls who joined quite young. Crystal joined at age twelve, noting, "you see other people doing it and you just think it's cool." And Nikkie, who also joined at twelve, explained, "if you ain't in it you just be . . . you just be feelin' left out. You be like, 'oh they all in a gang and I'm just sittin' here.'" As a result, she said, "I was like, 'I wanna get in it.' And I got in it." Latisha joined at twelve and explained, "it's fun. That's why I joined, 'cause it was fun and I seen what they was doing and I thought it was fun and it was cool or whatever." Likewise Pam joined at thirteen, and noted:

> They just [were] having fun, going to parties, kickin' it, staying out all night, new clothes, new shoes, selling drugs and all that. I wanted to be like that too. I wanted to wear name brand shoes, name brand clothes, I wanted my hair done and everything just like that so that's what I done.

In addition, residential instability appeared to be a factor shaping the influence of neighborhood gangs on girls' decision making. Over half of the gang members in the sample (52 percent in both cities) described having moved within the year prior to our interview, and two-thirds had moved within the previous two years. In comparison, 28 percent of the nongang girls had moved in the last year, and 48 percent within the previous two years. Moreover, these figures do not include such things as running away from home or spending time in detention or placement facilities—experiences that a large number of girls reported and that are indicative of further residential instability. While this instability is likely related to other family and economic problems that may be linked to risks for gang involvement, it is also the case that, upon arrival in a new environment, becoming involved with a local gang provides young women with a means of fitting in with a new crowd and becoming known. As Shawanda described, "I just needed

some friends, [joining the gang] was a quick way to make me a friend." In fact, several girls explicitly described joining gangs upon moving to new places, and others decided to join when they met gang members in residential facilities.

For instance, Traci had only recently moved to Columbus when we spoke, and likewise had recently joined her gang. She explained that moving to a new city, she "wanted to be like other people." At the same time she began noticing "all these blue scarves and red scarves and stuff," she got to know the neighbor in the apartment above hers—a young man who was a member of a neighborhood Crips set. Shortly thereafter she joined the gang and began going out with the young man. Traci felt that joining the gang was a way both to make friends, and to fit into her new environment. LaShawna was sent to Columbus to live with relatives when she was thirteen, and had been gang-involved since age twelve in the large city where she previously lived. In Columbus she became gang-involved when she "hooked up with" another gang member in a residential facility, where her knowledge of "big-city" gangs provided her with status and reputation.

A handful of young women, mostly in Columbus, described becoming gang-involved as a result of friends' involvement, rather than through neighborhood peer networks. Jennifer, Leslie, and Heather joined their gangs after a close friend introduced them to other gang members. For instance, Heather said of her decision to join: "I [was] at my friend Chad's house and they [gang members] had just came over 'cause they was friends with Chad's, and we just started talkin' and hangin' out and then they started talkin' about a gang and it's like that, I just got in there." Likewise, Jennifer joined her gang after her best friend introduced her to the OG ("Original Gangster," e.g., leader). She explained, "my friend was already in it and she would come over and she'd talk about all the, how it's real, it's just real cool to be in and everything like that." Once Jennifer met the OG, she began spending time with the other gang members, and eventually was allowed to join.[9]

Leslie had run away from home, and became friends with a gang girl she met at a local shelter for teen runaways. She returned home, but later "ran away with my friend. And she took me down there and introduced me to [the gang]." Leslie talked to the OG, who "told me that I would, it was an easy way to be protected and, um, I wouldn't have any problems. I wouldn't have to worry about money, food, clothing, a place to stay, 'cause I'da have all that because I was in the gang." At the point we interviewed, Leslie was pregnant and planning to sever her ties to the gang. Her outlook on it was decidedly negative. Of her initial conversation with the OG and decision to join, she surmised, "it was a bunch of lies . . . and I fell into the trap and believed him."

> JM: And why do you say it was a lie now?
> LESLIE: Because I was almost in the gang for about a year and a half. And, just bein' in there, you didn't go anywhere. You, um, you really didn't, I mean, succeed in anything 'cause the stuff that you were doin' was wrong. And, half, that's why half of 'em, half the guys are in here [the detention center] now, it has to do with some kind of gang-related somethin'.

. . . Young women in St. Louis were more likely to describe their neighborhood gangs as wary of outsiders, and thus new people—unless they were the relatives or friends of youths in the neighborhood—were less able to quickly assimilate into the local gang as girls in Columbus described.[10] Pam, for instance, joined her neighborhood gang when she was thirteen. She said, "I grew up with some of them, went to school with some of them, and by me knowing them I just knew the other ones 'cause they used to be around." Much like Chantell, Pam joined because she'd "been knowing them anyway all my life for real." But she described a gang with somewhat tighter boundaries than what Chantell had described. Pam explained that for someone to join her gang:

> They just got to be known or something. You can't just be no anybody. They got to know you or they been knowing you or they grew up with you or something like that or you family. Other than that, they just don't put you in there like that. . . . 'Cause anybody that is in the gang, everybody grew up together for real. It's just not like no anybody, like they gonna get anybody. You want to be in this gang? It ain't like that. You got to know a person, you got to grow up around it or be around it.

Tyra articulated much the same beliefs as Pam, noting, "If you ain't in our streets or nothin', live on our streets, you ain't joining nothin'." She said she joined her gang because "I grew up in that neighborhood with them." Moreover, Tyra suggested that part of the nature of gangs in St. Louis is attributable to how dangerous many neighborhoods are. She explained: "Growing up on the North Side [of St. Louis], you got to be like that 'cause everywhere you look, you turn around and somebody is getting killed. I don't care what nobody say, I think the North Side worse than any side."

Very few of the young women described getting involved with their gangs because their boyfriend was a member. In fact, only three girls—Rhonda, Marie and Stephanie—described this as a specific motivating factor. This is not to suggest that young women didn't have boyfriends, including within their gangs. For instance, Traci became gang-involved at around the same time her gang-involved neighbor became her boyfriend. But she didn't attribute her desire or decision to join the gang as having to do with him. Instead she said, "I just wanted to join, I don't know why, when I moved out here [to Columbus] I just *had* to join a gang." It is significant that only a handful of girls described a relationship with a boyfriend as a factor influencing their decision to join a gang, with most describing broader neighborhood peer networks as having greater importance. This finding challenges some long-held beliefs about young women in gangs, but also is in keeping with other research which suggests that, despite being overlooked by many scholars, girls' friendships are an important factor for explaining both their gang involvement and their delinquency.[11]

While neighborhood and friendship networks help answer the question of how and why girls come to join gangs, these remain only a partial explanation. In fact, as Figure 8.1 illustrates, often there are other precipitating factors to consider. Many young women described problems in their family lives that led them to spend time away from home, out on the streets, and with gang members. In addition, like their relationships with friends in the neighborhood, having gang-involved family members was significantly related to girls' gang involvement in both Columbus and St. Louis. In the next section, I will discuss further the impact of family problems on girls' gang involvement; then I will return to the issue of gang-involved family members.

Family Problems as Precipitating Circumstances

The family has long been considered crucial for understanding delinquency and gang behavior among girls.[12] Problems such as weak supervision, lack of attachment to parents, family violence, and drug and alcohol abuse by family members all have been suggested as contributing to the likelihood that girls will join gangs.[13] My study provides additional support for these conclusions, based on comparative findings from survey interviews, and from young women's accounts of why they joined gangs.

As Table 8.2 illustrates, gang members were significantly more likely to come from homes with numerous problems than were the young women who were not in gangs. Gang girls were significantly more likely to have witnessed physical violence between adults in their homes, and to describe having been abused by adult family members. In addition, gang members were much more likely to report that there was regular drug use in their homes. Most important, gang members were significantly more likely to describe experiencing *multiple* family problems—with 60 percent describing three or more of the five problems listed in Table 8.2, and 44 percent reporting that four or more of these problems existed in their families. In

fact, only *three* gang members—Angie, Brenda, and Chantell—said there were none of these problems in their families, compared to nine (20 percent) of the nongang girls.

In addition, a number of gang girls had been sexually abused or raped in the context of their families.[14] In all, 25 (52 percent) of the gang members in my study reported having been sexually assaulted, and described a total of 35 instances of sexual assault. Of these 35 incidents, 23 of them (66 percent) were committed by family members or men whom young women were exposed to through their families. Eight of these assaults were committed by immediate family members (e.g., girls' fathers, brothers, and in one case her mother). Eight were committed by extended family (e.g., girls' cousins, grandfathers, uncles), and seven were committed by individuals that young women came into contact with through their families. For instance, Tamika was raped by her stepfather's brother, Vikkie by her mother's boyfriend's friend, Yolanda by her uncle's friend, and Brittany by her aunt's boyfriend. While fewer nongang girls had been sexually assaulted (10 of 46, or 22 percent), like the gang girls, two-thirds of these assaults (eight of twelve) occurred in the context of the family.

For many young women, home was not a particularly safe place. Turning to young women's descriptions of their decision to join a gang, it is not surprising that the majority (though by no means all) noted family problems as contributing factors. The ways in which family problems facilitated girls' gang involvement were varied, but they shared a common thread—young women began spending time away from home as a result of difficulties or dangers there, and consequently sought to get away, and to meet their social and emotional needs elsewhere. Often young women specifically said that their relationships with primary caregivers were problematic in some way. A number of researchers have suggested that "the gang can serve as a surrogate extended family for adolescents who do not see their own families as meeting their needs for belonging, nurturance, and acceptance."[15] Regardless of whether gangs actually fulfill these roles in young women's lives, it is clear that many young women believe that the gang will do so when they become involved. . . .

Table 8.2 Problems within the Family		
	Gang Members (*N* = 48)	Nongang (*N* = 46)
Witness to Physical Violence between Adults	27 (56%)	12 (26%)*
Abused by Family Member	22 (46%)	12 (26%)*
Regular Alcohol Use in Home	27 (56%)	17 (37%)
Regular Drug Use in Home	28 (58%)	8 (17%)*
Family Member in Prison/Jail	35 (73%)	31 (67%)
Three + Family Problems	29 (60%)	11 (24%)*
Four + Family Problems	21 (44%)	6 (13%)*
*p < .05		

The most common family-related themes described by young women as contributing to their gang involvement were drug addiction and abuse.[16] While 58 percent of the gang members described regular drug use in their homes, ten girls (21 percent) explicitly discussed the impact of their mothers' crack or heroin addiction. Drug-addicted parents, while not necessarily described as abusive, often were quite neglectful, leaving girls feeling abandoned and unloved, but also not providing necessary supervision over their time and activities. Moreover, given the intense degradation of many drug-addicted women on the streets, these particular young women likely dealt with the trauma of having knowledge of or even witnessing their mother's involvement in such situations.[17]

Keisha was fourteen when we spoke, and had joined her gang the previous year. She described her neighborhood as "nothin' but Folks and Crips," and attributed her decision to become a gang member to her sense of abandonment resulting from her mother's drug addiction. She explained: "My family wasn't there for me. My mom smokin' crack and she act like she didn't wanna be part of my life, so I just chose the negative family, you know what I'm saying?" Likewise, Crystal described joining her gang at a time when she was "fighting with my mama 'cause she was on drugs."

Shandra got to know members of her gang "walking to school, back and forth to school and I would see them in the mornings and after school and after awhile I just [started] hanging around smoking weed and just kicking it with them." She elaborated:

> Right around the time that I started hanging with them I had just got put out of school and had tried to kill myself not too long before that 'cause I was just, you know, I had run away from home and I was just dealing with a lot of stuff. 'Cause my mother is on drugs real bad, and her and her boyfriend used to be fighting all the time and I just, I don't know, I guess I just didn't want to be around that. So I chose to be around the gang.

Shandra said after she "just used to kick it with them [gang members] so much, one day I just woke up and I just say I wanna be one of them, and then I told them and then they jumped me in the 'hood." She was twelve when she joined her gang. Shandra's

mother knew she had become gang-involved, "because I started coming in late and I be high when I came in, I started dressing like a gang member, wearing all stars and khakis and stuff like that." But she explained, her mother "didn't really say nothing about it." At the time, Shandra said she "felt close to" the other gang members, and "bond[ed] with them like they [my] family." When she first joined, she continued, the gang was so "important for me that I did anything I could to get respect from the OGs and just, you know, be down for [the gang]. It was important because I wanted to feel, I guess accepted to the gang, accepted in the gang."

In addition to their belief that joining a gang would fill emotional voids, a number of these young women said that a lack of supervision attributable to their mothers' addiction also was a contributing factor. Veronica, for example, joined her gang when she was "gettin' ready to be twelve," after her older brothers had joined. She said the gang was "right there in my neighborhood . . . then I seen that my brothers, 'cause I seen my brothers get put in. So then I said I wanna be put in." At the time, she explained, "I was just doin' what I wanted to 'cause when I found out my mom was doin' drugs and stuff. So she wasn't never in the house, so she didn't know."

Likewise, Yvette explained, "My mama, she on drugs, [we] used to fight and stuff. Me and her don't get along . . . [and] my father, he just ain't been around." Yvette said because of her mother's drug habit, when she was growing up her mother often "made me stay out late and stuff like that." Eventually Yvette "just started hanging out with" gang members in her neighborhood, whom she described as also being unsupervised. "I just hung around with some people that can do what they want to do, stay out late, whatever, go home when they want to go home, I'm hanging out with them." She said "it was like, I wasn't going to school a lot so I got with them. We was having so much fun. Most of them didn't go to school so I felt like I didn't need to go to school. . . . I had fun with the gang so I became one of them." Though her mother was unhappy and threatened Yvette when she found out about her gang involvement, Yvette said, "it was like too late for her to try and change me."

Another theme that emerged in some girls' discussions of how they became gang involved was the impact of being physically or sexually abused by family members. In most of these cases, violence and victimization in the family precipitated girls' decisions to avoid home, and several girls described running away from home and living for extended periods with friends—often exposing them to gangs. In a few cases, being placed outside the home as a consequence of abuse also had the unintended consequence of exposing girls to gangs and gang members. Erica's story is a case in point.

Erica was seventeen when we spoke, and had joined her gang when she was fifteen. She lived with her father and stepmother for most of her childhood, until her father and uncle raped her at the age of eleven, whereupon she was removed from the home. Since that time she had been shuffled back and forth between foster homes, group homes, and residential facilities, and had little contact with her family because they turned their backs on her. Erica explained, "I didn't have *no* family. Because of the incidents with my dad and my uncle. After that, they just deserted me and I didn't, I had nothin' else." Though she said her stepmother was the primary person who raised her, their relationship was severely damaged by the rape. "She doesn't, she doesn't believe it. I mean, even after he [dad] pleaded guilty she still doesn't believe it."

Erica's childhood up to that point had been filled with violence. Her father was physically abusive toward her stepmother, herself, and her siblings, and as a young child, Erica had witnessed her biological mother being raped. Both her father and stepmother had spent time in jail, and there was heavy alcohol and drug use in the home as she was growing up. As a result, she described herself as a physically aggressive child. She explained, "in elementary school before I even knew anything about gangs, I'd just get in a lot of fights." In fact, her nickname in elementary school was "Iron Mike," in recognition of her Tyson-like characteristics. Her initial contact with gangs came when she was fourteen and living in a foster home. During her stay there, she met a group of kids and began spending time with them:

I didn't know 'em, but I just started talkin' to 'em. And, they always wore them blue rags and black rags and all that. And, I asked them, I said, "well you part of a gang?" And they tell me what they're a part of. So,

it was like, everywhere I went, I was with them. I was never by myself. If they went out to [a] club I went with them. If they did anything, I was with them. And, um, we went down to some club one night and it was like a whole bunch of 'em got together and um, I asked to join.

Erica said she joined the gang "just to be in somethin'," and so that it could be "like a family to me since I don't really have one of my own." She felt that being in the gang allowed her to develop meaningful relationships. She explained, "people trust me and I trust them. It's like that bond that we have that some of us don't have outside of that. Or didn't have at all. That we have inside of that gang, or that set." Nonetheless, . . . Erica expressed some ambivalence about being in a gang, because it involved antisocial attitudes and behaviors that she didn't see as being part of who she really was, particularly as she neared adulthood. Her decision to join, though, was in part a search for belonging and attachment.

Likewise, Brittany described a terribly violent family life. She lived in a household with extended family—twelve people in all—including her mother, grandmother, stepfather, and an adolescent uncle who was physically abusive. Her aunt's boyfriend had sexually assaulted her at the age of five, but family members didn't believe her. Though she didn't know her father, who was in jail, she had early memories of him physically abusing her mother. Moreover, she felt very disconnected and unloved by her family, and also described being isolated at school: "I didn't have no friends, used to always get teased. . . . My grades started going down, I started getting real depressed, started skipping school, smoking weed after school and stuff." Brittany saw the gang as a means of finding love. She explained: "I felt that my family didn't care for me . . . that when I was on the streets I felt that I got more love than when I was in the house so I felt that that's where my love was, on the streets, so that's where I stayed." And though she did not admit to doing so herself, Brittany noted, "my best friend got initiated [into the gang] by having sex with twelve boys."

Other young women also focused on a myriad of family factors in explaining their gang involvement. Diane's experiences are exemplary of how family problems could compound in a way that ultimately leads to gang involvement. When we spoke Diane was fifteen, and among the most deeply entrenched gang members in the sample. She had joined her gang at eleven, but was only ten when she began hanging out with members, including the seventeen-year-old young man who lived next door:

> I think I was about ten and a half years old and we started hanging out over there, over at his house and all his friends would come over and I just got into, just hangin' out, just becomin' friends with everybody that was there. And then I started smokin' weed and doin' all that stuff and then when I turned eleven it was like, well, 'cause they seen me get in fights and they seen how my attitude was and they said, "Well I think that you would be, you would be a true, a very true Lady Crip."

The time she spent with the gang, and her decision to join, were predictable results of her life history up to that point. As a young child, the family moved around a lot because her father was on the run from the law. Her father dealt drugs out of their home, and had a steady stream of friends and clients moving in and out of the place. Exposed to crime and drugs at an early age, Diane tried marijuana for the first time at age nine. She noted, "I was just growin' up watchin' that stuff." Her life changed dramatically when she was ten and her father was sent to prison, leaving her care to her drug-addicted mother. Diane explained:

> We didn't have very much money at all. Like, my mom was on welfare. My dad had just gone to jail. My dad had just gone to prison for four years. . . . My mom was on drugs. My, see my dad, always sellin' acid, quaaludes, cocaine and my mom was on, just smokin' marijuana and doin' crack. Back then she was just real drugged out, had a lot of problems and it was just me and my little brother and my little sister and that's all that was goin' on, besides me goin' to school and comin' home to seein' my mom do whatever, hit the pipe, and goin' next door and hangin' out.

Diane remained very dedicated to her gang and fellow members, noting passionately, "I *love* my cousins [fellow Crips]. I *love* 'em." This was in large part because of what they provided her when she felt she had little else. She elaborated, "that neighborhood's not a good neighborhood anyway, so, I had nothin' to look forward to, but these people

they helped me out, you know? I mean, I was a young kid on my own. . . . I was just a little girl, my dad's gone and my mom's on drugs." Diane's father had been released from prison when we spoke, but was locked up again—as was Diane—for an armed robbery they had committed together. Ironically, her close bond with her father, and the knowledge she'd gained from him about how to commit crime, had resulted in a great deal of status for her among her gang peers. She noted, "my dad is just so cool. Everybody, everybody in my little clique, even people that aren't in my set, just my regular friends, they all love my dad."

As these young women's stories illustrate, a multitude of problems within families can increase young women's risk for gang involvement. This occurs through girls' attempts to avoid home, to meet social and emotional needs, as a result of ineffective supervision over their activities and, in cases like Diane's, by showing young women through example that criminal lifestyles are appropriate. These problems are exacerbated when young women live in neighborhoods with gangs, which provide a readily available alternative to life at home. Moreover, older gang members appear "cool," and their seemingly carefree lifestyle and reputed familial-like bonds to one another are an appealing draw for young girls with so many troubles at home.

Gang Involvement among Family Members

Some girls who lack close relationships with their primary caregivers can turn to siblings or extended family members to maintain a sense of belonging and attachment. However, if these family members are gang-involved, it is likely that girls will choose to join gangs themselves. Moreover, even when relationships with parents or other adults are strong, having adolescent gang members in the family often heightens the appeal of gangs.[18] As Table 8.3 illustrates, gang members were significantly more likely than nongang girls to report family members in gangs. Most importantly, gang members were much more likely to have siblings in gangs, and were more likely to have two or more gang-involved family members.

Table 8.3 Gang Membership among Family Members

	Gang Members (N = 48)	Nongang (N = 46)
Gang Member(s) in Family	38 (79%)	25 (54%)*
Sibling(s) in Gang	24 (50%)	8 (17%)*
Multiple Gang Members in Family	29 (60%)	13 (28%)*
*p < .05		

These relationships were actually somewhat different in the two sites—with the relationship between girls' gang membership and that of her family being most marked in St. Louis. In Columbus, gang girls were not significantly more likely than nongang girls to have a family member in a gang—57 percent of gang members had family in gangs, versus 48 percent of nongang girls. By comparison, all but one of the gang members in St. Louis (96 percent) reported having at least one gang-involved family member. In fact, a greater percentage of nongang girls in St. Louis (62 percent) described having a family member in a gang than did gang members in Columbus (57 percent). Moreover, St. Louis gang members were the only group for whom a majority reported having more than one gang-involved family member. In all, 21 St. Louis gang members (78 percent) described having multiple gang members in the family, compared to 38 percent of Columbus gang members, 29 percent of nongang girls in St. Louis, and 28 percent of nongang girls in Columbus.

However, gang members in both cities were significantly more likely to report a gang-involved sibling than nongang girls. In all, 52 percent of St. Louis gang members and 48 percent of Columbus gang members had siblings in gangs, compared to 19 and 16 percent of the nongang girls in these cities, respectively. In St. Louis, nine gang girls reported brothers in gangs, and ten reported sisters; in Columbus, eight gang girls had brothers in gangs and three had gang-involved sisters. Overall, 35 percent of the gang members had brothers who were gang members, and 27 percent had sisters in gangs. In addition, four gang members—two in each city—described having parents who had been in gangs.

Turning to young women's accounts of how they became gang-involved and the role family members played, there also are notable differences between the two sites. In Columbus, all of the young women who described the influence of a family member mentioned a sibling or siblings. In St. Louis, on the other hand, eight girls pointed to siblings, while twelve identified a cousin and/or aunt who prompted their decision to join. Gang girls in St. Louis also were more likely to talk about the influence of *female* family members, be they sisters, aunts or cousins. Perhaps as a consequence . . . , gang girls in St. Louis were more likely to talk about the importance of their friendships with other girls in the gang, while most gang girls in Columbus identified more with young men.

In general, the greater influence of extended family members on girls' gang involvement in St. Louis was striking. The likely explanation lies in the socioeconomic differences between the two cities and their effects on the strength of extended family networks. As I noted above, the young women in Columbus tended to live in neighborhoods with higher than average rates of poverty and racial segregation than the city as a whole. However the neighborhoods of girls in Columbus were somewhat better on social and economic indicators than the neighborhoods of girls in St. Louis. Moreover, while there are pockets of concentrated poverty in Columbus, St. Louis exhibits much larger geographic areas blighted by intense poverty, racial isolation, and population loss, resulting in large numbers of vacant lots and abandoned buildings in many of the poorest neighborhoods.

So how might these differences relate to the tendency for St. Louis gang members to say that extended family networks, rather than immediate family, drew them into gangs, while this simply was not the case in Columbus? I would suggest that the answer may lie in families' responses to entrenched poverty conditions. Research has shown that African American families living in poverty often rely to a great degree on extended family for economic, social, and emotional support.[19] Given the more detrimental economic conditions in St. Louis, it may be that extended family networks are stronger there than in Columbus. This would help explain why St. Louis gang members seemed to spend more time with their relatives outside the immediate family, and consequently, why those relatives had a stronger influence on girls' decision-making with regard to gangs. Regardless of which family members have an impact, it is clear that having family members who are in gangs increases the likelihood that girls will perceive gangs as an appropriate option for themselves as well.

More often than not, young women who joined gangs to be with or like their older siblings did so in the context of the types of family problems noted earlier. Veronica, who I discussed above, was a case in point. Her mother's drug addiction left her and her siblings unsupervised; when her older brothers began hanging out with the neighborhood gang, she followed suit. In fact, she went on to tell me, "then my *little* brother wanted to get put in it. And he was like only about six [laughs]. They told him no."

Similarly, Lisa was thirteen when we spoke, and only recently had joined her gang. Her brother Mike had been a member of a Folks gang for several years, and when the family relocated to another area of Columbus, he decided to start his own set of the gang in their new neighborhood. Lisa was among its members. Prior to Mike starting his own set, Lisa hadn't considered joining, but nonetheless said she "claimed [Folks] because that's what my brother was so I wanted to be like that too." Their mother had died when Lisa was eleven, and she described their father as physically abusive and distant. She felt very close to her brother, and said her desire to be with him was her primary reason for joining his gang.

Several weeks before Lisa joined, her brother's girlfriend Trish—who was also Lisa's best friend—was initiated. Lisa explained, "One day Trish was like, 'Well you wanna be true?' And I was like, 'Yeah.' And they was like, 'All right.' And they took me behind the railroad tracks and kicked the shit outta me and I was in it [laughs]." Lisa was initiated into the gang on the same day as her boyfriend and another male friend of theirs. A primary concern for her was to make a good impression on her brother. She explained:

The boys was scared. They was like, "Man, I don't know, I don't know." And then I was like, I just looked at my brother. Then I looked at my friend and I looked at them boys and I was like, "I'll go first." So I just did it, I think . . . why I did it then is just to be, I don't know. Just to show them, my brother, that I was stronger than them boys.

Although she enjoyed what she described as the "fun and games" that she had with her brother and the other gang members, Lisa was actually ambivalent about being in a gang. She told me, "Right now I wish, I kinda wish I never got into it but I'm already in it so, like, um, I just, I don't know. I don't think I'm gonna be that heavy as my brother is, like all the time, you know, yeah, yeah." Lisa was especially concerned for her brother, who took his gang involvement quite seriously, which she perceived as putting his physical safety at risk. She explained, "My brother, when he was little, he was a little geeky little kid that wore glasses. But now he's like, you know, and I don't understand it but uh, I wish he was still a little kid that wore glasses." Nonetheless, she felt being in the gang allowed her to spend time with him. She surmised, "We all just hang out all the time. We just are always together. If you see me you see my brother. If you see my brother you see his girlfriend. If you see me you see my boyfriend. I mean, it's just like that."

In fact, a number of young women described joining their gangs in order to be around and meet the approval of their older brothers regardless of whether—like Lisa and Veronica—they had family problems at home. When Tonya was younger, she said she noticed "my brother just started wearing red all the time, all the time." She continued, "then after school . . . he just kept going outside. All these dudes and girls used to have fun, selling drugs and having money and stuff. And then I just wanted to do it. I thought it would be fun so I joined. I tried to join and then my brother let me join." Tonya said her initiation into the gang involved "just a couple of my brother's friends, he didn't let nobody really [cause me] pain for real, like really beat me up. They was just beating me up so I would have to fight back. I had some bruises, busted lip, in another minute it was gone, it was cool." What wasn't gone was Tonya's belief that "I had gained my brother's respect and stuff." Only thirteen at the time, she said "in the beginning I was like a little shortie. I didn't sell drugs, I didn't run around shooting or none of that." Her involvement increased, though, when she began "going out with one of my brother's friends," who provided her with drugs, which, she said, was "how I started selling dope."

Monica was also thirteen when she joined her brothers' gang. She had four older brothers, between the ages of 20 and 28 at the time she joined, all of whom were members of the same Crips set. Sixteen at the time we spoke, she remained the youngest member of her gang, and said she joined because she "wanted to be like" her older brothers. Monica described that she "always followed them around," and explained, "all four of my brothers were in so I was like, 'all right, I wanna be in a gang.' So I used to ride around with them all the time. And then my brother asked me, he said, 'Do you wanna be down or what?' . . . And I was like, 'Fine, I'll do it.' So I did." Perhaps because of the adult role models in her family, and because she "grew up around it," Monica, like Diane, was one of the most committed—and consequently delinquent—gang members. She told me, "I'm down for real, I'm down for life." Diane's strong gang commitment resulted from gang members filling a caregiving niche unavailable to her from her family while her father was in jail. In contrast, Monica's commitment was the result of her close bonds to her family.

A number of the young women in St. Louis, as I noted above, described the influence of extended family members—most often cousins, but sometimes also aunts. All of these young women talked about spending quite a bit of their time at their relatives' homes, sometimes but not always when they lived in the same neighborhoods. Trina joined her gang when she was eleven; both her cousins and aunts were members, and she described "just being around over there, being around all of them" growing up. Trina said her aunts and cousins had dressed her in gang colors from the time she was young, and she surmised, "I just grew up into it."

Likewise, Shiree described her gang as "a family thing," and Alecia also said her gang involvement was "like a family thing." Alecia explained, "my auntie first moved on [the street] where I live now . . . [and] I started visiting my cousin." The gang evolved from "everyone that was growing up in that 'hood. . . . I seen all my relatives, not my father and mother, but you know, all my relatives in it and then I came over just like that." She said, "It ain't

like they talked me into it or nothing." But eventually she and her mother and siblings moved to the same block, further solidifying her gang affiliation.

Vashelle said she joined her gang "because my family, all of my cousins, my relatives, they was Bloods already and then I moved over there because my cousin was staying over there so I just started claiming [the gang]." While in general Vashelle believed that girls joined gangs for "little stuff, they want a family or something," she argued that these were not her own motives. She explained, "It's just something I wanted to do because my cousin was in it so I wanted to be hanging around. . . . I ain't no follower. It's something I wanted to do and by them doing it was just more influence on me."

In some cases conflict in girls' immediate families increased the time they spent with relatives. Vickie began spending time with a gang-involved cousin when she became frustrated at home and "just wanted to get out of the house." She explained, "My mama always wanted me to baby-sit. I got tired of doing that. She always yell and stuff, she come home from work and start yelling. Like that kind of stuff and I got tired of hearing that. I need somebody to hang out with where I wouldn't be home half of the time." She turned to her cousin and "just started hanging out with him." The members of his gang, she said, "was like, 'you gonna do something [to join]?' I was like, I just gotta do what I gotta do," and so she joined.

As the preceding stories have illustrated, in some cases girls' trajectories into gangs are more heavily influenced by neighborhood dynamics, in others by severe family problems, and in still others by close ties to gang-involved family members. Dionne is perhaps the best illustration of how all of the factors I've described thus far—neighborhood context, family problems, and gang-involved family members—can come together to fuel girls' gang involvement. Dionne grew up in a housing project with gangs, where she had four male cousins who were members. She had been physically and sexually abused repeatedly by her mother's boyfriend, who was also her father's brother.[20] She explained:

When [I] was little my uncle tried to have sex with me and stuff. I was like eight or seven, you know, and I told my mama in her sleep. I told my mama what happened, I woke her up out of sleep. You know she told me, she say, I'll get him when I wake up. For real, when she woke up, he ain't do nuttin' but tell her, "Aw, she lyin'. She just wants some attention." You know, and she hit me 'cause, you know, she thinkin' I'm just sayin' somethin'. I was mad though, and he thought he could take advantage by keep on doin' it.

There was also drug and alcohol abuse in the home, her mother had spent time in jail, and her mother and mother's boyfriend were violent toward one another. Dionne noted, "my mama, you know, me and my mama didn't get along. . . . My uncle [her mother's boyfriend], you know, we didn't get along. It was like, you know, he couldn't stand me, I don't know why. . . . He told me to my face, 'I hate you,' he say, 'I hope you die.' " Consequently, Dionne said, "I used to like goin' to school, 'cause to get away from home." Eventually she began running away and spending time on the streets around her housing project with her cousins and other gang members. "I just started hangin' with 'em and doin' what they did then, and they, it was like, they, you know, was used to me hangin' around." When she was eleven, one of her cousins tattooed the gang's name and her nickname on her forearm. Dionne was drunk when her cousin tattooed her, but she said that afterwards the tattoo "made me feel big and stuff, you know?" While she was abused and felt neglected and disparaged at home, Dionne said being with the gang "be kinda fun, you know, bein' around all your little friends, just chillin' or somethin'." . . .

Conclusion

This chapter has illustrated the range of circumstances that help pave girls' pathways into gangs. Notably, some of their discussions clearly parallel the discussions young men provide with regard to their decisions to join, particularly the strength of neighborhood peer networks. Young women join gangs because they perceive these groups as capable of meeting a variety of needs in their lives, both social and emotional, and sometimes economic as well. Previous research has suggested that a number of factors—among them socioeconomic context, family problems, and peer influences—contribute to girls' gang involvement. My research offers further support for these findings by comparing the experiences of gang and nongang girls, and also details in concrete ways the various trajectories through which some young women join gangs while others are able to avoid gang involvement.

My work suggests the strong influence of three overlapping factors—exposure to neighborhood gangs, problems within the family, and having gang-involved family members. The vast majority of gang girls described their decision to get into a gang as involving interactions between two or more of these factors. So for instance, girls who grew up in close proximity to gangs, particularly those with serious family problems, became aware of gangs and often chose these groups as a means of meeting social needs and avoiding home. In addition, my study found that (mostly adolescent) kinship networks had a strong relationship to girls' gang involvement. Girls with older siblings or relatives in gangs often looked up to those family members and, particularly but not always when there were other problems at home, sought to spend time with them on the streets and around their gangs. Notably, gang members in Columbus who said family members had an impact on their decision to join named siblings; in St. Louis they were more likely to mention cousins or other extended family members.

Finally, my research offers further support for the importance of family problems in facilitating many girls' gang involvement. Joan Moore's work found strong evidence, comparing male and female gang members, that young women recounted more cases of childhood abuse and neglect, and more frequently came from homes where wife abuse and other family problems were present.[21] My study fills in an additional piece of the puzzle by comparing female gang members with their nongang counterparts. Not only do female gang members come from more troubled families than their male counterparts, as Moore's work shows, but they also come from more troubled families than "at risk" girls who don't join gangs. Even among the handful of girls I interviewed who associated with gangs but didn't join, this appeared to be the case.

Moreover, my discussions with young women shed some light on how these family problems led to gang involvement. Often when relationships with primary caregivers were weak or ineffective, girls began spending time with the older adolescents who were hanging out on the street or around the neighborhood. For instance, drug-addicted parents led young women to feel neglected and abandoned, and did not provide needed supervision over their time and activities. For other young women, physical or sexual abuse or other conflicts in the household precipitated their spending time away from home. Given their likelihood of living in neighborhoods where gangs were present, and having older siblings or relatives in gangs, these groups were readily available for girls to hang out with and eventually, over time, step into.

Notes

1. See Decker and Van Winkle, *Life in the Gang*, chapter three.
2. See . . . Hagedorn, *People and Folks*; . . . Klein, *The American Street Gang*; Moore . . . *Going Down to the Barrio*; . . . Vigil, *Barrio Gangs*.
3. See Campbell, *The Girls in the Gang* and "Female Participation in Gangs"; Fishman, "The Vice Queens"; Joe and Chesney-Lind, "'Just Every Mother's Angel'"; Quicker, *Homegirls*. . . . Though not about young women in gangs, Baskin and Sommers also provide a useful account of how neighborhood and peer contexts facilitate women's involvement in violent crime. See their "Females' Initiation into Violent Street Crime."
4. Joe and Chesney-Lind, "'Just Every Mother's Angel,'" p. 411.
5. See Bursik and Grasmick, *Neighborhoods and Crime*; Wilson, *The Truly Disadvantaged*.
6. Significance levels are based on chi-square tests. It's important to note here that while I use statistics to make comparisons throughout the book, my sample is purposive in nature and thus violates key assumptions regarding random or representative sampling. While technically statistical methods are inappropriate for my sample, I use these methods not in an attempt to generalize to a larger population, but to highlight the strength of the patterns I uncovered.
7. Quicker, *Homegirls*, p. 80. See also Joe and Chesney-Lind, "'Just Every Mother's Angel.'"
8. See Decker, "Collective and Normative Features of Gang Violence"; Joe and Chesney-Lind, "'Just Every Mother's Angel'"; Lauderback et al., "'Sisters Are Doin' It for Themselves.'"
9. Jennifer was the only member of an all-female gang that I was able to interview in Columbus. She described the OG, who was in her mid-twenties and had started the gang several years before Jennifer joined, as very careful about who she allowed to join. This was not in keeping with the overall pattern in Columbus, where gangs tended to be fluid and loosely defined groups.
10. In their study of St. Louis gangs, Scott Decker and Barrik Van Winkle describe in similar ways the strength of neighborhood ties in the city, which they suggest have been quite longstanding—existing long before the recent re-emergence of gangs there. See their *Life in the Gang*.
11. See Bjerregaard and Smith, "Gender Differences in Gang Participation, Delinquency and Substance Use"; Bowker and Klein, "The Etiology of Female Juvenile Delinquency and Gang Membership"; Campbell, "On the Invisibility of the Female Delinquent Peer Group" and "Female Participation in Gangs." . . .
12. See Canter, "Family Correlates of Male and Female Delinquency"; Cernkovich and Giordano, "Family Relationships and Delinquency"; . . . Hagan et al., "Class in the Household"; Joe and Chesney-Lind, "'Just Every Mother's Angel'"; Moore, *Going Down to the Barrio*. . . .
13. Joan Moore documented a myriad of factors within families that contribute to the likelihood of gang involvement for young women. These include the following: childhood abuse and neglect, wife abuse, having alcohol or drug addicts in the family, witnessing the arrest of family members, having a family member who is chronically ill, and experiencing a death in the family during childhood. Her conclusion, based on comparisons of male and female gang members, is that young women in particular are likely to come from families that are troubled. See Moore, *Going Down to the Barrio*. . . .

    Joe and Chesney-Lind observed that the young women they spoke with sometimes had parents who worked long hours, or parents who were unemployed or underemployed—circumstances which they suggest affected girls' supervision and the quality of their family relationships. See their "'Just Every Mother's Angel.'" Esbensen and Deschenes, in a multi-site study of risk factors for delinquency and gang behavior, found that lack of parental supervision was associated with gang membership for male and female gang members, but that maternal attachment was more predictive of gang membership for males than females. See Esbensen and Deschenes, "A Multi-Site Examination of Gang Membership." . . .
14. These are included in my measure of abuse in Table 8.2 when a family member committed the assault, but not when it was someone else the girl was exposed to through her family.

15. Huff, "Gangs in the United States"; but see Decker and Van Winkle, *Life in the Gang.*
16. There is a growing body of literature that supports the link between childhood maltreatment and youths' subsequent involvement in delinquency. See Smith and Thornberry, "The Relationship between Childhood Maltreatment and Adolescent Involvement in Delinquency"; Widom, "Child Abuse, Neglect, and Violent Criminal Behavior."
17. See Bourgois and Dunlap, "Exorcising Sex-for-Crack"; Maher, *Sexed Work.*
18. Other research offers support for the relationship between girls' gang involvement and that of their family members. . . . See Moore, *Going Down to the Barrio*; Joe and Chesney-Lind, "'Just Every Mother's Angel'"; Lauderback et al., "'Sisters Are Doin' It for Themselves.'" Geoffrey Hunt made an important observation about gangs and "family" during my presentation of a paper based on this study at the 1998 meetings of the American Sociological Association. While scholars typically talk about the gang as a "surrogate" family for young people, in fact there are many cases in which both "real" and "fictive" kin are members of girls' gangs. Thus, when young women speak of the familial nature of their gang relationships, they sometimes are literally speaking about their blood relatives.
19. See Collins, *Black Feminist Thought.* . . .
20. Fortunately, when Dionne was interviewed for this project she was no longer living in her mother and uncle's home. She was living with her father, whom she described as "always giving me attention," and was in counseling to cope with what had happened to her.
21. Moore, *Going Down to the Barrio.* See note 13 above for more details.

References

Baskin, Deborah R. and Ira B. Sommers. 1993. "Females' Initiation into Violent Street Crime." *Justice Quarterly* 10: 559–581.

Bjerregaard, Beth and Carolyn Smith. 1993. "Gender Differences in Gang Participation, Delinquency, and Substance Use." *Journal of Quantitative Criminology* 4: 329–355.

Bourgois, Philippe and Eloise Dunlap. 1993. "Exorcising Sex-for-Crack: An Ethnographic Perspective from Harlem." Pp. 97–132 in *Crack Pipe as Pimp: An Ethnographic Investigation of Sex-for-Crack Exchanges*, edited by Mitchell S. Ratner. New York: Lexington Books.

Bowker, Lee H. and Malcolm W. Klein. 1983. "The Etiology of Female Juvenile Delinquency and Gang Membership: A Test of Psychological and Social Structural Explanations." *Adolescence* 18: 739–751.

Bursik, Robert J. Jr. and Harold G. Grasmick. 1993. *Neighborhoods and Crime: The Dimensions of Effective Community Control.* New York: Lexington Books.

Campbell, Anne. 1984. *The Girls in the Gang.* New York: Basil Blackwell.

——. 1990. "Female Participation in Gangs." Pp. 163–182 in *Gangs in America*, edited by C. Ronald Huff. Newbury Park: Sage Publications.

——. 1990. "On the Invisibility of the Female Delinquent Peer Group." *Women & Criminal Justice* 2: 41–62.

Canter, Rachelle J. 1982. "Family Correlates of Male and Female Delinquency." *Criminology* 20: 149–167.

Cernkovich, S. A. and Peggy C. Giordano. 1987. "Family Relationships and Delinquency." *Criminology* 25: 295–319.

Collins, Patricia Hill. 1990. *Black Feminist Thought: Knowledge, Consciousness, and the Politics of Empowerment.* Boston: Unwin Hyman.

Decker, Scott H. 1996. "Collective and Normative Features of Gang Violence." *Justice Quarterly* 13(2): 243–264.

Decker, Scott H. and Barrik Van Winkle. 1996. *Life in the Gang.* Cambridge: Cambridge University Press.

Esbensen, Finn-Aage and Elizabeth Piper Deschenes. 1998. "A Multi-Site Examination of Gang Membership: Does Gender Matter?" *Criminology* 36: 799–828.

Fishman, Laura T. 1995. "The Vice Queens: An Ethnographic Study of Black Female Gang Behavior." Pp. 83–92 in *The Modern Gang Reader*, edited by Malcolm W. Klein, Cheryl L. Maxson and Jody Miller. Los Angeles: Roxbury Publishing Company.

Hagan, John, John Simpson and A. R. Gillis. 1987. "Class in the Household: A Power-Control Theory of Gender and Delinquency." *American Journal of Sociology* 92: 788–816.

Hagedorn, John M. 1988. *People and Folks: Gangs, Crime and the Underclass in a Rustbelt City.* Chicago: Lake View Press.

Huff, C. Ronald. 1993. "Gangs in the United States." Pp. 3–20 in *The Gang Intervention Handbook*, edited by Arnold P. Goldstein and C. Ronald Huff. Champaign, IL: Research Press.

Joe, Karen A. and Meda Chesney-Lind. 1995. "'Just Every Mother's Angel': An Analysis of Gender and Ethnic Variations in Youth Gang Membership." *Gender & Society* 9: 408–430.

Klein, Malcolm W. 1995. *The American Street Gang: Its Nature, Prevalence and Control.* New York: Oxford University Press.

Lauderback, David, Joy Hansen, and Dan Waldorf. 1992. "'Sisters Are Doin' It for Themselves': A Black Female Gang in San Francisco." *The Gang Journal* 1: 57–70.

Maher, Lisa. 1997. *Sexed Work: Gender, Race and Resistance in a Brooklyn Drug Market.* Oxford: Clarendon Press.

Moore, Joan. 1991. *Going Down to the Barrio: Homeboys and Homegirls in Change.* Philadelphia: Temple University Press.

Quicker, John C. 1983. *Homegirls: Characterizing Chicana Gangs.* San Pedro, CA: International University Press.

Smith, Carolyn and Terence P. Thornberry. 1995. "The Relationship between Childhood Maltreatment and Adolescent Involvement in Delinquency." *Criminology* 33: 451–479.

Vigil, James Diego. 1988. *Barrio Gangs: Street Life and Identity in Southern California.* Austin: University of Texas Press.

Widom, Cathy Spatz. 1989. "Child Abuse, Neglect, and Violent Criminal Behavior." *Criminology* 27: 251–271.

Wilson, William Julius. 1987. *The Truly Disadvantaged: The Inner City, the Underclass, and Public Policy.* Chicago: University of Chicago Press.

CHAPTER 9

Longitudinal Perspectives on Adolescent Street Gangs

Marvin D. Krohn ■ Terence P. Thornberry

As was discussed throughout Section I, longitudinal research designs offer many advantages in studying important issues at the individual level of gang membership. Specifically, longitudinal research is better suited for identifying factors that increase the risk of gang joining, measuring patterns of gang membership duration, assessing the life-course consequences of gang membership, and explicating the causal relationship between gang membership and crime. This article expertly summarizes research findings on each of these topics (with the exception of the gang–crime connection, which is discussed in Section VII).

Street gangs have been of primary concern to the public, policy makers, and criminologists for well over a century. There is a very good reason for such concern: gang members contribute disproportionately to the overall level of crime, especially violent and serious offenses (Battin-Pearson, Thornberry, Hawkins, & Krohn, 1998; Curry, 2000; Curry, Ball, & Decker, 1996; Hill, Hawkins, Catalano, Maguin, & Kostennan, 1995; Howell, 2000; Huff, 1996; Klein & Maxson, 2006; Miller, 1975; Thornberry, Krohn, Lizotte, & Chard-Wierschem, 1993; Thornberry, Krohn, Lizotte, Smith, & Tobin, 2003; Thrasher, 1927). The research focus on gangs has led to important theoretical developments in the study of crime (Cloward & Ohlin, 1960; Cohen, 1955; Miller, 1958; Shaw & McKay, 1942; Thrasher, 1927) as well as

Reprinted from: Marvin D. Krohn and Terence P. Thornberry, "Longitudinal Perspectives on Adolescent Street Gangs," ed. A. Liberman, *The Long View of Crime: A Synthesis of Longitudinal Research*, 128–138, 147–151. Copyright © 2008 by Springer. Reprinted by permission.

being the impetus for many community-based prevention programs (e.g., Esbensen & Osgood, 1997; Howell, 1998; Kennedy, Piehl, & Braga, 1996; Klein, 1969; Kobrin, 1959; Mattick & Caplan, 1962; Miller, 1962; Thrasher, 1936).

In spite of these efforts gangs not only remain a significant problem, they have proliferated at an alarming rate in recent years. Klein and Maxson (2006) reviewed studies of gang proliferation and report that between 1980 and 1990 there was a dramatic increase in the number of large cities (100,000 population or more) that reported gang problems, increasing from 15% prior to 1980 to 70% by 1990. Gang problems spread to mid-sized and smaller cities from the mid 1980s through 1995 as well. Although there has been a slight reversal of the trend in less populated cities, the gang problem in larger cities remains stable.

With the rapid spread of gangs throughout the country, there has been an ever-increasing call for research to determine why individuals join gangs, the effects of gang membership on criminal behavior, why youth leave gangs once having joined, and the effects of gang membership on longer term life-course outcomes such as education and employment (Howell, 2000). Many of the more recent research efforts directed at answering these questions evidence a methodological shift from previous work on gangs. Earlier gang research either relied on observations of gang members during periods of membership or provided cross-sectional comparisons of gang members with non-gang members. More recent studies have introduced longitudinal panel designs to address questions concerning the reasons for and results of gang membership. The purpose of this paper is to examine the yield of longitudinal research on gangs in addressing these questions. Before doing so we briefly discuss the contributions of earlier research on gangs.

Early Gang Research

Almost all of the early work on gangs targeted youth who were currently in a gang, interviewing them and observing their interactions within the gang structure (Bursik & Grasmick, 1995). These studies have provided a wealth of very rich descriptive information on the life of gang members. From these studies we have learned much about the structure of gangs, gang members' perceptions of why they joined gangs, their feelings toward other gang members, and their gang-related activities (Hughes, 2005).

Although the information from these studies has made significant contributions to our understanding of gangs and gang members, there are a number of methodological limitations with them. By focusing on youth after they had already joined a gang, the only information they offer on the reasons for joining is necessarily retrospective. Retrospective data have long been recognized as likely to be distorted (Yarrow, Campbell, & Burton, 1970) and can be influenced by the experience of gang membership itself. Limiting the focus of inquiry to current gang members also makes it difficult to determine the effect of membership on behavior. For example, it is not possible to determine if gang membership produces an increase in criminal behavior over pre-gang involvement in crime. Studies that follow gang members through the years in which they are gang members provide some information on this issue but even they cannot distinguish between a gang effect and an age effect. For example, an increase in criminal behavior over the years that youth are in a gang may be due to the fact that they are entering into the years when the prevalence of crime is at its peak rather than due to the effect of the gang.

Also, most of the early research did not follow gang members once they left the gang. Therefore, few studies could address the question of whether gang membership has an impact on future criminality. Nor could they examine the potential

deleterious effect that gang membership has on life-course transitions and ultimately life chances. Some more recent qualitative studies of gang members have followed youth past the time when they were active gang members and have documented some of the adverse consequences of gang membership (Hagedorn, 1998; Moore, 1991).

Another common problem with early studies of gangs is the failure to include a comparison group of youth who do not join gangs. Many studies, especially observational ones, focus only on gang members and do not include subjects of similar age or background in order to determine if what is occurring in the lives of gang members is unique to them because of their membership or whether similar outcomes would occur to most youth who share similar background characteristics. Without such comparisons, it is impossible to determine if the gang is responsible for changes in behavior or other outcomes later in life (Hughes, 2005; Katz & Jackson-Jacobs, 2004).

Cross-sectional quantitative studies of gangs offer the advantage of including a comparison group with which to compare current gang members (e.g., Esbensen & Winfree, 1998; Klein, Gordon, & Maxson, 1986; Maxson, Whitlock, & Klein, 1997; Short & Strodtbeck, 1965). This study design allows researchers to directly contrast the characteristics and behavior of gang and non-gang youth at similar ages and having similar background characteristics in order to determine how they differ. From these differences, inferences can be made regarding the causes of gang membership and the effect of gang membership on behavior.

A major problem with cross-sectional studies, however, is that the temporal order of the variables is indefinite and therefore causal inferences are, at best, risky. For example, if we find that gang members have significantly poorer relations with their parents than non-gang members, we do not know whether those poor relations were a cause of or risk factor for joining the gang or if they are a consequence of being in a gang.

Qualitative studies have provided rich descriptive information on a number of issues regarding the characteristics of gang members and the processes that take place in the gang. Cross-sectional quantitative studies have added to our knowledge by identifying relationships between gang membership and a number of potential risk factors for joining a gang. However, there are a number of questions that cannot be adequately studied with either methodology. In the next section, we describe those issues and suggest how longitudinal panel analyses provide the best alternative for addressing them.

Advantages of Longitudinal Designs

A longitudinal study, as the term is used in this review, selects a sample of respondents and follows them forward in time as they age. The ideal design for investigating the impact of gang membership on life-course development would have several key features. First, it would be based on a community sample representative of a clearly definable population. By focusing on a community sample, both gang members and non-members are represented to allow for inter-individual comparisons. Second, assessment of the sample should begin at ages that are prior to the typical onset of gang membership. Since gang membership is primarily a mid- to late-adolescent phenomenon, studies that start in late childhood or early adolescence are well-suited to this task. Third, the full sample would be followed for longer rather than shorter periods of time, hopefully across multiple developmental stages—e.g., childhood, adolescence, and emerging adulthood. Fourth, repeated measures would be taken across the follow-up period, at multiple points in time. Repeated measures allow for the assessment of intra-individual change as each person develops. Finally, the study would have a broad measurement space to allow for the assessment of antecedents, correlates, and consequences of gang membership.

With regard to the study of gang membership, longitudinal designs as just described, especially when compared to cross-sectional designs, enhance our ability to investigate a number of important substantive issues. In particular, we identify six issues that can be more fully and accurately studied with longitudinal data. They are:

1. The Identification of Risk Factors
Identifying risk factors for gang membership is important for both theoretical and policy reasons.

Theoretically, the accurate identification of risk factors enhances our understanding of the origins of gang membership and helps structure more formal causal analyses. Practically, knowledge of major risk factors helps identify youth who may subsequently become gang members and aids in the development of intervention programs.

2. Separating Facilitation and Selection Effects
There is a well-established relationship between gang membership and involvement in delinquent behavior, especially serious delinquency and violence. This association has been observed in cross-sectional and longitudinal studies and studies based on surveys, direct observations, and official records (Thornberry et al., 2003). What is less clear, however, is the causal direction of this relationship. Does gang membership facilitate involvement in crime or are individuals already involved in criminal behavior attracted to the gang?

3. Tracing the Duration of Gang Membership
There is a commonsense notion that gang membership is a relatively stable phenomenon. That is, once an adolescent joins a street gang, he or she is likely to remain a gang member for quite a while. There is, however, relatively little research that follows representative samples of gang members over time to assess either this notion or the counter-notion, that gang membership is relatively fleeting.

4. Separating Causes and Consequences
Much of the work that has compared family and peer relationships among gang members to those of non-members has treated those relationships as risk factors or potential causes. With cross-sectional data, however, there is no way to determine the causal order among these variables. The observed relationship could have been due either to parental and peer variables leading to gang membership or to gang membership increasing the association with deviant others and the deterioration of the bond between the youth and the parent.

5. Establishing Short- and Long-Term Consequences of Gang Membership

One important area of research that has been advanced by both qualitative and quantitative longitudinal studies of gangs is the impact that participation in a gang has on the life course and life chances of gang members. What gang members do while they are in a gang and the status of being a gang member appear to impact their future direction, but whether the impact of gang membership on this outcome is real or spurious is less well understood.

6. Developmental Differences in Gang Membership

Developmental issues regarding gang membership and its impact on behavior and future outcomes have been largely unexplored. For example, we do not know if the risk factors for joining a gang differ for youth who join at different ages or if selection and facilitation effects are different at different ages.

A better understanding of these six issues has important theoretical and practical implications and, as we show in the following pages, these issues are more appropriately examined using longitudinal rather than cross-sectional study designs. The subsequent sections address these six issues, discussing first why longitudinal data are better suited for assessing them and then reviewing the results of longitudinal studies that have examined them. Some of these questions have been addressed rather fully, while for other questions, research is still in its infancy. We obviously focus on the former in the ensuing sections.

Risk Factors for Gang Membership

In the epidemiological tradition, we define risk factors as "individual or environmental hazards that increase an individual's vulnerability to negative developmental outcomes" (Small & Luster, 1994, p. 182). In the present case, risk factors for gang membership are attributes that significantly increase the chances or probability that a person possessing those attributes will subsequently become a gang member. Risk factors, by definition therefore, occur prior to the onset of the outcome.

Risk factors can be distinguished from other classes of concepts that also yield statistical associations with gang membership. These include causal variables which are also logically antecedent to gang membership but in addition to temporal order they exert a true causal impact. Risk factors are antecedent and may or may not be causal. Consequences are variables that occur after the onset of gang membership and may have been caused by gang membership. Correlates are variables that are contemporaneously related to gang membership but without temporal order being established. They merely co-occur with gang membership.

Causes, risk factors, correlates, and consequences will all yield a statistically significant association or correlation with gang membership. Thus, identifying risk factors, as opposed to any of these other types of variables, is less a matter of statistical analysis and more a matter of design.

Longitudinal designs with repeated measures are ideally suited to identifying risk factors. They follow the same people over time and first assess various individual and environmental hazards and then assess the onset of gang membership. With such a design it is relatively easy to see which earlier hazards are significantly related to later gang membership and which, therefore, can be considered risk factors.

In contrast, cross-sectional studies are severely challenged in their ability to identify risk factors. Since all data are collected simultaneously it is quite difficult to separate risk factors from correlates or consequences. For example, there is strong evidence in cross-sectional data that school failure is statistically associated with gang membership. Failure in school could lead youth to join gangs, that is, it would be a risk factor. But it is also plausible that gang membership leads to alienation from and failure in school, that is, school failure is a consequence of gang membership. Or, school failure and gang membership may be mere correlates, both generated by some common prior cause. Cross-sectional designs cannot logically distinguish among these possibilities.[1] Indeed, the very strong temporal dimension embedded in the definition of a risk factor suggests the superiority of longitudinal designs.

Even though risk factors are not necessarily causal, to properly identify risk factors, as opposed to correlates, is important for several reasons. First, absent accurate information on true causes, focusing intervention strategies on powerful risk factors is probably the most productive approach we have. Second, identifying risk factors is important to help target scarce prevention resources toward youth who are most likely to become gang members.

Turning to the empirical literature, a number of cross-sectional studies have identified correlates of gang membership. That is, they have identified attributes on which gang members and non-members differ, but, because of the cross-sectional design, they cannot determine if those attributes are antecedents, correlates, or consequences of gang membership. Reviews of this literature can be found in Thornberry et al. (2003, pp. 57–61) and Klein and Maxson (2006, Chapter 4).

In general, correlational studies show that gang membership is associated with deficits in a number of developmental domains. Although results are not entirely consistent across studies, and each study examines an idiosyncratic set of variables, these domains include neighborhood characteristics, family sociodemographic characteristics, parent-child relations, school factors, peer relations, individual traits, and prior deviance. The central question before us now is: which of these correlates are true risk factors, that is, which occur prior to gang membership?

The two most comprehensive assessments of risk factors are presented by Hill, Howell, Hawkins, and Battin-Pearson (1999) using data from the Seattle Social Development Project and by Thornberry et al. (2003) using data from the Rochester Youth Development Study. We start with these studies.

Hill et al. (1999) examined risk factors measured at ages 10–12 as predictors of gang membership between ages 13 and 18. Risk factors were drawn from five domains: neighborhood, family, school, peers, and individual characteristics. They found that "[21] of the 25 constructs measured at ages 10–12 predicted joining a gang at ages 13 to 18. Predictors of gang membership were found in all of the measured domains" (Hill et al., 1999, p. 308). The most potent risk factors are neighborhood youth in trouble and availability of marijuana;

family structure, especially living with one parent and other adults or with no parents; low achievement in elementary school or being identified as learning disabled; association with deviant peers; prior involvement in marijuana use or violence; and externalizing problem behaviors. Hill et al. (1999) also found that having multiple risk factors greatly increases the chances of joining a gang.

Thornberry et al. (2003) examined risk factors measured before age 14 on the probability of joining a gang between ages 14 and 17. Because of the relatively small number of female gang members available for this analysis, we concentrate on the results for males. The key findings are presented here in Table 9.1.

For the male participants in the Rochester study, gang members have significantly greater deficits as compared to non-members on 25 of the 40 measured risk factors. Risk is observed in all seven developmental domains. Although many antecedent variables are related to the odds of joining a gang, there are few variables that, independently, have a very large impact on gang membership. For example, there are only three variables in Table 9.1 that have an odds ratio of 3 or more: experiencing negative life events (OR = 3.25), prior delinquency (OR = 3.26), and prior violence (OR = 4.19).

While gang membership is not strongly related to many individual risk factors, it is strongly related to the accumulation of risk. Figure 9.1 presents the core results, in this case including female gang members because sample size is less of an issue for these cumulative risk analyses. For both males and females as the number of developmental domains in which risk is experienced increases, so too does the probability of gang membership. Youth, at least in Rochester, appear able to ward off the negative consequences of risk in a few domains, but, after that, the chances of gang membership increase rapidly. Hill et al. (1999) report similar results concerning the impact of accumulated risk on gang membership for the Seattle sample.

Several other longitudinal studies have identified risk factors for gang membership. Huizinga and colleagues (Esbensen & Huizinga, 1993; Huizinga, Weiher, Espiritu, & Esbensen, 2003; Huizinga, Weiher, Menard, Espiritu, & Esbensen, 1988) examined this issue in the Denver Youth Survey.

Table 9.1 Risk Factors for Gang Membership, Rochester Youth Development Study, Males Only

Risk Factors	Odds Ratios
Area Characteristics	
Percentage African American	1.59*
Percentage in Poverty	1.88**
Community Arrest Rate	1.79**
Neighborhood Disorganization	.95
Neighborhood Violence	.86
Neighborhood Drug Use	1.51*
Neighborhood Integration	.71
Family Sociodemographic Characteristics	
African American	2.28**
Hispanic	1.19
Parent Education	.53**
Family Disadvantage	1.39
Poverty Level Income	1.91**
Lives with Both Biological Parents	.47**
Family Transitions	1.42
Parent–Child Relations	
Attachment to Parent	1.02
Attachment to Child	.69*
Parental Involvement	.94
Parental Supervision	.53**
Positive Parenting	1.10
Report of Child Maltreatment	1.78*
Family Hostility	.77
School Factors	
Commitment to School	.64*
Attachment to Teacher	.48**
College Aspirations	1.09
Subject's College Expectations	.70
Parent's College Expectations for Subject	.64*
Math Score	.41**
Peer Relationships	
Delinquent Peers	1.97**
Early Dating	2.82**
Precocious Sexual Activity	1.58*
Unsupervised Time with Friends	1.41
Individual Characteristics	
Negative Life Events	3.25**
Depression	1.71**
Self-Esteem	.82
Externalizing Behaviors	1.98**
Delinquent Beliefs	2.15**
Early Delinquency	
General Delinquency	3.26**
Violent Delinquency	4.19**
Drug Use	2.49**
Age of Onset of General Delinquency	.78

*$p < .05$ (one-tailed test). **$p < .01$ (one-tailed test).
Source: Thornberry et al. (2003), Table 4.2. Reprinted with permission.

Figure 9.1 Cumulative Risk for Gang Membership

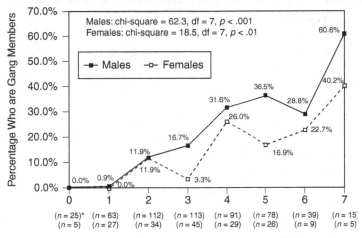

Note: Top *n* is for males; bottom *n* is for females
Source: Thornberry et al. (2003), Fig. 4.2. Reprinted with permission.

They found poor parental supervision, deviant peers, non-delinquent problem behaviors, and certain indicators of school attachment and performance to be related to later gang membership. In contrast, attachment to parents, self-esteem, and attitudes toward the future were not identified as risk factors. Huizinga et al. (1988) also report that the accumulation of risk is strongly related to gang membership.

Two studies (Craig, Vitaro, Gagnon, & Tremblay, 2002; Gatti, Tremblay, Vitaro, & McDuff, 2005) use data from the Montreal Longitudinal and Experimental Study to examine risk factors. Among the variables significantly related to gang membership are: low parental supervision, deviant peers, commitment to school, and non-delinquent problem behaviors.

Lahey, Gordon, Loeber, Stouthamer-Loeber, and Farrington (1999) examined predictors of first gang entry for males in the Pittsburgh Youth Study. Their study was restricted to African American males because of the small number of White male gang members available for analysis. In bivariate relationships, gang membership is predicted by prior conduct disorder behaviors, self-reported delinquency, and associations with delinquent peers. Gang membership is not related to household income, household structure, neighborhood crime level, or parental supervision, however.

Walker-Barnes and Mason (2001) identified ninth-graders who joined a gang during the course of that academic year. Parental warmth, parental control or monitoring, and peer deviance were all related to gang membership in the expected direction. Walker-Barnes and Mason also examined differences by race and ethnicity. In general, the parenting variables had a somewhat stronger impact for African American youth than for White or Hispanic youth. In particular, "higher levels of behavioral control and lower levels of lax and psychological control were related to decreases in gang involvement for Blacks . . . " (Walker-Barnes & Mason, 2001, p. 1826).

Bjerregaard and Lizotte (1995) used the Rochester data to look specifically at the impact of earlier delinquency and gun ownership on the likelihood of being a gang member. They found that prior involvement in serious delinquency and street delinquency, but not more general forms of delinquency, increases the likelihood of later gang membership. They also found that owning guns for protection, but not for sporting purposes, increases the chances of joining a gang.

One of the most thorough reviews of the risk factor literature was conducted by Howell and Egley (2005). They identified risk factors in five major domains or ecological levels. The significant risk factors to emerge from their systematic review are presented in Table 9.2. These results highlight

Table 9.2 Risk Factors for Gang Membership in Prospective Longitudinal Studies*

Community/Neighborhood Risk Factors

Availability/ perceived access to drugs (Hill et al., 1999)

Neighborhood youth in trouble (Hill et al., 1999)

Community arrest rate (Thornberry et al., 2003)

Feeling unsafe in the neighborhood (Kosterman et al., 1996)

Low neighborhood attachment (Hill et al., 1999)

Neighborhood residents in poverty or family poverty (Hill et al., 1999; Thornberry et al., 2003)

Availability of firearms (Bjerregaard & Lizotte, 1995; Lizotte et al., 2000; Lizotte et al., 1994; Thornberry et al., 2003)

Neighborhood disorganization (Thornberry, 1998; Thornberry et al., 2003)

Neighborhood drug use (Thornberry et al., 2003)

Family Risk Factors

Family structure (Hill et al., 1999**; Thornberry et al., 2003)

Family poverty (Hill et al., 1999; Thornberry et al., 2003)

Family transitions (Thornberry et al., 2003***)

Family financial stress (Eitle et al., 2004)

Sibling antisocial behavior (Hill et al., 1999)

Low attachment to parents/family (Eitle et al., 2004; Thornberry et al., 2003)

Child maltreatment (Thornberry et al., 2003)

Low parent education level (Thornberry et al., 2003)

Parent proviolent attitudes (Hill et al., 1999)

Family management: low parent supervision/control/monitoring (Hill et al., 1999; Lahey et al., 1999****; Thornberry et al., 2003)

Teenage fatherhood (Loeber, Farrington, Stouthamer-Loeber et al., 2003)

School Risk Factors

Low achievement in elementary school (Craig et al., 2002; Hill et al., 1999)

Negative labeling by teachers (as either bad or disturbed) (Esbensen et al., 1993)

Low academic aspirations (Bjerregaard & Smith, 1993; Hill et al., 1999; Thornberry et al., 2003)

Low school attachment (Hill et al., 1999)

Low attachment to teachers (Thornberry et al., 2003)

Low parent college expectations for subject (Bjerregaard & Smith, 1993; Thornberry et al., 2003)

Low degree of commitment to school (Thornberry et al., 2003)

Low math achievement test score (Thornberry et al., 2003)

Identified as learning disabled (Hill et al., 1999)

Peer Group Risk Factors

Association with peers who engage in delinquency or other problem behaviors (Bjerregaard & Smith, 1993; Bjerregaard & Lizotte, 1995; Eitle et al., 2004; Hill et al., 1999; Lahey et al., 1999****)

Association with aggressive peers (Craig et al., 2002; Lahey et al., 1999****)

Individual Risk Factors

Violence involvement (Hill et al., 1999; Thornberry et al., 2003)

General delinquency involvement (Curry, 2000; Hill et al., 1999; Thornberry et al., 2003; Esbensen & Huizinga, 1993)

Aggression/fighting (Craig et al., 2002; Lahey et al., 1999****)

Conduct disorders (Lahey et al., 1999)

Externalizing behaviors (disruptive, antisocial, & other conduct disorders) (Craig et al., 2002; Hill et al., 1999)

Early dating (Thornberry et al., 2003)

Precocious sexual activity (Bjerregaard & Smith, 1993; Thornberry et al., 2003)

(Continued)

Table 9.2 (*Continued*)
Antisocial/delinquent beliefs (Hill et al., 1999; Thornberry et al., 2003)
Hyperactive (Craig et al., 2002; Hill et al., 1999)
Alcohol/drug use (Thornberry et al., 2003; Bjerregaard & Smith, 1993; Thornberry et al., 1993; Hill et al., 1999)
Early marijuana use and early drinking (Hill et al., 1999)
Depression (Thornberry et al., 2003)
Life stressors (Eitle et al., 2004; Thornberry et al., 2003)
Poor refusal skills (Hill et al., 1999)
*Race/ethnicity and gender are excluded.
**The Social Development Research Group study compared three family structures: no parents in home, one parent only, and one parent plus other adults. The later structure was the strongest predictor.
***This risk factor predicted stability of gang membership.
****Significant effects were observed only in early adolescence.
Source: Howell & Egley (2005), Table 1. Reprinted with permission.

the multitude of risk factors in the backgrounds of gang members and the extensiveness of risk across domains. The core finding of accumulated risk is clearly evident in all the longitudinal studies included in their review.

Summary

Several general conclusions about the investigation of risk factors for gang membership appear warranted. First, there are only a relatively small number of longitudinal studies that have investigated this issue. There are even fewer studies that have used the same set of risk factors so there are few replicated results. Given the importance, both for theory and prevention, of understanding the antecedents of gang membership this is indeed unfortunate. One high priority for future study, and a relatively easy one given the bivariate nature of most risk factor analyses, would be more coordinated replication of these results across studies.

Second, that said, across the longitudinal analyses that have been conducted there are several risk factors that stand out as being of primary importance. They are involvement in prior delinquency and related problem behaviors, low parental supervision, and involvement in deviant peer networks. Less consistently, some aspects of poor school attachment and/or performance, and experiencing negative or stressful life events are also important.

Third, there are several variables that are often proposed as risk factors for gang membership that

enjoy little, if any, empirical support from longitudinal studies. They include family poverty and family structure, self-esteem, affective bonds with parents, and neighborhood crime. These findings remind us of the importance of basing theory and policy on empirically based observations and not supposition. They also remind us that not all aspects of a particular developmental domain need be equally related to an outcome. For example, in the area of the family, strong parental supervision and monitoring is consistently found to reduce gang membership, but affective ties are not related to gang membership. Zeroing in on the more central aspects, rather than adopting a blanket approach, is crucial for effective intervention.

Finally, as with many other problem behaviors, gang membership does not seem to be a product of a few central risk factors; none exerts a massive impact on the likelihood of being a gang member. But, the accumulation of risk is strongly related to the chances of becoming a gang member. Gang members have multiple deficits in multiple developmental domains, each one of which contributes in a small, but statistically significant, way to the chances of being a gang member. . . .

The Duration of Gang Membership

There is a general notion that once youth join a street gang they remain members for relatively long periods of time. In part, this view has been generated by popular culture and the mass media. For example, the lyrics in *West Side Story* claim that:

Once you're a Jet, you're a Jet all the way,
From your first cigarette to your last dyin' day.

In part this view is also generated by observational research that often focuses on traditional gangs in large cities with a long history of street gangs, like Chicago and Los Angeles (Thornberry & Porter, 2001). While the implied stability may be reflective of gang membership at the extreme end of the gang distribution, it may or may not represent the full range of street gangs.

Longitudinal studies, especially those based on community samples, are ideally suited for an examination of this issue. First, if the sample is representative of its locale, the gangs that the respondents belong to will be representative of the gangs that are found in that locale. Second, since the respondents are followed over time with repeated assessments of their gang involvement, direct estimates of the stability or the fluidity of gang membership can be obtained. Related issues, such as whether gang members join, leave, and re-join a gang or whether they move from one gang to another, can also be measured.

Thornberry et al. (2003) found that gang membership is quite fluid and transitory. Half of the male (50.4%) and two-thirds of the female gang members (66.0%) report being members of the gang for one year or less. In contrast, only 21.6% of the boys and 5.0% of the girls report being a gang member for 3 or 4 years. Moreover, very few of the gang members report joining a gang, leaving it, and then re-joining it or another gang. The predominant pattern is to join a gang, stay for a while (typically less than a year), and then leave the gang world. At least this is the pattern in Rochester.

Esbensen and Huizinga (1993) report very similar patterns in Denver. Over a four year period they found that of the 90 youths who reported being a member of a gang, 67% were members for only one year while only 3 percent belonged for all four years. Interestingly, when asked what role they expected to have in the gang in the near future, 60% reported that they would not want to be a member of the gang in the future.

The findings from the Pittsburgh Youth Study confirm the general patterns observed in both Rochester and Denver. Gordon et al. (2004) report 48% of the male gang members were in a gang for only one wave of data collection and 25% for only two waves of data collection.

The lack of stability in gang membership among youth in the Rochester, Denver, and Pittsburgh studies may be because all three research sites are characterized as emerging gang cities. That is, these cities did not have a long-standing tradition of gang behavior; rather the gang problem became recognized in the 1980s around the time that the three studies began. However, studies that have been done in more traditional gang cities also report that gang membership is a relatively temporary phenomenon among a majority of youth who participate in a gang (Hagedorn, 1998; Klein, 1971; Short & Strodtbeck, 1965; Vigil, 1988; Yablonsky, 1962).

Short- and Long-Term Consequences of Gang Membership

Over the past thirty years there has been an increasing recognition that behavior is constantly evolving as actors age (Baltes, 1987; Baltes & Brim, 1982). Behavior initiated during adolescence can have important consequences for successful entry into adult roles and responsibilities. The way actors navigate the transition to adulthood can, in turn, have an important and long-lasting impact on their life chances. The life-course perspective recognizes that as people move along trajectories, they make (or fail to make) transitions such as completing their education, getting married, or finding a job (see Siennick & Osgood, 2008). The success in making those transitions, for example, in completing one's education, is likely to have a significant impact on life chances. Disruption in or failure to complete major transitions will adversely affect subsequent development.

There is a growing body of research that finds that involvement in delinquent or drug-using behavior increases disruption in transitions along a number of important trajectories. Adolescents involved in delinquent behavior are more likely to drop out of school (Fagan & Pabon, 1990;

Kaplan & Liu, 1994; Krohn, Thornberry, Collins-Hall, & Lizotte, 1995; Mensch & Kandel, 1988), to become pregnant or impregnate someone else or become a teenage parent (Newcomb & Bentler, 1988; Smith, 1997; Thornberry, Smith, & Howard, 1997), and to be unemployed in their early adult years (Caspi, Wright, Moffitt, & Silva, 1998; Kandel, Chen, & Gill, 1995; Kandel, Davies, Karus, & Yamaguchi, 1986; Newcomb & Bentler, 1988). Since gang members are typically more involved in delinquent activities than non-gang members, it is reasonable to expect that being a member of a gang during adolescence will be associated with disrupted transitions from adolescence to adulthood and, ultimately, will adversely impact life chances. But there is relatively little direct evidence about the extent to which gang membership itself, over and above delinquent behavior, contributes to disorder in the life course.

To adequately examine the impact of gang membership on subsequent life-course transitions, it is necessary to follow former gang members over time and to compare them with non-gang members over that same period of time. Longitudinal panel studies are well suited to this task. They can determine if gang members, as opposed to similarly situated non-gang members, are more likely to have disorderly transitions such as dropping out of school and teenage parenthood. They can also examine the impact of such disorderly transitions on longer-term outcomes and determine if disorderly transitions mediate the relationship between gang membership and problematic outcomes in young adulthood. And, they can examine these issues controlling for levels of offending.

An added benefit of longitudinal studies that collect information at regular and relatively short intervals (e.g., one year or less) is their ability to identify short-term and more stable gang membership. Stability in gang membership may be expected to reflect greater commitment to the gang and the behavior and values represented therein. Hence, stable gang membership is expected to have an even greater impact on the life course than is short-term gang membership.

This issue is arguably one of the most important ones for gang researchers to address because of the long-term implications of the answers found. Yet,

there has been surprisingly little research on the impact of gang membership on life-course transitions. As early as 1971 Malcolm Klein observed, "Though the need is great, there has been no careful study of gang members as they move on into adult status" (1971, p. 136), a sentiment echoed by Hagedorn (1998) and Decker and Lauritsen (1996). Even as late as 2001, Levitt and Venkatesh stated that, "Little is known, however, about the long-run impact of adolescent street gang involvement on adult outcomes" (2001a, p. 1).

Some information about the impact of gang membership on life-course transitions has been generated by ethnographic studies that incorporated interviews in the design. For example, Hagedorn (1998) reinterviewed a sample of gang members originally studied as adolescents when they were in their early 20s. Of all male gang members, only a third had a high school diploma and about the same number were working. The rate of high school graduation for female gang members was about the same as male gang members. Almost all of the young women were mothers (88%) by their early 20s, with about 58% on welfare.

Moore (1991) found similar results in her ethnographic study. Only 40% of former gang members were employed as young adults. Female gang members had high rates of early parenthood and were more likely to be responsible for raising those children than were male gang members. Neither Hagedorn nor Moore had comparison groups; therefore, they could not control for factors other than gang membership that might have caused these outcomes.

Levitt and Venkatesh (2001 a,b) present data that suggests that gang membership might not have a direct effect on some problematic outcomes once other background characteristics are controlled. In 1990 they began an ethnographic study on a sample of 118 youths aged 16–26 that resided in one public housing complex in a disadvantaged neighborhood of Chicago. Of the 118 youth in the sample, 38 were active gang participants. Ten years later, they interviewed 94 of the original sample. In their initial study (2001a), they found that gang members obtained less education, had higher rates of arrest and incarceration, and earned a greater percentage of income from illegal sources than did non-gang members. However, once background factors such as GPA and drug use among their guardians were controlled, the effect of gang membership was not a significant predictor of high school graduation, being currently employed, or being currently incarcerated. Gang membership remained a significant predictor of ever having been incarcerated and the percentage of income from illegal sources. Levitt and Venkatesh (2001b) also report that once controlling for years of education and years incarcerated as well as a number of additional background variables, the effect of gang membership on illegal income is not significant. These findings suggest that gang membership is indirectly related to negative outcomes because membership results in less education and more years of being incarcerated which, in turn, affect the source of income in young adulthood. In spite of their limited sample size, their findings are suggestive of an important impact of gang membership.

Thornberry et al. (2003) provide the most extensive examination of the impact of gang membership on life-course transitions, following the sample in the Rochester Study from age 13 through age 22. Prospectively, they examined whether those youth who were gang members at any time during the teenage years were more likely to experience problematic transitions to adulthood including dropping out of school, early nest-leaving, early pregnancy, teenage parenthood, unstable employment (as young adults), cohabitation, and being arrested in young adulthood than were those youth who did not join a gang.

For males, Thornberry et al. (2003) distinguished between short-term gang members and stable gang members. Short-term members were more likely to impregnate a girl and to cohabit than were non-members. Stable gang members were more likely to drop out of school, impregnate a girl, be a teenage parent, experience unstable employment, and cohabit than were non-members. Because of the limited time in a gang for most females, it was not possible to differentiate between short-term and stable gang members. However, being a gang member was significantly related to all of the problematic transitions except for cohabitation. For both males and females, gang membership was also significantly related to a variable measuring the total number of problematic transitions experienced.

Thornberry et al. (2003) examined whether controlling for eight background variables, including prior delinquency, would eliminate the significant relationship between gang membership and each of the transitions. For males, stable gang membership remained significant for all the problematic transitions except for early nest-leaving. For females, gang membership was significantly related to early pregnancy, teenage parenthood, and unstable employment even after controlling for the other eight variables.

Finally, they examined whether gang membership in adolescence increased the probability of being arrested as a young adult. For males, they found that stable gang membership was significantly related to adult arrests even after controlling for the mean number of problematic transitions and the other eight control variables. Gang membership remained a significant predictor of female adult arrests as well.

In the first investigation of long-term consequences of gang membership, Krohn, Lizotte, Thornberry, Hall, and Chu (2006) examined the impact of adolescent gang membership on several outcomes at age 30. They used the male gang members of the Rochester sample and compared non-members to short-term and stable gang members.

The bivariate results indicate that stable gang members have significantly higher rates of unemployment and welfare receipt than either the non-members or the short-term members. Interestingly, the latter two groups are not significantly different from one another. In terms of criminal outcomes, both the short-term and stable gang members have significantly higher rates of self-reported crime, carrying a weapon, and being arrested. Multivariate models suggest that for employment and welfare the impact of adolescent gang membership is indirect, mediated by dropping out of school and unstable employment during the person's early 20s. For crime and arrest, the impact tends to be mediated by earlier delinquency. Interestingly, the impact of gang membership on weapons carrying is largely unmediated by these variables.

The results from the Rochester Study, along with results from ethnographic research, make a convincing case for the serious consequences of being a gang member on life-course transitions.

With the increasing availability of longitudinal data, these analyses can be replicated to determine if these relationships hold for other research sites. . . .

Note

1. Cross-sectional data can be used to assess whether a fairly limited subset of variables are risk factors for gang membership. Namely, they can assess the status of variables that cannot change over time (e.g., being adopted in childhood) or whose onset prior to gang membership can clearly be established (e.g., the age of school entry). Although there are these exceptions, cross-sectional designs generally do not provide strong assessments of risk factors.

References

Baltes, P. B. (1987). Theoretical propositions of life-span developmental psychology: On the dynamics between growth and decline. *Developmental Psychology, 23*, 611–626.

Baltes, P. B., & Brim, O. G. (1982). *Life span development and behavior* (Vol. 4). New York: Academic Press.

Battin-Pearson, S. R., Thornberry, T. P., Hawkins, J. D., & Krohn, M. D. (1998). Gang membership, delinquent peers, and delinquent behavior. *OJJDP Juvenile Justice Bulletin* (Vol. NCJ 171119).

Bjerregaard, B., & Lizotte, A. J. (1995). Gun ownership and gang membership. *The Journal of Criminal Law & Criminology, 86*, 37–58.

Bjerregaard, B., & Smith, C. A. (1993). Gender differences in gang participation, delinquency, and substance use. *Journal of Quantitative Criminology, 9*, 329–355.

Bursik, R. J., Jr., & Grasmick, H. G. (1995). The collection of data for gang research. In M. W. Klein, C. L. Maxson, & J. Miller (Eds.), *The modern gang reader* (pp. 154–157). Los Angeles, CA: Roxbury.

Caspi, A., Wright, B. R. E., Moffitt, T. E., & Silva, P. A. (1998). Early failure in the labor market: Childhood and adolescent predictors of unemployment in the transition to adulthood. *American Sociological Review, 63*, 424–451.

Cloward, R. A., & Ohlin, L. E. (1960). *Delinquency and opportunity*. Glencoe: Free Press.

Cohen, A. K. (1955). *Delinquent boys*. Glencoe: Free Press.

Craig, W. M., Vitaro, F., Gagnon, C., & Tremblay, R. E. (2002). The road to gang membership: Characteristics of male gang and non-gang members from ages 10–14. *Social Development, 11*, 53–68.

Curry, D. G. (2000). Self-reported gang involvement and officially recorded delinquency. *Criminology, 38*, 1253–1274.

Curry, D. G., Ball, R. E., & Decker, S. H. (1996). Estimating the national scope of gang crime from law enforcement data. *National Institute of Justice Research in Brief* (Vol. NCJ 161477).

Decker, S., & Lauritsen, J. (1996). Breaking the bonds of membership: Leaving the gang. In C. R. Huff (Ed.), *Gangs in America* (2nd ed., pp. 103–122). Thousand Oaks, CA: Sage.

Eitle, D., Gunkel, S., & Van Gundy, K. (2004). Cumulative exposure to stressful life events and male gang membership. *Journal of Criminal Justice, 32*, 95–111.

Esbensen, F. A., & Huizinga, D. (1993). Gangs, drugs, and delinquency in a survey of urban youth. *Criminology, 31*, 565–590.

Esbensen, F. A., Huizinga, D., & Weiher, A. W. (1993). Gang and non-gang youth: Differences in explanatory factors. *Journal of Contemporary Criminal Justice, 9*, 94–116.

Esbensen, F. A., & Osgood, D. W. (1997). National evaluation of G.R.E.A.T. *National Institute of Justice Research in Brief* (Vol. NCJ 167264).

Esbensen, F. A., & Winfree, L. T. (1998). Race and gender differences between gang and non-gang youths: Results from a multisite survey. *Justice Quarterly, 15*, 505–526.

Fagan, J., & Pabon, E. (1990). Contributions of delinquency and substance use to school dropout among inner-city youths. *Youth and Society, 21*, 306–354.

Gatti, U., Tremblay, R. E., Vitaro, F., & McDuff, P. (2005). Youth gangs, delinquency and drug use: A test of the selection, facilitation, and enhancement hypotheses. *Journal of Child Psychology, 46*, 1178–1190.

Gordon, R. A., Lahey, B. B., Kawai, E., Loeber, R., Stouthamer-Loeher, M., & Farrington, D. P. (2004). Antisocial behavior and youth gang membership: Selection and socialization. *Criminology, 42*, 55–87.

Hagedorn, J. H. (1998). *People and folks: Gangs, crime, and the underclass in a rustbelt city*. Chicago: Lakeview Press.

Hill, K. G., Hawkins, J. D., Catalano, R. F., Maguin, E., & Kosterman, R. (1995, November). *The role of gang membership in delinquency, substance use, and violent offending*. Paper presented at the annual meeting of the American Society of Criminology, Boston.

Hill, K. G., Howell, J. C., Hawkins, J. D., & Battin-Pearson, S. R. (1999). Childhood risk factors for adolescent gang membership: Results from the Seattle Social Development Project. *Journal of Research in Crime and Delinquency, 36*, 300–322.

Howell, J. C. (1998). Promising programs for youth gang violence prevention and intervention. In R. Loeber & D. P. Farrington (Eds.), *Serious and violent juvenile offenders: Risk factors and successful interventions* (pp. 284–312). Thousand Oaks, CA: Sage.

Howell, J. C. (2000). *Youth gang programs and strategies*. Washington, DC: U.S. Department of Justice, Office of Justice Programs, OJJDP.

Howell, J. C., & Egley, A., Jr. (2005). Moving risk factors into developmental theories of gang membership. *Youth Violence and Juvenile Justice, 3*, 334–354.

Huff, C. R. (1996). *Gangs in America*, Thousand Oaks, CA: Sage Publications.

Hughes, L. A. (2005). Studying youth gangs: Alternative methods and conclusions. *Journal of Contemporary Criminal Justice, 21*, 98–119.

Huizinga, D., Weiher, A. W., Espiritu, R., & Esbensen, F. A. (2003). Delinquency and crime: Some highlights from the Denver Youth Survey. In T. P. Thornberry & M. D. Krohn (Eds.), *Taking stock: An overview of findings from contemporary longitudinal studies*. New York, NY: Plenum Press.

Huizinga, D., Weiher, A. W., Menard, S., Espiritu, R., & Esbensen, F. A. (1988). *Some not so boring findings from the Denver Youth Survey*. Unpublished manuscript. Boulder: Institute of Behavioral Science, University of Colorado.

Kandel, D. B., Chen, K., & Gill, A. (1995). The impact of drug use on earnings: A life span perspective. *Social Forces, 74*, 243–270.

Kandel, D. B., Davies, M., Karus, D., & Yamaguchi, K. (1986). The consequences in young adulthood of adolescent drug involvement. *Archives of General Psychiatry, 43*, 746–754.

Kaplan, H. B., & Liu, X. (1994). A longitudinal analysis of mediating variables in the drug use–dropping out relationship. *Criminology, 32*, 415–439.

Katz, J., & Jackson-Jacobs, C. (2004). The criminologist's gang. In C. Summer (Ed.), *The Blackwell companion to criminology* (pp. 91–124). Malden, MA: Blackwell.

Kennedy, D. M., Piehl, A. M., & Braga, A. A. (1996). Youth violence in Boston: Gun markets, serious youth offenders, and a use-reduction strategy. *Law and Contemporary Problems, 59*, 147–196.

Klein, M. W. (1969). Gang cohesiveness, delinquency, and a street-work program. *Journal of Research in Crime and Delinquency, 6*, 135–166.

Klein, M. W. (1971). *Street gangs and street workers*. Englewood Cliffs, NJ: Prentice-Hall.

Klein, M. W., Gordon, M. A., & Maxson, C. A. (1986). The impact of police investigation on police reported rates of gang and non-gang homicides. *Criminology, 24*, 489–512.

Klein, M. K., & Maxson, C. L. (2006). *Street gang patterns and policies*. New York: Oxford University Press.

Kobrin, S. (1959). The Chicago area project: A twenty-five year assessment. *Annals of the American Academy of Political and Social Science, 322*, 19–29.

Kosterman, R., Hawkins, J. D., Hill, K. G., Abbott, R. D., Catalano, R. F., & Guo, J. (1996, November). *The developmental dynamics of gang initiation: When and why young people join gangs*. Paper presented at the annual meeting of the American Society of Criminology. Chicago.

Krohn, M. D., Thornberry, T. P., Collins-Hall, L., & Lizotte, A. J. (1995). School dropout, delinquent behavior, and drug use: An examination of the causes and consequences of dropping out of school. In H. B. Kaplan (Ed.), *Drugs, crime, and other deviant adaptations: Longitudinal studies* (pp. 163–183). New York: Plenum Press.

Krohn, M. D., Lizotte, A. J., Thornberry, T. P., Hall, G. P., & Chu, R. (2006). *The effect of gang membership on life-course transitions and early adult outcomes*. Los Angeles, CA: Paper presented at the American Society of Criminology.

Lahey, B. B., Gordon, R. A., Loeber, R., Stouthamer-Loeber, M., & Farrington, D. P. (1999). Boys who join gangs: A prospective study of predictors of first gang entry. *Journal of Abnormal Child Psychology, 27*, 261–276.

Levitt, S. D., & Venkatesh, S. A. (2001a). *An analysis of the long-run consequences of gang involvement*. Paper presented at the 2001 Harvard Inequality Summer Institute, Harvard University.

Levitt, S. D., & Venkatesh, S. A. (2001b). Growing up in the projects: The economic lives of a cohort of men who came of age in Chicago public housing. *American Economic Review, 91*, 79–84.

Lizotte, A. J., Krohn, M. D., Howell, J. C., Tobin, K. & Howard, G. J. (2000). Factors influencing gun carrying among young urban males over the adolescent-young adult life course. *Criminology, 38*, 811–834.

Lizotte, A. J., Tesoriero, J. M., Thornberry, T. P., & Krohn, M. D. (1994). Patterns of adolescent firearms ownership and use. *Justice Quarterly, 11*, 51–74.

Loeber, R., Farrington, D. P., Stouthamer-Loeber, M., Moffitt, T. E., Caspi, A., White, H. R., Wei, E. H., & Beyers, J. M. (2003). The development of male offending: Key findings from 14 years of the Pittsburgh Youth Study. In T. P. & M. D. Krohn (Eds.), *Taking stock of delinquency: An overview of findings from contemporary longitudinal studies* (pp. 93–136). New York: Kluwer Academic/Plenum Publishers.

Mattick, H., & Caplan, N. S. (1962). *Chicago youth development project: The Chicago boys' club*. Ann Arbor, MI: Institute of Social Research.

Maxson, C. L., Whitlock, M. L., & Klein, M. W. (1997). *A comparison of the risk factors associated with gang joining, violent behavior, and general delinquency.* San Diego, CA: Paper presented at the American Society of Criminology.

Mensch, B. S., & Kandel, D. B. (1988). Dropping out of high school and drug involvement. *Sociology of Education, 61,* 95–113.

Miller, W. B. (1958). Lower class culture as a generating milieu of gang delinquency. *Journal of Social Issues, 14,* 5–19.

Miller, W. B. (1962). The impact of a "total community" delinquency control project. *Social Problems, 10,* 168–191.

Miller, W. B. (1975). *Violence by youth gangs and youth groups as a crime problem in major American cities.* Washington, DC: U.S. Department of Justice, Office of Juvenile Justice and Delinquency Prevention.

Moore, J. W. (1991). *Going down to the barrio: Homeboys and homegirls in change.* Philadelphia: Temple University Press.

Newcomb, M. D., & Bentler, P. M. (1988). *Consequences of adolescent drug use: Impact on the lives of young adults.* Newbury Park, CA: Sage.

Siennick, S. E., & Osgood, D. W. (2008). A review of research on the impact on crime of transitions to adult roles. In A. Liberman (Ed.), The long view of crime: A synthesis of longitudinal research. New York: Springer.

Shaw, C. R., & McKay, H. D. (1942). *Juvenile delinquency and urban areas.* Chicago: University of Chicago Press.

Short, J. F., & Strodtbeck, F. L. (1965). *Group processes and gang delinquency.* Chicago: University of Chicago Press.

Small, S. A., & Luster, T. (1994). Adolescent sexual activity: An ecological, risk-factor approach. *Journal of Marriage and the Family, 56,* 181–192.

Smith, C. A. (1997). Factors associated with early sexual activity among urban adolescents. *Social Work, 42,* 334–346.

Thornberry, T. P. (1998). Membership in youth gangs and involvement in serious and violent offending. In R. Loeber & D. P. Farrington (Eds.), *Serious & violent juvenile offenders: Risk factors and successful interventions* (pp. 147–166). Thousand Oaks, CA: Sage.

Thornberry, T. P., Krohn, M. D., Lizotte, A. J., & Chard-Wierschem, D. (1993). The role of juvenile gangs in facilitating delinquent behavior. *Journal of Research in Crime and Delinquency, 30,* 55–87.

Thornberry, T. P., Krohn, M. D., Lizotte, A. J., Smith, C. A., & Tobin, K. (2003). *Gangs and delinquency in developmental perspective.* New York: Cambridge University Press.

Thornberry, T. P., & Porter, P. K. (2001). Advantages of longitudinal research designs in studying gang behavior. In M. W. Klein, H. J. Kerner, C. Maxson, & E. G. M. Weitekamp (Eds.), *The Eurogang paradox* (pp. 59–77). Dordrecht, The Netherlands: Kluwer Academic Publishers.

Thornberry, T. P., Smith, C. A., & Howard, G. J. (1997). Risk factors for teenage fatherhood. *Journal of Marriage and the Family, 59,* 505–522.

Thrasher, F. M. (1927). *The gang: A study of 1,313 gangs in Chicago.* Chicago: University of Chicago Press.

Thrasher, F. M. (1936). The boys' club and juvenile delinquency. *American Journal of Sociology, 41,* 66–80.

Vigil, J. D. (1988). *Barrio gangs: Street life and identity in Southern California.* Austin: University of Texas Press.

Walker-Barnes, C. J., & Mason, C. A. (2001). Ethnic differences in the effect of parenting on gang involvement and gang delinquency: A longitudinal, hierarchical linear modeling perspective. *Child Development, 72,* 1814–1831.

Yablonsky, L. (1962). *The violent gang.* New York, NY: Macmillan Press.

Yarrow, M. R., Campbell, J. D., & Burton, R. V. (1970). Recollections of childhood: A study of the retrospective method. *Monographs of the Society for Research in Child Development, 35,* 1–83.

CHAPTER 10

Motives and Methods for Leaving the Gang: Understanding the Process of Gang Desistance

David C. Pyrooz ■ Scott H. Decker

In the previous article, numerous risk factors for gang joining identified from a life-course research perspective were discussed. This article turns to the corollary aspect of gang joining: the process of leaving or exiting a gang. Outside the research arena it is widely repeated that there are only two ways out of a gang—death or prison. This is, however, simply inaccurate: the vast majority of youth who join a gang also, at some point, leave the gang. The authors here argue for the extension of the life-course perspective to the study of gang desistance as a means for understanding the precipitating factors and ways in which youth leave the gang. The reader should recognize the critical importance this area of research has for developing successful gang intervention strategies.

Introduction

The life-course perspective in criminology has required researchers to attend to the complexity of human development and change. Specifically, the perspective examines the onset, persistence, and desistance of involvement in crime throughout the life course. This has not been a simple task, as explaining how individuals desist from crime is quite different from how individuals initiate their involvement in crime (Laub & Sampson, 2001; Uggen & Piliavin, 1998). In addition, considerably more attention has been focused on initiation

than desistance. There are also difficulties in the operationalization of desistance, as it has been problematic to determine at what stage an individual truly has desisted from their involvement in crime (Kazemian, 2007; Piquero, Farrington, & Blumstein, 2007). Despite these challenges, the life-course perspective has proven valuable in a number of areas of inquiry, including the study of delinquent networks, adult offenders, and—the object of examination of the present study—gangs. The understanding of gang members, gangs, and the behavior of their members can benefit from the life-course perspective as it examines explanations for why adolescents join, persist, and desist from their involvement in gangs.

The problem, however, is that desisting from gangs has rarely been the object of study in gang research. With few exceptions (Decker & Lauritsen, 2002; Pyrooz, Decker, & Webb, 2010), the literature on desisting from gangs is limited to mostly indirect ethnographic observations, secondhand accounts, or reviews of the broader literature (Caldwell & Altschuler, 2001; Deane, Bracken, & Morrissette, 2007; Decker & Van Winkle, 1996; Rodgers, 2003; Spergel, 1995; Vigil, 1988, 2002). Most empirical gang research has focused on examining the impact of gang membership on criminological outcomes and identifying risk factors for gang membership (Krohn & Thornberry, 2008). As Klein and Maxson noted, "[s]urprisingly little research has been conducted on gang desistance and the processes of leaving gangs" (2006, p. 154). Given the strong facilitation effect of gang involvement on delinquency and victimization, it is imperative that researchers and practitioners alike learn more about gang desistance processes.

The present study sheds light on the life-course process of desistance as it applies to gang involvement. While there are a number of unanswered questions pertaining to gang desistance, our goal is to build on prior research by examining motivations and methods for leaving gangs. We do this by examining a sample of 84 former gang members, a relatively large sample of such individuals. We begin by discussing the applicability of existing theoretical models for explaining gang desistance. Next, in the course of reviewing the existing research that discusses why and how people leave groups such as gangs, we present a theoretical model of gang membership over the life course. Our analysis focuses on gang member motivations and methods for desisting with a series of descriptive models that highlight the role of enduring ties—or persisting social and emotional attachments—to the former gang network. We conclude with a discussion of the applicability of the life-course framework for studying gang desistance and introduce a typology for understanding gangs and gang desistance in the context of crime desistance. This typology identifies directions for future gang desistance research within the broader life-course framework, as well as the implications of the present study for desistance from other forms of crime.

Theoretical Framework

Life-Course Criminology and Desistance

The life-course perspective has a long history in the study of crime. Much of the work of the Chicago School had a life-course orientation, including the work of Clifford Shaw (*The Jack Roller*) and Edwin Sutherland (*The White Collar Offender*). Sheldon and Eleanor Glueck's longitudinal study of 500 delinquents in Boston laid the groundwork for much of the work that has followed in this area. Indeed, the work of Sampson and Laub (1993; Laub & Sampson, 2003) is based on follow-up analyses of the Glueck data. Farrington (2003) has traced a cohort of Cambridge offenders for forty years. Despite this historic research activity, the life-course perspective lost traction within the

discipline until the 1980s. After all, such research was expensive and had a long investment time before findings were available. The perfect storm for life-course research in criminology occurred with the "discovery" of the Glueck data by Sampson and Laub. Their two major works—Sampson and Laub (1993) and Laub and Sampson (2003)—revived both theoretical and methodological approaches that moved the discipline of criminology forward in important ways.

The core of the life-course argument rests with interpreting the age-crime curve. Hirschi and Gottfredson (1983; Gottfredson & Hirschi, 1990) argued that crime is invariant across the life course, such that the relationship between age and crime mediates our understanding of continuity and desistance in offending over time. The age-crime curve demonstrates that offending peaks in the late teens, and declines precipitously thereafter. This lays the groundwork for the desistance argument generally. The challenge for criminology is to account for the residual amount of crime not accounted for by age and maturational reform—in other words, identifying dynamic and variable factors that facilitate reductions in offending. Factors that describe desistance from crime, such as age-graded informal social control, cognitive transformation, identity reformulation, and role sets have much broader relevance and apply to a variety of groups. In other words, desistance from crime can bring meaning to desistance from groups.

Desistance from Delinquent and Criminal Groups

An important difference between desistance research based on career criminals and research on desisting from delinquent or criminal groups is that "group involvement" is often negatively associated with age. Younger offenders are more likely to occupy groups, and they are less entrenched in their ways and less likely to benefit from the gradual benefits of stable relationships and employment. These offenders would seem more subject to sudden changes in offending patterns that lead to desistance. Petersilia (2003) provided support for the role of stable relationships and employment in the re-entry process, citing them as key factors in the transition from lives of crime to lives of (relative) conformity. But juveniles and younger offenders—the age of most gang members—rarely benefit from these more gradual life-course corrections, as they typically are below the modal age at which Americans marry, and many of them are not eligible to work being below the age of sixteen. Thus it would not be surprising if more sudden departures from lives of crime and gang involvement characterize younger individuals who desist from crime.

Researchers such as Reiss (1988), Sarnecki (2001), and Warr (2002) held that the changing group nature of offending by age is crucial to understanding desistance. Warr's (1993, 1996, 1998) work focused on the group aspect of offending, and interpreted the meaning of turning points in the process of crime desistance differently from Sampson and Laub. Instead, Warr held that changing peer relations, rather than informal social control mechanisms, are responsible for understanding delinquency and crime desistance. Factors such as employment and marriage change peer group relationships, and peer changes then affect desistance (see also, Giordano, Cernkovich, & Holland, 2003; Schroeder, Giordano, & Cernkovich, 2007).

Bjorgo's (2002) research on racist groups in European countries (Finland, Germany, Norway, Sweden, and Switzerland) identified parallels with the crime desistance process described above. He described leaving racist groups as a culmination of "push" and "pull" factors (2002, 2009). Factors that pushed individuals away from racist groups included such things as a loss of belief in the ideology, social sanctions for belonging or believing (the "racist" stigma), disillusionment with inner group workings, status changes within the group, exhaustion from persistent pressure and threat, and acts that were deemed too radical or extreme. Factors that pulled individuals away from such groups included a desire for a conventional life, maturation, mitigated career opportunities, and family responsibilities (see also Bjorgo, 2009). These are consistent with the factors and processes identified by Laub and Sampson (2003), Petersilia (2003), and Maruna (2001) for criminal offenders.

Cronin's (2009) research on desistance from terrorist groups focused on changes in the nature of terrorist campaigns. Cronin identified eight different changes that lead to the decline and desistance of these groups, including: loss of leadership, unsuccessful generational transition, achievement of the cause, movement to a legitimate organization, loss of popular support, repression, or transitions toward criminality or a full insurgency. While Cronin spoke of desistance in the context of the group, these types of changes lead members of the group to forgo their current lifestyle in favor of another.

Bjorgo and Dorgan (2009) observed that group processes across criminal group types have more convergence across than divergence. Indeed, they held that religious cults, terrorist groups, gangs, right-wing hate groups and crime groups are similar with respect to group dynamics. This is true of the organizational characteristics, length of membership, commitment to ideology, and the commitment structure of the group. As Klein and Maxson (2006) emphasized, group processes within gangs trump the impact of ethnicity, gender, and neighborhood characteristics on criminological outcomes. As such, once those group processes are mitigated, outcomes such as desistance may manifest. Indeed, we conclude that the organizational characteristics of deviant groups and the desistance processes have more continuity across groups than they do discontinuity and extend this line of research to understanding life-course concepts such as desistance.

Key Life-Course Concepts in Desisting from Deviant Groups

We contend that the nature of groups is more concordant across deviant and criminal activities that involve groups (gangs, organized crime, cults, terrorism, hate groups) than it is discordant. As such, the social processes associated with exiting groups contain more similarities than differences.[1] Several key concepts guide our understanding of leaving deviant groups, including desistance, duration, motivation, method, and ties components. Because our study concentrates on leaving gangs, we use gang membership to highlight these concepts.

Fig. 10.1 presents a theoretical model of the key components of gang member desistance.[2] *Desistance* can be conceived as the declining probability of gang membership—the reduction from

Figure 10.1 The Life Course of Gang Membership in Relation to Key Desistance Concepts

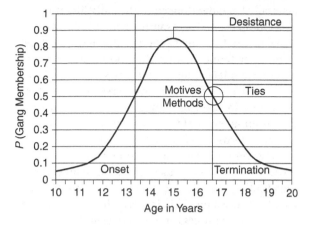

peak to trivial levels of gang membership. This process is consistent with Bushway et al.'s (2001) crime desistance framework as the reduced propensity to offend. Conceptually, desistance is the back half of the *duration* component; the other half consisting of the initiation or "ramping up" to peak levels of involvement. Operationally, onset and termination are marked by the identification and deidentification of gang membership, a well-established methodology in the criminological literature (Esbensen, Winfree, He, & Taylor, 2001; Webb, Katz, & Decker, 2006; Winfree, Full, Vigil, & Mays, 1992). These are important events, internally and externally, both to the individual and the gang, and mark the beginning and end of gang membership. But as we contend, a secondary component of gang membership duration involves a broader process of initiation and desistance—pre- and post-formal markers of onset and termination.

The *motivation* component is the subjective reasoning behind why former gang members decided to leave their gang. There are key factors that influence why gang members de-identify with a social network that was integral to one's life. The *method* component consists of how former gang members departed. In other words, the modes ex-gang members employed to leave their gang. To be sure, leaving the gang is not a one-party process or a one-way street, as the gang may influence this process. Leaving may trigger hard feelings among members of the gang leading to hostile "breakups," or the

process may involve ritual acts to make separation official. Finally, the *ties* component refers to lingering social and emotional attachments that remain post-departure or deidentification from the gang. Ties help us understand the residual connection to the former gang group and describe the broader process of associating and disassociating with the gang.

Desistance from Gangs

Decker and Lauritsen's (2002) study of 24 former St. Louis gang members is among the few direct examinations of the issue. Based on semi-structured interviews, they find that the process of leaving the gang occurred in two different manners: either gang members left the gang abruptly or gradually desisted from the group. These processes encompass the variability in the duration distribution, resembling life-course desistance concepts such as "knifing-off" and desistance as a "developmental process" (Bushway, Piquero, Broidy, Cauffman, & Mazerolle, 2001; Jacques & Wright, 2008). The knifing-off pattern has been detailed by Maruna and Roy (2007), and involves eliminating previous manners, social roles including associates, disadvantage, stigma, and opportunities. For gang members, knifing off applies to the process of severing ties with gang associates and thus eliminating (or reducing) criminal opportunities. The abrupt changes found by Decker and Lauritsen (2002) often involved physically leaving the neighborhood and/or moving to another city. Neighborhood ties are particularly important in this process, as these influences can be particularly troubling to those interested in leaving the gang.

A second pattern of desisting from their gang involved what Decker and Lauritsen (2002: 66) described as a more gradual departure. This process of gang desistance included developing beliefs and commitments that ran counter to those held by the gang. Similarly, Vigil (1988) described a succession quality that characterized the gang desistance process, where an accumulation of reasons or events that work together to de-identify a gang member with his or her gang, resulting in the decision to leave. Over time, the departure is officially sealed as the individual spends less time with fellow gang members, and becomes involved in conventional activities (Decker & Lauritsen, 2002; Vigil, 1988; see also, Spergel, 1995: 105).

Vigil (1988) and Decker and Lauritsen (2002) also examined the methods of leaving the gang. There is a popular belief that gang members have to "get jumped out" or "kill their mother" to leave the gang—a common feature of the "blood in, blood out" mantra of gangs and organized crime groups. Vigil's work in Los Angeles found that it was not uncommon for gang members to be beaten out of their gang. Decker and Lauritsen (2002) found some evidence of this in St. Louis, but exiting members were more often the targets of verbal abuse and threats of violence rather than actual violence. For the most part, gang members moved or just walked away from the gang. It is important to remember the maturation aspects of youth. Desistance is more likely as adolescents in these age-graded subgroups who once played and committed crimes together, mature and assume responsibilities such as getting jobs and having children (Bjorgo, 2002; Decker & Lauritsen, 2002; Sanchez-Jankowski, 1991; Vigil, 1988). In other words, peer groups naturally separate as people navigate into other social circles such as work.

The method of departure is often conditional on other factors, such as the motivation for leaving, position in the gang, and dependence on the gang. Experiencing a traumatic event, personally or vicariously, can be a motivation for leaving. Highly salient events such as being a victim of violence or witnessing violent victimizations can be an important part of the desistance process (Decker & Lauritsen, 2002; Vigil, 1988: 106–109). Decker and Lauritsen's sample of former gang members indicated that violence was the most frequently cited reason why youth chose to leave their gang. Decker and Van Winkle (1996: 272) observed that while violence often served to strengthen the bonds of gang membership, it did have an upper limit. Moreover, if one is deeply embedded within the gang, this may also have an impact on desistance. Since gang membership is structured and many gangs have both core and peripheral members spread across age-graded cliques, level of commitment can affect leaving. As Horowitz (1983) showed, core gang members can have more difficulty leaving than peripheral members due to group dependence and individual deficiencies

described by Klein (1971). Very little research has examined this thesis, however, as desistance has generally been overlooked in the gang literature.

Pyrooz et al. (2010) examined the social and emotional ties to the gang that persist after having left the gang. They found that neighborhood gang activity, school attendance, and length of separation from the gang were associated with persisting gang ties. Gang ties, in turn, had important implications for determining levels of victimization after desistance. In other words, ex-gang members who retained ties to the gang were more likely to be victimized than those who did not possess lingering connections. This finding was present even when controlling for length of desistance. Their research sheds light on the desistance process and is important for conceptualizing and operationalizing gang desistance.

The Current Study

We extend the understanding of desistance from gangs in the current study, drawing from the theoretical framework of life-course criminology. Desistance from gang membership is not well understood, certainly less well understood than criminal desistance generally. There is a parallel between this state of affairs and knowledge about desistance from crime a decade ago, as researchers held that crime desistance was understudied (Bushway, Thornberry, & Krohn, 2003; Piquero, Farrington, & Blumstein, 2003). Understanding why and how gang members leave their gang has important consequences for policymakers, law enforcement, and the juvenile justice system. Reducing the length of time individuals are in a gang would result in lower rates of offending and victimization, not to mention both the collateral and direct costs of imprisonment (Clear, Rose, & Ryder, 2001). The way that former gang members interact with individuals still in the gang can aid prevention, intervention and suppression efforts. But at this point in time, our state of knowledge has not advanced much further than when Klein (1971) first called attention to this issue.

Sample

The data for the present study were collected from interviews in local juvenile facilities as part of the

Arrestee Drug Abuse Monitoring (ADAM) program.[3] Local trained staff interviewed youth within 48 hours after booking. Data were collected over multiple quarters, generating a larger sample for analysis. We focused on one site based in Arizona—Maricopa County—because an addendum was administered to those with a history of gang membership.[4] By focusing on a recently detained group of adolescents, we have a sample that more closely reflects "the street" than a prison population that may be far removed from street gang activity, or a school population with a low prevalence of gang members (potentially excluding street gang youth due to absence or dropout). The key benefit to using the Arizona ADAM is that the gang addendum included a series of detailed questions specific to the gang desistance issues discussed above: duration, motives, methods, and ties.

While the gang addendum provides the opportunity to explore key issues in desisting from gangs, the cross-sectional nature of the data make it difficult to observe the unfolding process. However, the nature of our sample (age < 18) in combination with focusing on precise factors of the desistance process (motives, methods, ties) helps reduce the limitations of a cross-sectional sample. Respondents are less likely to retrospectively reconstruct events and processes that have occurred within the last year or so. That said, the data limit our ability to speak to the temporal processes of gang membership and should be interpreted as such.

Areas of Interest for Understanding Gang Desistance

Three key variables are the focus of our analysis: 1) the *motives* for leaving the gang, 2) the *method* of leaving the gang, and 3) the *ties* that endure after leaving the gang. What little evidence we have on these topics largely comes from ethnographic accounts of very small samples of ex-gang members (Decker & Lauritsen, 2002) or second-hand accounts from gang members who know individuals who have left their gang (Vigil, 1988). Consistent with life-course theory reviewed above, we looked for key desistance concepts (e.g., Giordano, Cernkovich, & Rudolph, 2002; Laub & Sampson, 2003; Maruna, 2001) in our examination of both motives and methods.

Self-nomination was used to operationalize gang membership status, consistent with a long line of individual level gang research (Esbensen et al., 2001; Katz, Webb, & Decker, 2005; Webb et al., 2006). Respondents were asked if they had ever been in a gang. For those responding "yes," a follow up question asked if they were currently in a gang. Those answering "yes" to the former and "no" to the latter were recorded as former or ex-gang members. The 84 respondents that fit this criterion were asked when they left the gang in order to capture the length of separation from the gang, as well as information specific to the areas central to the desistance process.[5]

Motives for leaving the gang was organized into push and pull factors. Motives are the subjective reasoning offered by former gang members for leaving their gang. Respondents were presented with a series of items for leaving their gang that were identified in the qualitative literature (e.g., Decker & Lauritsen, 2002; Vigil, 1988). *Pull* motives were characterized by changing social controls or turning point factors that fracture the "grip of the group" (van Gemert & Fleisher, 2005). Responses that included girlfriends, jobs, or children as the motivation for leaving the gang were recorded as pulls because they are external to the gang, acting as "hooks" to restructure the lifestyle of gang members. *Push* motives were characterized by cognitive shifts or transformations about gang life. Responses that included "I got tired of the gang lifestyle" or "I wanted to avoid trouble and violence" were recorded as pushes because they are internal to the gang, inspiring former gang members to seek out and select into other social arenas.

Methods for leaving the gang was organized into hostile and non-hostile factors. Gangs are often equated with a "blood in, blood out" mentality. Similar to how it is reported that individuals must get "jumped in" or complete missions that demonstrate fearlessness and/or allegiance to the gang in order to enter (Moore, 1991; Sanchez-Jankowski, 1991), it has been reported that leaving the gang entails some degree of ceremony as well (Decker & Lauritsen, 2002; Moore, Vigil, & Garcia, 1983; Vigil, 1988). *Hostile* departures involved events or ceremonies associated with leaving the gang, which included getting jumped out or having to commit a crime to leave. *Non-hostile* departures refer to former gang members that simply walked away from the gang without any fanfare or incident.[6]

Gang ties are social and emotional attachments to the former gang that persist despite having departed. Respondents were asked six questions tapping into the degree to which they retained such ties, including "would you respond if the gang was disrespected" (emotional) and "have you drank or got high with gang members" (social) (see Pyrooz et al., 2010). Respondents who maintain such ties are expected to display different motives and methods for leaving gangs, as well as different behavioral patterns due to the deviant influence of the gang.

We also explore the relationship between our key gang desistance variables with other factors, including gang organization, neighborhood gang activity, separation from the gang, serious offending, and violent victimization. *Gang organizational structure* tapped into the degree to which a gang is capable of controlling the behavior of members (Decker, Katz, & Webb, 2008). A series of seven binary items was summed to create this measure (e.g., "does the gang have regular meetings"). *Neighborhood gang activity* explores the presence of gangs and gang-related problems in respondents' neighborhoods. Five binary items were summed to create this measure (e.g., are there problems in your neighborhood because of gangs). *Separation from the gang* is time in months from leaving the gang until the interview date.[7] *Serious offending* was based on the arresting offense of the respondent. Serious offenses, such as violence or part 1 index offenses, were coded "1" and remaining offenses were coded "0." Finally, *violent victimization* is a prevalence score (yes or no) with regard to experiencing one of four types of victimization in the 30 days prior to arrest (e.g., robbery, assault).

Each of these measures should condition the motives and methods for leaving the gang. We hypothesize individuals who report being members of more organized gangs, who live in neighborhoods with a large number of gangs, who have a large number of gang ties, and who engage in serious offenses will find themselves in circumstances that make their departure from the gang more difficult. Alternatively, individuals who report being members of poorly organized gangs, who live in neighborhoods with the presence of few if any gangs, who commit few offenses with other gang members and who have few ties to gang members will find that leaving the gang requires far less formal effort.

Results

Descriptive Characteristics of the Sample

Table 10.1 displays the descriptive statistics for the study variables. Former gang members are mostly male (74 percent), Hispanic (57 percent), and under age 16, which is consistent with the dynamics of Maricopa County and the gang literature (Klein & Maxson, 2006). Respondents lived in neighborhoods where gang problems were evident. In addition, respondents reported that their former gang network could be described by at least two of the organizational structure variables. Former gang members reported having left the gang for twenty months on average. Despite this, many experienced violent victimization (35 percent) in the 30 days prior to their arrest, and their most recent arrest was a serious offense (33 percent). These findings are important because they provide a glimpse into the nature and lifestyle of the sample. In particular, these findings show that leaving the gang is not necessarily tied to exiting precarious social environments.

Turning to the key gang desistance variables—motives, methods, and ties—we found that leaving the gang is not as structured and ceremonial as one might expect. That is to say, the modal response for motives and methods for leaving the gang was that youth "just walked away" without incident and did so to avoid the nature of the gang lifestyle. Roughly two out of three former gang members reported exiting gangs to avoid the violence and trouble associated with gang membership. The remaining youth left because of important factors external to the gang lifestyle, such as family or employment. As we noted above, leaving the gang occurs prior to the introduction of important informal social controls for youth in this sample. Indeed, the median age of our sample was approximately 16, a developmental period when youth are just beginning to enter into relationships and employment. In this

Table 10.1 Univariate Statistics (*N* = 84)

	Mean or %	SD
Demographics		
Age	15.64	1.40
Male	74	–
Hispanic	57	–
Correlates		
Gang organization	3.15	2.03
Neighborhood gangs	2.14	1.66
Serious offending	33	–
Violent victimization	35	–
Gang desistance		
Separation from gang[1]	20.39	18.99
Gang ties	2.11	1.94
Pull motive	33	–
Hostile method	21	–

[1] In months.

sense, external controls may be more relevant to the desistance process for gang youth that persist into adulthood. This analysis is not meant to promote subjective factors over control factors; to the contrary, the implication of this finding is that youth leave for their own motivations and do not have to be coerced or persuaded to exit. This means that some of the factors that might make gangs qualitatively unique, such as their group processes and propensity for violence, may also be contributing to turnover in the ranks.

The method for exiting the gang, however, involved getting jumped out or committing crimes for about one of every five former gang members. While hostile departures may not be the norm, they are not uncommon enough to fuel the fire of popular gang imagery. Yet, after former gang members renounced their membership in gangs, many retained ties to their former gang. On average, former gang members in our sample reported at least two social and/or emotional attachments to the gang despite having been separated from the group for nearly two years. This suggests that de-identifying as a gang member does not mean disassociating with the gang, consistent with our theoretical model in Fig. 10.1. Over and above the motives and methods for leaving the gang, many former gang members stated that they would respond if their gang was disrespected or retaliate if a gang member was attacked. The "ties that bind" remain strong after leaving, and this is critical for researchers and practitioners alike to comprehend.

Interrelationships among the Study Variables

We begin our examination of the bivariate statistics by looking at separation from the gang due to the importance of distance between membership and non-membership. This is an important measure as the correlates of this measure provide indicators of the variables that can expedite the departure from a gang. Longitudinal gang research indicates that gang membership is associated strongly with higher and more serious levels of offending (Krohn & Thornberry, 2008). Thus, to the extent that gang membership can be truncated, savings in offending and victimization can be realized. The months of desistance is strongly correlated with age and gang ties. Not surprisingly, older gang members reported significantly longer time periods out of the gang. This is especially good news, as it indicates that there is a natural aging out process in gangs. This is consistent with the maturational reform argument that Klein (1967) and others report. There is no relationship between length of time out of the gang and a host of other measures, including gender, victimization, the level of gang organization, and the neighborhood gang index. This means that more organized gangs are no more likely to produce long lasting allegiance to the gang than are less organized gangs. This is a particularly salient finding, as it sheds light on the impact of the organizational structure of the gang on breaking the bonds of membership.

The gang ties measure is negatively correlated with the length of time out of the gang. This means the more ties to the gang that an individual has, the shorter the length of time they have been out of the gang. This makes sense, as over time gang ties would be expected to wane as an individual spends more time out of their gang. At the same time, we find that hostile methods for departure were positively related to neighborhood gang activity and negatively related to separation from gangs.[8] Gang members that seek to desist may experience greater hostility due to their proximity to the gang and attendant group processes. The relationship between hostile departure and separation may be a function of leaving gangs at different developmental stages, where non-hostile methods are treated differently at younger ages. As Krohn and Thornberry (2008) have suggested, the correlates and consequences of gang membership may not be invariant across age-graded or developmental stages.

A Deeper Look at Motives, Methods, and Ties

Based on the results of the bivariate correlations in Table 10.2, we further examined the relationship between motives, methods, and gang ties. The association between hostile departures and pull methods for leaving the gang was the largest in magnitude among all of the coefficients ($r = -.35$, $p < .05$). The negative relationship indicated that hostile methods of leaving the gang did not correspond with pull factor motives. To further explore this relationship we looked at the cross-classifications between motive and methods.

Table 10.3 displays the findings of the cross-classifications. This analysis is important as it allows for a consideration of the role of turning point events or hooks for change (marriage, employment, family, moving out of town) and the nature of the response to such motives by the gang. Based on our earlier discussion, we expect that motives should not be related to the method of departure. That is, the way that an individual exits their gang (method) should not be related to the motive for leaving the gang. This represents the null hypothesis, that there is no difference in the method of exit from the gang based on the motive for leaving the gang. Our results contradict such an expectation. Of the twenty-six members of the sample who reported that they left the gang because of pull factors external to the gang,

Table 10.2 Bivariate Statistics ($N = 84$)										
	1.	2.	3.	4.	5.	6.	7.	8.	9.	10.
1. Age	–	.	.	.	.	.	.	.	.	.
2. Male	.00	–	.	.	.	.	.	.	.	.
3. Hispanic	−.02	.13	–	.	.	.	.	.	.	.
4. Gang organization	−.04	−.33*	−.05	–	.	.	.	.	.	.
5. Neighborhood gangs	−.05	−.18	−.03	.06	–	.	.	.	.	.
6. Gang ties	−.28*	−.20	−.01	.19	.20	–	.	.	.	.
7. Separation from gang	.30*	−.15	−.01	.13	.08	−.24	–	.	.	.
8. Serious offending	−.10	−.07	.06	−.07	−.10	.13	.04	–	.	.
9. Violent victimization	−.18	.10	.20	.20	.04	.18	−.02	.08	–	.
10. Pull motive	.04	.06	−.08	.03	−.06	.10	−.03	−.02	.08	–
11. Hostile method	−.10	−.15	−.09	.12	.24*	.02	−.24*	.10	−.14	−.35*
* $p < .05$.										

Table 10.3 Cross-Classifications of Motive by Methods for Leaving the Gang

Motives		Hostile (N = 16)			Non-Hostile (N = 63)		
Push factor (N = 53)				100%			59%
			(N = 16)			(N = 37)	
		70%			30%		
Pull factor (N = 26)				0%			41%
			(N = 0)			(N = 26)	
		0%			100%		

Note: Five respondents did not provide a motive and/or method for classification. Parentheses indicate the number of former gang members fitting within that cell. Values in the upper right cells represent percentages within each column, or methods category (i.e., percent of the hostile and non-hostile methods leaving due to push and pull factors). Values in the lower left cells represent percentages within each row, or motives category (i.e., percent of push and pull desisters whose method of leaving the gang was hostile or non-hostile).

none of these individuals reported that their departure from the gang was hostile. In other words, fellow gang members did not meet individuals leaving the gang due to family or job obligations with resistance. On the other hand, those who left their gang because they grew tired of it or to avoid further trouble or violence or other push factors that were internal to the gang, did experience some ritual violence in leaving their gang. Upon leaving the gang, nearly one-third (30 percent) of those who were *pushed* away from the gang were met with violence by their gang.

Although this is a small sample, it represents the largest sample of ex-gang members reported to date. As such, this sample is important for understanding the process of desisting from gangs. While there has been little research on leaving the gang, there is no prior systematic research that reports on either the methods or motives for leaving the gang. These results indicate that when gang members face a turning point, they do not encounter resistance from leaving their gang. This suggests several things about the nature of the gang. First, the level of control of individual behavior by the gang may be more limited than some analyses suggest. Second, when individuals experience life changing events, such as marriage, family changes, employment, or moving to another town, gang members who sever their ties to the gang are not met with violence from their gangs. In many ways, the gang "understands" when important life events arise, and the gang

does not respond to those life events in a hostile manner. Correspondingly, former gang members who grew tired of the gang life or wanted to avoid violence often faced violent consequences in leaving their gang. The modal category for each of these groups was that they did not experience violence upon their departure from the gang.

We expanded on this relationship by examining desistance processes—motives and methods—in relation to gang ties. As detailed in Table 10.2, there was no relationship between the motive or method of leaving the gang and gang ties: everyone retained ties at the same rate. Yet, gang ties tell a more important story about the desistance process across motives and methods. When partitioning motives and methods for leaving the gang by gang ties,[9] we find that those who retained ties were at least twice as likely to be victimized violently or to be arrested for serious offenses regardless of why or how one left the gang (see Appendix B). These results indicate that leaving the gang is not automatically associated with reduced serious offending or violent victimization (see Pyrooz et al., 2010). Alternatively, those who left the gang in combination with attenuating or eliminating their ties were arrested for less serious offenses or experienced less violent victimization. These findings are important for both researchers and gang programmers, as examining the "back end" of gang membership provides clues into the conceptual as well as lifestyle factors. We develop this area of research further in the following section.

Discussion

Conceptualizing gang involvement under the purview of a life-course framework is beneficial for understanding gangs, gang membership, and gang-related behaviors. Gang membership, as well as the gang itself, operates within the three key life-course processes—onset, continuity, and change. Researchers have devoted considerable resources to identifying risk factors or predictors of gang joining; however, the efforts to understand the process of gang desistance, the impact of gang membership on later life events, and the aspects of former gang members' lives have received scant attention. The larger implication for this lack of research is clear: although we can speculate, we do not know if gang membership truly has a negative impact over the life course. While our data are unable to assess this question, our goal in general was to draw attention to the desistance process of gang membership. Our goal in particular was to examine gang desistance processes—motives and methods for desistance—while emphasizing the role of lingering ties to the gang. With this in mind, we introduce a typology for understanding the "back end" of gang membership.

In life-course criminological research, spearheaded mostly by Sampson and Laub (1993; Laub & Sampson, 2003), it was held that factors associated with onset of crime are unable to account for desistance from crime. "Gang membership" can be substituted fluidly for crime in this respect, as the forces that propel individuals to join their gang (respect, protection, opportunities for drug sales) are different than the motives for leaving the gang. The motives to leave the gang involve growing tired of gang life, the desire to avoid trouble or violence, family or work responsibilities. It is important to observe that leaving the gang is not simply the inverse or opposite of joining and is consistent with Uggen and Piliavin's (1998) notion of asymmetrical causation in the desistance process. In this context, we would note that if the chance to make money was a motive for joining the gang, replacing it with other money generating activities may not comprise a reason to leave the gang. We now move to a discussion of three important and related factors in understanding gang desistance—gang ties, gang membership, and involvement in crime.

Membership Ties, Involvement in Crime, Gang Involvement: A Typology

We attempt to develop a typology to understand the relationship between gang ties, gang membership, and involvement in crime. We believe that these are important variables in understanding the gang desistance process, though they are not completely overlapping. Determining when an individual is a "former" gang member is not altogether straightforward, even in the rare cases when there is a formal ceremony to memorialize that decision and make it public. It is possible for an individual to leave their gang but still retain ties to gang members and engage in crime, whether with members of their former gang, other individuals or on their own. Because gang membership and involvement in crime are closely linked, however, we expect that desistance from one's gang should be accompanied—in the main—by a reduction in involvement in crime, particularly with members of the former gang. However, as former gang members may retain ties to their former gang, such involvement may be inevitable particularly in the early stages of leaving. Thus we characterize leaving the gang in this case as a more gradual process, where an individual has left their gang, but retains a diminishing number and diminished intensity of ties to members of the former gang. In this scenario, their involvement in crime, particularly crime committed with members of the former gang, should wane over time. In cases where the former member "knifes off" the severing of ties and involvement in crime occur with more simultaneity and rather abruptly.

It is important to note that even once an individual has left their gang, criminal involvement may not cease. After all, not all crimes committed by gang members are motivated by the gang or committed in concert with other gang members. Desistance from crime is rarely sudden; there is no reason to suspect that desistance from gang crime will follow such a pattern. Indeed, given the boost to criminal involvement conveyed by gang membership, it is likely to be the opposite. That is, withdrawal from gang crime would be expected to occur over a more protracted time period owing to the higher levels of involvement produced by gang membership. Similarly, it is possible to leave one's gang and retain ties to the gang, as many members of the former gang may live in the neighborhood, or be friends or relatives. Thus the normal course of routine activities would bring a former gang member into contact with members of the gang. Gang ties are important for re-entry considerations, because of the high level of offending that characterizes gang membership. Neutralizing or severing those ties is often a difficult process because many of the ties to gangs reflect relationships that existed before the decision to join the gang. We also believe that "actions speak louder than words" in this process, so leaving the gang is more difficult than just saying "I left the gang." To be sure, cessation of gang membership involves both cognitive or identity shifts *and* restructured routine activities.

It is the combination of leaving the gang and leaving offending that we are really interested in promoting. After all, an individual who leaves their gang but continues to offend is not much of a desister. Moreover, an individual who has ceased offending yet is still a gang member, while rare, is still not a desister in this respect either. We believe that the two are linked given the strong facilitation effects produced by gangs; however, we also believe that gang ties are the key that may facilitate former gang members' continued involvement in crime.

We depict the relationships between leaving the gang and desisting from crime in Table 10.4. This table details the cross-classification of gang membership (current and former) with involvement in crime. Individuals who have not left the gang, and remain involved in crime are, simply put, gang members (Cell A). Individuals who have left the gang but remain involved in crime are tied to the gang (Cell B) via social and emotional connections to their former gang network. These ties keep them involved in crime, and these ties are

the primary means by which individuals remain enmeshed in their gang and criminal attachments. Cell C includes those who remain in the gang but are not involved in criminal activity. We refer to this group as "older members," but this can include Original Gangsters (OGs) or *veteranos*, in particular those who have aged through gang life and may be older. They resemble ritualists (Merton, 1938) in that individuals who remain a part of a group but are no longer committed to the mainstream goals of the group (see, however, Deane, Bracken, & Morrissette, 2007). Cell D includes those who have left the gang and no longer engage in criminality. These individuals are the true desisters in that they avoid criminal and deviant activities, and present the least complication in terms of gang definitional issues. None of our participants qualified as "true desisters" given that it was a juvenile detainee sample.

We believe that ties to gang members are the key explanatory variable in this formulation and account for a substantial amount of the variation across the typology. In the case of OGs/veteranos, the strength of ties is so great that individuals remain involved in the gang despite the fact that they no longer offend, largely a consequence of the aging out process displayed by the age-crime curve. Those who have left the gang and ended their involvement in crime have also cut their ties to the gang. Conceptually, gang ties condition this relationship. This is supported by research that upholds the facilitation perspective that gang membership enhances crime involvement. Leaving the gang—in particular cutting ties to the gang—produces a return to the pre-gang levels of offending. In some cases gang ties are so strong that despite an individual's decision to leave the gang, individuals remain involved in the criminal activities of their former gang members. Gang ties capture network intensity and duration, as well as variability in the social and emotional attachments to the gang among current and former gang members. These variables have important implications for future behavior. It is important to address the social issues of gangs that are reflected in ties, such as the persistence and intensity of membership.

It is our recommendation that future research employ both qualitative and quantitative methods

Table 10.4 A Typology of the Relationship between Leaving Gangs and Desisting from Crime			
		Left the gang	
		No	Yes
Desisted from crime	No	A. Gang member	B. Socially tied
	Yes	C. Older members	D. True desistance

Appendix A Sample Descriptive Statistics by Motives and Methods for Leaving the Gang

| | Motives (*N* = 79) | | | | Methods (*N* = 84) | | | |
| | Push | | Pull | | Hostile | | Non-Hostile | |
	Mean or %	(SD)	Mean or %	(SD)	Mean or %	(SD)	Mean or %	(SD)
Push motive	–	–	–	–	0	–	41	–*
Pull motive	–	–	–	–	100	–	59	–*
Hostile method	30	–	0	–*	–	–	–	–
Non-hostile method	70	–	100	–*	–	–	–	–
Gang ties	2.02	(1.89)	2.42	(2.16)	2.17	(1.94)	2.09	(1.95)
Age	15.60	(1.41)	15.73	(1.49)	15.39	(1.34)	15.71	(1.43)
Male	75	–	81	–	61	–	77	–
Hispanic	59	–	50	–	47	–	59	–
Gang organization	2.96	(1.90)	3.08	(2.12)	3.61	(2.12)	3.05	(2.01)
Neighborhood gangs	2.17	(1.63)	1.96	(1.66)	2.88	(1.32)	1.91	(1.69)*
Separation from gang	21.00	(20.19)	19.96	(17.67)	11.94	(8.96)	22.72	(20.38)*
Serious offending	33	–	31	–	33	–	32	–
Violent victimization	34	–	42	–	22	–	38	–

* $p < .05$. Statistical significance was assessed using chi square and independent sample *t*-tests.

Appendix B Examining the Role of Gang Ties by Desistance Processes

| | Motives | | | | Methods | | | |
| | Push | | Pull | | Hostile | | Non-Hostile | |
	Gang Ties	No Gang Ties	Gang Ties	No Gang Ties	Gang Ties	No Gang Ties	Gang Ties	No Gang Ties
N	36	16	17	9	5	13	44	21
Serious offense	39%	19	35	22	38	20	39	19
Violent victimization	42%	19	53	22	31	0	46	24

Note: Values in the bottom two rows are percentages.

to further examine both the desistance process and the "post-gang" lives of individuals. At this point in time, very few studies have examined gang desistance. In the case of qualitative approaches, more theoretical development is necessary to confirm findings such as those provided in Deane et al., Decker and Lauritsen, Pyrooz et al., and Vigil's research, as well as the current study. In the case of quantitative approaches, at this point in time, this present data is the largest sample examined on former gang members. This clearly poses problems with regard to generalization. To be sure, large longitudinal data sets with items specific to the gang desistance process would help understand temporal patterns while being able to generalize to larger populations; however, the problem is that items such as methods, motive, and gang ties are not available in these larger-scale data sets. It is only within these contexts that research can assess the gang desistance process and understand the aspects of gang involvement over the life course.

Note

1. One caveat must be offered in such comparisons, however. There is a dearth of research about desistance generally, whether it is the study of terrorists, cult members, hate group members, criminal offenders, or gang

members. For example, in one of the most important statements about criminal career research (Piquero et al., 2007) there are but a few pages devoted to desistance. Similarly, Cronin noted that "the question of how terrorist groups decline is insufficiently studied and the available research is virtually untapped" (2009: 49). So it would appear that desistance from criminal activity that takes place in groups is generally not well understood with regard to the desistance process.

2. Note that the slopes, intercept, and stability of the curve presented are hypothetical—the variability (invariability?) of gang membership trajectories are not well understood.

3. In the late 1980s, the National Institute of Justice established the Drug Use Forecasting (DUF) program, which came to be known as the Arrestee Drug Abuse Monitoring Program (ADAM). This program monitored a host of substance abuse–related issues among recent arrestees in 35 sites throughout the United States through the use of questionnaires and urinalysis.

4. Maricopa County is home to over three-fifths of Arizona's population and the city of Phoenix. Phoenix is the largest city in the state as well as being the sixth largest city in the United States. The metropolitan area is diverse, particularly with regard to the Hispanic population. The 2000 U.S. Census reported that Hispanics comprise 35 percent of the population. A recent study reported that among youth ages 12 to 18 in Arizona schools, nearly one out of every 10 students were currently in a gang (Arizona Criminal Justice Commission, 2007). The city of Phoenix and the state are home to a sizeable portion of gang youth and gang activity.

5. The cross-sectional nature of this study is a limitation to understanding gang desistance. Given that we are placing this phenomenon in a life-course theoretical framework and arguing gang desistance is a process, longitudinal data would be more fitting. That said, this is among the largest sample of former gang members examined systematically. The nature of the survey items helps tease out important features of the desistance process identified in previous research. Examining this process in a longitudinal framework should be a priority for future research.

6. Two independent coders examined open-ended responses to motives and methods for leaving the gang. In classifying these responses, the coders achieved 87 and 92 percent concordance. Divergent classifications were then discussed and placed in an agreed upon category. For Motives, four of the respondents did not report or could not be classified in a particular category. Pairwise rather than listwise deletion was used and this is reflected in the appropriate tables.

7. Nine subjects could recall the year they left the gang, but not the month. In these cases, the mid-point was used to reduce measurement error.

8. Appendix A details the difference by motive and method for leaving the gang. Neighborhood gang activity was nearly one unit greater for hostile methods of leaving, while separation from the gang was approximately 13 months greater for non-hostile methods.

9. Gang ties was dichotomized into whether the respondent did or did not have ties. Over 30 percent of the respondents reported having no ties to their former gang network.

References

Arizona Criminal Justice Commission. (2007). *2006 Gangs in Arizona*. Statistical Analysis Center Publication. Phoenix, AZ: Arizona Criminal Justice Commission.

Bjorgo, T. (2002). *Exit neo-Nazism: Reducing recruitment and promoting disengagement from racist groups*. Paper 627. Norwegian Institute of International Affairs.

Bjorgo, T. (2009). Processes of disengagement from violent groups of the extreme right. In T. Bjorgo & J. Horgan (Eds.), *Leaving terrorism behind* (pp. 30–48). New York: Routledge.

Bjorgo, T., & Dorgan, J. (2009). *Leaving terrorism behind: Individual and collective disengagement*. New York: Routledge.

Bushway, S. D., Piquero, A. R., Broidy, L. M., Cauffman, E., & Mazerolle, P. (2001). An empirical framework for studying desistance as a process. *Criminology, 39*, 491–516.

Bushway, S. D., Thornberry, T. P., & Krohn, M. D. (2003). Desistance as a developmental process: A comparison of static and dynamic approaches. *Journal of Quantitative Criminology, 19*, 129–153.

Caldwell, L., & Altschuler, D. M. (2001). Adolescents leaving gangs: An analysis of risk and protective factors, resiliency and desistence in a developmental context. *Journal of Gang Research, 8*, 21–34.

Clear, T. A., Rose, D. R., & Ryder, J. A. (2001). Incarceration and the community: The problem of removing and returning offenders. *Crime and Delinquency, 47*, 335–351.

Cronin, A. K. (2009). How terrorist campaigns end. In T. Bjorgo, & J. Horgan (Eds.), *Leaving terrorism behind* (pp. 49–65). New York: Routledge.

Deane, L., Bracken, D. C., & Morrissette, L. (2007). Desistance within an urban Aboriginal gang. *Probation Journal, 54*, 125–141.

Decker, S. H., Katz, C. M., & Webb, V. J. (2008). Understanding the black box of gang organization: Implications for involvement in violent crime, drug sales and violent victimization. *Crime and Delinquency,* *54,* 153–172.

Decker, S. H., & Lauritsen, J. (2002). Leaving the gang. In C. Ronald Huff (Ed.), *Gangs in America* (pp. 51–70). (3rd edition). Thousand Oaks, CA: Sage.

Decker, S. H., & Van Winkle, B. (1996). *Life in the gang: Family, friends, and violence.* Cambridge, UK: Cambridge University Press.

Esbensen, F. -A., Winfree, L. T., Jr., He, N., & Taylor, T. J. (2001). Youth gangs and definitional issues: When is a gang a gang and why does it matter? *Crime and Delinquency, 47,* 105–130.

Farrington, D. P. (2003). Key results from the first 40 years of the Cambridge study of delinquent development. In T. P. Thornberry & M. D. Krohn (Eds.), *Taking stock in delinquency: An overview of findings from contemporary longitudinal studies* (pp. 137–183). New York: Kluwer/Plenum.

Giordano, P. C., Cernkovich, S. A., & Holland, D. D. (2003). Changes in friendship relations over the life course: Implications for desistance from crime. *Criminology, 41,* 293–327.

Giordano, P. C., Cernkovich, S. A., & Rudolph, J. L. (2002). Gender, crime, and desistance: Toward a theory of cognitive transformation. *American Journal of Sociology, 107,* 990–1064.

Gottfredson, M. R., & Hirschi, T. (1990). *A general theory of crime.* Stanford, CA: Stanford University Press.

Hirschi, T., & Gottfredson, M. R. (1983). Age and the explanation of crime. *American Journal of Sociology, 89,* 553–584.

Horowitz, R. (1983). *Honor and the American dream: Culture and identity in a Chicano community.* New Brunswick, NJ: Rutgers University Press.

Jacques, S., & Wright, R. (2008). The victimization-termination link. *Criminology, 46,* 1009–1038.

Katz, C. M., Webb, V. J., & Decker, S. H. (2005). Using the Arrestee Drug Abuse Monitoring (ADAM) Program to further understand the relationship between drug use and gang membership. *Justice Quarterly, 22,* 58–88.

Kazemian, L. (2007). Desistance from crime: Theoretical, empirical, methodological, and policy considerations. *Journal of Contemporary Criminal Justice, 23,* 5–27.

Klein, M. W. (1967). *Criminological theories as seen by criminologists: An evaluative review of approaches to the causation of crime and delinquency.* Governor's Special Committee on the Criminal Offender. New York: Office of the Governor.

Klein, M. W. (1971). *Street gangs and street workers.* Englewood Cliffs, NJ: Prentice-Hall.

Klein, M. W., & Maxson, C. L. (2006). *Street gang patterns and policies.* New York: Oxford University Press.

Krohn, M. D., & Thornberry, T. P. (2008). Longitudinal perspectives on adolescent street gangs. In A. M. Liberman (Ed.), *The long view of crime: A synthesis of longitudinal research* (pp. 128–160). Washington, DC: National Institute of Justice.

Laub, J. H., & Sampson, R. J. (2001). Understanding desistance from crime. *Crime and Justice: A Review of Research, 28,* 1–69.

Laub, J., & Sampson, R. (2003). *Shared beginnings, divergent lives: Delinquent boys to age 70.* Boston: Harvard University Press.

Maruna, S. (2001). *Making good: How ex-convicts reform and rebuild their lives.* Washington, DC: American Psychological Association.

Maruna, S., & Roy, K. (2007). Amputation or reconstruction? Notes on the concept of "knifing off" and desistance from crime. *Journal of Contemporary Criminal Justice, 23,* 104–124.

Merton, R. K. (1938). Social structure and anomie. *American Sociological Review, 3,* 672–682.

Moore, J. (1991). *Going down to the barrio.* Philadelphia: Temple University Press.

Moore, J., Vigil, J. D., & Garcia, R. (1983). Residence and territoriality in Chicano gangs. *Social Problems, 31,* 182–194.

Petersilia, J. (2003). *When prisoners come home: Parole and prisoner re-entry.* New York: Oxford University Press.

Piquero, A. R., Farrington, D. P., & Blumstein, A. (2003). The criminal career paradigm: Background and recent developments. *Crime and Justice: A Review of Research, 30,* 359–506.

Piquero, A. R., Farrington, D. P., & Blumstein, A. (2007). *Key issues in criminal career research.* New York: Cambridge University Press.

Pyrooz, D. C., Decker, S. H., & Webb, V. J. (2010). The ties that bind: Desistance from gangs. *Crime and Delinquency.* doi: 10.1177/0011128710372191.

Reiss, A. J., Jr. (1988). Co-offending and criminal careers. In M. Tonry & N. Morris (Eds.), *Crime and Justice: A Review of Research, 10.* Chicago: University of Chicago Press.

Rodgers, D. (2003). *Dying for it: Gangs, violence, and social change in urban Nicaragua.* Work Papers Series 1, 35. London: Crisis States Research Centre, London School of Economics and Political Science.

Sampson, R. J., & Laub, J. H. (1993). *Crime in the making: Pathways and turning points through life.* Cambridge: Harvard University Press.

Sanchez-Jankowski, M. (1991). *Islands in the street: Gangs and American urban society.* Berkeley: University of California Press.

Sarnecki, J. (2001). *Delinquent networks: Youth co-offending in Stockholm.* Cambridge: Cambridge University Press.

Schroeder, R. D., Giordano, P. C., & Cernkovich, S. A. (2007). Drug use and desistance processes. *Criminology, 45*, 191–222.

Spergel, I. A. (1995). *The youth gang problem.* New York: Oxford University Press.

Uggen, C., & Piliavin, I. (1998). Asymmetrical causation and criminal desistance. *Journal of Criminal Law and Criminology, 88*, 1399–1422.

van Gernert, F., & Fleisher, M. S. (2005). In the grip of the group. In S. H. Decker & F. M. Weerman (Eds.), *European street gangs and troublesome youth groups* (pp. 11–30). Lanham, MD: AltaMira.

Vigil, J. D. (1988). *Barrio gangs: Street life and identity in Southern California.* Austin: University of Texas Press.

Vigil, J. D. (2002). *A rainbow of gangs: Street cultures in the mega-city.* Austin: University of Texas Press.

Warr, M. (1993). Age, peers, and delinquency. *Criminology, 31*, 17–40.

Warr, M. (1996). Organization and instigation in delinquent groups. *Criminology, 34*, 11–37.

Warr, M. (1998). Life-course transitions and desistance from crime. *Criminology, 36*, 183–215.

Warr, M. (2002). *Companions in crime: The social aspects of criminal conduct.* Cambridge: Cambridge University Press.

Webb, V. J., Katz, C. M., & Decker, S. H. (2006). Assessing the validity of self-reports by gang members: Results from the Arrestee Drug Abuse Monitoring program. *Crime and Delinquency, 52*, 232–252.

Winfree, L. T., Jr., Full, K., Vigil, T., & Mays, G. L. (1992). The definition and measurement of "gang status": Policy implications for juvenile justice. *Juvenile and Family Court Journal, 43*, 29–37.

Gang Structures and Group Processes

As noted consistently in the chapters in this section, street gangs are *groups*, not mere aggregations of individual gang members. Groups—and thus gangs—have group-level properties that shape and propel them beyond the specific attributes of their members. Research on street gangs must take into account these group qua group qualities, as the discussion in the following chapters does.

We can organize these group-level qualities into four categories:

- Gangs vary in the types of structures they exhibit

- Gangs vary in the levels and types of organization they exhibit

- Gangs are notable for the pivotal group processes they exhibit

- Gangs often go through transformations over time, almost independent of their member characteristics

What has become clear through decades of research on street gangs is that they are *qualitatively* different from most other youth groups. This is one of the reasons chapters in Section I of this volume stress the definition of street gangs: we need to distinguish these gangs from prison gangs, motorcycle gangs, drug-trafficking cartels and organized crime gangs, terrorist gangs, and the far more prevalent, socially based youth groups with which most young people affiliate as they grow up. All groups can be described by reference to such dimensions as social norms, leadership, cohesiveness, size, gender, age, ethnicity, group goals, levels of organization, and so on. These are shared dimensions, but different groups vary in how these dimensions play out in action. To study and differentiate one group type from another requires understanding how clusters of positions on these dimensions come together.

Street gangs, it seems, acquire their distinctiveness in part from the following salient features. First, their make-up is usually composed of marginalized ethnic, racial, national origin, and/or social class members. Second, they have developed an "oppositional culture" that exaggerates their we-versus-them orientation and turns attempts to influence them into reactions that solidify their gang identity. Third, they are characterized by a level of involvement in illegal activities that transcends that of nongang groups and individuals. Fourth, they are often unified by a rhetoric of violence that exceeds that of most youth groups. Fifth, processes of peer contagion and group identity lead to their own recognition that they are "special," which is often noted by special argot, clothing, hand signs, gang names, and territoriality.

It is worth adding that much of what makes street gangs so special and so different from other groups is often missed in media portrayals. These tend to exaggerate levels of violence, degree of organization, "control" of neighborhoods, involvement in drug trafficking, victimization of innocents, and so on. It is understandable, then, that most casual knowledge of gangs is stereotypical rather than accurate. Media portrayals are more often designed to excite than to explain. Yet, at the same time, research can also lead to misunderstandings of street gangs because different research methods can lead to different portrayals of gangs. Of particular importance to this section of this volume are the group structure and process issues.

Sad to say, much gang research overlooks the specific *group* nature of the gang phenomena. This "groupness," if you will, has too often been a given, not an object of study. This is due, at least in part, to the research methods used to study gangs.

Research based solely on police reports or court records is generally limited to individual suspects and accumulated single-crime incidents. Information on the group nature of offenses is often absent or amounts to little more than a check mark on a form that labels the offense as "gang related." Seldom is structure or process information available. Gang unit police officers often offer far more data from their field observations and interviews, but these are often subject to the stereotypes that also fuel media reports. Cops are not social psychologists.

Questionnaires administered to youth, both gang and nongang, have seldom delved into the complexities of gang structure and process because the survey questions are difficult to formulate and because youth are often unaware of the complexities of group experiences to which they are exposed. An exception can be noted in a few recent studies of gang organizational properties, an example of which is included in Section III. Personal interviews are a better source of data on group attributes because the interviewer is positioned to probe more fully into youths' understandings. But the researcher must be intrinsically interested in these attributes, and many are not. Like gang cops, most gang researchers are not social psychologists.

Traditionally, our best understanding of group attributes comes from gang ethnographers and field observers. These researchers see gangs in action: there is no escaping group processes when they are played out in front of the observer's eyes and when gang members are used to having research observers in their midst and are at ease with them. The problem here is that most (but clearly not all) gang ethnographies are single case studies, that is, one gang per researcher. This in-depth approach can be highly illuminating in regard to that gang, but not about gangs in general.[1]

What all this says is that there is an intersection between research methods and gang knowledge. Knowledge is affected by method. In the case of group-qua-group attributes, this is a serious problem and helps to explain why so much gang research appears to overlook the gang-as-group realities. Agreement on gang definitions and the elements of "groupness" that can be incorporated into multiple methods of gang research is badly needed. Given both kinds of agreement, a *science* of gangs can be produced, one that can discern common *patterns* of the phenomenon as well as the exemplars and exceptions. The chapters in this section exemplify movement in this direction with respect to gang structures, organization, and group processes.

Note

1. Published too late for inclusion in this volume, Walter Miller's 900-page volume, *City Gangs*, is worth the reader's attention. Edited and prepared posthumously by Scott Decker at Arizona State University, this exhaustive report on Boston street gangs reflects other findings from New York, Chicago, and Los Angeles in the 1950s, 1960s, and the present. Special attention should be given to the fruitful insights into clique structures, group processes, and criminal patterns in Chapter 5; see www.gangresearch.asu.edu/citygangs.

CHAPTER 11

Gang Structures

Malcolm W. Klein ■ Cheryl L. Maxson

The assumption that most street gangs are alike does not hold up. Nor does the assumption that no two gangs are alike. In the research reported in this chapter, the authors detail their development of a street gang typology that reveals five patterns of street gang structure. Derived originally from police information and then validated in a variety of settings in the United States and abroad, this typology brings coherence to what has been a mélange of street gang depictions. Such a typology of gangs also suggests that attempts to influence gangs and gang members should take into account their structural characteristics: what works with one type may not work with another. Further, research about one type may well yield data that do not apply well to others. Type-specific data may facilitate cross-community comparisons as well as community-specific approaches to gang control.

The Importance of Structure

The importance of understanding gang structures derives in large part from considering the dimensions of the structures and the relationships of these to other issues of concern. Let us consider several of these dimensions and issues.

Levels of Organization

It is assumed by most laypersons, public officials, and a surprising number of law enforcement

officers that street gangs are well organized—cohesive, hierarchically led, with clear codes of conduct. While this may be an accurate depiction of a small proportion of street gangs, it is not true for the large majority. We are misled by the images of such dramatic, fictional accounts as *West Side Story* (great musical, poor social science). In most street gangs, leadership is ephemeral, turnover is often high, and cohesiveness only moderate. Codes of conduct often exist in rhetoric but are easily avoided or broken. Many street gangs are more a loose collection of cliques or networks than a single, coherent whole. Further, in the majority of gangs, median individual membership lasts only about a year. This high level of turnover challenges any notion of stable structure (Esbensen and Huizinga, 1993; Thornberry et al., 2003).

A classical description of limited gang cohesiveness was provided by one of the authors more than 30 years ago (Klein, 1971: 109–123). Little has changed since that time. Decker and Curry have most recently (2000, 2002) described gangs' organization in St. Louis with respect to leadership, formal meetings, rules, subgroupings, connections to other gangs, and gang versus nongang friends. With the exception of generally accepted rules for behavior, the authors conclude that their street gangs are not well organized. Similar findings are reported by Hagedorn (1988) and Fleisher (1998), among others. In a separate analysis, Decker (2001) compared the two most-organized gangs (according to the police) in San Diego, St. Louis, and Chicago. He found that only one of these, Chicago's

Black Gangster Disciples, fit the "organized gang" stereotype.

For the social services worker attempting to establish rapport with a gang, this somewhat amorphous structure of street gangs will require extensive observation and interview before any individual interventions are possible. Detached worker programs often require literally *years* of work before gangs become responsive (which is often long after worker burnout takes over). Examples are found in the heyday of detached worker programs in New York (New York City Youth Board, 1960), Chicago (Carney et al., 1969; Spergel, 1966), and Los Angeles (Klein, 1971).

For the gang cop, this loose organization makes intelligence gathering quite idiosyncratic and defeats gang control via the arrest of hardcore leaders or the general harassment of members. Indeed, evidence suggests that concerted efforts at gang dissolution by social services workers or police may inadvertently increase gang cohesiveness through understandable mechanisms introduced elsewhere (Klein 1971, 1995) and discussed later in this chapter.

For the researcher, perhaps the most unrecognized but common problem raised by this loose gang structure is that gang informants, those willing and interested in bringing the researcher into their world, are likely to be atypical of the general membership. Failure to obtain observations or interviews with a representative sample of a gang's members or relying on archival data on those arrested or convicted are factors guaranteed to yield distorted images of gang structure and behavior. Many of the gang case studies in the criminological literature suffer from these faults.

Heterogeneity of Gang Structures

Later in this chapter, we will describe several different street gang structures that illustrate structural variability. But even within each of these, the range is wide along a number of important dimensions both structural and behavioral, to say nothing of the variations across gang communities and the institutions (social services, police, courts, schools) responding to them. There *are* generalizations that can fairly be made about street gangs—that's what science is for—but they are of value only as

we understand the variability that qualifies them. Within each category of street gangs, there can be wide differences in size, age ranges, gender proportions, centralized leadership, accepted codes, criminal behaviors, and so on. And *across* structures, these vary measurably.

The practitioner who ignores the structural variations, who thinks gangs are pretty much alike, will inevitably fail in attempting to intervene in multi-gang settings. The researcher who fails to seek the structural differences or who studies but one gang or one gang type will publish false generalizations and mislead his or her colleagues. The responses of many gang ethnographers to the narrow depictions offered by Yablonsky (1963), Taylor (1990), and Sanchez-Jankowski (1991) reveal that the levels of violence and of drug entrepreneurialism described by these authors have manifestly misled major public policy initiatives. We don't need more of these errors.

Structures and Functions

Groups persist in part because they fulfill certain needs of their members. In the case of street gangs, most prominent of these needs are the status, sense of identity, and perceived protection from rival groups that derive from membership. Secondarily, street gangs provide access to and social legitimization for antisocial attitudes and behaviors.

For the moment, however, the point to be made is that gang structure and function are interrelated, enough so that to ignore structural differences also yields misunderstanding of functional differences. Some gang structures, most notably the "traditional" and "compressed" forms to be described later, exist more for social than for criminal reasons. Especially in the case of traditional gangs, intergang rivalries and territorial disputes, whether violent or merely rhetorical, are often the hallmarks of gang existence, with criminal behaviors an important but secondary function. To attempt gang control in these instances merely through the enforcement of legal codes clearly misses the point; to attempt an understanding of these gangs through their variegated criminal patterns similarly overlooks the principal sources of their origin and persistence. That is, arrests and convictions usually do little to affect gang structure and function. It is the gang as a *unit* that requires intervention and control: gang structure and function should be the targets.

In a similar but contrasting fashion, there are "specialty" gangs, to be described later, whose principal function originated in or evolved into a primary focus on a narrow criminal pattern. Drug gangs, burglary rings, skinheads, and the like come to exist principally around these more narrow anti-social interests. This type of gang *can* be effectively controlled through selected enforcement procedures, and they can be understood and described by research using these interests as the focal point (Padilla, 1992; Hamm, 1993; Bjorgo, 1997; Valdez and Sifaneck, 2004). As we will demonstrate later, the contrasting functions bring with them important differences in gang size, leadership, duration, and other structural dimensions often overlooked in both practice and research.

It is our intent in this chapter to go beyond the consensus nominal definition offered in the introduction to more of an operational definition in which the measurement of gang patterns defines their nature. The patterns we choose here are those that reflect the *structural* characteristics of gangs—things like their age distribution, longevity, size, internal subgroupings, and crime patterns. We emphasize these structural components because other attempts to find gang patterns—gang typologies—have not done so and have failed in part due to this omission.

If we are successful in developing a structural typology of street gangs, we can offer an additional useful approach to gang definition. We want to attempt comparisons of gang situations across time and between cities and nations; such a typology might allow us to make progress in these directions. A recent example is the application of the structural typology to gangs in a dozen European cities. Where definitional consensus initially proved to be a barrier, the typology revealed much about the common and disparate gang patterns in these cities and many in the United States (Klein, 1996).

One final note; we recognize full well that in adopting this operational stance, we have not "solved" the definitional problem but merely surmounted it for our particular interest in facilitating street gang comparisons over time and space. For us, such comparisons are pivotal to drawing reliable generalizations about gangs and how to control them. It is a major goal of science, after all, to be able to draw forth generalizations about the phenomena it studies. Be these laws, principles, or patterns, science can neither summarize nor predict without them.

Past Efforts at Gang Typologies

Public images of gangs take some common forms. These include

- a group of youths lounging on the street corner, harassing passersby and disrupting local businesses

- the *West Side Story* image of cohesive, tightly organized rival collectivities whose principal concerns are minor crimes and territorial challenges

- super-gangs, Chicago-style, with memberships in the thousands, in control of neighborhoods and tightly entwined with organized-crime groups

- marauding cliques of a half dozen youths moving freely about other people's neighborhoods, randomly targeting people and facilities in almost senseless attacks "for the fun of it"

- bands of drug-selling, gun-toting thugs

So what does a street gang look like? Most thoughtful scholars have answered, first, that there is no one, single form of gang. Rather, gangs pattern themselves in stable and recognizable forms. It is this pattern of forms that has led to the attempts to typologize gangs. In a sense, the purpose of these typologies, and most certainly the one we shall describe as the result of our recent research, is to achieve an "ostensive definition" as described by Ball and Curry: "Although one has a clear or vivid idea of a thing when one can recognize examples of it immediately, the idea is not yet distinct until one can enumerate one-by-one the features that distinguish the thing from others" (1995: 226).

Attempts at gang typologies fall roughly into two time periods, which we will call the "classical" and "modern" periods of gang study. The former starts with Thrasher's 1927 work and ends with Klein's 1971 review of the classical works. The modern period starts with Walter Miller's mid-1970s national surveys and continues through the present.[1]

These attempts also fall roughly into two descriptive forms: gang typologies that are primarily behavioral and those that are primarily structural. Although some mixing of the two forms can be seen, they are usually quite distinct. The contrast is critical to our exposition later of our own research results. Behavioral typologies typify gangs by their purported tendency to manifest a predominant form of behavior. The most influential of these typologies was that of Cloward and Ohlin (1960), to which we will refer below. It was also typical of the behavioral typologies in that the behaviors noted were specifically criminal rather than more broadly social. The structural typologies, by contrast, largely bypass gang behaviors to find patterns in the social characteristics of the groups. Examples of structural dimensions are race and ethnicity (often used by police and the media), size (from small cliques to the super-gangs of Chicago), and type or level of organization (emphasizing leadership patterns or role differentiation).

The Classical Period

Serious attempts at typologizing started with Thrasher's 1927 work, *The Gang*, a monumental exercise in Chicago to catalog more than 1,000 youth groups through observations, interviews, secondhand reports, and other processes that seem loosely constructed in the hindsight of modern methods. The distinctions made were among (1) diffuse, (2) solidified, (3) conventionalized, (4) criminal, and (5) secret society groups. Four of these, at the least, may be seen as structural, although many of the groups subsumed under them would not today be classified as street gangs, many indeed being little more than common boys' play groups.

The only other original classification of gangs as structural entities during the classical period was that of the New York City Youth Board (1960), which mounted a major detached worker program on the streets of several boroughs. These gangs were (1) vertical, (2) horizontal, (3) self-contained, or (4) disintegrating. Here, the structure had to

do principally with organizational features and emerged from the experiences of the street workers rather than any a priori conceptual stance.

Four other classical period depictions, derived inductively from the researchers' observations in the field, stress behavioral rather than structural properties. Thus Cohen and Short (1958) reported a pattern of theft, conflict, and addict gangs based on the predominant crime orientations within the groups. Cloward and Ohlin (1960) followed with their highly influential depiction of criminal, conflict, and retreatist subcultures and gangs with the same emphases within them. Spergel (1964), a student of Ohlin, found a fourfold variation of racket, theft, conflict, and retreatist gangs. His was the only one of a half dozen early attempts at replication to confirm the basic behavioral/criminal pattern noted by his predecessors. Finally, we find Yablonsky's (1963) distinction among social, delinquent, and violent gangs in New York, although his emphasis was clearly on violent gangs as the major problem.

In his 1971 review of these major attempts and other gang writings of the classical period, Klein attempted to summarize the gangs described in both structural and behavioral typologies. He found the gang descriptions to be principally structural, with four dominant patterns: (1) traditional (age-graded subgroups, self-regenerating territorial gangs); (2) spontaneous (age-integrated short-term gangs); (3) specialty (short-term groups with specific rather than general criminal focuses, such as drug involvement); and (4) horizontal (short- or long-term alliances of gangs, usually manifest in times of extreme challenges by rival gangs, as in Chicago's early super-gangs).

Of the various typologies of the classical period, two had major influence. The Cloward and Ohlin typology, being theoretically integrated and based on social and cultural descriptions of lower-class urban life, was very appealing to scholars as a conceptual package. Failures to locate the pattern in other settings (e.g., Short and Strodtbeck, 1965; DeFleur, 1967; Vaz, 1962; Monod, 1967; Sherif and Sherif, 1967; and Downes, 1966) did little to discourage the acceptance of the criminal-conflict-retreatist typology.

The other influential attempt was Yablonsky's, although his social and delinquent gangs quickly faded in memory as his violent gang captured media and lay attention. Titling his dramatically written book *The Violent Gang* helped to solidify the image of street gangs not only as violent, but also as large, marauding congregations held together by megalomaniacal, sociopathic leaders. Focusing on the most feared of the behavioral patterns has set a pattern against which almost all future behavioral gang research has had to do battle. Most writers citing Yablonsky's descriptions have failed to note his exaggerations and the fact that the few gangs he observed were short-lived anomalies whose description has seldom if ever been replicated in any other time or place.

In a point to which we will return later, attempts to define gangs by dominant behaviors—violence, theft, graffiti, or other narrow criminal patterns— raise two problems. First, most gang members' crime is versatile; the members (and thus most of their gangs) engage in a wide variety of crimes. Thus the "violent gang" or the "theft gang" is an inaccurate depiction. Second, if one bases a gang control program on one type of crime, for example, violence, one will miss the true target of crime versatility. False assumptions can lead to misguided programming.

The Modern Period

Walter Miller entered into gang research in the 1950s with an anthropological thrust that distinguished his work from that of the dominant sociological paradigm. He viewed street gangs as reflections of lower working-class culture, rather than as distinct social entities, although his behavioral depictions are more those of traditional, territorial gang structures. Returning to gang work some 20 years later, Miller eschewed the ethnographic methods and undertook a survey of officials in many cities across the nation. He was led by this process to the need to distinguish gangs from other groups that he called "law violating youth groups."

In a strictly ad hoc procedure, W. Miller (1980) offered a list of 20 such groups of which only 3 are labeled "gangs": turf gangs, gain-oriented gangs, and fighting gangs. Most others are called rings, cliques, bands, or crowds, although they would by most scholars also be included as gangs. The arbitrariness of the system is obvious, yet the purpose

is laudatory as Miller hoped to delineate group differences that would facilitate comparisons across cities.

The labels applied by Miller to most of his other groups are almost solely behavioral rather than structural: disruptive, looting, burglary, robbery, larceny, extortion, drug dealing, and assaultive. The level of criminal specialization is highly unusual, and as we will indicate later, totally opposed to what has been almost universally demonstrated about gang crime, which is that it is versatile rather than specialized.

Several other behavioral typologies have been suggested during the modern period. Taylor's (1990) scheme for the development of gangs in Detroit, highly related to drug sales, claims an evolution from scavenger gangs to territorial gangs to corporate gangs. Others, such as DiChiara for Hartford, Connecticut (1997), and Salagaev for Kazan, Russia (2001), have similarly described case studies of criminal gang evolution from less- to more-organized states.

Huff (1989) and Fagan (1989) have also offered behavioral typologies. Huff described hedonistic, instrumental, and predatory gangs, while Fagan found younger members to form social, party, conflict, and delinquent gangs. Neither Taylor's, nor Huff's, nor Fagan's schemes articulate well with Miller's types—nor with each other's.

One can well ask how this can be. Especially given the three-city research undertaken by both Huff and Fagan (six cities in all), some general patterns should begin to emerge. That each behavioral typology provides a unique pattern raises two fundamental problems. The first of these is the suspicion that the typologies do *not* emerge naturally from systematic observations and analyses, but rather from some combination of different researcher perspectives, different methods, and unique gang locations. To surmount such problems would require the sharing of data and the coordination of research designs, a process almost unknown in American gang research. Without such coordinated, multisite research, we can expect to continue to see "unique" depictions of common phenomena.

The second problem with the behavioral, mostly crime-driven, typologies—as noted earlier—is that they fly in the face of what is known about crime patterns specifically. Klein's (1971) analysis of 1960s data, expanded from gangs to general delinquency in a later review (Klein, 1984), has since been replicated many times by other scholars to show that most offenders show a versatile rather than a specialized pattern of offending. Gang-specific studies of crime profiles are uniform in finding versatility patterns (Thornberry et al., 2003; Esbensen and Huizinga, 1993; Battin et al., 1998). Typically, youthful offenders *and* gangs show a variety of acts, including status offenses, theft, vandalism, burglary, robbery, drug use and selling, fighting, weapons possession, and assault. Klein referred to it as "cafeteria-style offending" (1995: 68). Given this absence of specialization, it is illogical to propose that gangs be delimited by any predominant crime pattern. Most gangs cannot be of that sort, although we will indicate later one specific but uncommon form of street gang, the "specialty" gang, that does fit that pattern.

It is precisely these sorts of problems of uncoordinated typologies that have led us to our own work on the structural typology reported in these pages. Interestingly, only one other structural attempt has appeared in the modern period, and it is one that gives us some trouble. From his observations in three major cities, Sanchez-Jankowski (1991) proposed the existence of three street gang structures: vertical, horizontal, and influential. The distinctions were based principally on forms of gang leadership or authority structure. Included as well are member rules and duties and codes of behavior, resulting in the author's claims of three *distinct* models.

One of our problems is that we can't find such distinct models in Jankowski's descriptions. More fundamentally, Jankowski has described rational, planned, organized, sophisticated gangs that defy almost all other researchers' findings, but he does not provide any data to support his position. We are, frankly, not convinced by Jankowski's descriptions that the gangs he observed would be similarly observed by others.

We should add that other researchers certainly have been aware of some of the structural dimensions of street gangs. Recent examples include James D. Vigil, Jody Miller, Scott Decker, and Finn-Aage Esbensen. However, their analyses did not refer to the gangs as *units* and did not attempt to delineate differences among gangs. Thus their descriptions do not help us to typologize gangs.

We are left, in sum, with two basic typological approaches that invite further work. The behavioral approach, despite its popularity, seems illogical given one of the few fully accepted generalizations about delinquency and gang crime: that it is versatile rather than specialized. Further, various scholars seem unable to arrive at common types. The structural typologies seem to us even less data based and, with the exception of Jankowski's proposal, have not emerged during the modern period.

Toward a Structural Typology

To develop a structural street gang typology that is clearly data based, one needs ready access to data on structural dimensions. These might include gang size, age ranges, gender, ethnicity, locations, leadership, subgroupings, cohesiveness, duration over time, and organizational norms. Further, one needs such data on many gangs in many settings in order to develop patterns and generalizations. Where could such data be located?

Ideally, a very large series of planned, coordinated ethnographies of street gangs would yield the structural data needed. A few single ethnographies or groups of long-term field observations have, in the past, provided some structural depictions (Klein, 1971; Moore, 1991; Padilla, 1992; J. Miller, 2001; Fleisher, 1998). But one needs far more than these, based on reasonably representative samples of street gangs, not the convenience samples that have been the rule until now. Such a major enterprise, for now, does not seem realistic.

Alternatively, one could undertake an archival analysis of already reported field studies, such as those listed above. But few of those deliberately collected data on structural dimensions, so that the results would at best be rather haphazard. But we shall return to them later to see what might emerge.

A third procedure would be to undertake large-scale, multisite interview or questionnaire surveys of gang-age respondents. Either household or school-based surveys would suffice, although each approach has problems of access and sampling. At this point, we are aware of only two such surveys. In the research undertaken by Esbensen and his colleagues to evaluate the G.R.E.A.T. program, its formulation did not include a deliberate gang structure investigation. Still the Esbensen model could be at some point adapted to our purpose. Surveys of St. Louis, Chicago, and San Diego gang members (Decker, 2001; Weisel, Decker, and Bynum, 1997) reveal very ambiguous perceptions of the members' own gang structures, even the highly structured Latin Kings and Black Gangster Disciples. Gang members are often poor informants on their own groups; they know their own cliques far better than the overall gang structure.

A fourth procedure would be to take advantage of the observations of street gang workers at various locations. Where they have existed (W. Miller, 1962; Short and Strodtbeck, 1965; Carney et al., 1969; Klein, 1971; New York City Youth Board, 1960; Spergel, 1966), gang workers have provided rich and often detailed pictures of relationships among gang members and the general characters of their gangs. (As with the ethnographic approach, one would have to mount a very large, planned program, in this case a multigang, multisite gang intervention program with the inclusion of gang workers as both interviewers and data providers. One model in five sites has recently been provided by Spergel, but that model, for our purposes, would have to be greatly expanded at enormous financial cost.)

While our search for a structural street gang pattern could not be accomplished in any of these forms with our limited resources, another source of appropriate data did seem available, namely, police observations. Clearly, one must approach police gang data with great caution. There are built-in biases, sampling problems, and limited perspectives to be recognized and overcome. Police roles and functions make the task difficult, but these same roles and functions are also unique in providing the data access needed. In every city, the police are the only group with broad exposure to street gangs. Officials in other social services agencies may be familiar with one or several gangs in their catchment areas, but they cannot

have close-at-hand, citywide exposure. This is especially true when contrasted with those many police departments that have special gang units or gang officers.

Even with knowledgeable gang officers as respondents, two problems have to be surmounted. The first is that gangs are *informal* groups. They do not provide the police with membership rosters, time cards, dues payment lists, membership cards, organizational charts, or constitutions and bylaws. The police data have to be observational, not inherently organizational. Second, some structural dimensions are more obvious than others; e.g., cohesiveness is less immediately observable than the existence of subgroups. Further, police perspectives sometimes ignore some dimensions—gender ratios is one example—and stereotype others, such as leadership. Thus the structural dimensions to be derived from police experts cannot be comprehensive but must be carefully selected. This is a limitation but not an insurmountable barrier.

Methods

We start by noting several dimensions *not* sought from our police respondents. Earlier interviews with 260 police gang experts across the country had made it clear that their style of thought did not yield consistent or realistic views of several matters. One of these was gang leadership. This tended to be stereotypic in form, stressing serious criminal involvement and older age, and thus missing age-graded leadership and leadership based on verbal capabilities, organizational skills, and athletic or social skills.

A second dimension was level of membership, again yielding rather stereotypical categories, such as core or hardcore and peripheral; actives, associates, and wannabes; confirmed, rostered, or certified. The terminology was not consistent, nor were the criteria for the differences very clear beyond the level of involvement in serious crime.

Most important, a direct question about gang structure proved fruitless. While many police experts correctly noted that street gangs tended to be loosely structured and poorly organized, others reported a dominant pattern of hierarchical structure and clear group rules. The notion of assessing gang cohesiveness, so critical to scholarly depictions of street gang structure, was foreign to many of our experts.

Two additional patterns became clear. In the absence of prior guidelines, police tended to think of street gangs in terms of two characteristics, ethnicity and violence. As to the first, it seemed to our experts that Hispanic gangs differed substantially from black gangs; both were different from Asian gangs; and white gangs were all but nonexistent. Most research data on street gangs did not support these clear distinctions.[2] For instance, Freng and Winfree (2004) found remarkable similarities overall among white, African-American, and Hispanic gang members with respect to their attitudes toward gangs, reasons for joining gangs, gang characteristics, illegal activities, and victimization rates. As we have noted elsewhere, group process trumps ethnicity.

The same is true of the violence issue, in that research data dispute the existence of predominantly violent gangs or violence as a meaningful dimension. Levels of gang violence are strongly correlated with the levels of the *amount* of gang offending. The more they offend, the more the pattern includes the less-common violent acts. This is a statistical pattern rather than a qualifying distinction among types of gangs. That police stress violence is certainly understandable, given their societal role, but it reflects a narrow view of what street gangs are all about.

For our purpose, this discussion meant two things. First, we could not ask police gang experts—"gang cops" in common parlance—to respond *directly* to questions about street gang leadership, levels of membership, structure and cohesiveness, ethnicity, or crime patterns. It also meant, however, that if we could establish gang types by reference to *other* dimensions, then we might be able to correlate these with some of the excluded dimensions in other ways. As will be seen in our data, this was indeed possible to some extent. We turn now to phase 1 of the research.

The Phase I Sample

Using as a database 792 cities with street gangs identified in our 1992 survey on gang proliferation and migration, a stratified sample of 60 cities was selected. Stratification was by period of gang onset in the cities (1970 and earlier, 1971–1984, and 1985–1992) in order to ensure adequate representation of older gang cities. Fifty-nine of the 60 cities yielded responses to our request for interviews with their best gang experts (some of whom had been our respondents in earlier research). We report here only the data that led to the street gang typology; other questions merely corroborated the problems of stereotypical or inconsistent perspectives alluded to above when questions about the many gangs in each city were posed.

The procedure which succeeded with the gang cops was to ask each to describe the single gang with which he or she was most familiar. Consistently useable responses were obtained on the dimensions of subgroups, size, age range, duration, territoriality, and crime versatility versus specialization. In other words, respondents described their best-known street gang as to whether or not it included significant subgroups, the size of its known membership, the range between youngest and oldest members, how long the gang had been in existence, whether it was a territorial gang or not, and whether its members engaged in a wide variety of offenses or mostly one or two types (and if the latter, what types).

These data came from the experts in the 59 cities, both new and old in their exposure to gangs, and were taken from all sections of the country. They included small, medium, and large jurisdictions, in rough proportion to the data set of 792 cities previously identified in our research. Thus we have some confidence in their national representativeness.

We undertook an analysis of the six dimensions across the 59 cities, looking for patterns of relationships among the dimensions. Five types of street gangs emerged from this analysis, as noted in Table 11.1.

The labels—traditional, neotraditional, compressed, collective, and specialty—represent our attempt to capture the more distinguishing features of each pattern.[3] The traditional, compressed, and specialty gang patterns correspond well to case descriptions already available in the scholarly literature about street gangs. For example, Weisel's (2002) violent gangs resemble our traditional and neotraditional gangs. Her delinquent gangs resemble our compressed gangs, while her income-generating

Table 11.1 Characteristics of Five Gang Types

Type	Subgroups	Size	Age Range	Duration	Territorial	Crime Versatility
Traditional	yes	large (> 100)	wide (20–30 years)	long (> 20 years)	yes	yes
Neotraditional	yes	medium-large (> 50)	no pattern	short (< 10 years)	yes	yes
Compressed	no	small (< 50)	narrow (< 10 years)	short (< 10 years)	no pattern	yes
Collective	no	medium-large (> 50)	medium-wide (> 10 years)	medium (10–15 years)	no pattern	yes
Specialty	no	small (< 50)	narrow (< 10 years)	short (< 10 years)	yes	no

gangs are similar to our specialty gangs. The neotraditional and collective gang patterns have been alluded to on occasion, but emerge more clearly here. In order to provide more meat to the bones of Table 11.1, we developed the five "gang scenarios" below, which also served in the second research phase to be reported next.

Five Street Gang Scenarios

The Traditional Gang. Traditional gangs have generally been in existence for 20 or more years: they keep regenerating themselves. They contain fairly clear subgroups, usually separated by age. O.G.s ("Original Gangsters") or Veteranos, Seniors, Juniors, Midgets, and various other names are applied to these different age-based cliques. Sometimes, the cliques are separated by neighborhood rather than age. More than other gangs, traditional gangs tend to have a wide age range of their members, sometimes as wide as from 9 or 10 years of age into the 30s. These are usually very large gangs, numbering a hundred or even several hundred members. Almost always, they are territorial in the sense that they identify strongly with their turf, 'hood, or barrio and claim it as theirs alone.

In sum, this is a large, enduring, territorial gang with a wide age range and several internal cliques based on age or area.

The Neotraditional Gang. The neotraditional gang resembles the traditional form, but has not been in existence as long—probably no more than 10 years and often less. It may be of medium size—say 50 to 100 members—or number its members in the hundreds. It probably has developed subgroups or cliques based on age or area, but sometimes may not. Like traditional gangs, it is also very territorial, claiming turf and defending it.

In sum, the neotraditional gang is a newer territorial gang that looks to be on its way to becoming traditional in time. Thus, at this point it is subgrouping, but may or may not have achieved territoriality, and its size suggests that it is evolving into the traditional form.

The Compressed Gang. The compressed gang is small—usually in the size range of up to 50 members—and has not formed subgroups. The age range is probably narrow—10 or fewer years between the younger and older members. The small size, absence of subgroups, and narrow age range may reflect the newness of the group, in existence less than 10 years and maybe for only a few years. Some of these compressed gangs have become territorial, but many have not.

In sum, compressed gangs have a relatively short history, short enough that by size, duration, subgrouping, and territoriality, it is unclear whether they will grow and solidify into the more traditional forms or simply remain as less complex groups.

The Collective Gang. The collective gang looks like the compressed form, but bigger and with a wider age range—maybe 10 or more years between younger and older members. Size can be under 100 but is probably larger. Surprisingly, given these numbers, it has not developed subgroups and may or may not be a territorial gang. It probably has a 10- to 15-year existence.

In sum, the collective gang resembles a kind of shapeless mass of adolescent and young adult members and has not developed the distinguishing characteristics of other gangs.

The Specialty Gang. Unlike the other gangs, which engage in a wide variety of criminal offenses, crime in this type of group is narrowly focused on a few offenses; the group comes to be characterized by the 'specialty. The specialty gang tends to be small—usually 50 or fewer members—without any subgroups in most cases (there are exceptions). It probably has a history of less than 10 years but has developed a well-defined territory. Its territory may be either residential or based on the opportunities for the particular form of crime in which it specializes. The age range of most specialty gangs is narrow, but in a few others is broad.

In sum, the specialty gang is crime-focused in a narrow way. Its principal purpose is more criminal than social, and its smaller size and form of territoriality may be a reflection of this focused crime pattern.

The two traditional types share subgroups and a strong territorial orientation. The compressed structure can be distinguished somewhat from the traditional types by smaller size and, most commonly, by more recent onset. The compressed, collective, and specialty types have no subgroups and have briefer durations (except the collective type). The reader will note that we have explicitly avoided mentioning crime patterns except in the case of the specialty type. In fact, crime specialization is what defines this type, and it's important for our research concerns to be able to distinguish drug gangs, burglary rings, and the like from other gang types.

We had some concern about the foundation of these scenarios, as they are built upon the "best-known" gangs. We couldn't assume that they are typical of the gangs in the country, and yet the content of the scenarios seems to make sense and have face validity. One exception is the collective type. Collective gangs are fairly large in size and age range and have been around for 10 to 15 years, yet have no subgroup structure. This was a residual category and that may explain some of the ambiguity in the structural characteristics of this type. Should data collection validate this as a meaningful gang type, it would certainly be interesting to know more about the organizational features that keep these gangs together.

The critical methodological problem with the phase I data was the need to fall back on our respondents' knowledge of the single gang that each knew best. If the attempts to measure the prevalence of the five structures nationally were to yield dissent, we wouldn't know whether to attribute this to structural variability or to the biases inherent in our phase I process. Thus the importance of a second research phase becomes obvious; we needed to validate these five types of groups in a totally independent sample of cities.[4]

The Phase II Sample

If consistent handling of the scenarios were to emerge in phase II, and if the five types did indeed encompass a good proportion of the gangs under the purview of our respondents, then we could feel more secure about the validity of the structural depictions. The phase II interviews allowed for data to invalidate our phase I finding of only five major types, because they sought not only the prevalence of the five types, but explicitly sought the existence of alternative structures as well.

We start our report of the phase II data with two promising results. First, while our phase II respondents did indeed offer descriptions of alternative structures, we found in coding these by the characteristics listed in Table 11.1 that the majority of the "alternative" structures were not alternatives at all; they fit neatly into the five structures. Return phone calls to the respondents revealed that these alternative listings were merely the result of some confusion about our instructions.

The second result is that the remaining alternative structures comprised only 5% of the total numbers of gangs enumerated by our respondents. In other words, the five scenarios representing types of street gangs seemed to have captured the vast bulk of gangs across the nation. We were surprised by how well the typology worked; we are no longer concerned about its derivation from the initial 59 best-known gangs.

The data on gang structure prevalence in phase II are taken from the 201 returns from a random sample of police gang experts in 250 cities out of the almost 800 identified in our earlier research. This return rate of 80%, although below the 90–95% return rate we have had in our prior law enforcement research, is nonetheless very substantial and not a source of concern. The instructions were as follows:

The enclosed survey should take only a few minutes to complete. The first two pages describe five types of gangs, based upon information we have received from law enforcement gang experts throughout the country. Please read all five descriptions first; then consider which type or types generally describe the gang forms in your city. The fit need not be perfect, but should be substantially correct. Then, answer the questions on page three. If some gangs do not fit any of the five descriptions, the questions on page four request information about these alternative gang forms. We'd like you to focus on the form or structure of your city's gangs first, without regard to crime. After you have completed page four, please turn the page and respond to the questions about crime on page five and about your records (page 6). Then, return the survey to us in the enclosed envelope.

Table 11.2 provides a summary of gang structures prevalence data for 2,860 gangs in 201 cities. We call attention to the following:

- In row 1, cities containing compressed gangs are the most common, and those with collective structures the least. Since most of the classic gang literature of the 1950s and 1960s was based principally on traditional, not compressed structures, it is immediately clear that a reconsideration of gang "knowledge" is called for in the modern era.

- In row 2, cities that are *predominantly* of one type of gang reveal an even stronger pattern of compressed gang prevalence. Both rows 1 and 2 reveal that most cities will typically be more familiar with non-subgrouped gangs.

- In row 3 (reading the percentages horizontally), we see that this general pattern also applies to the number of gangs. Gangs with age-graded or geographically based subgroups are less common than the three more homogeneous structural forms, particularly the compressed type.

- In the five subrows on ethnicity (now reading the percentages vertically), we see that, in line with most scholarly reports, the vast majority of gangs are composed of minority groups, principally and equally Hispanic and black. The marginal percentages (i.e., the final column) are 30% Hispanic, 31% black, 10% white, 13% Asian, and 16% mixed. The largest single percentage is for Hispanics in the traditional structure (57%), yet even here other ethnic groups are found in this structure. Neotraditional and compressed structures, the two most common types, show fairly similar patterns of ethnic composition, with Hispanics and blacks predominating as they do generally. Clearly the common stereotype among police and media reports of a generalized "black gang" or "Hispanic gang" form is incorrect and misleading. As we note repeatedly, group process trumps ethnicity in the world of street gangs.

- In the first table note (*), we list for cities with specialty gangs what their predominant crime type was (asked only with respect to specialty structures). Drug gangs, while a bit more prominent than other specialty types, certainly do not dominate the picture to

Table 11.2 Gang Structures in 201 Cities

	Traditional	Neotraditional	Compressed	Collective	Specialty	Totals
# cities	75	100	149	40	76*	
# cities with predominance**	15	24	86	6	14	
# of gangs across cities	316 (11%)	686 (24%)	1,111 (39%)	264 (9%)	483 (17%)	2,860
Hispanic	179 (57%)	229 (33%)	292 (26%)	62 (23%)	95 (20%)	857 (30%)
black	63 (20%)	191 (28%)	340 (31%)	125 (47%)	155 (32%)	874 (31%)
white	38 (12%)	34 (5%)	152 (14%)	10 (4%)	49 (10%)	283 (10%)
Asian	15 (5%)	73 (11%)	156 (14%)	49 (19%)	85 (18%)	378 (13%)
mixed & other	21 (7%)	159 (23%)	171 (15%)	18 (7%)	99 (20%)	468 (16%)

* Specialty focus: drugs (24), graffiti (20), assault (17). Others included burglary, auto, theft, robbery.
** Fifty-six cities showed no predominance of one gang structure, defined as a type appearing twice as often as any other.

the extent that law enforcement and media reports would suggest. Respondents in the 24 cities with drug gangs were asked how many such gangs there were; the result is an estimated maximum of 244 gangs with a drug focus, or about 8.5% of the 2,860 gangs reported in total. These data are at considerable variance with widely circulated reports in the media and many public statements made by prominent law enforcement officials and legislative members, state and federal, to the effect that street gangs have taken over much of the drug trade. They are in line, however, with other data produced by our earlier national surveys.

Not shown in Table 11.2 but of some interest is the relative "purity" of cities with respect to the five types of gang structure. Only one city reported having none of the five structures (but having an alternative structure). Fully a third of all cities reported having only one gang form, and another third reported two of the forms. Thus two-thirds of all 201 cities were relatively homogeneous with respect to the structural types. An additional 1 in 6 reported three types, and the rest reported four or all five types. A search for common pairings or groupings of structural types was not revealing, i.e., no pattern of combinations occurred that would not be predictable from their overall totals.

The five scenarios presented to our respondents, which encapsulate the "definers" of the five gang structures, do not include leadership patterns because we had little confidence in police views of gang leadership. They do not include the important dimension of group cohesiveness, because police responses on this dimension proved ambiguous; cohesiveness was not a common conception for our officers. Yet, other data were gathered that give us confidence that the five types are different in meaningful, indeed in validating, ways.

The ethnic differences, as suggested in Table 11.2, are in some cases very substantial. As we noted above, traditional gangs are more likely to be Hispanic while the collective and specialty gangs are more commonly composed of black members. We also noted that the two most common types—neotraditional and compressed—show far less ethnic or racial predominance.

Average gang size is another differentiating variable, as seen in Table 11.3. We note in particular the predicted large size of traditional gangs and small size of specialty gangs. Year of gang emergence in the city is somewhat differentiating (traditional gangs tend to be located in early onset cities), although not fully at the level we expected. The explosion in gang onsets in the 1980s probably puts limits on these differences. Size of the city shows some differences, but the common existence of two or more structures in the same city sets limits for these differences. The ambiguous collective gang is significantly a product of the largest cities.

The volume of crime attributed to the structures is also important, with the traditional and neotraditional gangs contributing the most, and specialty gangs contributing the least. Of course, this is a

Table 11.3 Selected Structural Dimensions					
	Traditional	Neotraditional	Compressed	Collective	Specialty
Average size	182	72	35	56	24
Year of onset*					
Through 1970	24%	13%	9%	15%	7%
1971–1984	28%	18%	16%	28%	15%
1985 & beyond	49%	68%	75%	56%	78%
City size > 100,000	35%	36%	28%	52%	33%
Average monthly arrests	10.9	9.2	6.1	7.4	5.7
Average monthly per member arrests	.16	.20	.22	.17	.29
*Year of onset refers to the year any gangs first appeared.					

function of average gang size. If we control for size as in the last row of Table 11.3, we see a considerable reversal; the average traditional gang member contributes the lowest number of reported arrests and the specialty gang member the highest. Specialty gangs, it should be remembered, are very much organized around their preferred crime type, be it drug sales, burglary, or some other, and are subjected to specialized law enforcement surveillance and pursuit. By contrast, the more crime-versatile traditional gang members engage in many activities which are of relatively little concern to the police. Thus, the reversed patterns of gang volume and per-member arrest rates are quite understandable and help to validate the nature of these gang structures.

We should draw special attention to the subgrouping that is typical of traditional and neotraditional gangs. In his studies of traditional gangs in Los Angeles in the 1960s, Klein (1971) based his conclusions on data describing 5 large gangs. He noted, however, that he preferred the term "gang cluster" because each contained several subgroups. If these separate cliques had been enumerated (each had its own separate name), Klein could have claimed the study not of 5 gangs but of 24 gangs.[5] Thirty years later, Alonso's comprehensive report on the Crips and Bloods in Los Angeles, one of the very few studies of the modern era to note the special subgrouping nature of traditional gangs, noted the same, continuing pattern:

> As a first step in identifying and counting gangs for this study, I identified general identities that were aligned with one of the two broad gang affiliations in Los Angeles; the Bloods or the Crips. . . . There were more specific identities observed within the gang called *clicks*. These subgroups were part of the larger gang or set. The territoriality of this analysis is based on the gang or set, not the individual subgroups or clicks. In Black gang culture of Los Angeles, a gang will develop subgroups within the gang to either distinguish different groups based on age in a hierarchical structure or based on geographic areas within the one gang. This analysis did not identify the subgroups or clicks as separate gangs and they should not be, but from reading the graffiti of these clicks, it would appear to the novice that multiple gangs were operating in any given area, when in fact all the different specific identities fall under one gang. For example the Grape Street Crips in Watts

are the same gang as the Watts Baby Loco Crips, but the latter represents a subgroup that is based on a younger group of members. The Park Village Crips in Compton have a click of younger members that operate under the name Original Tiny Gangsters that is also a part of the same gang. Gangs with large territories will also form subgroups to identify different geographic areas in the gang. For example the Eight Tray Gangster Crips divided their territory into four areas in the winter of 1980: the North Side, South Side, West Side and East Side. These specific identities were part of the larger gang and are not counted as independent groups. Similarly the East Coast Crips in Carson had different clicks based on streets, such as Tillman Ave Crips, and Leapwood Ave Crips, but these represent clicks in a non-hierarchical structure within the main gang of the Del Amo Block East Coast Crips. In some cases law enforcement will count a sub-click as a gang because it has reached a level of notoriety, and for this reason my gang counts may not be consistent with what the Los Angeles Police Department (LAPD) or the Los Angeles Sheriff's Department (LASD) have determined. (Alonso, 1999: 61–62)

We should also report that several variables do *not* reveal differences in our data. Most important, perhaps, is that our respondents did not report much of a difference in average arrests for serious crimes. We omit the data because, as we learned later in this project, their reports are necessarily based on inadequate data. . . . Region of the country did not differ; more gangs are to be found in the West and fewest in the Northeast, but this is true of all five gang types.

Additionally, we must recognize that with some of the variables noted above, including those we list as differentiating among the five types, statistical significance is not always achieved. We report the larger differences because this is an exploratory study overall, which clearly calls for further cross-validation of its findings. Equally important, many of the data are taken from police expert reports—these are *perceptions* of gang size, ethnicity, crime patterns, and so on. An officer reporting 5, 50, or 500 gangs in his jurisdiction cannot be close to a lot of the raw data at the street level. Differences that emerge do so over a miasma of informational noise and uncertainty. Those that emerge seem to "make sense"; they have construct validity, but they call for validation with other forms of data—gang by gang by gang. Such validation will prove to be expensive.

To say this does not mitigate the distinctions among the five gang structures. Rather, it calls attention to the need to assess what variables *reliably* characterize those structures. It also calls for considerable thought about the policy implications that derive from the very fact that there is a variety of structures. . . . Suffice to say at this point that to label a group a street gang does little to advance understanding of its nature or its impact in the community. Variety, not homogeneity, is the hallmark of the modern American gang.

For further clarification, it is worth noting certain kinds of gangs that do not fit within this typology of street gangs. Prison gangs do not; motorcycle gangs do not; terrorist groups do not; organized crime groups do not.

We emphasize this last group in particular because enforcement officials and the media too often place street gangs in the same category as drug cartels, La Cosa Nostra, the Mafia (Sicilian or Russian), and expanded prison gangs such as the Mexican Mafia ("la EME"). Street gangs are for the most part incapable of behaving like organized-crime groups, although there are a few large street gangs that occasionally bridge this gap, most notably Chicago's Black Gangster Disciples, Vice Lords, Latin Kings, and Black P Stone Nation or El Rukn (see Chicago Crime Commission, 1995, for a sensationalized version of these street gangs as organized-crime groups).

Organized-crime groups require mature, professionalized members—at least in the higher echelons—with organizational skills, well-defined leadership and specialized group roles, codes of conduct with clearly understood sanctions, and financial treasuries or other locations for profits to be used for group purposes; to survive, such crime groups often develop special relationships with legitimate businesses as well as political and legal institutions. Decker's (2001) comparison of street gangs and organized crime mentions a series of such characteristics of organized criminal gangs and how poorly they apply to street gangs in San Diego, St. Louis, and even Chicago. A common orientation to crime is, despite the narrow

enforcement viewpoint, hardly sufficient to classify street gangs as organized criminal groups or to suggest that forms of intervention or control for the latter are appropriate to the former.

Further Validation

Without developing new data on gangs to assess how well they are described and encompassed by our fivefold typology, we can provide tests by reviewing existing descriptions of street gangs. We do so by reference to two sets, the first from the United States and the second from Europe.

The first of these sets of descriptions are to be found in various American studies in which the authors have provided sufficient *structural* detail to allow an ex post facto categorization. Our reading of the descriptions by Klein (1971) in Los Angeles, Moore (1978) in East Los Angeles, Vigil (1988) in East Los Angeles, Short and Strodtbeck (1965) in Chicago, W. Miller (1962) in Boston, the New York City Youth Board (1960) in New York, Sanders (1994) in San Diego, and Hagedorn (1988) in Milwaukee all yield the common features of the traditional gang. The picture provided by Decker and Van Winkle (1996) in St. Louis suggests neotraditional gangs. Fleisher's (1998) ethnography of Kansas City male and female gang members provides a rare glimpse at a collective gang. Padilla's depiction of a Puerto Rican drug-selling gang in Chicago (1992), the Brightwood Gang in Indianapolis described by McGarrell and Chermak (2003), the description of a small group of Dominican drug sellers by Williams (1989), the depiction of drug gangs in south Texas offered by Valdez and Sifaneck (2004), and the unique financial analysis of a drug gang's operations in Chicago over four years presented by Venkatesh (1999) and Levitt and Venkatesh (1999) clearly illustrate the structure of specialty gangs. Jody Miller (2001), describing female-involved gangs in Columbus and St. Louis, deliberately applied the typology to the groups in those two cities to very good effect. Thus, where descriptions permit it, the typology seems applicable and useful. It is worth noting, nonetheless, that compressed gangs have not been described despite their ubiquitousness and are probably the forms from which the Rochester, Denver, and Seattle longitudinal data are taken (see

Thornberry and Porter, 2001, on gangs in traditional and emergent gang cities).

Two recent applications of the typology offer further support. Scott (2000) presented the typology to officials in 887 Illinois police agencies. Returns were received from 88% of these. Seventy-four percent of the street gangs in these jurisdictions fit within the typology[6] without further analysis. Similarly, the National Youth Gang Center (2000) analyzed data from a nationally representative sample of police jurisdictions. This sample of 265 agencies placed 74% of their gangs within the typology, in this case with neotraditional types accounting for 39% of the total and compressed following closely with 35%. In neither study were the 26% nonfitting gangs further analyzed, but our experience with our own 201 respondents suggests that some number of the nonfitters might well have fallen into the typology as well. In any case, these two applications of the typology provide evidence for its utility.

The second validation comes from views of street gangs in Europe. Perhaps the most famous of the European studies is James Patrick's 1973 ethnography, *A Glasgow Gang Observed*, in which the traditional structure is well illustrated. Klein's more recent review of reports and observations (Klein, 1996) found traditional gangs reported in Kazan, Berlin, and Brussels; specialty (drug) gangs in Manchester, Berlin (skinheads), and Stockholm; compressed gangs in Stockholm, Zurich, Frankfurt, and Stuttgart; and neotraditional gangs in Berlin. None of the cities visited reported gangs not fitting the typology, although various cities of course reported not having street gangs of any sort.

An additional opportunity is provided by Weitekamp (2001) in his review of reports on European gangs in a compendium of gang reports by various European authors in 1998 and 1999. This reading of these reports yields traditional gangs in Kazan; neotraditional gangs in Manchester; compressed gangs in Manchester, Copenhagen, Frankfurt, Oslo, and Paris; and specialty gangs in the Hague and Rotterdam. Descriptions not yielding data for placement in the typology came from Bremen and Slovenia. This review, like those above, is an after-the-fact exercise and has to be considered more as illustration than as proof. Nonetheless

the fact that the exercise "works" provides further confidence in the utility of the structural typology, far more so it seems to us than in the case with the earlier behavioral and structural typologies offered in the gang literature. . . .

Notes

1. We start the latter period with Miller, despite his major role during the classical period because his 1970s work was the first to make the attempt in more than one research site, a *sine qua non* of the comparative goal.
2. See also the rather strange ethnic "typology" presented to a national sample of prosecutors and reported by Johnson, Webster, and Connors (1995). It consisted of locally-based African-American gangs; gangs based in the Los Angeles area (e.g., Crips and Bloods); gangs with origins in the Caribbean; Hispanic gangs; Asian gangs; motorcycle gangs; hate gangs (e.g., KKK, Aryan Nation); other.
3. These materials were first reported by us in the *Journal of Gang Research*, 1995, 3(1): 33–40 and are reproduced here with permission.
4. Other typologies mentioned earlier have *not* been cross-validated in independent studies. Attempts have been made in the case of the Cloward and Ohlin categories, but successful replication has generally failed.
5. This included 16 male and 8 female "gangs."
6. Not surprisingly, given the dominance of Chicago's "supergangs," traditional gangs were reported to be most common in Illinois (about 30% of the cases reported). Next most common were compressed gangs at 24%.

References

Alonso, Alejandro A. 1999. Territoriality among African-American street gangs in Los Angeles. Master's thesis, Department of Geography, University of Southern California.

Ball, Richard and G. David Curry. 1995. The logic of definition in criminology: Purposes and methods for defining "gangs." *Criminology* 33(2): 225–245.

Battin, Sara R., Karl G. Hill, Robert D. Abbot, Richard F. Catalano, and J. David Hawkins. 1998. The contribution of gang membership to delinquency beyond delinquent friends. *Criminology* 36: 93–115.

Bjorgo, Tore. 1997. *Racist and right wing violence in Scandinavia*. Oslo: Tano Aschehoug.

Carney, Frank, Hans W. Mattick, and John D. Callaway. 1969. *Action on the streets*. New York: Associated Press.

Chicago Crime Commission. 1995. *Gangs: Public enemy number one*. Chicago: Chicago Crime Commission.

Cloward, Richard A. and Lloyd E. Ohlin. 1960. *Delinquency and opportunity: A theory of delinquent gangs*. New York: The Free Press.

Cohen, Albert K. and James F. Short, Jr. 1958. Research in delinquent subcultures. *Journal of Social Issues* 14: 20–37.

Decker, Scott H. 2001. The impact of organizational features on gang activities and relationships. In *The Eurogang paradox: Street gangs and youth groups in the U.S. and Europe*, ed. Malcolm W. Klein, Hans-Juergen Kerner, Cheryl L. Maxson, and Elmar G.M. Weitekamp. Dordrecht: Kluwer Academic Publishers.

Decker, Scott H. and G. David Curry. 2000. Addressing key features of gang membership: Measuring the involvement of young members. *Journal of Criminal Justice*, 28: 473–482.

Decker, Scott H. and G. David Curry. 2002. Gangs, gang homicides, and gang loyalty: Organized crimes of disorganized criminals? *Journal of Criminal Justice*, 30: 1–10.

Decker, Scott H. and Barrik Van Winkle. 1996. *Life in the gang: Family, friends, and violence*. Cambridge: Cambridge University Press.

DeFleur, Lois. 1967. Delinquent gangs in cross-cultural perspective: The case of Cordoba. *Journal of Research in Crime and Delinquency* 4: 132–141.

DiChiara, Albert. 1997. We ain't no gang, we a family!: Gangs as projects. Paper presented at the 1997 meeting of the American Society of Criminology. Hartford: University of Hartford, Department of Sociology.

Downes, David M. 1966. *The delinquent solution: A study in subcultural theory*. New York: The Free Press.

Esbensen, Finn-Aage and David Huizinga. 1993. Gangs, drugs, and delinquency in a survey of urban youth. *Criminology* 31(4): 565–587.

Fagan, Jeffrey. 1989. The social organization of drug use and dealing among urban gangs. *Criminology* 27: 633–669.

Fleisher, Mark. 1998. *Dead end kids: Gang girls and the boys they know*. Madison: University of Wisconsin Press.

Freng, Adrienne and L. Thomas Winfree. 2004. Exploring race and ethnic differences in a sample of middle school gang members. In *American youth gangs at the millennium*, ed. Finn-Aage Esbensen, Stephen G. Tibbetts and Larry Gaines, 142–162. Long Grove, IL: Waveland Press.

Hagedorn, John M. (with Perry Macon). 1988. *People and folks: Gangs, crime, and the underclass in a rustbelt city*. Chicago: Lakeview Press.

Hamm, Mark S. 1993. *American skinheads: The criminology and control of hate crime*. Westport, CT: Praeger.

Huff, C. Ronald. 1989. Youth gangs and public policy. *Crime and Delinquency* 35: 524–537.

Johnson, Claire, Barbara Webster, and Edward Connors. 1995. *Prosecuting Gangs: A National Assessment*. Washington, D.C. U.S: Department of Justice, Office of Justice Programs, National Institute of Justice.

Klein, Malcolm W. 1971. *Street gangs and street workers*. Englewood Cliffs, NJ: Prentice-Hall.

Klein, Malcolm W. 1984. Offense specialization and versatility among juveniles. *British Journal of Criminology* 24: 185–194.

Klein, Malcolm W. 1995. *The American street gang: Its nature, prevalence, and control*. New York: Oxford University Press.

Klein, Malcolm W. 1996. Gangs in the United States and Europe. *European Journal on Criminal Policy and Research* 4(2): 63–80.

Levitt, Steven D., and Sudhir Venkatesh. 1999. *An economic analysis of a drug-selling gang's finances*. Chicago: Department of Economics, University of Chicago.

McGarrell, Edmond F. and Steven Chermak. 2003. Problem solving to reduce gang and drug-related violence in Indianapolis. In *Policing gangs and youth violence*, ed. Scott H. Decker. Belmont, CA: Wadsworth.

Miller, Jody. 2001. *One of the guys: Girls, gangs, and gender*. New York: Oxford University Press.

Miller, Walter B. 1962. The impact of a "total community" delinquency control project. *Social Problems* 10(2): 168–191.

Miller, Walter B. 1980. Gangs, groups, and serious youth crime. In *Critical issues in juvenile delinquency*, ed. David Shichor and Delos H. Kelly, 115–138. Lexington: D.C. Heath.

Monod, Jean. 1967. Juvenile gangs in Paris: Toward a structural analysis. *Journal of Research in Crime and Delinquency* 4: 142–165.

Moore, Joan W. 1978. *Homeboys: Gangs, drugs, and prison in the barrios of Los Angeles*. Philadelphia: Temple University Press.

Moore, Joan W. 1991. *Going down to the barrio: Homeboys and homegirls in change*. Philadelphia: Temple University Press.

National Youth Gang Center. 2000. Special Survey Preliminary Results (unpublished). Tallahassee: National Youth Gang Center.

New York City Youth Board. 1960. *Reaching the fighting gang*. New York: New York City Youth Board.

Padilla, Felix M. 1992. *The gang as an American enterprise*. New Brunswick: Rutgers University Press.

Patrick, James. 1973. *A Glasgow gang observed*. London: Eyre Methuen.

Salagaev, Alexander. 2001. Evolution of delinquent gangs in Russia. In *The Eurogang paradox: Street gangs and youth groups in the U.S. and Europe*, ed. Malcolm W. Klein, Hans-Juergen Kerner, Cheryl L. Maxson, and Elmar G.M. Weitekamp, 195–202. Dordrecht: Kluwer Academic Publishers.

Sanchez-Jankowski, Martin. 1991. *Islands in the street: Gangs and American urban society*. Berkeley: University of California Press.

Sanders, William B. 1994. *Gangbangs and drive-bys: Grounded culture and juvenile gang violence*. New York: Aldine de Gruyter.

Scott, Greg. 2000. *Illinois law enforcement responses to street gangs: Interim report*. Chicago: Gang Crime Prevention Center, Office of the Illinois Attorney General.

Sherif, Muzafer, and Carolyn W. Sherif. 1967. Group process and collective interaction in delinquent activities. *Journal of Research in Crime and Delinquency* 4(1): 43–62.

Short, James F. Jr., and Fred L. Strodtbeck. 1965. *Group process and gang delinquency*. Chicago: University of Chicago Press.

Spergel, Irving. 1964. *Racketville, Slumtown, Haulburg: An exploratory study of delinquent subcultures*. Chicago: University of Chicago Press.

Spergel, Irving. 1966. *Street gang work: Theory and practice*. Reading, MA: Addison-Wesley.

Taylor, Carl S. 1990. *Dangerous society*. East Lansing: Michigan Sate University Press.

Thornberry, Terence P., Marvin D. Krohn, Alan J. Lizotte, Carolyn A. Smith, and Kimberly Tobin. 2003. *Gangs and delinquency in developmental perspective*. Cambridge: Cambridge University Press.

Thornberry, Terence P., and Pamela K. Porter. 2001. Advantages of longitudinal research designs in studying gang behavior. In *The Eurogang paradox: Street gangs and youth groups in the U.S. and Europe*, ed. Malcolm W. Klein, Hans-Juergen Kerner, Cheryl L.

Maxson, and Elmar G. Weitekamp, 59–78. Dordrecht: Kluwer Academic Publishers.

Thrasher, Frederic M. 1927. *The gang: A study of 1313 gangs in Chicago*. Chicago: University of Chicago Press.

Valdez, Avelardo, and Stephen Sifaneck. 2004. "Getting high and getting by": Dimensions of drug selling behavior among American Mexican gang members in South Texas. *Journal of Research in Crime and Delinquency* 41(1): 82–105.

Vaz, Edmond W. 1962. Juvenile gang delinquency in Paris. *Social Problems* 10(1): 23–31.

Venkatesh, Sudhir. 1999. The financial activity of a modern American street gang. *NIJ Research Forum* (November): 1–11.

Vigil, James D. 1988. *Barrio gangs: Street life and identity in Southern California*. Austin: University of Texas Press.

Weisel, Deborah Lamm. 2002. The evolution of street gangs: An examination of form and variation. In *Responding to gangs: Evaluation and research*, ed. Winnie L. Reed and Scott H. Decker, 25–65. Washington, D.C.: National Institute of Justice.

Weisel, Deborah Lamm, Scott H. Decker, and Timothy S. Bynum. 1997. *Gangs and organized crime groups: Connections and similarities*. Washington, D.C.: Police Executive Research Forum.

Weitekamp, Elmar G. M. 2001. Gangs in Europe: Assessments at the millennium. In *The Eurogang paradox: Street gangs and youth groups in the U.S. and Europe*, ed. Malcolm W. Klein, Hans-Juergen Kerner, Cheryl L. Maxson, and Elmar G. M. Weitekamp, 309–322. Dordrecht: Kluwer Academic Publishers.

Williams, Terry. 1989. *The cocaine kids: The inside story of a teenage drug ring*. Reading, MA: Addison-Wesley.

Yablonsky, Lewis. 1963. *The violent gang*. New York: The MacMillan Company.

CHAPTER 12

Hate Groups or Street Gangs? The Emergence of Racist Skinheads

Pete Simi

There was for a long time an assumption among gang researchers that skinhead gangs should not be considered "street gangs," any more than were prison gangs or motorcycle gangs. However, skinhead gangs, especially those with adolescent and young adult membership, can be seen in this chapter to fit well within the category of "specialty gangs," as described in the previous chapter. They share many of the structural characteristics of other specialty street groups such as drug gangs, tagger crews, auto theft cliques, and the like. Simi's description of his historical, observational, and interview procedures illustrates the advantage of getting "in close" measures of the group structures and processes that characterize street gangs. It is also clear that the racial ideology of the skinheads does not mean that they deserve to be studied separately: their racism is rather a dominant descriptor *of their nature, not a definer (as noted in Chapter 1 of this book).*

Although the emergence of racist skinheads during the 1980s provided gang researchers with a rich opportunity to examine one type of white gang, skinheads typically have been excluded from gang studies on the grounds that they are better understood as "hate groups" and/or "terrorists," sharing little in common with traditional street gangs (Curry and Decker 2003; Hamm 1993; Hicks 2004; Klein 1995; Moore 1993; Schneider 1999).[1]

In contrast to street gangs, racist skinheads have been portrayed as closely organized around an ideological system of "Aryan supremacy" (Hamm; Hicks; Klein)[2] and as lacking traditional gang territorial claims. Moreover, it is commonly believed that skinheads differ from traditional gangs in that they do not spend significant amounts of time "hanging out" on the streets; instead, they are said to be "inside . . . working on their materials; or if outside, they're looking for a target, not just lounging around. . . . Skinheads and bikers are focused, always planning. . . . Skins prefer narrower ranges of trouble" (Klein, 22).

A careful review of the literature suggests the inadequacy of conceptualizations of racist skinheads as distinct from traditional youth street gangs. Baron's (1997) study of Canadian racist skinheads and Anderson's (1987) study of San Francisco skinheads, for example, found these youth to be neither highly organized nor politicized. Skinhead youth lived on the streets or in other transient circumstances (e.g., crash pads) and often used violent and other criminal means for survival and the settlement of disputes with other urban and suburban youth cliques.[3]

This chapter examines the early development of Southern California skinheads (1981–1985) in relation to the larger sociohistorical context of gang formation.[4] Racist skinheads are shown to parallel conventional gangs along three dimensions: (1) organizational structure, (2) territoriality and group conflict, and (3) participation in nonspecialized criminal activity.[5]

Defining Skinheads as Gangs

A gang is defined here as an age-graded peer group that exhibits some permanence and establishes a sense of boundaries through gang-identified territory, style, and such oppositional practices as fighting and criminal activity (Decker and Van Winkle 1996; Klein 1995; Short and Strodtbeck 1965/1974). Although I share reservations about the inclusion of criminal activity in the definition of gangs, I argue that regardless of whether the street, youth, or criminal dimension is emphasized, skinhead groups meet the criteria commonly used to define gangs and thus fall within the same conceptual rubric. Some observers (Anderson, Mangels, and Dyson 2001) argue further that all "hate groups" should be viewed as gangs. This overly broad position, however, ignores the overtly political nature of hate groups such as the Ku Klux Klan.[6] While the Klan has consistently used racial intimidation and violence throughout its long history, it is more accurately conceptualized as a social movement organization (McAdam and Snow 1997) rather than a street or youth gang. Most members are adults, their territorial claims have always been broader than the local neighborhood, and throughout most of its history the Klan has sought political power in order to enact a broad platform of ideals that include conservative traditional patriarchal family forms, prohibitions against "race mixing," extreme anti-Semitism, and militant Aryan nationalism (Ferber 1998). In contrast, most skinheads become involved between the ages of twelve and nineteen (Anti-Defamation League 1995; Moore 1993; Wooden and Blazak 2001),[7] and they tend to coalesce around a unique music, style, argot, and set of practices that are autonomous and distinct from adult hate groups such as the Klan (Bjorgo 1998; Wooden and Blazak).

History of U.S. Skinheads

British scholars analyzed the original skinheads in England during the late 1960s using a neo-Marxist-inspired conception of youth subculture (Brake 1974; Clarke 1976; Hebdige 1979; Knight 1982). These studies tend to focus exclusively upon style, which they explain as an attempt to resolve a marginal working-class status in a class-based society.[8] Following the emergence of skinheads in the United States during the late 1970s, most American observers—like their British predecessors—also portrayed skinheads as qualitatively distinct from traditional gangs (Curry and Decker 2003; Hamm 1993; Hicks 2004; Klein 1995; Moore 1993; Schneider 1999).

The relatively small literature examining U.S. skinheads describes their emergence, development, and organizational characteristics at the broadest possible level, offering little specificity regarding the ground level of social action (for example, see Etter 1999; Hamm 1993; Hicks 2004; Kaplan 1995; Knox 2000; McCurrie 1998; Moore 1993; Wood 1999; Wooden and Blazak 2001; for an exception, see Anderson 1987). These broad depictions of skinheads have not been well suited to examining issues related to the local dimensions of skinhead emergence and development. Additionally, conceptualization of American skinheads has been divorced from the historical precedence of racial antagonism typical of many conventional gangs (see Curry and Decker 2003; Hagedorn 1988; Schneider 1999; Short and Strodtbeck 1965/1974).

The development of skinhead gangs was directly related to conflict with other youth groups (jocks, cowboys, rockers, minority gangs, etc.). This is not to say, as claimed by some observers, that early skinheads were "nonracist" (Sarabia and Shriver 2004; Wood 1999). My data clearly indicate that racism has been a component of skinhead identity from the beginning (see also Moore 1993); however, it was not initially attached to a broader political agenda and did not include participation in racist political activism.

Methods and Data

Between 1999 and 2004, I conducted participant observation and in-depth interviews in a variety of settings in order to examine the emergence and development of Southern California skinheads. I used a snowball sampling technique to locate skinheads in the Los Angles area, where the largest number have been thought to exist (Anti-Defamation League 1989). In all, I obtained data regarding seventeen Southern California skinhead gangs and their members.

My analysis is based primarily on 127 interviews conducted with forty-three current and former racist skinheads. These interviews were supplemented with data from interviews that I conducted with fourteen law enforcement officers and several "nonskinhead" white-power movement leaders (e.g., Tom Metzger and Richard Butler), who were among the first to promote the importance of recruiting skinheads to the white supremacist movement.[9] Skinhead interviewees were selected by means of purposive snowball sampling strategies, which enabled me to access a wide range of skinheads from various different groups (e.g., Orange County Skins, Norwalk Skins, American Firm, etc.). Most of the skinhead interviewees were male, reflecting the predominance of males in the skinhead subculture (Blee 2002). No clear social class pattern was found among interviewees, which is not surprising in view of the cross-section of social classes represented among skinheads in general (Anderson 1987; Hamm 1993). Interviews focused primarily on group history, how individuals became skinheads, group activities and practices, organizational characteristics, and recruitment strategies.

The range of events I observed with skinheads in Southern California included house parties and other social gatherings, white-power music concerts, and twenty-three home visits, ranging in length from one day to three weeks. Participant observation provided data regarding group practices and allowed me to build rapport with key informants who served as gatekeepers, introducing me to other skinheads and providing much-needed references for further interviews. Participant observation and interviewing allowed for close examination of a wide range of information that is impossible to obtain solely through secondary sources (Blee 2002).

Secondary data sources included antiracist watchdog organizations' (e.g., Anti-Defamation League) official reports, newspaper accounts, court documents, and various types of documentary evidence that law enforcement officials provided (e.g., videotaped interviews of skinheads conducted by law enforcement personnel, written correspondence among skinheads, etc.). These documents, as well as skinhead texts, such as newsletters, websites, and Internet discussion groups, were content analyzed and studied for corroboration or contradiction of insights gleaned from primary interview data.[10] This multimethod approach allowed for triangulation across an array of data (Denzin 1978).

There are methodological difficulties with studying skinheads. Because I am not a member of these groups, entree was difficult. Skinheads are often antagonistic toward outsiders and tend to prefer secrecy. Moreover, skinhead networks are diverse and loosely structured. After meeting a skinhead in his midthirties who was originally from Long Beach, California, at an Aryan Nations gathering in northern Idaho, I obtained e-mail access to several other relatively older skinheads from Southern California. I made contact with these skinheads (via e-mail) requesting, as a sociologist, opportunities to observe various skinhead events and to conduct life history interviews. Eventually these requests were granted, the only condition being that I was white. The first meeting occurred at a bar in Orange County, at which time contacts were made for further observations and interviews. The initial contacts led to further communication with other skinheads from various groups. These contacts snowballed into the sample described above. Reliance on nonprobability sampling was necessary, due to the hidden character of the population (see Heckathorn 1997, 2002 for an alternate respondent-driven sampling approach for hidden populations). At times my status was challenged, and I was accused of working in concert with law enforcement agencies or as an agent provocateur. Some of these challenges resulted in threats of bodily harm, although none occurred. Clearly these obstacles prevented me from gathering certain types of data (e.g., gang rosters), as did the refusal by certain skinheads to participate in the study.[11] My generalizations about racist skinhead gangs must, therefore, remain modest and tentative.

Subcultural Schism and the Transition from Punk to Skin

Although the skinhead style spread to America through a process of international cultural diffusion, Southern California skinheads formed in response to microlevel changes in the local punk rock scene and macrolevel changes in the wider social structure. In the late 1970s, Southern California punk started getting "hardcore" (Blush 2001; Spitz and Mullen 2001), signaling a more violent and suburban trend in punk rock. *Hardcore* referred to a faster style of music and a hostile attitude, which was expressed through random violence directed at other punks during music shows. For young suburban kids, hardcore aggressiveness provided an important security device against those antagonistic toward punk style:

> Around that time [late 1970s] there were a lot of kids [punks] who were getting seriously fucked up by these long-haired redneck hicks in their 4x4 vehicles, real Lynyrd Skynyrd kind of guys. They were going to punk shows and hiding out in the parking lot and ambushing us, and I think a couple of people died. . . . Nobody was doing anything about it. No disrespect against the Hollywood party punks . . . but they just weren't prepared to defend us out in the 'burbs where kids were getting beaten on all the time. . . . (quoted in Spitz and Mullen 2001, 192)

By the late 1970s, individuals were experimenting with the skinhead style (Moore 1993); however, these youths were submerged within the punk rock scene, and a "skinhead collective identity" had not yet developed. As hardcore continued to radicalize the punk scene, some punks merged hardcore with a "cholo" style to form punk gangs (e.g., the Suicidals, some sets of the Los Angeles Death Squad, etc.), while others formed skinhead gangs by building on the hardcore style, emphasizing a hypermasculine, clean-cut, working-class identity:

> Hardcore and skinheads were definitely connected. Hardcore took punk to a different level, to a more extreme level. You could see it with the music, the dress. . . . That's where there was a lot of overlap between skinhead and punk, and there was an overlap in members. . . . (Order Skinhead interview, 11/20/02)

One historian of punk also notes the stylistic connection between hardcore and skinhead:

> The rise of Hardcore coincided with the rise of Skinhead culture. In some ways the scenes overlapped. Edgier HC [Hardcore] types adopted Skinhead style. A shaved head provided the perfect

fuck you to Hippies. . . . Very few embraced the style and remained unfazed by the politics. Some racists' hatred was heartfelt; for others it was just a confrontational tool. . . . (quoted in Blush 2001, 31)

As these quotes suggest, there were stylistic and ideological overlaps between hardcore and skinheads, as well as important organizational linkages (Wood 1999).

Skinhead Organizational Characteristics, Social Gangs, and Street Socialization

The first skinhead gangs formed around 1981, after hardcore began splintering the punk scene. Skinhead gangs like the Northside Firm, the South Bay Skins, and the Order Skins formed across Los Angeles, Orange, San Bernardino, and Riverside counties. The early skinhead gangs were, as one member put it, "identity groups"; skinhead gangs bonded around identity markers and shared interests (e.g., shaved heads, clothing styles, musical preferences, slang, tattoos, etc.). Skinheads were building an identity with organizational names, initiation rites, semihierarchical social roles, and participation in the same type of nonspecialized, garden-variety delinquency that characterizes traditional street gangs (e.g., vandalism, underage drinking, petty theft, and, perhaps most importantly, fighting). Skinhead identity was loose, unstructured, and tied to social gatherings that were relatively unregulated, allowing for the innovation needed to create oppositional identities.

Early skinhead gangs were organized primarily around fraternal relations among members and conflict with other gangs, resembling what various observers describe as social gangs (see Fagan 1989; Maxson and Klein 1995; Schneider 1999; Short and Strodtbeck 1965/1974; Yablonsky 1962). They did not adhere to an explicit political ideology and did not engage in the conventional political activities (marches, leafleting, rallies, etc.) that eventually came to characterize some of the later skinhead gangs. Unlike Pinderhughes's (1997) Brooklyn white ethnic youth groups, which he differentiates from gangs on the basis of their lack of official names and clearly established leadership positions, the skinheads that I studied used initiation rites to mark group membership and, in some cases, established relatively formal leadership positions and other organizational roles. The level of involvement among skinheads ranged from core to peripheral, mirroring what others have found among traditional gangs (Decker and Van Winkle 1996; Klein 1995).

Skinhead gangs were part of a larger youth scene (Bennett and Petersen 2004; Cavan 1972; Gaines 1994; Irwin 1977; Polsky 1967) organized around a particular style, music, specialized language, and a range of oppositional practices that included violence (e.g., fighting) and garden-variety crime (e.g., vandalism, petty theft, drugs). The early skinhead scene was an umbrella without clearly demarcated boundaries, allowing fluid forms of participation; yet there emerged within the scene subgroups with clearer boundaries of membership (skinheads often refer to these as "crews").

> Yeah there were all the different crews and that's who you ran with. . . . Some of us got along pretty well and others didn't and we would fight with each other all the time. Back then it didn't matter if you were skinheads or not; if there was a problem between different crews we brawled. . . . They [crews] were usually about 20 or 30 skins; some were bigger and some got a lot bigger after they started recruiting heavy in the late 1980s. . . . (American Firm interview, 6/14/04)

While resembling Los Angeles Latino gang klikas, early skinhead crews had less age-graded organization than the much older Latino gangs (see J. Moore 1978, 1991; Vigil 1988, 2002); they were also less hierarchical. Such differences, however, may disappear if recent trends continue. The older traditional gang structures with age-graded subgroups and relatively well-defined territorial boundaries seem to be giving way "to relatively autonomous, smaller, independent groups, poorly organized and less territorial than used to be the case" (Klein 1995, 36). "Gangs are more mobile now and their territories may include a shopping mall rather than (or in addition to) a street or neighborhood or an area drug market" (Short 1996, 238). To some extent, the emergence of skinhead gangs reflects these changes. Although skinheads attempted to establish turf claims similar to traditional gangs, the development of high levels of mobility was necessary for attendance at hardcore music concerts and other functions of special significance to these youth. Thus early skinhead gangs included a combination of new trends (increasingly found among gangs in general) and traditional patterns of gang organization.

Street socialization is a street-based process involving peer guidance and the adoption of an alternate set of values and norms by youth who lack parental supervision and positive school experiences (Vigil 2002). Most skinheads describe their early participation as street socialization within urban and suburban locales, such as malls, parks, and music shows. Most reported spending evenings and nights walking the streets with other young skinheads and congregating at music shows and neighborhood schools and parks. In many cases this process began prior to formal affiliation with any one particular skinhead group. Subjects reported that these experiences were vital to forming bonds with other skinheads and loosening attachments to family and school, hence lessening these institutions' ability to regulate their behavior.

> We would meet up pretty much every night at the park or the school over by our house. A lot of us lived out here in Anaheim Hills or nearby so it wasn't hard for us to get together and hang out. We'd raise all kinds a hell once we were together, you know spray painting shit about skinheads ruling the streets, all kinds of shit. We'd go over and beer raid the 7–11 and go down and start fucking with other kids hanging around the park. . . . It was a blast. I wouldn't come home 'til the middle of the night and my parents would yell at me and shit, but I didn't care. . . . I stopped listening after a while. After that I started missing school and when I did go I was usually in trouble. . . . (White Aryan Resistance Skinhead interview, 6/21/04)

> I remember going out and hanging out on the street all night with "Popeye" and "Snake" you know before they started PENI [Public Enemy Number One] and before I got hooked up with WAR [White Aryan Resistance] Skins. . . . I was probably fifteen or so and we all lived pretty close. We just ran the streets getting into fights with punk gangs like the LADS [Los Angeles Death Squad] and doing all that stupid gang shit. (White Aryan Resistance Skinhead interview, 2/3/00)

Social Change, Skinhead Discontent, and Violent Territoriality

In addition to schisms in the local punk scene, skinhead formation was related to macrolevel changes involving the larger sociopolitical environment. Since the mid-1960s, increasing "nonwhite" immigration has been significantly altering California's demographics (Waldinger and Bozorgmehr 1996).[12] The initial skinhead response to these rapid social changes resembled the kind of conflict that ethnic/racial migration spurred in New York and other large urban centers a few decades earlier (see Adamson 2000; Meyer 2000; Schneider 1999; Suttles 1968). As Schneider explains regarding New York gangs:

> After World War II, the massive expansion of African-American and Puerto Rican communities redefined these conflicts, created unity among Euro-American groups around their "whiteness" and focused resentment on the newcomers . . . while efforts by African-Americans to integrate New York's schools in the 1950s led to boycotts and threats of violence by Euro-American parents. (9)

A Huntington Beach Skinhead describes in similar fashion more recent conflict between skinheads and "nonwhites":

> The blacks, we don't like the blacks. . . . We get along with some Chicanos, we don't like the Iranians, the Pakistanis, Afghanistanis, we don't like people. . . . These immigrants coming to our country that's who we're against. We didn't want them here . . . get them out if they moved into our neighborhood. We encouraged them to leave and they usually did. . . . We would burn crosses, uh Molotov cocktails, whatever it took. (Huntington Beach Skinhead interview, 3/12/89 [referring to the early and mid 1980s])

Other skinheads echo the effect of immigration on skinhead formation:

> You had all these beaners and other muds coming in here and we didn't have a chance. Jobs that should have been filled by white Americans were getting taken away and given to illegals under the table. . . . (American Front Skinhead interview, 7/19/99)

> [Orange County] was still predominantly white when I was a kid but my parents moved out here

in '73 from Chicago and it was pretty white, you know. It was right about the time they started shipping boatloads of Vietnamese refugees over here and then the Hispanics, illegal aliens, started coming up in droves and you saw the neighborhoods . . . crime-free white areas go to nonwhite cesspools. (White Aryan Resistance Skinhead interview, 3/17/02)

These statements express the social and economic anxiety and frustration that is often associated with waves of immigration (see Green, Strolovitch, and Wong 1998). Skinhead perceptions of this "social problem" were not monolithic, however. The Huntington Beach Skin expresses a degree of "tolerance" for "some Chicanos," while the American Front Skin views Hispanics as a significant threat. Thus, even among racist skinheads, ideology has important variations rather than being homogenous. In a city where they are greatly outnumbered by Hispanic gangs, white gangs that "tolerate" Hispanics are far more likely to develop ties and even alliances with Hispanic gangs. This occasionally results in "crossover" membership. What is most curious about these types of relationships is that they do not necessarily spell an end to racist beliefs. For example, in the city and surrounding areas of La Mirada (located in southern Los Angeles County), the racist skinhead gang La Mirada Punk (LMP) began in the mid-1980s as a multiethnic gang (white and Latino). As racism became a stable feature of the gang, some Latino members were purged. Today, LMP remains an active racist skinhead gang with links to various other skinhead gangs (some of whom maintain a strict "whites-only" policy of membership); yet LMP retains a membership that both a law enforcement interviewee (5/11/02) and an LMP interviewee (6/14/04) estimate is 40 percent Latino (including at least one Latino member who is in a leadership position).

Some skinhead gangs were formed to provide refuge from the perceived threat posed by minorities. This perception was related to larger structural changes, such as shifting neighborhood composition, increasing numbers of minority street gangs, and the anxiety-provoking policies surrounding busing (see also DeSena 1990; Hagedorn 1988; Meyer 2000; Rieder 1985; Schneider 1999). Each of these changes heightened interracial hostility and fear of minority-generated aggression being directed toward white youths:

> In my opinion nonwhite street gangs led to the rise of skinheads. Many whites growing up in gang-afflicted areas become victims. After being victimized or *feeling as if you are* [my italics], it's not a huge step to begin to hate that tormentor and to soon begin to hate his whole race. (White Aryan Resistance Skinhead interview, 9/10/02)

> I grew up in a pretty dark neighborhood and most of my homeboys did too. . . . We were surrounded by mostly spic gangs and all we had was each other and if we didn't want to get punked all the time then we needed to have some reinforcements to fight back . . . so yeah that [racial conflict] played a big role in how we got started and I think that was true for other skinhead gangs as well you know maybe not so much for some of the ones down in OC [Orange County] but even they were starting to get invaded by all these nonwhite gangs trying to take over neighborhoods and all that bullshit. (Norwalk Skinhead interview, 3/16/01)

These comments articulate sentiments widely shared among skinheads. Even those who did not directly experience racial antagonism were informed by the fear and resentment such conflicts engendered. From this vantage point, skinheads were not only necessary, but were a rational response to an environment that violated white youths on the basis of skin color.[13] The "victim status" (Berbrier 2000; Holstein and Miller 1990) evident in skinheads' self-definition as "working-class, white kids" who were the "new minority" tapped into the cultural heritage of working and minority populations' claims for social justice. These identities did not always correspond with objective conditions, however, as revealed by examples of kids from relatively affluent areas (e.g., Anaheim Hills) appropriating a working-class identity.[14] In this respect, skinhead gangs illustrate the elasticity of identities built around feelings of disaffection from the status quo (de Certean 1984).

Schneider (1999) argues that protecting turf and engaging in a pattern of conflict distinguish other youth formations from gangs. Defending turf, honor, and racial/ethnic pride helps gang members construct a framework for understanding their world by identifying "enemies" and crystallizing core values. The skinhead gangs I examined were not devoid of local neighborhood-based forms of territoriality, as some observers contend (Hamm 1993; Klein 1995; Moore 1993). Reflecting the tradition of street gang culture, skinheads attempted to claim territory, which could be seen in their choice of gang names (e.g., Huntington Beach Skins, Chino Hills Skins, South Bay Skins, Norwalk Skins, etc.) and their claims of specific locations (such as parks or music clubs) through the use of graffiti "tags" and other more physically aggressive means. Of the seventeen skinhead gangs I studied, thirteen attempted to claim territory by such methods as graffiti, hanging out, and/or accosting individuals who entered their turf.

Skinhead identity was formed in part around notions of protecting and defending local symbolic or turf boundaries. Situational conflict was directed toward two types of targets: First, racist skinheads attacked members of minority groups when they transgressed perceived boundaries (e.g., an African American family moving into a predominantly white neighborhood); second, racist skinheads developed rivalries with other gangs (both white and "nonwhite") primarily as a result of interpersonal disputes. A member of the American Front Skins and a member of the Huntington Beach Skins explain each type of territorial conflict:

> Well if a nigger moved in, we'd start fucking with 'em right away you know, like we'd drive by and shout, "Niggers, go back to Africa" or we'd spray paint their garage or somewhere else nearby their house to just let 'em know that we wanted them to get the fuck out. . . . (American Front Skin, 7/12/00)

> INTERVIEWER: In regards to territory, if someone from a rival gang comes into that territory, do skinheads protect that territory? And how would you do that?
>
> SKINHEAD: They tell 'em to leave, only they wouldn't do it that kindly. . . . They'd usually beat that person up you know. If it was someone from a gang, we didn't . . . like say if a LAD [predominantly white punk gang] member came into the territory in Huntington Beach that LAD would get jumped. . . . (Huntington Beach Skinhead interview, 3/12/89)

Although early skinhead violence was sometimes racially motivated, there is little evidence to suggest that these early skinhead gangs went beyond the longstanding pattern of white gangs' defense of racial neighborhood boundaries (see Adamson 2000; Meyer 2000; Rieder 1985; Short and Strodtbeck 1965/1974; Thrasher 1927). Skinhead racial identity was oppositional in localized terms, but there was no clear political program for broad social change along racial lines that is typically associated with adult hate groups like the Klan or Aryan Nations. As indicated above, much skinhead violence was directed toward other subcultural groups (e.g., other skin gangs, punks, surfers, etc.) that were also willing participants in the action. Skinheads defined their violence as a means of protecting themselves from aggressive nonskinhead groups.

> We went to all the different punk shows and mainly just fought with anyone who tried us, 'cause you had a lot of punk gangs thinking they were all cholo, like the Suis [the Suicidals gang] who were always looking to start shit. So we just went at it at pretty much every show back then. Back then we were pretty loosely organized. You know, we were a tight crew, you know, when it came to fighting, but we weren't politically organized like we were later. (Boot Boy Skinhead interview, 9/12/01)

Despite some efforts to build a neighborhood base in communities, skinheads have not developed into "quasi institutions" or even fundamental components of local neighborhoods. In this respect, early skinhead gangs resembled what Cloward and Ohlin (1960) refer to as "conflict subcultures" that lack strong neighborhood ties and engage in high levels of violence in order to gain status. Although skinheads clearly did not have the same kind of neighborhood ties as some Latino gangs that have existed in their barrios for several generations (J. Moore 1978, 1991; Vigil 1988, 2002), this difference may be due largely to historical circumstance. As these change—and if skinheads continue to maintain a presence in neighborhoods—it is possible that such ties between skinheads and their communities may develop.[15]

Conclusion

In this chapter I discuss the early development of Southern California racist skinheads and their parallels to conventional gangs. The focus on persistent and pervasive poverty has led to the view of gangs as "quasi institutions" (Hagedorn 1988; J. Moore 1991; Vigil 2002) within traditionally marginalized communities. The "underclass" emphasis, however, has neglected gang formations that are not associated with impoverished economic conditions (Horowitz 1987) and has inadvertently reproduced a narrower conception of gang membership than can be sustained in view of the economic, ethnic, and racial diversity of gangs.

At the same time, while the shaven-headed, swastika-tattooed, jackbooted youths who spew racist venom have become a powerful image associated with contemporary hate groups, few ground-level case studies explain the development and organizational characteristics of skinheads. Viewing racist skinheads primarily as terrorists and hate groups obscures their similarities to traditional minority street gangs. Overemphasis on the politicized character of racist skinheads ignores three important findings: (1) Most of the early skinhead groups meet criteria widely used for defining youth and/ or street gangs; (2) although some skinhead gangs gravitated toward a political orientation, this transition did not include all racist skinheads, and even among politicized gangs not all members shared the same level of commitment to this orientation; and (3) currently the two largest racist skinhead gangs in Southern California are entrepreneurially organized primarily around the increasingly lucrative methamphetamine trade rather than a political agenda (Simi and Smith 2004).

Observers speculate that the total number of skinheads nationwide remains relatively small; however, recent developments among skinhead gangs in Southern California demonstrate how quickly these gangs can change. Between 1996 and 2000, the Nazi Low Riders (NLR) grew from twenty-eight confirmed members to over 1,500 members in California alone (Anti-Defamation League 2004). Another Southern California–based skinhead gang, Public Enemy Number One (PENI), has grown from a few dozen members in the mid-1990s to more than five hundred current members. Despite these gangs' white supremacist orientation, their predominant focus is on profit-motivated criminal activity (e.g., methamphetamine production and distribution, identity theft, home invasions, and counterfeiting) designed for personal gain. There is no evidence that either gang uses the profits derived from these enterprises for funding larger political endeavors related to the white supremacist movement. Like early racist skinhead gangs, the NLR and PENI do not participate in racist political activism, and while their violence is sometimes racially motivated, they are more likely to engage in instrumentally motivated violence related to criminal operations or spontaneous violence related to interpersonal disputes (Simi and Smith 2004). Some skinhead gangs have become branches of the contemporary white supremacist movement, yet many other skinhead gangs remain oppositional in localized terms without a clear political program for broad social change along racial lines.

Notes

1. Adamson's (2000) analysis points to both similarities and differences between black and white gangs but does not address skinheads. A national estimate of skinheads is extremely difficult to ascertain, but most estimates suggest that skinheads are a relatively small portion of the overall gang picture (Etter 1999; Kaplan 1995). Despite small numbers, skinheads have maintained a continuous presence in the United States for the past twenty-five years and can be found in every region of the country.

2. Although antiracist and nonracist skinheads exist, this article focuses on racist skinheads (see Sarabia and Shriver 2004; Wood 1999). The distinction between racist and antiracist skinheads is relatively clear-cut; however, this was not the case initially, as factions along lines of racial ideology were originally much blurrier. Some ambiguity continues to persist as skinheads change allegiances between racist and antiracist (Blazak 2001; Finnegan 1999). Stereotyping and sound-bite terms like *racist* and *antiracist* actually obscure the process of becoming racist and encourage overly simplified explanations for this process.

3. There are far more empirical studies of European skinheads, and European scholars often distinguish between street-level skinhead youth cliques (gangs) and right-wing youth who possess an organized ideology and are actively involved in extremist political movements (Bjorgo 1998; Fangen 1998; Kersten 2001).

4. In this chapter, I focus on skinheads in Southern California. During the course of fieldwork, I conducted interviews with early skinheads in Chicago, Dallas, Denver, Detroit, Las Vegas, New York City, Philadelphia, Phoenix, Portland, Salt Lake City, and Seattle (*n* = 18). The data obtained from these interviews suggest important similarities between the emergence of skinheads in Southern California and in other locales; however, these impressions must be confirmed with in-depth case studies of skinheads in locales outside of Southern California. One interesting comparison would be skinheads' self-identification. In Southern California it is common for skinheads to describe their group as a "gang," while in other areas there is a strong stigma attached to using the term.

5. I am not arguing that no differences exist between racist skinheads and minority gangs, merely that empirical evidence suggests that conceptualizing skinheads as gangs is warranted.

6. The Klan has existed since 1865. By the 1920s, Klan membership reached a high of between 1.5 and 5 million followers, including high-ranking political figures (MacLean 1994; L. Moore 1991).

7. Because skinheads have maintained a presence in the United States since the late 1970s, there are now skinheads in their forties. However, we know very little about these "O.G." (Original Gangster) skinheads or more generally about how aging affects a skinhead's identity or life course trajectory.

8. This focus upon subcultural style has been criticized by several observers for lacking a solid ethnographic foundation (Cohen 1980; Leong 1992; Moore 1994).

9. This approach departs from previous studies of skinheads, in that I combine law enforcement data with primary interviews of skinheads. Hamm (1993) did not conduct law enforcement interviews, and his interviews of skinheads were more akin to survey questionnaires, which are not well suited to obtaining historical data. Other researchers have claimed that, because of the difficulty accessing skinheads, it is necessary to rely primarily on secondary sources in order to compile a history of skinheads (see Blee 2002; Wood 1999).

10. While some might claim that skinheads' presence on the Internet differentiates them from conventional gangs, this would be a mistake, as various gangs have developed a presence in cyberspace (e.g., 18th Street, Crips, etc.). Newspaper articles on the skinheads were drawn primarily from the *Los Angeles Times*, the *Orange County Register*, the *Los Angeles Weekly*, and the *San Bernardino Tribune*. I selected these articles through a structured, exhaustive search of the Lexis-Nexis database and microfilm indexes of the *Los Angeles Times* to

1980 using the following search terms: *skinhead, neo-Nazi, white supremacy, white power, hate* (including *hate crime, hate group,* etc.).

11. For example, one former skinhead, who was a founding member of one of the first skinhead gangs in Southern California and who is now a corporate attorney, refused to talk with me when I phoned him at his home.

12. This analysis does not posit that the predominantly suburban white neighborhoods where skinheads emerged were objectively under attack; rather, white youth who formed and joined skinhead gangs perceived that such conditions existed and were a threat—a perception with significant precedent among the larger white population (Meyer 2000).

13. Skinheads' "folk devil" status has obscured some of the motivating factors that led to their increasing racialization and has prevented a fuller understanding of the effects of external forces on skinheads' racial sentiments. While some research tends to portray skinheads as dominated by violent and irrational tendencies (see Hamm 1993; Moore 1993), skinhead grievances and violence resemble a long tradition of "normative" racial conflict in the United States (Meyer 2000).

14. Interestingly, appropriating a working-class identity can become a self-fulfilling prophecy (Merton 1968). After adopting the skinhead identity, some youth from middle-and upper-middle-class families experience downward mobility resulting from the loss of educational and economic opportunities that often accompany the skinhead emphasis on "toughness," "getting into trouble," and "anti-intellectualism" (Blee 2002; for an explanation of "how working-class kids get working-class jobs," see Willis 1981).

15. This question will be especially interesting to monitor as national demographic changes continue and "whites" become a numerical minority in the United States.

References

Adamson, Christopher. 2000. Defensive localism in white and black: A comparative history of Euro-American and African-American youth gangs. *Ethnic and Racial Studies* 23:272–98.

Anderson, Erik. 1987. Skinheads: From Britain to San Francisco via punk rock. M.A. thesis, Washington State University.

Anderson, James F., Nancie J. Mangels, and Laronistine Dyson. 2001. A gang by any other name is just a gang: Towards an expanded definition of gangs. *Journal of Gang Research* 8:19–34.

Anti-Defamation League. 1989. Annual Report. New York: Anti-Defamation League.

———. 1995. Annual Report. New York: Anti-Defamation League.

———. 2004. Nazi Lowriders. www.adl.org/learn.exr.us/nlr (accessed March 12, 2004).

Baron, Steven. 1997. Canadian male street skinheads: Street gang or street terrorist? *Canadian Review of Sociology and Anthropology* 34:125–54.

Bennett, Andy, and Richard Peterson. 2004. *Music scenes: Local, translocal, and virtual.* Nashville, TN: Vanderbilt University Press.

Berbrier, Mitch. 2000. The victim ideology of white supremacists and white separatists in the United States. *Sociological Focus* 33:175–91.

Bjorgo, Tore. 1998. Entry, bridge burning, and exit options: What happens to young people who join racist groups. In *Nation and race: The developing Euro-American racist subculture,* eds. Jeffrey Kaplan and Tore Bjorgo, 231–58. Boston: Northeastern University Press.

Blazak, Randy. 2001. White boys to terrorist men: Target recruitment of Nazi skinheads. *The American Behavioral Scientist* 44:982–1000.

Blee, Kathleen. 2002. *Inside organized racism: Women in the hate movement.* Berkeley: University of California Press.

Blush, Steven. 2001. *American hardcore: A tribal history.* Los Angeles: Feral.

Brake, Michael. 1974. The skinheads: An English working class subculture. *Youth and Society* 6:179–99.

Cavan, Shari. 1972. *Hippies of the Haight.* St. Louis: New Critics.

Clarke, John. 1976. The skinheads and the magical recovery of community. In *Resistance through rituals,* eds. Stuart Hall and Tony Jefferson, 99–102. London: Hutchinson.

Cloward, Richard A., and Lloyd F. Ohlin. 1960. *Delinquency and opportunity: A theory of delinquent gangs.* Glencoe, IL: The Free Press.

Cohen, Stanley. 1980. *Folk devils and moral panics: The creation of mods and rockers.* 2nd ed. New York: St. Martin's Press.

Curry, G. David, and Scott H. Decker. 2003. *Confronting gangs: Crime and community.* 2nd ed. Los Angeles: Roxbury Publishing.

de Certeau, Michel. 1984. *The practice of everyday life.* Translated by Steven Randall. Berkeley: University of California Press.

Decker, Scott H., and Barrik Van Winkle. 1990. *Life in the gang: Family, friends, and violence.* Cambridge, UK: Cambridge University Press.

Denzin, Norman. 1978. *The research act: A theoretical introduction to sociological methods.* New York: McGraw-Hill.

DeSena, Judith. 1990. *Protecting one's turf: Social strategies for maintaining urban neighborhoods*. Lanham, MD: University Press of America

Etter, Greg. 1999. Skinheads: Manifestations of the warrior culture of the new urban tribes. *Journal of Gang Research* 6:9–21.

Fagan, Jeffrey. 1989. The social organization of drug use and drug dealing among urban gangs. *Criminology* 27:633–69.

Fangen, Katrine. 1998. Living out ethnic instincts: Ideological beliefs among right-wing activists in Norway. In *Nation and race: The developing Euro-American racist subculture*, eds. Jeffrey Kaplan and Tore Bjorgo, 202–30. Boston: Northeastern University Press.

Ferber, Abby. 1998. *White man falling: Race, gender, and white supremacy*. Lanham, MD: Rowman and Littlefield.

Finnegan, William. 1999. *Cold new world: Growing up in a harder country*. New York: Random House.

Gaines, Donna. 1994. The local economy of suburban scenes. In *Adolescents and their music: If it's too loud, you're too old*, ed. Jonathon Epstein, 47–65. New York: Garland.

Green, Donald P., Dara Z. Strolovitch, and Janelle S. Wong. 1998. Defended neighborhoods, integration, and racially motivated crime. *American Journal of Sociology* 104:372–403.

Hagedorn, John M. 1988. *People and folks: Gangs, crime, and the underclass in a rustbelt city*. With Perry Macon. Chicago: Lake View.

Hamm, Mark. 1993. *American skinheads*. Boston: Northeastern University Press.

Hebdige, Dick. 1979. *Subculture, the meaning of style*. London: Methuen.

Heckathorn, Douglas D. 1997. Respondent-driven sampling: A new approach to the study of hidden populations. *Social Problems* 44:174–99.

———. 2002. Respondent-driven sampling II: Deriving valid population estimates from chain referral samples of hidden populations. *Social Problems* 49:11–34.

Hicks, Wendy. 2004. Skinheads: A three nation comparison. *Journal of Gang Research* 11:51–74.

Holstein, James, and Gale Miller. 1990. Rethinking victimization: An interactional approach to victimology. *Symbolic Interaction* 13:103–22.

Horowitz, Ruth. 1987. Community tolerance of gang violence. *Social Problems* 34:437–50.

Irwin, John. 1977. *Scenes*. Beverly Hills, CA: Sage.

Kaplan, Jeffrey. 1995. Right-wing violence in North America. In *Terror from the extreme right*, ed. Tore Bjorgo, 44–95. London: Frank Cass.

Kersten, Joachim. 2001. Groups of violent young males in Germany. In *The Eurogang paradox: Street gangs and youth groups in the U.S. and Europe*, eds. Malcolm W. Klein, Hans J. Kerner, Cheryl L. Maxson, and Elmar G. M. Weitekamp, 247–55. Dordrecht, The Netherlands: Kluwer.

Klein, Malcolm W. 1995. *The American street gang: Its nature, prevalence, and control*. New York: Oxford University Press.

Knight, Nick. 1982. *Skinhead*. London: Omnibus.

Knox, George. 2000. *An introduction to gangs*. 5th ed. Peotone, IL: New Chicago School.

Leong, Laurence Wei Teng. 1992. Cultural resistance: The cultural terrorism of British male working-class youth. *Current Perspectives in Social Theory* 12:29–58.

MacLean, Nancy. 1994. *Behind the mask of chivalry: The making of the second Ku Klux Klan*. Oxford: Oxford University Press.

Maxson, Cheryl L., and Malcolm W. Klein. 1995. Investigating gang structures. *Journal of Gang Research* 3:33–40.

McAdam, Douglas, and David A. Snow. 1997. *Social movements*. Los Angeles: Roxbury.

McCurrie, Thomas. 1998. White racist extremist gang members: A behavioral profile. *Journal of Gang Research* 5:51–60.

Merton, Robert K. 1957. *Social theory and social structure*. Glencoe, IL: The Free Press.

———. 1968. Self-fulfilling prophecy. In *Social theory and social structure*, ed. Robert Merton, 475–90. New York: The Free Press.

Meyer, Stephen. 2000. *As long as they don't move next door: Segregation and racial conflict in American neighborhoods*. Lanham, MD: Rowman and Littlefield.

Moore, David. 1994. *Lads in action: Social process in an urban youth subculture*. Brookfield, VT: Ashgate.

Moore, Jack. 1993. *Skinheads shaved for battle: A cultural history of American skinheads*. Bowling Green, OH: Bowling Green State University Popular Press.

Moore, Joan W. 1978. *Homeboys: Gangs, drugs, and prison in the barrios of Los Angeles*. Philadelphia: Temple University Press.

———. 1991. *Going down to the barrio: Homeboys and homegirls in change*. Philadelphia: Temple University Press.

Moore, Leonard J. 1991. *Citizen Klansmen: The Ku Klux Klan in Indiana, 1921–1928*. Chapel Hill: University of North Carolina Press.

Pinderhughes, Howard. 1997. *Race in the hood: Conflict and violence among urban youth*. Minneapolis: University of Minnesota Press.

Polsky, Ned. 1967. *Hustlers, beats, and others*. Chicago: Aldine Publishing Company.

Rieder, Jonathan. 1985. *Canarsie: The Jews and Italians of Brooklyn against liberalism*. Cambridge, MA: Harvard University Press.

Sarabia, Daniel, and Thomas F. Shriver. 2004. Maintaining collective identity in a hostile environment: Confronting negative public perception and factional divisions within the skinhead subculture. *Sociological Spectrum* 24:267–94.

Schneider, Eric. 1999. *Vampires, dragons, and Egyptian kings: Youth gangs in postwar New York*. Princeton, NJ: Princeton University Press.

Short, James F., Jr. 1996. Personal, gang, and community careers. In *Gangs in America*, ed. C. Ronald Huff, 221–40. 2nd ed. Thousand Oaks, CA: Sage.

Short, James, F., Jr., and Fred L. Strodtbeck. 1965/1974. *Group process and gang delinquency*. Chicago: University of Chicago Press.

Simi, Pete, and Lowell Smith. 2004. Public enemy number one: A natural history. Paper presented at the Academy of Criminal Justice Sciences meetings, March 9–13, in Las Vegas, NV.

Spitz, Marc, and Brendan Mullen. 2001. *We got the neutron bomb: The untold story of L.A. punk*. New York: Three Rivers Press.

Suttles, Gerald D. 1968. *The social order of the slum: Ethnicity and territory in the inner city*. Chicago, IL: University of Chicago Press.

Thrasher, Frederic M. 1927 (abridged 1963). *The gang: A study of 1,313 gangs in Chicago*. Chicago: University of Chicago Press.

Vigil, James D. 1988. *Barrio gangs: Street life and identity in Southern California*. Austin: University of Texas Press.

———. 2002. *A rainbow of gangs: Street cultures in the mega-city*. Austin: University of Texas Press.

Waldinger, Roger, and Mehdi Bozorgmehr, eds. 1990. *Ethnic Los Angeles*. New York: Russell Sage Foundation.

Willis, Paul. 1981. *Learning to labor: How working class kids get working class jobs*. New York: Columbia University Press.

Wood, Robert. 1999. The indigenous, nonracist origins of the American skinhead subculture. *Youth and Society* 31(2):131–51.

Wooden, Wayne, and Randy Blazak. 2001. *Renegade kids, suburban outlaws: From youth culture to delinquency*. 2nd ed. Belmont, CA: Wadsworth.

Yablonsky, Lewis. 1962. *The violent gang*. New York: Penguin.

CHAPTER 13

Understanding the Black Box of Gang Organization: Implications for Involvement in Violent Crime, Drug Sales, and Violent Victimization

Scott H. Decker ■ Charles M. Katz ■ Vincent J. Webb

Despite the image of street gangs as tightly and hierarchically organized groups, most research on most gangs has revealed that this portrayal is more stereotypic than realistic. Levels and forms of organization can vary widely across gangs, so there is room to study and understand what effects such variation may have on gang member behavior. In the following article, the authors tackle the effects of gang organization on the two categories of criminal behavior that have usually captured public, media, and official attention: violence and drug trafficking. The reader should note that this research was carried out on incarcerated gang members and thus concerns older and more seriously involved youth than are typical. The validity of generalizing to all gang members from particular categories of youth must be carefully considered in judging the value and limits of research on specific gangs or categories of gang members such as age group, ethnicity, gender, geographic location, and so on. Very good research can still be limited in its application.

The role of gangs in crime has been examined in a large body of research (Esbensen & Huizinga, 1993; Thornberry, Krohn, Lizotte, & Chard-Wierschem, 1993). At the individual level, a growing body of research has documented that gang membership has a disproportionate impact on crime. Individuals commit more crimes while in a gang, and those crimes tend to be more serious

than when individuals are not gang members. On the intervention side, there is ample evidence that dealing with gang members is more difficult than dealing with nongang offenders (Klein, 1995). Gang members who end up in prison also have longer and more serious involvement in crime than comparable nongang individuals (Fleisher & Decker, 2001).

Research on the aggregate impact of gangs in many large cities has been equally consistent. This research finds that cities with more gangs have more crimes of violence concentrated in those neighborhoods with high levels of gang presence (Klein, 1995). In addition, this research finds that the longer cities have gangs, the more difficult it is to eradicate those gangs (Spergel, 1995). Gangs also provide impediments to prevention, intervention, and suppression efforts.

These consistent findings about the salience of the relationship between gang membership and crime raise an important issue about the nature of the gang itself. Despite the considerable knowledge that has accumulated regarding the impact of gangs on crime, there is considerably less knowledge about the organizational and structural characteristics of gangs themselves. In a sense, gangs largely have been a "black box"; that is, little is known about the nature of the gang with regard to its structure and organization. Given the current dearth of knowledge of these characteristics, it comes as little surprise that there is a lack of knowledge of the relationship between such characteristics and the behavior of members. The current study attempts to fill these gaps, focusing on

Reprinted from: Scott H. Decker, Charles M. Katz, and Vincent J. Webb, "Understanding the Black Box of Gang Organization: Implications for Involvement in Violent Crime, Drug Sales, and Violent Victimization," *Crime & Delinquency*, 54(1): 153–172. Copyright © 2008 by Sage Publications. Reprinted with permission from Sage Publications.

the structural and organizational features of gangs and the influence of these characteristics on the behavior of gang members. In this sense, we seek to better understand the role of structural and organizational aspects of the gang on gang member behavior.

Background

Two views of the organizational features of gangs have dominated the discussion of the nature of gang organization.[1] The first is the instrumental–rational view. This view argues that gangs are rational organizations that act in ways to enhance their self-interest and behave in rational ways. This view finds its strongest support in the work of Mieczkowski (1986) and Taylor (1990) in Detroit; Padilla for some gangs in Chicago (1992); Sanchez-Jankowski in a number of cities (1991); and Skolnick, Correl, Navarro, and Rabb for California (1988). These works argue that the view of gang organizational and structural features can best be seen in the area of drug sales, though it extends to other areas such as the use of violence, neighborhood intimidation including graffiti—and some property offenses. This perspective would argue that gangs embrace common goals, motivate others to join in a common enterprise, and structure monetary activities. Such a way of looking at the organizational and structural characteristics of gangs emphasizes the formal, rational, and instrumental aspects of the organization. This view of gangs emphasizes their vertical nature and the role of internal controls on gang member behavior in creating discipline around well-established goals.

The second view of gang structure sees gangs as not well organized and less focused than the instrumental–rational view. This perspective argues that although gangs are united by several common features (names, symbols, and opposition), they are best understood by their diffuse organizational and structural characteristics. The research that supports this view points to the age range of most gang members, ages that are in the upper teens, and the developmental factors that inhibit high levels of organization among such members. In addition, this research points to the use of money generated by drug sales, robbery, and property crime among gang members, noting that most profits from such activities are used for individual purposes. The absence of a corporate use of such funds, from this perspective, is evidence of the somewhat disorganized, unstructured nature of gang organization. Research from diverse locales, including Milwaukee (Hagedorn, 1988); San Diego, Los Angeles, and Chicago (Fagan, 1989); St. Louis (Decker & Van Winkle, 1996); and Los Angeles (Maxson, Klein, & Cunningham, 1992) supports this view.

The debate about the organizational and structural characteristics of gangs is not new. Indeed, Thrasher (1929) placed the gang in the broader context of social groups. He contrasted the gang to "crowds" at the least formal level of organization to the political machine at its most formal level. Thrasher locates the gang in the middle of a larger discussion of the "Natural History" of the gang that emphasizes organizational characteristics and features of gangs (p. 70). Surprisingly, there has been little attention to the internal dynamics of the gang. Several notable exceptions exist. Hagedorn's (1994a, 1994b) study of gangs in Milwaukee examined the nature of gang organizational characteristics as well as the impact of that structure on behavior. Importantly, he found that the nature of the community as well as individual member characteristics had an impact on behavior. In most instances, drug sales were consistent with the individual–diffused model. In both studies, Hagedorn makes a compelling argument that gang members are individual entrepreneurs rather than part of well-organized groups. McGloin (2004) reports that Newark street gangs generally lack strong evidence of cohesion, despite the presence of small subgroups that have higher levels of affiliation with each other. That said, there is little evidence that the degree of organization is related to levels or types of crime. Similarly, Decker and Van Winkle (1995) report for St. Louis that gangs are generally disorganized with regard to drug sales and the profits generated from drug sales. Decker, Bynum, and Weisel (1998) found that gangs in San Diego and St. Louis are more diffuse and have weaker internal structures, whereas those in Chicago are more organized. These investigators examined the following organizational characteristics of gangs in their analysis: the presence and nature of subgroups, leaders, meetings, written rules, dues, political activities, involvement in legitimate businesses, and whether there were consequences for leaving the gang. They drew a specific link between the organizational structure of the gang and the level of organization in offending. Decker et al. (1998) also examined gang activities, but there was no specific attempt to link the organizational features of gangs to the behavior of gang members.

Maxson and Klein (1995) engineered another attempt to describe characteristics of the gang as an organizational unit. They built a typology of gang organization based on a large number (260) of telephone interviews with law enforcement officials that resulted in the identification of gang structures in 60 cities. It is important to note that this typology is based on a police sample, an approach that is different than interviews conducted with gang members. This survey built on Klein's earlier work (1971) and established four organizational structures of gangs: (1) spontaneous gangs that were small in size, lasted only a short time, and often specialized in crime types; (2) violent gangs, where the major emphasis of the gang was on fighting and stranger assaults; (3) traditional (also known as vertical) gangs that are intergenerational, include a large age range, and have versatile criminality; and (4) horizontal alliances that are temporary, cross-neighborhood alliances. The goal of the updated work was to identify *gang structures*, that is, the primary characteristics of gangs that would allow researchers and public policy to appreciate the differences across gangs. The characteristics of gangs included presence of subgroups, size, age range, duration, territoriality, and versatility. Their results identified five different types of gangs. Traditional gangs have been in existence for a long time and have clear subgroups. They have a wide age range, with territorial claims. Neotraditional gangs have much in common with traditional gangs but have a shorter life span. Compressed gangs are small, typically under 50 members, but are diverse in their criminal activities. Collective gangs are larger and have a broader age range than do compressed gangs but are not well developed. Finally, specialty gangs focus on a narrow range of offenses and have a small membership. The Maxson–Klein typology is important because of its consideration of

the influence of organizational characteristics on criminal behavior. However, this typology has yet to be tested empirically as an empirical measure of gang behavior.

Perhaps the best test of the relationship between gang structure and behavior is found in the work of Peterson, Miller, and Esbensen (2001). Using the 11-city GREAT database, they report that the organizational structure of gangs, measured in part by compositional measures such as gender, has an impact on gang behavior. Gender composition was related to the level of gang organization; notably, males in all-male gangs reported the lowest levels of organization, whereas males in gangs that had balanced gender composition had higher levels of organization. Gender compositional differences are important both for characteristics of the gang and such behavioral measures as involvement in property crime, violent crime, and drug crime.

The Present Study

Despite these advances in our understanding of the structural and organizational features of gangs, there is not enough information to specify how the organizational and structural characteristics of gangs affect criminal behavior and victimization. Stated differently, we know a fair amount about gang structures but very little about their relationship to behavior. This is a crucial omission from our understanding of gangs. After all, understanding gang structures and gang behavior without knowing their influence on behavior and victimization falls short of providing an explanation of the influence of such characteristics. Although this may seem obvious, gang research has provided more descriptive literature than analyses of relationships between gang characteristics and behavior, a notable omission. This article provides evidence about and examines in greater detail the relationship between gang structure and the behavior of gang members.

We hypothesize that members of gangs with stronger organizational structures will have higher levels of involvement in crime, commit more serious offenses, be arrested more often, and be victims of violent crime more often. These hypotheses are consistent with the enhancement approaches outlined by Thornberry, Krohn, Lizotte, Smith, and Tobin (2003), who suggest that group norms and group processes work together to increase involvement in offending while individuals are in a gang (p. 99). Group norms and group processes have a locus, which we suggest can be found in the organizational structure of the gang. We propose a similar link between gang membership and victimization. One of the most important findings in criminology in the past decade is the link between victimization and offending. Using multiple waves from the National Youth Survey, Lauritsen, Sampson, and Laub (1991) note a strong relationship between involvement in a delinquent lifestyle and victimization, particularly for males. We hypothesize that membership in a gang is a suitable proxy for involvement in a delinquent lifestyle, particularly as gang membership enhances involvement in offending.

It is important to point out from the start that this is not a test of gang member versus nongang member behavior, as much of the empirical work on gangs tends to be. Rather, this is a test of the influence of gang organization on several relevant behaviors as reported by individual gang members. The data used for the current study are particularly appropriate for this task in several ways. First, because the interviews were collected from arrestees, they represent more seriously involved juvenile offenders than school- or community-based samples. This may truncate the lower end of the distribution of gang involvement compared to at-large gang members, but is more likely to include more serious gang members. Second, the interviews were collected in three different sites in Arizona (Mesa, Phoenix, and Tucson), so the interview participants reflect more than just local enforcement practice. Finally, the demographic characteristics of gang members in this sample (race and ethnicity, gender, violent offending, drug sales, gang organization, victimization) are consistent with national trends reported by the National Youth Gang Center (Egley, 2002). The Arizona sites have a historic presence of gangs (Zatz, 1987; Zatz & Portillos, 2000), yet are not dominated by Los Angeles gangs. Finally, to provide the strongest test of these concepts, we examine the responses of current and former gang members separately. If there

is consistency in the responses of these two groups, we can more strongly conclude that the findings accurately depict the relationship between organizational structure and behavior. Because there is some evidence that current and former gang members differ in their assessment of the gang (Curry, Decker, & Egley, 2002; Thornberry, Krohn, Lizotte, Smith, & Tobin, 2003), this is an important addition to any analysis of gang structure and gang behavior. Although these data provide important measures of these concepts, they are not perfect. The data are cross-sectional, making it impossible to attribute causality. In addition, the measures of criminal involvement, arrest, and victimization are reported for the gang. Thus we are using measures of gang behavior as reported by individual members of the gang, a common characteristic of gang research, and indeed of research about collectives as reported by individual members of such collectives. Despite these limitations, however, these data provide important descriptive indicators of the influence of gang structure and organizational characteristics on behavioral outcomes.

To test these general hypotheses, we first constructed a measure of gang organization. We used a count index to assess the organizational structure of the gang, summing across dichotomous measures such as the presence of leaders, meetings, rules, punishment for violating the rules, symbols of membership, whether money is given to the group, and whether membership in the gang confers additional responsibilities for members. Each of these measures has been implicated in prior research (Decker, Bynum, & Weisel, 1998; Decker & Van Winkle, 1996; Peterson, Miller, & Esbensen, 2001) for its role in establishing more organized gangs.

We examine two indices of offense categories: an index of involvement in violent crime and an index of drug sales. The violent crime index is a count of the number of violent offenses that the gang commits, including threatening or intimidating others, committing robbery, jumping or attacking people, committing drive-by shootings, or killing people. The drug sale index is a count of the number of different kinds of drug sales that the gang is involved in, including marijuana, crack cocaine, powder cocaine, heroin, methamphetamines, and selling drugs to other drug dealers. It is important to note here that these are measures of *gang* involvement, not individuals who may be gang members. As such, these are direct measures of the influence of gang structure on the behavior of gang members, not the criminal behavior of gang members that may occur outside the direction or control of the gang. There is a large volume of gang research that documents the increased involvement of gangs and gang members in violent acts (Klein, 1995; Spergel, 1995; Thornberry, Krohn, Lizotte, Smith, & Tobin, 2003). The involvement of gangs in drug sales has a solid foundation in the literature (Decker, 2000; Decker & Van Winkle, 1995; Esbensen & Huizinga, 1993; Fagan, 1989; Maxson, Klein, & Cunningham, 1992; Skolnick, 1990). Because gang members are involved so extensively in violence, we also examine patterns of violent victimization of their members. Decker and Van Winkle (1996) and Lauritsen, Sampson, and Laub (1991) document the strong relationship between violence and victimization, particularly among gang members. Based on this literature, we include being shot at, being shot, being threatened with a gun, being threatened with another weapon, being robbed, being jumped, or being injured with another weapon. Finally, we examine an incidence measure of the number of arrests in the year prior to the interview. This index captures the extent of involvement with the criminal justice system. Indeed, there is empirical support for the hypothesis that gang members have extensive involvement with the criminal justice system, particularly at the arrest stage (Esbensen & Huizinga, 1993; Fagan, 1989; Katz, Webb, & Schaefer, 2000; Thornberry et al., 2003).

Method

The present study uses data collected as part of the Arrestee Drug Abuse Monitoring (ADAM) program. The ADAM program, originally established in 1987 by the National Institute of Justice,[2] was created to monitor drug use trends, treatment needs, and at-risk behavior among recently booked arrestees. The ADAM program collected data from recently booked arrestees in 35 sites across the United States.[3] The data used here are from two sites, Maricopa and Pima County, Arizona (aka

Arizona ADAM), that sample male and female juveniles.[4] For 14 days each quarter, trained local staff at each site conducted voluntary and anonymous interviews with juveniles who had been arrested within the last 48 hrs. At both the Maricopa and Pima County sites the catchment area for the sample encompasses the entire county. However, only those juveniles who have been detained and booked by the police are available for the study. Just over 96% of approached juvenile arrestees agreed to participate in the study.

The core ADAM juvenile data collection instrument generates self-report data on a variety of sociodemographic and behavior variables. In this article, we focus on three demographic variables (gender, ethnicity, and age), exposure to gang activity and membership, gang crime (violent offending, drug sales), violent victimization, and gang organizational measures measured by the instrument. Gang membership was determined through self-nomination, a technique that has received strong support in the research literature (Curry, 2000; Curry, Decker, & Egley, 2002; Esbensen & Huizinga, 1993; Esbensen, Winfree, He, & Taylor, 2001; Klein, 1995). We further validated our definition of gang membership by asking respondents to name the gang they belonged to. This procedure helped distinguish between those who were members of informal peer groups and those who were members of actual gangs. Only respondents who provided the name of a gang were considered gang members for this study. As such, our final sample of gang members consisted of those who self-reported association with a gang and who could name the gang.

The Arizona Sample

Juvenile data in Arizona were collected between 1999 and 2003 in three different booking facilities located in Phoenix, Tucson, and Mesa.[5] We combine data over multiple quarters of data collection and multiple catchment areas because of the need for large samples.[6] However, there are considerable similarities across the three catchment areas, justifying the aggregation of data across multiple years and sites. The descriptive characteristics of the sample are presented in Table 13.1. Table 13.1 presents a format followed in subsequent tables in that data from current gang members are contrasted to results from individuals who report ever being a member, though not currently. With regard to gender, both current and former members are overwhelmingly male, with 87% of current members and 74% of former members being males. There is consistency between current and former gang members with regard to ethnic composition. The modal category for each group is Hispanic, with roughly 60% of each group falling into this category. Whites are the next largest group, 21% of current and 31% of former members. African Americans comprised 15% of current gang members and 8% of former members. With regard to age, roughly equal percentages of 15- (23%), 16- (27%), and 17-year-olds (24%) were found among current gang members. Former gang members were a little older with 17-year-olds (37%) and 16-year-olds (24%) being the two largest categories. Every individual who self-reported gang membership identified the name of their gang, adding additional validity to the self-nomination procedure.

For the majority of individuals in the sample, a misdemeanor was the most serious offense that

Table 13.1 Characteristics of the Arizona ADAM Gang Samples		
	Current Gang Member (N = 156; percentage)	Ever a Gang Member (N = 85; percentage)
Gender		
Male	87	74
Female	13	26
Ethnicity		
Hispanic	60	57
African American	15	8
White	21	31
American Indian	3	4
Other	1	
Age		
≤ 13	9	8
14	17	13
15	23	19
16	27	24
17	24	37
Most serious charge		
Felony	24	31
Misdemeanor	43	56
Status	7	13
Other	26	
Is there gang activity in your neighborhood? (percentage responding yes)	81	65
Are people who live on your street members of a gang? (percentage responding yes)	76	51
Are there rival gangs in your neighborhood? (percentage responding yes)	55	50
In your neighborhood, is there pressure to join a gang? (percentage responding yes)	26	14
Are there problems in your neighborhood because of gangs? (percentage responding yes)	55	37
During the past 12 months, have you been arrested and booked for breaking a law whether or not you were guilty? (percentage responding yes)		75

led to their referral to the detention facility where they were interviewed. That said, 24% of current members and 31% of former gang members were referred for a felony. In addition, three quarters of each group reported that they had been arrested and booked for breaking the law at some time in the prior 12 months. Individuals in this sample were very familiar with gang activity. The majority of each group reported that there was gang activity in their neighborhood (81% of current, and 65% of former members), that people who lived on their street were members of a gang (76% and 51%, respectively), and that there were rival gangs in their neighborhood (55% and 50%). Though relatively small percentages of respondents indicated that there was pressure to join a gang in their neighborhood (26% and 14%), higher proportions reported that there were problems in their neighborhood because of gangs (55% and 37%). In sum, these two samples of youth were heavily involved in offending, and found themselves surrounded and influenced by gangs and gang activities. As such, these are appropriate samples with which to begin to understand the role of internal gang structure for gang behavior.

Findings

In Table 13.2, we examine the four indices described above. The first index includes the measure of Gang Organization. Drawing from the earlier work of Decker, Bynum, and Weisel (1998) and Peterson, Miller, and Esbensen (2001), seven measures of gang organization were used to form an index of the level of gang organization. These measures include the presence of leaders, whether the gang had regular meetings, rules, punishment for breaking the rules, symbols of membership, responsibilities to the gang, and whether or not the members give money to the gang. These seven measures tap both the structure of the gang (leaders, rules, meetings, symbols) as well as behavior (punishment,[7] responsibilities, and giving money) and represent important dimensions of how well organized a gang is. For both current and former members, symbols drew the largest percentage of positive responses (89% and 84%), with giving money to the gang drawing the lowest percentage

of positive responses (33% and 30%). Interestingly, the next smallest categories were for leaders (33% and 40%) and responsibilities to the gang (37% and 36%). A count index was constructed for these seven measures in which a "yes" response to each question about the organizational complexity of the gang was scored a "1" and summed across the seven measures. The mean for current members was 3.2 and for former members it was 4.5. This indicates a somewhat higher level of organizational complexity among gangs that former members were a part of, but in general a rather low level of organizational complexity. This is consistent with earlier work (Decker et al., 1998; Klein, 1995; Peterson et al., 2001; Zatz & Portillos, 2000), particularly because the individuals in this sample are juveniles.

The second index presented in Table 13.2 is Violent Victimization. We include seven variables: being threatened with a gun, being shot at, being shot, being threatened with another weapon, being injured with another weapon, being jumped or beaten up, and being robbed. These seven indicators tap into the major risks for violent victimization faced by gang members (Decker, 1996; Decker & Van Winkle, 1996; Sanders, 1994) and provide a measure of the extent to which gang members are at risk for being victims of violence. This is an important variable to examine in the context of the current analysis given our interest in the role of gang organization for involvement in criminal activities, and the link between violent offending and violent victimization (Lauritsen, Sampson, & Laub, 1991). Overall, these two samples were exposed to high levels of violent victimization. Seventy-five percent of current gang members and 62% of former gang members report being threatened with a gun. Being jumped or beaten up represented the modal category for each group with 82% of current members and 71% of former gang members reporting that they had experienced this form of victimization. These results provide continued support for the observation that gang members are involved in a substantial amount of violence, certainly in this case as victims. The level of victimization as measured by this seven-item index is modestly higher for current gang members (3.9) than former members (3.2).

Table 13.2 Organization, Violent Victimization, Drug Sale, and Violent Offending Index Measures

	Current Member	Ever Member
Gang organization index measures		
Does the gang have a leader?	33%	40%
Does the gang have regular meetings?	36%	46%
Does the gang have rules?	54%	46%
Is there punishment if rules are broken?	86%	79%
Does the gang have colors, symbols, signs, or clothes?	89%	84%
Do members have responsibilities to the gang?	37%	36%
Do members give money to the gang?	33%	30%
Range	0–7	0–7
Mean	3.2	4.5
Median	3.0	5.0
SD	1.9	1.9
Violent victimization index measures		
Have you ever been threatened with a gun?	75%	62%
Have you ever been shot at?	74%	57%
Have you ever been shot?	14%	11%
Have you ever been threatened with another weapon?	67%	59%
Have you ever been injured with some other weapon?	48%	31%
Have you ever been jumped or beaten up?	82%	71%
Have you ever been robbed?	28%	32%
Range	0–7	0–7
Mean	3.9	3.2
Median	4.0	3.0
SD	1.8	1.8
Drug sale index measures		
Does the gang sell marijuana?	80%	81%
Does the gang sell crack cocaine?	51%	50%
Does the gang sell powder cocaine?	53%	44%
Does the gang sell heroin?	17%	18%
Does the gang sell methamphetamine?	31%	30%
Does the gang sell drugs to other dealers?	56%	42%
Range	0–6	0–6
Mean	2.8	2.6
Median	3.0	3.0
SD	1.9	1.8
Violent crime index measures		
Does the gang intimidate or threaten others?	75%	80%
Does the gang rob people?	72%	57%
Does the gang jump or attack people?	80%	81%
Does the gang do drive-by shootings?	61%	50%
Does the gang kill people?	51%	37%
Range	0–5	0–5
Mean	2.8	3.0
Median	3.0	3.0
SD	1.9	1.5

The third index provides a measure of involvement in drug sales. The involvement of gangs and gang members in drug sales has been a consistent theme in the research about gangs (Decker & Van Winkle, 1995; Fagan, 1989; Hagedorn, 1988, 1994a, 1994b; Maxson, Klein, & Cunningham, 1992; Skolnick, 1990). We employ six indicators of involvement in drug sales to measure this dimension of gang behavior. Five of them ask specifically whether or not the gang sells a specific drug, including marijuana, powder cocaine, crack cocaine, heroin, and methamphetamines. The sixth measure asks whether the gang sells drugs to other drug dealers. It is important to note that in each case the question is whether the *gang* sells a particular type of drug rather than individual gang members. Not surprisingly, marijuana was the drug most likely to be sold by gangs (80%, 81%), followed by crack cocaine (51%, 50%) and powder cocaine (53%, 44%). The mean number of drugs sold was 2.8 for current gang members and 2.6 for former gang members. It is interesting to note that a majority of current gang members, 56%, report that their gang was involved in the sale of drugs to other dealers.

The fourth and final index that was developed for this analysis was an indicator of involvement in violent offending. Again, there is strong evidence in the literature that gangs are heavily involved in the commission of acts of violence (Decker, 2000; Maxson & Klein, 1990; Thornberry, Krohn, Lizotte, Smith, & Tobin, 2003; Tita & Abrahamse, 2004). Five specific offenses were used in constructing this scale. Gang members were asked whether the gang intimidated or threatened others, robbed people, jumped or attacked people, did drive-by shootings, or killed people. The majority of current gang members reported that their gang engaged in these activities, ranging from 80% of gang members who agreed with the statement that their gang jumped or attacked people, to a low of 51% who acknowledged that their gang killed people. For former gang members, the figures were generally lower, particularly for the fraction of former members who acknowledged that their gang killed people (37%). The mean score for current gang members on this five-point index was 2.8, and for former gang members it was 3.0.

We next examine the correlations between these four indices and one additional interval measure, the number of self-reported arrests in the past 12 months. We consider the correlations for each subgroup (current members and former members) separately in Table 13.3. We interpret these results as largely descriptive in nature, given the cross-sectional design of the data.

Correlations between the gang organization index and three of the other scales are significant

	Organization	Violent Victimization	Drug Sale	Violent Offending	Arrests
Current gang member					
Organization		.32**	.27**	.26**	.11
Violent victimization			.41**	.32**	.25**
Drug sale				.41**	.20*
Violent offending					.12
Ever a gang member					
Organization		.47*	.35*	.56**	−.25
Violent victimization			.44**	.66**	−.09
Drug sale				.56**	−.27*
Violent offending					−.14

Table 13.3 Correlation between Organization, Violent Victimization, Drug Sale, and Violent Offending Index Measures

*p = .05. **p = .01.

at the .01 level. Individuals who were members of more organized gangs report higher victimization counts, more gang sales of different kinds of drugs, and more violent offending by the gang than do members of less organized gangs.[8] This can be seen in the significant and positive correlations between the gang organization index and each of these indices. The correlation between the gang organization index and violent victimizations is the strongest of the three, .32. But it is also important to note from the top panel of Table 13.3 that the level of gang organization is significantly and positively related to the number of different violent and drug crimes that a gang engages in. These results run contrary to the findings from earlier work that the level of gang organization is not sufficiently complex to have implications for how gangs behave particularly in offending patterns largely described as "cafeteria style" (Decker, Bynum, & Weisel, 1998; Klein, 1995; McGloin, 2004; Peterson, Miller, & Esbensen, 2001).

The violent victimization index is positively related to gang drug sales, gang violent offending, and being arrested. Each of these correlations is strong for individual level data (.41, .32, and .25, respectively) and significant at the .01 level. These results are consistent with a growing body of research (Lauritsen, Sampson, & Laub, 1991; Loeber, Kalb, & Huizinga, 2001; Peterson, Taylor, & Esbensen, 2004) that documents the role of involvement in crime as an offender for victimization among adolescents. Although these are cross-sectional interview data and the time order of this relationship cannot be established, it is nonetheless important to point out the role of offending for victimization for current gang members, particularly in light of the consistent finding in gang ethnographies that gang members often join the gang for "protection" (Decker & Van Winkle, 1996; Hagedorn, 1988).

The pattern of relationships for former gang members is found in the bottom panel of Table 13.3. These relationships follow the general pattern found for current gang members, though where they deviate from this pattern, the relationships are stronger. Perhaps some of these differences are attributable to the fact that the former

gang members are somewhat older than the current members. Specifically, the gang organization index is strongly and positively related to violent victimizations, gang drug sales, and violent offending committed by the gang. Most notable is the strength of the relationship between the degree of gang organization and violent offending for this group of former gang members. This relationship is quite strong (.56) and significant at the .01 level. These results clearly suggest that despite the relatively low overall levels of gang organization observed for this sample, what organization does exist is related to increased involvement in drug sales, violent offending, and violent victimization. We are not able to identify the specific mechanisms through which the nature of gang organization is related to increases in these forms of offending and victimization. We believe that more organized groups are effective in pursuing individual and group goals, most often offending in the case of the gang. Organizational complexity can also increase the efficacy of the organization. In this context, organizational efficacy is the extent to which an organization can influence the behavior of its members and successfully compel them to pursue group goals. Prior research (Esbensen & Huizinga, 1993; Thornberry, Krohn, Lizotte, & Chard-Wierschem, 1993) has documented the extent to which offending increases during periods of gang membership compared to the time prior to becoming a member and the extent to which offending declines after individuals leave the gang. Our results suggest it is the organizational structure of the gang (weak as it may be) that accounts for changes in behavior. However, as our results are based on cross-sectional data, they are suggestive, offering hypotheses for future research.

Conclusions and Implications

A key issue in understanding the behavior of individuals who are members of a group is to know how well organized their group is. This is important for understanding offenders, as well as groups as diverse as corporate officers, doctors, and courtroom workgroups. A large body of research has argued that offenders are generally not well organized (Adler,

1985; Irwin, 1972; Wright & Decker, 1994, 1997), and generally lack the capacity to work together in an effective manner. This research is especially important to the study of gangs, because gangs are groups and as such exhibit some of the characteristics of social organizations. One ongoing debate in the understanding of gangs is the extent to which they are organized, and if so the degree to which the gang controls or directs involvement in crime. A substantial body of research in the area of gang control of drug sales has been conducted. Here the research has found that gangs are not effective mechanisms for controlling drug sales—particularly at the retail level—and that the degree of gang organization has little effect on participation in drug sales. To date, however, there have been few specific tests of the role of gang organization and organizational characteristics on offending and victimization. This article used a seven-item index of gang structure to construct an aggregate measure of gang organization that uses the key features of complex organizations, including leaders, rules, punishments for violating the rules, meetings, symbols of membership, responsibilities, and giving money to the gang. Whether current or former gang members were analyzed, significant positive relationships between the level of gang organization and involvement of the gang in violence and drug sales were found. Because these results are inconsistent with the expectations from the literature, they merit elaboration.

This research addressed two specific questions: (1) how organized are gangs? and (2) to what extent does gang organization affect involvement in violent crime, drug sales, violent victimization, and arrests?

Our answer to the first question is that gangs are not very well organized. Both current and former gang members expressed similar levels of organization for their gangs, one that was clearly in the middle of the range of organizational complexity. These scores on the gang organization index may reflect the age of respondents. After all, the interviews that provided the data for this study were collected in juvenile detention facilities, and it may be that juveniles have less knowledge of the organizational features of gangs or that they are not as involved in the more organized activities of gangs. On the other hand, the bulk of gang research indicates that the organizational structures of street gangs are not highly complex.

Our response to the second question is that even the low level of organization of gangs reported by this sample has important implications for the criminal behavior and victimization experiences of gang members. We reported above that the gangs represented by the current and former members of the Arizona ADAM sample were not particularly well organized. That said, the most important finding from this research is that even relatively low levels of gang organization have important implications for involvement in crime and victimization. This finding has significant consequences for understanding the effect that the gang has on the behavior of gang members. The more organized the gang, even at low levels of organization, the more likely it is that members will be involved in violent offenses, drug sales, and violent victimizations. These findings hold across current and former gang members, increasing their validity.

The answers to the two questions that frame our analysis are generally inconsistent with most prior research on gangs. Perhaps prior work has not had a good measure of gang organization. Indeed, we noted at the outset of this article that the gang has largely been a "black box" about which little is known. After all, nearly two decades ago James F. Short Jr. (1985) exhorted gang researchers to better understand the role of the gang in gang behavior. There has been very little work of that sort, and prior work has been with very small samples and not had direct measures of the level of gang organization. Prior work on gang organization in the past has been built on a single measure of gang organization or has viewed organization as a dichotomous variable—organized or not organized.

Perhaps the most important finding from this research is the finding that even incremental increases in gang organization result in more group process and congregate behavior among gang members. When more evidence of gang organization was present, elevated levels of involvement in crime and victimization were observed, a finding consistent with some prior gang research (Decker & Van Winkle, 1996; Klein, 1971). These results have two important policy implications. First, suppression and intervention efforts must pay more attention to the gangs that are the most organized. A large body of research on gangs has argued that gangs have a weak organizational structure or that gang organization doesn't matter (Decker, Bynum, & Weisel, 1998; Klein, 1995). This research has not considered the influence of different levels of gang organization or the influence of gang organization on behavior. The finding that gang organization, even at a low level, has important effects on behavior suggests that research and policy pay more attention to the characteristics of gang organization. Second, we suggest that responses to gangs on the part of police and social service agencies be reconsidered. The results of the current research suggest that interventions that reinforce the organizational structure of the gang are likely to produce negative consequences, particularly higher levels of victimization and offending. Avoiding interventions whose latent or manifest function is to strengthen the organization of the gang must be paramount in any gang strategy. Furthermore, steps that reduce the organizational complexity of a gang may pay dividends in reducing crime and victimization.

Notes

1. It should be noted that although the research cited here is for the situations studied in the particular cities, there is no claim made by the researchers that their research is representative of all gangs in their cities.
2. At its inception, the program was known as the Drug Use Forecasting (DUF) program.
3. At the time of the writing of this article, the Arrestee Drug Abuse Monitoring (ADAM) operations had been suspended due to federal spending constraints.
4. These two sites were selected because they were the only two sites that used the ADAM Gang Addendum.
5. As part of the National Institute of Justice gang addendum pilot project, Phoenix gang addendum data were collected in 1999, 2000, and 2002 and in Tucson they were collected in 1999 and 2000. In Mesa, data were collected in 2003 as part of a Motorola Corporation–funded study to examine the scope and nature of the gang problem in Mesa, Arizona.
6. It is possible that the same individuals were interviewed on multiple occasions, though we suspect that the number of such individuals would be small, and unlikely to influence the results.
7. This percentage is a subset of all individuals who report that their gang had rules.
8. It is important to note that the measure of gang offending is an aggregate measure and mostly "current" whereas the measure of victimization is "ever."

References

Adler, P. (1985). *Wheeling and dealing*. New York: Columbia.

Curry, D. (2000). Self-reported gang involvement and officially recorded delinquency. *Criminology, 38*(4), 1253–1274.

Curry, G. D., Decker, S. H., & Egley, A. H. (2002). Gang involvement and delinquency in a middle school population. *Justice Quarterly, 19*, 301–318.

Decker, S. H. (1996). Gangs and violence: The expressive character of collective involvement. *Justice Quarterly, 11*, 231–250.

Decker, S. (2000). Legitimating drug use: A note on the impact of gang membership and drug sales on the use of illicit drugs. *Justice Quarterly, 17*(2), 393–410.

Decker, S. H., Bynum, T. S., & Weisel, D. L. (1998). A tale of two cities: Gangs as organized crime groups. *Justice Quarterly, 15*, 395–425.

Decker, S., & Van Winkle, B. (1995). Slingin' dope: The role of gangs and gang members in drug sales. *Justice Quarterly, 11*, 1001–1022.

Decker, S., & Van Winkle, B. (1996). *Life in the gang: Family, friends, and violence*. New York: Cambridge University Press.

Egley, A. H. (2002). *National youth gang survey trends from 1996 to 2000*. OJJDP Fact Sheet No. 03. Washington, DC: U.S. Department of Justice.

Esbensen, F., & Huizinga, D. (1993). Gangs, drugs, and delinquency in a survey of urban youth. *Criminology, 31*, 565–590.

Esbensen, F., Winfree, T., He, N., & Taylor, T. (2001). Youth gangs and definitional issues: When is a gang a gang, and why does it matter. *Crime and Delinquency, 47*(1), 105–130.

Fagan, J. (1989). The social organization of drug use and drug dealing among urban gangs. *Criminology, 27*, 633–669.

Fleisher, M. S., & Decker, S. H. (2001). Going home, staying home: Integrating prison gang members into the community. *Corrections Management Quarterly, 5*, 65–77.

Hagedorn, J. H. (1988). *People and folks*. Chicago: Lakeview Press.

Hagedorn, J. H. (1994a). Homeboys, dope fiends, legits, and new jacks. *Criminology, 32*, 197–219.

Hagedorn, J. H. (1994b). Neighborhoods, markets, and gang drug organization. *Journal of Research in Crime and Delinquency, 31,* 264–294.

Irwin, J. (1972). The inmate's perspective. In J. Douglas (Ed.), *Research on deviance* (pp. 117–137). New York: Random House.

Katz, C. M., Webb, V., & Schaefer, D. (2000). The validity of police gang intelligence lists: Examining differences in delinquency between documented gang members and non-documented delinquent youth. *Police Quarterly, 3*(4), 413–437.

Klein, M. W. (1971). *Street gangs and street workers.* Englewood Cliffs, NJ: Prentice-Hall.

Klein, M. W. (1995). *The American street gang.* New York: Oxford University Press.

Lauritsen, J., Sampson, R. J., & Laub, J. (1991). The link between offending and victimization among adolescents. *Criminology, 29,* 265–292.

Loeber, R., Kalb, L., & Huizinga, D. (2001). *Juvenile delinquency and serious injury victimization.* Juvenile Justice Bulletin. Washington, DC: Office of Juvenile Justice and Delinquency Prevention.

Maxson, C. L., & Klein, M. W. (1990). Street gang violence: Twice as great, or half as great. In. C. R. Huff (Ed.), *Gangs in America* (pp. 71–100). Newbury Park, CA: Sage.

Maxson, C., & Klein, M. W. (1995). Investigating gang structures. *Journal of Gang Research, 3*(1), 33–40.

Maxson, C. L., Klein, M. W., & Cunningham, L. (1992). *Street gangs and drug sales.* Report to the National Institute of Justice.

McGloin, J. M. (2004). *Associations among criminal gang members as a defining factor of organization and as a predictor of criminal behavior: The gang landscape in Newark, New Jersey.* Ann Arbor, MI: UMI.

Mieczkowski, T. (1986). Geeking up and throwing down: Heroin street life in Detroit. *Criminology, 24,* 645–666.

Padilla, F. (1992). *The gang as an American enterprise.* New Brunswick, NJ: Rutgers.

Peterson, D., Miller, J., & Esbensen, F.-A. (2001). The impact of sex composition on gangs and gang member delinquency. *Criminology, 39,* 411–440.

Peterson, D., Taylor, T. J., & Esbensen, F.-A. (2004). Gang membership and violent victimization. *Justice Quarterly, 21*(4), 793–815.

Sanchez-Jankowski, M. (1991). *Islands in the street.* Berkeley, CA: University of California Press.

Sanders, W. B. (1994). *Gang bangs and drive-bys: Grounded culture and juvenile gang violence.* New York: De Gruyter.

Short, J. F., Jr. (1985). The level of explanation problem in criminology. In R. Meier (Ed.), *Theoretical methods in criminology* (pp. 51–72). Beverly Hills, CA: Sage.

Skolnick, J. H. (1990). The social structure of street drug dealing. *American Journal of Police, 9,* 1–41.

Skolnick, J., Correl, T., Navarro, E., & Rabb, R. (1988). *The social structure of street drug dealing.* BCS Forum, Office of the Attorney General, State of California.

Spergel, I. A. (1995). *The youth gang problem: A community approach.* New York: Oxford University Press.

Taylor, C. (1990). *Dangerous society.* East Lansing, MI: Michigan State University Press.

Thornberry, T., Krohn, M., Lizotte, A., & Chard-Wierschem, D. (1993). The role of juvenile gangs in facilitating delinquent behavior. *Journal of Research in Crime and Delinquency, 30,* 55–87.

Thornberry, T., Krohn, M. D., Lizotte, A. J., Smith, C. A., & Tobin, R. (2003). *Gangs and delinquency in developmental perspective.* New York: Cambridge.

Thrasher, F. (1929). *The gang.* Chicago: University of Chicago Press.

Tita, G., & Abrahamse, A. (2004, March). *Gang homicide in LA, 1981–2001: Perspectives on violence prevention* (No. 3). Sacramento, CA: California Attorney General's Office.

Wright, R., & Decker, S. H. (1994). *Burglars on the job.* Boston: Northeastern.

Wright, R., & Decker, S. H. (1997). *Armed robbers in action.* Boston: Northeastern.

Zatz, M. S. (1987). Chicano youth gangs and crime: The creation of a moral panic. *Contemporary Crises, 11,* 129–158.

Zatz, M., & Portillos, E. L. (2000). Voices from the barrio: Chicano/a gangs, families, and communities. *Criminology, 38,* 369–401.

CHAPTER 14

Gang Dynamics through the Lens of Social Identity Theory

Karen Hennigan ■ Marija Spanovic

In the academic world, street gang research has traditionally been carried out by sociologists, anthropologists, and criminologists. It is has been rare that social psychologists have been involved, even though groups and group dynamics have been core concerns in their discipline. Thus it is not surprising that group processes have not been highlighted in the history of gang research. The following chapter is a clear exception to this pattern, as the authors turn their special social psychological perspective, concepts, and language to the street gang world. The concept of "social identity" is spelled out, discussed, and then applied to research on how gang members respond to legal constraints applied directly to the gangs that frame their social identities. Comparing gang to nongang youth responses reveals insights into both gang member responses to legal constraints and the limits of those same restraints, based on group processes in gangs.

The gang as a form of human association and a social problem, an object of curiosity and commentary is at once ancient and contemporary. . . . Reports suggest that collective forms of delinquency have become cause for alarm in such widely separated areas as Western Europe and the Iron Curtain countries, the Far East, in Australia, and in such rapidly changing underdeveloped countries as Ghana and Kenya. Picturesque names establish the public identity of

these young people . . . names like "zoot-suiters" and "boppers" in the U.S., "Teddy boys" in England, "blousons noir" in France, "vitelloni" in Italy, "Halbstarke" in Germany, "bodgies" (boys) and "widgies" (girls) in Australia and New Zealand, "tsotsio" in South Africa, "mambo" boys and girls in Japan, "hooligans" in Poland and Russia, the "tap-karoschi" of Yugoslavia, and the "lui-mang" and "tai-pau" of Taiwan (Short and Strodtbeck 1965, p. 1).

This is the opening paragraph of one of the first detailed studies of group processes observed in street gangs.[1] Published in 1965, Short and Strodtbeck's work documents the ubiquitous nature of delinquent adolescent groups in many parts of the world, now going back five decades or more. Over the years, the descriptors used to depict such groups have changed, but their presence has been continuous and expanding. Efforts to understand the impact of street gangs have been continuous and expanding as well. A street gang is foremost a group. Young men and women all over the world attach importance to becoming part of such a group, gaining part of their identity from belonging to it. Relatively little academic and professional work on street gangs has taken advantage of the development of social psychological theories on social identity to understand how the street gang as a group influences its members.

The purpose of this chapter is to use the framework of social identity theory (Tajfel 1978; Tajfel and Turner 1979, 1986), self-categorization theory (Turner 1985, 1987), and related work (Brewer 1991; Hogg 2001; Pickett et al. 2002; Postmes and Spears 1998) to enrich our understanding of group processes in adolescent street gangs. The hope is to stimulate further exploration of gang group processes through the lens of these theories that have been developed over the last several decades by social psychologists in many parts of the world, especially in Europe, the United States, and Australia. We argue that this particular framework, mostly ignored in recent gang research and applied practice, holds promise for furthering our understanding of the dynamics of these groups and may also bring new insights to the work of formulating effective prevention and intervention strategies that heretofore have had disappointingly little impact on the continuity and growth of street gangs (see Klein and Maxson 2006, Chap. 3 for a review). We begin by laying out key theoretical components that we use to derive hypotheses about group-based mediators of gang violence. We test these hypotheses using data from a recent study of gang social identity among the youth living in Los Angeles, California (Hennigan and Sloane 2011).

Social identity theory is quite distinct from other identity-based theories (e.g., Erikson 1963; Stryker 1987; Stryker and Burke 2000) because of its focus on *intergroup* dynamics rather than *interpersonal* dynamics. Several authors have reviewed these differences in detail[2] which we will not repeat here. The common ground among these theories is a focus on the self in general, but the processes described are quite different and operate at different levels. Social identity theory is based on the model of a layered self-concept that includes layers defined by social characteristics that arise from identification with social groups or categories that are distinct from personal or individual characteristics. The personal layer of one's self-concept is defined in the context of *interpersonal* relations. In contrast, the social layers of one's self-concept are defined in the context of *intergroup* relations.

Gang ethnographers use working definitions of the concept of identity or gang identity that may or may not overlap with the social identity model discussed below. For example, much of Vigil's (1988a, 1988b) discussion on gang identity is conceptualized through an interpersonal lens from the point of view of Erikson's (1963) work and others (Wallace and Fogelson 1965; Whiting 1980). However, he explicitly develops his discussion

beyond personal identity to encompass the notion of group identity. His description of group processes highlights aspects of the group context of gang membership that overlaps with the social identity perspective, though he does not explicitly refer to this theoretical orientation. In his treatise, Vigil (1988b) emphasizes the contribution that gang membership makes to one's self-definition. He observes that "to gain acceptance from peers, an individual will adopt behavior patterns that initially have little intrinsic meaning to him, and perhaps might even be repugnant, but nevertheless are requisites for gang membership: for example, showing that one can feel, act, and look hard and uncaring" (pp. 427–428). "Growing up in the barrio and becoming socialized and enculturated to street peer networks and beliefs makes an individual *group-oriented* (emphasis added) early in life" (p. 435). "A person learns to feel what the group feels," and he must "learn the expectations of the group" (p. 437). "The barrio group . . . provides [its own] norms and patterns for emotional stability, social interaction and friendship, protection and street survival" (Vigil 1988b, p. 432). Overall, "for those who become members, the gang norms help shape what a person thinks about himself and others and provides models for how to look and act" (Vigil 1988b, p. 421).

The Social Identity Perspective

Social identity theory focuses on the way people think about themselves and others in an intergroup context. By identifying oneself as a member of a particular group (like a sports team, a school band, or a street-oriented group such as a street gang), one is accepting or taking on a social identity that has powerful implications *cognitively* for how an individual views himself and others and *behaviorally* for how an individual acts within his group and toward members of other groups. Tajfel (1978) defined social identity as "that *part* of an individual's self concept which derives from knowledge of his membership in a social group (or groups) together with the emotional value and significance attached to that membership" (p. 63). His definition is deliberately more specific and more limited than a general definition of identity which typically refers to an overall concept of self from an individual or interpersonal point of view. Social identities are specific to intergroup contexts as opposed to interpersonal ones. In the discussion below, social identity is defined in reference to a particular group or social category. Most individuals have multiple social identities related to multiple social categories or groups with which the person identifies, all of which may become part of the individual's overall self-concept.

Tajfel and Turner's (1979, 1986) work was in the context of intergroup relations involving real or perceived competition or conflict between social groups and categories. Studies have documented that even the simple awareness that there are two groups or categories, including one that I belong to and another that I do not, gives rise to ingroup favoritism and often outgroup derogation in terms of stereotyping and distributing rewards (Allport 1954; Billig and Tajfel 1973; Brewer 1999; Tajfel et al. 1971; Turner 1975). Research on social identity and related theories describe the dynamics by which we commonly perceive that our own group is better and more deserving than other groups, a perception that is continually reinforced by selectively comparing one's ingroup with an outgroup on whichever evaluative criteria come to mind. Research has documented that the criteria that typically come to mind are those by which the outgroup falls short in relation to the ingroup (and not vice versa). In short, we are motivated to make comparisons that support the perception that our ingroup is superior to an outgroup in important ways because it promotes a sense of positive distinctiveness, self-definition, and self-esteem.

Continuum of Behavior: From Individual-Level to Group-Level Behavior

From the point of view of social identity theory, an individual's social behavior falls between two extremes defined as interpersonal or intergroup behavior. At the interpersonal end of the continuum, the behavior between two or more individuals is fully determined by their interpersonal relationships and individual characteristics, where social

identity has little or no influence. At the intergroup end of the continuum, the behavior between two or more individuals is fully determined by their membership in a particular social group or category; here, personal values and characteristics are not influential. Social behavior rarely actually falls at one extreme or the other, but varies somewhere in between these two extremes, depending on the salience of group (intergroup) or individual (interpersonal) concerns. Tajfel (1978, p. 41) used soldiers at war as an example of behavior at the intergroup end of the continuum. A poem written by an American infantryman, James Lenihan, provides a poignant example of this. His poem expresses his shift from the group end of the continuum to the individual end of the continuum after he shot and killed a German soldier during World War II.[3] The poem begins:

> I shot a man yesterday
> And much to my surprise,
> The strangest thing happened to me
> I began to cry.
>   He was so young, so very young
> And Fear was in his eyes,
> He had left his home in Germany
> And came to Holland to die.
>   And what about his Family
> Were they not praying for him?
> Thank God they couldn't see their son
> And the man that had murdered him.

Murdered is a powerful word and it conveys perspective from the individual end of the continuum. Viewed from the group end of the continuum, the soldier's action was likely viewed as duty:

> It was the War
> And he was the enemy
> If I hadn't shot him
> He would have shot me.
>   I saw he was dying
> And I called him "Brother"
> But he gasped out one word
> And that word was "Mother."

His "surprise" is based on switching perspectives from the group end of the continuum (it was my duty as much as it was his duty) to the individual end (I saw him dying and called him brother).

Figure 14.1 Tajfel's Continuum of Behavior

Individual-Level Behavior	Group-Level Behavior
Personally responsible	Personally anonymous (not responsible)
Further personal goals	Further group goals

A soldier's training is meant to support "group behavior" and avoid the individual end of the continuum. The notion of a continuum is a heuristic that conveys how behavior toward another person may be controlled or influenced by the social identity-relevant aspects of an interaction (Fig. 14.1).

One of the corollary predictions of this model is that when a given social identity is controlling (at the group end of the continuum), the individual avoids feeling personally responsible for his actions. This is accomplished by depersonalizing the outgroup individuals involved as well as depersonalizing oneself, viewing each generically as a prototype of their group (Postmes and Spears 1998; Reicher et al. 1995). In this depersonalized state, the influence exerted by the social group through its normative expectations is paramount, meaning that the group-level expectations or norms outweigh one's own individual behavioral preferences.

It is interesting to reflect on stories that speculate as to how a person who showed no signs of aggression growing up became involved in group-based violence. From a social identity point of view, even persons who would be unlikely to be involved in violent acts at an interpersonal level may well be influenced to do so at the inter-group level. This is consistent with the finding in longitudinal studies that criminal activities heighten when the youth become involved in street gangs and recede after they leave the gang (Esbensen and Huizinga 1993; Gordon et al. 2004; Thornberry et al. 2003). There also is evidence that persons with aggressive tendencies are more likely to be drawn to join a street gang group (Thornberry et al. 2003), presumably in the same way that empathic persons are more likely to be drawn to groups involved in community service. However, the collective norms of street gangs support and expect aggressive action when the gang is challenged and individuals that identify with a street gang can be expected to increase this

type of behavior above levels motivated by individual proclivities.

Gang members and members of other groups are clearly not behaving near the group end of the continuum all of the time. A comment made by one respondent in a recent study illustrates this point.[4] This respondent related an incident where he had helped a friend that was jumped (beat-up) on the playground at school, even though the friend was involved with a rival gang. Then he cautioned the interviewer, "please don't tell anyone this because if my homies knew they would kill me." This young man engaged in interpersonal behavior (at the individual end of Tajfel's continuum) to help a friend and was concerned that the incident not be viewed in an intergroup context because if it was, there would be consequences for violating his group's normative expectations.

What factors mediate shifts in focus along this hypothetical continuum from interpersonal behavior to intergroup behavior? In short, the salience of interpersonal versus intergroup aspects in any given situation are affected *externally* by the particulars of the social context (including a history of intergroup conflict or competition, the location, who is present, etc.), but also *internally* by the individual's strength of identification with his relevant ingroup, as well as his level of ingroup cohesion or perceived "groupness." In the next sections, we will briefly review the literature on these concepts as they relate to internal or psychological factors that affect the consistency and extremity of intergroup behavior in general and gang behavior in particular.

Strength of Social Identity

Most of us are involved in various groups or social activities, yet not all of these inform our social identity. We identify strongly with some groups and less so with others, and this calculus may shift over time in reaction to circumstances and events. For example, there are those for whom identification with a political party strengthens around election time but otherwise remains relatively weak or unimportant. As a result, most of the time the normative expectations associated with political activism are inconsequential with little or no routine influence on behavior. For others, this social identity may be front and center and influential much of the time.

One way to understand how strongly a person actively identifies with one particular social group or another is to consider what one gains from doing so, a concept called social identity value (Sherman et al. 1999). Research supports the notion that social identities are assimilated because (1) they help one feel good about oneself and achieve positive self-esteem (Tajfel 1978; Tajfel and Turner 1979, 1986); (2) they help reduce the uncertainty about who you are and who you are not, based on a generic or prototypical understanding of the characteristics and behavioral norms of members of specific groups or categories[5] (Hogg 2000, 2007); and (3) they help fulfill basic human needs (i.e., needs to both fit in socially and at the same time be distinct or stand out in some unique way; Brewer 1991). Brewer maintains that both of these seemingly contradictory needs can be achieved through social identity. Being part of a group or category allows each of us to fit in or belong, and at the same time, we are motivated to view our own group, and by extension ourselves, as being unique or distinctive in some positive way. Other things being equal, the strength of identification with a particular social group predicts or explains the extent to which an individual's behavior is consonant with the normative expectations of that particular social group or category (Hogg and Abrams 1988; Hogg and Reid 2006; Smith et al. 2007). In other words, groups with which one is weakly identified (chronically or in certain situations) will have little normative influence. Among gang members, one would expect to find more correspondence between an individual's behavior and the gang's behavioral norms when social identification with the gang is high. Individuals that strongly identify with a group are expected to operate toward the group end of Tajfel's behavioral continuum much more frequently than individuals with weaker group identification.

Ingroup Cohesion and Intergroup Conflict

Other factors that affect how much group membership influences one's behavior include group cohesion and intergroup conflict. Early research in the area of group dynamics (c.f., Cartwright and Zander 1968; Gerard and Miller 1967) identified key processes that support group cohesion. Group cohesion, conceptualized as an attribute of the group, has been defined as "the total field of forces which act on members to remain in the group" (Festinger et al. 1950, p. 164). A group may be more or less cohesive depending on the interconnectedness of the individuals involved. The level of group cohesion has important implications for a group's capacity for effectively responding to intergroup challenges. Research supports the view that group cohesion facilitates concerted action and aggressive response to conflict with another group. The reverse, that intergroup conflict promotes cohesion, is also empirically supported (Brewer 1999; Dion 1979; Grant and Brown 1995; Sherif 1967). As early as 1906, Sumner observed that "intergroup conflict and in-group solidarity may form a mutually reinforcing feedback system in which hostility between groups becomes a self-sustaining cycle" (Sumner 1906 as cited in Dion 1979).

Early on, gang researchers focused on this aspect of group processes. Klein and Crawford (1967) and Short and Strodtbeck (1965) observed that street gangs were not highly cohesive groups. They observed that gang membership and gang leadership were generally relatively unstable. Maintaining a focus on group behavior was difficult. To be effective, leaders needed to direct the members' focus toward threats or challenges from outside of the group. Outside threats or challenges motivated participation in violent and criminal activities directed toward defending the group's turf or honor and at the same time played a central role in maintaining the group's cohesion as well as a leader's own status. Spergel (1995), Klein (1995), and Decker (1996; Decker and Van Winkle 1996) have all made similar observations. They observed that it is competition with nearby street gangs that draws local gang members together and gang cohesiveness thrives on gang-on-gang hostility. Consistent with social psychological research, conflict or threats from the outside increases a group's cohesion. In turn, strong group cohesion supports increased hostility toward persons outside the group. For street gang members, both group cohesion and intergroup conflict can be expected to strengthen identification with the gang and thereby increase the likelihood that gang members will behave near the group end of Tajfel's continuum.

Ingroup Entitativity or "Groupness"

A related but separate line of research also sheds light on factors that support a shift toward group behavior. This research focuses on whether or not a collection of individuals is perceived to be a group (a social entity) or merely an aggregate of people. For example, if the youth are gathered in a local park, impressions and reactions to the gathering (made by onlookers and by the participants themselves) may well depend on the extent to which the gathering is perceived to be a group or just a gathering. Campbell (1958) used the term "entitativity" to denote the degree of "groupness" inferred for an aggregate of people.[6]

Several cues have been found to underlie the inference that a collection of people is a group. Brewer et al. (2004) suggest that two general types of cues are often used to make inferences about groupness. One type of cue has to do with essence. A collection of individuals is more likely to be perceived as a group if they have similar traits or trait-related behaviors that define an essence for the group. Another aspect that conveys an essence is the sense that there are clear boundaries as to who is or is not part of the group. A second type of cue has to do with factors related to agency. Confirmation of a group's agency includes indications of interdependence, interaction, or coordinated efforts among the individuals involved. Group cohesion is a key attribute of this type of entitativity. The more a collection of persons gather together, interact in concert, or convey a sense of interdependence, the higher the perceived groupness of that collection of people. In a recent study, Ip et al. (2006) characterized these two approaches to making

inferences about groupness as being based on "birds of a feather" (essence) or on "flocking together" (agency). And other dichotomies have been suggested.[7] Whichever approach is used, the degree of groupness a person infers for their own ingroup has implications for just where on Tajfel's continuum their behavior is likely to fall. This inference of groupness underlies the basis for intergroup behavior linked to a social identity because behavior at the group end of his continuum requires that at least a minimal degree of groupness be perceived. An individual's strength of identification with a collection of people is predicated in part by the extent to which that individual infers some level of groupness among the individuals involved. Spears et al. (2004) argue that both "group distinctiveness and entitativity play an important role in creating social identity and putting it to use" (p. 293).

Outside observers generally infer that street gangs have a high level of entitativity or group cohesion (see Lickel et al. 2000),[8] but research findings on inside observations are at odds with this (Decker and Van Winkle 1996; Klein and Crawford 1967). Inside observers document relatively low levels of cohesion among traditional street gang members themselves (i.e., low ingroup entitativity). We can speculate that some of the reasons for this have to do with a street orientation common among traditional street gangs that is open to a variety of youth hanging out together. Like most adolescents, street gang youth spend most of their time hanging out, engaged in activities that are not uncommon among adolescents such as drinking, using recreational drugs, trespassing, loitering, and vandalism. Violence is rare in proportion to all gang activities (Battin et al. 1998; Decker and Van Winkle 1996; Esbensen et al. 1993; Klein 1995; Short and Strodtbeck 1965). And not all of the youth hanging out together will join in the violent gang activities. In fact, it is sometimes difficult for researchers to determine just who is or is not a member of a street gang. Ethnographers, including Vigil (1988a), have categorized gang-involved youth as regularly, peripherally, situationally, or temporarily engaged in gang activities (p. 99). Similarly, other gang researchers categorize gang-involved youth at various levels of commitment to gang life, such as hardcore, associates, fringe, or wannabe (Klein 1971, 1995). The point we are making is that despite an easy consensus among observers that street gangs have high entitativity or groupness (from an outgroup perspective), there is less consensus among the youth hanging out themselves (from an ingroup perspective) about just how cohesive the membership is or even how clear the boundaries of the gang are. Vigil (1988b, p. 429) offers these perspectives from two youth who were fringe members for a short time during high school. One said that he joined to "feel good because someone is behind you," but "I never made it as a true gang member." The other youth said that he became part of the gang to blend in to the social environment. He would "dress and act like a cholo" and "act cool and not stare at anybody" to avoid being in fights. He stated that he left the group in high school as the coping strategy of gang identification brought more problems than it solved.

Can a Social Identity Perspective Help Explain Involvement in Group-Level Behaviors?

Our review of a mix of social psychological and gang research findings suggests that two factors contribute to the influence that an ingroup such as a street gang has on an individual's behavior. These are the strength of identification with one's group (How integral is this group in a person's definition of who he is?) and perceptions of the groupness (How strongly defined is the group to that person?). Both of these factors promote depersonalization (i.e., seeing oneself as a prototypical member of the ingroup which facilitates compliance with ingroup norms). We expect that ingroup identification and ingroup entitativity are among the key mediators of group behavior (i.e., behavior that is consistent with the group's normative expectations—the group end of Tajfel's continuum).

If our goal is to understand the behavior of gang members in social situations, we should find that an individual's level of identification with his gang as well as his perception of the gang's groupness (e.g., cohesion and clarity of the gang's boundary)

help explain or predict group behavior defined as behaviors that are consistent with the gang's normative expectations. For most street gangs, normative group behavior includes involvement in criminal and violent activities. The same principle should be true for nongang youth, but in their case, criminal and violent activities are generally not part of the normative expectations for their peer group. So no relationship between these types of behaviors and markers of group identification or group entitativity within nongang peer groups is expected.

Other variables studied by criminologists may explain an individual's involvement in criminal activities and violence. A large body of research has focused on the deterrent value of individually held perceptions of the likelihood of getting caught and punished for delinquent or criminal activities. All things being equal, the more likely an individual believes it is that he may be caught and punished, the less likely he is to engage in criminal or violent activity (see Pratt et al. 2006 for a meta-analytic review; see also Maxson et al. 2011). These deterrence-related factors should be negatively associated with participation in delinquent and criminal activities when personal interests are salient (i.e., when the person is behaving close to the individual end of Tajfel's continuum). Because serious delinquency and violence are generally not normative behavior within nongang peer groups, we predict that individually held beliefs about the likelihood of getting caught and punished will be associated with participation in these activities and strength of identification with the peer group should have nothing to do with it. On the other hand, for gang-involved youth, we make the opposite prediction. Criminal and violent activities are strongly normative for gang members (see Decker 1996; Klein 1995). We predict that gang members' participation in these highly normative behaviors should be more strongly related to ingroup identification and group cohesion than to individual-level concerns such as the likelihood of getting caught and punished. In short, group-level expectations are expected to trump any individual-level concerns gang members may have for getting caught, but not so for the nongang youth.

Methods

Hennigan and Sloane (2011) interviewed the youth in areas claimed by local street gangs to study their reactions to civil gang injunctions in Los Angeles, California. The youth were interviewed in areas that were roughly matched on gang prevalence and sociodemographics. Some of the areas were involved in gang injunction efforts and some were not. Over a 10-month period, interviewers recruited male youth between the ages of 14 and 21 in designated gang neighborhoods in Los Angeles, California, by going door to door initially, then by engaging the youth hanging out on the street. Informed consent was obtained for all respondents and also from a parent for those who were less than 18 years old. As intended, this sampling approach resulted in oversampling street-oriented youth in the selected gang neighborhoods.

Of the 416 respondents, 97% were Hispanic, and 87% were born in the United States. Thirty-nine percent (39%) of the gang-involved youth had been held in custody overnight relative to 7% of the nongang respondents. Eighty-four percent of the gang and 59% of nongang youth had been the victim of violence.[9] Early in the interview, each respondent was asked to name various types of groups in which someone his age could become involved in his neighborhood including leadership groups, competitive teams, other organized clubs or activity groups, street gangs, tagger or skater groups, or party posses or crews. The interviewer then asked each respondent to list his own important peer groups. Interviewers were instructed to work with each youth to identify the respondent's primary unconventional (i.e., not adult organized or sponsored) informal peer group in addition to one or more conventional groups.[10]

The analyses here are organized solely around the primary unconventional informal peer group that each respondent identified, which included street gangs (27%), other crews or posses (27%), or informal groups of friends (46%). In the middle part of the interview, respondents answered a series of questions about their group. Social identity was measured using four items from the Identity Subscale of Luhtanen and Crocker's (1992) Scale of Collective Self-Esteem.[11] The four items were highly correlated (alpha = 0.79) and were combined to form a scale score with higher scores indicating stronger identification with one's group. Focusing on the same construct used by Klein in his work (Klein and Crawford 1967; Klein 1971), cohesion with a peer group was operationalized as the frequency of meeting or getting together. Group cohesion was measured with a single item. "In some groups, the members meet or get together frequently, but in other groups the members rarely meet or get together at all. Recently, how often do you meet or get together with members of <your group>?"[12] Perception of group boundaries was also measured with a single question. "For some groups it is really clear who is in the group and who is not. These groups have clear boundaries. In others, it is not very clear just who is in the group and who is not. These have fuzzy boundaries. How clear or fuzzy are the boundaries in <your group>?"[13]

In the second half of the interview, each respondent's involvement in criminal activities and violence was measured with a frequently used self-report protocol based on the one developed for the National Youth Study (Huizinga and Elliot 1986) that was subsequently revised and used in the Causes and Correlates studies (see Esbensen and Huizinga 1993; Loeber et al. 1998; Thornberry et al. 2003). For the analyses presented here, level of involvement in criminal activities was defined using the same list of activities employed by Thornberry et al. (2003, Appendix A), except that the index of 31 items here which includes two rather than four items for theft, sexual assault, and prostitution were omitted, and questions about tagging, intimidation, and extortion were added. The subset of six violent activities included here were the same as those used by Thornberry et al. (2003), except that sexual assault was omitted and witness intimidation was added. A variety index of criminal activities was formed by counting how many activities on the list the youth admitted doing in the last 6 months. Similarly, a variety index of violence was created by counting how many violent activities the youth did in the last 6 months. (See Thornberry and Krohn 2000 for a discussion of the validity of this measurement approach.)

Views of deterrence were measured by asking the youth to estimate how many times they would be caught and punished if they were to commit various types of crimes in their neighborhood on ten different occasions. The youth made estimates for 11 different criminal activities including three violent ones.[14] For each activity, the youth indicated his expectation of being caught and punished—from zero to ten times. While the level of consequences expected varied for different kinds of criminal activities, across respondents there were significant correlations among these estimates (Pearson's values were all statistically significant ranging from 0.22 to 0.60). This indicates that the youth who estimated a higher likelihood (relative to other respondents) on one type of crime tended to do the same for other crimes, even though the absolute level of their expectations varied across crimes. For this reason, we chose to combine these estimates to form a general scale of expected consequences across a variety of 11 criminal activities and for the subset of three violent activities. There was a high correspondence in the responses across these 11 items (alpha = 0.86) and the subset of aggressive or violent items (alpha = 0.72).

Results

Means and Standard Deviations of Criminal and Violent Activities and Proposed Mediators

The means and standard deviations of the indices of criminal behavior and of the subset of violent activities self-reported by gang and nongang youth are given in Table 14.1. Involvement in these types of behaviors is significantly higher for gang-involved youth than nongang youth. This is consistent with the supposition that these types of behaviors are normative for gang-involved youth but much less so for nongang youth.

Further, as suggested by our review of gang-related ethnographic and empirical research, on average gang-involved youth have weaker ingroup identification and more diffuse inferences about groupness, measured here as group cohesion and clear boundaries, than the youth involved in nongang peer groups. Nonetheless, there is considerable variability within both types of groups.

Similarly, the means for deterrence-related expectations associated with criminal and violent activities vary by gang status. Higher expectations for being caught and punished are expressed by the nongang than by the gang respondents. However, considerable variation in perceived deterrence is evident within both groups.

Correlations among Criminal and Violent Activities and Proposed Explanatory Variables

The bivariate correlations between the proposed explanatory variables and criminal and violent behavior of gang and nongang respondents are given in Table 14.2. As predicted, the table shows that both group identification and cohesion were significantly related to criminal activity in general (0.32, $p < 0.01$, and 0.22, $p < 0.05$, respectively) and with violent activities in particular (0.49, $p < 0.01$ and 0.22, $p < 0.05$) among gang members but not among nongang members where none of these correlations were statistically significant (−0.04 and −0.06 for criminal activity and −0.05 and 0.03 for violence). The measure of clear boundaries was not related to these behaviors for either group. The data confirm that despite overall lower levels of group identification and cohesion among gang respondents relative to nongang respondents, these ingroup characteristics were significantly related to the gang respondents' criminal and violent behaviors. On the other hand, none of these ingroup characteristics were related to criminal or violent behaviors among nongang respondents for whom these behaviors are not socially normative.

Among nongang youth, deterrence-related concerns were significantly related to both general criminal and violent activities (−0.32, $p < 0.01$ and −0.20, $p < 0.01$) and unrelated to ingroup identification or cohesion among the nongang respondents as predicted. Among gang-involved youth, there were simple bivariate correlations between deterrence-related concerns and general criminal activity (−0.24, $p < 0.05$) and violence (−0.21, $p < 0.05$). There was also a significant bivariate correlation between deterrence concerns and gang identification (−0.21, $p < 0.05$) but not between deterrence concerns and violence (−0.16, ns). The data were then tested using structural equation modeling to

Table 14.1 Means and Standard Deviations of the Study Variables

	Gang (N = 112)	Nongang (N = 304)
	Mean (S.D.)	Mean (S.D.)
Criminal activity (logged)	2.18 (0.058)	1.39 (0.72)***
Violence (logged)	0.90 (0.58)	0.41 (0.47)***
Identification	3.06 (1.39)	4.19 (1.13)***
Cohesion	4.01 (1.89)	4.97 (1.27)***
Clear boundaries	3.65 (1.29)	3.96 (0.92)*
Deterrence—criminal activities	3.30 (1.99)	4.96 (2.43)***
Deterrence—violence	2.82 (2.40)	4.35 (2.82)***

*The mean difference is significant at the .05 level
***The mean difference is significant at the .001 level

Table 14.2 Intercorrelations of Criminal Activity and Violence and Their Predictors

	1a	1b	2	3	4	5a	5b
Gang (N = 112)							
Criminal activity (logged) (1a)		0.71**	0.32**	0.22*	−0.04	−0.24*	NA
Violence (logged) (1b)			0.49**	0.22*	0.02	NA	−0.21*
Identification (2)				0.50**	0.22*	−0.21*	−0.16
Cohesion (3)					0.30**	−0.15	−0.06
Clear boundaries (4)						−0.02	0.01
Deterrence—criminal activities (5a)							0.81**
Deterrence—violence (5b)							
Nongang (N = 304)							
Criminal activity (logged) (1a)		0.64**	−0.04	−0.06	−0.08	−0.32**	NA
Violence (logged) (1b)			−0.05	0.03	−0.01	NA	−0.20**
Identification (2)				0.16**	0.21**	0.05	0.02
Cohesion (3)					0.16**	0.04	0.02
Clear boundaries (4)						0.01	0.03
Deterrence—criminal activities (5a)							0.84**
Deterrence—violence (5b)							

*Correlation is significant at the .05 level
**Correlation is significant at the .01 level

take the multivariate relationships into account to determine the best fitting model.

Structural Equation Modeling (SEM)

SEM was used to simultaneously test the relationships between cohesion, clear boundaries, deterrence, identification, and criminal and violent activity. Models were fit separately for gang-involved and nongang respondents to determine the best fitting models for each. Goodness-of-fit was evaluated using criteria recommended by Hu and Bentler (1999).[15]

Gang Models. In the first model shown in Figure 14.2, we predicted the index of general criminal activity using the proposed explanatory variables. The model was an excellent fit to the

Figure 14.2 Gang-Involved Respondents Only

This structural equation model tests predictors of criminal activity among gang-involved youth. Paths with *single-headed arrows* represent directional effects, and paths with *double-headed arrows* represent nondirectional correlations. The model reports standardized regression weights. Bolded paths are significant (*p* < .05)

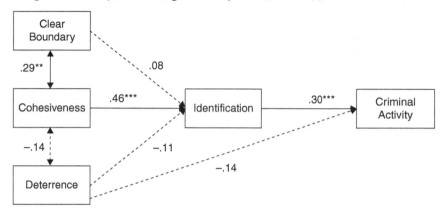

Figure 14.3 Gang-Involved Respondents Only

This structural equation model tests predictors of violent activities among gang-involved youth. Paths with *single-headed arrows* represent directional effects, and paths with *double-headed arrows* represent nondirectional correlations. The model reports standardized regression weights. Bolded paths are significant (*p* < .05)

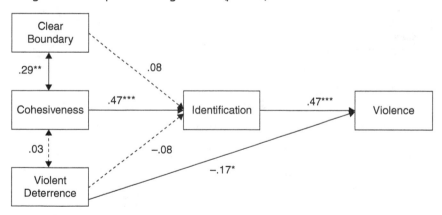

data: $\chi^2(3) = 2.94$, $p = 0.40$, RMSEA $= 0.00$, CFI $= 1.00$.[16] Cohesion was related to identification, and identification was related to criminal activity. The clear boundaries variable was associated with cohesion, but not related to identification or the criminal index. As predicted, deterrence-related concerns were not significantly related to criminal activity in this model.

Figure 14.3 shows that the best fitting model predicting violence as a dependent variable yielded a similar structure, with cohesion related to identification which was related to violence. It was also

Figure 14.4 Nongang Respondents Only

This structural equation model tests predictors of criminal activity among youth involved in nongang peer groups. Paths with *single-headed arrows* represent directional effects, and paths with *double-headed arrows* represent nondirectional correlations. The model reports standardized regression weights. Bolded paths are significant ($p < .05$)

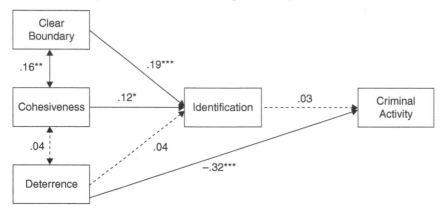

Figure 14.5 Nongang Respondents Only

This structural equation model tests predictors of violent activities among youth involved in nongang peer groups. Paths with *single-headed arrows* represent directional effects, and paths with *double-headed arrows* represent nondirectional correlations. The model reports standardized regression weights. Bolded paths are significant ($p < .05$)

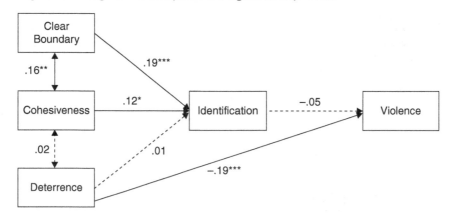

an excellent fit to the data: $\chi^2(3) = 1.96$, $p = 0.58$, RMSEA = 0.00, CFI = 1.00.[17] In this model however, a weak but statistically significant relationship with deterrence concerns was also indicated. Preacher and Hayes' (2004) SPSS macro was used to assess the extent to which identification mediated the relationship between cohesiveness and criminal activities among gang members as suggested in these models. This analysis indicated that full mediation occurred for both the criminal activity index (Sobel $Z = 2.49$, $p < 0.05$) and for violence (Sobel $Z = 3.96$, $p < 0.001$). Models wherein identification was entered as an independent variable and cohesiveness as a mediator were not significant, indicating that all of the influence gang cohesion had on these dependent variables was mediated through social identification and not vice versa.

Nongang Models. The same models were tested with nongang respondents. The resulting models provided an excellent fit to the data for criminal activity in Fig. 14.4: $\chi^2(3) = 2.07$, $p = 0.56$, RMSEA = 0.00, CFI = 1.00;[18] and violence in Fig. 14.5: $\chi^2(3) = 0.87$, $p = 0.83$, RMSEA = 0.00, CFI = 1.00.[19] Among the nongang respondents, groupness variables (clear boundaries and cohesion) were related to group identification but group identification was not related to criminal or violent activities. Instead, we observed that the criminal activity index (see Fig. 14.3) and the violence index (see Fig. 14.4) were negatively related to the personal estimates of the likelihood of getting caught and punished for such activities (deterrence). Deterrence had a strong negative relationship with both dependent variables among the nongang youth (Fig. 14.4 and Fig. 14.5) and only a weak relationship with violence among the gang-involved respondents (Fig. 14.3).

Discussion and Conclusions

We found support for the notion that groupness defined as group cohesion (frequency of getting together) and group identification (or strength of social identity) are associated with criminal and violent behavior among gang members, but not among members of other kinds of peer groups in the same neighborhoods. In the SEM models with gang-involved respondents, the association between group cohesion and both crime and violence was fully mediated by strength of social identity. These relationships were not found in the models with nongang respondents. We maintain that this disparity is due to widely different normative expectations within street gangs versus within nongang peer groups. Based on the tenets of social identity theory, we interpret criminal and violent behavior among gang members as a group-based phenomenon, not in terms of engaging in these behaviors together at the same time (which may or may not happen), but rather in terms of one's motivation to

act. The stronger one's identification with the gang, the stronger the individual is focused on the gang's normative expectations (i.e., behavior at the group end of Tajfel's continuum), regardless of individual concerns. Research suggests that a person engaged in group behavior depersonalizes himself and his victims, seeing each more in terms of a generic representative or prototype of their respective group than as individuals. These findings support the value of using this theoretical framework as a model in future research and strategic thinking about gang violence reduction and gang reduction strategies. The findings support framing the motivational context for gang violence in terms of social identity theory in general and Tajfel's continuum in particular.

This study also contributes to our understanding of why the process of weighing the likelihood of personal costs for engaging in illegal activities[20] does less to deter gang members than it appears to for nongang youth. Among the nongang respondents, the data suggest that the higher a respondent's estimate of the likelihood of getting caught and punished, the less involvement in criminal and violent activities. However, among the gang-involved youth, the data suggest that identification with the gang can trump or drastically reduce personal interests such as concerns about getting caught and punished when the behaviors in question are normative and group identification is strong. Since crime and violence are normative among gang-involved youth, personal estimates of getting caught and punished have little or no influence on their criminal and violent behaviors. Among nongang youth, however, serious crime and violence are rarely part of their groups' normative expectations, so personal interests such as avoiding risks of punishment carry more weight.

Gang researchers have observed that gang cohesion is less a function of internal factors such as affective ties or individual similarities than external factors that spawn social interaction in reaction to gang rivalries (Decker 1996; Klein and Crawford 1967). The findings for gang-involved youth in this study are consistent with this view.[21] This preoccupation with group rivalries has been described as a unique characteristic of street gangs, even as one example of ways that street gangs are qualitatively different from other groups. It is our contention that this and other aspects of group dynamics in gangs may be largely predicted or explained through the lens of social identity and related theories. Below, we present examples of approaches that researchers might take toward using social identity and related theories to generate explanations that may extend our understanding of gang dynamics in ways that could be useful for gang prevention and intervention.

Instead of treating social identity as a unitary concept, Leach et al. (2008) demonstrated that there may be value in examining multiple aspects of social identity. They confirmed a two-component model of group identification: self-definition and self-investment that predicted different reactions to ingroup transgressions. Specifically, when facing apparent misdeeds undertaken by group members, the *self-investment component* was prospectively associated with cognitively legitimizing the role of the group to the point of denying apparent incriminating evidence that the group's actions were wrong and embracing interpretations that their group's actions were just and warranted. Self-investment was associated with defending the group and supporting the group's actions, regardless of the objective circumstances. Three of the four items in the measure of social identity used in the study presented here were included in the self-investment component of the Leach et al. model. We suspect that it is the self-investment component of gang identification that is strongly related to violence and intergang rivalries. In contrast, the stronger the *self-definition component* of social identity, the more likely it was that individuals viewed apparent misdeeds by their group as unfortunate and even felt guilty about their own (indirect) association with it. Leach et al. reasoned that when a person identifies with his group primarily on the basis of being similar to others in the group, then the person may feel personal guilt or misgivings about the group's misbehavior and is less likely to defend the group's questionable actions. We wonder if this might describe the reactions of former gang members who now work with programs to discourage gang violence and help prevent the youth from joining or help the youth leave the gang. Is it possible that these former gang

members have transitioned from a self-investment style of social identity to a self-definitional style and their reactions to gang violence have evolved accordingly? If so, future research could examine the possibility of creating intervention strategies that minimize the self-investment component among gang members without being concerned about a lasting self-definition component of social identification.

A second line of research undertaken to test social identity–related hypotheses that may be relevant to street gang dynamics has focused on which rival outgroups are likely to command the most attention or concern. Based on the reactive distinctiveness hypothesis (see Tajfel and Turner 1979; Jetten et al. 2004), it is predicted that a group will be highly motivated to distinguish itself from other relevant groups that are minimally distinct from (i.e., are very similar to) the ingroup. The implication is that the most serious conflict for a street gang should be directed toward objectively similar groups (i.e., nearby local street gangs), because this kind of outgroup threatens the ingroup's reputed superiority on valued characteristics (e.g., toughness and hardness). In other words, driven by competition for the superior social identity, the outgroups that would be predicted to elicit the most competition (and galvanize ingroup cohesion) are nearby street gangs seen as having similar attributes (close to equals). Striving for a superior social identity (reputation, status), gangs engage in delinquent or violent activities to distinguish themselves from similar rival outgroups. Could this motive for positive distinctiveness be met in some more socially appropriate ways?[22]

A third example of the way a social identity framework could be useful is suggested by research on conflicting social identities. Consider the case of conflicting social identities articulated by Lien (2005) in her interviews with a young emerging gang member in Oslo. Lien describes the internal conflict a young man felt as he committed robbery with other gang members for the first time. He explained how he had acted with steely resolve together with others in his group and assumed the role of ruthless criminal well enough to scare the victim and obtain the victim's money. But later, at home and out of the group context, he felt remorse and feared that his family or school buddies would find out how he obtained the money. He continued his gang affiliation by compartmentalizing the activities, stealing from victims (expected in the gang context), and generously treating his friends and family to gifts (respected within his family and conventional group of friends). He told the interviewer, "I would die of shame if my girl friend and friends knew." From a social identity perspective, opposing or conflicting social identities (e.g., antisocial versus prosocial) may be unstable. Social identities are conceptualized as layers of one's self-definition. While many people have multiple layers of social definitions of themselves, identities with opposing normative expectations such as those with antisocial versus prosocial or conventional norms may be difficult to sustain. Recent work by Brook et al. (2008) suggests that incompatibility among the normative expectations of multiple identities *that are strongly held and important to the individual* is related to depression, anxiety, and unhappiness. We suspect that maintaining strong opposing social identities is not tenable for most people. This suggests that gang prevention programs that find a way to assist the youth in developing strong identification[23] with a peer group that has conventional normative expectations could offer some protection against the temptations of gang involvement. If group affiliation is driven by social identity value as argued by social psychologists (Sherman et al. 1999), then the affiliation that brings the greater value should dominate.

In closing, we are optimistic that using the theoretical framework and empirical knowledge accumulated on the cognitive and behavioral implications of social identity and related theories can contribute new ideas to the challenge of gang reduction.

Notes

1. Here, we will use the term "street gangs," following Malcolm Klein's lead (Klein 1995). In this discussion, we will be referring primarily to traditional street gangs that are structured around a territory or turf that is claimed by the gang. This discussion may or may not apply to other types of gangs such as prison gangs, drug gangs, or other gangs.

2. See Brewer (2001), Hogg et al. (1995), and Stets and Burke (2000).

3. Written after he returned home, the poem was found by James Lenihan's children after his death. They shared the poem with CNN on May 28, 2010. To view the complete poem, use the link http://articles.cnn .com/2010–05-28/us/soldier.poem_1_poem-soldier-holland?_s=PM:US.

4. Documented by an interviewer in the Hennigan and Sloane (2011) study.

5. Though clearly relevant to social identity, we have excluded from this discussion identification with social categories such as male or female, gay or straight, and broad groups based on wealth, political affiliation, country of residence or origin, etc. and focused in this article on groups of people, such as peer groups, teams, activity groups, and street gangs.

6. In this chapter, we will use the word "groupness" in place of the somewhat awkward term entitativity.

7. Other researchers have defined the mechanisms that characterize groups in different ways including dynamic and categorical (Wilder and Simon 1998), inductive or deductive (Postmes et al. 2005), and common bond versus common identity (Prentice et al. 1994).

8. Brian Lickel and his colleagues (Lickel et al. 2000) found in separate studies that college students in the United States and in Poland rated the level of entitativity or groupness of "a local street gang" as being quite high, near the top of the scale, similar to the levels rated for a rock band or a professional sports team. This is consistent with the "Westside Story" stereotype prevalent in the USA that gangs are highly cohesive groups.

9. For additional methodological details, see Hennigan and Sloane (2011).

10. Conventional peer groups were defined as youth groups sponsored or organized by adults in the context of school, community, or religious organizations. "Unconventional" peer groups were defined as a clique or crew that was part of the street gang, a tagger or skater or party group, or some other informal group of peers (friends).

11. The items included were the following: "Overall <group> has very little to do with how I feel about myself. <Group> is an important reflection of who I am. <Group> is unimportant to my sense of what kind of person I am. In general, belonging to <group> is an important part of my self-image." Six response options ranged from strongly agree to strongly disagree.

12. Response options used were the following: 6 = almost every day, 5 = two to five times a week, 4 = about once

a week, 3 = two or three times a month, 2 = about once a month, or 1 = less than that.

13. Five response options ranged from very fuzzy to very clear.

14. The activities were drinking in public, shoplifting, driving while drunk or high, tagging or writing graffiti, stealing a car, breaking into a building to steal something, trespassing on private properly, selling drugs in your neighborhood, hitting someone in a fight, seriously beating someone up, intimidating or challenging someone that might tell authorities about something illegal that they or a friend did.

15. A chi-square value that is nonsignificant, an RMSEA < 0.08, and a CFI > 0.95 represents a good fit (Hu and Bentler 1999).

16. Alternative models were also tested. Specifically, identification was entered as an independent variable and cohesion, clear boundaries, and deterrence were entered as mediators. This model provided a poor fit, $\chi^2(3) = 7.87$, $p = 0.05$, RMSEA = 0.12, CFI = 0.90. It also seemed plausible that delinquency predicted cohesion which in turn predicted identification. This model was not a good fit for the data, $\chi^2(3) = 7.97$, $p = 0.05$, RMSEA = 0.14, CFI = 0.68.

17. Entering identification as an independent variable and cohesion, clear boundaries, and deterrence as mediators provided a worse fit compared to the fit of the model presented in Fig. 14.2, $\chi^2(3) = 5.27$, $p = 0.15$, RMSEA = 0.08, CFI = 0.96. An alternative model wherein violence was entered as an independent variable and identification as a dependent variable did not fit the data well, $\chi^2(3) = 7.11$, $p = 0.07$, RMSEA = 0.13, CFI = 0.88.

18. Reversing the order of independent and dependent variable also resulted in a good fit, $\chi^2(2) = .22$, $p = 0.89$, RMSEA = 0.00, CFI = 1.00.

19. Reversing the order of independent and dependent variable also provided a good fit, $\chi^2(2) = 0.38$, $p = 0.83$, RMSEA = 0.00, CF1 = 1.00.

20. Note that studies that include measures of the social costs of criminal offending blur the distinction made here between individual estimates of the likelihood of getting caught and punished and social identity (i.e., the social costs bleed into group identification). Presumably, the stronger one's identification with a social group, the more likely concerns about a comember's views of offending will be correlated with shared normative expectations.

21. The findings are consistent though not all of the alternative definitions were tested here.

22. This observation should not be confused with the kind of organizing that street workers used in the past to attempt to guide gang members toward more conventional activities (see Klein 1995). Clearly, this kind of

approach would have to be undertaken in ways that would avoid increasing gang cohesion and avoid fueling traditional gang rivalries.

23. With emphasis on "strong" because Brook et al. (2008) found that social identities that were not strongly held had little or no influence on psychological well-being at all.

References

Allport G (1954) The nature of prejudice. Addison-Wesley, Cambridge

Battin SR, Hill KG, Abbott RD, Catalano RF, Hawkins JD (1998) The contribution of gang membership to delinquency beyond delinquent friends. *Criminology* 36:93–115

Billig M, Tajfel H (1973) Social categorization and similarity in intergroup behavior. *Eur J Soc Psychol* 3:27–52

Brewer M (1991) The social self: on being the same and different at the same time. *Pers Soc Psychol Bull* 17:475–482

Brewer M (1999) The psychology of prejudice: ingroup love or outgroup hate? *J Soc Issues* 55:429–444

Brewer M (2001) The many faces of social identity: implications for political psychology. *Polit Psychol* 22:115–125

Brewer M, Hong Y, Li Q (2004) Dynamic entitativity: perceiving groups as actors. In: Judd C, Yzerbyt V, Corneille O (eds) *The psychology of group perception: perceived variability, entitativity, and essentialism.* Psychology Press, Philadelphia, pp. 25–38

Brook AT, Garcia J, Fleming M (2008) The effects of multiple identities on psychological well-being. *Pers Soc Psychol Bull* 34:1588–1600

Campbell DT (1958) Common fate, similarity, and other indices of the status of aggregates of persons as social entities. *Behav Sci* 3:14–24

Cartwright D, Zander A (eds) (1968) *Group dynamics*, 3rd edn. Harper and Row, New York

Decker SH (1996) Collective and normative features of gang violence. *Justice Q* 13:243–264

Decker SH, Van Winkle B (1996) *Life in the gang: family, friends and violence.* Cambridge University Press, New York

Dion KL (1979) Intergroup conflict and intragroup cohesiveness. In: Austin W, Worchel S (eds) *The social psychology of intergroup relations.* Brooks/Cole, Monterey, pp 211–224

Erikson EH (1963) *Childhood and society.* Norton, New York

Esbensen F-A, Huizinga D (1993) Gangs, drugs, and delinquency in a survey of urban youth. *Criminology* 31:565–589

Esbensen F-A, Huizinga D, Weiher A (1993) Gang and non-gang youth: differences in explanatory factors, *J Contemp Crim Just* 9:94–116

Festinger L, Schachter S, Back K (1950) *Social pressures in informal groups.* Harpers, New York

Gerard HB, Miller N (1967) Group dynamics. *Annu Rev Psychol* 18:287–332

Gordon RA, Lahey BB, Kawai E, Loeber R, Stouthamer-Loeber M, Farrington DP (2004) Antisocial behavior and youth gang membership: selection and socialization. *Criminology* 42:55–87

Grant PR, Brown R (1995) From ethnocentrism, to collective protest: responses to relative deprivation and threats to social identity. *Soc Psychol Q* 58:195–211

Hennigan KM, Sloane DC (2011) Effects of civil gang injunctions on street gang-involved youth: acquiescence or defiance. Unpublished manuscript, Department of Psychology, University of Southern California, Los Angeles

Hogg MA (2000) Subjective uncertainty reduction through self-categorization: a motivational theory of social identity processes. *Eur Rev Soc Psychol* 11:223–255

Hogg MA (2001) Social categorization, depersonalization, and group behavior. In: Hogg M, Tinsdale TS (eds) *Handbook of social psychology: group processes.* Blackwell, Malden, pp 57–85

Hogg MA (2007) Uncertainty-identity theory. In: Zanna MP (ed) *Advances in experimental social psychology*, vol 39. Academic, San Diego, pp 69–126

Hogg MA, Abrams D (1988) *Social identifications: a social psychology of intergroup relations and group processes.* Routledge, London

Hogg MA, Reid SA (2006) Social identity, self-categorization, and the communication of group norms. *Commun Theory* 16:7–30

Hogg M, Terry D, White K (1995) A tale of two theories: a critical comparison of identity theory with social identity theory. *Soc Psychol Q* 58:255–269

Hu LT, Bentler PM (1999) Cutoff criteria for fit indexes in covariance structure analysis: conventional criteria versus new alternatives. *Struct Equation Model* 6:1–55

Huizinga D, Elliot DS (1986) Reassessing the reliability and validity of self-report delinquency measures. *J Quant Criminol* 2:293–327

Ip GW, Chiu C, Wan C (2006) Birds of a feather and birds flocking together: physical versus behavioral cues may lead to trait- versus goal-based group perception. *J Pers Soc Psychol* 90:368–380

Jetten J, Spears R, Postmes T (2004) Intergroup distinctiveness and differentiation: a meta-analytic integration. *J Pers Soc Psychol* 86:862–879

Klein M (1971) *Street gangs and street workers.* Prentice-Hall, Englewood Cliffs

Klein M (1995) *The American street gang: its nature, prevalence, and control.* Oxford University Press, New York

Klein M, Crawford LY (1967) Groups, gangs and cohesiveness. *J Res Crime & Del* 4:63–75

Klein M, Maxson C (2006) *Street gang patterns and policies.* Oxford University Press, New York

Leach CW, Zomeren M, Zebel S, Vliek M, Pennekamp SF, Doosje B, Ouwerkerk JW, Spears R (2008) Group-level self-definition and self-investment: a hierarchical (multicomponent) model of in-group identification. *J Pers Soc Psychol* 95:144–165

Lickel B, Hamilton D, Wieczorkowska G, Lewis A, Sherman S, Uhles AN (2000) Varieties of groups and the perception of group entitativity. *J Pers Soc Psychol* 78:223–246

Lien I-L (2005) The role of crime acts in constituting the gang's mentality. In: Decker S, Weerman F (eds) *European street gangs and troublesome youth groups.* Alta Mira Press, Lanham, pp 31–50

Loeber R, Farrington DP, Stouthamer-Loeber M, Moffitt TE, Caspi A (1998) The development of male offending: key findings from the first decade of the Pittsburgh youth study. *Stud Crime and Crime Prev* 7:141–172

Luhtanen R, Crocker J (1992) A collective self-esteem scale: self-evaluation of one's social identity. *Pers Soc Psychol Bull* 18:302–318

Maxson C, Matsuda K, Hennigan K (2011) Deterrability among gang and nongang juvenile offenders: are gang members more (or less) deterrable than other juvenile offenders? *Crime Delinquency* 57:516–543

Pickett CL, Bonner B, Coleman JM (2002) Motivated self-stereotyping: heightened assimilation and differentiation needs result in increased levels of positive and negative stereotyping. *J Pers Soc Psychol* 82:543–562

Postmes T, Spears R (1998) Deindividuation and anti-normative behavior: a meta-analysis. *Psychol Bull* 123:238–259

Postmes T, Spears R, Lee T, Novak R (2005) Individuality and social influence in groups: inductive and deductive routes to group identity. *J Pers Soc Psychol* 89:747–763

Pratt T, Cullen F, Blevins K, Daigle L, Madensen T (2006) The empirical status of deterrence theory: a meta-analysis. In: Cullen F, Paul J, Blevins K (eds) *Taking stock: the status of criminological theories.* Transaction Publishers, New Brunswick, pp 367–395

Preacher KJ, Hayes AF (2004) SPSS and SAS procedures for estimating indirect effects in simple mediation models. *Behav Res Methods Instrum Comput* 36:717–731

Prentice DA, Miller DT, Lightdale JR (1994) Asymmetries in attachments to groups and to their members: distinguishing between common-interest and common-bond groups. *Pers Soc Psychol Bull* 20:484–493

Reicher S, Spears R, Postmes T (1995) A social identity model of deindividuation phenomena. *Eur Rev Soc Psychol* 6:161–198

Sherif M (1967) *Group conflict and cooperation: their social psychology*. Routledge, London

Sherif M, Sherif CW (1979) Research on intergroup relations. In: Austin WG, Worchel S (eds) *The social psychology of intergroup relations*. Brooks/Cole Publishing, Monterey, CA

Sherman SJ, Hamilton DL, Lewis AC (1999) Perceived entitativity and the social identity value of group memberships. In: Abrams D, Hogg MA (eds) *Social identity and social cognition*. Blackwell, Malden, pp 80–110

Short JF, Strodtbeck FL (1965) *Group process and gang delinquency*. University of Chicago Press, Chicago

Smith JR, Terry DJ, Hogg MA (2007) Social identity and the attitude-behavior relationship: effects of anonymity and accountability. *Eur J Soc Psychol* 36:239–257

Spears R, Scheepers D, Jetten J, Doosje B, Ellemers N, Postmes T (2004) Group homogeneity, entitativity and social identity: dealing with/in social structure. In: Yzerbyt V, Judd CM, Corneille O (eds) *The psychology of group perception: contributions to the study of homogeneity, entitativity and essentialism*. Psychology Press, New York, pp 293–316

Spergel IA (1995) *The youth gang problem*. Oxford University Press, New York

Stets JE, Burke P (2000) Identity theory and social identity theory. *Soc Psychol Q* 63:224–237

Stryker S (1987) Identity theory: developments and extensions. In: Yardley K, Honess T (eds) *Self and identity: psychosocial perspectives*. Wiley, New York

Stryker S, Burke P (2000) The past, present, and future of an identity theory. *Soc Psychol Q* 63:284–297

Tajfel H (1978) *Differentiation between social groups*. Academic, London

Tajfel H, Turner JC (1979) An integrative theory of intergroup conflict. In: Austin WG, Worchel S (eds) *The social psychology of intergroup relations*. Brooks-Cole, Monterey

Tajfel H, Turner JC (1986) The social identity theory of inter-group behavior. In: Worchel S, Austin LW (eds) *Psychology of intergroup relations*. Nelson-Hall, Chicago

Tajfel H, Flament C, Billig M, Bundy RP (1971) Social categorization and intergroup behaviour. *Eur J Soc Psychol* 1:149–178

Thornberry TP, Krohn MD (2000) The self-report method for measuring delinquency and crime. In: Duffee D, Crutchfield RD, Mastrofski S, Mazerolle L, McDowall D, Ostrom B (eds) *CJ2000: innovations in measurement and analysis*, vol 4. US Department of Justice, Washington, DC, pp 33–83

Thornberry TP, Krohn MD, Lizotte AJ, Smith CA, Tobin K (2003) *Gangs and delinquency in developmental perspective*. Cambridge University Press, New York

Turner JC (1975) Social comparison and social identity: some prospects for intergroup behaviour. *Eur J Soc Psychol* 5:5–34

Turner JC (1985) Social categorization and the self-concept: a social cognitive theory of group behavior. In: Lawler EJ (ed) *Advances in group processes: theory and research*, vol 2. JAI Press, Greenwich, pp 77–121

Turner JC, Hogg MA, Oakes PJ, Reicher SD, Wetherell M (1987) *Rediscovering the social group: a self-categorization theory*. Basil Blackwell, Oxford, England

Vigil JD (1988a) *Barrio gangs: street life and identity in southern California*. University of Texas Press, Austin

Vigil JD (1988b) Group processes and street identity: adolescent Chicano gang members. *Ethos* 16:421–445

Wallace AFC, Fogelson R (1965) The identity struggle. In: Boszomeniji-Nagy I, Framo JL (eds) *Intensive family therapy: theoretical and practical aspects*. Harper and Row, New York

Whiting BB (1980) Culture and social behavior: a model for the development of social behavior. *Ethos* 8:95–116

Wilder D, Simon AF (1998) Categorical and dynamic groups: implication for social perception and intergroup behavior. In: Sedikides C, Schopler I, Insko C (eds) *Intergroup cognition and intergroup behavior*. Erlbaum, Mahwah, pp 27–44

CHAPTER 15

Gang Transformation, Changes or Demise: Evidence from an English City

Juanjo Medina ▪ Judith Aldridge ▪ Robert Ralphs

We tend to think of gangs as static entities; once established, they are thought to remain as they are, where they are. This is probably not a reasonable image. Gangs often change in nature and location. Indeed, many street gangs disappear over time and may or may not be replaced by new versions of themselves. How and why gangs undergo transformations has not been thoroughly researched, but could tell us much about their character and the situations that impinge upon them. The following chapter sheds light on significant gang changes in a major English city. While the location is overseas, this report reveals many similarities between these English street gangs and the street gangs familiar to American researchers. Comparative research of this sort strengthens our capacity to draw generalized conclusions about our objects of study.

Introduction

There is ample recognition within the criminological literature that gangs come and go and that those sustaining longer periods of existence may undergo important transformations (Klein and Maxson, 2006). Thus, "as types of criminal opportunities and social and institutional circumstances change, different types of criminal organisations develop" (Arias, 2006: p. 55). There are, however, very few empirical studies that assess gang stability, document the process of transformation that

gangs experience, or provide explanations for these changes (Rodgers 2006).

Some evidence suggests that (1) transformation rather than dissolution is the modal way in which gangs change and that (2) these transformations have more to do with external community characteristics than with the characteristics of the individual gang members or the group itself (Klein and Maxson, 2006).[1] Most of this research, however, is based only on police data. On the other hand, some ethnographic studies have supported the view that individual gang member trajectories in relation to "maturing out" of crime are key to understanding the process of gang transformation (Jenssen, 2008). As contested as to what drives gang changes is the pattern of transformation that gangs experience. Some have argued that gangs naturally evolve from turf street groups, to market-oriented drug gangs, and finally to groups that mix political and mercenary elements (Sullivan and Bunker, 2002). However, there are too few empirical studies of gang transformations to make general claims of this nature. It is also far from certain that once drugs come into the equation there is only one possible path of evolution: towards greater organisation and sophistication.

In this chapter we aim to address the question of gang transformations using data from an ethnographic study of gangs in an English city.[2] Fieldwork took place between 2005 and 2008 but we gathered considerable retrospective information about local gang history through interviews with individuals involved in gangs back in the 80s and have, after completion of fieldwork, managed to keep in touch

---

**** This is the first printing of this article ****

with key informants. The longitudinal aspects to the research design allow us to reflect on some of the intergenerational and intragenerational changes in relation to gangs and transformations of two specific gangs. Although our ethnographic study was focused on a variety of neighbourhoods across Research City, here we only report about gangs (Upperside and Lowerside) in Inner West (a corridor of historically marginalised neighbourhoods with a substantial black and minority ethnic population) since they are the ones about which we are in a stronger position to discuss transformations. Most lethal firearm violence in Research City is considered by the police to be "gang-related" and involves conflict within and between gangs from Inner West. Inner West gangs are often presented by media and authorities as the archetypal "contemporary" violent and profit-oriented street gang in the UK.

Before we describe our findings we describe the terms of the debate about gangs in the UK. This is relevant insofar as it raises questions about changes in the UK gang landscape over the last few decades. Gangs, as specific groups, do not experience processes of transformation in a vacuum. We can only understand within-gang transformation in the context of more general societal changes. Some commentators, as we show, have argued that cultural and economic changes have resulted in key cohort-related changes to gangs in the UK over the last few decades. We then explain how these macro-level changes have interacted with micro-level changes within gangs in Research City. In particular, we discuss how the proliferation of drug markets and the police response to this proliferation in Research City contributed to foster a gang culture that has continued to today. The degree to which this gang culture allows us to speak of articulated "supergangs" hierarchically organised around drug dealing, as some have argued (Pitts, 2008), is however more questionable. Equally, we will question the degree to which we can always assume gang stability exists when particular gang names continue to be used in certain localities.

Context: The Changing Gang Landscape in the UK

The dominant view of youth gangs until recently in Britain was established during the 1960 and 1970s.

Downes, in his influential *The Delinquent Solution*, argued that delinquent groups in the east end of London lacked "structured cohesion," institutional permanence and a group commitment to delinquency similar to that described by contemporary American criminologists such as Cloward, Ohlin and Yablonsky. Downes concluded that at most, he found street-corner groups or "small cliques whose members committed illegal acts sometimes collectively, sometimes in pairs, sometimes individually, in some cases regularly, in others only rarely" and for which delinquent engagement was not more central than "sexual prowess." These groups did not either "obtrude, let alone dominate an area" (Downes, 1966: 199). Despite the fact that his work was grounded in only a particular area of London and Downes himself suggested that "gangs" with leaders and territorial disputes had historically been present in the East End, his research was interpreted as evidence by the British criminological community that there have never been gangs in the UK. Similarly, Howard Parker's (1974) ethnographic account of delinquent youth networks concluded there were no gangs in Liverpool, insofar as the delinquent groups he described did not "possess such rigid defining criteria." Despite their persistent offending involvement, their *raison d'etre* was primarily social. These observations and descriptions are not dissimilar from many descriptions of gangs in the US; however, these findings have been widely interpreted to offer support for the notion that gangs were an American anomaly. What the UK had instead was groups of rowdy working-class adolescents involved in a succession of youth subcultures (teddy boys, punks, skinheads, rude boys, etc) that, according to the dominant view, were not gangs (Pitts, 2008). They were loosely structured groups for which fighting, crime and anti-social behaviour were incidental and secondary to their social and developmental functions. The only research from this period that had no difficulty attaching the descriptor "gang" to these groups was Patrick's (1973) ethnographic account in Glasgow, a city perceived in the criminological literature as an outlier.

Things began to change during the late 1980s and early 1990s. A number of shootings of young black people involved in drug dealing in Manchester at the time were said to be linked to "gang wars" (Walsh, 2003) and to control of the lucrative drug markets provided by heroin outbreaks and the emerging night time economy. So unusual were these events that they received considerable media attention and Manchester was dubbed "Gangchester" and "Gunchester" in the press. A research report carried out by Bullock and Tilley (2002) evaluating Manchester's responses to these problems offered further support for the notion that gangs were responsible for this escalation into firearm violence. Since this time, similar developments have been reported by the media in Birmingham, and later in London, Liverpool and Nottingham. Alongside this, a number of often controversial journalistic and biographical accounts about these new British gangs began to appear in the "true crime" section of bookstores.

The academic community in the UK was slow to respond to the emerging moral panic about gangs. A number of ethnographic accounts of marginalised young people or young offenders, published early in this decade, continued to assert the view that Asian, female or youth gangs did not exist in British marginalised areas (respectively, Alexander, 2000; Batchelor, 2001; Sanders, 2005), and that the problem was a media construction. These contributors noted serious concerns that media discourses misrepresented the experiences of young people (Batchelor, 2001), contributing to the stigmatisation of ethnic minority youth in the UK and imposing "a conservative culturalist perspective on black youth identifications" (Alexander, 2000: 238). These studies were correct in pointing out the excesses and tone of the media reporting, but may have been premature in some of their conclusions. Given this reluctance in the British academic community to directly engage in the study of gangs, it is perhaps not surprising that it took a young Dutch ethnographer to come to Manchester to carry out the first contemporary ethnographic study of gangs in Britain (Mares, 2001). His research, often neglected by subsequent reviews of British "gang" studies (e.g., Centre for Social Justice, 2009), questioned the established view by providing a detailed ethnographic description of some gangs in Manchester and a theoretical account of their development.

Mares's research was followed by a number of self report surveys with samples of arrestees (Bennett & Holloway, 2004) and young people (Communities that Care, 2004; Hayden, 2008; Bradshaw, 2005; Sharp et al., 2005) with a specific focus on measuring gang membership. These surveys document a level of gang involvement in the UK that is similar to those levels encountered in other advanced capitalist societies, including the US (see Klein and Maxson, 2006). These surveys also suggest that young people identified as gang-involved present a more serious offending profile and problematic background than other young people. This developing body of survey evidence also suggests that British gangs show a less pronounced institutional identity than those encountered in the USA (Winfree et al., 2007) and that their offending profile is far removed from the gun- or knife-toting and drug dealing projected in the media and by law enforcement agencies.

Are these surveys simply rebranding the long-standing phenomenon of neighbourhood based groups of young people involved in low-level offending? Is the term gang simply a new label being used to designate the—not radically changed—experiences of marginalised urban youth? Or did something really change during the late 1980s in the nature and dynamics of these groups? Can we assume that significant changes in political economy and culture from the 1970s to today (e.g. deindustrialisation, globalisation, consumerism, increased spatial polarisation of poverty and wealth, new philosophies of local government and urban development) have not had an impact on youth group dynamics, as they have in other neighbourhood-rooted criminal networks (Hobbs, 2001) and gun culture (Hallsworth and Silverstone, 2009)? A new generation of ethnographic or qualitative studies of gangs has emerged over the last five years in Cardiff and surrounding areas (Maher, 2007), London (Pitts, 2008), the anonymous "Research City" about which we report here (Aldridge and Medina, 2008), the five main Scottish cities (Bannister et al., forthcoming) and other areas that are considered to be hotspots for gang violence (Youth Justice Board, 2008). All have aimed to further clarify these questions.

The author that is most often associated with the assertion that we have witnessed a transformation of delinquent youth groups in the UK is Pitts (2008). Pitts claims that we are witnessing the development of new articulated "supergangs" with long histories of involvement in organised crime, clear subgroups, role differentiation, established territories and neighbourhood control, vertical links into higher echelon organised crime, and highly organised drug dealing activity. Pitts moreover identifies a new phenomenon of more institutionalised gangs with higher levels of organisation, more formalised structures, and greater hold on young peoples lives, which are more embedded in neighbourhoods' economic and social life. These supergangs, according to Pitts, developed from conditions of marginalisation and flourishing drugs markets. This explanation echoes accounts about the spread of gangs during the 1980s in the USA (see Fagan, 1996) and is consistent with research suggesting that during the first heroin outbreaks in the 1980s in the UK, young people were increasingly drawn into the informal economy and drug dealing to secure "a standard of living better than mere survival" (Auld et al., 1986: 173) and to achieve status, identity and meaning in contexts of marginalisation (Pearson, 1987).

A similarly debated point is whether these emerging gangs have been responsible for changing trends in violence (Hallsworth and Young, 2008). But regardless of whether gangs have contributed significantly to overall levels of violence, evidence suggests gang violence has a highly localised character (Home Office, 2008; Bannister et al, forthcoming). Police sources suggest diverse scenarios across cities. In Manchester and Birmingham, for example, drugs gangs developed with shootings linked to entrenched but highly fluctuating "tit-for-tat" violence around issues of "respect." In Glasgow, the weapons of choice are knives. Hales et al. (2006) suggests that gun violence is closely tied to illegal drug markets and gangs. Both police intelligence and independent research suggest a close tie between gangs and firearm violence in affected communities (Bullock and Tilley, 2002). Although fatalities from firearms are exceptionally rare in England and Wales (59 in 2006/2007, or 0.15 deaths per 100,000), precisely because of

their rarity they raise significant public alarm. In England and Wales these disproportionately affect black young people as both perpetrators and victims. This research suggests that gangs often underlie a changing criminal culture in which guns are becoming increasingly significant.

The development of policy responses to the media's increasingly sensationalist reporting of gangs and gang violence was slow at first. As Pitts (2008) has highlighted, this is particularly curious for a government that has exploited fear of youth crime for electoral advantage. This sluggishness changed significantly in 2007. Then Prime Minister Tony Blair presided over Britain's first "gun crime summit" as a response to new shootings of very young innocent bystanders in what were presented as gang related incidents. Later that year, one of the first measures adopted by Gordon Brown as new Prime Minister was the formation of the Home Office's *Tackling Gangs Action Programme* (TGAP) to identify good practice in dealing with gangs and gun crime. This resulted in the toolkit: *Tackling Gangs* (Home Office, 2008) and a government guidance leaflet for parents on how to detect children's involvement in gangs. Increasingly, police forces and local authorities are drawing on US interventions, importing models developed in Los Angeles and Boston of dedicated firearm/gang units and gang databases, as well as multi-agency gang intervention teams. Recent legislation introduced gang injunctions as a new tool in the police arsenal against young people suspected of gang membership. At the policy level, the term "gang" has now become entrenched in both national and local crime and disorder strategies (e.g. Home Office, 2008). However, considerable confusion still remains as to what a gang is. A serious concern for civil liberty advocates and gang researchers is how the "gang" label is both being used in a rather indiscriminate manner and disproportionally applied to ethnic minority youth (Bullock and Tilley, 2008; Ralphs et al., 2009).

In sum, media, policy and some academic accounts recognised that delinquent youth groups in Britain experienced change during the 1980s that continues today. These groups were seen to have become more institutionalised, more oriented toward profit activities built around participation in drug markets, and to have increased their level of participation in serious injurious violence, particularly firearm-related violence. In a parallel fashion, policy and programmatic responses to gangs have also changed and become more intrusive in the lives of young people (Ralphs et al., 2009; Medina et al., 2010; Aldridge et al., 2010). In the remainder of this chapter we focus on changes in the gang landscape in Research City in order to try to understand the reasons for such transformations.

The Origins of *Inner West* Gangs: From Peer Street Groups to Violent Drug Dealing Networks

It is probably fair to say that groups meeting the broad Eurogang definition[3] have existed in socially excluded parts of urban Britain for a very long time (Patrick, 1973; Parker, 1974; Mares, 2001; Hallsworth and Young, 2004), with accounts even going back to the nineteenth century (Davies, 2008). Our research confirms that gangs are not a recent phenomenon in Research City. Some of our older informants (now in their 50s) described their experiences in street-oriented, territorial, offending and fighting groups as part of their growing up in poor areas of Research City during the 1970s, and police we spoke to likewise described enforcement tactics used with these groups dating from around this time.

Were there any changes in the attributes and behaviours of groups of this type that may have made them more likely to be labelled as gangs? Consistent with Pitts' observations (2008), we saw evidence in Inner West of the impact of changing drug market conditions in the development of new gang identities. Inner West was traditionally an important focus for distribution of cannabis partially tolerated by local law enforcement, and the dealing of heroin in closed drugs markets by user-dealers. When crack cocaine hit the street, dealers from Inner West capitalised on this *laissez faire* climate in this more profitable merchandise. We have clear evidence that during the 1980s and 1990s, territorial peer groups of ethnic minority youth facing significant discrimination in education and the labour market were becoming increasingly involved in minor offending and the retail sale of heroin and crack in very successful open drug markets: "*There were mainly street markets whereby anybody could go to that market place and buy drugs basically, mainly heroin, and people would travel great distances to Research City to buy from these open markets simply because the reputation was of good quality gear and good, reasonable prices*" (K19).

In Inner West, these two groups (Upperside and Lowerside) soon started to be identified as gangs in media reports and by the police, and eventually adopted for themselves the "gang" names the police had assigned them. In a context of marginalisation and ethnic discrimination, young people involved in these groups saw these emerging illegal opportunities as key in explaining the transition of their informal delinquent peer groups into "gangs." This Inner West gang member explains: "*There were always gangs, but they weren't selling drugs. People just used to hang around together in groups. Before Upperside and Lowerside appeared. . . . My brother is 8 years older, so when he was younger they did go out and commit petty crimes, they were gangs, but they were doing different things.*" External labelling by media and the police played a pivotal role in reinforcing the group identity of these gangs. These peer groups became, or perhaps following local lore about criminal groups aspired to become, what the drug literature describes as structural pyramidical distribution systems (May et al., 2008) and the gang literature as specialist "drug gangs." In sum, changing drug markets and the societal response to them contributed to foster the encroachment of a gang culture in Inner West.

Apart from the growing significance of drugs in the informal economy and social organisation of the street in these neighbourhoods, a second key development during the 1980s and the 1990s was the emergence and stabilisation of comparatively high levels of gun violence. We found considerable evidence of conflict that arose from within the illegal open drugs markets in which these gang members participated. This conflict in Inner West was not, however (as commonly supposed), over the markets themselves, but tended to result from dealers stealing from or "taxing" one another, and often members of their own gang. In this context, dealers and gang members in *Inner West* began to arm themselves with guns. Violence linked to these market conditions and personal disputes from interpersonal conflict resulted in a spiral of retaliatory, primarily gun, homicides: "*We just wanted to make money, sell drugs, get rich. And, we was getting robbed, getting shot at, and then what are you gonna do, shoot back, innit? . . . All of sudden you start to sell drugs obviously and it starts to be like jealousy, we were clashing with each other so before you knew it everybody had like beef with each other.*"

In a context of tight gun controls and very low national levels of gun violence, these events made the phenomenon of "gang" violence particularly visible. This violence, although of an order of magnitude many times lower than that found in the US, continues to fluctuate today and marks Inner West as separate from other gang areas in Research City. The introduction of guns, as documented elsewhere (e.g., Jensen, 2008), had a significant impact in the lived experience of gang involved young people. References to violence and exposure to violent events as victims, perpetrators and witnesses, became part of everyday conversation and of growing up for many of the young people we spoke to. As this former girlfriend and relative of key Inner West gang members described to us: "*There was that many shootings at the time that it was just normal, it did become normal, you didn't even really think about the value of life, it was sad an everything, but then a couple of days later you would have forgotten about it and somebody else would have been shot*" (BE-A2). Our ethnographic work in Research City offers consistent support to these observations. Gangs in the Inner West area of the city developed and armed themselves during the late 1980s and 1990s in a context in which predatory attacks on dealers, as well as dealing activities, were increasing. The two dominant gangs at the time then initiated a long irregular cycle of retaliatory violence. As Klein has noted, there is no city with just one gang. Conflict is essential to the development of gang identities and, although a good deal of the violent conflict we registered was intra-gang rather than inter-gang, the clash between Upperside and Lowerside contributed to reinforce their respective group identities and brand names.

Changes in Inner West

As suggested in the previous section, explanations referring to ethnic discrimination, social exclusion, the role of drug markets, the international arms trade, and police labelling, then, have some value when understanding the transformation of delinquent youth groups in Inner West into quasi-specialist drug gangs in the late 1980s and early 1990s. Our data suggests that was the case. More questionable, as we will see, is the degree to which these processes during the late 1980s and early 1990s have led to the continued organisational institutionalisation of the gangs we studied. Although important changes have taken place in Inner West from the late 1990s to today, we cannot conclude that these changes have resulted in Inner West gangs achieving greater formal organisation (whichever way you define this). In this section we discuss these more recent changes.

The Decline of Open Drug Markets and the Factors Facilitating This Decline

Changing market conditions and successful police operations during the 1990s disrupted these specialist drugs gangs. As in other parts of Britain, we find the transition from a "highly structured pyramidical distribution system" into a "fragmented, non-hierarchical market with little structure" (May and Hough, 2001: 555). A combination of factors conspired to change the significance of Inner West as the place for the successful sale of drugs in open markets. This sort of market was particularly vulnerable to surveillance police operations, as TV dramas like *The Wire* have popularised. As a result of these operations a number of Inner West gang members received custodial sentences. The architectural redesign of the locations where these markets operated and the re-housing of numerous families also played a role in disrupting these markets. Other factors external to the activity of the authorities (e.g., mobile phones) also played a key role to the transition from open markets to distribution through personal networks. The breakdown of the street markets facilitated the move from gang co-ordinated drug dealing to individuals trading as free agents: "*Back in the day there was a structure of you know, you'd have your leader, you have the little second person and then you would have your workers and that. But nowadays it's more like you make your own money and do your own thing. Whereas back in the day you used to like go out and earn money for the gang and put it in and then you know you'd share it between them but nowadays it's everyone for themselves basically."* This picture contrasts starkly with the recent evidence of Pitts (2008) in London, where it is asserted that many "supergangs" have only recently evolved into these highly co-ordinated entities; in fact the reverse seems to be the case in Inner West.

Police intelligence officers spoke of the lessening importance of drug dealing amongst gang members, noting a diversification into other earning opportunities like stealing from cars or (armed) robberies. Nevertheless, even today, most gang members we spoke to were involved to some degree in dealing—though now primarily of cannabis instead of heroin and crack cocaine—even if their gangs did not specialise in this way. Although drug sales are now fundamentally individual activity, we still find some cooperation and division of labour amongst gang members (primarily between retail level dealers and their delivery focussed "runners").

The declining significance of Inner West as an open drug market had an impact on the level of profit for gang involved individuals. Inner West gang members active 15–20 years ago often quoted large incomes of £1–2,000 a week working in open heroin markets. However, these amounts incorporate an element of romantic reconstruction of the past, often referred to turnover rather than profit, were rarely secure and reliable, and tended not to result in financial stability. Indeed, most previously high-earning ex-gang members we learned about, today were in prison or living on state benefit.

Criminal income within gangs today, therefore, is not considerable, at least in part as a consequence of declining open markets. Gang members today earn money from a combination of legal and illegal opportunities in what could be described as "cafeteria-style" earning. An exclusive focus on illicit incomes is misleading because legitimate earnings (e.g. paid employment, business, state benefits) are as important. As the work and crime literature has established, legal and illegal economic activities are not mutually exclusive and "doubling up" in crime and other earning activities is common (Fagan, 1997).

Only a small minority of older gang involved individuals appear to have established consistently successful "illegal only" incomes by using their gang reputation and contacts to get involved in more serious criminal enterprises (e.g., prostitution, importation, and multi kilo drug distribution). However, whether these individuals can be considered any longer to be "gang members" is in question as we discuss below.

Gang Transformation or Gang Demise?

What is really left of the gangs of Inner West that developed during the 1980s? For a gang to have "transformed" assumes that the gang continues to exist in some form. But how meaningful is it to speak of these gangs still existing as subsequent generations come along? This section examines the extent to which the Upperside and Lowerside gangs can be seen as having a continuing existence.

These gang names in Belmont have continued to be used by the media and law enforcement agencies and have become part of the popular folklore of Research City. The police often identify delinquent groups formed by younger siblings and relatives of individuals formerly affiliated to either Upperside or Lowerside as if they were subgroups of these entities. These new subgroups, according to the official view, can be considered a "confederation of cliques" that share a *common* identity with older members. As one city official put it to us: *"Today a lot of our kids weren't even born at that time when these gangs started. And they've grown up knowing only of 'the war,' as they like to call it. And they don't know why it started, and they don't know what it's all about, they just know that it goes on and they're on one side of it."* The official and popular position on whether Upperside and Lowerside gangs remain in existence today is therefore clear. However, it is worth thinking systematically as to whether this is actually the case by examining our evidence. In order to answer this question, we separately consider (1) whether original members, twenty and thirty years on, are rightly still considered members; and (2) to what extent younger individuals are members of these original groups or somehow affiliated to them.

Original Members: Community Merchants and Criminal Merchants

We begin with those who were affiliated to the Upperside and Lowerside Belmont gangs from the 1980s and 1990s, now in their thirties and forties. Although some of these have moved away or in other ways cut former connections, many retain gang connections through the myriad friendship and family links that run through gangs and their neighbourhoods. Police tend to treat those who have maintained links with suspicion (for example by keeping their names on existing "gang" databases, and their photographs on the wall of the specialist gang unit). However, the extent to which these individuals have completely desisted from gang-connected and other criminal activities varies considerably. One typical "route out" of gang activity was in becoming (or aiming to become) community activists or community workers. We refer to these individuals as "community merchants."[4] We found that these individuals were able to use their past (or existing) connections to gangs as a way to acquire credibility in their roles as those who "know whereof they speak." Community merchants were sometimes put into service informally within the community, where their past reputations are turned to as a leveller in the resolution of conflict involving younger siblings or other gang members. We got to know well four individuals over the course of our research who, as a result of taking on community-oriented roles like these whilst retaining gang connections, could sometimes become embroiled in current-day gang dramas. Some of these individuals may even use their gang contacts to engage in activities in the informal economy to supplement their legal income (most often, this was through retail level drug dealing). Whilst we identify something of a blurring of the boundaries between "outside" and "inside" the gang amongst individuals like these, we are clear that it would be misleading to see these individuals as sitting at the top of a hierarchy trying to preserve the legacy of a common gang identity.

But what about those who persist in more dedicated criminal careers—does it make sense to consider any of these individuals as retaining gang membership today? As highlighted in the previous section, only a small minority of older individuals that were part of Upperside or Lowerside appear to have established consistently successful "illegal only" (or primary) incomes. However, we question whether they can be considered "gang members," given the extent to which their contacts and operations spread across Research City, and involve dealings with a wide range of what they may previously have considered "rival" gangs and family firms. Although they may retain social and family connections to their former peers and amongst the younger generation, and even rely on some of them for "backup" in criminal enterprises, critically, they do not restrict their criminal collaborations to current or former members of their gangs. Criminal merchants are often still proud of their past gang affiliation and invoke it as something that gives them street capital (Sandberg and Pedersen, 2009). However, they do not appear to get involved in everyday "gang dramas," for example, involving tit-for-tat retaliations or in relation to perceived slights. We refer to these individuals as "criminal merchants." We have argued that gangs first and foremost are groups with a reputation for a willingness to resort to violence, even if rarely enacted (Medina et al., in submission). Upperside and Lowerside as "brand names" still retain these associations and are likely to prove useful as street capital amongst these merchants. Thus, as with the community merchants, criminal merchants may retain some superficial features of gang membership insofar as doing so facilitates their trade, and is anyway a natural part of continuing to live in a city without severing long-standing friendship and family ties. But on this we are clear: it is misleading to see them as leaders of their former gang or any of its younger cliques, as Pitts may in relation to the London "super-gangs" he observed (Pitts, 2008). Indeed, we go even further: not only are community merchants and criminal merchants not leaders of Upperside and Lowerside today (in spite of police insistence to the contrary), it makes very little sense to even consider them members.

The Newer Generations

There are a number of gangs that are believed by local law enforcement to be younger off-shoots or cliques within Upperside and Lowerside. From Upperside, these cliques include Shankleytown's Crestside Man Dem (only a few streets' distance from the Upperside neighbourhood) and Fairview's Fairview Crew a few miles further afield and outside of Belmont. In relation to Lowerside, the Belmont Bloods reside in areas that overlap with the Lowerside neighbourhood, and, a few miles further afield, Ravenna's Ravenna Bloods gang, again, outside of Belmont. The "official" view about these younger groups is that they can alternatively be read: (1) as integral parts of Upperside and Lowerside in a hierarchical organisation scheme, (2) as "proxies" of Upperside or Lowerside (younger groups being manipulated in a war by proxy), or (3) as "projects" being sponsored by Upperside or Lowerside as venture capitalist firms. The image of some Chicago gangs underpins some of these police interpretations. Explanations of gang proliferation in the research literature, however, have emphasised processes around local community factors and cultural mimicking spawning new gangs rather than as the result of imperialist or capitalist gang broadening of their geographical scope (Klein and Maxson, 2006).[5] In this sense, alternatively, these youth offending groups could be interpreted as simply reproducing the cultural template laid out by Upperside and Lowerside. This cultural template would have been known in many cases to younger gang involved individuals through intimate or family connections to key individuals in these groups but also as reinvented by media accounts that have heavily popularised these two gangs.

So what do we find in Inner West? Are these younger groups in fact younger "cliques" or subgroups connected to Upperside and Lowerside in the ways that law enforcement suggest, or are they simply new gangs? Our evidence on this question is mixed. Both of the same-neighbourhood "doorstep" cliques for each gang—Crestside Man Dem and Belmont Bloods—have clear familial and social links to Upperside and Lowerside respectively. Members are the children, cousins, family friends, and neighbours of original members of Upperside and Lowerside. Although the young people in these cliques sometimes refer to themselves by their clique name, at other times they refer to themselves by the "parent" gang name, especially, for example, using the parent gang name for credibility when travelling further afield in Research City or outside of it, where the parent gang names are more widely known. The situation is slightly different, however, for the cliques whose members reside outside of Belmont—Fairview Crew and Ravenna Bloods. These cliques are made up of members who, like the doorstep cliques, include individuals who are children, cousins, family friends and neighbours of Upperside and Lowerside. The reasons for their "residential outsider" status in relation to Belmont are varied, and described elsewhere (Aldridge et al., 2010). However, these cliques also contain individuals born and bred in the neighbourhoods in which they are located—Fairview and Ravenna, without the same familial and social connections to Upperside and Lowerside. These young people are aware of and acknowledge the connections to the original gangs, but are much less likely to use the names, see themselves as representing them, or show respect to original Upperside or Lowerside gangsters. When referring to themselves, they prefer instead to identify with their home-grown neighbourhood gangs' names (but like those in the doorstep cliques, however, they may use the parent gang names as and when it suits to do so). In summary, then, the young people in both doorstep cliques and those further afield identify with the "parent" gangs, although the extent of this identification seems to vary depending on the extent to which the social networks of these groups overlap.

Original and older Belmont gangsters also recognise these cliques as "belonging" to one or the other of Upperside or Lowerside. But to suggest that the lines of connection between "parent" and "child" gangs are clear and unequivocal would be ill-advised. Our research makes clear that gangs all over Research City—Upperside and Lowerside included—are messy social networks that often overlap, including within families and friendship groups. We found the same to apply amongst these younger cliques. We have ample evidence that kinship does not strictly—or even primarily—determine with which cliques gang affiliated young people will identify. Even teenage children of well-known and respected Upperside and Lowerside individuals from the 1980s and 1990s are known to affiliate with cliques affiliated to a father's ostensibly "rival" gang.

We see only minimal—or at best mixed—evidence of hierarchical obedience and respect amongst young people in these cliques to the older generation of Upperside and Lowerside gang members (amongst its current members, as well as to both the community merchants and criminal merchants we describe in this chapter). To the extent that we do find a vertical deference, this is primarily amongst the "doorstep" cliques (Belmont Bloods and Crestside Man Dem); even here, however, our evidence is suggestive that control by older members over younger members appears to be declining over generations. We have, however, encountered situations of exploitation of younger members by some of the older generation.

The police imagine these cliques as part of the Upperside or Lowerside confederations and as part of two violently rival "supergangs." We return therefore to our question in light of the evidence presented. Does it make sense to talk about "gang transformation"? Or are we simply documenting a case of Upperside and Lowerside demise and the development of new gangs that are better understood as distinct and autonomous entities? As we have shown, we have evidence for both of these possibilities. The answer to these questions, however, is not only empirically complicated, but complicated in the very asking, because of the assumption contained in the question that gangs—as a concept—are, primarily, *organisations*. It is clear that Upperside and Lowerside continue to have some kind of existence, but it is not clear that this existence refers to a concrete criminal organisation with clear *institutional* connection to the past. Today these gangs continue to exist as objects to the police, but also more widely as symbols of status and street capital, as cultural referents for younger residents of these communities, and many other things besides. The criminological angle of most gang research means that when we talk of transformation, the focus is on organisational change or on change in the criminal careers of gang involved

individuals. From that limited organisational viewpoint, we see evidence of demise of the groups as active criminal networks, as well as evidence of ongoing existence, primarily through the cliques that have been spawned from them.

Final Thoughts

This chapter has described some of the basic changes that have taken place amongst Inner West gangs over the last 30 years. Our data support the view that profound cultural and socio-economic changes (e.g., globalisation of firearms and illegal drug trade, increasing spatial polarisation of poverty, etc.) shaped the experiences of young people participating in social networks with a group identity built around participation in criminal activities. This was a significant break from the past. Policing practices that were too keen to emphasise the distinctiveness of the criminal activities of the mostly-ethnic minority youth associated with these networks also contributed to raise their visibility and group identity.

However, the evolution of these groups does not conform to common stereotypes in Britain. We found little evidence of the appearance of supergangs that others have reported and that law enforcement agencies often mobilise as an image for strategic and political reasons; instead we find a much more complex picture. Why did Upperside and Lowerside not become supergangs? Visions of the gang as cohesive entities tend to overlook the high level of internal and violent conflict that may predate the lives of these groups. A good deal of the violence we encountered, as also reported about gangs elsewhere, emanated from interpersonal disputes regarding friends, family, and especially romantic relationships. More significantly we found conflict *within gangs* to be as important as conflict *between gangs*, and more important on a day-to-day level, consistent with the view that most violence takes place between people who know each other. Jealousy and the recovery of debt were important sources of this sometimes violent within-gang conflict (Medina et al., forthcoming). The interaction of this level of internal conflict, the lost role of Inner West in drug markets, the "heat" associated with being a member of these gangs (in terms of elevated police pressure and risk of victimisation: see Ralphs et al., 2009 and Aldridge et al., 2010) as a pressure to "leave the game," death and incarceration of key individuals, and individual trajectories of aging out of crime or progressing toward other profit making criminal activities requiring different forms of cooperation are explanatory candidates that may account for this process. In sum, we find then that both social and community external to the group, alongside factors linked to the developmental trajectories of gang members are significant to understand the process of change in gangs.

Yet, despite the dubious institutionalisation of supergangs in Inner West, we do find that, as reported above, some young people in these communities today display a greater familiarity with and use of gang iconography. Whether these groups can be considered part of the previously existing gangs is difficult to ascertain. Nonetheless, this is the way that is interpreted by local agencies to justify their actions: considerably greater intrusion and proclivity among local social services and law enforcement to treat ethnic minority young people in these communities as suspect or potential gang members and to label their peer groups as gangs. As Jensen (2008) has highlighted gangs are neither simply sociological facts, nor constructions; rather they are co-produced by state institutions, civil society and young men's practices. In this sense, the state, almost by definition, continues to play an important role in processes of recognition, transformation and disappearance of gangs.

Notes

1. Klein and Maxson (2006) argue that "traditional" and "compressed" gangs are the more stable gang formations, with "specialty," "collective," and "neotraditional" gangs more likely to change their nature or disappear. They speculate that "specialty gangs" are particularly vulnerable to police suppression and undercover efforts and, thus, likely to disappear as a result.
2. For a detailed description of the methodology of the research project and the research site see Aldridge and Medina (2008). We deliberately avoid naming the city to further protect the confidentiality of participants, as a way of addressing the problems of stigmatisation of

the neighbourhoods we observed, and to foster greater community support. All names we use for places, gangs or individuals are fictitious.
3. The Eurogang Project defines street gangs as "any durable, street-oriented youth group whose involvement in illegal activity is part of its group identity" (Klein and Maxson, 2006).
4. Jensen (2000) attempts to distinguish between street gangsters and drug dealers in Cape Town through a case study of "Kelly," a former street gang member who became a "big time" drug dealer: in local parlance, a "merchant." Jensen does not take up the term merchant to imply only those who have made the transition from street gang to big-time dealing. However, we like the term "merchant" as applied to those both in and making the transition out of street gangs, as so much of their roles involve "trade"—whether legitimately, in the informal economy, or in more organised criminal enterprises. Although inspired by Jensen's use of the term, we recognise that we take it up in a slightly different way. In this chapter, we describe both "community merchants" and "criminal merchants."
5. Some of this debate is resonant of conflicting views on Al-Qaeda. Interpretations of this terrorist group have also portrayed it as some form of super-organisation. Investigative journalist Jason Burke (2003) has argued in relation to Al-Qaeda that an alternative interpretation is to think of Al-Qaeda as an idea, a worldview that can be subscribed to and serve as inspiration for terrorist action.

References

Arias, E. D. 2006. *Drugs and democracy in Rio de Janeiro: trafficking, social networks and public security.* University of North Carolina Press.

Aldridge, J. and Medina, J. Youth gangs in an English city: Full Research Report. ESRC End of Award Report, RES-000–23-0615. Swindon: ESRC.

Aldridge, J., Medina, J., and Ralphs, R. 2010. "Collateral damage: territory and policing in an English gang city" in Goldson, B. (ed.) *Youth in crisis? "Gangs," territoriality and violence.* Cullompton: Willan.

Alexander, C. 2000. *The Asian gang.* Oxford: Berg.

Auld, J., Dorn, N. and South, N. 1984 "Heroin now: bringing it all back home" *Youth and Policy* 9:1–7.

Bannister, J., Pickering, J., Batchelor, S., Burman, M., Kintrea, K., and McVie, S. Forthcoming. *Troublesome youth groups, gangs and knife carrying in Scotland.* Edinburgh: Scottish Centre for Crime and Justice Research.

Batchelor, S. 2001. "The myth of girl gangs" *Criminal Justice Matter* 43(1):26–27.

Bennett, T. and Holloway, K. 2004. "Gang membership, drugs and crime in the UK," *British Journal of Criminology* 44:305–323.

Bradshaw, P. 2005. "Terrors and young teams" in S. H. Decker and F.W. Weerman (eds.) *European street gangs and troublesome youth groups*. Walnut Creek: Altamira Press.

Bullock, K. and Tilley, N. 2002. "Shootings, gangs and violent incidents in Manchester," *Crime Reduction Research Series*, Paper 13. London: Home Office.

———. 2008. "Understanding and tackling gang violence" *Crime Prevention and Community Safety* 10:36–47.

Burke, J. 2003. *Al-Qaeda: casting a shadow of terror*. London: IB Tauries.

Communities that Care. 2005. *Findings from the Safer London Youth Survey 2004*. London: Metropolitan Police Service.

Davies, A. 2008. *The gangs of Manchester: the story of the Scuttlers, Britain's first youth cult*. Preston: Milo Books.

Downes, D. 1966. *The delinquent solution: a study in subcultural theory*. London, Routledge and Kegan Paul.

Fagan, J. 1996. "Gangs, drugs and neighbourhood change" in C.R. Huff (ed.) *Gangs in America*, 2nd ed. Thousand Oaks: Sage.

———. "Legal and illegal work. Crime, work and unemployment" in Burton A. Weisbrod and James C. Worthy (eds.) *The urban crisis*. Northwestern University Press.

Hales, G., Lewis, C., and Silverstone, D. 2006. *Gun crime: the market in and use of illegal firearms*. London: Home Office.

Hallsworth, S. and Silverstone, D. 2009. "'That's life innit': A British perspective on guns, crime and social order" *Criminology and Criminal Justice* 9(3): 359–377.

Hallsworth, S. and Young, T. 2004. "Getting real about gangs" *Criminal Justice Matters* 5: 12–13.

———. 2008. "Gang talk and gang talkers: a critique" *Crime, Media and Culture* 4(2):175–195.

Hallsworth, S. 2006. "Racial targeting and social control: looking behind the police" *Critical Criminology* 14:293–311.

———. 2008. "Reasons not to be cheerful: New Labour's action plan for targeting violence" *Criminal Justice Matters* 72: 2–3.

Hayden, C. 2008. *Staying safe and out of trouble*. ICJS, University of Portsmouth.

Hobbs, D. 2001. "The Firm" *British Journal of Criminology* 41: 549–560.

Hobbs, D., Hadfield, P., Lister, S., and Winlow, S. 2003. *Bouncers: violence and governance in the night-time economy*. Oxford University Press.

Home Office. 2008. *Tackling gangs*. London: HO.

Jensen, S. 2000. "Of drug dealers and street gangs: power, mobility and violence on the Cape Flats" *Focaal* (36):105–116.

Jensen, S. 2008. *Gangs, politics and dignity in Cape Town*. The University of Chicago Press.

Klein, M. W. and Maxson, C. L. 2006. *Street gang patterns and policies*. Oxford University Press.

Maher, J. 2009. "Gangs? What gangs? Street-based youth groups and gangs in South Wales" *Contemporary Wales* 22(1):178–195.

Mares, D. 2001. "Gangstas or lager louts? Working class street gang in Manchester" in M. W. Klein, H. J. Kerner, C. L. Maxson, and E. G. M. Weitekamp (eds.) *The Eurogang paradox: street gangs and youth groups in the US and Europe*. London: Kluwer Academic Publishers.

May, T., Duffy, M., Few, B. and Hough, M. 2008. *Understanding drug selling in communities*. York: Joseph Rowntree Foundation.

May, T. and Hough, M. 2004. "Drug markets and distribution systems" *Addiction Research and Theory* 12(6): 549–563.

Medina, J., Aldridge, J. and Ralphs, R. Forthcoming. "Spectre or 'Super Gangs'? Youth gangs as messy social networks."

Medina, J., Ralphs, and Aldridge J. 2010. "Mentoring siblings of gang members: a template for reaching families of gang members?" *Children and Society*.

Parker, H. J. 1974. *View from the boys: a sociology of downtown adolescents*. Newton Abbot: David and Charles.

Patrick, J. 1973. *A Glasgow gang observed*. London, Eyre Methuen.

Pearson, G. 1987. "Social deprivation, unemployment and patterns of heroin use" in Dorn, N., South, N. (eds) *A Land Fit for Heroin?* London: MacMillan.

Pitts, J. 2008. *Reluctant gangsters: the changing face of youth crime*. Cullompton: Willan.

Ralphs, R., Medina, J., and Aldridge, J. 2009. "Who needs enemies with friends like these? The importance of place for young people living in known gang areas" *Journal of Youth Studies* 12(5):483–500.

Rodgers, D. 2006. "Living in the shadow of death: gangs, violence and social order in urban Nicaragua 1996–2002" *Journal of Latin American Studies* 38(2):267–292.

Sanders, B. 2005. *Youth crime and youth culture in the inner city*. London: Routledge.

Sandberg, S. and Pedersen, W. 2009. *Street capital: black cannabis dealers in a white welfare state*. Bristol: Policy Press.

Sharp, C., Aldridge, J. and Medina, J. *2006. Delinquent youth groups and offending behaviour: findings from the*

2004 Offending, Crime and Justice Survey. Home Office Online Report 14/06.

Sullivan, J. P. and Bunker, R. 2002. "Drug cartels, street gangs, and warlords" *Small War and Insurgencies* 13(2):40–53.

Walsh, P. 2003. *Gang wars: the inside story of the Manchester gangs.* Bidford on Avon: Milo Books.

Winfree, T., Weitekamp, E., Kerner, H-J., Weerman, F., Medina, J., Aldridge, J. and Maljevic, A. 2007. "Youth gangs in five nations" Annual Meeting of the American Society of Criminology, Atlanta (USA), November, 2007.

Youth Justice Board. 2007. *Groups, gangs and weapons.* London: Youth Justice Board.

Race and Ethnicity

While self-report studies consistently identify some portion of gang members as white, the majority of gang youth are racial and ethnic minorities, and a disproportionate share are immigrants (see Esbensen and Carson's chapter in Section II for an overview). These patterns are not accidental: gangs most often emerge in minority communities that are overwhelmed by poverty, unemployment, and low levels of social services. Institutional racism—including the racism of social neglect—can have devastating effects in disadvantaged communities and is especially challenging to combat. Gangs are often a product of these forms of multiple marginalization. As a consequence, numerous scholars have linked gang patterns to neighborhood disadvantage and associated inequalities (which the reader will learn more about in Section VI), recognizing that such social conditions are themselves patterned by racial exclusion.

In the United States, perhaps the strongest evidence of the broad import of marginalization—across race and ethnicity—comes by looking at historical patterns of gang formation. Early gang studies in the late nineteenth and early twentieth centuries emphasized social conditions associated with immigration, urbanization, and poverty in explaining the development and prevalence of gangs in particular communities. The groups in question, however, were largely white immigrants from Western Europe: Irish, German, Polish, and Italian, for example. This suggests that community-level processes—embedded in more macro-level patterns of inequality—are more significant for explaining gang patterns than are cultural variations across racial and ethnic groups. It also helps clarify why available research suggests that while there appear to be some striking gang patterns across race and ethnicity, these groups and their members tend to exhibit far more similarities than differences.

Nonetheless, distinct patterns of racial exclusion, immigration, community and neighborhood characteristics, and culture do suggest the utility of research on variations in gangs and gang members' experiences across race and ethnicity, both in the United States and in Western Europe (which has witnessed gang growth in the last decades, particularly among immigrant youth). Such investigations, unfortunately, are quite limited. James Diego Vigil's 2002 book *A Rainbow of Gangs* may be the only intentionally comparative study of this kind. Overall, while there is a large body of U.S. scholarship on Latino gangs, there are considerably fewer studies of Asian gangs and surprisingly little research explicitly about the potentially distinct features of African American gangs. Even less is known about white gangs (which are quite uncommon, particularly when distinguished from skinhead groups; see Chapter 12) or racially and ethnically mixed gangs—the groups in which white youth gang membership appears to be most common. The relative absence of such comparative work is particularly true when it comes to investigating the differential roles that racial formation and racism may have across groups in patterns of gang development, organization and group processes, and gang youths' experiences.

Prior research is nonetheless suggestive of several patterns. For example, in the United States, gang territoriality may be most pronounced among Latino gangs and least pronounced among Asian gangs (though there are likely variations in such patterns across community contexts). Research on Latino gangs tends to emphasize cultural heritage, while research on Asian gangs often focuses on national histories; neither theme is predominant in research on African American gangs. In addition, particularly in the 1990s, African American gang members have been more involved in the sale of crack cocaine than were other gang youth, while some Asian gangs appear to exhibit more crime specialization than groups that are predominantly Latino or African American, which have more versatile patterns of delinquency. But these differences may have as much to do with the theoretical lenses, methodological choices, and gang definitions employed by different researchers as they do with distinct racial/ethnic patterns.

The chapters selected for this section are intended to illustrate some of these complexities. Vigil first introduced the concept of multiple marginality in his 1988 book *Barrio Gangs.* The term was meant to capture the interrelated forms of marginality—cultural stressors as well as institutional barriers to upward mobility—that are experienced by Chicano youth and can lead to gang participation as a social adaptation. Krohn and his colleagues' chapter represents one of the few efforts to test the generalizability of this concept,

and their findings give credence to the significance of the layers of marginality that often impact gang youths' lives. Other chapters focus purposely on specific groups, including African Americans (Alonso), Mexican Americans (Duran), and Moroccan youth in Holland (de Jong). Each represents an effort to investigate distinct patterns—including those present in gang formation, gang joining, group processes in gangs, and experiences of social control—for gang youth in specific racial and/or ethnic groups. Not included here but much needed is additional research on gangs in Latin America, including the important role that U.S. immigration and deportation policies can have on gang formation and growth in these settings.[1]

The reader is reminded of our caution about the importance of systematic comparative research between groups and settings for drawing strong conclusions about distinct patterns across race and ethnicity. Nonetheless, clear patterns of racial/ethnic exclusion are prominent throughout. It is difficult to imagine that we can ever ameliorate the problems associated with gangs and gang membership without comprehensive strategies that address these inequalities.

Notes

1. For an overview of these issues, the reader can see the Washington Office on Latin America (WOLA) report, "Youth Gangs in Central America: Issues in Human Rights, Effective Policing, and Prevention." This report can be found online at http://www.wola.org/publications/youth_gangs_in_central_america.

CHAPTER 16

The Impact of Multiple Marginality on Gang Membership and Delinquent Behavior for Hispanic, African American, and White Male Adolescents

Marvin D. Krohn ■ Nicole M. Schmidt ■ Alan J. Lizotte ■ Julie M. Baldwin

James Diego Vigil's multiple marginality framework emerged from his inductive ethnographic work with Chicano gang members in the barrios of Los Angeles. One of the key strengths of such research, however, is its generative theoretical quality. Using self-report data from the Rochester Youth Development Study, Krohn and his colleagues test the explanatory value of multiple marginality for Hispanic youth, as compared to African American and white youth. While their quantitative measures cannot fully assess all dimensions of the multiple marginality framework, their findings suggest that Vigil's model holds particular promise for understanding gang membership, especially in light of the cultural stressors and institutional barriers that Hispanic youth face. The reader should keep in mind that the majority of Hispanic youth, including immigrants, do not join gangs. Most often, it is those who suffer multiple and overlapping forms of marginalization who are at the greatest risk for gang participation.

Editors' Note: The interpretation of Table 16.3 has been modified slightly with the permission of the authors.

Introduction

Over the past 20 years, there has been an increasing interest in crime and delinquency among individuals of Hispanic origin living in the United States.

Reprinted from: Marvin D. Krohn, Nicole M. Schmidt, Alan J. Lizotte, and Julie M. Baldwin, "The Impact of Multiple Marginality on Gang Membership and Delinquent Behavior for Hispanic, African American, and White Male Adolescents," *Journal of Contemporary Criminal Justice*, 27(1), 18–42. Copyright © 2011 by Sage Publications. Reprinted with permission from Sage Publications.

This is not surprising as the Hispanic population is now the largest ethnic or racial minority in the country (Malec, 2006; U.S. Census Bureau, 2008), is growing at a faster rate than all other groups (U.S. Census Bureau, 2008), and is expected to constitute almost a third of the population by 2050 (U.S. Census Bureau, 2008). In addition, compared with other groups, the Hispanic population is disproportionately young, male, and urban dwelling. These demographic characteristics, coupled with educational and economic disadvantages, are particularly conducive for high rates of crime.

Hispanic gang members are of particular concern. It is estimated that approximately one sixth of the Hispanic population are gang members, and in some communities, that figure is much higher (Arfaniarromo, 2001; Malec, 2006; Vigil, 1999). Gang membership facilitates participation in crime and increases its seriousness (Esbensen & Huizinga, 1993; Hill et al., 1996; Rosenfeld, Bray, & Egley, 1999; Thornberry, 1998; Thornberry, Krohn, Lizotte, & Chard-Wierschem, 1993; Thornberry, Krohn, Lizotte, Smith, & Tobin, 2003). If the rate of gang membership stays relatively constant and the overall population growth rate continues to be high among Hispanics, the crime problem in our urban areas can be expected to escalate dramatically.

Much of what we know about Hispanic gangs comes from ethnographic work that focuses on specific gangs of mostly Hispanic membership (Brotherton & Barrios, 2004; Hagedorn, 1988; Horowitz, 1983; Moore, 1978, 1991; Moore & Pachon, 1985; Moore & Vigil, 1987; Padilla, 1992; Vigil, 1988a, 1988b, 1999; Vigil & Long, 1990). These studies provide rich descriptions of the process of joining a gang and the daily lives of gang members. Most of these studies make the argument that there are reasons specific to the experience of being Hispanic in a non-Hispanic culture, along with the resultant educational and economic disadvantages, that lead Hispanic youth to join and participate in gang life. In some cases, these reasons have been incorporated into well-developed theoretical explanations on why Hispanics join gangs and the purposes that gangs serve in their lives (e.g., Vigil, 1988a, 1999, 2002).

These ethnographic studies typically focus on only one or a very limited number of gangs in the same geographic area whose members are from the same ethnic or racial group. Therefore, they are unable to examine whether the hypothesized reasons for Hispanic youths' gang initiation are any different than the reasons why other ethnic or racial group youths join gangs. Freng and Esbensen (2007) suggested that literature on gangs " . . . lacks an extensive comparison of differences between gang members from various racial/ethnic groups" resulting in the "inability to assess whether the same or different factors explain gang involvement for all racial/ethnic groups" (p. 603). To do so requires the same data be gathered on gangs with different ethnic or racial compositions.

In this study, we compare Hispanic, African American, and White youth to determine if different factors explain why they join gangs. Specifically, we focus on factors that fall under Vigil's (1988a, 1999, 2002) multiple marginality perspective. We use these factors and gang membership to predict subsequent involvement in crime.

Explaining Hispanic Gang Membership

Hispanic youth growing up in the United States face many difficulties. As Malec (2006) stated, the typical instability in adolescence is heightened for Hispanic youth because they "find themselves in a position of socio-cultural disconnection, stranded between the traditional Latino culture and the dominant mainstream culture" (p. 82). This dual disconnect increases in generations that are further removed from their native culture but not yet fully acculturated (Arfaniarromo, 2001). Several studies

focusing on the Hispanic population in the United States have found a positive relationship between levels of acculturation and rates of substance use (Amaro, Whitaker, Coffman, & Heeren, 1990; Barrett, Joe, & Simpson, 1991; Black & Markides, 1993; Caetano, 1987; De La Rosa, 2002; Farabee, Wallisch, & Maxwell, 1995; Gilbert, 1987; Gilbert & Cervantes, 1986; Marin, Perez-Stable, & Marin, 1989; Miller, Miller, Zapata, & Yin, 2008; Neff, Hoppe, & Perea, 1987). The cultural marginalization of Hispanic youth coupled with the disadvantaged economic conditions that many minorities face in this country create conditions that undermine traditional social control institutions, for example, family and school (Arfaniarromo, 2001; Malec, 2006; Vigil, 1988a, 1999, 2002). Vigil (1988a, 1999, 2002) has referred to this as "multiple marginality." His multiple marginality framework holds that the precarious position of Hispanics in this country can only be understood by taking into account the different layers of marginality and disadvantage that they face, for example, cultural, ecological, economical, and structural.

Vigil (1988a, 1999, 2002) suggested that macrohistorical (racism and repression) and macrostructural (immigration and ghetto/barrio living) forces combine to create different types of strain and undermine social control and bonds with the family and school as well as respect for law enforcement. Traditionally, family life is very important within Hispanic cultures (Castro, Sharp, Barrington, Walton, & Rawson, 1991; Moore, 1970; Murillo, 1976; Vega, 1990). However, due to marginalization, the family spends less time together and is less able to supervise children, which, in part, strains relationships between parents and teenagers (Arfaniarromo, 2001; Malec, 2006; Vigil, 1999). Hispanic youth may face particular problems in school. They may be at a disadvantage in terms of English language skills and are often faced with prejudicial attitudes from their peers (Murguia, Chen, & Kaplan, 1998). Suarez-Orozco and Suarez-Orozco (1995) provided particularly revealing results concerning the importance that Hispanics (Mexican Americans) place on education. They compared first- and second-generation Mexican Americans in terms of their attitude toward school. They found that first-generation

Mexican Americans felt education was essential to a successful future. However, second-generation Mexican Americans experienced disillusionment with and a lowering of expectations for what education could help them achieve. The Hispanic population possesses the highest school drop-out rate (Malec, 2006; Pabon, 1998), completes the least amount of years in school (Murguia et al., 1998), and receives lower grades on average (Murguia & Telles, 1996). Law enforcement agents are unable to step in effectively for the family and school because multiple marginality has eroded respect for law enforcement among Hispanic youth (Vigil, 2002).

In addition, marginality is linked to difficulties in establishing a self-identity and having low self-esteem (Arfaniarromo, 2001; Malec, 2006; Vigil, 1988a, 1988b). Not only is the adolescent self-identity development stage the most vulnerable time with regard to gang initiation (Vigil, 1988a, 1988b) but also gang membership is seen as an adaptation to multiple marginality for youth. The emergence of the street culture of the gang provides these youth with socialization and a self-identity that are absent due to their marginalization from traditional institutions, for example, family and school (Vigil, 1988a, 1988b, 1999, 2002). Self-identity can be created through developmental roles in gangs, and the gang becomes a type of "surrogate family" (Arfaniarromo, 2001; Belitz & Valdez, 1994; Moore, 1991; Vigil, 1988a, 1999). Gang ideals are adopted in lieu of family or school ideals (Arfaniarromo, 2001; Lopez & O'Donnell-Brummett, 2009; Vigil, 1988a, 1988b, 1999).

Vigil (1988a, 1988b, 1999) originally applied the multiple marginality perspective to Hispanics living in the barrios of Los Angeles. Arfaniarromo (2001) and Malec (2006) also talked exclusively about these factors affecting Hispanics because of their particular macrohistorical background. However, more recently, Vigil has extended the range of this perspective to account for gang membership among African Americans, Hispanics, Salvadorans, and Vietnamese (Vigil, 2002; Vigil & Yun, 2002). This raises an interesting question: does multiple marginality, or particular aspects of it, better account for Hispanic gang membership than for other demographic groups? Although there is a paucity of literature comparing gang

members from different racial/ethnic groups, the few studies that have done so, coupled with others that have examined whether there are differences in risk factors of delinquent behavior and drug use for different racial/ethnic groups, suggest that there is reason to explore this possibility.

Prior Research

Very few studies have explicitly compared youth gangs composed primarily of Hispanics with gangs composed of other racial or minority groups. Hagedorn (1988) attributed this to the lack of minority researchers involved in gang research. Although this undoubtedly was a contributing factor, there are methodological reasons as well. An ethnographic study comparing different ethnic/racial gangs requires building a rapport with several groups from various cultures that may even speak different languages. The time investment in such studies is substantial. The most appropriate way to perform a study focusing on the reasons for gang membership among different ethnic groups is to survey a sample from the general population (Thornberry et al., 2003). The difficulty encountered here is not only to generate sufficiently large samples of the different ethnic/racial groups of interest but also to include an adequate number of gang members within each ethnic/racial group. Few studies meet these requirements.

Although there is a scarcity of studies comparing Hispanic gangs to non-Hispanic gangs, a good deal of research has examined the causes of delinquent and drug-using behavior among different racial/ethnic groups. Before looking at the gang-specific research, we review studies that have focused on more general delinquent and drug-using behavior.

Theoretical explanations and research have focused on three primary aspects of Hispanics living in the United States that may be particularly important in the etiology of delinquent and drug-using behavior among this group: family relationships, school problems, and acculturation. Although family relationships and school problems can be said to affect other ethnic/racial groups,[1] the argument is that the emphasis within Hispanic culture on the family and the specific problems that Hispanics encounter in school make these factors especially important in accounting for delinquency among Hispanics.

Family

Several studies have suggested that the family plays a distinctly important role in Hispanic populations (Recio Adrados, 1975; Roberts & Stefani, 1949; Rogler & Cooney, 1984; Rogler & Hollingshead, 1985). Family norms and values are thought to exert a stronger influence on Hispanics, and they rely on their families for emotional and financial support more so than youths of other ethnic and racial groups. In addition, Hispanic youth are expected to engage in more joint activities with other family members (Rodriguez, Recio Adrados, & De La Rosa, 1993; Smith & Krohn, 1995). Although some studies do not support the hypothesis that family factors play a more important role in the etiology of delinquency and drug use for Hispanics than for other ethnic/racial groups (Brook, 1993; McCluskey & Tovar, 2003), most studies do find support (Gil, Bega, Biafora, 1998; McCluskey, 2001; Murguia et al., 1998; Pabon, 1998; Rodriguez et al., 1993; Rodriguez & Weisburd, 1991; Smith & Krohn, 1995). However, these studies do not all concur on which family-related variables are more important for Hispanics. Rodriguez et al. (1993) compared results from the National Youth Study (NYS; Elliott, Huizinga, & Ageton, 1985) with those based on a sample of inner-city Puerto Rican male adolescents. In both analyses, family involvement, family normlessness, and family strain were included. For the Puerto Rican male adolescents, family involvement had a significant effect on drug use and delinquency, whereas it did not have a significant impact in the more racially mixed NYS sample. Murguia et al. (1998) found family factors to be more important than school factors in association with drug-using peers for Hispanics; the opposite was true for Whites. For Hispanics, family warmth directly decreased association with drug-using peers.

Smith and Krohn (1995) confirmed that finding in a more direct comparison of Hispanic and non-Hispanic youth. Based on a sample of approximately 1,000 inner-city youth, Smith and Krohn found that, for Hispanic youth, parent–child

involvement and coming from a single-parent family were significantly related to delinquency but parental attachment and control were not. In contrast, attachment and control were significant predictors of delinquent behavior for Whites and African Americans, whereas involvement and single-parent family were not. In a more extensive analysis using data from the Rochester Youth Development Study (RYDS) and the Denver Youth Study, McCluskey (2001) found that family involvement influenced the delinquent values and association with delinquent peers for Hispanics but not for White youth in both data sets. In the Denver data, family involvement also was significantly related to these two variables for African American youth.

The bulk of the studies comparing Hispanic with non-Hispanic youth have found that family factors are more important in predicting delinquency (either directly or indirectly) for Hispanics than for other youth. Some variation exists in which family factors are significant predictors, but family involvement has been the most consistent.

School

Hispanics have the highest drop-out rate of any racial/ethnic group in the country (Malec, 2006; McCluskey, Krohn, Lizotte, & Rodriguez, 2002; Pabon, 1998), and although there has been an improvement in high school completion rates in recent years, there has not been any for Hispanics. Del Pinal and Singer (1997) attributed the underachievement of Hispanics to the relatively low levels of parental education. Less education among Hispanic parents, in turn, may result in parents not being aware of the benefits of education and having lower educational expectations for their children. Murguia et al. (1998) also mentioned that the deficiency of educational resources in Mexico and the majority of nonelites in the population perpetuate a lack of "a strong tradition of scholarship and schooling" among Mexican American immigrants (p. 346). Then too, the benefits of education for Hispanics may not be as great as they are for other racial/ethnic groups (Rumberger, 1991).

Language and the differences in Hispanic culture also have been implicated in lower achievement rates among Hispanic youth (Blea, 1988; Mirande,

1985; Moore & Pachon, 1985; Padilla, 1992; Vigil, 1988a). Many Hispanic youth come from homes in which Spanish is the primary language spoken, making the transition to the English-speaking school system more difficult. Hispanic experience in the educational system may be further marginalizing (Vigil, 1988a, 1999).

Given the problems encountered by Hispanics within the educational system that do not affect similarly members of other racial/ethnic groups, researchers have examined whether school and educational variables are more predictive of Hispanic delinquency and drug use (Brook, 1993; McCluskey, 2001; McCluskey et al., 2002; Murguia et al., 1998). Hispanic youth do not differ from others with respect to the impact of school-related variables on delinquency and drug use. Murguia et al. (1998) discovered that positive school experience decreased young adult substance abuse for both Hispanics and Whites. Brook (1993) found that a variable called *school environment* was a significant predictor of both Hispanic and African American drug use. In their comparison of inner-city Puerto Rican male adolescents within the NYS sample, Rodriguez et al. (1993) looked at school normlessness, school strain, and school involvement and found that only school involvement was a significant predictor of both drug use and delinquency for Puerto Ricans but not the general NYS sample.

Although the results that compare the impact of school-related variables on delinquency and drug use do not generally show that those variables are more predictive for Hispanics than other racial/ethnic groups, these studies do not examine whether these variables are more predictive of Hispanic gang membership. In his early work, Vigil (1988a, 1999) suggested that they should be, so we incorporate school-related measures in our analysis.

Acculturation

Cultural ties among new Hispanic immigrants to the United States often are very strong (Vigil, 1990). These ties serve to maintain strong family ties among Hispanics and, in turn, decrease the probability of problematic behavior. A number of studies have found that second- and third-generation Hispanic immigrants have a higher rate of delinquent behavior than do first-generation immigrants (Caetano, 1987; Gilbert, 1987). These findings are interpreted as evidence of the problematic aspects of acculturation. Specifically, the duality of the cultural situation that Hispanic adolescents experience as they begin to adopt the values and behaviors of the larger culture while still being pulled to maintain ties with the traditional culture of their parents strains the family relationship. In turn, this may lead to a higher likelihood that Hispanic youth will interact with friends in unsupervised, risky situations that perpetuate participation in delinquent behavior (Krohn & Thornberry, 1993; Recio Adrados, 1993; Rodriguez et al., 1993; Vega, Zimmerman, Gil, Warheit, & Asospori, 1993). In addition, the ambiguous cultural identity coupled with being the victim of prejudice and discrimination often leads to problems with self-identity and self-concept (Malec, 2006; Oetting, 1993; Vigil, 1999).

Although the predominant assumption in the literature is that acculturation will be positively related to delinquent and drug-using behavior, some scholars have recognized that acculturation may actually decrease the probability of problematic behavior (Miller, Barnes, & Hartley, 2009; Rodriguez et al., 1993; Recio Adrados, 1993; Rogler, Cortes, & Malgady, 1991). Strong ties to the Hispanic culture, including speaking Spanish at home, may make it more difficult for youth to meet the challenges of the English-speaking school system, and they may be subjected to more prejudice and discrimination. A strong cultural identity may also increase the likelihood of forming a cohesive network, which may behave in ways contrary to the laws. Rogler et al. (1991) reviewed the research on acculturation and psychological distress and found an equal number of studies discovering a positive relationship as those discovering a negative relationship. Miller et al. (2008) found that when acculturation was measured by the use of Spanish, the probability of drug use increased. However, when acculturation was measured by patterns of social interaction (whether Mexican American youth preferred to interact with youth of the same ethnic identity), it decreased the likelihood of drug use.

The research on delinquent and drug-using behavior suggests that certain correlates of delinquent and drug-using behavior such as family- and school-related variables may be more predictive of Hispanic behavior than they are of other racial/ethnic groups. The marginal situation caused by their acculturation to the dominant culture may adversely affect these factors. Although a number of studies throughout the past 20 years have investigated these hypotheses, few have examined explicitly whether there are differences in the predictors of gang membership across racial/ethnic groups.

Factors Affecting Gang Membership

Much of what we know of the differences in the reasons why members of various racial/ethnic groups join gangs has come from the excellent ethnographic studies on inner-city gangs (Hagedorn, 1988; Moore & Pachon, 1985; Moore & Vigil, 1987; Vigil, 1988a, 1999, 2002; Vigil & Long, 1990). Vigil has been formally and informally working with the Chicano community since the early 1950s (Vigil, 1988a) and, as previously mentioned, has developed the multiple marginality framework (Vigil, 1988a, 1999, 2002) through decades of formal studies, fieldwork, consultations, interviews, and observations. Some support has been found for the multiple marginality hypothesis with regard to Hispanic gang involvement (Hagedorn, 1988; Moore & Vigil, 1987; Vigil, 1988a; Vigil & Long, 1990; Vigil & Yun, 2002).

Two studies that examined the impact of acculturation on gang membership among Hispanic youth found that measures of acculturation decreased the likelihood of gang participation (Lopez & O'Donnell-Brummett, 2009; Miller et al., 2009). Particularly noteworthy is the study by Miller et al. (2009) as they found that acculturation decreased the probability of gang membership. Moreover, they found that the impact of acculturation was mediated by their measure of ethnic marginalization. They interpreted these results as suggesting that it was the individuals' perceptions of their marginalized position in the social order that was predictive of gang membership.

Although these studies are suggestive of differences across race and ethnicity on why youth

join gangs, they do not focus explicitly on these concerns. Few studies have compared the correlates of gang membership for different racial and ethnic groups primarily because it requires a fairly large sample within each group so that a sufficient number of gang members are involved in the study.

Curry and Spergel (1992) compared 139 Hispanic sixth- to eighth-grade male adolescents with 300 African American male adolescents in an inner-city school in Chicago. They found that educational frustration and low peer- and school-based self-esteem predicted gang involvement among Hispanics, whereas hanging out with friends who use drugs in areas of high drug use and having other family members involved in gangs predicted gang membership among African Americans. They concluded that prevention programs should focus on the difficulties that Hispanics have in school and aid in acculturating parents of these youth to get them more involved in their child's education.

Freng and Esbensen (2007) provided a comparison from a large, nationally representative sample of 4,997 eighth-grade students participating in the Gang Resistance Education and Training (G.R.E.A.T.) program. Freng and Esbensen sought to examine Vigil's (1988a, 1999, 2002) multiple marginality theory. They included indicators of acculturation, family relationships and processes, family background, school commitment, and street socialization. They found that there were more similarities in significant predictors across the racial/ethnic groups than differences when "ever in a gang" was the dependent variable. However, when current gang membership was assessed, differences emerged. For Hispanics and African Americans, school commitment, police factors, and street socialization were the main predictors; for Whites, ecological, economic factors, and techniques of neutralization were the most effective predictors.

Freng and Esbensen (2007) recognized that, given the very few studies comparing the correlates of gang membership for different racial and ethnic groups, many questions have gone unanswered. The current study seeks to address some of these issues. Using data from a longitudinal panel study of inner-city youth, we examine variables that represent key constructs in Vigil's multiple marginality theory to determine if there are differences in those that significantly predict gang membership for Hispanic, African American, and White youth. We then use these variables and gang membership to predict participation in three types of delinquent behavior.

Data and Sample

The current study uses data from the RYDS. The RYDS is an ongoing longitudinal study of the causes, correlates, and consequences of delinquency that spans over 20 years. A total of 1,000 seventh- and eighth-grade students were identified through the Rochester (New York) Public School system to participate in the study. Beginning in 1988, participants (called G2) and a primary caregiver (called G1) were interviewed every 6 months for nine interview periods (called Phase 1). Although data were collected in two additional phases, this study focuses on this time frame because participants were on average 14- to 18-years old, the primary age during which youth belong to gangs.

As the RYDS intended to investigate serious, chronic delinquents, a stratified sample was selected to ensure that the entire school population was represented but that high-risk youth were overrepresented. The sample was stratified on two dimensions to ensure high-risk youth were targeted. First, male adolescents were oversampled (75% vs. 25%) because they are more likely to engage in serious delinquency (Blumstein, Cohen, Roth, & Visher, 1986; Huizinga, Morse, & Elliott, 1992). Second, students living in areas of the city where criminal offenders live were oversampled based on the assumption that youth living in these areas are at a greater risk for offending than those areas where relatively few offenders live.

The subsequent analyses are based on the sample of 640 male adolescents interviewed through Wave 9. The baseline sample is composed of 687 male adolescents, which is a 93% retention rate.[2] The sample is restricted to male participants because too few female participants reported gang membership during Phase 1. Of the 640 male participants in the sample, 17.5% are Hispanic ($n = 112$), 63.1% are African American ($n = 404$), and 18.4% are White ($n = 118$). Overall, 31% of the sample reported ever being in a gang ($n = 199$). Twenty-two percent of gang members are Hispanic ($n = 44$), 67% are African American ($n = 134$), and 11% are White ($n = 21$). Within race, 39% of Hispanic participants reported ever being in a gang compared with 33% of African American participants and 18% of White participants.[3]

Measurement

Table 16.1 depicts how the explanatory variables, gang membership, and outcomes of interest are coded. As previously mentioned, we draw on the multiple marginality perspective in selecting factors that may explain Hispanic gang membership. G1 age at first birth is the age at which the participant's primary female caregiver reported having her first biological child. Young mothers not only may be at an economic disadvantage compared with older mothers but also may experience parenting deficits that could affect delinquent behavior of G1's children (Pogarsky, Lizotte, & Thornberry, 2003). Educational expectations for G2 measures whether G1 expects G2 to attend college at Wave 2 (when participants are 14.5 years old on average).[4] Parental expectations likely have an effect on participants' school bonds, which is an important component of the multiple marginality framework. A number of studies have incorporated some measure of language use as an indicator of acculturation (Amaro et al., 1990; Miller et al., 2008, 2009; Neff et al., 1987). The only measure contained in the RYDS data set is whether Spanish was spoken at home. It was only asked of Hispanic G1 participants at Wave 10 (when G2 was on average 21 years of age). However, it can be assumed that if the primary caregiver spoke Spanish at home at Wave 10, then they did at Wave 2 as well, so we include this as a measure of acculturation.

As the multiple marginality perspective suggests that macrohistorical and macrostructural forces combine to undermine social bonds like the family and school, measures of each are included here. Four measures of the quality of the parent–child relationship are examined. All are measured

Table 16.1 Variable Coding

Variable	Coding	Wave
G1 age first birth	Age at which G1 (primary female caregiver) reported having first biological child	–
Educational expectations for G2	G1 report of their expectations for G2 attending college; 1 = *No*, 2 = *Depends*, 3 = *Yes*	2
Spanish spoken at home	G1 report of Spanish spoken at home; 0 = *No*, 1 = *Yes*	10
Parental supervision	Four-item scale, higher scores indicate more parental supervision; α = .56	2
Positive parenting	Five-item scale, higher scores indicate more positive parenting; α = .79	2
Attachment to parent	11-item scale, higher scores indicate more attachment to parent; α = .87	2
Parental involvement	10-item scale, higher scores indicate more parental involvement; α = .77	2
Academic achievement	Self-reported average grade: 1 = *E/F*, 2 = *D*, 3 = *C*, 4 = *B*, 5 = *A*	4
Attachment to teacher	Five-item scale, higher scores indicate more attachment to teacher; α = .87	2
Commitment to school	10-item scale, higher scores indicate more commitment to school; α = .81	2
Self-esteem	Nine-item scale, higher scores indicate higher self-esteem; α = .79	2
Risky time with friends	Nine-item scale assessing amount of risky time spent with three closest friends, higher scores indicate more risky time; α = .77	2
Ever a gang member	Subject ever reported being a gang member from Waves 2 through 9	2–9
General delinquency	Incidence of general delinquency from Waves 2 through 9	2–9
Serious delinquency	Incidence of serious delinquency from Waves 2 through 9	2–9
Drug sales	Incidence of drug sales from Waves 2 through 9	2–9

at Wave 2 (when participants are 14.5) and are reported by the participant. Parental Supervision is a four-item scale (α = .56), Positive Parenting is a five-item scale (α = .79), Attachment to Parent is an 11-item scale (α = .87), and Parental Involvement is a 10-item scale (α = .77). For each scale, a higher score indicates better quality parenting.

Academic achievement is measured as the participant's self-reported average letter grade at Wave 4 (when participants were 15.5), the first wave at which we collect information on grades. A higher score indicates better grades. Two additional school measures at Wave 2 (age 14.5) are included in the analyses, namely, attachment to teacher and commitment to school. Attachment to Teacher is a five-item scale where higher scores indicate more attachment to the participant's teacher (α = .87), whereas Commitment to School is a 10-item scale where higher scores indicate a higher commitment to school (α = .81).

Self-esteem also has been linked to multiple marginality. We measure self-esteem using a nine-item scale with higher scores indicating more self-esteem (α = .79). Risky Time With Friends is a nine-item scale assessing the amount of risky time spent with the participant's three closest friends at Wave 2 (age 14.5; α = .77). Higher scores indicate more risky time with friends. Gang membership is a dichotomous measure of whether the participant reported being a member of a gang at any wave from 2 through 9, when respondents were on average age 14.5- to 18-years old.[5] As mentioned above, 39% of Hispanic participants, 33% of African American participants, and 18% of White participants report ever being a gang member. Overall, this amounts to 31% of the sample.

Three outcome measures are examined in this article, all of which are incidence measures of delinquency across Waves 2 through 9 when respondents were on average 14.5 to 18 years old.[6] General delinquency is a measure of the number of times participants reported committing any of 32 delinquent behaviors. Serious delinquency is a measure of the number of times participants reported committing any of eight more serious delinquent behaviors, such as breaking and entering or attacking someone with a weapon. Finally, we examine drug sales, which is a measure of the number of times participants reported selling marijuana or another hard drug.

Results

Zero-order relationships between race/ethnicity, gang membership, and the explanatory and outcome measures are displayed in Table 16.2. Within race, an asterisk next to a mean/proportion indicates a statistically significant difference between nongang and gang members on that particular measure. For Hispanic participants, the mean age of the primary female caregiver (95% mothers) when they had their first child is 19.6 for nongang members and 17.6 for gang members. The mean ages of the primary caregiver of nongang and gang members are very similar for African American participants, 18.8 and 18.7, respectively. White primary caregivers are generally older at first birth with a mean of 22.0 for nongang members and 19.2 for gang members. Within race, G1 age at first birth significantly differs between nongang and gang members for Hispanic and White participants but not for African American participants. Gang members tend to have parents who were younger when they first gave birth to a child.

For Hispanic and African American participants, a statistically significant difference exists in the primary caregiver's educational expectations between nongang and gang members; primary caregivers of nongang members are more likely to expect that G2 will attend college than those of gang members. Although the difference for White participants did not reach significance, it was close, and the mean is higher for nongang members, indicating higher educational expectations. Spanish language spoken at home is only available for Hispanic participants. Eighty-seven percent of Hispanic nongang members experienced Spanish spoken at home compared with 68% of Hispanic gang members. This is a statistically significant difference. So, speaking Spanish at home seems to insulate one from gang membership.

Both nongang and gang members across all races have good parent–child relationships (averaging around three or more on a four-point scale for each measure). Only one significant difference exists between nongang and gang members among African American participants: parental

Table 16.2 Descriptive Statistics by Race and Gang Membership						
	Hispanic		African American		White	
	Nongang	Gang	Nongang	Gang	Nongang	Gang
	Mean	Mean	Mean	Mean	Mean	Mean
G1 age first birth	19.56 ($N = 59$)	17.64* ($N = 39$)	18.81 ($N = 252$)	18.65 ($N = 123$)	22.04 ($N = 91$)	19.21* ($N = 19$)
Educational expectations for G2	2.45 ($N = 66$)	1.93* ($N = 44$)	2.41 ($N = 266$)	2.19* ($N = 134$)	2.30 ($N = 97$)	1.86 ($N = 21$)
Spanish spoken at home	0.87 ($N = 60$)	0.68* ($N = 40$)	–	–	–	–
Parental supervision	3.70 ($N = 67$)	3.61 ($N = 41$)	3.61 ($N = 267$)	3.51* ($N = 134$)	3.63 ($N = 96$)	3.40 ($N = 20$)
Positive parenting	3.14 ($N = 67$)	3.10 ($N = 41$)	3.23 ($N = 267$)	3.17 ($N = 134$)	3.15 ($N = 96$)	3.04 ($N = 20$)
Attachment to parent	3.40 ($N = 67$)	3.41 ($N = 41$)	3.45 ($N = 267$)	3.36 ($N = 134$)	3.40 ($N = 96$)	3.27 ($N = 20$)
Parental involvement	2.96 ($N = 67$)	2.86 ($N = 41$)	3.10 ($N = 267$)	3.05 ($N = 134$)	3.05 ($N = 96$)	3.08 ($N = 20$)
Academic achievement	3.30 ($N = 66$)	2.80* ($N = 41$)	3.32 ($N = 268$)	3.30 ($N = 129$)	3.56 ($N = 95$)	2.58* ($N = 19$)
Attachment to teacher	2.91 ($N = 67$)	2.75 ($N = 41$)	2.93 ($N = 264$)	2.82* ($N = 133$)	2.91 ($N = 96$)	2.71 ($N = 19$)
Commitment to school	3.00 ($N = 67$)	2.91 ($N = 41$)	3.16 ($N = 264$)	3.03* ($N = 133$)	3.06 ($N = 96$)	2.84 ($N = 19$)
Self-esteem	2.97 ($N = 67$)	2.83 ($N = 41$)	3.19 ($N = 267$)	3.05* ($N = 134$)	3.05 ($N = 96$)	2.92 ($N = 20$)
Risky time with friends	1.76 ($N = 67$)	2.13* ($N = 41$)	1.94 ($N = 263$)	2.35* ($N = 134$)	1.89 ($N = 95$)	2.13 ($N = 20$)
General delinquency	33.47 ($N = 68$)	193.47* ($N = 44$)	40.97 ($N = 270$)	167.20* ($N = 131$)	53.38 ($N = 97$)	79.74 ($N = 21$)
Serious delinquency	0.35 ($N = 68$)	17.77* ($N = 44$)	0.71 ($N = 270$)	16.32* ($N = 131$)	1.68 ($N = 97$)	7.95* ($N = 21$)
Drug sales	4.53 ($N = 68$)	30.82* ($N = 44$)	9.19 ($N = 270$)	38.46* ($N = 131$)	8.28 ($N = 97$)	2.21 ($N = 21$)
*$p < .05$.						

supervision is lower among gang members. Hispanic and White nongang members report significantly higher grades (between a C and a B) compared with gang members (between a D and a C). African American participants' reported grades do not differ across nongang and gang members with both averaging grades between a C and a B. With respect to the other school measures, Hispanic and White nongang and gang members report similar levels of attachment to teacher and commitment to school on average. These measures do not significantly differ across nongang and gang members for either race. However, African American nongang members report significantly higher average levels of attachment to teacher and commitment to school than gang members.

Hispanic nongang members report slightly higher levels of self-esteem on average (2.97 vs. 2.83), but this difference is not statistically significant. African American participants do significantly differ on levels of self-esteem with nongang members averaging 3.19 compared with 3.05 for gang members. White nongang members also report slightly higher levels of self-esteem than gang members (3.05 vs. 2.92), but similar to Hispanic participants, this difference is not statistically significant. Both Hispanic and African American gang members report significantly more risky time with friends than nongang members. White nongang and gang members do not significantly differ in the amount of risky time with friends, but nongang members do report slightly lower levels on average.

For general delinquency, Hispanic nongang members report an average of 33.5 incidences, whereas gang members report an average of 193.5. This difference is statistically significant. The results are similar for African American participants. On average, nongang members report 41 incidences compared with 167.2 for gang members; again, this is a statistically significant difference. White nongang and gang members do not significantly differ on their reported general delinquency, with means of 53.4 and 79.7, respectively. Statistically significant differences in serious delinquency exist between nongang and gang members for all races. On average, Hispanic and African American nongang members report fewer than one serious delinquency incident compared with 17.8 and

16.3 incidences, respectively, for gang members. White nongang members report an average of 1.7 incidences compared with 7.95 for gang members. Finally, Hispanic nongang members report selling drugs 4.5 times on average compared with 30.8 for gang members. This difference is statistically significant, as is the difference for African American participants. Nongang members report 9.2 incidences compared with 38.5 for gang members. No statistically significant difference exists between White nongang and gang members, with averages of 8.3 and 2.2, respectively.

The first step in the multivariate analysis is to estimate race-specific logistic regression models predicting gang membership using the explanatory variables discussed above. The second step involves predicting the three outcomes discussed above from the explanatory variables and gang membership, again using race-specific OLS regression models.

Table 16.3 shows the odds ratios for variables predicting gang membership for each of the three racial/ethnic groups. During preliminary analyses, we incorporated all of the explanatory variables displayed in Table 16.2. However, given the reduced sample size with race-specific equations and some strong correlations among explanatory variables, we reduced the number of explanatory variables to those displayed in Table 16.3.[7] Each of these equations fit the data quite well. We use the Wald test to look for statistically significant differences in coefficients across groups.

For Hispanics, we find that family factors and relationships, school problems, and speaking Spanish at home all affect gang membership. For example, Hispanic participants' female caregiver's age at first birth is a statistically significant predictor of gang membership; the higher the age at first birth, the less likely participants are to be gang members. In addition, high educational aspirations reduce the odds of gang membership by half. Risky time with friends significantly increases the likelihood of gang membership for Hispanic participants. When we include Spanish spoken at home, the impact of risky time with friends is reduced to insignificance. Speaking Spanish at home dramatically reduces the odds of gang membership by more than 70%, and it does so because it reduces the impact of risky time

Table 16.3 Odds Ratios Predicting Gang Membership

	Hispanic		African American	White
G1 age first birth[a,b]	0.80*	0.78*	0.98	0.74*
Educational expectations for G2	0.52*	0.50*	0.86	0.52
Spanish spoken at home	–	0.27*	–	–
Parental supervision	0.65	0.42	0.70	0.74
Commitment to school	0.61	0.81	0.44	0.18
Self-esteem[b]	0.96	0.63	0.51*	1.99
Risky time with friends[b]	2.35*	1.91	2.63***	1.18
χ^2	24.29***	28.64***	48.92***	21.19***
N	93	84	354	105

[a] Statistically significant difference in coefficients for Hispanic and African American models using Wald χ^2.
[b] Statistically significant difference in coefficients for African American and White models using Wald χ^2.
*$p < .05$. **$p < .01$. ***$p < .001$.

with friends. This finding is consistent with studies that have examined drug-using behavior and some of the theoretical discussions for Hispanic gang membership (Arfaniarromo, 2001; Malec, 2006) but is inconsistent with the few studies that have focused on gang membership (Lopez & O'Donnell-Brummett, 2009; Miller et al., 2009).

For African Americans, high self-esteem produces a significantly lower likelihood of gang membership than for Whites. However, there is no statistically significant difference in the effect of self-esteem between Hispanics, African Americans or White participants. Like Hispanic participants, risky time with friends predicts gang membership for African Americans, and the size of these effects are not different from each other. However, this effect is significantly larger for African Americans than for Whites.

Finally, for White participants, the primary female caregiver's age at first birth is the only significant predictor of gang membership, and its size is not different from that of Hispanic participants. However, for both Hispanics and Whites, the primary female caregiver's age at first birth shows significantly stronger reductions in gang membership than for African Americans.

Table 16.4 shows OLS equations predicting general delinquency, serious delinquency, and drug sales for each of the three racial/ethnic groups. With the exception of drug sales for Whites, gang membership always predicts delinquent outcomes.

For Hispanic participants, this means that there are indirect effects of age at first birth, educational aspirations, and Spanish being spoken at home on all three forms of delinquency through gang membership. Although the indirect effect of educational aspirations through gang membership to delinquency is unique to Hispanic participants, we cannot say that the links in this causal chain are different than for Whites.[8] Furthermore, although there are different predictors of the various kinds of delinquency across the three racial/ethnic groups, we cannot say that they are due to those groups' unique connection to gang membership.

For Hispanic participants, commitment to school reduces each delinquency measure, and risky time with friends also positively predicts general delinquency and drug sales (independent of Spanish spoken at home). For African Americans, high educational expectations lower general and serious delinquency, and commitment to school lowers general delinquency and drug sales. Risky time with friends also predicts drug sales for African Americans. Other than gang membership, nothing predicts delinquency for Whites.

Discussion and Conclusion

Hispanics are the fastest growing minority in the United States and there is reason to believe that, because of their economic and cultural marginality, they may become the fastest growing ethnic

Table 16.4 Equations Predicting Outcomes by Race

	Hispanic		African American		White	
	b	SE	b	SE	b	SE
General delinquency						
G1 age first birth	−0.09	0.05	−0.01	0.03	−0.07	0.05
Educational expectations	−0.37	0.22	−0.36**	0.12	−0.06	0.22
Spanish spoken at home	−0.23	0.43	–	–	–	–
Parental supervision	−0.66	0.57	−0.18	0.22	−0.45	0.48
Commitment to school	−1.39*	0.57	−0.85**	0.31	0.23	0.60
Self-esteem	0.81	0.53	−0.46	0.24	−0.32	0.62
Risky time with friends	0.87**	0.27	0.27	0.15	0.50	0.33
Ever a gang member	1.57***	0.41	1.80***	0.20	1.78***	0.50
Adjusted R^2	.49		.33		.20	
N	84		347		104	
Serious delinquency						
G1 age first birth	−0.04	0.03	−0.00	0.01	0.01	0.02
Educational expectations	−0.35**	0.13	−0.25***	0.06	−0.03	0.09
Spanish spoken at home	0.18	0.25	–	–	–	–
Parental supervision	0.09	0.34	−0.17	0.11	−0.11	0.19
Commitment to school	−0.85*	0.34	0.01	0.16	0.29	0.23
Self-esteem	0.28	0.31	−0.14	0.13	−0.48	0.24
Risky time with friends	0.32	0.16	0.11	0.08	0.08	0.13
Ever a gang member	1.46***	0.24	1.59***	0.11	1.62***	0.19
Adjusted R^2	.55		.49		.45	
N	84		347		104	
Drug sales						
G1 age first birth	0.01	0.05	0.00	0.02	0.01	0.02
Educational expectations	−0.06	0.18	−0.11	0.10	−0.17	0.10
Spanish spoken at home	0.62	0.36	–	–	–	–
Parental supervision	−0.62	0.48	−0.07	0.19	−0.14	0.22
Commitment to school	−1.01*	0.49	−0.54*	0.27	−0.09	0.27
Self-esteem	0.76	0.45	−0.01	0.21	−0.08	0.28
Risky time with friends	0.78**	0.23	0.28*	0.13	0.16	0.15
Ever a gang member	1.23***	0.35	1.27***	0.18	0.09	0.23
Adjusted R^2	.36		.20		.01	
N	84		347		104	

$*p < .05. **p < .01. ***p < .001.$

group in terms of gang membership as well. It is, therefore, important that we discover the particular reasons for Hispanic gang membership and determine if these reasons differ from those that lead to gang membership among African Americans and Whites. Although different correlates and causes of delinquency and drug use by racial/ethnic groups have been explored, there are very few studies examining differences in the correlates of gang membership.

The current study was informed by Vigil's (1988a, 1999) multiple marginality perspective. This perspective suggests that the combined effects of economic disadvantage, discrimination due to minority status, and being raised in one cultural tradition while dealing with a different dominant culture in our society creates multiple marginality. This, in turn, impacts the effectiveness of the family, the role that education plays in adolescents' lives, their adoption of and interaction in street life, and their self-esteem. Because of the limitations of our sample size and the number of Hispanic gang members included, we could not incorporate indicators of all of the constructs suggested by Vigil's perspective. Rather, we included variables that represent the domains he identifies.

The findings indicate that some of the dimensions suggested by Vigil are related to ever having been in a gang for Hispanic youth. The parental background variables, age at which the primary female caregiver had her first child and the parents' expectations for their children's education are significant predictors of ever having been in a gang for Hispanics. The age at which the female caregiver had her first birth is an important indicator of the disadvantage that the family (parent and child) will face during their lives. Age at first birth also was significant for White youth, but it was not for African American youth.

Parental expectation of their children's education is a significant predictor only for Hispanics. This suggests that Hispanics, as a result of multiple marginality and experiences within the school system, may not see education as an avenue for achievement. Thus, for some Hispanics, specifically Hispanic youth who join gangs, parents may not expect their children to go very far in the educational system. It is interesting to note that, among those Hispanic male adolescents who do not join gangs, the educational expectations of the parents are the highest of any racial group by gang membership group.

Surprisingly, neither family-process measures nor school-related measures were significant predictors of Hispanic gang membership. Although we examined multiple indicators of both constructs, none of them were significant when included in multivariate analyses. This is contrary to Vigil's suggestion that the strains caused by multiple marginality should make it more difficult for Hispanics to function effectively within the family and to be committed to the school. It should be noted that

these variables also were not significantly related to gang membership for African Americans and Whites in the multivariate equations.

Hanging around with friends in unsupervised, risky situations significantly predicted both Hispanic and African American but not White gang membership. As we did not examine the temporal order of gang membership and our measure of risky time with friends, we cannot determine whether hanging around with risky friends leads to becoming involved in gangs or if it is simply a result of joining the gang. Given other research indicating that youth associate with delinquent others prior to joining a gang, we suspect that it is the former. In any event, it appears that Vigil's description of minority youth experiencing street socialization is true for our Hispanic and African American male adolescents.

We had only one indicator of the very important construct of acculturation, Spanish speaking at home. This proved to be a significant predictor of ever having been in a gang for Hispanic male adolescents. It is interesting to note that when this variable is included in multivariate analysis, the effect of risky time with friends is no longer significant. We interpret these findings as being supportive of the predicted effect of acculturation. Those youth who come from homes where Spanish is no longer spoken likely are more acculturated to the dominant American culture than those whose families still speak Spanish at home. As suggested by some scholars (Arfaniarromo, 2001; Belitz & Valdez, 1994; Moore, 1991; Vigil, 1988a, 1988b, 1999, 2002), strong ties to traditional Hispanic culture insulates youth from negative influences they may find on the streets, whereas subculture and gangs tend to fill the void for Hispanic youth who are lacking those ties.[9] However, some research has found that measures of speaking Spanish (at home and elsewhere) increased the chances of gang membership (Miller et al., 2009), although they decreased the chances of drug use (Miller et al., 2008). The inconsistency in our results suggests that the direction of the relationship may be influenced by a number of factors including the specific Hispanic group that is being studied, the way in which acculturation is measured, and the geographical context in which the respondents reside. Clearly, further research is needed to clarify the impact of acculturation on gang membership.

After examining the predictors of gang membership, we incorporated those variables along with ever having been in a gang to predict participation in general delinquency, serious delinquency, and drug sales. Ever having been in a gang was a significant predictor of the three types of delinquency for all racial/ethnic groups except for drug sales among Whites. Risky time with friends had a significant direct effect on general delinquency and drug sales for Hispanics but only drug sales for African Americans and not at all for Whites. Perhaps the most interesting finding from this analysis was that commitment to school, which did not significantly predict ever being in a gang, had a significant direct effect on the three types of crime for Hispanics and on two of the three types of crime for African Americans. Female caregiver's age at first birth, Spanish speaking at home, and parental educational expectations are indirectly related to the three forms of delinquent behavior for Hispanics.

Research in this area is limited by the difficulty in acquiring a sufficient number of adolescents within each racial and ethnic group who have ever been in a gang. The one exception to this is the Freng and Esbensen (2007) study using the G.R.E.A.T. data. Our research also is limited in this respect. Because of this, we were restricted in the number of variables we could include and in the models that we could estimate. However, the findings do underscore the importance of acculturation (speaking Spanish at home) in ever having been in a gang. In addition, parental attitudes toward their children's education appear to be an important predictor of gang membership. Both of these variables can be interpreted as reflecting the difficulties Hispanic families face in making the transition to a new culture and language, especially in the educational arena. Those who suggest that efforts should be made to assist families with such a transition and to focus in particular on involving parents in their child's educational efforts find support from our results.

It is evident that more work needs to be conducted to determine the factors related to Hispanic gang membership that differentiate the etiological process from that of other ethnic/racial groups. To accomplish this, research should be designed specifically to acquire a sufficient number of Hispanic youth to enable a focus on gang members within racial and ethnic categories. Given the demographic trends, such research is essential if we want to understand the continuing gang problem in the United States.

Authors' Note

Points of view or opinions in this document are those of the authors and do not necessarily represent the official position or policies of the funding agencies.

Declaration of Conflicting Interests

The authors declared that they had no conflicts of interest with respect to their authorship or the publication of this article.

Funding

Support for the Rochester Youth Development Study has been provided by the Office of Juvenile Justice and Delinquency Prevention (86-JN-CX-0007), the National Institute on Drug Abuse (DA005512), and the National Science Foundation (SBR-9123299, SES-9123299). Work on this project was also aided by grants to the Center for Social and Demographic Analysis at the University at Albany from NICHD (P30-HD32041) and NSF (SBR-9512290).

Notes

1. Social structural factors like poverty and discrimination are also seen as important factors in predicting delinquent behavior and gang membership among Hispanics. However, these factors are not seen to be more important for Hispanics than they are for other minority groups.
2. The baseline sample is 687 because not all of the 750 identified boys were interviewed initially or they dropped out of the study after Wave 1.
3. Results of a chi-square test show statistically significant differences in gang membership across race. Hispanic and African American subjects are significantly more likely to be gang members than are Whites.
4. Missing data on this measure at Wave 2 were replaced by educational expectations at Wave 3. If both Wave 2 and Wave 3 were missing, it was replaced by educational

expectations at Wave 4. This was done to retain as many cases as possible for the multivariate analyses because of the smaller number of cases within race.

5. If a subject was missing at one wave, their gang membership status was calculated based on the information provided at the other seven waves.

6. Due to the skewed nature of the incidence measures, they will be logged in the multivariate analyses.

7. For example, attachment to teacher and commitment to school were highly correlated ($r = .55$ for Hispanic subjects, .57 for African American subjects, and .57 for White subjects). As a result, these variables were cancelling each other out in the multivariate analyses, so we only included commitment to school in the equation. All zero-order correlations are available on request.

8. This is because the parts of the indirect effects are not different across the racial/ethnic groups.

9. Strong cultural identity also strengthens self-identity (Berry, 1980; Buriel, 1984).

References

Amaro, H., Whitaker, R., Coffman, G., & Heeren, T. (1990). Acculturation and marijuana and cocaine use: Findings from HHANES 1982–84. *American Journal of Public Health, 80*, 54–60.

Arfaniarromo, A. (2001). Toward a psychosocial sociocultural understanding of achievement motivation among Latino gang members in U.S. schools. *Journal of Instructional Psychology, 28*(3), 123–136.

Barrett, M. E., Joe, G. W., & Simpson, D. D. (1991). Acculturation influences on inhalant use. *Hispanic Journal of Behavioral Sciences, 13*, 276–296.

Belitz, J., & Valdez, D. (1994). Clinical issues in the treatment of Chicano male gang youth. *Hispanic Journal of Behavioral Sciences, 16*, 57–74.

Berry, J. W. (1980). Acculturation as varieties of adaptation. In A. M. Amado (Ed.), *Acculturation: Theory, models and some new findings* (pp. 9–25). Boulder, CO: Westview.

Black, S. A., & Markides, K. S. (1993). Acculturation and alcohol consumption in Puerto Rican, Cuban-American, and Mexican-American women in the United States. *American Journal of Public Health, 83*(6), 890–893.

Blea, I. I. (1988). *Toward a Chicano social science.* New York, NY: Praeger.

Blumstein, A. J., Cohen, J., Roth, J., & Visher, C. A. (1986). *Criminal careers and "career criminals."* Washington, DC: National Academy Press.

Brook, J. S. (1993). Interactional theory: Its utility in explaining drug use behavior among African-American and Puerto Rican youth. In M. R. De La Rosa & J. L. Recio Adrados (Eds.), *Drug abuse among minority youth: Methodological issues and recent research advances, National Institute on Drug Abuse Research Monograph Series 130* (pp. 79–101). Rockville, MD: National Institute on Drug Abuse.

Brotherton, D. C., & Barrios, L. (2004). *The Almighty Latin king and queen nation: Street politics and the transformation of a New York gang.* New York, NY: Columbia University Press.

Buriel, R. (1984). Integration with traditional Mexican-American culture and sociocultural adjustment. In J. L. Martinez, Jr. & R. H. Mendoza (Eds.), *Chicano psychology* (pp. 95–130). Orlando, FL: Academic Press.

Caetano, R. (1987). Acculturation and drinking patterns among U.S. Hispanics. *British Journal of Addiction, 82*, 789–799.

Castro, F. G., Sharp, E. V., Barrington, E. H, Walton, M., & Rawson, R. A. (1991). Drug abuse and identity in Mexican Americans: Theoretical and empirical considerations. *Hispanic Journal of Behavioral Sciences, 13*, 209–225.

Curry, G. D., & Spergel, I. (1992). Gang involvement and delinquency among Hispanic and African-American males. *Journal of Research in Crime and Delinquency, 29*, 271–291.

De La Rosa, M. (2002). Acculturation and Latino adolescents' substance use: A research agenda for the future. *Substance Use and Misuse, 37*, 429–456.

Del Pinal, J., & Singer, A. (1997). Generations of diversity: Latinos in the United States. *Population Bulletin, 52*(3), 2–48.

Elliott, D. S., Huizinga, D., & Ageton, S. S. (1985). *Explaining delinquency and drug use.* Beverly Hills, CA: Sage Publications.

Esbensen, F. A., & Huizinga, D. (1993). Gangs, drugs, and delinquency in a survey of urban youth. *Criminology, 31*, 565–590.

Farabee, D., Wallisch, L., & Maxwell, J. C. (1995). Substance use among Texas Hispanics and non-Hispanics: Who's using, who's not, and why. *Hispanic Journal of Behavioral Sciences, 17*, 523–536.

Freng, A., & Esbensen, F. A. (2007). Race and gang affiliation: An examination of multiple marginality. *Justice Quarterly, 24*, 600–628.

Gil, A. G., Bega, W. A., & Biafora, F. (1998). Temporal influences of family structure and family risk factors on drug use initiation in a multiethnic sample of adolescent boys. *Journal of Youth and Adolescence, 27*, 373–393.

Gilbert, M. J. (1987). Alcohol consumption patterns in immigrant and later generation Mexican American women. *Hispanic Journal of Behavioral Sciences, 9*, 299–313.

Gilbert, M. J., & Cervanies, R. C. (1986). Patterns and practices of alcohol use among Mexican Americans: A comprehensive review. *Hispanic Journal of Behavioral Sciences, 8*, 1–60.

Hagedorn, J. M. (1988). *People and folks: Gangs, crime and the underclass in a rustbelt city*. Chicago, IL: Lake View Press.

Hill, K. G., Hawkins, J. D., Catalano, R. F., Kosterman, R., Abbott, R. D., & Edwards, T. (1996, November). *The longitudinal dynamics of gang membership and problem behavior: A replication and extension of the Denver and Rochester gang studies in Seattle*. Paper presented at the annual meeting of the American Society of Criminology, Chicago, IL.

Horowitz, R. (1983). *Honor and the American dream*. New Brunswick, NJ: Rutgers University Press.

Huizinga, D., Morse, B. J., & Elliott, D. S. (1992). *The National Youth Survey: An overview and description of recent findings*. Boulder, CO: Institute of Behavioral Science, University of Colorado.

Krohn, M. D., & Thornberry, T. P. (1993). Network theory: A model for understanding drug abuse among African-American and Hispanic youth. In M. R. De La Rosa & J. L. Recio Adrados (Eds.), *Drug abuse among minority youth: Methodological issues and recent research advances, National Institute on Drug Abuse Research Monograph Series 130* (pp. 102–128). Rockville, MD: National Institute on Drug Abuse.

Lopez, D. A., & O'Donnell-Brummett, P. (2009). Gang membership and acculturation: ARSMA-II and choloization. *Crime and Delinquency, 49*, 627–642.

Malec, D. (2006). Transforming Latino gang violence in the United States. *Peace Review: A Journal of Social Justice, 18*, 81–89.

Marin, G., Perez-Stable, E. J., & Marin, B. V. (1989). Cigarette smoking among San Francisco Hispanics: The role of acculturation and gender. *American Journal of Public Health, 79*, 196–198.

McCluskey, C. P. (2001). *Understanding Latino delinquency: The applicability of strain theory across ethnic groups*. New York, NY: LFB Scholarly Publishing.

McCluskey, C. P., Krohn, M. D., Lizotte, A. J., & Rodriguez, M. L. (2002). Early substance use and school achievement: An examination of Latino, White and African-American youth. *Journal of Drug Issues, 32*, 921–944.

McCluskey, C. P, & Tovar, S. (2003). Family processes and delinquency: The consistency of relationships by ethnicity and gender. *Journal of Ethnicity in Criminal Justice, 1*(1), 37–62.

Miller, H. V., Barnes, J. C., & Hartley, R. D. (2009). Reconsidering Hispanic gang membership and acculturation in a multivariate context. *Crime & Delinquency, 30*(10), 1–25.

Miller, J. M., Miller, H. V., Zapata, J. T., & Yin, Z. (2008). Mexican-American youth drug use and acculturation: A note on the mitigating effects of contextual dynamics. *Journal of Drug Issues, 38*, 199–214.

Mirande, A. (1985). *The Chicano experience: An alternative perspective*. Notre Dame, IN: University of Notre Dame Press.

Moore, J. (1978). *Homeboys: Gangs, drugs, and prison in the barrios of Los Angeles*. Philadelphia, PA: Temple University Press.

Moore, J. W. (1991). *Going down to the barrio: Homeboys and homegirls in change*. Philadelphia, PA: Temple University Press.

Moore, J. W., & Pachon, H. (1985). *Hispanics in the United States*. Englewood Cliffs, NJ: Prentice-Hall.

Moore, J., & Vigil, D. (1987). Chicano gangs: Groups norms and individual factors related to adult criminality. *Aztlan, 18*, 27–44.

Murguia, E., Chen, Z., & Kaplan, H. B. (1998). A comparison of causal factors in drug use among Mexican Americans and non-Hispanic Whites. *Social Science Quarterly, 79*, 341–360.

Murguia, E., & Telles, E. E. (1996). Phenotype and schooling among Mexican Americans. *Sociology of Education, 69*, 276–289.

Murillo, N. (1976). The American family. In C. A. Hernandez, M. J. Haug, & N. N. Wagner (Eds.), *Chicanos: Social and psychological perspectives* (2nd ed.). Saint Louis, MO: C. V. Mosby.

Neff, J. A., Hoppe, S. K., & Perea, P. (1987). Acculturation and alcohol use: Drinking patterns and problems among Anglo and Mexican American male drinkers. *Hispanic Journal of Behavioral Sciences, 9*, 151–181.

Oetting, E. R. (1993). Orthogonal cultural identification: Theoretical links between cultural identification and substance use. In M. R. De La Rosa & J. L. Recio Adrados (Eds.), *Drug abuse among minority youth: Methodological issues and recent research advances, National Institute on Drug Abuse Research Monograph Series 130* (pp. 32–56). Rockville, MD: National Institute on Drug Abuse.

Pabon, E. (1998). Hispanic adolescent delinquency and the family: A discussion of sociocultural influences. *Adolescence, 33*, 941–956.

Padilla, F. M. (1992). *The gang as a cultural enterprise*. New Brunswick, NJ: Rutgers University Press.

Pogarsky, G., Lizotte, A. J., & Thornberry, T. P. (2003). The delinquency of children born to young mothers: Results from the Rochester Youth Development Study. *Criminology, 41*, 1249–1286.

Recio Adrados, J. L. (1975). *Family as a unit and larger society: The adaptation of the Puerto Rican migrant family to the mainland suburban setting* (Doctoral dissertation, Graduate Center of the City University of New York, New York).

Recio Adrados, J. L. (1993). Acculturation: The broader view. Theoretical framework of the acculturation scales. In M. R. De La Rosa & J. L. Recio Adrados (Eds.), *Drug abuse among minority youth: Methodological issues and recent research advances, National Institute on Drug Abuse Research Monograph Series 130* (pp. 57–78). Rockville, MD: National Institute on Drug Abuse.

Roberts, L., & Stefani, L. R. (1949). *Patterns of living in Puerto Rican families*. Rio Piedras, Puerto Rico: Editorial Universitaria.

Rodriguez, O., Recio Adrados, J. L., & De La Rosa, M. R. (1993). Integrating mainstream and subcultural explanations of drug use among Puerto Rican youth. In M. R. De La Rosa & J. L. Recio Adrados (Eds.), *Drug abuse among minority youth: Methodological issues and recent research advances, National Institute on Drug Abuse Research Monograph Series 130* (pp. 8–31). Rockville, MD: National Institute on Drug Abuse.

Rodriguez, O., & Weisburd, D. (1991). The integrated social control model and ethnicity: The case of Puerto Rican delinquency. *Criminal Justice Behavior, 18*, 464–479.

Rogler, L. H., & Cooney, R. S. (1984). *Puerto Rican families in New York City: Intergenerational processes* (Hispanic Research Center Monograph No. 11). Maplewood, NJ: Waterfront Press.

Rogler, L. H., Cortes, D. E., & Malgady, R. G. (1991). Acculturation and mental health among Hispanics: Convergence and new directions. *American Psychology, 46*, 585–597.

Rogler, L. H., & Hollingshead, A. B. (1985). *Trapped: Puerto Rican families and schizophrenia* (3rd ed.). Maplewood, NJ: Waterfront Press.

Rosenfeld, R., Bray, T. M., & Egley, A., Jr. (1999). Facilitating violence: A comparison of gang-motivated, gang-affiliated, and nongang youth homicides. *Journal of Quantitative Criminology, 15*, 495–516.

Rumberger, R. W. (1991). Chicano dropouts: A review of research and policy issues. In R. R. Valencia (Ed.), *Chicano school failure and success: Research and policy agendas for the 1990s* (pp. 64–89). New York, NY: Falmer.

Smith, C., & Krohn, M. D. (1995). Delinquency and family life among male adolescents: The role of ethnicity. *Journal of Youth and Adolescence, 24*(1), 69–93.

Suarez-Orozco, C., & Suarez-Orozco, M. M. (1995). *Transformations: Immigration, family life, and achievement motivation among Latino adolescents*. Stanford, CA: Stanford University Press.

Thornberry, T. P. (1998). Membership in youth gangs and involvement in serious and violent offending. In R. Loeber & D. P. Farrington (Eds.), *Serious and violent juvenile offenders: Risk factors and successful interventions* (pp. 147–166). Rockville, MD: National Institute on Drug Abuse.

Thornberry, T. P., Krohn, M. D., Lizotte, A. J., & Chard-Wierschem, D. (1993). The role of juvenile gangs in facilitating delinquent behavior. *Journal of Research in Crime and Delinquency, 30*, 55–87.

Thornberry, T. P., Krohn, M. D., Lizotte, A. J., Smith, C. A., & Tobin, K. (2003). *Gangs and delinquency in developmental perspective*. Cambridge, UK: Cambridge University Press.

U.S. Census Bureau. (2008). *Hispanic Americans by the numbers from the U.S. Census Bureau*. Retrieved from http://www.infoplease.com/spot/hhmcensus1.hmtl

Vega, W. A. (1990). Hispanic families in the 1980s: A decade of research. *Journal of Marriage and the Family, 52*, 1015–1024.

Vega, W. A., Zimmerman, R., Gil, A., Warheit, G. J., & Asospori, E. (1993). Acculturation strain theory: Its application in explaining drug use behavior among Cuban and other Hispanic youth. In M. R. De La Rosa & J. L. Recio Adrados (Eds.), *Drug abuse among minority youth: Methodological issues and recent research advances, National Institute on Drug Abuse Research Monograph Series 130* (pp. 144–166). Rockville, MD: National Institute on Drug Abuse.

Vigil, J. D. (1990). Cholos and gangs: Culture change and street youth in Los Angeles. In C. R. Huff (Ed.), *Gangs in America* (pp. 116–128). Newbury Park, CA: SAGE.

Vigil, J. D. (1988a). *Barrio gangs*. Austin: University of Texas Press.

Vigil, J. D. (1988b). Group processes and street identity: Adolescent Chicano gang members. *Ethos, 16*, 421–445.

Vigil, J. D. (1999). Streets and schools: How educators can help Chicano marginalized gang youth. *Harvard Educational Review, 69*, 270–288.

Vigil, J. D. (2002). *A rainbow of gangs: Street cultures in the mega-city*. Austin: University of Texas Press.

Vigil, J. D., & Long, J. M. (1990). Emic and etic perspective on gang culture: The Chicano case. In C. R. Huff (Ed.), *Gangs in America* (pp. 55–68). Newbury Park, CA: SAGE.

Vigil, J. D., & Yun, S. C. (2002). A cross-cultural framework for understanding gangs: Multiple marginality and Los Angeles. In C. R. Huff (Ed.), *Gangs in America*, (3rd ed., pp. 161–174). Thousand Oaks, CA: SAGE.

CHAPTER 17

Racialized Identities and the Formation of Black Gangs in Los Angeles

Alejandro A. Alonso

Few contemporary studies specifically investigate the question of how and why particular gangs in specific locations come about, focusing more attention on gang maintenance or proliferation. Alonso's chapter thus provides a unique contribution, in tracing the formation of black gangs in Los Angeles, linking their formation to historical trends of social, economic, and political exclusion. In addition, it is one of the only investigations that specifically applies theories of racial formation and exclusion to the question of gang formation. The reader will notice that this historical analysis involves different methodological strategies than are typically employed by criminologists, the vast majority of whom use sociological or social psychological methods. This approach provides unique insights for understanding the larger social contexts in which gangs develop.

To explain the formation of urban gangs in Los Angeles (LA) and other cities in the United States, many researchers have emphasized the need to understand behavioral characteristics of gangs as groups and those of individual members. Results of these studies suggest that youths join gangs for safety, material access, a valued identity, and status as well as the result of peer pressures. Many gang studies consider the characteristics of already existing gangs to explain gang membership and organization (Vigil, 1996; Venkatesh, 1997; Decker

and Curry, 2000; Rumble and Turner, 2000) while others provide compelling evidence regarding the factors that sustain gangs or what is termed *gang persistence* (Vigil, 1988; Klein, 1995). Throughout the 1950s and 1960s academic research seeking to explain gangs flourished, stimulated by the perceived growth in violence and social disorganization of urban communities as key explanatory factors for a rise in gangs. The specific reasons for joining gangs cited by scholars has changed over time, generally becoming more complex since Frederic Thrasher's (1927) classic gang study that posited gangs as a spontaneously forming territorial group integrated through conflict. A study by Malcolm Klein, for example, identified 77 variables that distinguished gang members from the general population (1995, p. 77).

The arrival of immigrants and emergence of multiple communities of color in the metropolis, on the one hand, and an influx of cheap narcotics and easy access to weapons, on the other, make today's gang world a complex and dynamic environment, increasingly difficult to explain or generalize. This article traces the onset of Black gang formation in LA, using a sociohistorical and political analysis based on archival records and other published reports to explain *gang formation*. Most such studies do not necessarily shed light on questions of gang formation, namely, how and why do gangs form in specific communities and what spatial processes foster such formation? This analysis makes clear that at the root of *gang formation* are certain precipitating factors and suggests why specific geographical locales, as opposed to others, have been vulnerable to gang formation.

By focusing on gang formation I attempt to show how *the racialization of identities* played a major role in the gang formation process during two different post–World War II periods in LA. I argue that racialized identities and structural constraints contributed to early formation processes of traditional gangs.[1] Several classic and contemporary theories on gangs have shown the spatial linkages between immigrant and minority communities on the one hand, and gangs on the other, but existing theories have yet to make the connections between institutional practices, blatant societal prejudice, and the racialization of minorities as major factors toward gang formation. Generally, the literature fails to connect gang formation directly to racial inequality (Spergel, 1995, p. 161–162) but this paper will reveal how the racialization of Blacks played a critical role in the early formation of LA street gangs.

Two periods of gang formation in South LA are addressed here: the late 1940s and early 1970s. This paper links early gang formation in LA among Black youths in the 1940s to processes of residential segregation, police brutality and racially motivated violence and the aftermath of the civil rights period of the 1960s that led to the assassinations of many national and local LA activists that created a breeding ground for gang formation in the early 1970s. Although factors such as economic restructuring, deindustrialization, population shifts and poverty explain recent gang phenomena and have contributed to understanding *gang maintenance* and *proliferation* (Padilla, 1992; Shelden et al., 2001), I argue that these factors played a minimal role in early gang formation processes. Rather racial intimidation, school and residential segregation, extreme marginalization and racial exclusion from mainstream LA all played more significant roles in early gang formation among Blacks.

The following section of this paper briefly sketches the most widely recognized gang theories to date. Many of these explanations are useful as a means of understanding gang maintenance and proliferation, but do not provide enough explanation regarding gang formation in a place where gangs did not previously exist. Then, I provide a history of LA's Black gangs based on archival information and published reports. Lastly, I suggest a conceptual model of gang formation in LA.

Theories of Gang Formation

Early literature from the turn of the 20th century emphasized a biological basis for the development of gangs (Puffer, 1912). By the 1920s, followers of the Chicago School relied on cultural ecological models (Thrasher, 1927), while some more recent analyses using the underclass theory stress the urban economic as well as social bases for gang activity (Hagedorn, 1988; Klein, 1995). One of the shortcomings shared by many of these approaches is how race, immigrant status and social structure shape the place where gangs form. Most gang formation theory discusses at some length how communities of racial minorities are affected without much discussion about the racialization processes involved. Race is usually reduced to poverty, culture and behavior in explanations of higher rates of gang activity in minority neighborhoods.

Nature as Culture and Evolutionary Perspectives

John Puffer's analysis of gangs in the Boston area found that they engaged in outdoor activities, but several commonly embraced what he called shadier activities—smoking, drinking, and fighting (1912, p. 40). Puffer's gangs were "play groups" that spontaneously formed due to what he termed the "gang-forming instinct" present only in boys, acquired from ancestral relatives and prehistoric peoples that had ancestral ties (p. 25).

Frederic Thrasher published an empirical sociological gang study 15 years later that was rooted in the Chicago School tradition that used a *natural history* model to explain gang formation. Rather than using Puffer's gang instinct approach, Thrasher articulated an *ecological theory*, suggesting that gangs developed from specific conditions and experiences (1927, p. 44).

He argued that gang formation was a spatial and social process most prevalent in places that he characterized as "geographically and socially interstitial" places of the city (Thrasher, 1927,

p. 22), areas of social disorganization that included deteriorating homes, demographic change, and high immigrant populations. Because of isolation, competition, and conflict occurring in these places, they had been "naturally selected" for gang formation. Gangs formed as the result of the interaction between youths and the physical and social environment.

Also working in the Chicago School tradition, Clifford Shaw and Henry McKay examined gangs in the early 1930s in the "natural" urban areas of Chicago, as defined by the concentric zone and ecological models.[2] Pioneers of *cultural deviance theory*, they suggested that gangs formed from "learned behaviors" that emerged by means of weak societal controls in socially disorganized communities. These neighborhoods were characterized by extreme poverty and isolation, but more importantly an inability to inculcate common values of health, life, law, education and family to younger residents. The level of disorganization depended on economic conditions, land-use change, population shifts (especially immigration), and the share of Blacks and immigrants within the community (Empey, 1982, p. 191; Kornhauser, 1978, p. 63). These conditions encouraged the formation of gangs, whose traditions were transmitted to new generations of youths, continuing the cycle and leading to the persistence of gangs as an element in social structure (Kornhouser, 1978, p. 64).

Lower-Class Status and Culture

Albert Cohen (1955) outlined a *social strain model* of gang etiology that challenged the social disorganization approach. According to Cohen, communities classified as socially disorganized actually consisted of a vast network of informal institutions and associations that exhibited defects in organization (p. 32). Moreover, he questioned the root of gang formation, suggesting instead that the emergence of a "delinquent subculture" was behind the creation of gangs, utilizing a psychogenic approach to explain delinquency: all human action is an ongoing effort to problem-solve (p. 50).

Working class youths had status problems when operating within a middle class social system of values. Because the middle class evaluated the working class in a discriminatory way, marginalization was the source for strain and adjustment problems for working class youth. This strain engendered the development of a distinct subculture, which helped working class boys and young men to construct their own solutions in response to the failure of institutionalized approaches, such as formal schooling (p. 59).

In contrast, Walter Miller stated that gangs did not form as a reaction to achieve middle class values, but from *"focal concerns"* of lower class culture and everyday life (1958, p. 6). A specific cultural system operating in the lower class community influenced certain behavioral patterns that contributed to gang formation independent from (and not in reaction against) middle class values. These focal concerns included toughness, trouble, smartness, excitement, fate, and autonomy (p. 7). The gang was a product of the broken family and lower class culture, stressing reputation, status and masculinity, that were disconnected and unaffected by the middle class measuring rod.

Underclass Theory and Gang Formation

William Julius Wilson (1987) linked the existence of an urban "underclass" to economic dislocations, deindustrialization, lower class values (similar to Miller's analysis of the gang culture), prevalence of female-headed families (p. 26), joblessness and high incidences of criminal behavior and high rates of gang violence (1996, p. 59). According to Wilson, an isolated underclass population formed as the result of the out-migration of the middle class from the inner city, leaving a socially unstable and politically powerless community spiraling into persistent poverty.

Wilson's underclass model has been challenged for being disconnected to historical events, failing to explain the disproportionate incidence of pathology in communities of color, and lacking empirical grounding (Omi and Winant, 1994; Steinberg, 1995). Moreover, according to Hughes (1989), the underclass phenomenon is rooted in geographical/spatial categories such as ghetto, community, mismatch, suburbanization and neighborhood—categories left unproblematized in Wilson's analysis. Additionally, the underclass theory has not been able to explain fluctuations in gang crime as they rise and drop (Spergel, 1992, p. 128). Nevertheless, Wilson's ideas became influential and not surprisingly figured into contemporary gang formation theory.

For example, John Hagedorn (1988) drew on Wilson's underclass thesis to explain Black gang activity in Milwaukee during the 1980s, emphasizing economic restructuring, poverty concentration, and concomitant diminished sense of community stimulating suburbanization of more middle class Blacks, leaving older neighborhoods prone to gang formation. Similarly, Malcolm Klein (1995) used underclass theory to explain gang formation as well as aspects of gang persistence. Gang persistence, according to Klein, was linked to deindustrialization, economic changes in the inner city, the failure of the education system, suburbanization of middle class Blacks, and residential segregation (p. 194). A second category of variables related to gang maintenance was linked to psychological aspects of gangs such as status, identity, and belonging (p. 198). Klein offered an additional class of indicators to explain gang formation linked to structural and community features such as number of minority youth and absence of jobs. In short, Klein saw a burgeoning underclass community causing gang "onset" variables to emerge that were in turn connected to the psychological features that perpetuated gang traditions. As the urban underclass population grew so would gangs.

Multiple Marginality

While accepting some aspects of earlier theories, in his study of Latino gangs in LA, James Diego Vigil (1988) emphasized that the interaction of several pressures together determined the life chances of barrio youths in his *multiple marginality* thesis. Thus there was no single cause of gang formation, but rather multidimensional pathways that differed for each individual. Vigil's multiple marginality approach rested on a synthesis of variables including mother-centered homes, lack of male adult guidance, and low-income status that led youth toward poor school performance, increased contact

with law enforcement, and the beginnings of an aggressive lifestyle. In addition, Vigil emphasized the need for an historical consideration of barrio life (p. 172) that focused on the social history and context of settlement and residential patterns, low immigrant wages, poor community planning, and racial discrimination, which were all tied to gang formation. A combination of these processes led to an entrenched low-income population living in spatially isolated communities in inferior housing (p. 65).

Summary and Critique

What is most striking about the corpus of gang formation research is the limited discussion of how race and structure have worked together to create communities that have produced gangs. This apparent omission leads to some major shortcomings in both contemporary and traditional gang formation theory. The slum conditions, extreme poverty, and deteriorating homes that Thrasher observed in Chicago were never directly linked to racial status, residential segregation, or any form of racial discrimination that may have contributed to and fostered a climate conducive to gang formation. Additionally Shaw and McKay made no mention of the structural constraints and prejudices in their theoretical construction. Albert Cohen's social strain model was more associated with class status than race and Walter Miller's lower-culture thesis made no direct link to race.

Klein's model provides a thorough explanation of gang sustenance and proliferation but early formation processes were not rigorously explored. His mention of minority segregation (p. 199) is only marginally linked to race. Gangs existed in many urban communities long before the deindustrialization in the mid-1970 and 1980s and Black middle class suburbanization occurred.

To fully understand the dynamics of these gangs, we must view them from an historical perspective that illuminates the roles of race, place and social structure in early gang formation. Vigil's multiple marginality theory explains how gangs emerged in the barrios of LA by emphasizing how the historical circumstances of residential segregation, community isolation, low socioeconomic status and racism were contributing factors in early gang formation. Although Vigil's thesis integrates the underclass argument, he does not gloss over the effects of race but he does not provide a specific example of a gang forming.

Black Gang Formation in Los Angeles

What about the Black gangs that emerged in LA in the postwar period? The academic literature is largely silent on this question, despite the extensive publicity accorded to LA's Black gangs. In what follows, I provide an account of their formation, giving special consideration to the historical record, archival research and a series of in-depth interviews. In addition, I draw on earlier research (Alonso, 1999) that mapped the historical geography of Black street gang territories in LA, using law enforcement reports, extensive ethnographic analysis, and a territorial delimitation technique based on a gang graffiti analysis. . . .

This narrative draws on an extensive body of literature, including newspaper articles, unpublished papers, doctoral dissertations, scholarly articles and books, and a variety of law enforcement documents. In addition, this story incorporates information from in-depth interviews with key figures that participated in gangs during the period under scrutiny. Many of these interviews were conducted during annual reunion picnics in Los Angeles, where several hundred former gang members, going back to the late 1940s, would congregate. The open-ended interviews focused on gang history, and life in the community. More than 25 individuals were interviewed on multiple occasions (see Alonso, 1999, pp. 71–96).

This historically grounded and place-based approach allows us to see how Black migration into LA, school and residential segregation, political struggle, and other structural factors contributing to the profound ghettoization of South LA laid the foundation for the city's Black gangs. It is only within this context of intense racialization, marginalization, a deeply rooted racial social order and overt acts of racial violence that we can understand what triggered successive waves of Black gang formation in LA.

Gang formation among Blacks occurred during two periods, following WWII in the late 1940s and during the early 1970s. There was a lull of Black gang activity from 1965, after the Watts insurrection, up until the early 1970s when the contemporary Black gangs formed. This marked the beginning of the second phase of gang formation, which saw the rise of LA's newest gangs that continued to grow during the 1970s, reaching epidemic proportions in the late 1980s and early 1990s.

Post–World War II to 1965

The first major period of Black gang formation in LA began in the late 1940s after thousands of Blacks migrated from the South to fill WWII jobs. Restrictive covenants, legalized in the 1920s, maintained social and racial homogeneity of neighborhoods by denying non-Whites access to property ownership (Bunch, 1990, p. 114). By the 1940s such exclusionary practices had rendered much of LA off-limits to most minorities (Bond, 1936; Davis, 1990, pp. 161, 273; Dymski and Veitch, 1996, p. 40). Chronic overcrowding was taking a toll, and housing congestion became a serious problem as Blacks were forced to live in substandard housing confined by specific boundaries (Collins, 1980, p. 26; Bunch, 1990, p. 117). By the 1940s, Black residents continually challenged restrictive covenants in court, in an effort to leave their overcrowded Central Avenue neighborhood. These attempts resulted in violent clashes between Whites and Blacks (Collins, 1980, p. 30).

Throughout the 1940s, White resentment and racial paranoia grew as the Black population did, and especially as Blacks attempted to integrate into public schools while challenging the housing discrimination laws that prevented them from purchasing homes outside the original Black settlement area. In nearby areas of Huntington Park, Bell and South Gate some White Angelenos maliciously reacted against the growing Black population. Here White teenagers formed street clubs during the 1940s to terrorize Black youth. One of the most infamous was the *Spook Hunters*, a group of White teenagers that often attacked Black youths in the neighboring communities (Alonso, 1999, p. 74). Blacks seen outside of their neighborhoods were often physically attacked (Horne, 1995, p. 190). These White street clubs focused their efforts at spatially confining Blacks in "their" neighborhoods, fighting school integration and protecting racial purity in the community (Bunch, 1990, p. 117). The *Spook Hunters* would work toward these goals by instigating fights and intimidating Black youths.

This type of racial confrontation was not uncommon, nor was it restricted to LA. Thrasher (1927, p. 37), for example, identified a White gang in Chicago during the 1920s called the *Dirty Dozens* that often attacked Black youths with knives, blackjacks, and revolvers because of racial differences. In Steven Gregory's historical analysis of Black migration into Queens, New York he found that intensified racial segregation transformed the neighborhood of Corona, Queens and that a rigid color line developed in the early 1950s. The *Dukes*, a White gang, were intimidating Black residents and exacerbating racial conflict (Gregory, 1998, p. 63). It was also found that one of the major factors contributing to gang formation in Chicago was the race riot of 1919 that ignited many Black males to unite together to confront hostile White hoodlums who were terrorizing the Black community (Spear, 1967, p. 201; Perkins, 1987, p. 40).

In LA, Raymond Wright, one of the founders of the *Businessmen*[3] stated "you couldn't pass Alameda Blvd, because those White boys in South Gate would set you on fire" (Alonso, 1999, p. 75). Fear of attack from Whites was widespread and this intimidation led to the early formation of Black social street clubs aimed at protecting Black youths against persistent White violence directed against the growing Black community. Again, similar club formation patterns were seen in other cities. For example, Suttles observed that Black gangs in Chicago acted as guardians and served a useful social function in the community. He also observed an alliance between Blacks and Mexicans, in anticipation of conflicts with local Whites (1968, pp. 135–136).

The first major Black gangs surfaced on the Eastside of LA near Jefferson High School in the Central Avenue area, and began to spread south and westward (Fig. 17.1). As Black clubs began to negotiate strategies to combat White intimidation

and violence, the effectiveness of White efforts to combat integration and residential segregation began to fail. White Angelenos viewed the burgeoning minority population as a threat (Hahn, 1996, p. 79) while many Blacks viewed Black gang formation as a legitimate defense against violence. Eventually White flight set in and Anglo residents took advantage of new suburban developments, leaving South LA behind. This left the central district of LA as a Black enclave that represented 71% of the inner-city population (Brunn et al., 1993, p. 53) and by 1960, the three Black communities of Watts, Central Ave., and West Adams, previously islands of Black residence, had consolidated into one large continuous Black community with low, middle and upper class districts (Alonso, 1999, p. 77; Robinson, 2000, p. 158).

During the early 1960s conflict among Black clubs was growing as White residents continued to move out. As White clubs began to fade from the scene, eventually the Black clubs, which were first organized as protectors of the community, began to engage in conflicts with other Black clubs. Black gang activity represented a significant proportion of gang incidents (Los Angeles County Probation Department and Youth Studies Center, 1962, p. 1), and by 1960 club rivalry led to six murders (Los Angeles Police Department, 1961, p. 28) a figure considered extremely high at that time, making Black-on-Black violence between the clubs a serious concern in LA. In 1965, however, after the Watts Rebellion and under the leadership of several socially conscious organizations, most of this rivalry and violence among Black gangs ended. Black youths became politically mobilized and turned their attention toward the social problems that plagued their community. Gang members were successful in transforming several Black youths of South LA into "revolutionary soldiers" against police brutality (Hilliard and Cole, 1993, p. 218). The Rebellion of 1965 was considered "the Last Great Rumble," as members of these groups dismissed old rivalries and supported each other against heightened police brutality (Baker, 1988, p. 28; Davis, 1990, p. 297), thus Watts epitomized the emergence of a movement to build institutions led by and entirely responsible to the [Black] community (Bullock, 1969, p. 69).

Figure 17.1 Black Gang Territories in Los Angeles, 1960

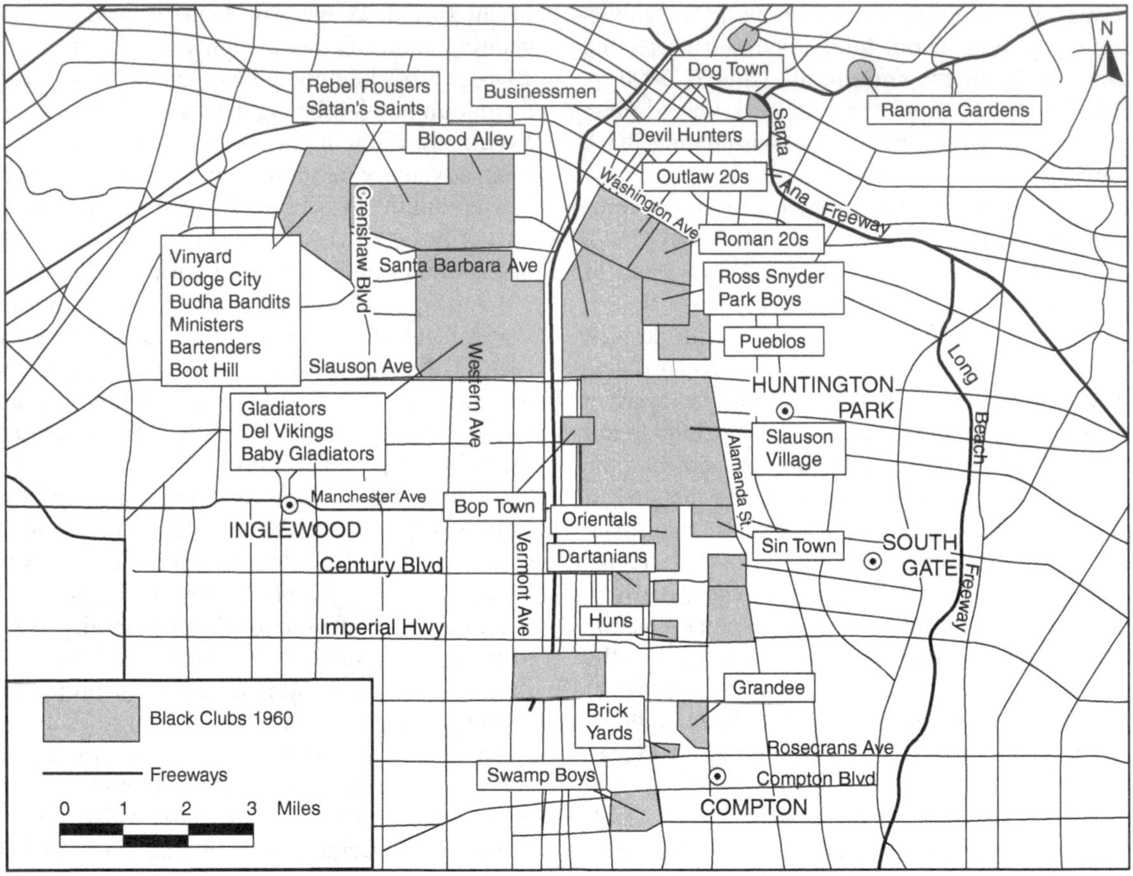

Sociopolitical Period, 1965–1970

In the aftermath of the rebellion, young people, including gang members began to build political institutions to contest social injustices, specifically police brutality. Until the decade's end, Black political groups were organizing and during these years Black street gang activity lessened. Reports that Black gang activity was on the decline began to circulate (Klein, 1971, p. 22) and according to one Los Angeles Police Sergeant, during the mid- and late-1960s, juvenile gang activity in Black neighborhoods was scarcely visible to the public at large and of minimal concern to South-Central residents (Cohen, 1972). The formation of new political and social movements, especially the Black

Panther Party (BPP) and the civil rights–oriented U.S. Organization,[4] offered Black youths vehicles for building self-esteem and self-affirmation, occupying time and energies that might otherwise have been spent engaging in destructive activities (Alonso, 1999, p. 81). After the Rebellion, a sense of cohesiveness began to form, along with self worth and positive identification as pride pervaded the Black community (Horne, 1995, p. 196). So too in other cities, even in Chicago, Black nationalism began to influence rival gangs and calm gang conflict (Keiser, 1969, p. 7).

Police abuses in LA became a rising concern for the Black community under Chief William Parker and Mayor Samuel Yorty who became an enthusiastic supporter of Parker and his tactics. Although Parker reformed the LAPD away from the corruption, he often resorted to unconstitutional methods of police investigation (Bollens and Geyer, 1973, p. 131; Tyler, 1983, pp. 124–138) and was warned in court about his procedures and methods. He was instructed to conduct his force in accordance with Constitutional law but Parker's actions created a divide between the police and the Black residents of South LA and in 1960 over $1 million in brutality and police misconduct claims were filed against the LAPD (Domanick, 1994, p. 163).

Parker's notorious insensitivity toward inner-city residents during the 1950s and early 1960s polarized the community and was largely responsible for the Rebellion of 1965 (Cannon, 1997, p. 69), and the year before, Parker claimed that Los Angeles did not have segregation problems (Domanick, 1994, p. 179). He opposed the civil rights movement and denied that police tactics contributed to deteriorating race relations in the city (Cannon, 1997, p. 70). Parker placed all blame on the California Highway Patrol's handling of the arrest that preceded the riot. When asked what sparked the riot, Parker replied, "someone threw a rock, and like monkeys in a zoo, they all started throwing rocks" (Domanick, 1994, p. 182). Throughout his 16-year tenure, up until his death in 1966, Parker and the LAPD operated without effective restraint (Tyler, 1983, p. 136) and relations between the LAPD and the Black community became deeply troubled.

During the 1960s, the United States government, along with local and state law enforcement agencies began paying close attention to Black political groups that they viewed as a subversive threat to society (Churchill and Vander Wall, 1990, p. 37). The emerging Black consciousness of the 1960s that fueled the political movement was viewed as hostile. The efforts of militant groups to organize young Blacks against police brutality were repressed by the FBI, which specifically viewed the BPP as a threat to national security. Chief Thomas Reddin, Parker's successor, retained the military model and police tactics of Parker and believed that Black radicals represented a major threat to the safety of his officers and their authority on the streets (Schiesl and Klein, 1990, p. 168).

By 1967, the BPP was one of the most influential Black political groups in the nation, and, by 1968, FBI director J. Edgar Hoover dispatched a memorandum calling his field agents to exploit all avenues of creating dissension within the ranks of the BPP (Churchill and Vander Wall, 1990, p. 63). Counterintelligence programs (COINTELPRO) used between 1968–1971 by the FBI were successful at weakening and neutralizing the BPP. The most vicious and unrestrained applications of COINTELPRO techniques during the late 1960s and early 1970s were clearly reserved for the BPP (Churchill and Vander Wall, 1990, p. 61; Horne, 1995, p. 13). Differences between the BPP and US Organization were exacerbated by COINTELPRO (Ngozi-Brown, 1997, p. 167), which sought to capitalize on the ideological differences between the BPP and the United States.

The FBI's COINTELPRO tactics included distribution of fabricated publications, leaflets, and cartoons, written by agents and designed to create further conflict between the two groups. The propaganda literature, purporting to be from one group, defamed and ridiculed the other group, leading to physical confrontations that escalated to gun violence. The FBI was clearly aware of this conflict and wrote that a struggle between the BPP and the US Organization should be more rigorously instigated and instructed field offices to submit imaginative hard-hitting counterintelligence measures aimed at crippling the BPP (Churchill and Vander Wall, 1990, p. 41).

Several BPP members were assaulted and killed by law enforcement officers around the nation during COINTELPRO. The FBI, along with the LAPD organized a four-hour police assault on the office of the BPP on Central Avenue in 1968 (Harris and Main, 1968; Torgerson, 1969), but the incident that had the most profound impact on Blacks in LA and truly marked the beginning of the end of the BPP era in Southern California and the end of the civil rights movement in LA was the assassination of BPP leaders Bunchy Carter[5] and John Huggins at UCLA's campus in 1969 (Drummond and Reich, 1969).

The end of 1960s was the last chapter of the political, social and civil rights movement by Black groups in LA, and a turning point away from the development of positive Black identity in the city. Several events followed close upon the assassinations at UCLA, including the imprisonment (until his vindication in 1997) of another BPP affiliate, Geronimo Pratt. Pratt, a Vietnam veteran with 18 combat decorations, was targeted for "neutralization" by the FBI (Churchill and Vander Wall, 1990, p. 41). By the late 1960s, COINTELPRO had obliterated the Black revolution in LA (Swearingen, 1995, p. 82), orchestrating the assassinations of 29 BPP members nation wide, and the imprisonment of hundreds of others (Robinson, 1997, p. 152). Thus the Panthers flashed across the western sky like a meteor; their own mistakes combined with repression meant that they were virtually extinct about five years after their beginnings (Horne, 1995, p. 197; Cannon, 1997, p. 97).

Gang Resurgence, 1970–1972

The eradication of Black consciousness and political leadership in LA created both a power vacuum in the community and a large void in the lives of youths in the late 1960s. This deeply racialized context coincided with the resurgence of new emerging street groups. A generation of Black teens saw their role models and leadership decimated, as the local backlash set in against Black nationalism and political organizing. Similarly, top national Black leaders—Medgar Evers, James Meredith, Malcolm X, and Dr. Martin Luther King Jr.—had been assassinated by the end of the 1960s. Through COINTELPRO tactics by the FBI, Black identity groups were rendered ineffective. Simultaneously Black youths in LA searching for a new identity began to mobilize as street gangs as they had in the late 1940s (Alonso, 1999, p. 89).

Shortly after much of the BPP power base was eliminated and as other social and political groups became ineffective, teenagers in South LA started a small street group to serve as a quasi-political organization. Teens too young to participate in the BPP movement during the 1960s had nonetheless absorbed much of the rhetoric of community control of neighborhoods (Baker, 1988, p. 28). What started off as a quasi-political unit slowly developed into a group of misguided teens.

Because of immaturity and a lack of leadership, the revolutionary rhetoric and goals did not endure. Compounded by the racialization of Black organizations during the 1960s new groups were never able to develop an effective political agenda for social change within the community. Increasingly, early social objectives became obscure, and by 1972 many members had become involved in criminal activities, including robberies and assaults. Such behavior led to one of the first gang murders of this time, when a 16-year-old high school athlete was beaten to death over a leather coat in 1972 at the Hollywood Palladium.[6]

Sensational media coverage of the event plus continued assaults by these new gangs attracted other youths to join. For youths marginalized on several fronts, association with such gangs reinforced a masculine identity and projected it onto self and others, fueling gang growth (Vigil and Yun, 1990, p. 64). The increased attention paid by the police and community to these early Black gangs, which later became known as the *Crips*,[7] attracted more youths to join in. The original intentions of group leaders were to serve as community leaders and protectors of their neighborhoods; however, because of a weak resource base, an unplanned agenda, lack of support, immaturity and perhaps most important, severe racialization of the late 1960s, left a generation of youths clueless about their future. Gang violence was in the early stages of what would soon become an epidemic in LA.

Throughout the mid-1970s gang rivalry grew as the number of gangs grew. Crip identity took over the streets of South LA and swept Southside schools in an epidemic of gang shootings and street fights by 1972 (Davis, 1990, p. 300) when there were 18 Black gangs in LA County. By 1978 that had multiplied to 60 gangs, and by the 1990s there were more than 270 gangs in the county (Alonso, 1999, p. 104; Fig. 17.2). With the proliferation of gangs came an increase of conflict and homicides, and by the late 1980s and early 1990s homicides reached epidemic levels (Hutson et al., 1995).

Toward a New Model of Gang Formation

The early attempts of Black gangs to continue the BPP legacy dramatically evolved into mischievous and ultimately criminal youth groups. At a time when economic opportunity was disappearing from South LA, the *Crips* were becoming the

Figure 17.2 Black Gang Territories in Los Angeles, 1972 and 1996

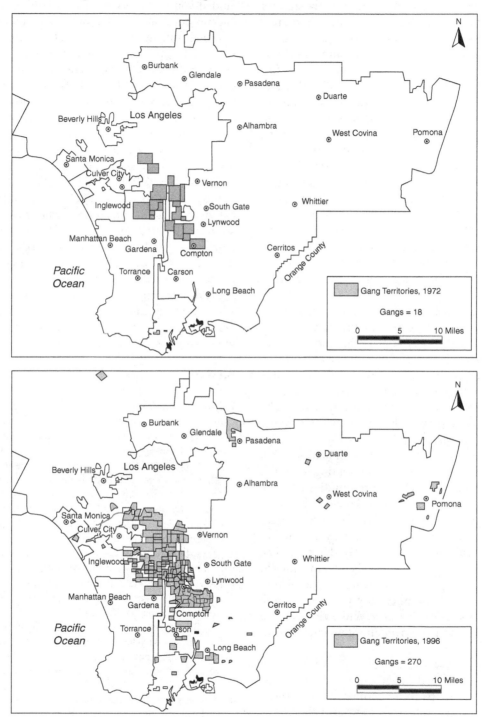

Source: Alonso, 1999, pp. 125–127.

power resource of last resort for thousands of abandoned youth (Davis, 1990, p. 300). Early signs of social disorganization had gripped the community with serious consequences but segregation, overcrowding, and racial violence had unquestionably had an enormous impact on the fate of South LA. The COINTELPRO activities of the FBI and abuses by the LAPD, and their disruption of community-based political and social organizations led to debilitating effects that greatly contributed to the formation of gangs. These activities resulted in the violent and tragic end to the civil rights movement and the removal of community leaders that inevitably had detrimental psychological effects on Black youths. In understanding the formation of these traditional gangs, race is central as an etiological factor. Alienation from the political consciousness that began in the 1960s heightened and became increasingly marginalized with successive generations.

Economic dislocations that contributed to elements of social organization were evident, but this history clearly reveals that the racialization and disenfranchisement of Black youths in specific geographic locales was a driving force behind initial gang formation during both periods.[8] Racism, built into the legal system, policing practices, and everyday White life in postwar LA turned increasingly violent as White groups organized to intimidate Black populations that were rapidly growing and attempting to settle into predominately White communities (Bunch, 1990, p. 118). The response was a defensive reaction formation that triggered the formation of gangs. Such gangs did not form as a result of lower class culture, mother-centered households, deindustrialization or middle class flight. Nor did they form in response to pressures to conform to middle class values. Rather they arose in response to much less subtle dynamics: White violence and intimidation, and the deepening racialization of inner-city youths.

Although there was a significant lull of Black gang activity during the 1960s, when youthful energies were channeled into legitimate social protest movements, gangs were only to form again following the state-perpetrated, deeply racist eradication of Black political organizations. This left a power

vacuum in the Black community that allowed misguided youths to form quasi-political groups that had no political direction and were vulnerable to criminal influences. Groups that are subjected to sustained exploitation eventually develop illicit and harmful characteristics and behaviors as a way to cope (Patterson, 1997, p. 142). These stresses led group members to victimize other group members, in this case other Black groups, which eventually became the agents of subjugation. The gangs that later developed became etched into an already existing racialized geography that was enforced and maintained by deindustrialization, a poor political economy, out-migration of Whites, and single-parent households. Such factors exacerbated a situation originally rooted in school and residential segregation, and the intensification of racial conflict. This was the case with the groups that formed in the late 1940s and again in the early 1970s. Thus at the root of gang formation lie efforts to maintain White privilege and racial exclusion throughout a period of turbulent social and geographic change in Los Angeles.

Notes

1. This overview is only relevant to understanding the formation of the older traditional gangs in Los Angeles. These processes do not relate to the formation of emergent and newer gangs that formed in the 1980s and 1990s. For a descriptive explanation of traditional and other types of gangs, see Klein and Maxson, 1996.

2. The 1942 text by Clifford Shaw and Henry McKay titled *Juvenile Delinquency and Urban Areas: A Study of Rates of Delinquency in Relation to Differential Characteristics of Local Communities in American Cities* did not include gangs, but all of the work regarding social disorganization, community control, and cultural transmission present in the 1942 study is evident in the work from 1931 on gangs. For a detailed descriptive analysis of the two publications, see Knox, 1998.

3. The Businessmen were one of the first Black clubs to form in Los Angeles during the late 1940s. They were based in the Central Vernon area of Los Angeles and were also known as the Bossmen (Alonso, 1999, pp. 72–76).

4. Members of U.S. Organization were cultural nationalists headed by Ron "Maulana" Karenga, forming in the 1960s. They promoted cultural awareness and knowledge through education of Africa, language, wardrobe,

and other cultural traits as a disciplined nonmilitant group. Their philosophy on civil rights was different from the BPP's position and they did not advocate self-defense and weapon use. Both groups vied for approval and support from the Black community in Los Angeles; therefore, they rarely worked together but rather worked against each other.

5. Bunchy Carter was a member of the Slausons during the 1960s and spent some time in prison before the 1965 Watts Rebellion. After the Rebellion and during the late 1960s, he became an influential local political figure in Los Angeles' civil rights movement and headed the LA chapter of the Black Panther Party. He was considered one of the preeminent local street leaders of the Black community in the late 1960s and was well respected because of his street reputation (see Tyler, 1983; Churchill and Vander Wall, 1990).

6. *Los Angeles Times*, March 19, 1972.

7. The Crips became a loose affiliation of several gangs that formed in South LA in the early 1970s. The first Crip gang formed near Freemont High School in South LA around late 1969 but then quickly spread into other areas of South LA, including Compton and Inglewood. By 1972, there were about eight independent Crip gangs.

8. Research on Hispanic gangs in LA reveals a similar pattern of gang formation that emphasizes the impact of race (Gonzalez, 1981, p. 81; Espinoza, 1984; Vigil, 1990, p. 118), while work on Asian gang formation in Los Angeles also uncovers its roots in racial conflict (Yu, 1987, p. 18; Kang, 1999).

References

Alonso, A. A., 1999, Territoriality among African American Street Gangs in Los Angeles. Unpublished master's thesis, Department of Geography, University of Southern California.

Baker, B., 1988, Cold killers and fearful innocents; Homeboys: Players in a deadly drama. *Los Angeles Times*, June 26, p. A1.

Bond, M., 1936, The Negro in Los Angeles. Unpublished dissertation, Department of History, University of Southern California, Los Angeles.

Bollens, J. C. and Geyer, G., 1973, *Yorty: Politics of a Constant Candidate*. Palisades, CA: Palisades.

Brunn, S., Yeates, M., and Zeigler, D., 1993, Cities of the United States and Canada. In S. Brunn and J. Williams, editors, *Cities of the World: World Regional Urban Development*. New York, NY: HarperCollins, 39–83.

Bullock, P., 1969, *Watts: The Aftermath*. New York, NY: Grove.

Bunch, L. G., 1990, A past not necessarily prologue: The Afro-American in Los Angeles. In N. M. Klein and M. J. Schiesl, editors, *20th Century Los Angeles: Power, Promotion and Social Conflict*. Claremont, CA: Regina, 101–130.

Cannon, L., 1997, *Official Negligence: How Rodney King and the Riots Changed Los Angeles and the LAPD*. New York, NY: Times Book.

Churchill, W. and Vander Wall, J., 1990, *Agents of Repression: The FBI's Secret Wars against the Black Panther Party and the American Indian Movement*. Boston, MA: South End.

Cohen, A. K., 1955, *Delinquent Boys: The Culture of the Gang*. Glencoe, IL: Free Press.

Cohen, J., 1972, Theories vary on the rise of Black youth gangs. *Los Angeles Times*, March 19, pp. B1–3.

Collins, K., 1980, *Black Los Angeles: The Maturing of the Ghetto, 1940-1950*. Saratoga, CA: Century Twenty-One.

Davis, M., 1990, *City of Quartz: Excavating the Future in Los Angeles*. New York, NY: Vintage.

Decker, S. H. and Curry, D.C., 2000, Addressing key features of gang membership: Measuring the involvement of young members. *Journal of Criminal Justice*, Vol. 28, 473–482.

Domanick, J., 1994, *To Protect and to Serve: The LAPD at War in the City of Dreams*. New York, NY: Pocket.

Drummond, W. J. and Reich, K., 1969, Two Black Panthers slain in UCLA hall. *Los Angeles Times*, January 18, p. A1.

Dymski, G. A. and Veitch, J. M., 1996, Financing the future of Los Angeles: From Depression to 21st century. In M. J. Dear, H. E. Stockman, and G. Hise, editors, *Rethinking Los Angeles*. Thousand Oaks, CA: Sage, 35–55.

Empey, L. T., 1982, *American Delinquency: Its Meaning and Construction*. Homewood, IL: Dorsey.

Espinoza, F. G., 1984, An Historical Perspective on the Growth of Hispanic Gangs in Los Angeles. Unpublished dissertation, Department of History, University of California, Los Angeles.

Gonzalez, A. G., 1981, *Mexican/Chicano Gangs in Los Angeles: A Sociohistorical Case Study*. Doctoral dissertation, University of California, Berkeley.

Gregory, S., 1998, *Black Corona: Race and the Politics of Place in an Urban Community*. Princeton, NJ: Princeton University Press.

Hagedorn, J. M., 1988, *People and the Folks: The Underclass in a Rustbelt City*. Chicago, IL: Lake View.

Hahn, H., 1996, Los Angeles and the future: Uprisings, identity, and new institutions. In M. J. Dear, H. E. Shockman, and G. Hise, editors, *Rethinking Los Angeles*. Thousand Oaks, CA: Sage, 77–95.

Harris, R. and Main, D., 1968, Policeman shot, 3 suspects slain near Adams, Crenshaw. *Los Angeles Times*, August 6, p. A1.

Hilliard, D. and Cole, L., 1993, *This Side of Glory: The Autobiography of David Hilliard and the Story of the Black Panther Party*. New York, NY: Back Bay.

Horne, G., 1995, *Fire This Time: The Watts Uprising and the 1960s*. New York, NY: Da Capo.

Hughes, M. A., 1989, Misspeaking truth to power: A geographical perspective on the "underclass" fallacy. *Economic Geography*, Vol. 65, 187–207.

Hutson, H. R., Anglin, D., Kyriacou, D. N., Hart, H., and Spears, H., 1995. The epidemic of gang related homicides in Los Angeles County from 1979 to 1994. *The Journal of the American Medical Association*, Vol. 274, 1031–1036.

Kang, K. E. S., 1999, Acculturation Styles and Struggles of Cambodian Gang Members. Unpublished thesis, Department of Social Work, California State University, Long Beach, Long Beach.

Keiser, R. L., 1969, *The Vice Lords: Warriors of the Streets*. New York, NY: Holt, Reinhart, and Winston.

Klein, M. W., 1971, *Street Gangs and Street Workers*. Englewood Cliffs, NJ: Prentice-Hall.

Klein, M. W., 1995, *The American Street Gang: Its Nature, Prevalence, and Control*. New York, NY: Oxford.

Klein, M. W. and Maxson, C., 1996, *Gang Structures, Crime Patterns, and Police Responses*. Social Science Research Institute.

Knox, G. W., 1998, *An Introduction to Gangs* (4th ed.). Chicago, IL: New Chicago School.

Kornhauser, R., 1978, *Social Sources of Delinquency: An Appraisal of Analytical Models*. Chicago, IL: University of Chicago Press.

Los Angeles County Probation Department and Youth Studies Center, 1962, *Study of Delinquent Gangs: Progress Report*. Los Angeles, CA: University of Southern California.

Los Angeles Police Department, 1961, *1960 Annual Report*. Los Angeles, CA: Author.

Miller, W., 1958, Lower class culture as a generating milieu of gang delinquency. *Journal of Social Issues*, Vol. 14, 5–20.

Ngozi-Brown, S., 1997, The US Organization, Maulana Karenga, and conflict with the Black Panther Party. *Journal of Black Studies*, Vol. 28, 157–170.

Omi, M. and Winant, H., 1994, *Racial Formation in the United States: From the 1960s to the 1990s* (2nd ed.). New York, NY: Routledge and Kegan Paul.

Padilla, F., 1992, *The Gang as an American Enterprise*. New Bruswick, NJ: Rutgers University Press.

Patterson, O., 1997, *The Ordeal of Integration: Progress and Resentment in America's "Racial" Crisis*. Washington, DC: Civitas Counter Point.

Perkins, U., 1987, *Explosion of Chicago Street Gangs*. Chicago, IL: Third World.

Puffer, J. A., 1912, *The Boy and His Gang*. Boston, MA: Houghton Mifflin.

Robinson, C., 1997, *Black Movements in America*. New York, NY: Routledge.

Robinson, P. L., 2000, Class and Place within the African American Community 1940–1990. Unpublished dissertation, Department of Geography, University of Southern California.

Rumble, N. M. and Turner, W. L., 2000, A systemic analysis of the dynamics and organization of urban street gangs. *The American Journal of Family Therapy*, Vol. 28, 117–132.

Schiesl, M. J. and Klein, N. M., editors, 1990, *20th Century Los Angeles: Power, Promotion, and Social Conflict*. Claremont, CA: Regina.

Shaw, C. and McKay, H., 1942, *Juvenile Delinquency and Urban Areas: A Study of Rates of Delinquency in Relation to Differential Characteristics of Local Communities in American Cities*. Chicago, IL: University of Chicago Press.

Shelden, R. G., Tracy, S. K., and Brown, W. B., 2001, *Youth Gangs in American Society*. Belmont, CA: Wadsworth.

Spear, A., 1967, *Black Chicago: The Making of Negro Ghetto (1890–1920)*. Chicago, IL: University of Chicago Press.

Spergel, I. A., 1992, The youth gangs: An essay review. *Social Service Review*, Vol. 66, 121–139.

Spergel, I. A., 1995, *The Youth Gang Problem: A Community Approach*. New York, NY: Oxford University Press.

Steinberg, S., 1995, *Turning Back: The Retreat from Racial Justice in American Thought and Policy*. Boston, MA: Beacon.

Suttles, G., 1968, *The Social Order of the Slum: Ethnicity and Territory in the Inner City*. Chicago, IL: University of Chicago Press.

Swearingen, M. W., 1995, *FBI Secrets: An Agent Exposé*. Boston, MA: South End.

Thrasher, F. M., 1927, *The Gang: A Study of 1,313 Gangs in Chicago*. Chicago, IL: University of Chicago Press.

Torgerson, D., 1969, Police seize Panther fortress in gunfights. *Los Angeles Times*, December 9, p. A1.

Tyler, B. M., 1983, Black Radicalism in Southern California, 1950–1982. Unpublished dissertation, Department of History, University of California, Los Angeles.

Venkatesh, S. A., 1997, The social organization of street gang activity in an urban ghetto. *American Journal of Sociology*, Vol. 103, 82–111.

Vigil, J. D., 1988, *Barrio Gangs: Street Life and Identity in Southern California*. Austin, TX: University of Texas Press.

Vigil, J. D., 1990, Cholos and gangs: Culture change and street youth in Los Angeles. In C. R. Huff, editor, *Gangs in America*. Newbury Park, NJ: Sage, 146–152.

Vigil, J. D., 1996, Street baptism: Chicano gang initiation. *Human Organization*, Vol. 55, 149–152.

Vigil, J. D., and Yun, S. C., 1990, Vietnamese youth gangs in Southern California. In C. R. Huff, editor, *Gangs in America*. Newbury Park, NJ: Sage, 146–152.

Wilson, W. J., 1987, *The Truly Disadvantaged: The Inner City, the Underclass, and Public Policy*. Chicago, IL: University of Chicago Press.

Wilson, W. J., 1996, *When Work Disappears: The World of the New Urban Poor*. New York, NY: Vintage Books.

Yu, E. Y., 1987, *Juvenile Delinquency in the Korean Community of Los Angeles*. Los Angeles, CA: The Korean Times.

CHAPTER 18

Typically Moroccan? A Group Dynamic Explanation of Nuisance and Criminal Behavior

Jan Dirk de Jong

Our inclusion of de Jong's insightful chapter from the Netherlands is useful for several reasons. Many Western European cities have become increasingly concerned with gang involvement among youth from immigrant communities, many of whom originate from Southern Europe, the Middle East, and Northern Africa. De Jong's analysis of the experiences of young Moroccan men in Holland highlights their experiences of multiple marginality, revealing important parallels with the experiences of immigrant gang youth in the United States. Thus, the reader will be reminded of our earlier point that gangs and gang members tend to exhibit far more similarities than differences across distinct minority groups. In addition, de Jong's chapter provides yet another highly illuminating account of group processes within gangs, including how peer dynamics serve to intensify an "us versus them" identity that can facilitate gang offending.

A Moroccan Gang Problem

In the Netherlands, troublesome "Moroccan" youth groups[1] have become a symbol of nuisance and criminal behavior and are depicted in the media as gangs. The media refer to a Moroccan gang problem (also known as the "Moroccan drama"), and in politics, there is talk of a "Moroccan debate" (*NRC Handelsblad* 2006). In this debate, it is stated

that gangs consisting of boys of Moroccan descent pose a nuisance to the larger society and are often engaged in (serious) criminal behavior. In recent years, these groups of Moroccan young men have also been alleged to be involved in street terrorism. The media and politicians have labeled the behavior of these Moroccan boys as "typically Moroccan" (*NRC Handelsblad* 2008).

What this means is that the delinquent behavior of these boys is interpreted as a reflection of values that have been identified by anthropologists as typically Moroccan. They refer to Moroccan values such as distrust, shame, family honor, and an appreciation of a warrior mentality (van Gemert 1998; Werdmölder 1986, 1990, 2005). In their view, the groups of Moroccan boys in the Netherlands reproduce these typically Moroccan values. This reproduction process is said to explain the extreme amount of the nuisance and criminal behavior for which the gangs are known.

This labeling of (serious) delinquent behavior as "typically Moroccan" and of the groups as gangs has taken place in a social and political context during the past few years in which right-wing parties have gained power based on naming and shaming. These parties openly point their fingers at the Moroccan community in the Netherlands and hold them accountable for safety issues in public spaces. To be precise, they state that Moroccan parents are unable and unwilling to raise their children properly and that they do not care what the young boys are up to when they are outside in the streets. They also blame the Moroccan community for breeding gangs of young street terrorists based

Reprinted from: Jan Dirk De Jong, "Typically Moroccan? A Group Dynamic Explanation of Nuisance and Criminal Behavior," eds. Finn-Aage Esbensen and Cheryl L. Maxson, *Youth Gangs in International Perspective: Results from the Eurogang Program of Research*, 225–236. Copyright © 2012 by Springer. Reprinted by permission.

on a view of Islam as a violent and fascistic religion (*Algemeen Dagblad* 2008). The fact that the Moroccan community occupies a low rung on the social-economic ladder of society is not mentioned very often as an explanatory factor for the group delinquent behavior of the boys, but their cultural heritage is (*Trouw* 2010).

That Moroccan gangs are now the symbol for nuisance and criminal behavior is based not only on stereotypical images in the media and politics but also on practical experiences of victims and bystanders. What surprises victims and bystanders is the extremely bold and aggressive behavior that the Moroccan boys display compared to other groups of young boys that cause nuisance and commit crimes (*NRC Handelsblad* 2009). It is this extreme behavior that calls for an explanation. Why do the boys in these groups behave in this manner? It is the purpose of this chapter to deliver an explanation for this matter, though not a cultural one. A cultural explanation (like the one offered above) would have us believe that the reproduction of typically Moroccan values accounts for the extreme nuisance and criminal behavior. This explanation, however, is lacking an empirical foundation. The anthropologists that hold this opinion only point at similarities between what they perceive to be traditional Moroccan values and the behavior of Moroccan boys in the Netherlands. They do not show properly how and why these values are being reproduced in group behavior. The research described in this chapter, therefore, takes a different approach and looks at the group processes that underlie the extreme delinquent behavior of Moroccan boys in the Netherlands. These processes offer a different explanation than a cultural one, as we shall see.

A second question that is raised in this chapter is whether it is justified to classify the groups of Moroccan boys that are responsible for the nuisance and criminal behavior as gangs. In order to address this question, the Eurogang definition of a youth gang (or troublesome youth group) is used: a durable, street-oriented youth group whose involvement in illegal activity is part of their group identity (Klein et al. 2000; Decker and Weerman 2005). As we shall see, the answer to this question is complex as they are street oriented and their involvement in illegal activity is part of their group identity, but the durability of the group constitutes a problem.

In order to answer these questions, I conducted ethnographic field research from August 1999 until January 2007. First, I recruited boys for interviews by offering them coupons for the movies and McDonalds. Later, after I had earned their trust, I just hung around in the streets with them and even accompanied them on a trip to Morocco. I have gotten to know most boys of the neighborhood, and about 30 of them quite well.[2] I have spent as much time as possible with the boys and have used the Eurogang ethnography protocol as a guideline in my interviews and participant observation (Weerman et al. 2009). In this chapter, I will take one incident, which is typical for the Moroccan gang problem in the Netherlands, from my field notes and analyze it from a group dynamic perspective.

An Incident in Zandvoort

A typical case highlighting the Moroccan gang problem is an incident known as the Zandvoort case. In this case, a troublesome youth group of about 30 Moroccan boys from Amsterdam were responsible for extreme nuisance and criminal behavior in Zandvoort. After spending a day at the beach, they committed acts of vandalism, theft, robbery, and assault (*Het Parool* 2003). The newspaper, *Het Parool*, branded the group a gang and offered an account of the events based on the case brought against one of the boys called Achmed[3]:

> At Zandvoort train station, some boys of the gang had stolen a radio, a football and a mobile phone from assorted youths. Achmed had ripped the mobile phone from the hands of the owner. Others were kicking the football across the platforms, whilst the rest of them took care of the radio. While the victims were reporting the crimes to the police, the gang stepped onto the train. There were four girls in the first class compartment. First Achmed and a tall friend went into that compartment to check things out, but suddenly about thirty others joined them. (*Het Parool* 2003, p. 1)
>
> Some boys climbed the luggage racks, others went to sit on the girls' laps. While screaming "tits, tits," they pinched the girls on their buttocks and

breasts, also groping them in the crotch. At Haarlem station, eight or nine boys chased the girls onto the platform, pinned two of them down against a candy machine and started again with their pawing. Later at the police station, Achmed with his white jersey wrapped around his naked upper body and in his green tracksuit, was identified by the girls as one of the ringleaders. They stated that he had dropped his tracksuit bottoms revealing grey underpants with pink hearts and proceeded to sit on one of the girls' laps. In court Achmed couldn't recall the event. "Maybe they have me confused with one of the other boys," was his reaction to the allegations. (*Het Parool* 2003, p. 3)

In many reactions to the events of that day, the group of Moroccan boys was defined as a gang, and their nuisance and criminal behavior was explained by pointing out that these boys were of Moroccan descent (even though most of them were born and raised in Amsterdam). This raises the question of whether or not the behavior of these Moroccan boys can be explained by the culture of their forbears from the Rif mountains in northern Morocco. Conversely, could the behavior of these young Amsterdam boys be better explained by general group dynamics that take place within the circumstances in which these boys grew up? In other words, is it typically a Moroccan problem or is this a case of marginalization more generally?

Are there unique processes of group formation among Moroccan boys that contribute to the classification of their behavior as extreme delinquent behavior in general and their group as a gang more specifically? Do the same behaviors among other groups result in the same labeling? Is there something fundamentally different within the Moroccan boys' group that contributes to their social ostracism? My specific research questions are: How and why do Moroccan boys form troublesome youth groups in the streets? What is it about their behavior that leads them to be labeled as the extreme nuisance and criminal behavior for which they are notorious? And, is there a reason to label these groups gangs? In this study, an attempt is made to answer these questions by validating a theoretical model based on empirical ethnographic research.

A Theoretical Model of Group Dynamics

In order to explain the nuisance and criminal behavior of a Moroccan group like the one in Zandvoort, a theoretical model combining microsociological and social psychological theories is proposed. This integrated theoretical model helps us to understand group formation, development of group culture, and behavioral adaptations that can explain serious and violent delinquent behavior of Moroccan boys.

Turner (2002) developed a theory explaining that group formation is a useful and even necessary condition for humans to satisfy certain (interactive) needs. The need for recognition and appreciation, for example, is satisfied by friendships and loving relationships. People also seek out each other to meet their needs for safety and security. The desire to satisfy social needs leads people to seek out others and to form new groups or join existing ones. Turner also maintains that, in order to be accepted into a group, a person will adapt his or her behavior to what he or she perceives to be the group's values and norms. In addition to this internal urge to conform to the group norms, the individual will also experience external pressure in the form of peer pressure. Out of fear of rejection or a negative sanction from other group members, a person will act in accordance with the demands placed on him by others (Turner 2002).

Individual expectations of normative behavior for members are created through group processes in which they judge each other's behaviors: They react positively to conformist behavior and negatively to deviant behavior (according to the group norms). Group members do not only adapt their own behavior to the expectations of the group, but they also contribute to determining the group's values and norms. In group processes that are partly influenced by their environment, group members confirm their shared values and norms and contribute to the social identity of the group (Tuckman and Jensen 1977).

According to Turner (1985, 1987, 1999), all people preferably identify themselves with groups that match their interests and values, that are accessible (i.e., in which they are accepted as a member), and that cater to their specific (interactive) needs. According to the self-categorization theory advanced by Turner, the processes by which a person identifies with a group take place on an individual level and on a social level.

At the individual level, identification with a group leads to a sense of group membership and awareness of a social identity. The extent to which a person will identify with a group and adapt his or her behavior to the expectations of other group members depends on three factors: (1) how important group membership is to the individual, (2) the degree of freedom the individual has to claim group identity, and (3) the existence of alternative groups to which the individual can affiliate. The stronger someone identifies with a group, the more his or her self-image will depend on the valuation given by other group members. A person will experience this as peer pressure and will feel forced to adapt to the values and norms of the group.

At the social level, group dynamics arise in which us-them relationships develop between group members and outsiders. This means that group members and outsiders are oppositional. If this is the case, someone will be quick to bond with a group when membership depends on external recognition (e.g., skin color, symbols, or a uniform dress code) and when the group is considered a minority (Vigil 1988, 2002). A person will also quickly and strongly identify with a group when there is a conflict with outsiders (Turner 1987).

The social identity theory posited by Tajfel and Turner (1979, 1986) explains the origins of deviant group values and norms. They also maintain the importance of environmental influences on behavioral adaptations within the group and the importance that group members attach to the social identity of the group. The social identity of a group is derived from shared experiences, meanings, values, and norms of the group. In addition, the social identity also reflects the status of a group compared to rival groups (Tajfel 1978, 1981). A group that performs better or is otherwise regarded as successful will provide not only more satisfaction of collective needs but also a higher status and a positive social identity.

Members of groups with low status and a negative social identity—such as Moroccan boys in the Netherlands—face negative consequences for members' self-image. Insofar as individual self-image is dependent on the group and its social identity, the individual will be negatively influenced by the negative reactions of the group. The collective need to defend themselves from external attacks on the group's status and identity forces members to align themselves with the values and norms of the group.

A theoretical model in which the discussed theories are combined should explain how and why Moroccan boys form troublesome youth groups, adapt their behavior within the group, and collectively react when the self-image of their group is under attack. I will test this hypothesis by analyzing the aforementioned incident in the summer of 2001 in Zandvoort.

The Zandvoort case is a striking example of the kind of nuisance and criminal behavior that the media portrays as typically Moroccan and therefore self-evidently is explained by their Moroccan descent. The media spoke of a Moroccan youth gang from Amsterdam, even though the police were not familiar with this gang. In the eyes of the police, it was not clear what brought these boys, who came from different neighborhoods in Amsterdam-West, to form a gang in Zandvoort and unite to commit such a large number of serious crimes.[4]

Later, I will discuss whether or not this troublesome youth group should be called a gang. In what follows, I will reconstruct what happened that day and make clear how the boys themselves experienced the day's events. This will be done using insights obtained during years of fieldwork in Amsterdam-West. Based on my field research, I shall show how such extreme delinquent behavior of Moroccan boys as took place in Zandvoort can be explained by the theoretical model. First, I shall recount the events of that day at the beach and the group interpretations of the events of that day.

Back to Zandvoort

On that particular day in May 2001, warm weather lured sun lovers from all parts of the country to Zandvoort. Among them, a number of Moroccan boys from Amsterdam went to the beach in search of fun. When the boys meet, they give each other a "box" by way of greeting and have a chat in their street language, as they are accustomed.[5] Some guys are real "matties" (friends), but most know each other only superficially through family, friends, and acquaintances, or through school, work, sports, or entertainment. They hang together on the street or "chill" together in the center of town. Usually, they go with guys from their own neighborhood, but on these occasions, they simply join up with Moroccan boys from other neighborhoods also looking for fun.

In the beginning of the day, the boys conduct themselves the way they would on the streets of Amsterdam: they reproduce a street culture with its own values and standards. They tell each other tough "tories" (stories) about "fitties" (fights) and "sick actions" (exciting adventures), talk about "dope pokoes" (nice rap songs) and "vette kinos" (great movies), and boast about "chickies" (girls) and driving (too fast) in "dikke waggies" (expensive cars). They also "diss" (belittle) each other and give each other "props" (appreciation) for hairstyles, (brand) clothes, "pattas" (shoes), and "pockets" (mobile phones).

Some of the boys "tappen" (drink alcohol), others smoke "jonkos" (joints) with "wirie" or "assi" (marijuana or hashish). The boys with sufficient "doekoe" (money) share their "tabacca" (cigarettes), alcohol, and drugs with the boys who are "skeer" (broke). They do not want to be called a "Jew" (stingy) or let bystanders think they hang around with "zwervers" (losers). What they do not want to share with others, they make sure to hide from the rest in order to prevent that they will be "genakt" (robbed) or "geflasht" (cheated) by one of their "gabbers" (friends and acquaintances).

The boys try to outdo each other with "wise-cracking" remarks, cursing each other, threatening each other, and pushing and fighting for the "fatoe" (as a joke). But when a fight threatens to turn into something serious, often one of the older boys calms the situation down. Their way of "gek doen" (acting crazy) also means provoking and challenging passersby. Boys that "schijt hebben" (do not give a shit) and "flikken" (dare to do) something are loudly applauded and are told they are "moe-ilijk" (tough). Sometimes one of the older boys gets a headache from this kind of behavior, and he stops

it by shouting or threatening (or, if it becomes too much, he takes a step away from the group). In other cases, the tough street behavior the boys use to impress each other can suddenly get seriously out of hand.

Some guys try "lullen" (picking up girls) with an intimidating macho attitude: "Hey there, baby. Come here! Come listen to me!" When one of these "players" fails in his attempts, the rest of the group will call him a "zwerver" (loser). The failure is recouped by calling the girl a "whore" or something along those lines and by shouting that he was not interested in those "kaolo tangas" (bitches) anyway because they are arrogant or ugly. The other guys interpret this as gaining stripes for being disrespectful toward women, and they dare each other to grab sunbathing girls' bare breasts. Eventually, one of the boys shows that he really is completely "loco" (crazy). He jumps on a woman's lap and pulls his pants down to show her his "bana" (penis), while the rest of the group jeers.

However, not all the guys are involved in this kind of behavior. Some find what the others do kind of "faya" (annoying). Such a doubter had better keep his mouth shut because if he publicly criticizes something one member of the group does, the streets will soon hear stories that will make him a "bitch," a "zemmel" (gay), or a "shekem" (traitor). Then he will be laughed at, scolded, or maybe even get hit. Nor can he allow his "bradas" (brothers) to be left in the lurch when they get into "problemen" (real trouble). For his own safety, he must be able to count on the fact that they will be there for him as well when trouble finds him.

As the events of the day unfold, the boys eventually notice that their group is increasingly attracting attention by the way they are "chilling" and "spacing" (lounging). They see the people around them looking annoyed, and some of bystanders appear scared or intimidated. The boys, however, feel that they have every right to be at the beach, and they convince each other that they are really not doing anything wrong. They find those "cheese-heads" (Dutch people) are "dooie" (boring) losers, and they complain to each other about the dirty looks they are getting. In their eyes, these Dutch people are all "homos" (cowards), "Nazis" (racists), and "Jews" (anti-Muslims) who hate Moroccans because they have black hair. And when one of these "tattas" (Dutch people) dares to say something to them, it is never "normal" (friendly) but always patronizing and without respect. If bystanders cause problems, the boys back each other up without asking who is responsible or at fault. They think the "cheese-heads" with their racist attitude deserve to be bothered or hit.

Yet the way they are treated does not sit well with the boys. They become "para" (agitated) by the idea they are thought of as criminals and will not allow anyone to make remarks about their behavior. On the other hand, they find it "moeilijk" (cool or tough) that adult people fear their "clique" (gang). It gives them a sense of power to intimidate others. To a certain extent, they enjoy it when others see them as "thugs" (street boys), who—when it comes to a fight—always display courage and do not hesitate to "bossen" (hit) or "punteren" (kick).

Nuisance and Criminal Behavior Explained by Group Dynamics

The description of the events in Zandvoort from the perspective of the Moroccan street boys illustrates several group processes. The boys get together to have fun, to gain recognition within the group, and to feel protected. They develop a specific street culture with its own values and norms (Fleisher 1995). The boys adapt their behavior to these values and norms not only because they want to satisfy their needs. They also try to live up to the expectations of the group because of peer pressure, in other words, out of fear of negative reactions from other group members.

These group processes are general to all problematic youth groups and can explain how and why Moroccan street boys form groups, how and why they adapt their behavior to the group, and how and why delinquent behavior can arise. In the case of the Moroccan boys in Zandvoort, however, there was delinquent behavior that escalated, and the nuisance and criminal behavior is characterized as extremely challenging and aggressive. In the following sections, I argue that the strengthening of group identity, the increasing peer pressure, and an intensification of us-them contrasts explain how and why the delinquent behavior of Moroccan boys can get so out of hand.

The Strengthening of Group Identity

Moroccan boys in the Netherlands realize that many people see them as a minority and as an inferior group (they are referred to as "kut-Marokkanen," which means something like awful Moroccans). The feeling of rejection by the Dutch strengthens their identification with other Moroccan boys. This identification is intensified further by their external recognition based on innate ethnic characteristics. Negative characteristics stemming from their Moroccan culture, such as aggressiveness and a lack of consciousness and responsibility, are ascribed to them. The boys experience such negative and stigmatizing reactions as threatening because it compromises their self-esteem (Vigil 2002).

In order to neutralize this threat, they embrace the negative stigma as a positive group identity and behave accordingly. This is why negative reactions from the public serve to strengthen the group identity, which is expressed by showing behavior that bystanders perceive as disruptive and threatening. The boys themselves appreciate this challenging and aggressive behavior as "kapot moeilijk" (very tough) and regard it as appropriate under the circumstances.

Increasing Peer Pressure

Because they identify so strongly with each other, Moroccan boys feel they have little choice but to pull together if they want to enjoy themselves; this is why they align themselves so easily and naturally with other Moroccan boys, even those they barely know. This creates large, loose group affiliations with constantly changing compositions. There is often confusion regarding what expectations exist with respect to each other's behavior in such groups. Because of the strong sense of interdependence and the uncertainty about the group norms, boys sometimes get entangled in the assumptions about what behavior other group members expect. In the uncertainty, they resort to the street culture they know and in which several forms of delinquent behavior are appreciated. Under these circumstances, this can give rise to (delinquent) behavior that no one requested nor expected from another group member.

The feeling that they can only count on other Moroccan boys increases the pressure to display desired behavior and to be accepted and valued by the group. Increasing peer pressure and confusion about shared group norms lead then—partly unintended and unforeseen—to delinquent behavior. If boys seek acceptance within the group by creating nuisance and displaying criminal behavior, other group members in turn see this as an incentive to display similar behavior (or even outdo the others). In this manner, conflicts can escalate so that afterward, the boys involved cannot explain how things got so out of hand.[6]

Intensification of Us-Them Contrasts

In such conflict situations, the strengthening of group identity and increasing peer pressure lead to an intensification of us-them contrasts between gangs of Moroccan boys and (random) outsiders. Conversely, the intensification of us-them attitudes leads to the strengthening of group identity and increasing peer pressure to engage in delinquent behaviors. Boys who know little of each other will quickly rally for each other, even when they know full well that their friends are the instigators of the conflict. The more they can rely on positive feedback from their peers, the more the boys will be motivated to choose sides in any (alleged) conflict with outsiders.

External recognition (not only because of ethnic characteristics but also because of clothing and hairstyles), frequently hanging around each other in close proximity, a sense of belonging to a minority, and their awareness of the fact that Moroccan youth are in conflict with Dutch society lead to an intensification of us-them contrasts. The Moroccan boys confirm each other in seeing outsiders as the enemy or as racists, and they experience strong feelings of mutual loyalty. In conflicts with outsiders, this means that, as a group, they have a more challenging attitude, they fiercely back up each other, and they respond aggressively to outsiders.

A Typically Moroccan Problem?

The nuisance and criminal behavior of Moroccan youth groups in general and that of the Moroccan boys during the incident at Zandvoort in particular can be understood and explained by group processes. Nevertheless, the behavior of Moroccan boys in the media and political debate is labeled as typically Moroccan. The behavior of the group of Moroccan boys in the Zandvoort incident was attributed to their alleged Moroccan descent. This view is supported by cultural anthropologists who explain the behavior of Moroccan boys by identifying cultural characteristics of their forbearers: in particular distrust, shame, family honor, and an appreciation of a warrior mentality (van Gemert 1998; Werdmölder 1986, 1990, 2005). Apart from the question of whether these cultural characteristics are indeed representative of the Moroccan culture, questions can be raised as to the extent to which these cultural characteristics have been transferred to the Moroccan boys who grew up in the Netherlands. It is assumed that cultural factors determine their behavior in the streets, but this has not been proven empirically.

My group dynamic model, on the other hand, does provide insight into the ways in which the group culture of Moroccan boys evolves and is reproduced in their interactions with each other in the streets. My field research has granted me the opportunity to conduct a detailed analysis of the group dynamics in which their street culture evolves. The Zandvoort incident provides an illustration of three aspects of Moroccan youth groups which were evident in my field research. First, these boys form groups for their interactive needs for recognition, security, and enjoyment. Second, they develop a street culture in which delinquent behavior is positively valued. Third, they adapt their behavior to the group in order to receive positive responses from other group members and especially to avoid negative reactions. Strengthening group identity, increasing peer pressure, and intensification of us-them contrasts lead to nuisance and criminal behavior that shocks bystanders and leaves victims stunned. Taking into account these circumstances that intensify general processes of group formation and behavioral adaptation can explain why the group of Moroccan boys in Zandvoort backed each other up so fiercely and responded to bystanders so aggressively.

The theoretical model of group dynamic processes and behavioral adaptation clarifies how and why certain behavioral expectations of Moroccan boys emerge, how and why they adapt their individual behavior to the street culture of their group, and how and why general group dynamics intensify to such a degree that unusual nuisance and criminal behavior may result.

A Gang Problem?

This brings us to the final question that will be addressed in this chapter: Can a problematic youth group of Moroccan boys like the one in Zandvoort that engages in such extreme delinquent behavior be considered a gang? The media and politicians seem to think so, but if we take a close look at the group and use the Eurogang definition of a gang, the answer is not so clear. The group is street-oriented, and its involvement in illegal activity is part of the group identity, but the group is not durable. The group consisted of boys from different neighborhoods in Amsterdam-West, and this particular constellation collaborated only for a day. Therefore, we cannot say that this group is a gang according to the Eurogang definition.

The networks of street boys out of which these kinds of groups emerge, however, are a different story. These networks are durable. During my years in the field, I have identified over 100 Moroccan street boys that make up the network of the neighborhood Overtoomse Veld in Amsterdam-West. Everybody in the network knows each other at least a little bit. The Moroccan boys can identify who is a "boy from Allebé" (named after the central square in Overtoomse Veld) and who is not. The network of "boys from Allebé" gives rise to all kinds of different groups. There are groups that form for leisure activities such as hanging around the neighborhood swapping stories or playing soccer. Other groups form because the group members seek activities outside the neighborhood, like going to the movies or going clubbing. And there are the delinquent groups which are divided into work groups and riot groups.

A work group emerges from the network when a couple of neighborhood street boys decide they want to commit crimes in order to make some money (working is their slang word for committing instrumental crimes). Mostly, these groups are not very big (three to six boys), and they are not durable. Some only exist for one particular criminal

event. The reason for this lack of durability is that a lot of times the boys will have a falling out over the division of labor or the loot. Also, the network provides enough other boys with whom they can go out to work.

A riot group emerges from the network when there is something exciting to do. The boys will anticipate the fact that it is going to "kick off" somewhere, and they will want to be there for the action. The sheer anticipation of the fact that something is going down makes a lot of boys interested in joining a riot group. Riot groups are usually quite big (30 boys up to 100). The events that attract riot groups are demonstrations (e.g., against the war in Iraq), but also a simple event like a day at the beach. The group in the Zandvoort case can be considered a riot group.

Now that we know that different and dynamic delinquent groups emerge from a durable network, this sheds a new light on the Eurogang definition of a gang. The network as a whole could almost be considered a gang of over 100 boys because it is durable and the boys' involvement in illegal activity is part of their network identity. I say almost, because the particular groups that emerge from the durable network are not durable themselves but change all the time. Therefore, I think we should conclude that Amsterdam does not have a gang problem following the Eurogang definition. But how we should define such a durable network of potential gang-like groups is still open for debate and demands more research.

Notes

1. The Amsterdam boys included in this research have Moroccan parents, but are born and raised in the Netherlands, and in most cases have a hybrid identity. To emphasize this, I put the adjective "Moroccan" in quotation marks.
2. For a detailed description of my methods and findings, I refer to my dissertation (de Jong 2007).
3. The name Achmed is a pseudonym.
4. The crimes are considered serious crimes because of the amount of aggression (i.e., the boys threaten bystanders with violence or even death), the extent of the sexual harassment, and the property damage.
5. The correct spelling of slang words is borrowed from the slang dictionary on the Internet. On this site, young

people themselves decide how their spoken language can best be written. It is therefore possible that slang words that stem from the Surinamese or Moroccan language are spelled differently than in the original language.

6. The behavior in Zandvoort was extreme even from the boys' perspectives, as they have indicated in interviews.

References

Algemeen Daghlad (2008, March 28th) Retrieved from http://www.ad.nl/

de Jong JD (2007) Kapot moeilijk. Een etnografisch onderzoek naar opvallend delinquent groepsgedrag van "Marokkaanse" jongens. Aksant, Amsterdam

Decker SH, Weerman FM (eds) (2005) European street gangs and troublesome youth groups. AltaMira, Oxford

Fleisher MS (1995) Beggars and thieves: lives of urban street criminals. University of Wisconsin Press, Wisconsin

NRC Handelsblad (2006, February 16th) Retrieved from http://www.nrc.nl/

NRC Handelsblad (2008, October 11th) Retrieved from http://www.nrc.nl/

NRC Handelsblad (2009, May 23rd) Retrieved from http://www.nrc.nl/

Het Parool (2003, September 20th) Retrieved from http://www.parool.nl/

Klein MW, Kerner H-J, Maxson CL, Weitekamp EG (eds) (2000) The Eurogang paradox: street gangs and youth groups in the U.S. and Europe. Springer, New York

Tajfel H (1978) Differentiation between social groups: studies in social psychology of intergroup relations. Academic, London

Tajfel H (1981) Social stereotypes and social groups. In: Turner JC, Giles H (eds) Intergroup behaviour. Blackwell, Oxford, pp 144–167

Tajfel H, Turner JC (1979) A integrative theory of social conflict. In: Austin WG, Worchel S (eds) Psychology of intergroup relations. Brooks/Cole. Monterey, pp 33–47

Tajfel H, Turner JC (1986) The social identity theory of intergroup behavior. In: Worchel S, Austin WG (eds)

Psychology of intergroup relations. Nelson-Hall, Chicago, pp 7–24

Trouw (2010, November 27th) Retrieved from http://www.trouw.nl/

Tuckman BW, Jensen MAC (1977) Stages of small group development revisited. *Group Organ Stud* 2:419–427

Turner JC (1985) Social categorization and the self-concept. A social-cognitive theory of group behavior. In: Lawler FJ (ed) Advances in group processes, vol 2. JAI Press. Greenwich, pp 77–122

Turner JC (1987) Rediscovering the social group: a self-categorization theory. Blackwell, New York

Turner JC (1999) Some current issues in research on social identity and self categorization theories. In: Ellemers N, Spears R, Doosje BJ (eds) Social identity. Blackwell, Oxford, pp 6–34

Turner JH (2002) Face to face: toward a sociological theory of interpersonal behavior. Stanford University Press, Stanford

van Gemert F (1998) Ieder voor zich. Kansen, cultuur en criminaliteit van Marokkaunse jongens. Het Spinhuis, Amsterdam

Vigil JD (1988) Barrio gangs. Street life and identity in Southern California. University of Texas Press, Austin

Vigil JD (2002) A rainbow of gangs. Street cultures in the mega-city. University of Texas Press, Austin

Weerman FM, Maxson CL, Esbensen F, Aldridge J, Medina J, van Gemert F (2009) Eurogang program manual background, development, and use of the Eurogang instruments in multi-site, multi-method comparative research. Retrieved from the Eurogang Network website: http:// www.umsl.edu/~ccj/euro gang/Eurogang_20Manual.pdf

Werdmölder H (1986) Van vriendenkring tot randgroep Marokkaanse jongens in een oude stadswijk. Het Wereldvenster, Houten

Werdmölder H (1990) Een generatie op drift. De geschiedenis van een Marokkaanse randgroep. Gouda Quint, Arnhem

Werdmölder H (2005) Marokkaanse lieverdjes. Crimineel en hinderlijk gedrag onder Marokkaanse jongens. Balans, Amsterdam

Legitimated Oppression: Inner-City Mexican American Experiences with Police Gang Enforcement

Robert J. Durán

As will be discussed in Section VIII, gang intervention models in the last decades have disproportionately drawn from suppression strategies. Some of these—like Operation Ceasefire in Boston—are designed to work in tandem with prevention and intervention efforts, and intentionally target those gang youth who are involved in the most serious and chronic offending. Others tend to eschew the social situations of gang members and can lead to concentrated law enforcement efforts that employ racial profiling, harassment, selective enforcement, and even wholesale police sweeps of minority communities that are identified as having a large number of gangs or gang youth. Durán's chapter presents an insider's view of gang and other community members' experiences of this latter model of gang suppression. His ethnographic research was facilitated by his own history as a former gang member. Durán's chapter is notable as well for its thorough description of his field research procedures and its comparison across cities. The findings presented here also contribute to scholarly work on the import of procedural justice, particularly in racial and ethnic minority communities.

Nationwide law enforcement agencies have launched an aggressive offensive against gangs. Newspapers and nightly newscasts regularly depict shootings and murders that are labeled gang-related. Police officers regularly report through the media that gangs are growing in number and increasing in violence. A large number of cities since the mid-1980s have created specialized gang units to support a "war on gangs." As a society we are bombarded with a "law and order" view of gangs and their communities. Police officers routinely recognize how such a war on gangs is hindered by traditional constitutional protections, but have developed support to create methods and tactics to sidestep disapproval; in essence they have become legitimated.

For half a century, the relationship between gang members and the police received little scholarly attention (Huff and McBride 1993; Needle and Stapleton 1983; Werthman and Piliavin 1967). Since the 1980s, more than 360 gang units began operating nationwide to respond to the perceived and actual threat caused by gangs (Katz 2001). Several researchers began exploring the impact of this targeted enforcement (Katz 2003; Klein 2004). Katz and Webb (2006) have conducted the largest study on gang units in four cities (Albuquerque, Inglewood, Las Vegas, and Phoenix). These research studies on gang units share a similar theme of obtaining data by accompanying and interviewing gang unit officers.

This article presents results from a systematic, ethnographic study of Mexican American gang life in Ogden, Utah, and Denver, Colorado. The analysis in this article benefits from the researcher's experience in gangs and law enforcement to make sense of the data. I report and analyze two important facets of "legitimated oppression": (1) legitimated profiling, and (2) interacting with suspected gang members. The questionable tactics used by police officers against gangs has created further divisions between law enforcement and the Mexican American community.

Policing Gangs

The majority of gang members across the United States have been racially and ethnically labeled by police officers as Latino (47 percent) or African American (31 percent), and they have been mostly poor (85 percent) (Egley 2002). Self-reported data indicate that whites identify as gang members at a higher rate than is captured by police data (Esbensen and Osgood 1997; Esbensen and Winfree 1998). Many states legally define gangs as three or more people engaged in criminal activity either collectively or individually. This neutral definition has resulted in an application of the label to people who are considered nonwhite. Acknowledging the racial and ethnic focus is important because policing strategies have created serious social consequences for individuals involved or associated with gangs (Katz 2003; Klein 2004). Through a survey of 261 police departments, Klein (1995) found that intelligence gathering, crime investigation, and suppression were the most common police actions against gangs, and that many states had instituted increased consequences for gang-related crimes. Spergel (1995) agreed that a vigorous "lock-em-up" approach remained the key action of police departments, particularly in large cities with acknowledged gang problems.

Werthman and Piliavin's (1967, 57) early work suggested that underlying troubles between gang members and the police involved problems of law. These two groups occupy separate cultural and structural conditions, and thus they respond to and perceive each other differently. The "ecological contamination" from perceived gang neighborhoods could infect many suspicious persons who lived there and subject these residents to police officers' discretion and to their power to investigate. Terrill and Resig (2003) found support for Werthman and Piliavin's ecological contamination hypothesis in which officers were more likely to use high levels of force when encountering criminal suspects in high crime neighborhoods.

Supplementing ecological contamination, a growing number of research data indicate police resources and behavior have been influenced by the growing proportion of minorities in the city (Blalock 1967; Holmes 2000; Jacobs and O'Brien 1998; Jackson 1989; Liska, Lawrence, and Benson 1981; Liska 1992; Smith and Holmes 2003). This has been conceptualized as the "minority group threat hypothesis," which is based on majority group fears of losing dominance to a culturally dissimilar group. Liska (1992, 18) reports "the greater number of acts or people threatening to the interests of the powerful, the greater the level of deviance and crime control."

Police have supported gang enforcement tactics by adopting a perspective that gang members are unsympathetic, out of control, and in "need" of suppression tactics (Briggs and Gavin 1988; Haws 1999; Kirksey 1983; Klein 2004). These tactics are then promoted by research which has found gang members more violent (and criminal) than non-gang members (Battin et al. 1998; Bjerregaard and Smith 1993; Curry, Ball, and Decker 1996; Esbensen and Huizinga 1993; Miller 1992; Thornberry 1998). However, there is little empirical support for the "best" method for responding to gangs (Fritsch, Caeti, and Taylor 1999). Several researchers have concluded that many communities in southwestern states (Arizona, California, Nevada, and Texas) have been experiencing a "moral panic" about gangs (Jackson and Rudman 1993; McCorkle and Miethe 2002; Tovares 2002; Zatz 1987). In these circumstances the local police have responded to gangs in the same manner as large cities with hyper-aggressive enforcement. Cohen (1980) identified the term *moral panic* to denote a disjuncture between a perceived and an actual threat that becomes exaggerated. The groups or people that become targeted for being a threat are those with little social power.

This study began with the research question "How are the lives of people, who the police believe are involved in criminal groups, affected by law enforcement strategies to suppress gangs?" I chose two cities (Denver, Colorado, and Ogden, Utah) that are considered by community residents, media, and police departments to have a gang problem.

My work specifically focuses on people of Mexican descent who were born in the United States (i.e., the largest percentage of Latinos in the United States). Police departments in both cities consider this ethnic group to have the largest number of gangs and gang members. I begin by discussing the methods I used in gathering these data and the settings where I did the research. I describe the wide array of factors police gang units use in profiling and initially stopping a myriad of community members. I then provide a portrayal of how the police interact with suspected gang members. Finally, I offer a conclusion that expands on ecological contamination, moral panic, and minority group threat. This research is unique in its use of lived experience and inside access to a significant number of people who have remained hidden from traditional gang and police research.

Methods and Settings

The research reported in this article is part of a larger study of Mexican American gang life in two barrio communities (Denver and Ogden) conducted for five years (2001–2006) and, informally, throughout fourteen years of my life (1992–2006). I used ethnographic research methods such as direct observation, casual interaction, semi-structured interviews, introspection, photography, and video-taping to collect these data.

My goal with this research method was to capture the gang social world in these two cities with thick description (Geertz 1973) while maintaining longitudinal insight to move past the multiple fronts (Douglas 1976) presented by gang members, media, and the police. A significant part of conducting ethnographic research includes the biography and background of the researcher because he or she is the research tool (Adler and Adler 1987; Lofland and Lofland 1995). I was a gang member growing up in Ogden, Utah, and I later used my ex-gang member status to keep myself located inside this social world to begin gathering data. I benefited from my work experience and networks in child and family services, law enforcement, and youth corrections. As an individual gang member, it was impossible to understand gangs without a method that could

allow me to gather data and talk with the people directly involved in this lifestyle.

To gather research data on gangs in Denver, where I was never a gang member, I became involved with a variety of groups focused on gang prevention, high school reform, police observation, and community empowerment. I used my advantage for having special expertise on gangs to begin "opportunistic research" in a new setting (Reimer 1977). In particular, a significant part of my research in Denver was from a group called Area Support for All People (ASAP). (All names and groups in this article are pseudonyms.) Current and ex-gang members helped to start this group in 1991 with the goal of decreasing the escalating violence (ASAP pamphlet, field notes, and interviews). A group of five to fifteen gang members and adult mentors met once a week for three hours. The group included a variety of youth from around the city between the ages of thirteen to eighteen. I attended this group regularly for two and a half years (December of 2000 to September of 2003).

In the fall of 2001, I began conducting semi-structured interviews to capture members' and associates' perspectives on gang culture. I tape-recorded and transcribed thirty-two gang member/associate interviews. I paid these respondents $25 each for their time. I maintained ten "key partners" (six in Denver and four in Ogden) and interviewed them multiple times. Because of the pejorative connotations of informants, I found this term better reflected my working collaboration with people who knew gangs from actual experience. Overall, I engaged in non-taped interviews with ninety additional gang-involved members and associates regarding gangs in both cities (122 total number of taped and non-taped interviews). These interviews allowed me to maintain my informal insider role without distancing myself with a more formal outsider research posture. All interviews were conducted in English with some minor use of Spanish. Most of my respondents had been in the United States for two to six generations and thus spoke English as their first language. The interviews lasted between one and two hours. All respondents associated with Mexican American or Mexican gangs.

In both cities there were more associates in the gang scene, with only a small percentage who had actually been jumped in or recognized as members by the gangs. For these reasons, I made little use of snowball sampling (Biernacki and Waldorf 1981) and instead followed what I call "judgment sampling." I used my extensive knowledge of people in the communities acquired through my participant observation (Bernard 1988; Pelto and Pertti 1979), my inside knowledge of gangs, and the aid of my ten key partners to individually select each person for an interview.

During my research, I interviewed seven gang officers in both states. Six of these interviews were conducted inside police facilities and one was conducted over the telephone. I regularly requested the police departments' official statistics relating to gangs and the gang unit. I have also worked a year-and-a-half in two youth correction facilities both prior to graduate studies and during the completion of this research, and one year in law enforcement in the state of Utah before my doctoral work where I was allowed to attend law-enforcement-only sessions that outlined police gang tactics and intelligence gathering. To remain objective about how police interact with possible gang members, I chose to work with an ongoing group of residents who, when seeing a police stop, walked over and recorded the interactions with camcorders. We worked in teams of two or more people. I call this group People Observing the Police (POP). This group regularly met in Denver since 2000 and in Ogden during the summer of 2005. After the stop had ended, if possible, we talked with police officers and the person(s) of interest.

I observed over two hundred police stops, forty-seven of which included gang units, in all areas of these two cities for three years. Most of my time involved patrolling nightlife areas such as cruising boulevards and minority communities. The use of police scanners helped me travel to the segregated white communities when an infrequent stop was made. Observation of stops along cruising boulevards allowed me to witness a wide variety of racial and ethnic group encounters with the police. Overwhelmingly, these areas were adjacent to communities of color, which aided my ability to patrol both areas. All of the observed gang stops included

Latinos, followed by African Americans and Asians. I used this information to compare and contrast Mexican American gang members' and associates' claims with police officers and the media. I also had official local police documents relating to the purpose and policies of gang enforcement.

According to the U.S. Census (1940 to 2000) Denver, Colorado, and Ogden, Utah, are both cities with a growing Latino and decreasing non-Hispanic white population. Both cities have historical neighborhoods that have been primarily Latino (50 percent or more) and located near industrial places of employment and segregated from certain areas of the city and are thus known as barrios (Camarillo 1979; Garcia 1981; Romo 1983). The numbers of individuals below poverty and median household incomes are similar. These two cities are in geographical areas that were once part of Mexico before westward expansion (Acuña 2000), and the majority of Latinos living in these areas are born in the United States (U.S. Census 2000).

Systematic Suppression

According to gang unit officers, suppression tactics using intelligence gathering, and zero-tolerance policing (hereafter defined as gang enforcement) remained at the heart of both the Denver and Ogden gang units. The premise behind such police tactics is rooted in the *broken windows* theory, which focused enforcement efforts on minor offenses to prevent social and physical disorder and thus reduce the level of overall crime (Wilson and Kelling 1982). Gang officers used a variety of indicators to initiate a stop and develop intelligence through interaction. Hagan and Albonetti (1982) found that people's residence in a central city increased their perception of criminal injustice. In Denver and Ogden, barrio community members felt unfairly profiled and treated negatively based on police perceptions of gang membership, whether actual or perceived. Mexican American community claims of harassment by themselves were often met with disbelief by middle-class white residents in the city along with authority figures. Police officers continually justified these beliefs by pushing for a higher number of interactions with Mexican Americans to substantiate gang stereotypes.

Legitimated Profiling

In both Denver and Ogden, police officers were primarily deployed in high-crime districts (Sherman, Gartin, and Buerger 1989). These were more often neighborhoods with a higher concentration of Latinos and blacks (50 to 90 percent) and economic poverty (20 to 70 percent) (U.S. Census). The police departments' diversity paled in comparison with these neighborhoods. Approximately 20 percent of Denver police officers were Latino and 5 percent of Ogden police officers. Since most street crime did not occur in plain sight, police officers had to determine which people were engaging in criminal activity.

Police officers focused on making stops based on the legal justification of reasonable suspicion and probable cause. Probable cause includes a belief, based on objective facts, that supports the suspicion that a person was committing or about to commit a crime (Hall 1996). A lead prosecutor in northern Utah described reasonable suspicion as "facts and circumstances that would lead a reasonable officer to believe that there is a particular problem or indication of criminal activity" (2003 interview). Together, reasonable suspicion and probable cause legitimated a wide ranging assortment of stops.

However, this led to a confrontational relationship between police and many residents in Denver and Ogden's barrios because residents believed that police officers were using gang and criminal stereotypes to predicate stops. A little higher than 95 percent (thirty-one out of thirty-two) of the individuals formally interviewed reported that they had been stopped for a variety of reasons that were not criminally predicated; in other words, they were profiled. Mexican American youth reported that common reasons the police gave for the stop included, "It looked like I was wearing gang clothing (i.e., sports team and hip-hop clothing); I was assumed to be out too late; People matched my description; There were reports of shots fired; We had more than three people in the car; or We looked suspicious." Other reasons community members were stopped included minor traffic violations that could only be detected with strict scrutiny. If there were no traffic violations, police officers had the option of using vehicle safety ordinances such as being without a front license plate, violating noise ordinances, having over-tinted windows (Utah), hanging rosaries or objects from the rearview mirror (Colorado), standing or driving around in a known gang area, or driving a customized (i.e., lowrider) vehicle. In sum, police officers had a full range of reasons to initiate and later justify a "criminal" stop when speaking with barrio residents.

The wide array of justifications created confusion on the part of Mexican Americans to keep from getting harassed. D-loc, a mid-twenties articulate ex-gang member from Denver, described a meeting between community members and police officers. He attempted to learn more about the legal term of reasonable suspicion:

> We were really trying to have some meaningful conversation with 'em and say. Why you pull us over, because there are four of us in a car? [Police response is] agh, reasonable suspicion. What if we're just walking down a street? Agh, reasonable suspicion. Well how come you stop our little brothers and sisters on the street, they ain't doing nothing. Agh, reasonable suspicion. It could be anything. We started getting upset because every answer they gave us was reasonable suspicion. So I said, What's reasonable suspicion? They said, There could have been a crime in your community and the description they gave might fit the description of someone walking down the street. There was a robbery that happened in a house and the suspect was described as a possible Hispanic male between 5'6 and 5'9. Ugh, between 120 lbs and 170 lbs. Shit, that's almost every male in my community between those ages and that description. That's half of the population in my neighborhood. So that gives you any reason to stop any one of us and be a bunch of assholes to anybody walking down the street because you feel like it?

POP observations supported Mexican American claims of harassment. During their five years of watching the police in Denver, Randolph and Pam, two middle-aged white police observers, reported the countless times they witnessed gang unit officers searching suspected gang member vehicles for drugs and weapons. Pam reported that officers would stop young men for unclear reasons and take them all out of the vehicle. Randolph said the officers would then ID everyone in the car, check them for outstanding warrants, search their pockets, and then send them on their way. He explained:

So when that happens over and over again, and it's the same general age group, ethnic group, gender group that it happens to time and time again, and no one is arrested. Like detention and searches are supposed to be based on a reasonable suspicion that a crime has been or is about to be committed, so what is the crime here? It seems that being a Chicano youth for the Denver Gang Unit is reasonable suspicion of criminal activity.

Traffic violations were highly discretionary and also very difficult to prove or disprove. Several researchers have attempted to determine the role and significance of this practice as racial profiling and how this practice is used to further an investigation into the identity of occupants and search for possible contraband (Bass 2001; Browning et al. 1994; Cole 1999; Fagan and Davies 2000; Meehan and Ponder 2002). In November of 2000, Denver initiated a task force to assess racial profiling in the city by requiring officers to fill out contact cards. The study found that each racial and ethnic group was stopped similar to their numbers in the city population, but that Latinos were searched at two to three times the rate of whites (Thomas and Hansen 2004). Based on POP observations, the city of Ogden overwhelmingly used racial profiling more than Denver. Chicle, a twenty-six-year-old ex-gang associate from Ogden, said:

They would make up reasons for maybe going too fast or going too slow, or maybe you were swerving. I've been pulled over fifteen to twenty times and I haven't gotten a ticket.

Although happy to not receive a ticket, Chicle believed a legitimate stop by the police entailed a consequence whereas a fictitious reason included being released. Cola, a twenty-seven-year-old ex-gang member from Ogden, recalled:

They stopped me for everything. They even stopped me a couple times to tell me they liked my car. I'm not sure what that had to do with anything. At the time I thought it was nothing but now that I think back, I realize they would take down all of our names. We were just glad that we weren't in trouble for anything.

The observed and described police discretion produced an elusive standard for establishing reasonable suspicion and probable cause because it was highly influenced by extra legal factors (i.e., age,

class, gender, neighborhood, and race). Anderson (1990) found that police officers become "willing parties" to "color-coding" that entailed making race, age, class, and gender presuppositions as to who commits crime and who will be perceived as dangerous. While researching as a member of POP, I found gang unit stops were particularly influenced by age, gender, race, and local gang stereotypes in 100 percent of the observed police stops (forty-seven out of forty-seven). The rationale for many of these stops and subsequent detention appeared far-reaching. Compliance with picture taking and information resulted in release of custody. The rationale of gang officers would leave researchers believing that most people stopped were gang members. However, gang members in both cities were a small percentage of barrio youth. Vigil (2002) found in Los Angeles that only 4 to 14 percent of barrio youth joined gangs. Klein (1968) estimated that only 6 percent of ten to seventeen-year-old Los Angeles youth were affiliated with gangs. According to my data accumulation over five years, there were definitely a greater number of associates than actual members of the gang, probably a 20 to 80 ratio.

Barrio youth faced greater difficulty entering different parts of the city because law enforcement often associated this behavior with causing problems with rival gangs. Randolph, a middle-aged member of People Observing Police from Denver, described a situation in which a car was stopped:

And the officer will say, I recognized the people in the back seat of that car as being from east Denver and I wanted to know why they were in west Denver. Now that's not a reasonable suspicion of a crime. People in the United States are supposed to have freedom of movement. Obviously the reason they were there was because they were cruising during Cinco de Mayo. It's a famous event for a lot of youth and so they will go cruise Federal [Boulevard] because it's a big thing. So it's a ridiculous reason to say someone is from another jurisdiction and that's why I stopped them.

According to the Gallup Poll as cited in the *Sourcebook of Criminal Justice Statistics*, Latinos (63 percent) report a greater belief that racial profiling is widespread in motorist stops on roads and highways than whites (50 percent). Sixty percent (nineteen out of thirty-two) of the Mexican Americans in the barrio I studied believed they were stopped simply because of their profile, and 95 percent (thirty-one out of thirty-two) witnessed experiences where their white friends were treated more leniently. A large number of researchers have reported police harassment within Mexican American communities (Acuña 2000; Bayley and Mendelsohn 1968; Escobar 1999; Mazón 1984; Mirandé 1987; Moore 1991; Morales 1972; Rosenbaum 1981; Vigil 1988). Bayley and Mendelsohn (1968, 109) reported: "The police seem to play a role in the life of minority people out of all proportion to the role they play in the lives of the Dominant majority [whites]."

A third demographic factor community members believed they were stopped for was their gender. Men or teenage boys were perceived as more highly targeted than women or teenage girls. Thus the seven women interviewed described fewer negative interactions with the police than the men, but believed that the police would try to use them to gather information. The young women who attended ASAP thought the men were stopped and harassed more by the police. Randolph, the middle-aged member of POP from Denver, commented on this pattern:

> If it's a car full of girls, they are far less likely, we saw, to be stopped. So, like, for every car full of girls they stopped, they stopped ten cars full of guys and we know that multiple passengers were much more likely to be targeted.

If ascribed characteristics were not enough for police to profile individuals as gang members, many Mexican American youth matched the criteria by their clothes, haircuts, numbers, or tattoos (interviews with Denver and Ogden Gang Units and gang protocol). Most youth would dress in clothes that were fashionable with their peers. This created great confusion for the police and even for gang members when the majority of youth dressed in baggy clothes from urban hip-hop brands (i.e., Ben Davis, Dickies, Johnny Blaze, Karl Kani, Phat Farm, Roca Wear, and Sean John) and clothing with numbers (e.g., Fubu 05, Joker 77, and sports jerseys). Fine et al. (2003) reported that urban youth in general felt disrespected by police and that adults in positions of authority would often equate their urban clothing as a symbol of their

criminal inclination. Lucita, a twenty-five-year-old gang associate from Ogden, recalled seeing when the police would approach her Mexican American friends:

> They get harassed, they get questioned, they get pulled over for any reason because they got their sunglasses on, or their windows are too tinted, or because they are wearing their pants a certain way, which is funny because you catch these white kids trying to do the same thing but they never get asked those questions. They never get asked "Why you dress like that?" or "Where are you going?"

Mexican Americans who dressed in certain ways increased their differential treatment by both authority figures and peers. Urban attire had the possibility for negative treatment by authority figures, but it brought approval from peers. Whites on the other hand were more likely to escape the consequences that came from the negative gang connotations.

With gang officers making a high percentage of their stops based on extra legal factors relating to age, gender, neighborhood, race, and gang stereotypes, community members were skeptical about police officers' stated primary objective as targeting crime. Rather, a large number of residents believed that police officers were there to enforce social control over the neighborhood and the people who lived there (Fagan and Davies 2000). Police officers often faced difficulty legitimizing their actions with the people they were policing. The profiling increased conflict, but officers lacked the structural power to alter where they were deployed and how they prevented crime. Their structural vulnerability led officers to dismiss claims of racial profiling. Nevertheless, the everyday motions of police work legitimated a focus on extra legal factors.

Interacting with Suspected Gang Members

The interactions between police and the Mexican-American community members were very tense because of the vagueness of the encounters and their unknown outcomes. Several people who observed police officers interacting with suspected gang members noted that the police often attempted to incite provocations to justify a search or arrest. The U.S. Commission on Civil Rights (1970), one of the few empirical studies devoted to Latinos, found this ethnic group viewed the police with tension and fear because of frequent arrests on insufficient grounds for "investigation" and "stop and frisks."

A number of researchers have explored officers' negative preconceptions toward minorities (Westley 1953), gang members (Klein 2004), and police perceptions that stricter enforcement is required (Bayley and Mendelsohn 1968). Bridges and Steen (1998) reported that probation officers' divergent beliefs about white and black criminality shaped their assessment of dangerousness and sentencing recommendations. Bayley and Mendelsohn (1968) reported that officers' beliefs are similar to those held in the wider society. Through experience, those who associated with or were in gangs came to feel that they were treated the worst.

Intelligence Gathering

Intelligence gathering was a key component of police suppression tactics. Donner (1980) reported surveillance conducted on people and groups were justified on preventive grounds against violence. However, police intelligence gathering has allowed the labeling of entire racial and ethnic groups, especially men, as gang members (Lopez 1993; Johnson 1993). Once people land on such lists, it becomes more likely that their future acts will be discovered, prosecuted, and dealt with punitively (Anderson 1990). Denver and Ogden gang lists do not require criminal activity for admission and they remain in the file for at least five years.

For police officers to create these lists, Mexican American youth were repeatedly asked to what gang they belonged. According to the police department gang protocol, people who admitted gang membership satisfied the first and primary requirement for being placed on a gang list, yet most people denied membership. The police used different tactics to discover gang involvement ranging from talking nonchalantly to coercion. Most respondents interviewed who were not involved with gangs believed that officers suspected them of lying in denying membership. Officers would search for clues by asking individuals to pull up their shirts,

looking for tattoos, or asking what high school they attended, to denote possible gang membership. Tone, a twenty-eight-year-old "convict" who chose to stay away from a gang lifestyle, said:

> They [police] would throw a couple different gang names at me and ask me which one I belonged to and I would say none. But they would always look like they didn't believe me if you didn't tell them what they wanted to hear.

Anne, the twenty-four-year-old gang associate from Ogden, said:

> I was pregnant and me and my friend were cruising and we were just sitting there parked and the cops came over and a couple other people were parked there and they were in a gang but they said we couldn't be loitering around there. And right away they were yelling at us what gang were we in. I said, "I'm not in a gang," and he said, "Don't lie," like yelling at me, "don't lie." I was like, "I'm not in a gang." And then he asked, "Why you around all of these gang members if you're not in a gang?" I was pregnant and a girl hanging out with another girl and so it made me pretty mad. And frustrated too because I kept telling him but he wouldn't let it go. He kept saying, "You're in a gang! Tell me!"

Although Anne was associating with gang members, she was not a member. A large number of people in the barrio know someone in a gang, but this does not make them a member. Individual gang membership created a stereotype that spread to everyone living in the barrio of this particular racial or ethnic background. Police officers could then use the gang label to legitimate all interactions with the Mexican American community. These labels were then maintained by the presumption of clear and precise policies and guidelines that countered all forms of legal challenges and complaints, yet no one outside the gang unit had access to the police files to verify its accuracy.

Others whose family members were involved in gangs were often treated as members of the gang. Monique, a twenty-two-year-old from Ogden who had two brothers involved in gangs, mentioned how the police automatically assumed she was a member and treated her poorly. Lucita, a twenty-five-year-old associate with a traditional gang who had two brothers who were previously involved in gangs, concurred with this negative treatment when she said:

> For a while there I was getting pulled over a lot. They assumed I was affiliated with so and so, they see you one time with this one person, therefore you have information that you are withholding from them or they think you know the whereabouts of an individual. Stuff like that. You get harassed and you get them on your back you can't get them off. They are on you constantly and they will pull you over for anything. I think they put the word out, look for this vehicle with this person driving.

Frequent disrespect from the police was reported by more than 97 percent (thirty-one out of thirty-two) of the Mexican Americans interviewed, and they took little time to recall instances of verbal and body language abuse. Although Mastrofski, Resig, and McCluskey (2002) reported that police disrespect was very rare, 4 percent of all police stops, almost half of these incidents, were unprovoked. The police attempted to dominate these interactions with the power of the law, authority, and entrusted discretion. Mack-one, a twenty-four-year-old ex-gang associate from Denver, said:

> They treated me bad. They thought I was a gang member. They didn't do really do any physical harm to me but, ugh, verbally they definitely thought of me as a lower human being.

Although acting civil and cordial may not be a requirement for policing, these stops produced feelings of anger, distrust, and hopelessness particularly when police could do whatever they wished and get away with it. Everyone interviewed could cite examples of being treated like dirt and then simply told to go on their way once officers found no reason to take the stop further (the majority of the time). Police officers' "fishing expeditions" would not always pay off. Anne, the twenty-four-year-old gang associate from Ogden, said:

> They're dicks; they don't care, and they don't care if you're a girl. I had one of the gang cops search me, and I know that is against the law. Not search me but pat me down, like really pat me down! I know they are not supposed to do that, and I told him, "You can't pat me down." I'm like, "You're supposed to have a female officer." He was all, "You don't tell me what to do." You know, just their little attitude, they'll put you

down to your face. You're nothing, you're a piece of shit. They totally don't have any respect for anybody who is a gang member or who they think is a gang member. I don't know how they choose the gang task force but they don't seem to understand anything about gangs. All they focus on is getting them off the street and into jail. It's awful.

Mirandé (1987, 153) argued that, "perhaps the most persistent overriding concern expressed by Chicanos is that the police treat them with less respect and courtesy, and with less regard for their rights." Mastrofski, Resig, and McCluskey (2002) reported that minorities experienced disrespect at twice the rate of whites. Smiley, a twenty-three-year-old ex-gang associate, said:

> They treat you like you are lower than everybody you know, like you are a bad person, like you are always committing felonies or that you are involved in crime. They just treat you with no respect. They just treat you like you are scum or something, like you are a bad person.

The two interactions between Mexican American community members and the police highlight the perception that the police are attempting to gather intelligence to bring individuals down and disrespect them during the process.

Gang-labeled Mexican Americans, those who were on the gang list, were approached differently because they were seen and treated as constant criminals even when following the law. Police perceptions shaped gang membership as a "master status" (Hughes 1945) that combines ascribed and achieved statuses with the belief of lifelong gang involvement. Changing this image was very difficult for gang members, particularly those attempting to leave the gang lifestyle. D-loc thought gang members were treated three times worse than non-gang members. Police officials primarily applied the gang label to Latinos and African Americans and thus the only people who could be perceived as non-gang members were whites. Many police stops of gang members would begin with ordering these Mexican Americans out of their vehicle and telling them to put their hands up in the air or lie face down on the ground. The officers more frequently drew their guns and attempted to investigate assumed gang involvement and planned activities. Cyclone, a twenty-five-year-old ex-gang member and ex-prison inmate, said:

> I got labeled as a known violent gang member and never been caught of a gang crime with anybody and it's odd because they label you as that and it's not a good label because it sticks with you for life. When I get pulled over it doesn't matter who I am with they pull me out of the car and pat me down. Every time. I mean they run my name, the NCI report comes up that says I am a violent person and they wait for three or four more cops to show up and then they get me out of the car just to check me. While I am with my family, my kids, I am getting discriminated. They've embarrass me in huge way with the people I'm with. They will tell the people I'm with I'm a bad influence or I'm trouble.

Klein (2004, 42–45) found that gang officer perceptions of gangs often did not match research findings. Klein found that most gang crime is minor; most gang activity is noncriminal; street gangs were social groups; street life becomes a part of gang culture; and the community context in which gangs arise was often ignored. The police, on the other hand, portrayed gangs as violent criminal enterprises, fundamentally different from other social groups and divorced from local community problems. Raul, an eighteen-year-old ex-gang member from Denver, said:

> They [police] mess with you all of the time. Like if you are a gang member they be stopping you all of the time. Checking to see if you have any weapons, some of these police officers are racist, they think we are all violent and do bad crimes but I think we are different. One time they stopped us and they were taking off our shirts and checking if we had any gang tattoos. Writing things on their computer, about when they stopped you, what gang tattoos you have. They even took pictures of me one time, and I don't know why.

Gang intelligence gathering was blatantly discriminatory when gang unit officers would stop countless Mexican Americans and leave groups of whites alone. If there were whites involved in gangs, as the self-report studies (Esbensen and Osgood 1997) and my research confirmed, they continued to go unnoticed by law enforcement. Winfree, Bernat, and Esbensen (2001) found that "Hispanics are no more likely to be gang members than Anglo youths...." Conducting sweeps on groups of white

youth and justifying it with gang reasoning had the potential to put gang unit funding and continued operations in jeopardy. Police officers' repeated profiling based on stereotypical perceptions and coercive intelligence on Mexican Americans justified increased funding, increased gang legislation, and the movement to relocate greater numbers of this population to the penitentiary.

Serious Forms of Police Misconduct

Respondents interviewed claimed that both Denver and Ogden's police departments often used excessive physical force. Although researchers for the Bureau of Justice Statistics (Greenfeld, Langan, and Smith 1999) reported that the use of force occurred in less than 1 percent of all encounters with citizens during the year of their survey, at least 34 percent (eleven out of thirty-two) of my respondents had experienced physical abuse one or more times. Eighty percent of this misconduct occurred during an arrest and in an isolated area during evening hours. People were more likely to be victimized by police in impoverished black and Latino neighborhoods. The level of abuse and misconduct in these cities was different from that noted in the infamous Rampart Division case,[1] but currently remains underresearched and veiled in secrecy. Denver had a high rate of police shootings; from 1980 to 2007, 222 people were shot, and 103 people killed by the Denver Police Department. (I have gathered data from various newspaper reports, historical records, and the District Attorney's Office.) The captain of the Denver Gang Unit assured me that many policies and protections were instituted to prevent misconduct from happening within his city. Nevertheless, two Denver gang officers were charged for not logging at least eighty pieces of drug evidence into the police department property bureau after making numerous arrests and giving tickets for marijuana possession and paraphernalia (Vaughan 2000). One of these officers was accused of harassing and brutalizing gang members within the Denver area, and this was the likely reason he was shot by a suspected gang member during a questionable traffic stop (Ritter 2003; 2004 interviews). The alleged gang member was also shot to death during this incident.

In another Denver case, an off-duty gang officer was driving home late at night after getting off work and became involved in a road rage incident in which he fired six shots at a Salvadorian immigrant, who died at the scene. Forensic evidence contradicted the officer's testimony about whether the immigrant was holding a gun (Lowe 2001). An ex-military and highly decorated African American man filed a racial profiling complaint against the gang unit. He described how several gang officers stopped him without cause, crashed into his wife's car, and held him down at gunpoint while making lewd remarks toward his wife (Lindsay 2004). Nevertheless, the gang unit claimed they had few complaints (2004 interview). Rodney, an African American Latino resident who was a gang associate from Denver, told me:

> I wish every gang member would actually report the abuse that they would go through by the Denver Police Department. Then we would have a better picture of what the role is that unit plays. But the gang members don't feel like they have a right to report when they have been beat up. If they actually took the time to document this stuff we would actually see the Denver Police is putting in more work than anybody. They function as a gang. [Interviewer: They said they had low amounts of complaints that come from that unit.] They said they have a low amount of complaints; yeah they do, because the people they are attacking are scared to complain. A lot of times, I don't even want to say scared; they don't feel empowered to complain. They feel like they are a gang member so they just have to deal with what they got.

The Ogden Gang Unit was the least prepared for dealing with "harassment" practices by their officers because their white officers were rarely challenged or questioned about how they operated. Therefore, the Ogden Gang Unit practiced a higher number of profile stops than Denver. Jay, a twenty-seven-year-old ex-Ogden-gang member, said:

> I think that some of their methods and tactics are a little on the borderline of police brutality, or excessive force. One of my friends who works at the police department is in close contact with the gang unit, told me that this one officer hates little gang members. He calls them on whether it be a fist fight, a weapons fight, whatever. He will physically challenge them, you know, you bring your stick and I'll bring mine. I guess they figure they got to do what they got to do.

Several community members challenged Ogden Gang Unit officers for their role in inciting a riot with about seventy-five African Americans at a hip-hop concert. The officers had received a call that alcohol was present and when they attempted to enter the building security officials denied them entrance. As a result, several people were beaten with police batons and charged with felony rioting (Gurrister 2003). After this case was turned over to the FBI for investigation, one of the key officers suspected of brutality began to target the individual who filed the complaint (Gurrister 2004a, 2004b).

Human Rights Watch (1998, 2) argued that "race continues to play a central role in police brutality in the United States. Indeed, despite gains in many areas since the civil rights movement of the 1950s and 1960s, one area that has been stubbornly resistant to change has been the treatment afforded racial minorities by the police." Their research involving fourteen cities reported that habitually brutal officers, usually a small percentage on the force, might receive repeated complaints but were usually protected by other officers and poor internal police investigations. Cyclone, a twenty-five-year-old ex-gang member and ex-prison inmate, said:

> I've been beaten by cops before. I was running from the police and I was drunk. I wrecked a car and I got out and started to run and I noticed there were five different counties of cops. There were cops from every district surrounding me. I laid down on the ground and the cop that jumped on me started punching me in back of the head. I went into County [Jail] and let them know that I was having serious migraines and I showed them the bumps on my head. They took a report and that's all that was ever said. They didn't do anything to the officer that whupped my ass. I got charged with resisting arrest and was tied to the bumper of a car. [Question: How many times do you think he hit you in the back of the head?] Probably about four or five. [What were you doing?] I was in handcuffs on my stomach while his knee was in my back, and the other cops were watching. They know something happened. If I wasn't in cuffs when he was hitting me I would have defended myself. They have the reports on the bumps on my head, severe handcuff marks on my arms; I couldn't feel my left hand for nearly an hour after they took the cuffs off.

Several of the interviewees also believed that illegal immigrants were treated worse by police. Mirandé (1987) suggested that undocumented immigrants were especially vulnerable because they lacked resources and familiarity with the justice system. Immigrants also reported fewer instances of abuse because they feared deportation. Nite Owl, an undocumented seventeen-year-old gang member, said:

> One time I was walking, and they [police] told me stop, and I stopped, and they didn't tell me to turn around or anything; they just came up and tackled me. They hit me two times with their stick and put the cuffs on my hands. Maybe they could say I'm sorry we messed up or something, but they didn't say nothing like that. They just sorry, it wasn't you. I said it wasn't me and they said shut up, so I didn't say anything.

Problematic urban conditions and minority presence has resulted in police violence being used proactively rather than simply reacting to a criminal threat (Jacobs and O'Brien 1998; Terrill and Resig 2003). Nite Owl viewed his situation as being in the wrong place at the wrong time, but there was nothing he could have done to prevent his receiving a severe beating. The Mexican American community recognized that a simple stop or interaction with the police had a variety of outcomes that were seen as legally permissible, but that law enforcement officers were not going to treat whites living in their racially segregated neighborhoods with the same type of aggression. Holmes (2000) reported that there is reliable data to conclude that southwestern Latinos are targets of police brutality based on his study of civil rights complaints filed with the U.S. Department of Justice. Furthermore, Kane (2002) reported that an increase in the percent of the Latino population increased police misconduct.

Conclusion

In many ways, the gang enforcement experiences of Mexican American youth living in the barrios can be difficult to believe compared with traditional notions of policing and studies on gangs. The research reported here runs contrary to all of the legitimated claims given by law enforcement and routinely heard in the media. In these segregated barrios, gang units systematically targeted people

of Mexican descent by disguising their racial and ethnic implications, a new nonracial rhetoric discussed by Omi and Winant (1994) as *code-words*. The higher number of stops and coercive questioning dramatically increased the number of people labeled as gang members and associates. Donner (1980) reported that the language used by law enforcement shielded their tactics from attack. Suppression and intelligence gathering against the Mexican American community became legitimated when it was justified with the term *gang*. In this article, I did not find that gang unit officers or law enforcement officials were incorrect in all criminal stops, but rather the majority of gang enforcement stops were predicated on noncriminal activity and included more non-gang members. The barrio residents were not anti-police. They *were* against the profiling and demeaning treatment. The end result of aggressive differential policing was greater division between the barrio and law enforcement.

Werthman and Piliavin's (1967) early research on police interactions with gang members initiated some worthy theoretical advances. One, living in a social environment that occupied different cultural and structural conditions implicated a wide variety of people as being of interest to police officers. Second, the underlying troubles between gang members and police involved problems of the law. Since Werthman and Piliavin's (1967) research, the 1990s brought a new policing effort involving gang units that spread to cities around the nation targeting perceived criminality in poor and minority communities (Fagan and Davies 2000; Heymann 2000; Sherman, Gartin, and Buerger 1989). Katz (2003) found severe social consequences for being labeled a gang member. The gang unit he studied impacted gang-labeled individuals' opportunities for employment and education.

This research found that the actual practice of gang enforcement included: (1) racialized profiles, (2) fabricated intelligence, and (3) suppression of marginalized communities. The problem became not that of law, as suggested by Werthman and Piliavin, but rather the enforcement of laws. Gang units legitimated the social control of people beyond involvement in crime to include perceived criminality. Heymann (2000) found the effectiveness of this new policing problematic. He reported that the cumulative effect of stopping more blacks and

Latinos is to diminish their equal protection status in this country. An increasing number of research studies related to gangs and police questions the suppression tactics used by law enforcement to target groups of people living in racially and economically segregated social environments. Jackson and Rudman (1993) suggested that these suppression strategies were bound to fail because they negatively impacted impoverished communities and then spread gang influence by creating a link between the community and prison. Klein (2004, 194) has argued that police work with gangs is ineffective because it is driven by "selective personal experience, stereotypes, and ideology, and seldom by objectively gathered knowledge about their nature."

This research supports Werthman and Piliavin's (1967) theoretical proposition of "ecological contamination," as perceived gang neighborhoods infecting many suspicious persons to police officers' discretion and to their power to investigate. In addition, this research highlighted how suspicious persons were not anyone living within the city, but particularly poor and young Mexican American males. This focus supports the "minority group threat" hypothesis (Jackson 1989; Liska 1992; Smith and Holmes 2003). In both cities, Latinos were increasing in numbers and this growth increased perceptions of gang involvement. Moreover, there was a disjuncture between the perceived threat and the actual threat (i.e., moral panic).

In summary, gang enforcement by gang units and patrol officers involved several theoretical patterns. One, the increase in the young, poor, and urban Mexican population was seen as a threat for gang membership. Second, structurally vulnerable areas became targeted with concentrated aggressive gang enforcement that supported gang assumptions and fueled the moral panic by labeling non-gang members as gang members (ecological contamination). Third, aggressive policing of marginalized and oppressed communities did not eliminate crime, but rather led to greater divisions between barrio residents and law enforcement.

Notes

Author's Note: I have chosen to use the term Mexican American for the people interviewed in this research. My sample includes people of Mexican descent

who are second- to fourth-generation U.S. citizens. The interviewees identified themselves as Hispanic, Mexican, Mexican American, Chicano, and Mexicano. Acuña (2000, 462) reports, "Throughout Chicano history the question of identity has consumed a lot of time and space, which is natural given the legacy of colonialism. Even before the Chicano Student Movement of the 1960s, activists argued as to what to call themselves." The lack of political and educational access for the majority of the people interviewed prevented me from using Chicano. For more discussion on this topic see Muñoz (1989). Although national data indicates that most Latinos consider themselves racially as white, none of the inner-city respondents in these neighborhoods identified with this racial group. They considered their ethnicity as a race. I will use the term *Latino* in this article to represent individuals from Mexico, Puerto Rico, Cuba, and other Latin American countries. *White* will be used to denote people of European descent who do not have a Hispanic ethnic background. See Delgado (1995) and Roediger (1991).

1. On March 2, 1998, six pounds of cocaine were discovered missing from the property room of the Rampart, California, police. This led to the arrest of a CRASH officer, who later entered into a confidential plea agreement and received a reduced sentence on drug charges (Glover and Lait 1999). The testimony of this officer would later lead to the overturning of one hundred convictions of alleged gang members and others arrested by the LAPD. Nine officers were prosecuted, and more than a dozen were fired or resigned, for behavior including beatings, framing people, killing individuals, selling drugs, and engaging in various types of crimes while investigating and pursuing gang members (Glover and Lait 2003). This scandal cost city tax payers more than $40 million to settle claims by victims (Lait and Glover 2003).

References

Acuña, R. 2000. *Occupied America: A history of Chicanos.* New York: Longman.

Adler, P. A., and P. Adler. 1987. *Membership roles in field research.* Newbury Park, CA: Sage.

Anderson, E. 1990. *Streetwise: Race, class, and change in an urban community.* Chicago: University of Chicago Press.

Bass, S. 2001. Policing space, policing race: Social control imperatives and police discretionary decisions. *Social Justice* 28:156–76.

Battin, S. R., K. G. Hill, R. D. Abbott, R. F. Catalano, and D. Hawkins. 1988. The contribution of gang membership to delinquency beyond delinquent friends. *Criminology* 36:93–115.

Bayley, D. H., and H. Mendelsohn. 1968. *Minorities and the police: Confrontation in America.* New York: Free Press.

Bernard, R. H. 1988. *Research methods in cultural anthropology.* Newbury Park, CA: Sage.

Biernacki, P., and D. Waldorf. 1981. Snowball sampling. *Sociological Research and Methods* 10:141–63.

Bjerregaard, B., and C. Smith. 1993. Gender differences in gang participation, delinquency, and substance use. *Journal of Quantitative Criminology* 9:329–55.

Blalock, H. M. 1967. *Towards a theory of minority group relations.* New York: Capricorn Books.

Bridges, G. S., and S. Steen. 1998. Racial disparities in official assessments of juvenile offenders: Attributional stereotypes as mediating mechanisms. *American Sociological Review* 63:554–70.

Briggs, B., and J. Gavin. 1988. Pena hits back: "We won't put up with it." *Rocky Mountain News*, November 5.

Browning, S. L., F. T. Cullin, L. Cao, R. Kopache, and T. J. Stevenson. 1994. Race and getting hassled by the police: A research note. *Police Studies* 17:1–11.

Camarillo, A. 1979. *Chicanos in a changing society: From Mexican pueblos to American barrios in Santa Barbara and Southern California, 1848–1930.* MA: Harvard University Press.

Cohen, S. 1980. *Folk devils and moral panics: The creation of the mods and rockers.* New York: St. Martin's.

Cole, D. 1999. *No equal justice: Race and class in the American criminal justice system.* New York: New Press.

Curry, G. D., R. A. Ball, and S. H. Decker. 1996. Estimating the national scope of gang crime from law enforcement data. Research in brief. NCJ 161477. Washington, DC: U.S. Department of Justice, Office of Justice Programs, National Institute of Justice.

Delgado, R. 1995. *Critical race theory: The cutting edge.* Philadelphia, PA: Temple University Press.

Donner, F. J. 1980. *The age of surveillance: The aims and methods of America's political intelligence system.* New York: Knopf.

Douglas, J. D. 1976. *Investigative social research.* Beverly Hills, CA: Sage.

Egley, A. 2002. *National youth gang survey trends from 1996 to 2000.* Washington, DC: U.S. Department of Justice, Office of Justice Programs, Office of Juvenile Justice and Delinquency Prevention.

Esbensen, F., and D. Huizinga. 1993. Gangs, drugs, and delinquency in a survey of urban youth. *Criminology* 31:565–89.

Esbensen, F., and W. Osgood. 1997. National evaluation of GREAT (research in brief). Washington, DC: U.S. Department of Justice.

Esbensen, F., and L. T. Winfree. 1998. Race and gender differences between gang and nongang youth: Results from a multi-site survey. *Justice Quarterly* 15:505–25.

Escobar, E. J. 1999. *Race, police, and the making of a political identity: Mexican Americans and the Los Angeles Police Department 1900–1945.* Los Angeles, CA: University of California Press.

Fagan, J., and G. Davies. 2000. Street stops and broken windows: Terry, race and disorder in New York City. *Fordham Urban Law Journal* 28.

Fine, M., N. Freudenberg, Y. Payne, T. Perkins, K. Smith, and K. Wanzer. 2003. "Anything can happen with police around": Urban youth evaluate strategies of surveillance in public places. *Journal of Social Issues* 59:141–58.

Fritsch, E., T. Cacti, and R. Taylor. 1999. Gang suppression through saturation patrol, aggressive curfew, and truancy enforcement: A quasi-experimental test of the Dallas anti-gang initiative. *Crime and Delinquency* 45:122–39.

Garcia, M. T. 1981. *Desert immigrants: The Mexicans of El Paso, 1880–1920.* New Haven: Yale University Press.

Geertz, C. 1973. *The interpretation of cultures.* New York: Basic Books.

Greenfeld, L. A., P. A. Langan, and S. K. Smith. 1999. Police use of force: Collection of national data. NCJ 165040. Washington, DC: U.S. Department of Justice, Bureau of Justice Statistics and National Institute of Justice.

Gurrister, T. 2003. Police tactics queried: Union station case builds. *Standard Examiner*, October 23.

Gurrister, T. 2004a. FBI probing Ogden incident. *Standard Examiner*, February 22.

Gurrister, T. 2004b. Officer accused of payback arrest. *Standard Examiner*, April 1.

Hagan, J., and C. Albonetti. 1982. Race, class, and the perception of criminal injustice in America. *The American Journal of Sociology* 88:329–55.

Hall, D. E. 1996. *Criminal law and procedure.* New York: Delmar.

Haws, J. 1999. Meeting on gangs seeks zero tolerance. *Standard Examiner*, July 19.

Heymann, P. B. 2000. The new policing. *Fordham Urban Law Journal* 28.

Holmes, M. D. 2000. Minority threat and police brutality: Determinants of civil rights criminal complaints in U.S. municipalities. *Criminology* 38:343–67.

Huff, C. R., and W. McBride. 1993. Gangs and the police. In *Gang intervention handbook*, eds. Arnold P. Goldstein and C. Ronald Huff. Champaign, IL: Research Press.

Hughes, E. C. 1945. Dilemmas and contradictions of status. *American Journal of Sociology* 50:353–59.

Human Rights Watch. 1998. *Shielded from justice: Police brutality and accountability in the United States.* New York: Human Rights Watch.

Jackson, P. I. 1989. *Minority group threat, crime, and policing: Social context and social control.* New York: Praeger.

Jackson, P., and C. Rudman. 1993. Moral panics and the response to gangs in California. In *Gangs: The origins and impact of contemporary youth gangs in the United States*, eds. S. Cummings and D. J. Monti.

Jacobs, D., and R. M. O'Brien. 1998. The determinants of deadly force: A structural analysis of police violence. *American Journal of Sociology* 103:837–62.

Johnson, D. 1993. 2 out of 3 young black men in Denver are on gang suspect list. *New York Times*, December 11.

Kane, R. J. 2002. The social ecology of police misconduct. *Criminology* 40:867–96.

Katz, C. M. 2001. The establishment of a police gang unit: Organizational and environmental factors. *Criminology* 39:37–73.

Katz, C. M. 2003. Issues in the production and dissemination of gang statistics: An ethnographic study of a large Midwestern police gang unit. *Crime and Delinquency* 49:485–516.

Katz, C. M., and V. J. Webb. 2006. *Policing gangs in America.* New York: Cambridge University.

Kirksey, J. 1983. Denver DA backs gangs crackdown. *Denver Post*, June 20.

Klein, M. W. 1968. From association to guilt: The group guidance project in juvenile gang intervention. Los Angeles, CA: Youth Studies Center, University of Southern California and the Los Angeles County Probation Department.

Klein, M. W. 1995. *The American street gang: Its nature, prevalence, and control.* New York: Oxford University Press.

Klein, M. W. 2004. *Gang cop: The words and ways of Officer Paco Domingo.* Walnut Creek, CA: AltaMira.

Lindsay, S. 2004. Police acted "inappropriately." *Rocky Mountain News*, April 21.

Liska, A. E. 1992. Introduction to the study of social control. In *social threat and social control*, ed. Allen E. Liska. Albany, NY: State University of New York

Liska, A. E., J. J. Lawrence, and M. M. Benson. 1981. Perspectives on the legal order. *American Journal of Sociology* 87:412–26.

Lofland, J., and L. H. Lofland. 1995. *Analyzing social settings: A guide to qualitative observation and analysis.* Belmont, CA: Wadsworth.

Lopez, C. 1993. List brands 2 of 3 young black men. *Denver Post*, December 5.

Lowe, P. 2001. Panel, police see different theories in glass shards: Glass, gun and blood focus forensic battle. *Rocky Mountain News*, November 24.

Mastrofski, S. D., M. D. Resig, and J. D. McCluskey. 2002. Police disrespect toward the public: An encounter-based analysis. *Criminology* 40:515–51.

Mazón, M. 1984. *The zoot-suit riots: The psychology of symbolic annihilation.* TX: University of Texas.

McCorkle, R. C., and T. D. Miethe. 2002. *Panic: The social construction of the street gang problem.* Upper Saddle River, NJ: Prentice Hall.

Meehan, A. J., and M. C. Ponder. 2002. Race and place: The ecology of racial profiling African American motorists. *Justice Quarterly* 19:399–430.

Miller, W. B. 1992. Revised from 1982. Crime by youth gangs and groups in the United States. NCJ 156221. Washington, DC: U.S. Department of Justice, Office of Justice Programs, Office of Juvenile Justice and Delinquency Prevention.

Mirandé, A. 1987. *Gringo justice.* Notre Dame, IN: University of Notre Dame.

Moore, J. W. 1991. *Going down to the barrio: Homeboys and homegirls in change.* Philadelphia, PA: Temple University Press.

Morales, A. 1972. *Ando Sangrando: A study of Mexican American–police conflict.* La Puente, CA: Perspectiva Publications.

Muñoz, C. 1989. *Youth, identity, power: The Chicano movement.* New York: Verso.

Needle, J. A., and W. V. Stapleton. 1983. Police handling of youth gangs. Reports of the National Juvenile Justice Assessment Centers. U.S. Department of Justice.

Omi, M., and H. Winant. 1994. *Racial formation in the United States: From the 1960s to the 1990s.* New York: Routledge.

Pelto, G. H., and J. Pertti. 1979. *The cultural dimension of human adventure.* New York: Macmillan.

Reimer, J. W. 1977. Varieties of opportunistic research. *Urban Life* 5 (4): 467–77.

Ritter, B. 2003. Investigation of the shooting death of Anthony Ray Jefferson. [online]. March 7. Available: http://www.denverda.org/Decision_Letters/02Jefferson .htm.

Roediger, D. R. 1991. *The wages of whiteness: Race and the making of the American working class.* New York: Verso.

Romo, R. 1983. *East Los Angeles: History of a barrio.* Austin: University of Texas Press.

Rosenbaum, R. J. 1981. *Mexicano resistance in the southwest.* Dallas, TX: Southern Methodist University.

Sherman, L. W., P. R. Gartin, and M. E. Buerger. 1989. Hot spots of predatory crime: Routine activities and the criminology of place. *Criminology* 27:27–55.

Smith, B. W., and M. D. Holmes. 2003. Community accountability, minority threat, and police brutality: An examination of civil rights criminal complaints. *Criminology* 41:1035–64.

Spergel, I. A. 1995. *The youth gang problem: A community approach.* New York: Oxford University Press.

Terrill, W., and M. D. Resig. 2003. Neighborhood context and police use of force. *Journal of Research in Crime and Delinquency* 40:291–321.

Thomas, D., and R. Hansen. 2004. Second annual report, Denver Police Department, Contact Card Data Analysis. June 1, 2002, through May 31, 2003. Available: http://www.denvergov.org/Police/BiasedPolicingRacialProfiling/tabid/392249/Default.aspx.

Thornberry, T. P. 1998. Membership in youth gangs and involvement in serious and violent offending. In *Serious and violent offenders: Risk factors and successful interventions*, eds. R. Loeber and D. P. Farrington. Thousand Oaks, CA: Sage.

Tovares, R. D. 2002. *Manufacturing the gang: Mexican American youth gangs on local television news.* Westport, CT: Greenwood.

Vaughan, K. 2000. Charges filed against two cops. Veteran gang officers accused of destroying evidence in "at least" 80 criminal cases. *Rocky Mountain News*, section local, July 20:4A.

Vigil, J. D. 1988. *Barrio gangs: Street life and identity in southern California.* Austin, TX: University of Texas Press.

Vigil, J. D. 2002. *A rainbow of gangs: Street cultures in the mega-city.* Austin, TX: University of Texas Press.

Werthman, C., and I. Piliavin. 1967. Gang members and the police. In *The police: Six sociological essays*, ed. D. Bordua. New York: Wiley.

Westley, W. A. 1953. Violence and the police. *The American Journal of Sociology* 59:34–41.

Wilson, J. Q., and G. L. Kelling. 1982. The police and neighborhood safety: Broken windows. *Atlantic Monthly*: 29–38.

Winfree, T. L., F. P. Bernat, and F. Esbensen. 2001. Hispanic and Anglo gang membership in two southwestern cities. *The Social Science Journal* 38:105–17.

Zatz, M. S. 1987. Chicano youth gangs and crime: The creation of a moral panic. *Contemporary Crisis* 11:129–58.

Gender

Research on the role of gender in gangs most often focuses on better understanding girls' and young women's participation in these groups.[1] Thus, the chapters in this section will familiarize the reader with what we know about key issues such as:

- The level of female gang involvement

- Risk factors for gang membership for girls

- The extent and character of delinquency among gang-involved girls

- The short- and longer-term consequences of gang participation for young women and girls

This is a good place to start, as numerous commentators have lamented the limited attention that girls in gangs have received in the scholarly literature. In fact, compared to what we know about gangs generally and young men's participation in these groups, there remains a paucity of research on young women's experiences with gangs.

Gang research has a long history, beginning most systematically with Frederic Thrasher's 1927 publication *The Gang.* Unfortunately, this is primarily a history of research on young men in gangs, and virtually no attention was paid to young women in gangs until the 1970s. The first systematic investigations of girls in gangs did not appear until the publication, in the early 1980s, of John Quicker's *Homegirls: Characterizing Chicana Gangs* (1983) and Anne Campbell's *The Girls in the Gang* (1984). This has left us a good half-century behind in our understanding of young women's and girls'

experiences with gangs, and also limits our ability to draw compelling conclusions about continuities and changes in girls' participation in gangs, including with regard to the key questions listed above.[2] Fortunately, the 1990s and early 2000s witnessed quite a bit of research on young women in gangs, including Joan Moore's (1991) *Going Down to the Barrio: Homeboys and Homegirls in Change,* a historical analysis of women's and men's gang experiences in the 1950s and 1970s; Jody Miller's *One of the Guys: Girls, Gangs and Gender,* an investigation of girls' and young women's gang participation in the midwestern United States; and numerous research articles (an excellent overview can be found in Dana Peterson's opening chapter of this section).

The growth in research on girls and gangs during this period is likely attributable to three historical shifts in the field. Probably most significant was the expansion of feminist criminology and its requisite attention to the experiences of women and girls, with young women's gang involvement one of many areas of research that benefited from the broadening of perspectives in the field. In addition, the dramatic proliferation of gangs across the United States in the 1980s and 1990s led to tremendous growth in gang research more generally during this period. This expansion was coupled with methodological innovations as well. The growing popularity of adolescent self-report studies—including, for example, the Denver Youth Survey, the Rochester Youth Development Study, the Seattle Social Development Project, and the Gang Resistance, Education, and Training

(G.R.E.A.T.) Program—began collecting data from samples that included both girls and boys, often following them longitudinally.

All of this research has provided us with much better foundational knowledge about young women's and girls' participation in gangs, as well as information about how their gang involvement compares to that of boys and young men. In addition, there is a small but slowly growing body of comparative research that investigates the extent and nature of girls' gang participation outside of the United States. What is most striking about this research, as noted by Dutch criminologist Frank Weerman, is that European survey results about girls in gangs show "remarkable similarities" to the findings of U.S. studies. Haymoz and Gatti's report, based on comparative survey results from Italy and Switzerland, is included in this section to highlight these patterns. Yet despite these important strides, overall, the last decade has not continued to keep pace with the flurry of research on the topic we witnessed around the turn of the new millennium. Thus, the reader will notice a mix of newer and older studies represented in this section.

In addition, to truly understand the role and impact of gender in gangs requires going beyond investigating young women's participation in these groups. Gender is a relational concept; it is not simply about women and girls, but also about men and boys, relations within and between these groups, normative expectations for the behaviors of girls/women and boys/men (often referred to as femininities and masculinities), and symbolism about gender (including stereotyping). Gender is a sociological concept, which means gender is also implicated in patterns of social organization and group processes, and as such, it shapes life trajectories and opportunities and is grounded in inequality. Moreover, gender is implicated in the behaviors and experiences of men and boys, and should not simply apply to studies of women and girls.

Several of the chapters in this section were selected precisely because they highlight these key points. For example, Peterson draws important attention to research demonstrating that the gender composition of gangs—the proportion of members that are male

versus female—patterns group members' behaviors. That is, group processes in gangs are shaped by their gendered organizational features, and these have implications for gang youths' behavior, regardless of whether they are girls or boys. Likewise, given the entrenched nature of gender inequality—in society, but also in gangs—scholars have long investigated whether gang membership is liberating for girls or causes further social injury. The answer, it appears, is both. Miller's study of young women's victimization risks in gangs illustrates these tensions well. Finally, Moloney and her colleagues' chapter is one of the few studies of male gang members that explicitly considers gender issues for young men, in this case investigating the role that fatherhood may have on transitions out of gangs and patterns of desistance.[3] Continued research on the roles of gender and gender inequality in gangs is much needed and offers promise for better understanding these groups and the experiences of the young women and young men within them.

Notes

1. While we use the terms "girls" and "young women" here interchangeably, the reader should note that most survey research on gangs suggests that girls tend to join and exit gangs in early adolescence, while boys' gang membership is more likely to occur or extend into mid- or late adolescence (see Esbensen and Carson's chapter in Section II). Qualitative studies, on the other hand, often include those young women whose gang participation has also extended into mid- or late adolescence.

2. That said, the information we do have available suggests that while there has been both continuity and change in young women's gang participation, the overall proportion of gang members who are girls and the nature of girls' gang involvement do not appear to have shifted substantially over the years. Importantly, these findings temper the popular claims of "girls gone wild" and "the new violent female offender" that so often surface in contemporary reports of girls' gang involvement.

3. For a striking comparison, the reader may wish to read these authors' investigation of motherhood among female gang members: "Young Mother (in) the Hood: Gang Girls' Negotiation of New Identities" in *Journal of Youth Studies,* 2011, vol. 14, pp. 1–19.

CHAPTER 20

Girlfriends, Gun-Holders, and Ghetto-Rats? Moving Beyond Narrow Views of Girls in Gangs

Dana Peterson

Popular understandings of female gang involvement sometimes rely on and reinforce gender stereotypes. In this chapter, Peterson provides an assessment of the ways these stereotypes present an inaccurate picture of girls in gangs and presents a detailed overview of the state of our research knowledge on several important topics. These include the prevalence, proportion, and roles of girls in gangs; the extent of their involvement in gang delinquency and violence; the impact of gender inequality in gangs; girls' gang joining and gang leaving; and the consequences of gang involvement for young women. The reader will come away with a thorough grounding in the fundamentals of our knowledge about female participation in gangs.

Introduction

What is the role of girls in gangs? Are girls "real" gang members? As with many questions, it depends upon whom you ask. The director of a multi-agency gang task force in southern New Mexico talked at length with me in 1996 about gangs and gang members in the area, but when I asked him about females' involvement, he replied, "Oh, there aren't any female gang members." His answer surprised me, as a recent survey that our Gang Resistance Education and Training (G.R.E.A.T.) program evaluation team conducted in Las Cruces middle

schools showed that 40% of self-reported gang members in that sample were female (Esbensen and Peterson Lynskey 2001). Law enforcement data over time consistently report that females make up less than 10% of gang members (see, e.g., Curry et al. 1994; National Youth Gang Center 2007). Similarly, several (though certainly not all) male gang members interviewed in Miller and Brunson's (2000) study voiced their opinions that whereas girls hung around the gang, they were not to be considered gang members: "There ain't no girls in our gang. Like the girls we talk to, they'll try to say they from our 'hood, but... they ain't from our gang" (p. 431). Such beliefs evoke early research and journalistic accounts that type-cast young women as either "sex objects or tomboys" with roles limited to the service of gang males: "One important duty . . . is to act as weapons carriers to the boys. . . . The girls also supply alibis. . . . Principally, however, the young ladies . . . suppl(y) the lads with such sex as they require— and (fulfill) duties such as lures and spies" (Bernard 1999, p. 45). Contemporary research with broader foci, however, documents that young females are indeed gang members, and they are not just girlfriends, groupies, gun/drug-holders, ghetto-rats, "guy-like" (i.e., tomboys), or gays (i.e., lesbians). This chapter integrates knowledge from both quantitative and qualitative research, providing an overview of a number of issues regarding female gang involvement captured in these general assertions: first, girls are gang members, and their presence in and contribution to gangs is significant; second, we should be concerned about their gang involvement because of injury not just to society but also (and

Reprinted from: Dana Peterson, "Girlfriends, Gun-Holders, and Ghetto-Rats? Moving Beyond Narrow Views of Girls in Gangs," eds. Shari Miller, Leslie D. Leve, and Patricia K. Kerig, *Delinquent Girls: Contexts, Relationships, and Adaption,* 71–84. Copyright © 2012 by Springer. Reprinted by permission.

perhaps more importantly) to the girls themselves; and third, we can learn a good deal about how to minimize this harm and help girls avoid or desist from gangs by listening to their reasons and risk factors for gang involvement and their reasons and methods for leaving their gangs.

Girls' Presence in Gangs

We now know that girls in gangs are not a "new" phenomenon, but what is the scope of this phenomenon? Self-report surveys of youth provide a different picture than the law enforcement data mentioned above. To illustrate, using recent data from seven diverse cities across the USA in the current national evaluation (or "G.R.E.A.T. II") of the revised G.R.E.A.T. program, we find that about two-fifths (41.4%) of gang members are female. This proportion represents 4.3% of girls (6.2% of boys) in the sample who self-reported being gang members in 2007–2008, when most of the sample was in 7th grade. These numbers are slightly above the percentages from Fall 1995, when the six-city sample in the previous national evaluation (or "G.R.E.A.T. I") of the original G.R.E.A.T. curriculum was of comparable age: females made up 35% of gang members, representing 2% of girls in the total sample. Although these figures suggest that the proportion of females in gangs and proportion of gang members who are female increased over the past decade or so, two caveats are in order: first, different sites and schools were included in the two evaluations, and second, the G.R.E.A.T. II sample is slightly older than the G.R.E.A.T. I sample.

These numbers raise the question, however, of whether girls in gangs are "on the rise," as recent newspaper articles would suggest, for example, "The feral sex: The terrifying rise of violent girl gangs" (Bracchi 2008). The answer is difficult to determine because for much of the last century, there has been inadequate *systematic* information about gangs and gang members in general and even less about gang girls. Although some surveys to estimate prevalence existed (Miller, W. B. 2001; Klein 1995; Curry et al. 1994), it was not until 1996 that the newly established National Youth Gang Center began annual surveys of a representative sample of law enforcement agencies. Despite a lack of consistent historical data, it is worth noting that Klein and Crawford reported in 1967 that 26% of gang members in their LA study were female. We thus have some evidence that not only is females' gang involvement not just a contemporary phenomenon, their presence in gangs is fairly high, 40 years ago as today.

Other self-report studies report estimates similar to the two G.R.E.A.T. evaluations' findings, and greater than those reported in law enforcement-based data. In the Rochester Youth Development Study, for instance, females were just under half of all gang members (Thornberry et al. 2003). These inconsistencies do not mean that one source of information is correct, and others are invalid; they simply offer different parts of the same picture, and there are several valid reasons for the differences in prevalence. First, law enforcement policies and strategies help shape their depiction of gang members as primarily male and older. In a report from their survey of law enforcement agencies that estimated females at just 3.65% of gang members, Curry et al. (1994) note that, "in a number of cities females, as a matter of policy, were never classified as gang members. In other jurisdictions, females were relegated statistically to the status of 'associate' members" (p. 8). Second, law enforcement agents focus upon certain behaviors (i.e., more serious delinquency) and locations (i.e., the streets) that are the purview of males more than females and of older more than younger youths; that is, their statistics reflect what they see (for further discussion, see . . . results of NIBRS data outlining gender differences in arrest characteristics). Third, there is some evidence that females age in and out of gangs earlier than do males, due in part to differential rates of adolescent maturity and to their associations with older gang-involved males, either family members or boyfriends. In the Denver Youth Survey, for example, females made up 46% of gang members at ages 11–15, but just 20–25% at older ages (Esbensen and Huizinga 1993; see also Thornberry et al. 2003). The fact that many self-report samples are young means that the proportion of gang members who are female will be higher in these data than in law enforcement data.

The proportion of gang members that is female also varies by such aspects as location and race/ethnicity. We found in G.R.E.A.T. I, for example, that females made up just one-quarter of gang members in Philadelphia, but over 40% of gang members in Las Cruces, Orlando, Phoenix, Pocatello, ID, and Will County, IL, and nearly 50% of gang members in Torrance, CA (Esbensen and Peterson Lynskey 2001). Disaggregating by race/ethnicity showed that among white and African American youths who were gang members, about 35% were female; among Hispanic and Asian gang members, the proportion of females was higher, at 44% (Esbensen et al. 1999).

These female gang members are not just "associates"; in some research, the proportion of females and males who report being "core" members of their gang is approximately equal (Esbensen et al. 1999; Peterson et al. 2001). This proportion appears to differ, however, by the sex composition of the gang. In all- or majority-female gangs, 67% of females report being core gang members, compared to 57% of girls in sex-balanced gangs and just 39% of girls in majority-male gangs (Peterson et al. 2001). Race/ethnicity may also structure the role of girls in gangs. Although studies with samples that allow such comparisons are rare, the limited evidence suggests that African American females may be more likely than Hispanic/Latina and Asian Pacific American females to both form independent female gangs and to state that females played a role in decision-making aspects of the gang (e.g., Hagedorn and Devitt 1999; Joe-Laidler and Hunt 1997; Miller, J. 2001). There are finer distinctions to be made, though, when it comes to race/ethnic differences. For instance, among Latinas in Hagedorn and Devitt's study, Mexican-American females were more likely than Puerto Ricans to describe females as calling the shots, making decisions about who could join the gang, and having meetings on their own. Such findings suggest that there may be important differences in the culture and experiences of different groups to be appreciated in understanding the presence and roles of girls in gangs. Unfortunately, most gang samples do not allow for such distinctions to be made, but a few important studies described in this chapter provide an excellent starting point and direction for future research.

Girls' Experiences Within and After the Gang

There are several interrelated reasons why we should be concerned with girls' involvement in gangs. First is that girls' involvement in gangs means greater involvement in the commission of delinquency and violence. But, it is not just the societal impact of girls' gang involvement that concerns us; it is also the deleterious effects that gang involvement has on girls themselves. Their experiences within the gang and potential long-term consequences even after leaving the gang highlight the fact that gang membership represents not just an opportunity for escaping or attempting to alleviate various social injuries, but also a mechanism for additional injury.

While comparatively little of gang members' time is spent in law-violating activity (Fleisher 1998; Klein 1995), they do commit more than their fair share of delinquent acts (Esbensen et al. 2010; Esbensen and Huizinga 1993; Thornberry et al. 2003), and girls' contributions are not absent. Although gang girls' levels of property and violent crime are lower than gang boys', they are greater than non-gang girls' and even non-gang boys' delinquency (Deschenes and Esbensen 1999; Esbensen et al. 1999; Esbensen and Huizinga 1993; Miller, J. 2001). For example, Esbensen and Winfree (1998) found that female gang members' property offenses outnumbered non-gang boys' offenses by 2.5 to 1, and for every one violent offense committed by a non-gang male, gang females committed 2.34. For drug use and drug sales, the ratios were even higher, at 3.23 and 5.24, respectively.

Females' criminal involvement differs slightly by the sex composition of their gangs. Girls in majority-male gangs had the highest frequencies of both personal and property offending, followed by girls in sex-balanced gangs, and, lastly, girls in majority- or all-female gangs (Peterson et al. 2001). Comparing girls and boys within gang type, more gender similarity in delinquency frequency was seen in majority-male gangs than in sex-balanced gangs, in which females' offending was significantly lower than males'.

Several explanations for these differences emerge from extant research. In sex-balanced gangs, females appear to be excluded by males from many serious forms of violence that represent status-enhancing activities within the gang (Miller, J. 2001; Miller and Brunson 2000; Peterson et al. 2001). Females' greater numbers may be seen by males as a threat to the perceived male-dominated world of gangs; thus, girls are kept from engaging in activities that confer status in these settings (Bowker et al. 1980; Miller, J. 2001; Miller and Brunson 2000 . . .). Meanwhile, females in majority-male gangs, because of their fewer numbers, are not seen as a threat to male power structure within the gang; rather, they are seen as "one of the guys" and allowed to more fully participate in criminal endeavors (Miller, J. 2001; Miller and Brunson 2000). Girls also may be excluded because they pose an additional "burden" for males during crime commission, as a young man in Miller and Brunson's (2000) study describes: "cause we didn't want nobody to blame us because something happen to them, if something would have happened to them" (p. 436). Finally, it is also the case that girls do not lack agency and sometimes actively use their gender to exclude themselves from certain activities (Miller, J. 2001).

These differences in delinquency between gang girls and boys illustrate a larger dynamic present in gangs that provides particular experiences for gang girls. That is, the gender oppression and sexual double standards present in society often are amplified in the gang context, where masculinities play out and intersect with the female gang experience (Brotherton and Salazar-Atias 2003; Messerschmidt 1999; Miller and Brunson 2000; Joe and Chesney-Lind 1995; Joe-Laidler and Hunt 1997; Portillos 1999). In their struggle to define and command their own identities as individuals and as women, girls find themselves constrained by cultural and societal expectations adhered to not only by males in the gang, but by themselves and other females. To gain and maintain respect, to demonstrate strength and independence, is to negotiate competing aspects of femininity and gang identity, a delicate balance that can lead to violence and victimization. Many girls want to explore feminine aspects of their identity, but must also not appear physically weak or too sexually available or they risk victimization, ridicule, or exclusion.

Because their behavior is under scrutiny by both males and other females, girls may act aggressively to demonstrate "heart" and gain respect; at the same time, however, they are disrespected, viewed as sex objects, and constrained based on their gender (Miller, J. 2001; Miller and Brunson 2000). In addition, despite joining gangs for protection, many girls find themselves to be victims of exploitation or violence, often sexual, at the hands of fellow gang members (Fishman 1999; Fleisher 1998; Hagedorn 1998; Harris 1994; Joe-Laidler and Hunt 1997; Miller, J. 2001; Moore 1991).

Finally, girls' gang involvement has potential long-term consequences, even after they leave gang life. In one of few studies able to examine the issue, Thornberry et al. (2003) report that gang membership significantly increased girls' odds of early pregnancy, teen motherhood, unstable employment, and adult arrests, as well as their number of off-time transitions. Such consequences are also described in qualitative research (Hagedorn 1998; Moore 1991). In an unfortunate contrast to their lofty career and family aspirations, ex-gang females in Milwaukee were likely to have dropped out of school, to be on welfare, to be overwhelmed with the burdens of motherhood, and to have turned to drug use to cope (Hagedorn 1998). Further, Latinas' outcomes were worse than those of African American former gang members, perhaps due to cultural values about women's roles (Hagedorn and Devitt 1999; Moore and Hagedorn 1996). In contrast, former female gang members in Nurge's (2003) Boston study did not appear to suffer long-term consequences from their gang involvement. They were all either employed or in school, and overall they were "happy, healthy, and well-adjusted" (p. 177), although several spoke of members who had died, were incarcerated, drug-addicted, or prostituting. Without non-gang comparison samples, however, it is unknown how well these former gang members were doing compared to non-gang females, a strength of Thornberry et al.'s (2003) study.

These findings highlight the paradox inherent in the "liberation" vs. "social injury" debate about girls' gang involvement. Rather than one or the other, girls find both in gangs, and there is a complex interplay, balance, and payoff between the two

(Campbell 1987; Chesney-Lind et al. 1996; Curry 1998; Miller, J. 2001; Nurge 2003; Peterson et al. 2001). Given these potentially deleterious effects, in and after the gang, it is important to examine ways in which we can prevent or intervene with girls' gang involvement. Research on joining and leaving the gang provides us with insight into why girls "choose" gang life and why and how they exit, giving us guidance to better assist or support them.

Girls' Gang Joining and Leaving

Sex Differences in Risk Factors for Gang Joining

Although there is growing understanding of risk factors for gang membership, our knowledge is limited as to whether risk factors for girls' gang involvement differ from boys', as not much youth gang research has systematically compared females and males. Further, as Klein and Maxson (2006) point out, the studies that do exist do not examine the same factors or use the same methods, so we cannot adequately compare findings or identify risk factors for gang membership that are consistently supported across studies. In addition, much of the scant research relies on cross-sectional data, inhibiting our ability to draw confident conclusions about causation over correlation.

Across 20 studies, Klein and Maxson (2006) identified six factors that were consistently or mostly supported as risk factors for gang membership: lack of parental supervision, negative life events (e.g., serious illness, school suspension, and intimate relationship disruption), early problem behaviors (e.g., reactivity, aggression, and impulsivity), antisocial beliefs, delinquent peers, and commitment to deviant peers. Different findings emerge from the very few quantitative studies comparing girls and boys on some or all of these six factors. Evidence is mixed as to whether parental monitoring is a risk factor for both sexes; in one study, monitoring decreased odds of gang joining for boys but not girls (Thornberry et al. 2003); in another, lack of monitoring predicted gang membership for both sexes (Esbensen and Deschenes 1998), while in others, it was not associated with gang membership for either sex (Esbensen et al.

2010; Maxson and Whitlock 2002). Negative life events and delinquent peers were associated with males' but not females' gang joining (Maxson and Whitlock 2002; Esbensen et al. 2010; Thornberry et al. 2003), and the other three factors have been found to predict both sexes' gang involvement (Esbensen and Deschenes 1998; Maxson and Whitlock 2002; Esbensen et al. 2010; Thornberry et al. 2003).

Although these studies found some shared risk factors, most also found factors unique to females. Factors that predicted girls' but not boys' gang involvement included being Hispanic (Bell 2009; Esbensen et al. 2010), having risk-seeking tendencies and few pro-social friends (Esbensen and Deschenes 1998), low commitment to school (Esbensen and Deschenes 1998; Esbensen et al. 2010), and neighborhood disorganization (Thornberry et al. 2003). Reducing likelihood of gang involvement for girls but not boys were involvement in community sports, receiving an award at school, being attached to a teacher (Maxson and Whitlock 2002), and college aspirations and expectations (Thornberry et al. 2003). These few studies do not include the same measures, so we cannot determine whether these patterns are consistently supported in the research. In addition, some of them report bivariate results (e.g., the increase in odds of gang membership associated with the presence of a risk factor; Maxson and Whitlock 2002; Thornberry et al. 2003), while others report multivariate results (i.e., odds of gang joining associated with a risk factor while holding other factors constant; Bell 2009; Esbensen and Deschenes 1998; Esbensen et al. 2010; Maxson and Whitlock 2002). Further complicating our ability to draw solid conclusions is that some studies are longitudinal (Thornberry et al. 2003), whereas others are cross-sectional (Bell 2009; Esbensen and Deschenes 1998; Esbensen et al. 2010; Maxson and Whitlock 2002). Keeping these limitations in mind, three tentative conclusions can be drawn from the research to date comparing females and males: (1) many risk factors appear to be shared by girls and boys, (2) we have as yet identified fewer factors associated with gang involvement for females than for males, and (3) there are factors unique to each gender, with a potential pattern of school factors being more influential for girls than for boys.

Admittedly, however, we are probably omitting in these quantitative studies important factors that may be specific to girls. Qualitative research, for example, identifies abuse, domestic violence, sexual assault, and parental criminality, substance use, and mental health issues as important influences in lives of girls who join gangs (e.g., Fleisher 1998; Miller, J. 2001). Because such factors are not often tapped in self-report surveys conducted in school settings and because much qualitative research lacks comparative samples, it is unclear whether these factors are unique to girls or are influential for boys' gang involvement as well.

What Reasons Do Girls Give?

How do the girls themselves explain their reasons for gang joining, and what can we draw from their descriptions of the contexts in which they live? Both quantitative and qualitative research demonstrate that there is no one reason why girls join gangs—not all girls join for the same reasons, and there is generally not just one reason an individual girl becomes gang-involved. No matter how varied the experiences that bring girls to the gang, however, there are patterns that can be ascertained.

Data from three separate samples from the two G.R.E.A.T. evaluations reveal that the top four reasons for gang joining consistently mentioned by both girls and boys are as follows: for fun, for protection, because a friend was in the gang, and to get respect (Esbensen and Peterson Lynskey 2001; Freng and Winfree 2004; Peterson et al. 2004; Peterson 2009). These reasons suggest a promise of benefits youth expect to gain from their gang involvement, and they are supported in other quantitative studies of youth. Some studies show that certain reasons may be more important for girls than for boys and vice versa. For example, Maxson and Whitlock's (2002) study of a high-risk sample in San Diego indicated that girls joined because of family (73%) or friend (62%) involvement and/or to get a reputation (58%), whereas boys joined for excitement (78%), territory or protection (71%), and belonging (61%).

Qualitative studies provide additional insight into girls' reasons for joining a gang, illuminating what might lie behind their responses to quantitative measures such as joining "for fun" or "for protection." Gang members in Joe and Chesney-Lind's (1995) study, for instance, described their neighborhoods as devoid of resources and activities, and thus the gang provided an important "social outlet," combating boredom and frustration. Miller, J. (2001) and Fleisher (1998) relayed experiences of girls whose family life of violence and discord left them to fend for themselves; in those situations, girls found the gang environment to be preferable, providing a safe haven, a mechanism for coping, an opportunity for empowerment, and a means of economic survival, both licit and illicit (Brotherton and Salazar-Atias 2003). In numerous studies, a large proportion of gang girls had histories of physical and/or sexual abuse or assault and running away from home (Fleisher 1998; Harris 1994; Joe and Chesney-Lind 1995; Miller, J. 2001; Moore 1991; Nurge 2003; Portillos 1999). The gang also provided a surrogate or alternate family; many girls describe both having family members who were gang members and/or feeling as though the gang were a substitute family for the biological families that were failing them (see Brotherton and Salazar-Atias 2003; Joe and Chesney-Lind 1995; Miller, J. 2001; Nurge 2003).

Girls also describe their gang joining in terms of finding respect and identity during an already-tumultuous adolescent period and pushing back against societally prescribed roles and stereotypes. For many girls, it is their own culture's roles against which they are rebelling. Girls of Mexican, Puerto Rican, and Dominican heritage, for example, describe their gang membership as a means of casting off or distancing themselves from various aspects of their culture while simultaneously creating new identities that may incorporate some but not other aspects of their culture (Brotherton and Salazar-Atias 2003; Campbell 1987; Harris 1994; Moore 1991; Portillos 1999). Through their gang membership, they may reject such values as passivity and subordinance to males, even extolling the pleasures of fighting, but maintain acceptance of the ideals of being a good mother (Campbell 1987).

Jody Miller's (2001) qualitative research provides an important contrast between gang and non-gang girls, demonstrating that the life experiences of girls who join gangs are consistently more negative than those of girls who avoid gang life. Gang girls were more likely to be exposed to gangs in their neighborhoods and families and to have more problem-prone families with parental substance use, domestic violence, physical and sexual abuse. Although gender comparisons are rare, there is also some evidence that gang girls come from more troubled backgrounds and families than do gang boys. Joan Moore's (1991) research on two LA Chicano gangs, for example, reveals that females are more likely than males to have experienced familial unemployment, addiction, arrests, gang member siblings, abuse, physical handicap, chronic illness, and/or death.

The body of qualitative work paints a complex picture of limited opportunity for young women as a function of gender, race/ethnicity, class, and culture, coupled with oppression and abuse, all of which push and pull them into gangs. This research also helps to elaborate on the reasons girls give in quantitative studies for joining gangs. Chesney-Lind et al. (1996) write that "their choice of gang membership is heavily shaped by the array of economic, educational, familial, and social conditions and constraints that exist in their families and communities" (p. 204). But it is also true that girls' "choices" to become gang-involved and the perceived "benefits" of gang membership must be viewed in terms of the structural constraints that make the gang appear to girls a "viable option" (see Brotherton and Salazar-Atias 2003).

Leaving the Gang

Whereas the gang serves a variety of functions for girls at particular points in their lives, for most girls, this involvement is a temporary "way station" of sorts (Brotherton and Salazar-Atias 2003, p. 195; see too Campbell 1984; Hagedorn 1998; Nurge 2003). Many girls have mixed thoughts and feelings about their gang membership, appreciating the benefits they received, but also lamenting the costs (Campbell 1984; Miller, J. 2001; Nurge 2003). Nurge (2003) writes that "the gang was able to meet

these young women's immediate needs, but was not a long-term solution to their problems" (p. 172). We know from extant research that gang membership is not necessarily "forever." Although there are individuals, especially males, who maintain their involvement for extended periods or for life (see e.g., Decker and Van Winkle 1996; Hagedorn 1998; Moore 1991), there are also many for whom gang membership is a transitory status. In G.R.E.A.T. I, for example, we found that 69% of adolescent gang members (77% of girls and 67% of boys) were members for 1 year or less; 22% (18% of girls and 25% of boys) were members for two consecutive years; only 7% (all boys) were gang-involved for more than 2 years; and just one respondent, a female, reported membership in all 5 years of the study (Peterson et al. 2003; 2004). Similar figures are reported by Thornberry et al. (2003).

A few studies provide insight into the why and how of leaving gangs, although the research here is more limited than that on gang joining. According to ex-gang members in St. Louis, for example, violence was an important push to leave the gang, with two-thirds stating that threats of or actual violence to themselves or family were the key reason to make the move out of the gang (Decker and Lauritsen 1996). Others left their gangs because they had moved or due to family reasons. Importantly, all of the gang members in Decker and Lauritsen's study were males; females may have different reasons for exiting the gang. One reason commonly espoused is motherhood (Fleisher and Krienert 2004); it is thought that many young women do not want their children involved in the gang lifestyle, and that having a child can provide a "pass" out of the gang. The extent to which this reason is common, however, is in question (e.g., Campbell 1987; Fishman 1999; Hagedorn and Devitt 1999; Varriale 2008). Research by Hagedorn and Devitt (1999) indicates that just 16% of females in their Milwaukee study left their gangs due to motherhood. More often (44%), they "just stopped," and a third indicated that their families had moved to get them away from the gang.

Quicker (1999) classifies Chicana gang members' exits as either "active" or "passive." Active departures, initiated either by the gang or the individual member, include violent beat-outs, while passive departures, the more frequent occurrence, are non-ceremonial and are developmental or result from status changes. That is, departures may occur over time as girls age and desist from interaction with the gang; or when a change such as marriage, the arrival of a child, or job perpetuates lessened interaction. Researchers such as Harris (1994) also document these processes, describing how some gang girls undergo specific exit rituals, such as being beaten or "jumped" out (i.e., fighting other members of the gang, just as in initiation), while others just back out of the gang, distancing themselves from gang activities.

In G.R.E.A.T. II, three questions allowed us to add to the scant literature on youths' desistance from the gang. First, former gang members were asked to identify, from a list of reasons, why they left their gangs. The most common reason given by both females (37%) and males (33%) was that they "just felt like it." The role of violence found in prior research is also evident: nearly one-third (30%) left because a friend was hurt or killed. Almost a quarter of girls said they had made new friends, and a similar proportion (22%) left because being in a gang "wasn't what I thought it was going to be." For one in five girls, an adult encouraged them to get out of the gang. Importantly, there were no statistically significant gender differences in reasons for leaving the gang. A second question allowed us to explore common myths about how youths leave gangs. Consistent with some prior research and in contrast to commonly held notions of "blood in, blood out," most (45% of girls and 44% boys) responded they "just left." Being "jumped/beaten out" was not absent in their responses, but it was a distant second (18% of girls and 21% of boys). No girls (and just 5% of boys) reported having to commit a crime to get out of their gangs. Again, no differences were found between girls and boys in the ways in which they left their gangs. Finally, respondents were asked if there were any consequences that resulted from leaving the gang. Interestingly, most former gang members of both sexes (56% of girls and 54% of boys) reported no consequences from leaving their gangs. Of those girls who did report consequences, the most common was that they had lost their gang friends (35%), a salient finding

given the social reasons many girls have for joining their gangs. One-quarter also indicated they had been beaten up by members of their former gangs, that a friend was hurt or killed, and/or that their family or friends were threatened, highlighting the potential for violent experiences even after they have left the gang to avoid them.

There are at least three key points to be taken from these collective findings. First, girls do leave gangs. Second, many just leave, without fanfare or consequences. They decide they do not want to be involved, they drift away, they make new friends. This departure does not mean, though, that we should just let nature take its course because, third, we know that gang life can pose additional risk for young women, and if we can use knowledge about desistance to encourage youths to choose alternatives, we can hope to avert or alleviate some of these risks.

Gang Girls Provide Guidance for the Future

Interest in females' gang involvement is intensifying, but research is not keeping pace. We now know much about the scope and nature of girls' gang involvement, enough to combat the images of girls as appendages of gang males, as girlfriends, gun-holders, and ghetto-rats (and other "g"-words mentioned previously). There is, however, the need to better understand whether girls' risk factors and reasons for gang joining are similar or different than boys'; how gender dynamics in the gang structure girls' experiences; what longer-term effects the gang experience has; why and how they leave their gangs; how all of these differ by race/ethnicity; and how we can use this information to prevent and intervene effectively. For the latter, we can take some guidance from extant research and what girls have told us about why they join and leave.

Quantitative research consistently identifies several overlapping reasons by both genders for their gang joining: for fun, for protection, because a friend or family member was in the gang, and to get respect—needs and desires sought by many, if not most, people in our lives. Qualitative data allow us to further understand these findings by providing rich and detailed illustrations of girls' experiences not tapped in surveys or structured interviews. From all of this is demonstrated what we already know, or should know, as it has been argued by scholars many times over: To prevent girls from joining gangs, we need, at the very least, to protect girls from physical and sexual abuse, sexual double standards, exploitation, and assault; break the cycle of familial gang involvement; provide affordable, available pro-social activities that are structured and supervised; encourage and support girls to make healthy choices about peers and activities; support girls in school and make available meaningful work; and provide opportunities for empowerment, growth, and explorations of identity. There are obvious structural conditions (sexism, racism, classism; educational, economic, social, and political barriers or constraints) that produce environments for young women that make the gang an "attractive option." Short of changing these conditions, the least we can do is better equip girls to negotiate these conditions and barriers in order to achieve healthier results. And, when we fail to protect girls from negative life events, we should work to ameliorate the effects of those events. In terms of prevention programming, given the apparent similarities in girls' and boys' reasons and risk factors for gang joining (though more research on this is needed), general programs targeted at both sexes may suffice. But, there is also cause to recommend gender-specific elements to address issues that may be more influential for females, such as sexual abuse, troubled families, and school-related factors.

We can take hope from the fact that girls do leave gangs. In large part, this may be due to natural processes of development and change, but this does not mean we should not do anything to try to speed the desistance process. Anything we can do to assist girls to leave their gangs can help reduce the gang's harmful consequences, such as crime commission, victimization, and long-term effects of membership on girls' lives, disadvantages that may accumulate the longer their membership. Girls' responses reveal possible intervention points, as they do not always find the benefits they hoped to gain. We can facilitate association with alternative peer groups and activities; some girls join gangs to find friendship, belonging, and fun, and they leave by making other friends or finding other activities to fill their time. We can ensure that girls have supportive adults engaged in their lives who will encourage them to choose these other options and ensure those options are available. We can continue to combat the "gang lore" perpetuating the ideas that the gang is a safe haven and that one cannot leave without serious consequences to self, family, or friends. Despite joining for protection, girls are victimized in gangs, and violence is a key motivating factor out of the gang. If we can intervene when violent incidents occur, we can reduce potential for retaliatory violence, as well as seize an opportunity to provide exit from the gang (Decker and Lauritsen 1996). Ceasefire Chicago (2009), for example, utilizes a Hospital Response team that visits hospital emergency rooms to speak with victims of violence and to refer them to services (education and job placement, in addition to support services).

We need also to remember, though, that leaving (as well as joining) the gang is a process (Vigil 1988), just like the process of change in any peer group. That is, gang members may not just suddenly quit (or join) their gangs; rather, their decision to leave is solidified over time and experiences, both within and outside of the gang. Further, clear distinctions cannot always be made between "gang members" and "ex-gang members" (Decker and Lauritsen 1996). Even after relinquishing their gang member status, girls may still associate with members of the gang; these are their neighbors, friends, and family members, after all.

Acknowledgments

Some of the research reported in this chapter was supported by two grants from the National Institute of Justice, Office of Justice Programs, US Department of Justice: Award #94-IJ-CX-0058 and Award #2006-JV-FX-0011. The research conducted under the latter grant was made possible, in part, by the support and participation of seven school districts, including the School District of Philadelphia. The opinions, findings, and conclusions or recommendations expressed in this manuscript are those of the author and do not necessarily reflect the views of the Department of Justice or of the seven participating school districts.

References

Bell, K. E. (2009). Gender and gangs: A quantitative analysis. *Crime & Delinquency, 55*(3), 363–387.

Bernard, W. (1999). Jailbait: The story of juvenile delinquency. In M. Chesney-Lind & J. M. Hagedorn (Eds.), *Female gangs in America: Essays on girls, gangs, and gender* (pp. 45–47). Chicago, IL: Lakeview Press.

Bowker, L. H., Gross, H. S., & Klein, M. W. (1980). Female participation in delinquent gang activities. *Adolescence, 15,* 509–519.

Bracchi, P. (2008, May 16). The feral sex: The terrifying rise of violent girl gangs. *The Daily Mail.* Retrieved June 10, 2008 from http://www.dailymail.co.uk/news/article-566919/The-Feral-Sex-The-terrifying-rise-violent-girl-gangs.html.

Brotherton, D., & Salazar-Atias, C. (2003). Amor de Reina! The pushes and pulls of group membership among the Latin Queens. In L. Kontos, D. Brotherton, & L. Barrios (Eds.), *Gangs and society: Alternative perspectives* (pp. 183–209). New York: Columbia University Press.

Campbell, A. (1984). *The girls in the gang.* Cambridge, MA: Basil Blackwood.

Campbell, A. (1987). Self-definition by rejection. *Social Problems, 34*(5), 451–466.

Ceasefire Chicago. (2009). *Hospital emergency room responses.* Retrieved July 17, 2009 from http://www.ceasefirechicago.org/ER_response.shtml.

Chesney-Lind, M., Shelden, R. G., & Joe, K. A. (1996). Girls, delinquency, and gang membership. In C. R. Huff (Ed.), *Gangs in America* (2nd ed., pp. 185–204). Thousand Oaks, CA: Sage.

Curry, G. D. (1998). Female gang involvement. *Journal of Research in Crime and Delinquency, 35,* 100–118.

Curry, G. D., Ball, R. A., & Fox, R. J. (1994). *Gang crime and law enforcement record keeping. Research in brief.* Washington, DC: Department of Justice.

Decker, S. H., & Lauritsen, J. L. (1996). Breaking the bonds of membership: Leaving the gang. In C. R. Huff (Ed.), *Gangs in America* (2nd ed., pp. 103–122). Thousand Oaks, CA: Sage Publications.

Decker, S. H., & Van Winkle, B. (1996). *Life in the gang: Family, friends, and violence.* New York: Cambridge University Press.

Deschenes, E. P., & Esbensen, F.-A. (1999). Violence and gangs: Gender differences in perceptions and behavior. *Journal of Quantitative Criminology, 15,* 63–96.

Esbensen, F.-A., & Deschenes, E. P. (1998). A multisite examination of youth gang membership: Does gender matter? *Criminology, 36,* 799–828.

Esbensen, F.-A., Deschenes, E. P., & Winfree, L. T., Jr. (1999). Differences between gang girls and gang boys: Results from a multisite study. *Youth & Society, 31*(1), 27–53.

Esbensen, F.-A., & Huizinga, D. (1993). Gangs, drugs, and delinquency in a survey of urban youth. *Criminology, 31,* 565–589.

Esbensen, F.-A., & Peterson Lynskey, D. (2001). Young gang members in a school survey. In M. W. Klein, H.-J. Kerner, C. L. Maxson, & E. G. M. Weitekamp (Eds.), *The Eurogang paradox: Street gangs and youth groups in the U.S. and Europe* (pp. 93–114). Amsterdam: Kluwer.

Esbensen, F.-A., Peterson, D., Taylor, T. J., & Freng, A. (2010). *Youth violence: Sex and race differences in offending, victimization, and gang membership.* Philadelphia, PA: Temple University Press.

Esbensen, F.-A., & Winfree, L. T., Jr. (1998). Race and gender differences between gang and nongang youths: Results from a multisite survey. *Justice Quarterly, 15*(3), 505–526.

Fishman, L. T. (1999). Black female gang behavior: An historical and ethnographic perspective. In M. Chesney-Lind & J. M. Hagedorn (Eds.), *Female gangs in America: Essays on girls, gangs, and gender* (pp. 64–84). Chicago, IL: Lakeview Press.

Fleisher, M. (1998). *Dead end kids: Gang girls and the boys they know.* Madison, WI: University of Wisconsin Press.

Fleisher, M. S., & Krienert, J. L. (2004). Life course events, social networks, and the emergence of violence among female gang members. *Journal of Community Psychology, 32*(5), 607–622.

Freng, A., & Winfree, L. T., Jr. (2004). Exploring race and ethnic differences in a sample of middle school gang members. In F.-A. Esbensen, S. G. Tibbetts, & L. K. Gaines (Eds.), *American youth gangs at the millennium* (pp. 142–162). Long Grove, IL: Waveland Press.

Hagedorn, J. M. (1998). *People and folks: Gangs, crime, and the underclass in a rustbelt city* (2nd ed.). Chicago, IL: Lakeview Press.

Hagedorn, J. M., & Devitt, M. L. (1999). Fighting female: The social construction of female gangs. In M. Chesney-Lind & J. M. Hagedorn (Eds.), *Female gangs in America: Essays on girls, gangs, and gender* (pp. 256–276). Chicago, IL: Lake View Press.

Harris, M. G. (1994). Cholas, Mexican-American girls, and gangs. *Sex Roles, 30*(3/4), 289–301.

Joe, K. A., & Chesney-Lind, M. (1995). Just every mother's angel: An analysis of gender and ethnic variations in youth gang membership. *Gender & Society, 9,* 408–430.

Joe-Laidler, K., & Hunt, G. P. (1997). Violence and social organization in female gangs. *Social Justice, 24*(4), 148–169.

Klein, M. W. (1995). *The American street gang. Its nature, prevalence, and control.* New York, NY: Oxford University Press.

Klein, M. W., & Crawford. L. Y. (1967). Groups, gangs, and cohesiveness. *Journal of Research in Crime and Delinquency, 4,* 63–75.

Klein, M. W., & Maxson, C. L. (2006). *Street gang patterns and policies.* New York, NY: Oxford University Press.

Maxson, C. L., & Whitlock, M. L. (2002). Joining the gang: Gender differences in risk factors for gang membership. In C. R. Huff (Ed.), *Gangs in America* (3rd ed., pp. 19–36). Thousand Oaks, CA: Sage Publications.

Messerschmidt, J. (1999). From patriarchy to gender: Feminist theory, criminology, and the challenge of diversity. In M. Chesney-Lind & J. M. Hagedorn (Eds.), *Female gangs in America: Essays on girls, gangs, and gender* (pp. 118–132). Chicago, IL: Lake View Press.

Miller, J. (2001). *One of the guys: Girls, gangs and gender.* New York: Oxford University Press.

Miller, J., & Brunson, R. K. (2000). Gender dynamics in youth gangs: A comparison of males' and females' accounts. *Justice Quarterly, 17,* 419–448.

Miller, W. B. (2001). *The growth of youth gang problems in the United States: 1970-98.* Washington, DC: Office of Juvenile Justice and Delinquency Prevention.

Moore, J. (1991). *Going down to the barrio: Homeboys and homegirls in change.* Philadelphia, PA: Temple University Press.

Moore, J. W., & Hagedorn, J. M. (1996). What happens to girls in the gang? In C. R. Huff (Ed.), *Gangs in America* (2nd ed., pp. 205–220). Thousand Oaks, CA: Sage.

National Youth Gang Center (2007). *National Youth Gang Survey analysis.* Retrieved May 17, 2008 from http://www.iir.com/nygc/nygsa/.

Nurge. D. (2003). Liberating yet limiting: The paradox of female gang membership. In L. Kontos, D. Brotherton, & L. Barrios (Eds.), *Gangs and society: Alternative perspectives* (pp. 161–182). New York: Columbia University Press.

Peterson, D. (2009). The many ways of knowing: Multi-method comparative research to enhance our understanding of and responses to youth street gangs. In M. D. Krohn, A. J. Lizotte, & G. Penly Hall (Eds.), *Handbook on crime and deviance* (pp. 405–432). New York: Springer Science and Business Media.

Peterson, D., Miller, J., & Esbensen, F.-A. (2001). The impact of sex composition on gangs and gang member delinquency. *Criminology, 39*(2), 411–440.

Peterson, D., Taylor, T. J., & Esbensen, F.-A. (2003). *Gang girls, gang boys, and the victimization dimension.* Paper presented at the Annual Meeting of the Academy of Criminal Justice Sciences, Boston, MA.

Peterson, D., Taylor, T. J., & Esbensen, F.-A. (2004). Gang membership and violent victimization. *Justice Quarterly, 21*(4), 793–815.

Portillos, E. L. (1999). Women, men, and gangs: The social construction of gender in the barrio. In M. Chesney-Lind & J. M. Hagedorn (Eds.), *Female gangs in America: Essays on girls, gangs, and gender* (pp. 232–247). Chicago: Lakeview Press.

Quicker, J. C. (1999). The Chicana gang: A preliminary description. In M. Chesney-Lind & J. M. Hagedorn (Eds.), *Female gangs in America: Essays on girls, gangs, and gender* (pp. 48–56). Chicago, IL: Lake View Press.

Thornberry, T. P., Krohn, M. D., Lizotte, A. J., Smith, C. A., & Tobin, K. (2003). *Gangs and delinquency in developmental perspective.* New York: Cambridge University Press.

Varriale, J. A. (2008). Female gang members and desistance: Pregnancy as a possible exit strategy? *Journal of Gang Research, 15*(4), 35–64.

Vigil, J. D. (1988). *Barrio gangs: Street life and identity in Southern California.* Austin, TX: University of Texas Press.

CHAPTER 21

Gender and Victimization Risk among Young Women in Gangs

Jody Miller

Research has shown a strong relationship between participation in delinquency and victimization risk, with Taylor's chapter in Section VII revealing that gang membership also has important links to risks for victimization. Miller's chapter extends this line of inquiry by investigating how the relationships among delinquency, gang participation, and victimization are shaped by gender. Exploring the experiences of gang girls, she finds that by limiting their involvement in gang-related crime, girls can decrease risks for victimization by rival group members. However, they sometimes face considerable risks within their gangs of both physical and sexual mistreatment. This chapter demonstrates the importance of investigating the role of gender inequality in shaping group processes in gangs.

An underdeveloped area in the gang literature is the relationship between gang participation and victimization risk. There are notable reasons to consider the issue significant. We now have strong evidence that delinquent lifestyles are associated with increased risk of victimization (Lauritsen, Sampson, and Laub 1991). Gangs are social groups that are organized around delinquency (see Klein 1995), and participation in gangs has been shown to escalate youths' involvement in crime, including violent crime (Esbensen and Huizinga 1993; Esbensen, Huizinga, and Weiher 1993; Fagan 1989, 1990; Thornberry et al., 1993). Moreover, research

Reprinted from: Jody Miller, "Gender and Victimization Risk among Young Women in Gangs," *Journal of Research in Crime and Delinquency*, 35: 429–453. Copyright © 1998 by Sage Publications, Inc. Reprinted by permission.

on gang violence indicates that the primary targets of this violence are other gang members (Block and Block 1993; Decker 1996; Klein and Maxson 1989; Sanders 1993). As such, gang participation can be recognized as a delinquent lifestyle that is likely to involve high risks of victimization (see Huff 1996:97). Although research on female gang involvement has expanded in recent years and includes the examination of issues such as violence and victimization, the oversight regarding the relationship between gang participation and violent victimization extends to this work as well. . . .

Based on in-depth interviews with female gang members, this article examines the ways in which gender shapes victimization risk within street gangs.

Gender, Violence, and Victimization

Feminist scholars have played a significant role in bringing attention to the overlapping nature of women's criminal offending and patterns of victimization, emphasizing the relationships of gender inequality and sexual exploitation to women's participation in crime (Arnold 1990; Campbell 1984; Chesney-Lind and Rodriguez 1983; Daly 1992; Gilfus 1992). In regard to female gang involvement, recent research suggests that young women in gangs have disproportionate histories of victimization before gang involvement as compared with nongang females (Miller 1996) and gang males (Joe and Chesney-Lind 1995; Moore 1991). Moreover, there is evidence that young women turn to gangs, in part, as a means of protecting themselves from violence and other problems in their families and from mistreatment at the hands of men in their lives (Joe and Chesney-Lind 1995; Lauderback et al., 1992).

This is not surprising, given the social contexts these young women face. Many young women in gangs are living in impoverished urban "underclass" communities where violence is both extensive and a "sanctioned response to [the] oppressive material conditions" associated with inequality, segregation, and isolation (Simpson 1991:129; see also Sampson and Wilson 1995; Wilson 1996). Moreover, violence against women is heightened by the nature of the urban street world, where gendered power relations are played out (Connell 1987), crack markets have intensified the degradation of women (Bourgois and Dunlap 1993; Maher and Curtis 1992), and structural changes may have increased cultural support for violence against women (Wilson 1996).

The social world of adolescence is highly gendered as well (Eder 1995; Lees 1993; Thorne 1993). It is a period in which peer relationships increase in significance for youths, and this is magnified, especially for girls, with increased self-consciousness and sensitivity to others' perceptions of them (Pesce and Harding 1986). In addition, it is characterized by a "shift from the relatively asexual gender system of childhood to the overtly sexualized gender systems of adolescence and adulthood" (Thorne 1993:135). Young women find themselves in a contradictory position. Increasingly, they receive status from their peers via their association with, and attractiveness to, young men, but they are denigrated for their sexual activity and threatened with the labels slut and ho (Eder 1995; Lees 1993). The contexts of adolescence and the urban street world, then, have unique features likely to make young women particularly vulnerable to victimization. Thus, for some young women, gang involvement may appear to be a useful means of negotiating within these environments.

However, as Bourgois (1995) notes, actions taken to resist oppression can ultimately result in increased harm. Among young women in gangs, an important question to examine is how participation in gangs itself shapes young women's risk of victimization, including the question of whether gang involvement places girls at higher risks of victimization because of a potential increased involvement in crime. Lauritsen et al. (1991) found that "adolescent involvement in delinquent lifestyles strongly increases the risk of both personal and property victimization" (p. 265). Moreover, gender as a predictor of victimization risk among adolescents decreases when participation in delinquent lifestyles is controlled for (Lauritsen et al., 1991). That is, much of young men's greater victimization risk can be accounted for by their greater participation in offending behaviors. Among gang members, then, involvement in crime is likely associated with increased risk for victimization. Gang girls' participation in crime is thus an important consideration if we hope to understand the relationship between their gang membership and victimization risk.

Girls, Gangs, and Crime

. . . Few would dispute that when it comes to serious delinquency, male gang members are involved more frequently than their female counterparts. However, evidence suggests that young women in gangs are more involved in serious criminal activities than was previously believed and also tend to be more involved than nongang youths—male or female. As such, they likely are exposed to greater victimization risk than nongang youths as well.

In addition, given the social contexts described above, it is reasonable to assume that young women's victimization risk within gangs is also shaped by gender. Gang activities (such as fighting for status and retaliation) create a particular set of factors that increase gang members' victimization risk and repeat victimization risk. Constructions of gender identity may shape these risks in particular ways for girls. For instance, young women's adoption of masculine attributes may provide a means of participating and gaining status within gangs but may also lead to increased risk of victimization as a result of deeper immersion in delinquent activities. On the other hand, experiences of victimization may contribute to girls' denigration and thus increase their risk for repeat victimization through gendered responses and labeling—for example, when sexual victimization leads to perceptions of sexual availability or when victimization leads an individual to be viewed as weak. In addition, femaleness is an individual attribute that has the capacity to mark young women as "safe" crime victims (e.g., easy targets) or, conversely, to deem them "off limits." My goal here is to examine the gendered nature of violence within gangs, with a specific focus on how gender shapes young women's victimization risk.

Methodology

Data presented in this article come from survey and semistructured in-depth interviews with 20 female members of mixed-gender gangs in Columbus, Ohio. The interviewees ranged in age from 12 to 17; just over three-quarters were African American or multiracial (16 of 20), and the rest (4 of 20) were white. The sample was drawn primarily from several local agencies in Columbus working with at-risk youths, including the county juvenile detention center, a shelter care facility for adolescent girls, a day school within the same institution, and a local community agency.[1] The project was structured as a gang/nongang comparison, and I interviewed a total of 46 girls. Gang membership was determined during the survey interview by self-definition: About one-quarter of the way through the 50+ page interview, young women were asked a series of questions about the friends they spent time with. They then were asked whether these friends were gang involved and whether they themselves were gang members. Of the 46 girls interviewed, 21 reported that they were gang members,[2] and an additional 3 reported being gang involved (hanging out primarily with gangs or gang members) but not gang members. The rest reported no gang involvement.

A great deal of recent research suggests that self-report data provide comparatively reliable and valid measures of youths' gang membership (see Bjerregaard and Smith 1993; Fagan 1990; Thornberry et al., 1993; Winfree et al., 1992). This research suggests that using more restrictive measures (such as initiation rituals, a gang name, symbolic systems such as colors or signs) does not change substantive conclusions concerning gang members' behaviors when comparing self-defined

gang members to those members who meet these more restrictive definitions.

Although most researchers agree that the group should be involved in illegal activities in order for the youth to be classified as a gang member (see Esbensen et al., 1993; Esbensen and Huizinga 1993; Fagan 1989), other research that has used self-nomination without specifying crime as a defining feature has nonetheless consistently found serious criminal involvement as a feature that distinguishes gangs from other groups of youths (Fagan 1990; Thornberry et al., 1993; Winfree et al., 1992). All the gang members in my sample were members of groups they described as delinquent.

Cooperation from agency personnel generally proves successful for accessing gang members (see Bowker et al., 1980; Fagan 1989; Short and Strodtbeck 1965). However, these referrals pose the problem of targeting only officially labeled gang youth. I took several steps to temper this problem. First, I did not choose agencies that dealt specifically with gang members, and I did not rely on agency rosters of "known" gang members for my sample. As a result of the gang/nongang comparative research design, I was able to avoid oversampling girls who were labeled as gang members by asking agency personnel to refer me not just to girls believed to be gang involved but also any other girls living in areas in Columbus where they might have contact with gangs. Second, although I was only moderately successful, throughout the project I attempted to expand my sample on the basis of snowball techniques (see Fagan 1989; Hagedorn 1988). I only generated one successful referral outside of the agency contexts. However, I was successful at snowballing within agencies. Several girls I interviewed were gang involved but without staff knowledge, and they were referred to me by other girls I interviewed within the facilities. Thus, in a limited capacity, I was able to interview gang members who had not been detected by officials. Nonetheless, my sample is still limited to youths who have experienced intervention in some capacity, whether formal or informal, and thus it may not be representative of gang-involved girls in the community at large.

The survey interview was a variation of several instruments currently being used in research in a number of cities across the United States and included a broad range of questions and scales measuring factors that may be related to gang membership.[3] On issues related to violence, it included questions about peer activities and delinquency, individual delinquent involvement, family violence and abuse, and victimization. When young women responded affirmatively to being gang members, I followed with a series of questions about the nature of their gang, including its size, leadership, activities, symbols, and so on. Girls who admitted gang involvement during the survey participated in a follow-up interview to talk in more depth about their gangs and gang activities. The goal of the in-depth interview was to gain a greater understanding of the nature and meanings of gang life from the point of view of its female members. A strength of qualitative interviewing is its ability to shed light on this aspect of the social world, highlighting the meanings individuals attribute to their experiences (Adler and Adler 1987; Glassner and Longhlin 1987; Miller and Glassner 1997). In addition, using multiple methods, including follow-up interviews, provided me with a means of detecting inconsistencies in young women's accounts of their experiences. Fortunately, no serious contradictions arose. However, a limitation of the data is that only young women were interviewed. Thus, I make inferences about gender dynamics, and young men's behavior, based only on young women's perspectives.

The in-depth interviews were open-ended and all but one were audiotaped. They were structured around several groupings of questions. We began by discussing girls' entry into their gangs—when and how they became involved, and what other things were going on in their lives at the time. Then we discussed the structure of the gang—its history, size, leadership, and organization, and their place in the group. The next series of questions concerned gender within the gang; for example, how girls get involved, what activities they engage in and whether these are the same as the young men's activities, and what kind of males and females have the most influence in the gang and why. The next series of questions explored gang involvement more generally—what being in the gang means, what kinds of things they do together, and so on. Then, I asked how safe or dangerous they feel gang membership is and how

they deal with risk. I concluded by asking them to speculate about why people their age join gangs, what things they like, what they dislike and have learned by being in the gang, and what they like best about themselves. This basic guideline was followed for each interview subject, although when additional topics arose in the context of the interview we often deviated from the interview guide to pursue them. Throughout the interviews, issues related to violence emerged; these issues form the core of the discussion that follows.

Setting

Columbus is a particular type of gang city. Gangs are a relatively new phenomenon there, with their emergence dated around 1985 (Maxson, Woods, and Klein 1995). In addition, it is thriving economically, experiencing both population and economic growth over the last decade (Rusk 1995). As such, it is representative of a recent pattern of gang proliferation into numerous cities, suburbs, and towns that do not have many of the long-standing problems associated with traditional gang cities, such as deindustrialization, population loss, and the deterioration of social support networks (see Curry et al., 1996; Hagedorn 1988; Klein 1995; Maxson et al., 1995; Spergel and Curry 1993). Even as Columbus has prospered, however, its racial disparities have grown (Columbus Metropolitan Human Services Commission 1995:17). In fact, in relative terms (comparing the gap between African Americans and whites), racial disparities in measures such as income and percentage poverty in Columbus are equal to or even greater than in many cities experiencing economic and population declines.[4]

According to recent police estimates, Columbus has about 30 active gangs, with 400 to 1,000 members (LaLonde 1995). Most of these groups are small in size (20 or fewer members) and are either African American or racially mixed with a majority of African American members (Mayhood and LaLonde 1995). Gangs in Columbus have adopted "big-city" gang names such as Crips, Bloods, and Folks, along with the dress styles, signs, and graffiti of these groups, although gangs are and have been primarily a "homegrown" problem in Columbus rather than a result of organized gang migration

(Huff 1989). Local police view these groups as criminally oriented, but not especially sophisticated. On the whole, gangs in Columbus seem to match those described in other cities with emergent gang problems—best characterized as "relatively autonomous, smaller, independent groups, poorly organized and less territorial" than in older gang cities (Klein 1995:36).

The young women I interviewed described their gangs in ways that are very much in keeping with these findings. All 20 are members of Folks, Crips, or Bloods sets.[5] All but 3 described gangs with fewer than 30 members, and most reported relatively narrow age ranges between members. Half were in gangs with members who were 21 or over, but almost without exception, their gangs were made up primarily of teenagers, with either one adult who was considered the OG ("Original Gangster," leader) or just a handful of young adults. The majority (14 of 20) reported that their gangs did not include members under the age of 13.

Although the gangs these young women were members of were composed of both female and male members, they varied in their gender composition, with the vast majority being predominantly male. Six girls reported that girls were one-fifth or fewer of the members of their gang; 8 were in gangs in which girls were between a quarter and a third of the overall membership; 4 said girls were between 44 and 50 percent of the members; and 1 girl reported that her gang was two-thirds female and one-third male. Overall, girls were typically a minority within these groups numerically, with 11 girls reporting that there were 5 or fewer girls in their set.

This structure—male-dominated, integrated mixed-gender gangs—likely shapes gender dynamics in particular ways. Much past gang research has assumed that female members of gangs are in auxiliary subgroups of male gangs, but there is increasing evidence—including from the young women I spoke with—that many gangs can be characterized as integrated, mixed-gender groups. For example, from interviews with 110 female gang members in three sites (Boston, Seattle, and Pueblo, Colorado), Curry (1997) found integrated mixed-gender gangs to be the predominant gang structure of female gang members, with 57.3 percent of girls

describing their gangs as mixed-gender.[6] It is likely that gang structure shapes both status orientations and criminal involvement among gang members (Brotherton 1996), and that these differences may also be mediated by ethnicity (Brotherton 1996; Joe and Chesney-Lind 1995; Moore and Hagedorn 1996). Generalizability beyond mixed-gender, predominantly African American gangs in emergent gang cities, then is questionable.

Gender, Gangs, and Violence

Gangs as Protection and Risk

An irony of gang involvement is that although many members suggest one thing they get out of the gang is a sense of protection (see also Decker 1996; Joe and Chesney-Lind 1995; Lauderback et al., 1992), gang membership itself means exposure to victimization risk and even a willingness to be victimized. These contradictions are apparent when girls talk about what they get out of the gang, and what being in the gang means in terms of other members' expectations of their behavior. In general, a number of girls suggested that being a gang member is a source of protection around the neighborhood. Erica[7], a 17-year-old African American, explained. "It's like people look at us and that's exactly what they think, there's a gang, and they respect us for that. They won't bother us. . . . It's like you put that intimidation in somebody." Likewise, Lisa, a 14-year-old white girl, described being in the gang as empowering: "You just feel like, oh my God, you know, they got my back. I don't need to worry about it." Given the violence endemic in many inner-city communities, these beliefs are understandable, and to a certain extent, accurate.

In addition, some young women articulated a specifically gendered sense of protection that they felt as a result of being a member of a group that was predominantly male. Gangs operate within larger social milieu that are characterized by gender inequality and sexual exploitation. Being in a gang with young men means at least the semblance of protection from, and retaliation against, predatory men in the social environment. Heather, a 15-year-old white girl, noted, "You feel more secure when, you know, a guy's around protectin' you, you know, than you would a girl." She explained that as a gang member, because "you get protected by guys . . . not as many people mess with you." Other young women concurred and also described that male gang members could retaliate against specific acts of violence against girls in the gang. Nikkie, a 13-year-old African American girl, had a friend who was raped by a rival gang member, and she said, "It was a Crab [Crip] that raped my girl in Miller Ales, and um, they was ready to kill him." Keisha, an African American 14-year-old, explained, "if I got beat up by a guy, all I gotta do is go tell one of the niggers, you know what I'm sayin'? Or one of the guys, they'd take care of it."

At the same time, members recognized that they may be targets of rival gang members and were expected to "be down" for their gang at those times even when it meant being physically hurt. In addition, initiation rites and internal rules were structured in ways that required individuals to submit to, and be exposed to, violence. For example, young women's descriptions of the qualities they valued in members revealed the extent to which exposure to violence was an expected element of gang involvement. Potential members, they explained, should be tough, able to fight and to engage in criminal activities, and also should be loyal to the group and willing to put themselves at risk for it. Erica explained that they didn't want "punks" in her gang: "When you join something like that, you might as well expect that there's gonna be fights. . . . And, if you're a punk, or if you're scared of stuff like that, then don't join." Likewise, the following dialogue with Cathy, a white 16-year-old, reveals similar themes. I asked her what her gang expected out of members and she responded, "to be true to our gang and to have our backs." When I asked her to elaborate, she explained.

> CATHY: Like, uh, if you say you're a Blood, you be a Blood. You wear your rag even when you're by yourself. You know, don't let anybody intimidate you and be like, "Take that rag off." You know, "you better get with our set." Or something like that.
>
> JM: Ok. Anything else that being true to the set means?
>
> CATHY: Um. Yeah. I mean, just, just, you know. I mean it's, you got a whole bunch of people

comin', up in your face and if you're by yourself they ask you what's your claimin', you tell 'em. Don't say nothin.

> JM: Even if it means getting beat up or something?
>
> CATHY: Mmhmm.

One measure of these qualities came through the initiation process, which involved the individual submitting to victimization at the hands of the gang's members. Typically this entailed either taking a fixed number of "blows" to the head and/or chest or being "beaten in" by members for a given duration (e.g., 60 seconds). Heather described the initiation as an important event for determining whether someone would make a good member:

> When you get beat in if you don't fight back and if you just like stop and you start cryin' or somethin' or beggin' 'em to stop and stuff like that, then, they ain't gonna, they'll just stop and they'll say that you're not gang material because you gotta be hard, gotta be able to fight, take punches.

In addition to the initiation, and threats from rival gangs, members were expected to adhere to the gang's internal rules (which included such things as not fighting with one another, being "true" to the gang, respecting the leader, not spreading gang business outside the gang, and not dating members of rival gangs). Breaking the rules was grounds for physical punishment, either in the form of a spontaneous assault or a formal "violation," which involved taking a specified number of blows to the head. For example, Keisha reported that she talked back to the leader of her set and "got slapped pretty hard" for doing so. Likewise, Veronica, an African American 15-year-old described her leader as "crazy, but we gotta listen to 'im. He's just the type that if you don't listen to 'im, he gonna blow your head off. He's just crazy."

It is clear that regardless of members' perceptions of the gang as a form of "protection," being a gang member also involves a willingness to open oneself up to the possibility of victimization. Gang victimization is governed by rules and expectations, however, and thus does not involve the random vulnerability that being out on the streets without a gang might entail in high-crime neighborhoods. Because of its structured nature, this victimization risk may be perceived as more palatable by gang members. For young women in particular, the gendered nature of the streets may make the empowerment available through gang involvement an appealing alternative to the individualized vulnerability they otherwise would face. However, as the next sections highlight, girls' victimization risks continue to be shaped by gender, even within their gangs, because these groups are structured around gender hierarchies as well.

Gender and Status, Crime and Victimization

Status hierarchies within Columbus gangs, like elsewhere, were male dominated (Bowker et al., 1980; Campbell 1990). Again, it is important to highlight that the structure of the gangs these young women belonged to—that is, male-dominated, integrated mixed-gender gangs—likely shaped the particular ways in which gender dynamics played themselves out. Autonomous female gangs, as well as gangs in which girls are in auxiliary subgroups, may be shaped by different gender relations, as well as differences in orientations toward status, and criminal involvement.

All the young women reported having established leaders in their gang, and this leadership was almost exclusively male. While LaShawna, a 17-year-old African American, reported being the leader of her set (which had a membership that is two-thirds girls, many of whom resided in the same residential facility as her), all the other girls in mixed-gender gangs reported that their OG was male. In fact, a number of young women stated explicitly that only male gang members could be leaders. Leadership qualities, and qualities attributed to high-status members of the gangs—being tough, able to fight, and willing to "do dirt" (e.g., commit crime, engage in violence) for the gang—were perceived as characteristically masculine. Keisha noted, "The guys, they just harder." She explained, "Guys is more rougher. We have our G's back but, it ain't gonna be like the guys, they just don't give a fuck. They gonna shoot you in a minute."

For the most part, status in the gang was related to traits such as the willingness to use serious violence and commit dangerous crimes and, though not exclusively, these traits were viewed primarily as qualities more likely and more intensely located among male gang members.

Because these respected traits were characterized specifically as masculine, young women actually may have had greater flexibility in their gang involvement than young men. Young women had fewer expectations placed on them—by both their male and female peers—in regard to involvement in criminal activities such as fighting, using weapons, and committing other crimes. This tended to decrease girls' exposure to victimization risk comparable to male members, because they were able to avoid activities likely to place them in danger. Girls could gain status in the gang by being particularly hard and true to the set. Heather, for example, described the most influential girl in her set as "the hardest girl, the one that don't take no crap, will stand up to anybody." Likewise, Diane, a white 15-year-old, described a highly respected female member in her set as follows:

> People look up to Janeen just 'cause she's so crazy. People just look up to her 'cause she don't care about nothin'. She don't even care about makin' money. Her, her thing is, "Oh, you're a Slob [Blood]? You're a Slob? You talkin' to me? You talkin' shit to me?" Pow, pow! And that's it. That's it.

However, young women also had a second route to status that was less available to young men. This came via their connections—as sisters, girlfriends, cousins—to influential, high-status young men.[8] In Veronica's set, for example, the girl with the most power was the OG's "sister or his cousin, one of 'em." His girlfriend also had status, although Veronica noted that "most of us just look up to our OG." Monica, a 16-year-old African American, and Tamika, a 15-year-old African American, both had older brothers in their gangs, and both reported getting respect, recognition, and protection because of this connection. This route to status and the masculinization of high-status traits functioned to maintain gender inequality within gangs, but they also could put young women at less risk of victimization than young men. This was both because young women were perceived as less threatening and thus were less likely to be targeted by rivals, and because they were not expected to prove themselves in the ways that young men were, thus decreasing their participation in those delinquent activities likely to increase exposure to violence. Thus, gender inequality could have a protective edge for young women.

Young men's perceptions of girls as lesser members typically functioned to keep girls from being targets of serious violence at the hands of rival young men, who instead left routine confrontations with rival female gang members to the girls in their own gang. Diane said that young men in her gang "don't wanna waste their time hittin' on some little girls. They're gonna go get their little cats [females] to go get 'em." Lisa remarked, "girls don't face as much violence as [guys]. They see a girl, they say, 'we'll just smack her and send her on.' They see a guy—'cause guys are like a lot more into it than girls are, I've noticed that—and they like, 'well, we'll shoot him.'" In addition, the girls I interviewed suggested that, in comparison with young men, young women were less likely to resort to serious violence, such as that involving a weapon, when confronting rivals. Thus, when girls' routine confrontations were more likely to be female on female than male on female, girls' risk of serious victimization was lessened further.

Also, because participation in serious and violent crime was defined primarily as a masculine endeavor, young women could use gender as a means of avoiding participation in those aspects of gang life they found risky, threatening, or morally troubling. Of the young women I interviewed, about one-fifth were involved in serious gang violence: A few had been involved in aggravated assaults on rival gang members, and one admitted to having killed a rival gang member, but they were by far the exception. Most girls tended not to be involved in serious gang crime, and some reported that they chose to exclude themselves because they felt ambivalent about this aspect of gang life. Angie, an African American 15-year-old explained,

> I don't get involved like that, be out there goin' and just beat up people like that or go stealin', things like that. That's not me. The boys, mostly the boys do all that, the girls we just sit back and chill, you know.

Likewise, Diane noted,

For maybe a drive-by they might wanna have a bunch of dudes. They might not put the females in that. Maybe the females might be weak inside, not strong enough to do something like that, just on the insides.... If a female wants to go forward and doin' that, and she wants to risk her whole life for doin' that, then she can. But the majority of the time, that job is given to a man.

Diane was not just alluding to the idea that young men were stronger than young women. She also inferred that young women were able to get out of committing serious crime, more so than young men, because a girl shouldn't have to "risk her whole life" for the gang. In accepting that young men were more central members of the gang, young women could more easily participate in gangs without putting themselves in jeopardy—they could engage in the more routine, everyday activities of the gang, like hanging out, listening to music, and smoking bud (marijuana). These male-dominated mixed-gender gangs thus appeared to provide young women with flexibility in their involvement in gang activities. As a result, it is likely that their risk of victimization at the hands of rivals was less than that of young men in gangs who were engaged in greater amounts of crime.

Girls' Devaluation and Victimization

In addition to girls choosing not to participate in serious gang crimes, they also faced exclusion at the hands of young men or the gang as a whole (see also Bowker et al., 1980). In particular, the two types of crime mentioned most frequently as "off-limits" for girls were drug sales and drive-by shootings. LaShawna explained, "We don't really let our females [sell drugs] unless they really wanna and they know how to do it and not to get caught and everything." Veronica described a drive-by that her gang participated in and said, "They wouldn't let us [females] go. But we wanted to go, but they wouldn't let us." Often, the exclusion was couched in terms of protection. When I asked Veronica why the girls couldn't go, she said, "so we won't go to jail if they was to get caught. Or if one of 'em was to get shot, they wouldn't want it to happen to us." Likewise, Sonita, a 13-year-old African American, noted, "If they gonna do somethin' bad and they think one of the females gonna get hurt they don't let 'em do it with them. . . . Like if they involved with shooting or whatever, [girls] can't go."

Although girls' exclusion from some gang crime may be framed as protective (and may reduce their victimization risk vis-à-vis rival gangs), it also served to perpetuate the devaluation of female members as less significant to the gang—not as tough, true, or "down" for the gang as male members. When LaShawna said her gang blocked girls' involvement in serious crime, I pointed out that she was actively involved herself. She explained, "Yeah, I do a lot of stuff 'cause I'm tough. I likes, I likes messin' with boys. I fight boys. Girls ain't nothin' to me." Similarly, Tamika said, "girls, they little peons."

Some young women found the perception of them as weak a frustrating one. Brandi, an African American 13-year-old, explained, "Sometimes I dislike that the boys, sometimes, always gotta take charge and they think sometimes, that the girls don't know how to take charge 'cause we're like girls, we're females, and like that." And Chantell, an African American 14-year-old, noted that rival gang members "think that you're more of a punk." Beliefs that girls were weaker than boys meant that young women had a harder time proving that they were serious about their commitment to the gang. Diane explained,

> A female has to show that she's tough. A guy can just, you can just look at him. But a female, she's gotta show. She's gotta go out and do some dirt. She's gotta go whip some girl's ass, shoot somebody, rob somebody or something. To show that she is tough.

In terms of gender-specific victimization risk, the devaluation of young women suggests several things. It could lead to the mistreatment and victimization of girls by members of their own gang when they didn't have specific male protection (i.e., a brother, boyfriend) in the gang or when they weren't able to stand up for themselves to male members. This was exacerbated by activities that led young women to be viewed as sexually available. In addition, because young women typically were not seen as a threat by young men, when they did pose one, they could be punished even more harshly than young men, not only for having challenged a rival gang or gang member but also for having overstepped "appropriate" gender boundaries.

Monica had status and respect in her gang, both because she had proven herself through fights and criminal activities, and because her older brothers were members of her set. She contrasted her own treatment with that of other young women in the gang:

> They just be puttin' the other girls off. Like Andrea, man. Oh my God, they dog Andrea so bad. They like, "Bitch, go to the store." She like, "All right, I be right back." She will go to the store and go and get them whatever they want and come back with it. If she don't get it right, they be like, "Why you do that bitch." I mean, and one dude even smacked her. And, I mean, and, I don't, I told my brother once, I was like, "Man, it ain't even like that. If you ever see someone tryin' to disrespect me like that or hit me, if you do not hit them or at least say somethin' to them. . . . " So my brothers, they kinda watch out for me.

However, Monica put the responsibility for Andrea's treatment squarely on the young woman: "I put that on her. They ain't gotta do her like that, but she don't gotta let them do her like that either." Andrea was seen as "weak" because she did not stand up to the male members in the gang; thus, her mistreatment was framed as partially deserved because she did not exhibit the valued traits of toughness and willingness to fight that would allow her to defend herself.

An additional but related problem was when the devaluation of young women within gangs was sexual in nature. Girls, but not boys, could be initiated into the gang by being "sexed in"—having sexual relations with multiple male members of the gang. Other members viewed the young women initiated in this way as sexually available and promiscuous, thus increasing their subsequent mistreatment. In addition, the stigma could extend to female members in general, creating a sexual devaluation that all girls had to contend with.

The dynamics of "sexing in" as a form of gang initiation placed young women in a position that increased their risk of ongoing mistreatment at the hands of their gang peers. According to Keisha, "If you get sexed in, you have no respect. That means you gotta go ho' in' for 'em; when they say you give 'em the pussy, you gotta give it to 'em. If you don't, you gonna get your ass beat. I ain't down for that." One girl in her set was sexed in and Keisha said the girl "just do everything they tell her to do, like a dummy." Nikkie reported that two girls who were sexed into her set eventually quit hanging around with the gang because they were harassed so much. In fact, Veronica said the young men in her set purposely tricked girls into believing they were being sexed into the gang and targeted girls they did not like:

> If some girls wanted to get in, if they don't like the girl they have sex with 'em. They run trains on 'em or either have the girl suck their thang. And then they used to, the girls used to think they was in. So, then the girls used to just come try to hang around us and all this little bull, just 'cause, 'cause thinkin' they in.

Young women who were sexed into the gang were viewed as sexually promiscuous, weak, and not "true" members. They were subject to revictimization and mistreatment, and were viewed as deserving of abuse by other members, both male and female. Veronica continued, "They [girls who are sexed in] gotta do whatever, whatever the boys tell 'em to do when they want 'em to do it, right then and there, in front of whoever. And, I think, that's just sick. That's nasty, that's dumb." Keisha concurred, "She brought that on herself, by bein' the fact, bein' sexed in." There was evidence, however, that girls could overcome the stigma of having been sexed in through their subsequent behavior, by challenging members that disrespect them and being willing to fight. Tamika described a girl in her set who was sexed in, and stigmatized as a result, but successfully fought to rebuild her reputation:

> Some people, at first, they call her "little ho" and all that. But then, now she startin' to get bold. . . . Like, like, they be like, "Ooh, look at the little ho. She fucked me and my boy." She be like, "Man, forget y'all. Man, what? What?" She be ready to squat [fight] with 'em. I be like, "Ah, look at her!" Uh huh. . . . At first we looked at her like, "Ooh, man, she a ho, man." But now we look at her like she just our kickin' it partner. You know, however she got in that's her business.

The fact that there was such an option as "sexing in" served to keep girls disempowered, because they

always faced the question of how they got in and of whether they were "true" members. In addition, it contributed to a milieu in which young women's sexuality was seen as exploitable. This may help explain why young women were so harshly judgmental of those girls who were sexed in. Young women who were privy to male gang members' conversations reported that male members routinely disrespect girls in the gang by disparaging them sexually. Monica explained,

> I mean the guys, they have their little comments about 'em [girls in the gang] because, I hear more because my brothers are all up there with the guys and everything and I hear more just sittin' around, just listenin'. And they'll have their little jokes about "Well, ha I had her," and then and everybody else will jump in and say, "Well, I had her, too." And then they'll laugh about it.

In general, because gender constructions defined young women as weaker than young men, young women were often seen as lesser members of the gang. In addition to the mistreatment these perceptions entailed, young women also faced particularly harsh sanctions for crossing gender boundaries—causing harm to rival male members when they had been viewed as nonthreatening. One young woman[9] participated in the assault of a rival female gang member, who had set up a member of the girl's gang. She explained, "The female was supposingly goin' out with one of ours, went back and told a bunch of [rivals] what was goin' on and got the [rivals] to jump my boy. And he ended up in the hospital." The story she told was unique but nonetheless significant for what it indicates about the gendered nature of gang violence and victimization. Several young men in her set saw the girl walking down the street, kidnapped her, then brought her to a member's house. The young woman I interviewed, along with several other girls in her set, viciously beat the girl, then to their surprise the young men took over the beating, ripped off the girl's clothes, brutally gang-raped her, then dumped her in a park. The interviewee noted, "I don't know what happened to her. Maybe she died. Maybe, maybe someone came and helped her. I mean, I don't know." The experience scared the young woman who told me about it. She explained,

I don't never want anythin' like that to happen to me. And I pray to God that it doesn't. 'Cause God said that whatever you sow you're gonna reap. And like, you know, beatin' a girl up and then sittin' there watchin' somethin' like that happen, well, Jesus that could come back on me. I mean, I felt, I really did feel sorry for her even though my boy was in the hospital and was really hurt. I mean, we coulda just shot her. You know, and it coulda been just over. We coulda just taken her life. But they went farther than that.

This young woman described the gang rape she witnessed as "the most brutal thing I've ever seen in my life." While the gang rape itself was an unusual event, it remained a specifically gendered act that could take place precisely because young women were not perceived as equals. Had the victim been an "equal," the attack would have remained a physical one. As the interviewee herself noted, "we coulda just shot her." Instead, the young men who gang-raped the girl were not just enacting revenge on a rival but on a young woman who had dared to treat a young man in this way. The issue is not the question of which is worse—to be shot and killed, or gang-raped and left for dead. Rather, this particular act sheds light on how gender may function to structure victimization risk within gangs.

Discussion

Gender dynamics in mixed-gender gangs are complex and thus may have multiple and contradictory effects on young women's risk of victimization and repeat victimization. My findings suggest that participation in the delinquent lifestyles associated with gangs clearly places young women at risk for victimization. The act of joining a gang involves the initiate's submission to victimization at the hands of her gang peers. In addition, the rules governing gang members' activities place them in situations in which they are vulnerable to assaults that are specifically gang related. Many acts of violence that girls described would not have occurred had they not been in gangs.

It seems, though, that young women in gangs believed they have traded unknown risks for known ones—that victimization at the hands of friends, or at least under specified conditions, was

an alternative preferable to the potential of random, unknown victimization by strangers. Moreover, the gang offered both a semblance of protection from others on the streets, especially young men, and a means of achieving retaliation when victimization did occur.

Lauritsen and Quinet (1995) suggest that both individual-specific heterogeneity (unchanging attributes of individuals that contribute to a propensity for victimization, such as physical size or temperament) and state-dependent factors (factors that can alter individuals' victimization risks over time, such as labeling or behavior changes that are a consequence of victimization) are related to youths' victimization and repeat victimization risk. My findings here suggest that, within gangs, gender can function in both capacities to shape girls' risks of victimization.

Girls' gender, as an individual attribute, can function to lessen their exposure to victimization risk by defining them as inappropriate targets of rival male gang members' assaults. The young women I interviewed repeatedly commented that young men were typically not as violent in their routine confrontations with rival young women as with rival young men. On the other hand, when young women are targets of serious assault, they may face brutality that is particularly harsh and sexual in nature because they are female—thus, particular types of assault, such as rape, are deemed more appropriate when young women are the victims.

Gender can also function as a state-dependent factor, because constructions of gender and the enactment of gender identities are fluid. On the one hand, young women can call upon gender as a means of avoiding exposure to activities they find risky, threatening, or morally troubling. Doing so does not expose them to the sanctions likely faced by male gang members who attempt to avoid participation in violence. Although these choices may insulate young women from the risk of assault at the hands of rival gang members, perceptions of female gang members—and of women in general—as weak may contribute to more routinized victimization at the hands of the male members of their gangs. Moreover, sexual exploitation in the form of "sexing in" as an initiation ritual may define young women as sexually available, contributing to a likelihood of repeat victimization unless the young woman can stand up for herself and fight to gain other members' respect.

Finally, given constructions of gender that define young women as nonthreatening, when young women do pose a threat to male gang members, the sanctions they face may be particularly harsh because they not only have caused harm to rival gang members but also have crossed appropriate gender boundaries in doing so. In sum, my findings suggest that gender may function to insulate young women from some types of physical assault and lessen their exposure to risks from rival gang members, but also to make them vulnerable to particular types of violence, including routine victimization by their male peers, sexual exploitation, and sexual assault.

This article has offered preliminary evidence of how gender may shape victimization risk for female gang members. A great deal more work needs to be done in this area. Specifically, gang scholars need to address more systematically the relationships between gang involvement and victimization risk rather than focusing exclusively on gang members' participation in violence as offenders. My research suggests two questions to be examined further, for both female and male gang members. First, are gang members more likely to be victimized than nongang members living in the same areas? Second, how does victimization risk fluctuate for gang members before, during, and after their gang involvement? Information about these questions will allow us to address whether and how gang involvement has an enhancement effect on youths' victimization, as well as their delinquency.

With the growing interest in masculinities and crime (see Messerschmidt 1993; Newburn and Stanko 1994), an important corollary question to be examined is how masculinities shape victimization risk among male gang members. The young women I interviewed clearly associated serious gang violence with the enactment of masculinity and used gender constructions to avoid involvement in those activities they perceived as threatening. Young men thus may be at greater risk of serious physical assaults, because of their greater involvement in serious gang crime and violence,

and because gender constructions within the gang make these activities more imperative for young men than for young women.

Notes

1. I contacted numerous additional agency personnel in an effort to draw the sample from a larger population base, but many efforts remained unsuccessful despite repeated attempts and promises of assistance. These included persons at the probation department, a shelter and outreach agency for runaways, police personnel, a private residential facility for juveniles, and three additional community agencies. None of the agencies I contacted openly denied me permission to interview young women: they simply chose not to follow up. I do not believe that much bias resulted from the nonparticipation of these organizations. Each has a client base of "at-risk" youths, and the young women I interviewed report overlap with some of these same agencies. For example, a number had been or were on probation, and several reported staying at the shelter for runaways.

2. One young woman was a member of an all-female gang. Because the focus of this article is gender dynamics in mixed-gender gangs, her interview is not included in the analysis.

3. These include the Gang Membership Resistance Surveys in Long Beach and San Diego, the Denver Youth Survey, and the Rochester Youth Development Study.

4. For example, Cleveland, Ohio, provides a striking contrast with Columbus on social and economic indicators, including a poverty rate double that found in Columbus. But the poverty rate for African Americans in Cleveland is just over twice that for whites, and it is more than three times higher in Columbus.

5. The term set was used by the gang members I interviewed to refer to their gangs. Because they adopted nationally recognized gang names (e.g., Crips, Bloods, Folks), they saw themselves as loosely aligned with other groups of the same name. This term was used to distinguish their particular gang (which has its own distinct name, e.g., Rolling 60s Crips) from other gangs that adopted the broader gang name. I will use the terms set and gang interchangeably.

6. This was compared to 36.4 percent who described their gangs as female auxiliaries of male gangs, and only 6.4 percent who described being in independent female gangs (Curry 1997; see also Decker and Van Winkle 1996).

7. All names are fictitious.

8. This is not to suggest that male members cannot gain status via their connections to high-status men, but that

to maintain status, they will have to successfully exhibit masculine traits such as toughness. Young women appear to be held to more flexible standards.

9. Because this excerpt provides a detailed description of a specific serious crime, and because demographic information on respondents is available, I have chosen to conceal both the pseudonym and gang affiliation of the young woman who told me the story.

References

Adler, Patricia A., and Peter Adler. 1987. *Membership Roles in Field Research*. Newbury Park, CA: Sage.

Arnold, Regina. 1990. "Processes of Victimization and Criminalization of Black Women." *Social Justice* 17(3):153–100.

Block, Carolyn Rebecca and Richard Block. 1993. "Street Gang Crime in Chicago." *Research in Brief*. Washington, D.C.: National Institute of Justice.

Bourgois, Philippe. 1995. *In Search of Respect: Selling Crack in El Barrio*. Cambridge, UK: Cambridge University Press.

Bourgois, Philippe and Eloise Dunlap. 1993. "Exorcising Sex-for-Crack: An Ethnographic Perspective from Harlem." Pp. 97–132 in *Crack Pipe as Pimp: An Ethnographic Investigation of Sex-for-Crack Exchanges*, edited by Mitchell S. Ratner. New York: Lexington Books.

Bowker, Lee H., Helen Shimota Gross, and Malcolm W. Klein. 1980. "Female Participation in Delinquent Gang Activities." *Adolescence* 15 (59):509–519.

Brotherton, David C. 1996. "'Smartness,' 'Toughness,' and 'Autonomy': Drug Use in the Context of Gang Female Delinquency." *Journal of Drug Issues* 26(1):261–277.

Campbell, Anne. 1984. *The Girls in the Gang*. New York: Basil Blackwell.

———. 1990. "Female Participation in Gangs." Pp. 163–182 in *Gangs in America*, edited by C. Ronald Huff. Beverly Hills, CA: Sage.

Chesney-Lind, Meda and Noelie Rodriguez. 1983. "Women under Lock and Key: A View from the Inside." *The Prison Journal* 63(2):47–65.

Columbus Metropolitan Human Services Commission. 1995. *State of Human Services Report. 1995*. Columbus, OH: Columbus Metropolitan Human Services Commission.

Connell, R. W. 1987. *Gender and Power*. Stanford, CA: Stanford University Press.

Curry, G. David. 1997. "Selected Statistics on Female Gang Involvement." Paper presented at the Fifth Joint National Conference on Gangs, Schools, and Community, March, Orlando, FL.

Curry, G. David, Richard A. Ball, and Scott H. Decker. 1996. "Estimating the National Scope of Gang Crime from Law Enforcement Data." *Research in Brief*. Washington, D.C.: National Institute of Justice.

Daly, Kathleen. 1992. "Women's Pathways to Felony Court: Feminist Theories of Lawbreaking and Problems of Representation." *Review of Law and Women's Studies* 2(11):111–52.

Decker, Scott H. 1996. "Collective and Normative Features of Gang Violence." *Justice Quarterly* 13 (2):243–264.

Eder, Donna. 1995. *School Talk: Gender and Adolescent Culture*. New Brunswick, NJ: Rutgers University Press.

Esbensen, Finn-Aage, and David Huizinga. 1993. "Gangs, Drugs, and Delinquency in a Survey of Urban Youth." *Criminology* 31(4):565–589.

Esbensen, Finn-Aage, David Huizinga, and Anne W. Weiher. 1993. "Gang and Non-Gang Youth: Differences in Explanatory Factors." *Journal of Contemporary Criminal Justice* 9(2):94–116.

Fagan, Jeffrey. 1989. "The Social Organization of Drug Use and Drug Dealing among Urban Gangs." *Criminology* 27(4):633–667.

———. 1990. "Social Processes of Delinquency and Drug Use among Urban Gangs." Pp. 183–219 in *Gangs in America*, edited by C. Ronald Huff. Newbury Park, CA: Sage.

Gilfus, Mary. 1992. "From Victims to Survivors to Offenders: Women's Routes of Entry and Immersion into Street Crime." *Women and Criminal Justice* 4(1):63–89.

Glassner, Barry and Julia Loughlin. 1987. *Drugs of Adolescent Worlds: Burnouts to Straights*. New York: St. Martin's.

Hagedorn, John M. 1988. *People and Folks: Gangs, Crime and the Underclass in a Rustbelt City*. Chicago: Lake View Press.

Huff, C. Ronald. 1989. "Youth Gangs and Public Policy." *Crime and Delinquency* 35(4):524–537.

———. 1996. "The Criminal Behavior of Gang Members and Nongang At-Risk Youth." Pp. 75–102 in *Gangs in America*, 2nd ed., edited by C. Ronald Huff. Thousand Oaks, CA: Sage.

Joe, Karen A. and Meda Chesney-Lind. 1995. "Just Every Mother's Angel: An Analysis of Gender and Ethnic Variations in Youth Gang Membership." *Gender & Society* 9(4):408–430.

Klein, Malcolm W. 1995. *The American Street Gang: Its Nature, Prevalence and Control*. New York: Oxford University Press.

Klein, Malcolm W. and Cheryl L. Maxson. 1989. "Street Gang Violence." Pp. 198–213 in *Violent Crime, Violent Criminals*, edited by Neil Weiner and Marvin Wollgang. Newbury Park, CA: Sage.

LaLonde, Brent. 1995. "Police Trying to Contain Gang Problem." *The Columbus Dispatch*, September 3, p. 2A.

Lauderback, David, Joy Hansen, and Dan Waldorf. 1992. "'Sisters Are Doin' It for Themselves': A Black Female Gang in San Francisco." *The Gang Journal* 1(1):57–70.

Lauritsen, Janet L. and Kenna F. Davis Quinet. 1995. "Repeat Victimization among Adolescents and Young Adults." *Journal of Quantitative Criminology* 1(2):143–166.

Lauritsen, Janet L., Robert J. Sampson, and John H. Laub. 1991. "The Link between Offending and Victimization among Adolescents." *Criminology* 29(2):265–292.

Lees, Sue. 1993. *Sugar and Spice: Sexuality and Adolescent Girls.* New York: Penguin.

Maher, Lisa and Richard Curtis. 1992. "Women on the Edge of Crime: Crack Cocaine and the Changing Contexts of Street-Level Sex Work in New York City." *Crime, Law and Social Change* 18:221–258.

Maxson, Cheryl L., Kristi Woods, and Malcolm W. Klein. 1995. *Street Gang Migration in the United States.* Final Report to the National Institute of Justice.

Mayhood, Kevin and Brent LaLonde. 1995. "A Show of Colors: A Local Look." *The Columbus Dispatch,* September 3, pp. 1–2A.

Messerschmidt, James W. 1993. *Masculinities and Crime: Critique and Reconceptualization of Theory.* Lanham, MD: Rowman and Littlefield.

Miller, Jody. 1996. "The Dynamics of Female Gang Involvement in Columbus, Ohio." Paper presented at the National Youth Gang Symposium, June, Dallas, TX.

Miller, Jody and Barry Glassner. 1997. "The 'Inside' and the 'Outside': Finding Realities in Interviews." Pp. 99–112 in *Qualitative Research,* edited by David Silverman. London: Sage.

Moore, Joan. 1991. *Going Down to the Barrio: Homeboys and Homegirls in Change.* Philadelphia: Temple University Press.

Moore, Joan and John M. Hagedorn. 1996. "What Happens to Girls in the Gang?" Pp. 205–218 in *Gangs in America,* 2nd ed., edited by C. Ronald Huff. Thousand Oaks, CA: Sage.

Newburn, Tim and Elizabeth Stanko. 1994. *Just Boys Doing Business?: Men. Masculinities and Crime.* New York: Routledge.

Pesce, Rosario C. and Carol Gibb Harding. 1986. "Imaginary Audience Behavior and Its Relationship to Operational Thought and Social Experience." *Journal of Early Adolescence* 6(1):83–94.

Rusk, David. 1995. *Cities without Suburbs.* 2nd ed. Washington, D.C.: The Woodrow Wilson Center Press.

Sampson, Robert J. and William Julius Wilson. 1995. "Toward a Theory of Race, Crime, and Urban Inequality." Pp. 37–54 in *Crime and Inequality,* edited by John Hagan and Ruth D. Peterson. Stanford, CA: Stanford University Press.

Sanders, William. 1993. *Drive-Bys and Gang Bangs: Gangs and Grounded Culture.* Chicago: Aldine.

Short, James E. and Fred L. Strodtbeck. 1965. *Group Process and Gang Delinquency.* Chicago: University of Chicago Press.

Simpson, Sally. 1991. "Caste, Class and Violent Crime: Explaining Differences in Female Offending." *Criminology* 29(1):115–135.

Spergel, Irving A. and G. David Curry. 1993. "The National Youth Gang Survey: A Research and Development Process." Pp. 359–400 in *The Gang Intervention Handbook,* edited by Arnold P. Goldstein and C. Ronald Huff. Champaign, IL: Research Press.

Thornberry, Terence R., Marvin D. Krohn, Alan J. Lizotte, and Deborah Chard-Weirschem. 1993. "The Role of Juvenile Gangs in Facilitating Delinquent Behavior." *Journal of Research in Crime and Delinquency* 30(1):75–85.

Thorne, Barrie. 1993. *Gender Play: Girls and Boys in School.* New Brunswick. NJ: Rutgers University Press.

Wilson, William Julius. 1996. *When Work Disappears: The World of the New Urban Poor.* New York: Knopf.

Winfree, L. Thomas, Jr., Kathy Fuller, Teresa Vigil, and G. Larry Mays. 1992. "The Definition and Measurement of 'Gang Status': Policy Implications for Juvenile Justice." *Juvenile and Family Court Journal* 43:29–37.

CHAPTER 22

The Path and Promise of Fatherhood for Gang Members

Molly Moloney ▪ Kathleen MacKenzie ▪ Geoffrey Hunt ▪ Karen Joe-Laidler

Life-course criminology investigates how transitions and turning points in individuals' lives contribute to the onset, stability, and change in antisocial and criminal behavior over time. In this chapter, Moloney and her colleagues investigate gang-involved young men's transitions to fatherhood, investigating how it can lead these young men to reevaluate their self-image and priorities, as well as how external factors such as access to employment can enable or thwart successful transitions away from gang life. Because so many scholars equate studying gender with studying girls, most research on parenthood among gang members focuses on young gang mothers. This study reveals how gender expectations play an important role in gang fathers' lives and parenting experiences. While a potent predictor of gang desistance was the purposive discontinuation of spending time with fellow gang members, which fatherhood could help promote, many young men found this difficult to sustain due to the strong social ties, support, and camaraderie gangs provide.

Introduction

Over the past 20 years, scholarship on youth gangs has grown significantly and, with the emergence of youth groups around the globe, a more culturally informed awareness is taking place (Decker and Weerman 2005; Hagedorn 2007; Klein et al. 2006). Following the tradition of American gang

studies, much gang research in other countries has focused on questions of prevalence, formation, organization, and drug and crime involvement. The United Kingdom is no exception as researchers try to counter media frenzy while also working with communities to establish a knowledge base on youth groups with characteristics of street gangs. A small but growing body of research points to the emergence of street gangs in many UK cities, with members being predominantly male, criminally active and carrying weapons (Bullock and Tilley 2008; Mares 2001). However, the application of the "American-style gang label" may reify and further stigmatize marginalized youth when researchers focus principally on gang members' criminal activity (Aldridge et al. 2008).

Because so much work on gangs has focused on criminal involvement, it is difficult to imagine life beyond the gang context. For example, what role does parenthood play in gang life? Anecdotal evidence shows that many gang members in America become parents at an early age and the risk factors associated with early fatherhood are abundantly present in gangs. Indeed, gang membership itself is a risk factor for early pregnancy and teenage parenthood (Thornberry et al. 2003: 169). Beyond this link, however, little is known about the process and context of parenthood, and fatherhood in particular.[1] Specifically, we know little about how gang involvement shapes parenting or how becoming a parent shapes involvement in gangs.

Drawing on the experiences of 91 gang members in San Francisco who became fathers, we explore the meaning of fatherhood for them and the role

Reprinted from: Molly Moloney, Kathleen MacKenzie, Geoffrey Hunt, and Karen Joe-Laidler, "The Path and Promise of Fatherhood for Gang Members," *British Journal of Criminology*, 49(3): 305–325. Copyright © 2009 by Oxford University Press, Inc. Reprinted by permission of Oxford University Press, Inc.

it plays in decisions to persist or desist in gang life and associated risky behaviours. We examine fatherhood as a potential key turning point in these young men's lives. *How does becoming a young father shape their life-course trajectories? What is the relationship between fatherhood and desistance from crime, substance abuse and other risky activities? What is the impact of fatherhood on their gang involvement? How do they navigate between the conflicting models of masculinity connected to their roles as gang members and as fathers?* For many of the young men, fatherhood acts as a significant turning point, facilitating a shift away from gang involvement, crime and drug sales; a decline in substance use; and engagement with education and legitimate employment. Many, though not intending to become fathers, and often initially dismayed by that development, describe the experience of fatherhood as radically changing (or even saving) their lives. While most of the young men credit fatherhood with this transformational capacity and see it as a turning point, not all are able to turn away from risky activities. Even for those who are successful, the desistance process is often a gradual one, fraught with pitfalls. We examine some of the structural and subjective factors that aid or hinder these efforts. Finally, we consider potential policy implications of their struggles and successes.

Turning Points and Desistance from Crime

Criminologists have sought to explain why crime tends to decrease with age, why some people desist from crime earlier or later than others, and what factors contribute to desistance or persistence in criminal careers. The life-course perspective has arguably emerged as the dominant paradigm on desistance, particularly Sampson and Laub's age-graded theory of informal social control in which stable employment and good marriages mark significant turning points in the life courses of previously crime-involved men, enabling them to desist from crime (Laub and Sampson 2001; Sampson and Laub 1993; 2005). Drawing on social-control theory, they argue that the social bonds engendered by strong marriage and/or employment can counteract juvenile trajectories of delinquency and crime.

This work emphasizes these exogenous turning points as catalysts that redirect behaviours and trajectories, thereby commencing the process of desistance. The effect of marriage on desistance has been one of the most consistent findings in the field (see also Farrington and West 1995; Horney et al. 1995; Rand 1987; for contrary evidence, see Giordano et al. 2002), although some suggest that the results are spurious, due to selection biases (Gottfredson and Hirschi 1994) or due to decreased exposure to delinquent peers after marriage (Warr 1998). The relationship between work and desistance is also well documented, although the specific nature of this relationship remains a contested issue (Pezzin 1995; Uggen 2000; Wadsworth 2006).

Despite these advances, a number of areas need further development. First, many seminal works in desistance studies are based on individuals who came of age decades ago (e.g. Sampson and Laub's use of data on white men who came of age in 1950s United States) and the meanings of key social institutions—marriage, parenting and employment—have since undergone dramatic transformations in America and in Europe. Second, while some research focuses on external turning points for desistance, as in institutions of social control, other researchers now emphasize subjective, emotional or cognitive changes for facilitating desistance (see, e.g. Barry 2007; Bottoms et al. 2004; Giordano et al. 2002; 2007; Maruna 1997; Rumgay 2004). Is the effect of turning points such as marriage, work or parenthood primarily the result of these as constraining institutions or is it the result of changes in identity, self and subjectivity? The interplay between external constraints and the subjective require further investigation and the need for contextual understanding. Third, some researchers (Forrest 2007; Giordano et al. 2002) have called for more analysis of why particular turning points contribute to the desistance of some people but not others.

This article attempts to contribute in these areas. In examining the experiences of racially diverse men who came of age in the 1990s and early 2000s in San Francisco, we build on these theoretical perspectives to account for current societal conditions and heterogeneous populations. We explore subjective and objective barriers to desistance, emphasizing the interplay between structure and agency, and examine the differential impact of the same turning point (fatherhood) on different men's trajectories. In particular, we focus on two substantive areas that are understudied in this life-course research on desistance: fatherhood and gang membership.

Unlike marriage and employment, the effect of *fatherhood* has been much less studied in desistance scholarship. There is conflicting evidence about the relationship between fatherhood, crime and desistance. Rand (1987) found that fatherhood had no effect on desistance. Farrington and West's (1995) study of working-class men in London found that marriage decreased chances of offending, whereas having a child outside of marriage increased rates of offending. Stouthamer-Loeber and Wei (1998) show an association between teen fatherhood and prior delinquency and the latter did not decrease after becoming a father. Massoglia and Uggen (2007) found that the effect of children on desistance depends on how desistance is conceptualized or measured—using varying measures, they find fatherhood increasing, decreasing or having no effect on desistance rates. We argue that one reason for the confusion about this relationship is that, while fatherhood *can* act as a turning point leading to desistance, this is far from an automatic process. Inability to support one's child through legitimate work and difficulties in "knifing off" from peers may be major obstacles in fathers' desistance. Edin, Nelson and Paranal's (2004) research on unskilled working-class men in the eastern United States is one of the few studies to examine the role incarceration and fatherhood play in desistance. They find that "the event of fatherhood can sharply alter how men perceive the risk and rewards of criminal activity. . . . Fatherhood in and of itself can prove a powerful turning point that leads men away from crime and toward a more mainstream trajectory" (Edin et al. 2004: 53).

To date, neither the desistance literature nor the life-course perspective has been well integrated into gang research. Gang involvement is one of many variables within some desistance studies (with the somewhat unsurprising finding that being a gang member decreases one's chances of desistance (Rand 1987)), but gang membership has not been

a central focus of desistance scholarship. Evidence suggests that gang membership not only selects for delinquent youth, but also facilitates delinquency and decreases the chances of desistance from crime (Gordon et al. 2004) and that increased time spent in a gang has increasing and compounding negative ramifications (Thornberry et al. 2003). These findings highlight the need for further work integrating gang and desistance research.

The life-course perspective is woefully underdeveloped within gang research. As Venkatesh (2003) argues, an individual's motivations for, and investments in time and energy into the gang may change over time, "especially over the life course as youth mature and move in and through other social institutions. This basic principle of sociological reasoning, the hallmark in life-course research, has been missing in street gang scholarship" (Venkatesh 2003:9). While once assumed to be a transitory experience in the life course, with aging out as an almost definitional aspect of gang experience (see, e.g. Thornberry et al. 2003), for many today in the United States, gang membership is no longer a fleeting youthful period. Within post-industrial economies, many manufacturing and trade opportunities, once available to young working-class men, have eroded or disappeared. The lack of opportunities as they mature into adulthood compels many to carry on gang activities well into their twenties and beyond (Fagan and Freeman 1999; Venkatesh 1997; for a cross-national comparison, see Hagedorn 2007). This diminution of the age-out effect in gangs further points to the need to examine the relationship between gang membership and life-course trajectories.

Thornberry and colleagues' (2003) longitudinal study of teenagers and gang members does connect the life-course and gang research,[2] examining risk factors leading to gang involvement and consequences stemming from it: " . . . in the short term, gang membership facilitates deviant behavior: delinquency and related behaviors increase when boys join gangs and decrease when they leave them. In the long term, gang membership increases disorderly transitions to adulthood and decreases the likelihood of desisting from crime" (Thornberry et al. 2003: 187).

Among the "disorderly transitions" they examine are early pregnancy and teen fatherhood. Though parenthood has not been a central issue in desistance literature, it is prominent in life-course research. The life course is generally expected to unfold in a set of culturally normative, age-graded stages. In the United States, this means that one completes high school before starting a career and one marries before parenting. Of course, some transitions happen out of order (parenthood before marriage) or are off-time, too early or too late. A basic premise of the life-course perspective is that off-time transitions are likely to be disruptive, leading to problems at later stages. This approach has been applied to early/teen parenting, underscoring the difficulties and negative consequences associated with early fatherhood due to the stress of navigating the parenting role before one is developmentally ready (Buzi et al. 2004) or because early fatherhood requires economic contributions before one has completed schooling or secured employment (Marsiglio and Pleck 2004). Scholarship on early fatherhood and the life course tends to emphasize the potential for this precocious transition to disrupt life-course trajectories, leading to diminished economic potential and increased chances of delinquency, crime or incarceration (Pirog-Good 1996).

But what about those who are already on a disrupted life course, or whose trajectories already seem to be negative, as in the case of many young gang members? Can fatherhood disrupt the trajectories of crime or substance abuse? Do early transitions to the adult role of fatherhood aid in speeding up the age- or developmental-related desistance process?

We explore how this new circumstance may be a turning point in which decisions are weighed differently and new responsibilities, opportunities and constraints add to their life choices and identities. There are a number of possible responses. First, unable or unwilling to perform this role effectively, gang fathers may give up on responsible fathering and continue their involvement with crime, gangs or substance use unaffected. Second, they may consider gang activity as a viable life-course opportunity, driving them further into an underground economy, to support their children. Third, they may

drop out of or lessen their gang involvement as part of becoming a father. We consider these and other responses among 91 young gang-involved fathers. As this is an exploratory study, we cannot fully disentangle issues of cause, effect and selection here. Yet, this qualitative analysis has much to contribute to this typically quantitative field of study. We offer an extended exploration of the *meaning* of these young men's experiences with fatherhood and its implications for desistance.

Research Methods and Sample

San Francisco, California, is an important location for conducting research on youth gangs due to its concentrated ethnic and cultural diversity. Of the total population of 776,733, 44 per cent are white (non-Hispanic origin), 31 per cent are Asian, slightly more that 14 per cent are of Hispanic origin, and 8 per cent are African-American (US Census Bureau 2002). National estimates of gang membership are diverse and some of the estimation difficulties are related to the perennial problems of gang definitions (Bursik and Grasmick 2006; Esbensen et al. 2001; Joe 1993; Maxson and Klein 1995).

The 91 men interviewed for this study between 2004 and 2006 were of ethnic minorities from low-income backgrounds. Most lived in one of ten neighbourhoods (especially Mission, Bayview Hunters Point, Potrero Hill, Tenderloin, Chinatown), with distinctive ethnic cultures, a strong working-class presence, public housing and a high concentration of gang activity.

All of the men are self-described current or former gang members and fathers. We have adopted self-nomination as the most reliable way of assessing gang membership (Esbensen et al. 2001: 124), although we also use additional information from our fieldworkers and community key informants to verify gang involvement of potential respondents. Self-identification poses some challenges, particularly for cross-cultural comparisons where the meaning of "gangs" varies dramatically from that in the American context (and from one American city to the next) (see Aldridge et al. 2008 for more on the difficulties faced when applying the label "gang"—particularly in the British context). However, almost all of the gang-identified men we interviewed participated in groups that fit under the Eurogang project's definition of gang or troublesome youth group (Klein and Maxson 2006) used by one of the largest sets of comparative, cross-national gang research: "Durable and street-oriented youth groups whose involvement in illegal activity is part of their group identity" (Klein et al. 2006: 415). While this definition is not without problems (Pitts 2008), it does establish a common framework and vocabulary for comparisons. Viewed through the lens of Maxson and Klein's (1995) five-part typology of gang membership, the men we interviewed were involved primarily in "compressed gangs" (adolescent group of a few years' duration, 10–50 members, with versatile criminal patterns), which Klein and colleagues (2006) describe as the most common in Europe and the United States, as well as to a lesser extent the traditional or neotraditional gangs (larger, multigenerational groups with denotable subgroups), which, though found in the United States (and comprising the dominant stereotype of American gangs), are as of yet uncommon in Europe (Klein et al. 2006).

Gang members who are fathers were recruited using snowball-sampling (Biernacki and Waldorf 1981), growing out of our long-standing research on and contact with gangs in San Francisco. The interviews were conducted by fieldworkers who were matched to the groups they were sampling, either by their knowledge of the specific communities, their ethnic background or their own experiences with gangs. We gave respondents a US$75 honorarium in recognition of their participation and time.

The face-to-face interviews consisted of a combination of quantitative and qualitative interview methods and most interviews took approximately 2.5 hours to complete. Open-ended questions focused on life histories and an in-depth examination of activities in three key moments: a year prior to the pregnancy; the year during the pregnancy; and what happened after they became fathers.

The respondents ranged in age from 16 to 44 years, with a median age of 23 years. The majority first became fathers between the ages of 14 and 28, with a median age of first birth at 18. Thirty-seven became fathers as minors (under 18) and 13 became fathers after the age of 21. We interviewed

men who recently faced the potential turning point of fatherhood but also men who faced this turning point quite a while ago, allowing us to trace the life-course trajectories for those men, and get a sense of long-term effects of fatherhood on their desistance efforts.

Education, Income and Employment

Overall, the respondents reported limited education. Less than half received a high-school diploma, and more than one-quarter dropped out of school and never returned. Sixty per cent of respondents were not attending school, but more than one-quarter were attending college, primarily through re-entry programmes after dropping out.

Close to half of the fathers had jobs, although the overall median job income was relatively low, at US$1,300 per month. Additional income among gang fathers came from a variety of sources, especially drug sales. Two-thirds of respondents admitted to drug sales and hustles, and more than 40 per cent provided details on drug sales earnings, with median sales of US$800 per month.

Family Patterns

The majority of the men were neither married nor cohabiting with a partner; only three men reported being married. Though some respondents denied paternity early in the pregnancy, all ultimately admitted their paternity and claimed their children. Slightly more than one-third of the fathers lived in households with their children at the time of the interview, although many more had tried and failed to live as a family with their child and the mother in the past. In general, the number of fathers who resided with their children declined with age. Among non-custodial fathers, parental involvement varied widely. Some were heavily involved in their children's lives, providing financial and childcare support and seeing them regularly. About 15 per cent of them, however, no longer had any contact with their children.

Our sample comprises multiple ethnic groups and gangs. Latinos/Hispanics represented the largest group in the sample (31 per cent),[3] followed by African-Americans (30 per cent) and Filipino-Americans (27 per cent). The remaining 13 per cent were of other backgrounds, including Cambodian,

Samoan, white, Chinese and mixed ethnic groups. Slightly more than 15 per cent of respondents were immigrants. This dataset presented us with a somewhat unique opportunity to make comparisons between different ethnic groups vis-à-vis fatherhood and gang involvement. Comparative research on young fathers of different ethnicities within the United States has found that cultural differences may play a role in the involvement of young fathers with their children (Anderson 1999; Cochran 1997; Hernandez 2002: Marsiglio et al. 2000). If the experience of young fatherhood is mediated by ethnicity and culture, we might expect the effect of becoming a young father on desistance also to vary by ethnicity.

We found some important variations within our sample along ethnic lines, although we recognize the statistical limits given our sample size and non-random sample. Latino fathers were more likely to have dropped out of high school (about one-third of Latinos as compared to 15 per cent of African-Americans and 25 per cent of Filipinos) yet had the highest employment (64 per cent) followed by more than half of Filipino fathers and 45 per cent of African-Americans. Some differences exist in family formations—Latinos were most likely to have more than one child (28 versus 22 per cent of African-Americans and eight percent of Filipinos) and had a higher incidence of having children with more than one woman. Nearly 60 per cent of the men interviewed fathered their first child with a partner from their same ethnic group, with African-Americans and Filipinos more likely to have multi-ethnic relationships than Latinos.

Despite these differences, what we found more striking in our data were the fundamental commonalities among the fathers across racial/ethnic lines—particularly in the men's narratives about the role that fatherhood played in shaping and changing their lives. Though there is significant variation in levels of desistance from gang life and the way different men perceive fatherhood, these variations did not largely break down along racial/ethnic lines.

Gang Involvement and Risk Behaviours

As gang research in the United States and internationally have shown, there is much variability in levels of gang participation and organization ranging from highly organized criminal gangs with clear hierarchies and involvement in criminal activities to non-hierarchical collectives with intermittent participation in crime (Klein and Maxson 2006; see Marshall et al. 2005 for a UK meta-analysis). Our respondents hail from multiple gangs and the nature of gang involvement varied considerably, with some heavily involved in large, structured gangs and others in loosely structured gangs of a more transient nature.

There were common threads among diverse gangs: loyalty and defending the honour of their gang, often through violence; participation in a variety of criminal activities and hustles, including drug sales; displays of street smarts; and drug and alcohol consumption. Approximately two-thirds had participated in drug sales at some point in their lives, with close to half still selling, either to supplement their income or as a primary income source. Smaller, but not insignificant, numbers reported involvement in robberies, carjackings, home invasions or weapons-carrying. More than 80 per cent had been arrested previously and more than two-thirds reported multiple arrests. All reported marijuana use in their lifetime and almost two-thirds were current users. The second most frequent drug tried was cocaine (56 per cent) followed by ecstasy (52 per cent). Fewer than 5 per cent of respondents had used either of these substances in the past week. Twenty-two respondents said that they had not used any drugs within one year or more, and 49 respondents indicated that they had used drugs within the past week.

Narratives of Transformation

These young men were heavily involved in gang life prior to fatherhood. Some dropped out of school or were regularly truant. They struggled to find employment, and even those who completed high school found good jobs difficult to obtain. Early education and employment experiences did little to promote a sense of masculinity and competence. Instead, they were left with a sense of inadequacy and disconnection from legitimate social structures that might foster their future success as a man and as a father. Street gang life was the most common "career" path. The cool, tough image of gang life was attractive as a financial opportunity and as a masculine identity. Most of the men describe their pre-fatherhood life as one largely organized around life on the street. Typically, they spent most days and every evening out on the streets with fellow gang members—hustling for drug sales or just hanging out with their friends, drinking alcohol or smoking marijuana.

Life Changes: Fatherhood Means Change

By conventional standards—and by the accounts of the men—their life trajectories, pre-fatherhood, were fraught with peril. Most faced futures of incarceration or possibly violent death—fates met by many of their friends. Indeed, fatherhood was credited with not only *changing* their lives, but, literally, *saving* their lives. As one man bluntly put it "I woulda been dead or in jail if I wouldn't have my kids" (Angel, 25, Latino[4]). Yet, that was life "before." Fatherhood introduced dramatic differences in their lives. While a few claim that fatherhood didn't change their lives at all, the vast majority of young men recount fatherhood as a turning point. Xavier (19, Latino) describes radical changes in his lifestyle brought about by his girlfriend's pregnancy:

> I didn't even wanna be out there [anymore]. I wanted to get a legal job. . . . Instead of being out on the street, I was in the house or the hospital. . . . I wasn't smoking weed or doin' drugs. . . . Bein' more responsible, more disciplined. And stopped chillin' outside as much. . . . I stopped robbin' people, stealin' cars.

Some men explained that the responsibilities of fatherhood (and in some cases the demands of the baby's mother) necessitated a reorganization of their time that led to fewer opportunities to participate in criminal activities; they were simply too busy to get into trouble: "I didn't have it in me no more to be violent and go out and do shit no more. 'Cause I was too busy thinking about what the fuck I was gonna do" (Andre, 22, African-American).

Spatial reorientation was a recurring theme, with fatherhood leading to movement from the streets into the home. Roy (23, Filipino) notes:

> Before that, the only thing I really actually would do every day would be kick it with the homies [fellow gang members] . . . [but after the pregnancy] I didn't kick it with them at all. . . . I was kickin' it hella much indoors with [the mother]. I was hella indoors.

Here is a shift away from time spent with gang peers—an issue further discussed below. Fatherhood leads to busier lives, moving inside, with little time or opportunity to get into fights or criminal activities that were previously endemic to their lives.

Some men argue that fatherhood motivated them to change their lives and desist from crime because they wanted to become positive role models for their children—role models they themselves lacked when younger:

> [Fatherhood] changed me a whole lot as far as being more responsible, being more true. And knowin' that I have to take a different road. I can't be out there on the streets drinkin' all the time. I can't be gettin' high. . . . I can't be doin' stupid stuff. Because if I'm incarcerated, who's to watch my two boys? Where would they be? They need a role model. (Jesus, 34, Latino)

Other researchers have dismissed such motivations for non-custodial fathers: " . . . it is likely that a relatively small proportion of men in [Roche's study] actually lived with their children. Thus parenthood would not inspire males to act responsibly or as positive role models" (Roche et al. 2006: 255). Our findings, however, suggest that even fathers who don't reside with their children take pride in and place importance on their father identity and are motivated to change. These and other subjective aspects of becoming a father appear to be as determinative of fatherhood's potential as a turning point as does the objective fact of becoming a father itself and the related structural constraints. Pride in and prioritization of their children doesn't mean that they always fulfilled their paternal responsibilities or met the expectations of their children's mothers for financial, emotional or physical/childcare support. Indeed, in a separate on-going research project interviewing female gang members, one-third of whom were themselves mothers, a lack of sufficient support or even regular contact from their children's fathers (who were often gang members) was a consistent theme (Hunt et al. 2005).

Subjective Transformations

Some men's explanations of how fatherhood acted as a turning point seem straight out of social control theory, in which the fathers describe the constraining effects of fatherhood and related social institutions externally pressuring them. Efren (22, Filipino) describes his imposed curfew: "Sometimes I gotta be home 'cause she [his baby's mother] be checkin'. It's like you got a curfew all the time." As in this example and others, the effect of fatherhood interacts with or is mediated through the role of the baby's mother in exerting social control. Also significant are the internal and subjective transformations linked to fatherhood, especially to personal identity and emotional transformation (see Giordano et al. 2007). Numerous respondents describe themselves as becoming "calmer" as a result of being a father, while others say that now they are more peaceful: "I'm more relaxed, calm. And I love bein' a father.... I was a bad little motherfucker before. Now I'm just mellow" (Raja, 22, Samoan). With this affective transformation, new fathers become calmer, less impulsive, less prone to violence and are more able to resist temptations to get caught up in the vagaries of gang life.

New Priorities and Future

Becoming a father led many to re-evaluate their past activities and their priorities. Alejandro (21, Latino) contrasts his priorities before his girlfriend's pregnancy ("My priorities was my gang") with life afterwards:

> Fatherhood's changed me a lot. I don't think about gangs no more. I think of my kids if anything. Before I do anything negative I always think twice.... I love my kids to the death.... They get me goin' everyday every time I wake up.... They keep me motivated.

Some fathers reported that this was the first time in their life that they felt *any* sense of priorities: "I didn't have no priorities then [before the pregnancy]. I just thought I was the best thing that got on this earth" (Sean, 22, African-American). Whereas before, they say they didn't care about anything, fatherhood has now provided them with something or someone to care for and about. Fatherhood facilitates a reorientation to a life with a future and new possibilities.

Some scholars argue that the erosion of viable economic opportunities for inner-city men has led to alienation and feelings of hopelessness about the future (Anderson 1999). Life-course scholars believe the possession of a future-orientation is a key factor in predicting which high-risk youth most successfully transition to adulthood or obtain social mobility (McCabe and Barnett 2000). For some gang fathers, the fact that they can see a future is new:

> I had never thought about a future before. My future was never important to me just besides day-to-day. It didn't matter. Now I had to start thinkin' about, "Oh my God, I got a kid. I gotta start thinkin' about a future." (Deangelo, 29, African-American)

There seems to be a fundamental shift in outlook from a present-oriented life in which they never looked beyond today to one that includes a future orientation.

By beginning to look at the future—"something to live for"—many men re-evaluate the risks and benefits of their gang and crime involvement. This change may be partly due to general maturational processes, but certainly this maturation is related to impending fatherhood. The consequences of enacting gang masculinity (including incarceration, violent injury or death) are costly for any young man, but these consequences may become more serious to young fathers, who now have more to lose:

> [I] started thinkin' about my [friend] who had died .... And if I keep puttin' myself out here in this trap, I can really just die out here.... Man, I gotta think about my child. (Gregory, 25, African-American)

Fathers describe a new situation in which the risks of gang life, which they often had discounted or not worried about previously, are now too great for them. Such worries don't always lead to desistance. In some cases, this leads to less risky illegal income-generating strategies. Leo (21, Latino) says that he continues selling drugs, but that "it's more careful now." He and other fathers may be more likely to take their drug sales off the streets or to limit their clientele, or which drugs they sell, as was the case for Gregory, who continues to sell marijuana but says that he has completely "dropped slingin' crack. I choose never to sell no crack again," so that he can be there for his son. In other cases, though, young fathers attempted to forego criminal pursuits entirely and navigate the legitimate economy to provide for themselves and their children. As a result, fatherhood provides a significant turning point to their desistance from crime.

The Timing of Changes

Although these fathers' narratives of change are often dramatic, with descriptions of sudden changes in *outlook*, actual changes in *behaviours* were gradual, suggesting that desistance is best understood as a *process*—gradual and cumulative—rather than as an abrupt or discrete phenomenon (Bottoms et al. 2004; Kazemian 2007; Laub and Sampson 2001). Despite the sometimes sudden change in priorities brought on by fatherhood, it often took considerable time and effort for the men to reorient their day-to-day practices, to find legal means of financial support, or to shift away from gang-dominated peers. Joel (27, Filipino) describes his gradual move from drug use and hustling to sobriety and legitimate work: "About six months into her pregnancy I cut down a lot. I wasn't even smoking [marijuana]. I mean, I was still smokin' but not . . . regularly. . . . I stopped hustling more. I started working more." In the early days of his son's life, he continued selling to pay bills, but eventually stopped selling and using.

The beginning of the turning point also varied, with some motivated to change immediately upon learning about the pregnancy or the mother's decision to keep the baby. Others didn't change their lifestyles at all during the pregnancy, but reported a new desire to change after the baby's birth. Serge (30, Latino) comments that, during the pregnancy:

> I was still off the hook, hella violent. And I didn't give a fuck if I lived or died. . . . When she was pregnant I didn't feel shit! When he was born and I seen his little face, that's when I got a lotta feelins like, "that's my little man right here."

It was when he saw his child that he felt motivated to change. Yet, some men, who eventually were motivated to change, took considerably longer, making changes only when faced with the possibility of losing their children due to state intervention or blocked access by their child's mother. Pablo (23, Latino) not only continued dealing, but brought his infant son to the corner where he would sell drugs. But when he got arrested for drug sales while with the baby, he faced the threat of losing custody. This was his turning point:

> Because I have my kids, because I'm not in jail, I'm working. . . . [Child Protective Services] almost took [my child]. . . . And I was . . . "No, I gotta stop selling dope." . . . It scared me, because they tried to send me to prison for five years.

The prospect of prison scared him, but no more so than the thought of losing his son—and the threat of prison became more serious now that he was a father. Fatherhood didn't operate directly or independently to cause his desistance, but instead reflected the interaction between fatherhood and incarceration threats.

In other cases, it was not the birth of their first child that marked the turning point, but subsequent children or even a step-child. Sometimes, becoming a father for a second or third time is the trigger, after which they attempt to avoid earlier, much regretted mistakes. Eddie (30, Latino) admits that he has had little contact with his first three children (the first of whom was born when he was 15) or their respective mothers. But, with this fourth child:

> I really didn't start bein' a real father until my last daughter. . . . But I was older by then. I was tired of doin' all the shit I was already doin'. But she's changed me a lot. . . . My last daughter is when I consider myself becomin' a father. [Before] my life had no purpose. I didn't care about anything.

Clearly, fatherhood alone was not sufficient to change, and Eddie himself points to the importance of age. Yet, as he recognizes, it is not merely age that brings change, but the "age readiness" of taking on the role of being a "real" father. It's not merely fatherhood as a biological fact that acts as the turning point, but "activating the father role"—something that requires choice and agency (Edin et al. 2004).

The gradual effect of fatherhood as a turning point may initially seem to undermine it as an explanatory mechanism. It may be helpful to think of turning points as exogenous "triggering events" that begin the gradual desistance process (Laub et al. 1998). Giordano and colleagues (2002) question the term "turning point," preferring instead "hooks for change," to highlight the individual's role and agency in grasping the opportunities from these hooks. This agency is apparent here, as some do and some don't respond to these hooks for change in their decisions to continue or desist. Similarly, Maruna (1997) argues against the concept "turning point" because change is not automatic; instead, agency must be emphasized in the desistance process. The turning-point concept may be more robust than this, and may allow for more agentic accounts than those critiques would imply. However, our analysis leads us to agree about the importance of agency and contingency in the desistance process. The agency and decisions of each man, and his subjective interpretations of fatherhood, are a crucial determinative factor in shaping the efficacy of this potential turning point.

Limits to the Effectiveness of Fatherhood on Desistance

These men's narratives make it seem as if fatherhood is a magical cure—an incredibly strong cause of desistance. A young gang member becomes a father, his outlook on life and his priorities are dramatically reoriented, his life-course trajectory is forever changed. Yet, if we look beyond their self-descriptions of transformation and place these narratives in the context of their ongoing experiences, even their own self-reports of continued gang-related activity belies the notion of fatherhood as panacea. Though fatherhood acts as a *potential* turning point for the majority, not all are able to successfully navigate this new life course. With the youngest of the fathers, it's not possible to gauge the permanence of the fatherhood effect on their desistance; " . . . what makes a turning point a turning point rather than a minor ripple is the passage of sufficient time 'on the new course' such that it becomes clear that direction has indeed been changed" (Abbott 1997: 89). However, with older fathers, for whom the initial turning point is now years behind them, we have better purchase for charting these changes and will examine some of the obstacles to fatherhood and desistance.

When a gang member becomes a father, an additional dimension of masculinity—with its choices,

responsibilities and significance—is interpreted and added to his repertoire of identities (Kimmel et al. 2004). While gang involvement provided one form of masculinity—marked by aggression, violence or drug use—fatherhood offers alternative scripts of masculinity—the breadwinner and good provider, the protector and teacher. Fatherhood is also understood as a measure of a man (Marsiglio and Pleck 2004). "Fatherhood has changed me a lot. . . . It turned me into a man basically" (Chris, 31, African-American). Affirmation of the masculine identity of father enabled some respondents to dissociate from the more destructive modes of masculinity connected with gang life. "It helped me grow into a man and, I guess, stop doin' all that violent stuff I was doin" (Jorge, 34, Latino).

Yet, fatherhood as a route to masculine identity is not unproblematic. The expectations associated with competently enacting a father identity were often at odds with those associated with their gang identities. Masculinity is negotiated and enacted differentially in different situations and different spaces (Connell and Messerschmidt 2005). Public masculine displays on the streets may vary from those in the privacy of the home, and various stages in an individual's life course may reflect different expressions of masculinities (Collier 1998). One area of particular difficulty for many men was in negotiating the role of breadwinner. Although their motivations and self-concept may have changed, along with their newfound desire to earn legitimate incomes and provide, young fathers were often no better positioned than before to become the breadwinner.

The Challenges of Economic Provision, Fatherhood and Desistance

The streets provided a variety of opportunities to assert their manhood and to earn money, most of them risky and illegal. With a child, there was added pressure on the young men to provide. Indeed, financial pressures were most frequently cited as the most difficult aspect of being a father: "I'm stuck in a box, you know, that I cannot move. . . . I try to save money, I try to take care of my family at the same time. Try to get certification. . . . I just feel I'm . . . tied up, you know" (Pablo, 23, Latino). These pressures make the idea of returning to drug sales tempting. To meet these financial expectations, most men carried on with familiar money-making strategies, at least early on in their fatherhood. James (23, Filipino) engaged in legal work but did not find his earnings sufficient in the long term. After his baby's birth, he and the mother worked. They began to set goals for themselves—getting their own place and the mother going back to school. He supplemented his delivery-driver income by drug selling. While his girlfriend was unhappy about this, she eventually relented: "You gotta do what you gotta do."

The decision to continue hustling brought a variety of reactions from the babies' mothers. Some were kept in the dark, others accepted or even expected the father to support the child through illicit means, but often, this was a source of conflict. Bryon (34, African-American) who was making "a lot of money" from drug dealing when his girlfriend got pregnant, "had it all figured out," that he could keep on as before, and things would work out. His girlfriend, however, thought differently and wanted him to get a legal job, which he thought was completely unrealistic. Looking back, though, he regrets his decisions, because he wound up going to prison and losing years with his child. While Bryon was eventually able to turn things around, renew his relationship with his son and has not used or sold drugs for years now, other respondents were never able to shift to a conventional life-course trajectory. Despite wanting to move into a legitimate lifestyle, many men, with criminal records, low education and limited job training, find it difficult to secure stable legitimate work, and rely on drug sales to support their children. For example, Jefe (29, Latino), who supports himself almost exclusively through drug sales, has completely lost access to one of his children and has only sporadic interaction with his second. He remains involved in the gang today.

The desistance process, even for those who were successful, was rarely linear and the boundaries between legal and illegal income were elastic and dynamic, with a "doubling up" of legal work and crime (Fagan and Freeman 1999):

INTERVIEWER: What sorts of things do you do to take care of your child?

EARL: What sorts of things? Work. If it comes real down to the bottom of the barrel like it's been lately, I'll hustle some trees [sell marijuana]. . . . (Earl, 25, African-American)

Still, his drug dealing has greatly decreased since becoming a father and is now "the last resort." Almost half of the fathers indicated that they currently sold drugs, including almost one-quarter who secured the majority of their monthly income from drug sales. More than half reported some sort of employment income in the last month, but less than one-quarter of the fathers relied solely on a job as their means of support. Employment rose and drug sales declined over time and age, but almost 30 per cent of working fathers supplemented their legitimate income with dealing. While money wasn't the only motivator for crime or gang involvement, most men expressed a desire to shift more fully toward legal work, but found it difficult because of low wages. Most of these young gang fathers, even though motivated to earn money legitimately, have far greater reserves of what McCarthy and Hagan (2001) refer to as criminal social capital (arising from associations within the gang) and criminal human capital (skills for hustles) than conventional human capital or social capital (ties to legitimate income networks, years of education or vocational training).

But most men venture into legitimate work, with varying levels of success. Many tried multiple jobs and most made an even greater attempt when they became fathers. Among fathers with jobs, approximately 20 per cent were employed in counselling and educational capacities with youth gang members. This work conferred a sense of pride, useful contribution and economic viability. When they managed to break into a job in which they had a sense of dignity, gang fathers were more likely to sustain those jobs longer. Other job types supporting their masculine expectations and economic needs included security work and trades. On the other hand, employment in menial jobs such as janitorial, restaurant work, retail sales and telemarketing was often short-lived, inconsistent and instrumentally and intrinsically unfulfilling.

Many of these gang members, though lacking work opportunities and experience, aspire to lead a "conventional" life, particularly to obtain legitimate employment, to have their own place and to have a family. They are cognizant of their limited educational background and lack of technical training and realize that their future employment prospects lie in low-paid occupations unless they can obtain further education. The fathers are also fully aware that attempts to go "legit" are further stymied by their criminal histories. Thus, economic structural realities represent the biggest barriers to a gang father's ability to care for his own family and perhaps to desist. Where they once may have been uninterested in or disdainful of various job-opportunity, training or educational programmes, after fatherhood, many were increasingly desirous of such supports, but sometimes found them difficult to access. As young men, they come into the work force with an already deficient educational foundation, alternative and illegal income sources may become normalized strategies for obtaining success and status as well as important for supporting children (Pirog-Good 1996).

Gangs, Peers and the Difficulties of Knifing Off

While financial problems may be the greatest difficulty in fatherhood expressed, the question of continuing involvement with fellow gang members appears to be one of the greatest predictors of success or problems with desisting from crime and transitioning into the legal job market. Cause, effect and selection issues are difficult to disentangle, but most respondents who most fully desisted from crime and began to rely on formal work are also those who began to spend the least time with their fellow gang members. Although it is too simplistic to blame the men's peers for their own decisions to engage in risky behaviours, it is in their company that opportunities arise to get involved in fights with rival gangs, robberies and other crimes that they seldom commit on their own. For many men, fatherhood ushers in a profound change in whom they spend time with and where they spend it. This withdrawal from the street and the gang is fundamental to desistance.

Fatherhood initiates for many a reorientation of where their fellow gang members fall in their list of priorities:

It switched from spending a couple of hours with her and most of the day with my friends to spending the whole day with her and not spending any time with my friends. (Diego, 23, Latino)

Some describe simply drifting away from their gang peers, but, for others, it was a more conscious decision to disengage for their child's sake. Arvin (25, Filipino) says that he quit hanging out with his friends and started spending more time with his family " 'Cause I knew what I was doin' was gonna catch up to me. I was gonna end up finally gettin' caught, or end up in the cemetery somehow." Carlos (26, Latino) avoided his former friends and others from the neighbourhood because "the negative impact wasn't gonna be on me anymore it was gonna be on my daughter."

But ending, or even decreasing, involvement with gang friends is not always easy and can take an emotional toll on the fathers. Roy associates fatherhood with loneliness:

Before I used to always be around a lot of people from like being on the streets and stuff. So it feels lonely now 'cause it's just me, me and [my son], or me and my best friend.

Part of what makes this so difficult is the important social supports that the gang represented for the fathers. While gang life is clearly associated with risky and criminal practices and connected to negative life-course trajectories, being part of the gang also had positive features in their often otherwise troubled lives. The gang provides protection in their violent neighbourhoods. Being part of the gang meant having "that feeling of people being there for you and watchin' your back" (Russell, 22, African-American). Indeed, many men describe the gang as a surrogate family.

"Knifing off" from the gang seems to be a key for those who successfully desist. But, knifing off successfully may be dependent upon finding new sources of respect and a strong identity—based on fatherhood, on newfound work status and/or in a relationship.[5] An affirmative alternative is necessary to replace their previous peer involvement.

The ability for fatherhood to act as a significant turning point appears to be heavily mediated by changes in peer relationships and social networks. Warr (1998) reported similar findings regarding the relationship between marriage (though not fatherhood) and desistance. It is important to understand the mechanisms by which fatherhood may influence desistance, such as in this peer effect. Fatherhood's effect on desistance may not always be direct, but rather mediated through shifts in peers, relationships with girlfriends or involvement in work, education or other social institutions. But these shifts may never have come about, and certainly not when they did, if not for the (generally unplanned) fact of fatherhood. Thus, the importance of fatherhood for enabling desistance, though far from guaranteed and often indirect, should not be underestimated. It can be the small but significant nudge that makes all the difference in these men's life-course trajectories—a trigger that allows for new possibilities.

Conclusion

A number of comparative lessons can be learned from this analysis. In the United Kingdom, scholars have long resisted examining youth group dynamics in the context of "gangs," preferring instead to focus on youth subculture where crime is one of a number of key areas of investigation (Aldridge et al. 2008; Campbell and Muncer 1989; Sanders 2002). The United Kingdom had no tradition of "gangbanging" with claims of territory and violent rivalries like the United States, and, for some British youth, the gangster image would only bring unwanted attention from authorities (Sanders 2002).

Such a gang label serves only to further mark, isolate and exclude groups of young people who, by their very place in the social structure, are already marginalized. The media's negative gangster portrayals of young Bengali men had a negative impact in East London, as the community, often unintentionally, further contributed to these young men being categorized as dangerous (Alexander 2000). Bullock and Tilley (2008) similarly found the "gang" problematic, as practitioners in Manchester faced difficulties in identifying who exactly was a gang member and feared such references would not only stigmatize youth, but also lead to the expected gangster identity. Moreover, youth and parents resisted the gang label. This resistance is

indeed instructive to American gang research. As we illustrated here, the impact of such labels is difficult, but not impossible, to overcome.

Fatherhood itself introduces a new label to the identity of a young gang member. With the new identity conferred following the birth of a child, new motivations and opportunities arose. Many were innovative in their strategies to get their needs met and become more responsible. Low earning capacity and an inability to hold jobs conflicted with and threatened these gang-involved fathers' masculine identities as breadwinners, leaving other masculine traits of the streets, such as aggression, dominance and hustling, as measures of masculinity. Illegal income sources became normalized strategies for obtaining success and status. Most gang fathers combined a variety of resources for their monthly income, legitimate and illegitimate—a choice that could backfire and lead to incarceration.

But for some men, fatherhood appears to have triggered important and long-lasting changes, enabling them to desist from criminal activities, reduce their risky practices and shift to a more sustainable life-course trajectory. For fatherhood to serve as this turning point, a variety of factors, structural and subjective, needed to come together. The ability for fatherhood to lead to desistance hinges on structural or material transformations in their lives—in which they move from the streets and gangs/delinquent peers to the home and workplace—but also on subjective or identity-based changes—in which fatherhood initiates a transformation in priorities, outlook and affect. Becoming a father does not automatically lead to lasting changes and the men's own agency and decisions are essential. Yet, neither is this a situation of unfettered agency, for the real structural and material barriers that limit the men's abilities to fully invest in their new father identities and desist from crime are ever present and immense.

The precariousness of new fatherhood as a potential turning point marks it as an important moment for possible intervention efforts and efforts should focus on understanding the appropriate timing for assistance. Rumgay (2004) argues that "for an opportunity for desistance to be seized it not only must present itself to the offender but also must be both recognized and valued as such—successful desistance from crime may be rooted in recognition of an opportunity to claim an alternative, desired, and socially approved identity" (Rumgay 2004: 405). Gang members may have been previously uninterested in intervention and treatment; with fatherhood comes a change in outlook and priorities—returning to school, entering the legal workforce and engaging in conventional activities. This may be a particularly opportune moment for intervention. Fatherhood may give them just the "alternative, desired, and socially approved identity" to enable them to successfully desist.

But these motivational issues are not enough—it is also necessary for the men to be able to competently enact this role. This competency is tied to the ability to successfully earn a supportive wage in the legal economy—made difficult by their low education and training and criminal records—and this is likely to grow worse in these times of global economic crises. Training and job programmes may be helpful at this point but with the caution that employment means more than just a job. Job quality is a bigger determinant of criminal and non-criminal practices than is income, job stability or education (Wadsworth 2006). Our respondents expressed frustration with un-meaningful service jobs that provide little satisfaction or competence, which may be necessary for work involvement to replace gang involvement.

Employment programmes typically have a positive effect on desistance for older but not for younger men (Uggen 2000). But, perhaps for young *fathers*, this age effect is modified—for even quite young fathers may perceive benefits from these programmes in ways that other young men, without parenting responsibilities, do not. In common discussions of the effect of early parenthood, there is the idea that this causes the young parents to "grow up too fast," to take on adult roles before they are ready. Analyses of early parenting focus on the role that this may play in tragically disrupting the life-course trajectories of young parents. But what about those whose life-course trajectories were previously less than bright? Is disruption in *these* trajectories unambiguously negative? If age and maturation are so strongly associated with desistance, then perhaps, in the cases of those already heavily involved in criminal and other risky practices, the speed-up

of social age can have positive effects, too. We are not suggesting that early fatherhood among young gang men is something to be celebrated, promoted or encouraged. But, in the none-too-rare occasions of its occurrence, those interested in intervention, desistance and prevention should be alert to this group as both more open to and needing of support than generally acknowledged.

Funding

National Institute of Child Health and Human Development (R01-HD053369).

Notes

1. Of course, both male and female gang members become young parents. However, it is important not to conflate the experiences of men and women in gangs, so we focus on gang fathers in this study and explore the experiences of gang mothers elsewhere (see Hunt et al. 2005).
2. See Laub and Sampson (2001) for a discussion of key differences between psychological/developmental and sociological/institutional life-course approaches.
3. The ethnic category Hispanic/Latino is a broad classification that includes immigrants from throughout Latin America, Puerto Rico and Cuba. In our sample, 21 of the 28 Hispanic/Latinos were born in the United States. Of the remaining seven, three were born in Mexico, three in Nicaragua and one in Ecuador.
4. The names of all participants have been changed to protect anonymity.
5. For a discussion of the limits of the "knifing off" concept, see Maruna and Roy (2007).

References

Abbott, A. (1997), "On the Concept of Turning Point," *Comparative Social Research*, 16: 85–105.

Aldridge, J., Medina, J. and Ralphs, R. (2008), "Dangers and Problems of Doing 'Gang' Research in the U.K.," in F. Van Gemert, D. Peterson and I.-L. Lien, eds, *Street Gangs, Migration and Ethnicity*, 31–46. Portland, OR: Willan Publishing.

Alexander, C. (2000), *The Asian Gang: Ethnicity, Identity and Masculinity*. Oxford, UK: Berg.

Anderson, E. (1999), *Code of the Street: Decency, Violence, and the Moral Life of the Inner City*. New York, NY: W.W. Norton & Company.

Barry, M. (2007), "Youth Offending and Youth Transitions: The Power of Capital in Influencing Change," *Critical Criminology*, 15: 185–98.

Biernacki, P. and Waldorf, D. (1981), "Snowball Sampling: Problems and Techniques of Chain Referral Sampling," *Sociological Methods and Research*, 10: 141–63.

Bottoms, A., Shapland, J., Costello, A., Holmes, D. and Muir, G. (2004), "Towards Desistance: Theoretical Underpinnings for an Empirical Study," *The Howard Journal of Criminal Justice*, 43: 368–89.

Bullock, K. and Tilley, N. (2008), "Understanding and Tackling Gang Violence," *Crime Prevention and Community Safety*, 10: 36–47.

Bursik, R. J. and Grasmick, H. G. (2006), "Defining and Researching Gangs," in A. Egley, C. L. Maxson, J. Miller and M. W. Klein, eds, *The Modern Gang Reader*. 3rd edn, 2–13. Los Angeles, CA: Roxbury Publishing Company.

Buzi, R. S., Saleh, M., Weinman, M. L. and Smith, P. B. (2004), "Young Fathers Participating in a Fatherhood Program: Their Expectations and Perceived Benefits," *The Prevention Researcher*, 11: 18–20.

Campbell, A. and Muncer, S. (1989), "Them and Us: A Comparison of the Cultural Context of American Gangs and British Subcultures," *Deviant Behavior*, 10: 271–88.

Cochran, D. L. (1997), "African-American Fathers: A Decade Review of the Literature," *Families in Society: Journal of Contemporary Human Services*, 78: 340–50.

Collier, R. (1998), *Masculinities, Crime and Criminology*. Thousand Oaks, CA: Sage Publications.

Connell, R. W. and Messerschmidt, J. W. (2005), "Hegemonic Masculinity: Rethinking the Concept," *Gender & Society*, 19: 829–59.

Decker, S. H. and Weerman, F. M., eds, (2005), *European Street Gangs and Troublesome Youth Groups*. Lanham, MD: AltaMira Press.

Edin, K., Nelson, T. J. and Paranal, R. (2004), "Fatherhood and Incarceration as Potential Turning Points in the Criminal Careers of Unskilled Men," in M. Pattillo, D. Weiman and B. Western, eds, *Imprisoning America: The Social Effects of Massive Incarceration*, 46–75. New York, NY: Russell Sage Foundation.

Esbensen, F-A, Winfree, L. T., He, N. and Taylor, T. J. (2001), "Youth Gangs and Definitional Issues: When Is a Gang a Gang, and Why Does It Matter?," *Crime & Delinquency*, 47: 105–30.

Fagan, J. and Freeman, R. B. (1999), "Crime and Work," *Crime and Justice*, 25: 225–90.

Farrington, D. P. and West, D. J. (1995), "Effects of Marriage, Separation, and Children on Offending by Adult Males," *Current Perspectives on Aging and the Life Cycle*, 4: 249–81.

Forrest, W. (2007), "Adult Family Relationships and Desistance from Crime," unpublished dissertation. Florida State University.

Giordano, P. C., Cernkovich, S. A. and Rudolph, J. L. (2002), "Gender, Crime, and Desistance: Toward a Theory of Cognitive Transformation," *American Journal of Sociology*, 107: 990–1064.

Giordano, P. C., Schroeder, R. D. and Cernkovich, S. A. (2007), "Emotions and Crime over the Life Course: A Neo-Meadian Perspective on Criminal Continuity and Change," *American Journal of Sociology*, 112: 1603–61.

Gordon, R. A., Lahey, B. B., Kawai, E., Loeber, R., Stouthamer-Loeber, M. and Farrington, D. P. (2004), "Antisocial Behavior and Youth Gang Membership: Selection and Socialization," *Criminology*, 42: 55–87.

Gottfredson, M. R. and Hirschi, T. (1994), "A General Theory of Adolescent Problem Behavior: Problems and Prospects," in R. D. Ketterlinus and M. E. Lamb, eds, *Adolescent Problem Behaviors*, 41–56. Hillsdale, NJ: Lawrence Erlbaum Associates.

Hagedorn, J. M., ed. (2007), *Gangs in the Global City: Alternatives to Criminology*. Chicago, IL: University of Illinois Press.

Hernandez, R. (2002), "Fatherhood in the Crossfire: Chicano Teen Fathers Struggling to 'Take Care of Business,'" JSRI Working Paper No. 58. East Lansing, Michigan: The Julian Samora Research Institute, Michigan State University.

Horney, J., Osgood, D. W. and Marshall, I. H. (1995), "Criminal Careers in the Short-Term: Intra-Individual Variability in Crime and Its Relation to Local Life Circumstances," *American Sociological Review*, 60: 655–73.

Hunt, G., Joe-Laidler, K. and MacKenzie, K. (2005), "Moving into Motherhood: Gang Girls and Controlled Risk," *Youth & Society*, 36: 333–73.

Joe, K. (1993), "Issues in Accessing and Studying Ethnic Youth Gangs," *The Gang Journal*, 1: 9–23.

Kazemian, L. (2007), "Desistance from Crime: Theoretical, Empirical, Methodological, and Policy Considerations," *Journal of Contemporary Criminal Justice*, 23: 5–27.

Kimmel, M. S., Hearn, J. and Connell, R. W., eds, (2004), *Handbook of Studies on Men and Masculinities*. Thousand Oaks, CA: Sage Publications.

Klein, M. W. and Maxson, C. L. (2006), *Street Gang Patterns and Policies*. Oxford: Oxford University Press.

Klein, M. W., Weerman, F. and Thornberry, T. (2006), "Street Gang Violence in Europe," *European Journal of Criminology*, 3: 413–37.

Laub, J. A., Nagin, D. S. and Sampson, R. J. (1998), "Trajectories of Change in Criminal Offending: Good Marriages and the Desistance Process," *American Sociological Review*, 63: 225–38.

Laub, J. H. and Sampson, R. J. (2001), "Understanding Desistance from Crime," *Crime and Justice*, 28: 1–69.

Mares, D. (2001), "Gangstas or Lager Louts? Working Class Street Gangs in Manchester," in M. W. Klein, H. J. Kerner, C. L. Maxson and E. G. M Weitekamp, eds, *The Eurogang Paradox: Street Gangs and Youth Groups in the U.S. and Europe*, 153–64. London: Kluwer Academic Publishers.

Marshall, B., Webb, B. and Tilley, N. (2005), *Rationalisation of Current Research on Guns, Gangs and Other Weapons: Phase 1*. London: Jill Dando Institute of Crime Science.

Marsiglio, W., Amato, P., Day, R. D. and Lamb, M. E. (2000), "Scholarship on Fatherhood in the 1990s and Beyond," *Journal of Marriage and the Family*, 62: 1173–91.

Marsiglio, W. and Pleck, J. H. (2004), "Fatherhood and Masculinities," in M. S. Kimmel, J. Hearn and R. W. Connell, eds, *Handbook of Studies on Men and Masculinities*, 249–69. Thousand Oaks, CA: Sage Publications.

Maruna, S. (1997), "Going Straight: Desistance from Crime and Life Narratives of Reform," *The Narrative Study of Lives*, 5: 59–93.

Maruna, S. and Roy, K. (2007), "Amputation or Reconstruction: Notes on the Concept of 'Knifing Off' and Desistance from Crime," *Journal of Contemporary Criminal Justice*, 23: 104–24.

Massoglia, M. and Uggen, C. (2007), "Subjective Desistance and the Transition to Adulthood," *Journal of Contemporary Criminal Justice*, 23: 90–103.

Maxson, C. L. and Klein, M. W. (1995), "Investigating Gang Structures," *Journal of Gang Research*, 3: 33–40.

McCabe, K. and Barnett, D. (2000), "First Comes Work, Then Comes Marriage: Future Orientation among African-American Young Adolescents," *Family Relations*, 49: 63–70.

McCarthy, B. and Hagan, J. (2001), "When Crime Pays: Capital, Competence, and Criminal Success," *Social Forces*, 79: 1035–60.

Pezzin, L. E. (1995), "Earnings Prospects, Matching Effects, and the Decision to Terminate a Criminal Career," *Journal of Quantitative Criminology*, 11: 29–50.

Pirog-Good, M. A. (1996), "The Education and Labor Market Outcomes of Adolescent Fathers," *Youth & Society*, 28: 236–62.

Pitts, J. (2008), *Reluctant Gangsters: The Changing Face of Youth Crime*. Portland, OR: Willan Publishing.

Rand, A. (1987), "Transitional Life Events and Desistance from Delinquency and Crime," in M. E. Wolfgang, T. P. Thornberry and R. M. Figlio, eds, *From Boy to Man, from Delinquency to Crime*, 134–62. Chicago, IL: University of Chicago Press.

Roche, K. M., Ensminger, M. E., Ialongo, N., Poduska, J. M. and Kellam, S. G. (2006), "Early Entries into Adult Roles: Associations with Aggressive Behavior from Early Adolescence into Young Adulthood," *Youth & Society*, 38: 236–61.

Rumgay, J. (2004), "Scripts for Safer Survival: Pathways out of Female Crime," *The Howard Journal of Criminal Justice*, 43: 405–19.

Sampson, R. J. and Laub, J. H. (1993), *Crime in the Making: Pathways and Turning Points through Life*. Thousand Oaks, CA: Sage Publications.

——. (2005), "A Life-Course View of the Development of Crime," *Annals of the American Academy of Political and Social Science*, 602: 12–45.

Sanders, J. M. (2002), "Ethnic Boundaries and Identity in Plural Societies," *The Annual Review of Sociology*, 28: 327–57.

Stouthamer-Loeber, M. and Wei, E. H. (1998), "The Precursors of Young Fatherhood and Its Effect on Delinquency of Teenage Males," *Journal of Adolescent Health*, 22: 56–65.

Thornberry, T. P., Krohn, M. D., Lizotte, A. J., Smith, C. A. and Tobin, K. (2003), *Gangs and Delinquency in Developmental Perspective*. Cambridge, UK: Cambridge University Press.

Uggen, C. (2000), "Work as a Turning Point in the Life Course of Criminals: A Duration Model of Age, Employment, and Recidivism," *American Sociological Review*, 67: 529–46.

US Census Bureau (2002), "DP-1. Profile of General Demographic Characteristics: 2000," Quick Tables, available online at http://factfinder.census.gov/servlet/QTTable?_bm=n&_lang=en&qr_name=DEC_2000_SFI_U_DPI&ds_name=DEC_2000_SFI_U&geo_id=05000US06075 (accessed 10 December 2008).

Venkatesh, S. A. (1997), "The Social Organization of Street Gang Activity in an Urban Ghetto," *American Journal of Sociology*, 103: 82–111.

——. (2003), "A Note on Social Theory and the American Street Gang," in L. Kontos, D. Brotherton and L. Barrios, eds, *Gangs and Society: Alternative Perspectives*, 3–11. New York, NY: Columbia University Press.

Wadsworth, T. (2006), "The Meaning of Work: Conceptualizing the Deterrent Effect of Employment on Crime among Young Adults," *Sociological Perspectives*, 49: 343–68.

Warr, M. (1998), "Life-Course Transitions and Desistance from Crime," *Criminology*, 36: 183–216.

CHAPTER 23

Girl Members of Deviant Youth Groups, Offending Behaviour and Victimisation: Results from the ISRD2 in Italy and Switzerland

Sandrine Haymoz ■ Uberto Gatti

Haymoz and Gatti's chapter represents one of the first attempts to examine female gang involvement cross-nationally. Their findings are significant on several fronts. They demonstrate the utility of both the Eurogang definition of gangs and comparative cross-national investigations (as discussed in Section I). In addition, they reveal notable similarities in gendered patterns across sites. For example, across locale, most youths are involved in mixed-gender gangs, and girls constitute approximately one-third of gang members. In addition, gang-involved girls—like their male gang peers—are involved in significantly more delinquency than their nongang peers, both male and female, and are at greater risk of victimization than nongang youth. Both of these findings are consistent with research in the United States, suggesting the generalizability of these patterns cross-nationally.

The aims of the present research were to evaluate the involvement of girls in youth gangs, to assess the degree of impact gang membership has on various types of deviant behaviour among girls, and to ascertain whether the relationships between gang membership and the behaviour of these girls differ between Italy and Switzerland.

The sample was made up of equal percentages of male and female students, between the ages of 13 and 16, attending different types of schools in Italy and Switzerland. The Italian cohort was made up of representative samples of students in 15 cities and towns of different sizes in different geographical areas; the Swiss cohort was representative of the school population in Switzerland. All students were asked to fill in the ISRD2 questionnaire—in electronic format in Switzerland and on paper in Italy. As it has already been shown in several studies, the method of data collection (electronic or on paper) does not significantly influence the results (Lucia et al. 2007; Killias 1989). The Italian sample was made up of 7th, 8th, 9th and 10th grade students, while the Swiss sample comprised students in the 7th, 8th and 9th grades. Examination of the age distribution of the students revealed that eliminating 10th grade students from the Italian sample would not have yielded homogeneity in terms of age; rather, this was achieved by eliminating, from both samples, subjects younger than 13 years of age or older than 16 years of age. At the end of this operation, the Italian sample comprised 5784 students and the Swiss sample 3459 students, all between 13 and 16 years of age.

The definition of street gang that we used was the one drawn up by the Eurogang group (Klein et al. 2001): "*A street gang is any durable, street-oriented youth group whose own identity includes involvement in illegal activity.*" Initially, we considered to be a gang member any subject who replied affirmatively to the following six questions:

Do you have a group of friends?

How long has this group existed? (>3 months)

Does this group spend a lot of time together in public places?

Is doing illegal things accepted by your group?

Do people in your group actually do illegal things together?

Do you consider your group a gang?

To better assess the meaning of the replies to these questions, we first recorded the frequency of affirmative answers in Italy and Switzerland (Table 23.1). It should be pointed out that all the percentages shown in the table refer to the whole sample and not only to those who have a group of friends.

Table 23.2 shows the percentage of deviant youth group members.

As can be seen from the table, a larger number of Italian youths stated that they had a stable, street-oriented group of friends; this in itself has no connotation of illegality. However, the percentages of Italian respondents who belonged to a group that considered illegal activities as acceptable and who considered their group to be a gang were also higher.

In order to assess the appropriateness of the definition based on the six questions, we cross-referenced the various replies; this operation revealed that, among youths who considered their group to be a gang, about half (55% of Italians and 44% of Swiss) also stated that their group did not indulge in illegal activities, and more than 40% (44% in Italy and 41% in Switzerland) claimed that their group did not consider illegal activities acceptable. For many youths, therefore, the term gang simply means a group of friends, though for others it may mean a delinquent group.

These results indicate the usefulness of a composite definition based on several questions concerning the characteristics of the group (Sharp et al. 2006) and reveal the unreliability of research based on a single question regarding gang membership. In Italy and Switzerland, therefore, and probably in other countries (Weerman and Esbensen 2005), a very different picture is seen from that observed in the United States, where the question "Do you belong to a gang?" or "Have you been a member of a gang in the past?" is regarded as sufficient in order to identify "gang members" (Curry et al. 2002), and where "self-nomination" is considered to be a "particularly robust measure of gang membership capable of distinguishing

Table 23.1 Percentages of Youths Who Replied Affirmatively to the Questions relating to the Eurogang Definition

	Italy (N = 5784)	Switzerland (N = 3459)
27. Do you have a group of friends?	83.7[b]	63.2
30. How long has this group existed? (>3 months)	78.7[b]	59.5
29. Does this group spend a lot of time together in public places?	64.0[b]	41.8
31. Is doing illegal things accepted by your group?	27.3[a]	24.4
32. Do people in your group actually do illegal things together?	21.1	22.1
33. Do you consider your group a gang?	16.3[b]	11.9

[a] Significant difference between Italy and Switzerland: $p < .01$
[b] Significant difference between Italy and Switzerland: $p < .001$

Table 23.2 Percentage of Deviant Youth Group Members

	Italy (N = 5784)	Switzerland (N = 3459)
Deviant youth group members (girls and boys)	5.7[a] (331)	4.7 (165)
Girl members of deviant youth groups	3.9 (117)	3.1 (55)
Boy members of deviant youth groups	7.8 (214)	6.4 (110)

[a] Significant differences between Italy and Switzerland at $p < .05$

gang from non-gang youth" (Esbensen et al. 2001, p. 124).

On the other hand, in Europe there is a certain reluctance to use the term "gang," which often evokes a stereotyped image imported from the US, and which is associated with the idea of an extremely violent and dangerous armed group that controls the neighbourhood. Alternative terms have therefore been proposed, such as "troublesome youth group" (Klein and Maxson 2006) or "delinquent youth group" (Sharp et al. 2006). For these reasons, instead of the term "gang" we prefer to use the expression "deviant youth group," which is less evocative and more suited to the fact that, as will be seen, the youths who belong to these groups not only commit more crimes, but are also more involved in other types of deviant behaviour (alcohol and drug abuse, risky behaviour, etc.).

Therefore, for the remainder of our analysis, we will consider those subjects who provided affirmative answers to the six questions above as being "deviant youth group members." We will then look at how they differ from the other subjects before focusing on gender issues and examining how the phenomenon of "deviant youth groups" affects both boys and girls. Apart from the question of terminology, it should be pointed out that the definition adopted by the Eurogang group, which is based on the six above-mentioned criteria and is widely accepted internationally, facilitates the organisation of very interesting comparative analyses of the relationship between juvenile delinquency and group membership in different social and cultural contexts.

Results

Table 23.3 shows the percentages of youths who belong to a gang according to the Eurogang definition, and whom we have preferred to define as Deviant Youth Group Members.

First of all, it can be seen that the percentages of youths belonging to Deviant Youth Groups (DYG) are fairly similar in Italy (5.7%) and Switzerland (4.7%), although the prevalence is significantly higher in Italy. It can also be seen that, both in Italy and Switzerland, one DYG member out of three is a girl. This level of female participation, which at first sight is very high, has also been recorded in other systematic investigations carried out in the United States and in England. In a recent English study, Sharp et al. (2006) actually found that girls and boys had the same probability (about 6%) of being delinquent youth group members.

The respondents who belonged to deviant youth groups were asked to indicate the composition of their group in terms of gender (Table 23.3); this composition may be of some relevance in categorising the features of the groups in the two countries (Peterson et al. 2001; Joe-Laidler and Hunt 1997).

A difference between Italy and Switzerland can be seen with regard to the composition of the deviant youth groups. Indeed, mixed groups are significantly more numerous in Italy (almost 80%) than in Switzerland (65.5%). Gender separation is therefore more marked in Switzerland than in Italy. It should, however, be pointed out that this differentiation is equally observable with regard to the membership of "normal" groups, i.e. those which are unrelated to deviance. Indeed, the tendency to form mixed groups is more marked in Italy, where a 71.7% rate has been recorded in contrast to a 54.4% rate in Switzerland. Conversely, the formation of groups made up exclusively of girls reaches 10.1% in Italy and 20% in Switzerland. It therefore seems that these differences in group composition

Table 23.3 Gender Composition of Deviant Youth Groups in Percent		
	Italy (*N* = 331)	Switzerland (*N* = 165)
All boys	19.0[a]	28.5
All girls	1.2[a]	6.1
Mixed group	79.8[b]	65.5
[a] Significant difference between Italy and Switzerland: $p < .05$ [b] Significant difference between Italy and Switzerland: $p < .001$		

stem from cultural peculiarities regarding boys and girls in the countries observed. Table 23.4 shows some characteristics of the "deviant youth groups."

In Italy, the percentage of both boys and girls who belong to deviant youth groups increases with age. At the age of 13, 5.3% of boys are members of deviant youth groups, a percentage which rises to 12.1% at the age of 16. Girls show a similar pattern, though the percentages are lower, rising from 2.2% at the age of 13, to 7.4% at the age of 16. In Switzerland, the situation is somewhat different; the percentages of boys who belong to such groups varies little, though a peak can be seen at the age of 14 (6.9%). Among Swiss girls, the percentage peaks at 15 years of age, but then declines at the age of 16 (2%). The proportion of young people who belong to deviant youth groups therefore seems to increase with age among both boys and girls in Italy, while in Switzerland membership of such groups is more stable among boys, whereas it declines with age among girls.

Immigration is more important in Switzerland than in Italy. Indeed, almost 40% of the Swiss respondents in our sample were immigrants. Specifically, 9.7% were first-generation immigrants

and 30.1% second-generation. In Italy, the proportion of immigrants was significantly lower, being 11% (5.2% first-generation and 5.8% second-generation). The relationship between immigration and DYG membership is important in Switzerland, where a markedly higher proportion of immigrants, both first- and second-generation, belong to DYG. The relationships between immigration and deviant youth groups are similar for both boys and girls. In Italy, a certain relationship can be seen between the respondents' family situation and their membership of deviant youth groups, the highest rate of DYG membership being found among boys from single-parent families.

We will first consider juvenile delinquency as a function of deviant youth group membership (Table 23.5), followed by delinquency among boys and girls, and finally the delinquency of deviant youth group members according to gender.

As shown in Table 23.5, deviant youth group members are much more involved in delinquent acts than youths who are not members of such groups. Indeed, the percentages of deviant youth group members involved in all of the delinquent behaviours, whether they be crimes against the

Table 23.4 Percentage of DYG Members among Students of Different Ages, Immigration Status and Family Configuration in Italy and Switzerland

| | Italy (N = 5784) | | Switzerland (N = 3459) | |
| | % of DYG members | | % of DYG members | |
	Boys	Girls	Boys	Girls
Age				
13 years	5.3	2.2	5.7	2.8
14 years	7.1	2.9	6.9	2.6
15 years	8.7	4.4	5.9	4.3
16 years	12.1	7.4	6.5	2.0
Immigration				
Natives	7.7	3.9	3.9	2.3
2nd generation	9.7	5.8	9.8	4.3
1st generation	5.3	1.8	10.7	4.8
Families				
Both biological parents	7.3	3.6	5.8	2.5
Single parent	11.5[a]	4.6	9.2	5.1
Reconstituted	7.0	5.8	7.3	5.0
[a] Significant difference between boys and girls: $p < .05$				

Table 23.5 Percentages of Youths Who Have Committed a Crime as a Function of Deviant Youth Group Membership (Prevalence Rate over 12 Months) and Ratios between Deviant Youth Group Members and Non-Members

	Italy (N = 5784)			Switzerland (N = 3459)		
	DYG members	Non-DYG members	Ratio (DYG members/Non-members)	DYG members	Non-DYG members	Ratio (DYG members/Non-members)
Theft of bicycle, moped, scooter	12.7[a]	1.9	6.7	19.3[a]	2.9	6.7
Theft of a motorcycle or a car	2.8[a]	0.5	5.6	3.8[a]	0.2	19.0
Theft from a car	9.6[a]	1.8	5.3	8.1[a]	0.7	11.6
Shoplifting	26.5[a]	8.2	3.2[b]	36.8[a]	8.1	4.5
Bag snatching	8.7[a]	1.5	5.8	8.1[a]	0.8	10.1
Vandalism	37.7[a]	9.6	3.9[c]	40.5[a]	6.4	6.3
Burglary	6.9[a]	1.6	4.3	5.0[a]	0.6	8.3
Hacking	20.6[a]	8.2	2.5	20.1[a]	4.4	4.6
Assault	9.7[a]	1.3	7.5	7.6[a]	0.9	8.4
Robbery	8.1[a]	1.4	5.8	7.5[a]	0.6	12.5
Group fight	45.5[a]	14.0	3.3[c]	42.3[a]	6.9	6.1
Carrying a weapon	26.9[a]	4.7	5.7	38.6[a]	6.4	6.0
Drug dealing	11.5[a]	2.0	5.8	16.2[a]	2.2	7.4
At least one illegal act[d]	72.1[a]	29.9	2.4[b]	76.3[a]	23.8	3.2

[a] Significant difference between deviant youth group members and non-members: $p < .001$
[b] Significant difference between the Italian and Swiss ratios: $p < .05$
[c] Significant difference between the Italian and Swiss ratios: $p < .01$
[d] Hacking is not included in this variable

person, property offences or drug dealing, are significantly higher. The fact of belonging to a deviant youth group is therefore strongly associated with the commission of crimes. Roughly speaking, almost three out of four members of deviant youth groups reported having committed a crime over the 12 months prior to the survey, while the corresponding figure for non-members was about one in four. The offence committed by the largest proportion of deviant youth group members was group fighting: 45.5% in Italy and 42.3% in Switzerland. Similarly, acts of vandalism were committed by a large proportion of deviant youth group members; almost 38% of DYG members in Italy and almost 41% in Switzerland reported that they had committed an act of vandalism in the previous 12 months, while the figure for non-DYG members was from 4-to 6-fold lower.

The table above (Table 23.5) indicates the ratios between the percentages of DYG members and non-members who reported committing crimes. In Switzerland, the ratios range from 4.5:1 (shoplifting) to 19:1 (vehicle theft); in Italy, the ratios are lower, ranging from 2.5:1 to 7.5:1. An important difference emerges between the two countries in terms of the effect of belonging to a deviant youth group; DYG membership has a greater impact on delinquency in Switzerland than in Italy, as is shown by the higher ratios recorded in Switzerland with regard to all forms of delinquent behaviour except for the theft of bicycles, mopeds and scooters. In order to evaluate the significance of the effect of DYG membership in both countries, we carried out a logistical regression analysis of the interaction between the countries and the deviant youth group membership. This revealed that the effect was significantly greater in Switzerland with regard to shoplifting, vandalism, hacking, group fights and general delinquency, as measured by the fact of having committed a least one crime in the previous 12 months. Thus, it seems that the DYG factor is more criminogenic in Switzerland than in Italy. Table 23.6 shows the prevalence rates of delinquency as a function of gender.

Overall, delinquency proved to be almost twice as high among boys as among girls, both in Italy and in Switzerland. In Italy, 41.7% of boys and 23.7% of girls reported having committed a crime in the previous 12 months; in Switzerland, the corresponding figures were 34.7% and 18%. Boys therefore commit significantly more crimes than girls; this is true for all types of crime except for shoplifting, which displayed similar percentages among boys and girls in both countries. Indeed, shoplifting proved to be the most common crime among girls, being committed by almost 1 in 10, in the 12-month period considered.

As a whole, the male-to-female ratios are fairly similar in Italy and Switzerland, except for burglary and hacking for which gender seems to exert a more marked influence in Switzerland than in Italy. Table 23.7 shows the delinquency of male and female members of deviant youth groups.

As already seen in the previous table, girls are generally less delinquent than boys. Indeed, with the exception of shoplifting, which seems to be committed more or less equally by males and females, the prevalence rates of girls who commit crimes are lower than those of boys in both countries. A similar pattern can be observed among male and female DYG members: 58.6% of female DYG members in Italy and 71.7% in Switzerland reported committing at least one delinquent act in the previous 12 months, while the corresponding figures among male DYG members were 79.7% in Italy and 77.6% in Switzerland. Interestingly, girls who belong to deviant youth groups are seen to commit more delinquent acts than boys who are not members of such groups. Indeed, 58.6% of female DYG members in Italy and 71.7% in Switzerland reported committing at least one offence in the previous 12 months, while the corresponding figures for boys who are not members

Table 23.6 Percentages of Youths Committing Crimes as a Function of Gender (Prevalence Rates over 12 Months) and Ratios between Boys and Girls

	Italy (*N* = 5784)			Switzerland (*N* = 3459)		
	Boys	Girls	Ratio (Boys/Girls)	Boys	Girls	Ratio (Boys/Girls)
Theft of bicycle, moped, scooter	4.2[b]	0.9	4.7	5.5[b]	2.0	2.8
Theft of a motorcycle or car	1.1[b]	0.1	11.0	0.7[b]	0.1	7.0
Theft from a car	3.9[b]	0.7	5.6	1.8[a]	0.3	6.0
Shoplifting	9.5	9.0	1.1	9.8	9.1	1.1
Bag snatching	3.2[b]	0.7	4.6	1.7[a]	0.6	2.8
Vandalism	15.7[b]	7.0	2.2	11.6[b]	4.6	2.5
Burglary	2.6[b]	1.2	2.2[c]	1.5[b]	0.2	7.5
Hacking	12.7[b]	5.5	2.3[c]	8.2[b]	2.0	4.1
Assault	2.9[b]	0.7	4.1	2.2[a]	0.2	11.0
Robbery	2.9[b]	0.7	4.1	1.4[b]	0.5	2.8
Group fight	23.7[b]	8.5	2.8	13.4[b]	3.9	3.4
Carrying a weapon	10.8[b]	1.7	6.4	13.8[b]	2.1	6.6
Drug dealing	3.8[b]	1.5	2.5	4.5[b]	1.2	3.8
At least one illegal act[d]	41.7[b]	23.7	1.8	34.7[b]	18.0	1.9

[a] Significant difference between boys and girls: $p < .01$
[b] Significant difference between boys and girls: $p < .001$
[c] Significant difference between the Italian and Swiss ratios: $p < .05$
[d] Hacking is not included in this variable

Table 23.7 Percentages of Youths Committing a Crime as a Function of DYG Membership and Gender (Prevalence Rates over 12 Months)

	Italy				Switzerland			
	DYG members		Non-DYG members		DYG members		Non-DYG members	
	Boys	Girls	Boys	Girls	Boys	Girls	Boys	Girls
Theft of bicycle, moped, scooter	15.9	6.9	3.3	0.6	25.5	7.4	4.2	1.8
Theft of a motorcycle or car	3.8	0.9	0.9	0.1	5.6	0.0	0.4	0.1
Theft from a car	12.6	4.3	3.2	0.6	12.1	0.0	1.1	0.4
Shoplifting	28.0	23.9	7.9	8.4	31.8	47.2	8.0	8.3
Bag snatching	9.7	6.9	2.7	0.5	12.3	0.0	1.0	0.7
Vandalism	43.9	26.7	13.4	6.2	50.5	21.8	8.9	4.0
Burglary	9.9	1.7	2.0	1.2	7.7	0.0	1.1	0.2
Hacking	25.5	12.0	11.6	5.2	23.6	11.3	7.1	1.7
Assault	13.6	2.6	2.0	0.6	10.7	1.9	1.6	0.1
Robbery	10.7	3.5	2.2	0.6	10.3	0.0	0.8	0.5
Group fight	56.1	26.3	21.0	7.8	50.0	26.9	11.0	3.1
Carrying a weapon	36.7	9.5	8.6	1.4	49.5	15.4	11.4	1.7
Drug dealing	12.6	9.5	3.0	1.2	19.6	9.6	3.4	1.0
At least one illegal act[a]	79.7	58.6	38.6	22.3	77.6	71.7	31.8	16.3

[a]Hacking is not included in this variable

of deviant youth groups were 39% in Italy and 32% in Switzerland.

As shown in Table 23.5, the effect of being a member of a deviant youth group is more marked in Switzerland than in Italy. However, in light of the results presented in the above table (Table 23.7), it appears that the stronger effect of DYG membership in Switzerland concerns the female members of such groups. Indeed, the percentages of male DYG members who reported committing at least one crime, unlike those of the female members, are seen to be similar in Switzerland and Italy. It therefore seems clear that the fact of being a member of a deviant youth group is more criminogenic among Swiss girls than Italian girls. The following tables present the results concerning the victimisation. Table 23.8 reports the victimisation suffered by DYG members and non-members.

As can be seen from the table, the members of deviant youth groups are more often the victims of assault, robbery and theft both in Italy and in Switzerland. The ratios of DYG members to non-members range from 1.4:1 (theft) to 2.5:1 (assault) in Italy and from 1.4:1 (theft) to 5.4:1 (robbery) in

Switzerland. Those who belong to deviant youth groups are therefore at greater risk of victimisation, especially violent victimisation, than those who are not members of such groups. With regard to bullying, which corresponds to violence at school, the situation in the two countries seems to be different. It is interesting that in Italy the members of deviant youth groups are less likely to be bullied than other youths. A possible explanation for this may be that these groups are present in the school environment, and that this may protect their members against victimisation at school. This explanation is not, however, applicable in Switzerland, where youths who are members of deviant groups are just as likely to be victimised as those who are not.

As far as the differences between the two countries are concerned, it emerges that membership of a deviant youth group has a greater effect in Switzerland than in Italy with regard to robbery and bullying. Thus, belonging to a deviant youth group increases the probability of suffering these two types of victimisation in Switzerland. The influence of DYG membership on the other two

Table 23.8 Percentages of Youths Who Have Been Victims of Crime as a Function of DYG Membership (Prevalence Rates over 12 Months) and Ratios of DYG Members to Non-Members

	Italy (N = 5784)			Switzerland (N = 3459)		
	DYG members	Non-DYG members	Ratio (DYG members/Non-members)	DYG members	Non-DYG members	Ratio (DYG members/Non-members)
Assault	7.2[c]	2.9	2.5	8.5[c]	2.1	4.0
Robbery	5.5[b]	2.5	2.2[d]	9.8[c]	1.8	5.4
Theft	22.7[b]	16.7	1.4	30.1[a]	22.0	1.4
Bullying	7.5[a]	12.1	0.6[d]	15.8	12.3	1.3
Victims of at least one act	26.6[c]	18.3	1.5	37.6[c]	23.7	1.6

[a] Significant difference between deviant youth group members and non-members: $p < .05$
[b] Significant difference between deviant youth group members and non-members: $p < .01$
[c] Significant difference between deviant youth group members and non-members: $p < .001$
[d] Significant difference between the Italian and Swiss ratios: $p < .05$

Table 23.9 Percentages of Youths Who Have Been Victims of Crimes as a Function of Gender (Prevalence Rates over 12 Months) and Ratios of Boys to Girls

	Italy (N = 5784)			Switzerland (N = 3459)		
	Male	Female	Ratio (Male/Female)	Male	Female	Ratio (Male/Female)
Assault	4.3[c]	2.1	2.0	2.9	1.9	1.5
Robbery	4.1[c]	1.3	3.2	2.9[b]	1.4	2.1
Theft	17.9	16.4	1.1	23.2	21.6	1.1
Bullying	10.7[a]	12.7	0.8	11.7	13.3	0.9
Victims of at least one act	20.8[c]	16.9	1.2	25.7	22.9	1.1

[a] Significant difference between boys and girls: $p < .05$
[b] Significant difference between boys and girls: $p < .01$
[c] Significant difference between boys and girls: $p < .001$

types of victimisation is similar in Switzerland and Italy. Table 23.9 shows the rates of victimisation as a function of gender.

Gender does not have such a marked effect on victimisation as on delinquency. Nevertheless, in Italy, boys are still significantly more often the victims of assault and robbery than girls are; by contrast, girls are more often the victims of bullying. In Switzerland, the differences between boys and girls are a little less accentuated, though boys are still significantly more often the victims of robbery than girls are. Thus, boys seem to be at greater risk of crimes of violence. No significant difference emerges between the two countries with regard to the effect of gender on victimisation. Table 23.10

shows the victimisation of members of deviant youth groups according to gender.

Generally speaking, the members of deviant youth groups are at greater risk of victimisation. Indeed, both female and male DYG members in both countries are more often the victims of assault, robbery and theft than those who are not members of such groups. It is interesting that male members of deviant youth groups in Italy are decidedly less likely to be bullied than other boys, while female members are just as likely to be bullied as other girls. It therefore seems that DYG membership protects boys against this form of victimisation, i.e. victimisation in the school environment. However, this characteristic is not found

Table 23.10 Percentages of Youths Who Have Been the Victims of Crime as a Function of DYG Membership and Gender (Prevalence Rates over 12 Months)

	Italy				Switzerland			
	DYG members		Non-DYG members		DYG members		Non-DYG members	
	Boys	Girls	Boys	Girls	Boys	Girls	Boys	Girls
Assault	6.5	8.3	4.1	1.8	8.3	7.3	2.5	1.7
Robbery	6.5	3.7	3.9	1.2	10.1	8.9	2.4	1.2
Theft	21.1	25.5	17.6	16.0	31.2	28.3	22.6	21.4
Bullying	4.5	13.0	11.3	12.7	14.5	18.2	11.5	13.1
Victims of at least one act	25.2	29.1	20.4	16.4	39.1	33.9	24.8	22.6

in Switzerland, where the pertinent rates are fairly similar.

Conclusions

As a whole, the phenomenon of deviant youth group membership was found to be fairly similar in Italy and Switzerland. Some differences did, however, emerge. Deviant youth group membership proved to be more frequent in Italy (5.7%) than in Switzerland (4.7%), a difference which, albeit limited, reached statistical significance. Deviant youth groups are more frequently mixed in Italy than in Switzerland; however, since this pattern can also be observed in other types of groups, it may be attributable to more generalised cultural features of the two countries. The age of deviant youth group members also differs. In Italy, the percentage of members, whether male or female, increases with age, while in Switzerland the prevalence rates remain relatively stable for boys and decline with age for girls. Generally speaking, immigration is a more important factor in Switzerland than in Italy, with first-generation immigrants being more involved in deviant youth groups in the former country. The relationship between immigration and membership of such groups is, however, similar for both boys and girls.

The present study demonstrated not only that crime rates are higher among members of deviant youth groups in general, but also that they are higher among female members, who account for about one third of deviant youth group members

in both countries. Overall, almost 75% of deviant youth group members reported having committed a crime during the 12 months prior to the study, compared to 25% of youths who are not members of such groups. The effect of deviant youth group membership on offending proved to be higher in Switzerland than in Italy with regard to vandalism, hacking, group fights and "at least one offence," while the gender effect on offending was seen to be similar in both countries (greater male effect in Switzerland only for hacking).

Delinquency among girl members of deviant youth groups is considerably higher than among other girls, reaching a higher level than that of boys who do not belong to such groups. In addition, it clearly emerges that membership of a deviant youth group exerts a more criminogenic effect on Swiss girls than on Italian girls.

With regard to victimisation, and particularly violent victimisation, the members of deviant youth groups are at greater risk than youths who are not members of such groups; in fact, they are more frequently the victims of assault, robbery and theft. This pattern was observed both in Italy and in Switzerland. As far as bullying is concerned, the situation is different in the two countries. In Italy, the male members of deviant youth groups are less likely to be bullied than other youths; this may be explained by the presence of such groups in schools, which might protect group members against any such victimisation within the school setting. In Switzerland, however, the members of deviant youth groups are just as likely to be bullied as non-member youths. It also seems that being a member of a deviant youth group exerts a stronger effect on victimisation in Switzerland than it does in Italy as far as robbery and bullying are concerned. With regard to the girl members of deviant youth groups, their level of victimisation is higher than that of non-member girls and equal to that of boys who are not members of such groups. Moreover, they seem to be particularly vulnerable to crimes of violence. All in all, membership of a deviant youth group implies greater involvement in delinquency and a greater risk of victimisation. The factor "deviant group" seems to be stronger than the factor "gender," in that girls who are members of deviant groups display a higher level of delinquency than boys who are not members of such groups.

As our study had a cross-sectional design, it does not enable us to determine whether the higher level of delinquency precedes or follows entry into the group, i.e. whether a selection process is at work, whereby those youths who are already more delinquent are induced to join a deviant group (selection model), or whether a facilitation process is operating, whereby the group exerts a criminogenic effect (facilitation model). The results of studies that have dealt with this issue in other countries (Esbensen et al. 2001; Thornberry et al. 2002; Gatti et al. 2005; Farrington and Loeber 2000) suggest that both processes are involved (enhancement model).

References

Curry, G. D., Decker, S., & Egley, A., Jr. (2002). Gang involvement and delinquency in a middle school population. *Justice Quarterly, 19*(2), 275–292.

Esbensen, F.-A., Winfree, L. T., He, N., & Taylor, T. J. (2001). Youth gangs and definitional issues: When is a gang a gang, and why does it matter? *Crime and Delinquency, 47*, 105–130.

Farrington, D. P., & Loeber, R. (2000). Epidemiology of juvenile violence. *Child and Adolescent Psychiatric Clinic of North America, 9*(4), 733–748.

Gatti, U., Tremblay, R. E., Vitaro, F., & McDuff, P. (2005). Youth gangs, delinquency and drug use: A test of the selection, facilitation, and enhancement hypotheses. *Journal of Child Psychology and Psychiatry, 46*(11), 1178–1190.

Joe-Laidler, K., & Hunt, G. (1997). Violence and social organization in female gangs. *Social Justice, 24*, 148–169.

Killias, M. (1989). *Les Suisses face au crime: Leurs expériences et attitudes à la lumière des sondages suisses de victimisation.* Grüsch (Grisons): Rüegger.

Klein, M. W., Kerner, H. J., Maxson, C. L., & Weitekamp, E. (Eds.). (2001). *The Eurogang paradox: Street gangs and youth groups in the U.S. and Europe.* Dordrecht, The Netherlands: Kluwer.

Klein, M. W., & Maxson, C. L. (2006). *Street gang patterns and policies.* Oxford: Oxford University Press.

Lucia, S., Herrmann, L., & Killias, M. (2007). How important are interview methods and questionnaire designs in research on self-reported juvenile delinquency? An experimental comparison of Internet vs. paper-and-pencil questionnaires and different definitions of the reference period. *Journal of Experimental Criminology, 3*(1), 39–64.

Peterson, D., Miller, J., & Esbensen, F.-A. (2001). The impact of sex composition on gangs and gang member delinquency. *Criminology: 39*(2), 411–439.

Sharp, C., Aldridge, J., & Medina, J. (2006). *Delinquent youth groups and offending behaviour: Findings from the 2004 Offending Crime and Justice Survey.* London: Home Office Research Development and Statistics Directorate.

Thornberry, T. P., Krohn, M. D., Lizotte, A. J., Smith, C. A., & Tobin, K. (2002). *The toll of gang membership: Gangs and delinquency in developmental perspective.* New York: Cambridge University Press.

Weerman, F. M., & Esbensen, F.-A. (2005). A cross-national comparison of youth gangs. In S. H. Decker & F. M. Weerman (Eds.), *European street gangs and troublesome youth groups* (pp. 219–255). Lanham: AltaMira Press.

Community Contexts

Among all the domains of risk factors for joining gangs, community characteristics are the least studied. Hence, we know a great deal more about individual, family, peer, and school features that are related to gang participation than about the characteristics of the communities that appear to foster gangs. As a result of the advent of annual law enforcement surveys conducted by the National Gang Center (described in Section II), we have regular trend data on the relationships between gang prevalence (e.g., whether or not a place has gangs, estimates of number of gangs and gang members, year-to-year changes) and city population, geographic location, and a host of other characteristics of cities. Indeed, a few scholars have employed these data to compare gang problems in rural versus urban environments. While we have learned about broad trends in the proliferation and location of street gangs in the United States from these data, they tell us little about the variation in community contexts that is important for gang emergence or persistence. Aside from the criticisms of relying on police estimates and the lack of a specified definition of a gang (see Section I), the major limitation of the National Youth Gang Survey data is that it doesn't capture variation within a city. Of course, every city with gangs has many neighborhoods without them, so it is critical that we have a better understanding of the features of neighborhoods that produce gangs of various types and promote youth's participation in them. It is also important that we conduct such studies in more than one city so that we can better understand these neighborhood variations in different city contexts.

The lack of studies on community characteristics is attributable to the difficulty of obtaining valid data on gangs at the neighborhood level. We can draw on the US Census and other established datasets to provide economic and social data that describe each neighborhood's population, household, commercial, and land use characteristics. But where do we find information on gang membership or activity? Some scholars obtain gang residential information or gang territories from the police (as, for example, the Katz and Schnebly study reported in this section), while others use address information from police designations of gang-related crime or violence as a proxy for gang activity. Even if such information were available from many gang cities, we would be concerned about variation in definitional policies or recording practices in different cities, which would limit the validity of comparisons. A different opportunity to study neighborhood variation derives from interview studies that employ representative samples of youth subjects to obtain gang, residential, and a host of other relevant characteristics, sometimes in a longitudinal manner that allows changes over time to be captured. A handful of these studies exist, but they are expensive to conduct and only provide data from a few select cities. Until we can benefit from planned, comparative interview studies utilizing representative sampling techniques, we must rely heavily on the perspectives generated by qualitative studies of gang neighborhoods. These have the advantage of providing rich narratives on the ways in which gangs and their members intersect with other neighborhood residents and social institutions, but they rarely include more than a few neighborhoods and therefore lack sufficient neighborhood variation to generate broad conclusions.

Several theories of crime and delinquency emphasize the importance of community contexts. Social disorganization, strain, differential opportunity, and subcultural deviance theories have influenced gang scholars. In particular, social disorganization theory forms the base for several of the studies presented in this section. This theory suggests that social structural factors such as economic and social disadvantage influence community processes like the development of social ties, trust among neighbors, and willingness to intervene to resolve community problems (what some scholars call "collective efficacy"). Residents of such communities are less likely to exert informal social control that keeps neighborhood youth in check and reinforces norms and values of law-abiding behavior. This, then, provides fertile ground for the growth of gangs, or perhaps gangs might offer a means of control that is otherwise lacking in the community. This is just one illustration of the way that criminological

theories offer guidance about the types of community contexts that may be important to the emergence and persistence of street gangs.

In addition to theory and methods, community contexts have important ramifications for programmatic and policy responses to gangs. We can well imagine that the efficacy of prevention and intervention programs would vary considerably depending on the features of the individual communities in which they are implemented. Furthermore, a narrow programmatic focus on individual or family factors that dismisses the gang-promoting features of the community would appear to be doomed to failure. Several of the articles in the final section of this volume grapple with this problem, but few interventions are as focused on place as the civil gang injunction. This intervention severely circumscribes the behavior of gang members within a bounded area, without taking into account the neighborhood factors that fostered gang problems in the first place. This is but one example of the way in which gang theory, research, and practice would benefit from paying closer heed to the importance of community contexts.

CHAPTER 24

Sweet Mothers and Gangbangers: Managing Crime in a Black Middle-Class Neighborhood

Mary E. Pattillo

This article advances our knowledge about the dynamics of formal and informal social control in communities. In her ethnographic study of a black middle-class neighborhood in Chicago, Pattillo illustrates the intricate web of social networks and how these social ties contribute to—and also undermine—social control efforts. Gang members that are long-term residents can be invested in dominant neighborhood norms and reinforce social control even while their dense social ties with nongang residents can sometimes preclude activation of control efforts. It is important to keep in mind that the gangs in Groveland specialize in drug sales and therefore are likely more organized and can exert more control over their own members than gangs in other community contexts.

The research on African Americans is dominated by inquiries into the lives of the black poor. Contemporary ethnographies and journalistic descriptions have thoroughly described deviance, gangs, drugs, intergender relations and sexuality, stymied aspirations, and family patterns in poor neighborhoods (Dash 1989; Hagedorn 1988; Kotlowitz 1991; Lemann 1991; MacLeod 1995; Sullivan 1989; Williams 1989). Yet, the majority of African Americans are not poor (Billingsley 1992). A significant part of the black experience, namely that of working and middle-class blacks, remains unexplored. We have little information about what black middle-class neighborhoods look like and

how social life is organized within them. In the tradition of grounded, sociological community studies (Anderson 1978, 1990; Suttles 1968; Whyte 1943), this article begins to fill this empirical and theoretical gap using ethnographic data collected in Groveland, a middle-class black neighborhood in Chicago.[1]

Groveland is home to one of the top gang leaders and drug dealers in Chicago, as well as to one of the highest ranking black officials in city government. The young people who grow up in the neighborhood are as easily introduced to the gangs and their drug business as they are to the neighborhood political organization. This article explores how the two co-exist and maintain what residents refer to as a "quiet neighborhood." I argue that variables shown to affect neighborhood social organization— especially residential stability and the strong informal ties that stability fosters—have not been sufficiently unpacked to illustrate why and how they help or hinder social organization. In Groveland, stability and dense networks do not prevent criminal behaviors. Instead, they work to circumscribe the criminal activity that does exist by holding the neighborhood delinquents within the bonds of familial and neighborhood associations. There exists a system of interlocking networks of responsible and deviant residents that sometimes paradoxically, and always precariously, keeps the peace.

Theories of Social (Dis)organization

Social organization is goal-oriented. *Social disorganization* is defined as "the inability of a community structure to realize the common values of its residents and maintain effective social controls" (Sampson & Wilson 1995:45); hence, social organization refers to the effective efforts of neighborhood actors toward common ends. These ends are similar across populations. Regardless of the social class or racial composition of a neighborhood, most people share a "common goal of living in an area relatively free from the threat of crime" (Bursik & Grasmick 1993:15). Moreover, disorder—public drinking, loitering, street harassment, corner drug selling, vandalism, abandonment, and litter—is neither desired nor condoned in any kind of neighborhood. There is a consistent, positive relationship between disorder and neighborhood dissatisfaction, citizen withdrawal, and crime levels (Skogan 1990). Because proscriptions against crime and disorder are similar across neighborhoods, including Groveland, the more interesting issues are the types of neighborhood contexts in which residents enact these values and their organizational strategies.

Social (dis)organization theory contends that a neighborhood's socioeconomic status is negatively related to ethnic heterogeneity and residential instability, both of which are positively related to crime (Byrne & Sampson 1986; Shaw & McKay 1942). Heterogeneity and instability work through their negative impact on informal and formal social control, where *social control* is defined as "the effort of the community to regulate itself and the behavior of residents and visitors to the neighborhood" (Bursik & Grasmick 1993:15). Both heterogeneity and instability hamper communication, decrease residents' familiarity with one another, and decrease their attachment to the neighborhood and its organizations, all important components of social control. A later reformulation of social organization theory—the systemic model—also stresses the importance of kin and neighborly ties for the social control of crime and disorder (Berry & Kasarda 1977; Bursik & Grasmick 1993; Sampson 1992).

One of the persistent challenges to social organization theory has been the existence of residentially stable neighborhoods with continuing high rates of crime (Suttles 1968; Whyte 1943). The systemic model's explanation for these apparent anomalies is that, while internally integrated, these neighborhoods lack essential ties to public forms of social control such as the police, government bureaucrats, and social service agencies. Low-income neighborhoods also have weak internal economies and lack sufficient connections to mainstream employment. Finally, the neighborhood's low status decreases its bargaining power in securing valuable city services, further impeding residents' attempts at social control. Thus, the disadvantaged social class make-up and the lack of ties to nonneighborhood actors cancel out whatever internal organization may exist (Bursik & Grasmick 1993; Guest & Lee 1983; Logan & Molotch 1987; Oliver 1988; Warren 1975).

Stable low-income areas may develop organized criminal subcultures where the "neighborhood milieu [is] characterized by close bonds between different age-levels of offenders, and between criminal and conventional elements" (Cloward & Ohlin 1960:171). In such locales, neighborhood stability can foster the formation of an alternative opportunity structure based on organized crime, which benefits both criminal and law-abiding residents. These relationships across the law provided the basis for organized crime among Irish, Italian, and Jewish immigrants alike (Ianni 1971, 1974; O'Kane 1992). More recent studies of poor neighborhoods also find that neighborhood delinquents provide important social and economic resources to their lawful friends, kin, and neighbors (Jankowski 1991; Sullivan 1989; Venkatesh 1996, 1997). These arrangements mirror the processes described in this article. However, crime and the subsequent alliances between criminals and noncriminals develop in these neighborhoods only because of "the pressures generated by restrictions on legitimate access to success-goals" (Cloward & Ohlin 1960:171). In other words, "Poverty and powerlessness are the root of both community acceptance of organized crime and recruitment into its networks" (Ianni 1974:38). It would follow that such pressures do not exist in middle-class neighborhoods where residents have the human and social capital to prosper in the legitimate occupational structure. How, then, can we account for an extensively organized and visible criminal element in a stable middle-class neighborhood such as Groveland?

The Unique Black Middle-Class Neighborhood

Groveland is a black neighborhood on the South Side of Chicago with a population of just under 12,000 residents, over 95% of whom are African American. The official community area covers approximately 91 square blocks. Ridge Lake Avenue, a six-lane thoroughfare, cuts through the middle of the neighborhood, and most residents refer to only the western half as "Groveland" proper, even though the sections are very similar. The fact that Ridge Lake Avenue separates gang territories is one explanation for the local understandings of neighborhood boundaries.[2]

The median family income in Groveland is nearly $40,000 annually, while the comparable figure for Chicago is just over $30,000. Over 60% of the population are white-collar workers. The majority of the dwellings are owner-occupied, single-family brick homes with modest front and back yards; there are very few apartment buildings. Most residents work diligently to keep the neighborhood clean and their yards and houses attractive.

There are two public grammar schools, a Catholic grammar school and one public high school. There are eleven churches in Groveland representing ten Christian denominations; six of these churches belong to the Groveland Clergy Association. Within Groveland there is a park—Groveland Park—that is a part of the Chicago Park District. There are three commercial streets within the neighborhood reported to be "the busiest predominantly black shopping district in the state."

Although there are sizeable physical boundaries on the east and west that enclose the neighborhood, and somewhat restricted access at the north and south borders, Groveland is integrally tied to its surrounding neighborhoods. It is a part of a larger black middle-class population residing on the city's South Side. Within the official community area of Groveland is the subdivision Cedarcove where the motto is "suburban living in the inner city."

By income and occupational criteria, as well as the American value of home ownership, Groveland is a middle-class neighborhood, and residents refer to it as such. Yet Grovelandites are not doctors, lawyers, and corporate executives (Cose 1993). The black class structure is truncated at the high end such that in 1993, only 18% of black families nationally had incomes over $50,000, whereas 37% of white families had such incomes (Smith & Horton 1997). The black middle class resembles the white lower-middle class (Collins 1983; Landry 1987; Wilson 1995). They are administrative assistants, small business owners, police officers, teachers, and government bureaucrats; and in 1990, nearly 12% of Groveland's residents were unemployed.

Geographically, black middle-class neighborhoods tend to be nestled between areas that are less economically stable and have higher crime rates. Figure 24.1 provides three statistics for Groveland and the surrounding neighborhoods. Below each neighborhood's pseudonym is the neighborhood's (rounded) median family income; next is the percent of families with incomes below the poverty line; the third figure is the 1990 homicide rate per 10,000 residents.

Figure 24.1 shows that all but one of the neighborhoods bordering Groveland have lower median family incomes. The poverty rate is also higher in four of the six adjacent neighborhoods. Taking this exercise one (geographic) step further, the Treelawn community area—north of both Trainer

Figure 24.1 Median Family Income, Poverty Rate, and Homicide Rate, Groveland and Surrounding Neighborhoods, 1990

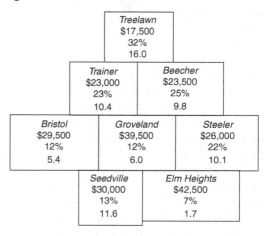

Sources: *Local Community Fact Book Chicago Metropolitan Area, 1990*; and Illinois Criminal Justice Information Authority 1994. Morenoff provided the homicide statistics.

and Beecher—has a median family income of just under $18,000, not even half the median family income in Groveland. Its poverty rate of over 30% is nearly triple that of Groveland. All these contiguous neighborhoods are over 90% black, illustrating Chicago's hypersegregation (Massey & Denton 1993).

Finally, using a measure of the most violent kind of crime, Figure 24.1 clearly illustrates the perils associated with living in a black middle-class neighborhood. All but two of the adjacent neighborhoods have higher homicide rates. For comparison, a white middle-class neighborhood in Chicago (Beltway) was also included in the larger project of which the present study is a part (see Methods section). The homicide rate for Beltway is only 1.4/10,000. Furthermore, the rates for the three community areas that surround Beltway are 1.8, 2.4, and 0.4 homicides per 10,000 residents, barely overlapping with the levels of violence in the Groveland area. The poverty rates in and around Beltway are similarly low when compared to the community surrounding Groveland.

The proximity of Groveland to poorer, less stable neighborhoods underscores the importance of the spatial context of black middle-class areas. While the black middle class has attempted to leave poor neighborhoods (Wilson 1987), they have not gotten very far. The higher poverty and higher crime areas nearby are constant reminders of what could happen if Groveland residents' efforts at social control fail (Morenoff & Sampson 1997). Black middle-class residents must struggle to remain in the majority and define the norms of public conduct and social order. The larger community depicted in Figure 24.1 also represents a dangerous training ground for Groveland's youth who are not confined to the small area of the neighborhood.

The ecological patterns observed in Groveland are not unique. African Americans of every socioeconomic status live in qualitatively different kinds of neighborhoods than their white counterparts. In a revealing exercise, Sampson and Wilson (1995) use census data to locate similar black and white ecological contexts. They find the following: "In not one city over 100,000 in the United States do blacks live in ecological equality with whites. . . . *The 'worst' urban contexts in which whites reside are*

considerably better than the average context of black communities" (42, emphasis added).

The residential returns to middle-class blacks are far smaller than those to middle-class whites. Massey, Condran & Denton (1987) compare similar black and white families in Philadelphia and the kinds of neighborhoods in which they live. Focusing on indicators such as the proportion of out-of-wedlock births, median home values, neighborhood poverty, and the educational performance of students in the local high school, the authors find dramatic differences between neighborhoods. For example, the probability for neighborhood contact with a family on welfare for college educated blacks was 22%, whereas college educated whites had only an 8% chance of such contact. This pattern was repeated for contact with blue-collar workers, high school dropouts, unemployed workers, and female-headed families.

With regards to exposure to crime, the black middle class is again at a disadvantage, even in the suburbs. "Even the most affluent blacks are not able to escape from crime, for they reside in communities as crime-prone as those housing the poorest whites" (Alba, Logan & Bellair 1994:427). Other studies have found similar disparities (Darden 1987; Erbe 1975; Farley 1991; Grossman & White 1997; Landry 1987; Massey, Gross & Shibuya 1994; Villemez 1980). Massey & Denton (1993) conclude that for blacks, "high incomes do not buy entrée to residential circumstances that can serve as springboards for future socioeconomic mobility" (153). Finally, being black and middle class does not allow for much excess in terms of either meeting ordinary expenses (Landry 1987) or accumulated wealth (Jaynes & Williams 1989; Oliver & Shapiro 1995). As one Groveland resident put it: "I think the average black person nowadays are all middle class mostly. They're struggling everyday to make it. You could go any way any day."

All these obstacles affect the ability of these residents to realize common goals and values. These spatial and social particularities also begin to answer the question of how a visible criminal element could persist in a predominately middle-class neighborhood. Segregation has ensured the continued confinement of blacks of various socioeconomic statuses into fixed geographic areas. These segregated black neighborhoods bear the full burden of disproportionate poverty among African Americans. All families in black middle-class neighborhoods are not equally endowed with the resources to steer their children in positive directions (e.g., paying for music lessons, sports leagues, and equipment) or to buy for their youngsters the status symbols of contemporary youth consumer culture. Socioeconomic disadvantage assists in making mainstream values "existentially irrelevant" for a portion of the population (Sampson & Wilson 1995). Economically marginal adults are equally captivated by the fast money that crime promises. These orientations are easily taken on by middle-class youth whose parents could provide some luxuries, but never enough to satisfy the wants of most American adolescents.

Crime in Groveland and the middle-class origin of many of its deviants require a complex incorporation of structure—the changing employment market, the differential allocation of municipal resources, and the effects of segregation—and culture, such as the appeal of popular media "gangsters." These factors impact social organization and social control in Groveland, but are largely exogenous to local interactions and events. (See Figure 24.2.)

The neighborhood-level focus of this article guides attention toward the way in which social connections between residents affect the management of crime. The mix of residents and lifestyles has consequences for the proximate sources of social organization, such as the collective supervision of neighborhood youth and organizational

participation and activism (Bursik & Grasmick 1993; Freudenberg 1986; Kasarda & Janowitz 1974; Sampson & Groves 1989). Ethnography is an appropriate method for investigating these microlevel processes.

Drawing from the systemic model, I reiterate the importance of residential stability for the creation and maintenance of social networks. The first empirical section of this article highlights the thick kin, neighborly, and friendship ties that exist in Groveland, across the boundaries of legitimacy. The second section describes how these networks positively impact both the informal and formal supervision of youth. Informal social control refers to the daily management of behaviors in casual settings, whereas formal social control involves actors who represent local institutions as well as official law enforcement agents. My argument departs from both social organization theory and the systemic model, however, in the explanation of how these networks facilitate control. As Figure 24.2 illustrates, dense social networks have both positive and negative effects for social control through specific mediating processes.

Neighborhood familiarity does not stop residents from getting involved in gangs and drug dealing. It does, however, keep them connected to nongang adults and youth who constantly monitor their illegal operations, demanding that they conform to neighborhood norms of order. Groveland's criminal element also constitutes a valid local organization in the neighborhood and levies considerable social control on its members. This

Figure 24.2 A Grounded Model of Neighborhood Social Control

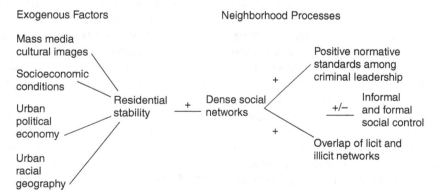

structure is described in the third empirical section of this article. Groveland's gang leaders were raised in the neighborhood. They often concur with the norms of the church and block club members and hold their youthful charges to similar standards. Both factions spurn disorder, actively combat graffiti, and show disdain for activities that may invite negative attention, such as loitering or public fighting. Also, both groups explicitly desire economic prosperity. The "occupational status" of the neighborhood drug dealers mirrors that of neighborhood residents who work in the legal sector. At the same time, these interlocking networks and the similarities in interests and behaviors make it difficult for law-abiding residents to totally rid their neighborhood of the criminal element, thus negatively affecting social control.

For the most part, the two groups agree on goals, but disagree on strategies. Living in a black middle-class neighborhood requires that law-abiding residents compromise some of their attitudes—such as the scorn for drug dealing and the violent enforcement that goes with it—for the achievement of a "quiet neighborhood." This unique, adaptive strategy for social organization rests on a tenuous integration of and intermittent truce between the networks of gang members and the business of drug dealing on the one hand, and the activism of church leaders, block club members, and local political officials on the other.

Method and Data

This research used the participant observation method (Lofland & Lofland 1984). The primary data were collected over a two and a half year period in the early 1990s for the Comparative Neighborhood Study (CNS) conducted at the University of Chicago. The CNS investigated racial discourse, culture, and social organization in four neighborhoods of different racial and ethnic composition—one white (Beltway), one Mexican American, one in transition from white to Mexican American, and Groveland. A second field worker worked in Groveland, although the majority of the field notes presented here were collected by the author.

The research included intensive participant observation in informal settings in the neighborhood such as Groveland Park and the local churches. I also conducted interviews with key leaders and lay residents, and regularly attended meetings of the Chicago Area Policing Strategy program, the Chicago Park District, Groveland's political organization, and the Chamber of Commerce. I minimized the problem of selectivity by getting involved in a wide range of activities and social networks, which yielded substantive conversations with gang leaders as well as social service providers, grandparents, and toddlers. Although limited to those people who did actually leave their own homes, the participant observation component of this project tapped a rich cross-section of Groveland residents. Demographic information, newspaper clippings, photographs, neighborhood flyers, and other supportive data were also collected throughout the study.

After the completion of the CNS, I moved to Groveland, continued the participant observation, and conducted 28 taped, in-depth interviews. Three pilot interviews also contained useful data. Interviewees were identified by a snowball sample and were chosen to represent residents from across the social class and age spectrum. The breakdown of social class positions was formulated taking into account the literature on the black class structure (Blackwell 1985; Landry 1987; Vanneman & Cannon 1987; Wilson 1978). Because the goal of interviewing was to gather a variety of residents' opinions, rather than have quantifiable data, the relaxed method of sampling was satisfactory.

All the interview and participant observation data were coded into over 30 general themes of interest. The coding process substantially increased my familiarity with the material by guaranteeing at least three layers of experience with the data: (1) the social interaction itself (interview or participant observation), (2) writing field notes or transcribing an interview, and (3) re-reading the notes for coding purposes. This article draws primarily from the inspection and organization of the following codes: gangs, drugs, guns, recollections of crime, intergenerational interaction, social networks, political participation, and the role of churches.

The arguments in this article should be read as a conversation between the specificity of people's words and actions in Groveland and the grand declarations of sociological theory. Following the methods of grounded theory (Glaser & Strauss 1967), existing sociological theories and categories were used as "sensitizing concepts" (Schwartz & Jacobs 1979). I had introductory knowledge of theories of social (dis)organization and social control as laid out by early Chicago School theorists and as refined by contemporary scholars. As a result, I focused on the informal ways that adults controlled the behavior of younger residents. Hence, some of the codes used to analyze the data, such as intergenerational interaction and social networks, reflect particular concerns raised by the literature.

Nevertheless, much emerges from the process of field work itself that cannot be anticipated by existing theories. As Lofland and Lofland (1984) point out:

> The researcher does not only (or mainly) wait for "significant" (sociologically or otherwise) events to occur or words to be said and then write them down. An enormous amount of information about the settings under observation or the interview in process can be apprehended in apparently trivial happenings or utterances, and these are indispensable grist for the logging mill (46).

Hence, analytic codes like "discussions of guns" or "the role of churches" became particularly salient only after being in the field and logging the minutiae of everyday interactions. Moreover, because neither the CNS nor the present author was interested exclusively in social control in Groveland, the plan for writing field notes was to be as exhaustive as possible. It was only through the constant re-inspection of the notes that significant themes grew out of mundane and unrelated interactions. The conclusions for this article were reached through the simultaneous processes of collecting data and coding it, and then going back to the field to further explore those codes; that is, the ideas were reached inductively through theoretical sampling (Glaser & Strauss 1967).

Social Organization in Groveland

Networks Intertwined

"GANG BUSTED" read the headline of a Chicago newspaper:[3]

In a blitzkrieg of police work reminiscent of the lightning attacks of the 1980s on the El Rukn street gang and the Herrera family of heroin peddlers, about 250 law-enforcement officers swooped down Thursday to make arrests after the indictment of 39 alleged Black Mobsters.

This "victory" for Chicago law enforcement—the article's subtitle read, "We Ripped Off the Head of the Snake"—has had less than predictable results in the neighborhoods on Chicago's South Side, including Groveland, much of which is Black Mobster territory. Social organization in Groveland is partially dependent upon the social control levied by neighborhood gang leaders on their local troops. Keith, a 26 year-old resident, described the neighborhood before the bust as follows:[4]

> One of the biggest gang leaders in Chicago, on the South Side, live right around the corner. And he ain't gon' let nothin' happen in his neighborhood. He don't want a lotta stuff goin' on 'cause he don't wanna lose his house. He control alla these little gangbangers. Like he got together with some of the churches and stuff and got that liquor store closed over there. You know, I won't say he all bad, 'cause he does do a lot of good things for the community. But he do 'em for the wrong reasons.

The former supervisor at Groveland Park also talked about the complex position occupied by the Black Mobsters in organizing the neighborhood:

> The kids really protect this building. No graffiti, well sometimes we'll get some, but they don't let that go on. No fighting, no break-ins. 'Cause there are gangs around here. I forget what they call themselves. Black somethings. But this is like a neutral zone. The gym show this weekend, Friday and Saturday, they [the gang] did security. They bought blue security t-shirts to match the kids' and they were all over the building. They had walkie-talkies and everything. They were in the front halls and all around the back. There were about thirty of 'em and we didn't even have to use the police. 'Cause, you know, I had called the police to provide security 'cause we must have had about two thousand people in here over the weekend. But they were better than the police.

Gangs are a reality of neighborhood life in Groveland. Both comments above illustrate that gangs are not uniformly depicted as the scourge of the community. Residents must reconcile the "good things" that gangs do (and the good people within gangs) with their "wrong reasons."

The density of neighborhood networks and the prevalence of family and fictive kin ties underlie the tangled relationship between gangs, drugs, and the forces that fight against them. Intimate networks are created and maintained when people live near one another for long periods of time (Sampson 1992). Seventy percent of the housing units in Groveland are owner occupied, serving to economically tie residents to the present and future of the neighborhood. A full 70% of the residents in Groveland moved into their homes before 1980, which means they had lived there at least ten years at the time of the 1990 census. In the area of Black Mobster rule (west of Ridge Lake Avenue) almost half of the residents moved into their current residence before 1970. These demographics indicate the stability necessary to form intimate social bonds, and bonds from childhood remain very much alive among adults in the neighborhood.[5]

The Vincent Family illustrates these enduring ties. Husband and wife Kim and Joseph Vincent both grew up in Groveland, although Kim lived in the neighborhood first. "Where I grew up we were like a family on the whole block," Kim describes. "You know, the next door neighbors babysat me and now I babysit their kids, you know. I'm their godmother and their mama's my godmother. So it's like a family."

Before Joseph Vincent moved to Groveland himself, he would come to visit his cousins who lived on Kim's block. When Joseph first saw Kim, he told his cousins he would marry her. Kim and Joseph both agree that it was love at first sight, although it took nearly fifteen years of off-and-on dating before they finally got married. After getting married, they bought a two-flat building in the neighborhood, rented the bottom and basement apartments, and Kim opened a day care in their top floor apartment. When their family grew, they bought a single-family house four blocks away (still in Groveland) and rented the apartments in the two-flat. Some days after school, their 8-year-old son drops his bags with his mother at her day care and walks the three blocks to visit his grandparents who continue to live in the house where Kim grew up. Many residents in Groveland have these kinds of close extended and spatially proximate family ties.

Fictive kin networks also flourish in Groveland (Anderson 1978; Chatters, Taylor & Jayakody 1994; Stack 1974). Neisha Morris's description of a part of her family tree illustrates how time erases the lines between blood and nonblood relatives. Neisha explains, "My uncle was her godfather. So that's why I say we cousins. It was like we've been knowing each other since little babies. You know, on pictures together. I been knowin' her forever, so that's why I say she my cousin."

Not only are families connected horizontally through siblings or cousins, intergenerational networks (often in one household) are also very common. Nearly 8% of children in households live with a grandparent (City of Chicago 1994), and 18% of Groveland families are "subfamilies"—usually childless married couples, or married or single parents who live in the household of another family unit. This commonly refers to a multigenerational or extended family household.[6] Reverend Darnell Johns, pastor of St. Timothy's Episcopal Church in Groveland, described this phenomena:

> Let's say a young woman who used to live in this neighborhood, she gets married and goes on her own. She has two or three children. She and her husband are having a difficult time and they break up and she moves back home with her parents. And so what happens is that she ends up being here with the children, and then the grandparents end up having to extend the whole parenting again.

Reverend Johns pondered aloud the effects of this type of family organization, concerned that the "cultural difference between a grandmother and a grandchild" would hamper communication and weaken the parental authority of the grandparent. This lapse in control, argued the Reverend, "creates a whole host of new issues and problems." Particularly, the break in communication is a break in social control. Johns noted:

> These people who are speaking [about problems in the community], it often is many of their children and many of their grandchildren who are contributing, you know, to the problems of the community. And what it is is it's just, it's just denial. It really is. You've kinda given me some food for thought. Maybe that's a good forum or workshop, you know,

to have at church—the generational dilemma in our community.

The "generational dilemma" that Reverend Johns refers to points to a complication in child rearing and supervision in the neighborhood. The extended family network has long been a positive feature of African American families (Billingsley 1968; Stack 1974). Yet having numerous adults in a household does not always translate into more or better supervision of youth. Instead, the role ambiguity of grandparents and parents, and the lower energy levels and limited financial resources of grandparents strain the familial relationship, grandparents' love and commitment notwithstanding (Chase-Lansdale, Brooks-Gunn & Zamsky 1994). At the same time, Reverend Johns's comments foreshadow how dense networks can connect upstanding members of the community to neighborhood delinquents. These relationships make it difficult to uniformly crack down on neighborhood crime because few parents and grandparents are able to see their own child or grandchild as being a bad apple and deserving of punishment.

Numerous extended family networks, specifically those spanning generations do, however, increase levels of familiarity within the neighborhood. In turn, mutual familiarity means that residents, especially youth, are exposed to antisocial networks as well as legitimate ones. The schools provide one local arena where disparate groups come together. Because the lives of classmates can take different trajectories, many Groveland adults have acquaintances on the other side of the law, if only by default. Thirty-three-year-old Kelly is in his second year of an M.B.A. program at a private Chicago university, while a childhood friend of his was caught in the city's round-up of the Black Mobsters. Kelly reports:

> I actually went to school with one of the top [Black Mobster] lieutenants who graduated, who lived on Third and Granger. I knew that family very well. Ah, but now he's in jail. The top lieutenant whose name was, whose nickname was Lance, is in jail. He's facing an array of charges, so he's gonna be there for a while. But his little street minions are still there.

In Groveland, everybody knows Lance. He went to the local public schools; he and his siblings participated in activities at Groveland Park, and now their children also attend Groveland School and frequent the park. Lance's position in the neighborhood is more multifaceted than the narrow title "gang leader" might imply. He is a father, uncle, neighbor, former classmate, and as was already mentioned, Lance has been a community activist, participating in the successful effort to close down neighborhood liquor stores.

Each of Lance's "minions" also shares this plurality of roles, thereby making some residents feel safer. Strangers are a certain cause of fear (Anderson 1990; Merry 1983). Yet, as Charisse described, gang members in Groveland are rarely strangers.

> I know most of 'em. Because it's not like anybody came into the neighborhood. Most of the people in this neighborhood are like grandparents now, so they've been here a long time. And it's a lot of their kids and grandkids. So it's still people that I grew up with, and people that I saw all the time. People I went to school with. So, it's not a change. I mean, I see them more and I realize what's going on more. But it's not a case, I don't feel unsafe, you know.

Forty-year-old Alberta Gordon echoes these sentiments:

> I don't carry a knife. I don't carry mace. I don't feel that this is something [I need to do]. And I feel that if anything happens to me coming home it will not be someone in this neighborhood because they know me. They know my sister. They know my brother.

Ms. Gordon got agreement from her teenaged son who chimed in: "They gotta deal with my grandmother."

Grandparents, grandchildren, cousins, neighbors, classmates—this density of relationships in the neighborhood forged through high levels of home ownership and long-term residence has created an intricate system of socialization that produces top-level city politicians as well as high-ranking gang leaders. Moreover, for many residents, this web of networks, and their embedded position within it, generally makes for a "quiet neighborhood."

The structure, however, does break down. Fifteen-year-old Brandon Johnson was shot and killed one January afternoon on one of Groveland's quiet streets. His obituary chronicled his activities, listed his affiliations with local institutions, and illustrated his intense involvement in neighborhood networks:

> He confessed his belief in Christ at an early age. He was a member of St. Timothy's Church under the direction of Reverend Darnell C. Johns. He was a youth member at St. Timothy's Church. He attended Benton High School as a sophomore. He played Basketball/Football at Benton. He was a member of the YMCA where he played Basketball. He had just started a part time job at Ridge Lake Groceries. He was a counselor for the City Wide Program during the summer.

This description shows that Brandon was actively involved in positive local and city-wide activities. One involvement the obituary did not mention, however, was Brandon's peripheral gang affiliation. As one of his peers described him, "Brandon was like a real good person. He wasn't really *too into gangs* or whatever." Another youth said, "He was trying to change. You know, he was a little, he was bad. Really bad. I mean, not he, I mean, well he got killed. He was changing his life around and he was actually good, you know. He was turning it around."

The details surrounding Brandon's death were as sketchy as his gang affiliation, yet both point to the intricacies of overlapping neighborhood networks. Brandon lived with his mother, stepfather, grandparents and siblings in the house that his grandparents moved into nearly 30 years ago. Both his mother and grandparents were church-going people and clearly passed on that orientation to Brandon. His grandparents had been involved in the church-sponsored "March Against Drugs." Ironically, Brandon was killed in an identified drug house where he had been visiting his girlfriend. His funeral was attended by a mix of members of his church youth group, classmates from his high school, and a group of young men who, in other locales, had been known to flash gang signs, wear gang paraphernalia, and use gang-member greetings. All these associations, however, did not alter the perception of Brandon as "like a real good person" who was "turning it around." This plurality of associations and roles that is characteristic of the Groveland networks affects social control efforts.

Informal and Formal Social Control in Groveland

Brandon's death prompted a special community meeting called by the pastor of his church. Nearly thirty neighbors and family members attended to discuss the need for increased police presence in the neighborhood, expanded activities at the park, and reinvigoration of the block clubs. These concerns are repeatedly raised in casual conversations and neighborhood meetings, and there are ongoing efforts by a number of individuals and community groups to further this agenda. These efforts, and the players involved in carrying them out, rest on one side of the see-saw of Groveland's social organization. The consensus in these groups and the approach they take to working on problems was expressed at a Local School Council meeting by Mr. Wilson who pointed out, "We have to take responsibility for all of our children. The same children that are beating up on our children are also our children. They go right around the corner when they go home. They are our children."

Most responsibility for "our children" is taken on informally using the strong extended family and friendship ties within the neighborhood. Alberta Gordon discussed this informal control:

> Some of the kids call me Ms. Gordon. Some of 'em call me Mama G. And I told them the reason I want them to feel comfortable in calling me Mama G is because I grew up calling people on this block by their last name or "Aunt" whoever the person was. For instance, Tanya's mother, I still to this day call Aunt Sarah. It was a respect and extended family [kind of thing]. So there are a lot of young people that I do know that call me Mama G. And I have no problem in telling them that they're wrong about doing something. And no problem in going to their parents because I know their parents. . . . [And I] have told their parents in return, if [my son] Michael is doing something and you know it's wrong, correct him and then let me know so that I can deal with it.

At Groveland Park, Ms. Spears put Ms. Gordon's sentiments into action:

> A teenaged girl walked to Ms. Spears to ask a question, but before she could get it out Ms. Spears spotted that the girl was wearing an electronic pager. Ms. Spears asked her sternly, "Whose beeper is that?"

The girl responded, "It's my father's."

Ms. Spears continued with a barrage of questions and directives, "What are you doing with a beeper? You don't need a beeper. Give it back to your father. I don't care if it's yo' brother's, mother's, father's—you don't need a beeper. It's not becoming. Take that beeper back to your father right now!"

The girl responded, "He's right in there. He knows I got it."

Ms Spears said in a serious voice, "Take it to him right now."

The girl turned around to do as she was told.

In associating a pager with drug dealing, Ms. Spears thought it was inappropriate for a respectable young girl to be wearing one. Being a neighborhood disciplinarian requires a certain amount of respect and renown that Ms. Spears has cultivated in the nearly 20 years she has lived in Groveland, raising her children and now her grandchildren there. She is also an employee of the Chicago Park District and for many years has worked in Groveland Park, which is across the street from her home. She is seen by many of the youth as a grandmotherly figure, and she addresses most people, young and old, with the sugary pleasantries "honey" and "baby." Her long-time residence means that she can intervene in children's inappropriate behaviors, confident that her intervention will be acceptable with the children's parents.

Similarly, Spider has lived in the neighborhood most of his 30 years, went to the local schools, and works as a recreation leader at Groveland Park. He uses this neighborhood-level legitimacy to coordinate men's pick-up basketball on Sunday mornings. Spider is the keeper of "the list"—the roster of names used to determine the next team to play. He frequently deviates from the list, moving up his friends' names or giving some players special choice in their teammates. His final decisions are respected. When tempers flare and the playing rules are ignored, Spider always has the last word. Once, after a controversy over a personal foul, Spider ordered, "All you mothafuckas that lost, get the fuck off the court." When the losing team did not move from the court, Spider responded, "Fuck that. The mothafucka is closed. Gimme my gotdamn ball." He took the basketball and turned off the lights in the gym announcing, "Shop is closed!"

Spider always handles conflict with this same blunt and direct swiftness. Furthermore, his amiable relationship with Lance and the Black Mobsters augments his status as an official park employee and gives him authorization to settle disputes and make decisions within the park, especially among young people. The key to promoting comfort and feelings of safety is to lessen anonymity. Yet the more people are familiar with one another, the more illicit networks are absorbed into mainstream connections and thereby normalized. This is the conundrum that plagues social control efforts in Groveland.

"Concerned residents" are enraged by gangs and drug activity. When informal mechanisms fail to control these activities, residents turn to the next level of social control—local organizations and institutions (Hunter 1995). These two levels are not separate, as the above examples illustrate. Employees of the local park are also long-time neighborhood residents, as are church leaders, business people, and police officers. Local organizations and institutions are only aggregations of the informal private ties that individual residents possess, increasing the ability to address the concerns that residents cannot tackle individually.

Residents air their complaints in community meetings (of block clubs, police beats, the Local School Council, church groups, the Chamber of Commerce). Gangs and gangbangers top the list of their concerns. According to an older man at a local police beat meeting, gangs are "worse than anything. They can just take over!" The formal neighborhood institutions direct their efforts at preventing this takeover.[7]

The residents who express their concern and anger over changes in their community—young people playing loud music, leaving trash on their lawns, stealing backyard furniture—frequently recognize that putting up gates around the entire neighborhood would not rid Groveland of the problems they are experiencing because the troublemakers are natives. One woman at a beat meeting complained of young men "gangbanging" (i.e., congregating) on her corner and of one man in particular who she thought was in charge. But, she said, "I didn't wanna give this young man's name [to the police] because his mama is such a sweet lady." This comment illustrates that while dense neighborhood networks and the resulting familiarity can improve some informal efforts at social control, it can thwart the use of public or formal means of control.

Many local institutions do, however, boast successes. The Chamber of Commerce has been active in efforts to keep the main commercial strip and the entire neighborhood thriving. One member of the executive board of the chamber talked about how the organization "got the pay phones out on the streets set up so that there are no incoming calls and no coin-generated calls after a certain time. This was particularly to stop any drug dealers from using the phone."[8] The chamber has also been successful in using the city's "Graffiti Blasters" program to promptly remove any graffiti from area businesses.

In addition to their proactive efforts, businesses are also supportive of other local organizations and institutions. When a group of block clubs teamed up with the Alderman's office to plan an anti-drug march, many businesses donated materials and food to help out. One organizer announced, "Mr. Brown over at Diamond Groceries is donating all the hot dogs, buns, and relish we need." The president of a Groveland block club said he could always count on the local grocery stores to donate food for his annual block party, and the area bank to donate money. Similarly, when the Catholic church's youth group planned an overnight retreat, two fast food restaurants donated food; and when the same group planned a career fair, a local record store donated door prizes. Residents and organizers depend on the businesses to support their efforts to provide positive activities in the neighborhood.

The churches spearhead social organization efforts in Groveland. Groveland United Church of Christ hosted a string of community meetings at which they made specific demands of the alderman, the police, and the public school principal. They targeted three drug houses in the neighborhood, two of which were eventually closed by the city. The church also complained of gang activity on the public elementary school playground and demanded that the police monitor the playground to make it unattractive to gang recruiters. At the next meeting, the police sergeant responded to these demands: "Immediately following the last month's meeting, we made arrests of some kids with spray cans on the school grounds. We will continue to work toward these goals," he assured. St. Mary's Catholic Church was successful in getting a security guard placed at Groveland Park, as well as more programs and activities for teenagers.[9]

Concerned residents focus their energies and activities on curbing youth delinquency. Nearly all the projects they propose are concerned with connecting young people to positive activities and groups, and deterring deviant behavior. Residents also discuss the physical maintenance of the neighborhood, but this is frequently connected to the irresponsibility of idle young people, "gang-bangers" who trash the neighborhood. Yet, for all the institutional support and commitment of key leaders, the force against which they are fighting also has a strong organization, powerful leaders, and the buffer of actors who negotiate both networks.

The Black Mobsters: Organization of a Different Sort

"Folks" is the gang "nation" under which the Black Mobsters are positioned (see Hagedorn 1988 for a discussion of the "People" and "Folks" nations in Milwaukee). The Groveland Park field house was a gang stronghold for much of this research. "What up, Folks?" was a conspicuous greeting at the field house. So, too, were six-pointed stars, hats tilted to the right, t-shirts with the picture of their jailed gang leader, and the color blue. Despite these signs, members of the "organization," as they called it, consistently declared:

> Ain't no gang problem around here. You come up to the park and you don't see no graffiti or nothin' like that. These people around here think we got a gang problem. This ain't nothin' like Lorry Park (another park on the South Side). I used to work up at Lorry, and say you used to bring your son up there to play. The boys would come up to him and take his ball and jump on him. And when he started to fight back because you taught him to stand up for hisself, they would be talkin' about, "You don't need nobody else. Come git wit us [our gang]."

Groveland's Black Mobsters stop short of bullying the nongang members who use the park. In routine park activities, however, there are many times when "Folks" use their organizational strength to control the park. For example, during a league basketball game a member of the "organization" was not getting much playing time. Someone from the stands called out, "All us over here came to see Pope play. Pope, go on in there and get you some time, man. Folks don't sit on the bench. They play. You B-Mobster ain't you? Then use yo' Mobster weight." Pope moved to the scorers table and checked himself into the game.

These shows of dominance are relatively harmless activities. In more than three years of fieldwork that included extensive visits to the park, two field workers together documented only one fight, no graffiti, and three cases of vandalism at the park. Blatant signs of disorder are absent from the park, and explicit gang-related activities, such as organizational meetings, are infrequent and always inconspicuous. This low profile allows gang members to use the park without eliciting much attention. As Cloward & Ohlin (1960) point out in their description of criminal elements in stable communities: "Social controls over the conduct of the young are effectively exercised, limiting expressive behavior and constraining the discontented to adopt instrumental, if criminalistic, styles of life" (171). When Lance and his employees and bodyguards congregated at Groveland Park (before the "gang bust"), they sometimes talked in hushed tones and acted in ways that betrayed their innocent veneer—making several trips to their cars, leaving abruptly in the middle of a conversation, or casting frequent and alert glances out of the window. But most often the young men played basketball, joined in on volleyball games, coached the younger boys, played dominoes, or just socialized. In effect, they were neighborhood residents using their neighborhood park, and this is how the supervisor treated them:

I don't know, well I do know, but I can't be sure of what any one does. So I'm not going to be telling people they have to leave. My supervisors come down here and they tell me not to let 'em sit out in front there. But, again, what am I going to say? I can't tell them to leave because they're just sitting out there. I mean, I do understand the concern. You know since I've been here there hasn't been one fight. I don't hear a lot of profanity. I mean, I know people curse, but there haven't been any problems. I mean, they all grew up together. They live here. Plus, some of 'em have kids here, so that's an extra part of it. I mean, I can't tell people to leave.

As an official of Groveland Park the supervisor is a part of the formal social control apparatus. Yet, she is reticent to condemn the gang members who frequent the park because of their claims to neighborhood legitimacy. They have children in park activities and friends throughout the neighborhood, which justifies their presence.

The "civility" of the Black Mobsters at Groveland Park is part of their more expansive efforts to legitimize their illegal businesses. Newspapers describe the Black Mobsters as Chicago's largest street gang, and its tentacles span the Midwest. One resident described Lance's dominion as spanning the country, claiming, "This [the park] Lance's spot. Tell 'em Reggie, Lance is the man over alla them. He the man in the city. He a real Mobster. He run the Mobsters in the city, down south, Texas, and up north in Minnesota." The "organization" has been involved in assorted endeavors. The police investigation of their activities uncovered money laundering schemes through music concert promotions, political organizations, neighborhood restaurants, and even social service establishments.

While their city-wide strength is considerable, their territorial hold in the Groveland area is limited to a four-block by ten-block area. To the south and east are four other neighborhood-based gangs, all of which belong to a rival gang nation. To the north and west are Ruthless Mobsters, also Folks, but a different faction from those in Groveland. While this territorial crunch produces some turf battles, the organization is concerned with turf primarily as it affects drug sales. Lance manages the Black Mobsters' business on the South Side of the city, but keeps Groveland relatively clean—partially because he wants his family safe, and partially because residents are active in fighting against such activity. As a result, there is almost no corner drug selling and few drug houses in the neighborhood. Linda Brewer, who grew up on the same block as Lance, described what happened when a family tried to sell drugs in the neighborhood outside of Lance's organization:

Lance told them they couldn't sell the drugs. It really really got bad and people was comin' [from] outside the neighborhood. A coupla people got robbed and raped and beat up, you know. And a coupla people got in there and started drive by shootin's and stuff like that. So he told 'em they couldn't sell it. 'Cause he was worried about his, now he was worried about his mom, you know. So, now alla the sudden he said they couldn't sell drugs around here.

Faced with the unsupervised sale of drugs in Groveland, and the disorder that it was causing, Lance put a stop to this upstart enterprise. These prohibitions illustrate Lance's centrality as an agent of neighborhood social control.

Ironically, having an organized gang in the neighborhood has, in some respects, translated into fewer visible signs of disorder, less violence, and more social control. Lance operates from a profit motive, albeit an illegal one. Aside from that, he wants his family safe, he wants his neighborhood clean, and he wants his children to have healthy activities. Lance and his minions' indigenousness to Groveland plays a role in these parallel interests of gangs and the upstanding citizens that fight against them.

Middle-Class Mobsters

If there is a system of occupational stratification within organized crime similar to that which exists in the legitimate sector, Groveland represents the middle managers in both milieus. Nineteen-year-old Neisha Morris described the activities of her boyfriend, Tim, who sold drugs:

> Well, see, Tim don't sell drugs on the corner. He did do that type of stuff but he got a pager, people can just page him. He don't sell drugs to people. He sell drugs to the niggahs that sell drugs. He not at the stage no more where he just sell to "hypes" [drug addicts] $10 bags, little bags. You know, one of his friends like wanna buy some "work" [drugs] and they'll like pay $800 for something and they work what they got from him. He say they bag it up and they sell it to hypes, like that. I guess he done moved up in the world. And it's like people that he buy his stuff from [that] got mo' money than him.

In her explanation of Tim's duties, Neisha described an occupational hierarchy (Padilla 1992). Tim was promoted from selling drugs on the corner to buying in bulk and selling to independent distributors who work the corners he once occupied. Above Tim are suppliers even more wealthy than he, who are likely to be subordinate to some even more powerful and wealthy drug dealer. In this occupational chain, Tim is not a laborer at the bottom of the totem pole. Having moved off of the corner, he is now able to work from his home. His job description fits that of a lower-level manager, or small-business owner, making him comparable to his neighbors who work similar jobs in the legitimate employment sector. Most Groveland residents have "clean jobs."

Another middle-class characteristic of Groveland is that the neighborhood is a bedroom community. Most drug selling takes place outside of the neighborhood and the profits are brought home to families like Neisha's. At the park, there were never drug exchanges, drugs present, or even obvious drug users or addicts. Corner drug selling is rare in the section of Groveland controlled by the Black Mobsters. The drug houses that are allowed to exist in the neighborhood were described by one resident as "drug salons," highlighting a hierarchy of drug-selling establishments. In drug salons, customers buy their drugs and leave, rather than congregating and creating the social disorder that accompanies drug use (Williams 1992). The money is to be made elsewhere, outside of Groveland. One ex-dealer reports, "I'll say all the people over here go to the other side [of the railroad tracks] to sell drugs. That's where all the places to do it. They'll go on the other side."[10] The proximity of Groveland to low-income markets attests to the primacy of geography in explaining crime in Groveland. Like the residents in Groveland who commute to their legal jobs, Groveland's drug dealers do most of their business outside of the neighborhood, but the violent repercussions of the drug trade often spill over into their own territory.

Within the drug-selling world, as in the legitimate sector, there is also a visible lifestyle hierarchy. Those at the top, like Lance, drive fancy cars, wear expensive watches and jewelry, and are surrounded by helpful underlings. Over the years, those underlings (or minions) acquire fancier (but used) cars, begin to wear more brand-named clothing, and make more frequent trips to the barber. As the Groveland Park supervisor relayed to her white friends who had a particular image of gang members, "These guys wear Fila and shop at Burberry's [designer brand and upscale clothing store, respectively]. This is not like, you know, guys hanging on the corner smoking."

In addition to the accouterments of middle-class status, on some issues Lance's behavior borders on prudery, as illustrated in a conversation about one of Lance's parties.

> "We had all kinds of food and shit," Spider boasted. "I stuffed myself. Man, I was full as hell. We had all kinds of waters too."
>
> A friend who was eager to hear what one of Lance's parties was like asked Spider, "Y'all didn't have no liquor?"
>
> Spider answered, "Naw. You know Lance don't have that kind of shit."

Lance's distaste for alcohol is common knowledge around the neighborhood. Also, as a good businessman he especially prohibits drug use by his "employees" and associates as well (Taylor 1990).

Much of this insistence on order stems from the organization's concern for the safety of their own parents, grandparents, siblings, sons, and daughters. Even more importantly, however, Lance was raised in this middle-class neighborhood. His behaviors illustrate his own desire to comply with the social norms. As Tracy Harris described, "At Groveland Park, they [Black Mobsters] were the ones outside every morning to make sure that the kids got to the park safely. And they stopped traffic and directed traffic. And got the kids in the park." She believed that the members of the Black Mobsters in Groveland were taught to be successful, and they are now passing on those middle-class orientations to their children:

> They got themselves in a situation and they used that situation to the best of their advantage. And they're working it. And that's what it's about. It's like any other job. They're working the situation to their advantage. And because they have some semblance of class, intelligence and some decent upbringing, they bring that back into the group in which they're in. And when they raise their children, they raise their children with the same effects as they were raised—to achieve something, to go somewhere.

The homologous class position of many of the Black Mobsters and their law-abiding neighbors makes getting rid of them even more difficult for concerned residents. They share many of the same values for an attractive and safe neighborhood, and both groups want socioeconomic security, but they have divergent strategies for achieving those values. Yet, because the outcomes are often similar, the neighborhood's betterment groups have a difficult time convincing their less-involved neighbors that there is even a problem. Apathy, based on what one resident called a "false sense of security," plagues organizational efforts in Groveland.

Many residents feel secure precisely because much of the illicit activity is kept within the bounds of acceptable neighborhood behavior. Neighborhood fights, for example, are rare, a fact that makes rallying the troops difficult. As one older resident put it, "I never seen one. 'Cause I call a fight several blows exchanged. Now wait a minute, there was a fight maybe about twenty-five years ago." The paucity of incidents is partially a function of the gang's deliberate control of such behavior, yet any incidents that do occur are usually gang related. There is a twist to the semi-effectiveness of gang organization: If no gangs existed, there would be no need for the protection that gangs provide. The same ironic logic holds for the coordinated, yet competitive, sale of drugs.

Conclusion

The fact that a high ranking gang leader lives in Groveland does not significantly distinguish it from other neighborhoods regarding the integration of licit and illicit networks. Low-income neighborhoods have frequently supported, and often defended, their crime bosses as fervently as they would any other product of the neighborhood. Gang members everywhere are connected to parents, cousins, teachers, and even pastors, although to varying degrees in different neighborhoods. These connections require further investigation into how residential stability and network density can both facilitate and impede social control. What is particular about Groveland as a middle-class neighborhood are the people to whom the illicit networks are linked, the unique strategies of organizing a diverse neighborhood that sits near higher crime areas, and the particular forms of illicit activities. The neighborhood organizers have myriad attachments to the neighborhood trouble-makers. These links help in informally influencing behavior, but can hinder involving public agents of social control. Simultaneously, the social position of gang members and those involved in selling drugs mirrors the legitimate occupational status of other neighborhood residents. With some "reminders" by legitimate community organizations, they also operate under similar rules of conduct, and with similar goals.

Neighborhood social organization does not exist as an absolute value, but represents a continuum, the ends of which are complete chaos or utopia. Without denying the successes guaranteed by middle-class resources, this article highlights the unique obstacles that black middle-class neighborhoods face in maintaining stability and realizing common values.

The conclusions are summarized as follows. First, black middle-class neighborhoods have higher poverty rates, and are closer to poverty areas than white middle class neighborhoods, creating unique forms of social organization. Second, higher proportions of low-income residents, along with the unstable middle-class footing of many others, means that crime may be an attractive option to a significant minority of residents within the neighborhood and in nearby areas. Concerned residents are aware that there will be widespread disorder if they do not actively manage the criminal enterprises fostered by economic insecurity. The criminal leadership shares the mainstream desires for neighborhood order, albeit by different means. The third argument advanced here is that residents of Groveland have formed strong primary and institutional ties based on high rates of home ownership and residential stability. These ties promote neighborhood-level familiarity, integrate disparate networks, and facilitate informal and formal social control. Fourth and finally, however, these ties also thwart efforts to totally rid the neighborhood of gangs and drugs. The criminal minority—already a part of the kin and neighborly networks that exist, and often contributing to the support of local families—is given a degree of latitude to operate in the neighborhood.

This research advances social organization theory by elucidating the mechanisms through which the proximate sources of social organization work. Dense friendship and kin ties and institutional strength and participation allow for the integration of licit and illicit networks both working toward common goals, but with variant strategies. For theories of race and social mobility, focusing on the context within which black middle-class families live is important for understanding enduring racial differences in social indicators as diverse as educational performance and mortality rates. Investigating these processes in Groveland is a step toward ameliorating the dearth of research on the black middle class.

Notes

1. All names of people and places have been changed to preserve anonymity.
2. With a few noted exceptions, demographic statistics in this article refer to the entire community area and are taken from the *Local Community Fact Book, Chicago Metropolitan Area, 1990* (1995).
3. The exact citation for this article is not in the References because the article contains the real names of people and places in Groveland.
4. Because interviews and especially field interactions were quite informal, many respondents used the Black English Vernacular. While I have edited some false sentence starts and rhetorical fillers (e.g., um, you know), I have not translated conversations into Standard English.
5. I asked interviewees about their "close friends." Respondents were allowed to name as many close friends as they wished. I then asked where these friends lived, their occupation, race and how the respondent met them. From these data I was able to determine the mean proportion of close friends who lived in the neighborhood across all interviewees, which was 49.1%. This nearly even proportion of local and non-local friendship ties is similar to what Oliver (1988) found in his study of three black communities in Los Angeles. However, working from ethnographic field data and the open-ended interviews used in this study, I have limited confidence in the above measure of the spatial dimension of network ties. I am much more convinced of the strong local ties by the experiential knowledge recorded in over three years of participant observation, and by hearing interviewees elaborate on their friendships and kin. My data are even less amenable to quantitatively analyzing the density of neighborhood ties.

6. For comparison, in predominately white Beltway, not even 2% of the children live with their grandparents, and only 3.7% of families are subfamilies.

7. Venkatesh (1997) describes a poor community in which the local gang had essentially taken over, replacing the previous authority of tenants' groups. The middle class organizational and financial resources in Groveland have inhibited such an absolute displacement of legitimate control.

8. While new technology has meant that drug dealers now have their own cellular phones from which to do business, when this initiative was first undertaken it would have limited the ability to use public phones for illegal business.

9. Both Groveland United Church of Christ and St. Mary's Catholic Church received the assistance of a nonprofit agency that specialized in organizing churches. Each church invited this agency to work with them, and paid a membership fee. The outside agency provided only training and technical assistance; it did not give specific directions or targets for social action. The proactive efforts on the part of the churches illustrate the independent commitment to getting involved in the neighborhood.

10. "The other side" refers to a small portion of the Bristol neighborhood (see Figure 24.1) with a high concentration of apartment buildings, and a much lower median family income and higher percent poor than other census tracts in the area.

References

Alba, Richard D., John R. Logan, and Paul E. Bellair. 1994. "Living with Crime: The Implications of Racial/Ethnic Differences in Suburban Location." *Social Forces* 73:395–434.

Anderson, Elijah. 1978. *A Place on the Corner*. University of Chicago Press.

———. 1990. *Streetwise: Race, Class and Change in an Urban Community*. University of Chicago Press.

Berry, Brian J.L., and John D. Kasarda. 1977. *Contemporary Urban Ecology*. Macmillan.

Billingsley, Andrew. 1968. *Black Families in White America*. Prentice-Hall.

———. 1992. *Climbing Jacob's Ladder: The Enduring Legacy of African-American Families*. Simon & Schuster.

Blackwell, James E. 1985. *The Black Community: Diversity and Unity*. 2d ed. Harper & Row.

Bursik, Robert J., and Harold Grasmick. 1993. *Neighborhoods and Crime*. Lexington Books.

Byrne, James, and Robert Sampson (eds.). 1986. *The Social Ecology of Crime*. Springer-Verlag.

Chase-Lansdale, Lindsey, Jeanne Brooks-Gunn, and Elise Zamsky. 1994. "Young African-American Multigenerational Families in Poverty: Quality of Mothering and Grandmothering." *Child Development* 65:373–93.

Charters, Linda, Robert Joseph Taylor, and Rukmali Jayakody. 1994. "Fictive Kinship Relations in Black Extended Families." *Journal of Comparative Family Studies* 25:297–312.

Chicago Fact Book Consortium (eds.). 1995. *Local Community Fact Book, Chicago Metropolitan Area, 1990*. University of Illinois.

City of Chicago, Department of Planning and Development. 1994. Demographic and Housing Characteristics of Chicago and Community Area Profiles. Report no. 5, City of Chicago.

Cloward, Richard A., and Lloyd E. Ohlin. 1960. *Delinquency and Opportunity: A Theory of Delinquent Gangs*. Free Press.

Collins, Sharon M. 1983. "The Making of the Black Middle Class." *Social Problems* 30:369–82.

Cose, Ellis. 1993. *The Rage of a Privileged Class*. Harper Collins.

Darden, Joe T. 1987. "Socioeconomic Status and Racial Residential Segregation: Blacks and Hispanics in Chicago." *International Journal of Comparative Sociology* 28:1–13.

Dash, Leon. 1989. *When Children Want Children*. William Morrow.

Erbe, Brigitte Mach. 1975. "Race and Socioeconomic Segregation." *American Sociological Review* 40:801–12.

Farley, Reynolds. 1991. "Residential Segregation of Social and Economic Groups among Blacks, 1970–80." Pp. 274–98 in *The Urban Underclass*, edited by Christopher Jencks and Paul E. Peterson. Brookings Institution.

Freudenberg, William. 1986. "The Density of Acquaintanceship: An Overlooked Variable in Community Research." *American Journal of Sociology* 92:27–63.

Glaser, Barney G., and Anselm Strauss. 1967. *The Discovery of Grounded Theory: Strategies for Qualitative Research*. Aldine.

Grossman, Ron, and Byron P. White. 1997. "Poverty Surrounds Black Middle Class: Upscale Neighborhood Virtually an Island." *Chicago Tribune*. 7 Feb., Section C, p. 1.

Guest, Avery, and Barrett Lee. 1983. "The Social Organization of Local Areas." *Urban Affairs Quarterly* 19:217–40.

Hagedorn, John M. 1988. *People and Folks: Gangs, Crime and the Underclass in a Rustbelt City*. Lakeview Press.

Hunter, Albert. 1995. "Private, Parochial and Public Social Orders: The Problem of Crime and Incivility in Urban Communities." Pp. 209–25 in *Metropolis: Center and Symbol of Our Times*, edited by Philip Kasinitz. New York University Press.

Ianni, Francis A. J. 1971. "The Mafia and the Web of Kinship." *The Public Interest* 22:78–100.

———. 1974. "New Mafia: Black, Hispanic, and Italian Styles." *Society* 11:26–39.

Jankowski, Martin Sánchez. 1991. *Islands in the Street: Gangs and American Urban Society*. University of California Press.

Jaynes, Gerald, and Robin M. Williams (eds.). 1989. *A Common Destiny: Blacks and American Society*. National Academy Press.

Kasarda, John D., and Morris Janowitz. 1974. "Community Attachment in Mass Society." *American Sociological Review* 39:328–39.

Kotlowitz, Alex. 1991. *There Are No Children Here*. Doubleday.

Landry, Bart. 1987. *The New Black Middle Class*. University of California Press.

Lemann, Nicholas. 1991. *The Promised Land: The Great Black Migration and How It Changed America*. Vintage Books.

Lofland, John, and Lyn H. Lofland. 1984. *Analyzing Social Settings: A Guide to Qualitative Observation and Analysis*. 2d ed. Wadsworth.

Logan, John R., and Harvey L. Molotch. 1987. *Urban Fortunes: The Political Economy of Place*. University of California Press.

MacLeod, Jay. 1995. *Ain't No Makin' It: Aspirations and Attainment in a Low-Income Neighborhood*. 2d ed. Westview.

Massey, Douglas, Gretchen A. Condran, and Nancy A. Denton. 1987. "The Effect of Residential Segregation on Black Social and Economic Well-Being." *Social Forces* 66:29–57.

Massey, Douglas, and Nancy Denton. 1993. *American Apartheid: Segregation and the Making of the Underclass*. Harvard University Press.

Massey, Douglas, Andrew Gross, and Kumiko Shibuya. 1994. "Migration, Segregation and the Concentration of Poverty." *American Sociological Review* 59:425–45.

Merry, Sally Engle. 1983. "Urban Danger: Life in a Neighborhood of Strangers." Pp. 63–72 in *Urban Life: Readings in Urban Anthropology*, edited by George Gmelch and Walter P. Zenner. Waveland.

Morenoff, Jeffrey, and Robert J. Sampson. 1997. "Violent Crime and the Spatial Dynamics of Neighborhood Transition—Chicago, 1970–1990." *Social Forces* 76:31–64.

O'Kane, James M. 1992. *The Crooked Ladder: Gangsters, Ethnicity, and the American Dream*. Transaction.

Oliver, Melvin. 1988. "The Urban Black Community as Network: Toward a Social Network Perspective." *Sociological Quarterly* 29:623–45.

Oliver, Melvin L., and Thomas M. Shapiro. 1995. *Black Wealth/White Wealth: A New Perspective on Racial Inequality*. Routledge.

Padilla, Felix M. 1992. *The Gang as an American Enterprise*. Rutgers University Press.

Sampson, Robert J. 1992. "Family Management and Child Development: Insights from Social Disorganization Theory." Pp. 63–93 in *Advances in Criminological Theory*, Vol. 3 (Facts, Fragments and Forecasts), edited by Joan McCord. Transaction.

Sampson, Robert J., and W. B. Groves. 1989. "Community Structure and Crime: Testing Social-Disorganization Theory." *American Journal of Sociology* 94:774–802.

Sampson, Robert J., and William Julius Wilson. 1995. "Toward a Theory of Race, Crime and Urban Inequality." Pp. 37–54 in *Crime and Inequality*, edited by John Hagan and Ruth D. Peterson. Stanford University Press.

Schwartz, Howard, and Jerry Jacobs. 1979. *Qualitative Sociology: A Method to the Madness*. Free Press.

Shaw, Clifford, and Henry McKay. 1942. *Juvenile Delinquency and Urban Areas*. University of Chicago Press.

Skogan, Wesley. 1990. *Disorder and Decline: Crime and the Spiral of Decay in American Neighborhoods*. Free Press.

Smith, Jessie Carney, and Carrell P. Horton. 1997. *Statistical Record of Black America*. 4th ed. Gale Research Press.

Stack, Carol. 1974. *All Our Kin: Strategies for Survival in a Black Community*. Harper & Row.

Sullivan, Mercer L. 1989. *"Getting Paid": Youth Crime and Work in the Inner City*. Cornell University Press.

Suttles, Gerald. 1968. *The Social Order of the Slum: Ethnicity and Territory in the Inner City*. University of Chicago Press.

Taylor, Carl S. 1990. *Dangerous Society*. Michigan State University Press.

Vanneman, Reeve, and Lynn Weber Cannon. 1987. *The American Perception of Class*. Temple University Press.

Venkatesh, Sudhir Alladi. 1996. "The Gang in the Community." Pp. 241–55 in *Gangs in America*, edited by C. Ronald Huff. Sage Publications.

———. 1997. "The Social Organization of Street Gang Activity in an Urban Ghetto." *American Journal of Sociology* 103:82–111.

Villemez, Wayne. 1980. "Race, Class, and Neighborhood: Differences in the Residential Return on Individual Resources." *Social Forces* 59:414–30.

Warren, Donald. 1975. *Black Neighborhoods: An Assessment of Community Power*. University of Michigan Press.

Whyte, William Foote. 1943. *Street Corner Society. The Social Structure of an Italian Slum*. University of Chicago Press.

Williams, Terry. 1989. *The Cocaine Kids: The Inside Story of a Teenage Drug Ring*. Addison-Wesley.

———. 1992. *Crackhouse: Notes from the End of the Line*. Addison-Wesley.

Wilson, Frank Harold. 1995. "Rising Tide or Ebb Tide? Recent Changes in the Black Middle Class in the U.S., 1980–1990." *Research in Race and Ethnic Relations* 8:21–55.

Wilson, William Julius. 1978. *The Declining Significance of Race: Blacks and Changing American Institutions*. University of Chicago Press.

———. 1987. *The Truly Disadvantaged: The Inner City, the Underclass and Public Policy*. University of Chicago Press.

CHAPTER 25

Gangs, Neighborhoods, and Public Policy

John M. Hagedorn

As with the previous article by Pattillo, the gangs Hagedorn studied are African American and heavily involved in drug distribution. He attributes changes in Milwaukee gang dynamics to the lack of effective social institutions and poverty that stemmed from deindustrialization in Milwaukee during the 1980s. The neighborhoods Hagedorn studied contain heterogeneous populations of working-class and poor families, along with gang members; he argues that these segmented neighborhoods experience conflict, alienation, and social distrust as a result of weakened social institutions. Hagedorn argues for investing in gang communities rather than using suppression strategies as a means of combating gangs, a point revisited in the articles included in the final section of this volume.

Are today's youth part of an "underclass"? What policies should communities adopt to control their gang problem? Based on recent gang research and experience in reforming Milwaukee's human service bureaucracy, we can address these questions and suggest practical local policies that go beyond the usual nostrums of "more cops" and "more jobs."

In the last few years a number of researchers have suggested that today's gangs have changed in some fundamental ways and may be part of an urban minority "underclass" (Moore 1985, Short 1990b, Taylor 1990, Vigil 1988). The nature of the

Reprinted from: John M. Hagedorn, "Gangs, Neighborhoods, and Public Policy," *Social Problems*, 38(4): 529–542. Copyright © 1991 by the Society for the Study of Social Problems. Reprinted by permission.

"underclass," however, has been the subject of controversy (Aponte 1988, Gans 1990, Jencks 1989, Ricketts, Mincy, and Sawhill 1988, Wilson 1991). This paper uses data gathered from three different Milwaukee studies over the past five years to examine the changing nature of Milwaukee's gangs, the characteristics of Milwaukee's poorest African-American neighborhoods, and the relationship between gangs and neighborhoods.

For the first study, completed in 1986, 47 of the founding members of Milwaukee's 19 major gangs, including 11 of the 19 recognized leaders, were interviewed (Hagedorn 1988). That study described the origins of Milwaukee gangs, their structure and activities, and documented how gangs came to be seen as a social problem. It also tracked the education, employment, drug use, incarceration experience, and the level of gang participation of the 260 young people who founded the 19 gangs, including the 175 founders of 12 African-American male gangs.

A brief follow-up study in spring of 1990 looked at the patterns of drug abuse and the structure of gang drug dealing in three African-American gangs. This pilot study tracked the employment, incarceration, and drug use status of the 37 founding members of the three gangs since the original study. It began a process of exploring the relationship between Milwaukee gangs and drug dealing businesses or "drug posses."

Finally, as part of a human services reform plan, Milwaukee County commissioned a needs assessment in two neighborhoods where several of Milwaukee's gangs persist (Moore and Edari

1990b). Residents were hired to survey heads of households drawn from a probability sample of 300 households in ten census tracts in two neighborhoods. These neighborhoods had a high percentage of residents living in poverty and a clustering of social problems associated with the "underclass."

This article first looks at how Milwaukee gangs have changed due to deindustrialization. Second, the paper explores some volatile social dynamics occurring within poor but still heterogeneous African-American neighborhoods. . . .

Macro-Economic Trends and Gangs in Milwaukee

The underclass has been conceptualized as a product of economic restructuring that has mismatched African-Americans and other minority workers with radically changed employment climates (Bluestone and Harrison 1982, Kasarda 1985, Sullivan 1989). Milwaukee epitomizes this mismatch: between 1979 and 1986 over 50,000 jobs were lost or 23 percent of Milwaukee's manufacturing employment (White et al. 1988:2–6). African-American workers were hit especially hard. In 1980 prior to the downturn, 40 percent of all African-American workers were concentrated in manufacturing (compared to 31 percent of all city workers). By 1989 research in five all-black Milwaukee census tracts found that only about one quarter of all black workers were still employed in manufacturing (Moore and Edari 1990b). African-American unemployment rates in Milwaukee have reached as high as 27 percent over the past few years.

Another way to view economic changes in the African-American community is to look at social welfare over the last thirty years. Like European immigrants before them, African-Americans came to Milwaukee with the hopes of landing good factory jobs (Trotter 1985) and large numbers succeeded. But as industrial employment declined and good jobs were less available, reliance on welfare increased (Piven and Cloward 1987:83). In 1963, when black migration to Milwaukee was still rising, fewer than one in six of Milwaukee's African-Americans were supported by AFDC. However by 1987, nearly half of all Milwaukee

African-Americans and two thirds of their children received AFDC benefits. Seven out of every ten Milwaukee African-Americans in 1987 were supported by transfer payments of some kind accounting for half of all 1987 black income in Milwaukee County (Hagedorn 1989).

Coinciding with reduced economic prospects for African-Americans, Hispanics, and other working people, gangs reemerged in Milwaukee and other small and medium-sized cities across the Midwest. While the popular notion at the time was that these gangs had diffused from Chicago, gangs in Milwaukee and the Midwest developed from corner groups and break-dancing groups in processes nearly identical to those described by Thrasher fifty years before (Hagedorn 1988, Huff 1989). The economy may have been changing, but the way gangs formed had not.

In 1986 we interviewed 47 of the 260 Milwaukee gang founders or members of the initial groups of young people who started the 19 major gangs in the early 1980s. At the time of our interviews, the founders were all in their early twenties and at an age when young people typically "mature out" of gang life. We asked the 47 founders to report on the current status of all the members who were part of the gang when it started. To our surprise, more than 80 percent of all male gang founders were reported as still involved with the gang as twenty to twenty-five year old adults.

We concluded at the time that the *economic basis* for "maturing out" of a gang—those good paying factory jobs that take little education, few skills, and only hard work—was just not there any more. As Short wrote in a recent review of gang literature, "There is no reason to believe that boys hang together in friendship groups for reasons that are very different now than in the past. . . . What has changed are the structural economic conditions . . . " (Short 1990a).

Moore (1991) has also documented economic effects of deindustrialization on the "maturing out" process of Chicano gangs. She finds that members of recent gang cliques in East Los Angeles are less likely to have found good jobs than members of older gang cliques. She concludes, "It is not that the men from recent cliques were more likely to have dropped out of the labor market, nor were they

Table 25.1 Employment and Adult Gang Involvement				
	% Black Male	% Hisp. Male	% Wh. Male	% Female
Full Time	9.7	10	10	8.6
Part Time	14.0	0	40	11.4
Unemployed	70.3	82.5	40	63.0
Involved with the Gang as an Adult	81.1	70	100	8.6
Totals	N = 175	N = 40	N = 10	N = 35

Table 25.2 1990 Status of 37 Founding Members of Three African-American Gangs				
Involved in Regular Sales of Cocaine	Used Cocaine Routinely since 1987	Spent Time in Prison	Presently Working Full Time	Murdered
59%	76%	86%	19%	8%
N = 22	N = 28	N = 32	N = 7	N = 3

more likely to be imprisoned. It may be that they could not get full-time stable jobs."

The difficulty in finding a good job today is off-set by the abundance of part-time jobs in the illegal drug economy. In preparation for a proposal to the National Institute on Drug Abuse to examine the impact of drug abuse and drug dealing on Milwaukee's gangs, we updated our rosters on the current status of the 37 founding members of three African-American gangs. By 1990, less than one in five (19 percent) of the founders, now in their mid to late twenties, were engaged in full-time work. However, three times as many of the founders (59 percent) graduated from the gang into drug "posses" or high-risk small businesses selling drugs. "High risk" is perhaps an understatement. Almost all of the 37 (86 percent) had spent significant time in prison since 1986, most for drug offenses. Three quarters (76 percent) had used cocaine regularly within the last three years and three had been murdered. While five of the 37 were said to be working as entrepreneurs (called "hittin' 'em hard"), the others involved with drug distribution worked part time ("makin' it") or sporadically ("day one") and continued to live on the margins.

As Don, a leader of the 1-9 Deacons told us in 1985: "I can make it for two or three more years. But then what's gonna happen?" The answer to Don's question is now clear. The lack of access to good jobs has had a direct effect of making illegal drug sales, no matter how risky, more attractive to Milwaukee's gang founders as an occupation for their young adult years.

Frederick Thrasher pointed out sixty years ago: "As gang boys grow up, a selective process takes place; many of them become reincorporated into family and community life, but there remains a certain criminal residue upon whom gang training has for one reason or another taken hold" (Thrasher 1963:287). The loss of entry level manufacturing jobs appears to have turned Thrasher's "selective process" on its head. Today most of the young adult gang founders rely on the illegal economy for guarantees of survival. It is only the "residue" who, at this time in Milwaukee, are being "reincorporated into family and community life."

There are also some indirect effects of economic changes. In Milwaukee most of the founders still identify somewhat with their old gang and often hang out in the same neighborhoods where they grew up, coexisting with a new generation of gang youth. This mixing of older members of drug "posses" with younger siblings and other young gang members has produced disturbing intergenerational effects. Older gang members with a street reputation employed in the fast life of drug dealing are modeling dangerous career paths for neighborhood youth. These intergenerational effects also appear in Anderson's latest work (1990). He finds that "old heads," older residents who upheld and disseminated traditional values, are being replaced by new "old heads" who "may be the product of a street gang" and who promote values of "hustling," drugs, and sexual promiscuity (103). This "street socialization" may contribute to reproducing an underclass rather than socializing young people into conventional lifestyles (Short 1990b, Vigil 1988).[1]

In summary, contemporary gangs have changed from the "delinquent boys" of fifties literature: There is a growing relationship between the youth gang, illegal drug-based distribution, and survival of young adult gang members in a post-industrial segmented economy. Clearly, powerful economic forces are affecting contemporary gangs as Wilson and other underclass theorists would predict. But when we take a closer look at the impact of economic, demographic, and institutional changes on processes within Milwaukee's poorest African-American neighborhoods, the situation becomes more complicated.

Gangs and Neighborhood Segmentation

Gangs have always been associated with neighborhoods and African-American gangs have been no exception. Thrasher found "Negroes" had "more than their share" of gangs (Thrasher 1963:132) as far back as the 1920s. In the neighborhood that Suttles studied, gangs were functional "markers" or signs by which neighborhood youth could know who may be harmful and who is not and thus were an important part of a neighborhood's search for order. Suttles' black gangs were not in any significant way distinct from white ethnic gangs (Suttles 1968:157). Similarly, the black Chicago gang members that Short and Strodtbeck (1965:108) studied were quite similar to nongang black youth though they were more lower class than white gang members. Until the 1960s, the sociological literature largely viewed black gangs as functional parts of black neighborhoods.

But things have been changing. Perkins, summarizing the history of black Chicago gangs, wrote that gangs first became disruptive to their communities in the late 1960s due to the influence of drugs, corrupting prison experiences, and the failure of community-based programs (Perkins 1987:40–42). Cloward and Ohlin theorized that housing projects and other big city "slums" tended to be disorganized and "produce powerful pressures for violent behavior among the young in these areas" (Cloward and Ohlin 1960:172). They correctly predicted that "delinquency will become increasingly violent in the future as a result of the disintegration of slum organization" (203).

Increasing violence in central cities has prompted angry responses from residents. Cooperation by broad elements of the black community with police sweeps of gang members in Los Angeles and elsewhere and the founding of "mothers against gangs" and similar organizations throughout the country are examples of community hostility to gangs. Gangs today are seen by both law enforcement and many community residents as basically dysfunctional. Today's gangs are a far cry from the "Negro" street gangs of Suttles' Addams area which contained the "best-known and most popular boys in the neighborhood" (Suttles 1968:172).

Based on our Milwaukee interviews, we concluded that gang members reciprocated the hostility of "respectables." While the gang founders were hostile toward police and schools as expected, they also severely criticized African-American community agencies which they felt were mainly "phoney." The black founders agreed their gangs were dysfunctional for their neighborhoods: two thirds of those we interviewed insisted that their gang was "not at all" about trying to help the black community. Some were shocked at even the suggestion that their gang would be concerned about anything but "green power" (i.e., money). The role model of choice for many of the founders we interviewed was not Dr. Martin Luther King, Jesse Jackson, or any African-American leader, but Al Capone.

One explanation for this intracommunity alienation in Milwaukee is the peculiar way black gangs formed. Gang formation in Milwaukee coincided with desegregation of the schools: a one-way desegregation plan that mandatorily bused only black children. While gangs originally formed from neighborhood groups of youth in conflict with youth from other neighborhoods, busing complicated the situation. School buses picking up African-American students often stopped in many different neighborhoods, mixing youth from rival gangs and transforming the buses into battlegrounds. Gang recruitment took place on the buses and in the schools as well as from the neighborhood. The black founders told us in 1985–86 that a majority of the members of their gangs no longer came from the original neighborhood where the gang formed.

Consequently, when the gang hung out on neighborhood corners, they were not seen by residents as just the "neighbors' kids" messing up. "I'll tell your Mama" did not work when no one knew who "mama" was or where she lived. Informal social controls were ineffective, so calling the police became the basic method to handle rowdiness and misbehavior as well as more serious delinquency. Hostility between the gangs and the neighborhood increased with each squad car arriving on the block.

A second explanation for intra-community hostility is provided by 1989 research in five of Milwaukee's poorest and all-black census tracts (Moore and Edari 1990b) where several of the gangs I had studied were founded. These neighborhoods exhibit many of the criteria of an "underclass" area, but they also differ in many respects from very poor ghetto neighborhoods described by Wilson and others.

Household income of the tracts was very low—1980 census data (before the eighties downturn) show more than 30 percent of the families in the five tracts living below poverty. The five tracts experienced a 42 percent population loss between 1960 and 1985. In 1989, when the interviews were completed, most (53.8 percent) respondents received AFDC and nearly twenty percent (19 percent) did not have a phone. A majority of residents in the five tracts presently live below the poverty line. The tracts certainly qualify as "underclass" areas by standard definitions (Ricketts and Mincy 1988).

But these neighborhoods are not uniformly poor. One quarter of the residents (28.6 percent) owned their own home—fifteen percent less than the citywide average, but still a stable base within a very poor neighborhood. Half of the household heads lived at their current residence for five or more years. While stable employment had drastically declined in these tracts since 1980, still nearly one third of working respondents had held their current job for 10 or more years. Unlike the "densely settled ghetto areas" Sampson describes (1987:357) where residents have "difficulty recognizing their neighbors," 80 percent of the Milwaukee respondents said the best thing about their neighborhood *was* their "neighbors." Nearly three in five (59.2 percent) visited with neighbors at least once a week.

More striking were strong kinship ties, supporting earlier work by Stack (1974) and others. Nearly half of all respondents visited their parents every day and over ninety percent visited their parents monthly. An even higher percentage visited siblings at least once a month. Finally, more than three quarters belonged to families that held family reunions—and 77 percent of those respondents regularly attended those reunions. Even child protective clients, who are among the most transient residents, had extensive kinship networks (Moore and Edari 1990a).[2]

But the neighborhoods are not regarded positively by most residents. Less than one fifth (19.7 percent) said the neighborhood was a "good place to live," and 52 percent said they would move if they could. While the respondents liked their neighbors as the best thing about their community, the top three worst things were said to be drugs (64 percent), violence (52 percent), and gangs (20 percent). About half said things had gotten worse the past two years, and a majority (54.5 percent) believed things will continue to get worse. And the problems were not "around the corner" or in an adjacent neighborhood, but right on the blocks where the interviews took place. The interviewers were often told by respondents to not go to a certain house or to avoid a certain side of the street because of dangerous drug or gang problems.

The area also has few basic social institutions. Zip code 53206 is a 20 by 20 square block area with 40,000 residents in the heart of Milwaukee, containing the census tracts where the interviews took place. This area has no large chain grocery stores. There are no banks or check-cashing stores in the entire zip code area. Bars and drug houses are in plentiful supply and the area has the highest number of Milwaukee drug arrests. Still, in 1989, this zip code area did not have a single alcohol/drug treatment facility. Even community agencies are located overwhelmingly on the periphery of 53206, circling the neighborhoods they serve, but not a part of them.[3] Community programs, churches, and social workers were seldom mentioned by survey respondents as a resource to call in times of neighborhood trouble.[4]

In summary, while these poor African-American neighborhoods have characteristics of Wilson's notion of the underclass, they also exhibit important differences. On the one hand, central city Milwaukee neighborhoods have been getting poorer due to deindustrialization and have experienced substantial population loss. They are home to the poorest and most troubled of all Milwaukee's residents. The area's lack of basic institutions is reminiscent of descriptions by Thrasher (1963) and Shaw and McKay (1969) and supports aspects of Wilson's underclass thesis.

On the other hand, large numbers of working class African-American families still reside in these neighborhoods. Some want to leave but cannot because of residential segregation (Massey and Eggers 1990) or lack of affordable housing. But many stay because they want to. Rather than neighborhoods populated overwhelmingly by a residue left behind by a fleeing middle and working class, as Wilson described, Milwaukee's "underclass" neighborhoods are a checkerboard of struggling working class and poor families, coexisting, even on the same block, with drug houses, gangs, and routine violence.

This ecological coexistence explains much of the intra-community tension between poor and working families and underclass gangs. Clearly when drug deals gone bad turn into midnight shoot-outs, residents of a neighborhood will be scared and angry. Contrary to Wilson's claim, events in one part of the block or neighborhood are often of vital concern to those residing in other parts (Wilson 1987:38). With a lack of effective community institutions, residents can either ignore the gunshots in the night, arm themselves for self-protection, call "911"—or give in to the fear and despair by moving out.[5]

While Milwaukee neighborhoods are not the socially disorganized underclass area reported by Wilson, neither are they the highly organized neighborhoods described by Whyte (1943) or Suttles (1968). Milwaukee's poor neighborhoods have segmented and an uneasy peace reigns between nervous factions. Suttles (1968) saw the 1960s Addams area as representing "ordered segmentation," where firm boundaries between ethnic neighborhoods helped make "a decent world within which people can live" (234). Instead, Milwaukee's neighborhood segments have become a prime source of instability.

This picture of neighborhood segmentation is consistent with Anderson's portrait of "Northton," a poor African-American community in a large eastern city (Anderson 1990). "Old heads" in Northton are not so much missing, as they have become demoralized and their advice shunned (78–80). Respectable residents are confronted by a growing street culture that increases community distrust of young people, victimizes neighborhood residents, and lures children into dangerous activities (92). Police simplistically divide the neighborhood between the "good people" and those linked to drug trafficking (202–3). Conflict between neighborhood segments inevitably increases, and "solidarity" is sacrificed to the imposed order of police patrols, vigilante justice, and prisons.

These heterogeneous but segmented neighborhoods in "Northton" and Milwaukee may be characteristic of many "underclass" communities across the United States (Jencks 1989). How to stabilize such neighborhoods is one of the major policy debates of the nineties. . . .

Conclusion

Deindustrialization has altered the nature of gangs, creating a new association between the youth gang, illegal drug-based distribution, and survival of young adult gang members in a post-industrial segmented economy. While it would be a mistake to see all gangs as drug-dealing organizations, the lack of opportunity for unskilled delinquents creates powerful strains on gang members to become involved in the illegal economy. Without a major jobs program, illegal traffic in drugs and related violence seem likely to continue at unacceptable levels (Goldstein 1985, Johnson et al. 1989).

Although neighborhood changes are clearly relevant to gang activities, Wilson's characterization of the underclass as living in neighborhoods from which middle and working class African-Americans have fled and abandoned social institutions (Wilson 1987:56) does not fully apply in cities like Milwaukee. Instead, there are deteriorating neighborhoods with declining resources and fractured internal cohesion. In cities like Milwaukee, it is not the absence of working people that define underclass neighborhoods but more the absence of effective social institutions. Without community controlled institutions, conventional values will have diminished appeal, neighborhoods will segment, solidarity will weaken, and working residents will continue to flee. The research on Milwaukee is consistent with the basic tenet of social theory, that the lack of effective institutions is related to crime and delinquency. The data support Spergel and others who call for "community mobilization and more resources for and reform of the educational system and job market" (Spergel and Curry 1990:309) as the most effective approach to gang control.

This article does support Wilson and others who call for massive new federal job programs. While lobbying for new state and federal job programs, social scientists should also focus on ways to encourage private and public investment in poor neighborhoods and advocate for more community control of social institutions. This means a stepped up involvement by academics in the workings of the large public bureaucracies which control resources needed to rebuild these communities.[6]

In the words of C. Wright Mills, bureaucracies "often carry out series of apparently rational actions without any ideas of the ends they serve" (Mills 1959:168). All too often the ends public bureaucracies serve are not helpful for poor communities. This article can be read as a call for social scientists to step up the struggle to make public bureaucracies more rational for the truly disadvantaged.[7]

Notes

1. Moore (1991) also finds a mixing of gang cliques in Los Angeles gangs. Short's (1990) 1960 Nobles were mainly employed in the early 1970s when they were restudied, in contrast to Vicelords, virtually all of whom had more prison experience, many of whom still identified with the Vicelords and were involved in illegal operations more than a decade after they were first studied.

2. Child protective clients, however, more than other residents, turned to police for help with problems than asking help from their relatives or neighbors.

3. In contrast, zip code 53204, a predominantly Hispanic area home to several Hispanic gangs, is dotted with community agencies, banks, merchants, and grocery stores. While this area is a neighborhood of first settlement for Mexican immigrants, it does not have the characteristics of social disorganization of the predominantly African-American 53206 neighborhoods. Those who use "percent Hispanic" as a proxy for social disorganization should take note of these findings (cf. Curry and Spergel 1988:387).

4. There are other institutions in the area with a high profile, particularly law enforcement. But the strong police presence plays to a mixed review. While most residents (38.3 percent) called the police for any serious problems in the neighborhood before they called relatives or friends, one in eight (12.1 percent) listed police as one of the three top "bad things" about the neighborhood. Police are still viewed with suspicion and fear in African-American communities.

5. It must be remembered, however, that the illegal drug economy, while disruptive, is also sustained by a local demand. Workers in drug houses assert that most Milwaukee cocaine sales are to people within the neighborhood, not to outsiders (in contrast to Kornblum and Williams [1985:11]). But when illegal activities bring trouble to the neighborhood, particularly violence, police are often welcomed in ousting drug dealers and combatting gang problems (Sullivan 1989:128).

6. This recommendation is not a call for revisiting the Chicago Area Project which relied on private financing and performed a "mediating role" with local institutions (Schlossman and Sedlak 1983, Sorrentino 1959), nor is it a call for a new war on poverty with built in antagonism between city hall and short lived federally funded agencies (Marris and Rein 1967, Moynihan 1969). Rather, it is a call for academics to directly engage in local struggles over how and where large public bureaucracies distribute existing resources.

7. This article is based on several previous papers. The first was presented on April 24, 1990, to the U.S. Conference of Mayors in Washington, D.C. Two others were presented at the 85th Annual ASA Meetings, also in Washington D.C., August, 1990. Joan Moore, Carl Taylor, Howard Fuller, and Clinton Holloway made helpful comments on various earlier drafts. *Social Problems'* anonymous reviewers also added valuable insights. . . .

References

Anderson, Elijah. 1990. *Streetwise: Race, Class, and Change in an Urban Community.* Chicago: University of Chicago Press.

Aponte, Robert. 1988 "Conceptualizing the underclass: An alternative perspective." Paper presented at Annual Meetings of the American Sociological Association. August. Atlanta, Georgia.

Bluestone, Barry, and Bennett Harrison. 1982. *The Deindustrialization of America: Plant Closings, Community Abandonment, and the Dismantling of Basic Industry*. New York: Basic Books.

Cloward, Richard, and Lloyd Ohlin. 1960. *Delinquency and Opportunity*. Glencoe, Ill: Free Press.

Curry, G. David, and Irving A. Spergel. 1988 "Gang homicide, delinquency, and community." *Criminology* 26:381–405.

Gans, Herbert J. 1990. "The dangers of the underclass: Its harmfulness as a planning concept." New York: Russell Sage Foundation, Working Paper #4.

Goldstein, Paul J. 1985. "The drugs-violence nexus: A tripartite conceptual framework." *Journal of Drug Issues* 15:493–506.

Hagedorn, John M. 1988. *People and Folks: Gangs, Crime, and the Underclass in a Rustbelt City*. Chicago: Lakeview.

———. 1989. "Roots of Milwaukee's underclass." Milwaukee, Wis.: Milwaukee County Department of Health and Human Services.

Huff, C. Ronald. 1989. "Youth gangs and public policy." *Crime and Delinquency* 35:52–537.

Jencks, Christopher. 1989. "Who is the underclass—and is it growing." *Focus* 12:14–31.

Johnson, Bruce, Terry Williams, Kojo Dei, and Harry Sanabria. 1989. "Drug abuse in the inner city." In *Drugs and the Criminal Justice System*, ed. Michael Tonry and James Q. Wilson, Chicago: University of Chicago.

Kasarda, John D. 1985. "Urban change and minority opportunities." In *The New Urban Reality*, ed. Paul E. Peterson, 33–65. Washington, D.C.: The Brookings Institute.

Kornblum, William, and Terry Williams. 1985. *Growing Up Poor*. Lexington, Mass: Lexington Books.

Marris, Peter, and Martin Rein. 1967. *Dilemmas of Social Reform, Poverty, and Community Action in the United States*. Chicago: University of Chicago.

Massey, Douglas S., and Mitchell L. Eggers. 1990. "The ecology of inequality: Minorities and the concentration of poverty, 1970–1980." *American Journal of Sociology* 95:1153–1188.

Mills, C. Wright. 1959. *The Sociological Imagination*. London: Oxford University Press.

Moore, Joan W. 1985. "Isolation and stigmatization in the development of an underclass: The case of Chicano gangs in East Los Angeles." *Social Problems* 33:1–10.

———. 1991. *Going Down to the Barrio*. Philadelphia: Temple University Press.

Moore, Joan W., and Ronald Edari. 1990a. "Survey of Chips clients: Final report." Milwaukee, Wis.: University of Wisconsin—Milwaukee Urban Research Center.

———. 1990b. "Youth initiative needs assessment survey. Final report." Milwaukee, Wis.: University of Wisconsin–Milwaukee.

Moynihan, Daniel P. 1969. *Maximum Feasible Misunderstanding: Community Action in the War on Poverty*. New York: The Free Press.

Perkins, Useni Eugene. 1987. *Explosion of Chicago's Street Gangs*. Chicago: Third World Press.

Piven, Frances Fox, and Richard A. Cloward. 1987. "The contemporary relief debate." In *The Mean Season: The Attack on the Welfare State*, ed. Fred Block, Richard A. Cloward, Barbara Ehrenreich, and Frances Fox Piven, 45–108. New York: Pantheon.

Ricketts, Erol, and Ronald Mincy. 1988. "Growth of the underclass: 1970–1980." Washington, D.C.: Changing Domestic Priorities Project, The Urban Institute.

Ricketts, Erol, Ronald Mincy, and Isabel V. Sawhill. 1988. "Defining and measuring the underclass." *Journal of Policy Analysis and Management* 7:316–325.

Sampson, Robert J. 1987. "Urban black violence: The effect of male joblessness and family disruption." *American Journal of Sociology* 93:348–382.

Schlossman, Steven, and Michael Sedlak. 1983. "The Chicago Area Project revisited." Santa Monica, Calif.: Rand Corporation.

Shaw, Clifford R., and Henry D. McKay. 1969. *Juvenile Delinquency and Urban Areas*. Chicago: University of Chicago.

Short, James F. 1990a. "Gangs, neighborhoods, and youth crime." Houston, Tex.: Sam Houston State University Criminal Justice Center.

———. 1990b. "New wine in old bottles? Change and continuity in American gangs." In *Gangs in America*, ed. C. Ronald Huff, 223–239. Beverly Hills, Calif: Sage.

Short, James F., and Fred L. Strodtbeck. 1965. *Group Process and Gang Delinquency*. Chicago: University of Chicago.

Sorrentino, Anthony. 1959. "The Chicago Area Project after 25 years." *Federal Probation* 23:40–45.

Spergel, Irving A., and G. David Curry. 1990. "Strategies and perceived agency effectiveness in dealing with the youth gang problem." In *Gangs in America*, ed. C. Ronald Huff, 288–309. Beverly Hills, Calif.: Sage.

Stack, Carol B. 1974. *All Our Kin*. New York: Harper Torchback.

Sullivan, Mercer L. 1989. *Getting Paid: Youth Crime and Work in the Inner City*. Ithaca, N.Y: Cornell University Press.

Suttles, Gerald D. 1968. *The Social Order of the Slum*. Chicago: University of Chicago.

Taylor, Carl. 1990. *Dangerous Society*. East Lansing, Mich: Michigan State University Press.

Thrasher, Frederick. [1927] 1963. *The Gang*. Chicago: University of Chicago.

Trotter, Joe William. 1985. *Black Milwaukee: The Making of an Industrial Proletariat 1915–1945*. Chicago: University of Illinois.

Vigil, Diego. 1988. *Barrio Gangs*. Austin, Tex: University of Texas Press.

White, Sammis, John F. Zipp, Peter Reynolds, and James R. Paetsch. 1988. "The Changing Milwaukee Industrial Structure." Milwaukee, Wis.: University of Wisconsin–Milwaukee, Urban Research Center.

Whyte, William Foote. 1943. *Street Corner Society*. Chicago: University of Chicago.

Wilson, William Julius. 1987. *The Truly Disadvantaged*. Chicago: University of Chicago.

———. 1991. "Studying inner-city social dislocations: The challenge of public agenda research." *American Sociological Review* 56:1–14.

CHAPTER 26

Neighborhood Variation in Gang Member Concentrations

Charles M. Katz ■ Stephen M. Schnebly

This article also highlights community disorganization theory, but in contrast to the two previous articles, this study adopts a quantitative approach to investigate how economic and social disadvantage is related to the rate of gang membership in 93 census tracts in Mesa, Arizona. While the authors find that disadvantage predicts a higher concentration of gang members, it also appears that there are lower rates of gang participation in extremely challenged neighborhoods. Drawing from disorganization theory and other research, the authors speculate that some stability of social ties in neighborhoods is necessary to transmit and support the negative social norms and antisocial behaviors on which gangs depend.

Editor's Note: *Table 26.3 has been modified slightly with permission from the authors.*

Over the past 30 years, street gangs have garnered considerable attention from criminal justice officials, policy makers, and academics. Consequently, these three decades have been witness to considerable investment in understanding both the scope and nature of the gang problem. For example, gang researchers routinely conduct costly annual surveys of police organizations to estimate the number of gangs, gang members, and gang crimes in cities across the country (Egley & Ritz, 2006; Klein, 1995; Maxson, 1998; Needle & Stapleton, 1983; Office of Juvenile Justice and

Reprinted from: Charles M. Katz and Stephen M. Schnebly, "Neighborhood Variation in Gang Member Concentrations," *Crime & Delinquency*, 57(3): 377–407. Copyright © 2011 by Sage Publications. Reprinted by permission of Sage Publications.

Delinquency Prevention, 2004). Several efforts to understand the gang phenomenon have utilized official records from police agencies and courts to examine how gang members differ from matched nongang criminally involved populations (Chesney-Lind, Rockwell, Marker, & Reyes, 1994; Huff, 1998; Katz, Webb, & Schaefer, 2000; McCorckle & Miethe, 1998; Zatz, 1987). Still others have employed self-report data collected from school-based samples to determine the individual-level correlates and consequences of gang membership (e.g., Esbensen & Deschenes, 1998; Gordon et al., 2004; Hill, Howell, Hawkins, & Battin-Pearson, 1999; Thornberry, Krohn, Lizotte, Smith, & Tobin, 2003).

Although this body of literature has enhanced substantially our understanding of gangs, gang members, and gang crime, some researchers note that gang research has focused almost exclusively on two general issues: (a) city-level variation in the magnitude of the "gang problem," and (b) individual-level outcomes such as the causes and correlates of gang membership and ties between gang involvement and crime (Hall, Thornberry, & Lizotte, 2006; Hughes, 2006; Klein & Maxson, 2006; Tita, Cohen, & Engberg, 2005). As a result of this focus on variability across cities and individuals, gang researchers have done little to address an issue with arguably greater theoretical and policy relevance—the role that community context plays in shaping *neighborhood-level* variation in youth gang involvement.

For example, how well do neighborhood-level structural conditions account for variability in gang member concentrations? What impact, if any, do levels of crime or community dynamics have on the concentration of gang members in a neighborhood? This study attempts to answer these and similar questions by exploring the relationships between neighborhood structure and gang member rates. We rely on official police gang-list data, police crime data, and two waves of decennial census data characterizing the socioeconomic and demographic conditions of 93 census tracts (neighborhoods) in the city of Mesa, Arizona.

In addition to being one of a handful of studies to explore neighborhood-level variation in gang member concentrations, this research extends prior work on this substantively important topic in several key ways. First, as previously noted, most macrolevel gang studies have focused solely on explaining city-level variations in gang presence and activity. The present study, however, draws both from ecological theories of crime and from prior gang research to examine the gang phenomenon at the more localized neighborhood level.

Second, although prior studies typically have used either gang presence or gang crime as indicators of community levels of gang involvement, we use an indicator that reflects not only whether gangs are present in a community but, more important, the rate of gang members per capita in a given neighborhood. Last, in addition to multiple measures of neighborhood-level structural conditions, our study incorporates indicators of both community dynamics (changes in neighborhood structure) and neighborhood crime conditions (e.g., violent crime rates), permitting a more thorough and theoretically driven examination of gang member concentrations than is found in the extant literature.

In the following section, we present the theoretical and research framework upon which this study is built, and we discuss our data and methods. Next, we present our analysis and findings regarding neighborhood-level variation in gang member concentrations. We conclude by discussing our findings in the context of prior research and theory.

Background

Early research from the Chicago school of criminology highlighted the importance of neighborhood disorganization in predicting crime in general and the formation of street gangs specifically (Shaw & McKay, 1931; Thrasher, 1927).[1] Ever since, criminologists have emphasized the utility of social disorganization theory for understanding the causal nexus that leads to the emergence of gangs and gang activity. A key tenet of social disorganization theory is that communities characterized by socioeconomic disadvantage, immigrant concentrations, and residential mobility tend also to be characterized by relatively lower levels of informal social control and higher levels of crime and deviance (Bursik & Grasmick, 1993; Kornhauser, 1978; Sampson, Raudenbush, & Earls, 1997; Shaw & McKay, 1942). More precisely, theorists postulate that these forms of structural disadvantage erode the foundations of normative authority and hinder the development of social cohesion and mutual trust.

Cohesion and trust are vitally important to a community because they allow cultivation of shared goals and provide impetus for collective action. This willingness and ability to develop and achieve shared goals—labeled "collective efficacy" by Sampson et al. (1997)—includes cooperative efforts to define, monitor, and condemn undesirable behaviors that occur within a community. Absent these social ties and mutual relationships, communities characterized by social disorganization find that they are unable to exercise control over their social and physical landscapes. As a result of this diminished capacity for control, disorganized communities tend to experience higher levels of crime and deviance than their more socially organized counterparts. Indeed, a growing body of recent community-level research provides evidence in support of theoretical linkages between crime, social control, and community structure (e.g., Bellair, 1997, 2000; Markowitz, Bellair, Liska, & Liu, 2001; Morenoff, Sampson, & Raudenbush, 2001; Sampson & Groves, 1989; Sampson et al., 1997).

Social disorganization theorists have explored other community-level characteristics that might also play a role in shaping levels of informal control across communities. Of particular importance are age composition of residential populations, population density, and characteristics of the physical landscape (Tita et al., 2005). In regard to age composition, informal-control theorists assert that a large proportion of youth residents in a community results in a diminished capacity for informal social control. The basis for this assertion is a reduction in the number and availability of adults capable of effectively exercising control. For instance, parents with multiple children are likely to be too preoccupied with familial responsibilities to effectively monitor (or intervene in) the activities of those in the community at-large.

Another key demographic attribute theorized to influence levels of social control is population density. More specifically, the density of the residential populace is thought to be negatively associated with levels of informal control. Theorists posit that high population density is typically accompanied by increased anonymity for individual community members (Roncek, 1981). The resulting estrangement between residents substantially impedes the cultivation of collective efficacy, which in turn reduces the capacity of the community to serve as an effective mechanism of social control.

Community-level theorists also have addressed the role that a community's physical landscape plays in shaping the effectiveness of mechanisms of informal social control. For example, vacant overgrown lots and dilapidated empty buildings not only represent physical deterioration but bestow upon community residents and visitors the impression of social deterioration and disorganization (e.g., J. Q. Wilson & Kelling, 1982). Furthermore, vacant buildings and lots are thought to diminish a community's capacity to exercise control by providing residents with a location to engage in criminal or deviant behaviors with little likelihood that such activities will be censured by neighborhood residents.

In addition to the relevance of social disorganization theory for community-level studies of crime, gang researchers have drawn from this theoretical model to explore variations in gang activity and gang behavior across communities. In a recent work, Papachristos and Kirk (2006) noted the ease with which the social disorganization framework can be extended to include the study of urban street gangs and gang behavior. The authors presented two succinct explanations for the genesis

and persistence of gangs in socially disorganized communities: "Gangs arise either to take the place of weak social institutions in socially disorganized areas, or because weak institutions fail to thwart the advent of unconventional value systems that often characterize street gangs" (p. 64).

Although each of these explanations posits a positive association between community disorganization and gang activity, the theoretical rationale for each, although not necessarily mutually exclusive, is different. One explanation emphasizes the notion that gangs are analogous to disease and that communities with a "gang problem" are simply those without the means (mechanisms of social control) to prevent or otherwise treat this particular social malady; the other emphasizes the notion that gangs represent a rational response to the conditions facing residents of socially disorganized communities.

The "underclass" narrative advanced by Wilson (1987) also supports the notion that the formation (and persistence) of gangs may be an attempt to replace ineffective community-based institutions. Underclass researchers argue that gangs and gang activity constitute an "adaptation" to the unique social, economic, and familial disadvantages experienced by the urban underclass (Hagedorn, 1988; Venkatesh, 1997; see also Papachristos & Kirk, 2006). Indeed, proponents of this position often argue that far from being a disease, street gangs can *benefit* their communities by providing residents with a much-desired mechanism of effective social control (e.g., protection from adverse events such as criminal victimization, attacks from rival gangs, and crooked landlords and business owners; Sanders, 1994; Venkatesh, 1997).

Prior Research

Regardless of social disorganization theory's relevance for gang research, relatively little empirical research has systematically examined the influence of neighborhood structure on gang presence and activity at the neighborhood level. Most empirical support for social disorganization theory and its numerous variants derive from studies examining the relationship between neighborhood structural factors and crime in general. In their review article, Sampson, Morenoff, and Gannon-Rowley (2002) assessed and synthesized the literature on neighborhood effects. They reported a strong and robust relationship between neighborhood structural disadvantage and delinquency, violence, and other high-risk behaviors. This body of research, however, has not determined whether gang problems are an etiologically similar phenomenon to crime or whether the same neighborhood structural factors that give rise to crime are the same as those that serve to promote gangs, as previously suggested.

Klein and Maxson (2006) noted that prior studies have failed to examine the relationship between gang presence and neighborhood structural disorganization net levels of neighborhood crime. It could be that gang presence is related to high levels of neighborhood crime because the facilitative effects of gang membership combined with a high concentration of gang members result in higher levels of neighborhood crime. Alternatively, it could be that high levels of neighborhood crime, which researchers have found to be significantly related to social disorganization, increase the number of gang members and gang crimes because of increased need for protection.

A review of prior literature suggests that research examining structural factors and their influence on gang phenomena generally falls into two broad categories: (a) that which examines how community structural factors influence varying levels of gang activity (e.g., crime) and (b) that which examines the influence of community structural factors on gang presence.

Community Structure and Gang Activity

Curry and Spergel (1988) examined the relationship between ethnicity and poverty on gang homicide and general forms of delinquency in 75 Chicago communities. The authors reported that gang homicide and delinquency rates were associated with different community structural factors. Delinquency rates were strongly associated with neighborhood poverty regardless of neighborhood ethnic composition, whereas gang homicides were differentially related to community ethnic composition. Specifically, gang homicides were significantly more likely to take place in communities with high concentrations of Hispanics. The authors

noted that although the data available were limited, their analysis suggested that unstable communities that undergo rapid population changes over time will likely face higher levels of gang violence than stable communities, even after controlling for the social and economic conditions of the community.

Results obtained by Rosenfeld, Bray, and Egley (1999), on the other hand, showed few differences between neighborhoods that had high levels of gang and nongang homicide. The analysis relied on case file data obtained from the St. Louis Metropolitan Police Department to identify whether homicides were gang affiliated, gang motivated, or nongang involved. It used census data from 588 census block groups. The authors examined whether neighborhood disadvantage, neighborhood instability, and racial composition (i.e., percentage Black) were associated with the distribution of gang-motivated, gang-affiliated, and nongang homicides. The authors found that little difference in neighborhood structural factors existed between the three types of homicide and that all three types of homicide were concentrated in predominately Black, disadvantaged, unstable neighborhoods (p. 505).

Block and Block (1993) used official police and census data to compare levels of gang and nongang homicide across 77 Chicago community areas. Their bivariate analysis showed that Black neighborhoods with high levels of gang homicide also experienced high levels of nongang homicide, whereas Hispanic and mixed-race neighborhoods with high levels of gang homicide experienced few nongang homicides. In addition, the authors reported that community structural factors had a strong and significant impact on the types of gang homicide occurring in communities. Communities that were experiencing substantial social and economic decline had higher levels of instrumental violence, whereas communities that were experiencing relative prosperity and increased population had higher levels of expressive violence.

Papachristos and Kirk (2006) conducted the most thorough examination of structural factors associated with gang crime in their analysis of data from the Project on Human Development in Chicago Neighborhoods. First, they aggregated surveys from 8,782 residents from 847 census tracts into 343 "neighborhood clusters" for measures of collective efficacy and informal social control. Second, they used census data from these same neighborhood clusters to create measures for concentrated disadvantage, immigrant concentration, and residential stability. Last, they relied on homicide data from the Chicago Police Department that indicated the location of each homicide and whether the homicide was gang or nongang related.

The authors reported that although collective efficacy mediated the effects of neighborhood structural factors on both gang and nongang violence, it did not do so differentially. In other words, they found that "collective efficacy operates similarly on violent gang behavior as it does on other forms of violent behavior" (p. 75). However, they did report that their findings were similar to those of Curry and Spergel (1988). Namely, area clusters with high rates of gang homicides, but low rates of nongang homicides, were typically associated with Hispanic neighborhoods with high levels of immigrant concentration.

Structural Conditions and Gang Presence

Sociologists have measured gang presence at varying levels of place and through different measures of "presence." Much of the early research on gang presence examined the number of gangs, gang members, and the proliferation of gangs through surveys of police organizations (Curry, Ball, & Fox, 1994; Klein, 1995; Miller, 1982; Needle & Stapleton, 1983). This body of work often relied on official police data (gang intelligence databases) to indicate the number of gangs and gang members in a city or relied on a police official's account of whether the city had a gang problem. Regardless of the researcher's measure, these studies consistently revealed that city size was significantly related to whether a community reported a gang problem, with larger cities significantly more likely to report a gang problem than smaller cities. Annual surveys conducted by the National Youth Gang Center have added support for this conclusion (Egley, 2005; National Youth Gang Center, 1998, 1999, 2000).

In the early 1990s, Jackson (1991) hypothesized that not all large cities would have an equal probability of having a gang problem but that cities experiencing demographic and economic transition were the most likely to have gang problems. Jackson argued that with the restructuring of society from a manufacturing to a service-based economy, the economic infrastructure of urban centers had declined substantially and necessarily had resulted in increased social disorganization. She hypothesized that economic instability and population decline were significantly related to the presence of gangs, even after controlling for crime rates.

Jackson examined all cities with populations of 25,000 or more using 1970 and 1980 U.S. census data to create measures reflecting the demographic and economic structure and transformation of cities, Uniform Crime Report data to create measures of crime, and data from the National Juvenile Assessment Survey to assess whether the city had a gang problem.[2] Jackson's analysis showed that gang presence was significantly more likely to be reported in cities experiencing declines in wholesale and resale employment and cities with large proportions of residents aged 15 to 24 years.

Wells and Weisheit (2001) further examined the relationship between gang presence and structural factors in both metropolitan and nonmetropolitan areas. They specifically were interested in understanding the relationship between gang presence and four general theoretical frameworks: ecology (social and economic stability), economic deprivation, population composition, and social diffusion (social and physical isolation). The researchers' measure of the county's gang problem was a police organizational self-report measure derived from the National Youth Gang Survey. Specifically, an official within each county's law enforcement agency reported whether the county had "no gangs," "transitory gangs," or "chronic gangs." Data for each of the four theoretical models were obtained from the Department of Commerce and Department of Agriculture. The authors reported that social stability and population composition were related to gang presence in both metropolitan and nonmetropolitan counties. However, economic stability and deprivation appeared to have a significant impact on gang presence only in metropolitan areas.

Building on the aforementioned research, Tita et al. (2005) examined the community characteristics of "gang set space." Tita et al. collected data from homicide files, street workers, and gang members to identify 35 hard-core violent urban street gangs in Pittsburgh and had a member of each street gang identify their set space. Using census data, the authors then examined the social structural factors that differentiated those areas where gangs did and those areas where gangs did not hang out. They found that population density, percentage of vacant residences, and percentage Black were related to gang set space. In addition, the authors reported that gangs were more likely to hang out in neighborhoods with high concentrations of underclass.

Limitations of Prior Literature

Although the research just reviewed has enhanced our understanding of the many factors that influence gang presence, it has been limited in several key ways. As previously pointed out by Tita et al. (2005), prior studies typically have examined gang presence at "gross units of observation," for example, at the city and county levels. Unfortunately, reliance on large units of analysis might mask important ecological conditions related to gangs and gang activity and does not necessarily allow for measurement of theoretically important constructs as envisioned by early gang scholars.

As previously discussed, many gang researchers have discussed the important role of neighborhood conditions in relationship to gangs, gang membership, and gang crime, and they argue that the social and physical characteristics of neighborhoods, not cities or counties as a whole, foster conditions that give rise to gangs. Therefore, the census tract serves as the unit of analysis for the study presented here. Although census tracts are only rough approximations of neighborhoods (Tienda, 1991), they are by far the most frequently used geographic unit to represent small communities in social science research on neighborhood effects (e.g., Brooks-Gunn, Duncan, & Aber, 1997; Jencks & Mayer, 1990).[3]

Prior research also has been restricted to examining gang presence. More specifically, the extant literature typically has examined gang presence through binary measures and has not more fully examined whether community structural factors are associated with the magnitude of a community's gang problem. For example, Jackson's (1991) measure of gang presence was whether the local

police agency self-reported having a gang problem, whereas Wells and Weisheit's (2001) measure of gang presence was the local law enforcement agency reporting whether "no gangs," "transitory gangs," or "chronic gangs" existed within their jurisdiction. Likewise, Tita et al. (2005) used a restricted measure of gang presence that reflected whether a geographic area was occupied by 1 of 35 hard-core violent street gangs. "Non-hard-core gangs" were excluded from their analysis.

These prior methods of measuring gangs at the neighborhood level are limited in several key ways. First, they necessarily restrict analysis to the presence of a gang or gangs in a neighborhood rather than the magnitude of the gang problem. Second, the use of a dichotomized measure increases the potential for measurement error. Much of the prior research on structural conditions and gang presence has relied on a single informant, typically a police official, to indicate whether a community or neighborhood had a gang problem or gangs were present. Third, the use of a dichotomous variable decreases variability and does not accurately reflect the realities of neighborhood-level gang problems. Recognizing these limitations, our study extends previous research through increased specification of the dependent variable. More specifically, we incorporate a more robust measure that reflects the concentration of documented gang members residing within a given neighborhood.

In addition, previous research exploring neighborhood variation in gang presence has failed to control for neighborhood levels of crime and violence or consider the potential influence of structural change on the prevalence of gangs and gang members. As discussed earlier, prior research has repeatedly shown that disadvantaged neighborhoods have fewer effective mechanisms of social control and have higher levels of crime and violence (Sampson et al., 2002; Sampson et al., 1997). Therefore, the significant relationship found in prior research between indicators of disadvantage and gang presence might have been a spurious relationship through crime and violence. Much prior research has shown that gang membership has a criminogenic effect on crime and violence (Hall et al., 2006; Klein & Maxson, 2006; Spergel, 1995) and that high numbers of gang members living in a neighborhood might significantly increase neighborhood levels of crime and violence, even after controlling for disadvantage. Alternatively, research examining gang joining has repeatedly found that youth often join gangs because they are fearful of being victimized and believe that gangs provide a source of guardianship and protection (Decker & Curry, 2000; Esbensen & Lynskey, 2001; Katz, 2004; Klein & Maxson, 2006; Peterson, Taylor, & Esbensen, 2004). Based on this body of literature, we might expect that neighborhoods with higher levels of violent crime also would have comparatively higher concentrations of gang members. Although our study does not attempt to examine the temporal ordering of this relationship, we include a measure of neighborhood violent crime so that we can assess whether there is a relationship between neighborhood structural factors and gang member concentrations, net levels of violent crime.

Last, although Shaw and McKay's (1942) ecological perspective emphasized the importance of changes in neighborhood structural conditions, prior studies examining gang presence have failed to incorporate indicators of community change (for exception, see Jackson, 1991). Of interest, the impact that structural change is expected to have on gang and gang membership is somewhat unclear. On one hand, changes in neighborhood structure (e.g., rising disadvantage) may result in diminished levels of social control and in turn be associated with high rates of membership and large concentrations of gang members (e.g., Jackson, 1991). On the other hand, gang joining and membership are group processes that likely require some degree of social stability to come to fruition. If so, rising levels of structural disadvantage, which likely disrupt the social ties and networks necessary for the formation and persistence of street gangs, may be associated with general reductions in gang membership at the neighborhood level. To explore both of these possibilities, we include in our study indicators of decennial changes in neighborhood-level structural conditions.

Data, Methods, and Analytic Strategy[4]

Three data sets were merged to conduct the analysis for our study. First, police gang-intelligence data

provided information on the prevalence of gang members at the neighborhood level. Second, police Records Management System (RMS) Computer Aided Dispatch (CAD) data were used to construct a neighborhood-level measure of violent crime. Third, data obtained from the 1990 and 2000 U.S. decennial censuses provided the study with numerous measures of neighborhood-level structural characteristics. We discuss each of these three data sources in greater detail next.

Gang Data

The Mesa Police Department's gang unit provided data from their gang-intelligence database. These data included the names of individuals documented as gang members by the Mesa Police Department as of December 31, 2002, as well as information related to each documented gang member's ethnicity, gender, date of birth, address, and gang affiliation.[5]

The documentation process can take place in any one of several different ways. Documentation may result from observations or questions raised by a patrol officer making a routine contact or by a detective in the course of an investigation. Officers document individuals as gang members using a gang documentation form that is forwarded to the gang unit. Gang unit personnel systematically screen these forms, and documented members are placed on the gang list.[6] Similarly, activity engaged in by the police gang unit serves as another important source for the documentation and placement of individuals on the gang list.[7]

Prior research by Curry (2000) examining the reliability and validity of police gang data has reported that there is "an overlap between the gang problem as it is observed by field studies and surveys and the gang problem as revealed by analyses of official records" (i.e., police gang lists; p. 1268). Curry further reported that individuals who are documented as gang members are significantly more criminally active than those identified as gang members in studies relying on self-report methodologies.[8]

Related, prior research using the Mesa Police Department's gang database has revealed that these data provide a valid measure of gang involvement.

Using gang list data and data from the Maricopa County Juvenile Probation Department, Katz et al. (2000) found that documented gang members were significantly more likely to engage in serious delinquency and were significantly more criminally active than a comparison group of delinquent youth. More specifically, documented gang members were arrested almost four times as often for violent offenses as individuals in the nondocumented comparison group and were arrested about three times as often for weapons offenses, property offenses, drug offenses, and status offenses.

For our study, the Mesa Police Department gang list provided the residential addresses for 1,064 documented gang members. These data were geocoded and summed within neighborhood boundaries to create counts of gang members residing in each of Mesa's neighborhoods. Because 150 addresses on the gang list fell beyond Mesa city borders, our analysis was based on 914 gang members residing in the city.

Census Data

Summary file 3 data from the 1990 and 2000 U.S. decennial censuses provided neighborhood-level measures of the social, economic, and physical characteristics of 93 census tracts in Mesa, Arizona. Described in detail below, some examples of census-tract level data used in the study include population and household totals, racial and ethnic composition, persons living in poverty, residential tenure, population density, and number of vacant housing units.

Crime Data

Police RMS/CAD data from the year 2002 were used to construct the study's neighborhood-level measure of violent crime. These crime data, which included calls for service and incidents arising from police-initiated field activities, were aggregated to the census-tract level and subsequently appended to the study's neighborhood-level gang data. All duplicate crime records, whether calls for service or police initiated, were eliminated from the data set. Thus, the final data set included 5,242 violent crimes in the City of Mesa for the year 2002.

Measures

The dependent variable examined in the study was constructed from official police gang-list data. Labeled *gang members*, this variable represents the number of officially documented gang members residing in each of Mesa's 93 census tracts.[9]

The study's indicators of neighborhood structure were created from census-tract-level measures obtained from the year 2000 decennial census. These neighborhood data included percentages in the following categories: African American persons, Hispanic persons, foreign-born persons, female-headed families with children, persons without a high school diploma, unemployed adults, persons living in poverty, households receiving public assistance income, males aged 12 to 24, renter-occupied housing units, persons living in a different house than 5 years ago, persons per square mile, and vacant housing units. Principle components analysis was used to reduce these highly correlated data into summary measures of neighborhood-level structural disadvantage (e.g., Land, McCall, & Cohen, 1990).[10]

The resulting component loadings are displayed in Table 26.1.[11] As the table reveals, two disadvantage components were extracted. The first component, designated *economic deprivation*, exhibits high loadings for percentage Hispanic and percentage foreign-born persons, as well as for the study's traditional measures of economic disadvantage, including the percentage of persons without a high school diploma, the adult unemployment rate, percentage of persons living in poverty, and percentage of households receiving public assistance income. The second component, labeled *social and familial disadvantage*, is associated with relatively high concentrations of African Americans, young male residents, single-parent families, and renter-occupied housing units. These two indicators of neighborhood disadvantage each are included as key independent variables in the study's analytic models.

Although excluded from the principle components analysis described earlier, the measures for persons in a different house than 5 years earlier, persons per square mile, and the proportion of vacant housing remain in the study as independent variables. Labeled *residential instability, population density*, and *vacant housing*, respectively, each of

Table 26.1 Factor Loadings from Principle Components Factor Analysis

Socioeconomic Disadvantage	Loading
% Latino	.852
% Foreign born	.873
% Residents without a H.S. diploma	.952
% Unemployed	.667
% In poverty	.862
% Households on public assistance	.805
Social/Familial Disadvantage	
% African American	.872
% Female-headed families with kids	.822
% Male residents aged 12–24	.776
% Renter-occupied housing units	.782

Extraction method: principle components with varimax rotation.

these measures was transformed into standardized z scores before inclusion in statistical models.

The study's indicators of neighborhood structural changes were computed from 1990 and year 2000 decennial census data. We began by conducting a principle components analysis of the study's pooled 1990 and 2000 census data.[12] This procedure resulted in two extracted disadvantage components (results not shown) with loadings nearly identical to those reported in Table 26.1. To construct measures of decennial changes in each disadvantage component (i.e., changes in economic deprivation and social/familial disadvantage), we subtracted the pooled 1990 component scores from their corresponding year 2000 pooled component scores. The resulting two variables are labeled *change in economic deprivation* and *change in social/familial disadvantage* and reflect the differences in neighborhood levels of economic deprivation and social/familial disadvantage between the years 1990 and 2000.[13]

In addition to indicators of neighborhood structure and structural change, the study also incorporates a measure of neighborhood crime. Constructed from police RMS/CAD data and labeled *violent crime*, this variable reflects the number of officially recorded incidents of violent crime per 1,000 neighborhood residents.[14]

Analytic Strategy

Because gang members compose only a small fraction of the total population in most communities, the analysis of neighborhood-level gang member rates requires the use of specialized estimation techniques.[15] An appropriate method for dealing with rare event data is the use of Poisson-based estimation procedures (Osgood, 2000). These procedures, which are well suited for analyzing rare events that occur in the context of relatively small base populations (e.g., neighborhoods), generally assume that the mean and the variance of the dependent variable are equivalent. When this assumption is violated, the data are considered overdispersed, and the use of the negative binomial estimator is necessary. Although Poisson-based regression can be used to analyze count data, a slight modification permits this class of estimators to examine variability in the rates of events. This is achieved by adding an exposure variable (or offset variable) to the model that is the natural log of the base population and then constraining the value of this variable to one. When such an exposure variable is added to a Poisson-based regression model, the resulting coefficients reflect proportional differences in rates per capita rather than counts (Osgood, 2000).

Because our analyses revealed overdispersion in our data (results not shown), we employed an overdispersed Poisson-based regression model (negative binomial model) that is appropriate for analyzing our aggregate-level count data (Osgood, 2000). For all models, the natural log of the residential population of each census tract was included as the exposure variable, and thus, all regression coefficients reflect proportional differences in the gang member rate across neighborhoods.[16]

Our analytic strategy involved estimation of a series of four regression models exploring the influence of structural conditions on neighborhood-level gang member rates. Model 1 incorporated the study's five indicators of neighborhood structure to explain variations in gang member rates across neighborhoods. In Models 2 and 3, respectively, we added violent crime rates and indicators of structural change to the model. Last, in Model 4 we explored the potential for nonlinear relationships between our dependent and independent variables.[17]

Results

Descriptive statistics for the study's neighborhood-level data are reported in Table 26.2. The typical Mesa neighborhood was populated by 9.83 gang members, which corresponds to an average of 2.06 gang members per 1,000 neighborhood residents (i.e., the gang membership rate). Because the study's key independent variables are standardized, the descriptive statistics for these measures do not readily convey the socioeconomic and demographic conditions in Mesa during the period under study. Thus, at the bottom of Table 26.2 we report summary statistics for the individual measures used to construct these standardized variables.

Table 26.2 Descriptive Statistics (*N* = 93)

Dependent Variable	Mean	SD	Min	Max
Number of gang members	9.83	13.70	0	68
Gang member rate per 1k	2.06	2.77	0	14.85
Independent variables				
Economic deprivation	0	1	−1.66	3.47
Social/familial disadvantage	0	1	−2.11	2.91
Residential instability	0	1	−2.44	2.84
Population density	0	1	−1.59	3.75
Vacant housing	0	1	−0.99	3.03
Violent crime rate per 100k	11.96	8.98	0	58.09
Change in economic deprivation[1]	0.17	0.71	−1.21	2.00
Change in social/family disadvantage[1]	0.40	0.46	−1.21	1.40
Neighborhood characteristics[2]				
% African American	2.83	2.05	0	10.03
% Latino	18.50	14.57	0.50	72.50
% Foreign born	10.34	8.55	1.17	44.30
% Female-headed families w/kids	8.50	5.15	0	20.37
% w/o high school diploma	15.46	10.06	2.83	51.75
% Unemployed	4.09	2.03	0	8.83
% In poverty	8.90	6.28	0	26.88
% Households on public assistance	5.16	3.03	0	14.06
% Males 12–24	11.34	4.01	0	20.67
% Renter-occupied housing	26.94	20.39	0	82.70
% Different house 5 years ago	58.71	13.18	26.60	96.11
Persons per square mile	4,971	3,103	35,89	16,603
% Households that are vacant	12.85	12.97	0	52.20

[1] *N* = 91 because 2 Mesa tracts did not exist in 1990
[2] These data were used to construct the factor scores and standardized independent variables listed above

Regarding levels of crime, Table 26.2 reveals that on average, approximately 12 incidents of violence per 1,000 residents occurred in neighborhoods across Mesa. Means for the measures of neighborhood change demonstrate that in the typical neighborhood, levels of both economic deprivation and social/familial disadvantage rose between 1990 and 2000. However, it is important to note the high levels of variability in the size and direction of these changes across neighborhoods. . . .

The results of a series of negative binomial regression models are reported in Table 26.3. The first model displayed in Table 26.3 explored the influence of neighborhood-level structural characteristics on concentrations of gang members residing in Mesa neighborhoods. Consistent with expectations and prior research, Model 1 reveals that neighborhoods characterized by relatively high levels of *economic deprivation* and *social/familial disadvantage* generally have higher rates of gang membership. These results also reveal that although population density and vacant housing were unrelated to gang member concentrations, *residential instability* was significantly and negatively associated with gang member rates.

Table 26.3 Results from Negative Binomial Regression Models ($N = 93$)				
Independent Variables	Model 1	Model 2	Model 3	Model 4
Economic deprivation	0.899**	0.864**	0.922**	1.069**
	(0.065)	(0.081)	(0.101)	(0.100)
Social/familial disadvantage	0.636**	0.578**	0.721**	0.646**
	(0.098)	(0.127)	(0.123)	(0.113)
Residential instability	−0.189*	−0.181*	−0.197*	−0.141
	(0.089)	(0.089)	(0.096)	(0.086)
Population density	−0.047	−0.024	−0.044	0.029
	(0.079)	(0.085)	(0.076)	(0.078)
Vacant housing	−0.016	−0.014	−0.004	−0.013
	(0.080)	(0.080)	(0.079)	(0.103)
Violent crime rate per 100k		0.008		
		(0.011)		
Change in economic deprivation			−0.063	
			(0.154)	
Change in social/familial disadvantage			−0.339	
			(0.183)	
Economic deprivation squared				−0.130**
				(0.041)
Social/familial disadvantage squared				−0.104
				(0.061)
Constant	−6.765**	−6.857**	−6.613**	−6.592**
	(0.066)	(0.147)	(0.110)	(0.080)
Log likelihood	−231.222	−230.972	−225.897	−224.663
Prob > χ^2	0.000	0.000	0.000	0.000
Pseudo R^2	0.226	0.223	0.231	0.248

Note: Standard errors in parentheses.
[1] $N = 91$
*$p < .05$, 2 tailed.
**$p < .01$, 2 tailed.

In Model 2, we present a model that accounts for not only the influence of neighborhood structure on gang member concentrations but also explores associations between gang member rates and neighborhood levels of violent crime. The results of this model revealed that net of structural conditions, levels of violent crime exert no significant influence on the gang member rate. In addition, neighborhood crime does little to mediate the influences of structural disadvantage on neighborhood levels of gang membership.[18]

In Model 3, we report the results of an analysis that addressed the influence of *changes* in neighborhood structural disadvantage on the concentration of gang members in a community. This model indicates that although both of the study's indicators of structural change are negatively associated with the gang member rate, neither reaches statistical significance in the model.[19]

The fourth and final model reported in Table 26.3 explored the potential for curvilinear associations between neighborhood structure and rates of gang membership. To do this, squared terms for both economic deprivation and social/familial disadvantage were added to the model to test for the quadratic functional form of nonlinearity. The results revealed significant nonlinearity in the association between economic deprivation and gang member concentrations. More specifically, the positive main effect of economic deprivation coupled with the negative coefficient for the squared economic deprivation term indicated that at extreme levels of economic deprivation, the magnitude of the positive association between these variables was significantly diminished.

Model 4 reveals similar evidence of a curvilinear association between social/familial disadvantage and the gang member rate, although this relationship fails to reach conventional levels of statistical significance ($p \leq .088$).

Summary and Discussion

Over the past 30 years, much prior research has examined individual-level correlates and consequences of gang membership, including the relationship between gang membership and crime. Although this body of research has had a profound influence on our understanding of gangs, gang membership, and gang crime in general, it rarely has addressed the role of community variation in the gang problem. Past research that has explored this issue typically has been limited by a variety of factors, including a reliance on large units of analysis, a focus on the presence of gangs as opposed to the magnitude of the gang problem, and the failure to account for potential associations between gang member rates, community structure, and crime. The study presented here addressed these limitations by exploring the influence of neighborhood structure, structural change, and neighborhood crime on gang member concentrations in 93 Mesa, Arizona, neighborhoods.

Consistent with expectations, preliminary statistical analyses revealed that neighborhoods characterized by comparatively high levels of economic deprivation or social/familial disadvantage also tended to have higher concentrations of gang members residing within their borders. Interpreted from the perspective of social disorganization theory and its variants, this evidence appears to suggest that high levels of gang membership in disadvantaged neighborhoods is the result of diminished capacity of social control in such places (e.g., Bursik & Grasmick, 1993; Sampson et al., 1997). Specifically, we postulate, as others before us have, that gangs flourish in more disadvantaged, socially disorganized neighborhoods where private, parochial, and public forms of social control are less effective (Papachristos & Kirk, 2006; Tita et al., 2005; Zatz & Portillos, 2000).

However, our analysis also revealed that the relationship between rates of gang membership and neighborhood disadvantage is neither as simplistic nor as linear as others before us have concluded. In particular, our findings indicate that the positive association between gang member concentrations and disadvantage is significantly diminished at extreme levels of structural disadvantage. This evidence of a nonlinear relationship suggests a point at which neighborhoods are so disadvantaged and disorganized, and social networks are so sparse, that they no longer possess the basic social structures necessary for youth residents to coalesce and form into gangs. For example, although residents in extremely disadvantaged communities lack the resources to support conventional youth activities, the disorganized nature of their communities also prohibits them from transmitting unconventional norms and behaviors—such as gang culture—to youth residents (e.g., Cloward & Ohlin, 1960).[20]

Unfortunately, our data do not permit us to explore more fully the exact nature of these associations between gang member concentrations and structural disadvantage. Although we find positive relationships between neighborhood disadvantage and the gang member rate, we are unable to determine whether these associations result from the inability of communities characterized by economic and social/familial disadvantage to defend themselves against gang formation or whether gangs arise and flourish in such places to fill the vacuum left by inadequate mechanisms of social control (e.g., Papachristos & Kirk, 2006). Furthermore, our data do not permit us to more thoroughly understand the causal mechanisms related to the point at which neighborhoods become so disadvantaged that they no longer foster the development and persistence of youth street gangs. Future research using longitudinal research methods might be particularly well suited to examine these issues (see, e.g., Hall et al., 2006).

In addition to the aforementioned findings, our analysis suggested that community factors may converge in different ways to contribute to the prevalence of gang members in neighborhoods, and that the importance of these community-level factors vary, depending on the ethnic composition of the neighborhood. For example, we found that neighborhoods with higher rates of Hispanics, foreign-born residents, and economic disadvantage (e.g., economic deprivation) had significantly higher concentrations of gang members residing within their borders. To a lesser extent, we also found higher concentrations of gang members among communities characterized by comparatively larger numbers of African Americans, female-headed households with kids, renter-occupied housing units, and young males (i.e., social/familial disadvantage). These findings suggest that the ethnic composition of neighborhoods might interact in unique ways with other neighborhood factors to contribute to the prevalence of gang membership at the neighborhood level.

Prior research has found repeatedly that gangs typically are organized around ethnic lines (Klein, 1995; Spergel, 1995) and that neighborhood ethnic composition has a significant effect on levels of gang violence (Rosenfeld et al., 1999). These findings combined with those of our study suggest that future research should closely examine the special role that ethnicity plays in gang membership at the neighborhood level, as well as the role that ethnicity plays within gangs and its contribution to violence. Although a burgeoning body of literature has focused on the role of females in gangs and their influence on gang behavior, the same level of attention has not been given to the role of ethnicity.

Our results also revealed that not all traditional indicators of neighborhood-level social disorganization are positively associated with gang member concentrations. For example, prior research has hypothesized that residential mobility is related to neighborhood social cohesion and the establishment of values and norms, which are necessary to enable effective informal social control at the neighborhood level. Neighborhoods with low levels of informal social control are thought to possess less capacity to prevent gang formation. Despite these empirical expectations, prior studies of communities and gangs have revealed a negative relationship between residential mobility and gangs at the neighborhood level (Tita et al., 2005; Wells & Weisheit, 2001).

Similar to these prior studies, our statistical models revealed a significant negative association between gang member rates and residential instability. This evidence, in conjunction with the findings just noted, suggests that although diminished social control is an important condition for the formation and growth of gangs, the presence of relatively stable social networks is also a key ingredient. Consistent with this notion are the study's findings regarding the influences of neighborhood structural change on gang member concentrations. Although these findings failed to reach statistical significance, our results indicated that neighborhoods that experienced the greatest structural changes over a 10-year period also tended to have lower rates of gang membership than their more static and structurally stable counterparts. Similar to the nonlinear findings previously discussed, this evidence suggests that the transmission of youth gang culture is more difficult—and thus less likely to occur—in social environments characterized by a rapidly changing residential populace.[21]

An additional finding of interest was that rates of gang membership were not significantly related to neighborhood levels of violence, net controls. There are several reasons one might expect that neighborhood levels of gang membership and violence would be associated with one another. Prior research has shown that on an individual level, gang members are responsible for a disproportionate amount of crime, and if enough gang members reside in a neighborhood we would expect that they would significantly increase neighborhood levels of crime and violence. For example, Block (2000) reported that the number of gangs present in an area was significantly related to the area's overall level of crime. Alternatively, some have hypothesized that gang membership might be the byproduct of neighborhood conflict and violence (Klein, 1995; Klein & Maxson, 2006). For example, those who live in neighborhoods with high levels of violence might be more inclined to fear being victimized and might choose to join a gang for protection, therefore increasing the prevalence of gang membership in the neighborhood. However, our findings were not supportive of these hypotheses. Instead, we found that neighborhoods with high concentrations of gang members were not necessarily those with comparatively high levels of officially recorded violence.

Our analyses also revealed that concentrations of gang members within neighborhoods was not significantly related to population density. This finding is contrary to previous research and theoretical assumptions (e.g., Tita et al., 2005; Wells & Weisheit, 2001). Our findings, in conjunction with Johnstone's (1981), suggest that population density may no longer be a necessary ecological precondition to gang formation. Since the 1980s, a significant transformation has swept through metropolitan communities. Urban centers that once were highly concentrated with urban poor began

to experience significant out-migration of their poor to suburban neighborhoods and an influx of middle- and upper-income residents to regentrified neighborhoods (Murphy, 2007). As this transformation took place, suburban neighborhoods across the nation experienced higher poverty rates. Several scholars have noted that by the year 2000, half of all people living below the poverty level lived in suburbs (Berube & Frey, 2002; Lucy & Phillips, 1995; see also Murphy, 2007). As a consequence, urban centers with their high levels of population density might no longer "hold a monopoly on the social conditions that foster ganging" (Johnstone, 1981, p. 376). Suburban neighborhoods characterized by economic deprivation or social/familial disadvantage might provide ample conditions to foster gangs.

Last, our analyses did not show a significant relationship between vacant housing and neighborhood-level gang member concentrations. Although past studies have found significant associations between the amount of vacant housing in a community and gang presence (Hagedorn, 1988; Jackson, 1991; Tita et al., 2005; Wells & Weisheit, 2001), this research has largely been conducted in industrial, rust-belt communities (for exception, see Jackson, 1991) where a major economic shift has occurred that negatively affected community structure (e.g., increases in vacant housing). Conversely, our study took place in Mesa, Arizona, which, like the rest of the Southwest, has experienced major economic growth. Consequently, such indicators may have qualitatively different sociological meaning based on geography.[22]

Two potential limitations should be noted before interpretation of the findings is complete. First, the findings of this study should not necessarily be generalized to other communities. A number of studies have demonstrated that a community's gang problem is unique and may not be similar to that of other communities. Accordingly, those neighborhood factors reflective of a local gang problem may be the result of characteristics that exist only within a given community. Second, our findings are reflective of the gang sample used for our study. In particular, we restricted our definition of gang members to those individuals officially documented as such by the local police agency. These individuals might be significantly more involved in criminality than other samples that might have been chosen for such a study, such as a sample drawn from school youth. Future research should examine the effect of different methodological strategies for sampling gang members and how they influence research.

Conclusion

The findings presented in this study indicated that neighborhood structural characteristics play an important role in determining the extent of the "gang problem" at the neighborhood level. Neighborhoods characterized by high levels of economic deprivation and social and familial disadvantage were found to have relatively larger concentrations of gang members than their more affluent counterparts. It is interesting that these positive associations between disadvantage and gang member concentrations are substantially reduced in neighborhoods characterized by extreme levels of economic and social/familial disadvantage. This evidence of nonlinear relationships suggests that at some point, neighborhoods are so disadvantaged and socially disorganized that they no longer provide a context suitable for the genesis or persistence of youth street gangs.

This study also reveals that neighborhood stability is an important concept for explaining variability in the rate of gang membership at the neighborhood level. Specifically, we find that gang membership is less common in unstable communities such as those characterized by residential mobility, population turnover, and rapidly changing structural conditions. Thus, it appears that gangs and gang membership are in part contingent on the presence of stable social ties and linkages that are necessary for virtually any social group (including gangs) to develop and persevere.

Although we are able to demonstrate the salience of neighborhood context for understanding variations in gang member concentrations at the neighborhood level, some important issues remain that are beyond the scope of this study and thus are left for future researchers to address. In particular, research is needed to address more fully the role that neighborhood characteristics play in the causal nexus that leads to the decision to join (or not join) a gang. For instance, although economic and social/familial disadvantage are positively associated with gang membership at the neighborhood level, do these contexts influence individual decision-making in the same way? Similarly, relative to individual-level characteristics, how strongly does community context influence the decision to join a gang?

Furthermore, future research should examine the broader impact of geographic region on neighborhood structure and gang member concentrations.[23] Over the past two decades, researchers have reported that the gang problem has grown and is significantly more pronounced in larger cities located in the western region of the United States (Klein & Maxson, 2006; Office of Juvenile Justice and Delinquency Prevention, 1999). Although this study contributes to our understanding of gang problems in a more typical gang city, it is unclear whether our findings are generalizable to other western cities. Since the 1980s, the western region of the United States has experienced massive growth due to (im)migration. This growth has in turn resulted in significant neighborhood structural change that is unique when compared to such cities as Chicago, St. Louis, and Pittsburgh, where much gang research has taken place. Future research should examine how the unique neighborhood structural changes that have taken place in the West might have impacted the region's gang problem. Answering these questions will require detailed multilevel data on gang members and their communities, as well as creative uses of both qualitative and quantitative research methodologies. Whatever the final answers will be, the results of the present study constitute an important step on the path to a more thorough understanding of the linkages between neighborhoods and gangs.

Declaration of Conflicting Interests

The author(s) declared no potential conflicts of interest with respect to the research, authorship, and/or publication of this article.

Funding

The author(s) received no financial support for the research, authorship, and/or publication of this article.

Notes

1. See also Short and Strodtbeck (1965).
2. Jackson (1991) indicated that the city was classified as having a gang problem if police "provided evidence of gangs" in the city (p. 385).
3. Census tracts are small, relatively permanent geographic entities located within counties or the statistical equivalent of counties that generally envelop an area of 2 square miles and contain approximately 4,000 individuals and 1,500 housing units. The geographic boundaries of census tracts typically follow enduring and easily visible elements of the physical landscape (e.g., streets, rivers, railroads). In addition, census tracts generally are defined so that each is relatively homogenous in terms of demographic and socioeconomic characteristics (Bureau of the Census, 1994, pp. 10-1 to 10-7).
4. The data we used were collected as part of an ongoing federal initiative aimed at reducing gang violence in the city of Mesa, Arizona. Mesa is located in the southeastern corner of the Phoenix–Mesa–Scottsdale metropolitan area and is bordered by such cities as Chandler, Tempe, and Apache Junction. It is the third largest city in Arizona, with a population of about 455,000. Mesa's crime rate is higher than some southwestern cities (e.g., Las Vegas, Los Angeles, and San Diego) but is lower than others (e.g., Albuquerque and Phoenix). For a thorough discussion of Mesa's gang problem, see Katz, Webb, & Armstrong, 2003; Katz et al., 2000; Spergel, Wa, & Sosa, 2002.
5. It should be noted that over the past several decades a large body of research has developed that has defined gang membership and examined the implications of the definition for researchers and policy makers. For a thorough review of this literature, see Esbensen, Winfree, He, & Taylor, 2001; Katz et al., 2000; Klein, 1995; Klein & Maxson, 2006; Spergel, 1995.
6. The Mesa Police Department uses seven criteria proscribed by the Arizona Revised Statutes Definitions, section 13-105, to determine whether an individual should be documented as a gang member. These criteria include self-proclamation, witness testimony, official statement, written or electronic correspondence, paraphernalia or photographs, tattoos, and clothing or colors. Although there is officer discretion in documenting gang members, officer discretion is confined significantly, which necessarily increases reliability. As discussed earlier, officers are not permitted to document an individual for any reason, but rather the individual must meet one of seven criteria. This information is then reviewed by a supervisor before they are placed into the gang database.
7. After an individual has been documented as a gang member that person's record would remain in the gang intelligence database for a specified period. In Mesa, records of associate gang members were purged after 1 year, and records of gang members were purged after 3 years. Mesa Police Department used an automated system to generate lists of documented gang members who had been in the system for the specified period. They check the listed names against police records, searching for any further police contacts that included evidence of continuing gang membership, involvement with a gang or gang members, or gang activity. If such evidence was found, that individual's record would be updated and replaced in the gang information system for another 1 to 3 years.
8. Much prior research has found that although self-report surveys of gang membership provide valid and reliable data, they tend to capture a greater number of marginally involved gang youth who are less delinquent than individuals found in police gang-list data. For a full discussion of this issue, see Curry (2000).
9. This measure reflects one of several possible methodological strategies for measuring the concentration of gang members in neighborhoods. Alternative strategies might include school-based surveys, field interviews, and citizen surveys. Although we recognize the value of these alternative approaches, prior research has shown that gang list data are valid and suitable for our purposes (e.g., Curry, 2000; Katz et al., 2000).
10. The criterion for component extraction was eigenvalues greater than 1. Varimax rotation was used to ensure that the extracted factors were uncorrelated with one another.
11. Because the variables for *persons living in a different house than 5 years ago, persons per square mile*, and *vacant housing units* initially failed to load on either of the two extracted components, these variables were excluded from the principle components analysis.
12. As was the case previously, the indicators for persons living in different house, persons per square mile, and

vacant housing failed to load strongly on any extracted component and were excluded from pooled principle components analysis.

13. We also computed structural change scores by running principle components analysis on 1990 data only and then subtracting the resulting component scores from those computed from year 2000 data only. The results from analyses that incorporated these alternative change scores were substantively identical to those reported next and thus are not reported in tabular format.

14. Incidents and calls for service that were coded as violent crimes include aggravated and simple assault, armed robbery, fighting, homicide, kidnapping, sexual assault, stabbing, strong arm robbery, and threatened violence.

15. In particular, rare event data pose three distinct problems that require special attention. First, such data typically are not normally distributed and thus violate a basic assumption of ordinary least squares estimation procedures. Second, rare event data typically are heteroskedastic because the variance of the error term grows as the base population shrinks. Third, rates for rare events are unstable and can be deceptive when computed from a small population base (Osgood, 2000).

16. We also estimated models using the population of male residents aged 12 to 24 as the exposure variable. The results of these models were substantively identical to those reported next and can be obtained from the authors upon request.

17. We also estimated spatial regression models to account for the potential problem of spatial dependence in the study's dependent variable. Although the Moran's I statistic initially revealed the presence of spatial autocorrelation (results not shown). the inclusion of the study's indicators of neighborhood structure into these models reduced the magnitude of residual autocorrelation to statistical nonsignificance. Of interest, this evidence is consistent with the structural similarity model presented by Baller, Anselin, Messner, Deane, and Hawkins (2001), in which "no remaining spatial dependence should be found once the structural similarity of neighboring [census tracts] has been explicitly controlled for" (p. 565).

18. We also ran a variation of Model 2 that, instead of violent crime, incorporated property crime rates per 1,000 residents (results not shown). This model revealed that neighborhood levels of property crime exert no significant influence on gang member rates net of neighborhood structural characteristics.

19. The inclusion of our measure of violent crime into Model 3 produced substantively identical results to those reported in Table 26.3.

20. It is worth noting that this theme has also been reported in the community policing literature. For example, as Walker and Katz (2008) repeatedly pointed out, in many extremely disadvantaged communities "the community" may simply be unable to participate in community policing processes because there is often no viable community to mobilize.

21. To further explore our findings regarding neighborhood instability and gang member concentrations, we estimated a series of models identical to those reported in Table 26.3 (results not shown) that included indicators of population change and percentage change in population from 1990 to 2000 for each Mesa neighborhood. The coefficients for these new indicators of population change were negative and failed to reach statistical significance. The remaining coefficients from these supplementary models closely mirrored those reported in Table 26.3.

22. For example, Mesa, Arizona, has undergone a substantial amount of housing development over the past few decades because of the fast-paced economy and population growth. Therefore, the substantial number of houses on the market (vacant houses) in many Mesa neighborhoods is positively associated with growth. However, in Pittsburgh and Illinois, where economic growth has not been as fast, and in fact has contracted in many communities, vacancy is associated with the downward spiral and decline of neighborhoods.

23. Related to this point, one anonymous reviewer noted that future researchers might also consider examining racially diverse adjoining communities such as those found in large metropolitan areas such as Los Angeles, Chicago, and New York. The reviewer's suggestion is intriguing in that such research would be able to test several community-oriented theoretical models.

References

Baller, R. D., Anselin, L., Messner, S. F., Deane, G., & Hawkins, D. F. (2001). Structural covariates of U.S. county homicide rates: Incorporating spatial effects. *Criminology, 39*, 561–590.

Bellair, P. E. (1997). Social interaction and community crime: Examining the importance of neighbor networks. *Criminology, 35*, 677–703.

Bellair, P. E. (2000). Informal surveillance and street crime: A complex relationship. *Criminology, 38*, 137–170.

Berube, A., & Frey, W. (2002). *A decade of mixed blessings: Urban and suburban poverty in Census 2000*. Washington, DC: Brookings Institution.

Block, R. (2000). Gang activity and overall levels of crime: A new mapping tool for defining areas of gang activity using police records. *Journal of Quantitative Criminology, 16*, 369–383.

Block, R., & Block, R. (1995). *Street gang crime in Chicago*. In M. Klein, C. Maxson, & J. Miller (Eds.), *The modern gang reader* (pp. 202–210). Los Angeles: Roxbury.

Brooks-Gunn, J., Duncan, G. J., & Aber, J. L. (1997). *Neighborhood poverty: Context and consequences for children* (Vol. 1). New York: Russell Sage Foundation.

Bureau of the Census (1994). *Geographic areas reference manual*. Washington, DC: U.S. Department of Commerce.

Bursik, R., & Grasmick, H. (1993). *Neighborhoods and crime: The dimensions of effective community control*. New York: Lexington.

Chesney-Lind, M., Rockwell, A., Marker, N., & Reyes, H. (1994). Gangs and delinquency. *Crime, Law, and Social Change, 21*, 201–208.

Cloward, R., & Ohlin, L. (1960). *Delinquency and opportunity: A theory of delinquent gangs*. New York: Free Press.

Curry, G. D. (2000). Self-reported gang involvement and officially recorded delinquency. *Criminology, 38*(4), 1253–1274.

Curry, G. D., Ball, R. A., & Fox, R. J. (1994). *Gang crime and law enforcement recordkeeping*. Washington, DC: National Institute of Justice.

Curry, G. D., & Spergel, I. (1988). Gang homicide, delinquency and community. *Criminology, 26*, 381–405.

Decker, S., & Curry, G. D. (2000). Addressing key features of gang membership. *Journal of Criminal Justice, 28*, 473–482.

Egley, A. (2005). *Highlights of the 2002–2003 National Youth Gang Surveys*. Washington, DC: Office of Juvenile Justice and Delinquency Prevention.

Egley, A., & Ritz, C. (2006). *Highlights of the 2004 National Youth Gang Survey*. Washington, DC: Office of Juvenile Justice and Delinquency Prevention.

Esbensen, F. A., & Deschenes, E. P. (1998). A multi-site examination of youth gang membership: Does gender matter? *Criminology, 36*(4), 799–827.

Esbensen, F. A., & Lynskey, D. (2001). *Youth gang members in a school survey*. In M. W. Klein, H. Kerner, C. L. Maxson, & E. Weitekamp (Eds.), *The Eurogang paradox: Street gangs and youth groups in the U.S. and Europe* (pp. 93–114). Dordrecht, the Netherlands: Kluwer Academic.

Esbensen, F. A., Winfree, L. T., He, N., & Taylor, T. J. (2001). Youth gangs and definitional issues: When is a gang a gang, and why does it matter? *Crime and Delinquency, 47*, 105–130.

Gordon, R., Lahey, B., Kawai, E., Loeber, R., Loeber, M., & Farrington, D. (2004). Antisocial behavior & youth gang membership: Selection and socialization. *Criminology, 42*(1), 55–88.

Hagedorn, J. H. (1988). *People and folks*. Chicago: Lakeview Press.

Hall, G. P., Thornberry, T. P., & Lizotte, A. J. (2006). The gang facilitation effect and neighborhood risk: Do gangs have a stronger influence on delinquency in disadvantaged areas? In J. F. Short & L. A. Hughes (Eds.), *Studying youth gangs* (pp. 47–61). Walnut Creek, CA: AltaMira.

Hill, K. G., Howell, J. C., Hawkins, J. D., & Battin-Pearson, S. R. (1999). Childhood risk factors for adolescent gang membership. *Journal of Research in Crime and Delinquency, 36*, 300–322.

Huff, C. R. (1998). *Comparing the criminal behavior of youth gangs and at-risk youths*. Washington, DC: U.S. Department of Justice.

Hughes, L. A. (2006). Studying youth gangs: The importance of context. In J. Short & L. A. Hughes (Eds.), *Studying youth gangs* (pp. 37–46). Walnut Creek, CA: AltaMira.

Jackson, P. I. (1991). Crime, youth gangs and urban transition: The social dislocation of postindustrial economic development. *Justice Quarterly, 8*(3), 379–397.

Jencks, C., & Mayer, E. (1990). The social consequences of growing up in a poor neighborhood. In L. J. Lynn & M. G. H. McGeary (Eds.), *Inner-city poverty in the United States* (pp. 111–186). Washington, DC: National Academy Press.

Johnstone, J. (1981) Youth gangs and the black suburbs. *Pacific Sociological Review, 24*(3), 355–375.

Katz, C. M. (2004). *Youth gangs in Arizona* (Publication prepared for the Arizona Criminal Justice Commission). Phoenix: Arizona State University West.

Katz, C. M., Webb, V. J., & Armstrong, T. A. (2003). Fear and gangs: A test of alternative theoretical models. *Justice Quarterly, 20*(1), 95–130.

Katz, C. M., Webb, V., & Schaefer, D. (2000). The validity of police gang intelligence lists: Examining differences in delinquency between documented gang members and non-documented delinquent youth. *Police Quarterly, 3*(4), 413–437.

Klein, M. W. (1995). *The American street gang*. New York: Oxford University Press.

Klein, M., & Maxson, C. (2006). *Street gang patterns and control*. New York: Oxford University Press.

Kornhauser, R. (1978). *Social sources of delinquency: An appraisal of analytic models.* Chicago: University of Chicago Press.

Land, K. C., McCall, P. L., & Cohen, L. E. (1990). Structural covariates of homicide rates: Are there any invariances across time and social space? *The American Journal of Sociology, 95*(4), 922–963.

Lucy, W., & Phillips, D. (1995). Why some suburbs thrive. *Planning, 61,* 20–21.

Markowitz, F., Bellair, A., Liska, A., & Liu, J. (2001). Extending social disorganization theory: Modeling the relationships between cohesion, disorder, and fear. *Criminology, 39,* 293–319.

Maxson, C. (1998). Gang homicide: A review and extension of the literature. In M. D. Smith & M. Zahn (Eds.), *Homicide studies: A sourcebook of social research* (pp. 199–220). Newbury Park: SAGE.

McCorckle, R., & Miethe, T. (1998). The political & organizational response to gangs. *Justice Quarterly, 15*(1), 41–64.

Miller, W. B. (1982). *Crime by youth gangs and groups in the United States.* Washington, DC: U.S. Department of Justice, Office of Juvenile Justice and Delinquency Prevention.

Morenoff, J., Sampson, R., & Raudenbush, S. (2001). Neighborhood inequality, collective efficacy, and the spatial dynamics of urban violence. *Criminology, 39,* 517–560.

Murphy, A. K. (2007). The suburban ghetto: The legacy of Herbert Gans in understanding the experience of poverty in recently impoverished American suburbs. *City and Community, 6*(1), 21–37.

National Youth Gang Center. (1998). *1996 National Youth Gang Survey program summary.* Washington, DC: Office of Juvenile Justice and Delinquency Prevention.

National Youth Gang Center. (1999). *1997 National Youth Gang Survey program summary.* Washington, DC: Office of Juvenile Justice and Delinquency Prevention.

National Youth Gang Center. (2000). *1998 National Youth Gang Survey program summary.* Washington, DC: Office of Juvenile Justice and Delinquency Prevention.

Needle, J., & Stapleton, W. (1983). *Report of the National Juvenile Justice Assessment Centers: Police handling of youth gangs.* Washington, DC: U.S. Department of Justice.

Office of Juvenile Justice and Delinquency Prevention. (2004). *2002 National Youth Gang Survey: Summary.* Washington, DC: Office of Juvenile Justice & Delinquency Prevention.

Osgood, D. W. (2000). Poisson-based regression analysis of aggregate crime rates. *Journal of Quantitative Criminology, 16,* 21–43.

Papachristos, A., & Kirk, D. (2006). Neighborhood effects on street gang behavior. In J. F. Short & L. A. Hughes (Eds.), *Studying youth gangs* (pp. 63–84). Walnut Creek, CA: AltaMira.

Peterson, D., Taylor, T., & Esbensen, F. (2004). Gang membership and violent victimization. *Justice Quarterly, 21*(4), 793–815.

Roncek, D. W. (1981). Dangerous places: Crime and residential environment. *Social Forces, 60,* 74–96.

Rosenfeld, R., Bray, T., & Egley, A. (1999). Facilitating violence: A comparison of gang-motivated, gang affiliated, and non-gang youth homicides. *Journal of Quantitative Criminology, 15*(4), 495–516.

Sampson, R., & Groves, B. (1989). Community structure and crime: Testing social-disorganization theory. *American Journal of Sociology, 94,* 774–802.

Sampson, R., Morenoff, J., & Gannon-Rowley, T. (2002). Assessing "neighborhood effects": Social processes and new directions in research. *Annual Review of Sociology, 28,* 443–478.

Sampson, R., Raudenbush, S., & Earls, F. (1997). Neighborhoods and violent crime: A multi-level study of collective efficacy. *Science, 277,* 918–924.

Sanders, W. (1994). *Gangbangs and drive-bys.* New York: Aldine De Gruyter.

Shaw, C., & McKay, H. (1931). *Social factors in juvenile delinquency: Report on the causes of crime (Vol. II).* National Commission on Law Observance and Enforcement. Washington, DC: U.S. Government Printing Office.

Shaw, C., & McKay, H. (1942). *Juvenile delinquency and urban areas.* Chicago: University of Chicago Press.

Short, J., & Strodtbeck, F. 1965. *Group process and gang delinquency.* Chicago: University of Chicago Press.

Spergel, I. (1995). *The youth gang problem.* New York: Oxford University Press.

Spergel, I., Wa, K., & Sosa, R. (2002). *Evaluation of the Mesa Gang Intervention Program (MGIP).* Chicago: University of Chicago.

Thornberry, T., Krohn, M., Lizotte, A., Smith, C., & Tobin, K. (2003). *Gangs and delinquency in developmental perspective.* New York: Cambridge University Press.

Thrasher, F. (1927). *The gang: A study of 1,313 gangs in Chicago.* Chicago: University of Chicago Press.

Tienda, M. (1991). Poor people and poor places: Deciphering neighborhood effects on poverty outcomes. In J. Huber (Ed.), *Macro-micro linkages in sociology* (pp. 244–262). Newbury Park, CA: SAGE.

Tita, G., Cohen, J., & Engberg, J. (2005). An ecological study of the location of gang "set space." *Social Problems, 52*(2), 272–299.

Venkatesh, S. (1997). The social organization of street gang activity in an urban ghetto. *American Journal of Sociology, 103,* 83–111.

Walker, S., & Katz, C. (2008). *The police in America.* New York: McGraw Hill.

Wells, L. E., & Weisheit, R. A. (2001). Gang problems in non-metropolitan areas: A longitudinal assessment. *Justice Quarterly, 18*(4), 791–823.

Wilson, J. Q., & Kelling, G. (1982, March). Broken windows: The police and neighborhood safety. *Atlantic Monthly,* pp. 29–38.

Wilson, W. J. (1987). *The truly disadvantaged: The inner city, the underclass, and public policy.* Chicago: University of Chicago Press.

Zatz, M. S. (1987). Chicano youth gangs and crime: The creation of a moral panic. *Contemporary Crises, 11,* 129–158.

Zatz, M., & Portillos, E. (2000). Voices from the barrio. *Criminology, 38*(2), 369–402.

CHAPTER 27

Who Needs Enemies with Friends Like These? The Importance of Place for Young People Living in Known Gang Areas

Robert Ralphs ▪ Juanjo Medina ▪ Judith Aldridge

Deriving from a study of gangs in an English city, this article focuses on the impact of living in a known gang area on youth who are not gang members. Using a variety of qualitative methods, Ralphs and colleagues find that youths' use of public space is severely constrained in gang neighborhoods. These youth are afraid to wander into other areas for fear of being victimized, even while they may be targeted in their own neighborhoods by rival gangs or police who seem all too willing to consider them as associated with gangs because of where they live. This study illustrates that the areas associated with gangs can be stigmatized and such labels can have a cascading effect on all neighborhood youth, leading to social exclusion and marginalization in school and work experiences.

Introduction

This paper explores the experiences of young people who live in places labelled as "gang areas" and who therefore are subject to surveillance and interventions by authorities as a result. It seeks to highlight the way that increasing official use of gang terminology impacts on the lives of non-gang-involved young people in their negotiations of the spaces where they live, in ways that are equally as (or more) damaging than peer-based negotiations of space (see Kintrea et al. 2008). We also focus on

Reprinted from: Robert Ralphs, Juanjo Medina, and Judith Aldridge, "Who Needs Enemies with Friends Like These?" *Journal of Youth Studies*, 12(5): 483–500. Copyright © 2009 by Taylor & Francis Ltd. Reprinted by permission.

the impact that gangs have on non-gang-involved young people. We illustrate how young people in Britain who reside in places that are recognized as having gang and related firearm problems are restricted in their use of space in ways that go beyond more general accounts of youth, space and territory (Hall et al. 1999, Cahill 2000, MacDonald et al. 2005, Kintrea et al. 2008). We begin with a brief overview of recent British developments of the use of gang terminology among the police, community agencies, and young people themselves; within government policy; and among academic researchers.

British Gangs: Media Hype, Public Fears and Official Responses

Young people, particularly young, working-class males, have long been the source of public fears and the target of the press (Cohen 1972). However, in recent years, Britain has been "gripped by gang fever" (Hallsworth and Young, 2004, p. 12); the latest British "folk devils" are undoubtedly youth gangs. Recent news headlines have included: "500,000 hoodies in gangs" (*The Sun* 2006), "The trials of living with the feral youths (*Guardian* 2005) and "Gun crime growing like cancer" (BBC 2003), as gun and knife crime becomes increasingly intertwined with fears of a growing British "gang problem."

In the absence of much recent research with a direct focus on British gangs, government, local authorities and the public are left to rely on these media accounts that "gang culture" is endemic in our cities and that these gangs resemble popular portrayals of gangs in the USA. This relentless media focus on gangs, alongside the violent deaths of several school-aged young people, has increased the public call for a political response. In February 2007, former Prime Minister Tony Blair presided over Britain's first "gun crime summit." This was swiftly followed with the formation of the Home Office's Tackling Gangs Action Programme (TGAP) to identify good practice in dealing with gangs and gun crime. This has resulted in the toolkit: "*Tackling gangs: practical guide for local authorities, Crime Disorder and Reduction Partnerships (CDRPS) and other local partners*" (Home Office 2008) and a government guidance leaflet for parents on how to detect children's involvement in gangs. In Britain, academics and public bodies such as the Youth Justice Board rightly warn against the dangers of a too liberal use of gang labels; yet, the term "gang" has become entrenched in both national and local crime and disorder strategies (e.g. Home Office 2008). Police forces and local authorities are increasingly drawing on US interventions by importing models developed in Los Angeles and Boston of dedicated firearm/gang units and multi-agency gang intervention teams, now firmly established within some British cities (Bullock and Tilley 2008, Home Office 2008).

The recent British government and local authority responses outlined here to the ostensibly increased threat posed by youth gangs—and their alleged increased use of firearms—can be understood within the theoretical discourses of risk. Many commentators have argued that we live in a society transfixed with risk (Beck 1992, Garland 2001). As a society, the management of risk is paramount to our ontological security (Giddens 1991). Reactionary policies around youth gangs can in part counter the public's fear (Garland 2001). The heightened level of risk deemed to result from youth gangs—primarily through the growing concern that they are increasingly using firearms—is new in a British context. This link between "gangs" and guns has elevated established concerns of youth as "troublesome" and "folk devils" (Cohen 1972) to their being viewed as "ruthless assassins"

and "high risk." This is particularly the case for young people residing in "gang areas," who are subject to labels and methods of "risk management" that are damaging in many ways. Indeed, we must be mindful not to label our young people (Lemert 1951, Becker 1963). In 2007, prior to resigning as Chair of England and Wales Youth Justice Board, Professor Rod Morgan warned that we risk demonizing a whole generation, by labelling young people as "thugs in hooded tops" and "gang members" (Youth Justice Board 2007).

Policing Gangs and Young People: The Story So Far

While the formation of dedicated firearm/gang units by police in Britain is a relatively new phenomenon, gang units have existed for two decades in the USA. During this time, many US researchers have questioned, in particular, the quality of gang-related intelligence and derived gang-members databases. Katz and Webb (2006) provide a useful and comprehensive overview. Some have suggested that police officials have arbitrarily classified individuals as gang members (Parachini and Crew 1996, cited in Katz et al. 2000). Others have noted how "hearsay information" about gang affiliation is incorporated into intelligence systems (Burrell 1990, Spergel 1995), resulting in individuals being unfairly labelled gang members solely as a consequence of the neighbourhood where they live, their relationship with a known gang member, or their style of dress (Hagedorn 1990, Chesney-Lind et al. 1994). Others are even more scathing: in their study of gangs in Las Vegas, McCorkle and Miethe (1998) concluded that the "gang problem" could be attributed to a moral panic constructed by the police department to obtain resources and regain legitimacy within the community. On the other hand, there are researchers who have argued that "gang information systems may be more helpful to police than first believed" and that they correctly identify criminally active individuals (Katz et al., 2000, p. 432). In Britain, these controversial US gang interventions have slipped unquestioned into mainstream policy and practice. It is probable that adopting a similar model of US gang interventions and surveillance will result in similar gang labelling practices. Indeed, in tracking the development of a Manchester-based gang intervention programme that was based on the Boston Gun Project, Bullock and Tilley (2008, p. 38) have noted "unresolved concerns about the risks of labelling and stereotyping young people," as well as poorly evidenced "gang membership."

Several studies have highlighted how the police construct populations of "permanent suspects" based on socio-economic status as much as on serious and persistent offending. These studies also note how "street life" places young people at greater risk of adversarial contact with authority (Aye-Maung 1995, Flood-Page et al. 2000, McAra and McVie 2005). There is a substantial body of literature that discusses how police "working rules" are used to construct a suspect population (McConville et al. 1991, 1997, Smith 1991, Reiner 1997, Quinton et al. 2000). These informal rules, based on police culture, are said to impact differently according to a range of demographics. One such important demographic, as we will discuss in this paper, is area of residence. The new policing of gangs and gang members, through the use of dedicated gang units with a remit to target youth gangs in particular areas, has the potential to intensify police attention on young people who have the misfortune to reside in known gang areas.

The links between gangs and gun crime is also significant for the policing of young people in known gang areas. There is a long history in Britain in relation to problematic police stop-and-search practices, particularly in relation to ethnic minorities (see Scarman 1981, Bowling and Phillips 2002, Sharp and Atherton 2007). Yet, despite the introduction of the Police and Criminal Evidence Act (PACE 1984) and subsequent amendments to the recording requirements for all stops—whether a search ensues or not (Home Office 2004)—due process is clouded by Section 60 of the Criminal Justice and Public Order Act 1994. Section 60, once authorized by an inspector (typically for a 24-hour period), allows officers to stop and search any individual within a defined area without "reasonable suspicion" when it is anticipated that serious violence may occur or that offensive weapons such as firearms may be carried.[1] The constant threat of gun crime in known gang areas, coupled with increased police surveillance by dedicated firearm and gang units, intensifies police attention on young people living in these areas and results in more vulnerability to excessive stop and search.

The Enduring Significance of Class and Place in Youth Experiences

In recent decades, it has been suggested that social class is of diminishing significance, as globalization has led to a more risk-based society (Beck 1992). Social theorists have similarly downplayed the importance of place, noting that growing geographical mobility has resulted in everyday experiences becoming increasingly disembedded from physical location (Calhoun 1991, Giddens 1991). In specific relation to youth studies, Blackman (2005) has been critical of postmodern, post-subcultural theory that places greater emphasis on agency and the individual at the expense of critical discussion of the structures and institutions that exist and continue to marginalize some sections of young people. He notes the lack of critical application to young people's social, economic and cultural realities. It is important that youth research seeks to address this omission, as Shildrick and MacDonald (2006, p. 126) argue: "A proper, holistic understanding of youth *requires* a closer appreciation of the ways in which young people's leisure and cultural lives intersect with wider aspects of their biographies." In these critiques of post-subcultural studies, both Blackman (2005) and Shildrick and MacDonald (2006) have pointed to the tendency to empirically ignore the lives and identities of less advantaged young people, while theoretically underplaying the potential significance of class and other social inequalities.[2]

In contrast, MacDonald et al. (2005) have stressed the continuing importance of class and place for young people. Kintrea et al. (2008) reached a similar conclusion in their study of territoriality and territorial conflict in six British cities, stating that all the areas they encountered with "territorial conflict" were areas containing multiple disadvantage. Significantly, they found this type of conflict to be much less evident in the more advantaged areas of each city. Kintrea and colleagues also suggest that the limitations that ensue as a result of young people's restricted spatial mobility actually inhibit transitions to adult life, as, for example, by restricting access to education. The lives of the young people presented in these recent British studies are highly bound up with their social class and the places they lived. Youth gangs similarly challenge the notion that class and place are not important in understanding young people's lives. Gang research has long associated gangs with the most deprived areas in inner cities (Thrasher 1927, Shaw and McKay 1942, Cohen 1955, Miller 1958, Cloward and Ohlin 1960, Parker 1974). Hagedorn (1988) uses an "urban underclass" framework while Venkatesh (1997, p. 82) similarly notes how street gangs, together with teenage pregnancy and welfare state dependency, have become a "signature attribute of ghetto life." More recently, Vigil (2002) refers to "multiple marginality" in his explanation of the existence of gangs across a range of diverse communities.

As with class, the links between gangs and space are important. Tita et al. (2005) have noted that not only are gangs spatially concentrated among disadvantaged neighbourhoods, but also, within this, they occupy what they term "gang set space." These are geographically defined areas within a neighbourhood where gang members "hang out." Klein (1995, p. 18) refers to these areas where gangs hang out as "the life space of the gang."

Kintrea et al. (2008) are the latest to note the bounded use of space by young people, due to (potential) conflict with other peers. For the most part, Kintrea et al. (2008) steer clear of using the term "gang," instead bypassing the problems of gang definitions by focusing on "territoriality." Hence, they take the well-trodden path in British academia of avoiding a direct focus on the "gang."[3] In contrast, the focus here is firmly on "gangs" and the implications of gang labels for places and the young people who live there. We do not refer here to "gangs" unproblematically. Indeed, what follows is a highly critical account of the dangers and impact on young people's lives that the over-liberal use of the terms "gang member" and "gang associate" can entail. This additional focus on official responses to "youth gangs" highlights a further dimension to young people's negotiations of space and place that goes beyond peer conflict.

This paper presents the experiences of non-gang-involved young people who live in areas of a city where gangs and gun crime are firmly established. We explore how the risks associated with gangs and gun crime lead young people wrongly identified as gang members or associates to develop coping strategies and how policy-level responses impact negatively on them, and in turn, on their identity, future aspirations and transitions to adulthood. As will be illustrated, in known gang areas the gang labels and treatment that follow form a central part of young people's experiences.

Methods

The findings presented in this paper are based upon the ESRC-funded YOGEC (Youth Gangs in an English City) ethnographic study, which involved 26 months of participant observation, nine focus groups and 107 formal interviews. Time was spent hanging around and socializing with gang members, their associates, ex-gang members and other young people in "gang" communities. Fieldwork also included attendance at community events, volunteering in youth centres frequented by gang- and non-gang-involved young people, and involvement in community groups concerned with gang violence. The data analysed here draw extensively on two focus group interviews with non-gang youth, interviews with "gang associates" and with senior police officers, and fieldwork observations of young people who live in known gang areas.

The research took place in an English city, and to maintain its anonymity it is referred to here as "Research City." This brief summary of the methods used glosses over many challenges and adaptations to the original research outline. For a more detailed discussion of the methodology and the rationale for the decision not to disclose the name of the city, see Aldridge et al. (2008). The research covered six "gang" areas of the city. The focus in this paper is on one area of the city where gangs were most entrenched, referred to here as *Inner West*. This area encompassed some of the most ethnically diverse and disadvantaged areas of the city and had a gang problem that was widely recognized by the police, young people, the local communities, the city council, and a range of statutory and voluntary sector organizations. When discussing "gangs" here, our starting point for a working definition in our research was the Eurogang definition: "Any durable street orientated youth group whose involvement in illegal activity is part of their group identity."[4] Although not explicit in this definition, the use of firearms was an important defining feature of gangs for city authorities. Some of the more established gangs associated with this area have been in existence for up to 20 years. They have been viewed as responsible for a series of fatal shootings and serious woundings of predominantly young males (aged 14 to 25). During the fieldwork, six young males from this area were fatally shot and many more shot at and injured.

Results

Everyone's a Target: Restrictions on the Use of Public Space as a Consequence of Fear and Gang Victimization

Living in known gang areas significantly limited the use of space for the non-gang young people in our research. When discussing the boundaries of the areas where they felt safe, several young people in one focus group described the space between two local fast-food takeaways—a mere 500 metres apart. When asked what they feared, these non-gang young people would typically cite the risk of street robbery and/or assault by gangs from rival areas and, in common with known gang members, they ultimately feared being shot. It was common for these young people to discuss the problems they experienced when venturing into an area whose gangs have established rivalries with gangs in their area. When young people encountered others from rival gang areas, typically they would be asked: "Who you down with?" and some young people reported that their mobile phone contact lists were searched through with repercussions possible depending on whom they were found to associate with. These confrontations occurred on public transport and in the city centre, shopping centres, and entertainment venues, as well as in rival gang areas. The fear of victimization that resulted restricted the mobility of these non-gang young people. The problems they encountered are discussed by participants in this focus group:

Yeah, if you go out of your own area, if you're dressed like some hot boy[5] and that, black clothing and that, then people will attack you and that and they ask you questions. [IWFG41: 16-year-old, white male]

We can't go to Main Road. [. . .] We go to Main Road, yeah, and straight away, "Yeah, there's a Upperside man, let's get him." [IWFG11: 15-year-old, white male]

The risk of being a victim of gun crime intensified young people's fears of venturing into rival gang areas:

I've got a brother, I fret when he leaves the estate. You understand where I'm coming from? Because he's going out to people that are not from around here, and might not like people off this estate. Do you understand where I'm coming from? And it makes you trapped; it makes you feel trapped anyway. Because you think, "Well if I move out, I'm gonna have to move way out." Because there are certain places, because your list or whatever is so long, there is gang members, and you might get to know them. And like there's people, you might have known them before they were gang members, and know them just as that person. And then you know all those people over there who want to kill him, you know what I mean, so you're not gonna go over there. But you've got to go over there to see your friends. [Interviewer: Because they might associate you with them, yeah?] And I'm not a gang member, but I might have friends. You get where I'm coming from? So therefore it would make me wary going in certain places. [IWFG42: 18-year-old, white female]

The fear of becoming embroiled in violent encounters led many young people to stay within particular areas within their neighbourhoods. However, as we discuss below, remaining within the confines of these areas did not offer complete protection either, as it could also lead to unwanted attention from both rival gangs and the police.

While gangs may be associated with an entire neighbourhood or housing estate, "set space" refers to the specific streets, spaces and buildings where gang members are known to congregate (Tita et al. 2005). In Research City, these set spaces were evident and of central importance in the process of labelling young people as gang members. Young people who attended certain youth and community buildings where gangs were known to go or who resided in these set spaces became labelled as gang members or gang associates by rival gangs—despite a lack of self-identification or criminality (two factors common to many gang definitions), as this white, male police intelligence officer discusses:

> West Park, I would say from experience, is the heart of Lowerside territory. Now rightly or wrongly, any male seen in that area, who frequents that area, would be regarded by opposing factions as being a gang member and that is very sad, but unfortunately that's how it's progressed. Likewise anyone on Long Lane. Upperside Gang, bang, they're going to be tarred with that brush, whether they've got allegiance and you know it's got to that extreme. [K112]

Young people had to navigate carefully the known gang places and spaces within their neighbourhoods. Gang set spaces became targets for rival gang attacks, with instances of drive-by shootings and one instance during fieldwork of a rival gang entering community buildings in balaclavas. These kinds of events resulted in local young people refusing to occupy these spaces, understandably deeming them "unsafe." This resulted in well-resourced, purpose-built facilities for young people remaining empty and underused. Many of the young people who lived close to youth facilities told us how they did not frequent them due to fear of harassment or even drive-by shootings from rival gangs. This view is summed up here by this young man:

> There are loads of people that ain't gang members that get shot. [. . .] "We've seen you speaking to so-and-so so we're coming for you." [. . .] I think everyone's a target; every young person in the area is a target really, if you're in the wrong place at the wrong time. [IWGA6: 15-year-old, black male]

This view is echoed here:

> They don't care who you are. As long as you're on that estate they'll just—they'll just shoot at anything. It could be even your little brother. There's been people playing on bouncy castles, and people driving by and shooting. The bouncy castle's getting popped and that. [IWFG41: 16-year-old, white male]

Young people living in these areas therefore perceived themselves to be at risk of serious violent attacks simply by being in the wrong place. Residing in these areas also had consequences in terms of how the police would view and subsequently police young people.

"By the Company that He Keeps": The Significance of Place for Police Applications of Gang Labels

Fearful of venturing into areas with gangs in rivalry to their own areas, non-gang young people would limit themselves to their local streets and places where they felt safer. This invariably brought them into contact with suspected gang members from their own areas. Their occupation of these spaces once more proved important in relation to police responses to them. The police employed similar strategies to those of rival gangs when evaluating whether somebody was a gang member, most often based on being seen in the company of known gang members. The way young people were labelled as "gang members" or "gang associates" is illustrated here by a police officer with over a decade of experience of working on gang-related crime in this part of the city:

> It's difficult to quantify gang members. I mean certainly there's like, you know, three or more engaged in criminal activity blah, blah, blah and all this business, and I always turn round and say, "OK," if somebody says to me, "Is Joe Bloggs a gang member?" And I will obviously look at what we know about him and say, "Well, if he's been stop-checked once or twice with a known gang member, he's on the periphery." But he's getting stop-checked regular, then you've got to say, "Well, look, by the company that he keeps we believe that he's a gang member." [KI12]

Consistent with previous accounts of police practice and "working rules" (see McConville et al. 1991, McAra and McVie 2005), young people attracted police attention as a result of keeping the wrong company rather than as a result of involvement in criminal activity. Indeed, being seen in the company of "known" gang members was crucial to the police application of the gang label in Research City. In the absence of a clear official definition of what constitutes a "gang member" in practice, association was both a necessary and sufficient condition for the application of the label, and despite a strong association in Research City between gangs and serious crime, criminal engagement was not a necessary official defining feature of gang membership for the police, let alone co-offending with known gang members. For those living or socializing in gang set spaces, it is inevitable that they will come into contact with gang members. Moreover, as a strategy of self-defence, to befriend "the gang" would seem logical. The non-gang young people we spoke to perceived behaving in a superficially friendly manner to gang members they knew (for example, greeting them in the street) was an effective strategy to avoid being victimized by them. Indeed, many young people who knew and had grown up with gang members, including siblings, often expressed negative views of gangs and the related activities gang members engaged in, especially serious violence and other forms of criminality. However, young people living in these areas were regularly stop-checked by police; the suspicion of gang involvement would result if they were in the company of those police considered to be "known" gang members. Because police designate gang affiliation on the basis of being seen with "known" gang members, it is inevitable that these observations will result in false positives.

Lemert (1951) and Becker (1963) describe the impact of deviant labels in relation to the potential for secondary deviance and further criminality. What we witnessed in our research was the potential for entire neighbourhoods (especially those living in gang set spaces) of young people to be labelled as "gang members" or "gang associates" and to receive high levels of police attention as a consequence of being born and raised in estates and streets with established gang associations. This young man describes being considered by the police to be a member of a 40-strong gang:

> I don't even think there really is a gang in Shanklytown. [*Interviewer*: So all the ones like I mentioned to you before, you know, the police have said there's about 40. . . .] 40 Crestside Crew and all that! [laughs] [*Interviewer*: So what would you say?] I would say there's about three, innit. . . . They aren't in Crestside Crew yeah, 'cause the police have said to me if you're seen speaking to a gang member, if they see you speaking to a gang member, automatically they put you in a gang. [*Interviewer*: So the police have said that to you?] Yeah, so the 40 people that they say, that could just be, they're young people from Crestside,

that like, these three gang members I spoke to. And then, like, if you say that I'm in a gang, if they see me speaking to a gang member now, who I speak to must be in a gang too and who they speak to. It's daft really. [IWGA8: 16-year-old, black male]

McAra and McVie (2005) have noted a similar cycle of police labelling of young people in Scotland, in which young people with friends known to the police are twice as likely to come into contact with the police, regardless of any criminality. In Research City, the specific association with gangs and gun crime elevates these more general police suspicions to another level. Many of the young people we got to know during the fieldwork became labelled as gang members or gang associates, even where they did not self-define as a gang member, held strongly anti-gang views, and did not engage in criminal activity. Nevertheless, once labelled, they were treated—by police and subsequently by other agencies such as schools—as capable of serious crimes, or as posing potential or actual risks as a result of the label. The following section outlines some of the repercussions of these gang labels.

Police Surveillance, Raids, Stops and Searches and Other Spatial Restrictions

Being labelled as a gang member or associate created a greater vulnerability to police attention and surveillance. Armed police raids on family homes in search for firearms were common and brought stigma, stress and feelings of violation to the families involved. Young people living in these areas and labelled as "gang associates" were often subjected to police checks and exclusion from community events including carnivals and family fun days. We regularly attended these events and witnessed how young people from the youth clubs where we worked were sometimes prevented from entering, and on occasion, overtly filmed by the police. Their access was denied due to apparent gang associations on the grounds of public safety and potential conflict between rival gangs. Again, many of these young people had no criminal history and did not view themselves as gang involved. Likewise, their peers did not see them as gang members, nor did members of the gangs that they were allegedly affiliated to, as we know from conversations and interviews with gang members and associates.

The police adopted a proactive method of harassment of people they identified as "gang members." When known gang members were visible on the streets where they live, they had to negotiate unwanted attention from the police as well as from rival gangs, who may target their hangouts with drive-by shootings, as this gang intelligence officer noted:

> If we suddenly see Crestside Crew emerging on Long Lane, bang, get over there, get our uniform lads to absolutely hammer them, harass them, do them for anything they can. So they basically think, "We've had enough of this," and we can dampen things down [. . .] but [hanging around on the streets] from our point of view makes them a target. Lowerside lads can drive by, so if we're dispersing them and displacing them, it's diminishing the problem again. [KI16]

Earlier, it was noted how streets and places become known as gang set spaces, and this is clearly evident in this account, as is the risk of drive-by shootings by rival gangs. This police "harassment" tactic was frequently discussed by the non-gang young people who lived in these areas, as this young man discusses:

> Like when the police say, "Where are you from?" and you say like, "Belmont," straight away, "Have you been in trouble?" "No." "Are you sure?" "Yeah." "Right, let me PNC[6] your ID. Are you sure you've not been in trouble before? I'll check. Have you got any guns on you?" Rear[7] always asking you. [IWFG12: 16-year-old, white male]

A focus group with non-gang youth in a rival gang area uncovered similar experiences:

IWFG43: *17-year-old, white male*: They judge everyone the same; they judge every person the same, no matter like how you dress and that.

IWFG42: *18-year-old, white female*: Yeah if you haven't got serial numbers on your shoulder, that's how they go on really, you know.

IWFG44: *16-year-old, Asian male*: Yeah and if you talk back to them, then they think he's Windham Gang.

IWFG43: *17-year-old, white male*: If you're dressed in all black, he'll see you as a gang member.

As this discussion indicates, young people viewed this type of unwanted (and in their view unwarranted) police attention and continued stop-checks—both formal and informal—as police harassment. Non-gang young people from these areas recounted being stopped by the police at least weekly, often two or three times per week, and on occasion, two or three times per day. Their experiences are typified in the following focus group discussion:

> [*Interviewer*: So how many times have you been stopped by the police?] It just depends. Say if I went to Ashland, yeah, I'd get pulled like twice a day. If you go into Ashland, yeah, they're just pulling you, "Where are you from? Where are you from?" "Belmont." "Yeah, what are you doing round here? Coming round causing trouble?" [IWFG11: 16-year-old, white male]

> [*Interviewer*: So on average, how many times do you get stopped?] Well, the most about three times a week. [IWFG12: 16-year-old, white male]

> [*Interviewer*: And what about other people, is that the same for everybody?] No, some are getting picked—like some are getting followed around all day long. [IWFG11: 16-year-old, white male]

> Well, about three weeks ago I got stopped and searched every day within like—for about seven days it was, but every day continuously. [IWFG43: 17-year-old, white male]

Previous studies have indicated that the type of repeated negative police contact documented here helps to reinforce young people's hostility to the police (Flood-Page et al. 2000, McAra and McVie 2005). These repeated altercations with the police resulted, for the young people in our research, in antagonistic relationships with the police and mistrust of them, as illustrated, for example, by their unwillingness to report crimes against them to the police or to assist the police in their enquiries. Not surprisingly then, many young people held a negative attitude to the police:

> INTERVIEWER: So how would you describe your relationship with the police, then?
> IWFG11: *16-year-old, white male*: Bastards.

IWFG15: *14-year-old, black male*: Sort of like bastards.

IWFG18: *15-year-old, white male*: Pests.

IWFG12: *15-year-old, black male*: Yeah.

IWFG16: *16-year-old, white male*: Like fucking cockroaches.

SEVERAL: [laugh]

This hostility shown to the police together with more general mistrust and lack of confidence in the local police force is consistent with recent research from both the USA (Brunson and Miller 2006) and Britain (Sharp and Atherton 2007). It is telling here that non-gang young people, regardless of ethnicity, reported similar experiences and perceptions of the police. However, while the police responded to all young people in these areas as potential gang members, regardless of ethnic origin, ethnicity was important in how police defined areas as "gang areas" and individuals as "gang members," as we will discuss in more depth in future publications.

The Impact of Living in Known Gang Areas: Gang Labelling and Its Consequences

Much of the literature on the labelling process (Lemert 1951, Becker 1963) and constructions of "suspect populations" (McConville et al. 1991, Quinton et al. 2000) has focused on how these deviant labels and associations can lead to further criminality. Setting aside the question of whether, or the extent to which, the application of labels can lead to actual gang joining,[8] here we describe a range of other consequences of the use of one specific kind of deviant label, the gang label—applied to both individuals and communities.

The labelling of young people as gang members or associates not only affected their experiences and use of public space but also their interactions with authorities. These gang association labels affected their experiences in secondary and further education, their aspirations, and ultimately their transitions to adulthood. To illustrate the magnitude of the consequences gang labels can have for young people, one young man's experience is discussed here as a case study. The problems he encountered including school exclusion, police raids and excessive police monitoring were recounted and experienced by several other young people known to the research team.

Dwain (not his real name), a 16-year-old black male, frequented a youth club where the lead author worked as a volunteer. He aspired to work in the music industry and to study law. He had never been arrested or charged with any offence. He was interviewed because of having several cousins involved in gangs. The youth clubs he frequented were also attended by gang members and he lived on the same street as several known gang members. Consequently, his street and local youth club were classed by police as "gang set spaces" (Tita et al. 2005). He expressed anti-gang attitudes: "Gang stuff is just daft" and condemned individual gang members: "There's only a few smart ones that make money. The rest of them are just daft." Nevertheless, he was considered to be a gang member or associate by the police and subsequently treated as a risk to his school. His response to this was damning: "If they're telling me that I'm in a gang, they don't know anything."

Yet, despite his denial and demands made to police to see the intelligence that led to this label, the association remained and resulted in a sequence of highly exclusionary events. During his final year of secondary school, a few months before his final exams, his school was informed by the police that he was a gang member, although they were unable to specify which gang due to insufficient evidence. Although never arrested for any offence or known to be involved in gang conflict in his school, he was temporarily suspended. The police evidence for this association was requested by his family but, at this stage, was not forthcoming.[9] He recalled how his school justified his suspension:

> They were saying to me that if I'm in a gang, that's bringing trouble for the school, 'cause that will bring the gang members to the school and that, after school and that, and kids will get robbed and all that, just talking rubbish. [*Interviewer*: They're saying that's down to you?] Yeah, that I'm a risk to the school if I'm in a gang and all that.

Being excluded from school was not an isolated occurrence for young people living in these known gang areas. Fortunately, Dwain was eventually able to return to school and sit his exams. The practice of excluding young people from schools highlights the emerging trend of a heightened sense of risk that schools, local authorities and police forces are alert to. At another school, a high-achieving student in his penultimate year, together with two school friends, was permanently excluded after a group of young men had gathered at the school gates and threatened to kill him. This event resulted in the school seeking guidance from local authority and police personnel who work on gang interventions. They labelled him as a "gang member," as a result of family links to gangs and subsequently, despite being a good student with no previous school warnings or involvement in crime, he was excluded because he posed a "serious risk to students and staff safety."[10] It is difficult to find a replacement school when a young person is deemed as posing a "high risk" to students and staff. In addition, his status as a victim of crime was ignored and his exclusion meant that he was once more victimized.

Exclusionary experiences like the ones illustrated here have wider implications for young people's transitions to employment. Young people in these areas frequently discussed the way that they felt excluded and marginalized because of the area where they lived. Others had fractious relationships with the education system as well as with the police. Non-gang young people discussed how teachers, aware of where they lived, would predict that they would end up a "drug dealer," a "gang member" or "dead." This may contribute to the low aspirations among young people we encountered in the research. Those who did pursue further education and job training recounted how they were negatively judged once they disclosed where they lived, as this 17-year-old, white male stated:

> Well, I've been like at Westside College, and all these teachers and that, they're all like from Westside [a suburban area], you know, all posh places like that. So when they go, "Where are you from?" and then like you mention Belmont, they look at you weird, they judge you weird, because they're used to like, you know, the posh areas, being able to walk around the streets and all that. [*Interviewer*: So even when you're out of the area like that and you're in college, you think you get treated ... ?] If you mention where you're from, they will judge you, the same as other people would, where you are. [IWFG43: 17-year-old, white male]

These experiences and perceptions had important consequences. During fieldwork, we encountered numerous examples of young people who had given up on seeking employment, long before they had reached the official school-leaving age of 16. Young people would refer to the stigma that their gang-affected area had and how nobody would give them a job once they knew their postcode. Regardless of whether these views hold true, their perceptions, enforced by negative interactions with police and other officials, were enough to make many young people give up trying. As noted earlier, young people (whether gang or non-gang affiliated) living in these known gang areas—gang or non-gang affiliated—experienced a curtailing of their geographical and social movement. This limited mobility consequently restricted their access to services. Hence, not all young people are able to access leisure and other services in the same way and therefore, as Ball et al. (2000) observe, the capacity to participate and consume varies among young people in dependence on structural factors, with social class and place clearly relevant here to these young people's experiences (see also Bose 2003, Blackman 2005, Shildrick and MacDonald 2006).

Discussion and Conclusions

Our findings confirm the view that the social construction and regulation of public space are further contributing to the social exclusion of marginalized young people (White 1996) and that this has become more of a problem with the development of new regulatory practices and powers (Collins and Kearns 2001). Policy responses to gangs may contribute to these exclusionary processes and lead to social control mechanisms with the characteristics outlined by Stanley Cohen (1979) in his well-known, dystopian essay "The Punitive City": blurred boundaries between inside and out, guilty and innocent; broadened and increasingly fuzzy definitions of crime; an expanded social control net; and dispersed state social control mechanisms beyond prison (or office) walls.

In the British context, recent academic discussion of gangs has tended to focus on definitions of what a gang is and whether they even exist (see

Hallsworth and Young 2004, Young et al. 2007, Pitts 2008). The experiences presented here of young people living in known gang areas has clearly demonstrated that a serious problem for many young people who reside in these areas concerns the individual level definition of who is a "gang member" or "gang associate." The accounts from non-gang-involved young people and those who dispute their gang-status labels illustrate that the less discriminate use of these terms by both gang-involved youth and officials has severe implications for the personal safety and exclusion of those who live in known gang areas.

It is commonly understood that the organization of youth gangs is fluid and their membership difficult to identify (Esbensen et al. 2001, Sullivan 2005). Yet, the evidence presented here demonstrates that local authorities and police forces often seem to apply the gang label based on association in gang-affected neighbourhoods—that is, observing a young person together with a "known gang member." These labels have serious consequences for those born and raised in such areas. We encountered a growing concern within these communities over the use of official gang labels with information of varying quality about individuals suspected of gang activity. Young people with family relationships to gang members, who attended the same schools, youth provisions or set spaces, or who lived on the same streets as gang members were in danger of being considered by police to be gang members themselves, or at least "gang associated" and subjected to increased surveillance and intervention, regardless of criminal involvement. This resulted in exclusion from community events and, more worryingly, exclusion from the education system.

In areas with established gang associations, it is difficult, if not impossible, for young people to avoid association with gang members. They attended the same local schools, youth and community centres; places of worship; and sports, music and drama groups, and hung out on the same streets. This was particularly the case for those young people who lived in gang set spaces. Hence, when spotted in conversation or stopped and searched by the police, they would often be labelled as "gang associated" if not as fully fledged "gang members." Rival gangs also interpreted these types of interactions with known gang members and sightings in gang set spaces as a sign of gang membership or allegiance. The result, as illustrated here, was as serious as permanent school exclusion, dawn raids by armed police and victimization. The young people who resided in these already marginalized areas were subsequently victims of further marginalization, exclusion and stigmatization, which increased their levels of disaffection and diminished their opportunities.

Place and class were central to these experiences. Young people encountered in these working-class areas associated with gangs were victimized, marginalized and excluded in many ways, as a consequence of this association—regardless of whether they were gang members or not. Historically, it has been widely accepted that gangs emerge under conditions of social exclusion. What these findings have highlighted is that further social exclusion of young people is a by-product of areas becoming firmly associated with gangs. We therefore need to identify strategies for the policing of gangs that are both successful and respectful of civil liberty concerns. With the increasing focus on risk management, the types of practices of some of our most marginalized young people that we have documented are likely not only to persist but also to expand and intensify. This is evident in the current climate of governmental concern around dealing with youth gangs (Home Office 2008) and continued investment and expansion of dedicated police units and other statutory agencies with a remit to target "youth gangs." Ironically, this type of persistent policing may well contribute to offending behaviour (McAra and McVie 2005), police mistrust (Sharp and Atherton 2007), poor legal socialization (Fagan and Tyler 2005) and perhaps reinforced gang identities.

The lived reality of the young people we encountered, regardless of their status as "gang member," "gang associate" or "non-gang," was one of marginalization and exclusion. This is in contrast to the picture painted in the British media of fearless young people marauding through our cities. They are instead highly *fearful*. Already living in deprived neighbourhoods, they are further excluded and victimized through association with gangs. MacDonald et al. (2005, p. 873) note how "Locally embedded social networks become part of the process whereby poverty and class inequalities are reproduced." In this instance, youth gangs can be seen as one form of social network that serves to reproduce inequalities. The interactions with authorities and other young people may further bolster "gang culture."

In line with both Kintrea et al. (2008) and Marshall et al. (2004), this paper has highlighted young people's fears of leaving the streets and estates where they live due to perceived threats of gangs from surrounding areas. For young people living in the most disadvantaged areas, this limited mobility can further reinforce their social exclusion and limit their access to services. As Kintrea et al. (2008, p. 14) note, "It is not just the fact of the negative impacts of territorial behaviour that appears to be the issue for young people, but also that they occur at a crucial stage in their lives." In this respect, their subsequent transitions to adulthood are affected by these social and physical restrictions.

Inner-city neighbourhood reputations can be extremely negative (e.g. Fraser 1996). In our research, we adopted the strategy of not disclosing publicly the neighbourhoods—even the city—in which our research was conducted, at least in part to avoid further stigmatizing what we anticipated would be communities already feeling stigmatized by "gang" reputations and by other markers of inner-city deprivation. We assess this strategy as vindicated in part by the results reported in this paper. We have shown that the gang label is indeed a dangerous one—and not just for young people involved in gangs but also for the young people living in gang-affected areas who are wrongly assumed to be gang members by the police and rival gangs based on their use of place and space, as well as more broadly for non-gang young people who are often victimized and stigmatized as they carry with them the reputations of having come from gang-affected neighbourhoods.

Acknowledgments

The research for this paper was funded by the ESRC (RES-000-23-0615), and entitled "Youth Gangs in an English City."

Notes

1. Section 60 was typically used in the days that followed a shooting incident. The use of Section 60 was also common at events such as carnivals or other community and musical events where the police anticipated attendance by gang members.

2. Shildrick and MacDonald (2006, p. 129) note the paradox that, in contrast to the popular media focus on young, working-class 'hoodies, "gangs" and general anti-social behaviour, discussed above, in much of the contemporary academic studies on youth and leisure, the cultural identities and practices of working-class youth—especially the most marginalized and disadvantaged sections—rarely feature.

3. This reluctance to use gang terminology in Britain dates back almost half a century (see Downes 1966), and the term remains highly contested to the present day (see also Young et al. 2007).

4. The Eurogang Network was formed with the remit of agreeing on consistent definition, questions and methodologies to allow comparative international gang research. For more information see its website at: http://www.umsl.edu/~ccj/eurogang/euroganghome.htm.

5. The term "hot boy" was used locally by young people to describe young males who were frequently talked about due to what they were involved in. This could mean they were regularly stopped by the police, or wanted/attacked by rival gangs, or known to carry a weapon such as a firearm. The term was also more generically used to refer to somebody who dressed and acted like a stereotypical gang member. Its origins may lie in the 1999 film Hot Boyz (also known as Gang Law), a US gangster movie starring the rap artist Snoop Dog.

6. "PNC" refers here to the Police National Computer. When the police stop a member of the public, this national computer system is used to check for any additional information such as outstanding warrants for arrest or previous convictions, or to confirm that the information provided is consistent.

7. "Rear" or more typically, "rear, rear, rear" was often used in conversation by many people when they were recounting an event or conversation in the same way that "etc., etc." or "and so on" are more commonly used.

8. The possible reasons why young people become involved in gangs will be discussed in future publications with a focus on onset of gang involvement/membership.

9. It took a subsequent official police complaint against his treatment and labelling as a gang member to ascertain

the police intelligence that led to this label. It emerged that on a couple of occasions when he had been routinely stopped by the police in his neighbourhood (a regular occurrence for him and other young people in his area), he was in the company of suspected gang members or "naughty lads," as one officer put it.

10. Ironically, a consistent theme that emerged through discussion and interviews with gang members was how the education system failed them. Leaving school was identified as a "critical moment" for either the onset of gang involvement or more sustained gang and offending involvement.

References

Aldridge, J., Medina, J., and Ralphs, R., 2008. Dangers and problems of doing "gang" research. In: F. van Gemert, D. Peterson and I. Lien, eds. *Street gangs, migration and ethnicity*. Cullompton: Willan Publishing, 31–46.

Aye-Maung, N., 1995. *Young people, victimisation and the police: British crime survey findings on experiences and attitudes of 12 to 15 year olds*. London: HMSO.

Ball, S., Maguire, M., and Macrae, S., 2000. *Choice, pathways and transitions post-16: new youth, new economies in the global city*. London: Routledge/Falmer.

BBC, 2003. Gun crime growing like cancer. BBC News, 21 May. Available from: http://news.bbc.co.uk/l/hi/england/3043701.stm [Accessed 8 April 2008].

Beck, U., 1992. *Risk society*. London: Sage.

Becker, H., 1963. *Outsiders: studies in the sociology of deviance*. New York: The Free Press.

Blackman, S., 2005. Youth subcultural theory: a critical engagement with the concept, its origins and politics, from the Chicago school to postmodernism. *Journal of youth studies*, 8 (1), 1–20.

Bose, M., 2003. "Race" and class in the post-industrial economy. In: D. Muggleton and R. Weinzierl. eds. *The post-subcultural reader*. Oxford: Berg, 167–180.

Bowling, B. and Phillips, C., 2002. *Racism, crime and justice*. Harlow: Pearson Education.

Brunson, R. and Miller, J., 2006. Young black men and urban policing in the United States. *British journal of criminology*, 46 (4), 613–640.

Bullock, K. and Tilley, N., 2008. Understanding and tackling gang violence. *Crime prevention and community safety*, 10, 36–47.

Burrell, S., 1990. Gang evidence: issues for criminal defense. *Santa Clara law review*, 30 (3), 739–790.

Cahill, C., 2000. Street literacy: urban teenagers' strategies for negotiating their neighbourhood. *Journal of youth studies*, 3 (3), 251–277.

Calhoun, C., 1991. Indirect relationships and imagined communities: large-scale social integration and the transformation of everyday life. In: P. Bourdieu and J. S. Coleman, eds. *Social theory for a changing society*. Boulder, CO: Westview, 95–121.

Chesney-Lind, M., Rockhill, A., Marker, N., and Reyes, H., 1994. Gangs and delinquency. *Crime, law, and social change*, 21 (3), 201–228.

Cloward, R. and Ohlin, L., 1960. *Delinquency and opportunity*. London: Routledge and Kegan Paul.

Cohen, A. K., 1955. *Delinquent boys*. Glencoe, IL: The Free Press.

Cohen, S., 1972. *Moral panics and folk devils*. London: McGibbon and Kee.

Cohen, S., 1979. The punitive city: notes on the dispersal of social control. *Crime, law and social change*, 3 (4), 339–363.

Collins, D. and Kearns, K., 2001. The safe journey of an enterprising school: negotiating landscapes of opportunity and risk. *Health and place*, 7, 293–306.

Downes, D., 1966. *The delinquent solution*. London: Routledge & Kegan Paul.

Esbensen, F., Winfree, L., He, N., and Taylor, T., 2001. Youth gangs and definitional issues: when is a gang a gang, and why does it matter? *Crime and delinquency*, 47 (1), 105–130.

Fagan, J. and Tyler, T.R., 2005. Legal socialization of children and adolescents. *Social justice research*, 18 (3), 217–241.

Flood-Page, C., Campbell, S., Harrington, V., and Miller, J., 2000. *Youth crime: findings from the 1998/99 youth lifestyles survey*. London: Home Office Research, Development and Statistics Directorate.

Fraser, P., 1996. Social and spatial relationships and the "problem" inner city. *Critical social policy*, 16 (49), 43–65.

Garland, D., 2001. *The culture of control*. Oxford: Oxford University Press.

Giddens, A., 1991. *Modernity and self-identity: self and society in the late modern age*. Cambridge: Polity.

Guardian, 2005. The trials of living with the feral youths of Salford. *Guardian*, 21 May. Available from: http://www.guardian.co.uk/society/2005/may/21/youthjustice.classroomviolence [Accessed 8 April 2008].

Hagedorn, J., 1988. *People and folks: gangs, crime and the underclass in a rust belt city*. Chicago: Lake View Press.

Hagedorn, J., 1990. Back in the field again: gang research in the nineties. In: C. R. Huff, ed. *Gangs in America*. Newbury Park, CA: Sage, 240–262.

Hall, T., Coffey, A., and Williamson, H., 1999. Self, space and place: youth identities and citizenship. *British journal of the sociology of education*, 20 (4), 501–513.

Hallsworth, S. and Young, T., 2004. Getting real about gangs. *Criminal justice matters*, 55 (1), 12–13.

Home Office, 2004. *Code of practice for the exercise by police officers of statutory powers of stop and search (Code A)*. London: Home Office.

Home Office, 2008. *Tackling gangs: a practical guide for local authorities, CDRPs and other local partners*. London: Home Office.

Katz, C. and Webb, V., 2006. *Policing gangs in America*. New York: Cambridge University Press.

Katz, C., Webb, V., and Schaefer, D., 2000. The validity of police gang intelligence lists: examining differences in delinquency between documented gang members and nondocumented delinquent youth. *Police quarterly*, 3 (4), 413–437.

Kintrea, K., Bannister, J., Pickering, J., Reid, M., and Suzuki, N. 2008. *Young people and territoriality in British cities*. York: Joseph Rowntree Foundation.

Klein, M., 1995. *The American street gang*. New York: Oxford University Press.

Lemert, E., 1951. *Social pathology*. New York: McGraw-Hill.

MacDonald, R., Shildrick. T., Webster, C., and Simpson, D., 2005. Growing up in poor neighbourhoods: the significance of class and place in the extended transitions of "socially excluded" adults. *Sociology*, 39 (5), 873–891.

Marshall, M., Frazer, S., Smith, I., Fuller, C., Geddes, M., Ardron, R., et al., 2004. *Young people in NDC areas: findings from six case studies*. Research Report 20, New Deal for Communities National Evaluation. Sheffield: Sheffield Hallam University.

McAra, L. and McVie, S., 2005. The usual suspects?: street-life, young people and the police. *Criminal justice*, 5 (1) 5–36.

McConville, M., Sanders, A., and Leng, R., 1991. *The case for the prosecution*. London: Routledge.

McConville, M., Sanders, A., and Leng, R., 1997. Descriptive or critical sociology—the choice is yours. *British journal of criminology*, 37 (4), 347–358.

McCorkle, R. and Miethe, T., 1998. The political and organizational response to gangs: an examination of a "moral panic" in Nevada. *Justice quarterly*, 15 (1), 41–64.

Miller, W., 1958. Lower class culture as a generating milieu for gang delinquency. *Journal of social issues*, 14, 5–19.

Parachini, A. and Crew, J., 1996. Memoranda to Mr. Erik S. Brown with the US Commission on Civil Rights (unpublished document).

Parker, H., 1974. *View from the boys: a sociology of downtown adolescents*. Newton Abbot: David and Charles Holding.

Pitts, J., 2008. Describing and defining youth gangs. *Community safety journal*, 7 (1), 26–31.

Quinton, P., Bland, N. and Miller, J., 2000. *Police stops, decision-making and practice*. Police Research Series Paper No. 130. London: Home Office.

Reiner, R., 1997. Policing and the police. In: M. Maguire, R. Morgan and R. Reiner, eds. *The Oxford handbook of criminology*. 2nd edn. Oxford: Oxford University Press, 997–1050.

Scarman, Lord, 1981. *The Scarman Report: the Brixton disorders*, Cmnd 8427. London: HMSO.

Sharp, D. and Atherton, S., 2007. To serve and protect?: The experiences of policing in the community of young people from black and other ethnic minority groups. *British journal of criminology*, 47 (4), 746–763.

Shaw, C. R. and McKay, H., 1942. *Juvenile delinquency and urban areas*. Chicago: University of Chicago Press.

Shildrick, T. and MacDonald, R., 2006. In defence of subculture: young people, leisure and social divisions. *Journal of youth studies*, 9 (2), 125–140.

Smith, D.J., 1991. Police and racial minorities. *Policing and society*, 2 (1), 1–16.

Spergel, I., 1995. *The youth gang problem*. New York: Oxford University Press.

Sullivan, M., 2005. Maybe we shouldn't study "gangs": does reification obscure youth violence? *Journal of contemporary criminal justice*, 21 (2), 170–190.

The Sun, 2006. 500,000 hoodies in gangs. 26 May.

Thrasher, F., 1927. *The gang*. Chicago: University of Chicago Press.

Tita, G., Cohen, J., and Engberg, J., 2005. An ecological study of the location of gang "set space." *Social problems*, 52 (2), 272–299.

Venkatesh, S. A., 1997. The social organization of street gang activity in an urban ghetto. *American journal of sociology*, 103 (1), 82–111.

Vigil, J. D., 2002. *A rainbow of gangs: street cultures in the mega-city*. Austin, TX: University of Texas Press.

White, R., 1996. No-go in the fortress city: young people, inequality and space. *Urban policy and research*, 14 (1), 37–50.

Young, T., FitzGerald, M., Hallsworth, S., and Joseph, I., 2007. *Groups, gangs and weapons*. London: Youth Justice Board.

Youth Justice Board, 2007. Rod Morgan leaves the Youth Justice Board, 26 January 2007. Available from: http://www.yjb.gov.uk/en-gb/News/RodMorganleavestheYJB.htm [Accessed 6 April 2008].

SECTION VII

Crime and Victimization

Gangs and their members are responsible for a disproportionate amount of crime and violence relative to other groups of adolescents and young adults. To the assertion that gangs are *qualitatively* different from other youth groups, it can also plainly be stated that, in terms of crime and delinquency levels, gangs are *quantitatively* different as well. Indeed, this universal and robust observation has been so consistently observed in research study after research study that it is practically an axiom. It is one of the primary reasons we have a specialized field of gang research in criminology, why there are specific undergraduate- and graduate-level courses solely devoted to the topic, why gang units (and gang investigator associations) exist in hundreds of law enforcement agencies across the United States, why many states have written and codified gang legislation laws (some of which include resonant terms such as "violent street gangs"), why there are special prosecutorial teams who handle only gang cases in their jurisdiction, and why print and broadcast media devote entire articles and television shows exclusively to gangs. In fact, simply using the word "gang" immediately conjures up images of crime and violence such that these concepts are loosely interchangeable, if not synonymous, in the vernacular of the general public. Go ahead, take a moment to think about gangs and gang activity to the complete exclusion of crime and violence. What other associations, if any, quickly come to mind? (Hopefully, the articles included in the other sections of this reader provide much more than this one-dimensional view of gang life.)

It is against this backdrop that we now turn to the topic of gang crime, violence, and victimization. However, first, it is important to recount a few key points for the reader to bear in mind while delving into the unadorned numbers and statistics of "gang homicides" and "gang violence"—which are typically devoid of individuation and humanization. These are intended mainly to provide contextualization and perspective for the research findings presented herein.

- Street gang members are primarily youth and young adults, and just like their nongang counterparts, they spend the majority of their time engaging in typical activities: hanging out, watching TV, riding around, eating, sleeping—the ordinary and mostly mundane stuff of life. They do not constantly sit around plotting their next drive-by or other retaliatory act, nor do they spend much time at all committing *any* criminal act—though they do have a tendency to *talk* a lot about it. Most of the time they are engaging in normal, law-abiding activities. And when criminal events do occur, they are most often spontaneous, requiring no forethought.

- Official crime statistics reveal that in the scope of all criminal activity, homicide is an extremely rare event; in the scope of all violent crime incidents, roughly 1 to 2 percent are homicides; and, since gang crime is by definition a subset of all crime, gang homicides are but a fraction of a fraction of violent crime. These points are by no means

387

intended to diminish the tragedy of these horrific events but are made for the purposes of perspective. All definitional issues aside (see Section I), the bulk of gang violence is concentrated in some cities in some communities throughout the United States.

- Stemming from the typology of gangs (discussed in Chapter 11), it follows that street gangs *as groups* vary in their propensities to commit acts of crime and violence. For example, among traditional gangs, long-established rivalries may lead to recurring cycles of violent acts of perpetration, retaliation, and escalation. For a specialty gang organized around drug trafficking, however, random violent acts would bring about unwanted law enforcement attention and threaten the success of its operation. A related point here is that cities comprise differing proportions of these various gang types. Thus, comparative studies of gang activity across cities would be greatly enhanced in terms of validity and reliability by accounting for these differences.

- With the possible exception of some specialty gangs, by and large, gangs do not specialize in any one type of offense or crime. Rather, gang members commit a variety of offenses, ranging from minor ones such as shoplifting, alcohol/drug use, and vandalism to serious crimes such as robbery, assault, and illegal firearm use/carrying. This tendency is typically referred to as a "cafeteria-style" offending pattern and is mentioned here because it is rarely, if ever, discussed outside criminological research circles. Relative to the latest gang drive-by shooting, this is not a very newsworthy topic for the media.

- Specifically covered in Krohn and Thornberry's chapter in this section, it is well established empirically that gangs facilitate or amplify individual offending rates. That is, gangs are not merely collections of highly delinquent individuals, but, separately and measurably, they contribute to members' delinquency rates. However, while research has significantly advanced our descriptive knowledge of the gang–crime link, *how* and *why* this occurs—our in-depth explanatory knowledge—remains deficient. Our best insights come from research on group-level processes, as discussed in Section III of this volume.

All of these points, we feel, are a useful lens through which to view the material in this section. The unit of analysis in this group of articles is intentionally diverse, comprising results at the citywide, incident, and individual level. All but one pertains to the commission of gang-related crime and violence, with the sole exception being Taylor's piece on victimization, reflecting the relative paucity of existing research on this aspect of gang involvement.

Two of the articles here concern gang-related homicides and, given our cautionary discussion above, we readily acknowledge this to be a limitation in scope. The reason for this, however, is simple: notwithstanding ongoing measurement concerns surrounding officially recorded gang crime, gang homicide data remains the most reliable official data available for research study. Indeed, it is almost certainly our *only* option at present, as very few law enforcement agencies record with any precision or regularity *any* other crime as gang related. Data contained in the FBI's *Uniform Crime Reports* (and associated *Supplemental Homicide Reports*) capture "juvenile gang killings" and "gangland killings" (organized crime). These two categories, separately or together, are insufficient to permit valid, reliable, or conclusive results—street gang homicides involve *both* juvenile and young adult participants, and Mafia and other organized crime groups are distinctly different from, and therefore beyond the scope of, street gangs and street gang research.

At present, the only systematic data collection effort on gang homicides nationally is performed by the National Gang Center (NGC) (see Chapter 5 for NGC findings on gang activity prevalence rates and trends). NGC results over the past 15 years demonstrate that gang homicides are exceedingly concentrated in highly populated areas—annually, roughly two-thirds of all gang homicides are reported by just 100 cities. Moreover, gang-related homicides do not rise and fall uniformly or in tandem across large cities. Some big cities exhibited little to no gang violence over the past decade, others experienced sporadic outbursts, and some endured such consistently high levels of gang violence that the local homicide problem was primarily a *gang* homicide problem.[1]

Unfortunately, because of the deficiencies and limitations of existing law enforcement records on gang violence, tracking incident counts and prevalence rates of gang homicide permits only a basic assessment of the national gang problem. More developed (and standardized) databases measuring gang participation rates and gang member and gang crime characteristics are necessarily needed to examine the problem at a deeper level, not only in the United States but in other countries as well. Two chapters in this section—one pertaining to a more expansive, systematic gang homicide database (Chapter 28) and the other pertaining to an ongoing effort to measure deviant youth (gang-like) groups across Europe (Chapter 31)—provide encouragement as to what can be gleaned from such data.

Notes

1. For those interested in reading more about national gang homicide trends, NGC's website (http://www .nationalgangcenter.gov/) contains publications and online analysis results pertaining to the topic. See especially the report "U.S. Gang Problem Trends and Seriousness, 1996–2009" by Howell and colleagues (http://www.nationalgangcenter.gov/Content/ Documents/Bulletin-6.pdf).

CHAPTER 28

Gang Homicides in Five U.S. Cities

Dawn McDaniel ■ Arlen Egley Jr. ■ J. Logan

This very brief, descriptive article presents findings from the Centers for Disease Control and Prevention's first analysis of the newly created National Violent Death Reporting System (NVDRS), which assembles and collates violent death data from multiple official sources beyond the standard police reports. Five cities were selected for inclusion in this study, which compares demographic and incident characteristics of gang homicides with those of nongang homicides. Important distinctions emerged between the two homicide types: gang homicides are more likely to occur in public places, involve younger participants and use of firearms, and, perhaps most notable to the reader, lack any drug connection whatsoever. These findings are remarkably consistent with those noted over 20 years ago in Los Angeles by two of the present editors.

Gang homicides account for a substantial proportion of homicides among youths in some U.S. cities; however, few surveillance systems collect data with the level of detail necessary to inform gang homicide prevention strategies. To compare characteristics of gang homicides with nongang homicides, CDC analyzed 2003–2008 data from the National Violent Death Reporting System (NVDRS) for five cities with high levels of gang homicide. This report describes the results of that

Reprinted from: Dawn McDaniel, Arlen Egley Jr., and J. Logan, "Gang Homicide – Five U.S. Cities, 2003–2008," *Morbidity and Mortality Weekly Report*, January 2012, 61(3): 46–51. Published by Centers for Disease Control and Prevention. Reprinted by permission of author.

analysis, which indicated that, consistent with similar previous research, a higher proportion of gang homicides than other homicides involved young adults and adolescents, racial and ethnic minorities, and males. Additionally, the proportion of gang homicides resulting from drug trade/use or with other crimes in progress was consistently low in the five cities, ranging from zero to 25%. Furthermore, this report found that gang homicides were more likely to occur with firearms and in public places, which suggests that gang homicides are quick, retaliatory reactions to ongoing gang-related conflict. These findings provide evidence for the need to prevent gang involvement early in adolescence and to increase youths' capacity to resolve conflict nonviolently.

NVDRS is an active, state-based surveillance system that collects violent death data from multiple sources, such as death certificates, coroner/medical examiner records, and various law enforcement reports (e.g., police reports and supplementary homicide reports [SHRs]). As of 2008, NVDRS has operated in 17 U.S. states.[1] This report includes 2003–2008 data from large cities in NVDRS states. Only cities ranked within the 100 largest in the United States were examined because gang problems more frequently occur in large cities (1–2). Cases of gang homicide were defined as homicides reported to have been either precipitated by gang rivalry or activity[2] or perpetrated by a rival gang member on the victim.

Because a city might be served by more than one law enforcement agency and each agency might have its own definition of gang-related crime, this analysis used only data from municipal police departments. Municipal police departments often have a jurisdiction congruent with city limits. Geographic areas matching municipal police jurisdictions were identified by geographic codes (either federal information processing standards or zip codes) for location of injury in NVDRS. U.S. Census Bureau 2000 population estimates were determined for each city using the *Law Enforcement Agency Identifiers Crosswalk* (3). For each of the 33 eligible large cities, gang homicide counts were averaged for the period 2003–2008 and divided by the population estimates to calculate an average annual gang-related mortality rate. Cities with gang-related mortality rates equal to or greater than one standard deviation above the average were selected for further analyses.

Five cities met the criterion for having a high prevalence of gang homicides: Los Angeles, California; Oklahoma City, Oklahoma; Long Beach,

California; Oakland, California; and Newark, New Jersey. In these cities, a total of 856 gang and 2,077 nongang homicides were identified and included in the analyses. Comparisons of the characteristics of gang and nongang homicides were made using Fisher's exact tests for all the variables except mean age, which required a t-test. The characteristics included basic demographics of the victims, descriptive information on the homicide event, and circumstances precipitating the event.

Gang homicide victims were significantly younger than nongang homicide victims in all five cities (Table 28.1). Whereas 27%–42% of the gang homicide victims were aged 15–19 years, only 9%–14% of the nongang homicide victims were in this age group. Approximately 80% of all homicide victims were male in each city; however, Los Angeles, Newark, and Oklahoma City still reported significantly higher proportions of male victims in gang homicide incidents compared with nongang

Table 28.1 Comparison of Gang and Nongang Homicide Victim Demographics—National Violent Death Reporting System, Five U.S. Cities

	Los Angeles, CA (2006–2008)				Long Beach, CA (2006–2008)				Oakland, CA (2005–2008)			
	Gang (N = 646)		Nongang (N = 892)		Gang (N = 52)		Nongang (N = 76)		Gang (N = 40)		Nongang (N = 358)	
Characteristic*	No.	(%)	No.	(%)	No.	(%)	No.	(%)	No.	(%)	No.	(%)
Mean age (yrs) (SD)	24.7	(9.0)†	34.3§	(15.8)	22.4	(7.4)†	35.3	(17.1)	23.4	(7.6)†	30.8	(12.3)
Age group (yrs)												
0–14	15	(2.3)†	43	(4.8)	2	(3.9)	6	(7.9)	2	(5.0)	4	(1.1)
15–19	199	(30.8)†	82	(9.2)	22	(42.3)†	7	(9.2)	14	(35.0)†	48	(13.4)
20–24	185	(28.6)†	159	(17.8)	15	(28.9)†	10	(13.2)	10	(25.0)	86	(24.0)
25–34	164	(25.4)	215	(24.1)	8	(15.4)	15	(19.7)	10	(25.0)	107	(29.9)
35–64	82	(12.7)†	353	(39.6)	5	(9.6)†	32	(42.1)	4	(10.0)†	109	(30.5)
≥65	1	(0.2)†	36	(4.0)	0	–	6	(7.9)	0	–	4	(1.1)
Unknown	0	–	4	(0.5)	0	–	0	–	0	–	0	–
Sex												
Male	615	(95.2)†	730	(81.8)	49	(94.2)	66	(86.8)	36	(90.0)	309	(86.3)
Female	31	(4.8)†	161	(18.1)	3	(5.8)	10	(13.2)	4	(10.0)	49	(13.7)
Unknown	0	–	1	(0.1)	0	–	0	–	0	–	0	–
Race/Ethnicity												
Hispanic	269	(41.6)†	278	(31.2)	19	(36.5)	19	(25.0)	29	(72.5)†	53	(14.8)
White, non-Hispanic	131	(20.3)†	254	(28.5)	10	(19.2)	21	(27.6)	4	(10.0)	25	(7.0)
Black, non-Hispanic	236	(36.5)	312	(35.0)	17	(32.7)	26	(34.2)	4	(10.0)†	262	(73.2)
Other/Unknown	10	(1.6)†	48	(5.4)	6	(11.5)	10	(13.2)	3	(7.5)	18	(5.0)

(Continued)

Table 28.1 (*Continued*)

| Characteristic* | Newark, NJ (2003–2008) | | | | Oklahoma City, OK (2004–2008) | | | |
| | Gang (*N* = 55) | | Nongang (*N* = 523) | | Gang (*N* = 63) | | Nongang (*N* = 228) | |
	No.	(%)	No.	(%)	No.	(%)	No.	(%)
Mean age (yrs) (SD)	23.8	(7.1)†	29.7	(11.9)	24.1	(8.7)†	35.7	(15.7)
Age group (yrs)								
0–14	0	–	15	(2.9)	4	(6.4)	12	(5.3)
15–19	18	(32.7)†	73	(14.0)	17	(27.0)†	23	(10.1)
20–24	15	(27.3)	96	(18.4)	18	(28.6)†	22	(9.7)
25–34	17	(30.9)	204	(39.0)	18	(28.6)	57	(25.0)
35–64	5	(9.1)†	127	(24.3)	6	(9.5)†	100	(43.9)
≥65	0	–	8	(1.5)	0	–†	14	(6.1)
Unknown	0	–	0	–	0	–	0	–
Sex								
Male	55	(100.0)†	458	(87.6)	60	(95.2)†	173	(75.9)
Female	0	–†	65	(12.4)	3	(4.8)†	55	(24.1)
Unknown	0	–	0	0	0	–	0	–
Race/Ethnicity								
Hispanic	4	(7.3)	60	(11.5)	14	(22.2)	37	(16.2)
White, non-Hispanic	0	–	30	(5.7)	2	(3.2)†	95	(41.7)
Black, non-Hispanic	51	(92.7)	430	(82.2)	44	(69.8)†	79	(34.7)
Other/Unknown	0	–	3	(0.6)	3	(4.8)	17	(7.5)

Abbreviation: SD = standard deviation.
*A t-test was used to compare mean ages. Fisher's exact tests were used to compare all other variables. When a variable had more than two levels, each level was compared with all the remaining levels.
†Denotes statistical difference ($p < 0.05$).
§Age was unknown for four of the nongang victims.

homicide incidents. In Los Angeles and Oakland, a significantly higher proportion of gang victims were Hispanic and, in Oklahoma City, a significantly higher proportion of gang victims were non-Hispanic black compared with nongang victims.

In at least three of the five cities, gang homicides were significantly more likely than nongang homicides to occur on a street and involve a firearm (Table 28.2). More than 90% of gang homicide incidents involved firearms in each city. For nongang homicides, firearms were involved in 57%–86% of the incidents. Gang homicides also were most likely to occur in afternoon/evening hours in the majority of the five cities; however, comparisons were not examined because the data were missing for 23% of nongang homicide incidents. In Los Angeles, Oakland, and Oklahoma City, gang homicides occurred significantly more frequently on weekends than did nongang homicides.

With regard to the circumstances preceding the homicide, drive-by shootings were significantly more likely to contribute to gang homicides than other types of homicide in Los Angeles and Oklahoma City (Table 28.2). Nearly one quarter of gang homicides in these cities were drive-by shootings, compared with 1%–6% of nongang homicides. A significantly smaller proportion of gang versus nongang homicides were precipitated by another crime in progress in the California cities, ranging from zero to 3% of gang homicides, compared with 9% to 15% of nongang homicides. Further, in Los Angeles and Long Beach, less than 5% of all homicides were associated with known drug trade/use. Although data for Newark and Oklahoma City indicated that 20%–25% of gang homicides involved drug trade/use, Newark was the only city that had a significantly higher proportion of gang versus non-gang homicides that involved drug trade/use.

Editorial Note

Homicide is the second leading cause of death among persons aged 15–24 years in the United States (4). In some cities, such as Los Angeles and Long Beach, gang homicides account for the majority of homicides in this age group (61% and 69%, respectively). The differences observed in gang versus nongang homicide incidents with regard to victim demographics, place of injury, and the use of drive-by shootings and firearms are consistent with previous reports (5). The finding that gang homicides commonly were not precipitated

Table 28.2 Comparison of Gang and Nongang Incident Characteristics—National Violent Death Reporting System, Five U.S. Cities

	Los Angeles, CA (2006–2008)				Long Beach, CA (2006–2008)				Oakland, CA (2005–2008)			
	Gang (*N* = 646)		Nongang (*N* = 892)		Gang (*N* = 52)		Nongang (*N* = 76)		Gang (*N* = 40)		Nongang (*N* = 358)	
Characteristic*	No.	(%)	No.	(%)	No.	(%)	No.	(%)	No.	(%)	No.	(%)
Weapon												
Firearm	619	(95.8)[†]	553	(62.0)	48	(92.3)[†]	46	(60.5)	38	(95.0)	308	(86.0)
Other	27	(4.2)[†]	277	(31.1)	4	(7.7)[†]	24	(31.6)	2	(5.0)	47	(13.1)
Unknown	0	–[†]	62	(7.0)	0	–	6	(7.9)	0	–	3	(0.8)
Location of injury												
Residence	90	(13.9)[†]	271	(30.4)	12	(23.0)	28	(36.4)	4	(10.0)	58	(16.2)
Street	418	(64.7)[†]	360	(40.4)	32	(61.5)[†]	30	(39.5)	27	(67.5)	219	(61.2)
Other	136	(21.1)	208	(23.3)	8	(15.4)	12	(15.8)	9	(22.5)	73	(20.4)
Unknown	2	(0.3)[†]	53	(5.9)	0	–	6	(7.9)	0	–	8	(2.2)
Time of injury[§]												
Day	147	(22.8)	148	(16.6)	5	(9.6)	11	(14.5)	7	(17.5)	68	(19.0)
Afternoon/Evening	259	(40.1)	239	(26.8)	27	(51.9)	16	(21.1)	18	(45.0)	128	(35.8)
Night	206	(31.9)	273	(30.6)	17	(32.7)	16	(21.1)	15	(37.5)	131	(36.6)
Unknown	34	(5.3)	232	(26.0)	3	(5.8)	33	(43.4)	0	–	31	(8.7)
Day of injury												
Mon/Tues/Wed	235	(36.4)	341	(39.2)	22	(42.3)	28	(36.8)	11	(27.5)	129	(36.0)
Thu/Fri	147	(22.8)	232	(26.0)	12	(23.1)	18	(23.7)	7	(17.5)	102	(28.5)
Sat/Sun	264	(40.9)[†]	319	(35.8)	18	(34.6)	30	(39.5)	22	(55.0)[†]	126	(35.2)
Unknown	0	–	0	–	0	–	0	–	0	–	1	(0.3)
Drive-by shooting	152	(23.5)[†]	57	(6.4)	9	(17.3)	5	(6.6)	9	(22.5)	50	(13.97)
No/Unknown	494	(76.5)	835	(93.6)	43	(82.7)	71	(93.4)	31	(77.5)	308	(86.0)
Any argument	105	(12.3)[†]	345	(16.6)	2	(3.9)	11	(14.5)	9	(22.5)	61	(17.0)
No/Unknown	751	(87.7)	1732	(83.4)	50	(96.2)	65	(85.5)	31	(77.5)	297	(83.0)
Crime in progress	20	(3.1)[†]	94	(10.5)	0	–[†]	7	(9.2)	1	(2.5)[†]	53	(14.8)
No/Unknown	626	(96.9)	798	(89.5)	52	(100.0)	69	(90.8)	39	(97.5)	305	(85.2)
Drug trade/use	5	(0.8)	11	(1.2)	0	–	4	(5.3)	5	(12.5)	59	(16.5)
No/Unknown	641	(99.2)	881	(98.8)	52	(100.0)	72	(94.7)	35	(87.5)	299	(83.5)
Bystander death	5	(0.8)	6	(0.7)	0	–	0	–	1	(2.5)	3	(0.8)
No/Unknown	641	(99.2)	886	(99.3)	52	(100.0)	76	(100.0)	39	(97.5)	355	(99.2)

(Continued)

Table 28.2 *(Continued)*

Characteristic*	Newark, NJ (2003–2008)				Oklahoma City, OK (2004–2008)			
	Gang (*N* = 55)		Nongang (*N* = 523)		Gang (*N* = 63)		Nongang (*N* = 228)	
	No.	(%)	No.	(%)	No.	(%)	No.	(%)
Weapon								
Firearm	53	(96.4)[†]	405	(77.4)	59	(93.7)[†]	130	(57.0)
Other	2	(3.6)[†]	110	(21.0)	4	(6.4)[†]	92	(40.4)
Unknown	0	–	8	(1.5)	0	–	6	(2.6)
Location of injury								
Residence	13	(23.6)	117	(22.4)	25	(39.7)[†]	131	(57.5)
Street	34	(61.8)	281	(53.7)	24	(38.1)[†]	41	(18.0)
Other	6	(10.9)	107	(20.5)	11	(17.5)	47	(20.6)
Unknown	2	(3.6)	18	(3.4)	3	(4.8)	9	(4.0)
Time of injury[§]								
Day	8	(14.6)	99	(18.9)	10	(15.9)	42	(18.4)
Afternoon/Evening	18	(32.7)	144	(27.5)	22	(34.9)	49	(21.5)
Night	23	(41.8)	175	(33.5)	29	(46.0)	63	(27.6)
Unknown	6	(10.9)	105	(20.1)	2	(3.2)	74	(32.5)
Day of injury								
Mon/Tues/Wed	22	(40.0)	208	(39.8)	21	(33.3)	89	(39.0)
Thu/Fri	11	(20.0)	129	(24.7)	15	(23.8)	73	(32.0)
Sat/Sun	22	(40.0)	186	(35.6)	27	(42.9)[†]	65	(28.5)
Unknown	0	–	0	–	0	–	1	(0.4)
Drive-by shooting	5	(9.1)	19	(3.6)	15	(23.8)[†]	3	(1.3)
No/Unknown	50	(90.9)	504	(96.4)	48	(76.2)	225	(98.7)
Any argument	8	(14.6)	49	(9.4)	20	(31.8)	80	(35.1)
No/Unknown	47	(85.5)	474	(90.6)	43	(68.3)	148	(64.9)
Crime in progress	4	(7.3)	49	(9.4)	15	(23.8)	71	(31.1)
No/Unknown	51	(92.7)	474	(90.6)	48	(76.2)	157	(68.9)
Drug trade/use	11	(20.0)[†]	29	(5.5)	16	(25.4)	52	(22.8)
No/Unknown	44	(80.0)	494	(94.5)	47	(74.6)	176	(77.2)
Bystander death	3	(5.5)[†]	6	(1.2)	2	(3.2)	3	(1.3)
No/Unknown	52	(94.6)	517	(98.9)	61	(96.8)	225	(98.7)

*Fisher's exact tests were conducted. When a variable had more than two levels, each level was compared with all the remaining levels. Because of missing data, statistical tests for time of injury were not conducted.
[†]Denotes statistical difference (*p* < 0.05).
[§]Day = 7:00 a.m. to 4:59 p.m. Afternoon/Evening = 5:00 p.m. to 11:59 p.m. Night = 12:00 a.m. to 6:59 a.m.

by drug trade/use or other crimes in progress also is similar to previous research; however, this finding challenges public perceptions on gang homicides (5). The public often has viewed gangs, drug trade/use, crime, and homicides as interconnected factors; however, studies have shown little connection between gang homicides and drug trade/use

and crime (5). Gangs and gang members are involved in a variety of high-risk behaviors that sometimes include drug and crime involvement, but gang-related homicides usually are attributed to other circumstances (6). Newark was an exception by having a higher proportion of gang homicides being drug-related. A possible explanation of this divergent finding could be that Newark is experiencing homicides by gangs formed specifically for drug trade. Overall, these findings support a view of gang homicides as retaliatory violence. These incidents most often result when contentious gang members pass each other in public places and a conflict quickly escalates into homicide with the use of firearms and drive-by shootings.

The findings in this report are subject to at least two limitations. First, the accuracy of gang homicide estimates in NVDRS and other surveillance systems is unknown. As a point of reference, CDC compared

NVDRS's gang homicide counts to another independent surveillance system, the National Youth Gang Survey (NYGS). NYGS[3] is a nationally representative annual survey of law enforcement agencies, including all large cities (2). Most cities included in this report also had high gang-related mortality rates in NYGS (Figure 28.1). Second, the gang homicide case definition can vary by law enforcement agency, which might introduce a misclassification bias. For instance, organized crime gangs, although distinct from youth street gangs are included in some but not all definitions of gang homicide. In

Figure 28.1 Estimated Gang-Related Mortality Rates among 33 U.S. Cities Included in the National Violence Death Reporting System (NVDRS) and/or the National Youth Gang Survey (NYGS), 2003–2008*

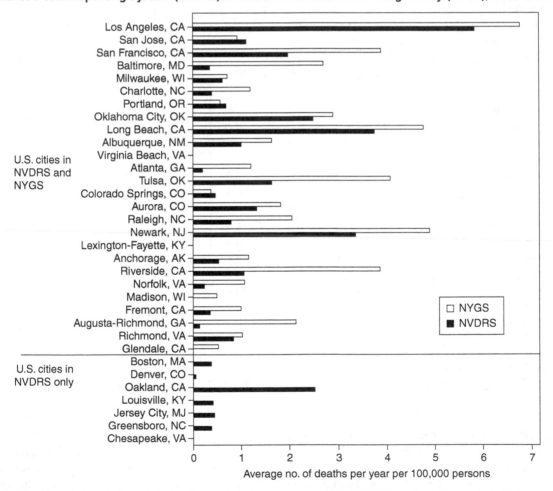

*Cities are listed in descending order by population size. City population estimates were determined by 2000 U.S. Census levels. Cities were in the 17 states participating in NVDRS during 2003–2008 and ranked among the 100 largest cities in the United States based on U.S. Census Bureau statistics. Surveillance years for participating cities vary.

What is already known on this topic?
Gang homicides account for a substantial proportion of homicides among youths in some U.S. cities; however, few surveillance systems collect the level of detail necessary to inform gang homicide prevention strategies.

What is added by this report?
This report was the first to use city-level data from CDC's National Violent Death Reporting System (NVDRS) to compare gang homicide to other homicide types. Results showed that gang homicides were more likely to occur on the street and involve young, racial/ethnic minority, male victims and firearms than other homicides. Additionally, data showed that gang homicides commonly were not preceded by drug trade and use or with other crimes in progress in Los Angeles, Long Beach, and Oakland, California.

What are the implications for public health practice?
Whereas many of the existing efforts directed at reducing gang homicide focus on suppression and control of gangs, drug trade, and other crimes, the results of this report indicate a need for complementary prevention efforts. Specifically, prevention programs should target adolescents before they reach the ages of 15–19 years to prevent them from joining gangs and being put at risk for gang violence in the first place. Further, to prevent the retaliation that results from gang conflict, programs might benefit from increasing youths' capacity to resolve conflict nonviolently. Although these prevention strategies seem promising, rigorous evaluation still is needed to support the effectiveness of these programs.

aimed specifically at gang processes. Preventing gang joining and increasing youths' capacity to resolve conflict nonviolently might reduce gang homicides (8). Rigorous evaluation of gang violence prevention programs is limited; however, many promising programs exist (9). In terms of primary prevention, the Prevention Treatment Program, which includes child training in prosocial skills and self-control, has shown reductions in gang affiliation among youths aged 15 years (10). Secondary prevention programs that intervene when youths have been injured by gang violence, such as hospital emergency department intervention programs, might interrupt the retaliatory nature of gang violence and promote youths leaving gangs. Finally, promising tertiary prevention programs for gang-involved youths might include evidence-based programs for delinquent youths that provide family therapy to increase the youths' capacity to resolve conflict.

Acknowledgments

The 17 states that collected 2003–2008 violent death data and their partners, including personnel from law enforcement, vital records, medical examiners/coroners, and crime laboratories; the National Gang Center and the law enforcement agencies that voluntarily report to their annual survey; Nimesh Patel, Div of Violence Prevention, National Center for Injury Prevention and Control, CDC.

Notes

1. Seven states joined in 2003 (Alaska, Maryland, Massachusetts, New Jersey, Oregon, South Carolina, and Virginia); six states joined in 2004 (Colorado, Georgia, North Carolina, Oklahoma, Rhode Island, and Wisconsin), and four states joined in 2005 (California, Kentucky, New Mexico, and Utah). Five California counties are included in NVDRS. The three counties in northern California began data collection in 2004. The two counties in southern California began data collection in 2005.
2. Homicides deemed to have been precipitated by gang rivalry and activity were identified based on variables captured in NVDRS or variables captured in SHRs, a data source for NVDRS. The relevant variables for

addition, some agencies report according to a gang member–based definition (i.e., homicides involving a gang member) whereas others report according to a gang motive–based definition (i.e., the homicide furthers the goals of a gang) (7).

In conclusion, gang homicides are unique violent events that require prevention strategies

NVDRS include "gang activity" or "gang rivalry" listed as a preceding circumstance. The relevant preceding circumstance variable in SHRs included "juvenile gang killing" and "gangland killing." Whereas standard NVDRS and SHR variables were used to capture cases, these variables are largely determined by the law enforcement narratives, and law enforcement agencies might have different criteria for listing gang activity on a report.

3. NYGS instructs respondents to provide the number of gang-related homicides recorded (not estimated) by each law enforcement agency and to use the following definition for a youth gang: "a group of youths or young adults in your jurisdiction that you or other responsible persons in your agency or community are willing to identify as a gang." This definition excludes motorcycle gangs, hate or ideology groups, prison gangs, and exclusively adult gangs.

References

1. US Census Bureau. Cities with 100,000 or more population in 2000 ranked by population. County and city data book 2000. Washington, DC: US Census Bureau; 2011. Available at http://www.census.gov/statab/ccdb/cityrank.htm. Accessed January 17, 2012.

2. Egley A Jr, Howell JC. Highlights of the 2009 National Youth Gang Survey: fact sheet. Washington, DC: US Department of Justice, Office of Juvenile Justice and Delinquency Prevention; 2011. Available at https://www.ncjrs.gov/pdffiles1/ojjdp/233581.pdf. Accessed January 17, 2012.

3. Inter-University Consortium for Political and Social Research. Law enforcement agency identifiers crosswalk [United States], 2005. Ann Arbor, MI: Inter-University Consortium for Political and Social Research; 2005. Available at http://data.nicar.org/files/active/0/04634-0001-Codebook.pdf. Accessed January 17, 2012.

4. CDC. Web-Based Injury Statistics Query and Reporting System (WISQARS). Atlanta, GA: US Department of Health and Human Services, CDC; 2012. Available at http://www.cdc.gov/injury/wisqars. Accessed January 17, 2012.

5. Howell JC. Youth gang homicides: a literature review. *Crime Delinquency* 1999;45:208–41.

6. Bjerregaard B. Gang membership and drug involvement: untangling the complex relationship. *Crime Delinquency* 2010;56:1–32.

7. Klein M, Maxson C. *Street gang patterns and policies.* New York, NY: Oxford University Press; 2006.

8. McDaniel, DD. Risk and protective factors associated with gang affiliation among high-risk youth: a public health approach. *Inj Prev* [Epub ahead of print, January 11, 2012].

9. Howell JC. Gang prevention: an overview of research and programs. Washington, DC: US Department of Justice, Office of Juvenile Justice and Delinquency Prevention; 2010. Available at https://www.ncjrs.gov/pdffiles1/ojjdp/231116.pdf. Accessed January 17, 2012.

10. Tremblay R, Masse L, Pagani L, Vitaro F. From childhood physical aggression to adolescent maladjustment: the Montreal prevention experiment. In: Peters RD, McMahon RJ, eds. *Preventing childhood disorders, substance abuse, and delinquency.* Thousand Oaks, CA: Sage; 1996:268–98.

CHAPTER 29

Homicidal Events among Mexican American Street Gangs: A Situational Analysis

Avelardo Valdez ■ Alice Cepeda ■ Charles Kaplan

The preceding chapter presented gang homicide data in terms of descriptive analysis. Of course, behind every gang homicide event are actual individuals, possessing varying degrees of social ties and association, as well as varying degrees of motives and circumstances. Gang homicide research at this situational level of analysis is virtually—but not entirely, thanks in part to this article—nonexistent. Here, the authors provide a rare qualitative account, including gang member interviews, of gang homicide events in a southern U.S. city. Emerging from their research is a greater recognition of such important situational factors in explaining gang homicide events as the existence of multiple motives, geographical boundaries between gang territories, and drug and firearm use.

Concerns have emerged about the association of United States (U.S.) Latinos and crime, especially because of the increased presence of street gangs among this population. However, many crime indicators for Latinos, including homicide, are often lower than for other socioeconomically comparable U.S. groups (Martinez, 2002; Sampson, 2008). This is often explained by the large proportion of immigrants compared with native-born counterparts that make-up the total Latino population, especially in urban areas. However, subgroups of Latinos, such as nonimmigrant street-oriented

youth, may be more susceptible to cultural value systems associated with homicide and other violent and antisocial behaviors (Umemoto, 2006). U.S. persons of Mexican origin may be more vulnerable to this process, given their persistent racialized status, than are other Latino groups (Telles & Ortiz, 2008). This article explores these interactions by examining quantitatively and qualitatively 28 homicides involving Mexican American gang members in a southwestern city.

As importantly, this article begins to delineate the complexity of homicide among Latinos by demonstrating how structural, subcultural, and situational factors differentially affect nonimmigrants and immigrants. Sampson and colleagues (2008) found that homicides were lower in U.S. urban areas with a high proportion of Mexican and other Latino immigrants. These studies argue that structural characteristics (poverty, unemployment, homeownership, etc.) in neighborhoods where immigrants live are distinct from those of African Americans and others. Expanding on this idea, Martinez (2002) argued that Latino homicide rates in particular are suppressed by a convergence of relative deprivation and structural conditions. However, even when controlling for neighborhood and other individual and family factors, immigrants in Chicago were 45% less likely to commit violence than were third-generation Latinos (Sampson, 2008). We hypothesize that among segments of United States born Latinos who live in structurally disorganized communities, the etiology of homicide events may be more socially multifaceted.

Reprinted from: Avelardo Valdez, Alice Cepeda, and Charles Kaplan, "Homicidal Events Among Mexican American Street Gangs: A Situational Analysis," *Homicide Studies*, 13(3): 288–306. Copyright © 2009 by Sage Publications. Reprinted by permission of Sage Publications.

The position of this study is that violence is often misunderstood because it is a highly interactive behavior that is often shaped by issues of reflexivity, such as the observer's own cultural and class biases (Sampson & Lauritsen, 1994). One of the unresolved issues in the area of violence is understanding the pivotal role of situational-level processes in the instigation of the violent act itself. Therefore, this study examines these processes by focusing on the violent episodes themselves, as well as on the nature of the gangs, their spatial ecology, and the social context in which they are embedded in the Mexican American population. As importantly, it explores within these homicidal situations victim–offender relations and the role of substance use and weapons in these homicides. Moreover, the study provides data, absent in many studies, on the meanings assigned to the language, behaviors, and symbols within the life context of individuals in these situations. This approach requires an understanding of individuals' own perception and subjective apprehensions. By examining the context and dynamics of these specific events, this analysis will expand our knowledge of criminal homicides generally and those related to youth gangs specifically.

Latino Homicides: Multilevel Perspectives

During the past decade, a great deal of national attention has focused on Latino adolescents and young adults associated with street gangs and violence. Evidence indicates that Latino youth street gangs have proliferated in the United States and have spread across the country in large and small cities and in suburban and rural areas. These Latinos often reside in neighborhoods characterized by unemployment, poverty, welfare dependency, single-headed households, and other characteristics that are traditionally associated with street gang formation.

This perspective corresponds to the structural analysis of crime and homicide that emphasizes the importance of social context or structural conditions in high rates of homicides and other crimes among the poor and other minority groups. Social disorganization theory, which has a long tradition in the social sciences, is a variant of this perspective,

with its emphasis on the socioeconomic and ecological variables as explanatory factors rather than on individual characteristics. When crime and interpersonal violence, particularly homicide, happen among Latino youth gangs, it will more likely occur in communities associated with structural characteristics such as poverty and social isolation.

Others argue that homicides and other types of interpersonal violence are more closely associated with subcultural factors. This perspective fosters the view that "lower-class communities generate a distinctive moral universe that glorifies and legitimates aggressive behavior, particularly among male juveniles" (Kubrin and Weitzer, 2003: p157). Ruth Horowitz (1983) found a prevailing "code of honor" shaping young Latino residents' values and behavior in Chicago. As well, Anderson (1999) identified a "code of the streets" in a disadvantaged Philadelphia neighborhood and two inner-city New York communities. Specifically, this subculture revolves around a street socialization process that emphasizes the development of collective and individual coping strategies that use violence as a means of resolving conflicts (Anderson, 1999).

Situational-level factors are those factors that have an immediate influence on the initiation or outcome of violence or other deviant behavior. Situational-level analyses treat the incident or event as the unit of analysis. Sampson and Lauritsen's (1994) discussion of violent events focuses on such factors as the presence and types of weapon, the presence of drugs or alcohol, the role of bystanders, and victims' degree of resistance and retaliation. Such micro-level factors and processes suggest mechanisms and properties that can contribute to a deeper understanding of violence. This situational approach is highly appropriate for violence and other behaviors among gang members who are involved in street gangs and marginalized and segmented from the majority society.

Gang-Related Homicide Research

Studies focusing on youth gang homicides have identified an increase in this trend across cities in the United States (Curry, Ball, & Decker, 1995). Law enforcement surveys have revealed that this increase in gang homicides is related to street gang–motivated events (Klein, 1995b). One specific characteristic associated with gang homicide research has been drive-by shootings (Hutson, Range, & Eckstein, 1996; Moore, 1991; Sanders, 1994). The use of automobiles to drive to opponents' homes or hangouts and to shoot at victims from a moving car has become a widely used tactic among youth gangs. Drive-by shootings, however, tend to vary among cities. For instance, Block, Antigone, Jacob, and Przybylski (1996) found that in Chicago, drive-by shootings were not as prevalent as in Los Angeles. In Los Angeles (1979–1994), approximately 25% of the gang-related homicides were a result of drive-by shootings (Hutson, Range, Kyriacou, Hart, & Spears, 1995).

Other important characteristics that distinguish gang homicides from other homicides are settings, participants, and firearms (Howell, 1999). In comparison with other homicides, gang-related homicides have been identified as generally involving more participants where the victim-offender had no prior contact (Maxson, Gordon, & Klein, 1985, p 220). This study concluded that "it is evident that gang incidents are generally more chaotic, with more people, weapons, offenses, and injuries." Other studies have provided further evidence that gang homicides were characterized by taking place in public spaces where the use of firearms was common (Klein & Maxson, 1989). It is clear that the growing availability of firearms has contributed to the increase in gang-related deaths among inner-city youth (Block & Block, 1993; Umemoto, 2006).

One of the unresolved issues in the study of street gang homicides is determination of whether homicide committed by gang members is gang related or a result of interpersonal conflict between individuals or groups who are affiliated with the gangs. That is, was the homicide a purposeful gang-related behavior related to the instrumental or expressive goals of the gang or a result of something much more personal that occurs in a collective transaction (Luckenbill, 1977)?

The unprecedented increase of youth involvement in gangs and homicide is a major concern in many Southwestern urban communities. While homicide is allegedly associated with street gangs more than other groups (the exception is intimate partner homicides), few studies have examined the complexity associated with this type of violence among this segment of the population. This article takes the theoretical perspective that although there are multiple-level factors that are continually interacting with each other, the situational factors remain the most challenging in understanding gang members' susceptibility to homicide. Approaching this subject from a situational perspective increases our opportunity to understand the homicides involving male gang members within the complex social system in which they are embedded. Moreover, these findings begin to explore the reasons this type of violence is concentrated among Mexican Americans rather than immigrants who live in the same neighborhoods.

Method

This article is derived from a National Institute on Drug Abuse investigation entitled Drug-Related Gang Violence in South Texas, which examines the epidemiology of violence and drug use among male gang members in San Antonio, Texas. The sample was randomly drawn by catchment area, gang types, and gang membership status from 26 gangs in San Antonio's West and neighborhood catchment areas. The sample consisted of 160 male gang members between 14 and 25 years old. The study used three data collection methods: focus groups, social and economic indicators, and *life history/intensive interviews* (Yin, Valdez, Mata, & Kaplan, 1996).

San Antonio, Texas, is located 140 miles from the U.S.–Mexico border. The population in 2000 was estimated to be 1.2 million, with approximately 60% of Mexican descent (U.S. Bureau of the Census, 2000). The West and South Side community in San Antonio is composed predominantly of Mexican-origin persons and is one of the poorest urban areas in the United States. According to the census data, the per capita income was $5,098, and the median household income was $14,352 for 22 census tracts that constitute this community. Some 55% of the families had children living in poverty, and only 23% of the families received public assistance. It is also an area that has a high concentration of crime, violence, and substance use (Yin et al., 1996). More relevant, in these neighborhoods is the highest concentration of delinquent behavior and gang activity in the city.

A life history/intensive interview was used to obtain data from the male gang members. The life history/intensive interview was designed to provide quantitative and qualitative data through the use of open- and closed-ended questions. The instrument consisted of the use of "scenarios," which are open-ended questions that allowed for "thick descriptions" of specific events, situations, and incidents. The structure of the scenario questions combines qualitative narratives with a matrix of closed-ended quantitative responses. The data used in this study were derived from a series of scenario questions that addressed the last time the participant saw someone get killed. This avoided the problem of having the participant admit to participating in a homicide but did allow him to discuss the homicide incident from a third-person perspective.

Analysis

For the purposes of this article, the homicide event is used as the unit of analysis. The qualitative analysis was based on the grounded theory approach. Open coding was accomplished by a line-by-line reading of the transcriptions. Each scenario narrative was read and coded for categories such as victim–offender relationship, circumstance, motive, drug relatedness, and weapons. Each of the interviews was conducted face-to-face with the eligible participants. The level of detail and the range of information elicited from the respondents resulted in the collection of descriptions of the same event from different respondents. In many instances, members of the victim's or offender's gang described the same homicide. Two or more respondents recounted 13 of the 28 homicides.

Results

The mean age of the participants ($N = 160$) was 19 years old, with approximately 26% enrolled in school at the time of the interview. The majority were unattached young men. About 31% reported having children. Poly-drug use was also characteristic of the respondents, with more than 90% reporting lifetime marijuana and cocaine use and 51% reporting having sold drugs within the past 3 months. Table 29.1 reflects the criminal involvement of the participants. As expected, a large percentage of the participants were involved in delinquent behavior. More than half of the respondents reported firing a gun or owning and/or carrying one within 30 days preceding the interview. Approximately 56% had been arrested for a violent or nonviolent crime.

Gang Types and Homicides

In a previous analysis, we created a typology of the gangs. Four classifications of Mexican American gangs were constructed (Valdez, 2003). These types included criminal adult dependent gangs, criminal non-adult dependent gangs, barrio-territorial gangs, and transitional gangs. It should be noted that this classification of these gangs is a sociological snapshot taken at the beginning of this study. The gang's place in this typology may have changed during the years, depending on a variety of factors that are addressed in previous publications.

Table 29.1 indicates that the largest numbers of homicides were committed by criminal non-adult

Table 29.1 Characteristics of Criminal Involvement and Homicides Committed by Gang Type				
Criminal Activities ($N = 160$)	%	Gang Type	No. of Gangs ($N = 14$)	No. of Homicides ($N = 28$)
Currently own gun	68	Criminal adult dependent (prison)	2	2
Carried a gun in past 30 days	56	Criminal adult dependent (nonprison)	1	1
Sold drugs in past 3 months	51	Criminal nonadult dependent	3	13
Arrested for violent crime	56	Barrio/territorial	4	6
Arrested for nonviolent crime	55	Transitional	4	6
Fired gun in gang-related fight	82			

dependent gangs, whereas the least numbers of homicides were committed by two criminal adult dependent types. The three gangs in the criminal non-adult dependent gangs classification were organized as a criminal enterprise with a distinct hierarchy and a distinct leadership structure. They are involved in more independent and personal (non-adult dependent) illegal activities such as drug dealing, car theft, robbery, and carjacking. The gangs offer an organizational structure to protect the interests of individual gang members, not as a centralized criminal enterprise. Members display high rates of drug and alcohol abuse. There is an absence of adult influence on these criminal gangs, which may explain the higher number of homicides.

The criminal non-adult dependent gang with the highest number of homicides was Varrio La Paloma (VLP), whose members were involved in 7 of the 28 murders. VLP is located in a public housing project and an older subdivision. There are approximately 100 hard-core and 80 marginal members in the VLP gang. During the 3 years of this study, the gang was involved in a war with a rival gang located in the residential neighborhood adjacent to the San Miguel projects. It was also involved in a serious conflict with a Chicano adult prison gang (the Brotherhood), which was attempting to take control of the heroin market in the projects. Two adult gang members were murdered by a VLP member when they refused to cooperate with him. Eventually, the VLP reached a compromise with the adult gang. The VLP would be allowed to sell cocaine and marijuana, but the heroin trade would be the exclusive right of the prison gang.

The least number of homicides was committed by the adult criminal dependent gangs (prison gang dependent and adult gang dependent). For instance, the Nine-Ball Crew is one of these types. During the course of the study, members from this gang committed only one murder. What distinguished this gang from the VLP is that it had direct ties to the Brotherhood, which controlled the heroin trade in this community. During the preceding two decades, this prison gang has established a criminal network outside the prison that controls the heroin trade in San Antonio and other South Texas cities. During the past few years, it has recruited several

youth gangs to sell heroin for it. The control it has over the Nine-Ball Crew is its most successful. The prison gang discourages random or episodic acts of violence by Nine-Ball Crew members or any of its other youth gang affiliates since those acts draw the attention of law enforcement, which could disrupt the prison gang's sophisticated drug-dealing operations. This may help explain why its members were involved in 1 of the 28 homicides identified in this study.

Twelve were committed by barrio/territorial and transitional gangs. Barrio/territorial gangs are located in various types of neighborhoods, ranging from public housing to residential single-family homes. Twelve gangs are categorized as this type. These are not as hierarchical as the above-mentioned groups. Criminal activities include drug dealing, auto theft, burglary, robbery, vandalism, criminal mischief, and other petty crime. These crimes tend to be more individual, less organized, and less gang directed. Violent behavior tends to be more random and personal. Except for gang turf disputes, most violence is centered on interpersonal fights and random situational acts of violence often associated with male bravado. Even gang drive-by shootings tend to be spontaneous and predicated on issues such as defending the gang's honor. These gang members use drugs similarly to the other groups, with the exception of a low prevalence of heroin use. They tend to operate independently of any adult gang influence. Most territorial gangs are in transition relative to a trajectory, that is, growing in membership and reputation or fading organizationally.

Spatial Ecology of Homicides

As mentioned earlier, the 26 gangs from the sample were located on the West and South Side communities of San Antonio. All the 26 gangs claimed territories within neighborhoods in these areas. These territories were separated by specific streets or natural boundaries such as public parks or creeks or ditches. Some of the larger gangs claimed physical spaces that included entire neighborhoods, often encompassing 5 to 10 city square blocks. Several of these larger gangs had subsets that controlled smaller areas of these larger territories. These were often smaller neighborhoods distinguished by clearly identified street boundaries. About a third of the gangs claimed territories that were based on public housing units. In some cases, some of the larger housing units were divided into 3 or 4 distinct gangs.

These 26 gangs had a history of conflict often centered on disputes over areas that each claimed or over criminal activities, particularly the sale of drugs. A large proportion of the homicides were between gangs whose territories were adjacent to each other. We argue that this spatial proximity between the victim's and offender's gang contributed to situations that led to the escalation of incidents leading to violence. For instance, while there were reports of circumstances in which a rival gang member would be allowed in a rival's territory (i.e., when he was just passing through or invited by a neutral nongang resident), acts such as wearing colors or throwing signs while in someone else's territory were a violation of the gang's ethos. The two gangs involved in the following homicide were from two distinct neighborhoods geographically divided by a natural boundary (major thoroughfare). Even with the presence of this boundary, these youth were in constant contact with each other. Pedro, a member of the Chicano Boyz, a criminal non-adult dependent gang, described the events that unfolded the night when a rival gang member was unexpectedly surprised in their territory sporting his colors:

> Yeah he was passing by there like nobody was around. But we were all inside the house. This guy didn't see nobody and he took out his black rag. Then my homeboy was passing by on his bike and he just started whistling. Everybody looked outside. We all just came outside and we got him. We just started kicking his ass. He was crying and shit. He was like, "Nah man, leave me alone. Just let me go." We then put him in the car and we took him somewhere else. We kicked his ass some more. We shanked (knifed) his ass a lot of times. After, we dropped him off in the street.

Similarly, Chris, a member of the Nine-Ball Crew, a prison-connected gang, recounted how he and his fellow gang member were caught "slipping" (i.e., unexpectedly caught with their guard down—not aware of surroundings) in a rival gang's territory.

> Me and RadioMan were walking over by the wall and didn't notice we went into their neighborhood. It was around Christmastime. At first I thought they were firecrackers, but then I saw they were shooting at us from the alley. I got shot in the stomach. When I turned around, RadioMan got shot too. All I remember was seeing him lying there, and he died in the ambulance.

The details of the homicide were recounted by several other respondents from RadioMan's gang. For instance, Mike recalled how he heard the shooting and ran over and saw his friend bleeding.

> I was at my mother-in-law's house, and my sister-in-law came in yelling that they had shot one of my friends. I ran over there. He was shot. He had a lot of blood, and it was coming out of his mouth. I think it hit him in the heart. It took a long time for the ambulance to get there.

Violence associated with gangs claiming streets in the same neighborhood was common. Most of these incidents were spontaneous, and typically the victim tended to be outnumbered by offenders. In one instance, the victim was walking down a street that was claimed by two well-known gangs in the neighborhood. He was recognized by members of the offending gang, and as Timoteo, a 17-year-old member of the VLP gang (criminal non-adult dependent) recalled, approximately 17 individuals were involved in the incident:

> He was walking in the hood. We recognized him. We just started beating the shit out of him. I don't know for how long, but it didn't seem to be too long. We were just kicking his ass, and then he just didn't make no more noises or nothing. There was about 17 or 18 of us. We just left him there, and the police came and found him.

It was observed that most of the gang territories were demarcated by gang graffiti on buildings and other locations that would identify the neighborhood with a respective gang (i.e., show that the gang claimed the area). However, this demarcation of physical territories was less prominent among the more adult criminal oriented gangs, who actually prohibited graffiti because it often attracted police attention and antagonized homeowners and small businesses. Also, within the larger community, there were social spaces that were considered neutral, such as some public recreational areas, community retail centers, downtown, and some night clubs and bars located outside the area. Nevertheless, the data above describe the risk these young men are exposed to as either victims or perpetrators, given the geographic proximity to rival territories.

Victim–Offender Personal Relationships

Data presented here reflect the nature of the victim–offender relationship as identified in the descriptions of each of the homicide events. Overall, the relationship between the victim and the offender for the reported homicides was primarily between rival gang members. That is, 19 of the 28 homicidal events were between members from adversary gangs in the neighborhood. For instance, the following describes the volatile relationship that had emerged between two transitional gangs (Killing Crew and AOS):

> It all started in high school. They [the offender's gang] were all jocks, and we [the victim's gang] were just ordinary people. They were all older than us and were in the 12th grade. We were only 9th graders. What started it all was because we knocked them down at school [in status]. We just took over, and they didn't like that. That's what started it all.
>
> The day it happened, we were going to a party. It was me, Patrick, Allen, Marc, and two other of my friends. We were getting ready to leave; we were in front of Marc's house. All of a sudden the AOS, they just started shooting at us. They hit Marc in the head and one of the other guys in the heart. They both died right on the spot. They also hit Patrick five times. He lost a lot of blood. He almost didn't make it at all. When it happened we ran, but when we looked back, there were three of them hit already on the floor.

The two gangs continued their feud for approximately another year until the AOS (offender's gang) fell apart. The Killing Crew (victim's gang) eventually became the dominant gang in the neighborhood.

Similarly, the following account details the events that led to the death of a 17-year-old who was part of a barrio/territorial gang (Hangers) that had been in constant disputes with a nearby rival gang. Antonio, a fellow Hangers member who was with the victim, recounted the events of that day:

> We were walking in the middle of the field in the courts [housing projects] where the playground is at. We were walking across it, and I guess they [rival gang] had fucking seen us and were waiting for us to pass by. We saw them, and they were going to start shooting at us. We just began running. Then my friend got it! He like fell then got back up and he started fucking running. He kept saying, "I'm hit. I'm hit." I said, "Don't fuck around dude." I didn't believe him. Then I saw him fall again. I just went over there and I tried to pick him up. He just kept saying he wanted his mom. There was chingos of blood.

For the remaining homicides, distinct relationships were observed between the victim and offender. For instance, five of the homicides were between acquaintances. In most of these, the victim and offender did not have a close personal relationship but knew each other from the neighborhood. One participant described how one of his fellow members (in Nine-Ball Crew) shot and killed a man that the offender knew from the neighborhood:

> We were in the neighborhood hanging out. T-Man was there, and then this guy showed up and started talking shit, saying he was a big time member of the adult prison gang. T-Man told him, "You're nobody" and shit, and then he kicked his ass in front of everybody. He told him to split, and the man didn't want to leave. He was with his girlfriend. T-Man told him to leave again, but he didn't want to. Then T-Man just took out a gun, and he just shot him with a gauge, and he just fell down. We were all freaking out. I just took off.

Two of the five cases were identified as drug acquaintances. That is, the victim and offender were familiar with one another through previous drug transactions. In one of these cases, a member of a transitional gang confronted a dealer who came into his neighborhood and was selling a bad product. Although the gang member did not have a close relationship with the dealer, he did admit to having scored from the victim in the past.

> This dude was from the North side, and that's why we started getting after him. You know, hey look, when you are buying drugs to sell drugs, you get good shit. You don't fuck around with these punk ass dealers.

As previously mentioned, although the majority of the relationships between the victim and offender were characterized as rival members, there were two incidents that involved members from the same gang. Sammy, a 19-year-old member of Chicano Boyz, describes the death of a member of his gang during one of their regular meetings:

> He was a homeboy, he wanted to get out. He told us that he wanted to get out because of his chick [girl-friend]. We told him, all right, well, we are going to have to roll you out because you don't dis [disrespect] a homeboy for a ho [girl]. We were all drunk, and he was dissing us for just to go with his chick. So they kicked his ass. He was just laying there, then they just cracked his head open with a rock. They killed him.

The above-mentioned incident was described by several members of this gang, including some of the victim's close friends, who were present and witnessed the incident.

In two additional homicides, a stranger was involved in one and a bystander in the other. Both of the victims in these separate homicides were residents of the respective neighborhood the gang involved was from. The first was an older man who happened to be waiting for the public bus at the time of the rival gang shootout. One of the targeted victims recalled, "We were just walking, and then we saw them and they tried to shoot at us, but some old man was just passing by, and they hit him." In the second, an African American man confronted a couple of members of the VLP and was shot and killed at the front doorsteps of his home. A member of the gang describes the details of the homicide:

> We were just there kicking back and stuff and the cops came around. We had just done a job [drug transaction], and we were packing [carrying a weapon]. When we saw the cops, we just took off, fuck it. Well Kid threw his gun on top of that man's house. I didn't throw away my gun. We then went to my homeboy's house, and we were smoking out there and getting all fucked up, and Kid said, "let's go for my gun." We went back, and one of my other homeboys told us that the Black man had gotten the gun. We knocked on his door but he didn't come out. Kid told him, "give me back my fucking gun; all we want is my gun." He then came out running at us with a bow and arrow and we started firing and shit. I don't know—the guy just fell down and he died.

Drug and Alcohol Relatedness of the Homicides

Of the 28 homicide incidents, 3 are identified as being intrinsically related to the system of drug distribution and use. For instance, one respondent described his confrontation with a dealer from the North side of San Antonio who was being accused of selling adulterated drugs. Pedro, a member of the transitional gang named VC Outlaws, discussed how the dealer did not know anything about the drug business in the neighborhood. He (the victim) did not even know he was dealing in a neighborhood where the adult prison gang controlled the business.

> Well my homeboy had bought some coke, and he said it wasn't good. So I told him I would go and fix it. I met the dude in my neighborhood, and it all went to shit. I told him, "Hey, if you're going to buy drugs to sell, you need to get good shit. You don't fuck around with this shit." He then pulled out a small gun, I think it was a 380. But I had the advantage because I think he was all fucked up on coke. I told him, "vato [man], what you did, I'm just coming over to fix it." That's when I slapped the gun and I already had mine on him and boom.

In yet another case, the homicide was committed within the context of a drug dealing hierarchy related to enforcing the norm of paying 10% to the adult prison gang. Goldy, a member of the VLP, who walks with the help of two crutches, described the violent confrontation he had with two members of the adult prison gang:

> They [adult prison gang] put a contract on me and sent two hit men. I did not want to pay 10% to them, so they came after me. They shot first but missed. I shot back and hit both of them. But they still shot at me and hit me in the thigh and knee. The knee is the one that still gives me a lot of trouble. But I killed both of them. A lot of my homeboys ran when the shit hit the fan.

Goldy went on to describe how he started out by selling dime bags, and then before he knew it, he was selling 3 or 4 ounces of heroin and coke a week. The adult prison gang attempted to recruit him to no avail, which escalated into the violent confrontation.

There were eight incidents in which the victim and/or offender was reportedly using drugs or alcohol. Specifically, in two of these homicides, both the victim and the offender were intoxicated. The victim was intoxicated in four and the offender in six of the eight homicide events. For instance, Abel, who was part of the Trece, a criminal adult (prison) dependent gang, recounted how his friend was murdered by a member of the rival Hangers gang:

> They just rolled up on Cat. We had been kicking back at his girlfriend's, getting high. But he was fine. He wasn't very stoned. He had just come out of the house. He was walking down the street then you just hear pop, pop, pop! I had to go and tell his mom. She came over and the ambulance got there. He was still alive but then died. I couldn't do shit.

In a couple of instances, the victim was drunk or high and was caught "slipping" by the offender. The following ongoing rivalry between two gangs in a housing project resulted in the death of a 19-year-old. The homicide occurred on New Year's Eve between the VLP and the Thugs. Apparently, earlier in the day, the Thugs had chased some VLP in a truck, but nothing happened. Later that night the VLP retaliated.

> I wasn't there, but I was across the street. Earlier that day five Characters had chased me in a minitruck. They were chasing me, and I ran to the other side, and I called my homeboys. Eight of us came back, and they were having a party, and everybody went inside because they saw us coming. One guy stayed outside. He was really drunk. It was the Character that was driving when they chased me. He was outside, he was taking a piss, and my homeboy just shot him in the neck, and he was going down, and they shot him in the back, and he was on the floor. He was twitching, and they shot him in the chest. It was like at 2-feet range with a 12-gauge.

Circumstance and Motives Associated with Homicides

Each homicide narrative was read and coded for circumstance and motives. Similar to Spunt et. al. (1998), the homicides were viewed as events that occurred over time (1998), that is, incidents that occurred over time, with two or more people experiencing a progression of interaction that resulted in death. Through the course of the interaction, the circumstances and motives changed. Thus, given the complexity of homicides, the narratives allowed for a preliminary examination of the multiple social circumstances and motives associated with the 28 gang homicide events.

This preliminary qualitative analysis revealed five distinct codes for circumstances and six different codes for motives. For coding purposes, *circumstance* was defined as the specific condition, situation, or event that was occurring at the time of the homicide. *Motives* were defined as the reason, cause, purpose, intention, drive, or object associated with the homicide. Analyses revealed that in many instances, there was a history associated either with the individual victim and offender or with their respective gangs. Most of the incidents had more than one circumstance or motive, which resulted in multiple codes for the incidents.

Circumstances

- Drug-related dispute: argument associated with drug transactions, use, or a combination

- Personal dispute: argument associated with personal issue

- Gang dispute: gang-related issues

- Assault: victim attacked and taken by surprise

- Rolling out: gang exit rite that entails a physical beating by several gang members

Motives

- Personal vendetta: feud between victim and offender

- Gang revenge or retaliation: retribution associated with specific gang incident

- Gang rivalry: ongoing feud between two gangs

- Territorial trespassing: intruding into rival gang's neighborhood, turf, barrio

- Gang solidarity: expression of shared goals, norms, and aims among gang members (camaraderie)

- Spontaneous retaliation: personal spontaneous (spur of the moment) retribution or defense

Since the majority of the victim–offender relationships involved rival gang members, the majority of the circumstances and motives were identified as gang revenge or rivalry. The following two narratives depict a gang dispute (circumstance) of an ongoing gang rivalry (motive) that resulted in the death of a 15-year-old who had just joined the gang 1 week before his death. Leo (of the Chicano Boyz) was in the car with the victim when the shooting happened and described how the events unfolded:

> We were in the cars, and we saw each other, and we talked shit to each [other], and they had stopped. That's when we stopped, and we had the cars facing backwards. We stopped and talked shit, and they stopped not even like 6 or 8 feet away from us, and that's when they started shooting, so we took off. They shot like eight times, and then that's when we all got down, and then that's when we snapped when Luc got shot. He wanted to like scream but he couldn't scream. They shot him from the back, and it came out through the front.

The feud continued for a number of months between members of the Chicano Boyz and Blasters Inc and resulted in several drive-by shootings. Juan, a member of the Chicano Boyz, informed us a few months after the killing of Luc that his family had to reinforce the front of the house with half-inch steel plates because of several drive-bys committed by the Blasters. Nine months after Juan's interview, our field staff learned that Juan's mother had been killed during a drive-by shooting at their home. After her death, the father and Juan's siblings moved out of state.

The following narrative is distinct from the previous one in that it describes a homicide associated with a gang dispute and assault (circumstances) caused by gang retaliation or revenge (motive). This killing was the beginning of an ongoing feud between the Trece and the Angeles. A member of the Trece recalled how he saw his friend get killed:

> Chuco was going to pick me up, but he offered some chick a ride. They got to by where I was. They got to like the corner before you turn where he was going to pick me up. Some car just pulled up and shot him at point blank with an AK in the head. The girl just jumped out the car; she knew what was going to happen. I hear the shot and then a couple of more shots, and that's when me and Gabe came out running, and we saw the car take off, and Chuco was shaking on the ground.

The rivalry continued, and a few weeks later, a member of the Angeles was shot and killed in retaliation for Chuco's death. A member of the Trece explained:

> Well that was for getting back at them for killing Chuco. I was with them, and this homeboy was all upset about Chuco. He rolled up on Ray; he saw him come out of a girl's house. He was walking down the street, and then he just shot him: pop.

There were several homicides that were characterized as being personal (circumstance) and spontaneous (motive) and that escalated into violent confrontations within the situational context of the gang subculture. In one incident, a respondent described how the behavior of an acquaintance who was not a gang member escalated into a confrontation resulting in his death. According to the respondent, the victim was a tecato (addict) who was hanging out with gang members one night while they were partying.

> We were in the courts (public housing) having a cookout. We were drinking and having fun. This guy started talking about my homeboy's chick. He didn't know it was his wife. He started looking at her and said he wanted to fuck her. My homeboy got up and went and got an ax and hit him across his head. My homeboy was fucking drunk.

Discussion and Conclusions

Increased street gang activity among San Antonio's Mexican-origin population is associated with a steady decline in structural conditions that has had a devastating impact on poor and working-class segments of this population and has led to increased levels of social disorganization. More specifically, Mexican American inner-city youth have become increasingly marginalized as a result of this economic transformation, which is accompanied by continual discrimination and unequal treatment, especially in the areas where these gang homicides occurred (Bauder, 2002). Confounding the issue is the fact that most of these gang members are from families with multigenerational involvement in poverty, crime, and residential instability, characteristics associated with persons involved in homicide and other violent behaviors (Moore, 1991). As important, many of these Mexican American youth have internalized those properties that socially define and devalue them as minorities.

On a situational level, our data show that the circumstances and motives of the majority of these homicides were predicated on the collective goals and activities of the gang, such as drive-bys or a dispute over turf. These gang homicides were distinct from those that were simply gang member homicides. The latter were homicides committed by gang members but not necessarily for the promotion of the gang's interests, such as retaliation (Tita & Abrahamse, 2006). Among the gang member homicides, the nature and intensity of the relationship between the perpetrator and the victim varied, from neighborhood associates to drug acquaintances to strangers. More importantly, these data clarify how all the homicides are associated with distinct street gang values. Social differences between adolescents are the bases for conflict among youth. However, for gang members the distinct context in which they find themselves tends to lead to more violent outcomes than other groups. The "code of the streets" dictates that a gang-affiliated youth in this street subculture is expected to be involved in violence, drug use, crime, and confrontational behaviors. In addition, the use of multiple circumstances and motives is an analytical tool that contributes to an understanding of the complex etiology of violence by moving beyond a classification of homicides that uses only single values.

Geographic proximity of gang territories emerged as an important characteristic in explaining these gang homicides. The fact that most of the homicides were between members of gangs bordering the same neighborhood or area may provide an understanding of the escalation of violent acts between these groups of youth in these neighborhoods. The spatial proximity of two gangs results in frequent contact and high visibility that create a volatile environment susceptible to aggression and violence. These findings are similar to the findings of others that gang homicide was more often turf related than drug related.

Other researchers have categorized gangs into street gangs and drug gangs (Klein, 1995a). Our findings reflect Goldstein's (1985) framework, which characterizes the relationship between drugs and violence as related to psychopharmacological, economic compulsive, and systemic factors. Based on this, three homicides were classified as systemically drug related, and eight were psychopharmacology related. In the majority of these cases, only one of the parties was pharmacologically impaired, usually the victim. In the majority of the cases, alcohol was the substance most likely to be associated with these homicides. This research supports our earlier findings that documented alcohol use, but not drug use, was associated with arrests for violent crime (Valdez, Kaplan, & Curtis, 2007). Our findings also suggest that criminal gangs are more likely to be involved in systemic forms of violence and discourage excessive drug use.

As others have found, our data indicate that firearms were used in almost all of these homicides (Block & Block, 1993). Of 28 cases, 23 involved the use of a gun, and in almost every type of victim–offender relationship. The use of weapons in these homicides is related to the large percentage of gang members who own, frequently carry, and have actually used one in a fight. This use of guns corresponds to other studies that report adolescent males are more likely than their non-gang peers to carry handguns if they are involved in gangs (Luster & Su Min, 2001). The ominous presence of these lethal weapons corresponds to the relatively high ownership of and easy access to guns in this state. However, as opposed to the general population, guns among this gang population are more likely to be used to settle disputes. This contradicts research that indicates that the use of firearms most often requires a purposive effort (casual relationships) rather than more spontaneous or episodic acts (personal/intimate relationships), in which the offender uses other types of objects. Moreover, our data have important implications, given that research has indicated that carrying a handgun as an early adolescent persists into later life and continual criminal behavior (Lizotte, Krohn, Howell, Tobin, & Howard, 2000).

In San Antonio, Latino homicides and other violent crimes have not been neutralized by a large influx of immigrants as in other cities (e.g., Los Angeles, Chicago, Miami, and Houston). However, this does not mean that Mexican immigrants are absent in this city. In fact, 13% of the total Mexican-origin population in San Antonio was composed of immigrants during the 1990s. Most of these Mexican immigrants and their families lived in the same disadvantaged neighborhoods as did the gang members described in this study. However, participation in gang activity and violence by similarly aged immigrant youth living in these neighborhoods and attending the same schools was almost nonexistent. What is the larger implication of these findings, given that nationally the U.S. foreign-born immigrant population (mostly Mexican) increased by nearly 50% in the past 10 years, to 31 million in 2000? If immigration status is a "protective" against violence, as Sampson has stated, can we expect crime to diminish in Latino neighborhoods? Our position is that it will, but this game will vanish rapidly in subsequent generations as the children of immigrants are socialized into society's racial hierarchy.

Future homicide research should focus on identifying predisposing factors and predictors by taking into consideration social structural differences and being sensitive to the situational processes that could lead to homicides within local contexts. Our findings begin to identify the etiology of youth gang homicides. Specifically, our data contribute to street gang mediation, dispute resolution, and crisis intervention programs by providing an understanding of how locally embedded social processes associated with specific gang types, ecology, drugs, circumstances, and motives unfold into homicidal events. Last, these findings point to the importance of developing crime prevention programs focused on the children of immigrants.

References

Anderson, E. (1999). *Code of the streets: Decency, violence and the moral life of the inner city*. New York: Norton.

Bauder, H. (2002). *Work on the west side: Urban neighborhoods and the cultural exclusion of youth*. Boulder, CO: Lexington Books.

Block, C., Antigone, C., Jacob, A., & Przybylski, R. (1996). *Street gangs and crime: Patterns and trends in Chicago*. Chicago: Illinois Criminal Justice Information Authority.

Block, R., & Block, C. (1993). *Street gang crime in Chicago: Research in brief*. Washington, DC: National Institute of Justice.

Curry, G., Ball, R. A., & Decker, S. H. (1995). *An update on gang crime and law enforcement recordkeeping*. St. Louis: University of Missouri, Department of Criminology and Criminal Justice.

Goldstein, P. J. (1985). The drugs/violence nexus: A tripartite conceptual framework. *Journal of Drug Issues, 15*(4), 493–506.

Horowitz, R. (1983). *Honor and the American dream: Culture and identity in a Chicano community*. New Brunswick, NJ: Rutgers University Press.

Howell, J. C. (1999). Youth gang homicide: A literature review. *Crime & Delinquency, 45*(2), 208–241.

Hutson, H., Range, D. A., & Eckstein, M. (1996) Drive-by shootings by violent street gangs in Los Angeles: A five year review from 1989 to 1993. *Academic Emergency Medicine, 3*, 300–303.

Hutson, H., Range, D. A., Kyriacou, D. N., Hart, J., & Spears, K. (1995). The epidemic of gang-related homicides in Los Angeles County from 1979 through 1994. *Journal of the American Medical Association, 274*, 1031–1036.

Klein, M. W. (1995a). *The American street gang: Its nature, prevalence, and control*. New York: Oxford University Press.

Klein, M. W. (1995b). Street gang cycles. In J. Q. Wilson & J. Petersilia (Eds.), *Crime* (pp. 217–236). San Francisco: Institute for Contemporary Studies.

Klein, M. W., & Maxson, C. L. (1989). Street gang violence. In M. E. Wolfgang & N. A. Weiner (Eds.), *Violent crime, violent criminals* (pp. 198–234). Newbury Park, CA: Sage.

Kubrin, C. E., & Weitzer, R. 2003. Retaliatory homicide: Concentrated disadvantage and neighborhood culture." *Social Problems, 50*(2): 157–180.

Lizotte, A. J., Krohn, M. D., Howell, J. C., Tobin, K., & Howard, G. J. (2000). Factors influencing gun carrying among young urban males over the adolescent–young adult life course. *Criminology, 38*(3), 811–834.

Luckenbill, D. (1977). Criminal homicide as a situated transaction. *Social Problems, 25*(2), 176–186.

Luster, T., & Su Min, O. (2001). Correlates of male adolescents carrying handguns among their peers. *Journal of Marriage & Family, 63*(3), 714.

Martinez, R., Jr. (2002). *Latino homicide: Immigration, violence and the community*. New York: Routledge.

Maxson, C. L., Gordon, M. A., & Klein, M. W. (1985). Differences between gang and nongang homicides. *Criminology, 23*(2), 209–222.

Moore, J. W. (1991). *Going down to the barrio: Homeboys and homegirls in change*. Philadelphia: Temple University Press.

Sampson, R. J. (2008). Rethinking crime and immigration. *Contexts, 7*(1), 28–33.

Sampson, R. J., & Lauritsen, J. L. (1994). Violent victimization and offending: Individual-, situational-, and community-level risk factors. In A. J. Reiss & J. A. Roth (Eds.), *Understanding and preventing violence: Social influences* (Vol. 3, pp. 1–114). Washington, DC: National Academy Press.

Sanders, W. B. (1994). *Gangbangs and drive-bys*. New York: Aldine.

Spunt, B., Brownstein, H., Crimmins, S., and Langley, S. 1996. "American women who kill: Self-reports of their homicides." *International Journal of Risk, Security and Crime Prevention, 1*(4): 293–303.

Telles, E. E., & Ortiz, V. (2008). *Generations of exclusion*. New York: Russell Sage.

Tita, G., & Abrahamse, A. (2006). Gang homicide in L.A., 1981–2001. In A. J. Egley, C. L. Maxson, J. Miller, & M. W. Klein (Eds.), *The modern gang reader* (3rd ed., pp. 291–305). Los Angeles: Roxbury.

Umemoto, K. (2006). *The truce: Lessons from an LA gang war*. Ithaca, NY: Cornell University.

U.S. Bureau of the Census. (2000). *Quick tables: QT-PL. Race, Hispanic or Latino, and age: 2000 for San Antonio city, Texas*. Retrieved July 16, 2003, from http://factfinder.census.gov

Valdez, A. (2003). Toward a typology of contemporary Mexican American youth gangs. In L. Kontos, D. Brotherton, & L. Barrios (Eds.), *Gangs and society: Alternative perspectives* (pp. 12–40). New York: Columbia University Press.

Valdez, A., Kaplan, C. D., & Curtis, R. L., Jr. (2007). Aggressive crime, alcohol and drug use, and concentrated poverty in 24 U.S. urban areas. *American Journal of Drug and Alcohol Abuse, 33*(4), 595–603.

Yin, Z., Valdez, A., Mata, A. G. J., & Kaplan, C. (1996). Developing a field-intensive methodology for generating a randomized sample for gang research [Special issue]. *Gang, Drugs and Violence, 24*(2), 195–204.

CHAPTER 30

Gang Membership and Offending Patterns

Marvin D. Krohn ▪ Terence P. Thornberry

Do gangs cause individuals to become highly delinquent (a facilitation effect)? Or do highly delinquent individuals join gangs (a selection effect)? Or is it a combination of both (mixed-model, or enhancement, effect)? This influential and innovative framework for examining the gang–crime connection was first proposed and tested by Thornberry and colleagues two decades ago. In this article, the authors provide a careful review of the numerous research projects—of varying places, times, subjects, sample characteristics, etc—that have since investigated this critical issue. Despite the diversity in research studies, the authors find uniformity in the results: gangs indisputably increase delinquent and violent offending rates among their members (i.e., a strong facilitation effect). More simply stated, group processes within the gang (discussed elsewhere in this book) contribute uniquely and decisively to the gang–crime connection.

Selection vs. Facilitation

. . .[T]here is no dispute about the association of gang membership and high rates of criminal involvement: gang members have much higher rates of crime than non-members. There is a dispute, however, about the interpretation of this relationship. Thornberry et al. (1993) identified three general models that could account for the strong statistical association between gang membership and high rates of crime.

The first is a "kind of person" model they labeled the *selection model*. A selection model argues that adolescents with a strong propensity for delinquency and violence seek out or are recruited into street gangs. They are likely to engage in delinquency regardless of their status as a gang member. Indeed, the observed statistical relationship between gang membership and delinquency is spurious, caused by some prior common cause. This model is most consistent with control theories of delinquency, especially those presented by Hirschi (1969) and Gottfredson and Hirschi (1990).

The second model identified by Thornberry et al. (1993) is the *facilitation model*. This is a "kind of group" model. Gang members do not have a higher propensity for delinquency and violence than non-members and, absent joining a gang, would not have higher rates of delinquency. When they join a gang, however, the normative structure of the gang along with group processes and dynamics facilitates increased involvement in delinquency. In this case, the delinquency of gang members should increase during periods of gang membership and be lower both before and after that period. This model is most consistent with learning theories (Akers, 1998) and life-course theories (Thornberry & Krohn, 2003).

These two views are not logically contradictory and both processes can occur. Thornberry et al. (1993) labeled this mixed model the *enhancement model*. Adolescents who are already involved in delinquency are most apt to join a gang (selection) but, after joining, their delinquency is likely to increase significantly (facilitation).

Although the enhancement model is quite plausible, it is not as interesting as the other two since the contrast between the first two approaches yields opposing hypotheses. Under the selection model, gang members would have higher rates of delinquency than non-members before, during, and after periods of membership. Also, among gang members, intra-individual change would not be systematically related to gang membership; if the impact of gang membership on delinquency is truly spurious (Gottfredson & Hirschi, 1990) an individual's rate of offending should not change as a function of gang membership. In contrast, under the facilitation model, gang members would have higher rates of delinquency than non-members only during periods of membership; before and after the groups would not differ. Also, the facilitation model predicts that intra-individual change is systematically related to gang membership; if gang membership is truly causal, an individual's rate of offending should increase when they become a gang member and decrease after they leave the gang.

Fully testing these competing approaches is impossible absent a true experimental design. Nevertheless, longitudinal studies that follow individuals across time offer the strongest feasible approach to examining them. The essence of the contrasting hypotheses just presented is temporal; in one case (selection) there should be no intra-individual change in delinquency as a function of gang membership, in the other (facilitation) there should be. Longitudinal studies with repeated measures are designed to capture intra-individual change and therefore assess this type of hypothesis.

Longitudinal designs have another advantage in this regard. By following the same individuals across time, each respondent acts as his or her own control and helps bring stable attributes under control (Farrington, Ohlin, & Wilson, 1986). Cross-sectional designs are limited to cross-person analyses and therefore can only statistically control for other variables. For example, if gang members have higher rates of delinquency than non-members that may be because males are more apt both to be gang members and to be delinquent. If an individual's delinquency increases during periods of membership and then declines, that cannot

be because of being male; the individual was male before, during, and after being a gang member. In general, longitudinal designs help control for stable characteristics, although time-varying characteristics remain a threat to validity.

Finally, longitudinal studies that are based on community samples with both gang members and non-members followed over time strengthen our ability to test these hypotheses. In particular, they can compare the delinquency of gang members to non-members at the same point in time, relative to periods of active membership for the gang members. The selection model hypothesizes that the gang members will always have significantly higher rates of delinquency than non-members; the facilitation model hypothesizes that the gang members will have higher rates than non-members only during the period of their active membership.

In sum, longitudinal designs that follow individuals across time offer many advantages over cross-sectional designs for testing causal hypotheses. While not as definitive as those from a true experiment, longitudinal results are far superior to those from cross-sectional data.

Initial Studies

Early studies of the gang facilitation effect focused on relatively simple analytic strategies comparing rates of criminal involvement for gang members and non-members over time. For example, the first assessment of these models using longitudinal panel data (Thornberry et al., 1993) relied on the Rochester Youth Development Study to compare gang members to non-members at three consecutive years, from when the respondents were 15 years of age until they were 17 years of age. Two types of comparisons were made: across time and across group. The first examined whether the delinquency of gang members changed as a function of their active gang membership. The second analytic strategy compared the gang members to non-members at each annual time point. Thornberry et al. (1993) conducted the analysis for five outcomes: general delinquency, violence, property crimes, drug use, and drug sales. They were also able to examine transient gang members, those who were members for no more than a single year, and more stable gang members, those who were members during at least two of the years. The analysis was limited to male respondents.

The results are quite consistent with the facilitation model. Focusing on violent delinquency where the patterns are clearest, Thornberry et al. (1993) found that rates of violence increased when the boys joined the gang and decreased when they left it. Also, gang members had significantly higher rates than non-members typically only during periods of active membership. The same basic pattern was observed for general delinquency, drug use, and drug sales. The only exception was for property crimes where none of the hypothesized models applied: " . . . gang membership seems to have little effect on the frequency of property crimes" (Thornberry et al., 1993, p. 80).

Bjerregaard and Lizotte (1995) also used data from the Rochester project to examine the impact of gang membership on patterns of gun ownership among members of the Rochester Youth Development Study. The analysis focused on later adolescence, roughly ages 16 to 18, and is limited to the male respondents because of the very low rate of gun ownership and use by adolescent females. The study distinguished between the ownership of guns for sporting purposes and for protection or illegal purposes.

Prior to joining a gang, gang members do not have significantly higher rates of protection gun ownership than non-members, nor are they more likely to engage in gun delinquency. Once in a gang, however, the rates of these two behaviors increase, only to fall after they leave the gang. For example, 30.9% of current gang members own a gun for protection as compared to 23.1% of future members and 13.2% of past members. Comparable percentages for gun delinquency are 13.6% versus 2.6% and 0%. These results, as well as multivariate logistic regressions, suggest that while there is a slight elevation in illegal gun involvement prior to membership, there is a substantial increase in involvement during the period of membership. Interestingly, there are no differences across the four groups—non-members, future, current, and past members—in terms of gun ownership for sporting purposes.

Empirical assessments of these competing conceptual models have also been conducted in several other longitudinal studies. Esbensen and Huizinga (1993) used data from the Denver Youth Survey and examined street offending, "serious crimes that occur on the street and are often of concern to citizens and policymakers, alike" (1993, p. 571). They were able to examine the impact of gang membership on behavior over a four-year period. Esbensen and Huizinga report results that are most consistent with the enhancement or mixed model. Involvement in street offending is considerably higher during periods of gang membership, than before or after. Nevertheless, gang members have a generally higher prevalence of street offending than the non-gang members, with some evidence of escalation in the year immediately prior to joining. Similar patterns were observed for serious offenses and illicit drug use, as well as when individual offending rates, instead of prevalence rates, are used as the indicator of delinquent involvement. Overall, in the Denver data there is some evidence of selection processes since prior delinquency is a risk factor for gang membership, but there is a stronger facilitation effect since the highest delinquency rates for the Denver gang members were observed during periods of active membership.

Hill et al. (1996) present data from the Seattle Social Development Project that are also generally consistent with the facilitation model. For gang members, violent delinquency is only slightly elevated in the year prior to active membership but once the adolescent joins the gang, violence increases substantially. After leaving the gang, rates of violence return to baseline. Interestingly, a somewhat different pattern is observed for drug sales in the Seattle sample. Involvement in drug sales increases substantially when adolescents become gang members but it remains high even after the individual leaves the gang. The latter pattern is not consistent with a selection model but it does suggest that the facilitative process of the gang may have contemporaneous effects for some behaviors, e.g., violence, and both contemporaneous and lagged effects for others, e.g., drug sales.

Zhang, Welte, and Wieczorek (1999) examined these issues in a set of regression models using data from the first two waves of the Buffalo Longitudinal Survey of Young Men. Support for the selection model was somewhat mixed: prior delinquency was related to gang membership but prior drug use was not. For both behaviors there is some support for the facilitation model, however. Current gang members report marginally higher levels of delinquency than non-members (p < .055) and significantly higher levels of drug use. Zhang et al. (1999) also found an interesting interaction between current gang membership and delinquency: "current gang membership had a relatively stronger effect on delinquency for youths who were classified in the low level of prior delinquency" (Zhang et al., 1999, p. 9). A similar interaction effect was observed for drug use. Thus, in the Buffalo data, the gang has a stronger impact on delinquency and drug use for those without a history of engaging in these behaviors as compared to those who had already initiated the behaviors.

Several analyses of this issue have been conducted using data from the Montreal Longitudinal and Experimental Study, an entirely French-speaking sample selected from low SES areas of Montreal (Tremblay, Vitaro, Nagin, Pagani, & Seguin, 2003). Early results were reported by Thornberry (1998) and Gatti, Vitaro, Tremblay, and McDuff (2002), but the fullest assessment is presented by Gatti et al. (2005). They examined the facilitation and selection effects at ages 14, 15, and 16 for four offense types—person offenses, property offenses, drug use, and drug sales—and for transient versus stable gang members.

For crimes against the person and for property crimes, the facilitation model appears to describe the behavior of the transient gang members while the enhancement model appears to describe the behavior of the stable gang members. The facilitative impact of the gang on property crimes in this Canadian sample differs from that found in Thornberry et al. (1993). Patterns of drug use and drug sales are somewhat less distinct in the Montreal sample. There is a tendency for the level of drug involvement to increase with the onset of gang membership. For example, in all of the six available comparisons (Gatti et al., 2005) drug sales and drug use increase during the first year of gang membership as compared to the prior year. Drug involvement remains high after periods of active membership, however, a finding similar to that reported by Hill et al. (1996).

Gatti et al. (2005) also examined the impact of current gang membership on a measure of total delinquency after they controlled for seven major risk factors for gang membership and delinquency, as well as current levels of delinquent friends. At all three ages current gang membership exerted a strong and significant impact on delinquency. Gatti et al. conclude that:

> The higher delinquency rates among gang members are largely linked to the experience of the gang itself, rather than to the social deficiencies that characterize its members, and that the apparent effect exerted by the gang is specific and goes beyond simply having delinquent friends.

Gordon et al. (2004) used data from the Pittsburgh Youth Study to examine these issues. They found stronger support for a selection effect than most of the other longitudinal studies. But even for this sample there are noticeable facilitation effects: " . . . we replicate prior findings of a substantial increase in drug selling, drug use, violent delinquency and property delinquency when boys are active gang members" (p. 78). They also report that these forms of delinquency decline after the boys leave the gang. Overall, the pattern of the Pittsburgh results is most consistent with an enhancement model.

The first European study using longitudinal data to examine these issues was conducted by Bendixen, Endresen, and Olweus (2006) using a sample from Bergen, Norway (see Olweus, 1993, for a general description). Bendixen et al. (2006) analyzed general antisocial behavior and violence at three time periods covering ages 13 to 16. They also examined the extent to which gang effects differed by gender.

For general antisocial behavior, which covered relatively minor acts of delinquency that focused on theft and vandalism, the Norwegian data are most consistent with the enhancement model. There are moderate-sized selection effects since gang members have higher rates of antisocial behavior than non-members prior to joining the gang. There are also moderate-sized facilitation effects as antisocial behavior for gang members is highest during periods of active membership. In all comparisons, antisocial behavior increases in the year of joining

SECTION VII: Crime and Victimization

a gang and decreases the year after leaving the gang (Bendixen et al., 2006). For violent delinquency, Bendixen et al. (2006) report a small selection effect and a large facilitation effect.

The size of the gang facilitation effect can be seen in Figure 30.1 reprinted from Bendixen et al. (2006). There is relatively little change in either general delinquency or violence from one time period to the next for the non-members. For the gang members however, there are substantial changes evident as a function of membership status. When an adolescent joined a gang, delinquency and violence increased substantially; when an adolescent left a gang, these behaviors declined substantially.

In the cross-time models just summarized, Bendixen et al. (2006) also included a time-by-sex interaction term. In general, the facilitative effect of gang membership on behavior was stronger for boys than for girls.

More Recent Investigations

Following these initial investigations, researchers have begun to use more sophisticated analytic strategies to see if the facilitation effect generally noted in those studies holds up under closer

Figure 30.1 The Impact of Joining and Leaving a Gang on (a) General Delinquency and (b) Violent Delinquency; Bergen, Norway Study

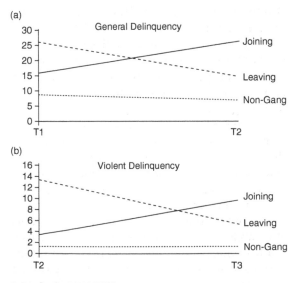

Source: Bendixen et al. (2006)

scrutiny. Thornberry et al. (2003) provide a more comprehensive investigation of these issues than in their original analysis (Thornberry et al., 1993). First, they examined the interplay of gang membership and delinquency across four, instead of three, years. Second, they held six major risk factors for delinquency, including prior delinquency, constant in multivariate models. Finally, they estimated a random effects model, which also included the six risk factors, to control for unmeasured population heterogeneity. All of these analyses suggest a strong facilitation effect and a rather modest selection effect:

> Net of the impact of family poverty, parental supervision, commitment to school, association with delinquent peers, negative life events, prior deviance, and unobserved population heterogeneity, [current gang membership is] statistically significant in predicting general delinquency, violence, drug use, and drug sales in all equations.

Hall, Thornberry, and Lizotte (2006) used the Rochester data to examine whether the impact of gang membership varies by level of neighborhood social disorganization. That is, does gang membership have a greater effect on delinquent behaviors for youth residing in areas with below-average levels of disorganization or for youth residing in more highly disorganized areas?

Given the lack of prior research on this question, Hall et al. (2006) point out that any of three models is possible. First, the gang facilitation effect could be greater in disorganized areas because of the lower levels of social control and protective factors in those areas. Second, the effect could be greater in more organized areas because youth from these areas are exposed to fewer risk factors in general so the impact of the gang may be more pronounced. Third, the potency of the gang effect may influence delinquency regardless of the level of area disorganization.

For general delinquency, violent delinquency, drug use, and drug sales, the results clearly supported the third, or null model. Of the 16 gang membership-by-neighborhood interaction terms (4 offense types × 4 years), 12 are not statistically significant and the other four are inconsistent, one supporting the first model and three supporting the second. Hall et al. (2006) conclude: "Overall, gang membership facilitates problem behaviors in both neighborhood contexts and does so at a similar magnitude" (p. 59).

Several studies have used the trajectory models developed by Nagin (1999; Nagin & Land, 1993; see Piquero, 2008 to examine the gang facilitation effect. These models, by tracing different trajectories of behavior over time, allow analysis to focus on relatively homogeneous offending groups thereby providing "a statistical basis to control for persistent unobserved individual differences that predispose individuals to follow a specific trajectory" (Lacourse, Nagin, Tremblay, Vitaro, & Claes, 2003, pp. 185 and 186). Lacourse et al. (2003) used the same Montreal data analyzed by Gatti et al. (2005). In this study, however, they started by identifying developmental trajectories of gang membership over a seven-year period covering ages 11 to 17.[1] Three trajectory groups emerged: adolescents who were never a gang member during this time (74% of the sample); a childhood onset group (13%) where the probability of gang membership was high from 11 to 14 and then dropped off; and, an adolescent onset group (13%) where the probability of gang membership was low at 11 and 12 and then escalated considerably to a peak at ages 15 and 16.

To test the gang facilitation effect they first hypothesized that patterns of violent delinquency should track the gang trajectories. That is exactly what they observed (Lacourse et al., 2003, pp. 190 and 191). For each gang trajectory group, violence is elevated at precisely the ages when gang membership is most prevalent.

Lacourse et al. (2003) then examined whether movement into and out of a gang was associated with increases and decreases in violence as the facilitation model predicts. Importantly, they conducted this analysis within trajectory groups to further control for unobserved heterogeneity. At all ages for all trajectory groups, the results are consistent with the facilitation model: "Transitions into a [gang] are associated with increased violent behaviors, and transition out of a [gang] is associated with decreased violent behaviors" (Lacourse et al., 2003, p. 193). For the trajectory group with childhood onset there is some evidence of a

selection effect and Lacourse et al. (2003) conclude that the enhancement model is most descriptive of their behavior but that the facilitation model is most descriptive of those who join gangs in adolescence.

In an interesting analytic reversal, Hill, Chung, Guo, and Hawkins (2002) first estimated trajectories of violent behavior from ages 13 to 18 and then examined whether gang membership facilitates violence within trajectory groups. They identified four groups characterized by different patterns of violence: non-offenders, desistors, late escalators, and chronics. They then entered gang membership as a time-varying covariate to see if, within trajectory groups, violence changed as a function of active gang membership. For the three offending trajectories, but not the non-offending group, violence increased when the youth joined the gang and decreased when they left the gang. This held at all time points and for both transient and stable members.

The facilitative effect of gang membership was stronger for the desistor and late escalator groups than it was for the chronic offender group. Indeed, in the year(s) they were active members, the members of the first two groups have rates of violent delinquency that were as high as those of the chronic offender group. In the other years, their non-active years, they were considerably lower.

Haviland and Nagin (2005) present the most sophisticated analysis to date of the selection and facilitation models. In an effort to increase the confidence we can place in causal inferences drawn from longitudinal survey data, they combined two recent advances in statistical modeling. The first is the trajectory method developed by Nagin (1999) that creates groups or classes of adolescents who are relatively homogeneous with respect to violent offending. The second are propensity or balance models (Rosenbaum, 2002; Rosenbaum & Rubin, 1983) that create as much balance as possible on covariates, including lagged measures of the outcome, between those who experience a "treatment" and those who do not. The uniqueness of the Haviland and Nagin (2005) approach is that the balancing scores are applied within the relatively homogeneous trajectory groups to minimize differences on the lagged outcome (and other covariates) between the treated and the untreated. This approach provides a much better approximation of experimental conditions than traditional methods for analyzing longitudinal data.

Haviland and Nagin used the Montreal data (Tremblay et al., 2003) in their investigation. They estimated trajectories of violent delinquency from ages 11 to 13 and then observed the impact of joining a gang at age 14, the "treatment," on subsequent violence. Within trajectory groups there is little if any evidence of selection effects. That is, the gang members do not differ from non-members on prior violence. There is, however, evidence of a facilitation effect in all three trajectory groups; adolescents who join a gang experience significant increases in subsequent violence. Interestingly, "for individuals in the chronic trajectory, who were already heavily engaged in violent delinquency, the point estimate for the increase is more than twice as large as that for low and declining trajectories" (Haviland & Nagin, 2005, p. 14). This is the opposite interaction to that reported by Zhang et al. (1999) and by Hill et al. (2002).

Summary

Since Thornberry et al. (1993) introduced the gang facilitation model, several longitudinal studies have examined it. They have used different data sets covering different sites, time periods, and countries, different measures of gang membership, different analytic strategies, and samples with different characteristics. Despite these differences, the uniformity of results is impressive.

First, there is no evidence that is supportive of a pure selection model as suggested by control theories (e.g., Gottfredson & Hirschi, 1990; Hirschi, 1969). That is, no study finds that gang members have uniformly higher rates of delinquency and related problem behaviors as compared to non-members.

Second, all studies find that delinquency varies as a function of gang membership status, a result consistent with a gang facilitation effect. That is, delinquency almost universally increases when adolescents join a gang and the greatest differences between gang members and non-members are observed during the gang members' period of membership. Also, delinquency typically declines after the member leaves the gang, with the exception of drug sales which appears to remain elevated.

Third, some studies (e.g., Esbensen & Huizinga, 1993; Zhang et al., 1999) also find evidence of a selection effect in addition to the facilitation effect. This pattern of results is most consistent with the enhancement or mixed model.

Overall, perhaps the safest conclusion to draw is that there is a minor selection effect, a major facilitation effect, and no evidence consistent with a pure selection model. The weight of the evidence suggests that street gangs do facilitate or elicit increased involvement in delinquency, violence, and drugs. There is no evidence to the contrary and abundant evidence in support of this view. These results greatly expand our understanding of the interplay between street gangs and delinquency, an expansion in knowledge that would not have been possible without longitudinal data on gang members and non-members. . . .

Note

1. Gang membership is based on the responses to the following question: " . . . were you part of a group or a gang that did reprehensible acts." This is the same measure Gatti et al. (2005) and Thornberry (1998) used in their analyses of gang effects in the Montreal data. Although Lacourse et al. (2003) refer to this as "delinquent group membership," to be consistent with the other studies that used this measure we refer to trajectories of gang membership.

References

Akers, R. L. (1998). *Social learning and social structure: A general theory of crime and deviance.* Boston: Northeastern University Press.

Bendixen, M., Endresen, I. M., & Olweus, D. (2006). Joining and leaving gangs: Selection and facilitation effects on self-reported antisocial behaviour in early adolescence. *European Journal of Criminology, 3,* 85–114.

Bjerregaard, B., & Lizotte, A. J. (1995). Gun ownership and gang membership. *The Journal of Criminal Law & Criminology, 86,* 37–58.

Esbensen, F. A., & Huizinga, D. (1993). Gangs, drugs, and delinquency in a survey of urban youth. *Criminology, 34,* 365–390.

Esbensen, F. A., Huizinga, D., & Weiher, A. W. (1993). Gang and non-gang youth: Differences in explanatory factors. *Journal of Contemporary Criminal Justice, 9,* 94–116.

Farrington, D. P., Ohlin, L. E., & Wilson, J. (1986). *Understanding and controlling crime: Toward a new research strategy*. New York: Springer-Verlag.

Gatti, U., Tremblay, R. E., Vitaro, F., & McDuff, P. (2005). Youth gangs, delinquency and drug use: A test of the selection, facilitation, and enhancement hypotheses. *Journal of Child Psychology, 46*, 1178–1190.

Gatti, U., Vitaro, F., Tremblay, R. E., & McDuff, P. (2002). *Youth gangs and violent behavior: Results from the Montreal Longitudinal Experimental Study*. Paper presented at the XV World Meeting of the International Society for Research on Aggression, Montreal, Canada.

Gordon, R. A., Lahey, B. B., Kawai, E., Loeber, R., Stouthamer-Loeher, M., & Farrington, D. P. (2004). Antisocial behavior and youth gang membership: Selection and socialization. *Criminology, 42*, 55–87.

Gottfredson, M. R., & Hirschi, T. (1990). *A general theory of crime*. Stanford: Stanford University Press.

Hall, G. P., Thornberry, T. P., & Lizotte, A. J. (2006). The gang facilitation effect and neighborhood risk: Do gangs have a stronger influence on delinquency in disadvantaged areas? In J. F. Short, Jr. & L. A. Hughes (Eds.), *Studying youth gangs* (pp. 47–61). New York: AltaMira Press.

Haviland, A. M., & Nagin, D. S. (2005). Causal inferences with group based trajectory models. *Psychometrika, 70*, 1–22.

Hill, K. G., Chung, I. J., Guo, J., & Hawkins, J. D. (2002). *The impact of gang membership on adolescent violence trajectories*. Paper presented at the International Society for Research on Aggression, Montreal, Canada.

Hill, K. G., Hawkins, J. D., Catalano, R. F., Kosterman, R., Abbott, R. D., & Edwards, T. (1996, November). *The longitudinal dynamics of gang membership and problem behavior: A replication and extension of the Denver and Rochester gang studies in Seattle*. Paper presented at the annual meeting of the American Society of Criminology, Chicago.

Hirschi, T. (1969). *Causes of delinquency*. Berkeley, CA: University of California Press.

Lacourse, E., Nagin, D., Tremblay, R. E., Vitaro, F., & Claes, M. (2003). Developmental trajectories of boys' delinquent group membership and facilitation of violent behaviors during adolescence. *Development and Psychopathology, 15*, 183–197.

Nagin, D. S. (1999). Analyzing developmental trajectories: A semiparametric, group-based approach. *Psychological Methods, 4*, 139–157.

Nagin, D. S., & Land, K. C. (1993). Age, criminal careers, and population heterogeneity: Specification and estimation of a nonparametric, mixed poisson model. *Criminology, 31*, 327–362.

Olweus, D. (1993). *Bullying at school: What we know and what we can do*. Oxford: Blackwell Publishers.

Piquero, A. R. (2008). Taking stock of developmental trajectories of criminal activity over the life course.

Rosenbaum, P. (2002). *Observational studies* (2nd ed.). New York: Springer-Verlag.

Rosenbaum, P., & Rubin, D. (1983). The central role of the propensity score in observational studies for causal effects. *Biometrika, 70*, 41–55.

Thornberry, T. P. (1998). Membership in youth gangs and involvement in serious and violent offending. In R. Loeber & D. P. Farrington (Eds.), *Serious & violent juvenile offenders: Risk factors and successful interventions* (pp. 147–166). Thousand Oaks, CA: Sage.

Thornberry, T. P., & Krohn, M. D. (2003). *Taking stock of delinquency: An overview of findings from contemporary longitudinal studies*. New York: Kluwer Academic/Plenum Publishers.

Thornberry, T. P., Krohn, M. D., Lizotte, A. J., & Chard-Wierschem, D. (1993). The role of juvenile gangs in facilitating delinquent behavior. *Journal of Research in Crime and Delinquency, 30*, 55–87.

Thornberry, T. P., Krohn, M. D., Lizotte, A. J., Smith, C. A., & Tobin, K. (2003). *Gangs and delinquency in developmental perspective*. New York: Cambridge University Press.

Tremblay, R. E., Vitaro, F., Nagin, D., Pagani, L., & Seguin, J. R. (2003). The Montreal Longitudinal and Experimental Study: Rediscovering the power of descriptions. In T. P. Thornberry & M. D. Krohn (Eds.), *Taking stock of delinquency: An overview of findings from contemporary longitudinal studies* (pp. 205–254). New York: Kluwer Academic/Plenum Publishers.

Zhang, L., Welte, J. W., & Wieczorek, W. F. (1999). Youth gangs, drug use, and delinquency. *Journal of Criminal Justice, 27*, 101–109.

CHAPTER 31

Deviant Youth Groups in 30 Countries: Results from the Second International Self-Report Delinquency Study

Uberto Gatti ▪ Sandrine Haymoz ▪ Hans M. A. Schadee

While the gang–crime association is well established in the United States, comparative results in other countries have historically been lacking. Arising out of the Eurogang project (discussed elsewhere in this book) and using the Eurogang network's definition of "gang" (i.e., deviant youth group, or DYG), this article investigates rates of youth involvement in these groups and corresponding offending rates by using data collected from over 40,000 adolescents in 62 cities across 30 countries. As anticipated, prevalence rates of gang membership and self-reported delinquency rates varied considerably across countries, but an unmistakable pattern emerged overall: membership in these types of groups is positively associated with delinquency, violence, and drug use.

Introduction

One of the most important predictors of juvenile delinquency is belonging to antisocial peer groups and particularly to gangs (Huizinga & Schumann, 2001; Klein, Kerner, Maxson, & Weitekamp, 2001; Lien, 2005; Weerman & Esbensen, 2005).

While youth gangs and their involvement in crime have been studied for over 80 years in the United States, in other countries research began much later. In Europe, the gang phenomenon exists, though the term "gang" is not frequently used (Klein

et al., 2001; Klein & Maxson, 2006). According to Klein, Kerner, Maxson, and Weitekamp (2001), European researchers are reluctant to use the word "gang" because of what they call the "*Eurogang paradox.*" This refers to a stereotyped view that Europeans have of American gangs, which are seen as being highly structured, close-knit, involved almost exclusively in serious crime, prone to using firearms and associated with territorial control and the running of the drug market.

In reality, however, according to Klein et al. (2001), these features, which European researchers regard as being typical of gangs, characterize only a small proportion of American gangs, which are more often loosely structured and similar to delinquent youth groups in Europe. For fear of evoking these stereotyped images, many European researchers avoid using the word "gang," preferring such terms as "troublesome youth group" (Decker & Weerman, 2005; Klein & Maxson, 2006) or "delinquent youth group" (Sharp, Aldridge, & Medina, 2006).

Deviant Youth Groups (DYGs) in the Second International Self-Report Delinquency Study

The analyses presented in this research are based on the second phase of the International Self-Report Delinquency Study (ISRD-2).[1] The first phase was implemented in 1992 in 13 countries, having been set up by the Research and Documentation Centre Wetenschappelijk Onderzoek-en Documentatie Centrum (WODC) of the Dutch Ministry of Justice (Aebi, 2009; Enzmann et al., 2010). The main aims of the ISRD-2 were to analyze differences in the rates of delinquency and victimization of youths between the ages of 12 and 15 years (corresponding to school grades 7, 8, and 9) among industrialized countries, to develop and standardize the methodology of self-reported questionnaires, and to test the generalizability of different theories, such as "self-control theory" and "lifestyle theory" (Enzmann et al., 2010). The survey questions pertaining to delinquency were fairly similar to those used in the "*National Youth Survey*" and the "*Denver Youth Study*" (Aebi, 2009).

The ISRD-2 survey was conducted in 30 countries between November 2005 and February 2007. In order to facilitate intercountry comparisons in the present study, the participating countries were grouped into the six clusters used by Enzmann et al. (2010) in their first publication regarding the ISRD-2. These clusters (which reflect different welfare regimes) are based on the groupings drawn up by Saint-Arnaud and Bernard (2003), to which the categories Eastern/Central European and Latin American have been added. The clusters are therefore: Anglo-Saxon countries: Ireland and United States (the latter represented by four states: Illinois, Massachusetts, New Hampshire, and Texas); Northern European countries: Denmark, Finland, Iceland, Norway, and Sweden; Western European countries: Austria, Belgium, France, Germany, Netherlands, and Switzerland; Mediterranean countries: Cyprus, Italy, Spain, and Portugal; Latin America: Aruba, Dutch Antilles, Suriname, and Venezuela; and Eastern and Central European countries: Armenia, Bosnia–Herzegovina, Czech Republic, Estonia, Hungary, Lithuania, Poland, Russia, and Slovenia. The ISRD-2 questionnaire is a revised version of the one administered during the first phase of the investigation; in response to an increased interest in the gang phenomenon and growing concern in European countries, new questions drawn up by the Eurogang network[2] with regard to this issue have been inserted.

Most participating countries constructed an urban sample based on a minimum of five cities/towns, while some countries[3] used national samples selected randomly from registers of all the classes in the country, with oversampling in at least one city, where 700 school pupils were interviewed. With regard to urban samples, it was decided that each sample would include at least 700 students from a large city or metropolitan area (about 500,000 inhabitants), a medium-sized city (120,000 inhabitants plus or minus 20%), and a cluster of small towns (10,000–75,000 inhabitants). However, it should be borne in mind that the urban samples (in those countries which adopted this sampling approach) are not representative of the nation as a whole but rather of the cities considered (Enzmann et al., 2010).

The samples used in this survey comprise a minimum of 2,100 7th-, 8th-, and 9th-grade students per country. It should, however, be pointed out that, in some countries, some of these grades were not considered,[4] while in others, students from higher grades were also included.[5]

In the present study, in order to facilitate comparisons among the countries, two selections were carried out: we took into consideration only 7th-, 8th-, and 9th-grade students and only classes from medium-sized towns (120,000 inhabitants plus or minus 20%) and large cities (about 500,000 inhabitants). Our total sample therefore comprises 40,678 students from 62 cities in 30 countries.

Another methodological difference between the countries concerns the method of data collection. In most countries, "pencil-and-paper" questionnaires were administered and were filled in by hand, while computers were used for data collection in some countries (Aebi, 2009). However, according to a rigorous study conducted in Switzerland, the method of data collection, whether it would be hand-written or electronic, does not significantly influence the results (Killias, 1989; Lucia, Herrmann, & Killias, 2007).

With the aim of analyzing the gang phenomenon, we adopted the definition drawn up by the Eurogang network, which facilitates the organization of very interesting comparative analyses of the relationship between juvenile delinquency and group membership in different social and cultural contexts. This definition is as follows: "*any durable street-oriented youth group whose involvement in illegal activity is part of their group identity*" (Klein et al., 2001). In our study, the notion of "durability" is taken to mean more than 3 months; the notion of "street-oriented" implies that the group spends a lot of time in public places, such as parks, streets, and shopping malls; the notion of "youth" refers to adolescents and young people; "illegal" refers to delinquent or criminal activities, and the term "identity" means the group identity, rather than the individual identity, of its members (Klein & Maxson, 2006). It must, however, be stressed that the Eurogang definition excludes the gangs that form in prisons, biker gangs, terrorist groups, drug cartels, and criminal organizations. We preferred the definition proposed by the Eurogang network to the self-designation, or self-nomination that is used in the United States as an indicator to identify gang members (Curry, Decker, & Egley, 2002; Esbensen, Winfree, He, & Taylor, 2001). Indeed, in the United States, simply answering such questions as *Do you belong to a gang?* or *Have you been a member of a gang in the past?* is often regarded as a "particularly robust measure of gang membership capable of distinguishing gang from nongang youth" (Esbensen et al., 2001, p. 124). Nevertheless, in the light of the results of several empirical studies (Haymoz, 2010; Sharp et al., 2006), this indicator is not considered valid in Europe.

The lack of clarity and the ambiguity of the term "gang" in the perception of the youths themselves were ascertained in the present study. Indeed, we noted that, among youths who considered their group to be a gang, about half (56%) stated that their group did not indulge in illegal activities and claimed that their group did not consider such activities acceptable (53%). According to the data yielded by our questionnaire, even in the United States 19% of those youths who consider their group to be a gang state that its members do not commit illegal acts, and 29% claim that committing crimes is regarded as unacceptable by their group. Thus, in some of the countries, a good percentage of respondents use the term "gang" merely to indicate a group of friends and without any particular antisocial connotation.

For this reason and also because the term of "gang" is evocative and bound to stereotyped images, we prefer to use the expression "deviant youth group" (DYG) instead of the term "gang." Therefore, in the remainder of our analysis, we will consider those subjects who provided affirmative

answers to the following six questions proposed by the Eurogang network to be "deviant youth group members" (DYGm):

- Do you have a group of friends?
- How long has this group existed? (>3 months)
- Does this group spend a lot of time together in public places?
- Is doing illegal things accepted by your group?
- Do people in your group actually do illegal things together?
- Do you consider your group to be a gang?

Having analyzed the frequency of the answers to these questions and having identified DYGm, we will evaluate the relationship between DYG membership and antisocial behaviors in the overall sample and in the 30 countries concerned.

Characteristics and Identification of DYGm

To better assess the meaning of the replies to the questions drawn up by the Eurogang network, we first recorded the frequency of affirmative answers in the 30 countries (Table 31.1). It should be pointed out that all the percentages shown in the table refer to the whole sample and not only to those who have a group of friends.

Most of the youths surveyed stated that they belonged to a stable peer group, which had existed for more than 3 months. Half of the respondents indicated that they spent a lot of time together in public places. The acceptance or commission of illegal acts proved to be less frequent: nevertheless, 17% (for acceptance) and 20% (for commission) replied affirmatively to these questions. Almost 15% of the youths considered their group to be a gang. The answers to all the questions differed markedly from one country to another (see minimum and maximum numbers of affirmative replies in Table 31.1); interestingly, all of the highest percentages were found in Ireland.

Table 31.1 Percentages of Youths Who Replied Affirmatively to the Questions Relating to the Eurogang Definition (N = 40,678)

	Mean	Maximum	Minimum
Do you have a group of friends?	75.6	94.5 (Ireland)	61.4 (Armenia)
How long has this group existed? (>3 months)	69.1	88.5 (Ireland)	51.5 (Suriname)
Does this group spend a lot of time together in public places?	49.7	80.4 (Ireland)	34.1 (Suriname)
Is doing illegal things accepted by your group?	19.5	41.7 (Ireland)	5.7 (Venezuela)
Do people in your group actually do illegal things together?	17.1	38 (Ireland)	4.2 (Bosnia/Herz)
Do you consider your group a gang?	14.7	44.2 (Ireland)	1.5 (Armenia)

Table 31.2 Prevalance Rate (%) of Deviant Youth Group Membership by Gender, Grade, Immigration, and Family Composition (N = 40,678)

	Percentage
Gender*	
Male	5.9
Female	3.0
Family*	
Complete	4.1
Noncomplete	5.1
Grade*	
Grade 7	3.5
Grade 8	4.1
Grade 9	5.4
Immigration*	
Native	4.0
First-generation migrant	4.6
Second-generation migrant	5.8

Note. *All differences significant at $p < .000$.

The percentage of youths who responded affirmatively to all six questions, and who can therefore be regarded as DYGm, proved to be 4.4% of the overall sample. Table 31.2 reports the demographic features of those youths who belong to a DYG. Significantly more boys than girls belong to a DYG. Indeed, 5.9% of males in our sample are DYG members compared with 3% of females. Female membership was nevertheless considerable, given that in our sample a third of DYG members were girls. This figure is similar to that seen in an investigation carried out in the United States by Bjerregaard and Smith (1993)

who found that girls accounted for about 30% of the gang members in their sample, while Esbensen and Huizinga (1993) observed that female gang membership varied from 20% to 46%, according to age. These figures have led researchers to believe that female gang membership has always been markedly underestimated (Hunt & Joe-Laidler, 2001). Indeed, two studies, one conducted in England and one in Russia, found that males and females were equally likely to be members of delinquent youth groups (Salagaev, Shashkin, Sherbakova, & Touriyansky, 2005; Sharp et al., 2006).

DYG membership has been seen to increase slightly as school grades increase, from 3.5% in the 7th grade to 5.4% in the 9th grade. Likewise, migrants, especially those of the second generation, were more frequently found to be DYG members. In addition, 5.1% of youths living in noncomplete families (not with both biological parents) were DYG members compared with 4.1% among youth in complete families. However, it should be stressed that these differences, albeit statistically significant, were only weakly so.

DYGs and Offending Behavior

For the purposes of the present study, we considered the respondents' answers to questions regarding 12 crimes—6 property offences (shoplifting, theft of a bicycle, moped, scooter, motorbike or car, theft from a car, breaking into a building with intent to steal, and selling drugs) and 6 violent offences (assault, robbery, bag-snatching, vandalism, carrying a weapon, and group fighting)—in addition to drug and alcohol use.

Table 31.3 shows the percentages of young people who reported committing at least one crime (delinquency), at least one violent crime (violence), at least three different types of crime (versatility) in the previous 12 months, and the percentages of those using alcohol and marijuana/hashish in the previous 4 weeks among DYG members and nonmembers. As can be seen, all of the behaviors considered are far more common among DYG members. With regard to delinquency, the greatest differences concern versatility, which can be considered an indicator of the seriousness of involvement in antisocial activities; with regard to the use of alcohol and marijuana/hashish, the greatest differences concern the latter substance.

Having ascertained that the prevalence of DYG membership is higher among males, slightly older subjects and those from noncomplete and immigrant families (the differences with regard to these last two features being slight, albeit significant), we investigated whether the differences in antisocial behavior between DYG members and nonmembers persisted after controlling for these demographic variables. To this end, we conducted five regressions with DYG and controls in each regression as independent variables; the dependent variables were delinquency, violence, versatility, alcohol, and marijuana/hashish use (see Table 31.4).

The odds ratio (OR) measures the (multiplicative) effects of different variables. The DYG membership has by far the largest effect of all variables considered. We note that no interactions between variables were considered in this regression and that values of 1 for the OR are neutral in their effect. A complete family protects to some extent

Table 31.3 Prevalence Rate (%) of Delinquency, Violence, Versatility (Last Year), Alcohol, and Marijuana–Hashish Use (Last Month) by Deviant Youth Group (DYG) Membership

	DYG Member (N = 1,720)	Nonmember (N = 38,899)	Total (N = 40,678)
Delinquency (one or more offences)	71.5	20.0	22.3
Violence (one or more violent offences)	57.3	14.5	16.3
Versatility (three or more different offences)	36.8	3.6	5.1
Alcohol use	63.1	26.0	25.4
Marijuana-hashish use	20.6	2.9	3.6

Table 31.4 Effect of Deviant Youth Group Membership on Delinquency, Violence, Versatility (Last Year), Alcohol, and Hashish Use (Last Month; N = 40,678, Logistic Regression)

	Delinquency (One or More Offences)	Violence (One or More Violent Offences)	Versatility (Three or More Different Offences)	Alcohol Use	Marijuana-Hashish Use
Odds ratio					
Deviant youth group membership	9.10**	7.12**	13.41**	4.93**	7.64**
Gender (male)	2.34**	2.91**	3.28**	1.08**	1.60**
Grades 7 to 9	1.22**	1.16**	1.17**	1.82**	2.01**
Complete family	.68**	.71**	.63**	.75**	.59**
Migration (first or second generation)	1.14**	1.13**	1.15*	.70**	1.04 n.s.
Nagelkerke R^2	.13	.13	.18	.11	.12

Note: The confidence interval of the odds ratio (OR) can be approximated by [.9 × OR – 1.1 × OR] n.s. = nonsignificant.
*$p \leq .001$.
**$p \leq .000$.

against the participation in these deviant or at risk activities (between 0.59 for use of hashish to 0.75 for alcohol use; conversely, an incomplete family increases the risk). Migration increases the relative frequency of offences somewhat (OR about 1.15), diminishes alcohol use, and has no effect on hashish use. As grade increases, the relative frequency of committing one or more offences increases (OR increases about 1.2 for each additional grade [year], and between 1.8 and 2.0 for substance use.). Males are more at risk than females for offences (from 2.3 to 3.3 increase in OR), but the effect of gender on alcohol use is limited (and the OR for use of hashish = 1.6 for males). But all these effects are relatively small when compared with the effect of membership in a DYG. For alcohol use, the OR is near 5.0, and for hashish use 7.5; this is similar to the OR for violent behavior, which increases to 9.1 for delinquency and reaches an overall height of 13.4 for three or more different offences. The control variables included with respect to such values represent relatively small effects and do not greatly influence the estimates of ORs without these controls.

For all these OR, the standard errors are about a tenth of the effect, so they are not given separately in the table.

DYGs in an International Perspective

As we have seen, DYGm accounted for 4.4% of the youths in the whole sample. This percentage, however, varies markedly from country to country: from a minimum of 0.4% in Armenia to a maximum of 16.8% in Ireland. Figure 31.1 shows the percentages of DYGm present in the cities of various countries. The horizontal lines in the figures subdivide the countries on the basis of the above-mentioned clusters (Anglo-Saxon countries, Northern European countries, Western European countries, Mediterranean countries, Latin American countries, and Eastern and Central European countries). Within each cluster, the countries are arranged in descending order of the prevalence of DYG membership.

The highest values can be seen in the Anglo-Saxon countries (8.7%). However, this is due exclusively to the extremely high prevalence of DYG members in Ireland; indeed, in the United States, the prevalence is fairly low. Prevalence rates proved to be somewhat high in Western European cities (5.6%), with the exception of Austria and the Netherlands, which display below-average values. The lowest values were recorded in the cluster of Latin American cities (2.5%). Low values can also be seen in the cluster of Central and Eastern European countries (3.2%), except for Hungary, Slovenia, and Estonia, where prevalence rates are high. The Mediterranean countries (4.1%) fall within, or below, the average values, while those of Northern Europe, though displaying the same prevalence levels (4.1%) as the Mediterranean, vary greatly from one to another (from a minimum of 0.7% in Iceland to a maximum of 6.8% in Sweden). In general, the prevalence rates of DYG membership are somewhat heterogeneous within various clusters; this would seem to indicate that the classification criteria of the clusters, which are based on various welfare regimes, do not constitute elements that can predict the prevalence of DYG.

After recording the prevalence of DYG membership in the cities of various countries, we made an intercountry comparison in order to verify the association between DYG membership and delinquency and alcohol and marijuana/hashish use in various contexts. The aim here was to ascertain whether the criminogenic effect of the DYG varies from country to country, and if so, to what extent. Although many researchers have examined the features and behaviors of DYG members, such studies have not systematically involved a large number of countries; moreover, they have utilized very diverse methods and parameters. It therefore seems opportune to investigate, by means of the same instrument of analysis, whether the DYG effect is present only in certain contexts or whether there is a constant and systematic association between such groups and antisocial behaviors. . . .

Numerous studies, especially in the United States, have documented higher rates of offending among gang members. As asserted by Battin-Pearson, Thornberry, Hawkins, and Krohn (1998, p. 1), "Gang membership intensifies delinquent behaviour. From the earliest to the most recent investigations, criminologists have consistently found that, when compared with youth who do

Figure 31.1 Prevalence rate (%) of Deviant Youth Group Members, by Country

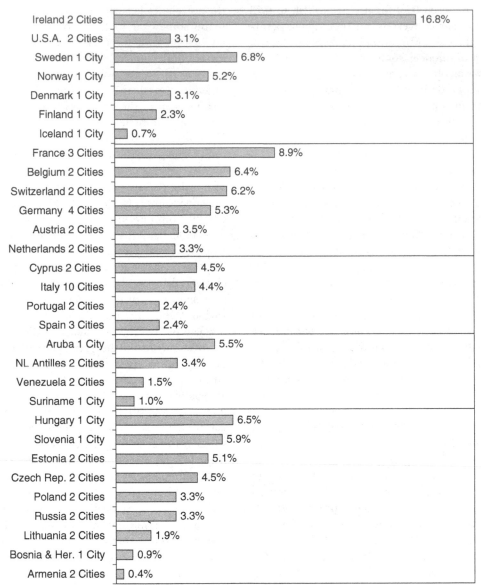

not belong to gangs, gang members are far more involved in delinquency, especially serious and violent delinquency." In all 30 of the countries that we considered, the prevalence rates of antisocial behaviors were significantly higher among DYG members than among nonmembers ($p < .05$). . . .

On the total sample, the ratio of DYG members to nonmembers offending is 3.6:1. In general, the ratios are fairly homogeneous (Pearson's correlation coefficient being .44, $p < .05$, two-tailed), and in most of the countries, the prevalence of delinquency is 3–4 times higher among DYG members than among nonmembers. A somewhat anomalous pattern emerges both in Ireland, where the relatively low ratio is due to the very high prevalence of delinquency among nonmembers, and in Spain, Armenia, and Iceland, where, as already mentioned, all DYG members reported committing at least one offence, while delinquency among nonmembers displays intermediate values. In Venezuela and Portugal, fairly high values among DYG members are accompanied by particularly low values among nonmembers. . . .

For [violent] offences, the values are lower than those of general delinquency; however, the ratio of offending DYG members to nonmembers in the whole sample (4:1) is slightly higher than for general delinquency.

The differences between DYGm and nonmembers proved to be significant in all countries ($p <$ .05), the correlation coefficient being similar to that seen for general delinquency (Pearson's correlation coefficient being .42, $p <$ .05, two-tailed). . . .

Most of the countries [indicate] a ratio of offending DYG members to nonmembers between 3:1 and 4.5:1. Higher ratios are to be seen in Iceland (9.6:1), Spain (6.6:1), Venezuela (6.4:1), and Slovenia (6:1). In Ireland, the ratio is particularly low (2.7:1), owing to the high frequency of violence among non-DYG members; thus, in this country, violence is not particularly closely linked to the DYG effect but is widespread throughout the young population.

The effect of belonging to a deviant group is particularly strong with regard to versatility (involvement in at least three different types of offence in the last 12 months), which we considered an indicator of the gravity of delinquent behavior.

In this case, the ratio of offending DYG members to nonmembers is 10:1 and shows that the criminogenic effect of the deviant group is much stronger with regard to serious delinquency than to situations of lesser gravity. The correlation coefficient for versatility (Pearson's correlation coefficient being .45, $p <$ .05, two-tailed) proved to be similar to the two previous coefficients. With regard to versatility, the scales . . . differ greatly: the scale referring to DYGm ranges from a minimum of 17.9 in Poland to 75 in Iceland; the scale referring to nonmembers displays far lower values, ranging from 1.5 (Lithuania, Venezuela, and Cyprus) to 9.1 in Ireland. The prevalence ratio of DYG members to nonmembers is particularly high in Venezuela (37.1:1), Bosnia-Herzegovina (26.3:1), and Portugal (23.8:1), while in Ireland (5.1) and Denmark (5.9), it is well below the average.

We subsequently analyzed the effect of belonging to a DYG on the consumption of beer, wine, or spirits within the last 4 weeks. It is acknowledged that the consumption of alcoholic beverages among minors, while not illegal in many countries, nevertheless constitutes an indicator of antisocial behavior and is statistically correlated with delinquency. Indeed, several researchers have reported that the link between gang membership and alcohol use, though less extensively studied than the link with drug use, constitutes a serious social problem; moreover, according to recent data, it is a problem that involves both males and females. In particular, binge drinking is more frequent among DYG members, as is initiation to alcohol use at an early age; indeed, in a recent study conducted on a population of students in the United States, 50.9% of DYG members reported having started drinking before the age of 13 years, while the figure among nonmembers was 22% (Swahn, Bossarte, West, & Topalli, 2010). Other authors have focused on the relationship between alcohol and violence among DYG members; these studies have shown that, in certain ethnic contexts, the use of alcohol acts as a kind of "social glue," helping to maintain group cohesion and to assert masculinity and male togetherness (Hunt & Joe-Laidler, 2001).

In our sample, too, the use of alcohol was associated with DYG membership, though the DYG effect proved to be less evident than in the behavioral categories examined above; in the total sample, the prevalence ratio of DYG members to nonmembers is 2.7:1, which, while indicative of a considerable and significant difference, is lower than the ratios recorded for delinquency, violence, and versatility.

Over the range of countries, the correlation between alcohol use and DYG membership is fairly high (Pearson's correlation coefficient being .54, $p <$ .01, two-tailed), the differences between members and nonmembers being significant in all countries except for Suriname, where belonging to a deviant group does not seem to influence alcohol use. The consumption of alcohol differs markedly, however, among various countries, as a result of cultural factors; among DYG members, the lowest prevalence is seen in France (29.6%) and the highest in Hungary (95.6%), while among nonmembers, the minimum and maximum values are 7.6% and 54.8%

in Iceland and Estonia, respectively. Rather surprisingly, alcohol consumption proved to be fairly limited in France, while in Estonia, the majority of youths, whether DYG members or not, reported drinking alcoholic beverages in the last 4 weeks. Despite the cultural differences and the different prevalence of alcohol consumption among young people, the DYG effect is seen to be fairly constant and quite homogeneous, though it appears to be particularly strong in Iceland, Bosnia-Herzegovina, and Portugal and somewhat modest in Estonia and Denmark.

. . . Several studies, especially in the United States, have revealed that young people who belong to DYGs are particularly likely to be involved in the use and sale of drugs (Battin-Pearson, Thornberry, Hawkins, & Krohn, 1998; Howell & Decker, 1999). Drug pushing chiefly concerns small-scale selling since control of the illegal drug market is in the hands of adult crime syndicates (Howell & Decker, 1999). According to Bjerregaard (2010), the use and sale of drugs by DYG members are therefore merely a manifestation of a general involvement in illegal activities of various kinds, rather than the expression of a veritable criminal organization.

According to our research data, the DYG effect on the use of marijuana/hashish appears to be particularly strong and homogeneous across the countries (the use of other drugs, such as ecstasy, heroin, cocaine, etc., also emerged and was again more frequent among DYG members; however, the extremely infrequent use of these substances did not allow us to make meaningful statistical analyses for all countries). The correlation coefficient between marijuana/hashish use and DYG membership is particularly high (Pearson's correlation coefficient being .85, $p < .001$, two-tailed).

The prevalence rates of marijuana/hashish use differ markedly between DYG members and nonmembers: 20.6 among the former versus 2.9 among the latter, with a ratio of 7.1:1 in the whole sample. Marijuana/hashish use among young people throughout the world therefore seems to be strongly conditioned by membership of a deviant group. The use of marijuana/hashish is particularly common among students in the United States and Spain. In the cities of five countries (Armenia, Poland, Portugal, Bosnia-Herzegovina,

and Finland), no significant differences emerged between DYG members and nonmembers, a finding that seems to be linked to the scant use of this substance by young people in these countries. In all the other countries, the differences proved significant ($p < .05$) and were particularly great in Iceland, Venezuela, Slovenia, the Dutch Antilles, and Norway, where a very low rate of marijuana/hashish use among nonmembers is coupled with a considerable use among DYGm.

Discussion

Our international investigation was made possible by the collaboration of 30 research teams. Supported by a committee coordinated by the criminologist Josine Junger-Tas, these teams drew up a single questionaire, which was then translated into numerous languages, and implemented it in such a way that the sample analyzed would be representative of the students in various countries, or at least, where it was not possible to construct a representative national sample of the students in a few cities situated in those countries. A volume describing the method adopted and the objectives of the study, and providing several national reports, has already been published (Junger-Tas et al., 2010), and a second volume dealing with comparative analyses of various issues is currently being prepared. The results of a first comparison of juvenile delinquency in the cities of the 30 countries considered have appeared in an article (Enzmann et al., 2010), which represents an investigative model and the beginning of what will be a long series of transversal analyses of specific issues.

It is important to underline the fact that the samples analyzed in our study are not representative of each country as a whole but only of a few cities. Our comparisons regard large- and medium-sized cities in 30 countries; we cannot therefore compare the different countries or draw up rank order lists. Another limitation of the present research is the fact that the samples were made up of students and not of all youths present in a given environment. This may give rise to some distortion; indeed, while in some countries all, or almost all, young people in the age groups considered attend school, in other, less organized countries, a certain percentage of subjects of obligatory school age do not actually attend school.

Our study investigated the phenomenon of DYGs, which are generally defined in the United States as "youth gangs." In line with European practice, we preferred not to use the term "gang," both because it is associated, albeit erroneously, with stereotyped images of armed, violent groups who control territorial areas, and because, as we have seen, it is used by many of the youths themselves simply to indicate a group of friends, without any antisocial connotation.

The prevalence of what we have called DYGm varies among the countries considered, ranging from less than 1% to more than 16%. The DYGm are found in Europe, the United States, and Latin America, and it is interesting that, although the frequency of DYG membership varies from one country to another, the effect that belonging to such groups has on antisocial behavior is observable, and indeed quite similar, in various environments investigated. The greatest impact is to be seen with regard to the more serious forms of delinquency, particularly, the versatility of delinquent behaviors; the effect is also much stronger with respect to marijuana/hashish use than alcohol use. Although we have used the term "effect," our data, which are of a cross-sectional nature, do not enable us to determine whether the higher level of delinquency precedes or follows entry into the group, whereby those youths who are already more delinquent are induced to join a deviant group (selection model), or whether a facilitation process is operating, whereby the group exerts a criminogenic effect (facilitation model). However, the results of longitudinal studies that have dealt with this issue (Gatti, Tremblay, Vitaro, & McDuff, 2005; Gordon et al., 2004; Thornberry, Krohn, Lizotte, Smith, & Tobin, 2002) suggest that both the processes are involved (enhancement model), but that the facilitation process often plays a greater role than the selection process.

The phenomenon of what we have defined as DYGs, which in other contexts are called gangs, is strictly relevant to our understanding of juvenile delinquency worldwide and must be taken into account in the planning of social and preventive intervention. The data from the ISRD-2 enable us

to confirm, for the first time, the importance of the relationship between DYG membership and various types of antisocial behavior in extremely different sociocultural environments. Moreover, they reveal that, to a great extent and in all environments, juvenile delinquency is an expression of specific group phenomena. The subject of youth gangs, which has been studied for many decades in the United States but for only a few years in Europe, is now becoming a focus of interesting comparative investigations at the international level, such as that conducted by Covey (2010) on the peculiar social and cultural aspects of gangs in five continents, and that of van Gemert, Peterson, and Lien (2008), who analyzed the issue of street gangs in relation to the growing phenomenon of migration in Europe and the United States. Nevertheless, the Second International Self-Report Delinquency study is the only investigation that has analyzed the phenomenon of DYGs in an extremely broad and diverse international setting and, above all, through a single instrument and a single method of investigation, which were the result of long and fruitful international collaboration.

Declaration of Conflicting Interests

The authors declared no potential conflicts of interest with respect to the research, authorship, and/or publication of this article.

Funding

The authors received no financial support for the research, authorship, and/or publication of this article.

Notes

1. The self-report method for measuring crime and delinquency of gang members is valid according to the research carried out by Webb, Katz, and Decker (2006). Indeed, they examined the self-report rates of recent drug use by gang members in comparison with their urinalysis outcomes, and they found that the disclosure rates of drug use by gang members did not differ significantly from those of nonmembers.
2. The Eurogang network, set up on the initiative of the criminologist Malcolm W. Klein, consists of leading

European and American researchers in the field. They are now working together to develop a common framework for comparative research based on standardized methodological instruments and a common research design. The Eurogang website is based on the webserver of the University of Missouri–St. Louis, http://www.umsl.edu/~ccj/eurogang/euroganghome.htm.

3. France, Portugal, Spain, Switzerland, the Czech Republic, Estonia, Hungary, Bosnia-Herzegovina, Aruba, Dutch Antilles, and Suriname.

4. In Iceland, only 8th-grade students were interviewed; in Poland, only 8th- and 9th-grade; in Slovenia, only 7th- and 9th-grade; in Bosnia-Herzegovina, only 7th- and 8th-grade students were interviewed.

5. Italy, Spain, and Poland.

References

Aebi, M. (2009). *Enquètes de délinquance autoreportée en Europe [Assessing deviance, crime and prevention in Europe].* Flémal: Communauté Européenne sur les presses de l'imprimerie.

Battin-Pearson, S. R., Thornberry, T. P., Hawkins, J. D., & Krohn, M. D. (1998, October). *Gang membership, delinquent peers, and delinquent behavior.* Washington, DC: Office of Juvenile Justice and Delinquency Prevention.

Bjerregaard, B. (2010). Gang membership and drug involvement: Untangling the complex relationship. *Crime Delinquency, 56,* 3–34.

Bjerregaard, B., & Smith C. (1993). Gender differences in gang participation, delinquency, and substance use. *Journal of Quantitative Criminology, 9,* 329–355.

Covey, R. (2010). *Street gangs throughout the world.* Springfield, IL: Charles C Thomas.

Curry, G. D., Decker, S. H., & Egley, A., Jr. (2002). Gang involvement and delinquency in a middle school population. *Justice Quarterly, 19,* 275–292.

Decker, S. H., & Weerman, F. M. (2005). *European street gangs and troublesome youth groups.* Lanham, MD: AltaMira.

Enzmann, D., Marshall, I. H., Killias, M., Junger-Tas, J., Steketee, M., & Gruszczynaka, B. (2010). Self-reported youth delinquency in Europe and beyond: First results of the Second International Self-Report Delinquency Study in the context of police and victimization data. *European Journal of Criminology, 7,* 159–183.

Esbensen, F. A., & Huizinga, D. (1993). Gangs, drugs, and delinquency in a survey of urban youth. *Criminology, 31,* 565–589.

Esbensen, F. A., Winfree, L. T., He, N., & Taylor, T. J. (2001). Youth gangs and definitional issues: When is a gang a gang, and why does it matter? *Crime and Delinquency, 47,* 105–130.

Gatti, U., Tremblay, R. E., Vitaro, F., & McDuff, P. (2005) Youth gangs, delinquency and drug use: A test of the selection, facilitation, and enhancement hypotheses. *Journal of Child Psychology and Psychiatry, 46,* 1178–1190.

Gordon, R. A., Lahey, B. B., Kawai, E., Loeber, R., Stouthamer-Loeber, M., & Farrington, D. P. (2004). Antisocial behavior and youth gang membership: Selection and socialization. *Criminology, 42,* 55–88.

Haymoz, S. (2010). *Les gangs en Suisse: délinquance, victimisation et facteurs de risques.* (Unpublished doctoral dissertation). University of Lausanne: Lausanne.

Howell, J. C., & Decker, S. H. (1999, January). *The youth gangs, drugs, and violence connection.* U.S. Department of Justice Programs, Office of Juvenile Justice and Delinquency Prevention. Washington, DC: USA.

Huizinga, D., & Schumann, K. F. (2001). Gang membership in Bremen and Denver. Comparative longitudinal data. In M. W. Klein, H.-J. Kerner, C. L. Maxson, & E. G. M. Weitekamp (Eds.), *The Eurogang paradox* (pp. 231–246). Dordrecht, Netherlands: Kluwer Academic.

Hunt, G., & Joe-Laidler, K. (2001). Situations of violence in the lives of girl gang members. *Health Care for Women International, 22,* 363–384.

Junger-Tas, J., Marshall, I. H., Enzmann, D., Killias, M., Steketee, M., & Gruszczynaka, B. (Eds.). (2010). *Juvenile delinquency in Europe and beyond: Results of the Second International Self-Report Delinquency Study (ISRD2).* Berlin: Springer.

Killias, M. (1989). *Les Suisses face au crime: Leurs expériences at attitudes à la lumière des sondages suisses de victimisation.* Grüach: Rüegger.

Klein, M. W., Kerner, H.-J., Maxson, C. L., & Weitekamp, E. G. M. (2001). *The Eurogang paradox.* Dordrecht, Netherlands: Kluwer Academic.

Klein, M. W., & Maxson, C. L. (2006). *Street gang patterns and policies.* Oxford, UK: Oxford University Press.

Lien, I.-L. (2005). Criminal gangs and their connections. In S. H. Decker & F. M. Weerman (Eds.), *European street gangs and troublesome youth groups* (pp. 31–50). Lanham, MD: AltaMira.

Lucia, S., Herrmann, L., & Killias, M. (2007). How important are interview methods and questionnaire designs in research on self-reported juvenile delinquency? An experimental comparison of Internet vs. paper-and-pencil questionnaires and different definitions of the reference period. *Journal of Experimental Criminology, 3,* 39–64.

Saint-Arnaud, S., & Bernard, P. (2003). Convergence or resilience? A hierarchical cluster analysis of the welfare regimes in advanced countries. *Current Sociology, 51,* 499–527.

Salagaev, A., Shashkin, A., Sherbakova, I., & Touriyansky, E. (2005). Contemporary Russian gangs: History, membership, and crime involvement. In S. H. Decker & F. M. Weerman (Eds.), *European street gangs and troublesome youth groups* (pp. 169–191). Lanham, MD: AltaMira.

Sharp, C., Aldridge, J., & Medina, J. (2006). *Delinquent youth groups and offending behaviour: Findings from the 2004 Offending Crime and Justice Survey.* London, England: Home Office Research Development and Statistics Directorate.

Swahn, M. H., Bossarte, R. M., West, B., & Topalli, V. (2010). Alcohol and drug use among gang members: Experiences of adolescents who attend school. *Journal of School Health, 80,* 353–360.

Thornberry, T. P., Krohn, M. D., Lizotte, A. J., Smith, C. A., & Tobin, K. (2002). *The toll of gang membership: Gangs and delinquency in developmental perspective.* New York, NY: Cambridge University Press.

Van Gemert, F., Peterson, D., & Lien, I.-L. (2008). *Street gangs, migration and ethnicity.* Portland, OR: Willan.

Webb, V. J., Katz, C. M., & Decker, S. H. (2006). Assessing the validity of self-reports by gang members: Results from the Arrestee Drug Abuse Monitoring Program. *Crime & Delinquency, 52,* 232–252.

Weerman, F. M., & Esbensen, F.-A. (2005). A cross-national comparison of youth gangs. In S. H. Decker & F. M. Weerman (Eds.), *European street gangs and troublesome youth groups* (pp. 219–255). Lanham, MD: AltaMira.

CHAPTER 32

The Boulevard Ain't Safe for Your Kids . . . [1]: Youth Gang Membership and Violent Victimization

Terrance J. Taylor

The link between gangs and crime, as well as criminal offending and victimization, has been firmly established in the research literature. Curiously, scholarly attention to the link between gang involvement and victimization has lagged behind considerably (but see Miller in Section V). In recent years, however, research has begun to carefully unravel the relationship between criminal victimization—in particular, violent victimization—and gang membership. Taylor's summary of the research findings to date underscores the paradox of gang involvement and victimization: youth's victimization experiences often motivate them to join a gang (e.g., for protection); however, once in the gang, the likelihood of being violently victimized increases substantially. Importantly, the reader should note the incongruity between what youth anticipate the gang will provide and entail versus what it actually does, and how this distinction has important implications for prevention and intervention efforts.

R ecent research has begun to examine the link between youth gang membership and violent victimization. Although studies of victimization in this area are sparse relative to those examining the link between gang membership and offending, the recent expansion to include victimization may be viewed as a promising development for a number of reasons. First, gang members'

Reprinted from: Terrance J. Taylor, "The Boulevard Ain't Safe for Your Kids . . . : Youth Gang Membership and Violent Victimization," *Journal of Contemporary Criminal Justice*, 24(2): 125–136. Copyright © 2008 by Sage Publications. Reprinted by permission of Sage Publications.

victimization has typically been hidden from public view or at least muted relative to their offending behaviors. Consequently, an entire group of victims have been virtually ignored, diminishing the impact of potentially life-changing experiences among a group of youths who disproportionately come into contact with the juvenile and adult justice systems. Second, youths who join gangs often report doing so for protection. Is this warranted? Do gangs reduce youths' victimization? Or do gangs actually enhance youths' victimization? Answers have real consequences for youths' future life chances.

The current essay looks at the research examining youth gang membership and violent victimization. . . . Three specific questions are examined. First, what does the extant research show regarding the linkage between gang membership and violent victimization? In other words, what do we know about the relationships between these phenomena? The essay is grouped into three sections, consistent with stages of gang membership: (a) victimization of gang members prior to their gang entry, (b) victimization during their time in the gang, and (c) victimization associated with gang exit and postgang membership. Second, what implications does this line of research have for practice (e.g., prevention and intervention programs)? We do have some knowledge on this topic, but what should we do? Specific policy recommendations are made in each section after the coverage of what we already know. Third, what questions remain unanswered? In other words, where do we go from here?

What Do We Know about the Gang Membership–Violent Victimization Link?

One early examination of the relationship between gang membership and victimization was conducted by Savitz, Rosen, and Lalli (1980). Their surveys of approximately 1,000 Philadelphia boys found no statistically significant differences between gang and nongang youths in terms of fear of victimization or actual victimization experiences. Since that time, research has consistently demonstrated the increased risk of victimization—particularly violent victimization—of gang members relative to their nongang peers. Results from a 1995 cross-sectional study of 8th grade public school students in 11 U.S. cities (Taylor, Peterson, Esbensen, & Freng, 2007) highlight the relationships between gang membership and victimization. Gang members were found to be significantly more likely to be violently victimized during the past year, as well as to experience significantly more annual victimizations, than nongang youths for several types of violence. Substantively, the differences have been found to be quite large. For example, 70% of gang youths reported being the victim of general violence (assault, aggravated assault, and/or robbery), compared to 46% of nongang youths. Although most of the general violent victimization consisted of assaults (60% of gang members, 43% of nongang youths), differences in serious violent victimization (i.e., aggravated assault and/or robbery) were even more pronounced. During the past year, 44% of gang youths reported being victims of serious violence, with 38% of gang members reporting one or more aggravated assaults and 21% reporting one or more robberies during this time. Corresponding figures for nongang members were 12% for any type of serious violent victimization, 8% for aggravated assault, and 7% for robbery. Gang members who were victims also experienced significantly more violent victimization incidents (4.9 assaults, 3.8 aggravated, 4.1 robberies) than did nongang members who were victims (3.4 assaults, 2.7 aggravated assaults, 2.4 robberies) during the prior year.

An interesting pattern to note involves the relationship between gang membership, sex, and violent victimization. Using data from the same cross-sectional study of 8th grade youths, Peterson, Taylor, and Esbensen (2003) found that for each type of victimization (except robbery), gang males had the highest annual prevalence, followed by gang females (nongang males for robbery), then nongang males (nongang females for robbery), and then nongang females. Note that gang girls were more likely to report having been victimized than nongang boys for assault and aggravated assault. Gang member homicides, however, primarily remain the domain of males (Howell, 1999; Maxson, 1999; Maxson, Curry, & Howell, 2002; Rosenfeld, Bray, & Egley, 1999).

Finally, youths' "affiliation" with gangs appears to increase the risk of experiencing violent victimization, even if they are not gang members themselves. Limited information is available concerning the extent to which being heavily "embedded" in the gang (i.e., being a "core" member) insulates or enhances victimization, although Curry, Decker, and Egley's (2002) study of middle school youths found that simply being associated with gangs enhanced violent victimization. Although self-reported gang members were the most likely to report being threatened with a gun, shot at with a gun, and/or injured by a gunshot, the percentage of "gang affiliated" youths who reported experiencing these things were much higher than youths who reported no gang involvement whatsoever.

Victimization Prior to Gang Membership

Youths often report joining gangs for protection. For example, a 5-year longitudinal panel study of adolescents in seven U.S. cities found that 28% to 57% of self-identified gang youths indicated that they joined their gangs for protection (Peterson, Taylor, & Esbensen, 2004). These percentages varied by the year of the survey/age of the respondents, with the lowest percentage reported among youths who joined gangs at the end of the study (when the average age was 16), and the highest reported during the third year (interestingly, the year most of the youths entered high school). From what are youths looking for protection?

Ethnographic studies on girl gang members provide some insight into this issue. Such studies have often found that girls join gangs to escape violently abusive home environments. For example, Miller's (2001) interviews with gang and nongang girls in Columbus, Ohio, and St. Louis, Missouri, found that gang girls were significantly more likely to have witnessed and personally experienced physical and sexual violence in their homes. Many of the gang girls stated that they had begun associating with gang members in their neighborhoods—and eventually becoming gang members themselves—after spending more time away from home to escape the violence.

From what are boys looking for protection? The answer to that question is more elusive. To date, this issue has received little attention. We are left with the following question: Are male gang members looking for protection from violent home environments, similar to those reported by girls? Or are boys looking to escape other types of victimization, such as from peers or community residents? Clearly, however, the answer is not that girls experience more violent victimization than boys, as official records (such as the Uniform Crime Reports), victimization surveys (such as the National Crime Victimization Survey), and surveys/interviews are quite consistent: Most forms of violent victimization (such as assault, aggravated assault, robbery, and homicide) are more common for young males than for young females. These sources also clearly illustrate that violent sexual offenses are more common for young females than for young males.

The answers to these questions are not only of interest to researchers—the recent increase in gender-specific programming information could benefit from it, as well. If boys and girls are joining gangs to escape similar forms of violence, more generalized prevention programs targeting the issue may be sufficient. However, if girls and boys are seeking protection from gangs for different forms of victimization, gender-specific prevention programming is vital. At this point, however, we do not know enough about sex differences in violent victimization prior to gang joining to definitively answer these questions.

Victimization Once in the Gang

Many studies have documented the violence associated with gangs. Gangs can be a haven for violence.

Decker (1996), for example, has suggested that gangs provide a "normative context" for violence, and despite gang members' statements that they joined gangs for protection, research findings generally illustrate that such wishes are not granted. Indeed, it appears that violent victimization actually increases once youths join gangs.

Peterson and colleagues (2004) examined this issue by comparing youths' self-reported victimization prior to joining a gang, when youths reported that they were in gangs, and after youths exited their gangs. Of import here is the finding that violent victimization was highest for gang youths (both males and females) in the year following their entry into the gang, that is, violent victimization was more likely to occur and occurred more frequently after youths joined their gang than prior to their gang membership.

Ethnographic studies have detailed the victimization experiences of gang members. Findings from these studies suggest that gang members may be at greatest risk of violence from members of their own gang. Members may be required to participate in violent initiation rituals when entering a gang. For example, approximately two thirds of the gang members in Decker and Van Winkle's (1996) ethnographic study of St. Louis gang members reported being "beat in" as part of their initiation process. Although the process varied from gang to gang, interviewees often recounted a process whereby prospective members were expected to fight against several current gang members, who were arranged in a line or a circle. Gang members may also be subjected to harsh discipline from members of their own gangs for violating gang rules. Padilla's (1995) research on one gang organized on drug sales uncovered the use of violence by the gang to sanction members for violations of collective rules, referred to as "Vs." The process Padilla outlined is similar to one Decker and Van Winkle describe, under which violators are expected to walk through a line of other gang members who take turns beating the transgressor. Although gang members may not perceive these experiences as violent victimization, gang members' accounts of these processes, however, leave little doubt that they must be classified as such.

Gang members may also become the victim of predatory offending by others. Previous research has found, for example, that gang members are more likely than nonmembers to be involved in drug-selling activities (Esbensen & Winfree, 1998; Howell & Decker, 1999; Howell & Gleason, 1999; Huff, 1998; Maxson, 1995) and possession of weapons (Bjerregaard & Lizotte, 1995; Blumstein, 1995), which may make them potential targets of robbers because of their reluctance to report victimizations to authorities (Jacobs, 2000).[2] In addition, gang members may become the targets of retaliation from rival gangs. Sanders' (1994) interviews with San Diego gang members, for example, found that drive-by shootings of other gang members were generally condoned, but shooting at "innocents" was generally prohibited. Indeed, gang members continue to be at increased risk relative to nongang members for homicide victimization (Howell, 1999; Maxson, 1999; Maxson et al., 2002; Rosenfeld et al., 1999).

What about sex differences in violent victimization of gang members? Research has generally highlighted the increased violent victimization risk of both male and female gang members while they are in their gangs. One issue which remains controversial, however, is whether the types of violent victimization differ for boys and girls when they are in their gangs, that is, research findings provide mixed support as to whether violent victimization experiences of male and female gang members are qualitatively similar or different. For example, are boys and girls both seeking protection from abusive home environments or are boys seeking protection from violent peers? Sexual victimization is perhaps the most controversial. Although many early ethnographic accounts of girls' role in gangs often portrayed them as "sex objects" to be used for male gang members' amusement, recent studies have begun to call this into question (see Miller, 2002a, for a review). For example, male gang members often describe initiation of female gang members as a process of being "sexed in"—that is, being required to have sex with multiple male gang members. Interviews with female gang members report that such experiences are rare and that female gang members who enter the gang in this way are generally accorded lower status within their gangs (Miller, 2001; Miller & Brunson, 2000).

Miller's work (1998, 2001, 2002b; Miller & Brunson, 2000; Miller & Decker, 2001) has also highlighted the ways in which gender serves to protect young women in gangs. Specifically, the "maleness" of gang norms leads to different experiences for boys and girls while they are in gangs. Female gang members often view themselves as integral parts of the gang, whereas male gang members are more likely to view girls as being peripheral members. This may enhance females' risk of victimization within their gang, such as from sexual exploitation by male gang members (see also Fleisher, 1998). It may, however, simultaneously reduce their risk from serious victimization outside the gang because female members may be excluded from some of the "highest risk" gang activities. Specifically, relative to male gang members, female gang members, to some extent, may be shielded from retaliatory attacks by members of rival gangs.

Victimization on Exiting the Gang

Contrary to media depictions, gang membership is a transitory state, that is, the old adage that "once you're in a gang, you're in for life" is typically untrue. For example, findings from longitudinal panel studies of adolescents in high-risk neighborhoods such as the Denver Youth Survey (Esbensen & Huizinga, 1993), Rochester Youth Development Study (Thornberry, Krohn, Lizotte, Smith, & Tobin, 2003), Seattle Social Development Study (Battin, Hill, Abbott, Catalano, & Hawkins, 1998), and public school students such as the National Evaluation of the Gang Resistance Education and Training (GREAT) program (Peterson et al., 2004) have found that the duration of gang membership typically lasts 1 year or less for both boys and girls. This is an important point, because it illustrates that gang members are not "lost causes" destined to experience a lifetime of increased violent victimization because they are forever embedded in their gangs.

In some cases, however, violent victimization is synonymous with gang exit. The most striking examples are homicide victimizations. By definition, homicide victimization results in the end of the gang experience (see Howell, 1999; Maxson, 1999; Maxson et al., 2002, for extensive reviews). More common, however, are instances where youths willingly exit gangs through a process of "aging out" (Klein, 1971) or "fading out" (Skolnick, 1988 [as cited in Decker & Lauritsen, 2002, p. 52]) by withdrawing from gang activities over a period of time once ties with other social institutions, such as jobs and family, are established. Interestingly, violent victimization of gang members themselves or of friends and/or family members was found to be the primary reason why St. Louis gang members exited their gangs (Decker & Lauritsen, 2002).

As Decker and Lauritsen (2002) point out, times directly following a serious violent experience for gang members, their friends, and/or family members may be a window of opportunity for intervention. Highlighting the victimization costs associated with gang membership at this point in time will provide concrete examples when they are fresh in the minds of youths. Conceptually, it seems that this would be an ideal time to reach these youths and to provide victim assistance services.

Tying It All Together: Potential Explanations for the Gang Membership–Victimization Link

Perhaps it is not surprising that gang members have been found to be at increased risk of victimization relative to their nongang peers. Lifestyle (Hindelang, Gottfredson, & Garofalo, 1978) and routine activities (Cohen & Felson, 1979; Cohen, Klugel, & Land, 1981) and perspectives suggest that this is to be expected. Gang members may be viewed as suitable targets lacking capable guardianship for serious violent victimization but who often have extensive interactions with motivated offenders. Exposure and proximity to high-risk situations abound. Involvement in delinquency and violence is more common among gang members than among their nongang peers.

Findings from two recent studies conducted by Taylor and colleagues (Taylor, Freng, Esbensen, & Peterson, 2008; Taylor, Peterson, Esbensen, & Freng, 2007) suggest that the routine activities and

lifestyles of gang members do, indeed, substantially explain the gang membership–victimization link. Gang membership was found to be associated with a slight decrease in the likelihood that youths experienced overall violent victimization, but this was primarily due to reductions in assault. Perhaps more important, gang members were found to be at greater likelihood of being the victims of serious violence (i.e., aggravated assault and robbery) than nongang members, once individual, family, and peer factors were taken into account, but gang victims were not found to experience any different levels of serious violent victimization than nongang victims in the presence of other factors, that is, the increased victimization risk for serious violent victimization found for gang members relative to their nongang peers was due primarily to gang members being more likely than other youths to engage in unsupervised hanging out with peers, to hang out where drugs and/or alcohol are available, and to engage in a substantially greater amount of delinquent behavior.

What does this mean for prevention and intervention? Prevention programs need to provide a realistic assessment of the increased likelihood of serious violent victimization associated with gang membership. For intervention programs, it seems clear that gang-involved youths' delinquent lifestyles need to be addressed, in addition to their gang membership. Specifically, getting youths to stop claiming gang affiliation may be an important step forward, because it could decrease the situations where youths are unsupervised, have drugs and/or alcohol readily available, and/or are involved in high levels of delinquent behavior. For real change to occur, however, getting youths out of these lifestyles—regardless of whether they are associated with gang membership—is critically important.

On a positive note, programs aimed at reducing delinquent activities should also result in reductions in serious violent victimization (and vice versa). This is not surprising, given the robust findings linking delinquency and victimization (Esbensen & Huizinga, 1991; Lauritsen, Sampson, & Laub, 1991; Loeber, Kalb, & Huizinga, 2001; Sampson & Lauritsen, 1990; Shaffer & Ruback, 2002; Zhang, Welte, & Wieczorek, 2001).

Where Do We Go from Here? Future Directions

Although we have gained substantial knowledge about the gang membership–violent victimization link, much remains unanswered. I will briefly highlight two points that seem to be particularly important: (a) community/regional differences and (b) differences between gang types.

Information from law enforcement agencies collected by the National Youth Gang Center (NYGC) documented an increase in the number of gangs and gang members throughout the country between 1980 and the mid-1990s, with numbers stabilizing or decreasing between the mid-1990s and early 2000s. Interestingly, the NYGC also documented the susceptibility of smaller locales to changes in larger cities' gang problems during this time, that is, when gang problems were increasing in larger cities, smaller communities also reported dramatic increases in gang problems; conversely, when gang problems in larger cities stabilized, smaller locales also reported stabilization or decreases (Egley, Howell, & Major, 2004). According to the most recent NYGC estimates (NYGC, 2007), there appears to be an increase in gangs. What this means for youth victimization remains to be seen, but it should be monitored closely.

One issue closely tied to this is gang member victimization in different types of gangs. Maxson and Klein (1995) developed a typology of five different types of gangs: (a) traditional (characterized by a long duration, a large number and wide age range of members, distinct subgroups, and a strong territorial orientation), (b) neotraditional (characterized by a duration of 10 years or less, medium-to-large in size, distinct subgroups, and a strong territorial orientation), (c) compressed (characterized by a short history, few members generally around the same age, with no subgroups), (d) collective (characterized by a duration of 10–15 years, medium-to-large number of members varying in age, with no subgroups), and (e) specialty (characterized by a duration of less than 10 years, small in size and similar in age composition, with a narrow criminal focus and territoriality related to this focus). Recent studies have illustrated the emergence of new types of "hybrid" gangs, which vary in function and form from previous gang types (Starbuck, Howell, & Lindquist, 2001).

How gang types influence gang members' violent victimization is difficult to assess at this point. One recent study of Arizona arrestees, for example, found that increased organization of gangs was moderately associated with gang members' violent victimization at the bivariate level (Decker, Katz, & Webb, 2008). In addition, Miller's work (1998, 2001, 2002b; Miller & Brunson, 2000; Miller & Decker, 2001) has illustrated key differences in gang members' victimization across gangs with different sex compositions. Given the differences in composition, structure, and focus, it will be important to continue to examine how gang members' victimization varies across gang types.

Conclusion

The current essay summarized the literature examining gang membership and victimization risk. Given the link between gang membership and violent victimization, it is important that gang members be viewed not only as offenders by criminal justice practitioners and researchers. Violent victimization is intertwined with gang membership before, during, and after youths are gang-involved.

I began with an examination of the literature examining gang members' victimization prior to joining their gangs. Findings from extant research suggest that youths' victimization experiences can increase the likelihood of their joining gangs. For example, girl gang members frequently report that they became affiliated with gangs to escape other types of abuse, such as that occurring within the family. This finding suggests that programs to reduce childhood abuse and family violence are likely to be critical for preventing adolescent victimization and gang membership because such efforts will reduce the motivations that girls have for joining gangs. Few studies have examined whether the same is true for male gang members, although youths of both sexes often report joining gangs for protection. Regardless of the initial source of the threat (i.e., family or other youth in the neighborhood or school), sources of protection other than gangs are needed to reduce victimization in the lives of these youth.

Next, victimization during the time youths are in the gang was examined. Once in the gang, youths appear to be at increased risk of violent victimization, relative to their nongang peers. These findings are in stark contrast to youths' desire to reduce victimization through their gang affiliations. It is worth noting, however, that the source of such victimization appears to be qualitatively different from that experienced prior to youths' gang membership. Although victimization preceding gang membership often comes from sources outside the gang, other gang members are often the ones inflicting the victimization once youths become involved with gangs. Violence involving group conflict is especially dangerous, and interventions designed to break cycles of retaliatory violence on the street are notoriously difficult to design.

Finally, this essay examined violent victimization associated with gang exit. Media depictions of gang membership have often painted a grim picture of youths' inability to escape the gang lifestyle for fear of violent victimization on exit. Extant research calls this into question. Although some youths are killed before getting out of gangs, gang membership appears to be a transitory state for youth gang members. Youths can successfully transition out of their gang membership status, and well-timed interventions can help with this process.

Notes

1. Quote taken from Method Man on the song "Rumble" (U-God, 1999, track 7).
2. Although weapons may be viewed as providing protection (thus reducing victimization risk), they may also be viewed as "valuable goods" attracting the attention of potential offenders (thus increasing victimization risk).

References

Battin, S. R., Hill, K. G., Abbott, R. D., Catalano, R. F., & Hawkins, J. D. (1998). The contribution of gang membership to delinquency beyond delinquent friends. *Criminology, 36*, 93–115.

Bjerregaard, B., & Lizotte, A. J. (1995). Gun ownership and gang membership. *Journal of Criminal Law and Criminology, 86*, 37–58.

Blumstein, A. (1995). Youth violence, guns, and the illicit-drug industry. *Journal of Criminal Law and Criminology, 86*, 10–36.

Cohen, L. E., & Felson, M. (1979). Social change and crime rate trends: A routine activity approach. *American Sociological Review, 44*, 588–608

Cohen, L. E., Kluegel, J. R., & Land, K. C. (1981). Social inequality and predatory criminal victimization: An exposition and test of a formal theory. *American Sociological Review, 46*, 505–524.

Curry, G. D., Decker, S. H., & Egley, A., Jr. (2002). Gang involvement and delinquency in a middle school population. *Justice Quarterly, 19*, 275–292.

Decker, S. H. (1996). Collective and normative features of gang violence. *Justice Quarterly, 13*, 243–264.

Decker, S. H., Katz, C. M., & Webb. V. J. (2008). Understanding the black box of gang organization. *Crime & Delinquency, 54*, 153–172.

Decker, S. H., & Lauritsen, J. L. (2002). Leaving the gang. In C. R. Huff (Ed.), *Gangs in America III* (pp. 51–67). Thousand Oaks, CA: Sage.

Decker, S. H., & Van Winkle, B. (1996). *Life in the gang: Family, friends, & violence*. New York: Cambridge University Press.

Egley, A., Howell, J. C., & Major, A. K. (2004). Recent patterns of gang problems in the United States: Results from the 1996–2002 National Youth Gang Survey. In F.-A. Esbensen, S. G. Tibbetts, & L. Gaines (Eds.), *American youth gangs at the millennium* (pp. 90–108). Long Grove, IL: Waveland Press.

Esbensen, F. A., & Huizinga, D. (1991). Juvenile victimization and delinquency. *Youth & Society, 23*, 202–228.

Esbensen, F. A., & Huizinga, D. (1993). Gangs, drugs, and delinquency in a survey of urban youth. *Criminology, 31*, 565–589.

Esbensen, F. A., & Winfree, L. T., Jr. (1998). Race and gender differences between gang and non-gang youth: Results from a multi-site survey. *Justice Quarterly, 15*, 505–526.

Fleisher, M. S. (1998). *Dead end kids: Gang girls and the boys they know*. Madison, WI: University of Wisconsin Press.

Hindelang, M., Gottfredson, M., & Garofalo, J. (1978). *Victims of personal crime: An empirical foundation for a theory of personal victimization*. Cambridge, MA: Ballinger.

Howell, J. C. (1999). Youth gang homicides: A literature review. *Crime & Delinquency, 45*, 208–241.

Howell, J. C., & Decker, S. H. (1999). *The youth gangs, drugs, and violence connection: OJJDP juvenile justice bulletin*. Washington, DC: U.S. Department of Justice, Office of Justice Programs, Office of Juvenile Justice & Delinquency Prevention.

Howell, J. C., & Gleason, D. K. (1999). *Youth gang drug trafficking: OJJDP juvenile justice bulletin*. Washington, DC: U.S. Department of Justice, Office of Justice Programs, Office of Juvenile Justice & Delinquency Prevention.

Huff, C. R. (1998). *Comparing the criminal behavior of youth gangs and at-risk youths: NIJ research in brief*. Washington, DC: U.S. Department of Justice, Office of Justice Programs, National Institute of Justice.

Jacobs, B. A. (2000). *Robbing drug dealers: Violence beyond the law*. New York: Aldine de Gruyter.

Klein, M. W. (1971). *Street gangs and street workers*. Englewood Cliffs, NJ: Prentice Hall.

Lauritsen, J. L., Sampson, R. J., & Laub. J. H. (1991). The link between offending and victimization among adolescents. *Criminology, 29*, 265–292.

Loeber, R., Kalb, L., & Huizinga, D. (2001). *Juvenile delinquency and serious injury victimization*. OJJDP juvenile justice bulletin. Washington, DC: U.S. Department of Justice, Office of Justice Programs, Office of Juvenile Justice & Delinquency Prevention.

Maxson, C. L. (1995). *Street gangs and drug sales in two suburban cities: NIJ research in brief*. Washington, DC: U.S. Department of Justice, Office of Justice Programs, National Institute of Justice.

Maxson, C. L. (1999). Gang homicide: A review and extension of the literature. In M. D. Smith & M. A. Zahn (Eds.), *Homicide: A sourcebook of social research* (pp. 239–254). Thousand Oaks, CA: Sage.

Maxson, C. L., Curry, G. D., & Howell, J. C. (2002). Youth gang homicides in the 1990s. In W. L. Reed & S. H. Decker (Eds.), *Responding to gangs: Evaluation and research* (pp. 107–137). Washington, DC: U.S. Department of Justice, National Institute of Justice.

Maxson, C. L., & Klein, M. W. (1995). Investigating gang structures. *Journal of Gang Research, 3*, 33–40.

Miller, J. (1998). Gender and victimization risk among young women in gangs. *Journal of Research in Crime and Delinquency, 35*, 429–453.

Miller, J. (2001). *One of the guys: Girls, gangs & gender*. New York: Oxford University Press.

Miller, J. (2002a). The girls in the gang: What we've learned from two decades of research. In C. R. Huff (Ed.), *Gangs in America III* (pp. 175–197). Thousand Oaks, CA: Sage.

Miller, J. (2002b). Young women in street gangs: Risk factors, delinquency, and victimization risk In W. L. Reed & S. H. Decker (Eds.), *Responding to gangs: Evaluation and research* (pp. 67–106). Washington, DC: U.S. Department of Justice, National Institute of Justice.

Miller, J., & Brunson, R. K. (2000). Gender dynamics in youth gangs: A comparison of males' and females' accounts. *Justice Quarterly, 17*, 419–448.

Miller, J., & Decker, S. H. (2001). Young women and gang violence: Gender, street offending, and violent victimization in gangs. *Justice Quarterly, 18*, 115–140.

National Youth Gang Center. (2007). *National Youth Gang Survey Analysis*. Retrieved January 6, 2008, from http://www.iir.com/nygc/nygsa/

Padilla, F. (1995). The working gang. In M. W. Klein, C. L. Maxson, & J. Miller (Eds.), *The modern gang reader* (pp. 53–61). Los Angeles: Roxbury.

Peterson, D., Taylor, T. J., & Esbensen, F. A. (2003). *Gang girls, gang boys, and the victimization dimension*. Paper presented at the Annual Meeting of the Academy of Criminal Justice Sciences, Boston, MA.

Peterson, D., Taylor, T. J., & Esbensen, F. A. (2004). Gang membership and violent victimization. *Justice Quarterly, 21*, 793–815.

Rosenfeld, R., Bray, T. M., & Egley, A. (1999). Facilitating violence: A comparison of gang-motivated, gang-affiliated, and non-gang youth homicides. *Journal of Quantitative Criminology, 15*, 495–516.

Sampson, R. J., & Lauritsen, J. L. (1990). Deviant lifestyles, proximity to crime, and the offender-victim link in personal violence. *Journal of Research in Crime and Delinquency, 27*, 110–139.

Sanders, W. B. (1994). *Gangbangs & drive-bys: Grounded culture & juvenile gang violence*. New York: Aldine de Gruyter.

Savitz, L., Rosen, L., & Lalli, M. (1980). Delinquency and gang membership as related to victimization. *Victimology: An International Journal, 5*, 152–160.

Shaffer, J. N., & Ruback, R. B. (2002). *Violent victimization as a risk factor for violent offending among juveniles*. Washington, DC: U.S. Department of Justice, Office of Justice Programs, Office of Juvenile Justice & Delinquency Prevention. (ERIC Document Reproduction Service No. ED474391)

Starbuck, D., Howell, J. C., & Lindquist, D. J. (2001). *Hybrid and other modern gangs*. Washington, DC: U.S. Department of Justice, Office of Justice Programs, Office of Juvenile Justice & Delinquency Prevention. (NCJ 189916)

Taylor, T. J., Freng, A., Esbensen, F.-A., & Peterson, D. (2008). Youth gang membership and serious violent victimization: The importance of lifestyles/routine activities. *Journal of Interpersonal Violence, 23*, XXX–XXX.

Taylor, T. J., Peterson, D., Esbensen, F.-A., & Freng, A. (2007). Gang membership as a risk factor for adolescent violent victimization. *Journal of Research in Crime and Delinquency, 44,* 351–380.

Thornberry, T. P., Krohn, M. D., Lizotte, A. J., Smith, C. A., & Tobin, K. (2003). *Gangs and delinquency in developmental perspective.* New York: Cambridge University Press.

Zhang, L., Welte, J. W., & Wieczorek, W. F. (2001). Deviant lifestyle and crime victimization. *Journal of Criminal Justice, 29,* 133–143.

Responses to Street Gangs, Programs, and Policies

Over roughly a half century, during which street gangs have increasingly become an issue of concern in the United States, there has been a general shift in dominant responses to gangs. A pattern was established in mid-twentieth-century institutions that favored a welfare approach. Social agencies developed outreach programs to engage gang members in prosocial pursuits while also encouraging local communities to absorb and provide opportunities for gang-oriented youth. Courts and probation departments took a "soft" approach, stressing engagement and rehabilitation over arrest and incarceration. Police departments that recognized gang problems tended to place responsibility for handling them in special juvenile divisions, stressing intelligence functions over enforcement activities.

Over time, these approaches did not seem to be sufficient, as gang problems (especially violence and drug trafficking) increased and political forces became more conservative, embracing a "war" on crime orientation. In terms that became more salient, gang prevention gave way to more intensive gang intervention and criminal justice suppression. Gangs came to be defined less as a community problem and more as a crime problem. One heard less of gang "work" and more of gang "control."

Currently, it is common rhetoric among gang researchers and practitioners alike to speak of the three prongs of gang programs and practices as prevention, intervention, and suppression. Prevention refers to targeting possibly gang-prone youth to discourage them from joining street gangs. Intervention offers various social and alternative opportunities to those who have already joined gangs with a view toward reducing their gang-related activity or inducing them to give up their membership. Suppression refers to criminal justice practices that go beyond normal arrest and punishment. The idea here is to deter gang crime for individual members and thus groups by such mechanisms as special enforcement teams, civil injunctions applied specifically in gang territories, gang "sweeps" by law enforcement task forces, and sentence enhancements for convicted gang members. A recent review of about 60 special programs in gang control (Klein and Maxson 2006, Chapter 8) revealed that they were about equally distributed among prevention, intervention, and suppression emphases, but that all were disproportionately targeted at individual members, not at gangs per se.

Adding to the complexity of this portrayal, Klein and Maxson's (2006) Chapter 7 outlines a set of 13 distinguishable goals of gang control spread out among prevention, intervention, and suppression practices and targeting individual gang members, gangs themselves, or gang-spawning communities. It is no small wonder, then, that gang programming has emerged as terribly complex both to conceptualize and to implement effectively. Each of the programs described in the chapters of this section of the *Modern Gang Reader* lays claim to achieving success in prevention, intervention, or suppression—but note how different are the goals they aim to achieve.

One of the more discouraging aspects of gang control efforts that is not well addressed in these chapters is the distinct possibility that inadequately conceived programs actually make things worse, by, for example, increasing gang recruitment and size, increasing gang cohesiveness, or increasing levels of gang-related crime. There are many ways by which this may occur, including:

- creating a "moral panic" about street gangs in communities;

- labeling excessive numbers of youth as gang members;

- applying practices that reinforce the "oppositional culture" already intrinsic to gang members;

- increasing the interpersonal bonds or cohesiveness among gang members;

- developing practices that are poorly coordinated among the prevention, intervention, and law enforcement agencies and have divergent or even conflicting goals (e.g., the common mistrust and antagonism between gang outreach workers and police gang officers); and

- providing media attention to street gangs that inadvertently makes them more attractive and exciting to potential new members.

In sum, it is worth considering that the damage done by inadequately conceived and implemented gang programs may exceed their promise for reducing gang problems. This potential for "boomerang effects" gives emphasis to the importance of combining street gang programs and practices with adequate scientific evaluations of their implementations and effectiveness. The implementation success is critical. A program model that is not properly implemented in the field or is seriously altered as the program is developed does not allow an evaluation of the model itself, thus negating our chance to assess its value and implement it elsewhere. After watching model programs being altered in action, one highly frustrated academic evaluator coined the acronym MILTFP, 4-1: "Make it like the frigging picture, for once."

As to the demonstrated success of street gang programs—whatever their goals—the aforementioned review by Klein and Maxson makes it clear that pitifully few of the 60 programs they catalogued were accompanied by adequate evaluations. As noted by the editors of the first edition of the *Modern Gang Reader*, "The saddest message of all is simply this; little that has been done can be demonstrated to be useful. Thus, the clues for the future have less to do with what might work, than with avoiding in the future what has not worked" (Klein, Maxson, and Miller, 1995: 249). Yet one can look on the bright side as well: if most efforts have not been adequately evaluated—if it's not yet clear what works and what does not—then many prevention, intervention, and suppression programs may hold promise. We can only know if they *do* hold promise by holding their implementers' feet to the fire, absolutely requiring them to engage in scientific assessments of both implementation and outcome. The reader of Section VIII may well consider how the programs described herein have met that challenge.

CHAPTER 33

Is G.R.E.A.T Effective? Results from the National Evaluation of the Gang Resistance Education and Training (G.R.E.A.T.) Program

Finn-Aage Esbensen ■ Dana Peterson ■ Terrance J. Taylor ■ D. Wayne Osgood

The Gang Resistance Education and Training (G.R.E.A.T.) Program

The Gang Resistance Education and Training (G.R.E.A.T.) program is a gang and delinquency prevention program delivered by law enforcement officers within a school setting. Developed as a local program in 1991 by Phoenix-area law enforcement agencies, the program quickly spread throughout the United States. The original G.R.E.A.T. program operated as a nine-lesson lecture-based curriculum taught primarily in middle-school settings. Results from an earlier National Evaluation of the G.R.E.A.T. program (1995–2001) found that the program had an effect on several mediating variables (factors commonly identified as risk factors) associated with gang membership and delinquency but found no differences between G.R.E.A.T. and non-G.R.E.A.T. youths in terms of these behaviors (i.e., gang membership and involvement in delinquent behavior).

Based in part on these findings, the G.R.E.A.T. program underwent a critical review that resulted in substantial program modifications. The revised

curriculum (see Box A) consists of 13 lessons aimed at teaching youths the life-skills (e.g., communication and refusal skills, as well as conflict resolution and anger management techniques) thought necessary to prevent involvement in gang behavior and delinquency. The revised G.R.E.A.T. curriculum was piloted in 2001, with full-scale implementation occurring in 2003. Currently, the program is taught in middle schools across the country as well as in other countries. In school districts with school-resource officers, the G.R.E.A.T. program is generally taught by the SROs. In other jurisdictions, law enforcement officers deliver the program as part of their assignment in community relations divisions, while elsewhere officers teach the program on an overtime basis. Regardless of officers' assignments, all instructors must complete G.R.E.A.T. Officer Training and be certified prior to their assignment to teach in the local schools. This training (one week for officers with prior teaching experience and two weeks for others), in addition to introducing the officers to the program, includes sections on gang trends, issues associated with the transition from an emphasis on enforcement to one of prevention, middle school student developmental stages, and teaching and classroom management techniques.

The program's two main goals are:

1. To help youths avoid gang membership, violence, and criminal activity.

2. To help youths develop a positive relationship with law enforcement.

Reprinted from: Finn-Aage Esbensen, Dana Peterson, and Terrance J. Taylor, "2009 Report to Schools and Communities: Program Implementation Quality and Preliminary Outcome Results," Finn-Aage Esbensen, Dana Peterson, Terrance J. Taylor, and D. Wayne Osgood, "Is G.R.E.A.T. Effective? Does the Program Prevent Gang Joining? Results from the National Evaluation of G.R.E.A.T," from the National G.R.E.A.T. Evaluation Reports & Publications. Published by the University of Missouri–St. Louis, 2009 and June 2012. Reprinted by permission.

Box A The G.R.E.A.T. Program

1. **Welcome to G.R.E.A.T.**—An introductory lesson designed to provide students with basic knowledge about the connection between gangs, violence, drug abuse, and crime

2. **What's the Real Deal?**—Designed to help students learn ways to analyze information sources and develop realistic beliefs about gangs and violence

3. **It's about Us**—A lesson to help students learn about their communities (e.g., family, school, residential area) and their responsibilities

4. **Where Do We Go from Here?**—Designed to help students learn ways of developing realistic and achievable goals

5. **Decisions, Decisions, Decisions**—A lesson to help students develop decision-making skills

6. **Do You Hear What I Am Saying?**—Designed to help students develop effective verbal and non-verbal communication skills

7. **Walk in Someone Else's Shoes**—A lesson to help students develop active listening and empathy skills, with a particular emphasis on understanding victims of crime and violence

8. **Say It Like You Mean It** – Designed to help students develop effective refusal skills

9. **Getting Along Without Going Along**—A lesson to reinforce and practice the refusal skills learned in Lesson 8

10. **Keeping Your Cool**—A lesson to help students understand signs of anger and ways to manage the emotion

11. **Keeping It Together**—Designed to help students use the anger-management skills learned in Lesson 10 and apply them to interpersonal situations where conflicts and violence are possible

12. **Working It Out**—A lesson to help students develop effective conflict resolution techniques

13. **Looking Back**—Designed to conclude the G.R.E.A.T. program with an emphasis on the importance of conflict resolution skills as a way to avoid gangs and violence; students also present their projects aimed at improving their schools

The National Evaluation of G.R.E.A.T.

In 2006, following a competitive peer review process, the National Institute of Justice awarded the University of Missouri–St. Louis funding to conduct the National Evaluation of the G.R.E.A.T. program. The evaluation consists of both process and outcome components that include student surveys, classroom observations in G.R.E.A.T. and non-G.R.E.A.T. classrooms, surveys of teachers, school administrators, and law enforcement officers, interviews with G.R.E.A.T. officers and G.R.E.A.T. supervisors, and observations of G.R.E.A.T. Officer

Training (G.O.T.). In this report we focus on findings of program effectiveness.

As will be detailed below, we surveyed students attending 31 public middle schools in seven cities across the country. Based upon student responses to multiple waves of questionnaires (pre-test, post-test, and annual follow-up surveys in each of the following four years), we are able to assess short- and long-term program effects. That is, we examine the extent to which students receiving G.R.E.A.T. differ from non-G.R.E.A.T. students in terms of their delinquent activity and gang involvement. Additionally, we examine the extent to which risk factors addressed in the G.R.E.A.T. program also differentiate the G.R.E.A.T. students from the control group.

Study Design

To implement an outcome evaluation of a school-based program that is offered in settings across the United States, it is important to select a sample that will be representative of the diversity of settings in which the overall program operates. Cost and logistics must also be factored into design decisions. Our overall strategy was to include four to six schools in six different cities. By including multiple schools in a single city we would reduce potential bias that could arise from including atypical schools. Having multiple cities in the evaluation would allow for inclusion of geographically diverse areas, different sized cities and school districts, differential levels of gang activity, and a diversity of racial and ethnic groups. Within each participating school, classrooms would be randomly assigned to receive G.R.E.A.T. or to be designated as a control classroom. While apprehension about the random assignment and subsequent exclusion of some classrooms from receiving G.R.E.A.T. was expressed by some principals and teachers, ultimately 31 schools agreed to the design specifics.[1] We now describe the site and school selection process of the evaluation.

Site Selection

During the summer of 2006, efforts were made to identify cities for inclusion in the National Evaluation of G.R.E.A.T. Site selection was based on three main criteria: 1) existence of the G.R.E.A.T. program, 2) geographic and demographic diversity, and 3) evidence of gang activity. This site selection process was carried out in a series of steps. First, the research staff contacted the G.R.E.A.T. Regional Administrators[2] and Bureau of Justice Assistance[3] personnel to identify locales with established programs. Consideration was given to factors such as the length of time the program had been in operation, number of G.R.E.A.T.-trained officers, and the number of schools in which the program was offered. Second, once this list of more than 50 potential agencies was constructed, the research staff contacted representatives in these cities to obtain more information about the delivery of the G.R.E.A.T. program. Third, given the focus of the program,

information about gang activity in these potential cities was obtained from the National Youth Gang Center. Ultimately, we selected seven cities (varying in size, region, and level of gang activity) as our primary target sites. Given the difficulties associated with securing permission to conduct evaluations in many school districts, we were hopeful that six of these seven cities would cooperate.

Once these seven cities were identified, the research staff worked with the primary local law enforcement agency and the school district in each city to seek their cooperation. Much to our surprise, all seven districts agreed to participate. Rather than exclude one of the sites, we decided to expand our design from six to seven cities. These participating cities are: Albuquerque, New Mexico; Chicago, Illinois; Greeley, Colorado; Nashville, Tennessee; Philadelphia, Pennsylvania; Portland, Oregon; and a Dallas–Fort Worth (DFW), Texas, area location. With school district approval, we then identified potential schools for study participation and contacted the principals. Our intent in the selection of schools was to include schools that, taken as a whole, would be representative of the districts. Once initial agreement to participate was obtained from the school administrator, more detailed discussions/meetings were held between school personnel, G.R.E.A.T. officers, and the research team. Whenever possible, face-to-face meetings were held, but in some instances final arrangements were made via telephone. School and police personnel were informed of the purpose of the evaluation, issues related to the random assignment of classrooms to the treatment or control condition (i.e., receive G.R.E.A.T./not receive G.R.E.A.T.), procedures to obtain active parental consent for students in these classrooms, scheduling G.R.E.A.T. program delivery, and other logistical issues associated with the study design.

Effectiveness of G.R.E.A.T.

The evaluation design of this project can best be described as an experimental longitudinal panel design. That is, classrooms in each of the participating schools were randomly assigned to the treatment (i.e., G.R.E.A.T.) or control condition (i.e., no program exposure), and students in these classrooms were scheduled to complete six waves of questionnaires (pre- and post-tests followed by four annual surveys). Thus, the final sample of students would be followed through their school experiences from 6th or 7th grade through 10th or 11th grade. Importantly, all students in the selected classrooms were eligible to participate in the evaluation. A total of 4,905 students were enrolled in the 195 participating classrooms (102 G.R.E.A.T. and 93 control classes) in the 31 middle schools at the beginning of the data collection process.

Active parental consent procedures were implemented in all sites. We worked closely with the principals and classroom teachers during the consent process. Teachers distributed and collected consent form packets. Each packet included a cover letter explaining the purpose of the evaluation as well as an informed consent form (explaining the risks and benefits of the students' participation) for parents/guardians to read, sign, and return to the teacher. When allowed by the districts, the research staff provided monetary compensation to the teachers directly for their assistance. In some instances, district regulations prohibited such compensation; in these cases, compensation was provided as a donation, made in honor of the teachers, to the school or district. Students were also given a small personal radio, calculator, or tote bag in exchange for returning a completed consent form. These rewards were provided to students regardless of whether the parent/guardian granted or withheld consent for the youth to participate in the study. Overall, 89.1 percent of youths ($N = 4,372$) returned a completed consent form, with 77.9 percent of parents/guardians ($N = 3,820$) allowing their child's participation.

Students completed pre-test surveys (prior to implementation of the G.R.E.A.T. program) with a completion rate of 98.3 percent and post-test surveys (shortly after completion of the G.R.E.A.T. program) with a completion rate of 94.6 percent. Students also completed annual follow-up surveys in each of the following four years, with completion rates of 87%, 83%, 75%, and 72%. These rates are quite impressive given the mobility of these students; we surveyed virtually all students still enrolled in schools within the original seven school districts, which meant we surveyed students in more than 200 different schools during each of the last two years of data collection. We obtained permission from principals at these schools to survey the transfer students—clearly, a time and labor intensive effort but one well worth achieving these high response rates.

Student Sample Characteristics

Table 33.1 presents the demographic information of the National Evaluation of G.R.E.A.T. sample for the entire group of youths, as well as separately by site, according to students' responses to the pre-test survey. The sample is evenly split between males and females; most (55%) youths reside with both biological parents; and the majority (88%) was born in the United States. The sample is racially/ethnically diverse, with Hispanic youths (37%), White youths (27%), and African-American (18%) youths accounting for 81 percent of the sample.

Approximately two-thirds of the youths (61%) were aged 11 or younger at the pre-test, representing the fact that 26 of the 31 schools delivered the G.R.E.A.T. program in 6th grade; three of the six Chicago schools and two of four schools in Albuquerque taught G.R.E.A.T. in 7th grade. Thus, the students in Chicago and Albuquerque were somewhat older than students in the other sites. Except in Chicago (in which Hispanics are overrepresented and African Americans under-represented), the sample is similar to the demographic composition of the respective school districts.[4]

Outcome Results

To reiterate, the G.R.E.A.T. program has two primary goals: 1) to help youths avoid gang membership, violence, and criminal activity, and 2) to help youths develop a positive relationship with law enforcement. The curriculum consists of 13 lessons aimed at teaching youths the life-skills (e.g., communication and refusal skills, conflict resolution and anger management techniques) thought necessary to prevent involvement in gangs and delinquency. To assess program effectiveness, we compare responses from students in the G.R.E.A.T. classes to the students in the control classrooms. First, we utilize the pre-test and the one-year follow-up questionnaires; these results, therefore, represent short-term program effects. The student questionnaire contains a number of questions that tap program components, including measures of

Table 33.1 Sample Characteristics at Wave 1, by Percentage

	Full Sample (N = 3,280)	ABQ (N = 591)	POR (N = 486)	DFW area (N = 614)	GRE (N = 582)	NSH (N = 590)	PHL (N = 457)	CHI (N = 500)
Sex								
Male	50	50	42	54	52	55	43	50
Female	50	50	58	46	48	46	57	50
Race/Ethnicity								
White	27	16	51	20	34	45	12	7
African American	18	4	7	21	2	23	44	29
Hispanic/Latino	37	49	13	46	50	17	20	56
American Indian	4	10	4	2	5	1	4	1
Asian	4	2	9	6	1	6	4	1
Multi-Racial	8	14	13	5	4	4	12	2
Other	4	5	3	1	5	5	5	2
Age								
11 or Younger	61	35	79	74	77	80	61	18
12	29	43	20	25	22	19	35	44
13 or Older	10	23	1	2	2	<1	4	38
Mean	11.48	11.87	11.21	11.27	11.23	11.19	11.42	12.22
Living Arrangement								
Both Biological Parents	55	52	58	60	58	60	38	57
Single Parent	20	20	15	15	14	18	24	19
1 Biological/1 Step-Parent	13	15	13	14	15	12	18	12
1 Biological/1 Other Adult	7	7	8	7	7	7	11	7
Other Relatives	3	6	5	3	4	2	8	3
Other Living Arrangement	2	1	1	1	3	2	2	1
Resident Status								
Born outside U.S.	12	10	9	13	11	15	11	15
Born in U.S.	88	90	91	87	89	85	89	85

gang membership, self-reported delinquency, and attitudes toward the police. Additionally the survey includes questions that were drawn from a variety of empirical studies assessing key risk and protective factors associated with youth problem behaviors.

In these analyses we included a subset of seven attitudinal measures and two behavioral measures. The two behavioral measures allow us to assess the extent to which the G.R.E.A.T. program impacts gang membership and involvement in illegal activity. Specifically, we ask the students to indicate whether they are in a gang (this approach has been found in research to be a valid and robust measure) as well as a 15-item self-reported delinquency inventory. To measure positive attitudes to the police, students were asked to respond to six questions tapping attitudes to the police. Additionally, we asked a series of questions measuring the students' attitudes about gangs. These four sets of questions allow us to directly assess the program's main goals.

G.R.E.A.T. was developed as a skills building program that identified a number of mediating risk factors; that is, skills such as conflict resolution, empathy, and resistance skills. We also examined the extent to which students exposed to the G.R.E.A.T. program (relative to those who had not received G.R.E.A.T.) had improved or enhanced skills that would enable them to better resist the lures of gang membership and resist peer pressure to engage in illegal activities. Among these skills are the following: empathy, risk-seeking, conflict resolution skills, resistance to peer pressure, and refusal skills. The G.R.E.A.T. program teaches lessons that directly address these particular skills.

Given the research design (individuals are nested within classrooms and classrooms are nested within schools), hierarchical linear modeling techniques were used to assess program effectiveness. We found statistically significant differences between the treatment (i.e., G.R.E.A.T.) and control students on 14 out of 33 attitudinal and behavioral outcomes. Specifically, the G.R.E.A.T. students compared to non-G.R.E.A.T. students reported:

- More positive attitudes about police (ES = .076)

- More positive attitudes about having police in classrooms (ES = .204)

- Less positive attitudes about gangs (ES = .114)

- More use of refusal skills (ES = .090)

- More resistance to peer pressure (ES = .079)

- Higher collective efficacy (ES = .125)

- Less use of hitting neutralizations (ES = .105)

- Fewer associations with delinquent peers (ES = .083)

- Less self-centeredness (ES = .054)

- Less anger (ES =. 057)

- Lower rates of gang membership (39% reduction in odds)

- Less use of lie neutralization (ES = .066; $p < .10$)

- More pro-social peers (ES = .051; $p < .10$)

- More pro-social involvement (ES = .047; $p < .10$)

These findings address the two main program goals: 1) to reduce delinquency and gang affiliation and 2) to improve youths' relationships with law enforcement. Additionally, several program-specific skills-building objectives appear to be met, especially refusal skills. These results can be considered quite favorable and reflect sustained program effects, one year post-program. That is, students completing the G.R.E.A.T. program had lower rates of gang affiliation than did students in the control group. Additionally, the G.R.E.A.T. students reported a number of more pro-social attitudes, including more positive attitudes to the police, than did the control students. There were, however, no statistically significant differences between the two groups of students on self-reported delinquency.

These results reflect only short-term program effect. An important question remains: are these short-term program effects sustained across time? To address this question, we continued to survey this group of students for three more years (most of the students were in 10th or 11th grade at the time of the last survey administration). Remarkably (in light of the rather small program dosage of 13 lessons that averaged 40 minutes per lesson), the analyses revealed results similar to the one-year post program effects, albeit with smaller effect sizes. Across four years post program the following 10 positive program effects were found:

- More positive attitudes to police (ES = .058)

- More positive attitudes about police in classrooms (ES = .144)

- Less positive attitudes about gangs (ES = .094)

- More use of refusal skills (ES = .049)

- Higher collective efficacy (ES = .096)

- Less use of hitting neutralizations (ES = .079)

- Less anger (ES = .049)

- Lower rates of gang membership (24% reduction in odds)

- Higher levels of altruism (ES = .058)

- Less risk seeking (ES = .053)

These effects are all in the direction of beneficial program effects, but again, the effect sizes are modest (some would say small). Importantly, although the other comparisons between the two groups were not statistically significant, all indicated more pro-social attitudes and behaviors among the G.R.E.A.T. students.

Some of these results might appear abstract to those not familiar with the G.R.E.A.T. program or with evaluation methodology. To help make sense of these findings, we provide examples of the actual questions that students were asked to measure these more general content areas.

Attitudes to police—a total of 5 questions including: "Police officers are honest." ("How much do you agree or disagree with these statements?")

Police in the classroom—3 questions including: "Police officers make good teachers." ("How much do you agree or disagree with these statements?")

Attitudes about gangs—3 questions including: "Getting involved with gangs will interfere with reaching my goals." ("How much do you agree or disagree with these statements?")

Refusal skills—5 questions including: "Every now and then we try to avoid doing things that our friends want us to do. How often have you done the following? Said no like I really mean it."

Collective efficacy—5 questions including: "It is my responsibility to do something about problems in our community." ("How much do you agree or disagree with these statements?")

Hitting neutralization—3 questions including: "It's okay to beat up someone if they hit you first." ("How much do you agree or disagree with these statements?")

Anger—4 questions including: "I lose my temper pretty easily." ("How much do you agree or disagree with these statements?")

Gang membership—1 question: "Are you now in a gang?"

Altruism—6 questions including: "It feels good to do something without expecting anything in return." ("How much do you agree or disagree with these statements?")

Risk seeking—4 questions including: "Sometimes I will take a risk just for the fun of it." ("How much do you agree or disagree with these statements?")

To recap, our multi-component evaluation found that the G.R.E.A.T. program is implemented as it is intended and has the intended program effects on youth gang membership and on a number of risk factors and social skills thought to be associated with gang membership. Results one year post-program showed a 39% reduction in odds of gang-joining among students who received the program compared to those who did not and an average of 24% reduction in odds of gang joining across the four years post-program. To learn more, please see the resources provided below.

Consult the following website for more information about the G.R.E.A.T. program: http://www.great-online.org/

Consult the following website for more information about the G.R.E.A.T. Evaluation, http://www.umsl.edu/ccj/About%20The%20Department/great_evaluation.html

G.R.E.A.T. has been identified as a promising program by Crime Solutions: http://www.crimesolutions.gov/ProgramDetails.aspx?ID=249

Acknowledgment

This research was made possible, in part, by the support and participation of seven school districts, including the School District of Philadelphia. This project was supported by Award No. 2006-JV-FX-

0011 awarded by the National Institute of Justice, Office of Justice Programs, U.S. Department of Justice. We would also like to thank the numerous school administrators, teachers, students, and law enforcement officers for their involvement and assistance in this study. The opinions, findings, and conclusions or recommendations expressed in this publication are those of the authors and do not necessarily reflect the views of the Department of Justice or of the seven participating school districts.

Notes

1. Two principals who were contacted declined their schools' participation. In one case, the principal had previously been a police gang investigator and, thus, knew the program worked. In the other case, the principal would not agree to our study design (i.e., random assignment of classrooms). In a third school, while the principal agreed to participate, there was resistance to the evaluation design, and this school was ultimately dropped from the study. In each instance, other schools were selected to replace the non-participating schools.

2. G.R.E.A.T. is a national program overseen by the G.R.E.A.T. National Policy Board (NPB). For administrative purposes, responsibilities for program oversight are held by (or given to) agencies operating in different geographic regions: Northeast, Midwest, Southeast, Southwest, and West. Additionally, two federal partners—the Bureau of Alcohol, Tobacco, Firearms, and Explosives (BATF) and the Federal Law Enforcement Training Center (FLETC)—are involved in program training and oversight.

3. The Bureau of Justice Assistance (BJA) oversees the allocation of federal funds and grant compliance associated with the G.R.E.A.T. program.

4. This disproportionate representation in Chicago occurred despite efforts by the research team to recruit schools that would be representative overall of Chicago Public Schools. One of the five originally-selected schools, which was comprised of nearly 100 percent African American students, was unable to meet the requirements of the study and was dropped from the sample. Given time constraints (i.e., too late in the school year to select a comparable school and implement the program with fidelity), we were unable to replace the excluded school during 2006–2007. Thus, the resulting sample was largely Hispanic, while the district was largely African American. To increase representativeness of the sample, the decision was made to add two primarily African American schools to the evaluation in the 2007–2008 school year, even though this meant that these schools would be one year behind other schools in the evaluation.

CHAPTER 34

The Comprehensive, Community-Wide Gang Program Model: Success and Failure

Irving A. Spergel ■ Kwai Ming Wa ■ Rolando Villarreal Sosa

Technically labeled the Comprehensive Community-Wide Approach to Gang Prevention, Intervention, and Suppression Program, but better known as "The Spergel Model" after its originator, Dr. Irving Spergel, the program described here is very complex. Although billed as prevention, intervention, and suppression, its principal thrust is gang intervention. As described here in six sites, the model has been replicated (with some variation) in many other locations. In some places, the program model has been reasonably well implemented; in others, this is not true. Even when adequately implemented, the model has been evaluated as somewhat successful in some instances but not in others. The cup is half-full and half-empty. In the eyes of many public officials, the Spergel Model stands as a major advance in gang control, although most officials couldn't describe the model to you. Further, most officials are not aware of its limitations in implementation and effectiveness. Yet it continues to receive support and is therefore important to be studied as described here by Spergel and his colleagues.

The focus of this study is a youth gang, social control program in Little Village that became a prototype for a comprehensive, community-wide approach to gang prevention, intervention, and suppression at five sites throughout the country. We indicate more briefly and schematically the process and impact of the model at the five other sites. Emphasis

is on elements of interorganizational relationships, program structure, and worker contacts and services that produced lower levels of arrests (and self-reported offenses) for program youth, particularly for violence and to some extent for drug activities. Our research design was quasi-experimental. The Little Village program (A) in Chicago, the prototype site, was sponsored by the Illinois Criminal Justice Information Authority, with funding from the U.S. Department of Justice's Violence in Urban Areas Program, 1992–1997. Five of the programs—Mesa, Arizona (B); Riverside, California (C); Bloomington-Normal, Illinois (D); San Antonio, Texas (E); and Tucson, Arizona (F)—were sponsored and funded by the Office of Juvenile Justice and Delinquency Prevention (OJJDP), Office of Justice Programs, U.S. Department of Justice, between 1995 and 2000 (FY 1994).[1]

Earlier comprehensive youth gang programs generally adopted some form of traditional street work, social, and athletic activities, mediation between gangs, and occasionally youth counseling and job referral, to reduce intergang conflict. Collaboration among social agencies and community groups sometimes occurred, but with little or no collaboration with criminal justice agencies as well. In more recent decades, law enforcement agencies developed extensive suppression strategies and tactics aimed at street gang control and limited rehabilitation or prevention, sometimes in alliance with probation, parole, and district attorneys. However, there was no integration or systematic coordination of their efforts across various types of organizations (including social agencies) for purposes of interrelated community protection and social development of targeted gang members or youth at high risk of criminal gang involvement. For the purpose of our discussion, we equate the terms *youth gang* and *street gang*.

Theory behind the Comprehensive Community-Wide Gang Program Model

The comprehensive gang program model was informed primarily by concepts from community social disorganization and, to some extent, by differential association, opportunity, anomie, social control, and group process theories. Our community-based model was sensitized by the ideas and research findings of Battin-Pearson and colleagues (1998); Bursik and Grasmick (1993); Cloward and Ohlin (1960); Cohen (1980); Curry and Spergel (1988); Haynie (2001); Hirschi (1969); Klein (1971, 1995); Kobrin (1951); Kornhauser (1978); Markowitz and colleagues (2001); Merton (1957); Morenoff, Sampson, and Raudenbush (2001); Sampson (1991); Sampson and Groves (1989); Sampson and Laub (1993); Shaw and McKay (1942); Short and Strodtbeck (1965/1974); Sullivan and Miller (1999); Sutherland and Cressey (1978); Suttles (1968); Thrasher (1927); Veysey and Messner (1999); and Zatz (1987).

Key assumptions of the model were that the youth gang problem, in its distinctive gang violence and drug-selling form, was increasingly present in marginal, low-income, minority, and socially isolated communities. It was not only represented by certain individual gang and gang member characteristics, but it was a response to the fragmentation of community and interorganizational efforts to adequately and interactively address the needs of youth for social development and social control and to protect the community through suppression of gang activity (Bursik and Grasmick 1993; Shaw and McKay 1942; Spergel 1995; Thrasher 1927). The model assumed that youth gangs were generally loosely structured, transitional organizations for the socialization of vulnerable youth between childhood and adulthood, particularly youth from disorganized or deviant families in socially and economically marginal neighborhoods (Klein

1971; J. Moore 1991; Vigil 1988). Local agencies and citizen organizations were often weak, with insufficient resources to address the gang problem in effective terms (Cloward and Ohlin 1960; Cohen 1955; Miller 1959; Sampson, Morenoff, and Earls 1999; Sampson, Raudenbush, and Earls 1997).

The comprehensive gang program model required criminal justice and social agencies to integrate and collaborate on key elements of control and social development, with participation from local neighborhood groups. Focus was not primarily directed to strategies of general community development, political or social reform, community policing, inclusive youth socialization, or even mediation of conflicts between gangs. These strategies were subsidiary to reducing the gang problem through an integrated social development, control, opportunities provision, and interorganizational mobilization approach. The model required the development of a lead agency and a street team of police, probation officers, and outreach youth workers (some former gang leaders)—interacting and working together—targeting delinquent/criminal gang youth and youth at high risk of gang membership who were also involved in delinquent activity (Figure 34.1).

Earlier interdisciplinary or interagency community-wide, gang social control programs were not well developed. They lacked an appropriate range of strategies and collaboration with key agencies or community groups concentrated on or related to the gang problem. Evaluation research was deficient in describing the strategies, services, and activities of the different workers and the nature of their effects on program youth. Analyses of outcome also may not have used comparable nonserved youth and multivariate controls, including race/ethnicity, age, prior arrest history, duration in the program, gang membership, and risk period (Klein 1995; Spergel 1995).

Our evaluation model (Figure 34.2) for the six program sites was created as a guide to collecting and analyzing data and to explaining the interrelationship of program processes, structures, and results. Special interest was in (1) policy and organizational changes and worker efforts that contributed to program development and (2) the program's effects on youth behavior, especially factors that contributed to reduced levels of violence

Figure 34.1 Comprehensive Gang Program Model (Goal 1: Improve Community Interagency Capacity to Address Youth Gang Crime; Goal 2: Reduce Gang Crime)

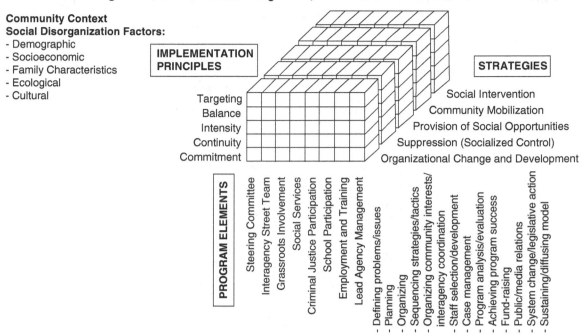

and drug crime arrests for program youth compared to similar nonserved youth in the same or comparable gang crime communities.

In order to explain changes in the targeted youth's behavior, data were collected at individual youth, program worker, and organizational levels (as well as, secondarily, at gang, family, and community levels). Key instruments used were individual youth interviews, individual youth police arrest histories, program worker records of service and contacts, organization administrator surveys, aggregate-level community crime statistics, U.S. census data, field observations, and program-related documents such as project applications for funding, progress reports, media reports, and local research studies. First we describe the program context in the prototype-A community, and then compare the nature of model implementation and results across all six communities.

Program Site A

The Little Village program (site A) took place in a very large metropolitan city, slightly earlier than

the programs at sites B through F. The Little Village community (about four square miles), located eight miles from Chicago's business center, comprised an almost exclusively Mexican and Mexican American population of sixty thousand (U.S. Census Bureau 1992), plus an estimated thirty thousand undocumented residents. The city had one of the highest per capita gang homicide and gang violence rates of all very large cities. Both the city and the program area had long been known for a tradition of chronic, serious, gang violence problems.

The site A program community and its immediate surrounding area contained well-established institutions, including major medical, educational, and religious organizations, social agencies, a variety of city service facilities, light industry, and a thriving retail business sector. The community had been a place of first or second settlement for many successive and different immigrant populations. Its present occupants—lower-middle-class and marginal-income Latinos (mainly Mexican Americans)—began to establish residency about thirty years ago, replacing a Central European population. Three aldermanic districts cut through the

Figure 34.2 Evaluation Model: Program and Comparison Areas, Gangs, Youth (Comparison Area Components = I, II, V [Partial], VI, VIII, IX)

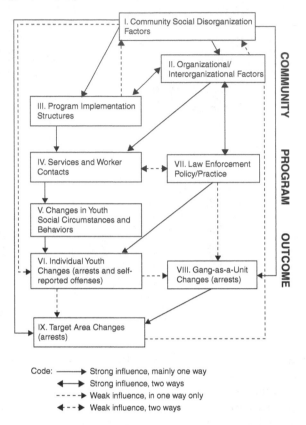

area. Several major community organizations and service agency coalitions were present and operated across several areas. Local neighborhood-group and organizational concerns were with city services, overcrowded schools, high school dropouts, and high gang violence.

The idea of a comprehensive, community-wide, integrated suppression and social intervention gang program did not arise from the ideas or pressures of local neighborhood or city leaders. However, a new mayor had been elected and a new police superintendent appointed, and the mayor and other city and county leaders were concerned with the rise in both domestic and gang violence in the city. The associate director of the state criminal justice planning agency encouraged the director of the new research and development (R&D) unit of the Chicago Police Department (CPD) to apply for funding from the

U.S. Justice Department's Urban Violence initiative. The senior author of this chapter, Irving Spergel, was asked to prepare a proposal for a demonstration community-based gang control project that focused on collaboration among agencies, including the police. The gang project was to be part of a set of violence control (including domestic violence) programs funded under the federal initiative. The gang project was initially required to target youth seventeen to twenty-four years of age.

The CPD agreed to be the lead agency of the project. The staff of the program was expected to comprise two full-time gang tactical officers and two part-time neighborhood relations officers, with three or four full-time adult probation officers and three youth workers who were part of the city's Department of Human Services gang outreach control program (located in the public schools). A local community advisory committee was also to be established. The project originally was to be administered by the commander of the Gang Crime Unit, with consultation from a liaison lieutenant from the police department's R&D unit. Spergel was expected to provide only initial technical assistance for developing the interagency collaboration but to have no program responsibility. He was also to undertake an evaluation of the program. However, because the CPD was busy preparing for a community policing initiative, and other city departments were in the midst of a series of reorganizations, neither had much time for the project. When the Department of Human Services decided not to participate in the project, Spergel (who had already become involved in getting the program started) assumed the role of project coordinator, with responsibility for coordinating the efforts of the police and adult probation officers, as well as developing a unit of outreach youth workers. In the CPD reorganization, the centralized citywide Gang Crime Unit was dissolved and its gang officers replaced by tactical officers located at the local police districts.

The coordinator was under pressure to get the project running as soon as possible, particularly the direct-service-work component aimed at older adolescent and young adult gang members who were responsible for most of the serious violence. Former gang members who had worked with him in two previous projects in another area of the city were recruited as outreach youth workers. The workers, who were familiar with many gangs, quickly made contact with youth from the two targeted violent gangs in the area, both of which were related to or in coalition with other gangs in the city. The tactical police and adult probation officers assigned to the project were new to the area, with little knowledge of local neighborhood gangs.

The Little Village community was divided into two adjacent gang turfs. One of the gangs—the Latin Kings—had an estimated 1,200 members; the other—the Two Six—had 800 members. There were other, smaller gangs in the program area. Police incident data suggested that the two major gangs were responsible for 75 percent of the felony gang violence, including twelve homicides, on average, in the community in each of the two years prior to project operations. Each gang was organized into

about fifteen subunits (or sections), operating on the streets of their respective territories. They engaged in a series of ongoing yet difficult-to-predict violent encounters with members of opposing gang sections. While most target gang youth used drugs, and about half sporadically sold drugs (particularly marijuana and powdered cocaine), they were not primarily or extensively involved in major drug-selling or drug transport operations. Other members of the same gangs were so involved, however.

The planned team approach was slow to get off the ground. Most of the outreach youth workers were from the two major gangs, had previously been arrested or served prison time, and were well known to members of each of the target gangs and to some of the veteran police in the district. Initially there was considerable suspicion and resistance among the project police, adult probation officers, and outreach youth workers to meeting with each other and sharing information about gang situations or gang youth. There was also no tradition of a close working relationship between county adult probation officers and city police. It took six months of weekly staff meetings, and many field contacts by project workers with each other, for them to feel comfortable and to gradually share information. Sharing names of targeted youth among the workers took three months and considerable prodding by the project coordinator.

Although coordination of information and collaboration of worker activity was essential, youth workers from the different gangs did not at first share information with other youth workers. Some were still somewhat identified with their respective gang groups, which may have been at war with each other in earlier years. Some, however, haltingly began to share a range of information about target youth gang violence. Probation and police officers more quickly exchanged information with each other about arrests and probation status of targeted youth. Such official information began gradually to be communicated to a few of the youth workers. In due course, youth workers, police, and probation officers were sharing information at biweekly staff meetings concerning violence occurring (or about to occur) in the community. After about a year, various project staff joined together to supervise graffiti paint-outs by target gang youth in their territories. Together they also supervised target youth in occasional basketball (and especially softball) games in neutral territory (usually on the University of Chicago's playing fields). Members of the gangs played against each other on opposing teams, with project staff participating.

Project workers were required to be on the street generally from 3:00 or 4:00 in the afternoon until midnight or later and engaged in crisis intervention, brief family and individual counseling and referrals, and surveillance and suppression activities. Workers did not necessarily perform their roles together, but they were in frequent communication by beeper and cell phone. At staff meetings, workers planned what to do with youth and how to handle crisis situations. Project efforts focused on individual gang youth who were active in carrying out or planning violent activities. The youth workers emphasized individual youth and family counseling, referrals for jobs, and social services. Little effort was directed to group services or conflict mediation between the gangs, that is, through peace and/or gang leadership meetings. Police and probation officers carried out their traditional law enforcement and supervision activities, targeting many of the same youth as the outreach youth workers and also referring target youth (and youth to be targeted) back to youth workers for services. Youth workers clarified information about serious gang assaults, aiding project police to determine who were, and were not, offenders. They also assisted probation officers in keeping abreast of information about youth and reminded youth to keep appointments with their probation officers.

A neighborhood advisory committee was formed, including representatives of several Catholic and Protestant churches, two Boys and Girls Clubs, a local community organization, a business group, other social agencies, the local alderman, and several local residents. Two large, local citizen meetings were held, but cohesion among the advisory committee members failed to develop. Local advisory committee leaders were unclear as to whether they wanted to develop individual service programs or an interagency coordinating group. Representatives of local community groups, social agencies, churches, and justice system agencies hardly communicated at all and were in varying degrees antagonistic to

each other. Key established community agency and justice system leaders did not support the advisory committee. A major stumbling block was the inability of local youth agencies and the police to jointly sustain the program. Ultimately the neighborhood advisory group dissolved.

The project lasted five years, with the coordinator continuing on a year-to-year basis. The original plan was for him not to continue in this role after the first year of operations. Although supportive of the officers assigned to the project, the CPD chose not to integrate the project into its regular operations or its community policing program. Top-level police division officers insisted that the department's primary mission was suppression and not community organization or social work. The CPD was not interested in joint relationships and operations with other agencies and community groups in regard to the gang problem. Its stated interest in establishing a collaborative relationship with the Cook County Department of Adult Probation failed to develop. The R&D liaison police lieutenant to the project, who favored continuation of the project, maintained that the department had "deep pockets" and did not need the program. In frustration, he transferred back to work at a local police district during the course of the project. Three years of funding—$1.5 million—remained at the end of the project period.

Program Findings

The site A program sample (n = 195) consisted of all youth who were contacted and provided with a combination of services and controls for a period of more than one month, over a two-to-four-year period. All targeted youth were male, ranging in age from fourteen to twenty-four years (averaging eighteen years), almost all were of Mexican American or Mexican origin, and all identified themselves as gang members.

The research design for program evaluation called for two comparison samples in Little Village: a comparison group of youth (n = 208) who were from the same gangs as the program youth and who had been arrested with them, but who had not been provided with services; and a "quasi-program" comparison group of youth (n = 90), also coarrestees of program youth, who were provided with only limited (mostly recreational) services. Complete criminal histories were collected for all youth in each sample—program, comparison, and quasi program. Sixty-five percent of program youth were interviewed three times, at intervals ranging from a year to a year and a half. Youth in other samples were not interviewed (due to a lack of resources).

The chief accomplishments of the project occurred mainly through the work of the interdisciplinary street team. An array of integrated services was provided: crisis intervention, brief counseling, family contacts, educational/job referral and job placement, police surveillance, warnings, arrests, and probation intensive counseling. By the end of the project, a statistically significant reduction in gang crime, particularly violence and drug arrests, was found among program youth compared to youth in the comparison samples. Area-level gang violence arrest rates (but not drug arrest rates) were reduced in the Little Village area compared to six other high gang violence areas of the city.

Focus of the analysis was on differences in arrest patterns of program youth, quasi-program youth, and comparison samples, during the program and matched preprogram periods (based on the targeted program youth's length of time in the program). Mean total arrests for youth in their preprogram periods were high: program sample = 4.5; comparison sample = 4.0; quasi-program sample = 7.8. The difference was statistically significant between the quasi program and each of the other two samples ($p \leq 0.05$). However, there were no statistically significant differences between the samples with respect to preprogram serious violence arrests (homicide, aggravated assault, aggravated battery, and robbery). The patterns of total arrests for violence (including simple assault, simple battery, and illegal possession of a weapon, as well as serious violence) were similar. There were also no statistically significant differences across the three samples in preprogram arrests for property crime, drug or alcohol arrests, and a range of relatively minor offenses (e.g., disorderly conduct and mob action).

Multivariate analyses were conducted to determine whether there were differences in arrest changes for each of the different categories of offenses in the program sample and the two comparison samples. Various statistical models used controls for type of arrest, number of preprogram arrests, age category, and length of time in confinement during the program and preprogram periods. Interaction terms included age categories and preprogram arrest levels for each sample.

All the general linear models were significant ($p \leq 0.0001$), with preprogram arrests the strongest effect among all independent variables—that is, a regression effect: Youth in each sample who had high levels of preprogram arrests reduced their numbers of arrests in the program period, while youth with no or low levels of preprogram arrests increased their arrests in the program period. Age was another significant strong effect: There were differences in all the models across all subsamples. In general, arrests of youth nineteen and older declined, but arrests of the youngest age category—sixteen and under—increased. There was no significant difference in change in total yearly arrests, property arrests, or arrests for minor offenses among the samples.

There were major differences, however, in arrest levels for serious violence, total violence (felony and misdemeanor), and drugs between program youth and quasi-program youth, and especially between program youth and the nonserved comparison youth. Reductions in serious violence arrests occurred for each of the samples, but were significantly different in the program sample compared to both the quasi-program and nonserved comparison samples: There was a 60 percent greater decrease (statistically significant) for the nineteen-and-older and seventeen-and-eighteen-year-old program youth subsamples than for the equivalent comparison and quasi-program subsamples. Reductions for program fourteen- to sixteen-year-olds were greater than those for the fourteen-to-sixteen-year-old quasi-program and comparison groups, but they were not statistically significant. The pattern of reduction was similar with respect to change in total violence arrests (see Table 34.2).

Project workers made special efforts to increase school attendance and to aid youth in seeking and holding jobs (including getting them up in the morning). Although workers referred youth for drug treatment and made brief counseling contacts toward reducing drug use, they focused less on drug crime than on violent behavior of program youth. While drug use was pervasive, drug-selling behavior among program youth was limited. Most arrests for drugs among youth in the three samples were for possession of marijuana and powdered cocaine. Information on major drug operations (mainly involving the Mexican Mafia) was passed to police by a few of the youth workers in a controlled, indirect manner, resulting in important drug raids, arrests, and the closure of at least one bar and several drug houses. An adult criminal organization, the Mexican Mafia, was the primary agent for drug distribution and transport, and occasionally used program youth (and/or their parents) to sell and carry drugs from Mexico to Chicago.

We expected that, if program youth reduced their levels of violence arrests (or self-reported violence offenses), there would be an increase in drug offenses. All gang-problem communities in Chicago were undergoing increases in gang drug arrests in this period. This seemed to be part of a process of further natural development of established gangs, from primary interest in turf-based violence to primary but not exclusive or even organized interest in drug selling.

While community area gang drug-related arrests increased by 1,000 percent (and area-level gang violence rates decreased) between the five-year preprogram period and five-year program period, they decreased for program youth over the same period (see Table 34.2). In contrast, drug arrests increased for quasi-program and nonserved comparison youth. The decrease was significant for the program seventeen-to-eighteen and sixteen-and-under age subgroups, compared to the equivalent quasi-program and comparison age subgroups ($p = 0.02$).

We know of no other crime control programs—for example, the initiation of community policing in the area—that could have accounted for these program youth changes (Skogan and Hartnett 1997). A series of logistic regression equations statistically accounted for different types of project worker effects on program youths' attitudes and behaviors, which in turn contributed to lower levels of violence and drug arrests. Effective suppression contacts, as perceived by project police (and indicated in worker activity reports), were related to a reduction in a program youth's degree of affiliation

with his gang. For example, compared to youth who did not change their affiliation, or changed to higher gang status, some youth changed from leaders to core members or regular members, peripherals, or nonmembers (odds ratio = 2.0; $p = 0.04$). Reduction in the youth's level of affiliation with the gang was significantly associated with lower violence and drug arrests. Suppression was also useful in persuading youth not to have unrealistically high income aspirations and to have more realistic ones (odds ratio = 2.71; $p = 0.006$).

Successful job referral and job placement of program youth (mainly by the outreach youth workers) simultaneously predicted the likelihood of youth spending less time with their gang friends (odds ratio 2.22; $p = 0.03$) and spending more time with wives or steady girlfriends (odds ratio = 2.48; $p \leq 0.01$). Worker success in getting youth back to school predicted a nonsignificant positive odds ratio of youth graduating or getting a GED (1.74; $p = 0.15$). The workers were more successful with older than younger youth in this regard (odds ratio 2.21; $p \leq 0.01$). Generally, holding a legitimate job was associated with significantly reduced levels of violence and drug arrests.

More program services and contacts—from all types of project personnel together, including youth workers, police, probation, and neighborhood organizers—predicted a reduced gap between the individual youth's income or job aspirations and expectations, that is, a more realistic appraisal of his chances for success in life. Similarly, the greater the dosage of worker contacts and services, the greater the reduction in the number of gang friends among these youth. Higher program dosage was also associated with reduced levels of violence arrests. Intensity and persistence in contacts and services clearly were required.

Collaborative project worker efforts—through interactive suppression, social support, and provision of social opportunities—effectively changed patterns of gang youth behavior, resulting in the pursuit of a more socially acceptable life course and the formation of relationships with more nongang peers. Such changes in the youth's behavior were highly predictive of lower rates of gang violence.[2]

At the Little Village community level, the project was associated with lower levels of arrests for gang-motivated aggravated battery and assault over the preprogram and program periods, compared to six similar high gang violence Latino (Mexican American and Puerto Rican) community areas in the city during the first three years of project operations. The rate of decline in gang violence arrests at the program-area level dropped off slightly during the last two years of the project, when staff were increasingly discouraged and frustrated as it became clear that the city administration and the police department were not prepared to institutionalize the project approach.

Cross-Site Community and Program Characteristics and Changes in Arrest Patterns

In this section we summarize and compare the characteristics, importance, and success in implementation of the program code (Figure 34.1) across the six sites (Table 34.1). We use numbers of asterisks to indicate the degree of general importance of the eighteen basic program characteristics in implementing the model. We also indicate, through use of symbols, the extent to which each of the program

	1.A. Program Implementation Characteristics (See also Figure 34.1)	Degree of Importance to Program Success[†]	Levels of Implementation by Project Site[‡]					
			A	B	C	D	E	F
Program Elements (Structure)	[a]City/County Leadership	***	2	4	4	1	1	1
	[b]Steering Committee	**	1	4	3	1	1	0
	[c]Interagency Street Team/Coordination	***	4	4	3	0	0	0
	[d]Grassroots Involvement	*	3	1	1	0	1	0
	Social Services: [e]Youth Work, [f]Individual Counseling, [g]Family Treatment, & [h]Recreation	**	3	3	3	2	3	3
	[i]Criminal Justice Participation	***	4	4	4	1	1	0
	[j]School Participation	**	1	3	3	3	2	0
	[k]Employment and Training	**	3	1	4	3	1	0
	[l]Lead Agency/Management/Commitment	***	4	4	4	0	0	0
Strategies	Social Intervention: [m]Outreach & [n]Crisis Intervention	**	4	3	3	1	1	0
	Community Mobilization: [o]Interagency & [p]Grassroot	**	1	3	2	1	0	0
	Provision of Social Opportunities: [q]Education, [r]Job, & [s]Cultural	**	3	2	2	2	1	0
	[t]Suppression	***	4	4	3	0	0	0
	[u]Organizational Change & Development	***	2	4	4	0	0	0
Operating Principles	Targeting [v]Gang Members/[w]At-Risk Gang Youth	***	4	2	3	1	3	3
	[x]Balance of Service	***	4	3	3	0	0	0
	[y]Intensity of Service	*	4	3	3	1	0	0
	[z]Continuity of Service	**	2	1	2	2	0	2
Key Factors Δ Contributing to . . .	1.B. Success in Program Implementation		c, i, l, t, x	a, c, i, l, t, u	a, c, i, k, l, u	—	—	—
	Failure in Program Implementation		—	—	—	c, l, t, u, x	c, l, t, u, x	c, i, l, t, u, x

[†]Importance of characteristics to success. ***= extremely, **= moderately, and *= somewhat.
[‡]Levels of implementation: 4 = excellent, 3 = good, 2 = fair, 1 = poor, and 0 = none. A = Chicago, B = Mesa, C = Riverside, D = Bloomington-Normal, E = San Antonio, F = Tucson. Δ refers to codes used in 1.A. Program Implementation Characteristics and Figure 34.1.

characteristics was implemented at each site. The degree of importance of these program characteristics, but not the level of their implementation, was determined by the senior author. The level of implementation was determined by the findings of an evaluation survey completed by five to seven of the program leaders at each site, and by two or three national program evaluators familiar with the particular programs. The results of the survey were summed but not weighted for each site. Key factors accounting for successful or failed implementation were also identified for the sites.

We also identify selected gang effect factors at each of the six sites (Table 34.2): level of the gang problem and its nature, gang structure, and race/ethnicity of gang members in the program and comparison youth samples, and in the program and comparison areas. Most attention is directed to a summary and comparison of key outcome factors from Figure 34.2, especially changes in youth behaviors (V), individual youth outcome/arrests (VI), and target area outcome/arrests (IX). Arrows in the last three sections of Table 34.2 indicate whether the individual youth in the program sample at each site significantly changed their arrest patterns, relative to youth in the comparison-sample. A similar determination of whether program-area arrests were reduced relative to comparison-area arrests is also made between the preprogram and program periods. The area arrest assessments were based on gross police arrest statistics, without demographic controls at the six sites.[3]

Factors Contributing to Program Implementation Success or Failure

A variety of interrelated program structures, strategies, and operating principles were assessed as necessary for the successful implementation of the comprehensive gang program model. At no site were all of the critical model factors fully implemented, although implementation appeared to have been more effective at site A, and to some extent at B and C, and less effective at sites D, E, and F. At sites A, B, and C, greater coordination of social intervention, services provision, and suppression contacts by workers predicted a reduction in violence and other types of arrests for individual youth. Certain program structure factors were

correlated with declines in arrests for violence (and less often for drugs).

It was important to assign degrees of importance to model factors and determine the degree of their successful adaptation across the sites. The following seemed especially important: city and county governmental leadership committed to the model; development of an interagency street team and use of indigenous former gang influentials; coordination and interrelationship of strategies of social intervention, suppression, and provision of socioeconomic opportunities by police, probation, and outreach youth workers; and optimal lead agency management capacity, with a substantial effort directed to the development of a steering committee. The presence of these factors across sites A, B, and C was associated with a significant level of success in the reduction of the gang violence problem for program youth. The absence of these factors, or the lack of their substantial development, appeared to account for failure at the individual program youth level, and possibly at the program-area level. Other types of delinquency (arrest) patterns of gang youth (with the exception of drug arrests for program youth at site A, and to some extent at site B) were not generally affected at any of the six sites. The comprehensive gang program model approach appeared to be more effective in addressing distinctive gang-related violence than other delinquency or crime problems (Table 34.2).

Gang Factors and Program Outcome

Gang-Problem Context Factors. The six project sites were located in a large metropolitan area, a medium-sized city, and smaller cities in the midwestern, southwestern, and far western parts of the country. The level of the gang problem, and especially the scope and severity of gang violence (but perhaps not drug-selling and drug-using activities of program youth), varied across the sites. Serious gang problems, particularly violence, were present in some cities but not in others. In none of the other five cities was the gang violence problem as severe and long-term as in the site A city. The gang drug problem existed with similar severity across all six cities, but without the presence of serious gang violence in the smaller cities. Youth gangs and/or delinquent groups were part of the history

Table 34.2 Summary of Program Effect Factors

Program Youth/Project Area Characteristics		A (Chicago)	B (Mesa)	C (Riverside)	D (Bloomington-Normal)	E (San Antonio)	F (Tucson)
Gang Factors	Level of site/problem	very high/chronic	low/emerging	moderate chronic/emerging	moderate/emerging	moderate chronic/emerging	high chronic/emerging
	Key problem(s)	violence & drugs	general delinquency	violence & drugs	drugs	property	violence & drugs
	Gang structure	large group, cohesive, decentralized	small group	large group, decentralized	large group, diffuse	small group, diffuse	small group, cohesive
	Race/ethnicity (gender)	Mex. Amer. (M)	Mex. Amer. (M & F)	Mex. & Afr. Amer. (M & F)	Afr. Amer. (M & F)	Mex. Amer. (M)	Mex. & Afr. Amer. (M & F)
Gang Membership Change	Program youth membership†	↓	↑	×	↑	×	↑
	Project area membership	×	×	×	↓	↓	NA
Individual Youth Arrest Changes Program vs. Comparison Youth†	Total arrests	×	(↓)	×	×	×	×
	Violence arrests	↓	(↓)	(↓)	×	×	×
	Drug arrests	↓	(↓)	↑	↑	×	×
	Property arrests	×	↑	×	×	×	×
	Other arrests	×	↓	×	×	×	×
Area Arrest Changes Program vs. Comparison Area‡	Total arrests	×	×	×	↑	↑	NA
	Violence arrests	↓	↓	↓	↑	↑	NA
	Drug arrests	↑	↓	↑	×	↑	NA
	Property arrests	×	↓	×	×	↑	NA
	Other arrests	×	×	×	×	↑	NA

Levels of change: ↑ = increase, ↓ = decrease, × = no change, NA = data not available.

†Significant statistical changes were determined only at the individual youth levels: ↑ = increase, ≤ 0.001 to ≤ 0.05; ↓ = decrease, ≤ 0.001 to ≤ 0.05; (↑) = increase, <0.06 to <0.015; (↓) = marginal decrease, <0.06 to <0.015; × = no significant change; NA = data not available.

‡Relative difference between program and comparison areas: ↑ = more increase; ↓ = more decrease.

461

of each of the cities, but lethal gang violence was identified as a problem only recently in the cities of sites B through F.

The youth gang problem addressed by all the projects was defined mainly by government and public agency leaders, based on police arrest and probation data. The problem was concentrated among low-income minority groups, especially among Latino male youth in socially isolated and marginal sectors of each of the cities, particularly in areas undergoing significant population change. The gang problem, however, was not necessarily located in the lowest-income or the highest general-crime-rate areas of the six cities.

At some sites, youth identified by the project as gang members could have been classified by other agencies as members of "tagger" groups or ephemeral delinquent groups. Youth sometimes became members of different gangs in the same local areas over time. Gang youth engaged in a range of unlawful acts in the program and comparison areas. Property, drug, and minor crimes predominated at sites B through F, yet program youth generally were distinctively more violent and chronically delinquent than other delinquent youth at each of the sites (Klein 1971; Thornberry et al. 2003). It was difficult to classify the gang problem simply as emerging or chronic. Somewhat benign gang traditions existed in sites B through F, but in each city the gang problem became more salient with the arrival (or increase) of a low-income, isolated minority population, particularly the youth sector.

While OJJDP's (1994) comprehensive gang program initiative was concerned primarily with reducing gang violence, the drug problem was viewed by local program agency administrators at sites B through F as the most serious of gang (and nongang) delinquency and crime problems (from surveys of eighty-six administrators at two program periods). The most frequent and serious gang-motivated and gang-related arrests for violence and drugs occurred only at site A. Large, cohesive, enduring gangs with many subunits were present only at site A. Gang members in four of the five other program sites were predominantly Mexican American; in one site they were predominantly African American. Across sites B through F, the minority youth—75 percent to 80 percent males—ranged in age from 12 to 20 years (median age about 16.5 years). The great majority of youth (85 percent) at these sites identified themselves as gang members, less often as associate or former gang members.

Arrest Changes. As in prototype site A, changes between the program and preprogram periods were the principal basis for determining program youth effects in sites B through F. Because of high interviewee dropout rates, self-report data were not as useful for program effect determinations as were police arrest data. Patterns of youth behavioral change (whether based on police arrest or self-report offense data) were similar over the same matched periods at each of the six sites.

The numbers of program and comparison youth at each site are shown in Table 34.3. In order to compare changes in arrest patterns of individually matched program and comparison youth—over matched program and preprogram periods—multivariate analyses were also conducted at sites B through F, with statistical controls for age, race/ethnicity, gender, gang membership status,

Table 34.3 Numbers of Youth at Each Site			
Site	Program Youth	Comparision Youth	Total
A	195	298	493
B	109	258	367
C	234	135	369
D	101	134	235
E	110	120	230
F	126	101	227
Total	875	1046	1921

preprogram arrest history, confinement period, and length of time in the program. Program youth had statistically significant reductions in total arrests only at site B. Program youth did better than comparison youth in non-statistically-significant reductions in violence and drug arrests at sites A and B, but only in violence arrests at site C. Drug arrests increased for program youth compared to comparison youth at sites C and D. Also, property arrests went up, but other minor crime arrests went down at site B.

In general, the most positive effects for program youth were reductions in violence and drug arrests, particularly at sites A and B, with a mixed effect at site C. Program youth did not fare as well at sites D, E, and F, where differences in arrests of program youth and comparison youth for most types of offenses were not statistically significant. At the successful sites (A, B, C), youth in the program for two or more years rather than for shorter periods of time had statistically significant reductions in arrests. Surprisingly, whether the youth was presently a gang member, an associate gang member, or a nongang youth did not account for changes in arrest patterns of youth for the different types of offenses, although gang members typically were more chronically and seriously delinquent than were associate gang members, who were in turn more chronically and seriously delinquent than nongang youth. The most powerful predictor of change in arrest patterns at all the sites was *preprogram arrests;* that is, those who had more arrests in the preprogram period had fewer arrests in the program period, and those who had fewer arrests in the preprogram period had more arrests in the program period. This regression pattern, however, applied equally to program and comparison youth. The next most powerful and consistent predictors of reduced arrests of all types were *age* and *gender.* Across all sites, older adolescents and young adults, as well as females, generally did better than younger youth and males in reducing arrests.

Area-Level Arrest Changes. We could not convincingly determine whether changes in arrest patterns of program youth at the individual level were related to (or predicted) changes in arrest patterns at the community-area levels, except possibly for violence arrests at sites A, B, and C.

We attempted to measure changes in gang arrests for program and comparison youth at the program and comparison area levels, at each of the sites. Separate high-gang-crime comparison areas were carefully selected and matched to the program areas (the program and comparison youth samples were from the respective program and comparison areas, except in site A). The comparison areas were equivalent (if not almost identical) to the respective program areas in size, as well as in population, socioeconomic, and high-gang-crime characteristics. We measured changes in area gang arrests as defined by the local police departments, aggregating offenses consistent with the individual youth arrest-category measures: *total arrests, violence* (serious and less serious), *drug, property,* and *other arrests* (mainly mob action, disorderly conduct, resisting/obstructing a police officer, status offense).

Changes in gang arrests at the matched area level at each site were not necessarily expected to closely parallel those at the individual youth level. Arrests for sample youth included gang and non-gang arrests; area-level arrests included only arrests defined by the local police as gang arrests. We could not control for age, race/ethnic, and gender factors but could for program and preprogram periods. The findings indicated that there were no changes in total gang arrests, gang property arrests, or gang "other" arrests that were different in the program areas than in the comparison areas. However, there was strong and consistent evidence that gang violence declined in the successful program sites (A, B, C), but did not in the unsuccessful sites (D, E, F). (We could not obtain local community-area gang arrest statistics at site F.) Gang drug arrests declined in the program areas relative to the comparison areas at sites B and C, but not at site A (where they rose in both the program and comparison areas—more in the program area than in four of the six comparison areas).

Implications for Policy and Theory

Evaluations of the demonstration programs and the utility of the comprehensive gang program el in the six different cities—large, medium, small—during the middle and latter part of the 1990s clarified the nature of, and what to do about, the gang problem within a theoretical framework oriented primarily toward community social disorganization. The character and context of the youth gang problem was somewhat different across the sites. The evaluations indicated that reductions of gang violence, and to some extent drug-related crime, could be achieved through strong local government interest and support, appropriate public policy change or development, interorganizational collaboration, and interdisciplinary team worker efforts (especially involving former gang influentials as outreach youth workers), all founded on effective interactive community/agency leadership mobilization, social intervention, opportunities provision, suppression, and organizational change and development strategies.

Program youth and area levels of gang-related violence were reduced at three of the six sites. The findings of project success at these sites contrast to the findings of project failure in evaluations of classic community-based gang programs (Gold and Mattick 1974; Klein 1971, 1995), and of a "total community" gang control project (Miller 1962). A more recent set of process evaluations of community-based but police-dominated gang suppression programs also indicate failure (Decker 2003). It is likely that all the failed projects lacked implementation of an adequate, combined, community-based, interorganizational, multistrategy, and interdisciplinary street-based intervention model to address the youth gang program.

The findings of the present evaluations also suggest that gang intervention theory may need to be modified. Gang and community theorists may have overemphasized the importance of single-dimensional individual, family, group, neighborhood, organizational, or larger societal factors relevant to the genesis and control of the delinquency gang problem (Bursik and Grasmick 1993; Hagedorn 1988; Klein 1971; Sampson, Morenoff, and Earls 1999; Skogan and Hartnett 1997). They may have insufficiently attended to government policies and especially to interorganizational relationships.

Gang program evaluations, when they exist, have been characterized by weak research designs; insufficient attention to use of comparison groups of individual, nonserved youth and comparable gang-problem areas; lack of use of individual- and area-level gang arrest histories (as well as individual youth self-reports of gang crime activities); inadequate definition of a "gang member," or level of gang involvement of youth; failure to specify services or controls provided to each program youth; and failure to use multivariate statistical models to assess individual youth outcome with attention to prior arrests (or self-reported offenses), age, and gender. Models to indicate causal routes between intervention, mediating, and outcome factors of program youth also need to be developed. A great deal more sophisticated, multidimensional research is required to understand the gang problem, and certainly to effectively evaluate gang program processes and outcomes (Decker 2003). We believe the evaluation research of the six sites we have described is a step in that direction.

Notes

Points of view in this chapter are those of the authors and do not necessarily represent the official positions or recommended policies of the U.S. Department of Justice or the Illinois Criminal Justice Information Authority, which were sponsors and funders of the particular program demonstrations and evaluations, or of the School of Social Service Administration of the University of Chicago, which provided supplementary support to complete the evaluations. For detailed case reports, including research methods, tables, and instruments, contact the Office of Juvenile Justice and Delinquency Prevention, Office of Justice Programs, U.S. Department of Justice, and the Illinois Criminal Justice Information Authority.

1. The lead agencies of the comprehensive community-wide interdisciplinary projects were (A) the Chicago Police Department; (B) the Mesa Police Department; (C) the Riverside Police Department (originally, the Office of Educational and Community Initiatives, University of California–Riverside); (D) Project Oz (youth-serving agency); (E) the San Antonio Police Department; and (F) Our Town Family Center (youth and family agency).

2. Gang violence was defined as any violence committed by youth in our samples (who were all gang youth)—whether the incident was of gang interest or not—based on arrest history and self-reports.

3. The site A area-level gang violence arrest reduction was also supported by additional measures and analyses, including a prevalence rate reduction of gang violence for seventeen- to twenty-five-year-old males (taken from U.S. census and CPD gang arrest data) and the perceptions of residents (n = 100) and organization representatives (n = 50) in Little Village compared to an adjoining, almost identical high gang-crime community, between the first and third years of the program.

References

Battin-Pearson, Sara R., Terrence P. Thornberry, J. David Hawkins, and Marvin D. Krohn. 1998. Gang membership, delinquent peers, and delinquent behavior. *OJJDP Juvenile Justice Bulletin.* Washington, DC: U.S. Department of Justice, Office of Justice Programs, Office of Juvenile Justice and Delinquency Prevention.

Bursik, Robert J., Jr., and Harold G. Grasmik. 1993. *Neighborhood, and crime: The dimensions of effective community control.* New York: Lexington.

Cloward, Richard A., and Lloyd F. Ohlin. 1960. *Delinquency and opportunity: A theory of delinquent gangs.* Glencoe, IL: The Free Press.

Cohen, Albert K 1955. *Delinquent boys: The culture of the gang.* Glencoe, IL: The Free Press.

Cohen, Stanley, 1980 *Folk devils and moral panics: The creation of mods and rockers.* 2nd ed. New York: St. Martin's Press.

Curry, G. David, and Irving A. Spergel. 1988. Gang homicide, delinquency and community. *Criminology* 26:381–407.

Decker, Scott H. 2003. *Policing Gangs and Youth Violence.* Belmont, CA: Wadsworth.

Gold, Martin, and Hans Mattick. 1974. *Experiment in the streets: The Chicago youth development project.* Ann Arbor: University of Michigan, Institute for Social Research.

Hagedorn, John M. 1988. *People and folks: Gangs, crime, and the underclass in a rustbelt city.* With Perry Maxon. Chicago: Lake View.

Haynie, Dana L. 2001. Delinquent peers revisited: Does network structure matter? *American Journal of Sociology,* 106:1013–1057.

Hirschi, Travis. 1969. *Crimes of delinquency.* Berkeley: University of California Press.

Klein, Malcolm W. 1971. *Street gangs and street workers.* Englewood Cliffs, NJ: Prentice Hall.

———. 1995. *The American street gang: Its nature, prevalence, and control.* New York: Oxford University Press.

Klein, M. W. and Maxson, C. L. (2006). *Street Gang Patterns and Policies.* New York: Oxford University Press.

Klein, M.W., Maxson, C.L., and Miller, J. (Eds). (1995). *The Modern Gang Reader.* Los Angeles: Roxbury Publishing Company.

Kobrin, Solomon. 1951. The conflict of values in delinquency areas. *American Sociological Review* 16:653–61.

Kornhauser, Ruth R. 1978. *Social sources of delinquency: An appraisal of analytic models.* Chicago: University of Chicago Press.

Markowitz, Fred F., Paul E. Bellair, Allen E. Liska, and Jianhong Liu. 2001. Extending social disorganization theory: Modeling the relationships between cohesion, disorder, and fear. *Criminology* 39:293–319.

Merton, Robert K. 1957. *Social theory and social structure.* Glencoe, IL: The Free Press.

Sampson, Robert J. 1991. Linking the micro and macrolevel dimensions of community social organization. *Social Forces* 70:43–64.

Sampson, Robert J., and W. Byron Groves. 1989. Community structure and crime: testing social disorganization theory. *American Journal of Sociology* 94:774–802.

Sampson, Robert J., and John H. Laub. 1993 *Crime in the making: Pathways and turning points through life.* Cambridge, MA: Harvard University Press.

Sampson, Robert J., Jeffrey D. Morenoff, and Felton Earls. 1999. Beyond social capital: Spatial dynamics of collective efficacy for children. *American Sociological Review* 64:633–60.

Sampson, Robert J., Stephen W. Raudenbush, and Felton Earls. 1997. Neighborhoods and violent crime: A multilevel study of collective efficacy. *Science* 277: 918–24.

Shaw, Clifford R., and Henry D. McKay. 1942. *Juvenile delinquency and urban areas.* Chicago: University of Chicago Press, 1969.

Short, James, F., Jr., and Fred L. Strodtbeck. 1965/1974. *Group process and gang delinquency.* Chicago: University of Chicago Press.

Skogan, Wesley G., and Susan M. Hartnett. 1997. *Community policing, Chicago style.* New York: Oxford University Press.

Spergel, Irving A. 1993. *The youth gang problem: A community approach.* New York: Oxford University Press.

Sullivan, Mercer L., and Barbara Miller. 1999. Adolescent violence, state processes, and the local context of moral panic. In *States and illegal practices.* ed. Josiah McC. Heyman, 261–83. New York: Berg.

Sutherland, Edwin, and Donald R. Cressey. 1978. *Principles of criminology.* 10th ed. New York: J.B. Lippincott.

Suttles, Gerald D. 1968. *The social order of the slum: Ethnicity and territory in the inner city.* Chicago, IL: University of Chicago Press.

Thornberry, Terence P., Marvin D. Krohn, Alan J. Lizotte, Carolyn A. Smith, and Kimberly Tobin. 2003. *Gangs and delinquency in developmental perspective.* Cambridge, UK: Cambridge University Press.

Thrasher, Frederic M. 1927, abridged 1963. *The gang: A study of 1,313 gangs in Chicago.* Chicago: University of Chicago Press.

U.S. Census Bureau. 1992. *Census of population and housing, 1990.* www.census.gov (accessed February 10, 2005).

Veysey, Bonita M., and Steven I. Messner. 1999. Further testing of social disorganization theory: An elaboration of Sampson's and Groves's "Community structure and Crime." *Journal of Research on Crime and Delinquency* 36:156–74.

Vigil, James D. 1988. *Barrio gangs: Street life and identity in southern California.* Austin: University of Texas Press.

Zatz, Marjorie S. 1987. Chicago youth gangs and crime: The creation of moral panic. *Contemporary Crisis* 11:129–58.

CHAPTER 35

A Study of Police Gang Units in Six Cities

Vincent J. Webb ▪ Charles M. Katz

The proliferation of street gangs throughout the nation has led understandably to a proliferation of gang-control programs, especially among law enforcement agencies. Prominent among these have been police gang units, elite groups of antigang police specialists. The "gang cop" is a new fixture in many departments. Webb and Katz have been at the forefront of efforts to understand and evaluate the place of gang units in gang-control efforts. In this chapter, the authors describe these units in a number of contrasting settings, including several different conceptions of why they developed as they did; there are different rationalities behind gang unit formation. The different functions that gang units serve are outlined; uniformity of approach is not found, suggesting a good deal of uncertainty about how gang units might best respond to gang problems.

The growth of gangs during the last two decades has been accompanied by the development and growth of specialized law enforcement responses to gangs. Traditionally, the police response to gangs and gang-related problems was to assign responsibility for gang control to existing units such as patrol, juvenile bureaus, community relations, investigations, and crime prevention (Huff, 1990; Needle and Stapleton, 1983). However, in the 1980s many police departments established specialized units for gang control, including what is commonly

referred to as the police gang unit. By 1999 over 55 percent of all large American police departments reported that they had a specialized gang unit for addressing local gang problems (Bureau of Justice Statistics, 1999). A police gang unit is a "secondary or tertiary functional division within a police organization, which has at least one sworn officer whose sole function is to engage in gang control efforts" (Katz, Maguire, and Roncek, 2000: 14). Therefore, by their very nature police gang units are specialized, have unique administrative policies and procedures, often distinct from those of the rest of the department, and have a front line of "experts" who are uniquely trained and dedicated to perform specific and focused duties. . . .

[T]his chapter reviews the extant research on police gang control efforts and makes use of data obtained from several ongoing research projects designed to examine the police response to gangs. In particular, we rely heavily on data that we collected as part of three federally funded studies that examined the police response to gangs in six cities: Albuquerque, New Mexico; Inglewood, California; Junction City (a pseudonym); Las Vegas, Nevada; Mesa, Arizona; and Phoenix, Arizona (Katz, 1997; Katz, Webb, and Haar, 1998; Katz, Webb, and Schaefer, 2000).

These sites provide several opportunities to examine police gang control efforts. First, as seen in Table 35.1, the sites provide the opportunity to examine the police response to gangs in cities of varying size, with different-sized gang units and diverse gang problems. Second, the selected sites provide the opportunity to examine a variety of

Reprinted from: Vincent J. Webb and Charles M. Katz, "Policing Gangs in an Era of Community Policing," *Policing Gangs and Youth Violence*, First Edition: 17–30, 239–251. Copyright © 2003 by Wadsworth, a division of Thomson Learning. Reprinted with permission.

Table 35.1 Site Characteristics

	Albuquerque	Inglewood	Junction City	Las Vegas	Mesa	Phoenix
Size of gang unit (sworn)	4	4	10	50	13	42
Size of city	431,027	113,015	351,745	929,940	350,592	1,172,538
UCR Part I crimes (per 1,000)	111.2	49.6	72.4	63.4	77.3	96.1
No. of gangs	100	33	15	201	25	336
No. of gang members	5,000	–	2,400	6,905	1,500	6,439

organizational configurations, allowing us to examine the implications of different configurations in shaping responses to the gang problem. Third, most of the sites studied are located in the Southwest region of the United States. While researchers have found that police departments across the country are claiming to have a gang problem, police departments in the Southwest have been found to be significantly more likely to respond to their gang problem by establishing specialized police gang units (Curry et al., 1992).

All of the studies involved a combination of observations of the gang unit officers and interviews with gang unit officers and key stakeholders from other parts of the police organization, the criminal justice system, and the community. Combined, these three studies involved a total of about 700 hours of observation, 62 interviews with gang unit officers, 21 interviews with police managers, and 120 interviews with stakeholders (for example, police agency personnel, other criminal justice officials, school administrators, and special interest group administrators). As part of these three studies we also reviewed official police documents and newspaper articles from local newspapers. In all, 237 official police documents and 349 newspaper articles were reviewed.

Our purpose in this chapter is to examine the nature, characteristics, and scope of police gang control efforts through a consideration of police gang units. The first section explores the establishment of police gang units and considers theoretical and policy rationales for police gang units as well as theoretical explanations of their growth. The second section reviews gang unit functions and patterns of functional specialization. . . .

Theoretical and Policy Rationales for the Establishment of Specialized Police Gang Units

Spergel and Curry (1993), from a survey of 254 professionals in 45 cities, identified five strategies that are used by communities to respond to gangs. They reported that suppression techniques employed by the police were the most commonly cited strategy. Some have noted that police gang units are perhaps the clearest embodiment of the gang suppression approach (Klein, 1995a: 161).

Under the suppression approach, Klein (1995a) argues, enforcement officials see their primary responsibility as responding to gang street crimes. In other words, officials are to deal with the crimes that are most likely to come to the attention of the public, such as assaults, drive-by shootings, drug sales, and graffiti. In turn, prevention and treatment strategies are not given high priority. In fact, police officials see these activities as outside the scope of their responsibility. Suppression strategy is based on deterrence theory. The idea is that swifter, severer, and more certain punishment will lead to a reduction of gang-related activity by those currently in gangs, as well as to a reduction in the number of individuals wishing to participate in gangs and gang behavior in the future. Accordingly, Klein argues that the "underlying assumption of all this is that the targets of suppression, the gang members and potential gang members, will respond 'rationally' to suppression efforts [and] will weigh the consequences of gang activity, redress the balance between cost and benefit, and withdraw from gang activity" (1995a: 160).

To understand the current response to the gang problem, it is helpful to first understand several developments that have shaped and justified the shift toward suppression-oriented strategies. First, policymakers no longer believe that the social intervention approaches of the 1960s and 1970s are a successful way to deal with the gang problem. Although this strategy took many forms, it was based on the assumption that gang membership is the by-product of a socially deprived community and that the values and norms of gang youths can be changed by reorienting the youths' attitudes, values, and expectations toward mainstream society. Social intervention approaches frequently relied on a detached worker who was assigned to work with gangs and gang members to steer youth away from delinquency and encourage them to pursue more socially acceptable activities such as athletic teams, club activities, and fund-raisers (President's Commission on Law Enforcement and Administration of Justice, 1967). However, many have argued that this approach did not lead to reduced delinquent activity and may in fact have led to increased group cohesiveness, which in turn may have led to increased delinquency. Additionally, some of these critics have claimed that the assignment of a caseworker increased the local reputation of particular gangs, which helped to attract new members and led to a growing gang problem in areas employing detached workers (Klein, 1971; Spergel, 1995).

Second, many believe that the scope and nature of the gang problem has dramatically changed over past years. In 1983 only 45 percent of cities with populations of 100,000 or more reported a gang problem (Needle and Stapleton, 1983), whereas by 1992 this figure had risen to over 90 percent (Curry, Ball, and Fox, 1994). These studies illustrate that gangs are no longer just a big-city problem but are also becoming prevalent in many small and medium-sized cities (Office of Juvenile Justice and Delinquency Prevention, 2000). A number of studies have also found that gang members are disproportionately responsible for delinquency, crime, drug use, and drug dealing when compared to non-gang members (Howell, 1999; Katz, Webb, and Schaefer, 2000; Klein, 1995a, b; Spergel, 1995). As a result, many local officials see the gang problem

as only getting worse in the future, and believe that the only way to stop the gang problem is by removing gang members from society through the criminal justice system.

The third reason for the shift to suppression-oriented strategies follows from the disenchantment with social intervention strategies and the belief that the gang problem has grown. Surveys of the public have illustrated that residents are fearful of the growing gang problem (Katz, 1990). Citizen surveys have consistently shown that one of the top priorities of the police should be dealing with gang-related problems (Webb and Katz, 1997). As a result, state and federal legislators have responded to public demands by allocating additional dollars toward suppression-oriented interventions (Klein, 1995a; McCorkle and Miethe, 1998). For example, many municipal and state agencies have received additional funding—usually through federal grants for interagency task forces, information tracking systems, and overtime pay for the police—to target hard-core gang members. Additionally, with the implementation of community policing in many police agencies, public pressures to address gang problems have forced many departments to make gang control efforts a top priority. . . .

Police Gang Unit Functions and Specialization

Police gang units generally engage in one or more of four principal functions: intelligence, enforcement/suppression, investigations, and prevention (Huff and McBride, 1990). The relative emphasis placed on each of these functions varies from one department to the next. Some gang units are single-function units and engage in only one activity—for example, intelligence or suppression. Other units engage in more than one of these functions, while others are very comprehensive and carry out all of these functions, which is the approach recommended by Huff and McBride (1990). How police agencies organize their resources to carry out these functions also varies from one department to the next. In some police departments the gang unit is a stand-alone bureau with status equivalent to other bureaus such as patrol and investigations, while in other departments the gang unit is a unit within a larger bureau such as the organized crime bureau. In the following section we briefly consider some of the different functions and organizational patterns characteristic of police gang units.

Intelligence Activities

Both police officials and researchers have identified intelligence gathering and the development and maintenance of gang tracking systems and databases as one of the most important functions carried out by specialized gang units (Bureau of Justice Assistance, 1997; Jackson and McBride, 1985; Katz, Webb, and Schaefer, 2000). Our research in the police departments of Albuquerque, Inglewood, Junction City, Las Vegas, Mesa, and Phoenix indicates that the gang units in each of these departments performed an intelligence function. This finding is consistent with that of Klein (1995b), who found that intelligence gathering, as opposed to enforcement, investigation, or prevention, was the primary function in 83 percent of the gang units across the country.

Although nearly every gang unit engages in some form of intelligence gathering, the importance of this function to the gang unit and to its respective department varies from one department to the next. For example, in Inglewood, purported to be the original home of the Bloods and Crips, intelligence gathering and dissemination is the sole activity performed by the department's gang unit. Key stakeholders in that department, such as detectives working in the robbery and burglary units, attribute substantial value to gang unit intelligence in supporting the investigative process. Information such as monikers (street names), legal names, addresses, known associates, photographs, and gang affiliation are useful in conducting investigations. Detectives are quick to cite instances in which intelligence from the gang unit was instrumental in solving a crime and leading to an arrest. On the other hand, the fact that a gang unit has an intelligence function does not necessarily mean that the function plays a central role within the unit. For example, in Las Vegas we found that a large gang unit carried out suppression, investigation, and intelligence functions. However, it was clear that in comparison to intelligence, suppression and investigation activities were given top priority and were

thought to be of greater importance to the functioning of the gang unit by the gang unit's officers. Relatively little emphasis was placed on the unit's computerized gang intelligence database, in part because there were few officers who could actually use the database. That gang unit's stakeholders articulated the need for good intelligence, but in contrast to Inglewood, for example, they were critical of the general unavailability and lack of access to information thought to be contained in the intelligence system.

Gang unit stakeholders in Albuquerque reaffirmed the importance of the intelligence function when they tied their assessment of the gang unit's value directly to the amount of information that the unit provided to other units. Stakeholders in patrol and area command units recalled that, in the early days, the original gang unit was valuable to the department because it was a dependable source of intelligence on gangs and gang members. However, it appears that as the unit became more autonomous and institutionalized, it focused less on intelligence and more on suppression, and as a result stakeholders tended to devalue the unit's contribution to gang control efforts. For stakeholders in Albuquerque, like those in the other departments we have studied, the gang unit's most valuable commodity is information gathered and shared as part of its intelligence function.

Suppression/Enforcement Activities

Suppression and enforcement gang unit activities are those most likely to capture the imagination of the public and the media as well as of police officers looking for action on the streets. Whereas the intelligence function and the sharing of information gives value to gang unit activities and legitimizes the existence of the unit from the perspective of many departmental stakeholders, it is suppression/enforcement that legitimizes the unit in the eyes of the public and the media, and gives them confidence that the unit is actively engaging in enforcement efforts directed at gangs and gang crime.

Suppression activities in the cities studied were typically restricted to directed patrol in known gang areas—meaning minority public housing districts as well as parks and parking lots that gang members were believed to frequent. Many of the officers explained that patrolling gang areas allows them to keep an eye on gang members and gang activity, and at the same time provides them with the opportunity to develop personal relationships with gang members for the purpose of establishing a thorough intelligence network.

Suppression activities are of central value in the gang unit's work group culture, even though the amount of time actually spent on such activities can vary immensely from one gang unit to the next. The one exception to the centrality of suppression in gang unit ethos is the situation where the unit performs a single nonsuppression function such as intelligence, as we found in Inglewood. The gang units in Las Vegas, Mesa, and Phoenix stand in marked contrast to Inglewood. Although they have responsibility for intelligence, most of their resources are focused on enforcement activities. Compared to intelligence gathering, suppression activities are highly visible, and when covered by the media they demonstrate that the department is combating the local gang problem.

We found that while most of the gang units emphasized enforcement as a core function of the gang unit, the amount of time spent engaging in suppression activities varied across the departments. For example, we found that members of the gang unit in Albuquerque, Las Vegas, and Phoenix on average spent over two hours per eight-hour shift on enforcement activities and had a relatively high number of enforcement-related contacts (for example, over two per eight-hour shift). However, observations of the Junction City gang unit indicated that the officers spent relatively little time on enforcement activities and had few contacts with gang members. Specifically, we found that the gang unit officers averaged only about 60 minutes per shift on enforcement-related activities and averaged only one contact for every 16 hours of work.

Criminal Investigation Activities

The gang units that we studied devoted relatively few resources and little time to carrying out criminal investigation activities. The most common involvement in criminal investigations tended to be indirect and performed largely as part of the intelligence function. As was previously mentioned, detectives in most of the sites studied were quick to point out the value and use of information provided by the gang intelligence unit in solving cases involving gang members. As a consequence, gang unit officers were occasionally found to be called in by other specialized investigative units to assist in the investigation of crimes involving gang members.

In two of the six sites, Las Vegas and Phoenix, the gang units had primary responsibility for investigating all "serious" gang-motivated crimes with the exception of homicide, kidnapping, and sexual assault. Gang unit officers in these units maintained that their expertise with gangs put them in a unique position to investigate and solve crimes. The officers also believed that it was essential for the unit to be involved in gang-related investigations in order to gather worthwhile and timely intelligence. For these reasons the Las Vegas Metropolitan Police Department's gang unit wanted investigative responsibility for gang-motivated homicides as well. However, the homicide bureau wanted to retain investigative responsibility, maintaining that their crime-specific expertise was required to investigate and solve homicides—gang motivated or not.

Interestingly, Klein, Gordon, and Maxson's (1985) study of gang and non-gang homicide investigations carried out by the Los Angeles County Sheriff's Department (LASD) and the Los Angeles Police Department (LAPD) bears directly on this issue. They found that in LASD cases investigative outcomes were enhanced when the gang unit was involved, but that in LAPD cases gang unit involvement made no difference in investigative outcomes.

Prevention Activities. Nearly all of the gang units that we have observed perform some prevention function, although, with the exception of Junction City, prevention received much less priority than intelligence, suppression, or investigations. In describing gang unit activity, prevention is probably at best a residual category that includes activities other than intelligence, suppression, or investigation. Prevention, when it does occur, frequently takes the form of public education. For example, in Junction City, a city with limited gang activity, the gang unit officers were directed by departmental order to spend 25 percent of their time on educational activities. Observations of

Junction City's gang unit's educational activities, such as presentations to local schools and community groups about the local gang problem, indicated that they were largely performed in order to gain support and help legitimize the unit's existence. Public educational appearances increased awareness of the unit and "promoted an image of operational effectiveness" (Katz, 2001: 32). Public education activities were found to provide a forum for the gang unit to convince the unconvinced that there is a gang problem that justifies the establishment and maintenance of a specialized gang unit.

Interestingly, none of the gang units studied participated in the best-known prevention effort, the Gang Resistance Education and Training (GREAT) program. Instead, in the departments studied we found that the community relations unit or bureau conducted these types of formalized prevention efforts. When we asked officers in the gang units why their units were not responsible for these prevention efforts, they stated that while they believed that these activities were worthwhile and "should be performed by someone in the department," they should not be the responsibility of the gang unit. Officers in all of the units studied agreed that enforcement-related activities should be the primary focus of the unit and not prevention or education-related activities. Some of the officers pointed out that such activities conflict with expectations of the purpose of the gang unit, while others stated that the unit's resources were already strained and that they could not afford to be distracted from their "real job" of combating gang-related crime.

Patterns of Specialization in Police Gang Units. Police gang units generally can be placed along a continuum of complexity based on the number of different functions that a unit performs. At one end of the continuum is the single-function gang unit, which focuses on one activity such as intelligence. As was mentioned previously, the Inglewood, California gang unit is an example of this type. Inglewood's unit consists of four officers who are assigned to collect, maintain, and disseminate gang intelligence. Further along the continuum is a somewhat more complex pattern of specialization characteristic of multiple-function gang units. This type of gang unit tends to perform two or three different functions such as intelligence

and suppression or intelligence and prevention, with one of the functions being primary and the other secondary. Here we define the primary function as the focal activity of the unit and the one on which most of the unit's efforts and resources are expended. The secondary function usually receives far less attention and resources and is viewed as being less important by gang unit officers. The Phoenix Police Department's gang unit is a good example of this type of unit. This unit engages in a combination of suppression, investigation, and intelligence activities, with emphasis placed on suppression. At the other end of the continuum, opposite the single-function gang unit, is the comprehensive unit, or a gang unit that performs intelligence, suppression/enforcement, investigation, and prevention, with each of these functions receiving differing levels of effort and resource investment. The Junction City unit is an example of a comprehensive gang unit.

This continuum of gang unit complexity based on specialization should be seen as a schematic, with different gang units placed at different points along the continuum. In reality, none of the gang units that we have studied fits one of the three points on the continuum perfectly; rather, each approximates a type. For example, although Inglewood's gang unit is considered to be a single-function unit, there are occasions when the unit will assist other units with suppression or investigative activity. Of all of the gang units observed, the Junction City unit came closest to approximating the comprehensive unit. Katz (2001) provides the following details on the formally assigned activities of that unit.

> Gang unit officers were instructed to allocate approximately 50 percent of their time toward intelligence activities, 25 percent toward enforcement activities, and 25 percent toward educational activities. The gang unit was also reconfigured as a support unit, and was mandated to assist other units and organizations with gang-related problems and issues (e.g., gang investigations, patrolling known gang areas). (p. 33)

In observing Junction City's gang unit activities, we found that 42 percent of the unit's time was allocated for enforcement, 24 percent for investigation, 20 percent for education, and 13 percent for intelligence (Katz, 1997).

With the exception of Inglewood, the single-function unit with responsibility for intelligence, the other gang units studied tended to place the greatest value, but not necessarily the greatest amount of effort, on suppression activities. This was the case in those departments where there was a serious gang problem (for example, Albuquerque, Las Vegas, and Phoenix), as well as those with a less serious gang problem (for example, Mesa, Junction City). We found that communities with serious gang problems present gang units with the greatest opportunities to devise and engage in suppression activities, whereas communities with less serious gang problems (for example, Junction City) present fewer such opportunities. Nevertheless, suppression is the most highly valued function among gang unit officers even in those departments with few opportunities to execute suppression activities. . . .

Toward Improving the Effectiveness of Police Gang Units

Our observation of police gang units convinces us that police organizations need to carefully reassess the organization configuration of their response to gangs as well as the investment of resources in that response. The starting point is a thoughtful and careful assessment of the local gang problem and of whether or not it is of sufficient magnitude to warrant a specialized unit to address the problem. With the possible exception of Junction City, the gang units that we have observed were in communities with substantial gang problems, and specialized gang units were a reasonable response to the local problem. However, we suspect that a substantial number of police gang units developed during the last decade were formed not in response to local gang problems, but were the result of mimetic processes (DiMaggio and Powell, 1991).

Mimetic processes occur when organizations model themselves after other organizations. DiMaggio and Powell (1991: 67–68) explain that mimetic processes may occur when (1) there is little consensus as to which organizational structures and operational activities are most efficient and effective, (2) organizational goals are unclear, or

(3) the "environment creates symbolic uncertainty" (for example, is there or is there not a gang problem in our community?). The authors argue that organizations mimic others in response to uncertainty. By adopting organizational structures and operational activities that are used by organizations that are considered successful, they themselves gain legitimacy. If anything, they argue, it illustrates to the organization's institutional environment that they are trying to do something to improve the (albeit ambiguous) situation.

In other words, we suspect that many police departments have created gang units for reasons related to institutional legitimacy rather than to respond to actual contingencies in their environment. Klein (1995a, b) alludes to this point in his discussion of Sergeant Wes McBride of the Los Angeles County Sheriff's Department (LASD). Many departments across the nation have adopted the structures and strategies recommended by McBride and the LASD because of their national reputation for gang control efforts, rather than because it is a model that is appropriate for a particular jurisdiction's gang problem.

While there is evidence that some police departments are eliminating their gang units (Katz, Maguire, and Roncek, 2000), it is unclear if this is in response to a diminished local gang problem, a growing awareness of problems stemming from the decoupling of gang units, or for other reasons. One would hope that it is a reflection of careful assessments of local gang problems that have in turn led to the elimination of police gang units. However, gangs remain a problem in jurisdictions throughout the country, and therefore warrant a continued response by the police. The challenge becomes one of reassessing present patterns of response and adjusting them to improve their effectiveness.

References

Bureau of Justice Assistance. 1997. *Urban Street Gang Enforcement*. Washington, D.C.: Bureau of Justice Assistance.

Bureau of Justice Statistics. 1999. *Law Enforcement Management and Administrative Statistics, 1997: Data for Individual State and Local Agencies with 100 or More Officers*. Washington, D.C.: U.S. Government Printing Office.

Curry, G. David, Richard A. Ball, and Robert J. Fox. 1994. *Gang Crime and Law Enforcement Record Keeping.* Washington, D.C.: National Institute of Justice.

Curry, G. David, Richard A. Ball, Robert J. Fox, and Darryl Stone. 1992. *National Assessment of Law Enforcement Anti-Gang Information Resources. Final Report.* Washington, D.C.: National Institute of Justice.

DiMaggio, Paul, and Walter Powell. 1991. "The Iron Cage Revisited: Institutional Isomorphism and Collective Rationality in Organizational Fields." In *The New Institutionalism in Organizational Analysis*, edited by Walter Powell and Paul DiMaggio. Chicago: University of Chicago Press.

Howell, James. 1999. "Youth Gang Homicides: A Literature Review." *Crime and Delinquency* 45 (2): 208–241.

Huff, C. Ronald. 1990. *Gangs in America.* Newbury Park, Calif.: Sage.

Huff, C. Ronald, and Wesley D. McBride. 1990. "Gangs and the Police." In *Gangs in America*, edited by C. Ronald Huff. Newbury Park, Calif.: Sage.

Jackson, Robert K., and Wesley D. McBride. 1985. *Understanding Street Gangs.* Sacramento, Calif.: Custom Publishing.

Katz, Charles M. 1997. "Police and Gangs: A Study of a Police Gang Unit." Ph.D. diss., University of Nebraska at Omaha.

———. 2001. "The Establishment of a Police Gang Unit: An Examination of Organizational and Environmental Factors." *Criminology* 39 (1): 301–337.

Katz, Charles M., Edward R. Maguire, and Dennis Roncek. 2000. "A Macro-Level Analysis of the Creation of Specialized Police Gang Units: An Examination of Rational, Social, Threat, and Resource Dependency Perspectives." Unpublished manuscript.

Katz, Charles M., Vincent J. Webb, and Robin Haar. 1998. *The Police Response to Gangs: A Multi-Site Study.* NIJ Research in Brief submitted to the National Institute of Justice, Office of Justice Programs. Washington, D.C.: U.S. Department of Justice.

Katz, Charles M., Vincent J. Webb, and David R. Schaefer. 2000. "The Validity of Police Gang Intelligence Lists: Examining the Differences in Delinquency between Documented Gang Members and Non-documented Delinquent Youth." *Police Quarterly* 3 (4): 413–437.

Katz, Jesse. 1990. "Officers' Folksy Tactics Pay Off in Gang Domain." *Los Angeles Times*, 5 November, p. B5.

Klein, Malcolm W. 1971. *Street Gangs and Street Workers.* Englewood Cliffs, N.J.: Prentice Hall.

———. 1995a. "Attempting Gang Control by Suppression: The Misuse of Deterrence Principles." In *The Modern Gang Reader*, by Malcolm W. Klein, Cheryl L. Maxson, and Jody Miller. Los Angeles: Roxbury.

———. 1995b. *The American Street Gang.* New York: Oxford University Press.

Klein, Malcolm W., M. A. Gordon, and C. L. Maxson. 1985. *Differences between Gang and Nongang Homicides. Criminology* 23: 209–222.

McCorkle, Richard, and Terance Miethe. 1998. "The Political and Organizational Response to Gangs: An Examination of a 'Moral Panic' in Nevada." *Justice Quarterly* 15: 41–64.

Needle, Jerome, and William Stapleton. 1983. *Police Handling of Youth Gangs. Reports of the National Juvenile Justice Assessment Centers.* Washington, D.C.: U.S. Government Printing Office.

Office of Juvenile Justice and Delinquency Prevention. 2000. *National Youth Gang Survey.* Washington, D.C.: Office of Juvenile Justice and Delinquency Prevention.

President's Commission on Law Enforcement and Administration of Justice. 1967. *The Challenge of Crime in a Free Society.* Washington, D.C.: U.S. Government Printing Office.

Spergel, Irving A. 1995. *The Youth Gang Problem: A Community Approach.* New York: Oxford University Press.

Spergel, Irving A., and G. David Curry, 1993. "The National Youth Gang Survey: A Research and Development Process." In *The Gang Intervention Handbook*, edited by Arnold P. Goldstein and C. Ronald Huff. Champaign, Ill.: Research Press.

Walker and Katz. 1995. "Less Than Meets the Eye: Police Department Bias-Crime Units." *American Journal of Police* 14: 29–47.

Webb, Vincent J., and Charles M. Katz. 1997. "Citizen Ratings of the Importance of Community Policing Activities." *Policing: An International Journal of Police Strategy and Management* 20: 7–23.

CHAPTER 36

Focused Deterrence Strategies and the Reduction of Gang and Group-Involved Violence

Anthony A. Braga

The Boston Gun Project (aka "Operation Ceasefire"), as described in this chapter, was not specifically designed as a gang suppression operation. But that's how it turned out, as most of the gun violence in the area was committed by gang members. The project was unusual in its adherence to the tenets of deterrence theory as its intellectual model. Like the Spergel Model described in Chapter 34, Operation Ceasefire has been somewhat modified and replicated in a number of locations. It has had much appeal to law enforcement agencies in particular. Because of its purported success, the model has been touted for its contribution to reducing violence, but a word of caution is in order (as noted by the author). Ceasefire is usually implemented at the height of an area's gun violence, when one might expect a reduction to follow anyway (the well-known "regression effect"). Because the project is usually implemented without predetermined control groups and areas, the ratio of regression effect to program effect is not clear.

Anumber of jurisdictions have been experimenting with new problem-oriented frameworks to understand and respond to gun violence among gang-related and criminally active group-involved offenders. These interventions are based on the "pulling levers" focused deterrence strategy, which directs criminal justice and social service attention toward the small number of chronic

offenders who are responsible for the bulk of urban gun violence problems (Braga, Kennedy, & Tita, 2002). While the research evidence on the crime prevention value associated with this approach is still developing, the pulling levers strategy has been embraced by the U.S. Department of Justice as an effective approach to crime prevention. In his address to the American Society of Criminology, former National Institute of Justice Director Jeremy Travis (1998) announced that the pulling levers approach has made "enormous theoretical and practical contributions to our thinking about deterrence and the role of the criminal justice system in producing safety."

Pioneered in Boston, Massachusetts, to halt youth violence, the pulling levers framework has been applied in many U.S. cities through federally sponsored violence prevention programs such as the Strategic Alternatives to Community Safety Initiative and Project Safe Neighborhoods (Coleman, Holton, Olson, Robinson, & Stewart, 1999; Dalton, 2002). In its simplest form, the approach consists of selecting a particular crime problem, such as youth homicide; convening an interagency working group of law enforcement practitioners; conducting research to identify key offenders, groups, and behavior patterns; framing a response to offenders and groups of offenders that uses a varied menu of sanctions ("pulling levers") to stop them from continuing their violent behavior; focusing social services and community resources on targeted offenders and groups to match law enforcement prevention efforts; and directly and repeatedly communicating with offenders to make them understand why they are receiving this special attention (Kennedy, 2006).

The first section of this chapter introduces the development of the pulling levers focused deterrence approach in Boston. The subsequent sections consider the available evaluation evidence on the effectiveness of pulling levers in Boston, speculate on the violence reduction mechanisms that may be associated with the Boston approach, and examine experiences with pulling levers focused deterrence strategies in other jurisdictions. The chapter concludes by reviewing the key elements that make up these promising gang and group-involved violence reduction strategies.

The Boston Gun Project and Operation Ceasefire

The Boston Gun Project was a problem-oriented policing enterprise expressly aimed at taking on a serious, large-scale crime problem—homicide victimization among young people in Boston. Like many large cities in the United States, Boston experienced a large sudden increase in youth homicide between the late 1980s and early 1990s. The Boston Gun Project began in early 1995 and implemented what is now known as the "Operation Ceasefire" intervention, which began in the late spring of 1996 (Kennedy, Piehl, & Braga, 1996). The working group of law enforcement personnel, youth workers, and Harvard University researchers diagnosed the youth violence problem in Boston as one of patterned, largely vendetta-like ("beef") hostility among a small population of chronic offenders, and particularly among those involved in some 61 loose, informal, mostly neighborhood-based groups. These 61 gangs included between 1100 and 1300 members, representing fewer than 1% of the city's youth between the ages of 14 and 24. Although small in number, these gangs were responsible for more than 60% of youth homicides in Boston.

The Operation Ceasefire focused deterrence strategy was designed to prevent violence by reaching out directly to gangs, saying explicitly that violence would no longer be tolerated, and backing up that message by "pulling every lever" legally available when violence occurred (Kennedy, 1997). The chronic involvement of gang members in a wide variety of offenses made them, and the gangs they formed, vulnerable to a coordinated criminal justice response. Authorities sought to disrupt street drug activity, focus police attention on low-level street crimes such as trespassing and public drinking, serve outstanding warrants, cultivate confidential informants for medium- and long-term investigations of gang activities, deliver strict probation and parole enforcement, seize drug proceeds and other assets, ensure stiffer plea bargains and sterner prosecutorial attention, request stronger bail terms (and enforce them), and bring potentially severe federal investigative and prosecutorial attention to gang-related drug and gun activity.

Simultaneously, youth workers, probation and parole officers, and later churches and other community groups offered gang members services and other kinds of help. These partners also delivered an explicit message that violence was unacceptable to the community and that "street" justifications for violence were mistaken. The Ceasefire Working Group disseminated this message in formal meetings with gang members (known as "forums" or "call-ins"), through individual police and probation contacts with gang members, through meetings with inmates at secure juvenile facilities in the city, and through gang outreach workers. The deterrence message was not a deal with gang members to stop violence. Rather, it was a promise to gang members that violent behavior would evoke an immediate and intense response. If gangs committed other crimes but refrained from violence, the normal workings of police, prosecutors, and the rest of the criminal justice system dealt with these matters. If gang members hurt people, however, the Working Group concentrated its enforcement actions on their gangs.

The Operation Ceasefire "crackdowns" were not designed to eliminate gangs or stop every aspect of gang activity, but rather to control and deter serious violence (Kennedy, 1997). To do so, the Working Group explained its actions against targeted gangs to other gangs: "This gang did violence, we responded with the following actions, and here is how to prevent anything similar from happening to you." The ongoing Working Group process regularly monitored the city for outbreaks of gang violence and framed any necessary responses in accord with the Ceasefire strategy. As the strategy unfolded, the Working Group continued communication with gangs and gang members to convey its determination to stop violence, to explain its actions to the target population, and to maximize both voluntary compliance and the strategy's deterrent power.

A central hypothesis within the Working Group was the idea that a meaningful period of substantially reduced youth violence might serve as a "firebreak" and result in a relatively long-lasting reduction in future youth violence. The idea was that youth violence in Boston had become a self-sustaining cycle among a relatively small number of youth, with objectively high levels of risk leading to nominally self-protective behaviors such as gun acquisition and use, gang formation, tough "street" behavior, and the like—behavior that then became an additional input into the cycle of violence. If this cycle could be interrupted, it was thought, a new equilibrium at a lower level of risk and violence might be established, perhaps without the need for continued high levels of either deterrent or facilitative intervention (Kennedy et al., 1996).

Evaluation Evidence

A large reduction in the annual number of youth homicides in Boston followed immediately after Operation Ceasefire was implemented in mid-1996. A U.S. Department of Justice (DOJ)–sponsored evaluation of Operation Ceasefire revealed that the intervention was associated with a 63% decrease in the monthly number of Boston youth homicides, a 32% decrease in the monthly number of shots-fired calls, a 25% decrease in the monthly number of gun assaults, and, in one high-risk police district given special attention in the evaluation, a 44% decrease in the monthly number of youth gun assault incidents. The evaluation also suggested that Boston's significant youth homicide reduction associated with Operation Ceasefire was distinct when compared to youth homicide trends in most major U.S. and New England cities (Braga, Kennedy, Waring, & Piehl, 2001).

In subsequent reviews of the evaluation, some researchers have been less certain about the magnitude of the violence reduction effect associated with Operation Ceasefire. Given the complexities

of analyzing city-level homicide trend data, Ludwig (2005) and Rosenfeld et al. (2005) urged caution in drawing strong conclusions about this program's effectiveness. Others reviewers, however, have been more supportive of the evaluation evidence on violence reductions associated with the Ceasefire intervention. The National Research Council's Panel on Improving Information and Data on Firearms acknowledged the uncertainty in specifying the size of violence reduction effect associated with Operation Ceasefire by virtue of its quasi-experimental evaluation design (Wilford, Pepper, & Petrie, 2005). Nonetheless, it concluded that the Ceasefire evaluation was "compelling" in associating the intervention with the subsequent decline in youth homicide. In their close review of the Ceasefire evaluation, Morgan and Winship (2007) found the analyses to be of very high methodological quality and to make a strong case for causal assertions.

Explaining the Effectiveness of Operation Ceasefire

The Harvard research team, unfortunately, did not collect the necessary pre-test and post-test data to shed light on the specific mechanisms responsible for the significant violence reductions associated with the Operation Ceasefire intervention. The research team focused on problem analysis and program development and, a priori, did not know which form the intervention would take and who the target audience of that intervention would be. Because the necessary evaluation data are not available, it is necessary to draw on the research literature on gang intervention programs to speculate on the effectiveness of the Operation Ceasefire approach to controlling gang violence (Braga & Kennedy, 2002).

As part of the Office of Juvenile Justice and Delinquency Prevention (OJJDP) National Youth Gang Suppression and Intervention Program, Spergel and Curry (1990, 1993) surveyed 254 law enforcement, school, and community representatives in 45 cities and 6 institutional sites on their gang intervention programs. From these survey data, Spergel and Curry developed a four-category typology of the interventions that these areas used to deal with gang problems: (1) suppression, (2) social intervention, (3) opportunity provision, and (4) community organization. Although Operation Ceasefire was a problem-oriented policing project centered on law enforcement interventions, the other elements of Operation Ceasefire that involved community organization, social intervention, and opportunity provision certainly supported and strengthened the ability of law enforcement to reduce gang violence. Beyond deterring violent behavior, Operation Ceasefire was designed to facilitate desired behaviors among gang members. As Spergel (1995) observed, coordinated strategies that integrate these varied domains are most likely to prove effective in dealing with chronic youth gang problems.

Suppression. The typical law enforcement suppression approach assumes that most street gangs are criminal associations that must be attacked through an efficient gang tracking, identification, and targeted enforcement strategy (Spergel, 1995). The basic premise of this approach is that improved data collection systems and coordination of information across different criminal justice agencies lead to more efficiency and to more gang members being removed from the streets, rapidly prosecuted, and sent to prison for longer sentences. Typical suppression programs included street sweeps in which police officers round up hundreds of suspected gang members, special gang probation and parole caseloads where gang members are subjected to heightened levels of surveillance and more stringent revocation rules, prosecution programs that target gang leaders and serious gang offenders, civil procedures that use gang membership to define arrest for conspiracy or unlawful associations, and school-based law enforcement programs that use surveillance and buy–bust operations (Klein, 1993).

These suppression approaches are loosely based on deterrence theory. Law enforcement agencies attempt to influence the behavior of gang members or eliminate gangs entirely by dramatically increasing the certainty, severity, and swiftness of criminal justice sanctions. Unfortunately, gangs and gang problems usually persist even in the wake of these intensive operations. Malcolm Klein (1993) suggests that law enforcement agencies do not generally have the capacity to "eliminate" all gangs in a gang-troubled jurisdiction, nor do they have the capacity to respond in a powerful way to all gang offending in such jurisdictions. Pledges to do so, though common, are simply not credible to gang members. Klein also observes that the emphasis on selective enforcement by deterrence-based gang suppression programs may increase the cohesiveness of gang members, who often perceive such actions as unwarranted harassment, rather than as cause to withdraw from gang activity. Therefore, suppression programs may have the perverse effect of strengthening gang solidarity.

Beyond the certainty, severity, and swiftness of sanctions, the effective operation of deterrence depends on the communication of punishment threats to the public. As Zimring and Hawkins (1973) observed, "The deterrence threat may best be viewed as a form of advertising" (p. 142). The Operation Ceasefire Working Group recognized that, for the strategy to be successful, it was crucial to deliver a *credible* deterrence message to Boston gangs. Therefore, its intervention targeted only those gangs who were engaged in violent behavior rather than wasting resources on those who were not. Spergel (1995) suggests that problem-solving approaches to gang problems based on more limited goals such as gang violence reduction rather than gang destruction are more likely to be effective in controlling gang problems. Operation Ceasefire did not attempt to eliminate all gangs or eliminate all gang offending in Boston. Despite the large reductions in youth violence, Boston still has gangs and Boston gangs still commit crimes. Nevertheless, Boston gangs now do not commit violent acts as frequently as they did in the past.

The Ceasefire focused deterrence approach attempted to prevent gang violence by making gang members believe that consequences would follow on the heels of violence and gun use, and encouraging them to choose to change their behavior. A key element of the strategy was the delivery of a direct and explicit "retail deterrence" message to a relatively small target audience regarding which kinds of behavior would provoke a special response and what that response would be. In addition to any increases in certainty, severity, and swiftness of sanctions associated with acts of violence, the Operation Ceasefire strategy sought to gain deterrence through the *advertising* of the law enforcement strategy and the personalized nature of its application. It was crucial that gang youth understood the new regime that the city was imposing. Beyond the particular gangs subjected to the intervention, the deterrence message was applied to a relatively small audience (all gang-involved youth in Boston) rather than diffused across a general audience (all youth in Boston), and it operated by making explicit cause-and-effect connections between the behavior of the target population and the behavior of the authorities. Knowledge of what happened to others in the target population was intended to prevent further acts of violence by gangs in Boston.

In the communication of the deterrence message, the Working Group also wanted to develop a common piece of shared moral ground with gang members. The Group wanted the gang members to understand that most victims of gang violence were gang members, that the strategy was designed to protect both gang members and the community in which they lived, and that the Working Group had gang members' best interests in mind even if the gang members' own actions required resorting to coercion in an effort to protect them. The Working Group also hoped that the process of communicating on a face-to-face basis with gangs and gang members would undercut any feelings of anonymity and invulnerability they might have, and that a clear demonstration of interagency solidarity would enhance offenders' sense that something new and powerful was happening.

Social Intervention and Opportunity Provision. Social intervention programs encompass both social services agency–based programs and detached "streetworker" programs; opportunity provision strategies attempt to offer gang members legitimate opportunities and means to success that are at least as appealing as the available illegitimate options (Curry & Decker, 1998; Klein, 1995; Spergel, 1995).

Boston streetworkers were key members of the Operation Ceasefire Working Group and, along with the Department of Youth Services (DYS) case workers, probation officers, and parole officers in the group, added a much needed social intervention and opportunity provision dimension to the

Ceasefire strategy. The mayor of the city of Boston established the Boston Community Centers' Streetworkers social services program in 1991. The streetworkers were charged with seeking out at-risk youth in Boston's neighborhoods and providing them with services such as job skills training, substance abuse counseling, and special education.

Many Boston streetworkers are themselves former gang members. Gang researchers have suggested that meaningful gang crime prevention programs should recruit gang members to participate in the program as staff and consultants (Bursik & Grasmick, 1993; Hagedorn, 1988).

Beyond their important roles as social service providers, streetworkers attempted to prevent outbreaks of violence by mediating disputes between gangs. Streetworkers also ran programs intended to keep gang-involved youth safely occupied and to bring them into contact with one another in ways that might breed tolerance, including a Peace League of gang-on-gang basketball games held at neutral, controlled sites.

Through the use of these resources, the Ceasefire Working Group was able to pair criminal justice sanctions, or the promise of sanctions, with help and with services. When the risk to drug-dealing gang members increases, legitimate work becomes more attractive. In turn, when legitimate work is more widely available, raising risks will be more effective in reducing violence. The expansion of social services and opportunities was intended to increase the Ceasefire strategy's preventive power by offering gang members any assistance they might want: protection from their enemies, drug treatment, access to education and job training programs, and the like.

Community Organization. Community organization strategies to cope with gang problems include attempts to create community solidarity, networking, education, and involvement (Spergel & Curry, 1993).

The Ten Point Coalition of activist black clergy played an important role in organizing Boston communities suffering from gang violence (Winship & Berrien, 1999). This organization was formed in 1992 after gang members invaded the Morningstar Baptist Church, where a slain rival gang member was being memorialized, and attacked mourners with knives and guns. In the wake of that watershed moment, the Ten Point Coalition decided to respond to violence in its community by reaching out to drug-involved and gang-involved youth and by organizing within Boston's black community.

Over time, the Ten Point clergy members came to work closely with the Boston Community Centers' streetworkers program to provide at-risk youth with opportunities. Although the Ten Point Coalition was initially very critical of the Boston law enforcement community, participants eventually forged a strong working relationship. Ten Point clergy and others involved in this faith-based organization accompanied police officers on home visits to the families of troubled youth and also acted as advocates for youth in the criminal justice system. These home visits and street work by the clergy were later incorporated into Operation Ceasefire's portfolio of interventions. Ten Point clergy also provided a strong moral voice at the gang forums in the presentation of Operation Ceasefire's antiviolence message.

Although its members did not become involved in Operation Ceasefire until after the strategy had been designed and implemented, the Ten Point Coalition played a crucial role in framing a discussion in Boston that made it much easier to speak directly about the nature of youth violence in Boston. Members of the Ceasefire Working Group could speak with relative safety about the painful realities of minority male offending and victimization, "gangs," and chronic offenders. The Ten Point clergy also made it possible for Boston's minority community to have an ongoing conversation with Boston's law enforcement agencies on legitimate and illegitimate means to control crime in the community.

Although the clergy supported Operation Ceasefire's tight focus on violent youth, they condemned any indiscriminate, highly aggressive law enforcement sweeps that might put nonviolent minority youth at risk of being swept into the criminal justice system. Before the Ten Point Coalition developed its role as an intermediary, Boston's black community viewed past activities of law enforcement agencies to monitor violent youth as illegitimate and with knee-jerk suspicion. As noted by Winship and Berrien (1999), the Ten Point Coalition evolved into an institution that provides an umbrella of legitimacy for the police to work under. With the Ten Point organization's approval of and involvement in Operation Ceasefire, the community supported the approach as a legitimate youth violence prevention campaign.

Experiences and Evaluation Evidence From Other Jurisdictions

At first blush, the effectiveness of the Operation Ceasefire intervention in preventing violence might seem unique to Boston. Operation Ceasefire was constructed largely from the assets and capacities available in Boston at the time and deliberately tailored to the city's specific gang violence problem. Operational capacities of criminal justice agencies in other cities will be different, of course, and gang violence problems in other cities will have important characteristics that distinguish them from the situation in Boston. Nevertheless, the basic working group problem-oriented policing process and the "pulling levers" approach to deterring chronic offenders are transferable to violence problems in other jurisdictions.

To date, a number of cities have experimented with these analytic frameworks and have reported noteworthy crime control gains. This section highlights gang violence reduction efforts in Los Angeles, California; Indianapolis, Indiana; Stockton, California; and Lowell, Massachusetts. Research evidence on some promising applications of focused deterrence strategies to individual offenders and overt drug markets is also presented. Consistent with the problem-oriented policing approach (Eck & Spelman, 1987; Goldstein, 1990), these cities have tailored the approach to fit their unique violence problems and operating environments.

Operation Ceasefire in Los Angeles

In March 1998, the U.S. National Institute of Justice (NIJ) funded the RAND Corporation to develop and test strategies for reducing gun violence among youth in Los Angeles. In part, the goal of this effort was to determine which parts of the Boston Gun Project might be replicable in Los Angeles. In designing the replication, RAND drew a clear distinction between the process governing the design and implementation of the strategy (data-driven policy development; problem-solving working groups) and the elements and design (pulling levers, collective accountability, retailing the message) of the Boston model. Processes, in theory, can be sustained and adaptive, and as such can be utilized to address dynamic problems. By singling out process as an important component, the RAND team hoped to clarify the point that process can affect program effectiveness independently of the program elements or the merits of the actual design (Tita, Riley, & Greenwood, 2003).

The Los Angeles replication was unique in several important ways. First, the implementation was not citywide, but rather was carried out only within a single neighborhood (Boyle Heights) within a single Los Angeles Police Department (LAPD) Division (Hollenbeck). The project site, Boyle Heights, had a population that was relatively homogenous. More than 80% of the residents were Latinos of Mexican origin. The same was true for the gangs operating in this area, many of which were formed prior to World War II. These gangs were clearly "traditional" gangs, with memberships exceeding 100 members or more. The gangs were strongly territorial, encompassed age-graded substructures, and were intergenerational in nature (Maxson & Klein, 1995).

Unlike in some other cities where gang and group-involved violence is a rather recent phenomenon, Los Angeles represented an attempt to reduce gun violence in a "chronic gang city" with a long history of gang violence, and an equally long history of gang reduction strategies. The research team had to first convince members of the local criminal justice community and the at-large community that the approach espoused differed in important ways from these previous efforts to combat gangs. In fact, it did: The RAND project was not about "doing something about gangs," but rather about "doing something about gun violence" in a community where gang members were responsible for an overwhelming proportion of gun violence.

The independent analysis of homicide files confirmed the perception held by police and community alike that gangs were highly over-represented in homicidal acts. From 1995 to 1998, 50% of all homicides in the area had a clear gang motivation. Another 25% of the homicides could be coded as "gang related" because they involved a gang member as victim or offender, but were motivated by reasons other than gang rivalries.

Given the social organization of violence in Boyle Heights, the multidisciplinary working group fully embraced the pulling levers focused deterrence strategy that had been developed in Boston. A high-profile gang shooting that resulted in a double homicide in Boyle Heights triggered the implementation of the Operation Ceasefire intervention in October 2000. The processes of retailing the message were formally adopted, although message delivery was mostly accomplished through personal contact rather than in a group setting. Police, probation, community advocates, street gang workers, a local hospital, and local clergy all passed along the message of collective accountability for gangs whose members continued to commit gang violence.

Unfortunately, as Tita, Riley, Ridgeway, and colleagues (2003) report, the Los Angeles pulling levers intervention was not fully implemented as planned. The implementation of the Ceasefire program in the Boyle Heights was negatively affected by the well-known Ramparts LAPD police corruption scandal and a lack of ownership of the intervention by the participating agencies.

Despite the implementation difficulties, the RAND research team was able to complete an impact evaluation of the violence prevention effects of the pulling levers focused deterrence strategy that was implemented. Using a variety of methods, the investigators determined that consistent, noteworthy short-term reductions in violent crime, gang crime, and gun crime were associated with the Ceasefire program. In addition to their analyses of the main effects of the intervention, RAND researchers examined the effects of the intervention on neighboring areas and gangs. Their analyses suggested a strong diffusion of violence prevention benefits emanating from the targeted areas and targeted gangs (Tita et al., 2003).

Indianapolis Violence Reduction Partnership

The Indianapolis Violence Reduction Partnership (IVRP) working group consisted of Indiana University researchers and federal, state, and local law enforcement agencies (McGarrell & Chermak, 2003). During the problem analysis phase, the researchers examined 258 homicides from 1997 and the first 8 months of 1998 and found that a majority of homicide victims (63%) and offenders (75%) had criminal and/or juvenile records. Those individuals with a prior record often had a substantial number of arrests. The working group members performed the same structured, qualitative data-gathering exercises used in Boston to gain insight into the nature of homicide incidents. The qualitative exercise revealed that 59% of the incidents involved "groups of known chronic offenders" and 53% involved drug-related motives such as settling business and turf disputes. The terminology "groups of known chronic offenders" was initially used in Indianapolis because, at that point in time, there was not a consensual definition of "gang" and the reality of much gang activity in Indianapolis was of a relatively loose structure.

The working group developed two sets of overlapping strategies. First, the most violent chronic offenders in Indianapolis were identified and targeted for heightened attention, leading to greater arrest, prosecution, and incarceration rates. Second, the working group adopted the pulling levers approach to reduce violent behavior by gangs and groups of known chronic offenders.

The IVRP strategy implemented by the Indianapolis working group closely resembled the Boston version of pulling levers. The communications strategy, however, differed in an important way. The deterrence and social services message was delivered in meetings with high-risk probationers and parolees organized by neighborhoods. Similarly, home visits by probation and parolees were generally organized by neighborhood. As the project progressed, when a homicide or series of homicides involved certain groups or gangs, the working group attempted to target meetings, enforcement activities, and home visits on the involved groups or gangs (McGarrell & Chermak, 2003).

A DOJ-funded evaluation revealed that the IVRP strategy was associated with a 34% reduction in Indianapolis homicides. The evaluation further revealed that the homicide reduction in Indianapolis differed from the homicide trends observed in six comparable Midwestern cities during the same time period (McGarrell, Chermak, Wilson, & Corsaro, 2006).

Operation Peacekeeper in Stockton

Beginning in mid-1997, criminal justice agencies in Stockton began experimenting with the pulling levers approach to address a sudden increase in youth homicide. The Stockton Police Department and other local, state, and federal law enforcement agencies believed that most of the youth violence problem was driven by gang conflicts and that the pulling levers approach used in Boston might be effective in reducing Stockton's gang violence problem. The strategy was implemented by the Stockton Police Department's Gang Street Enforcement Team and grew into what is now known as "Operation Peacekeeper" as more agencies joined the partnership (Wakeling, 2003).

The Peacekeeper intervention was managed by a working group of line-level criminal justice practitioners; social service providers also participated in the working group process as appropriate. When street gang violence erupted or when it came to the attention of a working group member that gang violence was imminent, the working group followed the Boston model by sending a direct message that gang violence would not be tolerated, pulling all available enforcement levers to prevent violence, engaging in communications, and providing social services and opportunities to gang members who wanted them.

To better document the nature of homicide and serious violence in Stockton, the working group retained Harvard University researchers to conduct ongoing problem analyses (Braga, 2005). Their results revealed that many offenders and victims involved in homicide incidents had noteworthy criminal histories and prior criminal justice system involvement. Gang-related conflicts were identified as the motive in 41% of homicides between 1997 and 1999.

The research analysis also revealed that the California city is home to 44 active gangs with a total known membership of 2100 individuals. Most conflicts among these gangs fall into three broad categories: Asian gang beefs, Hispanic gang beefs, and African American gang beefs. Within each broad set of ethnic antagonisms, particular gangs may form alliances with other gangs. Conflicts among Asian gangs involve clusters of different gangs comprising mostly Laotian and Cambodian youth. Conflicts among Hispanic gangs mainly involve a very violent rivalry between Norteño gangs from Northern California and Sureño gangs from Southern California. African American gangs tend to form fewer alliances and are divided along the well-known Blood and Crip lines.

An evaluation of Operation Peacekeeper found that this strategy was associated with a 42% decrease in gun homicide incidents. The same investigation also compared Stockton gun homicide trends to gun homicide trends in eight other midsized California cities, reporting that the large reduction in gun homicides in Stockton was not echoed in the comparison cities (Braga, 2008).

Project Safe Neighborhoods in Lowell

Supported by funds from the DOJ-sponsored Project Safe Neighborhoods initiative, an inter-agency task force implemented a pulling levers focused deterrence strategy to prevent gun violence among Hispanic and Asian gangs in Lowell, Massachusetts, in 2002 (Braga, McDevitt, & Pierce, 2006). While Lowell authorities felt very confident about their ability to prevent violence among Hispanic gangs by pursuing a general focused deterrence strategy, they were much less confident about their ability to prevent Asian gang violence by applying the same set of criminal justice levers to Asian gang members. As Malcolm Klein (1995) suggests, Asian gangs have some key differences from typical black, Hispanic, and white street gangs. Notably, they are more organized, have identifiable leaders, and are far more secretive. They also tend to be far less territorial and less openly visible, so their street presence is low compared to other ethnic gangs. Relationships between law enforcement agencies and the Asian community are often characterized by mistrust and a lack of communication (Chin, 1996). As such, it is often difficult for the police to develop information on the participants

in violent acts to hold offenders accountable for their actions.

During the intervention time period, the Lowell Police Department (LPD) had little reliable intelligence about Asian gangs in the city. The LPD had attempted to recruit informants in the past but most of these efforts had been unsuccessful. With the increased focus on Asian gang violence, the LPD increased its efforts to develop intelligence about the structure of the city's Asian gangs and particularly the relationship between Asian gang violence and ongoing gambling that was being run by local Asian businesses. Asian street gangs are sometimes connected to adult criminal organizations and assist older criminals in extortion activities and protecting illegal gambling enterprises (Chin, 1996). In many East Asian cultures, rituals and protocols guiding social interactions are well defined and reinforced through a variety of highly developed feelings of obligation, many of which are hierarchical in nature (Zhang, 2002). This factor facilitates some control over the behavior of younger Asian gang members by elders in the gang.

In Lowell, Cambodian and Laotian gangs consisted of youth whose street activities were influenced by "elders" of the gang. Elders were generally long-time gang members in their thirties and forties who no longer engaged in illegal activities on the street or participated in street-level violence with rival youth. Rather, these older gang members were heavily involved in running illegal gambling dens and informal casinos that were operated out of cafes, video stores, and warehouses located in the poor Asian neighborhoods of Lowell. The elders used young street gang members to protect their business interests and to collect any unpaid gambling debts. Illegal gaming was a very lucrative business that was much more important to the elders than any ongoing beefs the youth in their gang had with other youth (Braga et al., 2006). Relative to acquiring information on individuals responsible for gun crimes in Asian communities, it was much easier to detect the presence of gambling operations through surveillance or a simple visit to the suspected business establishment.

The importance of illegal gaming to influential members of Asian street gangs provided a potentially potent lever for law enforcement to exploit in preventing violence. The authorities in Lowell believed that they could systematically prevent street violence among gangs by targeting the gambling interests of older members. When a street gang was violent, the LPD targeted the gambling businesses run by the older members of the gang. The enforcement activities ranged from serving a search warrant on the business that housed the illegal enterprise and making arrests to simply placing a patrol car in front of the suspected gambling location to deter gamblers from entering. The LPD coupled these tactics with the delivery of a clear message: "When the young gang members associated with you act violently, we will shut down your gambling business. When violence erupts, no one makes money" (Braga et al., 2006). Between October 2002 and June 2003, during the height of the focused attention on Asian gangs, the LPD executed some 30 search warrants on illegal gambling dens that resulted in more than 100 gambling-related arrests.

An impact evaluation found that the Lowell pulling levers strategy was associated with a 43% decrease in the monthly number of gun homicide and gun aggravated assault incidents. A comparative analysis of gun homicide and gun aggravated assault trends in Lowell relative to other major Massachusetts cities also supported the contention that a unique program effect was associated with the pulling levers intervention (Braga, Pierce, McDevitt, Bond, & Cronin, 2008).

While this approach to preventing violence among Asian street gangs represents an innovation in policing, it is not an entirely new idea. The social control exerted by older Asian criminals over their younger counterparts is well documented in the literature. For example, in his study of Chinese gangs in New York City, Chin (1996) suggests that gang leaders exert influence over subordinate gang members to end violent confrontations so they can focus their energies on illegal enterprises that make money. The prospect of controlling street violence by cracking down on the interests of organized crime is also familiar to law enforcement. In his classic study of an Italian street gang in Boston's North End, Whyte (1943) described the activities of beat officers in dealing with outbreaks of violence by cracking down on

the gambling rackets run by organized crime in the neighborhood. Nevertheless, the systematic application of this approach, coupled with a communications campaign, represents an innovative way to deal with Asian street gang violence.

Applying Focused Deterrence to Individual Offenders. A variation of the Boston model was applied by Papachristos et al. (2007) in Chicago. Gun- and gang-involved parolees returning to selected highly dangerous Chicago neighborhoods went through "call-ins" where they were informed of their vulnerability as felons to federal firearms laws, with stiff mandatory minimum sentences for violating these laws; offered social services; and addressed by community members and ex-offenders. A rigorous evaluation showed a neighborhood-level homicide reduction impact of 37%. Individual-level effects were remarkable. For offenders with prior gun offenses but no evidence of gang involvement, for example, attendance at a call-in reduced the recidivism rate (i.e., return to prison) at around five years from release from approximately 50% to 10% (Fagan, Meares, Papachristos, & Wallace, 2008).

Applying Focused Deterrence to Overt Drug Markets. There is less experience in applying the focused deterrence approach to other crime and disorder problems. In High Point, North Carolina, a focused deterrence strategy was aimed at eliminating public forms of drug dealing such as street markets and crack houses by warning dealers, buyers, and their families that enforcement was imminent. With individual "overt" drug markets cited as the unit of work, the project employed a joint police–community partnership to identify individual offenders; notify them of the consequences of continued dealing; provide supportive services through a community-based resource coordinator; and convey an uncompromising community norm against drug dealing. This application of focused deterrence is generally referred to as the drug market intervention (DMI) strategy.

The DMI seeks to shut down overt drug markets entirely. Enforcement powers are used strategically and sparingly, with arrest and prosecution being enforced only against violent offenders and when nonviolent offenders have resisted all efforts to get them to desist and to provide them with help. Through the use of "banked" cases, the strategy makes the promise of law enforcement sanctions against dealers extremely direct and credible, so that dealers are in no doubt concerning the consequences of offending and have good reason to change their behavior. The strategy also brings powerful informal social control to bear on dealers from immediate family and community figures. The strategy organizes and focuses services, help, and support for dealers so that those who are willing to change their lives have what they need to do so. Each operation also includes a maintenance strategy.

A preliminary assessment of the High Point DMI found noteworthy reductions in drug and violent crime in the city's West End neighborhood (Frabutt, Gathings, Hunt, & Loggins, 2004). A more rigorous evaluation of the High Point DMI is currently being conducted.

An evaluation of a similar DMI strategy in Rockford, Illinois, found noteworthy crime prevention gains associated with the approach (Corsaro, Brunson, & McGarrell, 2011). Study findings suggest that the Rockford strategy was associated with a statistically significant and substantive reduction in crime, drug, and nuisance offenses in the target neighborhood.

Discussion

The available research evidence suggests that these new focused deterrence approaches to prevent gang and group-involved violence have generated promising results. Certain core elements of this approach seem to be the key ingredients in their apparent success. These key elements are delineated here (Braga et al., 2002).

Recognition of the Concentration of Urban Violence Problems among Groups of Chronic, Often but not Always Gang-Involved, Offenders

Research has demonstrated that the character of criminal and disorderly youth gangs and groups varies widely both within cities and across cities (Curry, Ball, & Fox, 1994). The diverse findings on the nature of criminally active groups and gangs in the jurisdictions described in this chapter certainly support this assertion. The research also suggests that the terminology used to describe the types of groups involved in urban violence matters less than their behavior. Gangs, their nature, and their behavior remain central questions for communities, police, and scholars.

At the same time, where violence prevention and public safety are concerned, the gang question is not the central one. The more important observation is that urban violence problems are, in large measure, concentrated among groups of chronic offenders; thus the dynamics between and within these groups have major implications for crime rates (Kennedy, 2001). This is an old observation in criminology, and one that is well known among line law enforcement personnel, prosecutors, probation and parole officers, and other authorities. The new crime prevention strategies offer a way of responding to this reality without setting the usually unattainable goals of eliminating chronic offending or eliminating criminal gangs and groups.

Recognition of Dynamic or Self-Reinforcing Positive Feedback Mechanisms among Group and Gang Violence

The research findings indicate that groups of chronic offenders are locked in a self-sustaining dynamic of violence often driven by fear, "respect" issues, and vendettas. The promising reductions observed in the cities employing these strategic crime prevention frameworks suggest that the "firebreak hypothesis" may be right. If this cycle of violence among these groups can be interrupted, perhaps a new equilibrium at a lower level of risk and violence can be established. This relationship may be one explanation for the rather dramatic impacts apparently associated with what are, in fact, relatively modest interventions.

The Utility of the Pulling Levers Approach

The pulling levers strategy at the heart of these new focused deterrence approaches was designed to influence the behavior, and the environment, of the groups of chronic offenders who were identified as the core of the cities' violence problems. The pulling levers approach attempts to prevent gang and group-involved violence by making these groups believe that dire consequences will follow from violence and gun use and choose to change their behavior. A key element of the strategy is the delivery of a direct and explicit "retail deterrence" message to a relatively small target audience regarding which kinds of behavior will provoke a special response and what that response will be.

Drawing on Practitioner Knowledge to Understand Violence Problems

The experiences, observations, local knowledge, and historical perspectives of police officers, streetworkers, and others with routine contact with offenders, communities, and criminal networks represent an underutilized resource for describing, understanding, and crafting interventions aimed at crime problems (Kennedy, Braga, & Piehl, 1997). The semi-structured qualitative research performed by the academics in these initiatives essentially refined and specified existing practitioner knowledge. Combining official data sources with street-level qualitative information helps to paint a dynamic, real-life picture of the violence problem.

An Interagency Working Group with a Locus of Responsibility

Criminal justice agencies work largely independently of one another, often at cross-purposes, often without coordination, and often in an atmosphere of distrust and dislike (Kennedy, 2001). Different elements operating within agencies may be plagued by the same problems. The ability of the cities profiled in this chapter to deliver a meaningful violence prevention intervention was created by convening an interagency working group of line-level personnel with decision-making power who could assemble a wide range of incentives and disincentives for the target audience. It was also important to place a locus of responsibility for reducing violence within the group. Prior to the creation of the working groups, no one in these cities was responsible for developing and implementing an overall strategy for reducing violence.

Researcher Involvement in an Action-Oriented Enterprise

The activities of the research partners in these initiatives departed from the traditional research and evaluation roles usually played by academics (Sherman, 1991). The integrated researcher–practitioner partnerships in the working group setting more closely resembled policy analysis exercises that blend research, policy design, action, and evaluation (Kennedy, 2009; Kennedy & Moore, 1995). Researchers have been important assets in all of the projects described in this chapter, providing what is essentially "real-time" social science aimed at refining the working group's understanding of the problem, creating information products for both strategic and tactical use, testing (often in a very elementary, but important, fashion) candidate intervention ideas, and maintaining a focus on clear outcomes and the evaluation of performance. They have begun to produce accounts of both basic findings and intervention designs and implementation processes, which will be helpful to other jurisdictions moving forward. In addition, in several sites, researchers played important roles in organizing the projects.

Conclusion

The cumulative experience described in this chapter appears supportive, at this preliminary stage, of the proposition that the basic Boston approach has now been replicated, with promising results, in a number of disparate sites. This extension suggests that there was nothing particularly unique about either the implementation or the impact of Operation Ceasefire in Boston. Further, it suggests that the fundamental pulling levers focused deterrence framework behind Ceasefire can be successfully applied in other jurisdictions, with other sets of partners, with different particular activities, and in the context of different basic types of gangs and groups. Further operational experience and more refined evaluation techniques will tell us more about these questions, as experience and analysis continue to accumulate. At the moment, there appears to be reason for continued optimism that serious violence by gangs and other groups is open to direct and powerful prevention.

References

Braga, A. A. (2005). Analyzing homicide problems: Practical approaches to developing a policy-relevant description of serious urban violence. *Security Journal, 18*, 17–32.

Braga, A. A. (2008). Pulling levers focused deterrence strategies and the prevention of gun homicide. *Journal of Criminal Justice, 36*, 332–343.

Braga, A. A., & Kennedy, D. M. (2002). Reducing gang violence in Boston. In W. Reed & S. H. Decker (Eds.), *Responding to gangs: Research and evaluation* (pp. 265–288). Washington, DC: National Institute of Justice, U.S. Department of Justice.

Braga, A. A., Kennedy, D. M., & Tita, G. (2002). New approaches to the strategic prevention of gang and group-involved violence. In C. R. Huff (Ed.), *Gangs in America* (pp. 271–286) (3rd ed.). Thousand Oaks, CA: Sage.

Braga, A. A., Kennedy, D. M., Waring, E. J., & Piehl, A. M. (2001). Problem-oriented policing, deterrence, and youth violence: An evaluation of Boston's Operation Ceasefire. *Journal of Research in Crime and Delinquency, 38*, 195–225.

Braga, A. A., McDevitt, J., & Pierce, G. L. (2006). Understanding and preventing gang violence: Problem analysis and response development in Lowell, Massachusetts. *Police Quarterly, 9*, 20–46.

Braga, A. A., Pierce, G. L., McDevitt, J., Bond, B. J., & Cronin, S. (2008). The strategic prevention of gun violence among gang-involved offenders. *Justice Quarterly, 25*, 132–162.

Bursik, R. J., & Grasmick, H. G. (1993). *Neighborhoods and crime: The dimensions of effective community control*. New York: Lexington Books.

Chin, K. (1996). *Chinatown gangs: Extortion, enterprise, and ethnicity*. New York: Oxford University Press.

Coleman, V., Holton, W. C., Olson, K., Robinson, S., & Stewart, J. (1999, October). Using knowledge and teamwork to reduce crime. *National Institute of Justice Journal*, 16–23.

Corsaro, N., Brunson, R. K., & McGarrell, F. (In press). Problem-oriented policing and open-air drug markets: Examining the Rockford pulling levers strategy. *Crime & Delinquency*.

Curry, G. D., Ball, R. A., & Fox, R. J. (1994). *Gang crime and law enforcement recordkeeping*. Research in Brief. Washington, DC: National Institute of Justice, U.S. Department of Justice.

Curry, G. D., & Decker, S. H. (1998). *Confronting gangs: Crime and community*. Los Angeles: Roxbury Press.

Dalton, E. (2002). Targeted crime reduction efforts in ten communities: Lessons for the Project Safe Neighborhoods Initiative. *U.S. Attorney's Bulletin, 50*, 16–25.

Eck, J. E., & Spelman, W. (1987). *Problem-solving: Problem-oriented policing in Newport News*. Washington, DC: Police Executive Research Forum.

Fagan, J., Meares, T., Papachristos, A. V., & Wallace, D. (2008, November). *Desistance and legitimacy: Effect heterogeneity in a field experiment with high-risk offenders*. Presented at the annual meeting of the American Society of Criminology, St. Louis, MO.

Frabutt, J., Gathings, M. J., Hunt, E. D., & Loggins, T. J. (2004). *High Point West End Initiative: Project description, log, and preliminary impact analysis*. Greensboro, NC: Center for Youth, Family, and Community Partnerships.

Goldstein, H. (1990). *Problem-oriented policing*. Philadelphia: Temple University Press.

Hagedorn, J. (1988). *People and folks: Gangs, crime, and the underclass in a Rustbelt city*. Chicago: Lakeview Press.

Kennedy, D. M. (1997). Pulling levers: Chronic offenders, high-crime settings, and a theory of prevention. *Valparaiso University Law Review, 31*, 449–484.

Kennedy, D. M. (2001). A tale of one city: Reflections on the Boston Gun Project. In G. Katzmann (Ed.), *Managing youth violence* (pp. 14–33). Washington, DC: Brookings Institution Press.

Kennedy, D. M. (2006). Old wine in new bottles: Policing and the lessons of pulling levers. In D. L. Weisburd & A. A. Braga (Eds.), *Police innovation: Contrasting perspectives* (pp. 155–170). New York: Cambridge University Press.

Kennedy, D. M. (2009). Drugs, race, and common ground: Reflections on the High Point Intervention. *National Institute of Justice Journal, 262*, 12–17.

Kennedy, D. M., Braga, A. A., & Piehl, A. M. (1997). The (un)known universe: Mapping gangs and gang violence in Boston. In D. L. Weisburd & J. T. McEwen (Eds.), *Crime mapping and crime prevention* (pp. 219–262). Monsey, NY: Criminal Justice Press.

Kennedy, D. M., & Moore, M. H. (1995). Underwriting the risky investment in community policing: What social science should be doing to evaluate community policing. *Justice System Journal, 17*, 271–290.

Kennedy, D. M., Piehl, A. M., & Braga, A. A. (1996). Youth violence in Boston: Gun markets, serious youth offenders, and a use-reduction strategy. *Law and Contemporary Problems, 59*, 147–196.

Klein, M. (1993). Attempting gang control by suppression: The misuse of deterrence principles. *Studies on Crime and Crime Prevention, 2*, 88–111.

Klein, M. (1995). *The American street gang: Its nature, prevalence, and control*. New York: Oxford University Press.

Ludwig, J. (2005). Better gun enforcement, less crime. *Crime and Public Policy, 4,* 677–716.

Maxson, C. L., & Klein, M. W. (1995). Investigating gang structures. *Journal of Gang Research, 3,* 33–38.

McGarrell, E. F., & Chermak, S. (2003). Problem solving to reduce gang and drug- related violence in Indianapolis. In S. H. Decker (Ed.), *Policing gangs and youth violence* (pp. 77–101). Belmont, CA: Wadsworth.

McGarrell, E. F., Chermak, S., Wilson, J., & Corsaro, N. (2006). Reducing homicide through a "lever-pulling" strategy. *Justice Quarterly, 23,* 214–229.

Morgan, S., & Winship, C. (2007). *Counterfactuals and causal models.* New York: Cambridge University Press.

Papachristos, A., Meares, T., & Fagan, J. (2007). Attention felons: Evaluating Project Safe Neighborhoods in Chicago. *Journal of Empirical Legal Studies, 4,* 223–272.

Rosenfeld, R., Fornango, R., & Baumer, E. (2005). Did Ceasefire, Compstat, and Exile reduce homicide? *Crime and Public Policy, 4,* 419–450.

Sherman, L. (1991). Herman Goldstein: Problem-oriented policing. *Journal of Criminal Law and Criminology, 82,* 693–702.

Spergel, I. A. (1995). *The youth gang problem: A community approach.* New York: Oxford University Press.

Spergel, I. A., & Curry, G. D. (1990). Strategies and perceived agency effectiveness in dealing with the youth gang problem. In C. R. Huff (Ed.), *Gangs in America* (pp. 254–265). Newbury Park, CA: Sage.

Spergel, I. A., & Curry, G. D. (1993). The National Youth Gang Survey: A research and development process. In A. Goldstein & C. R. Huff (Eds.), *Gang intervention handbook* (pp. 359–400). Champaign/Urbana, IL: Research Press.

Tita, G. E., Riley, K. J., & Greenwood, P. W. (2003). From Boston to Boyle Heights: The process and prospects of a "pulling levers" strategy in a Los Angeles barrio. In S. H. Decker (Ed.), *Policing gangs and youth violence* (pp. 102–130). Belmont, CA: Wadsworth.

Tita, G., Riley, K. J., Ridgeway, G., Grammich, C., Abrahamse, A., & Greenwood, P. (2003). *Reducing gun violence: Results from an intervention in East Los Angeles.* Santa Monica, CA: RAND Corporation.

Travis, J. (1998, November 12). *Crime, justice, and public policy.* Plenary presentation to the American Society of Criminology. Washington, DC. Retrieved January 21, 2011, from http://www.ojp.usdoj.gov/nij/speeches/asc.htm

Wakeling, S. (2003). *Ending gang homicide: Deterrence can work.* Perspectives on Violence Prevention, No. 1. Sacramento, CA: California Attorney General's Office/California Health and Human Services Agency.

Wellford, C., Pepper, J., & Petrie, C. (Eds.). (2005). *Firearms and violence: A critical review.* Committee to Improve Research Information and Data on Firearms. Committee on Law and Justice, Division of Behavioral and Social Sciences and Education. Washington, DC: National Academics Press.

Whyte, W. F. (1943). *Street corner society: The social structure of an Italian slum.* Chicago: University of Chicago Press.

Winship, C., & Berrien, J. (1999, Summer). Boston cops and black churches. *Public Interest,* 52–68.

Zhang, S. (2002). Chinese gangs: Familial and cultural dynamics. In C. R. Huff (Ed.), *Gangs in America* (pp. 219–236) (3rd ed.). Thousand Oaks, CA: Sage.

Zimring, F., & Hawkins, G. (1973). *Deterrence: The legal threat in crime control.* Chicago: University of Chicago Press.

CHAPTER 37

"It's Getting Crazy Out There": Can a Civil Gang Injunction Change a Community?

Cheryl L. Maxson ▪ Karen M. Hennigan ▪ David C. Sloane

Like police gang units and Operation Ceasefire described earlier, civil gang injunctions have become a gang suppression approach with much appeal to law enforcement and prosecution agencies. Yet there has been until now precious little adequate research designed to understand the value of the approach: anecdotal evidence ("I feel safer," "they say the gangs are intimidated by injunctions") is not a substitute for carefully designed research comparisons. In the case of this next chapter, the goal is not to test program effects directly on changes in gang crime, but rather to test effects on various responses of community residents to gang injunctions applied in their areas of residence. In addition to the reported results, the authors provide a discussion of competing theories that might explain injunction effects. More theory in place of practitioner ideologies can go far in improving our ability to mount effective gang control programs.

One weekend in November 2002, a drive-by shooting on the west side of San Bernardino, California left two teenagers and one adult wounded. A 15-year-old resident of the area told a reporter, "It's getting crazy out there" (Fisher et al., 2002). Living on a block where an 11-year-old recently had been stabbed during a burglary, she seemed to be stating the obvious. Police responded by instituting a civil gang injunction (CGI)—a process whereby selected gang members

are prohibited from engaging in such activities as loitering at schools, carrying pagers and riding bicycles, or face arrest—against a local gang. They hoped that by curtailing the gang's activities, they could diminish residents' sense of insecurity and promote a safer, healthier community. As a local newspaper editorialized, the injunction would help a neighborhood where residents "suffer emotional distress, their children cannot play outdoors, and their pets must be locked up inside" (Staff Reports, 2002).

The 2002 National Youth Gang Survey (NYGS) found active youth gangs in more than 2,300 cities and 550 other jurisdictions served by county law enforcement (Egley and Major, 2004). Youth that join gangs account for most serious and violent crimes committed by adolescents, and offending rates are elevated during active periods of membership (Thornberry et al., 2003). Gang members are notoriously resistant to intervention, and gang interventions are equally resistant to evaluation. In concluding a volume reporting nine separate police gang interventions. Decker (2003:290) warns "that we lack even basic knowledge about the impact of interventions on gangs and youth violence" and this ignorance "should be a clarion call to police, legislators, researchers, and policymakers" to critically evaluate interventions.

The CGI is an increasingly popular anti-gang strategy. Although civil court injunctions to prohibit gang activity at specific locations date back to 1980, the first injunction against a gang and its members is credited to the Los Angeles city attorney in 1987 (see Los Angeles City Attorney Gang

Prosecution Section, 1995).[1] Injunction activity increased at a moderate pace until the mid-1990s when it dramatically accelerated. Our interviews with gang officers and prosecutors and reviews of practitioner reports and media accounts yielded 37 separate CGIs in Southern California between 1980 and 2000. In the four-year period from 1996 to 1999, a Southern California gang was enjoined, on average, every two months. As of July 2004, at least 22 injunctions had been issued in the city of Los Angeles alone. This growth in injunction activity has been fostered by how-to workshops sponsored by the California Association of District Attorneys, detailed training manuals (see Los Angeles County District Attorney, 1996, for an early example), and local descriptions in practitioner publications (Cameron and Skipper, 1997; Genelin, 1998; Mazza, 1999). Gang injunctions have also received widespread attention in local and national media.

Although most injunctions have occurred in California, law enforcement agencies nationwide are searching for new tools to combat the growth and impact of gangs in their neighborhoods. A nationwide interview survey of police officers in jurisdictions that the 1999 NYGS indicated had developed a CGI found a high rate of confusion about the tactic and confirmed 11 jurisdictions in 7 states outside California have obtained a CGI (Maxson, 2004). Anecdotally, police and public officials claim the tactic is very effective in eliminating gang activity. Yet, relatively little systematic research on the effectiveness of injunctions has been completed.

This article presents the findings of an evaluation of the impact of a CGI implemented in the Verdugo Flats neighborhood of San Bernardino, California, in Fall 2002. The research focuses on changes in the quality of life in this neighborhood, rather than on the injunction's effects on the targeted gang members or on levels of crime. The study's findings have clear implications for gang and crime researchers, law enforcement agencies that anticipate using this strategy, civil court judges who are asked to limit the activities of gang members to achieve more community order, and community members wondering if this strategy can improve their neighborhoods.

Civil Gang Injunctions

After conducting interviews with law enforcement gang specialists and reviewing the practitioner literature, we concluded that the CGI is a relatively flexible tool to combat gangs (Maxson, et al., 2003). Allan examined the variation in provisions in 42 injunctions requested by prosecutors and found that injunctions addressed "local gang problems with customized provisions based on specific local circumstances" (2004:241). The procedures used vary among jurisdictions within and outside California, the state where most of them have been issued (Maxson, 2004). Here, we describe the process of obtaining and implementing CGIs as it is generally understood in California.

Implementing a CGI is an elaborate process. Police officers, often in collaboration with prosecutors, gather evidence that members of a street gang represent a public nuisance in their neighborhood, in violation of California Civil Code sections 3479 and 3480.[2] Evidence used to support an injunction includes the criminal history of gang members, written declarations by officers familiar with the neighborhood, and sometimes, declarations from community members that describe the effects of specific nuisance activities on neighborhood residents. The prosecutor uses the declarations and other materials to craft the injunction, working with officers to select the gang members to be named, the geographic area to be covered, and the specific behaviors that will be prohibited.[3]

The number of gang members, the size of the area, and the type of prohibited activities varies considerably.[4] The number of gang members can range from a handful to the hundreds, and the initial string of names often is followed by "and any other members."[5] The targeted area can be a housing complex, several square blocks, or an entire city, but most often CGIs are spatially based, neighborhood-level interventions intended to disrupt the gang's routine activities. Prohibited behaviors include illegal activities such as trespass, vandalism, drug selling, and public urination, as well as otherwise legal activities, such as wearing gang colors, displaying hand signs, and carrying a pager or signaling passing cars, behaviors associated with drug selling.

Nighttime curfews are often imposed. Most disturbing to legal scholars and advocates is the commonly applied prohibition against any two or more named gang members associating with one another (Bjerregaard, 2003; Geis, 2002; Stewart, 1998).

The prosecutor files the application for a temporary restraining order (TRO) in civil court, and a hearing is scheduled. All named gang members are served notice of the hearing and the injunction. At this hearing, the judge considers the submitted evidence, hears testimony, and entertains questions from targeted individuals. Occasionally, legal counsel represents individuals, but as a rule, defendants are not provided with public counsel in civil proceedings.[6] Judges have at times challenged the inclusion of certain individuals, the size of the targeted area, and the scope of prohibitions. If the preliminary injunction is issued at this hearing, targeted individuals must be served again with amended papers before the injunction can be enforced. Offenders can be prosecuted in either civil or criminal court for violation of a valid court order and fined up to $1000 and/or incarcerated for up to six months. Some prosecutors seek enhanced bail amounts for arrested offenders, which can translate into significant jail time. The preliminary injunction can be in effect for a limited time, such as a year, or indefinitely. Prosecutors may seek a permanent injunction and can add individuals or provisions to an existing injunction with relative ease. A few gang injunctions have been denied, but judges usually approve them, particularly because the California Supreme court upheld a San Jose injunction in the *Acuna* case (*People ex rel. Gallo v. Acuna*, 929 P.2d 596, 1997).

The tactics used for implementation vary from one injunction to the next. Sometimes a special unit is tasked with enforcement. In other instances, the whole patrol force is alerted to the conditions of the injunction. No registry records the number of arrests resulting from injunctions. Interviews with law enforcement officials suggest the number varies widely, from very few to as many as several hundred.

Theory: How CGIs Might Reduce Gang Activity

The criminological and social psychological literatures suggest several processes that might be relevant to understanding injunction effects on neighborhoods and gang members. First, social disorganization theory provides a foundation for predicting changes in social relationships. Resident participation in developing and implementing a gang injunction may spark a process of community engagement in efforts to build informal social control, social capital in the form of social networks, and supportive organizational structures (Bursik and Grasmick, 1993; Greene, 2004). Even if neighborhood residents are not engaged in the injunction activities directly, reducing the level of the immediate threat of the gang may lay a foundation for improving the quality of neighborhood life by strengthening collective efficacy (Sampson et al., 1997). As levels of intimidation and fear ease, a community may be able to organize and become involved in the process of reversing the deterioration of the physical and social order in their community, with its attendant effects on fear of crime and civic engagement.

Practitioners often note these anticipated effects (see excellent examples in Los Angeles City Attorney Gang Prosecution Section, 1995 and Los Angeles County District Attorney, 1996). The goals of injunctions typically are couched in community policing terms, such as solving specific community crime, disorder, and fear problems (Allan, 2004; Greene, 2003; Stewart, 1998). As Ventura County prosecutor Karen Wold envisioned when seeking an injunction against the Colonia Chiques gang in Oxnard, California, "Parents can take their kids to the park again" (Wolcott, 2004). Higher levels of community involvement and greater impact on community environments might be expected from injunctions developed and implemented with this philosophical orientation, as compared with other forms of gang enforcement (Decker, 2003).

Second, two theories address how injunctions might influence individual gang members. Deterrence theory predicts that sure, swift, and severe sanctions will deter criminal behavior. Although the penalties for injunction violations are not severe, the notifications of hearings and injunction papers might make targeted gang members believe that they are being closely watched and more likely to be apprehended and prosecuted for violations (Grogger, 2002; Klein, 1993).

Practitioners contend that issuance of the injunction has a profound effect on gang members. Longtime community gang intervention activist Father Greg Boyle was cited in a recent press report, "I mean, eight minutes after one was filed here on the Eastside, I had kids in my office saying, 'Get me a job'" (Fremon, 2003). Low arrest rates would presumably erode this perception.

In addition, social psychological theory suggests that group identity causes individuals to feel less responsible for their behavior, and influences them to conform to situation-specific group norms (cf., Postmes and Spears, 1998; Spears et al., 2001). In gangs, situation-specific norms promote violent and antisocial behavior (Decker and Van Winkle, 1996; Vigil, 1988, 2002). A gang injunction holds individuals personally accountable for their actions which could weaken gang identity and decrease levels of participation in gang-related behavior, especially among noncore members (cf., Ellemers et al., 2002). In this process of holding individuals responsible for their gang activities, identification with the gang might decline, as could the overall gang cohesiveness. Alternatively, if the injunction sends the message that law enforcement is targeting the group rather than individuals, fringe members might react with increased loyalty to fend off the perceived group level threat and gang cohesiveness might increase (Klein, 1995).

Each theoretical perspective points to different evaluation designs to assess potential outcomes of CGIs. Deterrence and individuation might be tested by interviews with targeted gang members and the examination of changes in crime patterns. Community social disorganization theory suggests the assessment of changes in community perceptions of intimidation, fear, disorder, and neighborhood efficacy. This latter approach is adopted in this study.

Proclamations of the success of gang injunctions surface regularly in practitioner publications and media accounts. Many jurisdictions have multiple injunctions, and presumably, repetition of the strategy follows a positive experience. We have illustrated these success claims and the anecdotal evidence marshaled to support them elsewhere (Maxson et al., 2003). In these accounts, changes in crime rates are sometimes noted, but without adequate comparison with equivalent areas or offenders.

Three independent evaluations of injunctions have used official crime data to measure outcomes. Maxson and Allen (1997) conducted a process evaluation of a CGI in Inglewood, California. Their brief assessment of reported crime in the target area suggested little support for a positive effect. A legal advocacy organization conducted a statistical analysis of various crime indicators in 19 reporting districts including and surrounding the Blythe Street injunction implemented by the Los Angeles Police Department in the San Fernando Valley (ACLU, 1997). The authors concluded that this injunction increased violent crime.

In the most rigorous study of crime patterns to date, Grogger (2002) assessed changes in reported serious violent and property crimes for 14 injunctions obtained in Los Angeles County between 1993 and 1998. Grogger compared crime trends in the injunction areas with those in matched comparison areas. Pooling the injunction areas, he found that violent crime decreased during the year after injunctions by roughly 5% to 10%. This effect was concentrated in reductions in assault, rather than in robbery. He found no effect in property crimes and no evidence that injunctions caused crime to increase in adjoining areas. Because all injunctions were aggregated in this analysis, it was unclear whether some injunctions were more effective than others. Moreover, he could not identify offenses committed by gang members or the specific individuals targeted by the injunctions. Still, this study is the first scholarly report of positive effects of injunctions on crime in neighborhoods targeted by CGIs.

The community disorganization perspective suggests that injunctions should improve patterns in community processes, such as neighborhood relationships, disorder, and informal social control. The evaluation in this study addresses community-level outcomes rather than the individual gang member outcomes suggested by deterrence and individuation. Because the few evaluations of injunctions conducted to date consider the impact on criminal behavior, this study is the first to focus on neighborhood processes.

Conceptually, we expect that community-level effects of an injunction would unfold over time. If injunctions cause gang members to modify their behavior in the community, then the more immediate effects for neighborhood residents should be reduced gang visibility, graffiti, instances of gang intimidation, and fear of gang victimization. Only later should these benefits result in reduced fear of crime more generally, less crime victimization, and improved community order. Long term, residents in neighborhoods may experience increased neighborhood social cohesion and informal social control, more collective and neighborhood social efficacy, more willingness to call police in threatening situations, and improved perceptions of police authority.

San Bernardino and the Verdugo Flats Injunction

An interview survey of more than two dozen Southern California police agencies with significant gang populations using multi-agency collaborations to combat them found that San Bernardino presented several advantages for the research. First, the San Bernardino Police Department (SBPD) had already conducted three injunctions (two against territorial street gangs and one against prostitutes along a main boulevard) before our first contact with them in Spring 2000. Second, the gangs that they were considering for further injunctions seemed excellent targets for studying the impact on communities. Third, the department welcomed our inquiry and proved very helpful in all regards.

San Bernardino is roughly 60 miles east of Los Angeles in the rapidly growing Inland Empire. In 2000, over 185,000 people lived in the city. Although the city is part of one of the fastest expanding economic areas in Southern California, it is also home to many poor minorities. Almost half of the population is Latino, roughly 18% are African Americans and about 30% are white. More than one in five of the residents in this city was born outside the United States, with another 20% born outside of California. Over one third of the population speaks only Spanish at home. The city has experienced gang activity for decades, and gangs have been expanding in the city throughout the last one third of a century. Although other Southern California cities were experiencing marked declines in violent and property crimes during the period of this study, reported crime in San Bernardino increased substantially between 2002 and 2003. San Bernardino police officials were quoted in local media reports as attributing the rise in crime rates to "continued economic problems, high rates of gang membership and a large number of parolees" (Warren, 2003: B5).

In Summer 2002, five shootings and one assault suggested that the Verdugo Flats gang was actively defending its territory against a failed intrusion by an African-American gang. Verdugo Flats is a large Latino gang that has claimed a sizeable swath of southwestern San Bernardino since the 1970s. SBPD reported that the gang had roughly 150 members as of August 2001, a 20% increase from two years before. They noted repeatedly that Verdugo Flats is "turf-oriented," claiming territory through extensive graffiti and intimidation of residents. SBPD officers stated that the combination of heightened violence and the inter-racial nature of the gang fight led San Bernardino authorities to move to file the long considered injunction on August 5, 2002.

Nineteen members of the gang were included in the requested injunction. The court instituted a TRO on September 24, 2002, prohibiting them from 22 activities. Prohibited activities included behaviors associated with selling drugs, trespass, a nighttime curfew, public order offenses (fighting, drinking, urinating, littering, vandalism, and graffiti), and public association with any other defendant.

SBPD officials implemented the injunction using procedures developed in their previous experiences. The enjoined individuals were named at patrol meetings, photographs of the individuals were placed on the wall of the room where patrol officers get their briefings, and Metropolitan Enforcement Team (MET) officers provided the primary enforcement for the injunction. As in earlier injunctions, the SBPD initiated a "sweep" of the injunction area right after they obtained the injunction. They searched homes of parolees and probationers and checked on outstanding warrants.

They catalogued paraphernalia, photographs, and clothing.

After the initial implementation activities, SBPD continued to monitor the individuals named in the injunction, kept patrol officers informed, and attempted to ensure that the injunction restrictions were enforced. MET officers trained patrol officers to use the appropriate forms to arrest enjoined gang members and made sure that the in-house computer would notify patrol officers if an injunction member was stopped and identified. One police informant noted that he came in several times on his day off to work with patrol officers who had apprehended an enjoined individual. From the inception of the Verdugo Flats CGI in September 2002 until January 2004, five individuals were arrested related to the injunction. Arrested individuals were liable for enhanced bail of up to $25,000.

Research Design and Methodology

A community assessment survey was conducted twice—once before the injunction and once shortly after the injunction was imposed—to test the impact of the immediate change on neighborhood residents' attitudes and perceptions. We predicted that specific experiences of gang intimidation, fear of gang members, and visibility of the gang members and graffiti would all decrease within the first six months after the injunction. We also tested the impact on more intermediate outcomes: fear of crime, crime victimization, and perceived level of social disorder. We included long-term survey measures of neighborhood social cohesion, informal social control, collective efficacy, neighborhood efficacy, and willingness to call the police and trust in the police, although we expected that these changes would evolve over a longer period of time. Table 37.1 summarizes the measures used for each outcome variable.[7]

In addition to the residents of the injunction area called Upper Flats, four other neighborhoods were surveyed to control for local history such as crime trends in the city between the first and second waves of the survey. Two comparison areas were chosen because they had similarly high levels of social disorder, but they varied in the level of territorial gang activities. These areas were suggested by two police informants who had focused on gang crime in San Bernardino for several years and were very familiar with gang activities in this part of the city. North Area, located about a mile northeast of Upper Flats, is high in crime and physical and social disorder, the latter confirmed both by the authors' visual tour of the area and by residents' responses on the Wave 1 survey.[8] SBPD sources repeatedly confirmed that North Area had no *territorial* gang presence over the course of the study. The second area, Seventh Street, is a territorial gang area, about a half-mile north of Upper Flats where a gang injunction had been filed in 1997. The two remaining areas, immediately south of Upper Flats, were defined as one area during the pre-injunction survey. When the Flats injunction was filed, part of this area was included in the injunction. We renamed that portion of the southern area Lower Flats, and the remaining comparison area was named South Area. The South Area served as a good comparison for the Lower Flats injunction area, because both had comparably lower social disorder before the injunction was filed (see Footnote 8). Beyond serving as comparisons for residents' perceptions about gangs, safety, and their community, these four comparison neighborhoods were also chosen as possible sites for displaced Verdugo Flats Gang activity because of the injunction.

Surveys were completed with 797 San Bernardino residents in five neighborhoods 18 months before and 1229 residents six months after the issuance of the injunction. Roughly two thirds were Latino, with the remainder equally distributed among other ethnic categories. All participants were adults (35–40% were 18–34 years, 40–45% were 35–54 years, and about 20% were over 54 years in the two surveys); two thirds were women. Census data were used to assess whether the achieved sample characteristics in Wave 1 roughly approximate the population it was designed to represent.[9]

A hybrid survey procedure[10] was used to promote response rates in these difficult-to-survey neighborhoods. After five contacts to sampled addresses in support of the self-administered survey, trained field staff approached remaining addresses for a doorstep interview using the same

Table 37.1 Summary of Measures for Immediate, Intermediate, and Long-Term Outcomes

	Item	Response Options
Immediate Outcomes		
See gang members hang out	How often have you seen gang members?[1]	Never/rarely/sometimes/monthly/more
See new graffiti	How often have you seen new graffiti or gang tags?	Never/rarely/sometimes/monthly/more
Been hassled by gang members	How often has someone you know been hassled by gang members?[1]	Never/rarely/sometimes/monthly/more
Young persons bullied by gang members	How often have young persons been bullied by gang members?[1]	Never/rarely/sometimes/monthly/more
Frightened by gang member	How often have you or a family member felt frightened by a gang member?[1]	Never/rarely/sometimes/monthly/more
Gang activities made you anxious	How often have gang activities made you feel anxious at home in the evening or night?[1]	Never/rarely/sometimes/monthly/more
Any intimidation by gang members	Count if any of the four items above happened[1]	Never/rarely/sometimes/monthly/more
Fear confrontation with gang member	How much do you fear that you or a member of your family will be confronted by a gang member in the neighborhood?	Not at all fearful set a little fearful/ fearful/very fearful
Intermediate Outcomes		
Fear of crime	How much do you fear that your home will be entered or damaged while you are away; that your car will be damaged or stolen; that you or a member of your family will be hurt by someone in the neighborhood; that you or a family member will be hurt even if you stay indoors?	Not at all fearful/a little fearful /fearful/very fearful alpha = .88 (W1); .90 (W2)
Perceived level of social disorder	How often has [13 possible problems] occurred?[1]	Never/rarely/sometimes/monthly/more
Any violent victimization (or attempted)	How many times has someone robbed or tried to steal something from you by force; physically attacked you or attempted to do so; threatened or attacked you with a weapon?[1]	Not at all/yes to any of 3 items
Any property victimization (or attempted)	How many times has someone damaged or vandalized your home, eg . . . ; stolen or tried to steal something belonging to you like your vehicle; something from inside your home or garage (not vehicle); something outside in your yard or in your vehicle?[1]	Not at all/yes to any of 4 items

[1] These questions included "in the last six months, in your neighborhood . . .

(Continued)

Table 37.1 (Continued)

	Item	Response Options
Long-Term Outcomes		
Social cohesion	People around here are willing to help their neighbors; This is a close-knit community; People in this neighborhood can be trusted; People in this neighborhood generally do not get along with each other; People in this neighborhood do not share the same values (r).	How strongly do you agree or disagree with these statements: strongly disagree/disagree/neither agree nor disagree/agree/strongly agree alpha = .71 (W1); .78 (W2)
Informal social control	How likely is it that a neighbor would do something: If someone was letting trash pile up in their yard or on their steps; if some young children were causing minor damage to a building in your neighborhood; if a suspicious stranger was hanging around the neighborhood; if youth in the neighborhood were getting into trouble?	Very unlikely/unlikely/neither likely nor unlikely/likely/very likely alpha = .83 (W1); .82 (W2)
Collective efficacy	Sum of standardized social cohesion and informal social control scales	
Believe neighborhood can solve problems	If there is a problem in this neighborhood, how likely is it that people who live here can get it solved?	Very unlikely/unlikely/neither likely nor unlikely/likely/very likely
Willing to call police if a gang member threatens	How likely or unlikely is it that you would call the police if a gang member threatened someone in your family?	Very unlikely/unlikely/neither likely nor unlikely/likely/very likely
Trust police	The police in my neighborhood can be trusted; the police in my neighborhood treat people fairly; the police in my neighborhood are respectful of people?	How strongly do you agree or disagree with these statements: strongly disagree/disagree/neither agree nor disagree/agree/strongly agree alpha = .86 (W1); .86 (W2)

protocol. Adjusted response rates were 64% for Wave 1 and 73% for Wave 2.[11]

Three sets of analyses were conducted. The first set compared the primary injunction area, Upper Flats, with North Area, the highly disordered neighborhood with no discernible territorial gang. The principal hypotheses for this first analysis predicted that residents in the primary injunction area would experience a positive change after the injunction on the immediate outcome variables relative to any change that occurred in its comparison area. We compared differences in the change over time in these two areas by examining their interaction in an analysis of variance using wave and area as factors. Significant interactions in the predicted direction were interpreted as support for the principal hypotheses. These analyses were repeated comparing change in the secondary injunction area, Lower Flats, with change in its control, South Area. A second set of analyses compared the same pairs of areas, testing whether similar change had occurred for each intermediate and long-term outcome.

A third set of analyses assumed that the Seventh Street area was characterized by similar neighborhood experiences before implementation of its injunction as those in the Upper Flats primary injunction area. Both areas, as described by police informants, had been high-crime, active gang territories before their injunctions. Outcomes from the Wave 2 survey were compared between the earlier injunction area and the new one. We predicted that long-term effects, unlikely to have developed in the recent injunction area, would evidence higher levels in the older injunction area. These effects were tested using t-tests and chi-square analyses.

Results

Immediate Outcomes

Our analyses supported the predictions that the gang injunction would have an impact on gang visibility almost immediately, and consequently they have an impact on the level of intimidation by gang members and the level of fear of gang members experienced by residents relatively soon after the injunction was filed and enforced. The top third of Table 37.2 shows the results of comparisons between Upper Flats and North Area, the two

high disorder neighborhoods. Respondents living in Upper Flats reported seeing gang members hanging out in their neighborhoods less often than respondents in North Area, after the injunction than before. Although graffiti decreased in both areas, no significant difference appeared between the two areas on change in the level of graffiti from Wave 1 to Wave 2.

Fewer respondents in Upper Flats reported being hassled, frightened, or made anxious by gang members after the injunction than respondents in North Area. From Wave 1 to Wave 2, the percent of residents who reported experiencing any kind of intimidation fell eight percentage points in Upper Flats and rose by six percentage points in North Area. Similarly, fear of confrontation with a gang member decreased in Upper Flats over this time while it increased in North Area.

A different pattern of results emerged among immediate outcomes in the low disordered areas. Comparing the secondary injunction area, Lower Flats, with South Area, the top third of Table 37.3 shows respondents in Lower Flats reported *more* rather than less gang visibility than the low-disorder comparison South Area, and were made to feel anxious by gang activity *more* rather than less often. The two low-disorder areas did not vary from wave-to-wave on any other immediate outcome measures.

Intermediate Outcomes

The gang injunction was also predicted to affect several intermediate outcomes if the influence of the injunction on gang intimidation and fear was strong and pervasive. Intermediate outcomes are less immediate because changes in gang behavior are just one of many factors in neighborhoods that may influence fear of crime, perceived level of disorder, and victimization. The analyses summarized in the middle of Table 37.2 showed little carryover of the injunction's impact to these more general outcomes. Residents of the primary injunction area, Upper Flats, reported less fear of crime than residents in North Area, but no significant differences on perceived social disorder or victimization.

Table 37.3 shows the results on these more general outcomes when comparing the secondary injunction area, Lower Flats, with its comparison, South Area. Both of these areas were low in

Table 37.2 Means and Tests of Area by Wave Interactions in Two High Disorder Areas on the Immediate, Intermediate, and Long-Term Outcomes

	Upper Flats		North Area		Main effect for area	Main effect for wave	Statistical test of predicted interaction
	W1 n = 287	W2 n = 384	W1 n = 227	W2 n = 322			
Immediate Outcomes							
See gang members hanging out	2.86	2.53	2.88	2.90	*		$F(1,1189) = 4.38, p = 0.037$
See new graffiti	2.54	2.44	2.95	2.67	*	*	ns
Been hassled	1.55	1.47	1.62	1.80	*		$F(1,1183) = 4.31, p = 0.038$
Young persons bullied	1.51	1.46	1.56	1.71	*		ns
Frightened by gang member	1.51	1.57	1.53	1.92	*	*	$F(1,1186) = 5.69, p = 0.017$
Gang activities made you anxious	1.95	1.76	1.88	2.02			$F(1,1183) = 4.18, p = 0.041$
Any intimidation by gang members	55%	47%	55%	61%			Wave 1 χ^2, ns; Wave 2 $\chi^2 = 13.18; df = 1,695; p < 0.001$
Fear confrontation with gang member	2.11	1.99	2.04	2.33	*		$F(1,1192) = 10.32, p = 0.001$
Intermediate Outcomes							
Fear of crime	2.14	2.03	2.17	2.28	*		$F(1,1213) = 5.16, p = 0.023$
Perceived level of social disorder	2.35	2.17	2.52	2.46		*	ns
Violent victimization (or attempted)	19%	23%	18%	29%		*	ns
Property victimization (or attempted)	48%	52%	54%	59%			ns
Long-Term Outcomes							
Social cohesion	2.95	3.04	2.84	2.80	*		ns
Informal social control	3.01	3.06	2.98	2.95			ns
Collective efficacy	2.98	3.05	2.91	2.87	*		ns
Belief neighborhood can solve problems	2.78	2.91	2.77	2.75			ns
Willing to call police if a gang member threatens	3.76	3.91	3.67	4.05		*	ns
Trust police	3.42	3.41	3.41	3.28			ns

disorder and victimization at Wave 1, but Lower Flats increased in perceived social disorder and victimization in the post-injunction survey relative to South Area.

Long-Term Outcomes

The long-term outcomes measured include neighborhood social cohesion, informal social control, collective efficacy, perceived neighborhood efficacy, and willingness to call and trust the police, which are indicators of the police's and community's ability to work together to combat crime. As a group, these outcomes might be influenced by changes set in motion by successful gang injunctions if the community became empowered as a result of changes in disorder, fear, and safety. However, statistical

Table 37.3 Means and Tests of Area by Wave Interactions in Two Low-Disorder Areas on the Immediate, Intermediate, and Long-Term Outcomes

	Lower Flats		South Area		Main effect for area	Main effect for wave	Statistical test of predicted interaction
	W1 n = 72	W2 n = 107	W1 n = 42	W2 n = 104			
Immediate Outcomes							
See gang members hanging out	1.72	2.06	1.73	1.51	*		$F(1,315) = 5.97, p = 0.015$
See new graffiti	2.11	2.23	1.82	1.62	*		ns
Been hassled	1.20	1.38	1.20	1.12			ns
Young persons bullied	1.23	1.43	1.23	1.14			ns
Frightened by gang member	1.22	1.41	1.27	1.20			ns
Gang activities made you anxious	1.37	1.56	1.56	1.28			$F(1,312) = 6.58, p = 0.011$
Any intimidation by gang members	38%	42%	41%	26%			ns
Fear confrontation with gang member	1.49	1.71	1.28	1.38	*		ns
Intermediate Outcomes							
Fear of crime	1.62	1.88	1.58	1.58	*		ns
Perceived level of social disorder	1.75	2.06	1.63	1.61	*		$F(1,321) = 4.44, p = 0.036$
Violent victimization (or attempted)	6%	23%	2%	8%		*	Wave 1 χ^2, ns; Wave 2 $\chi^2 = 9.27$; $df = 1, n = 209, p = 0.002$
Property victimization (or attempted)	28%	43%	36%	25%			Wave 1 χ^2, ns; Wave 2 $\chi^2 = 8.19$; $df = 1, n = 209, p = 0.004$
Long-Term Outcomes							
Social cohesion	3.36	3.24	3.50	3.40			ns
Informal social control	4.04	4.22	4.31	4.35			ns
Collective efficacy	3.43	3.32	3.46	3.47			ns
Belief neighborhood can solve problems	3.29	3.11	3.25	3.59			$F(1,315) = 4.28, p = 0.039$
Willing to call police if gang member threatens	3.50	3.39	3.41	3.54			ns
Trust police	3.61	3.59	3.45	3.64			ns

tests failed to reveal significant changes in the predicted direction on the long-term outcomes in the injunction areas relative to their comparison areas, as shown in Tables 37.2 and 37.3.

Contrary to predictions, perceived neighborhood efficacy decreased in the secondary injunction area, Lower Flats, relative to South Area. Residents here were less inclined to believe that the community could solve its problems after the injunction than before. Taken with the results of analyses in these areas above, lower neighborhood efficacy is consistent with the unexpected perceptions of higher gang visibility and disorder in the secondary injunction area.

As noted, Seventh Street is the territory of an active gang that had undergone an injunction five years before the second survey. Comparing the primary current injunction area, Upper Flats, with this area provides an opportunity to consider the impact on long-term outcomes as well as on immediate and intermediate ones. The results, as provided in Table 37.4, show that these two areas are not significantly different as regards immediate and intermediate outcomes when comparing the Wave 2 surveys. However, four of the six long-term outcomes showed significant differences between the two areas, with more favorable conditions in Seventh Street than in Upper Flats. One possible interpretation of these findings is that neighborhood social cohesion, collective efficacy, neighborhood efficacy, and willingness to call the police were higher in the Seventh Street Area than in Upper Flats because their gang injunction had been in place over a longer period of time. Although consistent with our hypotheses, the research design does not permit us to definitively rule out plausible alternative interpretations.

Outcomes By Age, Ethnicity, and Gender

Each of the analyses reported were repeated adding age (18 to 34 vs. 35 and older), ethnicity (Hispanic vs. Nonhispanic), and gender as factors. No significant interactions with these demographics qualified the findings reported in comparison within the high-disorder areas. One triple interaction was significant in comparisons of Upper Flats and South Area. Older respondents showed

Table 37.4 Means and Tests By Area Comparing Two High-Disorder Injunction Areas on Wave 2 Immediate, Intermediate, and Long-Term Outcomes

	Upper Flats W2 n = 384	Seventh Street W2 n = 312	Statistical Tests t-test or chi-square
Immediate Outcomes			
See gang members hanging out	2.53	2.49	ns
See new graffiti	2.44	2.4	ns
Been hassled	1.47	1.54	ns
Young persons bullied	1.46	1.55	ns
Frightened by gang member	1.57	1.56	ns
Gang activities made you anxious	1.76	1.8	ns
Any intimidation by gang members	47%	52%	ns
Fear confrontation with gang member	1.99	2.1	ns
Intermediate Outcomes			
Fear of crime	2.03	2.04	ns
Perceived level of social disorder	2.17	2.24	ns
Violent victimization (or attempted)	23%	20%	ns
Property victimization (or attempted)	52%	42%	$\chi^2(1) = 7.687, p = 0.006$
Long-Term Outcomes			
Social cohesion	3.04	3.16	$t(606)[1] = 2.132, p = 0.033$
Informal social control	3.06	3.2	ns
Collective efficacy	3.05	3.18	$t(622)[1] = 2.329, p = 0.020$
Belief neighborhood can solve problems	2.91	3.12	$t(620)[1] = 2.611, p = 0.009$
Willing to call police if a gang member threatens	3.91	4.16	$t(688) = 2.813, p = 0.005$
Trust police	3.41	3.46	ns

[1] adjusted for test with unequal variances.

an increase in trust, whereas younger respondents showed a decrease in trust in South Area, with little change from wave to wave in Upper Flats ($F = 6.88$; $df = 1,294$; $p = 0.009$). The findings reported in Tables 37.2–37.4 are robust across age, gender, and ethnicity.

Discussion of Findings

Our analyses provide evidence of short-term effects of a CGI on the primary neighborhood targeted. Our surveys of community residents reveal less gang presence in the neighborhood, as compared with changes in the primary control area. Furthermore, fewer residents report acts of gang intimidation and residents express less fear of confrontation with gang members.

Police reported no territorial gang presence in the primary comparison area, but residents reported substantial gang activity on the pre-injunction survey. As crime increased in the city over the two-year period between the surveys (Warren, 2003), gang fear and intimidation increased in the disordered control area (North Area) but not in the neighborhood with the new injunction (Upper Flats). Thus, this strategy seemed to yield salutary effects in the primary injunction area: Immediate benefits accrued to residents' experience of gang visibility, intimidation, and fear.

These immediate benefits did not extend to the intermediate or long-term outcome indicators. Only in fear of crime did the primary injunction area show a relative decrease. No significant relative changes were observed on the other intermediate outcomes, perceived social disorder or crime victimization. Little evidence was found that immediate effects on residents translated into larger improvements in neighborhood quality, such as neighborhood social cohesion, informal social control, collective efficacy, and police/community relationships, although reductions in fear of crime and gang visibility, fear, and intimidation may be precursors to such change in the long run.

We found tantalizing hints of such changes in the comparison of the new injunction area (Upper Flats) with a contiguous area in which an injunction had been implemented five years before the second survey (Seventh Street). The two areas had similar levels of gang visibility, fear, and intimidation, but the longstanding injunction area showed favorable levels of social cohesion, neighborhood and collective efficacy, and willingness to call the police if a gang member threatened residents. If we assume the two areas had similar neighborhood characteristics at baseline before their injunction, these results are consistent with the view that community improvements will accrue once fear and intimidation are mitigated by implementation of a CGI. However, as the similarity of immediate outcomes might indicate, these gains are continually threatened by the persistence of gang activities.

Theories of social disorganization provide a context for interpreting changes brought about by the injunction. There was no direct community involvement in the development or implementation of the Flats injunction—a typical pattern identified in other studies as well (Allan, 2004; Maxson, 2004)—so the absence of relative change in collective efficacy or relationships with police is not surprising. The immediate changes in gang intimidation and fear in the primary injunction area may yet spark a dynamic of community improvement, as would be predicted from social disorganization theory. In this near-term assessment, reducing intimidating gang activity did not net this community the broader benefits of neighborhood social capital. The community-level processes apparently heightened in the older injunction area may have been initiated by an earlier lowering of gang intimidation and fear there. The comparison between the two injunction communities is consistent with an interpretation of community change: willingness to engage with police in crime control efforts, a perspective that neighbors can and will intervene to resolve incipient crime problems, and greater social bonds among neighbors.

The decreases in gang visibility, gang intimidation, and fear of gang crime in Upper Flats also could be the result of individual level processes such as deterrence or social identity–mediated deindividuation spawned by the injunction. The apparent decrease in intimidating gang behavior suggests that this injunction did not spur an increase in gang cohesion over the short term, although it could be triggered at a later date.

The unexpected expansion of the territory covered by the Flats injunction into the less disordered injunction area (Lower Flats) provided the opportunity to investigate the impact on a neighborhood with considerably less gang activity. Our comparison of this secondary injunction area with a similarly low-disorder, contiguous community produced results that caution those who would promulgate the efficacy of gang injunctions in diverse settings. Lower Flats evidenced negative impacts, relative to its comparison area (South Area): more gang visibility, anxiety, social disorder, and property victimization, and less faith that a neighborhood can solve its problems. Why didn't this injunction work as well in this area? We can speculate about several possible explanations.

The secondary injunction area might have been the locale for the displacement of gang activity from the primary injunction area. This area was surveyed as a comparison area before the injunction because of its potential vulnerability to displacement. Analysis showed that the location of police contacts with named gang members before the issuance of the injunction took place almost exclusively in the primary injunction area. The increased gang activity in Lower Flats also might have reflected the unanticipated consequences of increased suppression activities. This view would argue that police over-reached by including this neighborhood with less gang activity and less social disorder in the injunction. Suppression activities may have backfired by building cohesiveness (Klein, 1995) or oppositional defiance (Sanchez-Jankowski, 1991) among the targeted gang members who lived or were active in this area.

Finally, these negative results may be a reflection of weaknesses in the study design or methodology that affected the secondary area comparisons in particular. The area experienced substantial demographic change, with generally more renters and less residential longevity in the neighborhood. Our controls for these demographic changes did not change our conclusions[12] but such transitions may foster neighborhood dynamics that increase gang activity, independent of intervention efforts. We are cautious about drawing broad generalizations about the negative outcomes detected in the secondary injunction area. . . .

Notes

1. The historical information on CGIs was gathered from documents prepared by prosecutors (see particularly Castorena, 1998 and Whitmer and Ancker, 1996), newspaper articles, and interviews with police gang experts and injunction practitioners.

2. Nuisance is defined by section 3479 as "Anything which is injurious to health, or is indecent or offensive to the senses, or an obstruction to the free use of property, so as to interfere with the comfortable enjoyment of life or property, or unlawfully obstructs the free passage or use, in the customary manner, of any navigable lake or river, bay, stream, canal, or basin, or any public park, square, street, or highway." According to section 3480, "A public nuisance is one which affects at the same time an entire community or neighborhood, or any other considerable number of persons, although the extent of the annoyance or damage inflicted upon individuals may be unequal."

3. Recent research on the formation of police gang units argues that law enforcement responses to gangs originate from a host of organizational factors, rather than from a rational assessment of the seriousness of local gang problems (Katz, 2001; Katz et al., 2002: see also, Decker, 2003). Any decision to pursue a CGI reflects these organizational, as well as other environmental, features.

4. Maxson et al. (2003) and Allan (2004) discuss the legal and procedural issues evident in the legal literature. For a detailed description of injunction forms in California and elsewhere, see also Maxson, 2004.

5. A recent CGI was issued against an estimated 1000 members of Oxnard's Colonia Chiques gang, precluding any identified gang member from congregating in a 6.6-square-mile area that covers more than a quarter of the city.

6. In addition to pro bono services sometimes offered by private attorneys, occasionally a judge will grant public counsel.

7. We consulted several surveys before beginning this one, including our sources for an earlier community policing survey for the Los Angeles Police Department (Maxson et al., 1999), among which were the New Jersey City Public Housing Resident Survey, University of Texas at Arlington Social Work Citizen Survey, University of Wisconsin Survey Research Laboratory Citizen Attitudes and Victimization Survey, the Chicago Community Policing Resident Survey, the Spokane Police Department and Washington State University Crime and Criminal Justice Survey, and the Joliet Police Department School Neighborhood

Questionnaire. Other surveys from which we adapted additional material include the Denver Youth Study, the National Crime Victimization Survey, the University of California at Irvine Fear of Crime and Gangs Survey, the Chicago Neighborhood Study (Sampson et al., 1997), and others. In the second wave, we added a series of questions regarding community organization; these were adapted from the Harvard Social Capital Benchmark. Table 37.1 reports the measures used in analyses reported here. In constructing these measures, we considered the distribution of individual items and assessed all scales for reliability.

8. Residents' perception of social disorder in the five study areas in the Wave 1 surveys confirmed the observations and opinions of the police informants. Two homogeneous subsets were identified post hoc by the Dunnett test. Upper Flats, North Area, and Seventh Street were equivalent in perceived level of social disorder before the injunction (M = 2.35, 2.52, and 2.27 respectively) and were higher than Lower Flats and South Area (M = 1.75 and 1.63).

9. Our ability to conduct a direct comparison to census data is limited to the five demographic variables for which there is a good match between our measurement categories and the census survey: age, gender, and education level of the respondent; home ownership; and the respondent's length of residency. Gender comparisons are rough approximations because the census data available are reported for the entire population, whereas our respondents were limited to adults. Our residential stability measure asked about length of time lived in the neighborhood, whereas the census asks if the respondent has moved within the last five years. We selected the Wave 1 sample as the best comparison because it was conducted just after the 2000 Census. Finally, the neighborhoods selected for our study are only roughly approximated by census block boundaries. Statistical comparisons of the two data sources reveal significant differences in all five areas on gender and educational attainment, and in a few areas on the other three variables. In all areas, survey respondents are disproportionately women and more educated when compared with the census population. It has implications for more limited generalizability of our findings to men and less educated persons. Beyond that, only scattered differences between the Census and the Wave 1 achieved sample were found. In Seventh Street, older individuals are more likely to respond to the survey. Homeowners disproportionately participated in the study in Upper Flats and North Area. In North Area and Lower Flats, survey respondents were less likely to have lived in the neighborhood for less than five years, but the Census incorporates any move, whereas our survey counted only moves from outside the neighborhood. In most areas, the match on age, homeownership, and residential stability between the Wave 1 and the census population was acceptable.

10. In our earlier work surveying highly disordered neighborhoods, we tested the efficacy of using a self-administered versus a telephonic personal interview survey approach. Anonymous self-administered surveys were more effective in these areas because residents seemed to be more forthcoming about their fears and perceptions than they were in personal interviews. (Explanations for survey mode differences are the subject of much debate, see Dillman, 2000 and Hennigan, Maxson et al., 2002). However, the self-administered approach in these communities resulted in lower than optimal response rates even after accruing responses over a three-month period according to Dillman's methods (Dillman, 1978, 1991). Consequently, for this work, we developed a hybrid approach for surveying in these areas that maximized the responses received from self-administered surveys (SA) and followed-up with face-to-face doorstep interviews (FTF) to achieve a higher response rate. Critical to the interpretation of comparisons across areas over time is the comparability of the ratio of SA to FTF achieved. In all except the South Area, the ratios were equivalent. More SA surveys were returned from the South Area in Wave 2 than in other areas, which created a bias toward less favorable neighborhood descriptions and more fear there. The direction of this bias, counter to the hypotheses and findings reported, suggests that differences between South and Lower Flats might be even stronger than indicated here. Furthermore, there were no interactions on any of the outcomes reported here between survey mode and wave. There were two significant mode by wave by area interactions on significant outcome effects. Testing the effects within survey mode revealed the reported differences were observed within both modes, but they were stronger within the FTF mode.

11. See Maxson et al., 2004, for a detailed statement of study areas, survey procedures, response rates, sample characteristics, the demographic comparability of the Wave 1 and Wave 2 achieved samples, and correspondence with U.S. Census data. We found no concern for methodological artifacts introduced by demographic shifts in any of the areas surveyed except for Lower Flats, where the Wave 2 demographics suggested an increase in renters and newcomers to the neighborhood.

12. The only difference was observed in the homeownership category and the intermediate outcome of perceived level of social disorder. The increase in social disorder in Lower Flats relative to South Area was observed only among renters.

References

Allan, Edward L. 2004. *Civil Gang Abatement: The Effectiveness and Implications of Policing by Injunction.* New York: LFB Scholarly Publishing LLC.

American Civil Liberties Union (ACLU) of Southern California. 1997. *False Premises, False Promises: The Blythe Street Gang Injunction and Its Aftermath.* Los Angeles: ACLU Foundation of Southern California.

Bjerregaard, Beth. 2003. Antigang legislation and its potential impact: The promises and pitfalls. *Criminal Justice Policy Review* 14:171–192.

Bursik, Robert J. and Harold G. Grasmick. 1993. *Neighborhoods and Crime: Dimensions of Effective Community Control.* Lexington, Mass.: Lexington Books.

Cameron, Jeffrey R. and John Skipper. 1997. The civil injunction: A preemptive strike against gangs. *The FBI Law Enforcement Bulletin* (November): 11–15.

Castorena, Deanne. 1998. *The History of the Gang Injunction in California.* Los Angeles: Los Angeles Police Department Hardcore Gang Division.

Decker, Scott H. 2003. *Policing Gangs and Youth Violence.* Belmont, Calif.: Wadsworth.

Decker, Scott H. and Barrick Van Winkle. 1996. *Life in the Gang: Family, Friends, and Violence.* New York: Cambridge University Press.

Dillman, Don A. 1978. *Mail and Telephone Survey: The Total Design Method.* New York: Wiley.

———. 1991. The design and administration of mail surveys. *Annual Review of Sociology* 17:225–249.

———. 2000. *Mail and Internet: The Tailored Design Method.* 2nd ed. New York: Wiley.

Ellemers, Naomi, Russell Spears, and Bertjan Doosje. 2002. Self and social identity. *Annual Review of Psychology* 53:161–186.

Egley, Arlen Jr. and Aline K. Major. 2004. *Highlights of the 2002 National Gang Survey.* OJJDP Fact Sheet. FS-200401. Washington, D.C.: Office of Justice Programs, U.S. Department of Justice.

Fisher, Michael, Ben Goad, and Lisa O'Neil Hill. 2002. Two areas face renewed violence. *The (Riverside) Press-Enterprise* (November 18).

Fremon, Celeste. 2003. Flying the flag: The debate over the latest gang crackdown. *LA Weekly* (July 18–24).

Geis, Gilbert. 2002. Ganging up against gangs: Anti-loitering and public nuisance laws. In C. Ronald Huff (ed.), *Gangs In America.* 3d ed. Thousand Oaks. Calif.: Sage.

Genelin, Michael. 1998. Community prosecution: A difference. *Prosecutor's Brief* 3:13–17.

Greene, Jack C. 2003. Gangs, community policing and problem solving. In Scott H. Decker (ed.), *Policing Gangs and Youth Violence.* Belmont, Calif.: Wadsworth.

———. 2004. Police youth violence interventions: Lessons to improve effectiveness. In Finn Esbensen, Larry Gaines and Steve Tibbetts (eds.), *American Youth Gangs at the Millennium.* Long Grove, Ill.: Waveland.

Grogger, Jeffrey. 2002. The effects of civil gang injunctions on reported violent crime: Evidence from Los Angeles County. *Journal of Law and Economics* 45:69–90.

Hennigan, Karen M., Cheryl L. Maxson, David Sloane, and Molly Ranney. 2002. Community views on crime and policing: Survey mode effects on bias in community surveys. *Justice Quarterly* 19:564–587.

Katz, Charles M. 2001. The establishment of a police gang unit: An examination of organizational and environmental factors. *Criminology* 39:301–338.

Katz, Charles M., Edward R. Maguire, and Dennis W. Roneek. 2002. The creation of specialized police gang units: A macro-level analysis of contingency, social threat and resource dependency explanations. *Policing* 25:472–506.

Klein, Malcolm W. 1993. Attempting gang control by suppression: A misuse of deterrence principles. *Studies in Crime and Crime Prevention.* Annual Review 88–111.

———. 1995. *The American Street Gang: Its Nature, Prevalence and Control.* New York: Oxford University Press.

Los Angeles City Attorney Gang Prosecution Section. 1995. Civil gang abatement: A community based policing tool of the office of the Los Angeles city attorney. In Malcolm W. Klein, Cheryl L. Maxson, and Jody Miller (eds.), *The Modern Gang Reader.* 1st ed. Los Angeles: Roxbury Publishing.

Los Angeles County District Attorney (LACDA). 1996. *SAGE: A Handbook for Community Prosecution.*

Maxson, Cheryl L. 2004. Civil gang injunctions: The ambiguous case of the national migration of a gang enforcement strategy. In Finn Esbensen, Larry Gaines, and Steve Tibbetts (eds.), *American Youth Gangs at the Millennium.* Long Grove, Ill.: Waveland.

Maxson, Cheryl L. and Theresa L. Allen. 1997. *An Evaluation of the City of Inglewood's Youth Firearms Violence Initiative.* Los Angeles: Social Science Research Institute, University of Southern California.

Maxson, Cheryl L., Karen Hennigan, and David C. Sloane. 2003. For the sake of the neighborhood? Civil gang injunctions as a gang intervention tool. In Scott H. Decker (ed.), *Policing Gangs and Youth Violence.* Belmont, Calif.: Wadsworth.

Maxson, Cheryl L., Karen Hennigan, David C. Sloane, and Kathy A. Kolnick. 2004. *Can Civil Gang Injunctions Change Communities? A Community Assessment of the Impact of Civil Gang Injunctions.* Draft Final Report to the National Institute of Justice. Los Angeles: Social Science Research Institute, University of Southern California (April).

Maxson, Cheryl L., Karen Hennigan, David C. Sloane, and Molly Ranney. 1999. *The Community Component of Community Policing in Los Angeles.* Final Report to the National Institute of Justice. Los Angeles: Social Science Research Institute, University of Southern California (August).

Mazza, Susan. 1999 Gang abatement. The San Diego experience. *Law Enforcement Quarterly* 288:11.

McGloin, Jean M. 2005. Policy and intervention: Consideration of a network analysis of street gangs. *Criminology & Public Policy.*

Postmes, Tom and Russell Spears. 1998. Deindividuation and antinormative behavior: A meta-analysis. *Psychological Bulletin* 123:238–259.

Sampson, Robert J., Stephen W. Raudenbush, and Felton Earls. 1997. Neighborhoods and violent crime: A multilevel study of collective efficacy. *Science* 277:918–924.

Sanchez-Jankowski, Martin. 1991. *Islands in the Street: Gangs and American Urban Society.* Berkeley, Calif.: University of California Press.

Spears, Russell, Tom Postmes, Martin Lea, and Susan E. Watt. 2001. A SIDE view of social influence. In Joseph P. Forgas and Kipling D. Williams (eds.), *Social Influence: Direct and Indirect Processes.* Philadelphia, Pa.: Psychology Press.

Staff Reports. 2002. Bernardino injunction issued against local gang. *San Bernardino County Sun Newspaper* (September 24).

Stewart, Gary. 1998. Black Codes and broken windows: The legacy of racial hegemony in antigang civil injunctions. *Yale Law Journal* 107:2249–2279.

Thornberry, Terence P., Marvin D. Krohn, Alan J. Lizotte, Carolyn A. Smith, and Kimberly Tobin. 2003. *Gangs and Delinquency in Developmental Perspective.* Cambridge, U.K.: Cambridge University Press.

Vigil, James Diego. 1988. *Barrio Gangs: Street Life and Identity in Southern California.* Austin: University of Texas Press.

———. 2002. *A Rainbow of Gangs.* Austin, Texas: University of Texas Press.

Warren, Jennifer. 2003. Decline in violent crime seen statewide. *Los Angeles Times* (October 16):B5.

Whitmer, John and Deanne Ancker. 1996. The history of the injunction in California. In LACDA (ed.), *SAGE: A Handbook for Community Prosecution.*

Wolcott, Holly. 2004. Officials seek injunction against Oxnard's Colonia Chiques gang. *Los Angeles Times* (March 25).